C0-ABH-738

BUSINESS LAW
PRINCIPLES AND CASES

BUSINESS LAW
PRINCIPLES AND CASES

HAROLD F. LUSK, S.J.D.
Professor Emeritus of Business Law

CHARLES M. HEWITT, J.D., D.B.A.
Dean, The University Division

JOHN D. DONNELL, J.D., D.B.A.
Associate Professor of Business Law

A. JAMES BARNES, J.D.
Assistant Professor of Business Law

All of Indiana University

Second U.C.C. Edition

1970   RICHARD D. IRWIN, INC. Homewood, Illinois
IRWIN-DORSEY LIMITED Georgetown, Ontario

© BUSINESS PUBLICATIONS, INC., 1935 and 1939
© RICHARD D. IRWIN, INC., 1946, 1951, 1955,
    1959, 1963, 1966, and 1970

ALL RIGHTS RESERVED. No part of this publication may
be reproduced, stored in a retrieval system, or transmitted, in any form or by any means, electronic, mechanical, photocopying, recording, or otherwise, without
the prior written permission of the publisher.

Second U.C.C. Edition

First Printing, January, 1970

Second Printing, August, 1970

Library of Congress Catalog Card No. 69–19982

Printed in the United States of America

Preface

This is the ninth revision of a text that was first published in 1935. The authors have tried to preserve the basic strengths of this highly successful book while at the same time incorporating many new features. Some of the major subject matter changes are: a substantial expansion of the coverage of torts, with a new chapter treating torts involving business relations, the addition of chapters giving an introduction to trade regulation, the addition of a chapter on legal problems associated with consumer credit, and an expansion of the material on corporations. The additions reflect recent changes in course content at Indiana University. Most of these changes, in turn, are the result of research which attempted to identify those areas of the law which businessmen indicated should be stressed in business law courses.[1]

Since many more court decisions based upon the Uniform Commercial Code have become available since the last edition, we have been able to use such cases as illustrations in all of the chapters to which the Code applies. Because Louisiana is now the only American jurisdiction which has not adopted the Code, most references to pre-Code law have been eliminated. They no longer seem necessary and only tend to confuse the student.

We have almost completely replaced older cases with current ones, although we have not hesitated to keep a few of the older cases which we thought were unusually effective for teaching purposes. In choosing cases, we have tried to limit ourselves to cases involving business relations and have looked for those whose fact situations might add depth and breadth to the business student's understanding of actual business operations. More importantly, some of the cases were specifically chosen because they are useful vehicles for discussing trends in law or for adopting an "environmental approach."

The problem cases at the end of each chapter are based upon decided cases except, of course, for the introductory questions at the end of the first two chapters. The problem cases are selected to supplement the cases in the chapters and sometimes illustrate different viewpoints than those represented by the cases in the text. We recommend their use to give the student experience in analyzing legal fact situations and in applying the principles and rules of law which they are learning.

We are pleased that a workbook prepared by Professors Phillip Scaletta of Purdue, John R. Goodwin of West Virginia University, and Thomas Dunfee of Illinois State University will be available for use beginning with this edition of the book.

---

[1] John D. Donnell, "The Businessman and the Business Law Curriculum," 6 *Amer. Business Law Journal* 451 (1968).

We appreciate the many suggestions we have received from instructors who have used previous editions and from students and former students. We solicit additional criticism and suggestions from users of this edition. We are especially indebted to Professor Clyde Carter of the University of North Carolina, who read the entire manuscript, and to Mr. Howard G. Rath, Jr., a member of the bar of Los Angeles, who read the chapters on corporations, for many helpful suggestions. Without the aid of James H. Grund, publication of this revision would have been long delayed. We also wish to express our appreciation to Professor John R. Goodwin of West Virginia University as well as to Robert A. Long and to Gary D. Spivey of Indiana University for their contributions to the book and to the Teacher's Manual and Test Manual. Our secretaries, Mrs. Lucinda Roenfeldt and Mrs. Nancy Valette, were indispensable, and their many hours of assistance on the manuscript are much appreciated. Lastly, the revision authors are particularly grateful to Harold F. Lusk not only for having created the fundamental structure upon which this revision was built, but also for having made many invaluable suggestions which were incorporated into this revision.

Bloomington, Indiana   CHARLES M. HEWITT, JR.
December, 1969   JOHN D. DONNELL
    A. JAMES BARNES

Contents

vii

Infliction of Mental Distress. RIGHTS OF PROPERTY: Nature of Property Rights. Trespass to Land. Trespass to Personal Property. Conversion. Deceit (Fraud). BUSINESS TORTS: Economic Relations.

EXISTING OBLIGATION: Nature of Preexisting Obligation. Criminal and Tortious Acts. Holder of an Office. Public Officers. Contractual Obligations. Exceptions. New Contract. DEBT, COMPROMISE, AND COMPOSITION: Liquidated Debt. Compromise (Accord and Satisfaction). Composition. FOREBEARANCE TO SUE: Right to Bring Suit. Valid Claims and Reasonable Claims. Party Making Promise. BARGAIN AND EXCHANGE: The Bargain. Adequacy of Consideration. Nominal Consideration. PAST CONSIDERATION: Nature of Past Consideration. Implied Promises to Compensate. CONSIDERATION IN BILATERAL CONTRACTS: Mutual Obligation. Illusory Promise. Right to Cancel Contract. WHEN CONSIDERATION UNNECESSARY: Promise Inducing Substantial Action. Charitable Subscriptions. Business Promises. Debts Barred by Statute of Limitations. Debts Dischargₑd in Bankruptcy. Promise to Perform a Conditional Duty. Sealed Promises. CONSIDERATION UNDER THE UNIFORM COMMERCIAL CODE: In General. Consideration in Franchising.

INTRODUCTION: Capacity. Parties to Contract. Presumption as to Capacity. INFANTS' CONTRACTS: Theory of Infants' Incapacity. Period of Infancy. Emancipation. General Rule. Business Contracts. State Statutes. Infant Partner. NECESSARIES: Liability for Necessaries. Nature of Necessaries. DISAFFIRMANCE OF CONTRACT: Right to Disaffirm. Time of Disaffirmance. Return of Consideration. Infants' Rights on Disaffirmance. Misrepresentation of Age. RATIFICATION: Nature of Ratification. Requirements for Ratification. Effect of Ratification. INFANTS' TORT LIABILITY: Nature of Liability. INSANE AND DRUNKEN PERSONS: Nature of Liability. Test of Insanity. Effect of Adjudication of Insanity. Necessaries. Disaffirmance of Contract. Ratification of Contract. MARRIED WOMEN'S CONTRACTS: Contractual Capacity at Common Law. Married Women's Statutes. ALIENS; CORPORATIONS: Aliens. Corporations. Trustees and Guardians. Governmental Units.

INTRODUCTION: Nature of Illegality. Classification. Presumption. BARGAINS IN VIOLATION OF POSITIVE LAW: Scope of Positive Law. Bargain to Commit a Crime. Bargain to Commit a Tort. BARGAINS MADE ILLEGAL BY STATUTES: Types of Statutes. Wagering Statutes. Stock and Commodity Market Transactions. Statutes Declaring Bargains Void. Regulatory Statutes. Revenue-Raising Statutes. PUBLIC POLICY: General Concept. Bargains Injurious to Public Service. Bargains to Influence Fiduciaries. Bargains Relieving from Liability for Negligence. Bargains in Restraint of Trade. Miscellaneous Illegal Bargains. EFFECT OF ILLEGALITY: General Rule. Ignorance of Fact or Special Regulation. Rights of Protected Parties. Knowledge of Illegal Use. Divisible Contracts. Rescission before Performance of Illegal Act. UNENFORCEABLE CONTRACTS AND THE UNIFORM COMMERCIAL CODE: Unconscionability.

STATUTE OF FRAUDS: Introduction. Provisions of Statute of Frauds. Interpretation of Statute of Frauds. Scope of the Statute of Frauds. COLLATERAL CONTRACTS: Nature of Collateral Contracts. Original Contracts. Exceptions.

INTEREST IN LAND: Scope of Provision. Contracts Coming within the Statute of Frauds. NOT TO BE PERFORMED WITHIN ONE YEAR: Scope of Provision. Computing Time. Contracts to Extend Time of Performance. An Indefinite Time Stated. THE WRITING: Nature of Writing Required. Content of the Memorandum. The Signing. Oral Variation of Contract. EFFECT OF FAILURE TO COMPLY: General Effect. Rights of Parties to Oral Contract. SALE OF GOODS AND THE CODE: The Memorandum. Part Payment or Part Delivery. Admissions in Pleadings or Court. Specially Manufactured Goods. Effect of Noncompliance. INTERPRETATION: Necessity for Interpretation. Basic Standards of Interpretation. Rules of Interpretation. Usage. PAROL EVIDENCE: Scope and Purpose of Parol Evidence Rule. Admissible Parol Evidence. Subsequent Contracts. Partial Writings. Ambiguous Contracts.

ASSIGNMENT OF CONTRACTS: Introduction. Contracts Not Assignable. Contracts Which Are Assignable. The Delegation of Duties. RIGHTS ACQUIRED BY ASSIGNEE: General Rule. Notice of Assignment. Successive Assignments. Assignment of Wages. ASSIGNOR'S LIABILITY TO ASSIGNEE: Implied Warranties. General Liability. THIRD-PARTY BENEFICIARY: Classes of Third-Party Beneficiary Contracts. Donee Beneficiaries. Creditor Beneficiaries. Incidental Beneficiaries. Municipal or Governmental Contracts. ASSIGNMENT UNDER THE UNIFORM COMMERCIAL CODE: Scope of Application. Assignment.

CONDITIONS: Introduction. Nature of Conditions. Creation of Conditions. Independent Promises. ARCHITECTS' AND ENGINEERS' CERTIFICATES: Requirement of Certificate. When Failure to Produce Certificate Is Excused. PERFORMANCE AND BREACH: Duty of Performance. Complete or Satisfactory Performance. Substantial Performance. Material Breach. Prevention of Performance. Time Is of the Essence. Performance to Personal Satisfaction. IMPOSSIBILITY OF PERFORMANCE: Nature of Impossibility. Illness or Death of Promisor. Performance Declared Illegal. Destruction of Subject Matter. Commercial Frustration. DISCHARGE: Nature of Discharge. Discharge by Agreement. Waiver. Discharge by Alteration. Discharge by Statute of Limitations. Uniform Commercial Code. NATURE OF REMEDIES: Objective in Granting Remedy. Enforcement of Remedy. Uniform Commercial Code. CLASSIFICATION OF DAMAGES: Introduction. Basis for Awarding Damages. Measure of Damages. Mitigation of Damages. Liquidated Damages. Nominal Damages. EQUITABLE REMEDIES: Specific Performance. Injunction.

Part IV.   AGENCY

INTRODUCTION: Nature of Relation. Early Development. English Law. Scope of Agency. CLASSIFICATION: Introduction. Master and Servant. Principal and Agent. General and Special Agents. Independent Contractor. CREATION OF RELATION: Requirement to Create Agency. Statutory Requirements. CAPACITY OF PARTIES: Infants and Insane Persons as Principals. Unincorporated Associations as Principals. Capacity to Act as Agent. Business Organizations as

Principals. AUTHORITY TO BIND PRINCIPAL: Authorization. Express Authority. Implied Authority. Apparent Authority. RATIFICATION: Nature of Ratification. Requirements for Ratification. What Acts May Be Ratified. Effect of Ratification. Ratification Must Be Entire.

DISCLOSED OR PARTIALLY DISCLOSED PRINCIPAL: Liability of Agent of Disclosed Principal. Liability of Agent of Partially Disclosed Principal. Execution of Writings. UNDISCLOSED PRINCIPAL: Nature of Relation. Rights of the Third Person. Scope of Liability of Undisclosed Principal. Rights of Undisclosed Principal. LIABILITY ON SPECIAL TRANSACTIONS: Basis of Liability. Liability for Agent's Representations. Liability for Agent's Warranties. Liability for Payment to Agent. Liability for Credit Contracted by Agent. Liability on Negotiable Instruments. NOTICE TO OR KNOWLEDGE OF AGENT: Effect of Notice to Agent. When Notice Is Not Binding on Principal. Knowledge of Agent. Limitations on the Rule. LIABILITY FOR ACTS OF SUBAGENTS: Appointments of Subagents. Liability of Principal for Acts of Subagents. LIABILITY FOR TORTS OF AGENT: General Rule. Scope and Course of Employment. Liability for Torts of Professional Agent. Liability for Deceit of Agent. Tort Liability Is Joint and Several.

LIABILITY ON AUTHORIZED CONTRACTS: Disclosed Principal. Contracts in Writing. Partially Disclosed Principal. Undisclosed Principal. Agent as Party to Contract. AGENT'S LIABILITY ON UNAUTHORIZED CONTRACTS: General Rule. Agent's Liability on the Contract. Agent's Liability on Implied Warranty of Authority. Agent's Liability for Deceit. Ratification or Knowledge of Third Person. Transactions Not Binding on Principal. LACK OR LIMITATION OF CAPACITY OF PRINCIPAL: Nonexistent Principal. Incompetent Principal. Principal Lacking Full Capacity. Defenses Available to Agent. AGENT'S LIABILITY FOR TORT: General Rule. Liability for Deceit and Duress. Liability for Conversion. Liability for Negligence. Liability to Third Persons for Breach of Duty to Principal. THIRD PERSON'S LIABILITY TO AGENT: Agent's Right of Action on Contract. Agent with Property Interest in Contract. Professional Agents. Agent's Right of Action for Possession. Agent's Action for Tort.

AGENT'S DUTY OF LOYALTY: Duty in General. Secret Communications. Duty Not to Buy from or Sell to Self. Duty to Act for Only One Party to Transaction. AGENT'S DUTY TO OBEY INSTRUCTIONS AND TO USE CARE AND SKILL: Duty to Obey Instructions. Standard of Care and Skill. Duty to Communicate Notice or Knowledge. Duty in Making Collections. Duty in Extending Credit. Duties of Professional Agent. AGENT'S DUTY TO ACCOUNT: Duty to Account for Money and Property. Duty to Keep Principal's Property Separate. Liability for Use of Principal's Property. PRINCIPAL'S DUTIES TO AGENT: Duty to Compensate Agent. Duty If Compensation Is Contingent. Compensating Professional Agents. Reimbursement for Expenditures. TERMINATION OF AGENT'S POWERS: General Rules. Termination by Will of Parties. Termination by Contract Provisions. Termination by Change of Circumstances. Termination of Powers Given as Security. Notice to Third Persons.

Part V.   PARTNERSHIPS

INTRODUCTION: Historical Background. Uniform Partnership Act. Nature of Partnership. Partnership Not an Entity. Partnership versus Corporation. CREATION OF PARTNERSHIP: No Formalities Required. Intent of Parties. Tests of Existence of Partnership. CAPACITY TO BE A PARTNER: Infants and Insane Persons. Corporations. CARRYING ON A BUSINESS: Requirements for Carrying on a Business. Co-owners of a Business. Co-owners Who Are not Partners. Business Must Be Carried on for Profit. PERSONS REPRESENTED TO BE PARTNERS: Effect of Holding out as Partner. Holding out or Consenting to Holding out. JOINT VENTURE: Nature of Joint Venture. LIMITED PARTNERSHIP: Nature of Limited Partnership. Necessity for Enabling Statute. Requirements for Creation of Limited Partnership.

INTRODUCTION: Nature of Relation. Articles of Partnership. Provisions of Articles of Partnership. PARTNERSHIP PROPERTY: What Is Partnership Property? Title to Partnership Property. Possession of Partnership Property. Incidents of Partnership Ownership. Creditors of Individual Partner. MANAGEMENT OF BUSINESS: Right to Voice in Management. Agreements as to Management. Voting Rights. Right to Resort to Courts. PROFITS AND LOSSES: Rights and Liabilities of Partner. RELATION BETWEEN PARTNERS: Nature of Duty Partner Owes to Partner. Duty in Transacting Partnership Business. Books of Partnership. Disclosure of Information. Right to Wages. Right to Sue Partner.

PARTNER AS AGENT OF PARTNERSHIP: General Powers of Partner. Relation of Third Persons to Partnership. Partner's Power to Convey Partnership Real Property. Special Situations. General Limitations on a Partner's Power. BORROWING ON PARTNERSHIP'S CREDIT: Partner's General Power to Borrow Money. Partner's Power to Pledge Firm Assets. Partner's Power to Bind Firm on Negotiable Instruments. Partnership's Liability for Money Borrowed. PARTNER'S INDIVIDUAL LIABILITY: Nature of Liability for Torts. Partner's Crimes. Suing the Partnership.

DISSOLUTION: Definition and Effect of Dissolution. Dissolution without Violation of Agreement. Dissolution in Violation of Agreement. Dissolution by Operation of Law or Court Decree. CHANGE IN MEMBERSHIP: Effect of Change in Membership. Acquisition of Partner's Interest by Copartners. A Partner Transfers His Interest to a Third Person. Addition of a Partner. The Common-Law Rule. NOTICE OF DISSOLUTION: Necessity of Notice. Who Is Entitled to Notice. WINDING UP PARTNERSHIP BUSINESS: Procedure in Winding Up. Who Winds up Business. Partner's Power in Winding Up. Rights of Estate of Bankrupt or Deceased Partner. DISTRIBUTION OF ASSETS: Order of Distribution. Distribution of Assets of Insolvent Partnership.

Part VI. CORPORATIONS

Subscription. Issuing Shares of Stock. Liability of Issuer under U.C.C. Transfer of Corporate Stock. Restrictions on Transfer. Corporation's Duty to Transfer. Redemption and Purchase of Stock by Corporation. FEDERAL AND STATE SECURITIES LEGISLATION: Securities Act of 1933. Securities Exchange Act of 1934. State "Blue-Sky" Laws.

INTRODUCTION: General. SHAREHOLDER MEETINGS: Exercise of Shareholder Functions. Annual Meetings. Special Meetings. Notice of Meetings. Quorum. Conduct of the Meeting. VOTING RIGHTS: Shareholders Entitled to Vote. Cumulative Voting. Proxy Voting. Voting Trust. DIVIDENDS: Introduction. Types of Dividends. Funds Available for Payment of Dividends. Tests of Validity of Dividend Payments. Directors' Discretion in Payment of Dividends. Payment of Dividends on Preferred Stock. Stock Dividends and Stock Splits. Distributions. Dividend Declaration. Effect of Transfer on Right to Dividend. INSPECTION OF BOOKS AND RECORDS: Common-Law Right to Inspect. Statutory Inspection Rights. PREEMPTIVE RIGHTS: General. Application of Preemptive Rights. Preemptive Rights under the Model Act. EXTRAORDINARY CORPORATE TRANSACTIONS: Introduction. Procedure for Amending Articles. Other Extraordinary Transactions. Appraisal Right. SHAREHOLDERS' SUITS: Shareholders' Individual Suits. Shareholders' Derivative Suits. Minority Shareholders' Suits. Dissolution at Suit of a Minority Shareholder. SHAREHOLDER LIABILITY: Shareholder Liability on Shares. Shareholder Liability on Illegal Dividends and Distributions. Other Bases for Shareholder Liability.

RIGHTS OF FOREIGN CORPORATIONS: Introduction. The Model Act. "DOING BUSINESS": Introduction. Subjecting Foreign Corporations to Suit. Taxing Foreign Corporations. Admission of a Foreign Corporation. Penalty for Failure to Obtain Permission.

Part VII. PROPERTY

NATURE AND CLASSIFICATION: Nature of Property. Possession. Real and Personal Property. Tangible and Intangible Property. Public and Private Property. ACQUISITION OF PERSONAL PROPERTY: Production or Purchase. Taking Possession. Gift. Lost Property. Confusion. Accession. NATURE AND CREATION OF BAILMENT: Essential Elements. Creation of Relation. Custody of Servant or Agent. RIGHTS AND LIABILITIES OF PARTIES: Bailee's Duty of Care. Alteration of Liability by Contract. Bailee's Duty to Return Property. Bailee's Right to Compensation. Bailor's Liability for Defects in Bailed Property. SPECIAL BAILMENT SITUATIONS: Bailment of Fungible Goods. Safe-Deposit Boxes. Involuntary Bailments. Common Carrier. Innkeepers.

FIXTURES: Nature of Fixture. Express Agreement. Mode of Attachment. Use with Real Property. Additions by Owner. Additions by Tenants. RIGHTS AND

INTERESTS IN REAL PROPERTY: Fee Simple. Life Estate. Leasehold. Easements. Licenses. CO-OWNERSHIP OF REAL PROPERTY: Nature of Co-ownership. Tenancy in Common. Joint Tenancy. Tenancy by the Entirety. Community Property. Tenancy in Partnership. ACQUISITION OF REAL PROPERTY: Origin of Title to Real Property. Acquisition by Purchase. Acquisition by Gift. Acquisition by Adverse Possession. Acquisition by Tax Sale. Acquisition by Will or Descent. TRANSFER BY DEED: Formalities of Transfer. Quitclaim and Warranty Deeds. Form and Execution of Deed. Recording Deeds. DISPOSITION ON DEATH OF OWNER: Statutes of Descent and Distribution. Right of Disposition by Will. Execution of Will. Limitations on Disposition by Will. Revocation of Will. LANDLORD AND TENANT: Nature of Lease. Execution of Lease. Rights, Duties and Liabilities of the Landlord. Rights and Duties of the Tenant. Termination of the Lease. PUBLIC CONTROLS ON THE USE OF LAND: Nuisance Control. Zoning and Subdivision Ordinances. Eminent Domain.

INTRODUCTION: Nature of Security. Unsecured Credit. Secured Credit. Development of Security. Uniform Commercial Code. Security Interests in Real Estate. COMMON-LAW AND STATUTORY LIENS ON PERSONAL PROPERTY: Persons Entitled to Common-Law Liens. Characteristics of a Common-Law Lien. Statutory Liens on Personal Property. Foreclosure of Lien. SECURITY INTERESTS IN PERSONAL PROPERTY: Obtaining an Enforceable Security Interest. ATTACHMENT OF THE SECURITY INTEREST: The Security Agreement. Future Advances. After-Acquired Property. Proceeds. PERFECTING THE SECURITY INTEREST: Public Filing. Possession by the Secured Party as Public Notice. Perfection by Attachment. PRIORITIES: Security Interest in Fixtures. DEFAULT AND FORECLOSURE: Contract Provisions. Right to Possession. Sale of Collateral. Distribution of Proceeds. Consumer Goods. Duties of Secured Party. REAL ESTATE MORTGAGES: Historical Development. Form, Execution, and Recording. Rights and Liabilities of Mortgagor and Purchasers. Mortgagee's Right to Assign Mortgage. Foreclosure of Real Estate Mortgage. Right of Redemption. TRUST DEEDS AND LAND CONTRACTS: Trust Deeds. Land Contracts. MECHANIC'S LIEN ON REAL ESTATE: Nature of Mechanic's Lien on Real Estate. Persons Entitled to a Lien. Rights of Subcontractors and Materialmen. Basis for Mechanic's Lien on Real Estate. Requirements for Obtaining Lien. Priorities and Foreclosure. Waiver of Lien. SURETYSHIP AND GUARANTEE: Surety and Guarantor. Creation of Relation. Defenses of Surety. Creditor's Duties to Surety. Subrogation and Contribution.

Part VIII. SALES

INTRODUCTION: Nature of Sales and the Law of Sales. Uniform Commercial Code—Sales. TERMS OF THE CONTRACT: General Terms. Delivery and Payment Terms. SALES ON TRIAL: Sale on Approval. Sale or Return. Sale on Consignment or on Memorandum. BULK TRANSFERS.

TITLE: Introduction. Provisions for Passing of Title. RIGHTS OF THIRD PARTIES: Introduction. Creditor's Rights. Transfer of Voidable Title. Purchaser in Ordinary Course of Business. RISKS: Introduction. Explicit Agreements. Identification and Insurable Interest. Risks of Loss—General Rules.

NATURE OF WARRANTIES: Representations. Warranties—General. EXPRESS WARRANTIES: Nature of Express Warranty. Creating an Express Warranty. WARRANTY OF TITLE: Nature of Warranty of Title. Scope of Warranty of Title. IMPLIED WARRANTIES: Nature of Implied Warranty. Implied Warranty of Merchantability. Implied Warranty of Fitness for Particular Purpose. EXCLUSIONS, MODIFICATION, OR CONFLICT OF WARRANTIES: Common-Law Rule. Exclusions or Modifications. Conflict of Warranties. WHO BENEFITS FROM WARRANTY: General Rule. Demise of the Privity Doctrine. Uniform Commercial Code. PRODUCT LIABILITY: Negligence. Strict Liability.

INTRODUCTION: General Rules. Course of Dealing and Usage of Trade. Modification, Rescission, and Waiver. Assignment and Delegation. Cooperation Respecting Performance. DELIVERY: General Rules. Seller's Duties of Delivery. INSPECTION AND PAYMENT: Buyer's Right of Inspection. Payment. ACCEPTANCE; REVOCATION; REJECTION: What Constitutes Acceptance. Effect of Acceptance. Revocation of Acceptance. Buyer's Rights on Improper Delivery. Manner of Rejection and Duties after Rejection. Failure to Particularize. ASSURANCE, REPUDIATION, BREACH, AND EXCUSE: Assurance. Anticipatory Repudiation. Excuse.

SELLERS' REMEDIES: Recovery of Purchase Price. Recovery of Damages for Breach. Resale as Measure of Damages. Seller's Remedies on Discovery of Buyer's Insolvency. Seller's Right to Stop Delivery. BUYERS' REMEDIES: Right to Recover Goods. Buyer's Right to Damages for Nondelivery. Damages for Defective Goods. GENERAL RULES: Buyer and Seller Agreements as to Damages. Proof of Market Price. Statute of Limitations.

Part IX.   COMMERCIAL PAPER

BACKGROUND: Historical Background. Uniform Commercial Code—Commercial Paper. FORMS OF COMMERCIAL MONEY: Nature of Commercial Paper. Draft. Check. Certificate of Deposit. Promissory Note. BENEFITS OF NEGOTIABILITY: Rights of Assignee of Contract. Rights Acquired by Negotiation.

FORMAL REQUIREMENTS: Basic Requirements. Importance of Form. Language of Negotiable Instrument. IN WRITING AND SIGNED: Writing. Signing. UNCON-

DITIONAL PROMISE OR ORDER: Requirement of Promise or Order. Promise or Order Must Be Unconditional. Express Conditions. Special Provisions of the Code. SUM CERTAIN IN MONEY: Sum Certain. Payable in Money. PAYABLE ON DEMAND OR AT DEFINITE TIME: Payable on Demand. Definite Time. PAYABLE TO ORDER OR BEARER: Necessity of Words of Negotiability. Payable to Order. Payable to Bearer. SPECIAL TERMS: Additional Terms and Omissions. Ambiguous Terms.

Part X.   MISCELLANEOUS

THE DEVELOPMENT OF OUR CREDIT SOCIETY: Legal and Social Problems of Credit. FEDERAL LEGISLATION: TRUTH IN LENDING: Introduction. Disclosure Requirements. Truth in Advertising. Requirements on Real Estate. Limitations on Garnishment. Enforcement of CCPA. Other Legislation. THE CREDIT CARD: The Risk of Loss. Personal Defenses of Card Holder.

THE INSURANCE CONTRACT: Nature of Contract. Kinds of Insurance. MAKING THE CONTRACT: General Requirements. The Application (Offer). When Application Is Contract of Insurance. Acceptance of Offer in Application. DELIVERY OF POLICY: Importance of Delivery of Policy. When Policy Is Delivered. REPRESENTATIONS AND WARRANTIES: Nature of Representations and Warranties. Effect of False Representations. Effect of False Warranty. Construing Representations and Warranties. INSURABLE INTEREST: Nature of Insurable Interest. Insurable Interest in Property Insurance. Insurable Interest in Personal Insurance. NOTICE AND PROOF OF LOSS: Notice of Loss. Proof of Death, Sickness, or Accident. Proof of Loss Required in Property Insurance. TERMINATION AND LAPSE: Nature of Termination and Lapse. Termination of Contract of Personal Insurance. Lapse of Contract of Personal Insurance. Termination of Standard Property Insurance. Termination by Increase of Risk. Special Provisions in Contracts of Property Insurance. ASSIGNMENT OF CONTRACT OF INSURANCE: Assignment of Personal Insurance. Assignment of Property Insurance.

BACKGROUND: Bankruptcy Laws in the United States. Purpose and Scope of Bankruptcy Act. BANKRUPTS: Voluntary Bankruptcy. Involuntary Bankrupts. ADMINISTRATION OF BANKRUPT'S ESTATE: Adjudication and Appointment of Trustee. Examination of Bankrupt. Rights and Duties of Trustee. DEBTS: Provable Debts. Allowable Debts. Debts Having Priority. Dischargeable Debts. PREFERENCES, LIENS, AND FRAUDULENT TRANSFERS: Preferential Payments. Preferential Liens. Fraudulent Transfers. DISCHARGE: Basis for Granting Discharge. Filing Objections to Discharge. Acts Which Bar Discharge. Who May File Objections.

Part XI.   ECONOMIC RELATIONS AND THE LAW

INTRODUCTION: Rights Protected. DECEITFUL DIVERSION OF PATRONAGE: Disparagement. Trademarks and Other Marks. TRADE SECRETS, PATENTS, AND COPYRIGHT: Trade Secrets. Patents. Copyrights. INTERFERENCE WITH CONTRACT OR ECONOMIC EXPECTATIONS: Interference with Contract. Interference with Economic Expectations.

APPENDIXES

PART | *Introduction*

chapter 1. The Nature and Role of Law and Its Development in America

Origins of Law

Development. It is difficult to discuss the origins of law in precise terms for two principal reasons. First, under some definitions "law" existed long before recorded history and thus the specific origins of law will never be known. Second, subsequent discussion will demonstrate that it is impossible to formulate a satisfactory definition of law which has general applicability. Certainly, no single definition can adequately reflect the many facets and dynamic character of the law.

The law of ancient civilizations usually was tied closely to religion, and religious leaders were the lawgivers and interpreters. The Babylonians believed the sun god gave their code law directly to Hammurabi. The Bible relates the origin of Jewish law in the Old Testament stating, "And Moses came and called for the elders of the people, and laid before their faces all these words which the Lord commanded him."

Most of the early laws reflected the taboos, customs, habits, and needs of the people. The early Greeks, for example, lived in one place and had home and hearth gods. They had a well-developed concept of private property in land but frequently treated growing crops as belonging to the entire community. In contrast, the early Germanic tribes were nomads and had well-developed concepts of personal property, but they viewed the land as free to all.[1]

The emphasis of the early law was on keeping the peace. Severe and sometimes brutal penalties were inflicted on those that engaged in conduct tending to breach the social equilibrium. Rights to use private force (particularly for purposes of revenge) were recognized, and the biblical maxim "an eye for an

---

[1] Rene A. Wormser, *The Story of the Law* (New York: Simon and Schuster, Inc., 1962), p. 156, revised paperback edition.

3

eye and a tooth for a tooth" was a commonly used standard for measuring punishment.

As people began to move into cities and trade and commerce arose, new more complicated law was needed. The law was put into writing and the administration of the law moved out of the hands of religious leaders into the hands of civil authorities. Although many of the moral and ethical concepts found in modern law can be traced to religion-related law of ancient times, the separation of law and religion probably increased the degree of objectivity and rationality in the law.

Concepts of Law

Legal Philosophy. From time immemorial men have discussed the nature of law, its sources and its functions, as well as that even more illusive concept —"justice." Writings are available by the thousands, including statements from the great philosophers of the ages such as Plato, Aristotle, and St. Thomas Aquinas, down to John Dewey of recent times. Others can be quoted from legal scholars and legal philosophers such as Cicero and Papinian of Rome, Henry de Bracton and Sir Edward Coke of England, Friedrich von Savigny and Rudolf von Jhering of Germany and the late Roscoe Pound of the United States. Until the reader has gained some familiarity with the materials of the law and more particularly some appreciation of the difficulties judges face as they deal with specific fact situations and seek to justify their decisions in specific disputes, a discussion of legal theories may be relatively meaningless to him. On the other hand, some general notion of the concepts of the law expounded by some of the great legal thinkers who have helped to shape our law is likely to be useful to the student as he reads a "case" and seeks to understand the judge's opinion.

Pound distinguishes and briefly outlines 12 different concepts of law in his *Introduction to the Philosophy of Law*.[2] However, there are four basic concepts, some encompassing several of those identified by Pound, which reappear most frequently in the writings of philosophers and scholars as well as entering into the thinking of judges as they decide specific disputes.

Law as What Is Right. The first of these is that law is "what is right" in a moral sense, whether the notion of right is derived directly from a divine source or from the nature of man. This concept suggests that laws may be bad because they are inconsistent with properly reasoned deductions from God's revealed will or man's inherent nature and that improvement of the law, and therefore of the society of men, may come from better reasoning and/or new revelations.

---

[2] Roscoe Pound, *Introduction to the Philosophy of Law* (New Haven, Conn.: Yale University Press, 1922), pp. 26–30, paperbound edition.

Critics of this view question the existence of any fixed code of right and wrong. They also question the ability of any person to set out such a code because as anthropologist Ruth Benedict says, "No man ever looks at the world with pristine eyes. He sees it edited by a definite set of customs and ways of thinking." [3]

Law as Custom.   Another concept is that law is a historical accretion, developed over ages from the traditions and customs of a society which reflects the peculiar nature of the people interacting with a particular environment. Some of the thinkers emphasizing this concept of law have visualized legal development as the unfolding of some basic idea. For example, Sir Henry Maine noted that under the rigid class hierarchy system that characterized feudalism, nearly all legal rights and duties that a person had depended upon his position in the hierarchy—or his status. The feudal structure was shattered by the expansion of trade and industry which involved the use of contract. This led to his famous generalization that the history of law is the progress from status to contract.

Law as Command.   A third basic concept of the law is that it is a body of rules which are essentially the commands of a political entity, backed by sanctions imposed by that entity. Under this view it is the will of the ruler or the ruling group rather than reason or morality which shapes and defines the law, and the influence of group character and tradition is minimized.

Law as Social Planning.   A fourth concept of law emphasizes its purpose rather than its source and views law as a means of social control which seeks to balance conflicting claims and values of the society and its various elements. Pound, the leader of the group called the sociological school of jurists, says:

Sociological jurists seek to enable and to compel lawmaking, whether legislative or judicial or administrative, and also the development, interpretation, and application of legal precepts, to take more complete and intelligent account of the social facts upon which law must proceed and to which it is to be applied. . . . (They) insist that we must look at law functionally. We must inquire how it operates, since the life of law is in its application and enforcement.[4]

Schools of Jurisprudence.   Although, of course, students of the law differ in the emphasis which they give to these four general concepts, the outstanding thinkers are frequently classified as belonging to a group which can be identified according to which of these concepts seems uppermost in their thinking. The metaphysical or natural law theory adherents stress the concept we have discussed first, law as "what is right." The historical group stresses the second concept, custom and tradition; the analytical group or positivists stress the third or imperative theory; and the sociological school is the name given to

---

[3] Ruth Benedict, *Patterns of Culture* (Boston: Houghton Mifflin Co., 1934), p. 18, Mentor Books edition.

[4] Roscoe Pound, *Jurisprudence* (St. Paul, Minn.: West Publishing Co., 1959), Vol. I, pp. 350–52.

those holding the fourth concept. As Roscoe Pound points out, these differences stem from concentration on different processes or phenomena which are lumped together as law. The precepts or rules are the focus of the analytical school. The technique of the law or the way judges find a basis for their decisions, which tends to be particularly tradition-bound and slow to change, is the central focus of the historical school. The metaphysical or natural law schools concentrate primarily on the ideal element of the law, that is, what the law ought to be. As we have indicated, the sociological school focuses on the balancing and compromising of interest in society to achieve social ends.

Many legal scholars are convinced that no theory or group of theories can adequately describe law. Some, often called the realists, prefer to focus on law as a process. For example, Llewellyn says: [5]

Actual disputes call for someone to do something about them. First, so that there may be peace . . . and secondly, so that the dispute may really be put to rest. . . . This doing of something about disputes, this doing of it reasonably, is the business of the law. And the people who have the doing in charge, whether they be judges or sheriffs or clerks or jailers or lawyers, are officials of the law. *What these officials do about disputes is, to my mind, the law itself.*

Still other writers attempt to define law in terms of the function it performs.

Summary

Writings of many great men have discussed the nature of law. Four major concepts can be identified. They are: (1) law is what is right, (2) law is custom, (3) law is the command of the ruler, and (4) law is an attempt at social planning.

Functions and Limits of Law

Changing Functions through Time.   If law cannot be adequately defined by theory, can it at least be described in terms of the major functions law performed for society? Roscoe Pound traced the development of law from ancient to modern times.[6] He concluded that in terms of major functions performed, the law has evolved through four stages.

In the first stage, found in primitive societies, the major function of law is to keep the peace, as discussed above. In more advanced societies, represented by Greek and Roman law and also by the law of medieval England where landholding was the major interest, the prime function of law tends to shift to maintenance of the "status quo." Pound characterizes this stage as, "An idea of justice as a device to . . . keep each man in his appointed groove and thus

---

[5] K. N. Llewellyn, *The Bramble Bush* (New York: Oceana Publications, Inc., 1960), p. 12.
[6] Roscoe Pound, "Liberty of Contract," 18 *Yale Law Journal* 454 (1909).

prevent friction with his fellows." The third stage was a product of the Age of Enlightenment, the appeal of reason against authority. The change in legal theory to the view that justice is a device to secure a maximum of individual self-assertion, especially through freedom of contract, followed similar thinking in religion, philosophy, politics, and economics and came as the emphasis in economic activity shifted from agriculture to trade and manufacture. Finally, the fourth and current stage emphasizes social justice. This is the stage that Pound himself helped to usher in.

The law today still performs the earlier three functions, and also others, despite the fact that there may frequently be conflict between these functions. We shall briefly discuss eight of the functions performed by modern law.

Peace Keeping.   One of the important functions of modern legal systems is keeping of the peace. Disruptions of the equilibrium in highly interdependent modern societies tend to spread and tend to penalize innocent nonparticipants. In addition, rising standards of education tend to militate against self-help and any form of unjustifiable injurious conduct by any members of society. Criminal law and tort law seek to maintain the peace and to punish or penalize those who disturb the social order. Tort law also seeks to provide reimbursement for the members of society who suffer losses due to the dangerous or unreasonable conduct of others.

Influence and Enforce Standards of Conduct.   Although legal standards often differ from moral standards, the law frequently influences or shapes the social consensus concerning standards of morality. Price-fixing agreements by businessmen, for example, were neither criminal nor immoral until after the passage of the Sherman Act in 1890. The failure of the National Prohibition experiment, however, would seem to indicate that there are limits on the power of law to shape and influence the moral standards of society.

The law sets standards as to what constitutes reasonable or acceptable performance of legal duties. For business this has meant that as more careful or efficient processes have been developed these improved processes tend to establish new higher legal standards for judging business conduct. Thus the modern businessman must exercise a great deal more care in making, advertising, and distributing his product than did his counterpart of the last century.

Maintenance of the "Status Quo."   Cohen gave an example of law functioning to maintain the status quo when he analyzed the British law of real property:

. . . back of the complicated law of settlement, fee-tails, copyhold estates, of the heir-at-law, of the postponement of women, and other feudal incidents, there was a great and well founded fear that by simplifying and modernizing the real property law of England the land might become more marketable. Once land becomes fully marketable it can no longer be counted on to remain in the hands of the landed aristocratic families; and this means the destinies of the British Empire. For if American experience has demonstrated anything, it is that the continued leadership by great families cannot be as well founded on a money as on a land economy. The same kind of talent which enables Jay Gould to acquire dominion over certain railroads enables Mr. Harriman to take it away from his sons. From the point of view of an establish land economy, a money economy thus seems a state of perpetual war instead of a social order where son succeeds father. . . .[7]

Rapidly changing modern law affords few clear examples of this "status quo" function.[8]

Facilitate Orderly Change.   A more important function of modern law is to facilitate orderly change in order to meet the changing needs of a dynamic society. American law paradoxically functions so as to preserve both stability in the law and yet to permit and facilitate change. Indeed, Whitehead states that, "The art of progress is to preserve order amidst change, and to preserve change amidst order." [9] Justice Holmes once stated that, "Every important principle is in fact at bottom the result of views of public policy." Subsequent chapters will disclose how the courts have initiated policy changes in many vital areas. These court-made changes have been especially important in antitrust, product liability, and other areas of vital concern to businessmen.

Maximum Individual Self-Assertion.   Although the concept of political democracy goes back to the Greeks, the ideas of individual freedom in terms of a minimum of external restraints was formalized into economic theory and had maximum impact on the law during the 19th century. Freedom for the individuals in society, however, must always be defined in relative terms. The total absence of restrictions means anarchy where no rights are recognized or protected by law. In legal terms absolute rights cannot exist because legal rights cannot be defined except in terms of the corresponding legal duties imposed upon others.

In absolute terms a businessman's "right" to run his factory on his own land as he pleases could become the duty of society to accept foul odors, loud noises, and perhaps even physical damage to property. The absolute right to strike could mean the legal duty of society to tolerate the stoppage of essential public services.

One of the vital functions of Western law has been the balancing of rights and duties of citizens in their relationships with government. The early emphasis was on protecting citizens from the exercise of arbitrary power by government.

Facilitate Planning and the Realization of Reasonable Expectations.   In a modern industrial society businessmen must, within limits, be able to plan ahead. This involves not only a basis for predicting the risks and consequences of alternative courses of action, but, also, some means for planning and seeing

---

[7] Morris R. Cohen, "Property and Sovereignty," 13 *Cornell Law Quar.* 8, 10 (1927).

[8] Zoning laws represent attempts to protect the status quo interests of property owners.

[9] A. N. Whitehead, *Process and Reality* (New York: The Macmillian Co., 1929), p. 515.

that reasonable expectations are realized. Tort law, insurance law, sales law, contract law, and other areas provide a basic legal framework to facilitate both the prediction of risks and the effectuation of economic plans.

Promotion of Social Justice.   Since the turn of the century the emphasis has shifted toward the positive use of governmental powers as a means of affording all citizens equal access to the benefits of our total economic and political life. Not only have our legislatures passed "laws" establishing a social security system, welfare payments to the poor, medical payments for the old, etc., but the courts have tended more and more to protect the disadvantaged. The U.S. Supreme Court decisions requiring school desegregation and furnishing legal counsel to impoverished persons accused of crime are two prime examples among many.

Provision of Compromise Solutions.   In a special sense American law usually functions so as to avoid extremes, which according to Aristotle, is the true path to justice. Freund summarizes this when he says of the U.S. Supreme Court:

By avoiding absolutes, by testing general maxims against concrete particulars, by deciding only in the context of specific controversies, by accommodating between polar principles, by holding itself open to reconsideration of dogma, the Court at its best provided a symbol of reconciliation. Perhaps it is this blend of idealism and pragmatism that constitutes, in the end, the most notable characteristic of the judicial process.[10]

Limits on the Law.   Although legal rules have been created concerning most aspects of our vital relationships, there are definite limits not only as to what law can do but also limits as to what the law will try to do. Some of these limits are imposed by the Constitution. Other limits have been self-imposed by the courts or are logically dictated by special circumstances.

The courts generally will refuse to deal with trifling or insignificant matters. Considerations of public expense and the prestige of the court system probably are behind this policy. In addition, the courts have evolved various hands-off policies in certain areas of the law such as certain types of internal family disputes, political questions, and social insults or affronts. There is, however, a modern tendency for the courts to intervene in many of these areas. In some states, for example, the courts now allow a minor son to sue his father (or rather his father's insurance company) for negligent injury. The Supreme Court recently reversed a long-standing hands-off policy with its reapportionment decision.[11]

Historically American courts have refused to answer hypothetical questions or to give advisory opinions by the requirement that there must be a bona fide case or controversy before the court. By refusing to address themselves to

---

[10] Paul A. Freund, "The Supreme Court," Harold J. Berman (ed.), *Talks on American Law* (NewYork: Random House, Inc. 1961), pp. 83–84, Vintage Books edition.
[11] *Baker* v. *Carr,* 396 U.S. 186 (1962).

hypothetical or feigned questions the courts both avoid unseen pitfalls and preserve maximum flexibility for the real controversies that may eventually arise.

For similar reasons American courts will not address themselves to moot issues. An issue becomes moot if later events render any decision by the court meaningless in regard to a specific case. Assume that a businessman files suit to have an action by an administrative agency enjoined and while this suit is pending the agency is abolished and its orders are negated by an act of Congress. The question of the action by the agency would then become moot.

Lastly, later chapters will disclose that there are many areas of the law where the courts either for practical or policy considerations in effect reach a decision which amounts to a refusal to take any action. For example, the courts usually will refuse to enforce gratuitous promises, grant any relief on illegal bargains, or grant relief where the defendant's wrongful act was only indirectly and remotely responsible for the harm suffered by the plaintiff. In many instances these self-imposed limits are primarily due to recognition by the courts that no human institution can or should be omnipresent in all affairs.

Summary

The main functions of modern law include: peace keeping; influencing and enforcing standards of conduct; maintaining the status quo; facilitating orderly change; providing for maximum individual self-assertion; facilitating planning and the realization of reasonable expectations; promotion of social justice; and the provision of compromise solutions.

The Constitution limits the application of law. Other limits have been self-imposed by the courts themselves, such as refusal to deal with insignificant matters, hypothetical questions and moot issues.

Law in the United States

Introduction.   When the government of the United States was organized, there were included certain features which influenced the evolution of the law. The separation of governmental powers into the executive, legislative, and judicial branches, and the granting of certain powers to the central government and the retention by the states of the powers not so granted, brought about a governmental organization not known to existing or earlier nations. The plan has worked well, and the evolution of the law has not been retarded.

The Constitution of the United States.   The Constitution of the United States is the basic law of the land. It defines the powers and sets out the organizational plan of the federal government. Any law—federal, state, or common —that is in violation of a provision of the Constitution of the United States is null and void. The provisions of the Constitution are, for the most part, broad and general in their terminology, and this leaves sufficient flexibility in our basic law to permit desirable development and evolution. The government of the United States is one of enumerated powers, and the enumeration of its powers is to be found in the Constitution.

State Constitutions. Each state has adopted a constitution which serves as the basic law of that state. Any provision in a state constitution which is in conflict with a provision of the Constitution of the United States is of no force and effect. In many respects the constitutions of the several states follow the provisions of the federal Constitution, but as a general rule the provisions of the state constitutions are more detailed. For example, Article I of the Constitution of Indiana, which is the Bill of Rights, has 37 clauses, whereas the Bill of Rights of the federal Constitution is set out in the first eight amendments. The state constitutions usually include such matters as the manner of conducting elections, the establishment and maintenance of schools, the financing of the state government, the chartering of corporations, and other similar matters which are not included in the federal Constitution.

Acts of Congress. Article I, Section 8, of the federal Constitution sets out the powers of Congress, and clause 18 of Section 8 confers on Congress the power: "To make all Laws which shall be necessary and proper for carrying into Execution the foregoing Powers, and all other Powers vested by this Constitution in the Government of the United States, or in any Department or Officer thereof." The 10th Amendment to the Constitution provides: "The powers not delegated to the United States by the Constitution, nor prohibited by it to the States, are reserved to the States respectively, or to the people." Consequently, the acts of Congress which fall within the scope of the powers conferred by the Constitution on the United States are "the law of the land"; that is, they have nationwide force. It does not necessarily follow that the legislature of a state is prohibited from enacting statutes which fall within the scope of the powers conferred on the United States, but it does mean that any state statute, the terms of which conflict with a lawful act of Congress, is a nullity insofar as it conflicts with the act of Congress.

In many areas, state legislatures have enacted statutes which supplement federal legislation in a particular area. For example, most states have enacted state antitrust laws. If Congress has not legislated in an area in which it has the power to do so, a state may legislate in that area, provided it is not prohibited by the federal Constitution from doing so.

State Legislation. The powers of a state legislature are exceedingly broad in their scope. In general, they include every area except those denied them by the state constitution and those prohibited to the states by the Constitution of the United States and those areas conferred by the Constitution of the United States on the federal government in which Congress has acted, in which case the state legislature is confined to legislation which does not conflict with acts of Congress.

The powers of the state are further narrowed by the provisions of the 13th and 14th Amendments to the Constitution of the United States. The 13th Amendment abolished slavery throughout the United States and its territories. The 14th Amendment confers citizenship on persons born or naturalized in the United States and makes them citizens of the United States and the state in which they reside. It further provides: "No State shall make or enforce any law which shall abridge the privileges or immunities of citizens of the United States; nor shall any State deprive any person of life, liberty, or property without due process of law; nor deny to any person within its jurisdiction the equal protection of the laws." This amendment to the Constitution has played a very important role in limiting the powers of both Congress and the state legislatures.

It is through acts of Congress and statutes enacted by the state legislatures that most major changes in the law are brought about and that the law is kept abreast of economic and social changes. Developments in the field of business, such as the carrying-on of a business by a corporation, are based on state statutes, and the business carried on by the corporation is regulated by both federal and state statutes.

Ordinances.   Each state had the power to create political subdivisions and to confer on such subdivisions the power to legislate. The power conferred can never exceed the powers of the state legislature which creates the governmental subdivision. The states have created many subdivisions such as counties, townships, municipal corporations, villages, school districts, irrigation districts, and drainage districts, all of which, as a general rule, have some powers to legislate. Any legislative act of such a subdivision will be enforceable provided it does not exceed the legislative power conferred on it by the state legislature and is not in violation of the provisions of the Constitution of the United States or of the constitution of the state.

Common Law.   The heavy and continuing outpourings of ordinances and state and federal statutes from thousands of lawmaking bodies in the United States tends to overshadow in the popular consciousness the basic underpinning of the American legal system—the common law. The common law is the system of law developed by the royal courts established in England in the two or three centuries after 1066 by William the Conqueror and his successors. They developed a body of nationwide or "common law"—in contrast to the preexisting local law which was largely based upon the customs of the village as enforced by local leaders.

Some of the early judges of the royal courts were clerics learned in the canon or papal law. At that time the church courts had jurisdiction over matters of marriage and inheritance as well as over offenses, such as perjury and defamation, which were considered wrongs against God rather than against society and also over controversies with respect to offices and membership in and property of the church. Through them, concepts from the canon law and also from Roman law, with which they were familiar, were introduced into and helped to shape the common law and to distinguish it from the less well-developed ideas of the preceding Saxon rulers of England.

The body of rules for settling disputes which is the common law grew primarily from the decisions of judges in settling actual disputes. This is in contrast to other sources such as the edicts of a ruler, acts of a legislative body or codes of law prepared by legal scholars. A strong legal profession developed in England as early as the Middle Ages, and legal apprentices or law students began to compile records of the decisions in the royal courts. These earlier decisions or precedents were then used by lawyers in support of clients' petitions for relief and by judges in justifying their decisions. Thus, the rule of *stare decisis,* a Latin phrase meaning to let the decision stand, developed, and once a court had decided a dispute it would decide later cases which were similar in the same way.

Equity.   The law of equity and the Court of Chancery grew out of the Norman Kings' Council as did the common law. Under the Normans the chancellor was the most powerful executive officer of the king and the chief law member of the King's Council. He not only issued writs which permitted an aggrieved person to bring an action in a common-law court, but he himself, as a personal representative of the king, heard pleas which the common-law courts were unable to handle. Especially after the period of designing new writs or forms of action had ended, it was to the chancellor that a petitioner came when his case did not fit the increasingly rigid writ system. Procedure, too, at least in the earlier period, was more flexible in Chancery. So a separate body of law, equity, with a separate court, the Court of Chancery, gradually developed. Equity had precedence over the common law because its decrees applied to the person of the defendant and disobedience to a decree was a contempt of court. Indeed, it was considered a direct disobedience of the king.

The remedies in equity were also more flexible. While a judgment of a law court was limited to money damages or recovery of property, courts of equity, for example, would grant an injunction (a decree forbidding the defendant to do some act, even a prohibition against pursuing a cause of action in a common-law court), specific performance (ordering the defendant to perform his contract), reformation (rewriting a contract or instrument to conform to the actual intent of the parties), partition (to divide disputed property). It might be said that the common-law courts emphasized form, while the Chancery Courts were more interested in the merits of the case and the justice of the decision. Another distinction was that juries were not used in equity.

The Law Merchant.   Even before the Middle Ages trading cities existed throughout Europe and the merchants and traders established their own courts and developed a set of rules which were international in origin and application governing trade and commerce. These courts existed outside of established systems of courts. It was in these courts that our law of sales of goods, negotiable instruments and other commercial law developed. It was not until the 18th century that the law merchant and the merchants' courts were absorbed into the common law.

Adoption of the Common Law.   Since the colonists were familiar with the English law and court system, it is not surprising that these were adopted after independence and that the judges in the new nation continued to look for guidance to the decisions of English judges. A single English legal writer, William Blackstone, probably had the greatest influence on American Law. His *Commentaries on the Laws of England,* written in the years from 1755 to 1765, is believed to have sold as many copies in America as in England, a thousand sets selling at £10 each, having been imported by colonists before 1771.[12] Since most lawyers were trained by a kind of apprenticeship system in which they "read law" with a practicing attorney, this four-volume work came to serve as the leading legal textbook. In fact, it was used in law schools too until the end of the 19th century.

However, a number of lawyers also read treatises based upon the French civil law and Roman law. Through them concepts from these bodies of law once again influenced the common law as it developed in America to serve the needs of a society rather different from that of England.

As additional states were admitted to the Union, they too, except for Louisiana, adopted the English legal system. Louisiana, as a French colony, had previously adopted and it continues to base its law upon the French civil law which culminated in the Code Napoléon, which, in turn, had its roots in the Justinian Code of Rome.

Roman law also has influenced the law of California and Texas through their Spanish heritage (Spain's law also is based upon Roman law).

Some states have codified, that is enacted as statutes, large parts of the common law. Most commonly this includes the criminal law. The legislature may, while compiling and systematizing, intentionally change certain rules of the common law, and subsequent legislatures may more or less frequently make additional changes.

Although some states established separate courts of chancery, in most of the states the same judges sat, often at separate periods, both as law judges and chancellors. Some states, such as Delaware and New Jersey continue to maintain courts of chancery, but in most states the distinction between law and equity has nearly been abolished and a petition for one of the remedies which developed in equity is filed in the same court and in the same manner as if it were a suit for damages. Also as the distinctions have been obliterated, many of the maxims of equity have come to influence judges' decisions in suits for damages.

---

[12] Charles M. Haar, preface to William Blackstone, *Commentaries on the Laws of England: Of Public Wrongs* (Boston: Beacon Press, 1962), p. xxii.

Place of the Courts. Although American courts, under the theory of separation of powers, cannot legislate, they do contribute materially to the evolution of the law. The courts function in three important respects: (1) they rule on claims that constitutional rights have been denied by a statute or a governmental act, (2) they interpret statutes in all cases coming before the courts in which the rights of the parties are determined by the application of a statute, and (3) they apply the common law rules to new but analogous situations which may arise. In the hearing and determining of controversies, the court will interpret applicable statutes in the light of changing social and economic conditions, and will expand the common law to cover new situations.

The line between the province of the legislature to enact new laws and the province of the courts in interpreting a constitution and extending the law to new situations is not easy to draw. The function of the Supreme Court of the United States in interpreting the Constitution not infrequently results in new law as this basic document is interpreted and reinterpreted in the light of new knowledge, new conditions and new thinking. Two recent examples of new interpretations of constitutional requirements are the school desegregation decision [13] and extension of the right of criminal defendants to counsel.[14]

In performing the third function the courts continue to develop and change the common- or judge-made law in much the same fashion as it originally grew. A court must decide a dispute properly brought before it. It cannot escape the task because no similar case or precedent can be found. For example, until the invention of lighter-than-aircraft and airplanes the old common-law rule that a landholder owned the space from the center of the earth to the heavens may have been sufficient to settle disputes, but utilization of this means of conveyance necessitated a different concept of real property. When airplanes came to be used to cause precipitation through chemical seeding of clouds, courts were petitioned to grant damages from the cloud seeders by those who got rain they didn't want or failed to get rain they believed they would otherwise have received.[15]

Private Law. Under our legal system, we have a vast area which we shall term "private law." Each individual in our society may, through his voluntary acts assume obligations which will be enforceable by court action. Salmond [16] stated this concept as follows:

There is an obvious analogy between agreement and legislation—the former being the private and the latter the public declaration and establishment of rights and duties. By way of legislation the state does for its subjects that which in other cases it allows them to do for themselves by way of agreement. . . . Save when the interests of the public at large

---

[13] *Brown* v. *Board of Education,* 347 U.S. 483 (1954).

[14] *Gideon* v. *Wainwright,* 372 U.S. 335 (1963).

[15] See *Southwest Weather Research* v. *Rounsaville,* 320 S.W.2d 211 (Ct. Civ. App. Tex., 1959).

[16] P. J. Fitzgerald, *Salmond on Jurisprudence* (London: Sweet & Maxwell, 1966), para. 121.

demand a different rule, the autonomy of consenting parties prevails over the legislative will of the state. . . . So far as possible, it contents itself with executing the rules which its subjects have made for themselves and in so doing it acts wisely.

The courts will enforce the terms of a contract, the provisions of the articles of incorporation or bylaws of a corporation, or other similar private agreements as readily as they enforce a rule of common law or the provisions of a statute, provided the circumstances are such that the agreements, articles, or bylaws comply with certain accepted standards.

Summary

The government of the United States was the first to be organized on the basis of separation of powers. The basic law of the land is the Constitution of the United States, and the basic law for those powers retained by the states is the constitution of each state. Acts of Congress, within its powers, are law throughout the United States, provided they are not in violation of the U.S. Constitution. Each state legislature has the power to enact laws for the state which are not violative of either the constitution of the state or the Constitution of the United States. Major changes in the common law are brought about by legislative action. Subdivisions of the state governments, particularly incorporated towns, villages, and cities, are empowered to legislate within defined limits. The newly organized states of the United States adopted the English common law insofar as it was suitable to the social and economic conditions of the states.

Our court system is unique in that we have a federal court system and each state has a separate court system. With the exception of federal constitutional questions and the interpretation of treaties, the state courts are not bound by the decisions of the United States Supreme Court.

Within limits, individuals may, in effect, legislate as to their private matters, since courts enforce contractual and other similar obligations created by the acts of the parties.

Recent American Legal Development

Although courts and legal procedure tended to be informal in colonial America and many of the judges were laymen, law became a popular study even before the Revolution. From that time forward lawyers played a leading role in forming the Union and in serving in the executive and legislative as well as judicial branches of the federal and state governments. Although laymen continue even today to serve as judges in the lowest level courts (the J.P. or justice of the peace courts) in many states, lawyers serve in most of the other courts and only those admitted to the bar are permitted to represent parties in the courts. Judgeships still are not infrequently rewards for political service where the office is appointive and the prize in a political contest where it is elective. However, raising judicial salary levels and the adoption of formal or informal systems for nominating or screening candidates for judicial qualifications before appointment or political nomination have tended to raise the level of ability of judges in most courts.

Improvement in Legal Procedure. The trend in legal procedure has been away from legal technicalities toward simplification, greater flexibility, and emphasis upon the merits of the case. One important development with this purpose is "discovery procedure." In civil cases (suits between private parties) rules of procedure adopted by the federal courts and by many of the states in the last few decades give the parties access to the facts upon which the other party relies. This permits a lawyer, in the presence of the opposing lawyer, to interrogate the other party's witnesses under oath prior to trial and to obtain copies of pertinent documents and other data. In an injury case the defendant would be permitted to have a physician of his choice examine the plaintiff and to have copies of such potentially pertinent evidence as Xrays and photographs. The pretrial interrogations, called depositions, may be used to impeach the testimony of the witness at the trial if there should be discrepancies. Either party may make use of depositions to bring into the trial testimony from a person who cannot be present in person.

Another recent procedural device of great importance is the pretrial conference during which the opposing attorneys are required to sit down with the judge to try to get agreement, a "stipulation," on as many of the pertinent facts as possible so that the time required to establish legal proof of them through witnesses in court may be eliminated. Also the judge will encourage the parties to try to settle the case by coming to an agreement disposing of the dispute so that it need not go to trial. Both efforts are directed at clearing the increasingly congested calendars of most courts so as to shorten the time between the filing of the pleadings (the complaint and answer) of the parties and the conclusion of the trial. Simplification of pleading procedure serves the same purpose as well as putting more emphasis on merit than form.

Uniform Statutes. Many efforts were made by state legislatures to codify various parts of commercial law. Each legislature tended to put its own imprint on the law which had derived from the law merchant through English common law. In addition, of course, courts added variety by their interpretation. Businessmen operating in many states found these differences inconvenient and irritating. Beginning late in the 19th century the Commissioners on Uniform State Laws drafted uniform acts which were adopted by most of the states. The first was the Uniform Negotiable Instruments Law in 1896. However, the provisions of the various separate uniform laws were not coordinated and there were conflicts and gaps between them.

The Uniform Commercial Code. The aim of the Uniform Commercial Code is to establish a coordinated code covering most of commercial law and to establish a means of continuing revision to improve it and keep it up to date. The Uniform Commercial Code is the product of the combined efforts of the American Law Institute and the National Conference of Commissioners on Uniform State Laws. Work was begun in 1942 and was carried on by committees composed of judges, lawyers, law teachers, and businessmen. A completed code was approved by the American Law Institute and the National Conference of Commissioners on Uniform State Laws in 1952. A revision of the 1952 Code was prepared and approved, and this revision was published as the *1958 Official Text*. Most of the states adopting the 1958 Code were making their own amendments, thus largely imperiling the primary objective of the Code which was uniformity.

Further study of the Code and the amendments made by the adopting states was carried on and certain amendments were adopted and included in the 1962 version of the Code. In addition the Permanent Editorial Board for the Uniform Commercial Code was established. The policy of the Board is to assist in attaining and maintaining uniformity in state statutes governing commercial transactions. By 1969 the Code had been adopted in all of the states except Louisiana. In addition, it had been adopted in the District of Columbia and in the Virgin Islands.

The Scope of the Code. The scope of the Code is stated in the comment to the title of the Code (P. 3, *1962 Official Text* with comments) as follows, "This Act purports to deal with all the phases which may ordinarily arise in handling a commercial transaction, from start to finish." The Code is divided into 10 articles: Article 1, General Provisions; Article 2, Sales; Article 3, Commercial Paper; Article 4, Bank Deposits and Collections; Article 5, Letters of Credit; Article 6, Bulk Transfers; Article 7, Warehouse Receipts, Bills of Lading and Other Documents of Title; Article 8, Investment Securities; Article 9, Secured Transactions, Sales of Accounts, Contract Rights and Chattel Paper; and Article 10, Effective Date and Repealer.

In Article 1 the general purpose of the Code is stated and general principles for the interpretation and application of the Code provisions are set out. In part 2 of Article 1 terms are defined and principles of interpretation are stated. Articles 2 and 3 are, primarily, a reorganization and modernization of the Uniform Sales Act and the Uniform Negotiable Instrument Law. In Article 7 the Uniform Warehouse Receipt Act and the Uniform Bill of Lading Act are combined, reorganized and modernized. Article 8 is an amendment of the Uniform Stock Transfer Act and includes as investment securities corporate bonds. The definition of an investment security is broad enough to include all types of stocks, bonds, notes, etc., issued by a corporation to obtain money to finance its operations.

Articles 4, 5, and 6 replaces either existing state statutes or model acts. In Article 9 a comprehensive scheme is set out for the regulation of security interests in personal property and fixtures. It replaces the Uniform Conditional Sales Act and the Uniform Trust Receipt Act and legislation dealing with chattel mortgages, factor's liens and assignments of accounts receivable.

Although the Code does not purport to affect any areas of the law other than those specifically stated, its adoption brings about some changes in other areas of law. The Code requires a higher standard of conduct for merchants by imposing a duty to act in "good faith." The duty to act in "good faith" is defined as honesty in fact including the observance of reasonable commercial standards of fair dealing in the trade. The duty to act in "good faith" is imposed on every contract or duty falling within the Code.

The Code recognizes that most contracting today is done by means of forms usually prepared by one of the parties. In some situations the terms may be one-sided or oppressive. The Code stipulates that the courts may find that such terms are "unconscionable" and deny enforcement. The Code further provides that the obligations of good faith and reasonableness may not be disclaimed by contract.

There are other sections of the Code which restrict the right of one or both parties as to the use of specific types of contract terms. In the case of certain types of terms the party signing a form must initial particular terms separately or he will not be bound.[17] In other cases disclaimer of liability terms must be in "conspicuous" print and specific words must be used or the disclaimer terms will not be effective.[18] These latter requirements reduce the possibility that a person will bind himself inadvertently in the signing of these form contracts.

Summary

The trend in legal procedure has been away from legal technicalities toward simplification, greater flexibility, and emphasis upon merits of the case. Modern discovery procedures mean that more accurate presentation of facts can occur. The pretrial conferences shorten the time taken in actual trial proceedings.

The Uniform Commercial Code sets out the law for a major part of all business transactions. The Code governs in every state but Louisiana. Topics covered are: sales; commercial paper; bank deposits and collections; letters of credit; bulk transfers; warehouse receipts and other documents of title; investment securities; secured transactions; sale of accounts, contract rights, and chattel paper; and some general provisions.

---

[17] See Secs. 2–205 and 2–209.
[18] See Sec. 2–316(2).

Questions

1. Can you give any modern examples where changing customs tend to bring about changes in law?
2. What are the major functions of the legal system in the United States?
3. Can you give some examples of laws which tend to promote social justice?
4. What is the role of the U.S. Constitution?
5. What is the common law?
6. Can you give a specific example of two people making private law?
7. What is the primary purpose of the U.C.C.?
8. What action on the part of the states adopting the U.C.C. has imperiled the primary objective of the Code?
9. What is the scope of the U.C.C.?

chapter 2. Law in Action

Introduction

Enforcement. A law is meaningless unless there are some methods by which it may be enforced. If a society is to have an effective legal system, it must develop a body of laws which set out the rules whereby the conduct of its members, both socially and economically, is guided and regulated. Also required is an organized and effective means of determining whether or not laws have been violated and what action should be taken by society to enforce its laws.

The courts play the major role in the performance of this function as they settle disputes brought before them. Administrative agencies and governmental commissions are playing an increasing role in lawmaking and in law enforcement, especially with respect to the conduct of business organizations. Administrative agencies frequently are not only vested with executive but also legislative and quasi-judicial powers. To prevent abuse of these powers, the decisions of administrative tribunals are subject to review in the courts.

Lawyers play a key role in enforcing the law in both the courts and the administrative agencies. Increasingly, however, lawyers are called upon to give advice which will permit businessmen and others to avoid becoming involved in disputes. This function is called the practice of preventive law. An alternative dispute settling device, the voluntary arbitration tribunal, often functions without any lawyers. Lawyers, however, are frequently chosen as arbitrators and are often used to present the cases of disputants. The use of arbitration has increased in recent years, and although these tribunals are not part of our judicial machinery, several states by statute have made their awards enforceable as court judgments.

Our court system differs from that of any other nation, in that we have 51 separate court systems—the federal and the 50 state systems—each of which functions independently of the others. They are, however, similar in their organizational patterns. Each is composed of courts having general jurisdiction and courts performing specialized functions. One power exercised by our courts, both state and federal, which is not exercised by the courts of any other country is that of declaring legislation to be unconstitutional and void. This gives our courts a place of special importance in our government.

Federal Court System

The Federal Courts.   Congress established a system of federal courts having general jurisdiction, and also established courts vested with more limited and more specialized jurisdiction. The system of courts having general jurisdiction is composed of the district courts, which are courts of record having general original jurisdiction; the courts of appeals, which are intermediate courts having only appellate jurisdiction; and the U.S. Supreme Court, which is the highest judicial tribunal. The special courts are the Court of Claims, the Court of Customs and Patent Appeals, and the Customs Court.[1]

The Court of Military Appeals and the Tax Court of the United States are not true courts but are quasi-judicial agencies. Congress also established many administrative tribunals, such as the Interstate Commerce Commission, Federal Trade Commission, Federal Communications Commission, National Labor Relations Board, and Securities and Exchange Commission which, although they have some judicial powers, are not courts.

Jurisdiction of Federal Courts.   The Constitution of the United States sets out the classes of cases over which the federal government has judicial power. It empowers Congress to create federal courts and vest in them "the judicial Power of the United States." The jurisdiction vested in the courts, with the exception of the original jurisdiction of the Supreme Court, is determined by Congress.

In regard to the Supreme Court the Constitution provides: "In all Cases affecting Ambassadors, other public Ministers and Consuls, and those in which a State shall be Party, the Supreme Court shall have original Jurisdiction. In all the other Cases before mentioned, the Supreme Court shall have appellate Jurisdiction, both as to Law and Fact, with such Exceptions, and under such Regulations as the Congress shall make."

The cases over which the United States has judicial powers are set out in the Constitution as follows:

---

[1] There is some controversy as to whether the Customs Court is a true court or an administrative tribunal having broad quasi-judicial powers.

The judicial Power shall extend to all Cases, in Law and Equity, arising under this Constitution, the Laws of the United States, and Treaties made, or which shall be made, under their Authority;—to all Cases affecting Ambassadors, other public Ministers and Consuls;—to all Cases of admiralty and maritime Jurisdiction;—to Controversies to which the United States shall be a Party;—to Controversies between two or more States;—between a State and Citizens of another State;—between Citizens of different States,—between Citizens of the same State claiming Lands under Grants of different States, and between a State, or the Citizens thereof, and foreign states, Citizens or Subjects (Article III, Section 2[1]).

Congress has given the federal courts exclusive jurisdiction over some of the classes of cases falling within the judicial powers of the United States; federal courts and state courts have concurrent jurisdiction over other classes of cases; and in some areas, Congress has failed to act, and, consequently, jurisdiction over these classes of cases is left in the state courts. In some instances, Congress has conferred jurisdiction on the state courts in actions arising under particular federal statutes, such as, for example, the Wages and Hours Act and the Taft-Hartley Act.

The federal courts have *exclusive* jurisdiction over admiralty, maritime, and prize cases. They also have exclusive jurisdiction over any civil action arising under any act of Congress relating to patents, copyrights, and trademarks; any proceeding for the recovery or enforcement of a fine, penalty, or forfeiture, pecuniary or otherwise; any seizure under any law of the United States on land or upon water not within the admiralty or maritime jurisdiction; and all matters and proceedings in bankruptcy.

The federal courts and the state courts have *concurrent* jurisdiction in the broad area of general civil actions. The federal district court has original jurisdiction of all civil actions where the matter in controversy exceeds the sum or value of $10,000, exclusive of interest and costs, and where the action arises under the Constitution or treaties of the United States. It also has original jurisdiction of all civil actions where the matter in controversy exceeds the sum or value of $10,000, exclusive of interest and costs, and where the action is between (1) citizens of different states; (2) citizens of a state and a foreign state or citizen, or subject thereof; and (3) citizens of different states and in which foreign states or citizens or subjects thereof are additional parties.[2]

Since the federal courts are not given exclusive jurisdiction over these cases, the state courts will also have jurisdiction over them. In such cases the plaintiff may, if he wishes, bring his action in the state court; however, if the defendant elects to do so, he may have the case removed to the federal court. Jurisdiction of all such cases in which the amount involved does not exceed $10,000, exclusive of interest and costs, is left in the state courts.

Federal District Courts. Under the federal system the district court is the court of original jurisdiction. With the exception of a very small class of cases

---

[2] United States Code, Annotated, Title 28,§§ 1331 and 1332, as amended July 25, 1958.

involving questions reserved to the Supreme Court, all cases must be brought in the district court. It is here that suits are started, and it is here that issues of fact are determined. Each court has one or more judges, depending on the amount of business coming before the court. These courts have criminal, civil, and equity jurisdiction, and are empowered to hear certain cases against the United States if the sum involved is not over $10,000. A three-judge court is required to pass on constitutional issues.

The district courts of the District of Columbia, the Canal Zone and of the Virgin Islands have local jurisdiction approximating that of state courts. All district courts are courts of record—that is, a permanent record is made and kept of the proceedings of the court, including the testimony of the witnesses given during a trial. They also have power to fine or imprison for contempt.

Bankruptcy Court and Master in Chancery. The bankruptcy court and the master in chancery are attached to, and are a part of, the district court. Cases in bankruptcy, after adjudication by the judge of the district court, are referred to the bankruptcy court for the purpose of having the estate administered. They are then returned to the district court, where the hearing on the petition for discharge is heard. The referee in bankruptcy has judicial powers, but his acts are reviewable by the district judge. The district judge may refer matters arising in equity cases to the master in chancery for hearing. The master in chancery reports his findings back to the district judge. The district judge is relieved of much detail in receivership cases and similar cases by referring certain matters, such as hearings on claims, to the master in chancery.

U.S. Commissioners. Each district court is empowered to appoint as many U.S. commissioners as it deems advisable. Provision is also made for the appointment of one or more commissioners for each of the national parks. The commissioners are officers attached to the federal district courts who have authority to hear and certify depositions, attend to matters referred to them in civil or admiralty cases, issue attachments and subsequent hearings in internal revenue cases, conduct preliminary proceedings to hold an accused person to answer in district court, set bail for accused persons, issue search warrants, and try persons accused of petty offenses committed in national parks or petty offenses against the United States. They are appointed for a term of four years.

Court of Appeals. After a case has been tried and determined by the district court, either party has the right to appeal to the Court of Appeals. There are a few matters which may be taken directly from the district court to the Supreme Court, but in the majority of cases an appeal from the district court must be taken to the Court of Appeals. The Court of Appeals does not have original jurisdiction in any case. Each court consists of from three to nine judges, and the district judges are competent to sit as judges in their respective circuits.

Supreme Court of the United States. Appeals may be taken from the Court of Appeals to the Supreme Court; but such appeals, as a general rule, are a matter of privilege and not a matter of right. The litigant wishing to take such an appeal must petition the Supreme Court for permission to appeal. The Court of Appeals may certify a question to the Supreme Court for decision. In such instances the Supreme Court may answer the question or may call for and hear the entire case. The Supreme Court also has the right to require the Court of Appeals, and also the highest court of a state, to transmit the records of the case to it for decision where the validity of a treaty or statute of the United States or the validity of a state statute is attacked on the grounds that it is repugnant to the Constitution, treaties, or laws of the United States or where either party to a controversy claims that his federal constitutional rights have been violated. Where the highest state court has held invalid a treaty or statute of the United States, or where a statute has been attacked on the grounds that it is repugnant to the Constitution or laws of the United States and has been held valid, an appeal may be taken to the Supreme Court by its permission. The Supreme Court has original jurisdiction in cases affecting ambassadors, public ministers, and consuls of foreign countries, and in cases where a state is a party.

Court of Claims.　The Court of Claims is a court of record and has jurisdiction to render judgment upon any claim against the United States (1) founded upon the Constitution, or (2) founded upon any act of Congress, or (3) founded upon any regulation of the executive department, or (4) founded upon any express or implied contract with the United States, or (5) for liquidated or unliquidated damages in cases not sounding in tort.[3] It also has jurisdiction over claims arising under the Contract Settlement Act of 1944 and over other special cases in which the United States is a party. It does not have jurisdiction over any claim for a pension or any claims growing out of treaties with foreign nations.

The district courts have concurrent jurisdiction with the Court of Claims over general claims against the United States if the amount involved does not exceed $10,000.

A bench of a chief judge and four associate judges constitutes the Court of Claims. Appeals from the Court of Claims are heard by the U.S. Supreme Court.

Court of Customs and Patent Appeals.　The Court of Customs and Patent Appeals is composed of a chief judge and four associate judges. It is a court of record. It is primarily an appellate court having jurisdiction over appeals from the decisions of the Customs Court, of the Board of Appeals (a board which rules on objections to decisions made by the Patent Office), of the Board of Interference, and of the Examiners of the Patent Office, and from decisions of the Commissioners of Patents as to trademark applications and proceedings. On appeal, it has jurisdiction to review, on questions of law only, the findings of the U.S. Tariff Commission as to unfair practices in import trade.

---

[3] United States Code, Annotated, Title 28, § 1491.

Appeals may be taken from the Court of Customs and Patent Appeals to the U.S. Supreme Court.

Customs Court. The U.S. Customs Court is composed of nine judges. Its office is located in the port of New York. It has exclusive jurisdiction of appeals for reappraisement, of applications for review of reappraisement of imported merchandise, and of petitions for remission of additional duties filed under the customs laws. It also has jurisdiction to review or protest the decisions of collectors of customs.

Appeals are taken from the decisions of the Customs Court to the Court of Customs and Patent Appeals.

Summary

In the United States we have 51 separate court systems—the federal system and the 50 state systems. The federal court system is made up of the Supreme Court of the United States provided for in the Constitution of the United States and inferior courts created by Congress. The jurisdiction of the federal courts is set out in the Constitution and in general they have jurisdiction over cases directly affecting the federal government, over matters which are interstate in character, and over cases between citizens of different states or of a state and a foreign country provided the amount involved exceeds the sum or value of $10,000, exclusive of interest and costs. The regular courts of the federal system are the federal district court, the Court of Appeals, and the Supreme Court of the United States. The bankruptcy court, the master in chancery, and the U.S. commissioners are special branches of the district court.

Litigants may, as a matter of right, appeal a case from the district court to the Court of Appeals which has only appellate jurisdiction. Appeals to the Supreme Court are by permission of the court. The Supreme Court has original jurisdiction in cases affecting ambassadors, public ministers, consuls of foreign countries, and cases in which a state is a party.

The Court of Claims was created to hear claims against the United States and in 1944 was given jurisdiction over claims arising under the Contract Settlement Act. The Court of Customs and Patent Appeals and the Customs Court are courts having limited jurisdiction as to subject matter—custom and patent cases. A number of administrative agencies have been created which have quasi-judicial powers.

State Court Systems

Introduction. The court systems of the several states are fundamentally the same, but they vary widely in the details of their organization. All the states have inferior courts, such as the justice of the peace courts, police courts, traffic courts, and small claims courts, and these are not courts of record. All the states have courts of record having general original jurisdiction. The functions of the courts of record having original jurisdiction may be vested in one court or may be distributed among various courts, such as (1) courts of law, (2) courts of equity, (3) criminal courts, and (4) probate courts. Where the jurisdiction of all types of cases is vested in one court, a separation of the various types of cases is, as a general rule, recognized within the court by the keeping of separate dockets and separate calendars, although the same judge may preside over all types of cases. For example, law cases are entered in the law docket and are placed for trial on the law calendar; equity cases are entered in the equity docket and are placed for trial on the equity calendar; and this same procedure is followed for criminal and probate cases or for whatever divisions may be made. All the states have courts of appeals. Most states have courts of intermediate appeals and courts of final appeals, but some states have only one Court of Appeals. All the states have special courts with limited jurisdiction either as to subject matter or as to territorial jurisdiction or as to both.

Jurisdiction of State Courts. The states have general jurisdiction over controversies arising between the citizens of the state. They have jurisdiction over all controversies involving the title to land, other than federally owned land, which is within their borders, and they have jurisdiction over all crimes committed within the state, except crimes against the federal government. The various courts of the state system have whatever jurisdiction is conferred on them by the constitution and statutes of the state.

Inferior Courts. The justice court, presided over by a justice of the peace and having a limited jurisdiction as to amount, territory, and subject matter, is at the base of most state systems. These courts, as a general rule, are established, and their jurisdiction is defined by statute; and so, although the part they play in the court systems of the various states is similar, they differ widely as to the details of their jurisdiction and methods of procedure.

In some states the justice of the peace need not be learned in the law, whereas in others he must be a member of the bar. He is appointed or elected by popular vote, has jurisdiction over petty criminal matters, can hold preliminary hearings in graver offenses and commit the accused, and in civil matters can hear controversies arising out of contract where the amount involved does not exceed a set limit. (This limit varies from $50 to $1,000.) In some states the justice has jurisdiction over tort cases where the damages claimed do not exceed a set amount. His territorial jurisdiction seldom exceeds the county and more often is confined to the township, city, or ward. He has no equity jurisdiction and cannot determine questions of title to land. No formal pleadings are required, and no record of testimony or proceedings is made. A record is kept of judgments rendered; executions, garnishments, etc., issued;

and payments made into court. An appeal may be taken from the justice court to the circuit court where the case is tried *de novo*. (This means the whole case is tried over again.)

Special inferior courts, not courts of record, generally have limited jurisdiction both as to subject matter and as to territory. As a general rule a police court has jurisdiction over minor crimes committed within a city. In some states a mayor's court handles the minor criminal cases. Many states have traffic courts which do little more than accept the payment of statutory or predetermined fines if the accused admits his guilt, or bind the accused over to the police or mayor's court if the accused denies his guilt.

Small claims courts, which have jurisdiction over controversies between individuals in which small sums are involved, have been established by some of the more populous states. The procedure in these courts is very informal. As a general rule the parties handle their own cases without the aid of an attorney. In some of these special inferior courts, judges must be members of the bar in good standing, whereas in others, especially in mayors' courts, the judge need not be a member of the bar. As a general rule an appeal may be taken from one of these inferior courts to a court of record of general jurisdiction, and the whole case will be tried over again.

Courts of Record.   The courts of record having general jurisdiction are the courts of original jurisdiction, frequently called "trial courts," and they handle the great majority of the cases disposed of by the courts of the country. In courts of record, written pleadings are required, and a record of the proceedings of the court is kept. In these courts the original trial of the case is conducted, the witnesses are heard, the facts of the case are determined, and judgment is entered. These courts are known as circuit, superior, district, or county courts. In New York state, they are called "supreme courts." As a general rule, they have territorial jurisdiction over a county and are not limited as to their jurisdiction of subject matter or as to the amount involved in the case. Usually, however, there is a lower limit as to the amount of damages claimed in tort and contract cases. For example, in some states, if the damages claimed are $50 or less, the case must be brought in one of the inferior courts.

In the more populous areas, special courts are established to handle particular types of cases. The jurisdiction of such courts is set out in the statutes creating the courts. As a general rule these courts have concurrent jurisdiction with the courts of general jurisdiction, and appeals are allowed from these special courts to the higher courts of appeals on the same grounds and under the same rules as govern appeals from the courts of general jurisdiction.

Courts of Appeal.   Three systems of higher courts of appeals have been adopted by the various states. In some states, there is only one court having general appellate jurisdiction. All appeals are taken from the court of original jurisdiction to the Court of Appeals, usually called the "supreme court"; and its decision is final unless the questions to be decided are such that the case may be carried to the U.S. Supreme Court. Other states have two courts having appellate jurisdiction. Under some state systems, one of the courts of appeals, usually called the "appellate court," is a court of intermediate jurisdiction; that is, an appeal from the court of original jurisdiction is taken to the appellate court, and after the matter has been passed on by this court, an appeal may be taken to the higher court of appeals, usually called the "supreme court." The federal system follows this plan. In other states having two courts of appellate jurisdiction, each court is a court of final appeal but is given jurisdiction over certain classes of appeal cases. Even though both courts have final jurisdiction, one court is considered inferior to the other. The one considered as inferior is given jurisdiction over cases of lesser importance, and its decisions are often subject to review by the superior court. Excepting the few questions which may be appealed to the U.S. Supreme Court, the decision of the highest state court of appeals is final.

The function of a Court of Appeals is to review the work of the trial court. To be granted an appeal, a party who is discontented with the judgment of the trial court, the appellant, must allege that an error of law was made during the course of the trial. Such an error might be an erroneous ruling on a motion or an incorrect statement of the law made in an instruction to the jury. The Court of Appeals reviews the record of the case, reads the briefs, hears the arguments of the attorneys for the parties to the suit, and decides the issues raised on the appeal. If no material error has been committed, the judgment of the trial court will be affirmed. If material error has been committed, the Court of Appeals may grant a judgment for the appellant, thus disposing of the case; or it may set aside the judgment of the lower court and send the case back for retrial, that is, the case is reversed and remanded or, as stated by some courts, reversed and a new trial ordered. In some instances the judgment of the lower court may be affirmed in part and reversed in part. If the case is an equity case, the Court of Appeals may modify the decree of the trial court, may set it aside and order a new trial, or may affirm it.

Summary

The court systems of the different states are composed of courts of general jurisdiction and special courts. Generally, in these state court systems there are inferior courts which are not courts of record and which have jurisdiction over minor criminal matters and over civil cases in which only a limited amount is involved. The principal court of the state systems is the court of record of original jurisdiction. It is called the circuit court in some states, the district court in other states, the supreme court in New York, and by other names in a few of the states. All the states have special courts. The jurisdictions of these special courts are defined by the statutes creating them. There is a wide variety of special courts, such as criminal courts, equity courts, probate courts, juvenile courts, superior courts, small claims courts. Some states have intermediate courts of appeals and a court of final appeals, whereas others have only one Court of Appeals. As a general rule, appeals may be taken from the judgments of all courts of record to the Court of Appeals. The statutes of the state will define the procedure to be followed in taking an appeal and will state the jurisdiction of the Courts of Appeals.

Administrative Agencies

Their Growth. In 1952 Mr. Justice Jackson asserted,

The rule of administrative bodies probably has been the most significant legal trend of the last century and perhaps more values today are affected by their decisions than by those of all the courts, review of administrative decisions apart.[4]

Starting with the predecessor to the Veterans Administration in 1789, the number and size of the administrative agencies established by acts of Congress have increased steadily. By 1930 nearly two thirds of all of the federal agencies now in existence were in operation, although some of those with which businessmen are most frequently involved, such as the National Labor Relations Board (NLRB) and the Securities and Exchange Commission (SEC), were not established until a few years later. The Interstate Commerce Commission (ICC), which was established in 1887, and became the model for many of those established later, and the Federal Trade Commission (FTC) are other federal administrative agencies whose rule making and quasi-judicial decision making frequently affect businessmen. States too have many administrative agencies regulating business activity such as commerce and industrial commissions which regulate transportation agencies and utilities, promote industrial safety and make compensation awards for industrial accidents.

By combining the power to adjudicate with powers to initiate proceedings, investigate, prosecute, and issue regulations having the force of law, several advantages could be gained. First, by specializing only in certain areas administrators gained expertise. Second, less-cumbersome procedures and rules could be developed and many determinations could be made by clerks rather than judges. Third, policy and rule making could be carried out on a continuous basis rather than case by case.

The major danger of the administrative agency approach to rule making and enforcement rests in the fact that it combines legislative, prosecutive and adjudicative functions within one agency, which gives the agency an enormous amount of power. The Administrative Procedures Act of 1946 was enacted to

---

[4] *FTC* v. *Ruberoid Co.,* 343 U.S. 470, 487 (1952).

require agencies to follow fair procedures and to afford better protection of the rights of persons appearing before them.

Summary

An administrative tribunal is an agency, outside the court system, having broad judicial powers. It is created by statute. An administrative tribunal may carry out investigating, prosecuting, and adjudicating functions. In all cases, a party against whom an administrative tribunal has proceeded has the right to appeal. The scope of the appeal depends on the provisions of the statute creating the administrative tribunal or agency. Administrative agencies are capable of specialization and can adopt flexible and economical methods of regulation.

Procedure

The Adversary System. Disputes are settled by courts under what is known as the adversary system. In this system the judge's role is viewed not only as unbiased but also as essentially passive.

It is up to the party who claims to have been injured or otherwise wronged to prove in court both that the facts he relies upon actually occurred and that the law entitles him to a recovery. The other party seeks to disprove one or both of these claims. It is the lawyer's job to present his client's version of the facts, to convince the judge (or jury if one is used) that they are true and to undermine confidence in the other party's allegations to the extent they are inconsistent. Each lawyer seeks to persuade the judge that his interpretation of the law applicable to the case is the correct one and he proposes jury instructions which state the law in the light most favorable to his client's case. If there is no jury the lawyer seeks to present the judge with a line of reasoning which, if accepted, will result in a decision favoring the lawyer's client. It is believed that this competition between counsel in presenting their competing versions of the facts and conceptions of the law will result in the judge, or jury, sorting out the true facts and the judge finding the soundest view of the law. Proponents believe that the principal advantage of the adversary system rests in the fact that it limits the role and power of judges. The facts and issues are developed by the competing parties and the system makes it difficult for a judge to control the outcome of the case.

However, the judge does not have to be entirely passive. He is responsible for the correct application of the law and he may ignore the legal reasoning of both of the opposing attorneys and base his rulings and decisions wholly on his own study of the law. Also, he may ask questions of witnesses and suggest types of evidence he would like to have presented. In certain types of disputes, especially in domestic relations matters, judges assume much more of the initiative and may even change character completely and engage in attempts at mediation.

The Functions of Procedure.   There is a large body of law which establishes the rules and standards for determining disputes in the courts. Much of this law is complex and technical. However, knowledge of some of the basic principles of the law of procedure is necessary if the student is to understand the reports of cases included in this text and for a businessman if he is to be able to cooperate effectively with his lawyer if he becomes a party to a legal controversy.

The law of procedure varies in different jurisdictions and in different types of cases. For example, the procedure followed in a criminal case is somewhat different from that applicable to a civil case. Equity, probate, and admiralty cases have still different rules. Since businessmen are most frequently involved in civil cases only civil procedure will be discussed.

Summons, Complaint, and Answer.   When suit is brought against a person, he is entitled to notice of the suit and must be given an opportunity to defend himself. In most jurisdictions the issuing and serving of a summons is the first step taken in the starting of a civil lawsuit. The summons is a writ of process which bears the seal of the court issuing it, and which notifies the defendant that suit has been started against him by the named plaintiff. The form of the summons in general use states briefly the nature of the suit, the time within which the defendant must enter his appearance, if he wishes to defend, or the day and the time of day when he must appear in court.

The rules relative to the service of the summons vary widely. At common law and generally in civil law cases the summons is served on the defendant personally by the sheriff or one of his deputies within the territorial limits of the court's jurisdiction. For instance, a summons issued out of a circuit or district court having jurisdiction over a county would have to be served on the defendant within the boundaries of that county. In some states the summons may be left at the defendant's residence or place of business; and in a few states, service may be made by mail. Other rules relative to service apply in cases such as divorce suits or suits to quiet title to land.

In order that the defendant may know the claims of the plaintiff and be prepared to defend against those claims, the plaintiff is required to file a complaint (also called a "declaration" or a "petition"). Under the rules generally in force, the plaintiff's complaint must state in separate, numbered paragraphs the plaintiff's claim in full. Any matter omitted from the complaint is not a part of the plaintiff's case; and evidence, in the case of trial, is not admissible to prove material facts not stated in the complaint. The complaint will also state the remedy requested by the plaintiff. In a civil law case the remedy requested is usually a stated sum of money as damages. It is of the utmost importance that the plaintiff state all the facts of his case to his attorney, since the omission of material facts from the complaint may be fatal to the plaintiff's case.

If the defendant wishes to defend, he must, within the permitted time, file his answer. It answers the plaintiff's complaint; paragraph by paragraph, either admitting or denying the matters stated in the paragraph or neither admitting nor denying the matters stated but leaving the plaintiff to his proof. The defendant may, in addition, state an affirmative defense to the plaintiff's case. For example, suppose the plaintiff bases his suit on a contract. The defendant may admit the contract but set up, by way of affirmative defense, facts which, if established, would prove that the defendant was induced to enter into the contract by fraudulent representations made by the plaintiff and therefore was not bound by the contract.

If the defendant sets up an affirmative defense, he must state the facts of the defense in the same form as that required of the plaintiff in his complaint, and the plaintiff must make an answer (called a "reply") to the defendant's statements in the same form as that required in the defendant's answer to the plaintiff's complaint.

The complaint and answer (called "pleadings") serve a twofold purpose: They inform the parties of their relative claims, and they form the basis for the trial of the case. Only those points which are matters in dispute or issues in the case will be considered on the trial of the case. Points which are not stated in the pleadings and points admitted in the pleadings are not issues in in the case, and no evidence will be admitted to prove such points. If a material point has been omitted from the pleadings, the trial judge may, after proper motion has been made, permit an amendment of the pleadings and allow the omitted matter to be added.

Demurrers. If the defendant's attorney, on reading the complaint, believes that the plaintiff has not stated facts which would entitle him to a judgment, he will file a demurrer instead of an answer. The demurrer is used for the purpose of testing the sufficiency of the complaint. If the defendant's attorney files a demurrer, a time will be set for a hearing before the judge, and at this time the attorneys for the plaintiff and defendant will argue the question of the sufficiency of the complaint. If the judge finds at this hearing that the complaint is insufficient (does not state a cause of action), the plaintiff's attorney will be given an opportunity to amend the complaint; but if the facts of the plaintiff's case do not warrant the granting of the remedy asked, the demurrer will be sustained, that is, the case will be dismissed without further proceedings.

Under federal rules demurrers are replaced with motions to dismiss. The opportunity to amend is at the judge's discretion.

Pretrial Hearing. A comparatively recent innovation is the pretrial hearing, which may be used in the federal courts and in the trial courts of some states. The purpose of the pretrial hearing is to dispose of a controversy without a formal trial or to reduce issues to bare essentials, to save trial court time. In such a hearing the attorneys representing the parties meet with the judge who will hear the case if it goes to trial and discuss with him the facts of the case as stated in the pleadings together with facts known to the attorneys.

During the discussion the judge will ask questions which will help to clarify the points in issue, and he may suggest a basis on which the case might be settled. An attorney in such a case does not, as a general rule, have the authority to bind his client to a settlement agreement; consequently, any proposed settlement worked out will have to be submitted by each attorney to his client. If such proposal is acceptable to both litigants, the case will be disposed of without formal trial; otherwise, the case will be tried.

Trial of Case.   When the pleadings are complete and the issue thereby determined, the case will be set for trial. The parties will decide whether or not they wish a trial by jury, unless the case is to be tried in equity, in which case a jury, as a general rule, will not be used. If a jury is desired, it must then be selected and sworn in, after which the attorneys will usually make statements to it, outlining the claims their clients make in regard to the controversy. The witnesses for the plaintiff will then be sworn, examined, and cross-examined. When all the evidence of the plaintiff has been presented, his attorney will so indicate, and the attorney for the defendant will take charge.

At this point the defendant's attorney may make a motion asking the judge to direct a judgment for the defendant. If the judge decides that the plaintiff has offered no evidence which would justify the granting of the remedy requested, he will grant the motion, and the trial will end at this point. However, if the judge feels that the plaintiff has offered any evidence which would support a judgment, he will deny the motion, and the trial will continue.

The defendant's witnesses will then be sworn and examined on direct examination by the defendant's attorney and cross-examined by the plaintiff's attorney. When all the testimony of the witnesses has been heard, the case is ready to be presented to the jury. At this point in the trial, either the defendant's attorney or the plaintiff's attorney, or both, may make a motion for a directed verdict. If both attorneys make motions for a directed verdict, the case will not, under the rules of procedure generally followed, be presented to the jury but will be decided by the judge. If only one motion for a directed verdict is made, the judge will deny the motion unless he feels that no credible evidence has been offered which would justify the jury in finding for the other party. If no motion for a directed verdict is made, or if such motion is made and denied, the case will be presented to the jury for its consideration.

The attorneys will sum up the case and give their arguments to the jury, after which the judge will instruct the jury as to the law which applies in the case. In his instructions the judge must not, under the laws of most states, comment on the weight of the evidence or credibility of the witnesses; he must confine himself to expounding the rules of law which the jury should apply in reaching its verdict.

Where the amount of the plaintiff's loss is in dispute, the jury not only finds for one of the parties but if it finds for the plaintiff, its verdict will state the amount of the recovery. The attorney for the losing party may make a motion for a judgment notwithstanding the verdict. If the judge finds no competent evidence to support the verdict, or decides that the law requires the opposite result, he will grant the motion; otherwise it will be denied.

If the verdict is not set aside, the judge will enter a judgment based on the verdict. The defeated party may make a motion for a new trial. This gives the trial judge an opportunity to correct material errors which may have been made during the trial; however, such motions are usually denied. If the unsuccessful party thinks a material error was committed during the trial, he may appeal the case.

If there is no jury the judge is the finder of facts and he enters his judgment in the record. His findings of fact will be accepted by an appeal court on the same basis as those of a jury, that is unless the appeal court finds no competent evidence supporting a finding of fact.

Procedure in Administrative Agencies. The procedure followed in administrative agencies is more informal than that followed in the courts. In general, the members of the agency investigate suspected and reported violations of the regulatory law over which agency has jurisdiction. If the members of the agency decide that there has been a violation, the accused will be prosecuted. The hearing is held before the members of the agency, who are invested with quasi-judicial powers, and who will impose sanctions if the accused is found guilty. The accused does have the right to appeal to the courts; but under the terms of the act creating the agency, this right is limited. In general, no appeal is allowed if the decision involves only the discretionary powers of the persons rendering the decision. However, the court will, as a general rule, hear and determine an appeal if it is based on the ground that the person making the decision acted capriciously or was guilty of discrimination, or that the subject matter of the case was not within the scope of the powers vested in the agency.

Summary

The rules and standards of procedure are complex and technical and are primarily within the province of the attorney. A knowledge of the basic principles of procedure will enable the businessman to cooperate with his attorney in the event he is sued or brings a suit.

Although the procedure followed in the several states is not uniform, there are certain basic practices followed by all states. The party defendant is notified that suit has been brought against him, usually by serving him with a summons. The next step is the preparation and filing of the complaint (also called a "declaration" or a "petition") which sets out in numbered paragraphs the facts on which the plaintiff bases his claim for a remedy.

If the defendant wishes to defend the suit he must file an answer to the plaintiff's complaint in which he answers the statements in the plaintiff's complaint. He may add special facts on which he bases his defense. If the facts stated in the plaintiff's complaint, even though they could be proved, would not be adequate to justify the granting of the remedy asked, the defendant may file a demurrer which if sustained ends the case. Motions to dismiss have replaced demurrers under federal rules.

A recent practice is to hold pretrial hearings in which the attorneys for the parties and the judge who will hear the case explore the facts and attempt to arrive at an out-of-court settlement.

On the trial of a case, the plaintiff's witnesses are sworn and examined first, then the defendant's witnesses are sworn and they testify. Rebuttal witnesses may testify but no new facts can be introduced on rebuttal. When all the witnesses have been heard, the lawyers argue the case, the judge charges the jury, and it then deliberates the case in secret and brings in a verdict. The judgment is entered by the judge. The judge has the power to set a verdict aside on proper motion provided no credible evidence has been offered which supports the verdict.

Arbitration

Nature of Arbitration. Arbitration is a method of settling controversies without resorting to the ordinary processes of law. The arbitration of disputes has been practiced from the earliest times, and some method of arbitration of disputes is known in nearly every country. We have evidence that disputes were arbitrated in England as early as 1224. In 1609, Lord Coke, in his decision in *Vynior's* case, stated that an agreement to arbitrate could be countermanded by either party to the agreement. Although the statement was not binding in that case, it was accepted by the English courts as law; and thereafter, either party to an arbitration could withdraw at any time before the award.

Arbitration Statutes. In the United States, arbitration statutes making agreements to arbitrate irrevocable have been adopted by over one half of the states and by the federal government. These statutes may be divided into two general classes: (1) statutes making agreements to arbitrate existing disputes irrevocable and (2) statutes making agreements to arbitrate future disputes as well as existing disputes irrevocable. The latter type of statutes are alike in their general provisions. They provide that the agreement shall constitute a defense to an action at law or in equity, that the court may appoint arbitrators if they are not named in the agreement to arbitrate, that the parties may be compelled to carry out their agreement to arbitrate, and that the courts shall enforce the awards. It is only in the event that a party refuses to fulfill his agreement to arbitrate or refuses to abide by the award that it is necessary to resort to the courts.

In a state having the latter type of statute, if either party, after entering into an agreement to arbitrate, brings suit at law or in equity, the suit will be dismissed on proof of the agreement. When arbitrators are not named in the agreement and the parties cannot agree or one of the parties refuses to act, the judge will, on application by the party to the court, appoint an arbitrator. If one of the parties refuses to participate in the arbitration, the aggrieved party notifies the other party to the agreement of the time and place of the hearing. If the other party does not appear and offer his evidence, the aggrieved party proceeds with his case, and an award is made by the arbitrator.

When an award is made and the losing party does not abide by the award, the winning party may apply to the court for an order confirming the award, and the court must grant such order, unless the award is vacated, modified, or corrected. Upon the granting of the order confirming the award, judgment is entered. The courts may vacate the award on a showing that it was procured by corruption, fraud, or other undue means.

Procedure in Arbitration. There is no set procedure which must be followed in an arbitration. The parties may adopt any procedure they wish; however, there must be some organization to the procedure if the arbitration is to prove successful. Trade associations and similar organizations have adopted rules for procedure in arbitrations which are followed by their members. In the United States the American Arbitration Association has encouraged the use of arbitration for the settlement of disputes and has set up an organization and compiled rules to aid in the arbitration of disputes.[5] This service is now used extensively throughout the United States.

The procedure recommended by the American Arbitration Association is as follows. When a claim arises under a contract containing an arbitration clause, the claimant gives written notice to the other party of his intention to arbitrate. The notice must set forth the nature of the dispute, the amount involved, if any, and the remedy sought. The parties may name the arbitrator or arbitrators, or may provide for their selection in the agreement. Under the rules of the American Arbitration Association a panel of arbitrators is sub-

---

[5] The American Arbitration Association is a voluntary group, operating under New York charter on a nonprofit basis, which maintains and administers "arbitration machinery" in over 1,500 cities serving practically every trading area in the United States.

mitted to the parties, and each party strikes from the panel the names of persons whom he does not wish to act and numbers the remaining names in order of his preference. The name having the lowest combined numbering is selected as arbitrator. For example, if one party numbers the name Smith "1," Wells "3," and Lewis "6," and the other party numbers the name Smith "6," Wells "2," and Lewis "1," Smith's total would be 7, Wells's total would be 5, and Lewis' total would be 7. Wells would be selected as arbitrator, since he has the lowest total.

The time and place of the hearing are determined by the parties. This is one of the advantages of arbitration. The parties can select the place which is most convenient for all participants and can hold the hearing at such time as they wish. They do not have to wait for a courtroom, nor do they have to await their turn on a crowded court calendar.

Evidence in Arbitration.   The evidence in the case is presented in an orderly manner, but the technical rules of evidence do not apply to the admissibility of evidence. The parties may call witnesses, submit letters and other documentary evidence, and use any type of exhibit they wish. The hearing is informal and is intended to be carried on in a friendly spirit. The objective of the hearing is to acquaint the arbitrator with all the facts of the case. If the parties wish, they may present their case in writing instead of orally.

The Award.   When the evidence has been presented, the arbitrator makes his award. The award is in the nature of a judgment. The arbitrator in his award may grant any remedy or relief which he deems just and equitable, provided the remedy or relief granted is within the scope of the agreement of the parties. The arbitrator in his award may assess the arbitration fees and expenses in favor of any party.

Summary

Arbitration is a method of settling disputes without resorting to the ordinary processes of law. At common law, an agreement to arbitrate disputes which might arise during the performance of a contract was held to be illegal. At the present time, most of the states have statutes making agreements to arbitrate future disputes legal. Many of the arbitration statutes also provide some aid in enforcing the award.

There is no set procedure which must be followed in an arbitration. The procedure recommended by the American Arbitration Association is followed in many arbitrations.

The rules of evidence which apply in the trial court cases are not applied in arbitration cases, but the evidence is presented in an orderly manner. When all of the evidence has been presented, the arbitrator makes his award, which is in the nature of a judgment.

The Legal Profession

Various Roles of the Lawyer. Although lawyers tend to be stereotyped as advocates who do battle in the courtroom, this is only one of several functions performed by lawyers for their clients. They also at various times serve as negotiators, as draftsmen, as investigators, as mediators or conciliators, and even as arbitrators. However, today most lawyers, especially those who serve businessmen, spend most of their time as counselors.

Preventive Law. In earlier times businessmen tended to call in a lawyer only in an emergency. When some event occurred such as the receipt of a summons or the default of a debtor, or when a supplier would not make good his warranty, the lawyer went to court to defend or assert the legal rights of his businessman client. Today businessmen employ lawyers primarily for counsel in advance of taking business action, rather than to rescue them afterwards from unexpected results. This new use of lawyers, for what is called preventive law practice, utilizes the lawyer's professional skills to manage the businessman's actions and the events in which he is involved so that their legal consequences will be favorable. This is because business activity is now subject to a myriad of statutes and regulations of administrative agencies. Also, as we shall see in the next chapters, the growth of the common law of tort has imposed increasing burdens upon businessmen. To avoid legal pitfalls, the businessman needs guidance from a lawyer in many of his everyday actions, such as in the pricing of his product, the buying and selling of securities, and in dealing with his employees as well in less-frequent transactions such as real estate or special equipment purchases.

Specialization. The law not only has become very complex but it is undergoing constant change. Therefore, no one individual can be up to date on the whole of the law. He can master only narrow areas of it. As a result there is a strong trend toward specialization of lawyers, although members of the profession have tended to think of themselves as generalists and to resist the trend. However, today even in small towns only a few of the practicing members of the bar conduct trials, one or two probably check the majority of the titles in real estate transactions and one or two do most of the tax work. In order to gain the advantages of individual specialization and mutual consultation as well as sharing the costs of an adequate law library and a competent clerical staff, lawyers are tending to enter partnerships with a number of other lawyers instead of practicing solo or in two-man partnerships, as was once typical of the profession.

The larger business corporations tend to employ the larger law firms because specialization, and hence often expertise, is greater but, nevertheless, a continuing personal relationship can be maintained with one partner who becomes intimately acquainted with the corporation's business and business practices. He then marshalls the appropriate expertise in the law firm to deal with specific legal problems of the corporation. Since legal opinion or a lawsuit is no better than the facts upon which it is based, this close and continuing association between the lawyer and the client may be as important as legal expertise in gaining highly competent legal service.

The advantages of such a close relationship and easy accessibility between lawyers and business executives is the reason for the rapid growth in the last two decades of another form of specialization—the corporate law department. The corporate counsel, a salaried lawyer who is an employee of the corporation, specializes in the legal affairs of a single client. The very large corporations often have law departments which function much like a large law firm, and a few employ as many as 100 lawyers.

A Good Client.   Good legal advice is the product of knowledge of the pertinent legal principles and decisions and knowledge of the relevant facts about the contemplated business action. Since the businessman usually has a better knowledge of or access to the relevant facts about the business, his cooperation with the lawyer is usually essential not only in carrying out but also in developing the advice of the lawyer. A recent study involving extensive interviews with corporate counsel and business executives by one of the authors identified four criteria for a client who is able to cooperate effectively with his lawyer.

The first criterion is that the client makes timely requests for legal advice. The lawyer may need time for legal research, for reflection and for consultation with his colleagues before he can do his best in practicing preventive law with respect to a contemplated business action. Often he can point out unrecognized legal pitfalls and find paths around them if he is kept generally informed well in advance of his client's business plans.

The second criterion is that the client discloses all pertinent facts to counsel. Since legal ethics pledge the lawyer to keep confidences and good advice is dependent upon knowledge of all legally significant facts, full disclosure by the client is essential if the legal counsel is to be sound.

Thirdly, the client has some understanding of the legal process, the lawyer's function, and the law pertinent to his business. Much time of both parties can be saved when the client has enough familiarity with the law to recognize what facts are legally significant. He can then make sure the lawyer is aware of those facts and avoid emphasizing matters that may be important to him but which will not help the lawyer identify or solve his legal problem. The study of business law should contribute to this understanding.

The fourth criterion is that the client demands high-quality legal service. A conscientious lawyer's main goal is to assist his client in attaining his business objectives. The client who accepts and follows unquestioningly legal advice that he doesn't understand and which he thinks impedes his business is foolish and does his counsel no favor. The advice may be due to lack of understanding or misunderstanding of business practices or other facts. Equally foolish is the client who believes that his lawyer is incompetent because he cannot find a legal way to accomplish his client's objective.

Summary

Many businessmen now take the preventive law approach and consult with counsel before taking action. Law is now so complex that specialization is required in many areas. To be a good client means: making timely requests for legal advice; full disclosure to counsel; some understanding of the law and the legal process; and demanding high-quality legal service.

Questions

1. Explain the two distinct grounds upon which civil suits originate in a federal district court.
2. May private citizens always have their cases heard by the U.S. Supreme Court?
3. What are some of the reasons for the growth of administrative agencies?
4. What are the major differences between trial courts and courts of appeal?
5. What is the adversary system in our law?
6. What is the main function of pleading?

PART II *Torts*

chapter 3. Crimes and Intentional Torts

Crimes

Introduction. A crime may be defined to be any act done by an individual which is considered a wrong by society and for the commission of which the law has provided that the wrongdoer shall make satisfaction to the public. This raises the question of what is a wrong. Acts which seriously disturbed the social equilibrium were defined as crimes as the common law evolved. Today our criminal law has been codified; consequently the elements of various crimes are defined in statutes.

The term "wrong" as used in its popular sense includes violation of moral or ethical standards, failure to perform social duties imposed by the group of which the individual is a member, and many other acts. However, under the legal definition of crime, such conduct is not necessarily classed as criminal. It is not criminal unless it is condemned by law and unless the wrongdoer is subject to punishment imposed by the state, in which case the state will bring an action in its own name against the wrongdoer. One of the problems confronting modern society is where to draw the line between conduct which will be punished as crime and conduct which will be merely condemned as a breach of a social duty.

Nature of Crime. What conduct will be held to be criminal and punishable as such will depend on the attitude of the particular society at a given time. Almost all societies have considered treason, murder, theft, and certain sex offenses as crimes; however, the nature and severity of the penalty imposed for the commission of these crimes has varied from country to country and from time to time. At one time in England, and in some countries today, any expression of disagreement with the policies of the rulers of the country was treason; and in England prior to the reform of the criminal law, the death penalty was imposed as punishment for substantially all crimes. During the early colonial period here in America, blasphemy and witchcraft were punished as crimes.

Every major social development has been accompanied by criminal statutes defining certain conduct as criminal. And as a general rule, there is a tendency on the part of some groups to feel that the legislation is not justified, that it discriminates against them, and that no wrong is committed if they violate the statute.

Relationship Involved. In the area of criminal law the relationship involved is that of the individual and the society of which he is a member. Society is represented by the organized government, and in the event the individual is accused of criminal conduct, the action brought against him will be brought by the state.

In the United States, criminal law is recognized as a separate division of the law. The rules of procedure followed in the trial of criminal cases differ in important respects from those followed in the trial of civil cases. For example, in criminal cases the accused is presumed to be innocent, and his guilt must be proven by the state beyond a reasonable doubt. Also, if the verdict of the jury in a criminal case is "not guilty," the state cannot appeal. All criminal cases are brought in the name of the state, as, for instance, *"State* v. *John Brown,"* or *"United States* v. *John Brown"* in the event the crime is punishable by the federal government.

In civil cases the action is brought by one individual in the society against another. There is no question of guilt involved. The only consideration is whether one party has invaded the rights of another under circumstances which justify the state in using its power to protect the rights of the injured party.

There is no presumption in favor of either party; and the party plaintiff, if he is to recover, must prove by a preponderance of the evidence—not beyond a reasonable doubt—that the defendant did wrongfully invade his (the plaintiff's) rights and that the plaintiff was injured thereby. The plaintiff must establish his right to the remedy asked. The remedy granted will be in the nature of compensation to the plaintiff, not as punishment of the defendant, except in some states punitive damages are allowed in some types of tort cases.

Scope of Criminal Law. The crime control problem is one of the most difficult and important tasks faced by society. In its broadest aspects, it transcends the law, but it is the function of the legislature and the courts to deal with the criminal on a down-to-earth, practical level. In the United States, we have an established system of criminal administration which includes the police, prosecutors, administrators of the prisons, and parole boards, together with the legislators and the courts. Too often, the courts and the personnel of the courts are criticized for failures in the administration of criminal justice when they are in no way responsible for such failures.

In the area of crime, it is the function of the legislature to define the criminal act and to state the punishment to be imposed on those guilty of the commission of such act. It is the function of the court to determine whether or not the accused is guilty and, if so, to impose the penalty set out in the criminal statute. In performing this function, the court must interpret the criminal statute, determine its scope, and decide whether or not the crime of which the party is accused comes within the provisions of the statute. It is the function of the prosecutor to investigate the case, prepare the indictment, and present the facts to the court. The failure of those performing the police function to obtain evidence, an error on the part of the prosecutor in the preparation of the indictment, or an unconvincing manner in the presentation of the facts of the case may result in the guilty party's escaping conviction.

Essentials of a Crime. At common law, two elements were considered essential to criminal liability: the criminal act accompanied by criminal intent (*mens rea*). Today, as a general rule, those acts which are declared to be crimes will be defined by the criminal statutes. Establishing the fact that a criminal act has been committed is, in most criminal cases, a relatively simple matter. Also, the identity of the person or persons who are guilty of performing the criminal act may be established with a reasonable degree of certainty by direct evidence. However, the accompanying criminal intent cannot be established by direct evidence. Intent is a state of mind.

We require the proof of criminal intent as a means of distinguishing between inevitable accident, for which those involved should not be held criminally liable, and willful conduct, in which case those involved should be held responsible. No means has as yet been devised whereby we can prove the state of a person's mind at any given time; consequently, intent is not a question of the state of the actor's mind at the time he acted.

Intent is established through the use of legal standards, and the standard applied is that of the "ordinary man." That is, what would one be justified in assuming that an ordinary man would have intended if he had been in the position of the accused and had acted as the accused did? If one voluntarily does a criminal act, he will be held to have intended the natural and probable consequences of his act. For example, if Amos deliberately strikes Bert with a heavy iron bar and in doing so kills him, Amos will be held to have intended the natural result of his act; that is, Amos' intent to kill Bert will be established.

Capacity to Commit a Crime. With the exception of certain exempt classes, all persons are held to be responsible for their criminal conduct. It may be argued that this places the greatest burden on those who are weakest; however, it is the weak whose conduct endangers society. In general, infants and persons who are insane or intoxicated are not held to be criminally liable, due to the fact that they do not have mental capacity to entertain the criminal intent which is an essential element of crime. However, self-induced intoxication offers only limited protection against punishment in automobile cases for instance.

In regard to infants the common-law concept of an infant's liability for crime has been replaced by a new theory. The age at which a person is considered an infant under the criminal law is, in many states, 16 or 17 years. Juvenile courts have been established in almost every state, new administrative procedures have been set up, and new methods of dealing with juveniles have been adopted. The prevailing philosophy is that a child is not a criminal and that it is the duty of society to guide an erring child in his conduct and to help him develop into a desirable citizen.

There are many stages of insanity. The generally accepted rule is that if the person committing the criminal act was, at the time the act was committed, insane and his insanity was such that he was incapable of distinguishing right from wrong, he cannot be held criminally liable for his conduct. In some states the courts have held that if the criminal act was done under an irresistible impulse, the person committing the act will not be criminally liable. If the accused, after the commission of the criminal act, becomes insane and, as a result of his insanity, is incapable of aiding in the conduct of his trial, the prosecution will be postponed or dismissed. If a person becomes insane after conviction but before sentence, he will not be sentenced again until he regains his sanity. As a general rule the insane person who has committed a crime will be confined in a mental hospital.

Fraudulent Acts. Many of the crimes against business involve some type of fraudulent conduct. In some states, it is a crime for an officer of a bank knowingly to overdraw his account with the bank without the written consent of the board of directors; and in some states, it is a crime for a banker or broker to receive deposits while insolvent. In substantially all states, it is a crime to obtain property by fraudulent pretenses, to issue fraudulent checks, to make false credit statements, to make false statements in advertisements, and to convey property for the purpose of defrauding one's creditors. The giving of short weights or measures is generally declared to be a criminal act.

Forgery. The crime of forgery pertains to the making of false writings. In general, the definition of the crime is sufficiently broad to include the false and fraudulent making or alteration of any writing which, if genuine, would, or on its face might, have some legal effect upon the rights of others. We usually think of forgery as the signing of another's name to negotiable instruments, but the crime is much broader than this. It includes counterfeiting, changing trademarks, falsifying public records, and altering wills, deeds, leases, or any other legal document. In fact, it includes all falsification of or tampering with any document of any kind or nature which is of legal significance.

Protecting the Accused.   Justice Holmes expressed a basic philosophy of the American criminal law system when he said: ". . . and for my part I think it less evil that some criminals should escape than that the Government should play an ignoble part." In a series of landmark decisions, the U.S. Supreme Court clarified and expanded the constitutional guarantees of people, particularly of poor people, accused of crimes.

Some of the recent landmark decisions established the following principles:

1. A suspect charged with a federal crime must be taken before a magistrate without "unnecessary delay" or any confession obtained will not be admissible.
2. Illegally obtained evidence may not be admitted in either federal or state courts.
3. Any indigent person charged with a serious crime has a right to be represented by court appointed counsel.
4. The Fifth Amendment protection against self-incrimination applies to both state and federal criminal proceedings.
5. When police questioning begins to focus on the accused for accusatory rather than for investigative purposes, the accused must be permitted to consult with counsel.
6. The police must advise the accused of his right to remain silent and his right to counsel prior to any questioning.[1]

Summary

A crime is a wrong forbidden by law which is subject to punishment by the state and which the state prosecutes in its own name. Not all wrongs are punishable as crimes. What conduct will be held to be criminal and punishable will depend on the attitude of the particular society at a given time. Many acts are declared to be criminal today which were unknown or were not so declared 50 or 75 years ago.

The relation involved in the area of criminal law is that of the individual and the society of which he is a member. In its broadest aspects, the area of crime transcends the law itself and includes the police, prosecutors, administrators of prisons, and parole boards, together with the legislators and courts. There are two essential elements to most crimes: the criminal act accompanied by criminal intent. Criminal intent is proven objectively through the use of legal standards.

---

[1] These principles were established in the following cases: *Mallory* v. *United States,* 354 U.S. 449 (1948); *Mapp* v. *Ohio,* 367 U.S. 643 (1961); *Gideon* v. *Wainwright,* 372 U.S. 335 (1963); *Malloy* v. *Hogan,* 378 U.S. 1 (1964); *Escobedo* v. *Illinois,* 378 U.S. 478 (1964); and *Miranda* v. *Arizona,* 384 U.S. 436 (1966).

With the exception of certain exempt classes, all persons are held responsible for their criminal conduct. Infants, insane persons and others who do not have the mental capacity to entertain a criminal intent cannot be held criminally liable.

Fraudulent acts and forgery have been declared to be crimes by statutory enactment.

There have been a series of landmark decisions expanding the constitutional rights of persons accused of crimes.

Torts

Introduction.   Under the Anglo-Saxon law, no distinction was made between crime, tort, and breach of contract; the present-day distinction came later. But even today, there is an overlap which points to their common origin, and one and the same act may be a crime, tort, or breach of contract. The first distinction to be recognized was that made between the act of crime and the other two acts: tort and breach of contract. At a somewhat later time the distinction between the act of tort and that of breach of contract was recognized. In the United States today the relation between crime and tort is closer than that between tort and breach of contract. The same act may be both a crime and a tort. The fact that a person has been convicted of the crime and punished by the state in no way relieves him from his liability in tort to the person injured by his wrongful conduct.

Under the early English law an individual's right to a remedy was based on the concept of right and wrong, and unless a person was guilty of wrongful conduct, he was not subject to punishment or to the imposition of a penalty. At an early date the breach of the king's peace was the basis for wrongful conduct, and the penalties for such conduct were imposed by the king for his benefit. The next step in the development of the law was the recognition of the individual's right to redress for his personal injuries. This gave rise to the concept of legal duty.

The basis of a person's liability in tort is his breach of a duty owed to a fellow member of society. In the development of the law of torts the courts at first recognized the duty of a person to refrain from an intentional aggression on another. At a somewhat later time, they began to recognize the duty of a person when engaged in a course of conduct to act with due care with respect to consequences which might reasonably be anticipated. As society developed, personal contacts increased, and the duties owed by members of society increased accordingly. Today the area of tort law is developing rapidly. Every new scientific invention has its impact on society and may give rise to new duties the breach of which will give rise to a remedy in tort.

For the most part the law of torts is based on concepts of legal standards of conduct. Each member in society is required, in his daily activities, to follow a course of conduct which does not fall below a recognized standard. If he fails to maintain this accepted standard of conduct and, as a result of such failure, another is injured, he will be required to repair the resulting damage unless he can establish a right to act as he has on the ground of privilege or recognized social interest.

Elements of Tort. A tort is a breach of a duty, other than a duty created by contract,[2] for which the wrongdoer is liable in damages to the injured party. The concept of duty shifts with social developments. In general, culpable conduct which causes injury to another person is an essential element of tort. Under some circumstances, failure to act may be a tort, but the law does not impose liability on a person who fails to play the part of the good Samaritan. Base ingratitude, cruel refusal of kindness, and discourtesy are not the basis of tort liability. One of the objectives of our society is to assure to each individual in society the greatest degree of freedom consistent with a like degree of freedom for others. Our law of torts aids materially in the accomplishment of this objective. The law of torts imposes on each individual in society a duty to give due consideration to the effect of his conduct on the personal welfare of others.

Nature of Tort. In general torts may be classified as intentional tortious conduct, negligence, and strict liability. Intentional torts may be subdivided into intentional interference with the person and intentional interference with property rights.

Summary

The basis of a person's liability in tort is his breach of a duty owed to a fellow member of society which breach causes harm to such member. For the most part the law of torts is based on standards of conduct. If a person fails to maintain the accepted standard of conduct and, as a result of such failure, another is injured, he will be required to answer for the resulting damage unless he can establish a right to act as he did on the ground of privilege or recognized social interest.

Torts may be classified as intentional breaches of duty and nonintentional breaches. Intentional breaches may be further subdivided into intentional interference with the person and intentional interference with property. The nonintentional torts are negligence and strict liability.

Interference with Personal Rights

Assault and Battery. An assault is the intentional act of putting another person in immediate fear for his physical safety. Actual physical contact is

---

[2] Some writers have termed the fulfillment of a contractual promise an obligation, reserving the term "duty" for use in the law of tort.

not an element of an assault, and neither is fear. For example, if Addison threatens Berry and shoots at Berry but misses him, Addison is liable to Berry in tort. Berry has not been physically injured and he may not have been frightened, but he was apprehensive that he would be injured.

Battery is the intentional touching of another without justification or without the consent of that person. This does not mean that a tort results every time one person touches another. In our everyday activities, especially in crowded cities, there are many physical contacts between persons which are not torts, since such contacts cannot be classed as intentional interference with the person of another.

False Imprisonment.   False imprisonment is the intentional confining of another for an appreciable time within limits fixed by the one causing the confinement. Unless the one confined knows that he is confined and has not consented to it, the act is not false imprisonment. Suppose a private detective mistakenly thinks a customer in a store is a shoplifter and, over the protests of the customer, locks him in the manager's office until the manager returns from lunch about an hour later. In such a case the customer, if not guilty, has a right of action against the store owner for false imprisonment.

Defamation.   Closely related to the protection of the person's body is the protection of the person's reputation and good name. The twin torts of libel and slander are based on defamation. A distinction is made between libel and slander, in that libel is written defamation whereas slander is oral defamation.

In both libel and slander the basis of the tort is the publication of statements which hold a person up to hatred, contempt, or ridicule. By publication is meant that the defamatory statements must have been made to one other than the defamed party. If you accuse a person to his face or write him a personal letter, these acts do not constitute publishing your statements. From a legal standpoint, statements made by a husband or wife to his or her spouse are not considered published. The courts have generally held that the dictation of a letter to a stenographer or the communication of statements by one corporate officer to another is publication, although a minority of courts do not so hold. If defamatory statements are made to the defamed person and overheard by another, the courts have held that this constitutes publication. A person who repeats or republishes defamatory statements is liable even though he gives the source of his statements.

As a general rule, although all written defamation (libel) may be actionable without proof of damage, oral defamation is divided into slander per se where no damages need be proved and slander *per quod*. It is slanderous per se to falsely state that a man has a loathsome disease or has committed a crime. It is also slander per se where the defamation affects a person in his trade or profession. Lesser forms of slander (*per quod*) require that the plaintiff prove the extent of his damage—often a difficult thing to do.

Truth is a complete defense to a defamation suit. In addition, false statements may be either absolutely privileged or conditionally privileged. Statements made by congressmen on the floor of Congress, official papers filed in court proceedings, statements made by judges or attorneys during a trial are examples where absolute privilege usually attaches. Reports made between corporate officials concerning matters pertinent to their jobs, statements made about politicians or controversial public figures, and credit bureau reports may be qualifiedly or conditionally privileged. Now, false and defamatory statements about public figures are privileged if made without malice. Conditional privileges may be lost if the defendant's conduct is malicious or he abuses the privilege in some way.

Malicious Prosecution and Abuse of Process.   Tort cases involving malicious prosecution are closely related to cases involving abuse of civil process. In the former the defendant "maliciously" instigates criminal proceedings against the plaintiff and the proceedings are later terminated in the plaintiff's favor. In the latter the defendant employs civil proceedings to harass or injure the plaintiff.

The presence of probable cause (grounds for reasonable suspicion) usually will excuse the defendant from liability in a malicious prosecution suit because of the broad public interest in encouraging people to report on suspected criminal conduct. The plaintiff must prove both the absence of probable cause and the presence of malice on the part of the defendant. Malice means that the defendant acted with an improper motive. Abuse of civil process evolved out of the tort of malicious prosecution. A sizable minority of jurisdictions still do not recognize this tort. The plaintiff must prove want of probable cause and malice although the requirements of proof are less stringent than in the case of malicious prosecution. In abuse of process suits the courts are balancing the interests of society in permitting wide use of civil process against the interests of people who are unduly harassed by people with improper motives.

Right of Privacy.   In very early times the law gave a remedy only for physical interference with person and property. Later came recognition of man's spiritual nature, of his feelings and of his intellect; and with the advance of civilization the common-law judges recognized that thoughts, emotions, and sensations demanded legal protection. A recent development in this area of the law is the granting of a remedy for the invasion of privacy. The boundaries in this area are not definitely determined, but the law is primarily concerned with the protection of a mental interest, such as freedom from mental anguish resulting from the invasion of one's privacy. The cases granting relief involve the use, without permission, of a picture of a person for advertising purposes, the tapping of telephone wires, and similar acts. A person who is currently in the public eye does not have the right of privacy in matters published concerning him if such matters would be classed as news.

Infliction of Mental Distress. Historically, the courts have been hesitant to grant redress for alleged mental injuries for fear of opening the floodgates to fictitious claims. Modern medical science has established the fact that traumatic experiences involving strong emotions such as rage, shock, fright, or shame can induce physical changes which can be detected. As a result, modern courts are more receptive to claims involving claimed mental injuries of various types. The courts try to contain this new type of liability by imposing requirements that the conduct causing the distress must be "outrageous" and the resulting physical injury must be of a substantial and serious nature.

Summary

The safety of the person is important to any society, and the wrongful interference with the person is a tort. Assault is the intentional act of putting a person in apprehension of physical injury. Battery is the intentional act of touching another without the consent of that person and without justification. False imprisonment is the intentional act of confining another for an appreciable time within limits fixed by the one causing the confinement.

Closely associated to these personal torts are the torts of libel, slander, malicious prosecution, and the invasion of the right of privacy. Libel and slander are the defamation of character or good name. Libel is written, and slander is spoken, defamation. The basis of both libel and slander is the publication of false statements which hold one up to hatred, contempt, or ridicule. Invasion of privacy involves using a person's picture for advertising without his consent, unwarranted publicity, and other similar acts which cause a person mental anguish. The intentional infliction of emotional distress may create tort liability where there is outrageous misconduct. The trend in tort law is for the courts to recognize an increasing variety of new torts thus making the law more sensitive to various types of harms.

Southwest Drug Stores of Mississippi, Inc. v. *Garner*
195 So.2d 837 (Sup. Ct. Miss. 1967)

Mrs. Garner (plaintiff) sued Southwest Drug Stores of Mississippi, Inc. (defendant), for damages for false imprisonment and slander. The jury returned a verdict for Mrs. Garner for $8,000. Southwest appealed. Affirmed.

Mrs. Garner and her sister stopped at Southwest Drug Store in the Gardiner Shopping Center in Laurel. They went into the drug store, leaving her father, who was ill, in the car in the parking lot in front of the drug store.

While Mrs. Garner was at the cosmetic counter looking at soap, Ratcliff, the store manager, approached her and asked if he could help her. She told him she wanted a bar of soap, and he said he would have one of the ladies wait on her. With the assistance of the saleslady Mrs. Garner found the soap, and with the saleslady went to the cashier and paid for it. She received a sales ticket and the soap was placed in a small paper bag.

Mrs. Garner's sister continued to shop, since she also wanted some soap. Mrs. Garner told her that she would go to the car to see about their father and would take some of the sister's packages with her. She walked out of the store, and before she reached the car Ratcliff hurried after her, calling in a loud voice to stop.

She testified that he said to her in a rude and loud manner, "Hey, wait there. . . . You stop there, I want to see what you got in that little bag. You stole a bar of soap." Mrs. Garner said further, "And I looked at him, I said, 'You mean you're accusing me of stealing this soap.' I pulled the soap out. He says, 'Yes, you stole the soap, and let's prove it, let's go back.' "

Mrs. Garner said a number of people were close by and heard the words, but that she did not know any of them. Ratcliff did not put a hand on her or her belongings, but he did demand that she return to the store.

When they got back in the store Mrs. Garner asked the cashier if she had bought the soap, and the cashier told her that she had paid for the soap. She told the cashier that Ratcliff was accusing her of stealing the soap. She then began to cry and was embarrassed. . . . Mrs. Garner said the incident made her sick and she had to go to the family doctor twice.

INZER, JUSTICE.   Southwest Drug urges that the lower court erred in not granting a requested peremptory instruction. They argue that the proof shows a qualified privilege existed and it was not exceeded; that Ratcliff investigated what he believed to be a case of shoplifting upon probable cause in a reasonable manner, and therefore under the laws of Mississippi such an investigation was privileged and no action was maintainable thereon. The statute relied upon is Mississippi Code Annotated section 2374–04 (Supp. 1964), which reads as follows:

If any person shall commit or attempt to commit the offense of shoplifting, as defined herein, or if any person shall wilfully conceal upon his person or otherwise any unpurchased goods, wares or merchandise held or owned by any store or mercantile establishment, the merchant or any employee thereof or any peace or police officer, acting in good faith and upon probable cause based upon reasonable grounds therefor, may question such person, in a reasonable manner for the purpose of ascertaining whether or not such person is guilty of shoplifting as defined herein. Such questioning of a person by a merchant, merchant's employee or peace or police officer shall not render such merchant, merchant's employee or peace or police officer civilly liable for slander, false arrest, false imprisonment, malicious prosecution, unlawful detention or otherwise in any case where such merchant, merchant's employee, or peace or police officer acts in good faith and upon reasonable grounds to believe that the person questioned is committing or attempting to commit the crime of shoplifting as defined in this act.

. . . .

Southwest argues that Ratcliff had observed Mrs. Garner and believed by her actions that she was committing an act of shoplifting; that her actions gave him probable cause to investigate, and that he acted in good faith and upon an occasion of privilege in carrying out his duties to protect his employer's property.

Although the occasion was one of qualified privilege, the privilege was lost by the manner in which it was exercised. Mrs. Garner testified, and the jury found that she was wrongfully accused of stealing in a rude and loud voice in the presence of other people outside the place of business. Granting that Ratcliff had reason to believe that Mrs. Garner had put a bar of soap in her purse and left the store without paying for it, and that he had probable cause to make inquiry, still he was careless and negligent in his method of ascertaining whether Mrs. Garner had paid for the soap.

Wehrman v. Liberty Petroleum Company
382 S.W.2d 56 (St. Louis Ct. App. 1964)

Wehrman (plaintiff) sued Liberty (defendant) for false arrest. The trial court jury brought in a verdict of $100 actual and $7,500 punitive damages and Liberty appealed. Affirmed.

Wehrman bought some gasoline from a Liberty station and began to have engine trouble. He complained to the station manager, Brown, and was told that water was in the gasoline and that the company would reimburse Wehrman $9.10 for the gas and expense he had incurred. That afternoon Wehrman had to spend another $4.05 getting his car fixed. He told Brown and Brown told him to write the company. After two weeks Wehrman asked Brown for his check but Brown was busy so Wehrman had his tank filled for $2.65 while waiting.

Brown thereupon told Wehrman that he would never get paid, and demanded payment of $2.65 for the gas. Wehrman replied that he hadn't come in to buy, that the sale had been solicited, that if Brown wanted the gas he could drain it out of his tank, or that Brown could deduct the amount from what was owed Wehrman. Brown said, ". . . 'I'm telling you for the last time it's pay or get off.' . . ." Wehrman said, ". . . 'Well, I'll get off.' . . ."

Brown then called the police and reported that Wehrman had bought gas without paying for it. He did not give any background facts. Wehrman was arrested for larceny but was released after about one hour.

DOERMER, JUDGE.   Liberty argues that all Brown did was to give the police information of the occurrence, and point to a line of cases, beginning with the decision of this court in 1877 in *Lark* v. *Bande,* which holds that the mere giving of wrong information to the police, even though it results in an arrest, cannot be the basis of an action for false arrest and imprisonment. . . . We are of the opinion, however, that a different rule should prevail where the informant knowingly and deliberately gives the police an incomplete and biased version of the occurrence which induces them to believe that another is a thief, and results in the latter's unwarranted arrest. It seems to us that from such evidence the jury could reasonably find that the informant instigated the arrest by stimulating or goading the police to take such action.

In the instant case, had Brown fully reported to the police *all* of the facts known to him we would have no hesitancy in holding that any arrest which followed could not be said to have been instigated by him. But Brown's own testimony, as well as that of Wehrman's, shows that the information which Brown gave to the police was incomplete, inaccurate, and highly misleading.

Jones v. *Walsh*
222 A.2d 830 (Sup. Ct. N.H. 1966)

Dolores Jones (plaintiff) sued John Walsh (defendant) for damages for slander and defendant Walsh appealed from an adverse ruling. Affirmed.

LAMPRON, JUSTICE. Jones' declaration reads in part as follows: "On or about Friday, May 22, 1964, at Exeter . . . at Tula's Restaurant . . . owned and operated by Walsh, Walsh did injure the character and good name of Jones who was at that time a waitress in the employ of Walsh and by his acts caused it to be believed that Jones was guilty of the crime of embezzlement in that in the course of a certain conversation, which Walsh had with Jones in the presence of a number of people in a crowded restaurant, falsely and maliciously accused Jones of embezzlement as follows to wit:

" 'You are not ringing the cash up in the cash register.' " Jones replied, " 'Are you accusing me of stealing?' " Walsh replied, " 'Well, you're not ringing in the cash.' "

If one falsely and without a privilege to do so publishes spoken words which imputes to another conduct constituting a criminal offense chargeable by indictment or information either at common law or by statute and of such a kind as to be characterized as morally reprehensible, he is liable to the person to whom such wrong doing is imputed without proof of special damage. A charge of the commission of embezzlement constitutes such a slander *per se*.

It is not necessary that the words used charge Jones with such a crime in a technical or direct manner. "A mere insinuation . . . the putting of words in the form of a question . . . a mere expression of opinion or of a suspicion or belief may be actionable." The test is whether the words used taken in the sense in which they are reasonably understood under the circumstances by persons familiar with the language used are capable of the defamatory construction of accusing Jones with a criminal offense of the type previously described.

We are of the opinion that hearers of common and reasonable understanding could ascribe such a meaning to Walsh's words. Whether they did under the circumstances of this case is a question to be decided as a fact.

"Not all slander, however, is actionable. Some spoken defamation may fall within a class which the law terms privileged, and for which no damages may be recovered." Walsh suggests in his brief that, having a legitimate interest in the receipts of his business, he "cannot be liable because the statements were made on a conditionally privileged occasion and nothing appears in the writ and declaration to indicate that the occasion was abused."

It is true that "an occasion is conditionally privileged when the circumstances induce a correct or reasonable belief that (a) facts exist which affect a sufficiently important interest of the publisher, and (b) the recipient's knowledge of the defamatory matter will be of service in the lawful protection of the interest." *Restatement, Torts,* s. 594. However, to come within that privilege "the defamatory communication must be made to a person whose knowledge of the defamatory matter because of his social or legal duty or his interest thereto is likely to prove useful in the protection of that interest." Furthermore such a "privilege may be so far abused by an unnecessary and excessive publication that the immunity is lost."

Medlin v. *Allied Investment Co.*
398 S.W.2d 270 (Sup. Ct. Tenn. 1966)

Medlin (plaintiff) sued Allied Investment Co. (defendant) alleging that Allied held a mortgage on Medlin's home and that the agents of Allied, erroneously thinking that Medlin was in default on mortgage payments, had made abusive phone calls, sent default notices to Medlin and to the Federal Housing Authority. As a result, Medlin claimed damages for mental anguish and emotional disturbance. The trial court sustained a demurrer to the complaint and Medlin appealed. Affirmed.

BURNETT, CHIEF JUDGE.   The common law rule that mental anguish without other actual injury will not support an action for damages has continued as a legal principle even though the reasons for maintaining such a rule have been rebutted. This principle, however, does not have the rigidity that it did at common law; the courts have allowed actions of this sort in very limited situations. The courthouse doors have not been flung open to redress injuries in the mental well-being of a person. The most valid objection to the protection of such interests lies in the "wide door" that might be open, not only to fictitious claims, but to trivialities and mere bad manners. The law cannot be responsible for absolute peace of mind, and many interferences must be left to other agencies of social control.

In the face of some strong policy consideration, recovery has been allowed for interference with peace of mind in certain situations only. Certain factors present in those cases in which recovery has been permitted outweighed the valid policy consideration against allowing such actions. These factors are set out in the *Restatement of Torts, Second,* Section 46, "Outrageous Conduct Causing Severe Emotional Distress."

Under the *Restatement* rule, two factors must concur in order to outweigh the policy against allowing an action for the infliction of mental disturbance: (1) The conduct complained of must have been outrageous, i.e., not tolerated in civilized society; and (2) as a result of the outrageous conduct, there must be serious mental injury. Stated another way, there are two valid policies fighting for recognition; the interest in a judicial climate that does not become burdened with the trivial lawsuits versus the interest a person has in being free from unreasonable emotional disturbances. The result of this policy conflict has been somewhat of a compromise.

Since the mortgagor has not alleged a course of conduct on the part of the mortgagee that could be classed as outrageous, the suit is barred. It is not enough in an action of this kind to allege a legal conclusion; the actionable conduct should be set out in the declaration. The mortgagee's conduct, as set out in the declaration, shows that the mortgagee was negligent in keeping his records and that because of this negligence, he caused two notices of default to be sent to the mortgagor. He was abusive to the mortgagor on the telephone, but the substance and severity of the abuse is not set out in the declaration. Therefore this court cannot ascribe the term "outrageous" to this alleged abuse.

Rights of Property

Nature of Property Rights. Property and property rights are of such importance to society that they are protected against unwarranted interference by others. In cases of tortious interference with property rights, any action brought to recover damages, as a general rule, is brought by the party in possession rather than by the owner. However, an action for trespass may be brought by the owner of land which is leased to another if the nature of the trespass is such that it results in damage to the owner's reversionary interests. The recognized torts against property are trespass to land, trespass to personal property, and conversion.

Trespass to Land. Any entry by a person onto the land in the possession of another, or the causing of anything to enter onto the land of another, or the remaining on the land or the permitting of anything to remain on the land in the possession of another is a trespass to that land unless permission is given or unless the entry is privileged. Actual pecuniary harm to the land is not an essential element of the tort. The interference with the right of possession is sufficient injury on which to base a suit. If no harm is done, only nominal damages can be recovered.

Walking across land in the possession of another, throwing water against a building in the possession of another, shooting across land in possession of another, or damming a stream and thus causing the water to back up on land in possession of another are trespasses to land. In fact, any interference with land in possession of another may be a trespass whether it is of short or long duration and whether or not pecuniary harm results. If no harm is done, it is a technical interference with the property rights of the possessor.

The early cases laid down the rule that the right to land extended from the center of the earth to the heavens. This rule has been modified since the advent of aircraft. Today the temporary invasion of the air space over the land by aircraft is privileged, provided it is done in a reasonable manner and in conformity with legislative requirements. The operation of aircraft, at the present time, is considered an extrahazardous activity; and if anything is dropped from an aircraft, or if a forced landing is made, the aviator is liable for any actual harm which results. The trend in the law is to impose greater duties on landowners to keep their premises in a reasonably safe condition even where trespassers are concerned.

Trespass to Personal Property.   Any intentional intermeddling with personal property which is in the possession of another is a trespass if the intermeddling does harm to the property or deprives the possessor of the use of the property for an appreciable time unless it is privileged or is done with the consent of the possessor. Suppose Adams moves an automobile a few feet to enable him to park his own automobile. He is not liable for trespass. However, if, as a joke, Adams moves the automobile around the corner, and the owner, although he uses reasonable diligence, cannot find it for some time, say an hour or more, Adams is liable for trespass. As a general rule, if one intermeddles with the personal property of another and the property is harmed in no way, no trespass has been committed. However, if the property is personal to the owner, say, for instance, an undergarment, and the owner refuses to use the property after the intermeddling, a trespass has been committed even though the property has not been damaged physically.

Conversion.   A conversion is an unlawful dominion over, or the unlawful appropriation of, the personal property of another. A conversion takes place when a distinct act of dominion is wrongfully exerted over another's personal property in denial of, or inconsistent with, his ownership or rights therein. Generally, the gist of a conversion is the wrongful deprivation of a person's personal property to the possession of which he is entitled. If a person unlawfully takes goods from the possession of another, he is guilty of conversion even though he mistakenly thought he was entitled to the possession of the goods. If a person wrongfully sells, pledges, mortgages, leases, or uses the goods of another, that person is guilty of conversion. A person is guilty of conversion if he wrongfully, even though by mistake, delivers goods of one person to another who is not entitled to the possession of the goods. In the case of a conversion of goods the owner, or the one entitled to the possession of the goods, is entitled to recover the reasonable value of the goods from the one guilty of the conversion.

Deceit (Fraud).   The tort of deceit, included in the broader term "fraud," is based on injury resulting from a misrepresentation of a material fact, knowingly made with intent to deceive, which is justifiably relied on to the injury of the defrauded party. The keystone of the tort is misrepresentation of a material fact; but misrepresentation is also the basis for equitable relief in fraud cases, and it also plays a major role in quasi-contract and restitution cases. There is no clear line of demarcation between these fields. A misrepresentation may be the basis for the rescission of a contract, relief in equity, recovery in quasi contract, or the remedy of restitution in law; but as a general rule, misrepresentation standing alone cannot be the basis for recovery of damages in tort.

Five elements are considered as essential to a recovery in deceit. There must be (1) misrepresentation of a material fact, (2) knowingly made or made in disregard of the truth of the representation, (3) with the intent to induce action, (4) justifiabily relied on, and (5) injury must result. The misrepresentation must be of an existing or past fact. A statement of opinion or a prediction of future events cannot be the basis of the tort of deceit. The person making the statement must know that it is false or must know that he does not have sufficient information to make a positive statement. An honest mistake of fact is not actionable. Intent is tested objectively, and a person is held to have intended the usual and normal results of his acts. If the party to whom the statement is made knows it is false or under the circumstances should know that it is false, he cannot recover in deceit. The relation of the parties and their experience and intelligence will be considered in determining whether a person has justifiably relied on a false representation. If no injury has resulted from the false representation, there can be no recovery in tort.

Summary

The torts for interfering with property rights are trespass to land, trespass to personal property, and conversion. Any wrongful interference with the possession of land is a trespass. Likewise, wrongful intermeddling with the possession of personal property is a trespass. Conversion is, basically, such a serious interference with a person's right to control or to dispose of personal property that the party who interferes is generally required to pay full value for the property and take title to it. Deceit is based on misrepresentation of a material fact knowingly made with the intent to mislead, justifiably relied on to one's injury. Through deceit one gains a wrongful economic advantage of another.

Franc v. *Pennsylvania RR*
225 A.2d 528 (Sup. Ct. Penn. 1967)

This was an action to recover damages for personal injuries brought by Franc (plaintiff) against the Pennsylvania Railroad (defendant). Franc was severely injured when she fell through a gap in the planking on a single track railroad bridge. The gap was covered by snow and had been in the bridge for about three weeks. The bridge was the private property of the railroad although the public had used it to cross the creek for many years. Franc sued and the trial court gave a judgment notwithstanding the jury verdict to Pennsylvania Railroad. Franc appealed. Reversed and the jury verdict for Franc reinstated.

MUSMANNO, JUSTICE.   The duty of the railroad company in situations such as the one here outlined is spelled out in the *Restatement of Torts,* Sec. 335:

"A possessor of land who knows' or from facts within his knowledge should know, that trespassers constantly intrude upon a limited area thereof, is subject to liability for bodily harm caused to them by an artificial condition, thereon, if (a) the condition (i) is one which the possessor has created or (ii) is, to his knowledge, likely to cause death or serious bodily harm to such trespasser and (iii) is of such a nature that he has reason to believe that such trespassers will not discover it; and (b) the possessor has failed to exercise reasonable care to warn such trespassers of the condition and the risk involved therein."

Comment (c):

". . . If, however, the condition, though obvious to adult trespasser, is such as not to disclose to him that there is a risk on its full extent, the possessor is under a duty to warn the trespasser of the risk and its extent."

"Comment (f):

". . . On the other hand, he (the possessor) is not entitled to assume that the trespassers will discover conditions which are unusual to land of the character upon which the trespasser intrudes, or which are due to carelessness in the maintenance of those conditions which are necessary to the use of the land. . . ."

As above stated, the railroad company knew or should have known of the defect in the floor of the bridge and it is clear that it failed to exercise reasonable care to warn users of the bridge of the condition and the risk involved in crossing the bridge. It displayed no signs on or near the structure, warning civilians away, nor did railroad employees inform civilians to keep off the bridge. On the contrary, the railroad employees joined with the civilians in the march across the missing-plank bridge.

Justices Roberts and Eagen agree that the result is correct but "without reliance on *Restatement 2d, Torts,* Section 335."

Dissent. "The majority opinion . . . invokes Section 335 of the *Restatement of Torts* to delineate the duty of the railroad in this situation, even if the plaintiff be considered a trespasser. Not only has Section 335 not been adopted by this court, but it is contrary to the long recognized rule in this Commonwealth, i.e., that a plaintiff who is a trespasser can recover only if the defendant is guilty of wanton or wilful misconduct."

Heuer v. *Wiese*

60 N.W. 2d 385 (Sup. Ct. Wisc. 1953)

This was an action by Ernest Heuer (plaintiff) against Marvin Wiese (defendant) to recover the purchase price of a clover crop. Wiese set up the conversion of the crop by Heuer as a defense. Motion of Wiese for summary judgment denied and Wiese appealed. Order denying summary judgment affirmed.

About July 8, 1951, Ernest Heuer and Marvin Wiese entered into an oral contract whereby Heuer agreed to sell and Wiese agreed to buy for $600 a clover crop then standing on Heuer's field. Heuer was to cut the crop when directed by Wiese. Heuer cut the crop on July 31, 1951. After Heuer had cut the crop, he notified Wiese by letter to remove the crop by August 10, 1951. Wiese failed to remove the crop by August 10, 1951, and a week later Heuer took possession of the cut crop and with a chopper cut the crop up on his field. On September 25, 1951, Heuer brought suit against Wiese to recover the unpaid balance of the purchase price of the crop and Wiese filed a counterclaim for damages for the conversion of the crop by Heuer.

FRITZ, CHIEF JUSTICE. Heuer's action is for breach of the contract by Wiese's failure to remove the crop from Heuer's field within a reasonable time after it was cut by Heuer as agreed upon; and thereby caused Heuer to be deprived of the value of the hay and to suffer damage to the field and seeding as a result of the clover not having been removed. When Heuer cut the crop on or about July 31, 1951, he notified Wiese by a letter, sent rural route, to remove the cut crop from his field by August 10, 1951, noontime, or he would commence an action for breach of contract. Heuer did not confine himself to the remedy which he stated in his letter to Wiese that he would take if the crop was not so removed, neither did he give any notice of an intention to rescind the contract. He chose to take possession of the crop and destroy it by cutting it and scattering it on his field. That is admitted, Wiese's ownership of the crop is admitted. The record is silent of any act on the part of Heuer whereby he re-invested himself with ownership prior to taking and destroying the crop. Wiese contends that the acts of Heuer were a conversion of Wiese's crop, which created an estoppel against Heuer to sue on the contract; resolving the issue in the case as only one of law that can be reached by a motion for summary judgment for dismissal of the complaint. As stated in *Adams* v. *Maxcy:*

"Conversion is any distinct act of dominion wrongfully exerted over another's personal property in denial of or inconsistent with his rights therein, such as a tortious taking of another's chattels, of any wrongful exercise or assumption of authority, personally or by procurement, over another's goods, depriving him of possession, permanently or for an indefinite time."

The conversion of the crop precludes Heuer from recovering for the balance of the purchase price which Wiese had agreed to pay.

(Note: The case was ordered tried in order to determine the validity of Heuer's claim for damage due to the fact he could not plant when Wiese failed to remove the crop.)

Business Torts

Economic Relations. The modern courts recognize interference with economic relations as a tort, but the boundaries of this field have not been definitely determined. The determination of the rights of the parties requires a fine balance between free competition which is the life of trade, the encouragement of individual initiative, and the general social welfare. The law relating to Business is discussed in Chapter 45.

Problem Cases

1. It was Kroger's policy to have its store manager, Letsinger, pick people at random and question each person so selected as a matter of routine at the check-out counter, as if he had stolen cigarettes or some other commonly pilfered item. Clark had her groceries at the check-out counter when Letsinger said, "Don't you want those Marlboro cigarettes?" Clark responded that she had stopped smoking some time ago but Letsinger told her that he would like to see her outside. He then told her in a forceful manner to follow him to a back room. She was in the back room about 20 minutes where she was interrogated repeatedly about cigarettes in the presence of another clerk. She showed Letsinger the contents of her purse and he finally told her to leave. Clark left the store in a hysterical condition. Clark sued for slander and for false imprisonment and the trial court awarded actual damages of $5,000 and punitive damages of $5,000. Should this judgment be sustained on appeal?

2. In 1959 Desilu sold to CBS a two-part drama called *The Untouchables* which was a dramatization of certain wholly fictional events supposed to have happened during the lifetime of Capone. These incidents were the pure invention of imaginative scriptwriters. Response to this drama was such that it was expanded into a weekly series which was broadcast for a period of five years. Another full-scale exploitation of Capone was created by Desilu in the episode "The Big Train." It, too, was completely fictitious.

   Because of the commercial exploitation of the Capone name, Capone's widow and son were forced to abandon their "peaceful life in comparative obscurity" by selling their home, their restaurant business, changing their name, and moving to another city. They brought suit against Desilu for a claim of invasion of privacy. Judgment for Desilu, and the Capones appealed. Should the decision be reversed?

3. Gray, a patient with severe back trouble, signed a hospital "consent form" for an operation. Gray was not informed of the dangerous risks (a 20 percent chance of paralysis) involved in the operation. Although done without negligence, the operation resulted in paralyses of both legs. Gray sued the doctor for damages for battery and the doctor set up the consent form which purported to waive all of Gray's rights to sue. Is this a good defense?

4. On December 6, 1963, four employees of the General Motors Acceptance Corporation entered the premises of the business owned by Towler's husband and insisted that Jackson, who worked there, phone Towler to determine her husband's whereabouts. He did so causing Towler to become alarmed for her husband who had a bad heart. Towler was pregnant at the time and suffered a miscarriage. Towler alleged Jackson knew such a call would cause her to become upset and sued him as well as the four others. Can Towler recover?

5. Urban purchased a hot water heater from Hartford Gas on an installment contract.

Later Hartford Gas employees appeared and repossessed the heater, erroneously believing that Urban was in default on payments. At the time of repossession the employees stated to a number of people that Mr. and Mrs. Urban were "deadbeats." Mrs. Urban became hysterical and an arrested diabetic condition flared up, causing prolonged illness. Mrs. Urban sued Hartford Gas for her emotional and physical injury. Can she recover?

6. Pond worked as an engineer in the foreign operations of General Electric Co. for 17 years. He resigned in 1950 and was given a "service letter" which outlined his various assignments. Pond unsuccessfully sought employment with several prospective employers and later discovered that each employer had written standard inquiries to G.E. requesting information about his honesty, loyalty, competency, etc., and in each case G.E. had sent the following letter in reply:

> This is in reply to your letter of March 12 in which you request information concerning Mr. Jules S. Pond.
>
> The official in International General Electric to whom Mr. Pond reported passed away several years ago, and I am unable to give you first-hand information concerning him. His personnel record with the Company indicates that he had approximately 17 years of service in the International General Electric family. . . .
>
> Insofar as I can determine from his records, we would not be prepared to consider him for re-engagement.
>
> Very truly yours, Charles Mentzer, Specialist-Personnel

Pond sued G.E. for damages for libel claiming that the official to whom he had reported was in fact alive and that G.E. was deliberately trying to give future employers a bad impression of his record. Can Pond recover damages?

7. Pauling, a scientist of international repute, won a Nobel prize in chemistry and later won a Nobel Peace Prize. He became a leader in a movement to promote a nuclear test-ban treaty and because of this became the subject of a defamatory editorial entitled "Glorification of Deceit" which appeared in the *Globe-Democrat* newspaper. The editorial falsely stated that he had been cited for contempt of Congress and contained other false statements. Pauling sued for libel and the defendant, *Globe-Democrat,* argued that proof of malice on its part was essential because Pauling was a "public figure." Is this a good defense?

8. Humble Oil called Harrison's employer and asked permission to speak to Harrison during work hours. Humble explained that Harrison was delinquent on an account owed to Humble. Harrison sued Humble for having violated his right of privacy. The defendant Humble made a motion for a summary judgment. Should this motion be granted?

9. Andoscia, while addressing a meeting of representatives of a credit union of which he was a member, was interrupted by the presiding officer, Coady, who told one Lynch to read a document. The document stated that Andoscia was in arrears in his loan account with the credit union, that the account had been turned over to an attorney for collection, and that Andoscia's membership in the union was thereby cancelled. The statement was false and Andoscia sued Lynch and Coady for defamation. Assuming that Andoscia can show no damages, can he recover?

10. Konas purchased some merchandise from Red Owl and gave a bad check in pay-

ment. The manager made several attempts to contact Konas but was unable to do so. He also sent a written notice to Konas advising her that the check had bounced. On two occasions he presented the check at the drawee bank and was informed that there were insufficient funds to cover the check. The manager than had criminal charges brought against Konas but Konas was acquitted by the jury. Konas sued Red Owl for damages for malicious prosecution. Can Konas collect damages?

chapter 4. Negligence and Strict Liability

Negligence

Nature of Negligence. In the law of torts, negligence occupies a position midway between intentional tort and strict liability. We subscribe to the philosophy that each person in society should be given the maximum of freedom of action consistent with the like freedom of other persons. If a person is given freedom to act, he is legally bound to give due consideration to the rights and welfare of other members of society and to exercise such a degree of self-control that his acts are not unduly injurious to others. Each member of society owes a duty to refrain from following a course of action which will result in foreseeable harm to another. As expressed by one judge, "You must take reasonable care to avoid acts or omissions which you can reasonably foresee would be likely to injure your neighbor."

To recover damages for negligence, a person must establish that (1) the defendant has been guilty of negligent conduct toward the plaintiff and (2) that plaintiff has suffered an injury as a result of such conduct. Negligence without resulting injury is not actionable.

Standards of Conduct. The presence or absence of negligence is determined by applying standards of conduct to the facts of the case. The standard which has been adopted is the conduct of a reasonable man of ordinary prudence under the same or similar circumstances. This standard is flexible and serves as a measuring stick in the infinite variety of situations arising in the negligence cases. It also satisfies the requirement that a standard be external and objective and that, as far as possible, it be the same for all persons. The standard is one which must be applied by the jury, or by the court in the absence of a jury. Since negligence is based on conduct, the court, in applying the standard, attempts to put itself in the place of the actor and to pose the following questions: "Did the actor, in the light of the existing conditions, act like a reasonable man of ordinary prudence? Should he, as a reasonable and prudent man, have foreseen the danger of harm and prevented it?"

Ignorance, honest mistakes, and physical defects of a person, do not relieve a person from his responsibility to persons whom he has injured. Under the law of negligence, each member of society is required to act in such a manner that he does not create unreasonable risks which endanger the person or property of others. To have negligence, there must be a recognizable risk, and the conduct of the person causing the injury must be unreasonable in relation to the foreseeable risk. That is, his conduct must be below the accepted standard, which is the conduct of a reasonable and prudent man under the circumstances. To have liability, there must be injury resulting from negligent conduct.

Suppose a person drives an automobile at 40 miles an hour through the main street of a city on a rainy, foggy night at the time the offices are closing and workers are going home. Such conduct is clearly negligent, since a reasonable man of ordinary prudence would foresee the risk of harm. However, if no one is injured and no property is damaged as the result of the negligent conduct, the person is not liable in tort for damages.

Proximate Cause.   When a person has acted, it is impossible to trace to the ultimate end all the consequences of the act. Therefore, it is necessary to place a limit on a person's responsibility for the results of his acts. Early in the development of the law of negligence the court adopted the rule that a person would not be held liable unless his act was the "proximate cause" of the injury. The choice of language was unfortunate because it connotes proximity in time and place. Under some circumstances a time and place limitation may aid in working out the limits of responsibility, but such a test is inadequate. Consequently, there is much disagreement in the law as to the tests which should be applied in marking the limitations of responsibility. Some courts have held that the person is not liable unless the harm is the natural and probable consequence of his act. Other courts have held that the act must have been a substantial factor in producing the harm. Attempts have been made to establish a fixed system of rules to cover all cases, but "proximate cause" cannot be reduced to a set of fixed rules. In all but a limited number of cases the question of "proximate cause" will be a question of fact for the jury or for the judge, in the absence of a jury, to solve by the application of good common sense to the facts of each case.

Defenses.   There are two principal defenses to a tort action for damages for negligence, namely, assumption of risk, and contributory negligence. A person may, either by express agreement or by his conduct, enter into a relation with another which involves danger to himself; and he may indicate his willingness to assume the risks of the known or foreseeable dangers, thereby relieving the other party from legal responsibility for injuries resulting from the known or foreseeable dangers.

In most cases, no express agreement to assume risks exists, but the assumption of the risks is implied from the conduct of the parties and from the surrounding circumstances. By voluntarily entering into a relationship which involves obvious danger, it may be taken as an assumption of the risks of the situation and relieve the other party from legal responsibility. If a person goes to a ball game, he will be held to have assumed the risk of being hit by a ball. Ordinarily, a person will be held to have assumed only those risks which are known to him or which are foreseeable. He will be held to know of those risks which a person of adult age would recognize.

Each person in society is required to exercise a reasonable degree of caution and to look out for himself. If one does not exercise a reasonable degree of caution and this failure combined with the negligence of another results in an injury, neither party can recover damages from the other. Each party has been negligent, and their combined negligence has caused the injury. If either party sues in tort for damages for negligence, the other party can set up "contributory negligence," which would be a complete defense under the rule followed in most states. Some courts have held that a child of immature years cannot be guilty of contributory negligence.

Last Clear Chance.   A confusing qualification to the defense of contributory negligence called the doctrine of "last clear chance" has been developed. The decision of the courts of the several states cannot be reconciled and in some instances the decisions of the courts within a state are not always in accord.

This doctrine applies where a plaintiff through initial negligence exposes himself to a risk of harm but then is helpless to avoid the harm. The defendant has a last clear chance to avoid the harm but fails to do so. Under these circumstances the plaintiff is allowed to recover in spite of the fact that his initial negligence was a contributing cause.

In criticizing the doctrine of "last clear chance" Prosser states: "The variety of irreconcilable rules, all purporting to be the same, and the lack of any fundamental theory to support them, suggests that the 'last clear chance' doctrine is more a matter of dissatisfaction with the defense of contributory negligence than anything else." [1]

Res Ipsa Loquitur.   The injured plaintiff normally has the sometimes difficult burden of proving how and when the defendant was negligent. The so-called *res ipsa* doctrine permits a plaintiff to establish a prima facie case of negligence simply by showing that: (*a*) the event which injured him would not ordinarily occur in the absence of negligence, and (*b*) the defendant was in exclusive charge of control of the instrumentalities causing the harm. The

---

[1] William L. Prosser, *Handbook of the Law of Torts* (3d ed.; St. Paul, Minn.: West Publishing Co., 1964).

Latin words *res ipsa loquitur* translated mean "the thing speaks for itself" and where the doctrine is held to apply the defendant must defend against the prima facie case thus made or run the risk of having a judgment rendered against him.

Summary

Liability for negligence is based on a breach of duty to refrain from following a course of action which will result in foreseeable harm to another. The standard of conduct in determining a person's duty to fellow members of society is the conduct of a reasonable man of ordinary prudence under the same or similar circumstances. There is no liability for mere negligent conduct. To have liability, there must be injury resulting from negligent conduct.

The courts have attempted to limit the scope of a person's liability for his negligent conduct. One theory for the limitation of liability is the theory of "proximate cause," that is, the injury must be the direct result of the negligent act.

The principle defenses to liability for negligence are (1) assumption of risk, and (2) contributory negligence. The *last clear chance* doctrine permits an injured plaintiff to recover under some circumstances even though he was guilty of contributory negligence.

The doctrine *res ipsa loquitur* in effect shifts the burden of proof from the plaintiff to the defendant. The defendant must rebut the prima facie case the plaintiff makes when the plaintiff proves his injury falls under circumstances where the doctrine applies.

Jiffy Markets, Inc. v. *Vogel*
340 F.2d 495 (8th Cir. 1965)

This was an action brought by Vogel (plaintiff) who received extensive lacerations as the result of walking into and through a large glass panel which formed the front of the building in which Jiffy Markets, Inc. (defendant) operated a supermarket. Vogel sued Jiffy and won a judgment in the federal district court and Jiffy appealed. Affirmed.

MATTHES, CIRCUIT JUDGE.   . . . There were no signs or markings of any kind on the glass panels on the night of the litigated occurrence and the glass was spotlessly clean. Vogel stopped his automobile with the front facing the vending machine. He turned off the lights, got out of the automobile eighteen or twenty feet from the front of the store and proceeded toward the building intending to enter the store and make a purchase. From the testimony, the jury was warranted in finding that as Vogel approached the store he was walking at a normal gait and with his head up; that although he was looking ahead, he did not see the glass or its bordering metal frame and saw no reflections from lights or identifying marks of any kind on the glass. He did not realize until he crashed through the glass that what he thought was the entrance to the store was, in fact, a solid plate glass panel.

Inasmuch as the litigated incident occurred in the State of Kansas, we look to the law of that state for ascertainment of the duty imposed on the proprietor of a business establishment toward his patron or business invitee. Both parties cite and rely upon *Little* v. *Butner* (1960). That case teaches that the business proprietor is under a duty to use care to keep in a reasonably safe condition the premises where guests or customers may be expected to come and go; if there is a dangerous place on the premises, the proprietor must safeguard those who come lawfully thereon by warning them of the condition and risk involved: "The true ground of liability is his *superior knowledge* over that of business invitees of the dangerous condition and his failure to give warning of the risk . . . however, he is not an insurer against all accidents which may befall them upon the premises."

Jiffy contends that under all of the evidence favorable to Vogel and giving to Vogel the benefit of all reasonable inferences, it conclusively appears that Jiffy did not breach any duty toward Vogel; that Jiffy was not guilty of any actionable negligence, and the issue of liability should not have been presented to the jury. To support this contention, Jiffy invokes and presses upon us the "superior knowledge" test enunciated in *Little,* supra. It insists (a) that the evidence clearly showed that the glass panels constituted an accepted method of construction, and the presence of the glass was clearly observable to a person in the exercise of ordinary care for his own safety; (b) that there was no duty on the part of Jiffy to warn Vogel of the claimed hazardous condition (glass panels) because the evidence conclusively established that the condition was apparent and would have been seen by Vogel if he had been giving reasonable attention to the surrounding physical conditions.

We are not so persuaded. To be sure, transparent plate glass is recognized as suitable and safe material for use in construction of buildings, indeed, it is common knowledge that such glass is used rather extensively in commercial buildings. However, it seems to us that the number of reported cases, some of which are cited infra, involving personal injuries from bodily contact with transparent glass doors and walls is some indication that with the advantages that may be derived from such construction are concomitant risks which the proprietor must assume. Of course, whether the proprietor is responsible to a patron who comes in contact with a glass door or wall and sustains injuries, depends on the facts and circumstances surrounding the incident judged in light of the controlling legal standards. . . . The jury was not required to speculate as to the dangerous and unsafe condition created by the glass front. There was evidence to that effect. A former employee of Jiffy testified that during a period of eight months he observed four or five persons come in contact with the glass front and "bounce off." A safety engineer testified it was a hazardous arrangement, and detailed the methods that could have been employed to correct the lack of visibility of the glass.

Without further discussion, we conclude and hold that there was substantial evidence from which the jury could find: (1) that the glass front constituted a dangerous and unsafe condition; (2) that Vogel was exercising ordinary care for his own safety; (3) that there was a duty on the part of Jiffy to warn its patrons of the condition and (4) that Jiffy breached its duty. . . .

Mick v. Kroger Co.
224 N.E.2d 859 (Sup. Ct. Ill. 1967)

Mrs. Mick (plaintiff) sued Kroger (defendant) for damages suffered in a fall she had while she was carrying out her groceries. The trial court awarded her a judgment for $4,000 and this verdict was sustained by the District Appellate Court. Kroger appealed to the Illinois Supreme Court. Reversed.

Throughout the several years during which Mrs. Mick had shopped at Kroger's it had maintained a carry-out service for its customers. On September 10, 1963, she purchased groceries which were placed in a large bag. When informed that no one was available to help her take the groceries out to the family car, she lifted the 30-pound bag and carried it outside. Finding that her husband, who had been waiting for her in their car, had left Kroger's parking lot to pick up their children from school, she rested the bag on the fender of a nearby car. When her husband returned, she picked up the bag and stepped off the sidewalk and onto the parking lot pavement. In doing so she fell, suffering the injuries for which she sued.

UNDERWOOD, JUSTICE.   The principal issue in this case is whether a merchant can be said to have a duty to assist customers in carrying large packages of groceries from its store by virtue of the fact that it customarily did so. In affirming, the appellate court ruled: "The Kroger Company owed to Mrs. Mick, an invitee on its premises, the duty to exercise reasonable care under the circumstances. From the evidence taken as a whole, a jury could and did find that the failure to provide a carry-out service for Mrs. Mick constituted an unreasonable risk of harm and a breach of its duty to exercise reasonable care for her protection as a customer. In this day and age, shoppers generally frequent the modern, self-service supermarkets, where they are furnished with a large cart which they wheel through the store and in which they place large amounts of groceries."

As prerequisite to a successful action for negligence, the plaintiff must establish that the defendant owed a duty to protect her from the injury alleged to have been sustained. Since Mick was a business invitee of Kroger's, the appellate court correctly ruled that it owed her the duty of exercising reasonable care for her safety. A storekeeper, however, is not the insurer of his customer's safety. Therefore, the question before us is whether, considering the allegations and proof herein, the jury should have been allowed to find that carrying groceries from the store building to a car in the adjacent parking lot involved a risk to the customer sufficient to require the merchant, in the exercise of this duty, to provide carry-out service. We think not.

The only allegation in support of Mick's claim that Kroger's duty to exercise reasonable care for her safety required it to furnish an employee to assist in carrying out her groceries is the assertion that it was customary both for her and for other customers. Mick simply asserts that since Kroger voluntarily engaged in the practice of having its employees aid continue to do so, and that its failure to perform that duty on this occasion constituted actionable negligence. While we have not heretofore considered the question of whether custom alone can establish a duty, the few cases which we have found on this issue say that it cannot. In our judgment, application of this rule is particularly appropriate here.

It may be conceded, as the appellate court held, that "under some circumstances, it would be the duty of a store to furnish assistance to its customers in carrying out their groceries," but the issue here is whether such duty existed under the facts of this case. Assuming that conditions might exist which because of their abnormal nature created an unusual risk to the safety of customers transporting groceries from a store to a parking lot, and that, therefore, a duty fell upon the merchant to assist the customer, is of no help to Mick here, for there is neither allegation nor proof of any such circumstances.

We may likewise concede that the carry-out services are an inducement to customers to trade with defendant, but the fact that a merchant voluntarily provides such services does not, in the absence of conditions giving rise to an unreasonable risk to the person who carries out his own purchases, create a duty upon that merchant to continue to provide such service if he chooses to discontinue it. It is, in our judgment, neither good law nor desirable public policy to discourage additions to or improvements in services rendered by those who serve the public by so expanding existing concepts that the voluntary institution of such services *per se* creates a duty to continue them wholly apart from the question as to whether such custom protects the customer from an unreasonable risk to which he is otherwise exposed. We conclude therefore that Mick cannot succeed in her action in the absence of evidence in the record from which the jury could properly have inferred that Kroger exposed her to an unreasonable risk of harm, either because it deviated from its customary practice or apart from the change.

Mick voluntarily purchased the groceries and chose to carry out a bag which she says she felt was too heavy for her, even though alternative courses of action were available. If the carrying of this bag increased the danger of injury to her, we believe she must be said to have exposed herself to the additional hazard.

There is no other evidence in the record of this case from which the jury could infer that Kroger's deviation from its customary practice exposed Mick to unreasonable risk, unless this can be inferred solely from the fact that she was injured. Such an inference would clearly be improper, as it would allow a duty to be shown merely by virtue of the fact that an injury occurred.

Scott v. John H. Hampshire, Inc.
227 A.2d 751 (Ct. App. Md. 1967)

This was an action brought by Scott (plaintiff) against John H. Hampshire, Inc. (defendant) for injuries sustained when Scott was hit by a chain. Judgment for Hampshire Co. and Scott appealed. Reversed and remanded.

On the date of the accident, Scott was working for a contractor in the construction of a regional library. He noticed that instead of a longer choker a piece of chain attached to a steel cable for the purpose of lengthening it was being used as a choker in the unloading of steel from a truck with a crane. Concerned about what he had observed, Scott came down from the building to warn nearby workmen of the dangerous situation. When the supervisor was informed that the use of the chain to unload steel was dangerous and that someone was likely to get hurt, he stated that they would move it further on and stop. And as the steel was moved ahead, the chain broke and struck Scott on his head and about his body while he was standing about twenty feet away. Hampshire, who was the roofing contractor, was the owner of the steel.

When Hampshire Co. moved for a directed verdict at the close of the case for Scott, the trial judge, assuming the existence of primary negligence, ruled that Scott had assumed the risk and was therefore guilty of contributing to the accident.

HORREN, JUDGE. While there is a difference between an assumed risk and contributory negligence in that an assumed risk implies an intentional exposure to a known danger whereas contributory negligence is the doing or failure to do something which directly contributes to the injury sustained, the distinction between the two is often difficult to draw and, as is the case here, is often without importance. So regardless of whether the defense was contributory negligence or assumption of risk, neither defense is applicable in this case where the conduct of Hampshire Co. appears to have created such a situation as to justify if not to compel Scott to undergo the risk of being injured in order to warn others and avert their harm.

This Court, in recognizing the principle that it is commendable to save life, has consistently held that a person who endeavors to avert the consequences of the negligence of another person, by an act which is dangerous but not reckless, is not precluded from recovering damages for injury suffered as a consequence of having interposed. In *Marney* it was said that the "law had so high a regard for human life that it will not impute negligence to an effort to preserve it, unless made under such circumstances as to constitute rashness."

J & Jay, Inc. v. E. Perry Iron & Metal Co.
210 A.2d 462 (Sup. Ct. Maine 1965)

J. & Jay, Inc. (plaintiff), owner of a truck, brought this action against E. Perry Iron & Metal Co. (defendant), charging that Perry negligently operated a crane so as to damage J. & Jay's truck. Jay appealed from a directed verdict in favor of Perry. Reversed.

J. & Jay, Inc. was employed by Nicholas DiPietro to move scrap metal and machinery purchased by the latter from the Bancroft & Martin yard to the junk yard of Perry Iron & Metal. The duties of Jay were limited solely to the transportation. The loading and unloading of the truck was carried out by or under the direction of DiPietro and others.

At Perry's yard Stephen Ham, J. & Jay's driver, placed the truck as instructed directly under the lifting cable of Perry's crane. Bridges hooked the sling, which had remained about the machine, to the cable of the crane in the same manner as the sling had been attached to the Bancroft & Martin crane. The plan was that Perry's crane operator would "take a strain on it," that is to say, would hoist the machine from the floor of the truck. The truck would then be driven from beneath the machine and the machine lowered to the ground.

The truck remained stationary at the point where the driver had been directed. The driver testified that no signal to move was given. As the machine was being hoisted, it struck the side of the truck, causing it to overturn with the resulting damage.

WILLIAMSON, CHIEF JUSTICE.   The doctrine of *res ispa loquitur* in our opinion is applicable. We are satisfied that damage does not ordinarily flow from the shifting or dropping of a load in the operation of a crane in the absence of negligence. It is not unreasonable, therefore, that the person charged with the operation of the crane should face an inference of negligence naturally drawn from the known facts, if he cannot explain his conduct.

We conclude that the evidence would warrant the inference and thus a finding of negligence on the part of someone between the placing of the machine on the truck at Bancroft & Martin and the accident in Perry's yard.

Res ipsa loquitur has been defined and applied repeatedly in our cases.

"The doctrine of *res ipsa loquitur* is not substantive law. It does not need to be alleged in the declaration. It is a rule of evidence which warrants, but does not compel an inference of negligence. The doctrine does not affect the burden of proof. It merely shifts the burden of evidence. The defendant, who knows or should know, must explain. The rule applies where the accident is unexplained and the instrument causing the injury was under the management and control of the defendant, and the unexplained accident is one which does not ordinarily occur if due care is used.

.   .   .

The inference, however, must be warranted. The rule does not apply, unless the unexplained accident is of a kind which does not, according to the common experience of mankind, occur if due care has been exercised. The basis of the inference is the doctrine of probabilities. Facts prove must, in their very nature, indicate such an unusual occurrence as to carry a strong inherent probability of negligence. Mere conjecture and surmise will not suffice."

We are not of the view, however, that under the circumstances responsibility for negligence, if any, on the part of Bridges in attaching the sling to the crane would fall upon Perry. We need not, and do not, determine the precise limits of "exclusive control" as a matter of law. It is sufficient here that the jury properly could have excluded negligence of others than Perry from the cause of the accident.

Strict Liability

Nature of Strict Liability.   Under some circumstances a person is held liable for the results of his acts without reference to the question of negligence. In such a situation the actor is an "insurer" of those who may be injured by his act. These cases involve a situation in which the undertaking is hazardous and harm is foreseeable even though the greatest of precaution is taken, yet the undertaking is of sufficient social benefit that it will be permitted. The actor is permitted to proceed but is required to assume all the risks of the undertaking. The keeping of wild or vicious animals, spraying crops from aircraft, blasting, and trespassing of domestic animals are examples of situations in which strict liability has been imposed. In addition, many legal authorities have noted a trend in the cases to expand the application of the doctrine of strict liability. This trend is particularly noticeable in the area of product liability as demonstrated in the case which follows. The product liability area is discussed extensively in Chapter 34.

Summary

Cases of strict liability may involve situations in which the undertaking is hazardous and harm is foreseeable yet the undertaking is of sufficient social benefit so as to make outright prohibition of such conduct not feasible. The full risk of injury is placed upon the person engaged in this type of conduct. The modern trend is to expand strict liability on the basis of social policy criteria.

Shone Coca-Cola Bottling Company v. *Dolinski*
420 P. 2d 855 (Sup. Ct. Nev. 1966)

Dolinski (plaintiff) brought this action for damages against Coca-Cola Bottling Company (defendant) claiming that he suffered physical and mental distress when he partially consumed the contents of a bottle of "Squirt" containing a decomposed mouse. Coca-Cola appealed from a verdict of $2,500 in favor of Dolinski. Affirmed.

THOMPSON, JUSTICE.   We affirm the verdict and judgment since, in our view, public policy demands that one who places upon the market a bottled beverage in a condition dangerous for use must be held strictly liable to the ultimate user for injuries resulting from such use, although the seller has exercised all reasonable care, and the user has not entered into a contractual relation with him. Perhaps the supporting policy reasons are best expressed by William L. Prosser in his article, "The Fall of the Citadel," (1966): "The public interest in human safety requires the maximum possible protection for the user of the product, and those best able to afford it are the suppliers of the chattel. By placing their goods upon the market, the suppliers represent to the public that they are suitable and safe for use; and by packaging, advertising, and otherwise, they do everything they can to induce that belief. The middleman is no more than a conduit, a mere mechanical device, through which the thing is to reach the ultimate user. The supplier has invited and solicited the use; and when it leads to disaster, he should not be permitted to avoid the responsibility by saying that he made no contract with the consumer, or that he used all reasonable care."

In *Escola* v. *Coca Cola Bottling Co.* (1944), Justice Traynor, in a concurring opinion, wrote: "Even if there is no negligence, however, public policy demands that responsibility be fixed wherever it will most effectively reduce the hazards to life and health inherent in defective products that reach the market." That point of view ultimately became the philosophy of the full court in *Greenman* v. *Yuba Power Products, Inc.* (1962) There Justice Traynor wrote: "The purpose of such liability is to insure that the cost of injuries resulting from defective products are borne by the manufacturer that put such products on the market rather than by the injured persons who are powerless to protect themselves."

We believe that the quoted expressions of policy are sound as applied to the manufacturer and distributor of a bottled beverage. Indeed, eighteen states have judiciously accepted strict liability, without negligence and without privity, as to manufacturers of all types of products; and six more have done so by statute. Though the appellant suggests that only the legislature may declare the policy of Nevada on this subject, the weight of case authority is contra. As indicated, most states approving the doctrine of strict liability have done so by court declaration.

Our acceptance of strict tort liability against the manufacturer and distributor of a bottled beverage does not mean that the plaintiff is relieved of the burden of proving a case. He must still establish that his injury was caused by a defect in the product, and that such defect existed when the product left the hands of the defendant. The concept of strict liability does not prove causation, nor does it trace cause to the defendant.

Affirmed.

Nuisance

Nature of Nuisance. Nuisances may be divided into private and public. A private nuisance is created when a landowner's use or enjoyment of his land is lessened substantially due to unjustifiable conduct on the part of another. The conduct creating the nuisance may be either intentional or negligent. In a few situations liability may be imposed due to the extra-hazardous activity of the defendant even though neither intent nor negligence are present. The fact that the conduct or use of land by a neighbor hinders an owner from putting his land to a special or "delicate use" does not mean the owner hindered can enjoin the conduct. Thus, where one owner operated a race track with the use of floodlights at night, and the adjacent owner operated an open air movie, it was held that the latter could not prevent the former from using the flood-lights.[2] With increasing population and urbanization nuisance litigation is on the increase.

---

[2] *Amphitheaters, Inc.* v. *Portland Meadows,* 198 P.2d 847 (1948).

Summary

Every person is entitled to have the peaceful use and enjoyment of his property free from unjustifiable interference by others. Nuisance law balances the various interests of society in determining which rights shall prevail.

Bie v. *Ingersoll*
135 N.W.2d 250 (Sup. Ct. Wisc. 1965)

This is an action brought by Willy Bie and Betty Bie (plaintiffs) to abate the operation of the plant operated by B. R. Amon & Sons (defendant). Judgment for Bies and Amon appealed. Affirmed.

The gravel pit was in existence and occasionally operated at and prior to the Bie's purchase of their home in 1951. However, operations as an asphalt plant did not commence until 1960. At the time that the plant commenced operations, the land on which it was located was later zoned as "residential," but the area was re-zoned as "industrial" for the specific purpose of accommodating the asphalt plant operations.

Mrs. Bie and other residents of the vicinity testified that the operation of the plant caused a noxious odor to spread over the area. Some witnesses also testified that the odor made them sick and nauseated. One of the residents testified that she could not stay outside when the wind carried the odor in the direction of her property. Some residents of the area also complained of the dust that blew over and into their homes.

HEFFERMAN, JUSTICE.   The only question raised on this appeal is whether the trial court's finding, that the asphalt plant's operation and the trucking in connection with it constituted a nuisance, is contrary to the great weight and clear preponderance of the evidence. The activity complained of must create more than an inconvenience, and must be offensive to the person of ordinary and normal sensibilities. The result is not to be measured by its effect upon those of extreme sensibilities.

The following finding by the trial court is in accord with the above tests for determining whether or not certain activity is a nuisance:

"That the smoke given off from the hot mix plant is a nuisance to the plaintiffs herein, in that it carries onto the property of the plaintiffs dirt, dust, and other unpleasant particles, and that it contains an odor of a noxious nature resembling that of tar and asphalt, and that the dirt and odor referred to substantially interfere with the comfort and enjoyment of the plaintiffs in the use of their property, and injures the use of their property;

"That the operation of trucks to and from the pit upon the roadway constructed therefore is a nuisance in that it creates excessive dust and dirt which is carried upon the property of the plaintiffs, and that it substantially interferes with the comfort and enjoyment of the plaintiffs in the use of their property, and injures the use of their property."

What we said in holding a tanning business a nuisance is applicable here.

"A business necessarily contaminating the atmosphere to the extent indicated should be located where it will not necessarily deprive others of the enjoyment of their property, or lessen their comfort while enjoying the same."

The appellant contends that findings are contrary to the great weight and clear preponderance of the evidence because the zoning authority has classified the property occupied by the asphalt plant as industrial. There are those cases that hold that if the local lawmakers have acted through a zoning ordinance, a court cannot thereafter hold a conforming use to be a nuisance. Other jurisdictions reason that a zoning ordinance and a use permitted by it does not give the property owner immunity from the consequences of maintaining a nuisance. We conclude that though an industrial use is permitted by the ordinance, the property must be used in such way that it will not deprive others of the use and enjoyment of their property. The operation of the asphalt plant, within the purview of the zoning ordinance, is lawful, but as we said in *Pennoyer* v. *Allen*:

". . . such interruption (of enjoyment) and destruction (of comfort) is an invasion of private rights, and to that extent unlawful. It is not so much the manner of doing as the proximity . . . to the adjacent occupant which causes the annoyance." (Parentheses ours.)

In *Dolata* v. *Berthelet Fuel & Supply Co.* we held that a coal yard constituted a nuisance as to neighboring residential properties even though the yard itself is located on the fringe of an industrial business district. Professor Jacob Beuscher of the Wisconsin Law School discusses that problem in an extensive law review article. We agree with the cases discussed there that hold that the zoning classification is not the controlling factor, though it is, of course, entitled to some weight. It is rather "the peculiar nature and the location of the business, not the fact that it is a business, that constitutes the private nuisance and ground for equitable relief."

The appellants argue that if this court agrees with the trial court in finding a nuisance, that the judgment nevertheless must be modified because it is so broad in scope that all further operation of the plant is prohibited. The appellants contend that the release of "one minute particle" of dust would be violative of the order. We do not find the terms of the judgment to be that broad. The trial court abated the plant operation only to the extent that it constituted a nuisance. If the asphalt plant can be operated in a way that odors and dust are not present to such a degree as to constitute a nuisance, then the order does not prohibit the operation of the plant.

Problem Cases

1. Augspurger went into Western Auto's service department to talk to the shop foreman about repairing his car. He heard pounding at the east or far end of the room. He walked to the stall from which the sound was coming and found the foreman trying to remove a steel bearing from a Ford axle with a cold chisel and a ball peen hammer. One end of the axle was on a hoist and a young man was holding the other end on the floor. He did not stand as close to the foreman as several other men who were also

watching the work. After engaging in general conversation for about five minutes, he told the foreman what he wanted. He replied, "Wait until I get this damn bearing off here and I will tell you."

The foreman "had the hammer in one hand, the chisel in the other and the young fellow seemed to be holding the axle up . . . because the axle seemed to be hopping around when it was propped up and he would whack away at that bearing."

Augspurger was injured when his leg was struck by a flying metallic particle. Suit was brought and the trial court sustained defendant's motion for directed verdict on the ground that plaintiff had failed to prove actionable negligence. Plaintiff appealed. Should the case be reversed?

2. Pewatts was a customer in Penney's store. As she was walking along the main aisle of the store with her family, she noticed a display of hats on a side aisle. After proceeding to the display and shopping she returned to the main aisle, tripped over a 6-inch high table holding a mannequin, and was injured. Pewatts filed suit to recover damages from Penney's on the theory that the "attractive display had caused her to walk without watching carefully." The trial court jury awarded $8,000 in damages. Will this be upheld on appeal?

3. Proctor Paint Co. had knowledge that children occasionally played on company grounds. Some employees of Proctor placed cans under fill pipes in a partially open yard to catch the fluid drippings which are the natural by-products of a paint manufacturing operation. Patterson, a 12-year-old, started playing "fireman" with one of the cans and suffered severe burns. Patterson sued Proctor and Proctor defended on the ground that property owners are not liable for mere negligent injury to trespassers. Is this a good defense?

4. Hergenrether sued a truck owner on the theory that the latter's employees had negligently left his truck parked, unattended on a dark "skid row" street with the key in the switch. Hergenrether claimed that this negligence was the cause of theft of the truck which led to his loss when his parked vehicle was struck by the thief. The jury found for Hergenrether and the trial judge gave a judgment notwithstanding the verdict to the defendant. Should the trial judge have let the jury verdict stand?

5. Richardson was shopping at Safeway Store in Kansas City. As he was walking by the meat counter, he suddenly fell backwards. He got up and saw a bone on the floor. He stated that this bone which caused his fall was "about two inches, two by two, was round, and had marrow in the center" and "meat around it." He reported the fall to a lady at the cashier's office and showed her the bone that he had fallen on. Richardson offered no evidence as to how long the bone had been there or how it got there. The lower court ruled for the plaintiff and the defendant appealed. Should the case be reversed?

6. Argo, a blind peddler, would visit every business on a certain street from time to time. He would enter every business where the door opened when he turned the knob. The defendant was having his business renovated and a stair was removed and the well temporarily left open just inside his doorway. Argo entered and fell 18 feet down the open stairwell. Argo probed with his cane and felt the ledge of the stairwell which he assumed to be floorway. Over a period of 12 years Argo had visited the defendant's business about 40 times. Argo sued for his injuries. The defendant argues that he owed no special duty to make his premises safe for blind people and that Argo was a trespasser. Are these arguments valid?

7. Sales Affiliates gave some advertising samples of a permanent wave solution to various

beauty parlor customers without providing any instructions as to how the samples were to be used. McKisson, a beauty parlor operator with bleached hair, put some on her head and her hair all came out. McKisson sued Sales Affiliates on the theory of strict liability. Sales Affiliates argues McKisson was guilty of contributory negligence because being in the trade she knew that wave solution should not be used on bleached hair. Is this a good defense?

8. Guthrie entered the defendant's cattle sale auction barn and a steer broke through the ceiling and fell upon Guthrie. Guthrie sued claiming that the *res ipsa* doctrine applied. Does *res ipsa* apply under these facts?

PART III Contracts

chapter 5. Introduction

Nature of Contract

Basis of Contract. The basis of a contract is a promise or a group of promises. A promise looks to the future, and the person to whom it is made is justified in expecting that it will be fulfilled. In our everyday relationships with our fellow members of society, we make many promises, some of which, for various reasons, will not be performed. The seriousness of one's failure to carry out his promise will depend on the nature of the justified expectation of the person to whom it is made and the importance of its fulfillment. Many promises made in the regular course of human relations may have material significance to the parties involved but have little or no effect on the welfare of society. The failure to discharge the duty created by a promise will not give rise to a right of action in court unless it has those characteristics which make its nonperformance injurious to the general welfare of society. In general, a promise, the performance of which has economic significance, gives rise to rights which will be protected by court action, whereas a promise which has only social significance does not give rise to such rights.

Evolution of the Contract. The courts and law writers have given us many definitions of a contract, all of which recognize the promise, or the agreement which is the result of promises, as an element. A generally accepted definition is: "A contract is a promise or a set of promises for the breach of which the law gives a remedy or the performance of which the law in some way recognizes as a duty." [1] The contract, as defined, has been accepted as the basis of commercial transactions from the earliest times. It was known to and enforced by the Egyptians and Mesopotamians 3,000 or 4,000 years before Christ. We have little reliable information relative to the law of contracts in England

---

[1] American Law Institute, *Restatement of the Law of Contracts* (1932), ¶ 1, p. 1.

during the Anglo-Saxon period. The legal historians agree that some forms of contract were known and used; but since the people did not engage extensively in commerce, the concept of contract was not developed, and there was no clear-cut distinction made between crime, tort, and contract.

After the Norman Conquest the formal contract—that is, the promise in writing and sealed—was enforced by court action, as was also the debt or the obligation to pay for goods sold and delivered to the payee. An informal promise was not enforceable in the regularly established courts. In general, commerce was carried on during this period at the fairs, and controversies growing out of commercial transactions were heard by the judge of the merchant's court, and the law merchant was applied in determining the rights of the parties.

As early as 1378 the courts of equity would give relief to a plaintiff if he had incurred detriment on the faith of the defendant's promise. Both in equity and in law a remediable breach of an oral promise was originally treated as deceit, that is, a tort. As trade expanded, the oral promise grew in importance; and by natural transition, actions upon oral promises came to be regarded as actions on a contract, and the remedy granted was compensation for failure to obtain the thing promised instead of reimbursement for the loss of the thing given for the promise. Also, the courts would enforce contractual promises against the estate of a deceased person, whereas liability for damages for tort ended with the life of the wrongdoer.

By 1603 the common-law courts recognized the enforceability of the simple contract, that is, a promise not under seal. The courts, however, recognized that it would be not only impractical but also undesirable to grant a remedy to the promisee in all instances in which a promise, not under seal, was not performed. After a long period of development the courts finally began to accept the presence of consideration as the test for the enforceability of the simple contract. Today the requirements for a valid contract are (1) an offer, (2) an acceptance of the offer, (3) supported by consideration (with some exceptions), (4) by parties having capacity to contract, and (5) the objective of the contract must be legal. In all cases the promise or promises (offer and acceptance) which are the basis of the contract must be made voluntarily. In addition, in some cases an otherwise valid contract is not enforceable unless it has been reduced to writing. Each of these elements will be discussed in subsequent chapters.

Classification of Contracts.   To aid in the analysis of contractual problems contracts have been classified according to their various characteristics. These classifications are not all-inclusive or all-exclusive and the same contract may be classified under more than one category.

Formal and Informal or Simple.   Contracts under seal, negotiable instruments, and recognizances are classified as formal contracts. All other contracts, whether oral or written, are classed as informal or simple contracts.

Unilateral and Bilateral. As the terms indicate, a unilateral contract is one in which only one of the parties makes a promise, whereas in a bilateral contract, both of the contracting parties make promises. A unilateral contract may be a promise for an act or an act for a promise. For example, a promise to pay a reward for the return of lost property is a promise for an act. The person offering the reward makes a promise and the person returning such property performs the requested act. And a promise to repay money loaned is an act for a promise. The lender performs the act of paying the borrower who in return promises to repay the money. A promise to sell and deliver goods given in exchange for a promise to pay the agreed purchase price at some future date is a bilateral contract or a promise for a promise.

Valid, Unenforceable, Voidable, Void. A valid contract is one which fulfills all the legal requirements for a contract. A court will lend its aid to the enforcement of a valid contract.

An unenforceable contract is one which satisfies the basic requirements for a valid contract, but which the courts, because of some statutory requirement or some rule of law, are denied the authority to enforce. Such a contract may create, in an indirect way, a duty of performance. A contract which is oral but which, if it is to be enforceable, is required by statute to be in writing, is an example of an unenforceable contract. Under some circumstances, such a contract, although not enforceable, may give rise to rights on which a cause of action may be based.

A voidable contract is one which binds one of the parties to the contract but gives to the other party the right, at his election, to withdraw from the contract. For example, a person who has been induced by fraudulent representation to make a promise is given the right to elect not to be bound by his promise. If he elects to perform his promise, however, he can hold the other party to the performance of his duties under the contract.

The term "void" is applied to a contract which is a nullity due to the lack of some essential element of a contract, that is, it has no legal force or effect. In some respects, it is inaccurate to call such a promise a contract. A promise to murder a person given in exchange for a promise to pay an agreed sum would be termed a void contract.

Executed and Executory. A contract becomes executed when all the parties to the contract have fulfilled all their legal obligations created by the contract. Until all such legal obligations have been fulfilled, the contract is executory. If one of the parties has partially fulfilled his obligations under the contract, the contract is often referred to as a partially executed contract. The contract might be executed as to one of the parties to the contract and executory as to the other party.

Express and Implied. An express contract is one in which the promise or promises are stated or declared in direct terms, that is, set forth in words. They may be stated orally or put in writing. An implied contract is one in which the promise or promises are not stated in direct words but are gathered by necessary implication or deduction from the circumstances, the general language, or the conduct of the parties. For example, suppose you go to the dentist and ask him to fill a tooth for you, and say nothing at the time about paying him. You would, under the circumstances, have impliedly promised to pay him the standard fee for such services. You would be bound by a contract implied in fact.

Summary

The basis of a contract is a promise but all promises do not give rise to contractual obligations. The modern concept of a contract was developed in the English law after the 15th century and the simple contract did not attain its present characteristics until the 19th century.

Contracts are divided into classes in order to aid in analysis of contractual problems. The recognized classifications are formal and informal or simple; unilateral and bilateral; valid, unenforceable, voidable and void; executed and executory; and express and implied.

Quasi Contracts

Historical Development. The judges in the common-law courts of England applied, without consideration of the justice of the result, the rules of law which were applicable. As the law developed, however, a gap was left between the law of tort and the law of contracts. In such a situation the party had no remedy since under the strict application of the rules of tort law he had no right to recover and under the strict rules of contract law the parties had not entered into a contract. Usually the essential element of a contract which was lacking was the making of a promise. To remedy this situation the common-law judges resorted to a fiction: they held that a promise had been made or was implied in law even though, as a matter of fact, no promise had been made. The cases were classed as contract cases, and the form of action was the same as that brought to enforce a promise. These obligations based on promises implied in law are known as "quasi contracts." The basis for a recovery in an action in quasi contract is the unjust enrichment of one party at the expense of another. In most cases the remedy is a money judgment for the amount of the unjust enrichment.

Pleadings. The party bringing a suit in quasi contract will state in his pleadings that the party defendant promised to pay or reimburse the plaintiff, and since the promise is implied in law, the party defendant will not be permitted to deny in his answer the making of the promise. The basis of recovery in quasi contract is the justice of the case rather than the application of technical rules of law.

Measure of Damages. The measure of damages for the breach of a contract is, as a general rule, the sum of money which is necessary to place the injured party in substantially the same position he would have occupied had the contract been performed. In quasi contract the court, as a general rule, awards a judgment for an amount equivalent to the unjust enrichment of the party defendant.

Basis for Recovery. The cases which come under the heading of quasi contracts are of infinite variety, and it is impossible to list the situations that may arise which will justify a recovery in quasi contract. In any situation in which a party is justified in believing that a binding contract exists and the party performs under such belief, thereby benefiting the other party, he may recover for the benefits conferred in a suit in quasi contract.

If the parties have entered into a valid contract, the courts will not add to or alter the terms of the contract or allow additional recovery by the application of the principles of quasi contract. For example, suppose Albert has contracted to work for Bill and Bill has contracted to pay Arthur $150 per week for a 40-hour week. And then some weeks Arthur works less and some weeks more than the 40 hours. If Arthur should bring suit in quasi contract to recover a judgment for payment for the hours in those weeks he had worked overtime he would be denied recovery.

One cannot recover in quasi contract for benefits voluntarily conferred on another without his knowledge or consent, or under circumstances which justify him in accepting the benefits believing them to be a gift. Suppose Parks paints Oren's house when Oren is away on his vacation. Parks cannot recover for the benefits conferred on Oren in a suit in quasi contract. One cannot force benefits on another without the knowledge and consent of the other person and then force him to pay for the benefits.

Summary

The purpose of granting a remedy in quasi contract is to prevent unjust enrichment of one party at the expense of another. The amount of the recovery is based on the amount of the unjust enrichment. Quasi contract cannot be brought where there is an express or implied valid contract covering the subject matter.

Gebhardt Bros., Inc. v. Brimmel
143 N.W.2d 479 (Sup. Ct. Wisc. 1966)

This was an action in quasi contract by Gebhardt Bros., Inc. (plaintiff) against Brimmel (defendant) for the value of fill delivered. Judgment for Gebhardt and Brimmel appealed. Reversed.

Gebhardt entered a subcontract with Semrow, a general contractor, whereby Gebhardt was to supply fill for construction work to be done by Semrow on Brimmel's land. The prime contract included the cost of this fill work. Semrow failed to pay Gebhardt for the fill delivered and Gebhardt sued Brimmel.

HEFFERMAN, JUDGE.   We have previously held that, though there is no express contract, there may be circumstances where, by conduct of the parties, it becomes unjust or inequitable for one party to fail to pay for the goods or services furnished by another. We have previously stated that three elements must be established in order that a plaintiff may establish a claim based on unjust enrichment. These elements are: (1) a benefit conferred upon the defendant by the plaintiff; (2) an appreciation or knowledge by the defendant of the benefit; and (3) the acceptance or retention by the defendant of the benefit under such circumstances as to make it inequitable for the defendant to retain the benefit without payment of its value.

The first of these two elements have been adequately proved, and the finding that 150 loads of earth were delivered to Brimmel's property is not contrary to the great weight and clear preponderance of the evidence. We cannot, however, concur with the learned trial judge's legal conclusion that under the circumstances it was inequitable for the defendant Brimmel to retain the benefit without the payment of its value. That conclusion overlooks the clear and undisputed testimony of Brimmel that the cost of the fill was included in the price agreed upon between him and the general contractor. The evidence could support no other finding. The facts also show that there was an express contract between Gebhardt and Semrow, the general contractor, for the payment of the fill. That Gebhardt recognized this is apparent from the fact that no effort was made to collect from Brimmel until efforts to collect on the express contract with Semrow had proved to be fruitless. . . .

. . . This case is directly governed by our decision in *Superior Plumbing Co.* v. *Tefs* (1965). We therein held that a subcontractor must resort for payment to the principal contractor and not to the owner of the property and that the owner is not liable on an implied contract simply because he has received goods or services or knows that the services have been rendered.

Questions and Problem Cases

1. Into what two general classes may we divide promises?
2. Define a contract.
3. What is the difference between a unilateral and a bilateral contract?
4. What is the difference between a unenforceable contract and a voidable contract?
5. In 1955, La Maita agreed on his retirement to sell his two-family house and garage to Misisco. At the time the two apartment parts of the house brought in $62.50 per month. Misisco moved into one of these units paying $30 per month. Later he rented both units paying $100 per month. Misisco spent about $5,000 over the next few years improving the property with the knowledge and consent of La Maita. In 1961, La Maita brought eviction proceedings and had Misisco evicted. Misisco brought a suit in quasi contract for the reasonable value of benefits conferred; but the trial court ruled that

since there was no written contract no recovery could be had by Misisco. Was this ruling correct?

6. In January, 1956, Smith and Morris sold stock in the First National Bank of Marion (Bank) to Stowell. At approximately the same time Stowell gave Morris an option to repurchase 10 shares of the stock of the bank at $305 per share at any time Stowell disposed of it. In 1958, 30 shares of the bank's stock was issued to Stowell as a stock dividend. About October 1, 1961, Stowell, who was an officer and cashier of the bank, decided to leave the bank and to dispose of his stock. He offered 10 shares of his stock to Morris at the option price, $305 per share. Morris claimed that under the option he was entitled to purchase the 30 shares issued to Stowell as a stock dividend. Morris based his claim on the theory that Stowell was unjustly enriched and that he had a right to recover the 30 shares of stock in an action of quasi contract. The court held that the option contract was complete and not ambiguous and that Morris had no right to the 30 shares of stock. Should this decision be reversed on appeal?

chapter 6. Offer

Introduction

Nature of Offer. Before parties enter into a contractual relationship they usually engage in informal negotiations. Whether these informal negotiations result in the creation of a contractual relationship will depend on whether the parties reach a mutual agreement and on the presence of other essential elements.[1] Although these informal negotiations may not be a part of the final agreement, they do point up the contractual intent of the parties.

To have an agreement, two or more persons must arrive at a mutual understanding with one another. Generally, this is accomplished by the making of a proposition by one party and the acceptance of that proposition by the other. A proposal or offer looks to the future and is an expression of what the party making the offer—the offeror—promises shall be done or happen or shall not be done or happen, provided the party to whom the offer is made—the offeree—complies with stated conditions.

An offer to contract is composed of two parts: (1) an expression by the offeror of what he promises shall be done or happen or shall not be done or happen, and (2) an expression of what the offeror demands in return.

Form of Offer. The expression by the offeror may be made in any form which will serve to communicate his proposition to the offeree. It may be made by acts, by spoken words, by written words, or by any combination of these. All that is necessary is that the one making the offer communicate his proposition, by some means, to the offeree.

Businessmen frequently use a standard form of purchase order in making an offer to buy. Such forms usually include a statement of the terms of the offer to purchase.

---

[1] Consideration, parties having capacity to contract, and a legal objective.

Intent. Since a contract is based on an obligation voluntarily assumed, the offeror must make his proposition with the intent to contract, thus making "intent" an essential element of an offer. In the law, intent is always tested by an objective standard. What either party to a contract may have honestly thought—a subjective test of intent—is immaterial. In determining the presence of intent, the circumstances surrounding the parties, their acts, their words, and any other facts which may aid the courts in reconstructing the situation are offered in evidence, and from this reconstruction of the entire happening, the court decides whether a reasonable man familiar with the business being transacted would be justified in believing that an offer had been made. Neither party will be permitted to offer as evidence what he thought, that is, what his mental reaction was; that is immaterial.

It is not essential that the party be conscious of the legal effect of his words and acts. It is essential, however, that the acts manifesting the making of the offer be done intentionally, and that they be done voluntarily.

Certainty of Terms. An offer, the terms of which are incomplete or vague, cannot serve as the basis for a contract. Judges frequently make the statement that if the parties have not made a contract, the courts will not make one for them. The offeror need not state the terms of his offer with absolute certainty. However, they must be sufficiently definite to enable the court to determine the intention of the parties and to fix the legal rights and duties arising therefrom. An offer need not state time, price, quantity, or other terms with mathematical exactness, but it must state a formula or basis whereby such matters can be determined with reasonable certainty.

For example, an offer to furnish all the coal the offeree will need in his business during a stated period of time is sufficiently certain, since the court can determine the amount of coal the offeree "needs" during the period. If the offeror, in making the offer, uses such vague expressions as "I will do right by you" or "I will make you a good price," the offer will, as a general rule, be held to be void for uncertainty of terms.

Omission of Terms. If the contracting parties omit from their agreement material terms or leave material terms for future agreement, the court will hold that because of uncertainty of terms, no contract results. The omission of minor or immaterial terms will not affect the validity of an offer; and under some circumstances, what appears to be an omitted term may be supplied by usage of trade. In a case involving a provision in a lease whereby the landlord agreed to sell the leased premises to the tenant for a stipulated price, "terms to be agreed upon," the tenant having the privilege to accept at any time before the expiration of the term of the lease, the court held that a contract to sell was concluded when the tenant tendered the full stipulated price in cash. However, in this case the tenant had expended substantial sums in improving the building in anticipation of accepting the offer, and the decision was based on the equities of the case, not on its technical aspects.[2]

Usage of Trade.   Usage of trade is defined in the Uniform Commercial Code (Section 1–205 [2]) as follows: "A usage of trade is any practice or method of dealing having such regularity of observance in a place, vocation or trade as to justify an expectation that it will be observed with respect to the transaction in question. The existence and scope of such a usage are to be proved as fact." When a contract is negotiated the presumption is that the parties intend any usage of trade to be a part of the contract. If the parties do not wish to be bound by an established usage of trade they must make it clear by their words or acts that they do not wish to be so bound. And they must make clear the result they wish to reach or the courts will hold in some instances that the parties intended the usage to be effective, or in other instances that the terms of the proposition are too uncertain to create a contract.

Preliminary Negotiations.   There are times when one may wish to enter into a contract with another person but, instead of making an offer, will try to induce the other party to make the offer. To accomplish this, he will extend an invitation to negotiate. Suppose Allen owns a house which he wishes to sell. He may approach Bailey and say, "I would like to sell my house to you. How much will you offer me for it?" Allen has not made an offer. Suppose Allen says, "I would like to sell my house. I think it is worth at least $15,000." Allen still has not made an offer.

In the negotiation of a sale, it is a common practice for the seller to make statements of what he thinks he should receive for the property, and for the buyer in turn to make statements as to his idea of the value of the property, without either party making a clear-cut proposition which would be interpreted as an offer. This is what is known as "dickering," and the courts have recognized that in the transaction of business it is often to the advantage of the parties to dicker. Such dickering is generally termed "preliminary negotiation" and is not an offer.

Advertisements.   As a general rule the courts have held that an advertisement of goods for sale at a stated price is not an offer to sell the goods at that price, that it is merely an invitation to negotiate for the sale of the goods. Likewise, they have held that the distribution of a price list, either through the mails or by general advertisement, or a mere quotation of a price is not an offer to sell the goods at the listed price. However, if an advertisement contains a positive promise and a positive statement of what the advertiser demands in return, the courts will generally hold that it is an offer.

Rewards.   Advertisements of rewards for the return of lost property or for

---

[2] *Morris* v. *Ballard,* 16 F.2d 175 (D.C. Cir. 1926).

the capture of criminals are common examples of offers made through advertising. Such offers are offers for unilateral contracts. The offer is accepted by the performance of the requested act—the return of the lost property or the capture of the criminal. The nature of the offer is such that there can be only one acceptance and only one resulting contract; consequently, it is logical to conclude that when a person advertises to pay a reward for the return of lost property or the capture of a criminal, he does so with the intent to make an offer.

Bids. When one advertises for bids on construction work, the nature of the contemplated contract is such that it is logical to assume that the advertiser is interested in soliciting offers and that the advertisement is an invitation to make offers. One may expressly state in the advertisement for bids that the job will be let to the lowest responsible bidder without reservation. In such a situation as this, the advertisement is an offer to let the job to the lowest bidder.

As a general rule the advertising for bids and the letting of contracts by governmental units are controlled by statute, and general contract law does not apply. Such statutes usually set out the method of advertising to be used and the form to be followed in making the bid, and provide that the contract is to be let to the lowest and *best* bidder.

Auctions. Unless, in the terms governing the auction, language is used which clearly expresses the intention to sell without reservation to the highest bidder or to the lowest bidder, as the case may be, the bidder will be the offeror, and the seller will be free to accept or reject bids, as the case may be. In the ordinary auction, no contract is made until the auctioneer strikes the goods off to the highest bidder. In Section 2–328 of the Uniform Commercial Code the rules of law which apply to an auction of goods are set out.

Summary

The offer must state (1) what the offeror promises and (2) what he demands in return. It may be made in any manner whereby the offeror can communicate his proposition to the offeree. It must be made with "intent" to contract, and its terms must be reasonably certain. General business practices and common usages play an important role in determining whether an offer has been made. Since dickering is common in the transaction of business, an indication of a willingness to negotiate will not be interpreted as an offer; and as a general rule, advertisement of goods for sale are not offers.

However, an advertisement offering to pay a reward is usually an offer. An advertisement for bids is, as a general rule, a solicitation of offers, and substantially the same rule applies to sales at auction. Whether or not an offer is made by an advertisement will depend on its wording.

Lefkowitz v. *Great Minneapolis Surplus Store, Inc.*
86 N.W. 2d 689 (Sup. Ct. Minn. 1957)

This was an action by Morris Lefkowitz (plaintiff) against Great Minneapolis Surplus Store, Inc. (defendant), to recover damages for breach of a contract to sell a certain fur piece which it had offered for sale through a newspaper advertisement. Judgment for Lefkowitz, and Surplus Store, Inc., appealed. Judgment affirmed.

On April 6, 1956, Surplus Store, Inc. published the following advertisement in a Minneapolis newspaper:

> "Saturday 9 A.M. Sharp
> 3 Brand New
> Fur
> Coats
> Worth to $100.00
> First Come
> First Served
> $1
> Each"

On April 13, Surplus Store again published an advertisement in the same newspaper as follows:

> "Saturday 9 A.M.
> 2 Brand New Pastel
> Mink 3-Skin Scarfs
> Selling for $89.50
> Out they go
> Saturday. Each . . . $1.00
> 1 Black Lapin Stole
> Beautiful,
> worth $139.50 . . . $1.00
> First Come
> First Served"

On each of the Saturdays following the publication of the above-described ads Lefkowitz was the first to present himself at the appropriate counter in the Surplus Store and on each occasion demanded the coat and the stole so advertised, and indicated his readiness to pay the sale price of $1. On both occasions, Surplus Store refused to sell the merchandise to him, stating on the first occasion that by a "house rule" the offer was intended for women only and sales would not be made to men, and on the second visit that Lefkowitz knew Surplus Store's house rules.

MURPHY, JUSTICE. The trial court properly disallowed Lefkowitz's claim for the value of the fur coats since the value of these articles was speculative and uncertain. The only evidence of value was the advertisement itself to the effect that the coats were "Worth to $100.00," how much less being speculative especially in view of the price for which they were offered for sale. With reference to the offer of Surplus Store on April 13, 1956, to sell the "1 Black Lapin Stole * * * worth $139.50 * * * "the trial court held that the value of this article was established and granted judgment in favor of Lefkowitz for that amount less the $1 quoted purchase price.

Surplus Store contends that a newspaper advertisement offering items of merchandise for sale at a named price is a "unilateral offer" which may be withdrawn without notice. It relies upon authorities which hold that, where an advertiser publishes in a newspaper that he had a certain quantity or quality of goods which he wants to dispose of at certain prices and on certain terms, such advertisements are not offers which become contracts as soon as any person to whose notice they may come signifies his acceptance by notifying the other that he will take a certain quantity of them. Such advertisements have been construed as an invitation for an offer of sale on the terms stated, which offer, when received, may be accepted or rejected and which therefore does not become a contract of sale until accepted by the seller; and until a contract has been so made, the seller may modify or revoke such prices or terms.

There are numerous authorities which hold that a particular advertisement in a newspaper or circular letter relating to a sale of articles may be construed by the court as constituting an offer, acceptance of which would complete a contract.

The test of whether a binding obligation may originate in advertisements addressed to the general public is "whether the facts show that some performance was promised in positive terms in return for something requested."

The authorities above cited emphasize that, where the offer is clear, definite, and explicit, and leaves nothing open for negotiation, it constitutes an offer, acceptance of which will complete the contract.

Whether in any individual instance a newspaper advertisement is an offer rather than an invitation to make an offer depends on the legal intention of the parties and the surrounding circumstances. We are of the view on the facts before us that the offer by Surplus Store of the sale of the Lapin fur was clear, definite, and explicit, and left nothing open for negotiation. Lefkowitz having successfully managed to be the first one to appear at the seller's place of business to be served, as requested by the advertisement, and having offered the stated purchase price of the article, he was entitled to performance on the part of Surplus Store.

Surplus Store contends that the offer was modified by a "house rule" to the effect that only women were qualified to receive the bargains advertised. The advertisement contained no such restriction. This objection may be disposed of briefly by stating that, while an advertiser has the right at any time before acceptance to modify his offer, he does not have the right, after acceptance, to impose new or arbitrary conditions not contained in the published offer.

Drew v. *John Deere Co. of Syracuse, Inc.*
241 N.Y.S.2d 267 (App. Div. N.Y. 1963)

This was an action by Drew (plaintiff) against John Deere Co. (defendant) for breach of a contract to sell a repossessed tractor. Drew appealed from an unfavorable ruling on his motion for a summary judgment. Affirmed.

HALPERN, JUSTICE. The theory of the complaint is that a contract by John Deere to sell a certain tractor to Drew had come into existence as the result of an auction sale conducted by John Deere and that Deere breached the contract by refusing to deliver the tractor upon the tender of the purchase price.

John Deere was the assignee of a conditional sales contract covering the tractor, which it had repossessed upon the vendee's default. More than 50% of the purchase price having been paid, John Deere was required to resell the repossessed tractor at public auction. John Deere advertised the auction sale, stating that the property would be sold to the highest bidder at the sale. Drew bid $1,500 at the sale but the auctioneer did not accept the bid; instead he announced that John Deere itself had bid $1,600 and accordingly the property was struck down to John Deere.

Drew claims that John Deere was disqualified to bid because it had not announced in advance that it intended to bid pursuant to section 102, subdivision 4, of the Personal Property Law. Hence, Drew argues, his bid was the highest lawful bid and therefore a contract of sale came into existence between Drew and John Deere for the sale of the tractor at the price bid.

Drew's whole case rests upon the theory that the auction was one "without reserve." At such an auction the owner of the property has no right to withdraw the property after bidding has commenced. It is also necessarily implicit in an auction "without reserve," that the owner of the property may not himself bid in the property, as this would be equivalent to withdrawing it from sale (*Restatement of Contracts,* §27). Various legal theories have been advanced for the holding that the announcement that the auction would be "without reserve" imposes a binding legal obligation upon the owner, but the best view seems to be that the owner, by making such an announcement, enters into a collateral contract with all persons bidding at the auction that he will not withdraw the property from sale, regardless of how low the highest bid might be. Therefore, the highest *bona fide* bidder at an auction "without reserve" may insist that the property be sold to him or that the owner answer to him in damages.

On the other hand, in an auction sale not expressly announced to be "without reserve," the owner may withdraw the property at any time before it is actually "knocked down" to a bidder by the auctioneer. There is no contract until the offer made by the bidder is accepted by the auctioneer's "knocking down" the property to him. . . .

In our case, there was no express statement that the auction would be "without reserve." The statement that the sale would be made to the highest bidder is not the equivalent of an announcement that the auction would be "without reserve." "An announcement that a person will sell his property at public auction to the highest bidder is a mere declaration of intention to hold an auction at which bids will be received."

Corbin writes that the auctioneer at an auction sale in asking for bids, does not make an operative offer. "This is true even though the seller or his representative has issued advertisements or made other statements that the article will be sold to the highest bidder, or is offered for sale to the highest bidder. Such statements are merely preliminary negotiations, not intended and not reasonably understood to be intended to affect legal relations. When such is the case, the seller or his representative is as free to reject the bids, highest to lowest, as are the bidders to withdraw them. The seller may at any time withdraw the article from sale, if he has not already accepted a bid. He need give no reasons; indeed, he rejects all bids by merely failing to accept them—by doing nothing at all. It is not necessary for him to say that 'the privilege is reserved to reject any and all bids.' Such a statement is merely evidence that the goods are not being offered 'without reserve.' "

Since, upon the present record, the auction sale appears to have been "with reserve," no contract of sale came into existence, even if we assume that Drew was the highest lawful bidder. . . .

Terms Included in Offers

Tags, Tickets, Folders, Etc. An offer has not been communicated until the offeree has knowledge of the proposition. The writing and mailing of a letter stating the offeror's proposition is not effective as an offer until it is received by the offeree. If one writes a letter in which he makes an offer but the letter is lost and never delivered, no offer has been made. A more difficult situation arises when the offeror prints his proposition on a tag attached to goods shipped, on a ticket delivered to the purchaser of a service, on an invoice sent for goods shipped, or on a folder delivered with monthly bills or distributed as handbills. When has a proposition made in some such manner been communicated to the offeree? No clear-cut rules can be extracted from the decided cases, but the courts have developed standards which aid in solving the problem. If the offeree actually reads the terms, or if he does not read them, but under the circumstances should know as a reasonable man that the tag, ticket, invoice, or handbill contains the terms of the offeror's proposition, the proposition has been communicated to him. However, if the offeree has no reason to know that the printed matter on the tag, ticket, invoice, or handbill contains a proposition and he does not read it, there has been no communication. There is presumption against the inclusion in contracts of terms located in unusual places or printed in microscopic print.

Summary

An offer must be communicated to be effective. Only the offeree has the right to accept an offer. Whether a proposition printed on a tag, ticket, invoice, or handbill has been communicated depends on the facts and circumstances of each individual case, but the test is what reasonable men would have intended.

Cutler Corp. v. *Latshaw*
97 A.2d 234 (Sup. Ct. Pa. 1954)

This was a petition by Jennie Latshaw (plaintiff) against Cutler Corp. (defendant) to set aside a judgment. Judgment for Cutler Corp. and Latshaw appealed. Reversed.

On November 20, 1951, Latshaw contracted in writing to pay the Cutler Corp. the sum of $6,456 for certain work to be done and material to be furnished in repairing her premises in Philadelphia. Dissatisfied with the manner in which the work was being performed, Latshaw ordered the employees of the Cutler Corp. to cease operation until defects in the work were corrected.

On July 23, 1952, the Cutler Corp. confessed judgment against Latshaw in the sum of $5,238.56 under an alleged warrant of attorney contained in the contract. Latshaw petitioned for a rule to show cause why the judgment should not be stricken from the record; the lower court made the rule absolute; and Cutler appealed.

The contract consisted of five form sheets carrying certain printed matter. The face of each sheet began with a standardized identification of the parties and the designative of Latshaw and Cutler, respectively, as "buyer" and "contractor."

Then followed in small type the wording: "Upon your acceptance below, you are hereby requested by the undersigned owner of the installation premises, hereinafter called 'Buyer,' to furnish and install the materials shown in the following specifications at the installation premises mentioned below (subject to conditions on reverse side)."

In the middle of the sheet, in large type, appeared the single word: Specifications. Beneath this word, *in handwriting,* followed a list of the various items of work to be done and materials to be supplied by Cutler.

The reverse side of each sheet carried in very small type eight paragraphs, No. 6 of which spelled out a warrant of attorney with confession of judgment. Although each reverse sheet also carried the word, "Specifications," with "continued" in parantheses, no specifications were listed—in spite of the fact that the entire list of the specifications could not be contained on the first sheet and had to go over to other sheets. In fact, with the exception of the printing indicated, the reverse sides of the sheets were blank.

MUSMANNO, JUSTICE.   A warrant of attorney authorizing judgment is perhaps the most powerful and drastic document known to civil law. The signer deprives himself of every defense and every delay of execution, he waives exemption of personal property from levy and sale under the exemption laws, he places his cause in the hands of a hostile defender. The signing of a warrant of attorney is equivalent to a warrior of old entering a combat by discarding his shield and breaking his sword. For that reason the law jealously insists on proof that this helplessness and impoverishment was voluntarily accepted and consciously assumed.

The case at bar falls short of producing evidence that Miss Latshaw was even aware that a warrant of attorney was remotely contemplated. The physical characteristics of the five-page document demonstrate that the reverse sides were entirely ignored. Although the sizeable blank spaces on the reverse pages could have been utilized for the continuing enumeration of specifications, the parties adopted additional sheets, writing only on the faces thereof, for that list. In the absence of any explanation as to why five pages were used when three would have sufficed (employing the reverse sides), the conclusion is inescapable that the parties purposely intended not to make the reverse sides of the sheets any part of the contract.

The mere physical inclusion of the warrant of attorney in a mass of fine type verbiage on each reverse sheet does not of itself make it part of the contract. In the case of *Summers* v. *Hibbard Co.,* the question arose as to whether certain printed phrases on a letterhead became part of the contract entered into between the involved parties. The Supreme Court of Illinois held:

"The mere fact that appellants wrote their acceptance on a blank form for letters at the top of which were printed the words, 'All sales subject to strikes and accidents' no more made those words a part of the contract than they made the words there printed, 'Summers Bros. & Co., Manufacturer of Box-Annealed Common & Refined Sheet Iron,' a part of the contract. The offer was absolute. The written acceptance which they themselves wrote, was just as absolute. The printed words were not in the body of the letter, or referred to therein. The fact that they were printed at the head of their letter heads would not have the effect of preventing appellants from entering into an unconditional contract for sale."

In the case of *Sturtevant Co.* v. *Fireproof Film Co.,* . . . The Court of Appeals of New York (stated:) "When an offer, proposal, or contract is expressed in clear and explicit terms, matter printed in small type at the top or bottom of the office stationery of the writer, where it is not easily seen, which is not in the body of the instrument or referred to therein, is not necessarily to be considered as a part of such offer, proposal, or contract."

One of the most hateful acts of the ill-famed Roman tyrant Caligula was that of having the laws inscribed upon pillars so high that the people could not read them. Although the warrant of attorney in the numerous sheets of the contract at bar was within the vision of Latshaw, it was so placed as to be completely beyond her contemplation of its purport. An inconspicuously printed legend on a contract form or letterhead which is obviously fortuitous, irrelevant or superfluous is no more part of the agreement entered into than the advertisements on the walls of the room in which the contract is signed.

Diminutive type grossly disproportionate to that used in the face body of a contract cannot be ignored; it has its place in law, and, where space is at a premium, it allows for instruction, guidance and protection which might otherwise be lost, but where it is used as an ambush to conceal legalistic spears to strike down other rights agreed upon, it will receive rigorous scrutinization by the courts for the ascertainment of the true meaning which may go beyond the literal import.

Termination of Offer

Duration of Offer. When an offeror makes an offer, he thereby confers on the offeree the power to create a contract by the acceptance of the offer; but for practical as well as legal reasons, such a power cannot exist for an indefinite period. The power to convert an offer into a contract may be terminated in the following ways: (1) by provisions in the offer, (2) by lapse of time, (3) by revocation, (4) by rejection of the offer, (5) by death or insanity of the offeror or offeree, (6) by destruction of the subject matter of the proposed contract, or (7) by the performance of the proposed contract becoming illegal.

Provisions in Offer. When the offeror states in his offer that the offer must be accepted within a designated time, the offeree does not have the privilege of accepting after the expiration of the designated time. After the stated time has elapsed, it is impossible for the offeree to comply with all the terms of the original offer. Often, in limiting the time for acceptance, the offeror will use such expressions as "by return mail," "for immediate acceptance," and "prompt wire acceptance." "By return mail" does not of necessity require the acceptance to go out by the next mail, especially in large cities where mails are leaving hourly; but it does require an answer the same day the offer is received unless received too late to be answered that day, and in that event the acceptance must be dispatched on the opening for business the succeeding day. "Immediate acceptance" and "prompt wire acceptance" give the offeree a shorter time than "by return mail." The time would depend to some extent on the nature of the transaction; in any event, a few hours at the longest would be the limit of time allowed in which to accept.

An offeror may state that the offer must be accepted within a specified number of days without expressly stating the date from which the time shall start to run. For example, an offer may contain a provision that the offer must be accepted or rejected within 10 days. This creates an ambiguity, and the courts have not been in accord in their holdings. One view is that the offer is not communicated until it is received and therefore the time does not start to run until the offer is received. The opposing view is that the offeror is imposing the time limit for his own benefit and that the time should begin to run from the date of the offer.

An attempt to accept an offer after it has terminated due to the lapse of the time stated therein is, in legal effect, an offer to contract on the terms of the original offer. If the original offeror is still willing to contract on the terms of his original offer and indicates his willingness to the original offeree, a contract will result.

Lapse of Time. If no time for acceptance is stated in the offer, the offer terminates on the lapse of a reasonable time. This rule of law has been developed by the courts and is based on practical grounds. In effect, it writes into an offer which contains no provision for its termination a provision that the offer must be accepted within a reasonable time. The length of time which is reasonable must depend on the circumstances of the case. Each case will have to be decided as a separate proposition, and general rules will be of little help.

If the parties are trading on the floor of the stock or commodity exchange, any offer made will have to be accepted immediately. Under such circumstances, trading is very rapid, and anyone trading on the exchange knows that offers made are not intended to be held open for more than a very short time. If the offer is made relative to the sale of real estate, a reasonable time for acceptance might well be counted in days. But if the offer is made relative to the sale of a commodity for which there is an established market, the court will hold that the offeree has waited an unreasonable time if he delays his acceptance until he can determine the price trends in the market.

If an offer is made when the parties are negotiating face to face, the time for acceptance will not extend beyond the period of the negotiations unless special words or circumstances clearly indicate that the offeror intends to hold his offer open after they part.

In cases of offers of reward for the capture of criminals, the offer may be open for acceptance for a very long time. In one case in which there was an offer to pay a reward for the capture of the person who had committed a particular crime, the court held that the offer would not lapse until the running of the statute of limitations on the crime. Offers made by trade associations to pay rewards to persons capturing criminals who have committed crimes against members of the association may continue for years.

Revocation. As a general rule the offeror may revoke his offer at any time before acceptance. This rule applies even though the offer states that it will remain open or the offeror promises to hold it open for a stated period of time. However, if the offeror contracts to hold the offer open for a stated period of time, that is, promises for a consideration to hold it open, the offer is irrevocable for the agreed period. This is known as an option. Also, in those states which enforce contracts under seal, a promise under seal to hold an offer open for a stated period is irrevocable for the stated period. The courts have, in some recent cases, held that if an offer is made under such circumstances that the offeror knows or should know that the offeree will change his position in reliance on the offer and he does change his position in justifiable reliance on the offer, the offeror will be estopped from withdrawing his offer for a reasonable time. This exception is usually treated as falling under the doctrine of promissory estoppel.

Communication of Revocation. If the offeror wishes to revoke his offer, he must communicate his revocation to the offeree. The rules which apply to the communication of an offer also apply to the communication of a revocation. In all but a few states, a letter, telegram, or message of revocation is not effective until it is received by the offeree. In a few states a revocation is effective when dispatched.

If the offeror has offered to sell designated property to the offeree and thereafter, but before the offer has terminated, the offeror sells the property to another and this is known to the offeree, the courts have held that the offeree cannot, by giving notice of acceptance, create a contract. The knowledge on the part of the offeree that the offeror has changed his position in such a manner that he can no longer perform the promise in his offer has been held as equivalent to notice of revocation.

Revocation of Offer to Public. An offer to the general public is communicated by making a general announcement of the offer. This announcement may be made through the newspapers, magazines, posters, handbills, radio, or any other means suitable to the purpose of the offeror. If the offerer, after having made the offer, wishes to withdraw it, he must announce his withdrawal in substantially the same manner as that used in announcing the offer. The fact that one read or heard the offer but did not read or hear the withdrawal is of no moment. If the same publicity has been given to the revocation as was given to the offer, the offer is revoked as to the entire public, and an attempt to accept after the publication of the withdrawal is ineffective.

Revocation of Offer for Unilateral Contracts. The general rule that an offer may be revoked at any time before acceptance applies to some types of offers for unilateral contracts, but there is some question whether the courts will apply the rule in all cases. If an offer for a reward is made and the offeror revokes the offer before the reward is claimed, the revocation will be effective.

If the act requested is of such a nature that an appreciable period of time is required for its performance, should the offeror be permitted to revoke the offer an instant before the act is performed and the offer accepted? If the nature of the act is such that the offeror receives benefits from the performance, a recovery for the benefits conferred will be allowed in a suit in quasi contract. If the act is such that, although the performance is detrimental to the offeree, it is not beneficial to the offeror, no recovery can be had in quasi contract. Justice would dictate in such a case that the offer should be held to be irrevocable until the offeree, having started performance, would have a reasonable time to complete the performance.

Cases involving the revocation of offers for unilateral contracts are not very common. Business contracts are generally bilateral; and the courts, if the facts permit, will interpret a contract to be bilateral rather than unilateral.

Rejection. When the offeree rejects an offer, it is terminated, and any subsequent attempt to accept it is inoperative. The offeree may reject the offer by expressly stating that he will not accept it, or he may indicate his rejection by acts or words or by conduct which will justify the offeror in believing that the offeree does not intend to accept the offer.

If the offeree replies to the offeror by making a counteroffer or a conditional acceptance, the offer is terminated. A counteroffer is a statement by the offeree that he will enter into the transaction only on the terms stated by him in his counteroffer. A conditional acceptance is a statement by the offeree that he will accept the offer only if certain changes are made in the terms of the offer. Both, by implication, are rejections of the original offer.

Inquiry Regarding Terms. An inquiry by the offeree regarding the terms of the offer is neither a counteroffer nor a conditional acceptance, and it will not terminate the offer. An unequivocal acceptance of an offer accompanied by statements that the terms of the offer are harsh or unreasonable or that better terms should be granted (a grumbling acceptance) is not a counteroffer or a conditional acceptance. Whether the offeree has made an inquiry as to the terms of an offer, a counteroffer, a conditional acceptance, or an unequivocal acceptance accompanied by statements regarding the terms of the offer is a matter of interpretation to be decided according to the facts of each case.

If an offeror makes an offer to be accepted within a certain time and then further states that he will consider counteroffers made within the time limit without such counteroffers terminating the offer, a counteroffer will not be a rejection if it comes within the terms of the offer.

Likewise, if an offeree states that he is holding the offer under advisement but is willing to close the deal before the time stated for the termination of the offer, provided the offeror will accept the terms of the offeree, such action will not terminate the offer, and on the refusal of the offeror to alter the terms of his offer, the offeree may still accept the original offer.

Death or Insanity. There are some situations over which the parties have no control which will terminate an offer. It is a well-established rule that the death or insanity of either party will terminate the offer. This rule was developed in the English courts at the time that a "meeting of the minds" of the parties was the test of the existence of a contract. After death there is no mind; and at the that time the courts held that an insane person had no mind. Consequently, if one of the parties died or became insane, it was impossible to have the essential "meeting of minds."

In the case of death the courts have held that the notice of the death is not necessary to terminate the offer. This rule is not in full accord with the general rules governing the termination of offers and sometimes results in injustice, but it is so well established that it will no doubt require legislative action to change it.

Destruction of Subject Matter. If the subject matter of a proposed contract or subject matter essential to the performance of a proposed contract is destroyed without the knowledge or fault of either party, after the making of an offer but before its acceptance, the offer is terminated. For example, suppose Ames has a stock of hay on his farm which he offers to sell to Ball and, without the knowledge or fault of either party, the stack of hay is destroyed by fire before Ball has accepted the offer. The courts will hold that when the stack of hay burned, the offer terminated.

Intervening Illegality. If the performance of a proposed contract becomes illegal after the making of the offer but before the acceptance, the offer is terminated. For example, suppose Ames offers to kill and sell to Ball 60 wild rabbits each week during the month of December, and before Ball accepts the offer the state legislature enacts a statute making the sale of wild rabbits illegal. The courts will hold that when the state made the sale of wild rabbits illegal, the offer was terminated.

Summary

An offer confers on the offeree the power to create a contract by acceptance of the offer. The duration of an offer is limited. It may be terminated by the terms of the offer. If the offer contains no stated time for acceptance, it terminates on the lapse of a reasonable time. Unless the offer is under seal, or unless there is a valid contract to hold the offer open for a stated period, the offeror may revoke the offer at any time before acceptance. With few exceptions a revocation is not effective until communicated to the offeree. An offer is terminated if rejected by the offeree. A counteroffer or conditioned acceptance terminates an offer, but an inquiry does not. Death or insanity of either the offeror or the offeree, destruction of the subject matter of the proposed contract, or intervening illegality terminates an offer.

Humble Oil & Refining Co.
v. *Westside Investment Corp.*
419 S.W.2d 448 (Ct. Civ. App. Tex. 1967)

This was a suit for specific performance of an option brought by Humble Oil & Refining Company (plaintiff) against Westside Investment Corporation (defendant). Judgment for Westside and Humble appeals. Affirmed.

KLINGEMAN, JUSTICE.   Westside and Humble entered into a written option agreement on April 5, 1963, wherein Humble, for the sum of $50.00, was given a 60-day option to purchase the real estate described therein. This option provided that the offer was irrevocable.

The only question before the Court is whether Humble validly exercised its option to purchase within the 60-day period provided in the option contract.

On May 2, 1963, Humble mailed a letter to Westside which stated:

"Humble Oil & Refining Company hereby exercises its option to purchase Lots 19, 20, 21, 22 and 23, Block 2, Lackland Heights Subdivision, in or near the City of San Antonio, Bexar County, Texas, granted in Option and Purchase Contract dated April 5, 1963. As additional inducement for Humble to exercise its option to purchase, you have agreed that all utilities (gas, water, sewer and electricity) will be extended to the property prior to the closing of the transaction. The contract of sale is hereby amended to provide that Seller shall extend all utility lines to the property before the date of closing.

"Please sign and return one copy of this letter in the space indicated below to signify your agreement to the amendment to the purchase contract."

Thereafter, on May 14, 1963, within the 60-day period, Humble mailed to Westside another letter reading as follows:

"Humble Oil & Refining Company hereby notifies you of its intention to exercise the option granted in Option and Purchase Contract dated April 5, 1963 covering Lots 19, 20, 21, 22, and 23, Block 2, Lackland Heights Subdivision, in or near the City of San Antonio, Bexar County, Texas. The exercise of said option is not qualified and you may disregard the proposed amendment to the contract suggested in letter dated May 2, 1963, from the undersigned as Agent and Attorney-in-Fact for Humble Oil & Refining Company Addressed to Westside Investment Corporation."

In the option agreement dated April 5, 1963, Westside did not agree to bring utilities to the site, and there is nothing in the record pertaining to such utilities except the reference thereto in Humble's letter of May 2, 1963.

Westside contends that, as a matter of law, Humble rejected the offer by its letter of May 2, 1963, and such offer could not be revived by a subsequent unconditional acceptance.

Humble's two points of error are:

First Point: "The trial court erred in holding that Humble's letter of May 2, 1963, had the effect of terminating the option contract."

Second Point: "Humble timely exercised the option granted to it in the contract of April 5, 1963."

Humble concedes that a mere offer is terminable by a conditional acceptance or counteroffer, but contends forcibly that an option to purchase, based upon a valid consideration, providing for the exercise thereof within a stated period of time, is basically different in law from a mere offer, and such option agreement is an enforcible contract distinct from the contract to which the option relates, and is not modified, abandoned or terminated in any manner or with less formalities than required to enter into a binding contract in the first place.

It is well settled and Westside concedes that where there is an option to purchase supported by a valid consideration, the offerer cannot revoke or terminate such option during the time fixed in the option. The material question to be determined by this Court is whether the offeree can, during the term of such an option agreement reject the offer, or do some act which in law constitutes a rejection, and thereafter, during the term provided in such option, make an unconditional acceptance which would be effective.

Humble, however, contends that even if such letter of May 2, 1963, be construed as a conditional acceptance, that it would not terminate the option agreement, and that it could thereafter, during the term provided in the option agreement, make an unconditional acceptance which would be valid and effective. We are not in agreement with Humble's contention. An option is a mere right of election, acquired by one under a contract, to *accept or reject* a present offer within the time therein fixed. In *Williston on Contracts,* 3rd Ed., Vol. 1, §77, pp. 251–252, it is stated: "A conditional acceptance is, therefore, itself a counter-offer and rejects the original offer, so that thereafter even a purportedly unqualified acceptance of that offer will not form a contract."

It is our conclusion that Humble's letter of May 2, 1963, constituted a counter-offer and rejection of Westside's offer, and terminated such offer, and that Humble's attempted unconditional acceptance thereafter had no effect and did not form a contract.

Jaybe Construction Co. v. Beco, Inc.
216 A.2d 208 (3 Conn. Cir. Ct. App. 1965)

This was an action to recover damages for breach of contract brought by Jaybe Construction Company (plaintiff) against Beco, Inc. (defendant). Judgment for Jaybe and Beco appealed. Affirmed.

Jaybe along with other contractors received from the state of Connecticut certain plans concerning renovations to be made at a state school. Beco, without solicitation, sent the following letter to Jaybe and other contractors:

"March 30, 1964

Re: Project BIR–61–B150 Southbury Training School Cottages 16, 17, 32 & 33-Dev. 18-Kitchen

In connection with the above job we are pleased to quote a job price of $14,450.00 covering items 4, 11, 11a, 12, 13, 14, 16, 17, & 23.

Price quoted includes delivery and setting in place, less faucets, valves, traps and appurtenances unless furnished by the manufacturer as standard equipment.

All electrical, plumbing & steam connections by others.

Yours truly,
Baron Equipment Company"

Jaybe received the contract from the state and for the first time communicated with Beco by telephone, stating that Jaybe had been awarded the contract and it had included the Beco figure of $14,450.00. Jaybe stated further that the offer and a formal contract would be sent for Beco's signature. A request was made to Beco to "shave" his original bid if possible.

After checking with the state concerning equipment desired, Beco found that it would be unable to complete the work at the original price and sent Jaybe a new price.

The work was eventually completed by a sub-contractor for $15,450.00. Jaybe sued for breach of contract and damages of $1,000.00.

KINMONTH, JUDGE. The determination whether a certain communication by one party to another is an operative offer, and not merely an inoperative step in the preliminary negotiations, is a matter of interpretation in the light of all the surrounding circumstances. From the nature of such communications, the question whether certain acts or conduct constitute a definite proposal, upon which a binding contract may be predicated without any further action on the part of the person from whom it proceeds, or a mere preliminary step which is not susceptible, without further action by that party, of being converted into a binding contract depends on the nature of the particular acts or conduct in question and the circumstances attending the transaction. It is impossible to formulate a general principle or criterion for the determination. Accordingly, whether a communication naming a price is a quotation or an offer depends on the intention of the party as it is manifested by the facts and circumstances of each particular case.

When Jaybe used Beco's figure in computing its own bid, it bound itself to perform in reliance on Beco's terms. Though Beco did not bargain for this use of its figure, neither did it make it idly indifferent as to whether the figure would be used or not. On the contrary, it is reasonable to assume that Beco submitted its bid to obtain the subcontract. It was bound to realize the substantial possibility that its bid would be the lowest and that it would be included by Jaybe in its bid. It was to Beco's interest that Jaybe be awarded the general contract. From all the evidence before it, the trier must determine what the intention was. Intention is an inference of fact, and the conclusion is not reviewable unless it was one which the trier could not reasonably make. From the facts, we cannot say that the court erred in concluding that Beco's letter of March 30, 1964, was an offer.

The right to revoke an ordinary offer before acceptance is unquestioned; but if the offer is accepted before its withdrawal, a binding contract will be created. A mere inquiry as to whether one proposing a contract will alter or modify its terms does not amount to a rejection. The finding of the court is clear that Jaybe in the telephone conversation of April 13, 1964, accepted Beco's offer and merely made an inquiry as to whether Beco could "shave" its figure. We cannot disturb finding. Jaybe accepted Beco's offer prior to Beco's withdrawal.

Changes under the Uniform Commercial Code

The Offer. Under the provisions of the Code an offer or a contract of sale does not fail for indefiniteness of terms even though one or more terms are left open if the parties have intended to make a contract and there is a reasonably certain basis for giving an appropriate remedy. (2–204 [3].)[3] As under the general rules of contract law, the contract may be made in any manner

---

[3] The numbers in the parentheses refer to the sections of the Uniform Commercial Code, 1962.

sufficient to show agreement, including conduct of both parties which recognizes the existence of such contract. (2–305 [1].)

The comment of the American Law Institute and the National Conference of Commissioners on Uniform Law states:

Subsection (3) states the principle as to "open terms" underlying later sections of the Article. If the parties intend to enter into a binding agreement, this subsection recognizes that agreement as valid in law, despite missing terms, if there is any reasonably certain basis for granting a remedy. The test is not certainty as to what the parties were to do nor as to the exact amount of damages due the plaintiff. Nor is the fact that one or more terms are left to be agreed upon enough of itself to defeat an otherwise adequate agreement. Rather, commercial standards on the point of "indefiniteness" are intended to be applied, This Act making provision elsewhere for missing terms needed for performance, open price, remedies and the like.

The more terms the parties leave open, the less likely it is that they have intended to conclude a binding agreement, but their actions may be frequently conclusive on the matter despite the omissions.

As was previously stated, a promise to hold an offer open which is not supported by consideration is unenforceable under the common law. Merchants in their dealings commonly rely on such a promise. In recognition of this, it is provided in the Code that an offer by a merchant to buy or sell goods in a signed writing which by its terms gives assurance that it will be held open is not revocable for lack of consideration during the time stated, or if no time is stated, for a reasonable time, but in no event may such period of irrevocability exceed three months. (2–205.) To assure that a promise to hold an offer open is consciously and intentionally made, the Code further provides that if the promise is included in a form supplied by the offeree it must be separately signed by the offeror.

E. A. Coronis Assocs. v. *M. Gordon Constr. Co.*
216 A.2d 246 (Sup. Ct. N.J. 1966)

This was an action for breach of contract brought by E. A. Coronis Associates (plaintiff) against M. Gordon Construction Co. (defendant). A summary judgment was entered in favor of E. A. Coronis Associates (Coronis) and M. Gordon Construction Co.'s (Gordon) appealed. Reversed.

COLLESTER, J. A. D. This litigation began when Coronis brought suit on three contracts not here pertinent. Gordon admitted liability thereon, but counterclaimed for breach of a contract to supply and erect structural steel on one of its projects. Gordon is a general contractor. In anticipation of making a bid to construct two buildings at the Port of New York Authority's Elizabeth Piers it sought bids from subcontractors. Coronis designs, fabricates, supplies and erects structural steel. On April 22, 1963 it sent the following letter to Gordon:

"April 22, 1963
Dear Mr. Ben Zvi:
   We regret very much that this estimate was so delayed. Be assured that the time con-
sumed was due to routing of the plans through our regular sources of fabrication.
   We are pleased to offer:
All structural steel including steel girts and purlins
Both Buildings delivered and erected. $155,413.50
All structural steel equipped with slips for wood girts & purlins
Both Buildings delivered and erected. 98,937.50
NOTE:
This price is predicated on an erected price of .1175 per Lb. of steel and we would expect
to adjust the price on this basis to conform to actual tonnage of steel used in the project.
   Thank you very much for this opportunity to quote.
                                 Very truly yours,
                                 E. A. CORONIS ASSOCIATES
                                 /s/ Arthur C. Pease
                                 Arthur C. Pease"

Gordon contends that at some date prior to April 22 the parties reached an oral
agreement and that the above letter was sent in confirmation.

   Bids were opened by the Port Authority on April 19, 1963, and Gordon's bid
was the lowest. He alleges that Coronis was informed the same day. The Port
Authority contract was officially awarded to Gordon on May 27, 1963 and executed about two weeks later. During this period Gordon never accepted the
alleged offer of Coronis. Meanwhile, on June 1, 1963, Coronis sent a telegram,
in pertinent part reading:

"Due to conditions beyond our control, we must withdraw our proposal of April 22nd
1963 for structural steel Dor Buildings 131 and 132 at the Elizabeth-Port Piers at the
earliest possible we will resubmit our proposal."

Two days later, on June 3, 1963, Gordon replied by telegram as follows:

"Ref your tel. 6-3 and for the record be advised that we are holding you to your bid of
April 22, 1963 for the structural steel of cargo bldgs 131 and 132."

Coronis never performed. Gordon employed the Elizabeth Iron Works to perform
the work and claims as damages the difference between Coronis' proposal of
$155,413.50 and Elizabeth Iron Works' charge of $208,000.

   Gordon contends that the April 22 letter was an offer and that Coronis had no
right to withdraw it. Two grounds are advanced in support. First, Gordon contends that the Uniform Commercial Code firm offer section, precludes withdrawal
and, second, it contends that withdrawal is prevented by the doctrine of promissory
estoppel.

   Prior to the enactment of the Uniform Commercial Code an offer not supported by consideration could be revoked at any time prior to acceptance. The
drafters of the Code recognized that the common law rule was contrary to modern
business practice and possessed the capability to produce unjust results. The response was section 2–205 which reverses the common law rule and states:

"An offer by a merchant to buy or sell goods in a *signed writing which by its terms gives assurance that it will be held open* is not revocable, for lack of consideration, during the time stated or if no time is stated for a reasonable time. . . . (Emphasis added.)

Coronis' letter contains no terms giving assurance it will be held open. We recognize that just as an offeree runs a risk in acting on an offer before accepting it, the offerer runs a risk if his offer is considered irrevocable. In their comments to section 2–205 of the Code the drafters anticipated these risks and stated:

"However, despite settled courses of dealing or usages of the trade whereby firm offers are made by oral communication and relied upon without more evidence, such offers remain revocable under this Article since authentication by a writing is the essence of this section." Uniform Commercial Code, comment, par. 2

We think it clear that Coronis' writing does not come within the provision of section 2–205 of a "signed writing which by its terms gives assurance that it will be held open."

Having so concluded, we need not consider the question of whether the Coronis letter was an offer or whether the letter dealt with "goods." We note in this connection that Coronis quoted the price for structural steel delivered and erected.

Gordon also argues that even if Coronis' writing of April 22 is not a firm offer within the meaning of section 2–205, justice requires that we apply the doctrine of promissory estoppel to preclude its revocation. *Restatement, Contracts,* § 90 provides:

"A promise which the promisor should reasonably expect to induce action of forbearance of a definite and substantial character on the part of the promisee and which does induce such action or forbearance is binding if injustice can be avoided only by enforcement of the promise."

Gordon argues that it relied on Coronis' bid in making its own bid and that injustice would result if Coronis could now revoke. Thus, Gordon contends that Coronis' bid is made irrevocable by application of the doctrine of promissory estoppel.

The authorities are not uniform in applying the doctrine of promissory estoppel to situations comparable to that before us. We believe the better line of authority applies the doctrine.

The *Drennan* case involved an oral bid by a subcontractor for paving work at a school project on which plaintiff general contractor was about to bid. Defendant's paving bid was the lowest, and the general contractor computed his own bid accordingly. Plaintiff was the successful bidder but the following day was informed by defendant it would not do the work at its bid price. The California Supreme Court, per Justice Traynor, applied the doctrine of promissory estoppel to prevent defendant's revocation of its bid, stating:

"When plaintiff used defendant's offer in computing his own bid, he bound himself to perform in reliance on defendant's terms. Though defendant did not bargain for this use of its bid neither did the defendant make it idly, indifferent to whether it would be used or not. On the contrary, it is reasonable to suppose that defendant submitted its bid to obtain the subcontract. It was bound to realize the substantial possibility that its bid would be the lowest, and that it would be included by plaintiff in his bid. It was to its own interest that the contractor be awarded the general contract; the lower the subcontract bid, the lower the general contractor's bid was likely to be and the greater its chance of acceptance and hence the greater defendant's chance of getting the paving subcontract. Defendant had reason not only to expect plaintiff to rely on his bid but to want him to. Clearly defendant had a stake in plaintiff's reliance on its bid. Given this interest and the fact that plaintiff is bound by his own bid, it is only fair that plaintiff should have at least an opportunity to accept defendant's bid after the general contract has been awarded to him." (333 P.2d at p. 760)

To successfully establish a cause of action based on promissory estoppel Gordon must prove that (1) it received a clear and definite offer from Coronis; (2) Coronis could expect reliance of a substantial nature; (3) actual reasonable reliance on Gordon's part, and (4) detriment. *Restatement, Contracts,* § 90.

The Law Division did not think promissory estoppel would apply in the situation *sub judice*. Therefore we reverse.

Problem Cases

1. John Woods, son of Susan Woods, several years before the death of his mother called on her regularly, giving her personal attention and aiding her in the managing of her property, which consisted of securities of the value of about $80,000. On several occasions during this period the mother told John that he would be paid for his trouble, and she also told several of her friends that "her son, John, was taking care of her business and that he would be paid for his services." During this period John never asked for pay for his services and was never paid. After the death of his mother John filed a claim in her estate for pay for services rendered and the executor refused to pay the claim. John Woods brought suit to enforce the claim. Susan Woods had willed one half of her estate to John and one half to a daughter. Is John entitled to pay for his services to his mother?

2. On December 15, 1925, Patrick wrote Kleine concerning a lot owned by her: "If you have not sold, I, of course, am the logical purchaser, as it is worth more to me than anybody else. . . . I hope I shall have the pleasure of hearing from you shortly."

   On the 16th day of December, Kleine acknowledged Patrick's letter and wrote: "If you should be interested in this (my lot) would be glad to hear from you. Size of lot 20 x 100, Price $1,000 (one thousand dollars)."

   Two days later Patrick telegraphed Kleine: "Will accept your proposition of one thousand dollars for lot thirty-five in block seventy-nine ought six and will get contract and check to you within a day or so."

   The next day, the following letter was written Kleine by Patrick: "Enclosed you will find contracts in the usual form and also my check for $100 as an evidence of good faith, and will you please sign and return one copy to me, so that the title company can institute search?"

   On the 23rd day of December Kleine returned the contract and check and advised Patrick that the lot had been sold. Patrick sued for specific performance. Can Patrick get the property?

3. Cohen contracted to sell and deliver to Udell "approximately 10,000 single heater and approximately 10,000 two-burner heaters, all in perfect condition." Cohen delivered 1,756 single heaters and 3,074 two-burner heaters. Udell sued Cohen to recover damages for breach of the contract and Cohen set up as a defense that the terms were too uncertain to be enforceable as a contract. Is the defense good?

4. Directors of X Corporation passed a resolution offering a reward of $500 to anyone who could and would furnish information regarding theft of tools. Brown, a janitor employed by X Corporation, was in the room and overheard the passing of the resolution. The next morning, before notice of the reward was posted, Brown gave the president of X Corporation the desired information. X Corporation refused to pay Brown the reward and Brown sued X Corporation to recover a judgment for the amount of the reward. Is Brown entitled to a judgment?

5. Kergald arrived with her trunk at a Boston station and turned it over to Armstrong Transfer Company, a common carrier, for delivery to her home. At the time she checked her trunk she was given a small pasteboard which she put into her purse without reading. Armstrong did not ask her about the value of the trunk. The pasteboard had an order number on one side and the words "Read contract on reverse side." On the other side was printed, "The holder of this check agrees that the value of the baggage checked does not exceed $100 unless a greater value has been declared at time of checking and additional payment made therefor. . . ." Armstrong lost the trunk and refused to pay more than $100. The trial court instructed the jury that the plaintiff was not bound by the disclaimer unless she had knowledge of it. The jury returned a verdict for $1,700 for Kergald and Armstrong appealed. Should the verdict be set aside?

6. Hansen entered a contract with Kelley through Kelley's agent, Bowles. The contract stated that upon the sale of a specific block of stock, Hansen would receive $169,000 "together with a reasonable share of the profits" made on the sale of the stock. The block was sold for $1,681,000. Hansen was paid only $169,000 and he sued Kelley for a "reasonable share" of the profits. Is Hansen entitled to more money?

7. In July, 1951, Walker leased a small lot to Keith for a 10-year term at a rent of $100 per month. Keith was given an option to extend the lease for an additional 10-year term, under the same terms and conditions except as to rental. The renewal option provided: "rental will be fixed in such amount as shall actually be agreed upon by the lessors and the lessee with the monthly rental fixed on the comparative basis of rental values as to the date of the renewal with rental values at this time reflected by the comparative business conditions of the two periods." Keith gave the proper notice but he and Walker were unable to agree upon the rent. Keith sued to enforce the lease. Was there a valid lease contract?

8. In 1961 Rogers, an officer of American Sand, Inc., was asked by Clark to quote a special rate for the possible purchase of 20,000 to 25,000 tons of bank-run sand. Rogers indicated that he would sell such an amount of the commodity at 45 cents per ton. In 1962 and 1963, Clark obtained various building contracts in the Hartford area and purchased sand, to the extent of about 20,000 tons, from other local dealers in the same commodity. On or about February 3, 1963, an occasion arose as a result of which Clark determined to purchase sand from American Sand and between February 4, 1963, and March 8, 1963, obtained some 1,538.30 tons of bank-run sand. The price charged by the American Sand to all customers, except those with whom special arrangement had been made, was 55 cents per ton, which is a reasonable price for the commodity. American demanded 55 cents per ton and Clark contends that he only has to pay 45 cents per ton. Is Clark right?

9. Wertheimer telegraphed Welke offering to sell him a definite quantity of whiskey at a stated price "for immediate acceptance." Three hours after the receipt of the order, Welke telegraphed an acceptance of the offer. Wertheimer refused to ship the whiskey and when sued set up as a defense that the offer had terminated before acceptance. Did a contract result?

10. Ramsey offered to sell certain real estate to Herndon and gave him until January 15, 1965, to accept the offer. Herndon was attempting to arrange a loan so that he could purchase the property, and this was known to Ramsey. Herndon had not completed the arrangements for his loan by January 15, 1965, and Ramsey sold the property to Armstrong. Herndon completed the arrangements for his loan on January 17, 1965, and tendered performance to Ramsey who informed Herndon of the sale to Armstrong. Herndon brought suit against Ramsey for damages for breach of contract. Is Herndon entitled to a judgment?

11. On September 21, 1942, Gentry executed to New Headley Tobacco Warehouse Company (Warehouse Co.) a lease of property in Lexington for a term of 21 years 6 months. The lease contained no provision for renewal or extension. On March 24, 1952, Gentry addressed the following letter to Warehouse Co.:

> In the event you build within the next five years (from March 1st, 1952) an addition to your warehouse at cost of not less than $25,000.00 on the property you have under lease from me, I agree,
>
> First, to extend your present lease so you will have a total term of twenty-two years (22 years) from March 1st of the year the addition is built.
>
> Second, the extended term of lease shall carry a net rental to me of Sixteen Hundred ($1,600.00) per annum instead of the present net rental of Twelve Hundred Dollars per annum.
>
> Third, in all other respects the terms and conditions of the extended lease shall be the same as the present lease.

Warehouse Co. had not made any response or started construction of the building before Gentry died on September 29, 1955. On April 16, 1956, Warehouse Co. communicated their acceptance of Gentry's offer to the executor of Gentry's estate. The executor refused to extend the lease, and Warehouse Co. brought an action to force the executor to extend the lease. Does Warehouse have a lease?

chapter 7. Acceptance

The Acceptance

The significant changes in the law of acceptance caused by the adoption of the Code will be discussed at the end of this chapter.

Requirements for Acceptance. The basis of a contract is the mutual consent of the parties to the contract. This consent is manifested by one party—the offeror—making an offer to another party—the offeree—and by the offeree indicating, either expressly or by implication, his willingness to be bound on the terms stated in the offer. The offeree has no legal right to insist that the proposition made to him be reasonable, practical, or sensible. The proposition is that of the offeror, and if the offeree wishes to accept it, he must agree to all of its terms. Any attempt on the part of the offeree, in his acceptance, to alter the terms of the offeror's proposition will terminate the offer.

The common-law rule is that the offeree's acceptance must correspond in all respects with the offer. This does not mean that the offeror must, in accepting an offer, repeat the words of the offer; but it does mean that he must, by his words or acts, clearly manifest his intent to comply in all respects with that which the offeror has stipulated as the return he demands for his promise or act.

Offer in Unilateral Contract. An offer in a unilateral contract is, as a general rule, a promise for an act. To accept such an offer, the offeree must perform the act as requested. Any material variance between the requested act and the tendered performance will result in no acceptance. If the nature of the requested act is such that it will take a substantial period of time for its completion, there will have been no acceptance of the offer until the act has been completed. Under some circumstances, if the offeree has started performance of the requested act, the offer is irrevocable until he has had a reasonable opportunity to complete the performance. If the offeree has started performance and the offeror revokes his offer before performance is completed, the offeree can recover in a suit in quasi contract for benefits conferred.

Offer in Bilateral Contract.   An offer for a bilateral contract states or implies the promise which the offeror requests the offeree to make if he wishes to accept the offer. Except for the provisions of the Uniform Commercial Code stated below relative to offers for contracts for the sale of goods, if the offeree wishes to accept the offer he must make the promise requested, as requested. No other or different promise than that stated in the offer will suffice as an acceptance. If the offeree, in attempting to accept the offer, makes a promise which adds to, subtracts from, or alters the terms of the promise requested, it is a counteroffer or conditional acceptance, and no contract results. In accepting an offer for a bilateral contract, it is not necessary for the offeree to repeat the promise requested by the offeror word for word. All that is necessary is that he indicate his intention to be bound by the requested promise.

When a Writing Is Anticipated.   Frequently, the parties negotiating a contract will have a written draft of the agreement drawn and signed. Whether a binding contract is entered into by the parties before they sign the written draft or at the time they sign depends entirely on the intentions of the parties. Their intention will be determined by the application of the objective standard of what a reasonable man familiar with the facts and circumstances would be justified in believing the parties intended.

As a general rule, where the parties have completed their negotiations and have reached an agreement on all the material provisions of their transaction, the courts have held that a binding contract results. A decision to have a written draft of the agreement drawn and signed by the parties will not affect the time at which the binding contract came into existence. If the parties do not agree on the terms of the written draft, their disagreement will not discharge them from their liability on the contract into which they have already entered. If they agree on the terms of the written draft and sign it, the writing will be accepted in court as the best evidence of the terms of their contract.

Where the parties are negotiating a complicated agreement and make rough drafts of the agreement for the purpose of correcting mistakes and making alterations, the courts will hold, as a general rule, that a binding contract does not result until the final written draft is approved by the parties. Such final approval is usually indicated by the signing of the written draft.

If the circumstances are such that it is clear that the parties do not intend to be bound until a written contract is signed, yet they begin to perform after the writing is drafted but before it is signed by one or both of the parties, the courts will hold that they are bound by the terms of the writing.

Silence as Acceptance.   The legal principle that one cannot impose a contractual obligation on another without the consent of that person, either expressed or implied, is well established. The application of this legal principle prevents the offeror from so wording his offer that the offeree will be forced to act or be bound by a contract. Mere silence on the part of the offeree, as a general rule, is not acceptance. For example, if a person makes an offer in which he states, "If I do not receive your rejection of this offer within ten days, I shall consider my offer accepted," and the offeree makes no reply, no contract will result, unless it can be established that the offeree remained silent with the intent to accept or unless previous dealings or other circumstances impose on the offeree a duty to reply.

The relation of the parties, the course of dealing, usage of trade, a prior agreement, or other special circumstances may impose on the offeree a duty to reject an offer or be bound by it. If this is true, the offeree's silence will amount to an acceptance, and a contract will result.

Likewise, if benefits are conferred on the offeree under circumstances where it is clear that the benefits are not conferred as a gift, and the offeree is aware of this, and yet accepts the benefits, he will be bound by a contract to pay for the benefits conferred. For example, if one continues to accept a newspaper or magazine after his subscription expires, he will be liable for the subscription price. His liability is on a contract, and the recovery is for the reasonable value of the goods or services furnished, not in quasi contract on the grounds of the unjust enrichment of the offeree.

Intention to Accept.   In order to have a valid acceptance of an offer, the offeree must have performed the act or made the promise requested in the offer with the intention of accepting the offer. The same standards are applied in determining the intentions of the offeree as are applied in determining the intentions of the offeror. The objective test of what a reasonably prudent man would be justified in believing under the circumstances is the test applied.

In the case of a unilateral contract, where an act is required for an acceptance, the offeree must have performed the act with the intention of accepting the offer, or the offeror will not be bound.

Some courts have held that the offer of a reward for the apprehension of a criminal is an offer to pay a bounty, not an offer to contract. These courts allow a recovery if the requested act is performed, and knowledge of the offer of a reward is immaterial. And a few courts have refused to apply the intent test in all reward cases, holding that if the person offering the reward received the benefits he desired, public policy would demand that he pay the promised reward.

In the case of a bilateral contract an offer is accepted when the offeree makes the promise requested in the offer. If the offeree's reply is not a definite statement that he accepts the offer, the court must determine whether or not his reply indicates an intention to accept.

Summary

An offeree, in order to accept an offer, must perform the requested act as requested or make the requested promise with the intent to accept the offer. In the case of a unilateral contract the offeree must perform the requested act, and in the case of a bilateral contract the offeree must make the requested promise. If a written draft of the agreement is anticipated, whether the parties are bound before the signing of the written draft or at the time of the signing will depend on the intention of the parties. As a general rule, silence on the part of the offeree is not an acceptance. However, by the agreement of the parties, by usage of trade, or by course of dealing, the offeree may owe a duty to reject an offer, in which case his failure to give notice of rejection will amount to an acceptance. In order to have an acceptance of an offer, the offeree must have performed the requested act or made the requested promise with the intention of accepting the offer. In determining intention, one must apply the objective test of what a reasonably prudent man would be justified in believing the offeree intended.

James v. *P. B. Price Construction Co.*

401 S.W.2d 206 (Sup. Ct. Ark. 1966)

This was an action by P. B. Price Construction Company (plaintiff) against Worth James (defendant). James appealed from a verdict for Price. Affirmed.

James obtained a contract to lay certain sewer lines for Base Line Sewer District. James then subcontracted to Price the cutting of the street and the replacing of the pavement, roads, and highways. This work was to be done after James had laid the sewer lines and tamped the dirt in the trenches to proper level. Price wrote a letter to James on May 24, 1963, stating terms of the subcontract. In a conversation on or about September 23, 1963, James told Price that he would not agree to the terms of Price's letter. James then submitted a letter to Price on September 23, 1963, restating terms of the subcontract. Price told James that he could not agree to the terms in the letter and that he would write a supplement to it and then would sign the letter with the supplement. Price then wrote James a letter dated September 30, 1963, which contained an additional supplement to James's previous letter as follows: "Any failure due to settlement is to be repaired at your expense and we hereby agree to perform such work for you at our actual cost." James received the letter but never indicated his acceptance of the additional quoted provision. Price proceeded with the work and after Price had completed the paving, he incurred additional costs of paving due to the subsequent settlement of the trench that James had tamped. Price sued James for the cost Price incurred in repairing this damage.

McFADDIN, JUSTICE. . . . [T]he question is whether the contract between the parties was that submitted by Worth James on September 23rd; or whether the contract between the parties was the Worth James letter of September 23rd, PLUS the Price letter of September 30th. That contracts can be made by correspondence is recognized in our opinions.

Furthermore, that a party, by knowingly accepting the benefits of a proposed contract, is bound by its terms, is likewise recognized in our cases. We hold that a question of fact was made for the jury as to what was the contract between the parties. The fact that Worth James never agreed—in the September 23rd conversation—to what is contained in the September 30th letter, is not a sufficient defense; also, the fact that Worth James says he did not sign anything agreeing to Price's letter of September 30th, is not a sufficient defense. If James, knowing of the letter of September 30th, accepted the benefits of refilling the sunken trenches, all the time knowing that Price had stated that it was to receive its actual expenses, then Worth James would be bound. It is textbook law that an offer may be accepted by conduct; and whether Worth James accepted by conduct the provisions of the Price letter of September 30th, was a question of fact for the jury.

Crouch v. Marrs
430 P.2d 204 (Sup. Ct. Kan. 1967)

This was a suit by Phillip Crouch (plaintiff) against Roy Marrs, Purex Corporation and others (defendants) to establish Crouch's rights in regard to a certain building. From a judgment for the defendants; Crouch appealed. Reversed.

On February 26, 1964, Crouch wrote to the Purex Corporation asking for their lowest price if they were interested in selling an old plant building and its contents located in Meade, Kansas. The letter read in part:

"I would be interested in buying the old building that housed the plant and what other items that are still left. The items that are still left are: two crushers, furnace and the elevator is about all that is left."

On March 4, 1964, Crouch received a letter of reply from Purex Corporation signed by Frank Knox which stated:

"We will sell this building and the equipment in and about that building for a total of $500."

On March 19, 1964, Crouch wrote to Frank Knox, Purex Corporation, stating that the building was in "pretty bad condition" and asking "would you consider taking $300.00 for what is left?" This letter was not answered.

Later, on April 16, 1964, Crouch addressed another letter to Frank Knox, Purex Corporation, which read:

"I guess we will try the building for the amount you quoted, $500.
I am sending you a personal check for this amount.
It will be 2 or 3 weeks before we can get started; and I presume that we will be allowed all the time that we need to remove the material."

On April 17, 1964, the Purex Corporation, through Frank Knox, wrote a letter to Martin Asche which stated:

"In answer to your inquiry about our property approximately six miles north of Meade, Kansas.

"We will sell for $500.00 the mine building and whatever machinery and equipment which remains in or about that building. A condition of sale will require that the property purchased be removed from the premises within forty-five days.

"If this price is acceptable we will be pleased to receive a cashier's check to cover."

On April 23, Knox, on behalf of Purex Corporation, indorsed and cashed the check which Crouch had mailed on April 16.

On April 24, 1964, Asche wrote a letter accepting the offer of April 17, which reads:

"We are enclosing a cashier's check for $500 and the bill of sale of mine buildings with the agreement of option to purchase property.

"If the corporation has any other property and machinery in this area for sale, we would be pleased to deal with the corporation. It was our pleasure to deal with the Purex Corporation."

On April 27, 1964, Frank Knox sent Crouch the following telegram:

"Your counter offer received April 23 is unacceptable. Your check mistakenly deposited by Purex will be recovered and returned to you or Purex check will be issued to you if your check cannot be located."

There followed a letter dated May 16, 1964, which read:

"This is a follow-up to our telegram to you of April 27, advising you that your check which we received on April 23 was not acceptable, but that it had been deposited by mistake. Since we were unable to recover your check, we herewith enclose our check for $500 to reimburse you.

"We wish to explain, that the reason we could not accept your counter-offer of $500 for the mine building and machinery at Meade, Kansas was because we had received and accepted an offer from another party prior to receipt of yours on April 23."

In the meantime Martin Asche had entered into a contract to sell the building to Roy Marrs who owned the land surrounding the building site for $500 and had entered into a contract to sell the equipment to the C. & D. Used Truck Parts for $800.

Crouch started to salvage the building but Roy Marrs put a lock on the gate and would not allow Crouch to enter.

Crouch then brought an action to enjoin Marrs from interfering with his salvage operations.

HATCHER, COMMISSIONER. Marrs contends that Crouch's check was cashed through inadvertence or an error in office procedure and under such circumstances the cashing of the check did not constitute an acceptance of Crouch's offer. The difficulty with this contention is that there was no evidence of any character as to why the check was cashed. Neither would the error void the contract unless mutual mistake was pleaded.

Crouch suggests that the statement in the letter of May 6, 1964, to the effect "we have received and accepted an offer from another party prior to receipt of yours" was a "falsehood" as Asche's acceptance was dated one day after Crouch's check was in the Los Angeles Clearing House. We need not speculate as to the binding effect of Purex Corporation's offer to Asche. The question is whether the endorsing and depositing of Crouch's check constituted an acceptance of his offer to buy. We think it did.

The endorsing and depositing of a check constitutes an acceptance of the offer to buy which accompanies it because the act itself indicates acceptance. An offer may be accepted by performing a specified act as well as by an affirmative answer. Also, where the offeree exercised dominion over the thing offered him—in this instance the check—such exercise constitutes an acceptance of the offer.

Brook v. Oberlander

199 N.E.2d 613 (Ill. App. Ct. 1964)

This was an action for breach of contract brought by Stanley Brook and Norman Rubin, both as a partnership and as a corporation (plantiffs), against Paul Oberlander (defendant). Judgment for Oberlander and Brook and Rubin appealed. Affirmed.

Brook and Rubin were the sole owners and operators of two construction companies; one was organized as a partnership, the other as a corporation. Oberlander sent a sub-contracting bid to the Brook and Rubin partnership in regard to a certain airport alteration contract which was later awarded to the Brook and Rubin corporation.

Oberlander then went to a meeting with Brook and an airline representative where he was told to start work and was given certain forms to be filled out which contained the following language:

". . . THESE FORMS MUST BE FILLED OUT COMPLETELY AND IN DETAIL AND WILL REPRESENT A COMMITMENT BY YOUR COMPANY AS TO THE TIME SCHEDULES TO WHICH YOU WILL CONFORM. *If you agree with the terms of this proposed contract, please sign and return it to us for our signature.*
The enclosed contract is not to be considered as an effective agreement until executed by you and by us. The data submitted by you in the aforementioned forms, if acceptable to us, shall be incorporated in a job coordinated progress schedule together with the other trades on this job. When this form has been prepared, a conference will be called on all the subcontractors involved and this schedule will then be adjusted and corrected to the mutual agreement of all parties. This document shall then also become a part of the contract and shall be duly executed by all parties concerned."

Oberlander refused to fill out the forms and Brook and Rubin had to arrange for another sub-contractor to do the work covered by the Oberlander bid.

SULLIVAN, JUSTICE.   Brook and Rubin further contend that when Mr. Brook and Oberlander met at O'Hare International Airport, and Oberlander was asked to commence work, that constituted an unequivocal acceptance of Oberlander's bid and a contract was thereby created. However, at the same time that Oberlander was asked to commence work he was given [the various forms] and he was also asked to execute [the contract], [which] stated that "if you agree with the terms of this proposed contract, please sign and return it to us for our signature." This letter further recited "The enclosed contract is not to be considered as an effective agreement until executed by you and by us." From the wording of this letter, which bore the name, [Brook and Rubin] corporation, both at the heading and at the end of the letter, it would appear that the [Brook and Rubin corporation], if it had the right to accept the proposal of [Oberlander] submitted to the [Brook and Rubin] partnership on March 16, 1962, specifically refused to accept said proposal and insisted upon the execution of the written contract and "general provision of sub-contract."

       . . . .

Oberlander raises the point that an offeror has the right to choose the person with whom he deals and the offer cannot be accepted by one to whom it was not addressed. . . . Since the offer was made to the Brook and Rubin partnership, the Brook and Rubin corporation had no right to accept the offer and thereby bind Oberlander. Oberlander made no offer to the Brook and Rubin corporation to induce it to bid on the general contract.

Communication of Acceptance

Requirements for Communication. The acceptance of a unilateral contract, as a general rule, requires the doing of an act, although under some circumstances it may require the making of a promise. The acceptance of a bilateral contract requires the making of the requested promise. The law does not recognize as valid an uncommunicated promise; consequently, if the acceptance of an offer requires the making of a promise, the acceptance is not effective until the promise is communicated to the offeror. If the offeror, in his offer, stipulates the time, place, or method of communicating the acceptance, the offeree must comply fully with these terms if he wishes to accept. An attempt to accept at a time or place or in a manner other than that stipulated would be, in legal effect, a counteroffer.

If a method or place of communication is merely suggested and not stipulated, acceptance may be communicated by a different method or at a different place, provided it is delivered to the offeror before the offer terminates.

If the offer is silent as to the time, place, or method of communicating the acceptance, the offeree may accept within a reasonable time, at any place, and by any recognized method of communication, provided the acceptance is received by the offeror before the offer terminates.

Under some circumstances, trade usage will imply that an acceptance of an offer which stipulates no place of acceptance must be accepted during business hours at the offeror's place of business.

When Acceptance Is Communicated.   Under some circumstances, it becomes important to determine the place and exact time at which a contract comes into existence. As a general rule a contract comes into existence at the time the offer is accepted and at the place in which the last act is performed which creates the contract. This raises the question of when an acceptance is communicated.

If the parties are dealing face to face, the contract comes into existence at the time the words or acts of acceptance are spoken or performed and at the location of the two parties at this time. If the parties are negotiating over the telephone, the contract comes into existence at the time the offeree speaks the words of acceptance into the telephone and at the location of the offeree at this time.[1]

If the parties are using some agency of communication such as the mails or telegraph, there will be a time lag between the dispatching and the receipt of the acceptance. There will also be a risk that the message of acceptance will never reach its destination—the offeror. Since the offeror is in a position to include any provisions in his offer he wishes, he may so word his offer that the acceptance is not operative—is not communicated—until it is actually received by him. If the offer is silent on this point, the courts have developed rules of law which apply.

Authorized Agency of Communication.   An acceptance is effective and a contract arises when the acceptance is dispatched, provided the offeree uses the means of communication authorized by the offeror. If the offer states no agency of communication, the agency of communication used by the offeror to communicate the offer is the authorized agency of communication. That is, if the offer is sent by mail, the offeree is authoried to use the mail to communicate his acceptance, and an acceptance sent by mail is effective, and a contract arises at the time the letter of acceptance is dropped into an official depository for mail. Likewise, if the offeror in his offer expressly authorizes the offeree to send his acceptance by a designated agency of communication, an acceptance sent by the designated agency of communication is effective, and a contract arises at the time the acceptance is dispatched.

In some instances an agency of communication other than that used by the offeror to communicate his offer may be authorized by usage of trade. If it is customary in a particular trade to send offers by letter and to accept by telegram, a telegraphic acceptance will be authorized by usage, and it will be effective when delivered to the telegraph office for transmission.

The courts have distinguished between a stipulated agency of communication and an authorized agency of communication. Whether an agency of communication mentioned in an offer is stipulated or authorized will depend

---

[1] *Wilson v. Scannavino,* 159 Cal. App.2d 369, 324 P.2d 350 (1958).

on the language of the offer interpreted in relation to trade usage and the surrounding circumstances. If the offeror has, in effect, stated in his offer *"you must"* use this agency of communication, the agency of communication is stipulated; but if the offeror has, in effect, stated in his offer *"you may"* use this agency of communication, the agency of communication is authorized. In all events the acceptance must be communicated before the offer terminates.

When Acceptance Is by Agency Not Authorized. If an acceptance is sent by an agency of communication other than that authorized by the offeror, the acceptance is not effective until it is received by him and then only if it is received by him within the time the acceptance would have been received had the authorized agency of communication been used. By using an agency of communication not authorized by the offeror, the offeree assumes all the risks of the agency he has selected. Suppose Bell sends an offer to Able by mail for acceptance by return mail. The letter is mailed on July 6 and is delivered in the regular course of the mail on July 10. Able mails an acceptance on July 11. The acceptance is effective, and a contract arises when the letter of acceptance is mailed, even though it is lost in the mail and is never received by Bell. Suppose Able, instead of mailing his acceptance, telegraphs an acceptance. The acceptance is not effective, and a contract does not arise until the telegram is delivered to Bell and then only if the telegram is delivered before July 15, the time within which a letter of acceptance would have reached Bell had Able accepted by the authorized agency of communication, the mail.

Summary

An acceptance is not effective until it has been communicated to the offeror. If, as a part of an offer, the time, place, and method of communication of the acceptance are stipulated, such stipulation must be complied with by the offeree in accepting the offer. If the offer is silent in respect to time, place, and method of communication of the acceptance, the offeree may communicate his acceptance to the offeror at any reasonable time, to any reasonable place, by a method of communication of his own choosing.

If an agency of communication is used by the offeror to communicate his offer, he, by implication, authorizes the offeree to use the same agency of communication to communicate the acceptance; and if the offeree uses such agency of communication, the acceptance is effective, and a contract results when the acceptance is delivered to the agency of communication. The offeror, in his offer, may expressly authorize the offeree to use a particular agency of communication to communicate his acceptance, or an agency of communication may be authorized by usage of trade. If the offeree uses the authorized agency of communication to communicate his acceptance, the acceptance is effective, and a contract results when the acceptance is delivered to such agency of communication. The offeror accepts all the risks of the agency of communication.

If the offeree uses an unauthorized agency of communication he assumes all the risk of the communication of the acceptance, and the acceptance is not effective until it is received and then only provided it is received within the time an acceptance by the authorized agency would have been received had it been delivered in the ordinary course.

Morello v. Growers Grape Products Assoc.
186 P.2d 463 (Ct. App. Calif. 1947)

This was an action by Euginio Morello (plaintiff) against Growers Grape Products Association and others (defendants) to recover damages for the breach of an alleged contract to sell brandy. Judgment on a directed verdict for Growers Grape Products Association, and Morello appealed. Judgment reversed.

Morello and Growers Grape Products Association (Association) entered into a contract under which Morello processed brandy for Association. This contract provided that Association would give Morello an opportunity to purchase the brandy which he processed. By the terms of this contract Association was to notify Morello when they had decided to sell the brandy and the price at which they were selling, and Morello was to have five days in which to accept the offer. On November 9, 1942, Association wrote Morello as follows: "The unsold brandy of your distillation remaining in the pool, according to our records, amounts to approximately 23,902—46 original proof gallons. This amount, which is subject to our final verification, or any quantity thereof, is offered to you at $1.25 cash, per original proof gallon, f.o.b. the storage racks within the Internal Revenue Bonded Warehouse where it is now held, provided:

"1. That you accept this offer in writing or by telegraphic notification delivered within five days from the date of this letter."

On November 13, 1942, Morello called Association by telephone and attempted to accept the offer but Association told Morello that his acceptance must be in writing or by telegraphic notification. On November 13, 1942, Morello mailed his acceptance at Fresno, California. Association claims that it did not receive the letter of acceptance until Monday, November 16, 1942. The offices of Association are in San Francisco and they were closed on Sunday, November 15. Association claims that no contract resulted because Morello did not accept its offer in writing within five days.

GOODELL, JUSTICE.   Morello testified that he telephoned his acceptance to Association on the 13th and was told that he must put it in writing. The offer called for either written or telegraphic notification, so the telephonic "acceptance" has to be disregarded. However, if Morello's letter dated the 13th was mailed even as late as the 14th—the fifth day—it was within time, although not *received* in San Francisco until Monday, the 16th. Neither paragraph 13 nor the offer itself specifies that the acceptance must be *received* within five days; they call for an acceptance *delivered* within five days.

It is elementary that a contract is complete when the letter of acceptance is posted. The word "delivered" in the offer creates only an apparent, not a real difficulty, because under the law dealing with the formation of contract *delivery of an acceptance to the post office operates as delivery to the person addressed*, except in unusual cases.

There are many cases holding substantially that the deposit by one party in the mails of an instrument properly addressed to the other party, with postage thereon prepaid, constitutes a *delivery* to the other party, *at the place where* and the *time when it is so deposited*.

The post office was clearly the agent of the offeror, for the offer was itself sent by mail and it called for an acceptance in writing and thereby invited the use of the same medium as that chosen for the offer.

Changes under the U.C.C.

The Code attempts to make the enforceability of business contracts depend more on the intent of the parties and less upon the meeting of common-law legal formalities. A contract for the sale of goods may be made in any manner sufficient to show agreement even though the moment of its making cannot be determined. A contract may exist even though many terms are left open. (2–308—2–311.)[2] The only requirement is that there must be a "reasonably certain basis" for giving an "appropriate" remedy. (2–204.)

The fact that the price is left unsettled, is later to be agreed upon, or is to be set by one of the parties does not defeat the contract. (2–305.) Output, requirements and exclusive dealing contracts, are rendered more enforceable. (2–305.) In all of these "loose" or informal contractual situations the basic duty to act in good faith and in accordance with standards of commercial reasonableness helps to define the obligations of the parties.

The mercantile practice of using forms in the buying and selling of goods has created some problems. For example, A may use a form in offering to buy goods from B and B may use a form in accepting the offer and the terms of acceptance may differ in some respects from those of the offer. Under the common law no contract resulted. However, with some exceptions, merchants were inclined to ignore these differences and proceed to perform.

The Code has been drafted on the assumption that agreements should be enforced if they have been consumated by commercial understanding. To implement this view the Code provides: A definite and seasonable expression

---

[2] The numbers in parentheses refer to the sections of the Uniform Commercial Code, 1962.

of acceptance or a written confirmation which is sent within a reasonable time operates as an acceptance even though it states terms as additional to or different from those offered or agreed upon, unless acceptance is expressly made conditional on assent to the additional or different terms. (2–207 [1].) Under this provision, if the offeree expressly states that his different or additional terms must be agreed to by the offeror such an attempt to accept would be a counteroffer and would terminate the original offer.

If the negotiating parties are merchants and the acceptance includes additional or different terms, such terms will be treated as proposals for additions to the contract and the offeror will be bound by such terms unless the offer expressly limits acceptance to the terms of the offer, or the proposed additional or different terms materially alter the terms of the offer, or the offeror gives seasonable notification of his objection to the changed terms. (2–207 [2].) If the parties, by their conduct, recognize the existence of a contract when their writings do not otherwise establish one, the terms of the particular contract consist of those terms on which the writing of the parties agree, together with any supplementary terms incorporated under any other provision of the Code. (2–207 [3].)

The rules relative to the means used to communicate an acceptance have been relaxed under the provisions of the Code. Unless the offeror expressly stipulates that a designated agency of communication must be used, the offeree may accept in any manner or by any medium reasonable under the circumstances. (2–206.) If an offer is made by mail and the acceptance is made by telegram, the acceptance would be effective and the contract would be consummated when the telegram was dispatched, provided a telegraphic acceptance was reasonable under the circumstances.

If a buyer orders goods for prompt shipment, his offer will be accepted either by a prompt promise to ship or by the shipment of conforming goods. A shipment of nonconforming goods is not an acceptance if the seller notifies the buyer that he is shipping nonconforming goods as an accommodation. (2–206–1 [b].) If a seller receives an order or offer to purchase goods for prompt shipment and the seller ships nonconforming goods without giving the buyer the required notice, the shipment of the goods is an acceptance and since the seller has shipped nonconforming goods, he will be liable for breach of the contract.

Summary

The Code gives greater weight to the intentions of businessmen and less weight to technical form requirements. The "matching terms" concept is replaced by (2–207) which permits a contract to exist even though no full agreement exists. Acceptance may be by any reasonable means and orders for immediate shipment must be handled promptly either by notice or by shipment. If a seller ships nonconforming goods in response to an order for immediate shipment, the seller will be deemed to have accepted the buyer's original order unless he notifies the buyer that the nonconforming goods are being shipped for the buyer's accommodation.

Euclid Engineering Corp. v. Illinois Power Co.
223 N.E.2d 409 (Ill. Ct. App. 1967)

This was an action brought by Euclid Engineering Corp. (plaintiff) against Illinois Power Co. (defendant) for damages for breach of contract. Judgment for Power Company and Euclid appealed. Affirmed.

Power Company, on May 14, 1963, wrote the following letter to Euclid:

"We are enclosing descriptive data on two diesel generator units recently retired in excellent condition at our Vandalia, Illinois, power plant. . . ."

"This equipment is offered for sale 'where is and as is' subject to prior disposal and subject to our acceptance of purchaser's assurance that the units will be used outside of the Illinois area. If you are interested please submit your best offer in writing to reach us on or before May 31, 1963."

"If you wish to inspect the equipment simply let us know when you will arrive so that we can have one of our engineers at the site to assist you."

One month later, on June 14, 1963, there was a long-distance telephone conversation between the vice-president of Euclid, George Kohn, and G. H. Wright of Power Company, followed by a letter from Euclid to Power Company which in part was as follows:

"Subject your prompt acceptance, we will pay the sum of $30,000.00 where is and as is, Vandalia, Illinois, the two 1000KW General Motors diesel engine generator units, with associated equipment, more fully described specifications attached your letter May 14, 1963.

"This offer is subject our inspection and approval."

A subsequent telephone conversation occurred on June 24, 1963, between J. W. Kohn, president of the Euclid and G. H. Wright of Power Company and was followed by a letter from Kraakevik (Power Co. executive) to Kohn which stated:

"Confirming telephone conversation this morning with our Mr. G. H. Wright, we accept your offer of thirty thousand dollars ($30,000.00), where is and as is, for the two 1,000KW General Motors diesel engine generator units and associated equipment at our Vandalia, Illinois, power plant, which you are buying for resale to a Montreal customer.

"We understand your offer is subject to your inspection and approval of the equipment and such inspection will be made promptly,—within the next week.

"Our acceptance is with the understanding you will handle removal and payment per the terms of our 'short form' contract which will be mailed within the next day or two."

Thereafter, on either July 1 or July 2, 1963, George Kohn met with Kraakevik and others at the power company and went to Vandalia to inspect the diesel

generators and equipment with a Mr. Gann from Power Company. Upon returning to Decatur from Vandalia, Kohn attempted to leave a check to pay for the
equipment in the amount of $30,000.00 with Kraakevik, who refused to take it
at that time. Later, on July 3, Euclid sent a letter to Power Company containing
a check for $30,000.00. This letter read as follows:

"Dear Mr. Kraakevik:
"Referring conferences in your office July 1 and 2 which confirmed acceptance of our
offer the two 1000KW General Motors Model 567-B diesel engine generator units with
associated equipment, located your Vandalia, Illinois plant, all in accordance with your
communication May 14, 1963, with specifications attached and our proposal of June 14,
1963. All this equipment having been inspected by me with your Mr. O. L. Gann. In
accordance your request, we are hereto attaching our check No. B-7717 in the amount of
Thirty Thousand Dollars ($30,000.00) in full payment of this machinery.
"It is regrettable that our negotiations for the purchase of this equipment should result in
controversy regarding our ultimate disposition for re-sale.
"We, therefore, wish to clarify our position that although we are negotiating and intend to
make disposition to a Canadian customer, we nevertheless want to be free making disposition within the United States, except the Illinois area, which you specified as restricted in
your proposal May 14. We also are not in accord with other conditions imposed by you,
namely:
    "a) Your acceptance of our purchase contingent upon permission from Illinois
    Power Commission;
    "b) Your acceptance of our purchase subject to release by your mortgage of bond
    holders;
    "c) Your acceptance of our purchase subject to final approval of your Board of
    Directors.
"The above conditions which you have emphasized very strongly are not part of our
agreement and never previously mentioned.
"We will furnish at our own expense liability insurance coverage and Illinois Workmen's
Compensation certificate."

                              . . .

CRAVEN, PRESIDING JUSTICE.   The Commercial Code is entitled to a liberal
construction. The provision relied upon by Euclid still requires an agreement or
a meeting of the minds between the negotiating parties. One of the tests provided
by the statute is conduct by both parties which recognizes the existence of such a
contract. The whole section states:

". . . (Sec. 2–204). *Formation in General.* (1) A contract for sale of goods may be made
in any manner sufficient to show agreement, including conduct by both parties which
recognizes the existence of such a contract.
"(2) An agreement sufficient to constitute a contract for sale may be found even though
the moment of its making is undetermined.
"(3) Even though one or more terms are left open a contract for sale does not fail for
indefiniteness if the parties have intended to make a contract and there is a reasonably
certain basis for giving an appropriate remedy."

The original letter to Euclid of May 14, 1963, was not an offer but was an
invitation for Euclid to make an offer. The letters of June 14, 1963, and June

24, 1963, standing alone, without further evidence, and without further disagreement between the parties, would have constituted a contract, but it is clear from the letter submitted by Euclid on July 3, 1963, that Euclid recognized that during all of this period of time negotiations had never terminated. Fundamental to Euclid's undertaking to purchase the equipment offered for sale was Power Company's acceptance of the terms under which Euclid would meet Power Company's requirement that Power Company be assured that the units, if purchased, "will be used outside of the Illinois area." Euclid's letter of July 3 clearly indicates that it believed that this requirement was satisfied by its assurance to Power Company that such a sale would not be made. However, it was not up to Euclid to decide whether such assurance, standing alone, was evidence satisfactory to Power Company of an offer within the scope of Power Company's request for assurance that the equipment would not be used in the Illinois area subsequent to its sale. Power Company was free to accept or reject any proposal made by Euclid designed to meet the requirement that the equipment, if sold, would be used elsewhere than in the Illinois area and it is manifest that Power Company was never satisfied that Euclid had given it sufficient assurance concerning to whom the equipment would be ultimately sold and where it would be placed for use, to allow Power Company to treat the offer as acceptable.

. . . .

. . . We believe the rule to be well stated in I.L.P., Vol. 12, *Contracts,* § 31, as follows:

'One of the essential elements for the formation of a contract, other than a contract implied in law or quasi contract, is a manifestation of assent by the parties to the terms thereof. It is essential that both parties assent to the same thing in the same sense and that their minds meet on the essential terms and conditions.' "

The Uniform Commercial Code has not made any change in the basic law.

Because we are unable to find agreement between the parties from their negotiations, we must affirm the finding of the trial court that no contract existed. . . .

In re Doughboy Industries, Inc.
233 N.Y.S.2d 488 (Sup. Ct. N.Y. App. Div. 1962)

Pantasote Company (plaintiff) brought suit to require Doughboy Industries, Inc. (defendant) to arbitrate a dispute. Doughboy appealed from the trial court's denial of its motion to stay arbitration. Reversed for Doughboy.

On two occasions prior to May 6, and on May 6, Doughboy ordered and received shipments of film from Pantasote. On each of these occasions Doughboy had used a purchase order form which stated: "ALTERATION OF TERMS—None of the terms and conditions contained in this Purchase Order may be added to, modified, superseded or otherwise altered except by a written instrument signed by an authorized representative of Buyer and delivered by Buyer to Seller, and each shipment received by Buyer from Seller shall be deemed to be only upon the terms and conditions contained in this Purchase Order except as they may be added to, modified, superseded or otherwise altered, notwithstanding Buyer's act of accepting or paying for any shipment or similar act of Buyer."

Pantasote accepted each order by sending an acknowledgment form which stated: "IMPORTANT—Buyer agrees he has full knowledge of conditions printed on the reverse side hereof, and that the same are part of the agreement between buyer and seller and shall be binding if either the goods referred to herein are delivered to and accepted by buyer, or if buyer does not within ten days from date hereof deliver to seller written object to said conditions or any part thereof."

The reverse side of Pantasote's acknowledgment form contained a general arbitration clause binding both parties to submit any dispute arising under the contract to arbitration. A dispute arose over the May 6 contract and Pantasote brought suit to require that Doughboy submit the dispute to arbitration.

BREITEL, J.   This case involves a conflict between a buyer's order form and a seller's acknowledgment form, each memorializing a purchase and sale of goods. The issue arises on whether the parties agreed to arbitrate future disputes. The seller's form had a general arbitration provision. The buyer's form did not. The buyer's form contained a provision that only a signed consent would bind the buyer to any terms thereafter transmitted in any commercial form of the seller. The seller's form, however, provided that silence or a failure to object in writing would be an acceptance of the terms and conditions of its acknowledgment form. The buyer never objected to the seller's acknowledgment, orally or in writing. In short, the buyer and seller accomplished a legal equivalent to the irresistible force colliding with the immovable object.

. . . .

The dispute, which has arisen and which the parties wish determined, the seller by arbitration, and the buyer by court litigation, is whether the buyer is bound to accept all the goods ordered on a "hold basis." The arbitration would take place in New York City. The litigation might have to be brought in Wisconsin, the buyer's home State.

. . . .

This case involves only the application of the arbitration clause. Arguably, a different principle from that applied here might, under present law, govern other of the terms and conditions in either of the commercial forms. The reason is the special rule that the courts have laid down with respect to arbitration clauses, namely, that the agreement to arbitrate must be direct and the intention made clear, without implication, inveiglement or subtlety. . . . The severability of arbitration clauses from other provisions in commercial documentation would, of course, follow, if it be true that the threshold for clarity of agreement to arbitrate is greater than with respect to other contractual terms. . . .

It should be evident, as the buyer argues, that a contract for the sale of goods came into existence on May 13, 1960 when the seller made a partial shipment. . . . The contract, at such time, was documented only by the buyer's purchase-order form. However, that is not dispositive. It is equally evident from the prior transactions between these parties, and general practices in trade, that more documents were to follow. Such documents may help make the contract, or modify it. Whether the subsequent documents were necessary to complete the making of the contract (as would be true if there had been no effective or valid acceptance by partial shipment), or whether they served only to modify or validate the terms of an existing contract (as would be true if there had been a less formal written acceptance, merely an oral acceptance, or an acceptance by partial shipment of goods) is not really too important once the commercial dealings have advanced as far as they had here. By that time, there is no question whether there was a contract, but only what was the contract.

Recognizing, as one should, that the businessmen in this case acted with complete disdain for the "lawyer's content" of the very commercial forms they were sending and receiving, the question is what obligation ought the law to attach to the arbitration clause. And in determining that question the traditional theory is applicable, namely, that of constructive knowledge and acceptance of contractual terms, based on prior transactions and the duty to read contractual instruments to which one is a party. . . .

But, and this is critical, it is not only the seller's form which should be given effect, but also the buyer's form, for it too was used in the prior transactions, and as to it too, there was a duty to read. Of course, if the two commercial forms are given effect, they cancel one another. (Certainly, the test is not which is the later form, because here the prior form said the buyer would not be bound by the later form unless it consented in writing. It needs little discussion that silence, a weak enough form of acceptance, effective only when misleading and there is a duty to speak, can be negatived as a misleading factor by announcing in advance that it shall have no effect as acceptance. . . .)

Consequently, as a matter of law there was no agreement to arbitrate in this case, if one applied existing principles.

But the problem of conflicting commercial forms is one with which there has been much concern before this, and a new effort at rational solution has been made. The solution would yield a similar result. The Uniform Commercial Code (L. 1962, ch. 553) takes effect in this State September 27, 1963 (§ 10–105). It reflects the latest legislative conclusions as to what the law ought to be.

. . . The draftsmen's comments to section 2–207 are in precise point. Thus, it is said:

"3. Whether or not additional or different terms will become part of the agreement depends upon the provisions of subsection (2). If they are such as materially to alter the original bargain, they will not be included unless expressly agreed to by the other party. If, however, they are terms which would not so change the bargain they will be incorporated unless notice of objection to them has already been given or if given within a reasonable time. . . .

"6. If no answer is received within a reasonable time after additional terms are proposed, it is both fair and commercially sound to asume that their inclusion has been assented to. Where clauses on confirming forms sent by both parties conflict each party must be assumed to object to a clause of the other conflicting with one on the confirmation sent by himself. As a result the requirement that there be notice of objection which is found in subsection (2) is satisfied and the conflicting terms do not become a part of the contract. The contract then consists of the terms originally expressly agreed to, terms on which the confirmations agree, and terms supplied by this Act, including subsection (2)."

On this exposition, the arbitration clause, whether viewed as a material alternation under subsection (2), or as a term nullified by a conflicting provision in the buyer's form, would fail to survive as a contract term. In the light of the New York cases, at least, there can be little question that an agreement to arbitrate is a material term, one not to be injected by implication, subtlety or inveiglement. And the conclusion is also the same if the limitation contained in the offer (the buyer's purchase order) is given effect, as required by paragraph (a) of subsection 2 of the new section.

Accordingly, the order denying Doughboy's motion to stay arbitration should be reversed, on the law, with costs to Doughboy and the motion should be granted.

Problem Cases

1. Baldwin placed an order with Peters, Writer and Christensen (Peters) stockbroker, for 50,000 shares of Acme Uranium Company stock at 2 cents a share. Peters contended that it was directed to buy the stock "as close to two cents as possible" but the trial court held that the order was to purchase the stock at 2 cents a share. Peters purchased 50,000 shares at 2⅛ cents per share. Baldwin refused to accept and pay for the stock and Peters brought suit to recover damages for breach of the contract. The trial court rendered a judgment for Peters for $1,000. Will this judgment be upheld on appeal?

2. Sierota signed an authorization to advertise his business for sale in two issues of two publications of Union Interchange, Inc. The authorization provided that Sierota would pay $150 for the advertising. The authorization contained the following clause: "This agreement shall become effective only when accepted by your office in Los Angeles, California. You shall notify me of such acceptance."
   Sierota testified that he signed the authorization believing it to be a listing of his business requiring him to pay only when Union Interchange, Inc. sold his business. Union Interchange, Inc. did not notify Sierota that it accepted the agreement. Was there a contract created?

3. Schwartz and the Shapiros purchased an apartment building. Prior to the purchase of the building the parties each signed a writing which provided "should either party agree to sell their 1/2 interest individually that sale of same shall first be offered to the remaining owner at the original purchase price." The parties later entered into oral agreements relative to the management and operation of the property. During the trial of the case the question of whether the writing and oral agreements constituted a binding contract was raised. The parties had indicated their intention of having a formal draft of the agreement prepared by an attorney, but this was never done. Does this mean no contract existed?

4. Fuller had stored hay in a barn on a farm leased by Bowley. Bowley contemplated purchasing the hay but decided not to do so. On March 11, Bowley gave Fuller written notices to remove the hay by March 15, and that a charge of $1 per day

storage would be made after that date. Fuller did not remove the hay until April 1. Bowley claims that he is entitled to $1 per day storage from March 15 to April 1. Is Bowley entitled to storage charges as claimed?

5. Chesebrough wrote Bayne, a broker, to purchase 2,000 bags of coffee at $8.53 per pound. Bayne purchased 2,000 bags of coffee at $8.54 per pound and telegraphed Chesebrough as follows: "Letter just received. Bought 2,000 bags at $8.54 subject to your approval. Must have immediate reply. Rush." This telegram was dispatched at noon but was not delivered to Chesebrough until 2:50 P.M. Immediately upon receipt of the telegram Chesebrough wired: "Telegram just received. Purchase approved at $8.54." This telegram was delivered to Bayne at 3:40 P.M., which was after the close of the commodity exchange. Bayne had sold the coffee just before the exchange closed. Did a contract for the coffee result?

6. Corlies wished to remodel his offices and talked with White, a contractor, about doing the work. On September 28, White discussed his estimate with Corlies. Later, that same day Corlies made some changes in his specificatons and sent the changes with the following note to White: "Upon an agreement to finish the fitting up of the offices at 57 Broadway in two weeks from date, you can begin at once. The writer will call again, probably between 5 and 6 this P.M."

   On receipt of this note White purchased lumber and began the work. The next day Corlies notified White of the withdrawal of his offer. White claims that he accepted the offer by the purchase of the lumber and the beginning of work on the offices. Is White's contention correct?

7. On May 27, Drexler placed an order for goods with Deering, one half to be shipped at once, one half of the remainder to be shipped in July, and the balance to be shipped before the last of August. The first shipment was made, and the goods were received and paid for.

   Before the second shipment, Deering mailed to Drexler a paper across which was printed in large letters, "Acceptance of Order" and at the bottom of which was printed, also in large letters, "please sign and return the accompanying confirmation." This form contained a clause providing that any dispute arising would be submitted to arbitration. Drexler retained the paper without signing it.

   There subsequently arose a dispute which Deering submitted to arbitration without the consent of Drexler. Drexler did not appear and took no part in the arbitration. Drexler contends that he did not agree to arbitrate and that he is not bound by the award. Deering contends that Drexler, by retaining the "Acceptance of Order," is bound by its terms. Is Drexler bound by the terms of the "Acceptance of Order?"

8. Fisher had advertised for bids for the furnishing of lumber to be used on a construction job. Cedar Rapids Lumber Company was low bidder. Fisher sent Cedar Rapids Lumber Company a telegram as follows: "You are low bidder. Come on the morning train." Was this telegram an acceptance of the bid?

9. Grafe-Week, subcontractor, made a bid to Leavell & Co., prime contractor, for the mechanical section of a missile project. This original bid was later accepted by Leavell with a condition that Grafe-Week obtain and bear the cost of a performance bond. Grafe-Week refused to do the job and Leavell sued contending it had accepted the bid. Is Leavell right?

10. Toro offered to purchase Geyer's business and put up a check for $5,000 to show her good faith. The purchase agreement provided that if the offer was not accepted by Geyer on or before March 1, the check for $5,000 "shall be returned." Prior to March 1, Geyer cashed the check but did not notify Toro of acceptance of his offer.

After March 1, Toro sued for the return of the $5,000 on the grounds that Geyer had failed to accept the offer within the specified time. Geyer answered that he had effectively accepted the offer when he cashed the check. Can Toro recover the $5,000?

11. On February 25, A & P held a lease on the premises at 3309 W. Madison Street. The lease was about to expire, and A & P wrote Geary, the owner, offering to lease the premises for the ensuing year.

   On March 7, at 10:30 A.M., Geary mailed a letter accepting A & P's offer. On the same day, at 9:30 P.M., A & P mailed a letter revoking its offer. At the time A & P mailed its letter of revocation, it did not know that Geary had mailed a letter of acceptance. Did a contract result?

12. A salesman of Harvester Company solicited from Hendrickson an order for a machine. The order was subject to the approval of Harvester Company at its home office. The order was received by Harvester Company, but it took no action thereon, and it did not ship the machine. After waiting a reasonable time, Hendrickson brought suit to recover damages for breach of the contract. Harvester set up as a defense that it never accepted Hendrickson's offer. Did a contract result?

chapter 8. Reality of Consent

Introduction

Nature of Real Consent.   One of the fundamental requirements for holding a person liable for the nonperformance of a contractual promise is that the promise must have been made voluntarily. Honesty and fair dealing are essential to the success of a free, competitive economy. Under our contract law the promisor is protected from sharp dealing and from the performance of an unconscionable promise by the ruling that a promise which has been induced by misrepresentation, fraud, duress or undue influence is voidable at the election of the injured party. In negotiating contracts the promisor will be required to exercise reasonable caution and judgment, and he will seldom be permitted to escape from promises carelessly made. Standards have been developed by the courts which are used as the basis for determining whether or not the promisor should be held to his promise. Stated in broad general terms the basic question posed by the court is: was the promisor, in the exercise of reasonable and prudent judgment, misled or coerced into making the promise by the conduct or promise of the promisee or someone acting in his behalf? If the court finds that he was misled or coerced he may have the right to elect not to perform his promise. Under some exceptional circumstances the courts have held that if a promise is induced by fraud or duress, it is void.

Closely related to a promise induced by misrepresentation, fraud, duress, or undue influence is the promise based on a mistake of fact. If both parties to an agreement have acted in the erroneous assumption as to the existence or nonexistence of a material fact relating to their agreement, the courts have, as a general rule, granted whatever relief the circumstances of the case warranted. The primary consideration in such a case is the equity of the situation. The courts attempt to render a decision which is fair to all parties involved.

Misrepresentation and Fraud

Misrepresentation.   If one person, by words or acts or by any other conduct, has created in the mind of another an impression which is not in accordance with the facts, such person is guilty of misrepresentation. Misrepresentation of a material fact justifiably relied on is ground for holding a contractual promise voidable. Knowledge of the falsity on the part of the person making the misrepresentation is not essential, and the method by which the misrepresentation is made is not material.

The misrepresentation must be of a material fact. To be material, the fact need not be the sole fact which induced the injured party to make the contractual promise, nor need it be the major inducement. It must be a contributing factor, however, and the circumstances must be such that it is reasonable to presume that the party would not have made the contractual promise had he known the true facts.

The misrepresentation must be of an existing or past fact. An expression of future happenings is prospective and is not a statement of fact. Likewise, arguments intended to convince a party that the transaction is a "good deal" are not statements of fact.

A party, in order to be entitled to a remedy, must have justifiably relied on the misrepresentations. If the party knows that the statements are erroneous, or if the facts and circumstances are such that, in the exercise of reasonable prudence, he should have investigated and discovered the falsity of the statements, he is not justified in relying on the statements.

As a general rule, if both parties have equal knowledge and equal opportunity to learn the true facts, neither party is justified in relying on statements made by the other party. But if the party making the misrepresentations has superior knowledge and is in a position to know the facts, the other party will, as a general rule, be justified in relying on the statements. For example, if the owner of an apartment building states that the apartments rent for from $55 to $75 per month, the prospective buyer will be justified in relying on the statement.

The remedy available to a party who is induced by misrepresentation to make a contractual promise is rescission—that is, the injured party may return what he has received and recover what he has given in performance of the contract, or its value. If no performance has been rendered, the injured party may give notice that he disaffirms the contract; and if suit is brought against him for breach of contract, he may set up the misrepresentation as a defense.

In all cases of misrepresentation the injured party must act seasonably. Failure to rescind or disaffirm within a reasonable time after the injured party learns of the misrepresentation amounts to waiver of the right to rescind or disaffirm.

Fraud. Fraud is an intentional misrepresentation of a material fact made for the purpose of inducing another, in reliance upon it, to part with some valuable thing belonging to him, or to surrender a legal right. If one party, through misrepresentations knowingly made, creates a mistaken belief as to the existence or nonexistence of a fact material to a transaction and thereby influences the action of the party to whom the representation is made, the party making the misrepresentation is guilty of fraudulent conduct.

The method used to create the mistaken belief is immaterial. It may be by words, acts, concealment, or any other method. The result is important, not the method whereby the result is attained. The terms "misrepresentation" and "fraud" are frequently used synonymously; however, misrepresentation, as used in law, signifies innocent misrepresentation, whereas fraud signifies intentional misrepresentation.

If a person is induced to make a contractual promise by fraudulent representations, he may rescind the contract, since the right to rescind is based on misrepresentation. However, if the elements of an actionable deceit are present—(1) misrepresentation of a material fact, (2) knowingly made, (3) with intent to defraud, (4) justifiably relied on, (5) with resulting injury—the injured party has an election of remedies. He may rescind the contract, or he may affirm the contract and bring an action in tort to recover damages for the deceit. Damages for deceit include compensation for all injury resulting directly from the deceit. As in misrepresentation, the injured person must act seasonably, and his failure to give notice within a reasonable time after he learns of the deceit will amount to a waiver of his rights.

Summary

Fairness and honesty are necessary for the efficient functioning of a free competitive economy. Consequently, an offer or an acceptance induced by innocent misrepresentations or by fraud is not binding on the party induced to make or accept an offer by such means. There may be no dishonesty in an innocent misrepresentation.

The remedy for misrepresentation is rescission. If the person making the erroneous statements knows that they are not true and makes them to mislead the other party to his injury, obviously the dishonest party should not be permitted to retain his ill-gotten gains.

Kennedy v. *Flo-Tronics, Inc.*
143 N.W.2d 827 (Sup. Ct. Minn. 1966)

This was an action for damages for alleged misrepresentation brought by Robert E. Kennedy (plaintiff) against Flo-Tronics, Inc., and others (defendants). Judgment for the plaintiff and the defendants appealed. Reversed.

OTIS, JUSTICE.   The contract out of which this litigation arose was entered February 23, 1961. By its terms Kennedy transferred to Flo-Tronics, Inc., all of the assets in a business he was conducting under the name of Kenco Plastics, in return for which Kennedy received 4,000 shares of stock in Flo-Tronics, having a market value of $8.50 per share. Under the contract, Kennedy was obliged to retire the debts he then owed. To that end the stock he received was pledged with a bank as collateral for a loan in the sum of $17,500. In addition he executed a second mortgage on his home for $5,000. Kennedy claims he was induced to enter the contract by the assurances of one of Flo-Tronics officers, Earl Nelson, that the value of Flo-Tronics stock would rise from $8.50 per share to $25 a share by January 1, 1962. The stock did increase in market value to $17 per share by April 18, 1961. However, Kennedy was advised that under S.E.C. regulations he was not permitted to sell it until he had retained it for six months. By March, 1962, the market value had fallen to approximately $3 a share. At that time the bank sold the stock for the sum of $10,367,65. In addition the second mortgage on Kennedy's home was foreclosed.

．． ． ．

In justifying his reliance on Nelson's opinion because of a disparity in their relationship, Kennedy cites *Stark* v. *Equitable Life Assur. Society* . . . :

"A fiduciary relation exists when confidence is reposed on one side and there is resulting superiority and influence on the other; and the relation and duties involved in it need not be legal, but may be moral, social, domestic, or merely personal."

We went on to say, however, that a fiduciary relationship is not established simply by a long acquaintance. . . .

A recent decision of this court on which Kennedy relies is *Hollerman* v. *F. H. Peavey & Co.* We there affirmed a judgment awarding damages against a vendor of poultry feed for misrepresenting future profits. The losses sustained by the growers were occasioned by air-sacculitis which decimated the flock. In referring to a brochure which guaranteed a profit, we stated:

"*If it is doubtful that the representations of the brochure amount to more than expressions of opinion or estimates,* it must be conceded that the affirmations of Peavey's representative to plaintiffs on the disease of chicks are material." (Italics supplied.)

We then held that a vendor's assurance that disease was a minor problem and need not give the producers any concern was a material misrepresentation of fact. In arriving at our decision, we observed:

". . . It is well established that if a person represents as true material facts *susceptible of knowledge,* to one who relies and acts thereon to his injury, the one making the representations cannot defeat recovery by showing that he did not know his representations were false or that he believed them to be true. . . .

．． ． ．

". . . Defendants had superior knowledge, or an opportunity for knowledge, of the problems which might be encountered in the conduct of the business. Because of their ignorance and inexperience in regard to matters concerning which material representations were made, plaintiffs had a right to rely upon the superior knowledge of defendants."

. . . . .

In the light of Kennedy's background, experience, and intelligence, we hold he was not justified in assuming that Nelson was omniscient or infallible in a matter as patently fraught with uncertainty as the state of the securities market at a given date in the future.

Perry v. *Woodall*
438 P.2d 813 (Sup. Ct. Utah 1968)

This was an action brought by Lowell Perry (plaintiff) against Earl Woodall (defendant) to collect payments due on a contract to purchase a drugstore. Woodall counterclaimed for damages for fraud. Perry appealed from a judgment against his payment claim and in favor of Woodall's counterclaim. Held reversed as to both claim and counterclaim.

Prior to April 1, 1964, Perry was the owner of all the corporate stock of Buy Wise Drugs, Inc., which operated a drugstore in the Rose Park area of Salt Lake City. Perry managed the business on behalf of the corporation and Woodall had been for a number of years a pharmacist employed at the drugstore. From time to time prior to April, 1964, Perry and Woodall discussed the possibility of Woodall purchasing the business. These discussions resulted in a written offer by Woodall dated March 13, 1964, to purchase Perry's stock upon certain terms set out in the offer. The offer was accepted on March 14, 1964, and Woodall took over the management and assumed control of the business on April 1, 1964.

. . . . .

Prior to the making of the contract of sale, Woodall had been furnished a report by an inventory service which reported the merchandise and physical assets of the store as being in excess of $47,000. Woodall had also been furnished a balance sheet as of February 10, 1964, prepared by the corporate bookkeeper, which showed liabilities of about $47,000, including current liabilities on trade accounts payable of over $20,000.

On July 18, 1964, Perry furnished to Woodall an affidavit which listed the liabilities of the business as being in the sum of approximately $61,000. After receipt of the affidavit, Woodall communicated to Perry through his attorney by letter, which communication pointed out that a number of items listed on the affidavit were personal debts rather than corporate liabilities. The communication also contained a new proposal by Woodall to purchase the business. In the new offer Woodall proposed to pay to Perry the sum of $10,000 for the latter's interest in the assets and inventory. Woodall had failed to pay to Perry all of the sums due under the first offer.

The negotiations between the parties did not result in a second agreement. Woodall continued to operate the business until September 7, 1964, at which time he was appointed receiver in an action commenced by one of the creditors of the business. Woodall continued to act as receiver until January 1966, at which time he resigned and a successor was appointed. Woodall continued to manage the business for the successor receiver until March 1966, at which time he purchased the assets of the business at a receiver's sale for the sum of about $45,000.

TUCKETT, JUDGE.   The court found that Woodall elected to rescind the purchase agreement in July after he had received the affidavit of Perry setting out all of the obligations of the business. We are of the opinion that the record does not support the finding of the court in this regard. One who claims he has been deceived and elects to rescind his contract by reason of the fraud or misrepresentation of the other contracting party must act promptly and unequivocally in announcing his intention. The facts in this case would indicate that Woodall, after learning of the extent of the indebtedness of the corporation he had purchased in July 1964, did not elect to rescind the contract at that time, but rather expressed dissatisfaction with his purchase of the business and offered to renegotiate the terms of that purchase agreement. Woodall, after learning all of the facts, if he then considered that he had been defrauded, had a duty to notify Perry promptly of his election to rescind the contract and to also tender back to Perry the assets of the corporation, as well as the corporate stock involved in the transaction. The law is well settled that one electing to rescind a contract must tender back to the other contracting party whatever property of value he has received. Woodall elected to retain possession of the corporate assets and to carry on the business until it was taken over in the receivership proceedings. We are of the opinion that Woodall waited too long, and that he cannot now rescind the contract. . . .

The judgment of the trial court is reversed and the case is remanded to that court for a new trial. Perry is entitled to costs.

Franchey v. Hannes

207 Atl. 2d 268 (Sup. Ct. Errors, Conn. 1965)

This was an action by Mr. and Mrs. Franchey (plaintiffs) against Mr. and Mrs. Hannes (defendants) for damages due to fraudulent nondisclosure. Judgment for Mr. and Mrs. Franchey and Mr. and Mrs. Hannes appealed. Affirmed.

Hannes owned a house located on 1.05 acres of land where it was found on a survey made that a large portion of the driveway and a foot of apron of the swimming pool encroached on neighbor's property. After owning the house for three years, Hannes decided to sell. In listing this house with the realtor, he did not disclose the encroachments.

Franchey became interested in buying the house and property and visited the property several times, but Hannes never did disclose the true boundaries. On the day on which the transfer of title took place, Mrs. Franchey found a map showing the property as surveyed and the encroachment on the neighbor, but she did not recognize it for what it was or realize its significance and went to the attorney's office for signing the transfer of title. She did remark that she had found a map but the attorney produced another which showed no encroachment, and he assured

Mrs. Franchey that everything was all right. In February, 1959, Franchey discovered the encroachment and filed suit for damages.

ALCORN, ASSOCIATE JUSTICE. We turn now to the court's ultimate conclusion that Hannes incurred a liability to Franchey for a fraudulent nondisclosure. As already indicated, the trial court concluded that Hannes had not made an actionable, deliberate or reckless misstatement of fact. . . . It concluded, however, that the facts bring the case within the exception to the rule that mere silence is not actionable in a transaction in which the parties deal at arm's length unless the circumstances or the existence of a confidential relationship gives rise to a duty to speak. . . . It then proceeded to find, in the circumstances of this case, a duty to speak. The operative factor producing this result seems to have been the physical appearance of the property. This factor alone was insufficient to give rise to a duty to disclose.

The facts of the case bring it, rather, within the widely accepted rule that, although a vendor may, under the circumstances, have no duty to speak, nevertheless, if he does assume to speak, he must make a full and fair disclosure as to the matters which he assumes to speak. He must then avoid a deliberate nondisclosure. . . . From the court's finding it is apparent that Franchey, upon viewing the property, reasonably was led to assume, from its physical appearance, that at least the driveway and the pool were within the boundaries of the land they were interested in buying. Instead of remaining silent, Hannes, at the conference in New York, represented that the broken stone wall was the northerly boundary. Later when the parties visited the premises together, Hannes disclaimed knowledge of the location of the boundary markers and Mrs. Hannes stated that she had planted the rock garden. Neither Mr. or Mrs. Hannes disclosed the encroachments of which they were then aware. Thus, there was a failure to diclose the whole truth about the very subject concerning which they had assumed to speak. The court found this action to be intentional and that its result was that Mr. and Mrs. Franchey were induced to buy the property. Mr. and Mrs. Hannes' conduct was the equivalent of a false representation.

Duress and Undue Influence

General Nature. Duress is unlawful constraint exercised upon a person whereby he is forced to do some act that he otherwise would not have done. As applied to contracts, it is the overcoming of the promisor's free will through threats of bodily or other harm, thereby inducing him to enter into a contract through force and fear.

Undue influence is closely related to duress. It exists where one party is under the domination of another and is induced, by the unfair persuasion of the dominant party, to follow a course of action which he would not have followed of his own free will.

A contractual promise made under duress or undue influence is voidable.

The reason for this is that since the party making the promise has been deprived of his ability to exercise a free choice, he should not be bound by his promise. In both duress and undue influence the parties are not bargaining on an equal basis. As a general rule the equality of the bargaining power of the parties to a contract is immaterial. The parties are presumed to be capable of protecting their own interests, and the courts will not assume the role of arbiters of the equality of bargaining powers in the everyday give-and-take of the marketplace. However, when the situation is such that the inequality cannot, in fairness and good conscience, be ignored, the courts will grant relief by declaring voidable the contractual promise made under the pressure of duress or induced by undue influence.

Duress.   Duress had its origin in the law of crimes and torts. In the early stages of its development the test of duress was the threat of physical injury sufficient to overcome the will of a constant man of ordinary courage made by one having the power to execute the threat.

We no longer require threat of physical injury as our test for duress, nor do we use the standard of the constant man of ordinary courage as the standard of resistance required of the person coerced. No simple test of the existence of duress has been developed. As a general rule the courts have stated that the means used must be wrongful. An analysis of the cases reveals that the word "wrongful" is not confined to criminal or tortious acts but may also include unconscionable conduct. In applying this test, the court must determine, in the exercise of its judicial discretion, where the line shall be drawn. Each case is treated as presenting a separate problem. If the act is wrongful, and if it deprives the coerced person of his ability to make a free choice, the courts will, as a general rule, grant relief.

Threats of criminal prosecution made to coerce a person into making payment of a claimed defalcation or to compensate for claimed unlawful gains have been held to be duress if the person making the threat gains thereby advantages to which he is not lawfully entitled.

The courts have generally held that the threat of a civil suit does not constitute duress. However, if the bringing of a civil suit is clearly an abuse of civil process, it may amount to duress. One of the functions of our courts is to hear and determine the disputes between individuals; consequently, a threat to bring suit on a disputed claim or to enforce a claimed right by court action cannot amount to duress. The threat to bring suit on an unfounded claim, when the person threatening suit knows that the financial situation of the person threatened is such that a suit would, in all probability, bring financial ruin to him, would be held by some courts to amount to duress.

The unjustified withholding of a person's goods for the purpose of forcing him to pay an unreasonable charge has been held to be duress. In the earlier cases the courts held that the refusal of a common carrier to deliver goods unless an unreasonable carriage charge was paid amounted to duress. This concept has been extended to other similar situations; and today, "duress of goods," the unjustified withholding of goods unless exorbitant charges are paid, is generally held to be duress, and the person paying the excessive charges to obtain possession of the goods is permitted to recover the amount of the overcharge.

Undue Influence. The objective of the defense of undue influence is to protect the aged, the timid, and the physically or mentally weak from the unscrupulous who succeed in gaining their confidence and take advantage of them. There is no precise definition of undue influence. It is a form of coercion. Before the courts will grant relief on the ground of undue influence, there must be a wide difference in the bargaining ability of the parties. The victim of undue influence must have the mental capacity to contract but at the same time not have the ability to protect himself against unscrupulous persons who gain his confidence.

In most of the cases involving undue influence, we generally have a situation in which a close relative or long-time friend takes advantage of the relationship and induces his weakened victim to make a gift or transfer property to him for a wholly inadequate consideration. The principal test is whether the confidential relationship has been used to divert property from its normal course, in view of all the circumstances, to the person exercising the undue influence.

Summary

Duress is the obtaining of an advantage over a person by means of pressure brought to bear which deprives that person of his ability to make a free choice. A contractual promise obtained by duress is voidable. In contract law, if the means of executing the pressure is wrongful and the contractual promise is unjust or unconscionable, the courts will grant relief. The relief granted may be rescission of the contract or the granting of a judgment for any sum obtained over and above that to which the coercing party was, in fairness and honesty, entitled.

Undue influence is based on a confidential relationship wherein one party dominates the other and wherein the dominant party owes a duty to look for the interests of the servient party. If such a relationship exists and the dominant party, in breach of his duty, uses his position to benefit himself at the expense of the servient party, the courts will hold the transaction voidable on the ground of undue influence.

In both duress and undue influence, the party with superior bargaining power takes advantage of the situation and gains an economic advantage which is so unequal and unfair that it is, as the courts frequently state, shocking to the conscience of man.

Hellenic Lines, Ltd. v. *Louis Dreyfus Corp.*
372 F.2d 753 (2nd Cir. 1967)

This was a petition to compel arbitration brought by Hellenic Lines, Ltd. (plaintiff) against Louis Dreyfus Corporation (defendant). Petition granted and Dreyfus appealed. Affirmed.

On November 9, 1964, Hellenic contracted with the Iranian Economic Mission to load, at Hellenic's expense, approximately 5,000 tons of wheat at a grain elevator in Baltimore, Maryland, and transport it to Iran. Dreyfus was not a party to this freight engagement. However, on the same day, Dreyfus had contracted to sell the wheat in question to the Iranian Mission. Dreyfus has a dual capacity in the transaction; it sold the grain and it operated the grain elevator where the wheat would be loaded on a vessel. Hellenic was not a party to this contract of sale.

Dreyfus had been trying for some time to collect elevator charges billed to Hellenic a few years before in connection with the loading of a Hellenic vessel. Therefore, when Dreyfus learned that the S.S. *Hellenic Star* would be loading the grain, Dreyfus notified Hellenic that it would require prepayment of loading charges. This request triggered a series of irascible telephone conversations and correspondence between Hellenic and Dreyfus. Nevertheless, several days later Hellenic sent its check of $24,096 in partial compliance with Dreyfus' demand. The S.S. *Hellenic Star* arrived at the grain elevator on December 2, but was not assigned a berth until December 6. Hellenic protested this detention because it was causing the vessel to miss commitments at other ports. On December 8, Dreyfus informed Hellenic that the sums already deposited did not cover overtime expenses in loading the vessel and asked for further prepayment. A further dispute arose as to who was causing the delay in loading and consequent overtime and other expenses. Hellenic, among other things, pointed out that it had a claim against the Iranian Mission because the wheat had not been bagged in advance. Finally, in response to a demand by Dreyfus that the ship accept overtime or get out, Hellenic under protest paid Dreyfus another $10,000 for the estimated costs of overtime. . . . Finally, in this charged atmosphere, Hellenic's ship left berth on December 15.

At this point the situation changed; Dreyfus, wearing its other hat as seller of the grain, was obliged to furnish a "clean" bill of lading against the letter of credit opened in its favor by the Iranian Mission. However, what was tendered to it by Hellenic was a bill of lading with the following legend thereon:

503 (Five hundred and three) bags shortshipped. Bags frail, contents of several bags spilling while loaded. Not responsible for spillage of contents. Detention in loading due in the amount of $10,653.12 as per attached statement. Amount refundable to Hellenic Lines Limited for overtime as demanded and paid $10,000.00 also overpayment of stevedoring $515.05. All other terms and conditions of freight engagement no. 4575 of Nov. 9, 1964 to apply.

Hellenic claimed that placing this information on the bill of lading was necessary to protect its rights against the cargo. At the time, Dreyfus objected strenuously to the notations, particularly the items of $10,653.12 detention damages and over-payment of overtime and stevedoring of $10,000 and $515.05, respectively. Some urgent correspondence and negotiation followed, resulting in a settlement of the dispute. As to certain of the items, e.g., the alleged shortage and condition of the bags, Dreyfus agreed to pay Hellenic "any amount which . . . (Hellenic) may be called upon to pay to the receivers of this parcel by reason of not having inserted these remarks in the Bill of Lading." As to the items of $10,653.12, $10,000, and $515.05, in return for their deletion from the bill of lading, Dreyfus agreed by letter of December 23, as follows:

> In consideration of your making these deletions, we agree to submit your claims to arbitration in New York and, to that effect, we nominate as our Arbitrartor Mr. Charles Nisi. Please nominate your Arbitrator so that the two may appoint an Umpire.
>
> We agree to pay any detention and any refunds of overtime and/or stevedoring charges which the Arbitrators may decide you are entitled to receive.

Therefore, a clean bill of lading was issued, the wheat was delivered, and Dreyfus collected the $378,000 due it from the Iranian Mission.

On December 30, 1964, Hellenic appointed its arbitrator, but Dreyfus refused to enter arbitration contending that the agreement to arbitrate was procured under duress.

FEINBERG, JUDGE. The early concept of duress had its roots in criminal and tort law as another sanction to control anti-social behavior that amounted to an assault on the person. The doctrine has changed and broadened over the years. For a while, it was said that the proscribed conduct had to throw fear into a man of "ordinary firmness" to amount to duress; now it may be enough if the complaining party actually is coerced, whether he be brave or timorous. It has also been pointed out that even a threat to do an otherwise lawful act may amount to duress under certain circumstances. Definitions of duress abound in the cases and literature. Thus, *Restatement, Contracts* (1932), characterizes duress as

(a) any wrongful act of one person that compels a manifestation of apparent assent by another to a transaction without his volition, or
(b) any wrongful threat of one person by words or other conduct that induces another to enter into a transaction under the influence of such fear as precludes him from exer-cising free will and judgment, if the threat was intended or should reasonably have been expected to operate as an inducement.

In *United States v. Bethlehem Steel Corp.,* Mr. Justice Frankfurter stated:

> These principles are not foreign to the law of contracts. Fraud and physical duress are not the only grounds upon which courts refuse to enforce contracts. The law is not so primitive that it sanctions every injustice except brute force and downright fraud. More specifically, the courts generally refuse to lend themselves to the enforcement of a "bargain" in which one party has unjustly taken advantage of the economic necessities of the other.

However duress may be defined, a key element today is the state of mind of the person threatened. This is not to say that the existence of choice necessarily disproves the existence of duress. In *Union Pac. R. R.* v. *Public Serv. Comm'n.* Mr. Justice Holmes pointed out that:

> It always is for the interest of a party under duress to choose the lesser of two evils. But the fact that a choice was made according to interest does not exclude duress. It is the characteristic of duress properly so called.

The question is one of degree. "As a practical matter it is obvious that there is no line of absolute demarcation between fear that deprives a person of free will and judgment and lesser degrees of fear. . . ." Moreover, the nature and extent of the pressure "is inseparable from the subject. The pressure must be improper and excessive in going beyond what is reasonable under the circumstances in order to constitute either duress or undue influence." Although it is not difficult to cite cases where extreme economic pressure was held not to be duress, we need not determine whether the limits of the doctrine are so narrow. A finding of duress at least must reflect a conviction that one party to a transaction has been so improperly imposed upon by the other that a court should intervene. After carefully reviewing the record, we have no such conviction here.

We turn again to the facts of this case. It is quite clear that at no time did Dreyfus exhibit the loss of judgment or severe impairment of bargaining power required to establish duress. Dreyfus, whose annual volume at the time was in the vicinity of $700 to $800 million, had the problem of satisfying the conditions of a letter of credit in order to obtain payment of $378,573. The claims raised by Hellenic amounted to slightly over $21,000. It is difficult to believe that Dreyfus could not have made some arrangement to obtain an amended letter of credit to cover a claim amounting to less than six percent of the sum due from the Iranian Mission. . . .

. . . It is evident that Dreyfus merely exercised its business judgment in a difficult situation. It had started a squabble under auspicious circumstances, but had to continue with it when the situation had changed. Dreyfus undoubtedly noted—as do we—that although the tables had been turned, Hellenic was not demanding immediate repayment but only a promise to arbitrate, hardly a shocking request. Finally, we regard as significant the taking by Dreyfus of preliminary steps to prepare for the arbitration, the two-month delay in claiming duress, and its sudden emergence only after a dispute as to the scope of the arbitration agreement. . . . Under all these circumstances, we agree with the district court's conclusion that "because the facts suggest that Dreyfus, a large company, was substantially in an equal bargaining position with Hellenic, it ill behooves Dreyfus to argue that it was the victim of serious economic duress in the classic legal sense."

Mistake

Nature of Mistake.   Mistake, as the word is used in the law of contracts, has a narrow meaning. It applies only to those situations where the contracting party or parties believe that a present or past fact which is material to their transaction exists when it does not, or believe that it does not exist when it does. Mistake must not be confused with ignorance, inability, or poor judgment. If a person offers his goods for sale at a price determined by him and after he has sold the goods learns that they were more valuable than he knew, the courts will not set the sale aside on the ground of mistake. This is not mistake; it is ignorance of the value of the goods.

Likewise, if a person makes a contractual promise to perform a service or bring about a designated result but finds that he is mistaken as to his capacity and that he is unable to perform the service or accomplish the promised result, the court will not relieve him from his obligation on the ground of mistake. This is not mistake but only inability.

When a person has entered into a transaction which is less beneficial than expected or which proves detrimental, the courts will not relieve the party from his obligations on the ground of mistake. This may be a mistake of judgment, but the courts do not relieve from mistakes of judgment.

The courts will not grant relief merely on the ground that one or both of the parties deem the contract a bad deal or, in other words, made a mistake when they entered into the agreement; nor is the court very apt to grant relief when the mistake is due to the negligence of the party. Owing to the great variety of factual situations arising, together with the diversity of the court decisions, it is difficult, if not impossible, to state concise rules whereby a person can determine the situations in which the court will grant relief from contractual promises on the ground of mistake.

Two closely related yet distinguishable situations have been recognized as justifying relief on the ground of mistake. One is a mistake resulting from ambiguity in the negotiation of the transaction. The other is a mistake as to a material fact which induced the making of the contractual promise.

Mistake Resulting from Ambiguity. In negotiating a contract, it may happen that the parties will use language which is susceptible equally to two interpretations. In such a situation, if one party honestly places one interpretation on the language and the other party, with equal honesty, places the other interpretation on it, the courts will generally hold that the parties did not, in fact, reach a mutual agreement, and as a result there was no contract. The classical example of this situation is the *Peerless* case. The parties in this case entered into an agreement for the purchase and sale of a cargo of cotton to be shipped from Bombay, India, to England on the ship *Peerless*. There were two ships *Peerless* sailing from Bombay to England; one sailed in October, the other in December. One party knew of the ship sailing in October and expected the cotton to be shipped then, whereas the other party knew of the ship sailing in December and expected the cotton to be shipped at that time. Neither party was aware of the fact that there were two ships *Peerless* sailing from Bombay to England. The court held that due to the misunderstanding, no contract resulted.

Mistaken as to Material Fact.   A mistake as to a material fact is fundamentally a matter of the mind. A person may believe that a fact exists which does not, or he may believe that a fact does not exist when it does. To justify the courts in granting relief, the fact must be material, and, as in fraud cases, it must be as to a present or past fact. A mistake as to the happening of future events is never ground for relief from the obligations of a contractual promise.

In deciding cases involving mistake of fact, the courts give great weight to the fact situation in each case. Although some general rules have been formulated and some attempt has been made to classify the cases, it is apparent that the justice of the individual case has played a more important role in deciding each case than has a formal rule.

Mutual Mistake.   Mutual mistake of material fact is ground for granting relief both in law and in equity. To come within this rule, both of the parties must have contracted in the mistaken belief that certain material facts existed. The mistake must be as to existing or past facts. A court might grant relief if the mistake was as to future happenings; but as a general rule, it is presumed that the contracting parties assume the risks of future events.

For example, suppose Austin agrees to sell his horse to Baker, and Baker agrees to buy the horse and pay Austin $300 for it. At the time the contract is entered into, the horse is dead. When the contract was entered into, both Austin and Baker believed that the horse was alive. The contract will not be enforced. A mistake as to the quality of the goods sold is not, as a general rule, ground for granting relief. In the foregoing example, if, at the time the contract was entered into, both Austin and Baker believed that the horse would develop into a first-class race horse but it did not, the mistake would not be ground for granting relief. In any situation, one of the parties may assume the risks of the existence of certain facts and take the risk of their nonexistence. If one of the parties assumes such risk, no relief will be granted in the event the facts do not exist.

Unilateral Mistake.   Whether or not the court will grant relief when only one of the contracting parties is in error as to the existence or nonexistence of a material fact depends on the surrounding circumstances. If one of the parties knows or should know that the other party is mistaken in his belief that certain facts exist and enters into the contract for the apparent purpose of taking advantage of the situation, the courts will grant relief. As a general rule, if the mistake is the result of the negligence of the party in error, the courts will not grant relief. However, even though the mistake is the result of slight negligence, if relief can be granted to the party in error without imposing material loss on the other party, the courts will grant relief, especially if the enforcement of the contract would impose unwarranted hardship on the party in error. In all mistake cases the courts attempt to render a decision which is fair and equitable to all parties involved. As in fraud cases, if a party wishes to be relieved of the burden of a mistake, he must act as soon as he discovers the mistake. An unreasonable delay in asking relief will amount to a waiver of the right to rescind the contract.

Mistakes in Drafting Writing. Courts of equity will grant relief in those cases in which a mistake has been made in drafting a written contract, deed, or other document. Suppose Arnold bargains to sell Barber a vacant lot which adjoins Arnold's home. The vacant lot is "Lot 3, block 1"; Arnold's house is on "Lot 2, block 1." In drawing the contract the stenographer strikes the wrong key, and the contract reads "Lot 2, block 1." Neither Arnold nor Barber notices this error when they read and sign the contract. A court of equity will reform the contract. Usually, no relief will be granted if one of the parties is mistaken as to the meaning of the language used in a contract; however, if the language is ambiguous, or both parties are mistaken as to the meaning and it does not express the intentions of the parties, no contract is formed.

Mistakes of Law. Mistake as to one's legal rights under a contract is not generally accepted as sufficient justification for granting relief. If the mistake of law is coupled with mistake of fact, relief may be granted. Some courts have attempted to distinguish between mistake of law—error of judgment as to legal rights—and ignorance of law—lack of knowledge of the existence of the law. Such a distinction is difficult to apply and has no secure foundation, because one's error in judgment as to his legal rights usually is the result of some degree of ignorance of the law.

Summary

Under some circumstances the courts will relieve a party of a contractual obligation on the ground of mistake. Mistake as to the subject matter of a contract is generally accepted as ground for holding that no contract came into existence, since the parties, as the result of the mistake, never reached an agreement. Mistake of fact is fundamentally a matter of mind. Relief will be granted only if the facts and circumstances make the enforcement of the contract unjust and if the parties can be restored to their original positions without injury to innocent third persons.

As a general rule the courts will grant either the remedy of rescission or the remedy of reformation of a contract entered into under a mutual mistake of a material fact. If the mistake is unilateral, that is, only one of the parties is negotiating under a mistaken conception of fact, the courts will grant no relief. However, the courts grant relief if the circumstances are such that justice and fair dealing demand it.

If one party is mistaken as to the existence or nonexistence of a material fact and the other party knows or should know of the mistake, he will not be permitted to take advantage of it. If the mistaken party has proceeded with reasonable care and the mistake is the result of a clerical error and not an error in judgment, relief will be granted if necessary to avoid grave injustice.

Mistakes made in drafting a writing will be corrected through the remedy of reformation. Before a writing will be reformed to correct a claimed mistake, there must be clear and convincing evidence that it was a mistake in drafting the instrument and not merely a lack of understanding of the language used. The statement frequently made that the courts will not relieve from mistakes of law is the generally accepted rule. However, the rule is subject to some exceptions, and relief may be granted if necessary to avoid serious injustice.

Anderson Brothers Corp. v. O'Meara
306 F.2d 672 (5th Cir. 1962)

This was an action to rescind a contract and to recover damages for mutual mistake brought by O'Meara (plaintiff) against Anderson Brothers Corporation (defendant). Judgment for O'Meara and Anderson Brothers appealed. Reversed.

Anderson Brothers Corporation was engaged in the business of building special dredges and constructing pipelines. Anderson built a specially designed dredge to perform the submarine trenching necessary for burying a pipeline under water. In particular it was designed to cut a relatively narrow trench in areas where submerged rocks, stumps and logs might be encountered. The design was copied from a dredge which Anderson had leased and successfully used in laying a pipeline across the Mississippi River.

After it was completed, the dredge was advertised for sale in a magazine. This advertisement came to O'Meara's attention in early December, 1955. O'Meara wanted to acquire a dredge capable of digging canals fifty to seventy-five or eighty feet wide and six to twelve feet deep to provide access to off-shore oil well sites in southern Louisiana.

On December 8, 1955, O'Meara contacted the Anderson's Houston, Texas, office by telephone and learned that the price of the dredge was $35,000. Terms of sale were discussed, and later that day Anderson sent a telegram to O'Meara who was then in Chicago, saying it accepted O'Meara's offer of $35,000 for the dredge to be delivered in Houston. The offer was made subject to an inspection. The next day Kennedy, one of O'Meara's employees, went to Houston from New Orleans and inspected the dredge. Kennedy, it appears, knew nothing about dredges but was familiar with engines. After inspecting the engines of the dredge, Kennedy reported his findings to O'Meara by telephone and then signed an agreement with Anderson on behalf of O'Meara. The agreement made provision for a down payment of $17,500 and for payment of the remaining $17,500 over a period of seventeen months. The dredge was delivered to O'Meara at Houston on December 11, 1955, and from there transported to southern Louisiana.

It soon became clear to O'Meara that he had bought a dredge which, because of its design, was incapable, without modification, of performing the sweep dredging operation he wanted done.

On July 10, 1956, about seven months after the sale and after O'Meara had made seven monthly payments pursuant to the agreement between the parties, O'Meara wrote Anderson stating he could not use the dredge without modification and suggesting that the differences between the parties could be settled amicably by Anderson contributing $10,000 toward the estimated $12,000 to $15,000 cost of converting the trenching dredge into a sweep dredge. Anderson rejected this offer and on July 23, 1956, O'Meara's counsel wrote Anderson tendering return of the dredge and demanding full restitution of the purchase price.

JONES, CIRCUIT JUDGE. The judgment for damages rests entirely upon the conclusion of mutual mistake. The dictrict court's conclusion that the parties were mutually mistaken "with respect to the capabilities of the subject dredge" is not supported by its findings. "A mutual mistake is one common to both parties to the contract, each laboring under the same misconception." O'Meara's mistake in believing that the dredge was capable, without modification, of performing sweep dredging was not a mistake shared by Anderson who had designed and built the dredge for use in trenching operations and knew its capabilities. The mistake on the part of Anderson's employee in assuming that O'Meara intended to use the dredge within its designed capabilities was certainly not one shared by O'Meara, who acquired the dredge for use in sweep dredging operations. O'Meara alone was mistaken in assuming that the dredge was adapted, without modification to the use he had in mind.

O'Meara insists that even if the findings do not support a conclusion of mutual mistake, he is entitled to relief under the well-established doctrine that knowledge by one party to a contract that the other is laboring under a mistake concerning the subject matter of the contract renders it voidable by the mistaken party. As a predicate to this contention, O'Meara urges that the trial court erred in finding that "none of Anderson's offices or employees knew that O'Meara intended to use the dredge for shallow sweep dredging operations."

. . . .

There is a conflict in the evidence on the question of Anderson's knowledge of O'Meara's intended use, and it cannot be held that the district court's finding is clearly erroneous.

. . . .

O'Meara makes a further contention that when he purchased the dredge he was laboring under a mistake so grave that allowing the sale to stand would be unconscionable. The ground urged is one which has apparently been recognized in some circumstances. However, the Texas courts have held that when unilateral mistake is asserted as a ground for relief, the care which the mistaken complainant exercised or failed to exercise in connection with the transaction sought to be avoided is a factor for consideration. It has been stated that "though a court of equity will relieve against mistake, it will not assist a man whose condition attributable to the want of due diligence which may be fairly expected from a reasonable person."

. . . .

O'Meara saw fit to purchase the dredge subject to inspection, yet he sent an employee to inspect it whom he knew had no experience with or knowledge of dredging equipment. It was found that someone familiar with such equipment could have seen that the dredge was then incapable of performing channel type dredging. Although, according to his own testimony, O'Meara was conscious of his own lack of knowledge concerning dredges, he took no steps, prior to purchase, to learn if the dredge which he saw pictured and described in some detail in the advertisement, was suited to his purpose. Admittedly he did not even inquire as to the use Anderson had made or intended to make of the dredge, and the district court found that he did not disclose to Anderson the use he intended to make of the dredge. The finding is supported by evidence. O'Meara did not attempt to obtain any sort of warranty as to the dredge's capabilities. The only conclusion possible is that O'Meara exercised no diligence, prior to the purchase, in determining the uses to which the dredge might be put. Had he sent a qualified person, such as the naval architect whom he later employed, to inspect the dredge he would have learned that it was not what he wanted, or had even made inquiry, he would have been informed as to the truth or have had a cause of action for misrepresentation if he had been given misinformation and relied upon it. O'Meara chose to act on assumption rather than upon inquiry or information obtained by investigation, and, having learned his assumption was wrong, he asks to be released from the resulting consequences on the ground that, because of his mistaken assumption, it would be unconscionable to allow the sale to stand.

Ryan v. *Vickers*
406 P.2d 794 (Sup. Ct. Colo. 1965)

Action for breach of a contract to pay rent and royalties brought by Ryan assignee of E. M. Johnson and Metallurgical Coals (plaintiff) against Jack Vickers and others (defendants). Judgment for the defendants appealed. Affirmed.

E. M. Johnson and Metallurgical Coals were the owners of certain land which was under lease to the J. F. Coal Corp., another West Virginia corporation. This land was leased to J. F. Coal for the purpose of mining coal therefrom, and under the terms of the several leases J. F. Coal was obliged to pay E. M. Johnson and Metallurgical Coals certain rents plus additional royalties on coal actually mined. Jack Vickers and other members of his family, as well as certain of his business associates, were stockholders in J. F. Coal. In the several months before September 9, 1959, J. F. Coal became hopelessly in debt to the tune of about one million dollars, as of that date owing, among others, E. J. Johnson and Metallurgical Coals about $75,000 in unpaid rent and royalties, and also owing the Small Business Administration some $250,000. On September 9, 1959, Jack Vickers and his lawyer, held a meeting with E. M. Johnson and representatives of Metallurgical

Coals, and Vickers said that he intended to form a new coal mining company and, in connection therewith, desired that E. M. Johnson and Metallurgical Coals lease to this new company, when formed, the same properties which were then under lease to the bankrupt J. F. Coal, such new leases to be on the same terms and conditions as the old ones. E. M. Johnson and Metallurgical Coals verbally agreed to lease these properties to the coal mining company which Jack Vickers was about to form, and as a part and parcel of the foregoing verbal agreement, Vickers also verbally agreed to make E. M. Johnson and Metallurgical Coals "whole" as to the amount of the indebtedness of J. F. Coal to them for the unpaid rent and royalties, this promise to cover not only existing indebtedness but such further and additional indebtedness as might accrue until such time as the existing leases to J. F. Coal could be cancelled and new leases given the company which Vickers proposed to form. At this same meeting E. M. Johnson and Metallurgical Coals and their lawyer had informed Vickers and his lawyer that as landlords they not only held a landlord's lien on the mining machinery and equipment of J. F. Coal, which machinery and equipment was estimated to have a value of $500,000, but also that their lien under local law took precedence over all other liens or claims, including that of the Small Business Administration.

It was on the basis of an alleged verbal contract entered into by the parties on September 9, 1959, Ryan, as assignee, made claim against Vickers for damage flowing from Vickers for breach contending that her assignors had performed all of their obligations under the verbal contract, but that Vickers had failed to pay them for the unpaid rent and royalties due them from J. F. Coal.

Upon trial it developed that the landlord's lien of E. M. Johnson and Metallurgical Coals was *not* prior to the lien of the Small Business Administration, and on the contrary that the lien of the Small Business Administration had priority over their lien.

The trial court's motion dismissed her claim, holding that all parties to the agreement were of the "mistaken belief that the plaintiffs held a first lien on the property of J. F. Coal Corp.," all of which was held to be a mutual mistake of "both law and fact" which excused Vickers from performing his promises as called for by their agreement.

McWILLIAMS, JUSTICE. We reject Ryan's contention that the foregoing represented a "change in the law"—as opposed to a mistake—and that being only a change in the law the general rule that a contract will not be set aside where a subsequent decision by a court of last resort overrules a prior decision of the same court must prevail. We do not so view the matter. At least our attention has not been directed to any judicial declaration antedating September 9, 1959—the date of the alleged verbal contract between the parties—which held that a West Virginia landlord's lien had priority over a lien of the Small Business Administration.

And as already noted, when Ryan's assignors later sought to foreclose their landlord's lien it was held that their lien was inferior to that of the Small Business Administration.

Hence, rather than any "change" in the law, we view this as a mutual mistake of law; or perhaps more accurately a mutual mistake as to the applicability of existing law to the factual situation here at hand, and that the mistake is of such nature as to constitute an exception to the general rule that a mistake of law will not vitiate a contract.

In 17 *C.J.S. Contracts* § 145, p. 900 such exception is discussed as follows:

"To the general rule . . . that mistake of law is no ground for relief there are certain exceptions or apparent exceptions. . . . Mistake as to particular private rights may be treated as a mistake of fact, or as a mixed mistake of law and fact. Private rights of property, although they are the result of rules of law, or depend on rules of law applied to the construction of legal instruments, are usually considered matters of fact. . . ."

The State of West Virginia would appear to be in accord with the foregoing principle that a mistake of law as to the nature or extent of one's private legal rights, interest or estates is deemed such a mistake of law and fact as to render unenforceable any agreement entered into with reliance thereon.

That the "mistake" in the instant case is of such a nature is believed to be at once obvious. All parties mistakenly believed that Johnson and Metallurgical Coals had a first and prior lien against the mining machinery and equipment of J. F. Coal. Such is clearly a mistake as to the nature and extent of the rights and interests of Johnson and Metallurgical Coals in and to the machinery and equipment and J. F. Coal. Accordingly, under the foregoing authority, we hold that the mistake is of such nature as to avoid the agreement there sought to be enforced.

Kenneth E. Curran, Inc. v. *State*
215 A.2d 702 (Sup. Ct. N.H. 1965)

Suit to set aside a contract on the ground that Kenneth E. Curran, Inc. (plaintiff) had made a mistake in computing a bid on a construction project for the State of New Hampshire. The trial court had the case transferred without a ruling to the State Supreme Court. Held Curran was entitled to rescission.

Curran submitted a bid of $102,171.98 on a project to add an addition to a campus building at Plymouth State Teachers College. The bid had been computed on a hand operated, ten key adding machine by an experienced employee. When the bids were opened on July 23, 1964, Curran's bid was over $55,000 under the next lowest bid. Realizing the possibility that a mistake had been made, Curran totalled the bids again that evening and discovered that the adding machine used would not add over $99,999.99 and thus omitted $100,000.00 in the cost estimates. On July 24, Curran notified the State of error and asked that his bid be cancelled. Curran was then informed that he would be held to his bid.

WHEELER, JUSTICE.   While there are a number of respectable authorities to the contrary the better view we think has been expressed in the following language: "Equitable relief by way of rescission will be granted by most courts, in the case of unilateral mistakes, when the following conditions are present: (1) The mistake is of such consequence that enforcement would be unconscionable. (2) The mistake must relate to the substance of the consideration, that is a material feature. (3) The mistake must have occurred regardless of the exercise of ordinary care. (4) It must be possible to place the other party in status quo."

Following this general rule it has been held that it is only when negligence of a contractor resulting in a mistake in submitting his bid amounts to such carelessness or lack of good faith in calculation as to violate a positive duty in making up a bid, taking into consideration the nature of the transaction and position of the offeree, that equitable relief will be denied.

. . . . .

Contractors do not work under ideal conditions in the rush to meet the deadline for submitting bids and equity recognizes that honest, sincere men, even in the exercise of ordinary care, under such pressure can make mistakes of such a fundamental character that enforcement of the apparently resulting agreement would be unconscionable. In such a situation, if the parties may still be placed in status quo, equitable relief will be granted.

Prior to advertising for bids the Department had estimated for its own purpose the expected cost of the project in the amount of $158,000. This figure was not published and was unknown to Curran's estimators at the time they compiled their bid figures. The disparity of over $50,000 between Curran's bid, the Department's own estimates, and that of the next lowest bidder was sufficient to charge it with notice of probable error.

. . . . .

We hold the agreed facts warrant a finding that Curran acted honestly, and in good faith in submitting his bid that this bid contained a material mistake of such grave consequence that its enforcement would be unconscionable, especially in view of the State's prior estimate of a cost of $158,000 for this project as compared to Curran's bid of $102,171.98; that this mistake having promptly been brought to the attention of the State it could without undue prejudice, accept the second low bid of $159,957.

We further hold that Curran on the agreed facts is entitled to a decree ordering the rescission of its bid, the cancellation of its bid bond or restitution of its penal sum of $4,000 if already collected by the State, and that the case be remanded for appropriate orders in accordance with this opinion.

Problem Cases

1. The Hassenstabs owned a motion-picture theater which they listed for sale with Zeeb, a real estate broker. Zeeb placed the following advertisement in a newspaper:

"If you are interested in a good theater that shows $20,000 per year net income and can be purchased on E.Z. terms, call for an appointment." Brown answered the advertisement and was told by Hassenstab that the theater produced a net income of $20,000. Brown signed an offer to purchase. The earnest money receipt provided: "Purchasers to look at books and approve them by August 23, 1952."

On the evening August 22, 1952, the Browns went to the theater to examine the books. Mrs. Hassenstab, who did the bookkeeping, had prepared a typewritten statement of receipts and expenses from her day book, payroll book and rental records. The books were displayed at the time, but it was the typewritten statement prepared by Mrs. Hassenstab that received attention. The books, lacking as they were in totals and other entries, were of little help to one who sought information. The statement showed that the net profits from the business would be about $22,000 per year.

The contract of purchase was signed in September. In December, the Browns began to suspect that the net profit from the business was substantially less than $20,000, and in March, they asked for and received the theater books for the years 1951 and 1952. From the books they learned that the net income from the business was $5,522.76 in 1951 and $229 in 1952. In May, the Browns tendered the keys to the theater to the Hassenstabs, gave notice of rescission of the contract and brought suit to recover what they had paid. Can the Browns recover their payments?

2. Askew was a mechanic who had never been engaged in business and was totally unfamiliar with vending machines and the law pertaining to the use of such machines. Smith had been engaged in the vending machine business for 16 years and represented to Askew that he (Smith) was an expert on vending machines and was familiar with all laws pertaining to the operation of such machines, particularly in the state of Virginia. Smith induced Askew to purchase 500 one-cent vending machines for the vending of gum and trinkets and to pay $12,500 for them. Askew was to have as his territory designated cities in the state of Virginia. Both Askew and Smith were residents of Texas at the time the contract was executed.

Smith represented to Askew that the machines could be legally operated in Virginia. Askew learned later that the operation of such machines was illegal under the laws of the United States, the state of Virginia and the cities in which he was to operate the machines. When Askew learned of the illegality of the operation of the machines in Virginia, he sold the machines for $1,000, their fair value, and brought suit to recover $11,500 damages. Smith defended on the ground: "That the representations as to the legality of vending machines within the State of Virginia made by a layman cannot be made the basis for a cause of action." Is Smith right?

3. Wolf and Marlton entered into a contract by the terms of which Marlton agreed to build a house for Wolf in an area which Marlton was developing. Wolf made a payment of $2,450 at the time of the signing of the contract. A clause in the contract provided for the forfeiture of the $2,450 payment in the event Wolf did not complete performance of the contract. Wolf later on notified Marlton that he cancelled the contract and demanded the return of the payment he had made. Marlton refused to return the money whereupon Wolf said that he would complete the performance of the contract but as soon as the house was completed, he would sell it to some undesirable person and ruin Marlton's building business. Was this threat duress?

4. Tucker Corporation was organized in July, 1946, under the laws of the state of Delaware for the purpose of manufacturing motor vehicles. In 1947, Bates (and other dealers) entered into a written agreement whereby Tucker . . . agrees to sell and Dealer [Bates] hereby agrees to purchase a Tucker Dealer Franchise which will entitle Dealer to sell at retail Tucker motor vehicles manufactured by the Company in the following described territory. . . ." Bates agreed to pay $4,000 for the franchise. He paid $2,000 down and executed a promissory note payable to Tucker for the balance. Subsequently, Bates paid $1,500 on account of the note indebtedness.

On November 22, 1948, an involuntary petition in bankruptcy was filed against Tucker Corporation. At the time of filing the bankruptcy and reorganization proceedings, Tucker Corporation had not proceeded sufficiently with the manufacture of automobiles so as to enable it to deliver Tucker automobiles to any Tucker dealers including Bates.

The trustee in bankruptcy brought suit against Bates to recover the $500 balance due on the note. Bates set up fraud as his defense. Is this defense good?

5. Gallagher and Lederer executed a written contract whereby Gallagher obligated himself to convey to Lederer an easement of right-of-way over lots owned by Gallagher to buildings which Lederer was erecting. Gallagher refused to execute the conveyance of the right-of-way, and Lederer told him that if he did not execute the conveyance she (Lederer) would sue him for damages for breach of the contract. Gallagher executed the conveyance. Later Gallagher brought this action to have the conveyance cancelled on the ground of duress and to have Lederer enjoined from using the right-of-way. Gallagher claims that he was not liable for damages for breach of the contract due to the fact that at the time Lederer threatened suit Gallagher's wife was seriously ill and he feared if such a suit were filed against him it would endanger her life, and he was thereby induced involuntarily to execute the conveyance of the right-of-way. Will Lederer be enjoined?

6. Creech bought certain real proper from Warr for $43 an acre. In negotiating the purchase, Creech told Warr that he intended to use the land for a tree farm and that he was paying from $25 to $60 per acre for the land whereas he was in fact purchasing the land as agent for Power & Light Co., which planned to use the land as a lake site. When Warr learned that Creech had paid as much as $200 an acre for some land, that Creech was acting for Power & Light Co., and that the land was to be used as a lake site, Warr sued Power & Light Co. in tort to recover for the claimed deceit. Is Warr entitled to a judgment?

7. Anna Voboril's husband owed International Harvester Company for machinery purchased. The account was past due, and an agent of the company told Anna that if she did not give her notes, payable to the company for the amount of her husband's debt, the company would have her husband arrested and put in jail. Anna was uneducated, a foreigner, and knew nothing about court procedure. She did not know that her husband could not be imprisoned for debt. Anna executed the notes and, on the due date, refused to pay them. When sued on the notes, she set up duress as a defense. Is the defense good?

8. Welsh was engaged in the business of selling automobile tires and accessories at retail. In 1931, he entered into a written contract with Kelly-Springfield Tire Company whereby Welsh agreed to purchase all his tires, tubes, and other automobile accessories from Tire Company. This contract contained a provision permitting Welsh, in the event of the termination of the contract, to return for credit at invoice price all goods purchased from Tire Company. Similar contracts were executed by the parties in subsequent years.

On January 2, 1934, Welsh executed a contract with Tire Company, but the contract did not include the clause providing for the return of goods in the event of termination. The contract was terminated, and Tire Company refused to accept returned goods. Tire Company brought suit to recover an unpaid balance for goods sold to Welsh. Welsh claimed credit for goods on hand, but Tire Company refused to accept them. No specific representations were made. Welsh did not read the contract, and Tire Company did not point out to him the change in the contract. Is Welsh entitled to credit for goods on hand?

9. Geremia requested Boyarsky to make a bid for the carpenter work and painting on a house which Geremia was building. Boyarsky called in the evening for the purpose of figuring his estimate but did not finish the work that evening. He had placed items on two separate pieces of paper and had not added the figures.

The next morning Geremia called on Boyarsky, who was on a job, and asked him to stop work and complete the estimate. Boyarsky sat down with Geremia at a workbench and proceed to add the items of the two sheets. In his haste Boyarsky totaled the items on one sheet at $99.10 when the correct total was $859.10. As a result of this error, a bid of $1,450.40 was submitted when a bid of $2,210.40 should have been submitted. Geremia accepted the bid. Later the same day, Boyarsky discovered the error and notified Geremia of it. Is Boyarsky bound by his bid?

10. Mendoza, a man of limited education, made a payment of $500 earnest money and signed a contract with Stapleton, a realtor, for the purchase of a house. The house was advertised as: ". . . $4,700 FHA and GI loan. $38 monthly payments takes care of all. Only $8,500." Mendoza signed the contract without reading it under the belief that the total price of the house was $8,500 at $38 per month when in fact the $8,500 represented the amount due over and above the outstanding mortgage of $4,000 which was to be paid at the rate of $38 per month. Thus, according to the contract, Mendoza owed Stapleton $13,200. Mendoza sued and asked for the return of the $500. Stapleton argues that Mendoza should have read the contract. Is this a good defense?

chapter 9. Consideration

History and Function of Consideration

Historical Development. During the early period of the development of the law of contracts in England, only those promises which were in writing and sealed were enforced. As trade expanded and the law merchant began to be absorbed into the common law of England, the courts were frequently called upon to determine the rights of the parties to a simple contract, and the law of covenants (promises under seal) was inadequate. The action available for the breach of duty under a simple contract was an action in tort for deceit in which case the injured promisee would allege that the promisor had made a promise which he did not fulfill and that the promisee had justifiably relied on the promise and had been thereby deceived by the promisor. This was an unsatisfactory solution to the problem.

At the beginning of the 18th century several tests for the determination of the enforceability of simple promises were tried. Out of this trial and error approach came one basic test which has proven to be satisfactory in most situations. It was borrowed from the law merchant and was termed the bargain theory of consideration. Today the general rule is, with some exceptions, that a promise is not enforceable by court action unless it is supported by consideration; and the general test for consideration applied by the courts is whether or not detriment to the promisee or benefit to the promisor has been bargained for and given in exchange for the promise.

Under some special circumstances, however, promises are enforced which are not supported by consideration as it is defined above. Two exceptions which are generally recognized are: (1) a situation in which the promisee has justifiably relied on the promise to his injury, termed injurious reliance or promissory estoppel, and (2) a situation in which the right to enforce the promise by court action is barred by operation of law and the obligor makes a promise which removes the bar to the enforcement of the obligation. Under the Code (2–209)[1] no consideration is required for an agreement to modify a contract involving the sale of goods.

Summary

During the early period of the development of contract law in England, only promises which were in writing and sealed were enforced. The only action available at this time for the breach of a promise not under seal was a suit in tort for damages for deceit. When the courts began to enforce informal promises, they were confronted with the task of devising some rule whereby they could distinguish between enforceable and unenforceable promises. About the middle of the 18th century the courts adopted the bargain theory of consideration as the primary test. Under some circumstances, however, promises not supported by consideration were enforced. Under the Code, provision is made for the enforcement of defined promises even though they are not supported by consideration.

Detriment or Benefit

Analysis of Test.   The test mentioned heretofore, "detriment to the promisee or benefit to the promisor," is an important guide in determining the presence or absence of consideration. But this test in no way aids us in determining what the nature of the detriment or of the benefit must be in order to satisfy the requirements for consideration. Obviously, not all those things and experiences which might be classed as detriment or benefit are included.

Legal Detriment.   Legal detriment is the surrendering of a legal right or the assuming of a legal burden. In our free society each individual has the right to do or not to do many things. When a person surrenders one of these rights or obligates himself to do something which he has a legal right not to do, he has suffered a legal detriment. In the transaction of business the parties to a deal are exchanging legal rights. In the ordinary business contract each party suffers a legal detriment, and each party enjoys a legal benefit. For example, suppose a customer buys a radio from a merchant for $50. The customer suffers a legal detriment—surrenders his right to keep the $50. The merchant also suffers a legal detriment—he surrenders his right to keep the radio. Each gains a benefit—the customer gains the right to the radio, and the merchant gains the right to the $50.

An exchange, to be consideration, need not be an exchange of things which have economic value. For example, suppose Able promises his nephew Beal

---

[1] The numbers in parentheses refer to the sections of the Uniform Commercial Code, 1962.

that he (Able) will pay Beal $1,000 if Beal does not smoke during the four years he is in college, and Beal, in payment for the promise, refrains from smoking during that itme. Able's promise is supported by consideration and is enforceable by court action. Beal has given up his right to smoke in exchange for the promise of Able to pay him $1,000. This right has no economic value, but the surrendering of the right is legal detriment.

Legal Benefit. In the majority of situations, if the promisee has suffered a legal detriment, the promisor has enjoyed a corresponding legal benefit. Although consideration under the bargain theory is usually defined as a detriment to the promisee or a benefit to the promisor, there are no cases in which a promise supported wholly by benefit to the promisor has been enforced by court action. Detriment to the promisee, without a corresponding benefit to the promisor, has been held by the courts to be sufficient as consideration. A simple and reasonable test of consideration sufficient to support a promise is "detriment to the promisee, bargained for and given in exchange for a promise."

Summary

Consideration under the bargain theory may be defined as "detriment to the promisee or benefit to the promisor, bargained for and given in exchange for a promise." Detriment, as used in this definition, is the surrendering of a legal right or the assumption of a legal obligation. As a general rule, when the promisee has suffered a detriment, the promisor has enjoyed a corresponding benefit. Detriment to the promisee, standing alone, has been held to be sufficient consideration; but benefit to the promisor, standing alone, has been held not to be sufficient consideration under the bargain theory.

Lowndes Cooperative Assoc. v. Lipsey
126 So.2d 276 (1961)

This was an action by Lipsey (plaintiff) against Lowndes Cooperative Association (defendant) to recover a judgment for payments allegedly due under a retirement agreement. Judgment for Lipsey and Lowndes Cooperative Association appealed. Judgment affirmed.

Lipsey managed Lowndes Cooperative Association (Cooperative) for thirty-one years. In 1956 Lipsey suffered a stroke but he recovered and returned to work. On June 6, 1958, the board of directors of Cooperative decided that Lipsey should be relieved of his duties as manager, effective June 30, 1958, and that he should be paid certain retirement benefits for the succeeding thirty months "provided he cooperates with the board of directors and the new management."

Lipsey was somewhat reluctant to accept retirement, but, in view of the offer made by the board of directors, he finally accepted it, and did not attempt to encourage any active opposition to the board's action among his friends who were members of Cooperative. He spent about an hour to an hour and a half each morning for a period of two months aiding the new manager. Cooperative discontinued payments to Lipsey in November 1958.

ETHRIDGE, JUSTICE.   Cooperative contends: (a) The retirement promises set forth in the minutes of June 13th were mere gifts to Lipsey, and there was no consideration for them; (b) If there were, the promises would be for past services, which would be legally insufficient.

A. L. I., *Restatement of the Law of Contracts,* Sec. 75, defines consideration as follows: "(1) Consideration for a promise is (a) an act other than a promise, or (b) a forbearance, or (c) the creation, modification or destruction of a legal relation, or (d) a return promise, bargained for and given in exchange for the promise."

Within the terms of this definition, there manifestly is legal consideration to support an obligation of Cooperative to pay the retirement benefits to Lipsey, as described in the resolution of June 13. Lipsey accepted the offer of Cooperative to retire. He retired without any active opposition from himself or his friends who were members of the organization. Furthermore, he gave a return promise to cooperate with the association, and the jury was warranted in finding that he did. He spent some time each day for about two months at Cooperative, advising and assisting the new, inexperienced manager in lining up details of his new job.

Hence there were several legally sufficient considerations to support Cooperative's promise to pay the retirement benefits, and to make it a binding obligation: A promise to cooperate, the act of retiring without objection, and the acts of advising and assisting the new manager. So there were forbearance, a return promise, and acts in accord with the agreement other than the promise. A benefit to the promisor or detriment to the promise is sufficient consideration for a contract. This may consist either in some interest, right, profit or benefit accruing to the one party, or some forbearance, detriment, loss or responsibility given, suffered or undertaken by the other. Detriment, as used in testing the sufficiency of considerations, means legal detriment as distinguished from detriment in fact. Since the sufficiency of the considerations for this contract is manifest, we do not reach the question of whether the elements of benefit to the promisor and detriment to the promisee are necessary to the sufficiency of a consideration.

Pitts v. McGraw-Edison Co.
329 F.2d 412 (Cir. 1964)

This was an action by Pitts (plaintiff) to recover retirement benefits from Mc-Graw-Edison Company (defendant). The trial court ruled for McGraw-Edison Company and Pitts appealed. Affirmed.

Pitts served McGraw and its predecessor for about 25 years as a manufacturer's representative. During this time, Pitts was in no way bound to McGraw, and Mc-Graw's only obligation was to compensate Pitts by commission on sales in the assigned territory. About a year prior to his retirement, Pitts voluntarily chose to represent McGraw exclusively and for the first time refrained from selling the products of McGraw's competitors. Both orally and in letters, McGraw promised to pay Pitts a 1% overwrite commission on all sales in his former territory after he retired. McGraw made the payments for five years, and at the end of the five years gave notice that that was the final payment. Pitts protested discontinuance of the payments and brought action on the grounds that he accepted an offer to receive the 1% overwrite commission in exchange for his retirement and passing on to his successor valuable information on active and inactive accounts accumulated over the years. McGraw contends that this was not an actual retirement, because Pitts was not their employee and that they had made no offer which Pitts accepted. They further contend that even if the payments were construed as a retirement contract, it was void and unenforceable for lack of consideration.

MILLER, JR., CIRCUIT JUDGE. In considering these contentions, it must be kept in mind that Pitts was an independent businessman, not an employee of McGraw-Edison. His relationship with McGraw could be terminated by either party at any time without notice and without liability therefore. Pitts in his testimony concedes this, and it was so found as a fact by the District Judge. Unless Pitts is able to establish a valid contract obligating McGraw to pay the "retirement" benefits claimed, he has no cause of action.

Assuming without so holding, that there was a promise by McGraw to pay Pitts the retirement benefits claimed, we are faced with the question of what consideration passed from Pitts to McGraw-Edison to make this promise enforceable.

Pitts vigorously argues that although he did not promise to do anything as plainly appears from the two letters, and so conceded by him, consideration nevertheless exists because of the action taken by him at the request of McGraw, namely, his retirement as a manufacturer's representative, including other manufacturers as well as McGraw, and his turning over to McGraw his personal records pertaining to customers and sales over a period of years in the past. There would be merit in this contention if it was supported by the facts.

However, these factual contentions of Pitts were disputed by the evidence of McGraw. The District Judge made findings of fact that Pitts was not required by the terms of the letters, or by any other statements on the part of McGraw or its agents to do anything whatsoever; that upon his retirement on July 1, 1955, Pitts was free to handle the products of any other manufacturer or competitor if he so desired, to seek other employment, or to do as he pleased; that nothing in the arrangement circumscribed Pitts's actions or rights in any manner; and that Pitts was not obligated to perform any duties on behalf of McGraw. These findings are fully supported by the evidence. In fact, they were substantially conceded by Pitts in the cross-examination of him as a witness, in which he apparently contended that he did certain things for McGraw after his retirement although he was not required to do so.

On the basis of these facts, the District Judge ruled that the payments to Pitts over the period of July 1, 1955, to July 1, 1960, were without consideration, were the result of voluntary action on the part of McGraw and were mere gratuities terminable by the defendant at will.

Pitts further contends that although McGraw's promise may not be supported by legal consideration, it is nevertheless enforceable under the doctrine of promissory estoppel, which, as explained by the authorities is different from the well recognized principle of estoppel in pais, based on misrepresentation of fact.

Promissory estoppel is defined in *Restatement, Contracts,* Section 90, as follows:

"A promise which the promisor should reasonably expect to induce action or forebearance of a definite and substantial character on the part of the promisee and which does induce such action or forebearance is binding if injustice can be avoided only by enforcement of the promise."

This principle appears to be of somewhat limited application in the United States.

Although there may be other facts in the present case which prevent it from coming within the scope of that definition, we believe that an important fact is that Pitts in no way altered his position for the worse by reason of McGraw's letters of July 1 and July 30, 1955. The District Judge found as a fact that Pitts gave up nothing to which he was legally entitled and was restricted in no way in his activities thereafter. Pitts gave up nothing in accepting retirement that he would not have lost if he had refused to accept it. We do not find in the present case the injustice required in order to enforce the alleged promise.

Preexisting Obligation

Nature of Preexisting Obligation.   A preexisting obligation, as used in the law of consideration, is an obligation which the promisor already owes at the time he makes a promise to assume such obligation. When a party promises to do or does that which he is already legally obligated to do, or promises to refrain or does refrain from doing that which he has no right to do, he is suffering no detriment, and his promise or act is not sufficient consideration to support a promise.

Although the question of a preexisting obligation may arise in an infinite variety of situations, such obligations fall roughly into four general groups: (1) acts which are criminal or tortious, (2) acts which the holder of an office is under a duty to perform, (3) acts which the promisee is under a contractual duty to the promisor to perform; and (4) acts which the promisee has already obligated himself by contract to perform, but the performance of which, owing to unforeseen and unforeseeable factors, is more burdensome than either of the contracting parties contemplated.

Criminal and Tortious Acts.   Since each individual in our society is under a duty to refrain from the commission of a crime or tort, a promise to refrain or a refraining from the commission of such an act cannot be sufficient consideration to support a promise. The commission of a criminal or tortious act or the promise to commit such an act cannot, for obvious social reasons, be considered sufficient consideration to support a promise. A contract to commit a crime or tort is void.

Holder of an Office. The cases in which the question of whether or not the performance of an official duty is sufficient consideration to support a promise have involved mostly holders of public office, although there have been cases which involved corporate officers, trustees, and others who were acting in an official capacity. Since the cases involving public officers predominate, and since the rules which apply to public offices also have general application, we shall simplify our discussion by confining it to situations involving public officers.

Public Officers. A person, by accepting a public office, obligates himself to perform those official acts which are incidental to the office. The performance of an act which the holder of a public office is obligated to perform is universally held not to be legal detriment and not sufficient consideration to support a promise. This position is supported by both logic and public policy. If the officeholder does only that which he is duty bound to do, he has given nothing in payment for a promise to compensate him—he has suffered no legal detriment in exchange for the promise. If holders of public office were permitted to accept pay from individuals for performing their official duties, there would be an incentive on the part of the officeholders to delay performance until they had received additional compensation or to render services to those who paid the most for the services.

If the holder of a public office does acts which are similar to, but not a part of, his official duties, the performance of the act will be legal detriment and will be sufficient consideration to support a promise. For example, suppose First Bank offers a reward for the arrest of a bank robber, and the sheriff of the county apprehends and arrests the robber in the regular course of the performance of his duties as sheriff. The sheriff has suffered no legal detriment in making the arrest and has not given sufficient consideration to support the bank's promise to pay the reward. But suppose the sheriff, while on vacation in a state other than that in which he holds office, should apprehend and cause the arrest of a criminal for whose apprehension a reward had been offered, the sheriff, in such a case, would be entitled to the reward. Since, as a general rule, a sheriff owes no duty to perform services in any bailiwick other than that in which he holds office, the act of apprehending and causing the arrest of the criminal would be legal detriment and would be sufficient consideration to support the promise to pay the reward.

Contractual Obligations. If a person has voluntarily assumed a legal obligation, he has no right to refuse to fulfill that obligation, and if he does, he is guilty of a wrong for which the courts will grant a remedy.

If a person is under a legal duty, created by contract, to perform an act, and the person to whom the duty is owed promises to pay additional compensation for the performance of that act, such performance is not a legal detriment to the person obligated to perform, since he already owes a duty to do so. The doing of that which a person is already legally bound to do is not sufficient consideration to support a promise. If such were recognized as sufficient consideration, fraudulent practices would be encouraged, in that if one of the parties to a contract were in a position where he would suffer serious injury in case performance was not completed, the other party could take advantage of the situation and force payment of additional compensation by refusing to perform.

Exceptions.   There are exceptional circumstances, however, under which the courts have enforced such promises. Suppose, for example, the parties enter into a contract on the assumption that certain conditions exist but, after performance is started, encounter unforeseen and unforeseeable difficulties. If a new promise is made to pay additional compensation for the performance of the contract, the courts will, as a general rule, enforce the new promise. Such cases are clearly exceptions to the general rule, and the decisions can be supported on the basis of justice and fair dealing.

New Contract.   The parties to a contract may, by mutual agreement, terminate a contract and enter into a new one whereby the obligations of one party are the same as under the terminated contract but the obligations of the other are greater. In such a situation the courts require clear and convincing evidence that the old contract was terminated by mutual agreement of the parties and that the entire transaction was free from fraud, duress, or undue influence. The fact that one of the parties did not assume any new burdens under the new contract whereas the other did is strong evidence that it was not entered into a good faith but was only an attempt to avoid the application of the rule that the doing of what one is already obligated to do is not sufficient consideration to support a promise.

Summary

The doing of an act which a person is already under a legal obligation to do is not sufficient consideration to support a promise. On the grounds of logic and public policy the courts have held that the performance of an act which is a part of the official duties of the holder of a public office is not sufficient consideration to support a promise. Likewise, the performance of contractual obligations by one of the parties to a contract is not sufficient consideration to support a promise on the part of the other party to pay additional compensation. The courts have recognized exceptions to this latter statement. If unforeseen and unforeseeable conditions are encountered in the performance of a contract and the promisor promises to pay additional compensation to offset the additional burden of performance resulting from such conditions, the courts will enforce the promise if justice and fair dealing demand that it be enforced. The parties may terminate a contract by mutual agreement and thereafter enter into a new contract covering the same subject matter as that covered by the terminated contract.

Robert Chuckrow Construction Co. v. Gough
159 S.E.2d 469 (Ct. App. Ga. 1968)

This was an action by Ralph Gough (plaintiff) against Robert Chuckrow Construction Company (defendant) to collect for work done on trusses. Judgment for Gough and Construction Company appealed. Reversed.

Gough was a sub-contractor of Construction Co. on a construction job known as the Kinney Shoe Store, having agreed with Construction Co. in a written contract dated April 30, 1965, to perform carpentry work required by the drawings and specification for that building. By the express provisions of the written contract, Gough undertook to "provide all labor and materials, scaffolding, tools, equipment and all other things necessary for the prosecution and completion of the work in strict accordance with the drawings and specification and job control chart." Gough's employees had erected approximately 38 trusses on May 15, 1965, when 32 of them fell off the building. On the following Monday, Gouch was told by Construction Co. representative to remove the fallen trusses from the building, disassemble, inspect, rebuild, and re-erect them and to submit an additional bill for this work. Gough proceeded to do so. He also erected the balance of the trusses required to complete the roof truss structure and completed the carpentry work on the project. He was paid by Construction Co. all sums owed under the written contract but given nothing for the costs incurred by him in connection with the fallen trusses.

QUILLIAN, JUDGE. The pivotal question on which the decision of the present case turns is whether the evidence adduced upon the trial showed the parol contract sued upon to be an enforceable agreement. Assent of the parties to the terms of the contract and a consideration for the performance of the same are essential requisites to its validity. Where either of these elements is lacking the contract is not binding or enforceable.

Gough, under the terms of the parol agreement, assumed no obligation or duty that he was not bound to perform under the written contract he had previously entered into with the defendant. Under both the written contract and the oral agreement Gough assumed the obligation to erect and properly place the same number of trusses to support the decking for the roof of the building.

The Supreme Court held in *Johnson* v. *Hinson*, "An agreement on the part of one to do what he is already legally bound to do is not a sufficient consideration for the promise of another."

It should be noted that the cause of the trusses' falling was unexplained and there was no evidence that their collapse was due to Construction Co.'s fault or any deficiency in the specifications as to how the trusses were to be erected.

Debt, Compromise, and Composition

Liquidated Debt. The courts have consistently held that a promise to discharge a liquidated debt on payment of part of the debt at the place where the debt is payable and at or after the time the debt is due is not enforceable because of lack of consideration. This rule is the result of following to its logical conclusion the rule that the performance of an act which one is already bound to perform is not sufficient consideration to support a promise. The courts have expressed dissatisfaction with the rule on the ground that it is contrary to general business practices; yet the rule is so firmly established that the courts hesitate to overrule it.

This rule applies only if all the following requirements are satisfied:

1. The debt must be liquidated; that is, the parties must be in complete agreement as to the amount. For example, suppose you receive a bill for $50 from your doctor for services he has rendered you while you were ill. You feel that the doctor has charged too much and tell him so. After some time, you and the doctor agree on $40 as the amount of the bill. The debt, which up to the time of the agreement was unliquidated, now becomes liquidated—the amount is certain and undisputed.

2. Payment must be made at or after the due date. If the debtor pays any part of the debt before the due date in exchange for the creditor's promise to accept a lesser sum in full payment, the debtor has done something he is not legally obligated to do—pay before due date—and this is sufficient consideration to support the promise of the creditor to accept a lesser sum.[2]

3. Payment must be made at the place where the debt is payable. Payment at any other place, if made in exchange for a promise by the creditor to accept a lesser sum, is sufficient to support such promise.

4. Payment must be made in the same medium of exchange as that provided for in the contract. Payment in any other medium, if done in exchange for a promise to accept such payment in discharge of the debt, is sufficient consideration to support such promise.

For example, suppose a creditor promises to discharge a debt payable in money if the debtor delivers goods or renders services. The delivery of the goods or the rendering of the services, irrespective of their economic value, will be sufficient consideration to support the promise to discharge the debt. Likewise, a part payment plus the delivery of goods or the performing of a service is sufficient consideration. The courts have consistently held that if the

---

[2] In some states payment must have been requested by the creditor.

promisor does anything which he is not legally obligated to do, it is sufficient consideration to support a promise to discharge the debt.

In those cases in which a creditor has promised (without new consideration) to extend the due date of an obligation, the courts have held that since the debtor (promisee) has suffered no detriment, the promise is unenforceable for lack of consideration. The rule has been applied only to contracts requiring the payment of money or the delivery of fungible goods—goods of which any unit is from its nature or by mercantile usage treated as the equivalent of any other unit.

A creditor may accept a lesser sum and make a gift of the unpaid balance. If the creditor does make a bona fide gift of the balance, he cannot at a later date repudiate the gift and recover the balance. To have a bona fide gift of property, there must be a delivery. Since a debt is intangible property, no physical delivery can be made, and some of the earlier decisions held that it was impossible to make a gift of a debt. However, the courts of today hold that a certificate of gift delivered to the debtor, or to someone representing the debtor, is sufficient delivery. The giving of a receipt marked "payment in full" is not a certificate of gift.

Compromise (Accord and Satisfaction). A compromise is the settlement of a disputed claim by the mutual agreement of the parties. In legal terminology an agreement to settle a disputed claim is an "accord," and the fulfillment of the agreement is a "satisfaction." A compromise is referred to as an "accord and satisfaction."

If there is an honest dispute as to the amount of a debt or as to the existence of a debt, the debt is unliquidated. In such a case the parties have the right to submit the dispute to the courts for adjudication. But if the parties arrive at a mutual agreement of settlement without court action, each has suffered a legal detriment, since each has surrendered his right to have the claim submitted to the courts for adjudication, and the surrender of this right is legal detriment and is sufficient consideration to support the mutual promises to pay and accept the agreed sum in full satisfaction of the disputed claim. Therefore a promise to pay an agreed sum in discharge of an unliquidated debt is supported by consideration and is enforceable by court action.

If a person has two claims against another, one admitted and the other disputed, payment of the admitted claim is not sufficient consideration to support a promise to discharge the disputed claim. In such a situation the debtor, in paying the admitted claim, has done nothing which he is not already obligated to do.

Composition. A composition is an agreement between a debtor and two or more of his creditors whereby the debtor agrees to pay each creditor who is a party to the agreement a pro rata portion of his claim, and the creditors agree to accept the amount in full satisfaction of their claims. Under such an agreement the debtor has discharged liquidated claims by the payment of a lesser sum at or after the due date. Some courts have held that the consideration to support the agreement is found in the mutual promises of the several creditors to accept the lesser sum. Under this reasoning the legal detriment is found in the surrendering of a portion of a creditor's claim, and this is accepted as sufficient consideration to support the promises of the other creditors who are parties to the agreement to surrender a like portion of their claims. Other courts have treated composition agreements as exceptions to the general rule. They have admitted that they are not supported by sufficient consideration, but have enforced them because sound business practices demand that they be enforced. A composition agreement which is free from misrepresentation and fraud will be enforced by court action.

Summary

A promise to discharge a liquidated debt on the payment of a lesser sum on the due date and at the place where the debt is payable is not supported by sufficient consideration and, consequently, is not enforceable by court action. An agreement to settle a disputed claim—an unliquidated debt—is supported by sufficient consideration and therefore is enforceable by court action. A composition agreement between a debtor and two or more of his creditors, if free of misrepresentation, fraud, duress, or undue influence, is enforceable by court action.

Industrial Life Insurance Co. v. *Finley*
382 S.W.2d 100 (Sup. Ct. Tex. 1964)

This was an action by Robert D. Finley (plaintiff) against Industrial Life Insurance Co. (defendant) for commission due. Judgment for Finley and Industrial Life appealed. Reversed and remanded.

Industrial Life Insurance Company entered a contract with Robert D. Finley, Jr., under the terms of which Finley agreed to solicit life insurance for Industrial from debtors of financial institutions and dealers located in the Midland area. The contract dated July 8, 1958, provided that Finley would be compensated for his services in two respects: First, he would receive 50 percent of the net premiums on insurance written by him and, in addition, he would be paid contingent commissions computed upon the basis of a formula outlined in the contract. The relationship continued until August 1, 1960, as of which date Finley ceased to write insurance for Industrial.

On July 7, 1961, the Agency Supervisor of Industrial wrote Finley as follows:

"Enclosed is your contingent statement of December 31, 1960. You will note that your statement is now in the black in the amount of $814.52. It is my understanding that Mr. Shepard has previously advised you that this money will not be payable to you until the business has run off the books.

"I hope this will give you the information you need and wish you the best of luck down in Austin."

At this point the final and exact amount of contingent commissions which would result from application of the contract formula to the policies written by Finley could not be known until the business had "run off the books," that is, until the full experience of the policies, and the application of the contract formula to them, could be known.

On December 8, 1961, the Vice President of Industrial wrote Finley the following letter:

"Our attorneys have examined our entire contingent commission program and have advised us that the wording which is controlled in the contingent commission portion of your original agency agreement which was dated July 9, 1958 covers only contingent commissions earned in 'each 12 month period for which premiums are received under this agreement.' They have advised that, whenever the agency agreement had been cancelled, the earning of any contingent commission ceases on that date. They have advised that your contingent commission should be computed August 1, 1960, since July, 1960, was the last month in which you issued coverage for our company. However, since your agency agreement also provides that the formula be computed for each 6 month period, *we furnished to you on July 7, 1961, a statement of the contingent commission which had accrued to you as of December 31, 1960.* In the event you have misplaced your copy of this statement, I am enclosing a photostatic copy of same which reflects that, *as of that date, your contingent commission amounted to $814.52.*

"Inasmuch as this is the last date that the contingent commission will be computed, I am enclosing herewith *our check in the amount of $814.52 which is full and final settlement for the contingent commission due under our contract which you terminated by letter dated August 16, 1960. . . ."*

The check of Industrial in the sum of $814.52 transmitted to Finley by the above letter also carried on its face a notation which read: "Received as full payment of all money due as contingent commission under an Agency Agreement between Robert D. Finley, Jr. and Industrial Life Insurance Company dated July 9, 1958." Finley cashed the check. Finley later wrote claiming that a balance of $9,835.62 was due.

STEAKLEY, JUSTICE.   In the solution of the problem of accord and satisfaction before us, we are not required to construe the basic contract of the parties, and we express no opinion thereof. The various possible constructions and the positions of the parties, reviewed above, are relevant only in the establishment of the fact that there existed a *bona fide* dispute between the parties at the time of Industrial's letter to Finley, dated December 8, 1961. This is the letter which transmitted Industrial's check in the sum of $814.52 with the statement that the check was tendered in "full and final settlement for the contingent commission due under our contract which you terminated by letter dated August 16, 1960"; and with the check bearing the corresponding notation, "Received as full payment of all money due as contingent commission under Agency Agreement between Robert D. Finley, Jr. and Industrial Life Insurance Company dated July 3, 1958."

Much has been written upon the defense of accord and satisfaction. There must be a new contract, express or implied, in which the parties agree to the discharge of the existing obligation by means of the lesser payment tendered and accepted. The defense may be established by part payment of an unliquidated demand; and [s]ufficient consideration for accord may inhere in or arise out of a dispute as to liability upon a liquidated claim. This presupposes that denial of liability, in whole or in part, is not merely factitious or *mala fides*. . . ."

In *Root & Fehl* v. *Murray Tool Co.,* the check from the debtor to the creditor was marked in full payment of the account. The jury found that it was not agreed between the parties that the check was in full satisfaction but the jury also found that the creditor knew the check was marked as a payment in full. The court said:

"We think, in view of the fact that there was no evidence in the record of any express agreement between the parties that the check was to be accepted only as partial payment, the legal effect of the acceptance with the knowledge of the recital on the check that it was tendered in full payment, as a matter of law, operated to sustain plaintiff in error's plea of accord and satisfaction, entitling it to the judgment rendered by the trial court."

Similarly, in *Call of Houston, Inc.* v. *Mulvey,* the court said:

"The doctrine under which a debt may be discharged by acceptance of a check in a smaller amount required that the check be tendered on the condition that its acceptance will be in full satisfaction of the debt. This condition may be expressed or inferred from circumstances and the debtor's conduct clearly indicating that acceptance of the check is to discharge the entire debt. . . ."

Forebearance To Sue

Right to Bring Suit. Every member of our society has the legal right to bring to the courts for enforcement any claim which he may have against other members of society. If a person has a claim which he reasonably and honestly believes is valid, he has a right to bring suit to enforce the claim, and the postponing of or refraining from bringing suit is sufficient consideration to support a promise.

Valid Claims and Reasonable Claims. The courts held in some of the early decisions that if the promisee did not have a valid claim against the promisor, postponing suit or refraining from bringing suit was not sufficient consideration to support a promise. Under this rule the validity of the promisee's claim would have to be determined by court action before the court could decide whether or not a promise to forbear bringing suit was supported by consideration. The generally accepted test today is the reasonableness of the promisee's belief that his claim is valid.

Forbearance to bring suit on a wholly spurious claim is not sufficient consideration to support a promise. The promisee must honestly believe that his claim is valid, and the circumstances must be such that a reasonable man in his position would be justified in believing the claim to be valid. The fact that the claim may be doubtful does not prevent forbearance to sue from being sufficient consideration to support a promise.

Party Making Promise. The promisor need not be the party threatened with suit. For example, suppose a son owes a debt which is past due and unpaid, and the son's creditor is preparing to bring suit to enforce the claim. The father promises the creditor that if he will forbear bringing suit for one year, he (the father) will pay the claim; and the creditor, in reliance on the father's promise, does not sue the son. The creditor has suffered legal detriment which is sufficient consideration to support the father's promise to pay the son's debt.

Summary

Forbearance to bring suit on a claim which the promisee is justified in believing is a valid claim is legal detriment and is sufficient consideration to support a promise. A promise made by a third party may be supported by the promisee's forbearance to sue.

Frasier v. Carter
437 P.2d 32 (Sup. Ct. Idaho 1968)

This was an action by Lena Frasier (plaintiff) against D. L. Carter (defendant) for damages for breach of contract. Judgment for the plaintiff and the defendant appealed. Affirmed.

Lena Frasier brought this action against Carter, a practicing attorney, upon the following letter agreement:

"D. L. Carter
Lawyer
May 12, 1962"

"Dear Lena

"This is to advise and confirm our agreement—that in the event the J. W. Frasier estate case now on appeal is not terminated so that you will receive settlement equal to your share of the estate as you would have done if your waiver had been filed in the estate in proper time, that I will make up any balance to you in payments as suits my convenience and will pay interest on your loss at 6%.

Sincerely
/s/ D. L. Carter"

By his will, her husband has devised and bequeathed all of the separate and community property to Lena and the three children. The specific devises and bequests to Lena were more valuable than her interest in the community property. However, the specific devises and bequests were conditioned upon a waiver by Lena of her interest in the community property, and the will provided that if she failed to waive her community property rights then she would receive her interest in the community property and nothing more.

No such waiver was executed by Lena and under the decree, distribution was made to Lena of her half share of the community property in lieu of the specific devises and bequests provided for by the will.

TAYLOR, JUSTICE.   The principal ground urged for reversal is that the promise of Mr. Carter to pay to Mrs. Frasier any loss she sustained by reason of failure to waive her community interest in the Frasier estate, was without consideration. We think consideration was sufficiently established. The promise was in writing, which is presumptive evidence of consideration, and the burden of showing want of consideration sufficient to support the written promise was upon Carter.

Mrs. Frasier contends that Carter's promise to pay was supported by her forbearance from prosecuting an action against him for his negligence in failing to advise her properly respecting her interest in the Frasier estate. Waiver of, or forbearance to exercise, a right which is not utterly groundless is sufficient consideration to support a contract made in reliance thereon.

"Mere forbearance without any request to forbear, or circumstances from which an agreement to forbear may be implied, is not a consideration which will support a promise."

However, an agreement to forbear may be implied, and actual forbearance is some evidence of an agreement to forbear.

Bargain and Exchange

The Bargain.   Under the generally accepted definition of consideration, the required detriment to the promisee or benefit to the promisor must be bargained for and given in exchange for the promise. Whether or not a detriment or benefit has been bargained for will depend on the intent of the parties. Nothing will be held to be consideration unless the parties intend it to be such. For example, suppose you should say to a friend, "If you will come by my house on your way home tonight, I will give you the extra copy of *Inside Asia* which I have." It is clear that the "coming by my house," which your friend is under no legal obligation to do, is not intended as consideration for your promise to give him a book. In determining intent, that is, in determining whether the promise or act has been bargained for and given in exchange for the promise, the same standards are applied as would be applied in determining the intent to make or accept an offer.

Adequacy of Consideration.   The statement that the courts will not inquire into the adequacy of the consideration is frequently made. However, this statement cannot be accepted as a rule of law which will be followed under all circumstances. It is true that if the parties are dealing on an equal basis and the transaction is free from misrepresentation, fraud, duress, undue influence, or mistake, the courts will not refuse to enforce the contract solely on the ground that a burdensome duty was assumed in exchange for a relatively small consideration. This is especially true if the exchange does not involve items of a readily determinable economic value. In general, each party to a contract has the right to judge the value of the exchange according to his own standards, and the court will not substitute its judgment of values for that of the parties to the contract.

The courts will take into consideration the relative value of the things exchanged in those cases in which a promise is made to exchange a larger amount of money or fungible goods for a lesser amount of the same medium of money or the same kind and quality of fungible goods at the same time and place. For example, suppose Ade promises that in consideration of Bill's paying him $10 in Chicago on July 1, he (Ade) will pay Bill $100 at the same time and place. Ade's promise is, in fact, a promise to make Bill a gift of the difference, $90. Promises to make gifts are not enforceable by court action.

If the purported consideration is of such a nature that it can have no value, the courts will hold that no consideration has been given. Also, if the difference in the value of the exchanges is great, this fact may be taken into consideration in determining the existence of fraud, duress, or undue influence; however, inadequacy of consideration standing alone is not sufficient to justify the setting aside of a transaction on the ground of fraud, duress, or undue influence.

The courts, in equity cases, have refused to grant specific performance of contracts on the ground of the inequality of the exchange. Since the granting of an equitable remedy rests in the sound discretion of the court, if the bargain imposes an unconscionable burden on one of the parties, or if it appears that one of the parties has a definite bargaining advantage over the other party and has taken advantage of his position to "drive a hard bargain," the court, in the exercise of its discretionary powers, will refuse to grant an equitable remedy to the party who has taken the unconscionable advantage of the other party.

Nominal Consideration. Nominal consideration refers to the recitation of consideration in a written agreement when, as a matter of fact, the consideration recited is not actually bargained for and given in exchange for the promise but is written into the contract to give the appearance of consideration when there is not sufficient consideration given to support the promise.

Writings which recite one dollar or other small sums as the consideration have given rise to many conflicting decisions by the courts. For example, in a written agreement the consideration for a promise made may be recited as "one dollar in hand paid, receipt of which is hereby acknowledged." If it is reasonably certain from the relation of the parties and the surrounding circumstances that the "one dollar" was actually bargained for and given in exchange for the promise, the courts are uniform in holding that the consideration is adequate. On the other hand, if it is reasonably clear that the recitation of consideration was included in the writing to give it the appearance of validity, and the consideration was not bargained for and given in exchange for the promise, a majority of the courts hold that the promise is not supported by sufficient consideration and that it is not enforceable by court action. In an early U.S. Supreme Court case,[3] Justice Story stated that the recitation of consideration, even though the recited consideration was not paid, was sufficient in that it gave rise to an obligation to pay which was a sufficient consideration to make the agreement enforceable. A minority of the courts still follow this rule.

Summary

If the parties do not intend as consideration the legal detriment given in exchange for a promise but intend it as a gratuity, it will not be sufficient consideration to support the promise. The courts will not inquire into the adequacy of the consideration so long as a sufficient consideration is given; but if in addition to the gross inequality of the exchange there is evidence of unfair dealing, the court will refuse to enforce the promise on the ground of misrepresentation, fraud, duress, or undue influence.

The recitation of a consideration in a writing is not sufficient to support a promise if no consideration has, in fact, been bargained for and given in exchange for the promise.

Past Consideration

Nature of Past Consideration.   The term "past consideration" is applied to a situation in which the parties attempt to support a present promise on a benefit conferred at some time in the past. This involves a consideration of terms, because, as a matter of fact, past consideration is not sufficient consideration. At the time the promise is made, the promisee is under no obligation to the promisor, and he suffers no legal detriment in exchange for the promise. The parties attempt to support a present promise on a legal detriment which was suffered at some time past.

Implied Promises to Compensate.   Past consideration cases must be distinguished from those cases in which a promise is made to pay a sum certain in discharge of an existing but unliquidated obligation. Such a promise is supported by sufficient consideration. It differs from an "accord and satisfaction" only in one respect: the claim is not a disputed claim. The promise merely makes definite the unliquidated obligation.

Summary

"Past consideration" is an attempt to support a present promise on a benefit conferred in the past. Past consideraiton will not support a present promise.

---

[3] *Lawrence* v. *McCalmot,* 2 Howard 426. 452: 11 L. Ed. 326.

Past consideration cases should not be confused with those cases in which a promise is made to pay a sum certain in discharge of an existing but unliquidated obligation. Such promises are supported by sufficient consideration and are enforceable.

Consideration in Bilateral Contracts

Mutual Obligation. The parties to a bilateral contract exchange promises, each is promisor and each is promisee. The test of consideration is not merely one of determining whether there has been an exchange of promises but whether the promises exchanged have created a binding obligation the performance of which will be a detriment to the promisee or a benefit to the promisor. If the obligation created by the promise is one which the promisor is already legally bound to perform, the promise cannot be sufficient consideration to support an exchange promise.

Illusory Promise. An illusory promise is one which is so worded that the fulfillment of the promise is left to the election of the promisor. It is not sufficient consideration to support a bilateral contract. Since the promisor may or may not fulfill the promise, depending on his own desires and wishes, he has not made a binding promise.

Right to Cancel Contract. If one or both parties to a contract reserve the right to cancel it at will, the contract is not a binding contract, since, by canceling the contract, one or both of the parties may avoid the binding effect of any promises made. If the contract provides that it will remain in force for a stipulated period of time after notice of cancellation is given, the promises are mutual, since both parties are bound for at least the time that elapses from the the time of the making of the contract until the notice of cancellation becomes effective. If one of the parties is given the right to cancel the contract on the happening of a stated event, such a provision does not give the promisor the right to cancel at will, and his promise is sufficient consideration to support the promise given in exchange.

The courts have also held that infants' contracts and contracts induced by misrepresentation, fraud, duress, or undue influence are not void for lack of consideration. Even though one of the parties has the right to disaffirm the contract and thereby escape liability, he is bound until he exercises his right to disaffirm, and he will be bound if he does not exercise his right to disaffirm within a reasonable time.

Summary

If a bilateral contract is to be valid, both contracting parties must make legally binding promises. If one of the parties is not bound, the other is not bound. If the promise of one of the parties to a bilateral contract is so worded that the performance of the promise depends on that party's will, wish, or desire, the promise is not a legally binding promise and cannot be sufficient consideration to support a bilateral contract. If the right to cancel a contract at will is reserved by either or both of the parties, the contract is void for lack of consideration.

Hanson v. Central Show Printing Co.
130 N.W.2d 654 (Sup. Ct. Iowa 1964)

This was an action by Harry Hanson (plaintiff) against Central Show Printing Co. (defendant) to recover damages for breach of an employment agreement. Judgment for the Central Show Printing Co. and Hanson appealed. Affirmed.

Hanson was a skilled pressman and had been in the employ of the Central Show Printing Co. for many years prior to 1959. In the autumn of that year he had an opportunity to obtain a steady job with the Stoyles Printing Company, also of Mason City. He knew that Central's business was often slack in the winter, and contacted G. C. Venz, the president of Central to learn whether he would have steady work with it. This resulted, after some negotiations, in an arrangement expressed in a letter from Benz to Hanson as follows:

"Oct. 21, 1959
Mr. Harry Hanson,
Starting today, Oct. 21, I will guarantee you 40 hours work per week through out the entire year each year until you retire of your own choosing.
/s/ G. C. Venz, Pres."

Hanson thereupon elected to remain in the employ of the Central and did so until October 21, 1961, when he was discharged, without cause.

THOMPSON, JUSTICE.   The question before us is essentially a simple one, and has been before the courts of the various jurisdictions many times. The rule which has been generally followed is thus set forth in 35 A.L.R. 1432: ". . . in the absence of additional express or implied stipulation as to the duration of the employment or of a good consideration additional to the services contracted to be rendered, a contract for permanent employment, for life employment, for as long as the employee chooses, or for other terms purporting permanent employment, is no more than an indefinite general hiring terminable at the will of either party." This rule fits the situation before us, where the employment was to be "until you retire of your own choosing."

In *Bixby* v. *Wilson & Company,* the plaintiffs had been employed by the defendant during a strike at its Cedar Rapids plant. They were informed that their employment would be permanent. In reliance upon this promise some gave up other jobs; some gave up farm leases; and some moved to Cedar Rapids. But the trial court held that these things were insufficient consideration to support the claimed contract for permanent employment, and rendered judgment for the defendant.

Hanson contends that he gave up the opportunity to take other employment; that this was a detriment to him, and so furnished consideration for the agreement. But it has been repeatedly held that this is not sufficient in contracts for permanent employment, or, as Hanson contends here, until he should "retire of your own choosing."

There is a class of cases in which sufficient consideration to uphold a contract for permanent, or life, employment, or employment so long as the employee chooses, has been found. These are cases in which the servant has been found to have paid something for the promise of the employment, in addition to his agreement to render services. A majority of them are cases in which the employer, faced with a claim for damages, agreed to give the claimant permanent employment in consideration of the release of his claim. . . . A case involving a different but also valid consideration is *Carnig* v. *Carr*. The factual situation there was that the plaintiff had been engaged in a competing business with the defendant, and had accepted permanent employment which involved the abandonment of his own enterprise. The defendant thereby received the benefit of removal of competition.

We think the real basis for the majority rule is that there is in fact no binding contract for life employment, when the employee has not agreed to it; that is, when he is free to abandon it at any time. So in the instant case, Hanson was bound only so long as he chose to work.

Streich v. *General Motors Corp.*

126 N.E.2d 389 (App. Ct. Ill. 1955)

Streich (plaintiff) brought this action for damages for breach of contract against General Motors. Judgment for General Motors and Streich appealed. Affirmed.

G.M. placed purchase order No. 11925, an order for air magnet valves, with Streich. The order provided as follows:

"This Purchase Order is issued to cover shipments of this part, to be received by us from September 1, 1948 to August 31, 1949 as released and scheduled on our series 48 'Purchase Order release and Shipping Schedule' No. 478412 attached and all subsequent Purchase Order releases."

This order provided that the order, including the terms and conditions on the face and reverse side, constitute "the complete and final agreement between Buyer and Seller and no other agreement in any way modifying any of said terms and conditions will be binding upon Buyer unless made in writing and signed by Buyer's representative."

On the reverse side art twenty-three provisions, among which are the following:

"Deliveries are to be made both in quantities and at times specified in schedules furnished by Buyer. Buyer will have no liability for payment for material or items delivered to Buyer which are in excess of quantities specified in the delivery schedules. Buyer may from time to time change delivery schedules or direct temporary suspension of scheduled shipments.

"Buyer reserves the right to cancel all or any of the undelivered portion of this order if Seller does not make deliveries as specified in the schedules, or if Seller breaches any of the terms hereof including the warranties of Seller."

On April 19, 1949, order No. 11925 was cancelled by the defendant.

McCORMICK, PRESIDING JUDGE.   There is no question but that under the law a contract properly entered into whereby the buyer agrees to buy all its requirements of a commodity for a certain period, and the seller agrees to sell the same as ordered, is a valid and enforceable contract and is not void for uncertainty and want of mutuality.

The contract in the instant case is not such a contract. Purchase Order No. 11925 states that it is issued to cover "shipments of this part, to be received by us from September 1, 1948 to August 31, 1949 as released and scheduled on our series 48 'Purchase Order release and Shipping Schedule' No. 478412 attached and all subsequent Purchase Order releases." Construing the letter of April 1, 1948 as an integral part of the contract, the provisions therein contained are merely that it "now becomes necessary to issue our 48 series 'Open End' purchase order for our requirements from September 1, 1948, through August 31, 1949." Reading and construing the two documents together, notwithstanding the detailed provisions contained on the reverse side of the purchase order, the result is an agreement on the part of the seller to sell a certain identified valve at a certain fixed price in such quantities as the buyer may designate, when and if it issues a purchase order for the same. The word "release" as used throughout these documents is treated by both parties as equivalent to "order."

In *Corbin on Contracts,* Vol. 1, Sec. 157, the author says:

"In what purports to be a bilateral contract, one party sometimes promises to supply another, on specified terms with all the goods or services that the other may order from time to time within a stated period. A mere statement by the other party that he assents to this, or 'accepts' it, is not a promise to order any goods or to pay anything. There is no consideration of any sort for the seller's promise; and he is not bound by it. This remains true, even though the parties think that a contract has been made and expressly label their agreement a 'contract.' In cases like this, there may be no good reason for implying any kind of promise by the offeree.

Here, the buyer proffers purchase order 11925, with its twenty-five or more clauses, to the seller for acceptance. In the instrument it makes no promise to do anything. On the surface it appears to be an attempt to initiate a valid bilateral contract. The seller accepts, and as by a flash of legerdemain the positions of the buyer and the seller shift. The buyer now becomes the promisee and the seller the promisor. The promise of the seller to furnish identified items at a stated price is merely an offer and cannot become a contract until the buyer issues a release or order for a designated number of items. Until this action is taken the buyer has made no promise to do anything, and either party may withdraw. The promise is illusory, and the chimerical contract vanishes. "An agreement to sell to another such of the seller's goods, wares, and merchandise as the other might from time to time desire to purchase is lacking in mutuality because it does not bind the buyer to purchase any of the goods of the seller, as such matter if left wholly at the option or pleasure of the buyer.

In the instant case, when the seller accepted purchase order No. 11925, no contract came into being.

In this case the use of the contract is extended to cover commodities which must be manufactured before they are available for sale. According to the admitted statements in the complaint, special tools had to be manufactured in order to produce the item herein involved. The seller here, misled by the law ordinarily applicable to an enforceable bilateral contract, undoubtedly, as he alleged in his complaint, did go to considerable expense in providing tools and machines, only to find that by the accepted agreement the buyer had promised to do absolutely nothing. A statement of expectation creates no duty. Courts are not clothed with the power to make contracts for parties, nor can they, under the guise of interpretation, supply provisions actually lacking or impose obligations not actually assumed.

Professor Fuller, in a note to *Alexander Hamilton Institute* v. *Jones, . . .* discussing insurance and correspondence school contracts, says:

"One often has the impression of a kind of running battle between draftsmen and the courts, with much shifting of ground on the part of both.

Back of this development lies a problem that touches the basic philosophy of contract law. The law of contracts is founded generally on the principle that it is the business of the courts to interpret and enforce the agreements that the parties have negotiated. This theory confronts the social reality that in many cases no real negotiations take place, and the terms of the contract are in fact set by the will of one party alone. This situation may arise where one party is indifferent or ignorant, or it may result from a superiority of bargaining power on one side. In such situations, there seems to be emerging a principle of law not yet frankly acknowledged which might be phrased something as follows: where one party to a contract has the power to dictate its terms, the terms of the contract are subject to judicial review, and may be modified by the court if they are unduly harsh." Fuller, *Basic Contract Law,* p. 260.

The agreement contained in purchase order No. 11925 was artfully prepared. It contains, in print so fine as to be scarcely legible, more than twenty-three clauses, most of which are applicable to bilateral contracts. It has all the indicia of a binding and enforceable contract, but it was not a binding and enforceable contract because the promise was defective. Behind the glittering facade is a void. This agreement was made in the higher echelons of business, overshadowed by the aura of business ethics. To say the least, the agreement was deceptive.

Nevertheless, as the law is today, on the pleadings in the instant case, the trial court could do nothing but sustain the motion to dismiss the complaint.

When Consideration Unnecessary

Promise Inducing Substantial Action. Where a promisor makes a promise which he, as a reasonable person, should expect would induce the promisee, in justifiable reliance thereon, to take some action or forbearance of a definite and substantial character, which would be detrimental to him, the courts will enforce the promise although it is not supported by consideration. The enforcement of such promises is based on broad concepts of equity and fair dealing and they are enforced to avoid injustice. The concept on which the enforcement of such promises is based had its origins in the law of tort. Today the enforcement of the promise is based on the principles of estoppel, that is, since the promisor's conduct has led the promisee, in justifiable reliance on the promisor's acts, to change his position and thereby suffer an injury, the promisor will not be permitted (will be estopped) to set up lack of consideration as a defense to a suit to enforce the promise.

Charitable Subscriptions. A charitable subscription is a promise to make a gift for a charitable, educational, or eleemosynary purpose. In England, such promises are held to be unenforceable; but in the United States, such promises are enforced provided the institution to which the promise is made has incurred obligations in reliance on the promise. Until obligations are incurred in reliance on the promise, the promisor may withdraw his promise without liability. The holdings of the courts are justified on the basis of public policy.

Business Promises. The courts have enforced promises made in business transactions on the ground that the promisee justifiably relied on the promise only in extreme cases where the dictates of justice and fair dealing demanded that the promise be enforced. Business contracts and business subscription agreements are, as a general rule, bilateral in nature and are supported by sufficient consideration. The general attitude of the courts toward promises made in business transactions has been that they are not enforceable unless they are supported by sufficient consideration as tested by the bargain theory of consideration.

Debts Barred by Statute of Limitations. The states are not in accord in their holdings relative to the enforceability of an unconditional promise to pay a debt barred by the statute of limitations. In general, such a promise is enforceable although the promise is not supported by consideration. In some, but not all states a voluntary payment on the debt or a securing of the debt will be held to be an unconditional promise to pay the debt and such new promise will be enforceable by court action until the statute of limitations has run against it. For example, suppose Alcorn owes Butler $500, and the statute of limitations on the debt is five years. If, after the five years has passed, Alcorn has not paid the debt and then promises Butler that he will pay it, such promises will be enforceable for a five-year period. If, after the debt has run for three years, Alcorn pays Butler part of the debt and promises to pay the balance, such promise will be enforceable for a period of five years from the time it is made. In many states a promise to pay a debt barred by the statute of limitations must be in writing if it is to be enforceable.

Debts Discharged in Bankruptcy. If a debtor makes an unconditional promise to pay a debt or some portion thereof after he has been adjudged a bankrupt or after the debt has been discharged in bankruptcy, such a promise will be binding only as to that debt. A few states require that such a promise, if it is to be enforceable, need be in writing. A promise to pay a debt discharged in a composition agreement is not enforceable unless it is supported by a new consideration.

Promise to Perform a Conditional Duty. If the happening of a condition or event is made a condition precedent to the promisor's duty to conform and the condition is not fulfilled and thereafter a promise is made by the promisor to perform, such promise will be enforced, and no new consideration will be required. For example, if Butler and Alcorn execute a contract in which the giving of notice by Alcorn is a condition precedent to Butler's obligation under the contract and Alcorn fails to give the required notice and thereafter Butler promises to perform, his promise will be binding even though it is not supported by consideration.

Sealed Promises. At one period in the development of our law the only promises which were enforceable by court action were promises in writing and sealed. At that period, great stress was placed on formality, and it was the formality of the sealing of the written promise which gave it its standing in court. Under the established rule in force at that time, the only seal recognized by the courts was a wax wafer bearing a distinguishing impression. Important personages had a private seal which was used to authenticate written documents. The form of the seal is no longer important. The word "seal" or the letters "L.S." (*locus sigilli,* meaning the place of the seal) following the signature are sufficient. A pen scroll, a paper wafer, and an impression stamped into the paper are commonly used.

Public officials, such as notaries public, have seals which are used to authenticate certain documents, and it is customary for corporations to adopt a seal which is used for the sealing of deeds to real estate and similar conveyances. No state requires a seal to validate a contractual promise, and the efficacy of the seal is recognized in only a few states. Several states have adopted statutes which declare, in effect, that there shall be no distinction made between the enforceability of sealed and unsealed promises. Other states have adopted statutes which provide that a seal shall be prima facie evidence of consideration, that is, that a party bringing suit to enforce a sealed promise will not have to allege and prove consideration; but if the contractual promise is not supported by consideration, the party defendant may set up in his answer the lack of consideration as a defense; and if lack of consideration is proven, the court will not enforce the promise.

Summary

To avoid injustice certain promises not supported by consideration are enforced. Promises justifiably relied on by the promisee, which induce substantial action on his part, will be enforced if a refusal to enforce would result in substantial injustice. In the United States charitable subscriptions are enforced provided the beneficiary of the promise has changed his position in reliance thereon. Promises made in business transactions are rarely enforced unless supported by sufficient consideration.

Promises to pay debts barred by the statute of limitations or discharged in bankruptcy are enforced. A promise to pay a debt discharged in a composition agreement will not be enforced unless supported by a new consideration.

No state requires a seal to validate a contractual promise, and the efficacy of the seal is recognized in only a few states.

Consideration under the Uniform Commercial Code

In General. It will be recalled that a promise in writing to hold open an offer made between merchants is enforceable even though it is not supported by consideration. (2–205.) And likewise an agreement modifying a contract to sell goods needs no consideration to be binding. (2–209.)

Lunsford v. *Wilson*
149 S.E.2d 515 (Ct. App. Ga. 1966)

This was an action by W. C. Lunsford, Jr. (plaintiff) against E. C. Wilson (defendant) for the purchase price of certain "furniture and fixtures" which Lunsford sold to Wilson under a written contract. Judgment for Lunsford and Wilson appealed. Reversed and remanded.

EBERHARDT, JUDGE.   Wilson alleged that the contract sued upon had been modified orally and there was testimony as to monthly payments inconsistent with the terms of the original agreement. He denied that demand had been made for strict performance of the original agreement. Lunsford challenged this defense on the ground that there was no allegation of consideration for the modification. Assuming that the items contracted for were "goods" as defined by the Sales Article of the Uniform Commercial Code (see 2–105(1) and 2–107(2)), no consideration was necessary for the agreement of modification (Code 2–209(1)), and Wilson raised a valid defense. If upon the trial of the case it is shown that some of the items were not "goods," 2–209(1) would not be applicable as the agreement sued upon was an entire contract.

Consideration in Franchising.   A franchise system has been defined in marketing-management terms as an organization composed of distributive units established and administered by a supplier as a medium for expanding and controlling the marketing of his products. It is an integrated business system. Franchised dealers are legally independent but economically dependent units of the system.

The franchise approach offers a supplier a highly effective means of gaining rapid market expansion with minimum capital outlay. The growth rate and profitability of many franchise systems has been fantastic. Since most franchised dealers have the major investment in their outlets strong profit and loss incentives are present.

The franchise method of distribution first gained national recognition and success in the automobile industry. The standard form of franchise contract formerly used by automobile manufacturers did not require the dealer to whom the franchise was given to represent the manufacturer for any specified period of time nor did it provide that the dealer would purchase any automobiles. These franchises provided that either party could cancel on relatively short notice "with or without cause" or on causes left to the sole judgment of the franchisor. Many franchises currently used in other industries were modeled after automobile dealer franchises.

Until recent times the courts, with few exceptions, ruled that such franchises were not enforceable as contracts.[4] This strict-enforcement-of-contracts approach allows franchisers to exercise a maximum of control over their franchises with a minimum of legal risks. Franchisees failing to follow policies can be canceled or threatened with cancellation. Dealers with highly specialized investments in particular franchises can ill-afford to have their franchise cancelled.

After extensive hearings concerning the one-sided nature of automobile dealer franchises, Congress in 1956 enacted legislation imposing liability on manufacturers of automobiles if they exercise coercion against a dealer to the damage of the dealer.[5] The U.C.C. (1–203) requires the exercise of "good faith" in franchise relationships involving the sale of goods. In addition, Section 2–309 of the Code requires the giving of reasonable notice of termination of a sales contract which provides for successive performances but is indefinite

---

[4] See the classic case, *Ford Motor Company* v. *Kirkmyer Motor Co., Inc.,* 65 F.2d 1001 (1933).

[5] United States Code, Annotated, Title 15, §§ 1221–25.

as to duration. An agreement dispensing with notice will not be enforced if it is unconscionable.

The trend in contract law, particularly in franchise relationships, appears to be away from the strict and technical application of the rules of contract law relative to consideration and requirements of definiteness. Rights may be granted even though, from a technical standpoint, the contract or franchise may be indefinite or lacking in consideration.

Summary

Many franchises have been held to be unenforceable as contracts because of indefiniteness and lack of consideration. The Code tends to make more of these loose informal arrangements enforceable as contracts. Franchisers with one-sided contracts may encounter difficulties under the Code provisions dealing with good faith, unconscionability, and reasonable notice requirements.

Tele-Controls, Inc. v. Ford Industries, Inc.
388 F.2d 48 (7th Cir. 1967)

This was an action by Tele-Controls, Inc. (plaintiff) against Ford Industries, Inc. (defendant), for damages and for injunctive relief against Ford Industries' termination of Tele-Controls' dealership. This appeal is from the District Court's denial of a preliminary injunction.

In 1966, Tele-Controls and Ford Industries entered into a dealer agreement making Tele-Controls the exclusive sales agent in the Chicago area for Code-a-phones, a telephone-answering device manufactured by Ford Industries. Paragraph 13(b) of the contract provided:

Either party hereto may terminate this Agreement at any time, with or without cause, by giving to the other party a written notice of intention to terminate at least thirty (30) days prior to the effective date of termination specified in such notice. In the event of termination by Code-a-phone, Dealer shall continue to maintain the sales and service facilities previously maintained until the effective date of the termination.

On February 1, 1967, Ford Industries sent a notice of termination to Tele-Controls effective at the close of business on March 10.

CUMMINGS, CIRCUIT JUDGE.   Tele-Controls' other reliance is upon the Uniform Commercial Code. . . . Section 1–203 of the Uniform Commercial Code provides: "Every contract or duty within this Act imposes an obligation of good faith in its performance or enforcement." This is an overriding provision that applied to the contract termination provisions found in Section 2–309(2) and (3) of the Uniform Commercial Code.

It is unnecessary to decide whether the Uniform Commercial Code governs this entire dealership contract, for Oregon case law required that termination must be in good faith. Under Oregon law, if Audio had been able to establish Ford Industries' bad faith, a preliminary injunction might have been appropriate. However, no sufficient showing of bad faith has yet been made. The record does show that Ford Industries considered Audio to be an unsatisfactory dealer, inadequately capitalized, not selling enough Code-a-phone units, and not maintaining a sufficient inventory. Of course, if Ford Industries' bad faith can be established at the trial, the District Court might then properly conclude to grant injunctive relief.

Problem Cases

1. In 1955, Kalkhurst was employed by Western Company, the predecessor of the National Outdoor Advertising Company. During that year Mr. Kalkhurst received a letter from Western informing him that he was being put on retirement at $200 a month for the remainder of his life. In 1956 the payments stopped. Mr. Kalkhurst brought an action against Western (now National Outdoor) alleging breach of contract and seeking restoration of his $200 retirement payments. Western set up no consideration as a defense. Is this a good defense?

2. Jones purchased a new Mercury automobile from Mercury, Inc. The contract of purchase and sale provided that Jones would not sell or transfer the title to the automobile during the following period of 12 months without first offering the automobile to Mercury, Inc., for purchase at the price at which it was sold less a handling charge of 10 percent. Jones sold the automobile in violation of the agreement, and Mercury, Inc., sued Jones to recover damages for breach of contract. Jones set up as a defense lack of consideration. Is the defense good?

3. Schaffer and Wolbe entered into an oral agreement by which Schaffer was to sell real estate for Wolbe, a real estate broker. Instead of salary, Schaffer was to receive 50 percent of the commission on all sales in which he participated—either by listing the property, drawing up the contract or showing the property to a prospective purchaser who subsequently purchased it. Schaffer later participated in the sale of property in which Wolbe, the broker, received a commission of $12,500. Schaffer brings this action on the oral agreement for 50 percent of Wolbe's commission. Wolbe contends that the oral contract sued upon is too vague and indefinite to be enforced, that it lacks mutuality and consequently is unenforceable. Is the agreement enforceable?

4. Payne Co., as general contractor, was building an apartment building and entered into a written subcontract with Hill Co. whereby the latter agreed, for a consideration of $2,397.50, to install certain paving for Payne Co. for parking areas which Payne Co. was obligated under its general contract to install.

   After the paving work was completed as agreed it was discovered that rain water drained from this property onto a neighbor's adjoining property. Payne Co. reentered and at its own expense erected a curbing that apparently corrected this condition. Payne Co. paid $2,000 to apply on Hill's claim but refused to pay the balance on the ground that Hill had made an oral agreement subsequent to the written agreement and had breached this oral agreement to build a curb for no extra money. Can Payne Co. hold Hill on this subsequent oral promise?

5. Betty Shirk, daughter of Gertrude Shirk, had been married and to this union had been born a daughter. Betty later obtained a divorce and was awarded the care and custody of the daughter. After the divorce Betty and her daughter lived with Betty's mother in McPherson, Kansas.

Betty's mother wanted to adopt the grandchild and rear her as her own. Betty and her mother then entered into a contract by the terms of which Betty agreed to give her consent to the adoption of her daughter by her mother who agreed to leave one third of her estate to Betty. After the adoption Betty moved to Dallas, Texas, where she remarried and established a home. Betty's mother died leaving a will by which she had devised her entire estate to Betty's brother, William. Betty brought this action to recover on the contract to leave one third of the estate to her. Lack of consideration was set up as a defense. Is this a good defense?

6. Addington, a nephew of William E. Brown, became homeless when eight years old. Although under no legal obligation to do so, Brown took Addington into his own home where during the next six years he was fed, clothed, educated in the public schools, and otherwise cared for by Brown. In 1929, Brown had reached an advanced age and at Brown's suggestion Addington promised in writing to pay Brown $100 "during each year that William E. Brown shall live."

Addington paid nothing during Brown's lifetime. The administrator of Brown's estate now sues to recover the amount due under the agreement. Addington sets up that the agreement is not supported by consideration. Is this a good defense?

7. On September 1, 1937, Monroe entered into a written contract to sell a house and lot to Bixby for $4,000. A payment of $60 was made at the time the contract was signed and the balance, with interest at the rate of 6 percent per annum, was to be paid in monthly installments of $30 or more per month the first year and $35 or more each month thereafter until the contract price was paid in full.

Sometime later Bixby asked to have the monthly payments reduced, and Monroe drew up a purported agreement as follows:

Agreement

First party, Anna V. Wiley Monroe; Second party, Hazel May Bixby;

First party agrees to accept 5% interest on contract. The first party agrees to accept Thirty ($30.00) Dollars a month payment instead of Thirty-five ($35.00) Dollars a month. The first party agrees to give the second party a deed when the first party has received Twenty-five Hundred ($2,500.00) Dollars from September 1, 1939.

The second party is not to transfer the contract unless the first party agrees to the transfer.

(S) Mrs. Anna V. Wiley Monroe"

This paper was signed by Monroe but not by Bixby.

Bixby made payments until January 25, 1950, when she refused to make further payments on the ground that she had paid $2,500 and was entitled to a deed, and that she was under no obligations to pay the balance of the $4,000. Monroe claims that there is an unpaid balance of $1,178.08 due on the original contract. Is Monroe right?

8. Middleton was engaged in the manufacture, installation and servicing of refrigeration machinery; and entered the following contract with Holecroft:

John Holecroft

Dear Sir:

I propose to employ you to work for me for 15 months *at my option,* under the following conditions:

hereafter, $300 per month 8½ hours per day

6 days per week   7¢ car mileage

Any training which you and I consider necessary will be given you on your own time, I will furnish material and instruction. You will furnish and maintain your own small hand tools. Overtime or undertime to be on a straight time basis. *If I fail to offer you work as follows you are free to seek employment elsewhere; Car mileage plus the equivalent of 160 hours in any 31 consecutive days.*

If any cause prevents you from working for me, it is assumed that such cause would prevent you from working for others. You agree to assign me any rights in any inventions you might make while in my employ or for 6 months thereafter. On any repair work that you originate and collect for in full upon completion you will receive 10% commission on the total amount you collect plus salary as stated.

Sincerely yours,
H. A. Middleton

Accepted *John Holecroft.*

Holecroft worked for Middleton for 5½ hours and then quit. Middleton sued for damages and Holecroft set up lack of mutuality as his defense. Is this defense good?

9. Mrs. O'Neil contracted with a contractor for the erection of a prefabricated home costing about $30,000. Mrs. O'Neill's stove, refrigerator, washing machine and dryer would not fit into the kitchen as designed, and this necessitated the replacement of some seven kitchen cabinets. The contractor ordered these from Frederick Trading Co. (Frederick). Before the contractor completed the house he became insolvent. Frederick prepared to file a mechanic's lien against the house, and Mrs. O'Neill promised Frederick if it would not file a mechanic's lien she would pay them for the cabinets. Frederick, in reliance on Mrs. O'Neill's promise, did not file a mechanic's lien on the house. Mrs. O'Neill then refused to pay for the cabinets and Frederick brought suit. Mrs. O'Neill set up lack of consideration as a defense. Is this a good defense?

10. In 1951, Western Star Mill Company (Mill Co.) entered into an oral contract with Burns to the effect that he should have the exclusive sales agency for Mill Co.'s products in Pontotoc County, Texas. Burns claims that he was to have an exclusive agency so long as he promoted or pushed Mill Co.'s feed and paid his bills. There was no mention of how long the contract would remain in effect. Burns was not required to handle Mill Co.'s feed only, and he continued to handle Purina Feeds. Burns was free to buy whatever amount he wanted and sell at any price he chose.

Mill Co. set up, as a defense to Burns's claim, that any agreement for an exclusive sales agency was void for lack of consideration. Is this a good defense?

11. Portland Gasoline Company entered into a contract with Superior Marketing Company, Inc., whereby Superior contracted to market all the butane-propane gas mixture produced by Portland at a natural gas processing plant owned by it. Superior failed and refused to market all the butane-propane gas mix produced by Portland, and Portland brought suit to recover damages for breach of contract. Superior set up lack of consideration as a defense. Is this a good defense?

12. During the years 1950, 1951, 1952, and 1953, Manwill made payments on behalf of Oyler aggregating $5,506.20 and in 1954 he transferred to Oyler a grazing permit worth $1,800 and 18 head of cattle worth $3,000. In October, 1957, Oyler orally promised Manwill that he would repay him $5,506.20. It is admitted that at the time the advances were made Oyler did not promise to repay and Manwill did not expect to be repaid. Manwill based his suit to recover on Oyler's moral obligation to repay and his oral promise to do so. Can Manwill recover?

13. National Chemsearch Corporation of New York, Inc. (Chemsearch), employed Bogatin as a salesman. Prior to employing Bogatin, Chemsearch gave him one week's training. After the contract of employment was executed Chemsearch gave Bogatin the customer list and other sales aids. The contract included a restrictive covenant which provided that Bogatin would not give the customer list to a competitor or use it for his own benefit, would not reveal secret information, and would not solicit for a competitor in the territory assigned to him for a period of one year after termination of his employment. The employment was terminable at will by either party. Bogatin, in breach of his contract, accepted employment with a competitor of Chemsearch and gave it the customer list and certain secret information. Bogatin contends that since the contract is terminable at will by either party it is void for lack of consideration. Is this contention correct?

14. On November 13, 1952, Long Investment Co. contracted to sell and O'Donnel contracted to buy a tract of land which was outside the corporate limits of the city of Milwaukee, but in close proximity thereto. The agreed purchase price was $8,250, and O'Donnel made a down payment of $1,500. The balance of the purchase price was to be paid by O'Donnel upon the land being annexed to the city of Milwaukee and a sewer installed, "but not later than July 1, 1953."

The land was not annexed to the city of Milwaukee until 1955, and the sewer had not been extended at the time suit was brought. Neither Long Investment Co. nor O'Donnel had taken any action either to terminate or to perform the contract.

On January 13, 1956, Long Investment Co. sold the land to a third party for $15,000 without first giving O'Donnel notice. O'Donnel brought suit to recover as damages the difference between the contract price, $8,250, and the sale price, $15,000, plus the $1,500 down payment. Long Investment Co. defended on the ground that since O'Donnel had the right to cancel the contract it was not binding. Is Long correct?

chapter 10. Capacity of Parties

Introduction

Capacity. The term "capacity" as used in the law denotes the ability to perform legally valid acts, that is, the ability to incur legal liability or to acquire legal rights. In ancient times, relatively few persons had full legal capacity, but modern law aims to confer such capacity as widely as possible.

Since some persons, due to natural incapacities, are considered incapable of protecting their interests in our free competitive economy, we have developed laws the objective of which is to protect such persons and prevent the dissipation of their estates.

Parties to Contract. Parties having capacity to contract are essential to the validity of a contract, and there must be at least two persons—the promisor and the promisee—as parties to a contract. An individual cannot contract with himself. Nor can he as an individual contract with himself as an official. For instance, Bell cannot contract in his individual capacity with himself in his official capacity as administrator or executor of an estate. A stockholder or officer of a corporation may contract in his individual capacity with the corporation since a corporation has an existence separate and apart from its officers and stockholders.

Although there are only two parties to a contract, there is no legal limit to the number of persons (individuals, corporations, etc.) who may join as promisors or promisees. There is a practical limit, however, since it must be possible to identify each party to the contract with reasonable certainty.

Presumption as to Capacity. Where suit is brought to enforce a contractual promise, the party plaintiff must allege in his complaint (1) the offer, (2) the acceptance, and (3) the consideration—the three essential elements of an enforceable contract. He must also allege and prove the failure to perform the promise and the resulting damages. The plaintiff need not allege and prove that the parties to the contract have capacity to contract, since lack of capacity to contract is the exception rather than the rule. If the pleadings are silent as to the capacity of the parties, the court will proceed with the case on the presumption that all parties have capacity to contract. If a party is under a disability and does not have capacity to contract, such fact must be set out specifically in the pleadings. If the party plaintiff lacks capacity to sue, the suit will be brought by his friend or someone having authority to act in his behalf; if the party defendant, in an action on a contract, lacks capacity to contract, it will be set up as matter of defense in the answer. The classes of persons who do not have full capacity to contract are (1) infants, (2) insane persons, (3) drunken persons, (4) married women, (5) aliens, and (6) corporations.

Summary

Capacity is the ability to perform legally valid acts. In modern society, persons with natural incapacities to perform legally valid acts are under legal incapacities. Aliens, corporations, and convicts, under some conditions, do not have full legal capacity.

To have a binding contract, there must be two parties to the contract—a promisor and a promisee. The same person cannot act in both capacities. There may be more than two promisors and more than two promisees. There is no legal limit to the number of persons who may be parties to a contract.

Everyone is presumed to have capacity to contract; consequently, in bringing suit on a contract, it is not necessary to allege and prove contractual capacity. Lack of capacity is a matter of defense and must be affirmatively set out as a defense in the pleadings.

Infants' Contracts

Theory of Infants' Incapacity.   Since the courts have recognized from an early date that a person of immature years does not have the capacity to compete on an equal basis with mature persons, they have granted to an infant the privilege of disaffirming his contracts. The rules of law which apply to infants' contracts have been developed to satisfy a social need and, in many respects, cannot be justified from the standpoint of legal logic.

At one period during the course of the development of the law relative to an infant's capacity to contract, the courts attempted to classify infants' contracts into three categories: (1) contracts clearly beneficial to the infant, (2) contracts possibly beneficial to the infant, and (3) contracts prejudicial to the infant. Contracts falling into class 1 were valid, those falling into class 2 were voidable, and those falling in class 3 were void. This classification has been abandoned, and now, with few exceptions, the contracts of infants are voidable at the election of the infant.

Period of Infancy. At common law the age of infancy was fixed at 21 years for both men and women. In counting time, the law generally disregards parts of days. Under this rule an infant becomes of age at the first moment of the day before the 21st anniversary of his birth. In a few states an infant becomes of age on his birthday. Several of the states have changed the common law in some respects by statute, but in the majority of states the age of infancy is 21 years. In some states the age of infancy for women is 18 years, and in some states the contractual incapacity of a female is removed by marriage.[1]

At common law, no distinction was made between an infant of tender years and one who had nearly attained his majority. Today, by statute, some states have provided that an infant may disaffirm his contracts, but if he is over a stated age, usually 18 years, he must, on disaffirmance, place the adult *in statu quo.*

As a general rule the statutes defining the period of infancy fix a definite age at which a person reaches his majority. From a practical standpoint, it is desirable to have a simple rule whereby the period of infancy may be determined with certainty.

Emancipation. As a general rule the father of an infant has the right to the infant's services and can collect the infant's wages. If the father is dead, the widowed mother succeeds to the father's rights in this respect. A person who employs an infant is not discharged of liability to the parent by payment of wages to the infant unless the infant is emancipated. When a parent emancipates a child, he surrenders his right to the child's wages. There are no formal requirements for emancipation. All that is necessary is that the parent expressly or impliedly consent to the infant's entering into a contract of employment. If an infant has been emancipated, he can recover, either on the contract or on the basis of quasi contract, for services rendered. Emancipation does not enlarge the infant's capacity to contract.

General Rule. An infant's contract binds both the infant and the adult unless the infant exercises his right to elect to disaffirm the contract; consequently, infants' contracts are voidable, not void. If the infant elects to be bound by the contract, the relation existing between the infant and the other contracting party is the same as that existing between contracting parties who have full capacity to contract. If an infant, on reaching his majority, elects to ratify a contract entered into while an infant, no new promises are involved, and no new consideration need be given. The infant, by ratifying the contract,

---

[1] Arkansas, California, Florida, Idaho, Illinois, Iowa, Maryland, Minnesota, Montana, Nevada, North Dakota, Oregon, South Dakota, and Utah.

has exercised his privilege of election, and thereafter both parties are bound by the contract.

Business Contracts. As a general rule an infant is not liable on his business contracts, even though he may be dependent on the income from the business for his living. In a few cases the courts have held infants liable for equipment which has been purchased for the purpose of aiding in earning a living, such as machinery necessary to operate a farm or a truck to be used in trucking operations, but these cases are clearly exceptions to the general rule. Undertakings such as these are generally classed as the operation of a business, and the contracts entered into in connection with these operations are, as a rule, held to be business contracts. The courts have usually held infants liable for the reasonable value of tools of a trade which have been purchased for the purpose of following a trade. Contracts for such equipment have been classed as contracts for necessaries and not as business contracts.

State Statutes. Many states have enacted statutes which have changed in some respects the common law relative to an infant's capacity to contract. These statutes are not uniform in their terms or coverage. In some states the infant's rights in regard to his capacity to convey or contract to convey an interest in real estate is defined by statute, and some states have enacted statutes making an infant engaged in business liable, under some circumstances, on his contracts entered into in connection with the operation of the business. An example of such a statute is Section 599.3 of the Iowa Code of 1946. It provides: "No contract can be thus disaffirmed in cases where, on account of the minor's own misrepresentation of his majority, or for having engaged in business as an adult, the other party had good reason to believe him capable of contracting."

In those states which have codified their laws, the capacity of an infant to contract, and his rights and liabilities under his contracts, are set out in detail. In general, such statutes follow the pattern of the common law, but they may differ from it in some of the details.[2]

Infant Partner. An infant may become a member of a partnership, or a partnership may be composed of members all of whom are infants, and it will in no way affect the validity of partnership contracts. An infant partner may withdraw from the partnership without liability to his copartner or copartners for damages for breach of the contract of partnership. However, the infant partner cannot withdraw his original investment in the partnership capital if such withdrawal will injure partnership creditors.

Although the courts are not in complete accord in their decisions, they have generally held that if an infant withdraws from a partnership that is solvent, he is entitled to the return of his original capital less any withdrawals

---

[2] See West's Annotated California Code, Civil Code, ¶ 25 to ¶37.

he may have made. If an infant withdraws from a partnership that is insolvent, he cannot withdraw any portion of his capital contribution until partnership creditors have been paid in full, in which case his withdrawal would be his capital investment less his share of the partnership losses. If the infant's share of the losses exceeds his capital investment, he is not individually liable to partnership creditors for any portion of the unpaid balance of their claims against the partnership. An infant's adult copartners are not obligated to reimburse him for loss of his capital investment resulting from partnership losses.

If an infant purchases the capital stock of a corporation, he has the right to disaffirm the purchase, return the stock, and recover the amount paid for it even though the capital of the corporation has been impaired in the interim.

Summary

An infant has the privilege of disaffirming his contracts. The period of infancy is, with few exceptions, 21 years.

A parent is entitled to the services of an infant child unless he emancipates the child—that is, unless he gives his consent to permit the infant child to enter into employment contracts and to collect his own wages. Emancipation does not enlarge an infant's capacity to contract.

An infant's contracts are voidable, not void, and they are held to be valid until the infant has exercised his privilege and disaffirmed the contract. The adult party to a contract is bound by the contract until the infant disaffirms it. As a general rule an infant may disaffirm his business contracts, even though he has engaged in the business as a means of supporting himself. Many states by statute have altered, in some respects, an infant's capacity to contract. These statutes are not uniform in their terms or coverage.

An infant may become a member of a partnership. An infant partner may disaffirm the partnership agreement without liability to his partners for breach of such agreement, and he may disaffirm his personal liability to partnership creditors, but he may not withdraw his capital investment to the injury of such creditors.

Necessaries

Liability for Necessaries. The statement that infants are liable on their contracts for necessaries is frequently made by the courts, but the statement is incorrect. An infant is liable for the reasonable value of necessaries furnished him, but his liability is quasi contractual in nature. If an infant contracts for necessaries and the contract price is greater than the reasonable value of necessaries furnished, the infant is liable only for their reasonable value. His liability is not based on his contractual promise.

Nature of Necessaries.   Necessaries are confined to those things which are personal to the infant, that is, things which are essential to the infant's continued existence and general welfare. Generally, necessaries are food, clothing, shelter, and medical care, suitable to the infant's station in life, and a basic education or vocational training and the tools of his trade.

In determining the liability of an infant for things furnished him which would fall into the class of necessaries, the courts take into consideration the standards of the stratum of society into which the child was born. For instance, things which might be held to be necessaries for an infant born into a wealthy, well-educated family might not be held to be necessaries for the infant child born into a poor, uneducated family. An infant is not liable for things which do not fall into the classification of necessaries, irrespective of his station in life.

An infant's liability for necessaries is limited to the reasonable value of necessaries actually furnished to the infant. For example, if an infant contracts to rent a room for one year and occupies it for only three months, the infant's liability would be the reasonable rent for the room for the three months he occupied it. Also, if an infant is furnished with adequate necessaries by his parent or guardian, the infant will not be liable for necessaries furnished him by other persons. Since his needs are already supplied by his parent or guardian, any items for which he contracts, even though they might fall into the classification of necessaries, will be held not to be necessaries.

Summary

An infant is liable for the reasonable value of necessaries actually furnished to him. Only those things that are necessary to the existence of the infant and to his future development are classed as necessaries. Generally, necessaries are limited to food, clothing, shelter, and medical care, suitable to his station in life, and basic education and training for a trade and tools of the trade. If an infant is adequately supplied with necessaries by his parents or guardian, he will not be liable for necessaries furnished him by other persons.

Spaulding v. New England Furniture Co.

147 A.2d 916 (Sup. Jud. Ct. Me. 1959)

This was an action by Norman Spaulding, by his next friend (plaintiff), against New England Furniture Company (defendant) to recover a judgment for payments paid for furniture. Judgment for Spaulding and New England Furniture Company appealed. Judgment affirmed.

Spaulding, an infant living with his wife and child, purchased from New England Furniture Company (Company) a number of items of household goods and furniture on a conditional sales contract. The purchase price of the items, including certain service charges, was $1,431.09. After paying the company $388 Spaulding defaulted, and Company repossessed the items. Spaulding brought this action to recover a judgment for the $388. Company contended that the household goods and furniture were necessaries and that Spaulding was liable on the contract.

SIDDALL, JUSTICE. One who defends a minor's suit to disaffirm a contract and to recover the amount paid thereon has the burden of proving that the articles sold were necessaries.

"In a suit by a minor to rescind a contract the burden is on the defendant to show that the article was a necessary."

What are necessaries? Our court in *Kilgore* v. *Rich,* said: ". . . Coke's enumeration of the kinds of necessaries has always been accepted as true doctrine, which are these: 'Necessary meat, drink, apparel, necessary physic, and such other necessaries, and likewise his good teaching, or instruction, whereby he may profit himself afterwards.' "

In *Utterstorm* v. *Kidder,* our court elaborated further upon the meaning of the term "necessaries" in the following language: "A minor is bound by and cannot disaffirm his contract for necessaries such as food, clothing, lodging, medical attendance and instruction suitable and requisite for the proper training and development of his mind. While the term 'necessaries' is not confined merely to such things as are required for bare subsistence, and is held to include those things useful, suitable and necessary for the minor's support, use and comfort, it is limited in its inclusion to articles of personal use necessary for the support of the body and improvement of the mind of the infant, and is not extended to articles purchased for business purposes, even though the minor earns his living by the use of them, and has no other means of support."

In the instant case Spaulding was married and living with his wife and child at the time of the delivery of the articles set forth in the conditional sales contract. He was obliged to support his family. Although an infant, he was liable for the value of necessaries furnished to him for his family.

Whether or not the articles set forth in the conditional sales contract were necessaries was a fact for the referee to determine. The determination of this question involved the interpretation of the testimony as to the financial situation of Spaulding, the social position and condition in life of Spaulding and his family, their requirements and needs, the nature and quality of the articles furnished and their adaptability to the needs of Spaulding and his family, and his supply, if any, from other sources. Articles which may be necessities for one family may well be luxuries for another. The record contains considerable testimony on this aspect of the case.

In its objections Furniture Co. contends that the referee expressly excluded from his findings the issue of whether or not the articles in question were necessaries. We do not so interpret the report of the referee. As we view the report, the referee specifically found that the goods sold were not necessaries.

Whether the articles sold to Spaulding were necessaries was for the referee to determine. He found they were not necessaries. His finding was justified by the evidence. The action of the presiding justice in overruling the company's objections was proper. The entry will be Exceptions overruled. [*Note: Spaulding would be liable in those states which, by statute, have declared that when an infant marries his incapacity to contract is removed.*]

Disaffirmance of Contract

Right to Disaffirm. An infant's right to disaffirm his contracts is absolute and is personal to the infant. As a general rule, the infant's right to disaffirm his contracts is not conditioned on the infant's ability to return the consideration he has received or on his ability to fulfill other conditions, and the infant or his personal representative (administrator of a deceased infant or a guardian) are the only ones who can exercise the right to disaffirm.

Time of Disaffirmance. The infant may exercise his right to disaffirm his executed contracts, except contracts affecting title to real estate, at any time from the time he enters into the contract until a reasonable time after he reaches his majority. He cannot disaffirm a contract affecting title to his real estate until he reaches his majority. In some states an infant may repossess real estate which he has sold and conveyed to another, but he cannot disaffirm the conveyance during infancy. If the infant, after he reaches his majority, disaffirms a sale of real estate, the adult must account to the infant for the rents and profits during the period he (the adult) was in possession.

If the infant does not disaffirm within a reasonable time after he reaches majority, he will be bound. The contracts of an infant are valid until he exercises his right to disaffirm, and if he does not exercise this right seasonably, he thereby waives the right. What is a reasonable time for disaffirmance is a question of fact, and the time allowed the infant to disaffirm will depend on the facts and circumstances of each case. No general rule can be stated.

Return of Consideration. The objective of the law in giving an infant the right to disaffirm his contracts is the protection of the infant's estate from dissipation during his infancy, but the courts will not permit the infant to use this right to defraud adults. There is considerable diversity in the decisions as to the relative rights of the parties if the infant disaffirms his contract.

If the disaffirmed contract is wholly executory, the disaffirmance cancels all the legal obligations brought into existence by the contract. If the infant has received consideration, he will be required, on disaffirmance of the contract, to return any of the consideration or the benefits from such consideration which he still has in his possession at the time he disaffirms the contract. However, his right to disaffirm his contract does not depend, as a general rule, on his ability to return the consideration he has received.

Infants' Rights on Disaffirmance. At common law, when an infant disaffirmed his contract, he had the right to recover from the adult any consideration which he had given or its value. This right was not conditioned on his returning the consideration he had received or on his placing the adult *in statu quo*. However, if the infant had in his possession at the time he disaffirmed his contract any of the consideration he had received, or if his estate had been enhanced by the transaction, he would not be permitted to retain the benefits and at the same time recover the consideration given. The courts in some states and the statutes of other states require the infant, on disaffirmance of his contract, to pay for the benefits received or to place the adult *in statu quo*. This duty is limited under some circumstances.

As a general rule, if an infant disaffirms his contract, he can recover what he has parted with, even though it has been transferred to an innocent third-party purchaser. This rule does not apply to goods sold by an infant in those states which have adopted the Uniform Commercial Code.

In determining the rights and liabilities of an infant on his contract, the courts in equity cases have not followed the strict rule of the common law. Generally, the courts have, in such cases, applied the equitable principle (he who asks equity must do equity) and have required the infant to do whatever is equitable and just under the circumstances of the case. The interests of the infant are protected by the court and are paramount to those of the adult. However, the adult's interests are also taken into consideration, and the courts endeavor to work out a solution as fair and equitable as the circumstances of the case permit. There is a tendency on the part of some courts to apply equitable principles to law cases.

Misrepresentation of Age. The misrepresentation of his age by the infant does not, as a general rule, estop the infant from exercising his right to disaffirm the contract induced by the fraud. In some cases in equity the courts have held that an infant, who by misrepresentation of his age has induced the adult to enter into the contract, will not be granted an equitable remedy on disaffirmance of the contract.

Some courts will permit an infant, who by misrepresenting his age has induced the adult to enter into a contract, to disaffirm the contract and recover what he has given without requiring the infant to account for benefits received. But the majority of the courts now require the infant to restore the consideration received and to account for its use and its depreciation in value.

Summary

An infant has the right to disaffirm his contracts, except those affecting title to his real estate. He may exercise this right at any time from the time he enters into the contract until a reasonable time after he reaches his majority. An infant will not be permitted to use his infancy as a means of enhancing his estate; consequently, on disaffirmance, he must return to the adult any consideration received which he still has or any amount by which his estate has been enhanced. However, the infant's right to disaffirm is not conditioned on his putting the adult *in statu quo.* If the infant has dissipated the consideration received, he can, under the majority rule, recover the consideration parted with without reimbursing the adult. In equity cases, as a general rule, the strict common-law rule is not followed, but the court, on disaffirmance by the infant, will work out a solution to the case which is fair and equitable to all parties involved. The courts have held, with few exceptions, that misrepresentation of his age does not estop an infant from disaffirming the contract induced by the misrepresentation. However, a majority of the courts will require the infant, on disaffirmance, to return the consideration received and to account for its depreciation and for the value of its use.

Kiefer v. *Fred Howe Motors, Inc.*
158 N.W.2d 288 (Sup. Ct. Wisc. 1968)

This was an action brought by an infant, Steven Kiefer (plaintiff), against Fred Howe Motors, Inc. (defendant) to recover payments made on the purchase of an automobile. Judgment for Kiefer and Howe Motors appealed. Affirmed.

WILKIE, JUSTICE.   Three issues are presented on this appeal. They are:

1. Should an emancipated minor over the age of eighteen be legally responsible for his contracts?
2. Was the contract effectively disaffirmed?
3. Is Kiefer liable in tort for misrepresentation?

The law governing agreements made during infancy reaches back over many centuries. The general rule is that ". . . the contract of a minor, other than for necessaries, is either void or voidable at his option." The only other exceptions to the rule permitting disaffirmance are statutory or involve contracts which deal with duties imposed by law such as a contract of marriage or an agreement to support an illegitimate child. The general rule is not affected by the minor's status as emancipated or unemancipated.

Howe Motors does not advance any argument that would put this case within one of the exceptions to the general rule, but rather urges that this court, as a matter of public policy, adopt a rule that an emancipated minor over eighteen years of age be made legally responsible for his contracts.

The underpinnings of the general rule allowing the minor to disaffirm his contracts were undoubtedly the protection of the minor. It was thought that the minor was immature in both mind and experience and that, therefore, he should be protected from his own bad judgments as well as from adults who would take advantage of him. The doctrine of the voidability of minors' contracts often seems commendable and just. . . . However, in today's modern and sophisticated society the "infancy doctrine" seems to lose some of its gloss.

Paradoxically, we declare the infant mature enough to shoulder arms in the military, but not mature enough to vote; mature enough to marry and be responsible for his torts and crimes, but not mature enough to assume the burden of his own contractual indiscretions. In Wisconsin, the infant is deemed mature enough to use a dangerous instrumentality—a motor vehicle—at sixteen, but not mature enough to purchase it with protection until he is twenty-one.

No one really questions that a line as to age must be drawn somewhere below which a legally defined minor must be able to disaffirm his contracts for nonnecessities. The law over the centuries has considered this age to be twenty-one. Legislatures in other states have lowered the age. We suggest that Howe Motors might better seek the change it proposes in the legislative halls rather than this court. A recent law review article in the *Indiana Law Journal* explores the problem of contractual disabilities of minors and points to three different legislative solutions leading to greater freedom to contract. The first approach is one gleaned from the statutes of California and New York, which would allow parties to submit a proposed contract to a court which would remove the infant's right to disaffirmance upon a finding that the particular contract is fair. This suggested approach appears to be extremely impractical in light of the expense and delay that would necessarily accompany the procedure. A second approach would be to establish a rebuttable presumption of incapacity to replace the strict rule. This alternative would be an open invitation to litigation. The third suggestion is a statutory procedure that would allow a minor to petition a court for the removal of disabilities. Under this procedure a minor would only have to go to court once, rather than once for each contract as in the first suggestion.

Undoubtedly, the infancy doctrine is an obstacle when a major purchase is involved. However, we believe that the reasons for allowing that obstacle to remain viable at this point outweigh those for casting it aside. Minors require some protection from the pitfalls of the marketplace. Reasonable minds will always differ on the extent of the protection that should be afforded. For this court to adopt a rule that the appellant suggests and remove the contractual disabilities from a minor simply because he becomes emancipated, which in most cases would be the result of marriage, would be to suggest that the married minor is somehow vested with more wisdom and maturity than his single counterpart. However, logic would not seem to dictate this result especially when today a youthful marriage is oftentimes indicative of a lack of wisdom and maturity.

Howe Motors questions whether there has been an effective disaffirmance of the contract in this case.

Williston, while discussing how a minor may disaffirm a contract, states:

"Any act which clearly shows an intent to disaffirm a contract or sale is sufficient for the purpose. Thus a notice by the infant of his purpose to disaffirm . . . a tender or even an offer to return the consideration or its proceeds to the vendor, . . . is sufficient."

The 19th-century view was that a minor's lying about his age was inconsequential because a fraudulent representation of capacity was not the equivalent of actual capacity. This rule has been altered by time. There appear to be two possible methods that now can be employed to bind the defrauding minor: He may be estopped from denying his alleged majority, in which case the contract will be enforced or contract damages will be allowed; or he may be allowed to disaffirm his contract but be liable in tort for damages. Wisconsin follows the latter approach.

The trial produced conflicting testimony regarding whether Kiefer had been asked his age or had replied that he was "twenty-one." Kiefer and his wife, Jacqueline, said "No," and Frank McHalsky, Howe Motors' salesman, said "Yes." Confronted with this conflict, the question of creditability was for the trial court to decide, which it did by holding that Kiefer did not orally represent that he was "twenty-one." This finding is not contrary to the great weight and clear preponderance of the evidence and must be affirmed.

Ratification

Nature of Ratification. An infant cannot ratify a contract until he reaches his majority. During infancy the infant is incapable of making a binding contractual promise. If he were permitted to ratify his contracts during the period of his infancy, he would be able to remove his disability by his own act. This the courts will not permit him to do.

Requirements for Ratification. There are no formal requirements for the ratification of an infant's contract. The infant's ratification, on reaching his majority, may be either expressed or implied. Any words or acts on the part of the infant, after reaching his majority, which indicate with reasonable clarity the infant's intent to be bound by the contract, are sufficient.

If the contract is executed, the retaining of the consideration by the infant for an unreasonable time after the infant attains his majority amounts to a ratification. If an infant accepts benefits or tendered performance, or if he performs his part of the contract after reaching majority, it will be evidence of intention to ratify, although anyone standing alone would not necessarily be conclusive. The courts have generally held that if an infant, after he becomes of age, indicates an intent to ratify his contract, he cannot escape the effects of his ratification by showing that he did not know that he had a right to disaffirm his contract. In this situation the courts have usually applied the rule that ignorance of the law is no excuse.

If the contract is executory, some courts have held that mere inaction on the part of the infant after he reaches his majority does not amount to a ratification. Other courts have held that since an infant's contract is valid until it is disaffirmed, failure to disaffirm within a reasonable time amount to a waiver of the rights to disaffirm and is a ratification.

The circumstances of the case are of major importance in determining whether or not a contract has been ratified. For example, an infant signed a note as surety. The note was not paid when due, but the infant was not given notice of default. Approximately 10 years after the infant reached his majority, suit was brought against him on the note. The defense of infancy was set. The court held that the infant had not ratified the contract.

In one real estate transaction the court held that failure to avoid the sale within a year amounted to a ratification, whereas in another case the court held that failure to avoid the sale for five years was not a ratification. Inaction for a period less than the running of the statute of limitations, standing alone, has been declared not to amount to a ratification; however, this cannot be accepted as an established rule.

Effect of Ratification. A ratification makes the contract valid from its inception. When an infant ratifies a contract after reaching his majority, he thereby exercises his right to elect whether or not he wishes to be bound by the contract. Having exercised his right to elect and having elected to be bound, he cannot thereafter disaffirm the contract. He is bound by his election.

Summary

An infant cannot ratify a contract until he reaches his majority. All that is necessary for ratification is an indication of an intention to be bound. If the contract is executed, inaction for an unreasonable time will, as a general rule, amount to a ratification. If the contract is executory, some courts have held that mere inaction will not amount to a ratification. Ratification makes the contract valid from its inception.

Adams v. *Barcomb*
216 A.2d 648 (Sup. Ct. Vt. 1966)

This was an action brought by Rose Adams (plaintiff) against Leonard Barcomb (defendant) to recover $975.00. Judgment for Barcomb and Adams appealed. Reversed.

In May, 1964, Adams, age 20, traded in an Opel and paid $975.00 in cash on a 1960 Chevrolet she purchased from Barcomb. About two weeks later Adams decided that she did not want the car and had her mother notify Barcomb to this effect. When Barcomb refused to return her money, she hired a lawyer. She operated the car for about two months after she reached her 21st birthday and since that time let it sit in her yard.

SHAMGRAW, JUSTICE. Barcomb contends that Adams' use of the automobile for about two months after she became of age constituted a ratification of the contract. This is the legal conclusion arrived at by the trial court in finding No. 5, wherein the court stated that Adams had "lost the benefits of her revocation."

The temporary use of the automobile by Adams for about two months, standing alone, in the face of a prior disaffirmance of the contract, and the continuance of this litigation to its final conclusion, does not demonstrate an intention on her part to ratify the contract.

Such use of the automobile by Adams during the pendency of this action to recover what she had paid for the vehicle, after Barcomb had flatly rejected her prior disaffirmance, does not constitute a ratification of the original contract as a matter of law. . . .

Infants' Tort Liability

Nature of Liability. An infant is liable for his torts and crimes. The general rule applied in determining an infant's liability for tort, including negligence, is whether or not he used that degree of care ordinarily exercised by children of like age, mental capacity, and experience. This is usually a question of fact for the jury. In determining an infant's criminal liability, the statutes of the state in which the crime is committed must be consulted.

An infant will not be held liable in tort if the tort action is based primarily on the breach of a contract. The nature of the tort liability must be such that the infant may be held liable without directly or indirectly enforcing his contractual promise.

For example, suppose Allen rented his boat to Boyer, an infant, and Boyer negligently damaged the boat. Boyer, as bailee of the boat, is liable to Allen, as bailor. If Allen sues Boyer to recover damages for breach of the bailment contract, the defense of infancy is good, and Allen cannot recover. Likewise, if instead of bringing suit on the contract, Allen brings suit in tort for the negligent damaging of the boat, the defense of infancy is again available to Boyer. But if Boyer sells the boat and absconds with the money, and Allen brings suit in tort for the conversion of the boat, the defense of infancy is not available to Boyer. A tort recovery for the conversion of the boat is not either a direct or an indirect enforcement of the bailment contract.

Insane and Drunken Persons

Nature of Liability. The basic theory of the liability of insane persons is the same as that of infants; that is, it is presumed that the insane person, like the infant, does not have the capacity to protect his interests in the give-and-take of a free competitive economy. As a general rule the drunken person is dealt with in the same manner as though he were insane, but before he will be considered drunk, he must be intoxicated to such an extent that he does not have the mental capacity to comprehend the business at hand.

Some states do not follow the general rule, and in such states the fact that one of the parties to the contract was drunk at the time he entered into the contract is not ground for the disaffirmance of the contract. In the states which recognize the right of a drunken person to disaffirm his contract, such person must prove that at the time he entered into the contract, he was so intoxicated that he could not comprehend the business at hand, that he was taken advantage of because of his condition, and that the contract was not a fair and just contract, and he must, on disaffirmance, put the other party *in statu quo.*

Test of Insanity. The courts recognize that persons have varying degrees of mental capacity and that no simple rule whereby mental capacity may be tested can be formulated. The test usually applied is whether or not the contracting party had, at the time the contract was entered into, sufficient mental capacity to comprehend the business involved. The same test is applied in determining the contractual capacity of drunken persons.

The nature of the mental weakness of the contracting party is immaterial. The incapacity may result from lunacy, idiocy, senility, or other defects or diseases of the mind. A person may have periods of insanity and be lucid at all other times. A contract made during a lucid interval is binding. A person may be laboring under insane delusions, but his contracts will be binding unless his insane delusions are so connected with the subject matter of the contract as to render him incapable of comprehending its nature.

Effect of Adjudication of Insanity. In most states the contracts of a person who has been adjudged insane are void. The statutes of some states expressly provide that the contracts of a person who has been adjudged insane are void, and in others the same result has been reached by judicial decision. This rule applies only where there has been a regular hearing before a court having jurisdiction over such cases, and where, after due investigation, the court has adjudged the person to be of unsound mind and incapable of managing his estate and has appointed a guardian or conservator of the estate. If a person is sued on a contract and he sets up as a defense insanity at the time he entered into the contract, a finding that he was insane at the time he entered into the contract would not be an adjudication of insanity. Such a finding is binding only as to the case being tried.

Necessaries. An insane person is liable for the reasonable value of necessaries furnished him. The rules relative to what are necessaries and the liability for necessaries generally are the same as those applying to infants.

Disaffirmance of Contract. If a person contracts with an insane person and does not know or does not have reasonable cause to know of the person's insanity, and if the contract is fair and entered into in good faith, the insane party cannot disaffirm the contract unless he can put the sane party *in statu quo.*

If the sane party knows or, in the exercise of reasonable care, should know, of the insanity of the other party, the insane party can disaffirm the contract without putting the sane party *in statu quo*. However, he must return to the sane person any portion of the consideration which he still has. The rule in such cases is the same as the rule governing infants' contracts.

Ratification of Contract.   A contract entered into by a person while he is insane may be ratified by that person if and when he regains his sanity, or it may be ratified by his personal representative in the event the insane person is adjudged insane or dies. The ratification of an insane person's contract has the same effect on the rights of the parties to the contract as has the ratification of an infant's contract. The contract will be considered as valid from its inception.

Summary

The contracts of an insane person entered into while insane are voidable unless the party has been adjudged insane by a court having jurisdiction of the case, in which event the majority of jurisdictions hold that the contract is void.

If a contracting party does not have sufficient mentality to comprehend the nature of the business being transacted, he is insane, irrespective of the cause of his mental weakness. An insane person cannot disaffirm a fair contract entered into with a person ignorant of the insanity unless he puts the party *in statu quo*. Knowledge of the insanity on the part of the sane person gives the insane party the same rights to disaffirm a contract as an infant has.

A person who, at the time he enters into a contract, is intoxicated to such a degree that he cannot comprehend the business at hand, is, in most states, treated the same as an insane person.

Cundick v. Broadbent
383 F.2d 157 (10th Cir. 1967)

This was an action brought by Irma Cundick (plaintiff) guardian *ad litem* for her husband, Darwin Cundick, to set aside an agreement for the sale of (1) livestock and equipment; (2) shares of stock in a development company; and (3) base range land in Wyoming to J. R. Broadbent (defendant). The alleged grounds for nullification were that at the time of the transaction Cundick was mentally incompetent to execute the agreement. Judgment for Broadbent and Cundick appealed. Affirmed.

MURRAH, CHIEF JUDGE.   At one time, in this country and in England, it was the law that since a lunatic or *non compos mentis* had no mind with which to make an agreement, his contract was wholly void and incapable of ratification. But, if his mind was merely confused or weak so that he knew what he was doing yet was incapable of fully understanding the terms and effect of his agreement, he could indeed contract, but such contract would be voidable at his option. But in recent times courts have tended away from the concept of absolutely void contracts toward the notion that even though a contract be said to be void for lack of capacity to make it, it is nevertheless ratifiable at the instance of the incompetent party. The modern rule, and the weight of authority, seems to be as stated in 2 Jaeger's *Williston on Contracts,* 3d ed., §251, ". . . the contractal act by one claiming to be mentally deficient, but not under guardianship, absent fraud, or knowledge of such asserted incapacity by the other contracting party, is not a void act but at most only voidable at the instance of the deficient party; and then only in accordance with certain equitable principles."

In recognition of different degrees of mental competency the weight of authority seems to hold that mental capacity to contract depends upon whether the allegedly disabled person possessed sufficient reason to enable him to understand the nature and effect of the act in issue. Even average intelligence is not essential to a valid bargain. In amplification of this principle, it has been said that if a maker of a contract ". . . has sufficient mental capacity to retain in his memory without prompting the extent and condition of his property and to comprehend how he is disposing of it and to whom and upon what consideration, then he possesses sufficient mental capacity to execute such instrument." The Wyoming court adheres to the general principle that "mere weakness of body or mind, or of both, do not constitute what the law regards as mental incompetency sufficient to render a contract voidable. . . . A condition which may be described by a physician as *senile dementia* may not be insanity in a legal sense."

Against the background of medical and lay evidence tending to show Cundick's incompetency on the crucial date, there is positive evidence to the effect that at the time in question he was 59 years old, married and operating a sheep ranch in Wyoming; that in previous years he had sold his lamb crop to Broadbent and on a date prior to this transaction the parties met at a midway point for the purpose of selling the current lamb crop. Although there is innuendo concerning what transpired at the meeting, neither party testified and no one else was present. We do know that the meeting resulted in a one page contract signed by both parties in which Cundick agreed to sell all of his ranching properties to Broadbent. It is undisputed that Cundick and his wife thereafter took this one page contract to their lawyer in Salt Lake City who refined and amplified it into an eleven page contract providing in detail the terms by which the sale was to be consummated. The contract was signed in the lawyer's office by Cundick and Broadbent in the presence of Cundick's wife and the lawyer. The lawyer testified that the contract had been explained in detail and that all parties apparently understood it.

The narrated facts of this case amply support the trial court's finding to the effect that Broadbent did not deceive or overreach Cundick. In the absence of any evidence that Broadbent knew of Cundick's mental deficiency, the only evidence from which it can be said that Broadbent took advantage or overreached him is the proof concerning the value of the property sold under the contract. As to that, there is positive evidence that the property was worth very much more than what Broadbent paid for it. But as we have noted, there was evidence to the effect that after the original contract was signed and some complaint made about the purchase price, the parties agreed to raise the price and the contract was so modified. . . .

Married Women's Contracts

Contractual Capacity at Common Law. At common law a married woman could not contract. When a woman married, her legal existence ceased, the husband being the sole representative of the family. It is often said that under the common law the husband and wife were one, and the husband was that one. At an early date the courts of equity recognized the right of the wife to a separate estate, and through equitable proceedings a separate estate could be created for the wife.

Married Women's Statutes. This disability has been partially or totally removed by statutes adopted by the various states. Some statutes give a married woman full power to contract, whereas others are so drafted that she cannot enter into contracts of suretyship or contracts with her husband. In interpreting these statutes, one should keep in mind the common-law rule that a married woman has no power to contract, because her power to contract is limited to the power granted in the statute. If the statute does not give her power to enter into a particular type of contract, she will continue to be under the old common-law disability. To determine the limits of married women's power to contract, one must consult the statutes of the various states.

Summary

At common law a married woman had no legal capacity. Her contracts were void. When a woman married, her legal identity was merged into that of her husband, and the husband exercised the legal rights of the unit. The common-law incapacity has been partially or totally removed by statute. The statutes of the several states are not uniform.

Aliens, Corporations

Aliens. As a general rule there are no restrictions on an alien's power to contract. During a war, under "trading with the enemy" legislation, one is not permitted to enter into contracts with alien enemies; yet these statutes do not prohibit all contracts with aliens of an enemy country who may be in the United States. Ownership of land and some other rights of certain aliens are controlled either by treaty or by state laws. Contracts in violation of such treaties or statutes are void.

Corporations. Today, under our general corporation statute, a corporation may be granted the authority to carry on any legitimate business. Although there is considerable diversity in the holdings of the courts, the trend is to hold a corporation bound by its contracts, if they are not illegal, even though the contract is not within the chartered authority of the corporation.

Trustees and Guardians.   Trustees of trust funds, trustees in bankruptcy, administrators or executors of the estates of deceased persons, guardians of infants and insane persons, receivers, etc., may enter into contracts in their official capacity. As a general rule the contracts of the trustee of a trust fund bind the trustee personally. If the contract is permitted under the terms of the trust agreement, the trustee may charge it against the trust on his accounting. The extent to which a trustee in bankruptcy, the administrator or executor of the estate of a deceased person, the guardian of an infant or insane person, or a receiver may enter into contracts is set out in the statutes of the various states.

Governmental Units.   The right to contract is an incident of the sovereign power of the U.S. government and of the government of the state. The right of a governmental unit, such as a county, township, or city, depends on the powers conferred on the unit when it is created. The power of governments and of governmental units to contract is limited to contracts which are in furtherance of the objectives of the government and is always subject to constitutional limitations.

A government and, as a general rule, a governmental unit may sue on their contracts, but they cannot be sued unless they consent thereto. The privilege of suing the U.S. government and the state governments is generally granted by statute. The Court of Claims was created to adjudicate claims against the U.S. government, and the federal district courts have jurisdiction over suits against the United States if the amount involved does not exceed $10,000.

The agents who have authority to negotiate contracts for governments and governmental units, the method of negotiating contracts, the scope of contractual liability, and the subject matter of the contracts are generally defined by statutes. If there are no statutes in regard to these matters general contract law will apply.

Summary

In the United States, there are no general restrictions on an alien's capacity to contract. The corporation, in theory, has authority to enter into only such contracts as its charter permits. Trustees, receivers, administrators, executors, guardians, and other fiduciaries may enter into contracts in their official capacity. The scope of their capacity is usually set out in the trust agreement or by statute. Governments and governmental units generally have capacity to contract. They can sue but cannot be sued without their consent. Consent to sue is generally granted by statute. The contractual rights and liabilities of governments and governmental units are controlled in many respects by statutes.

Problem Cases

1. Rotondo, on August 8, 1953, purchased a diamond ring from Kay Jewelry Company (Kay) informing the latter that he was a minor 19 years of age and that he was buying it as an engagement ring. Rotondo made a part payment of $94.49 on the ring. On that same day he presented the ring to his fiancée.

   On April 10, 1954, the engagement was terminated but the ring was not returned. Rotondo testified that he asked Kay to repossess the ring shortly after the engagement was broken, but there was no evidence that the ring was repossessed.

   On July 6, 1954, Rotondo, while still an infant, brought this suit to recover the payment made on the ring. Can Rotondo recover his payments?

2. Gillen, an infant of the age of 20 years, 10 months and 24 days, purchased from Doenges-Long Motors, Inc. (Motor Co.), a new 1956 Ford automobile for the agreed price of $2,852.98. As a down payment thereon, Gillen paid Motor Co. $452.98 in cash and turned over to it as a trade-in a 1949 Pontiac for which he was allowed $500, leaving an unpaid balance of $1,900. For this unpaid balance Gillen gave his note for the amount of $2,621.40, secured by a chattel mortgage on the Ford, payable in 30 equal monthly installments. When Gillen purchased the Ford he represented that his age was 21 years.

   Promptly after reaching his majority, Gillen advised Motor Co. that he disaffirmed the contract. He returned the Ford and demanded the return of his down payment of $452.98 and the Pontiac. His demand was refused and he brought this action to recover the Pontiac and $452.98 with interest. Motor Co. set up as a defense that since Gillen misrepresented his age he was estopped to disaffirm the contract, and that, if Gillen was entitled to disaffirm, Motor Co. was entitled to damages in the amount of $664.78. Is Motor Co. right?

3. Key, while an infant, purchased an automobile. He made a down payment and gave a note secured by a chattel mortgage for the balance. After reaching his majority Key made a payment on the note and thereafter defaulted. Southern Acceptance Corporation (Southern) repossessed the automobile and Key gave notice of disaffirmance of the contract. Southern Acceptance Corporation contended that Key had ratified the contract. Is Southern correct?

4. Hurley and his grandmother, Elizabeth Price, inherited as co-owners 676 shares of the common stock of Edison Company. At the time of inheritance, Hurley was a minor of the age of 20 years and lived with his grandmother. On December 11, 1928, the grandmother requested Hurley to sign a dividend order authorizing Edison Co. to pay all dividends due on the shares of stock to Elizabeth Price and Hurley signed the diivdend orders without receiving any consideration therefor and without knowing the nature of the document being signed. Elizabeth Price died December 27, 1943, and it was not until March 18, 1944, that Hurley first learned that he was co-owner of the stock. On March 20, 1944, Hurley gave notice to Edison Co. that he disaffirmed the dividend order which he had signed earlier and demanded that the Edison Co. pay his one half of all dividends paid on the stock since he became co-owner thereof. The Edison Co. refused to pay and Hurley brought suit. Edison Co. contends that Hurley did not disaffirm within a reasonable time after he became of age. Does Hurley have the right to disaffirm the contract?

5. Adamowski, an infant, contracted with Flying Service for a flying instruction course. Adamowski paid $300 as an initial payment and was to pay $3,200 for the complete course. After one month of lessons Adamowski withdrew and brought suit to recover the $300 payment. Flying Service contends since the lessons cannot be returned, Adamowski cannot recover his money. Flying Service also contends that the flying lessons were necessities. Is Flying Service correct on either one of these two contentions?

6. Gissen was working as a clerk at a Miami Beach hotel when Geraldine Goodwill, age eight, slammed a door so hard on his hand that his finger was cut off. Gissen sued Geraldine's parents. Are the parents liable for the injury to Gissen's finger?

7. Bender, a boy of eight, was set upon by a large 16-year-old boy and seriously injured. Bender sued the boy and his parents alleging that the parents knew of the vicious propensities of their son and had failed to exercise reasonable authority over him. Does this state a valid cause against the parents?

8. Gary, age 12, was riding with his brother Ralph, age 17, in the family car when Ralph negligently wrecked the car, injuring Gary. Gary sued Ralph for damages and the defenses are that: (*a*) sinee both parties are infants no cause exists, and (*b*) it is against public policy to allow an infant to sue his own brother. Are either of these defenses good?

9. Earlier in a criminal proceeding Davis had been found not guilty on the grounds of insanity. He was committed to a hospital for the criminally insane but in a mental health proceeding was not declared to be insane. He escaped from the hospital about five years before the bringing of this suit. During that time had married and had established a trucking business. In connection with the trucking business he had bought equipment from The Colorado Kenworth Corporation (Kenworth) as follows: Kenworth tractor $15,000—paid on purchase price $9,058.90; trailer—paid $8,693.74; refrigeration unit, purchase price $17,450; tires $1,125, paid $242.50. Davies sold his business, including this equipment for $1,600, the value of his equity in the equipment. Notice of disaffirmance was given but no offer was made to place the parties *in statu quo*. David contends that since he was found to be insane in the criminal proceedings all his contracts are void. Is David right?

chapter 11. Illegality

Introduction

Nature of Illegality. A bargain is illegal if either its formation or its performance is detrimental to the general public interest. We recognize and protect the individual's right to bargain, but public welfare is paramount to individual rights, and whenever the bargain of individuals, either in its formation or in its performance, is criminal, tortious, or contrary to accepted standards of morality, it will be declared to be illegal and will not be enforced by court action. In general, illegal bargains are void; however, there are exceptions to the rule. (Note: In legal treatises and judges' opinions, the term "illegal contract" is commonly used. We have used "bargain" in preference to "contract" because "bargain" is a neutral word. "Illegal contract' is a contradiction of terms, and its use tends to be confusing.)

Classification. There are an infinite number of situations which give rise to illegal bargains. However, for the purpose of discussion, illegal bargains may be roughly classified into the following categories: (1) bargains in violation of positive law,[1] (2) bargains made void by statute, and (3) bargains contrary to public policy.

Presumption. In determining the legality of a bargain, the courts will presume that the parties intended a legal result will interpret the bargain so as to hold it legal, unless it is clear that the parties intended an illegal bargain. All doubts are resolved in favor of the legality of the bargain.

---

[1] Law actually and specifically enacted or adopted by proper authority for the government of an organized jural society. Black *Law Dictionary* (4th ed.; St. Paul, Minn.: West Publishing Co., 1951), p. 1324.

Summary

A bargain is illegal if either its formation or its performance is detrimental to public policy. Bargains to commit a crime or tort, or bargains which are contrary to accepted standards of morality, are illegal. Such bargains are generally declared to be void; however, there are exceptions to this rule. The courts, in interpreting a bargain, will presume that the parties intended to negotiate a legal contract.

Mascari v. Raines

415 S.W.2d 874 (Sup. Ct. Tenn. 1967)

This was an action by Mrs. Mascari (plaintiff) against Joe Raines (defendant) to collect on a note. Judgment for Raines and Mascari appealed. Affirmed.

Raines, a beer retailer, signed a promissory note in the amount of $1,896.00 and delivered it to Mascari, a beer wholesaler, to secure payment of beer delivered by Mascari to Raines on credit. A state statute provided:

"In order to effectively collect the tax levied by this chapter all sales of beer by wholesalers to retailers or any other persons, except sales to duly licensed wholesalers and sales within military installations as set out in § 57–313, shall be for cash only. The intent of this provision is that wholesale sale of beer and delivery and payment therefor shall be a simultaneous transaction, and any maneuver, device or method of extending credit is expressly prohibited."

"Any person convicted of violating any provision of this chapter shall be subject to a fine of not over five hundred dollars ($500) or to imprisonment for not more than one (1) year, or to both such fine and imprisonment."

When sued on the note, Raines set up illegality as his defense.

CHATTIN, JUDGE.   In the case of *Biggs* v. *Reliance Life Insurance Company,* this Court said:

"The general rule, broadly stated, is that a contract explicitly prohibited by statute is void, and that a prohibition may be implied from the fact that a penalty is prescribed. But the rule is not an inflexible one, and mere imposition of a penalty does not of necessity, or in all circumstances, mean that a contract in contravention of the statute is so far void as to be unenforceable by anyone a party to it."

In arriving at the effect of the statute, the courts will look to the language of the statute, its subject matter, the object and reach of the statute, the wrong or evil which it seeks to remedy or prevent, and the purpose sought to be accomplished in its enactment; and if from all these it is manifest that it was not intended to imply a prohibition or to render the prohibited act void, the courts will so hold and will construe the statute accordingly.

By the clear and unambiguous terms of the Act, wholesalers of beer are prohibited from extending credit in the sale of beer to retailers or any other persons not excepted; and if he does so, his act is in violation of law for which he may be fined or imprisoned or both.

We are not bound by the holding of the trial judge that the legislative intent of this act is to effectively collect the tax levied and not to make void or unenforceable an obligation made in violation thereof.

Bargains in Violation of Positive Law

Scope of Positive Law. Under the classification of positive law, we shall discuss only those bargains the performance of which require the commission of a crime or tort and shall not include regulatory statutes, the violation of which may be declared to be a misdemeanor.

Bargain to Commit a Crime. It is axiomatic that a bargain which requires the commission of a crime is illegal. Also, a bargain which does not require the commission of a crime, but which is of such a nature that it tends to induce the commission of a crime, is illegal. The fact that a party to a bargain might benefit from the bargain if he commits a crime will not, as a general rule, make the bargain illegal, but if the inducement is strong enough to endanger the welfare of society, the bargain is illegal.

The nature of the bargain may be such that its formation is a crime. Connivance is a crime; and a bargain whereby one party, for a consideration, agrees to "look the other way" while the other party commits a crime is an illegal bargain. Also, if parties enter into a series of bargains, each innocent in itself but each a part of a plan to accomplish a criminal result, all of the bargains are illegal. For example, suppose the creation of a monopoly is made a crime under the statutes of the state. Arthur, Burton, Clayton, and Dyer own all the theaters in the area. They enter into a bargain to form a partnership to operate their theaters. The purpose of the partnership is to obtain a monopoly of the theater business in the area so that they can charge higher prices. The bargain is illegal, although a bargain to form a partnership to operate a theater is, standing by itself, legal, and the bargains to convey the theaters owned by the parties are, standing by themselves, legal. All of the bargains taken together are illegal, since the objective of the series of bargains is to create a monopoly in violation of positive law.

Bargain to Commit a Tort. The commission of a tort is clearly detrimental to the general public welfare; consequently, a bargain which cannot be performed without the commission of a tort is illegal. The fact that a tort may be committed during the performance of the bargain does not make it illegal. For example, suppose Adams contracts to build a large office building. During the course of the construction of the building an employee of Adams may negligently injure a pedestrian who is passing the building. The fact that such a tort may be committed in the performance of the construction contract does not make the contract illegal.

Summary

If the formation or the performance of a bargain requires a violation of positive law, it is illegal. The commission of a crime or a tort is a violation of positive law. If the formation or the performance of a bargain requires the commission of a crime or will induce the commission of a crime, the bargain is illegal. If a bargain cannot be performed without the commission of a tort, it is illegal.

Bargains Made Illegal by Statutes

Types of Statutes. The statutes affecting the legality of bargains may be divided into three classes: (1) criminal statutes, (2) statutes expressly declaring contracts void, and (3) regulatory statutes. All of these statutes are, as a general rule, so drafted that a penalty is imposed for the violation of the statute; consequently, they are basically criminal in nature. In our classification, we consider as criminal statutes only those statutes the violation of which involves moral turpitude.

Wagering Statutes. All states have enacted statutes prohibiting or regulating wagering. Such statutes are of special significance in the law of contracts. There is a thin line of distinction between wagering, risk shifting, and speculative bargaining. Risk shifting and speculative bargaining are legal; wagering is illegal. When the parties create a risk, which has no prior existence, for the purpose of bearing it, such a bargain is a wager or bet and is usually prohibited by wagering statutes. For example, suppose Able promises Bell that he will pay Bell $10 if State wins Saturday's football game, provided Bell will pay him $10 if University wins. This is a bet. Neither Able nor Bell would suffer an economic loss as the result of the outcome of the game. When they agree to pay $10, conditioned on the outcome of the game, they create a risk, which did not exist, for the purpose of bearing it.

A bargain for insurance is a typical example of a risk-shifting bargain and is, of course, legal. If the insured does not have an insurable interest in the insured property, then the bargain to insure is a wagering bargain and is illegal. In the case of property insurance the insured's relation to the property insured must be such that he will suffer pecuniary loss on the happening of the event against which the property is insured. The recovery of the insured is based on the principle of indemnity; and, as a general rule, his recovery cannot be greater than the pecuniary loss suffered. The pecuniary interest is not important in life insurance. In life insurance the relationship between the insured and the person obtaining the insurance must be such as to negate the existence of an intent to speculate in human life.

Stock and Commodity Market Transactions.   A good-faith transaction on the stock or commodity market is not illegal. It may be a speculative bargain, but it is not a wager. A wager based on the fluctuation in the price of a stock or commodity is illegal. The primary difference between the two is that in the valid stock or commodity market transaction, the stock or commodity is purchased, and the seller is bound to deliver the shares of stock or quantity of commodity bargained for, and the buyer is obligated to accept delivery and pay the agreed price; whereas in the wager transaction, no stock or commodity is purchased. It is merely a bargain to pay an amount based on the fluctuation in the price of a stock or commodity.

Marginal transactions are not illegal. In such a transaction the purchaser pays a portion of the purchase price to the broker who acts as his agent in buying the stock or commodity. When the broker buys the stock or commodity, he pays the purchase price in full. He then borrows the money to pay the difference between the margin paid by the purchaser and the full purchase price, and pledges the stock or commodity as security for the loan. The pledge agreement provides that if the market price of the stock or commodity declines below a certain point, the purchaser will pay additional margain to the broker, and on his failure to do so, the broker will sell the stock or commodity and from the proceeds pay the loan and pay over to the purchaser any surplus remaining. The purchaser may at any time order the broker to resell the stock or commodity, in which event he will do so, and from the proceeds discharge the loan and pay the balance over to the purchaser.

The fact that the purchaser may intend never to accept delivery of the stock or commodity does not affect the validity of the transaction. However, if there is an understanding between the broker and the purchaser to the effect that the purchaser will not be obligated to accept delivery of the stock or commodity, the transaction will be interpreted as a wager and will be illegal.

Statutes Declaring Bargains Void.   State legislatures have enacted statutes which declare certain defined classes of bargains or bargains made under certain circumstances to be void. In some instances, it is clear from the wording of the statute and the surrounding circumstances that the legislative intent is to declare the bargain to be voidable, not void. There is little uniformity in the provisions of such statutes or in the subject matter included. In general, there is no moral turpitude involved in the violation of such statutes, and, with some exceptions, no penalty is imposed for their violation.

Usury laws and Sunday laws are examples of such statutes. Both have been generally adopted. The usury laws provide that if a charge for the use of money is made which is in excess of a stated amount, the lender will be subject to a penalty. The penalty imposed ranges from forfeiture of principal and interest to forfeiture of any amount of interest charged in excess of the legal rate of interest. In several states the usury laws do not apply to loans to corporations.

The Sunday laws prohibit the performance of certain labors and the transaction of business on Sunday. These statutes are not uniform in their provisions. The commoner forms of Sunday statute prohibit all contracts and sales not of necessity or charity. The Sunday statutes of several states follow the pattern of the early English statute and prohibit bargains which are of the "ordinary calling" of the parties. Ordinarily, only bargains which are completed on Sunday come within the prohibitive provisions of these statutes. A bargain negotiated on Sunday but closed on a secular or business day is not illegal. The courts have generally held that a bargain closed on Sunday but renegotiated or adopted on a secular or business day is not illegal.

Regulatory Statutes. A variety of statutes have been passed by Congress and the state legislatures regulating the dealings in a particular article of commerce. These statutes are not uniform either in their wording or in their scope, but certain types of statutes predominate. The commonest type of regulatory statute requires the obtaining of a license before a person, partnership, or corporation engages in the regulated activity. The purpose of such statutes is to protect the public against dishonest and unskilled persons. Lawyers, doctors, dentists, and other professional men are required to pass examinations before they are granted a license to practice their profession. In most states, real estate brokers, salesmen, insurance agents, and others who are engaged in performing special services for the public are required to prove that they are of good character, and they may also be required to pass some type of examination or test of skill before they are granted a license.

Barbers, beauty parlor operators, building contractors, electricians, plumbers, and others performing skilled services may be required to obtain a license before they engage in their trade. In addition, some businessmen, such as pawnbrokers, retailers and wholesalers of liquor and tobacco, and sellers of other special commodities, are required to obtain a license before they engage in the regulated business.

As a general rule, these statutes impose a penalty on a person who engages in the business or practices the profession or skill without first having complied with the statute and obtained the required license. The applicant for a license is required to establish his right to the license, usually by proving his good character and by demonstrating in some manner that he has the training, education, and skill to perform the regulated service or to carry on the business in a manner which is not detrimental to the public. If a person bargains to perform services or engages in a regulated business without first having obtained a license, his bargain is illegal.

Revenue-Raising Statutes. Some licensing statutes have as their objective the raising of revenue. Whether a statute requiring the obtaining of a license is a regulatory statute or a revenue-raising statute depends on the intention of the legislature. Some statutes are so worded that the intent of the legislature is not clearly expressed. However, if the statute requires proof of character and skill and imposes a penalty on a person who engages in the regulated activity before he first obtains a license, the statute, as a general rule, will be interpreted as a regulatory statute. But if the statute imposes a substantial license fee and provides that a license shall be issued to anyone paying the fee, and if the penalty imposed is a percentage of the fee or an interest charge based on the fee, the statute, as a general rule, will be interpreted as a revenue-raising statute. The failure to obtain a license required by the provisions of a revenue-raising statute in no way affects the validity of the bargains of the unlicensed person.

Summary

There are three classes of statutes which affect the legality of bargains: (1) criminal statutes, (2) statutes expressly declaring the bargain to be void, and (3) regulatory statutes.

Wagering bargains are illegal. A wager is the creation of a risk for the purpose of bearing it. Risk-shifting bargains are not illegal. Stock market and commodity market transactions entered into in good faith are not illegal; and likewise, margin transactions entered into in good faith are not illegal. However, if the principal purpose of a bargain is to wager on the fluctuation in the market price of a stock or commodity, it is illegal.

A wide variety of bargains and especially those involving certain subject matter are made void by state statute. If a person bargains to perform any of the skilled services which require a license without first obtaining a license, his bargains are illegal. However, if the licensing statute is a revenue-raising statute instead of a regulatory statute, the bargains of the unlicensed person are not illegal.

Smith v. *Sherwood & Roberts, Spokane, Inc.*

441 P.2d 158 (Sup. Ct. Idaho 1968)

This was an action brought by Robert Smith (plaintiff) against Sherwood & Roberts, Spokane, Inc. (defendant) to recover penalties for usury and damages for wrongful repossession of a tractor. Judgment for Sherwood & Roberts and Smith appealed. Affirmed.

In 1963, Smith, as purchaser, and Dart Tractor Co., as seller, signed a conditional sales contract for a used tractor and angle dozer. The contract was on a form provided by Sherwood & Roberts, a finance company, and had its name in bold print at the top. The agreement stated a "TOTAL CASH PRICE" of

$2,350.00, less a down payment of $350.00, plus insurance of $47.51, for a "BALANCE TO BE FINANCED" of $2,047.51. To this balance was added a "FINANCE CHARGE" of $327.53, for a "TOTAL TIME PURCHASE PRICE" of $2,375.04, "which Purchaser agreed to pay "Seller" beginning May 25, 1963, in twenty-one monthly installments of $107.95 and one of $108.09, skipping March and April, 1964. The contract contained on its reverse side an assignment form, with "Sherwood & Roberts" printed as assignee. On the day of the contract's execution, it was assigned by Dart to Sherwood & Roberts.

Shortly after Smith took delivery of the tractor, it broke down and needed repairs. After a series of arguments Sherwood finally repossessed the tractor.

McQUADE, JUSTICE.   Under Washington law, twelve percent is the maximum legal rate of interest, "and no person shall directly or indirectly take or receive in money, goods or thing in action, or in any other way, any greater interest, sum or value for the loan or forbearance of any money, goods or thing in action than twelve percent per annum."

The finance charge on the "balance to be financed" of the conditional sales contract was at least 14.68% on the declining balance. Thus, if the contract was subject to the usury law of Washington, Sherwood violated that law by charging Smith an usurious rate for the use of Sherwood's money.

In the Washington case of *Hafer* v. *Spaeth,* a merchant sold a piano on an installment (conditional) sales contract. The balance of the agreed purchase price —$175.00 less $30.00 down payment—was to be paid in monthly installments of $5.00 "with $3.50 handling charge per month or a fraction thereof." The trial court found the conditional sales contract was a loan and the handling charge was interest, and determined the transaction was usurious. The Washington Supreme Court reversed saying:

The contract simply provided the terms upon which the vendor was willing to sell, and upon which the purchaser expressed his willingness to buy, the piano. In other words, the transaction was one which contemplated the sale of a chattel upon specified terms, and not one which exacted a consideration for the extension of payment of an existing or prospective, indebtedness.

· · ·

It is not the office of a conditional bill of sale to secure a loan of money, but, rather, only to permit an owner of personal property to make a *bona fide* sale on credit, reserving title in himself for security until the purchase price is fully paid.

In Idaho and the large majority of other jurisdictions, *bona fide* conditional sales contracts are not subject to usury laws. After careful consideration of Smith's arguments urging us to abandon this rule or to find the present action an exception, we have discovered no compelling reason why the general rule should not control here.

The record does not disclose if the seller, Dart, made *bona fide* oral offers to Smith of different prices for cash and for credit before they agreed to enter the conditional sales contract. However, the contract itself states a cash price, details adjustments and charges, and presents a time purchase price. Smith does not contend that these sums and computations had not been entered in the contract before he signed it. The contract clearly indicated a different price for cash and for credit, and Smith knowingly chose the credit price.

Kusche v. Vulcanized Rubber and Plastics Co.
206 A.2d 40 (Sup. Ct. Penn. 1965)

This was an action by Kusche (plaintiff) against Vulcanized Rubber Co. (defendant). Judgment for Vulcanized and Kusche appealed. Affirmed.

Kusche, with many years experience in banking and negotiating loans, entered into an oral agreement with Vulcanized Co. to negotiate a mortgage loan of $500,-000 on behalf of the Vulcanized at a fee of 3%. Kusche successfully secured a commitment for such a loan from a Philadelphia bank, which was submitted to the board of directors of Vulcanized, but Vulcanized used this commitment as an aid to obtain a loan with similar conditions from another banking institution, and then refused to pay Kusche the 3% commission.

Kusche sued for the commission and Vulcanized defended on the ground that Kusche was barred from recovery of any compensation by the Real Estate Brokers License Act of 1929, in that during the time involved he was not licensed as a real estate broker or salesman, and did not come within the exceptions for which no license was required.

EAGEN, JUSTICE.   The statute involved specifically prohibits any individual, association or corporation from acting "in the capacity of a real estate broker, or a real estate salesman," in the Commonwealth of Pennsylvania unless properly licensed by the State Real Estate Commission. It further specifically bars any individual, association or corporation from instituting suit for recovery *"for any act done or service rendered, the doing or rendering of which is prohibited under the provisions of this act to others than licensed real estate brokers, unless such person . . . was duly licensed . . . at the time of the doing of such act or the rendering of such service."* (Emphasis supplied). It further defines a real estate broker to include "all persons . . . who, for another and for a fee, commission, or other valuable consideration, shall . . . negotiate or offer or attempt to negotiate a loan, secured or to be secured by mortgage or other encumbrance upon . . . real estate."

Kusche's position is that the loan sought by Vulcanized was a working capital corporate loan in which the lien on the real estate was merely incidental and not the principal basis for the transaction. Hence, it is urged the loan is not of the nature contemplated by the real estate licensing act.

The loan to be negotiated by Kusche was to be secured by a mortgage on real estate. The loan agreement negotiated with the second bank also provides for the execution and delivery of a mortgage on the borrower's real estate. Therefore, under the clear language of the statute, Kusche in negotiating such a loan was acting in the capacity of a real estate broker, and the securing of a license was a condition precedent to any enforcement of a contract to pay commissions for such service.

Public Policy

General Concept. Public policy is one of those broad concepts which gives flexibility to the law where flexibility is needed. In many respects, it is comparable to the concept of the general public welfare. Public policy changes from time to time along with social and economic development. Conduct which may be acceptable in one era may not be acceptable in a later era, and vice versa. Also, the public policy of one state may differ in some degree from that of another.

Our concept of public policy goes beyond that of tortious or criminal conduct. A bargain, the performance of which would require the doing of an immoral or unethical act, would be illegal. There is no simple standard or rule which the court can use as the basis for determining whether or not a bargain is against public policy and illegal. Each case is treated as a separate problem, and the presiding judge has broad discretionary powers in determining the legality of the bargain. The public policy of a nation or state is reflected in its laws and judicial decisions.

Bargains Injurious to Public Service. Any bargain is illegal if it tends to induce a public servant to deviate in any degree from the duty he owes the public. A bargain is illegal if it is a bargain to pay additional compensation to a public servant or if it is a bargain to pay an amount less than the salary provided by law for the performance of the duties of a public office. Any bargain is illegal if it is a bargain by a public officer whereby his personal interests in the matter may conflict with his duty to the public. A person may make his desires regarding legislation known to a member of Congress or a state legislature, but it is illegal to offer a congressman or legislator presents or personal favors to influence his decision on legislative matters. Obviously, a bargain to pay a public servant a bribe is illegal.

Bargains to Influence Fiduciaries. Any bargain is illegal if it tends to induce a fiduciary—trustee, administrator, agent, or partner—to breach his fiduciary duties to his beneficiary or principal. Such a bargain is basically a fraud on the beneficiary or principal. In general, a fiduciary is not permitted to enter into any transactions whereby his personal interests will conflict with his fiduciary duties, unless he makes full disclosure of his interests to his beneficiary or principal and he effectively consents.

Bargains Relieving from Liability for Negligence. The legality of a bargain relieving a person from the consequences of his own negligence depends on the relation of the parties and the nature of the duties owed. As a general rule a bargain whereby one of the parties attempts to provide against liability for his willful negligence or for fraud is illegal. Also, as a general rule a bargain relieving a person from the consequences of his negligence in the performance of a duty owed to the public is illegal. For example, if a common carrier bargains to relieve himself from liability for damage to property while in transit, where such damage results from the negligence of his agents or servants, the bargain is illegal. However, the common carrier may bargain to limit, to a reasonable degree, the amount of damages recoverable for injury to property in transit, where the injury is not due to the willful negligence of his agents or servants, and such a bargain will not be illegal.

If no duty is owed to the public and the parties are bargaining on a fair and equal basis, free from duress and undue influence, a bargain relieving one of the parties from his nonwillful negligence is legal. Property damage and public liability insurance contracts are legal. The objective of such contracts is to protect the insured against his liability for negligent acts.

Bargains in Restraint of Trade.   Bargains in direct restraint of trade are illegal. Any bargain whereby a person, for a consideration, agrees not to compete in trade with another is illegal. If we wish to maintain our free competitive economy, we must permit persons to compete freely. If we enforced bargains not to compete, free competition could be destroyed.

We do permit bargains which restrain trade if the restraint is reasonable and if valid interests are protected by the restraint. For example, if a contract for the sale of a business or for employment contains a provision which provides that the seller or employee will not compete with the buyer or employer, such provision is legal, provided the restraint is reasonable. A bargain in restraint of trade, if it is to be legal, must be a part of a contract—that is, ancillary to the contract—, must be for the purpose of protecting interests created by the contract, and must be no greater than is reasonable to protect those interests. If the contract is an employment contract, the restraint must be limited as to both space and time. As a general rule the restraint in a contract for the sale of a business or other property must be limited as to space but need not be limited as to time. However, under some circumstances the limitation must be as to both space and time.

The courts are not in complete accord as to the rights of the parties to a contract which includes a restraint provision which imposes a greater restraint on a party than is reasonably necessary to protect the interests created by the contract. If the restraint provision is divisible, the courts have, as a general rule, enforced that part of the restraint which is reasonable and refused to enforce that part which is unreasonable. In such cases the controversy is usually whether or not the restraint provision is divisible.

If the restraint provision is indivisible and is greater than is reasonably necessary to protect the interests created by the contract, a majority of the courts hold that the provision is illegal and void in its entirety and that it affords the party no protection. A minority of the courts hold that, even though indivisible in terms, the restraint provision is enforceable for as much of the restraint as would be reasonable.

Bargains to create monopolies and bargains which prevent the free alienation of property are in restraint of trade and are illegal. For example, suppose Arnold sells his farm, Willow Brook, to Bates, and Bates, as a part of the contract of sale, promises never to sell or mortgage Willow Brook. This promise is illegal and void.

Miscellaneous Illegal Bargains. It is impossible to list and discuss all types of bargains which are against public policy and are illegal. Such bargains are limited only by the limitations of the ingenuity of man. Bargains to commit immoral acts, bargains which tend to interfere with marital relations or parental relations, collusive bargains to obtain a divorce, bargains to defraud, bargains which induce the breach of other contracts, and a variety of other bargains, the formation or performance of which would be detrimental to the general welfare, are illegal.

Summary

Bargains opposed to public policy vary so greatly that it is impossible to list them. The public policy of a state or nation is reflected in its constitution, laws, and judicial decisions. In general, any bargain is illegal if its formation or performance will be detrimental to the general welfare. Each case must be decided according to the facts of the case. Bargains are illegal if they tend to induce persons who owe a duty to serve the public to breach their duty to the public. Bargains are illegal if they tend to induce a fiduciary to breach his fiduciary duty to his beneficiary or principal. Bargains relieving a person from liability for his nonwillful negligence are legal, unless the duty of due care is owed to the public and unless the negligence will result in injury to the public.

From an early period, bargains in restraint of trade have been held to be illegal. However, a bargain in restraint of trade is legal if the restraint is ancillary and is no greater than is reasonably necessary to protect the interests created by the principal contract.

Adelson v. Wilson & Co.
398 P.2d 106 (Sup. Ct. Nev. 1965)

This was an action brought by Wilson & Co. (plaintiff) against Mervin and Nathan Adelson as guarantors (defendants). Judgment for Wilson & Co. Reversed on appeal.

Mervin and Nathan Adelson gave two written guarantees of payment to Wilson & Co. for goods sold to Adelson, Inc. The guarantees guaranteed "prompt and punctual payment to Wilson & Co., Inc., of any account now owing from purchaser (Adelson, Inc.) and for all goods, wares and merchandise hereafter sold and delivered by Wilson & Co., Inc., to said purchaser." The guarantee also included the following provision: "The records of Wilson & Co., Inc., shall be conclusive with respect to the amounts, times and places of delivery of any and all merchandise, and the balance due and owing to Wilson & Co., Inc., by said purchaser." Adelson, Inc. defaulted on its accounts owed to Wilson & Co. and the latter sued Mervin and Nathan Adelson on the guarantee.

BADT, JUSTICE.   Wilson & Co. relies on a combination of two circumstances to substantiate evidence of a sale to Adelson, Inc. The first circumstance is the provision in the guaranty which states: "The records of Wilson & Co., Inc. shall be conclusive with respect to the amounts, times and places of delivery of any and all merchandise, and the balance due and owing to Wilson & Co., Inc., by said Purchaser."

We are thus led to the effect of the contract clause as quoted. The authorities seem to be equally divided as to the legal effect of such a clause. Professor Wigmore sees no danger in it. Arnold, in his work on *Suretyship & Guaranty,* and Stearns on *Suretyship* hold such clause to be void as against public policy. The case of *Fidelity & Deposit Co. of Maryland* v. *Davis* adopts the view that an agreement of this nature between the principal and surety is void as against public policy. "A person cannot waive the protection which the law affords. The surety cannot, by his *ex parte* acts, conclusively determine his own cause of action. The courts cannot have rules of law prescribed by acts of the parties."

We are convinced by the reasoning of the Kansas court that the view taken by it is the correct one, and that the clause in question is void on the grounds of public policy.

Feldman v. Stein Building & Lumber Co.
148 N.W.2d 544 (Ct. App. Mich. 1967)

Opal Feldman (plaintiff) brought this action for damages against Stein Building Company (defendant) alleging that Stein, her landlord, negligently allowed snow and ice to accumulate in her apartment house parking lot and that this negligence was the cause of her fall. Feldman appealed from an adverse judgment. Reversed.

The lease Feldman signed contained an exculpatory clause excusing Stein from all liability for injuries suffered by tenants on the premises. The clause specifically excluded liability for injuries caused by ice or snow accumulations.

LESINSKI, CHIEF JUDGE.   Since we find that ice removal is one of the statutory duties imposed by a penal statute, and since Feldman is clearly within the protection thereof, we are brought by this determination to the ultimate issue of this case—the validity of a contractual agreement which would immunize the landlord from liability for breach of this statutory duty.

While affirming the principle of freedom of contract, we note the well-settled rule that where freedom of contract and declared public policy are in conflict, the former necessarily must yield to the latter.

It is relevant to inquire into the background of such legislation. Prior to its passage in New York, several decisions held that a lease clause exempting the landlord from his statutory duty would not enable said landlord to escape liability. However, prior case law had held such clauses valid. The need for a clear-cut statement to resolve this issue was imperative, and the legislation subsequently enacted clarified the intent.

. . . .

In *Eastern Avenue Corporation* v. *Hughes* (1962), the Maryland court of appeals, in upholding an exculpatory clause, listed the jurisdictions which found such exculpatory clauses valid, and followed this listing with the citation of the New York, Massachusetts and Illinois cases which had upheld such provisions as not against public policy, and then concluded with the statement:

"In the latter states the legislatures have subsequently enacted statutes invalidating some types of exculpatory clauses."

In 1964, the Maryland legislature took similar action.

. . . .

We cite 6A *Corbin, Contracts,* § 1515, "Power to Waive or Bargain Away Rights and Defenses Conferred by Statute," p. 728, wherein that eminent authority said:

It is obvious that when a right, a privilege, or a defense is conferred upon an individual by the law, it is conferred upon him because it is believed to be in the public interest to do so. In many such cases it is believed to be contrary to the public interest to permit him to waive or to bargain away the right, privilege, or defense; and when it is so believed the attempted waiver or bargain is inoperative.

In keeping with this philosophy, we hold that the attempted waiver or bargain here is inoperative as against public policy and therefore void.

Moreira Constr. Co., Inc. v. *Moretrench Corp.*
235 A.2d 211 (Super. Ct. App. Div. N.J. 1967)

This was an action by Moreira Construction Co. (plaintiff) against Moretrench Corp. (defendant) to collect damages caused by defective pumps which Moretrench allegedly leased to Moreira. Moretrench counterclaimed for rent due. Judgment for Moreira on both claim and counterclaim and Moretrench appealed. Reversed.

Moreira based its claim upon certain representations and warranties that the pumps leased were in good working order. Moretrench contended that (1) the representations and warranties which Moreira alleged, whether express or implied, "were expressly excluded" by the written contract, and (2) in any event, Moretrench was not liable for any interruption of Moreira's construction operations because the contract provided:

23. The liability of Lessor to Lessee is expressly limited to the free replacement (f.o.b. point of shipment) of any defective part or parts of the equipment furnished under or subsequent to this agreement on receipt by Lessor of said defective part or parts f.o.b. Rockaway, New Jersey, provided such defect is not caused by misuse or neglect on the part of Lessee.

The trial court ruled that a clause of this type is invalid because it is contrary to public policy.

PER CURIAM.   Initially, it should be pointed out that here the contract between the parties consisted of one page. Although Carlos Moreira testified that paragraph 23 was never brought to his attention nor read by him it is clear that, in the absence of fraud, one who does not choose to read a contract before signing it cannot later relieve himself of its burdens.

In *Henningsen* the manufacturer of an automobile gave an express warranty which sought to limit its liability to replacement of defective parts and which disclaimed all other warranties, express and implied. The court held that this provision was violative of public policy. But the underlying factor which led the court to that conclusion was the "gross inequality of bargaining position by the consumer in the automobile industry. . . ."

Unlike *Henningsen,* which dealt with a manufacturer and an ordinary layman, the instant matter deals with two corporations in a commercial setting. Although plaintiff Moreira is obviously a small corporation, its owner has been engaged in the construction business for 18 years.

Furthermore, in *Henningsen* the court noted that the clause in question was a standardized one used throughout the automobile industry, thus leaving the consumer with no alternative but to accept the terms of the contract as stated. In 1958 defendant Moretrench Corp. was the world's largest well point company. However, there was testimony to the effect that there were three competitors of Moretrench in the area and there was no showing that Moreira was precluded from negotiating a contract on more favorable terms.

Exculpatory clauses in apartment house leases also have been held to be invalid because of inequality of bargaining power, but such clauses are normally valid in leases of industrial property since no inequality of bargaining power exists.

Moreira also relies on *Myers* v. *Land,* a case cited in Henningsen. In that case plaintiff purchased from defendant a machine to manufacture concrete blocks. The contract of sale expressly disclaimed any warranties not contained therein and limited defendant's liability to the replacement of defective parts. When the machine failed to manufacture concrete blocks plaintiff instituted an action for the purchase price. The court held that the limitation of liability and disclaimer of warranties did not bar the suit. But the theory upon which the court based its holding is important. It held that the failure of the machine to accomplish the purpose for which it was designed amounted to more than a breach of warranty. Rather, "there has been no delivery of that which was bought." The court said that if defendant's disclaimers could prevent plaintiff from bringing an action for the price, "one would have no recourse where he got an automobile without a motor or wheels." Here Moreira did not allege a total failure of consideration, and it did not seek the return of the rental. It did not claim that the equipment did not work at all but that it worked poorly, particularly during the period from November 7 to November 15, and that the poor performance was due to a defective pump. But Moreira had used the pump continuously from August 1 to November 7, 24 hours a day. His claim was for the costs allegedly incurred because of the idleness of his work force from November 7 to November 15 caused by the failure of the pump to keep the job site free of water. In such an action the rationale of *Myers* does not apply, and paragraph 23 is a bar against such a claim.

Aristocrat Window Co. v. Randell
206 N.E.2d 545 (App. Ct. Ill. 1965)

This was an action for an injunction brought by Aristocrat Window Co. (plaintiff) against Ralph Randell (defendant). Judgment for Aristocrat and Randell appealed. Reversed.

In 1962 Aristocrat entered into a contract of employment with Randell making him a branch manager in charge of the company's operations at Chicago, Illinois. Paragraph VIII of the employment contract read in part as follows:

(b) For a period of five (5) years after the termination of this Agreement, the employee will not, within a radius of three hundred miles from the present place of business of the employer, directly or indirectly, own, manage, operate, control, be employed by, participate in, or be connected in any manner with the ownership, management, operation or control of any business similar to the type of business conducted by employer at the time of the termination of this Agreement.

On March 16, 1963, Aristocrat discharged Randell and later brought this suit to enjoin Randell under the no-competition provision.

SULLIVAN, JUSTICE.   Randell also raised the point that the negative covenant was unreasonable, in restraint of trade and against public policy. We deem it advisable to discuss this point. The negative covenant restricts the employee from future competition within 300 miles of the "present place of business of the employer for a period of five years." Whether a restriction from engaging in a particular business is reasonable, under all the circumstances of the case and is not in general restraint of trade or against public policy, is a question to be determined by the court under the particular facts of the case.

In *Hursen* v. *Gavin,* the court said:

A contract in restraint of trade is thus total and general, when by it a party binds himself not to carry on his trade or business at all, or not to pursue it within the limits of a particular country or state. Such a general contract in restraint of trade necessarily works an injury to the public at large, and to the party himself in the respects indicated, and is therefore against public policy.

By restricting the defendant Randell from engaging in his employment within 300 miles of the north side Chicago branch, the restrictive covenant included the major portion of the area of the state of Illinois, as well as parts of Iowa, Wisconsin, Indiana, and Michigan. Under the facts in this case the 300 mile limitation in the contract is unreasonable, against public policy and the contract therefore is unenforceable.

Effect of Illegality

General Rule. As a general rule a court will not enforce an illegal bargain but will leave the parties where it finds them. They cannot recover damages for breach of the illegal promises, cannot recover consideration from which they have parted, and cannot recover in quasi contract for benefits conferred. The courts do not follow this rule as a means of punishing one of the parties, but for the reason that the results obtained thereby best serve the interests of the public. If the facts and circumstances are such that the interests of the public are best served by allowing a recovery, such recovery as will best serve the interests of the public will be granted.

Ignorance of Fact or Special Regulation. Even though ignorance is, as a general rule, no excuse, the courts have, in exceptional cases, granted recovery to a party to an illegal bargain if the party has been ignorant of the facts which made the bargain illegal, provided the other party had knowledge of the illegality and provided the illegality does not involve moral turpitude. If both parties are ignorant of the facts which make the bargain illegal, the courts have, in some cases, permitted the parties to recover for performance rendered before they learned of the illegal nature of the bargain. In no case will the courts allow recovery for performance rendered after knowledge of the illegality.

In cases in which one of the parties is ignorant of a special statutory regulation of the other's business and of the violation thereof, the courts will allow recovery for performance rendered by the innocent party before he learns of the illegality. For example, suppose Alberts, an actor, contracts to perform for Bates, the operator of a theater. Bates has not obtained a license to operate the theater as required by a penal regulatory statute. Alberts, in ignorance of the violation of the statute by Bates, performs his part of the bargain. Alberts can recover the compensation promised by Bates.

Rights of Protected Parties. Most regulatory statutes have as their objective the protection of the public. As a general rule, if a bargain is entered into by a person who is guilty of the violation of a regulatory statute with another for whose protection the statute was adopted, such bargain will be declared void as to the party violating the statute but enforceable by the protected party. For example, suppose a foreign corporation does intrastate business in a state without obtaining a license, and the laws of the state expressly provide that the contracts of an unlicensed foreign corporation doing intrastate business in the state shall be void. The corporation, in such a case, cannot enforce a contract made by it while unlicensed, but the other party to the contract can enforce it against the corporation.

If the parties to an illegal bargain are not equally guilty but one of the parties has been induced to enter into the bargain by the other party, the courts will grant recovery to the less guilty person. For example, suppose a confidence man induces his victim to enter into a bargain which is illegal as a means of defrauding him. The victim can recover what he has parted with, unless the illegal act involved moral turpitude.

Knowledge of Illegal Use. Knowledge that an article sold will be used for an illegal purpose will not make the sale illegal, unless the use to be made of the article is a serious crime. If an article is sold or money is loaned for the purpose of aiding in the commission of a crime, the sale or the loan is illegal, and the party making the sale or the loan cannot recover the sale price of the article or the money loaned. For example, if Alberts loans Bates $50 knowing that Bates intends to play cards for money that evening, Alberts can recover a judgment for the $50 loaned. However, if Bates is at the card table gambling and Alberts loans Bates $50 to enable Bates to continue his gambling, the loan is illegal, and Alberts cannot recover a judgment for the $50 loaned.

Divisible Contracts. If part of a bargain is legal and part is illegal, the courts will enforce the legal part if the legal can be separated from the illegal. But if the bargain is an indivisible bargain and part of it is illegal, the illegal part will taint the entire bargain, and the whole will be void.

A contract is divisible when it consists of several promises or acts on the part of one party and each promise or act is matched by a corresponding promise or act on the part of the other party so that there is a separate consideration for each promise or act.

If a provision in a contract is illegal but the illegal provision does not affect the principal purpose of the contract, the principal portion will be enforced but the illegal provision will not. For example, suppose Alberts sells his barber shop to Bates. The contract of sale provides that Alberts will not engage in barbering during the remainder of his life. The restraint provision is illegal, but the sales contract, except the restraint provision, will be enforced.

Rescission before Performance of Illegal Act. If one of the parties to an illegal contract rescinds the contract before the performance of the illegal act, he may recover any consideration he has given. If a party to a bet gives notice of withdrawal and demands the return of his money before the stakeholder has paid it over, he can recover his money. However, if a stakeholder refuses to pay to the winner the money which has been bet, the winner can recover the money from him. The statutes of some states provide that one who has lost money gambling can recover it.

Summary

As a general rule, if parties have entered into an illegal bargain, neither can recover a judgment if the other party fails to fulfill his promises. No recovery is granted in quasi contract for the benefits conferred in the fulfillment of an illegal bargain. If the parties are not equally at fault, the courts may, if the circumstances demand it, grant one-party relief.

If one party is justifiably ignorant of the facts which make the bargain illegal or is ignorant of a special regulation, he may recover for consideration given. Also, the party protected by a regulatory statute may recover for breach of a contract entered into with a person who has not complied with the provisions of the statute.

As a general rule, knowledge that an article sold will be used illegally does not make the sale illegal, but if the use intended is the commission of a serious crime, the sale is illegal. Also, if the sale is for the purpose of aiding in the commission of a crime, it is illegal.

If a bargain is divisible and part is legal and part is illegal, the courts will enforce the legal parts and not the illegal parts, unless the illegal parts go to the principal objective of the contract. If the bargain is indivisible and part is illegal, the entire bargain is void. A party may rescind an executory illegal bargain before the performance of the illegal act and recover any consideration given.

United States v. Acme Process Equipment Co.
385 U.S. 158 (U.S. Sup. Ct. 1966)

Acme Process Equipment Company (plaintiff) brought this action against the United States (defendant) in the Court of Claims to recover damages for breach of a contract under which Acme undertook through itself and subcontractors to manufacture 2,751 75-mm. recoilless rifles for about $337 per rifle. Among other defenses, the United States alleged that it had rightfully cancelled its contract with Acme because three of Acme's principal employees had accepted compensation for awarding subcontracts in violation of the Anti-Kickback Act. The Court of Claims found, as facts, that the kickbacks had been paid as alleged and that this was the ground on which the United States had cancelled the prime contract with Acme, but construed the Act as not authorizing the cancellation. Reversed.

BLACK, JUSTICE. The Anti-Kickback Act, as originally passed in 1946 and as amended in 1960, provides two express sanctions for its violation: (1) fine or imprisonment for one who makes or receives a kickback, and (2) recovery of the kickback by the United States. The Court of Claims held, and it is argued here, that had Congress wanted "to provide the additional remedy of contract annulment, it could have done so" by express language, and of course it could have. But the fact that it did not see fit to provide for such a remedy by express language does not end the matter. The Anti-Kickback Act not only "prohibited" such payments, but clearly expressed a policy decidedly hostile to them. They were recognized as devices hurtful to the Government's procurement practices. Extra expenditures to get subcontracts necessarily add to government costs in cost-plus-a-fixed-fee and other cost reimbursable contracts. And this is also true where the prime contract is a negotiated fixed-price contract with a price redetermination clause, such as this prime contract is here. The kickbacks here are passed onto the Government in two stages. The prime contractor rarely submits his bid until after he has tentatively lined up his subcontractors. Indeed, as here, the subcontractors frequently participate in negotiation of the prime contract. The subcontractor's tentative bid will, of course, reflect the amount he contemplates paying as a kickback, and then his inflated bid will be reflected in the prime contractor's bid to the Government. At the renegotiation stage, where the prime contractor's actual cost experience is the basis for price redetermination, any kickbacks, paid by subcontractors and passed onto the prime contractor after the prime contract is awarded, will be passed onto the Government in the form of price redetermination upward.

Acme argues, however, that the express provision for recovery of kickbacks is enough to protect the Government from increased costs attributable to them. But this argument rests on two false assumptions. The first is that kickbacks can easily be detected and recovered. This is hardly the case. Kickbacks being made criminal means that they must be made—if at all—in secrecy. Though they necessarily inflate the price to the Government, this inflation is rarely detectable. This is particularly true as regards defense contracts where the products involved are not usually found on the commercial market and where there may not be effective competition. Such contracts are generally negotiated and awarded without formal advertising and competitive bidding, and there is often no opportunity to compare going prices with the price negotiated by the Government. Kickbacks will usually not be discovered, if at all, until after the prime contract is let. The second false assumption underlying Acme's argument is that the increased cost to the Government is necessarily equal to the amount of the kickback which is recoverable. Of course, a subcontractor who must pay a kickback is likely to include the amount of the kickback in his contract price. But this is not all. A subcontractor who anticipates obtaining a subcontract by virtue of a kickback has little incentive to stint on his cost estimates. Since he plans to obtain the subcontract without regard to the economic merits of his proposal, he will be tempted to inflate that proposal by more than the amount of the kickback. And even if the Government could isolate and recover the inflation attributable to the kickback, it would still be saddled with a subcontractor who, having obtained the job other than on merit, is perhaps entirely unreliable in other ways. This unreliability in turn undermines the security of the prime contractor's performance—a result which the public cannot tolerate, especially where, as here, important defense contracts are involved.

In *United States* v. *Mississippi Valley Co.* the Court recognized that "a statute frequently implies that a contract is not to be enforced when it arises out of circumstances that would lead enforcement to offend the essential purpose of the enactment." The Court there approved the cancellation of a government contract for violation of the conflict-of-interest statute on the ground that "the sanction of nonenforcement is consistent with and essential to effectuating the public policy embodied in" the statute. We think the same thing can be said about cancellation here.

Wilson v. Stearns
267 P.2d 59 (Dist. Ct. App. Calif. 1954)

This was an action by Wilson (plaintiff) against Stearns (defendant) to recover commissions. Judgment for Stearns and Wilson appealed. Reversed.

Wilson and Stearns entered into a contract with no specific termination date providing that Wilson was to sell real estate for Stearns in return for a percentage of the sale price. Wilson and his three employees proceeded to sell 85 houses for Stearns amounting to $671,900. The percentage earned by Wilson under the contract amounted to $17,089.06. Stearns refused to pay Wilson any commissions and when sued by Wilson, Stearns set up as a defense that Wilson had no license as a real estate broker.

WHITE, PRESIDING JUSTICE. As his first ground for reversal Wilson earnestly contends that in view of the findings of the court that he performed every service required of him by the contract in question; that George Stearns has received full benefit therefrom which he has retained, the conclusions arrived at by the court that Wilson was not entitled to recover because of the provisions of section 10176(f) of the Business and Professions Code was erroneous.

Insofar as here material, the code section in question provides:

Sec. 10176. The commissioner may, upon his own motion, and shall upon the verified complaint in writing of any person, investigate the actions of any person engaged in the business or acting in the capacity of a real estate licensee within this State, and he may temporarily suspend or permanently revoke a real estate license at any time where the licensee within the immediately preceding three years, while a real estate licensee, in performing or attempting to perform any of the acts within the scope of this chapter has been guilty of any of the following:

. . . (f) The practice of claiming, demanding, or receiving a fee, compensation or commission under any exclusive agreement authorizing or employing a licensee to sell, buy or exchange real estate for compensation or commission *where such agreement does not contain a definite, specified date of final and complete termination.* (Emphasis added.)

Stearns's contention is that a contract made contrary to the terms of the law designed for the protection of the public and prescribing a penalty for the violation thereof, is illegal and void, and that no action may be brought to enforce such a contract. Undoubtedly, the general rule in this state is that when it appears there is a violation of such a statute, the prescribed penalty contained therein is the equivalent of an express prohibition and, that a contract made contrary to the terms thereof is void.

The trial judge was in accord with our view of the legislative intent as evidenced by the language contained in his "Memorandum and Order for Judgment," as follows:

In enacting this section (§ 10176, Business and Professions Code), I think the evil which the legislature had in mind was the practice of some brokers to obtain contracts which placed themselves in a position to claim commissions for an indefinite time without performing any services, nor, perhaps ever intending to. It is difficult to see what evil there is in claiming or recovering commissions where, as in this case, valuable, timely and lawful services are rendered to the satisfaction of the seller, the seller claims no prejudice from the fact that the agency was exclusive or that the termination date was indefinite and there is no evidence that the broker ever before claimed a commission under or entered into such a contract.

A mere reading of the statute at once suggests that it is aimed at fraudulent or dishonest conduct by real estate brokers who engage in, *"The practice* of claiming, demanding, or receiving a fee, compensation or commission under any exclusive agreement . . . where such agreement does not contain a definite, specified, date of final and complete termination."

As was said by the trial judge and borne out by the record, there is not a scintilla of evidence that Wilson was engaged in the "practice" denounced by the statute. In truth and in fact, the evidence shows that this was the first tract sold by Wilson and that he had no previous experience in tract selling.

We are disposed to apply the rule announced in the case of *Norwood v. Judd,* wherein the court said:

The rule that the courts will not lend their aid to the enforcement of an illegal agreement or one against public policy is fundamentally sound. The rule was conceived for the purposes of protecting the public and the courts from imposition. It is a rule predicated upon sound public policy. But the courts should not be so enamored with the Latin phrase *'in pari delicto'* that they blindly extend the rule to every case where illegality appears somewhere in the transaction. The fundamental purpose of the rule must always be kept in mind, the realities of the situation must be considered. *Where, by applying the rule, the public cannot be protected because the transaction has been completed, where no serious moral turpitude is involved, where the defendant is the one guilty of the greatest moral fault, and where to apply the rule will be to permit the defendant to be unjustly enriched at the expense of the plaintiff, the rule should not be applied.* (Emphasis added.)

Unenforceable Contracts and the Uniform Commercial Code

Unconscionability. The court may refuse to enforce an unconscionable contract or an unconscionable clause in a contract for the sale of goods. The Code (2–302) provides:

(1) If the court as a matter of law finds the contract or any clause of the contract to have been unconscionable at the time it was made the court may refuse to enforce the contract, or it may enforce the remainder of the contract without the unconscionable clause, or it may so limit the application of the unconscionable clause as to avoid any unconscionable result.

(2) When it is claimed or appears to the court that the contract or any clause thereof may be unconscionable the parties shall be afforded a reasonable opportunity to present evidence as to its commercial setting, purpose and effect to aid the court in making the determination.

An unconscionable contract is one in which one of the parties being in a strategic position takes advantage of the situation and drives a bargain which is unfair and commercially unreasonable. In the past this concept has been applied in equity in that a court will not grant specific performance of an unconscionable contract. The expanded concept does not require that the situation involve fraud, duress, or undue influence although elements of fraud and duress frequently are present. The following illustrate some of the situations where various courts have applied Section 2–302 as a basis for denying enforcement of certain contract provisions.

1. Small print on the back of signature cards prepared by banks which waived the depositor's right to a jury trial in the event of litigation.[2]
2. A clause in a home improvement contract between a Maine corporation and a Massachusetts citizen which stipulated the New York law would apply.[3]
3. A clause disclaiming all liability on warranties where the goods were found to be worthless.[4]
4. Excessively high prices or excessive credit charges.[5]

Additional examples of the application of the "unconscionable" concept are discussed in the case which follows.

Summary

The court may find that a contract any part of it to be unconscionable and unenforceable as a matter of law. To be unconscionable a clause must be unfair and commercially unreasonable at the time of making of the contract. The principle is prevention of oppression and unfair surprise. The court may enforce the contract in part or limit the application of any unconscionable clause so as to avoid an unconscionable result.

Williams v. Walker-Thomas Furniture Co.
350 F.2d 145 (D.C. Cir. 1965)

Walker-Thomas Furniture Co. (plaintiff) brought these two separate actions (consolidated for purposes of appellate review) against Williams (defendant) to

---

[2] *David* v. *Manufacturers Hanover Trust Co.,* 4 U.C.C. Rep. 1145 (N.Y. Civ. Ct. 1968).
[3] *Paragon Homes, Inc.* v. *Carter,* 4 U.C.C. Rep. 1144 (N.Y. Sup. Ct. 1968).
[4] *Vlases* v. *Montgomery Ward & Co., Inc.,* 377 F.2d 846 (3rd Cir. 1967).
[5] *Central Budget Corp.* v. *Sanchez,* 279 N.Y.2d 391 (N.Y. Civ. Ct. 1967).

repossess certain furniture sold on credit. Judgment for Furniture Co. and Williams appealed. Reversed.

Furniture Co. operated a retail furniture store in the District of Columbia. During the period from 1957 to 1962, Williams purchased a number of household items from Furniture Co., for which payment was to be made in installments. The terms of each purchase were contained in a printed form contract which set forth the value of the purchased item and purported to lease the item to the customer for a stipulated monthly rent payment. The contract then provided that title would remain in Furniture Co. until the total of all the monthly payments made equaled the stated value of the item, at which time the customers could take title. In the event of a default in the payment of any monthly installment, Furniture Co. could repossess the item.

The contract further provided that

the amount of each periodical installment payment to be made by [purchaser] to the Company under this present lease shall be inclusive of and not in addition to the amount of each installment payment to be made by [purchaser] under such prior leases, bills or accounts; *and all payments now and hereafter made by [purchaser] shall be credited pro rata on all outstanding leases, bills and accounts* due the Company by [purchaser] at the time each such payment is made. (Emphasis added.)

The effect of this rather obscure provision was to keep a balance due on every item until the balance due on all items, whenever purchased, was liquidated. As a result, the debt incurred at the time of purchase of each item was secured by the right to repossess all the items previously purchased by the same purchaser, and each new item purchased automatically became subject to a security interest arising out of the previous dealings.

On April 17, 1962, Williams bought a stereo set of stated value of $514.95.[6] She defaulted shortly thereafter, and Walker-Thomas sought to replevy all the items purchased since December, 1957.

WRIGHT, CIRCUIT JUDGE. Williams' principal contention, rejected by both the trial and the appellate courts below, is that these contracts, or at least some of them are unconscionable and, hence, not enforceable. In its opinion the District of Columbia Court of Appeals explained its rejection of this contention as follows:

Williams' second argument presents a more serious question. The record reveals that prior to the last purchase appellant had reduced the balance in her account to $164. The last purchase, a stereo set, raised the balance due to $678. Significantly, at the time of this and the preceding purchases, Furniture Co. was aware of Williams' financial position. The reverse side of the stereo contract listed the name of Williams' social worker and her $218 monthly stipend from the government. Nevertheless, with full knowledge that Williams had to feed, clothe and support both herself and seven children on this amount, Furniture Co. sold her a $514 stereo set.

---

[6] At the time of this purchase her account showed a balance of $164 still owing from her prior purchases. The total of all the purchases made over the years in question came to $1,800. The total payments amounted to $1,400.

We cannot condemn too strongly Furniture Co.'s conduct. It raises serious questions of sharp practice and irresponsible business dealings. A review of the legislation in the District of Columbia affecting retail sales and the pertinent decisions of the highest court in this jurisdiction disclose, however, no ground upon which this court can declare the contracts in question contrary to public policy. We note that were the Maryland Retail Installment Sales Act, Art 83 §§ 128–153, or its equivalent, in force in the District of Columbia, we could grant appellant appropriate relief. We think Congress should consider corrective legislation to protect the public from such exploitive contracts as were utilized in the case at bar.

We do not agree that the court lacked the power to refuse enforcement to contracts found to be unconscionable. In other jurisdictions, it has been held as a matter of common law that unconscionable contracts are not enforceable. While no decision of this court so holding has been found, the notion that an unconscionable bargain should not be given full enforcement is by no means novel.

Congress has recently enacted the Uniform Commercial Code, which specifically provides that the court may refuse to enforce a contract which it finds to be unconscionable at the time it was made. The enactment of this section, which occurred subsequent to the contracts here in suit, does not mean that the common law of the District of Columbia was otherwise at the time of enactment, nor does it preclude the court from adopting a similar rule in the exercise of its powers to develop the common law for the District of Columbia. In fact, in view of the absence of prior authority on the point, we consider the congressional adoption of § 2–302 persuasive authority for following the rationale of the cases from which the section is explicitly derived. Accordingly, we hold that where the element of unconscionability is present at the time a contract is made, the contract should not be enforced.

Unconscionability has generally been recognized to include an absence of meaningful choice on the part of one of the parties together with contract terms which are unreasonably favorable to the other party. Whether a meaningful choice is present in a particular case can only be determined by consideration of all the circumstances surrounding the transaction. In many cases the meaningfulness of the choice is negated by a gross inequality of bargaining power. The manner in which the contract was entered is also relevant to this consideration. Did each party to the contract, considering his obvious education or lack of it, have a reasonable opportunity to understand the terms of the contract, or were the important terms hidden in a maze of fine print and minimized by deceptive sales practices? Ordinarily, one who signs an agreement without full knowledge of its terms might be held to assume the risk that he has entered a one-sided bargain. But when a party of little bargaining power, and hence little real choice, signs a commercially unreasonable contract with little or no knowledge of its terms, it is hardly likely that his consent, or even an objective manifestation of his consent, was ever given to all the terms. In such a case the usual rule that the terms of the agreement are not to be questioned should be abandoned and the court should consider whether the terms of the contract are so unfair that enforcement should be withheld.

In determining reasonableness or fairness, the primary concern must be with the terms of the contract considered in light of the circumstances existing when the contract was made. The test is not simple, nor can it be mechanically applied. The terms are to be considered "in the light of the general commercial background and the commercial needs of the particular trade or case." Corbin suggests the test as being whether the terms are "so extreme as to appear unconscionable according to the mores and business practices of the time and place." We think this formulation correctly states the test to be applied in those cases where no meaningful choice was exercised upon entering the contract.

Problem Cases

1. Thomas owned a farm on which there were some improvements, including a barn. Thomas leased the farm to Story. Story and Owens entered into a contract for the remodeling of the barn. Owens furnished the materials and performed the labor. The remodeling consisted of building in the barn an amphitheater with partition, bleachers, and pits. After the barn was remodeled Story used it to stage chicken fights. The conducting of chicken fights was a crime in the state. Story did not pay Owens for his work and materials, and Owens filed a mechanic's lien against the premises and brought this action to foreclose the lien and to recover a judgment for the amount owing to him. Story and Thomas set up illegality as a defense. Can Owens recover?

2. Harris, Upham and Company was a co-partnership engaged in the brokerage business and was a member of the New Orleans Cotton Exchange. Dr. Kahn authorized Harris, Upham and Company to buy for his account cotton contracts. A cotton contract is 100 bales or 50,000 pounds of cotton.

   On October 15 and 16, 1946, Harris, Upham and Company purchased on the New Orleans Cotton Exchange seven cotton contracts at prices ranging from 36.25 to 38.47 cents per pound. The cotton contracts were for December delivery. Dr. Kahn paid $3,000 of the purchase price but failed to pay the balance. After due notice, Harris, Upham and Company resold the cotton on October 17 and 21 at prices ranging from 35.89 to 32.60 cents per pound. Dr. Kahn refused to pay Harris, Upham and Company their brokerage fee and the loss sustained on the cotton contracts, and Harris, Upham and Company brought this suit. Dr. Kahn set up that he never intended to take delivery of the cotton, but only to pay differences based on the fluctuations in the market, and that the contract was a gambling contract and void. Is this a good defense?

3. A state statute reads in part as follows: "No contractor [as defined in this act] shall act as agent or bring or maintain any action in any court of the state for the collection of compensation for the performance of any act for which a license is required by this act without alleging and proving that such contractor was a duly licensed contractor at the time the alleged cause of action arose." Northern contracted to furnish material and perform labor for Elledge on a cost plus building contract. At the time of the contract Northern had a valid contractor's license. This license, however, expired before the contract was completed. Elledge refused to pay the agreed price. May Northern recover the agreed price in an action against Elledge?

4. Le Roy owned and operated a grocery store on Jackson Street, in Seattle. He made application to the Washington State Liquor Control Board for a license to sell beer, and paid $60 license fee; the license was denied and the license fee returned.

   Sinnar, a business machinery operator, told Le Roy that he knew someone at the license bureau and would arrange a license for $450. Le Roy paid Sinnar the $450 but never received the license. Le Roy sued Sinnar to recover the $450. Sinnar did not plead illegality as a defense and the trial court ruled in favor of Le Roy. Sinnar appealed and now seeks to raise the defense of illegality. Can Sinnar win?

5. Somerset owned and operated a business located in the city of Columbia. Somerset sold at retail silver, china, crystal, jewelry, and related articles. Ninety-five percent of his sales were in the area of Greater Columbia. He sold at discount to four or five florist shops in the lower part of the state which handled merchandise for brides. Somerset sold his business to Reyner. The sales agreement included a restrictive clause whereby Somerset agreed not to engage in a similar business in the state of South Carolina. At the time of the sale Somerset stated that he had no intention of reentering the business and told them they could include the entire state in the restrictive provision if they wished. Somerset now brings suit asking that the restrictive provision be declared void as being against public policy. Should Somerset's request be granted?

6. The Kuzmiaks were tenants of Brookchester, Inc. The lease included an exculpatory clause releasing the landlord from liability to the tenant for a large number of defaults on the part of the landlord including ". . . nor shall the landlord be liable for any latent defect in the building," and a broad general provision relieving the landlord or his agents or employees. Mrs. Kuzmiak fell down the stairway in the apartment and was injured. She contended that her fall was caused by a defect in the construction of the stairway and by the landlord's negligence in the care and maintenance of the stairway. Brookchester, Inc., set up the exculpatory clause in the lease as a defense. Is this a good defense?

7. Campbell Soup Company entered into a written contract with Wentz, a local farmer. Briefly summarized, the contract provided that Wentz would sell to Campbell all of the Chantenay carrots to be grown on Wentz's farm during the coming season. The contract contained many provisions most of which were drafted with the buyer's interest in mind. For example, Campbell's determination of conformance with specifications was to be conclusive; Campbell had the right to refuse carrots in excess of 12 tons to the acre; Wentz agreed not to sell carrots to anyone else without Campbell's approval; liquidated damages to the extent of $50 per acre for any breach by Wentz; and, under certain circumstances Campbell was excused from accepting carrots.

   The contract price for January was $30 a ton; the market price at that time was at least $90 a ton. Wentz sold approximately 62 tons of his carrots on the open market. Campbell enters a court of equity seeking equitable relief in the form of specific performance. Should a court of equity enjoin Wentz from selling his carrots on the open market?

8. Cataline entered into a conditional sales contract with O. K. Used Car Co. for the purchase of an automobile. Cataline later learned that the interest rate under the terms of the contract exceeded that allowed by state law and instituted an action to rescind (cancel) the contract for usury. As a defense O. K. Used Car asserts that the excess interest resulted from the mistaken use of the wrong interest rate in computing the payments under the contract. O. K. contends that the court should order

that the excess interest be remitted to Cataline and the complaint dismissed. Should the court rescind the contract?

9. Robins and Girardi, former employees of Magic Fingers, Inc., while employed by it signed an employment contract which provided that "for a period of three years after the termination of your employment with the Company for any cause, you will not directly or indirectly engage in any business which shall be in competition with the business of the Company." Robins and Girardi left Magic Fingers, Inc., and went with a corporation operating and selling in the same territory as Magic Fingers, Inc.

    Magic Fingers, Inc., brought this action asking that Robins and Girardi be enjoined from the violation of the postemployment restrictive covenant. They contend that the restrictive covenant, since it does not limit the territory in which they may work, is against public policy and illegal. Is this contention valid?

10. John Fox was employed by Rent-A-Car Systems, Inc. Under a contract which provided for a stock purchase option agreement and stipulated that Fox would "not engage in competition with Rent-A-Car Systems in any phase of the vehicle rental or leasing business or any other business in which the employee is engaged at the time of the termination of his employment with the employer for a period of two years after the termination date in any city in the United States wherein the employee was engaged in such business." Fox was employed by Rent-A-Car in the city of Atlanta where, shortly after acceptance by Fox of the Stock Purchase Option Agreement, he resigned and became executive vice president of General Truck Lease, Inc., located within the city of Atlanta. Is Rent-A-Car entitled to obtain an injunction to prevent Fox from becoming vice president of General Truck Lease, Inc.?

11. Georges, a local dry cleaners business, placed an order with the Telephone Company for an advertisement in the yellow pages of the directory. This order was merely a repeat of the text and content of an ad placed by Georges in a previous telephone directory of the same company. The Telephone Company made an error in printing the new book and listed an incorrect number for Georges' firm. The contract for the ad contained the following provision:

    In the case of error or in the case of omission of any item of advertising by the Telephone Company the extent of the Telephone Company's liability shall be limited to a pro rata abatement of the charge paid to the Telephone Company as the error or omission may affect the entire advertising item.

Georges sued Telephone Company claiming a substantial loss of profits due to omission of his ad. Should a motion to dismiss made by Telephone Company be granted?

12. Davis was employed by Bookkeepers Business Service, Inc., under a contract which in part provided that in the event of the termination of employment, the employee shall not for a period of two years canvass, solicit, or accept business of the employer's clients. Davis decided to quit Bookkeepers and to go into business for himself. Davis solicited several corporate accounts, which had been but no longer were affiliated with Bookkeepers Business Service. Bookkeepers filed a suit against Davis, endeavoring to obtain a preliminary injunction restraining him from violating the employment contract. Should the court grant such an injunction?

13. Lumber Co. entered into a contract with Johnson whereby it was to prepare the plans and specifications for a nursing home. If Johnson purchased all of the materials used in the construction of the home from Lumber Co. no charge was to be made for the preparation of the plans and specifications, otherwise Johnson was to pay it $1,000

for such services. Lumber Co. did not have an architect's license and it did not have an architect in its employ. In defense to a suit brought by Lumber Co. for its services in preparing the plans and specifications, Johnson set up illegality. Is this a good defense?

14. The Otis Elevator Company installed a passenger elevator in the Oil Exchange Building, a five-story, general office building and contracted to "repair, inspect, examine, clean, and lubricate it twice each month and to keep it in a safe condition as a passenger elevator." The contract contained a provision relieving Otis Elevator Company from all liability for injuries resulting from defects in the elevator and from the negligence of its officers, agents, servants and employees in the maintenance of the elevator. As the result of the failure of Otis Elevator Company to use due care in keeping the elevator in working order, the elevator fell from the third floor to the basement, injuring the passengers. Suit was brought against Otis Elevator Company to recover damages for the personal injuries suffered by the passengers and it set up as a defense the clause in the contract relieving it from liability for negligence. Is Otis Elevator Company liable?

15. Dias owned a two-story building which he wished remodeled. Houston was a building contractor. Dias and Houston entered into a contract by the terms of which Houston agreed to remodel the building for $4,000. Before the work was completed Dias and Houston had a dispute and Houston refused to complete the work. Dias engaged another contractor to complete the work and brought suit to recover a judgment against Houston for the damages resulting from his breach of the contract. After Houston quit the job, Dias discovered that Houston did not have a contractor's license. Houston set up as a defense that since he was unlicensed, the contract was void. Is this a good defense?

chapter 12. Writing

Statute of Frauds

Introduction. At common law a writing was not essential to the validity of an informal contract, and the same is true today. In England during the 17th century, and for a long period thereafter, any person having an interest in the outcome of a court action was disqualified as a witness and could not testify in the case. Most transactions between persons during this period were oral, since relatively few people could write; as a consequence, if a controversy arose wherein the rights of the parties were litigated, the parties in interest had to prove their case by the testimony of disinterested third-party witnesses. In many cases the only parties having knowledge of the facts of the case were the parties in interest, and since they were disqualified as witnesses, it was impossible for them to prove their case. As a result of such a condition the practice of offering perjured evidence grew up. This practice, together with other fraudulent practices, became so common that parliament found it necessary to pass laws aimed at correcting the existing abuses. These laws were comprehensive in their scope and included provisions regulating the making of wills, the creation of trusts involving real estate, and the enforceability of informal contracts.

These laws were enacted in 1677, and the statute embodying them was entitled "A Statute for the Prevention of Frauds and Perjuries" (29 Car. II, c. 3), popularly known as the Statute of Frauds. The principal means of accomplishing the desired reforms was by requiring written proof of an agreement and by denying the courts, in the absence of such written proof, the right to enforce the agreement. The statute defined five classes of contracts and provided that no action should be brought to enforce such contract unless it was evidenced by some note or memorandum in writing. In the United States the

243

several states have enacted statutes of frauds which have the same objective as the original English statute. These statutes are not uniform in their provisions, but they do follow the general pattern of the English statute.

Provisions of Statute of Frauds. We are interested only in those provisions of the statute of frauds which define certain classes of contracts and declare such to be unenforceable unless evidenced by a writing. The following are the classes of contracts generally included in the statute of frauds: (1) contracts by an executor or administrator to be answerable from his own estate for a duty of the decedent's estate; (2) contracts with an obligee to answer to him for the debt, default, or miscarriage of his obligor; (3) contracts in which the consideration is marriage or a promise to marry, except contracts consisting only of mutual promises by two persons to marry each other; (4) contracts for sale of an interest in land; (5) bilateral contracts, so long as they are not fully performed by either party, which are not capable of performance within a year from the time of their formation; and (6) contracts for the sale of goods or choses in action of a value above an amount variously fixed by the statutes of the several states.

In addition to these classes of contracts, the statutes of a substantial number of states require (1) a promise to pay a debt barred by the statute of limitations or by a discharge in bankruptcy and (2) a contract to pay a commission for the sale of real estate to be evidenced by a note or memorandum in writing and signed by the party to be bound thereby or his duly authorized agent.

Interpretation of Statute of Frauds. The common-law courts took an antagonistic attitude toward legislation which changed the existing common law. The rule of interpretation adopted was that any statute in derogation of the common law would be strictly construed, that is, it would be given no greater scope than a technical interpretation of the language of the statute demanded. This rule was applied in interpreting the statute of frauds; and as a result, many cases have been brought which have required the courts to determine whether the particular contract came within one of the defined classes and was unenforceable for the lack of the required note or memorandum. The Uniform Commercial Code provides "This Act shall be liberally construed and applied to promote its underlying purposes and policies." (Sec. 1–102.) This section of the Code controls the construction of the statute of frauds provisions of the Code.

Scope of the Statute of Frauds. The statute of frauds applies only to informal contracts. Consequently, before any question of its provisions; it merely makes it unenforceable. If one of the parties to the oral contract has performed, thereby conferring benefits on the other contracting party, and his right of action is barred by the statute, he can recover in quasi contract for the benefits conferred, and under special circumstances a court of equity will hold that part performance will justify the court in decreeing performance of the contract.

The statute of frauds of some states provides that the contract, unless evidenced by the required writing, is void. In most cases, however, the courts have interpreted the statute to mean that the contract will be unenforceable, not void.

Summary

The English parliament, in 1677, enacted a "Statute for the Prevention of Frauds and Perjuries," which provided that no action could be brought to enforce defined classes of informal contracts unless they were evidenced by a note or memorandum in writing signed by the party to be bound. The several states have enacted statutes which follow the general pattern of the English statute, but they are not uniform in their provisions. The statute of frauds provisions of the Uniform Commercial Code will bring about some changes in the statute of frauds of those states adopting the Code.

The courts have given a strict interpretation to these statutes. The parties must have entered into a valid contract before the statute of frauds applies. The statute makes an oral contract which falls within one of the defined classes unenforceable, not illegal.

Collateral Contracts

Nature of Collateral Contracts. A collateral or secondary contract is one made with an obligee (promisee) in which a third person promises to pay the debt, default, or miscarriage of the obligor (promisor) in the event the obligor fails to perform that duty. Since a contract by an executor or administrator to be answerable from his own estate for a duty of the decedent's estate is, under most circumstances, a collateral contract, we shall not discuss such contracts as a separate class.

Whether a contract is an original or a collateral contract is primarily a question of the intention of the parties. One must analyze the transaction and from the language used, the relation of the parties, and all the surrounding circumstances determine whether the obligor has contracted to perform in all events or only in the event that some other person fails to perform the duty owed to the obligee.

Original Contracts. Often a three-party transaction may appear to include a collateral contract—that is, a contract to answer for the debt, default, or miscarriage of another—when, in fact, it will include only an original contract. The following are examples of some such transactions:

1. Clark orders from Able flowers to be sent to Brown, Clark promising to pay Able for the flowers. The contract between Clark and Able is an original contract. The fact that Brown receives the consideration given in no way affects the character of the contract.

2. Clark has funds in his possession which he is administering for the benefit of Brown. Able sells a suit to Brown in reliance on Clark's contract to pay for the suit out of the funds which Clark is administering for the benefit of Brown if Brown does not pay for it. The contract between Able and Clark is an original contract. Clark is not obligating his own estate but is promising to use funds available for that purpose to discharge a debt owed by Brown.

3. Brown owns an automobile. Clark enters into a contract with Brown whereby Clark contracts to pay to Brown a sum sufficient to pay Able (or anyone else) the damages Brown may owe to Able in the event Brown, in the operation of the automobile, injures Able and becomes liable to him as a result of the injury. The contract is an original contract (an indemnity contract) between Clark and Brown, and the fact that Able may benefit indirectly does not affect the character of the contract.

4. Brown purchases an automobile from Able on a title-retaining contract by the terms of which Brown agrees to pay Able $100 per month until a $1,000 balance is paid in full. After paying $200 of the indebtedness, Brown sells the automobile to Clark, who contracts with Brown to pay to Able the unpaid balance of $800. The contract between Brown and Clark, whereby Clark promises to pay Able $800, is an original contract. Clark is obligated to pay Able in all events. Able is a third-party creditor beneficiary of the contract.

5. Able owes Brown $100, and Brown owes Clark $100. Able, Brown, and Clark enter into an agreement whereby Able agrees to pay Clark $100; Able discharges his $100 debt against Brown, and Brown discharges his $100 debt against Clark. The resulting Able-Clark contract is an original contract. Able is obligated to pay Clark $100 in all events. This type of transaction is termed a "novation."

6. Clark owns shares of the capital stock in the Brown Corporation. He sells the stock to Able and contracts to guarantee the payment, by Brown Corporation, of an annual dividend of not less than 5 percent. Clark's guarantee contract is an original contract. A corporation owes no obligation to its stockholders to pay a dividend; consequently, Clark's guarantee is not a contract to answer for the debt, default, or miscarriage of another. Instead, it is more in the nature of a warranty of the quality of goods sold.

Suppose, however, that Clark owns 5 percent corporate bonds issued by the Brown Corporation and he sells the bonds to Able and contracts to pay the 5 percent annual interest payment if Brown Corporation defaults. The Clark-Able contract is a collateral contract and is unenforceable unless evidenced by a note or memorandum in writing signed by Clark or his duly authorized agent. Brown Corporation is obligated to pay the interest on the bonds, and Clark's contract to pay in the event Brown Corporation defaults is a contract to answer for the debt, default, or miscarriage of another—in this case, Brown Corporation.

There are other transactions of this same general type which occur less frequently than those described. For example, if Clark contracts to pay Able a debt owed to Able by Brown in consideration of Able discharging Brown, such a contract is an original contract, or if Clark purchases from Able a debt owed to Able by Brown, the contract is an original contract.

Exceptions. An exception occurs in the following situation. If a third person has promised the obligee that he will answer for the debt, default, or miscarriage of another, but such promise is made to gain personal advantages resulting from the obligee's performance, and the promise to discharge the obligor's debt in the event of his default is merely incidental to the principal objective of the contract, some courts have interpreted such a promise as an original promise.

Summary

A collateral contract is one made with an obligee to pay the debt, default, or miscarriage of the obligor in the event he fails to perform that duty. Whether a contract is original or collateral will depend primarily on the intention of the parties to the contract.

An original contract is one in which a promisor obligates himself to perform in all events. Often a contract in which three persons are involved may appear to include a collateral contract, but an analysis of such a transaction will reveal that only an original contract is involved.

Guinn Co. v. *Mazza*
296 F.2d 441 (D.C. Cir. 1961)

This was an action by Guinn Company (plaintiff) against Mazza (defendant) to recover damages for breach of an oral agreement to advance money to Togor Publications. Judgment for Mazza and Guinn appealed. Affirmed.

Togor Publications was heavily indebted to Guinn for printing prior issues of *Bounty* magazine and Guinn refused to extend further credit unless payment or "acceptable assurances" were forthcoming. Mazza was a board member of Togor. On July 2 and 3, 1956, Mazza agreed to lend Togor $150,000 and communicated and expressed this promise to Guinn assuring the latter that Guinn could rely on this loan. Mazza told Guinn "to go ahead with printing the August 1956 issue of *Bounty*." Mazza was to get stock in Togor for making the advance of $150,000.

Guinn printed the magazine in reliance on the oral "promise, statements and assurances" of Mazza but Mazza has never advanced any money to Togor and Togor has not paid Guinn.

Guinn sued Mazza on his oral promises to advance the money and Mazza set up the statute of frauds as his defense.

BURGER, CIRCUIT JUDGE. To the extent Guinn relies on the oral communication from Mazza, whether we view this as an "assurance" or a "promise" or an "agreement" it is an undertaking which falls squarely within the controlling New York Statute of Frauds. There is no claim here that Mazza was to pay Guinn for printing costs; Mazza simply gave "assurances" or "guarantees" to Guinn that Mazza would advance money to Togor and that payment would ultimately be made by Togor. Togor remained originally liable on the debt. Since the authorities agree that if as between all the parties the original debtor remains primarily liable, the oral undertaking by the new promisor (here Mazza) is a promise to answer for the debt of another and thus is barred by the Statute of Frauds unless put in writing. . . .

The settled law of the matter is stated at 3 *Williston, Contracts*:

Ordinarily, there is no individual liability on the part of a stockholder for the debts of a corporation. His promise to pay such a debt is in a strict sense the promise to answer for the debt of another; and such a promise, if oral, is unenforceable under the Statute of Frauds.

In other words, where the oral promise of a stockholder to pay the debt of a corporation is collateral in form and effect, and the consideration, therefore, is not to secure or promote some personal object or advantage of the promisor, as distinguished from the indirect benefit to him from the mere fact of his being a stockholder of the corporation, the promise is within the statute.

Star Sales Co. v. Arnoult
169 So.2d 178 (Ct. App. La. 1964)

This was an action to recover on a debt brought by Star Sales Co. (plaintiff) against Arnoult (defendant). Judgment for Arnoult and Star Sales appealed. Affirmed.

Sometime in 1957 or 1958, Arnoult and Camet engaged as partners in a sundries business. Camet, it appears was the person in active charge; but Arnoult, a financially responsible man, was the financial backer of the enterprise. They conducted the business as a partnership under the trade name of Colonial Distributors and bought goods for resale from Star Sales Company, Inc.

For several months the purchases of the partnership from Star Sales were on a cash basis. In September 1958, Mr. Arnoult, Mr. Camet, and a Mr. Lawson, an employee of Colonial, who was taken in as a partner upon putting up $4,100.00 went to the office of Star Sales Company, Inc., and discussed with its secretary-treasurer, Howard Rabin, and bookkeeper, Mr. Lopez, the matter of opening an account for Colonial Distributors for purchase of its goods on credit. Star Sales was unwilling to extend credit to Colonial Distributors but was satisfied with the financial responsibility of Mr. Arnoult and proposed to bill Mr. Arnoult personally for goods delivered to Colonial.

All invoices were thereafter billed in the name of J. L. Arnoult. The merchandise was picked up at Star Sales's warehouse by an employee of Colonial Distributors. In 1959 Colonial Distributors was incorporated, with the former partners becoming stockholders.

Payments on the account were made by Colonial Distributors, before and after incorporation, and the checks were co-signed by Mr. Arnoult until sometime in 1959 or 1960 (the date is not certain) when Mr. Arnoult "got out" of the company. Thereafter Mr. Arnoult did not sign any checks given on this account. This was before June 1960, from which date the account in question runs. No change in the billing of the account was ever made.

In October 1960, Star Sales discontinued the account because of its delinquency of *$1,941.90*. In November, Colonial Distributors, Incorporated, went into bankruptcy, but before doing so notified Star Sales and allowed it to reclaim merchandise to the extent of $702.09, for which credit was given November 9, leaving a balance of *$1,239.81*. Star Sales sued Arnoult for this balance and Arnoult set up the statute of frauds.

BARNETTE, JUDGE.   There is no question whatever that Star Sales was unwilling to extend credit to Colonial Distributors, either as a partnership or corporation, and would not have done so except upon reliance on the financial responsibility of the defendant, James L. Arnoult. We do not question that the account was carried on Star Sales's books in the name of J. L. Arnoult, but it is equally certain that Star Sales knew that the actual purchaser of its goods was Colonial Distributors.

We are convinced that the credit would not have been extended except for the assurance given Star Sales by Mr. Arnoult, but this, in our opinion, was an agreement of surety; a promise to be responsible for; a guarantee or promise to pay the account of the purchaser, a third party. Parole evidence cannot be admitted to prove the debt. In the absence of some instrument in writing confirming the verbal agreement, which no doubt was made, Star Sales's suit cannot be maintained.

A distinction must be made between a promise to pay for goods delivered to another person, thus creating a primary obligation of the person making the promise, and one where the promiser stands good for the account as a guarantor. The question which must be determined is if the promise constitutes a primary or collateral obligation. An examination of the relationship of the parties and the motive and pecuniary interest of the party making the promise may throw light upon the intent and is therefore pertinent in deciding the question: to whom was the credit given?

We think a great deal of light is thrown on the intent of the parties from the fact that this was not a promise regarding a single transaction as in *Magee* v. *Crowe,* where the purchase of specific items were involved, but rather one running over a period of years in the form of an open account. It is apparent that notwithstanding Star Sales's billing system and its carrying the account in the name of Arnoult, its dealings in connection with the account were with Colonial Distributors. When it became apparent that Colonial was about to go into bankruptcy, Star Sales accepted the return of a substantial amount of goods from Colonial. This fact was pointed out by the trial judge as of significance. He reasoned that if Arnoult, a financially responsible person, was in fact the purchaser, the seller would have been more interested in letting the sale stand and looking to Arnoult, the purchaser, for payment.

Interest in Land

Scope of Provision. The provision of the statute of frauds requiring contracts for the sale of an interest in land to be evidenced by a memorandum in writing and signed by the party to be bound thereby or his duly authorized agent does not include deeds, mortgages, wills, and other conveyances of land.

Contracts Coming within the Statute of Frauds. Although the statute of frauds is worded "interest in land," the courts have interpreted land to mean real estate, and any contract, the performance of which will affect the ownership rights in real estate, comes within the statute of frauds. Contracts to sell, to mortgage, to permit the mining and removal of minerals on the land, and to give easements fall within this class. Leases fall within this class, but in most states, leases are provided for by a special provision of the statute. Contracts to insure buildings, to erect buildings, to organize a partnership to deal in real property, and similar contracts are not within this class because they do not affect an interest in the real property.

Summary

If the performance of the contract will require the transfer of any interest in real property, it comes within the provisions of the statute and is not enforceable unless it is evidenced by a writing. The distinction between real property and personal property is a part of the law of property and is not discussed in connection with our discussion of the statute of frauds.

Transport Man. Co. v. *American Radiator & Stand. San. Corp.*
326 F.2d 62 (3rd Cir. 1963)

Transport Co. (plaintiff) brought this action for breach of contract against American Radiator Corp. (defendant). Judgment for American and Transport appealed. Affirmed.

After considerable negotiations, American orally agreed to meet with Transport to work out the terms for the sale of a foundry plant owned by American to transport for $575,000.

A conference between the representatives of the principals was held on July 30, 1962. Though the testimony as to what was said at this meeting is in conflict, the parties agree that it terminated with the understanding that American would prepare the necessary documents for effectuating the sale and would submit them to Transport. American also suggested that Transport should attempt to lease space in the plant to the Hartz Mountain Products Corporation, which at that time was a tenant in other property owned by Transport. It was suggested that such a lease would be assigned to American as further security for the purchase-money mortgage. On August 17, 1962, Hartz Mountain advised American by letter that it contemplated entering into a five-year lease with Transport for 150,000 square feet of the Bayonne property at a rental of $100,000 per year.

The parties met again on August 23, 1962, at which time American requested some proof of Transport's financial responsibility and a draft of a letter of credit, dated August 28, 1962, in the amount of $100,000 from the Irving Trust Company was subsequently delivered to American.

In the meantime, Thompson, who had been hired to become American's real estate manager, inspected and evaluated the plant and concluded that the $575,000 figure was grossly inadequate. American informed Transport that negotiations at the price of $575,000 were out of the question, and that American would be willing to continue discussions only if Transport substantially increased its offer. When Transport refused to alter its position, American advised that negotiations for the sale were terminated. Transport sued for specific performance and American set up the statute of frauds as a defense. Transport argued that part performance removed the defense of the statute of frauds.

STALEY, CIRCUIT JUDGE.   The acts relied upon to support this argument consist of the procurement of the letter of credit from the Irving Trust Company and the efforts to secure a lease from the Hartz Mountain Products Corporation. But these are clearly legally insufficient to remove the bar of the statute for under the New Jersey cases, as under the general law, acts merely ancillary or preparatory to the contract cannot be deemed in part performance of it. Moreover, even when executed in direct pursuance of the contract, the acts must result in such an irretrievable change of position that invocation of the statute would constitute a fraud upon the performing party. In the case at bar, the letter of credit was furnished merely as evidence of Transport's financial ability to perform its promise. By its very terms, no amount was payable under it until the parties certified that a contract of sale had been executed.

With respect to the Hartz Mountain lease negotiations, Transport contends that its efforts in this regard were referable to the proposed agreement of sale. This is unquestionably true, but it is undisputed that the assignment of such a lease to American was intended to serve as further security for the purchase-money mortgage. Thus, though the efforts to secure a tenant were referable to the proposed agreement of sale, they were clearly ancillary to it. More important, Transport has cited nothing to indicate that these efforts resulted in an irretrievable change of position on its part, except to state that "failure to deliver such space would impair is reputation and business image in the area. . . ." Of course, this is not such a change of position as would bring it within the part-performance exception to the statute.

In the alternative, Transport argues that American should be equitably estopped from asserting the defense of the Statute of Frauds. . . .

There is no indication in the New Jersey authorities that the bar of the statute of frauds may be avoided on the theory of estoppel by circumstances which would not qualify as part performance within the case hereinabove discussed. In any event, estoppel required the showing of an assumption of a position by representation or act by one party upon which the other had rightfully relied to an extent which would render unjust its repudiation by the first party.

Not To Be Performed within One Year

Scope of Provision.   This provision applies only to executory bilateral contracts. If Allen loans Bates $100 and Bates orally promises to repay the loan in two years, the contract is a unilateral contract and need not be evidenced by a writing. Likewise, if a bilateral contract has been fully performed, the fact that the contract was oral and could not be performed within a year of the making thereof would in no way affect the rights acquired by the parties to the performed contract. Since the statute is worded in the negative, "*not* to be performed within one year," the courts have held that if, under the terms of the contract, it is possible to perform the contract within a year of the making thereof, it need not be evidenced by a writing to be enforceable. The fact that it is highly improbable that performance will be completed or that performance was not completed within one year is not controlling.

The one-year period is computed from the time the contract comes into existence, not from the time performance is to begin. For example, a contract entered into on July 1, 1965, whereby the promisor agrees to work for the promisee for one week, work to begin on July 3, 1966, cannot be performed within one year from the making thereof and, if it is to be enforceable, would have to be evidenced by a memorandum in writing signed by the party to be bound or his duly authorized agent.

Computing Time.   In computing time, as a general rule, parts of days are not counted. A contract entered into today to work for one year, work to begin tomorrow, can be performed within one year under the rule generally followed. However, if such a contract were entered into on Saturday, work to begin the following Monday, it could not be performed within one year from the making thereof. In a few states the day the contract is entered into is counted. In these states a contract to work for one year entered into today, work to begin tomorrow, cannot be performed within one year from the making thereof.

In some cases the courts have held that if a contract to work for one year is entered into this week, Monday, work to begin next week, Monday, and the promises are then repeated when the work begins, the time will be counted from the time the promises are repeated, and no writing will be required.

Contracts to Extend Time of Performance.   In determining whether or not a contract to extend the time for the performance of an existing contract can be performed within one year, time is computed from the day the contract to extend the time of performance is entered into to the time of performance under the extended time contract will be completed. For example, on July 1, 1965, Able contracts to work for Brown for six months beginning on July 2, 1965. on September 1, 1965, Able and Brown enter into a contract whereby Able agrees to work for Brown for an additional 11 months after the performance of the existing contract. The contract for the extension of time cannot be performed within one year from the making thereof.

An Indefinite Time Stated. When the time of performance of the contract is stated in indefinite terms, such as "for life" or "as long as needed," and under existing conditions it is possible to perform the contract within one year, it need not be evidenced by a writing to be enforceable, even though the actual time of performance is more than one year.

The courts are not in accord in their interpretation of contracts to support someone and contracts to refrain from action. All courts hold that a contract whereby Ames contracts to support Barnes for life need not be in writing. They reason that the contract will be fully performed on the death of Barnes and this may occur within a year. Most courts hold that no writing is required to make a contract enforceable whereby Ames contracts to support Barnes for five years. Some courts interpret it as a five-year contract and hold that a writing is required.

A majority of the courts hold that a contract whereby Ames contracts not to compete with Barnes for a period of five years must be evidenced by a writing to be enforceable whereas a few courts hold that the contract will be completely performed on the death of Ames and that this may occur within a year and that no writing is required.

The statutes of some states provide that any contract which, by its terms, is not to be completed before the end of a lifetime is unenforceable unless evidenced by a writing.[1]

Summary

The provision of the statute of frauds which requires that a contract must be in writing if it cannot be performed within one year from the making thereof applies only to bilateral contracts. Since it is worded in the negative, "not fully performed," no writing is required if it is possible, under the terms of the contract, to complete performance within one year. Time is computed from the time of the formation of the contract, not from the time the promisor is to begin performance. A contract to extend the time of performance of an existing contract must be evidenced by a writing if the time from the formation of the contract to extend time of performance to the time of complete performance of the contract, under the terms of the contract, exceeds one year. If the

---

[1] Personal Property Laws of New York, § 31 (1).

time for performance is stated in indefinite terms, such as "for life" or "for long as needed," the courts hold, in the absence of a special statute, that no writing is required, since the contract, under its terms, may be performed within one year.

White Lighting Co. v. Wolfson
438 P.2d 345 (Sup. Ct. Calif. 1968)

This was an action by White Lighting Company (plaintiff) against James Wolfson (defendant) for $850 claimed due and Wolfson counterclaimed damages for breach of an oral employment contract. The trial court sustained demurrers to the counterclaim and Wolfson appealed. Reversed.

Wolfson alleged as the first count of the cross-complaint that during October 1964 White promised him that if he would continue with White as vice president and sales manager he would receive a salary of $300 per week, automobile and other business expenses, and one percent of the annual gross sales of White exceeding one million dollars per year, payable quarterly commencing November 1, 1963. Although Wolfson relied to his detriment on these oral representations and performed all the conditions, White refused not only to comply with the promise as to the percentage of gross receipts but also to give Wolfson any information by which he could determine if any amount was owing to him. Although Wolfson's employment was to be on a "permanent" basis, it was not to continue for any specified period. To this count the trial court sustained a general demurrer without leave to amend on the ground that the alleged oral employment contract violated the statute of frauds.

TOBRINER, JUSTICE.   Even though part of an employee's compensation is to be measured by annual receipts of the employer, the statute of frauds does not apply to an employment contract unless its terms provide that the employee cannot completely perform it within one year from the making of the contract. Civil Code, section 1624, subdivision 1, invalidates "an agreement that by its terms is not to be performed within a year from the making thereof" unless the contract "or some note or memorandum thereof, is in writing and subscribed by the party to be charged or by his agent." The cases hold that section 1624, subdivision 1, applied only to those contracts which, by their terms, cannot possibly be performed within one year.

The contractual provision that Wolfson would receive one percent of the annual gross sales of White exceeding one million dollars per year does not in itself convert the oral employment contract into one which by its terms cannot be performed within a year. Decisions involving other oral employment contracts with similar terms as to compensation support this conclusion. Thus the statute of frauds does not apply to employment contracts for an indefinite period merely because the contract provides that payment will be forthcoming on termination of the employment relationship. Nor does the statute of frauds apply to employment contracts because the compensation for the services is to be measured by their value to the employer over a period of more than one year. Moreover, in *Pecarovich* v. *Becker,* the court held that the statute of frauds does not apply to an oral contract relating to the services and annual salary of a football coach for a three-year period; the court explained that the contract authorized the employer to terminate the employment relationship at the end of each year by payment of a named sum.

Our conclusion coincides with the position unanimously taken by the few courts that have dealt with oral employment contracts involving bonus or profit-sharing provisions. Thus in *Dennis* v. *Thermoid* the court held that a provision for a bonus payable at the end of the year did not render an oral employment contract not performable within that year.

Since in the instant case the alleged oral contract may be terminated at will by either party, it can, under its terms, be performed within one year. When Wolfson's employment relationship with White was terminated, Wolfson had completely performed; White's performance consisted of nothing more than compensating Wolfson. Moreover, as we have explained, the inclusion of the provision for a bonus ascertainable only after one year does not invalidate the oral agreement under the statute of frauds.

The Writing

Nature of Writing Required. The statutes of fraud of the several states are not uniform in their provisions for writing. In most of the states the statutes require "a memorandum," or "a note or memorandum," but in some of the states the statutes require "a contract in writing."

If a memorandum, or note or memorandum, is required, it may be made at any time up to the time suit is filed. If it has been signed but has been lost, its loss and its content may be proven by parol evidence. It may be in any form, such as, for instance, a formal contract, letters, telegrams, receipts, or any other writing accurately stating the material provisions of the contract.

The memorandum, or note or memorandum, may consist of several documents, in which case the documents must show, either by attachment physically or by the content or references in the documents themselves, that they all refer to the same transaction. If a contract in writing is required, it must include all the material provisions of the agreement, and must be made with the intent to bind the party signing it. The memorandum, or note or memorandum, need not be made with the intent that it be binding.

Content of the Memorandum. The note or memorandum, in order to be sufficient, must state the names of the parties, or designate them so that they can be identified from the content of the writing, must describe the subject matter of the contract with reasonable certainty (a more detailed description of real property than of personal property is required), must state the price to be paid (with some exceptions), and must state credit terms, if credit is extended, and all other terms that are material. The statutes of frauds of some states expressly provide that the consideration need not be stated in the memorandum; however, if price is a material term, it must be stated.

It is immaterial in what order the terms are stated or how the parties are indicated. The parties may be indicated by their signatures on the memorandum, by the appearance of their names in the heading of the memorandum, by an address on an envelope in which the memorandum is mailed, or by a statement in the memorandum expressly setting out the names of the parties.

Under the provisions of the Uniform Commercial Code, the requirements for the note or memorandum of a contract to sell goods [2] are not as strict as are those required in general.

The Signing.   The statute of frauds in force in most of the states provides that the memorandum must be signed by the *party* to be bound or his duly authorized agent. Since the statute is worded in the singular, the memorandum need not be signed by both parties but must be signed by the party who is being sued or by his agent. In some states the courts have held that the memorandum of a contract to sell an interest in real estate must be signed by both the vendor and the vendee.

Unless the statute expressly provides that the memorandum or contract must be signed at the end thereof, the signature may appear any place on the memorandum.

In a sale at auction the auctioneer and his clerk are impliedly authorized to sign the note or memorandum as agent for both the buyer and the seller. However, this implied authority continues only during the auction sale.

Oral Variation of Contract.   By the great weight of authority, an oral variation of a contract, for which contract a sufficient note or memorandum exists, is not enforceable. The contract may be enforced as originally negotiated, but the variation is not enforceable. However, a mutual oral agreement to cancel a contract, for which a sufficient memorandum exists, is effective.

Summary

A note or memorandum in writing is generally a sufficient writing to satisfy the statute of frauds. It may be made at any time prior to the bringing of suit to enforce the contract and need not be in any particular form. If several documents are relied on, they must be physically attached together, or it must be clearly indicated from their contents that they refer to the same transaction. The note or memorandum must include the names of the parties and describe the subject matter of the contract with reasonable certainty and in addition must contain all the material provisions of the contract.

---

[2] Uniform Commercial Code, Section 2–201 (1) and (2).

The note or memorandum must be signed by the party to be charged or his duly authorized agent; that is, it must be signed by the party defendant. No particular place or mode of signing is stipulated by the statute. An agent may sign in his principal's name or in his own name. An auctioneer or his clerk has implied authority to sign for both the buyer and the seller. An oral variation of a contract, where such contract is evidenced by a sufficient note or memorandum, is not enforceable.

Jennings v. Ruidoso Racing Assoc.
441 P.2d 42 (Sup. Ct. N.M. 1968)

Cecil Jennings (plaintiff) brought this action claiming that on April 28, 1963, he was hired as comptroller of the Ruidoso Racing Association (defendant) for the period May 1, 1963, to April 30, 1964, at a salary of $1,000 per month and was wrongfully discharged on May 18, 1963. Jennings appealed from a judgment denying recovery. What result?

NOBLE, JUSTICE. The complaint alleges that the employment for which the action is brought was to commence May 1, 1963, and continue for a period of one year. For the purpose of determining whether the period for performance brings the agreement within the statute of frauds, the time begins to run from the day the contract is entered into. It is thus generally held that a contract for a year beginning at a future date, as was this one, is within the statute.

We are thus concerned with whether the record discloses some memorandum or note in writing signed by an authorized person on behalf of Ruidoso Racing Association sufficient to satisfy the statute of frauds. Jennings strongly urges that the writings may consist of several instruments, and introduced excerpts of the minutes of the board of directors of March 15, 1963, and a check as writings sufficient to satisfy the statute. Thus, it is necessary for us to determine whether excerpts of the minutes of the March 15, 1963 meeting, together with a check subsequent thereto, will satisfy the statute of frauds.

The minutes of the March 15, 1963, meeting of the board of directors, admitted in evidence, contain the following:

"Director A. A. Bradford moved that in recognition of services performed, the corporate secretary, Cecil Jennings, be paid $1,000.00 as a bonus, and further that since the term of his original employment was near expiration, that he be hired as comptroller for the next succeeding year at his present rate of compensation. Ralph Nix seconded and it was so voted."

The parties agree that corporate minutes, if otherwise sufficient, may be used as a memorandum in writing to meet the requirements of the statute of frauds. Those minutes were signed by Jennings as secretary and by the president of the corporation. They were, accordingly, signed by the party to be charged with the contract.

Does the excerpt from the above minutes sufficiently describe the duties which Jennings was hired to perform and prescribe the salary he was to receive? The statute is not pressed "to the extreme of a literal and rigid logic." The statute of frauds is intended to protect against a fraud, but it is not intended to be taken as an escape for those seeking to avoid their obligations. It must be remembered that the memorandum, sufficient to satisfy the statute of frauds, need not in itself amount to a contract. The contract in this instance is an oral agreement. The statute of frauds only requires that there be written evidence to prove that the particular contract was made. Clearly, Jennings was employed as "comptroller" of the corporation. . . .

In *Fanney* v. *Virginia Inv. & Mortgage Corp.,* a memorandum describing the employment of the cross-complaint as "executive-secretary" was held to sufficiently describe the service to be performed.

Does the memorandum sufficiently fix Jennings' rate of pay? In *Marks* v. *Cowdin,* a recital in the written memorandum that the plaintiff's employment was to be continued for a term and stated salary was held to be sufficient.

"The tests to be applied in order to identify the employment are thus embodied in the writing. We are not left to gather the relation between the parties from executory promises. We are informed that the relation then existing is the one to be maintained. . . ."

. . . However, in addition to the excerpt from the minutes of the meeting of March 15, 1963, the record discloses a salary check signed by authorized persons on behalf of the corporation, and it clearly indicates that it relates to the salary paid Jennings for a portion of the period for which he claims employment pursuant to the minutes of the March 15, 1963 meeting. These writings together contain all the essential terms of the agreement between the parties necessary to satisfy the statute of frauds.

Effect of Failure to Comply

General Effect. The statute of frauds does not, as a general rule, declare an oral contract which comes within the scope of the statute's provisions void or voidable if it does not comply with the requirements of the statute; it declares such a contract unenforceable. If suit is brought to enforce an oral contract which comes within the provisions of the statute of frauds and the party defendant does not plead noncompliance with the statute as a defense, he thereby waives his defense, and the court will proceed in the same manner as though the statute of frauds had been complied with.

Rights of Parties to Oral Contract. If the parties have entered into an oral contract which comes within the provisions of the statute of frauds and one party has performed, thereby conferring benefits on the other party, he can recover for the benefits conferred in an action in quasi contract.

The courts of equity recognize and enforce the statute of frauds; yet a court of equity may refuse to permit a party to raise the defense of the statute of frauds if such refusal is necessary to prevent the perpetration of a fraud. The refusal to permit the defense of the statute of frauds is based on general concepts of fairness and justice. The idea is expressed in the equitable maxim that he who asks equity must do equity.

Part performance will take the contract out of the statute of frauds in cases involving the purchase of real property where the purchaser has been given possession of the property and has made extensive improvements to it. Part performance may also remove the statute of frauds defense in cases involving sale of goods (discussed next) to the extent that there is either part payment or part delivery. Absent special facts, part performance does not remove the statute of frauds defense where either the "one year" or "promises to answer" statutes are involved.

If an oral contract which comes within the statute of frauds has been fully performed, neither party will be permitted to rescind the contract and recover the consideration given. Once the contract has been performed, the transaction is a closed deal and cannot be reopened on the ground of noncompliance with the provisions of the statute of frauds.

Summary

An oral contract which comes within the provisions of the statute of frauds is unenforceable, not void or voidable. If one of the parties to an oral contract which is within the statute of frauds performs, thereby conferring benefits on the other party, the party who has performed can recover in quasi contract for the benefits conferred. In transactions concerning real estate, if there has been part performance of an oral contract, a court of equity may grant specific performance if the circumstances are such that specific performance is necessary to avoid an unjust result. If the parties have performed an oral contract which comes within the provisions of the statute of frauds, neither party can rescind the contract on the ground of noncompliance with the statute of frauds.

Sale of Goods and the Code

The Memorandum.   The statute of frauds does not apply to oral sale of goods contracts unless the price is $500 or more. Such an oral contract is not enforceable by way of action or defense unless the requirements of the statute of frauds are complied with. These requirements can be met by the execution of a memorandum signed by the party against whom enforcement is sought or by his authorized agent or broker. The memorandum satisfies the requirements of the statute of frauds if it is "some writing sufficient to indicate that a contract of sale has been entered into between the parties." It is not insufficient because it omits or incorrectly states a term agreed upon. A sales contract is not enforceable beyond the quantity of goods stated in the memorandum. (2–201 [1].) [3]

As between merchants, if an oral contract has been negotiated and one of the parties, within a reasonable time thereafter, sends a written confirmation, sufficient to bind him, to the other party, such writing is sufficient to bind the receiver, although he does not sign it, if he has reason to know its contents, unless written notice of objection to its contents is given within 10 days after it is received. (2–201 [2].)

Part Payment or Part Delivery.   Under the Code part payment or delivery of part of the goods satisfies the statute of frauds but only "with respect to goods for which payment has been made and accepted or which have been received and accepted." (2–201 [3] [c].) This provision of the statute makes the oral contract of the parties enforceable only to the extent that payment has been made and accepted or that the goods have been received and accepted; it does not make the oral contract enforceable in its entirety.

Admissions in Pleadings or Court.   Although a sufficient writing has not been executed and no part payment or part delivery has been made, if the party being sued admits in his pleadings or in court that an oral sales contract was entered into, he can be held liable. The oral contract is not enforceable, however, beyond the quantity of goods admitted. (2–201 [3] [b].)

Specially Manufactured Goods.   Oral contracts for goods to be specially manufactured are enforceable (1) if the goods are not suitable for sale in the ordinary course of the seller's business, and (2) if the seller, before notice of repudiation is received and under circumstances which reasonably indicate that the goods are for the buyer, has made a substantial beginning of their manufacture or commitment for their procurement. (2–201 [3] [a].) Under this section of the statute of frauds a wholly executory oral contract for goods to be specially manufactured is unenforceable.

Effect of Noncompliance.   The statute of frauds does not declare oral contracts which come within its scope void or voidable if they do not comply with the requirements of the statute, but it does declare such contracts unenforceable. If suit is brought to enforce an oral contract for the sale of goods for the price of $500 or more, the party sued, if he wishes to avail himself of the protection of the statute, must plead it specially in the trial court. If the contract has been completely performed, neither party will be permitted to rescind the contract and recover the consideration given.

Summary

An oral contract for the sale of goods for the price of $500 or more is unenforceable unless evidenced by a writing signed by the party against whom en-

---

[3] The numbers in the parentheses refer to the sections of the Uniform Commercial Code, 1962.

forcement is sought or his authorized agent or broker. The writing need not set out all the terms of the agreement but must be sufficient to indicate that a contract was entered into. It is not enforceable beyond the quantity stated. It may be satisfied by part payment or part delivery or by admission in the pleadings or in court but not for a quantity beyond payment made, goods received and accepted, or admitted. A written confirmation sufficient to bind the sender will bind the receiver unless he objects to its terms within 10 days of its receipt. The statute of frauds declares the contract coming within its provisions unenforceable and the party defendant must plead the statute as matter of defense in the trial court if he wishes to avail himself of its protection.

Starr v. *Freeport Dodge, Inc.*
282 NYS.2d 58 (N.Y. Dist. Ct. 1967)

This was an action by Starr (plaintiff) against Freeport Dodge, Inc. (defendant) for damages for breach of contract. Freeport made a motion for summary judgment. Motion denied.

. . . Starr signed an order form for a new automobile which described the subject matter of the sale, the price, which was in excess of $500, and the identity of both buyer and seller. The form is not signed by the dealer and bears the following printed statement, "This order is not valid unless signed and accepted by the dealer." Prefixing the line, above which the quoted statement appears, is the word "Approved."

Starr made a $25 down payment to the dealer, which was accepted by the dealer and for which deposit a credit was noted on the form. On the day scheduled for delivery of the car Starr was informed by Freeport's representative "that some error had been made" and that it would be necessary for Starr to pay an additional $175 over and above the price previously agreed upon in order to obtain delivery of the car.

Freeport argued that there was no contract between the parties and that the order form, unsigned as it is by the dealer, falls within the purview of Section 2–201 of the Uniform Commercial Code as unenforceable since it was not signed by the party to be charged.

TOMSON, JUDGE. In the *Williamson* case, the court . . . stated:

The Uniform Commercial Code repealed the Sales Act of 1951. Under the Code, part payment takes the case out of the statute only to the extent for which payment has been made. The Code therefore makes an important change by denying the enforcement of the contract where in the case of a single object the payment made is less than the full amount.

The *Williamson* case is discussed in Hawkland, *A Transactional Guide to the Uniform Commercial Code,* Sec. 1.1202, pp. 28, 29, as follows:

By failing to distinguish part payment from partial acceptance and receipt, the section does not create one problem, neatly illustrated by *Williamson* v. *Martz.* Here S orally agreed to sell to B two vats for a total price of $1,600, B paying $100 on account. Subsequently B refused to take the vats, and S sued for breach of contract. B set up section 2–201 of the Code as his defense, and S countered that the partial payment took the matter out of the statute of frauds. The court held for B. Subsection 2–201 (3)(c) removes the statute of frauds only to the extent of payment. Since the payment of $100 cannot be translated into one vat (worth $800), S cannot enforce the contract to the extent of one vat. There being no way to divide up a vat, S is barred completely by the Statute.

Though this case seems to follow the plain meaning of subsection 2–201 (3)(c), the result appears to be excessively restrictive. The payment of $100 indicates a contract whose quantity term must be at least one unit. The court, therefore, could safely enforce the agreement to the extent of one vat, and thus, give S a recovery of $800. The payment of $100, of course, does not necessarily prove a contract for two vats, and the court would not be justified in enforcing the contract for such an amount. But it is difficult to see how the contract could have contemplated less than one vat, assuming, as the court did, that vats are indivisible.

. . .

. . . The language of 2–201 (3)(c) does not require the Williamson result. Even if subparagraph (c) validates, as the writers seem unanimously to agree, a divisible contract only for as much of the goods as have been paid for, it does not necessarily follow that such a rule invalidates an indivisible oral contract where some payment has been made and accepted. To paraphrase Hawkland—It is difficult (here) to see how the contract could have contemplated less than one (automobile), assuming as the court did, that (automobiles) are indivisible. Any other conclusion would work an unconscionable result and would encourage rather than discourage fraud if the facts as pleaded (known as "low balling" in the trade) were proven at a trial.

Julian C. Cohen Salvage Corp. v. Eastern Electric Sales Co.
206 A.2d 331 (Super. Ct. Pa. 1965)

This was an action by Julian C. Cohen Salvage Corporation (plaintiff) against Eastern Electric Sales Company (defendant) to recover the purchase price of cable sold and delivered. Judgment for Julian C. Cohen Salvage Corporation and Eastern Electric Sales Company appealed. Judgment affirmed.

Julian C. Cohen Salvage Corporation (Cohen) operated a salvage business in Maryland. Eastern Electric Sales Company (Eastern) operated its business in Philadelphia. Cohen, in a telephone conversation, informed Eastern that it had a quantity of telephone cable for sale. An agent of Eastern inspected the cable and, as the result of a later telephone conversation, Cohen shipped the cable to Eastern at Philadelphia where the cable was run off Cohen's reels onto Eastern's reels and was taken by Eastern's employees to its warehouse where it remains. Eastern contends that that it agreed to buy only so much of the cable as it could use. Cohen introduced in evidence a written sales order which contained Cohen's name, the notation "SOLD TO: Eastern Electric," the date, the name of the shipper, the quantity, and the description of the goods, the weight of the goods, as well as the notation "Your Order Number" and "Our Sales Number." The form was signed by the authorized agent of Eastern. Eastern admitted that in the oral conversation the price was agreed upon. Eastern set up the Statute of Frauds as a defense.

ETHAN ALLEN DOTY, JUDGE. Eastern's reliance on the Statute of Frauds to vitiate this contract is misplaced. Section 2–201 (1) of the Uniform Commercial Code provides that a contract for the sale of goods in excess of $500 is not enforceable "Unless there is some writing sufficient to indicate that a contract for sale has been made between the parties and signed by the party against whom enforcement is sought, or by his authorized agent or broker."

In this case Cohen introduced into evidence a written sales order which contained Cohen's name, the notation, "SOLD TO: Eastern Electric," the date, the name of the shipper, the quantity and description of the goods, and the weight of the goods, as well as the notation, "Your Order Number," and "Our Sales Number." This form was admittedly signed by an authorized agent of Eastern. This writing was sufficient to satisfy the requirements of the Statute of Frauds.

All that is required is that the writing afford a basis that the offered oral evidence rests on a real transaction. Uniform Commercial Code, No. 1, to Section 201. See also *Harry Rubin & Sons, Inc.* v. *Consolidated Pipe Co. of America, Inc.* As stated in that case, "Its object is the elimination of certain formalistic requirements adherence to which often resulted in injustice, rather than the prevention of fraud."

This writing clearly afforded a basis for believing that the oral evidence rests on a real transaction. The fact that price was omitted (and it was the only relevant term omitted) is not fatal since "A writing is not insufficient because it omits . . . a term agreed upon. . . . 2–201 (1).

There is another reason why the Statute of Frauds does not preclude a verdict for Cohen in this case. Section 2–201 (3) (c) of the Code provides: "A contract which does not satisfy the requirements of subsection (1) but which is valid in other respects is enforceable with respect to goods which have been received and accepted."

That the cable was received there can be no doubt. After it was received by Eastern it was run from one reel to another by several of Eastern's employees who admitted they inspected it at that time. It was then tagged and placed in Eastern's warehouse, where it remains.

In order to avoid the conclusion that Eastern had accepted the cable, Eastern offered testimony that it had notified Cohen of its rejection shortly after the cable was received. However, there was no written notice of rejection. Moreover, the testimony that Eastern notified Cohen of the rejection of these goods is not credible, particularly in view of the fact that Eastern still has the cable in its possession and has never offered to return it or attempted to return it to Cohen.

Therefore, in view of its failure to act with respect to the cable it is clear that Eastern accepted the goods in question and a valid and enforceable contract exists between the parties. Section 2–606 (1) (b) and section 2–602 of the Uniform Commercial Code.

Cook Grains, Inc. v. Fallis
395 S.W.2d 555 (Sup. Ct. Ark. 1965)

This was an action by Cook Grains, Inc. (plaintiff) against Paul Fallis (defendant) for breach of an oral contract to sell and deliver 5,000 bushels of soybeans at $2.50 per bushel. Judgment for Fallis and Cook Grain appealed. Affirmed.

ROBINSON, ASSOCIATE JUSTICE.   Cook Grain argues that this written contract is sufficient as a confirmation under Sec. 2–201 (2).

Cook Grain concedes that ordinarily the alleged cause of action would be barred by the statute of frauds, but contends that here the alleged sale is taken out of the statute of frauds by the Uniform Commercial Code. Sec. 2–201 (2).

(2) Between merchants if within a reasonable time a writing in confirmation of the contract and sufficient against the sender is received and the party receiving it has reason to know its contents, it satisfies the requirements of subsection (1) against such party unless written notice of objection to its contents is given within ten [10] days after it is received. . . .

Thus, it will be seen that under the statute, if Fallis is a merchant he would be liable on the alleged contract because he did not, within ten days, give written notice that he rejected it.

The solution of the case turns on the point of whether Fallis is a "merchant" within the meaning of the statute. Ark. Stat. Ann. § 85–2–104 (1961 Addendum) provides:

'Merchant' means a person who deals in goods of the kind or otherwise by his occupation holds himself out as having knowledge or skill peculiar to the practices or goods involved in the transaction or to whom such knowledge or skill may be attributed by his employment of an agent or broker or other intermediary who by his occupation holds himself out as having such knowledge or skill. . . .

There is not a scintilla of evidence in the record, or proffered as evidence, that Fallis is a dealer in goods of the kind or by his occupation holds himself out as having knowledge or a skill peculiar to the practices of goods involved in the transaction, and no such knowledge or skill can be attributed to him.

The evidence in this case is that Fallis is a farmer and nothing else. He farms about 550 acres and there is no showing that he has any other occupation. . . .

Reich v. Helen Harper, Inc.
3 U.C.C. Rep. 1048 (Civ. Ct. N.Y. 1966)

This was an action brought by Reich (plaintiff) against Harper (defendant) for the breach of an oral contract to purchase 11,500 yards of India madras for 75 cents per yard. Held: Kaplan's motion to dismiss on grounds of the statute of frauds denied.

A document entitled "Rate Confirmation" was sent by Amtec to both Kaplan and Reich. It described the goods, stated the quantity, the price per yard, and that Amtec, upon whose printed stationery this appeared, was acting as sales agent for Ricky Fabrics (a designee of Reich) and that the goods were being sold to Kaplan. On January 9, 1966, Reich sent Kaplan a bill for 11,528 yards of Madras at 75 cents a yard on the printed bill form of Brian Mills, a name under which Reich does business. On February 18, 1966, Kaplan sent a letter to Brian Mills, attention of Mr. Reich, reading as follows:

Brian Mills, 152 W. 27th St., New York, N.Y.
  Att: Mr. Elliott Reich
Gentlemen:
  Replying to your letter of the 18th, please be advised that we examined a few pieces of merchandise that was billed to us against your invoice No. 10203, and found that it was not up to our standard.
  We are, therefore, unable to accept this shipment, and we also wish to advise that the few pieces that we examined are also being held for return to you.
                    Very truly yours,
                    /s/ Isidor Kaplan

GOLD, JUDGE. . . . [The Code] makes it necessary for a merchant buyer or merchant seller to watch his mail and to act promptly if he is not to be bound by a contract for sale with respect to which he has signed no writing. It deprives the party who fails to answer the confirmation, by rejecting it, of the defense of the statute of frauds. The burden of persuading the trier of the facts that a contract was in truth made orally prior to the written confirmation is unaffected.

In *Harry Rubin & Sons, Inc.* v. *Consolidated Pipe Company,* the Supreme Court of Pennsylvania stated:

As between merchants, the present statute of frauds provision (i.e., under § 2–201[2]) significantly changes the former law by obviating the necessity of having a memorandum signed by the party sought to be charged. The present statutory requirements are: (1) that, within a reasonable time, there be a writing in confirmation of the oral contract; (2) that the writing be sufficient to bind the sender; (3) that such writing be received; (4) that no reply thereto has been made although the recipient had reason to know of its contents. Section 2–201(2) penalizes a party who fails to 'answer a written confirmation of a contract within ten days' of the receipt of the writing by depriving such party of the defense of the statute of frauds.

It becomes necessary now to determine whether the document sent by Amtec is "sufficient against the sender." In short, would it bind Reich so that he, Reich, would be deprived of the statute of frauds as a defense were Kaplan the party suing herein? The court finds that the document would in and of itself so bind Reich to the transaction. Moreover, this commitment would be reinforced by Reich's invoice to Kaplan.

Whether examined together with Reich's invoice or standing alone, the sales confirmation would also bind Kaplan so as to deprive him of the defense of the statute of frauds in light of Kaplan's failure to give written notice of objection to its contents within ten days from the receipt thereof. The invoice rendered by Reich to Kaplan promptly after the sending of the sales confirmation would leave not the slightest doubt that the written confirmation was complete and that Kaplan would in effect forfeit the right to utilize the statute of frauds if he failed to make timely written objection to its contents.

The contention of Kaplan that the sales confirmation is not "signed" and is therefore not binding upon the sender and therefore cannot be binding upon the recipient is without basis in law. The authorities clearly hold to the contrary.

The term "signed," used in UCC, § 2–201, is defined in UCC, § 1–201 (39) in part as follows:

" 'Signed' includes any symbol executed or adopted by a party with present intention to authenticate a writing. . . ."

The question remaining then is whether the sale confirmation sent to Kaplan was "signed." In the context of the facts here present, the question may also be posed in the following manner: Was there an intent to authenticate the writing? This court believes so.

In the instant transaction not only was there the printed name of the agent, "Amtec," but in addition the name of the seller's principal was hand-lettered thereon.

The court is likewise of the opinion that the statute of frauds is not available to Kaplan for the further reason that Kaplan's letter, written some forty-five days after the receipt of the sale confirmation and some forty days after receipt of Reich's bill, may in and of itself constitute a sufficient memorandum to satisfy § 2–201 of the Uniform Commercial Code.

It has long been held that a memorandum sufficient to satisfy the statute of frauds need not be contained in one document but "It may be pieced together out of separate writings, connected with one another either expressly or by the internal evidence of subject matter and occasion." If the writings so conjoined meet the three requirements of the code, that a contract is evidenced, it is signed and the quantity of goods is specified, then the agreement is enforceable.

Interpretation

Necessity for Interpretation. Interpretation of a contract is the process of discovering and explaining the meaning of words and other manifestations used by the parties to the contract. If suit is brought to enforce a right claimed under a written contract, the court must interpret the meaning of the writing in order to determine the existence of a contract and the right and duties of the parties to the contract.

Basic Standards of Interpretation. The courts have adopted broad, basic standards of interpretation which they follow in determining the meaning of contracts and agreements which are expressed in writing. They will, as a general rule, give the writing the meaning that the contracting parties would be expected to give it under the circumstances surrounding the making of the contract. And they will give to the words and phrases used the meaning usually given to them by the business, trade, or profession in which the parties are engaged.

Rules of Interpretation. If the language used in a contract is clear and definite, the interpretation of the writing is a matter for the judge; but if the writing is uncertain and ambiguous, and parol evidence is introduced in aid of its interpretation, the question of its meaning should be left to a jury.

When the court is asked to interpret a writing which is being litigated it will attempt first to determine, by reading the writing in its entirety, the principal objective of the parties. Ordinary words will be given their usual meaning and technical words will be given their techninal meaning unless it clearly appears that a different meaning was intended. Each clause and provision will be interpreted with regard to its relation to the principal objective of the contract.

If the parties have used general terms followed by special terms, the court will assume that the special terms qualify the general terms. If the parties have used a form contract, or a contract which is partly printed and partly written, and there is a conflict between the printed and the written terms, the written terms will control. If there is an ambiguity in a contract and one of the parties has drawn the contract, the contract will be construed more strongly against the party who has drawn it.

Usage. Usage is a uniform practice or course of conduct which is followed in a line of business or profession or in a locality and which is either known to the parties or so well established that the parties must be presumed to have acted with reference thereto.

Usage may give to certain words a meaning different from the general meaning of the words. It may add to a written contract provisions not actually written into the writing. The courts have generally held in such cases that there is a presumption that the parties did not intend to reduce the entire agreement to writing but intended to contract with reference to those known usages. If both contracting parties live in the same community or are members of the same trade or association, the presumption is that they contract with reference to the usage of the community or trade and that they are both familiar with such usages. If the parties do not wish so to contract, they should express an intention not to be bound by such usages. Where the parties are not residents of the same community or members of the same trade group, the presumption is that they contract in regard to general usages and not in respect to local or special usages. It may be shown, however, that the local or special usages were known to both parties and that they contracted in reference to them. Where different usages prevail in different sections, the presumption is that the parties contracted in reference to the usage prevailing at the place where the contract was made and was to be performed.

Summary

Interpretation of a contract is the process of determining the meaning of words and other manifestations used by the parties to the contract. If an action is based on a writing, the writing must be interpreted in order to determine the rights and duties of the parties thereto. As guides to the court in the interpretation of written instruments, general standards and rules of interpretation have been adopted. Usage plays an important role in the interpretation of contracts. Usage is a uniform practice or course of conduct followed in a business or profession or in a locality, and may give to the language used a special meaning, or it may add terms to the contract.

United States v. *Essley*
284 F.2d 518 (10th Cir. 1960)

This was an action by the United States (plaintiff) against Irene Essley (defendant) to recover rent provided for in oil and gas leases on public land. Judgment for the United States for much less than claimed due and it appealed. Judgment reversed and cause remanded with instructions.

The Secretary of the Interior issued to Irene Essley four oil and gas leases on tracts of public lands in Colorado. Each lease was for a period of five years and contained a provision requiring that the lessee should pay "a rental of 50 cents for each acre or fraction thereof for the first lease year; and a rental of 25 cents for each subsequent lease year; Provided, That . . . no rental is required for the second and third years. . . ." In 1959, the United States brought this action to recover the rents for the 4th and 5th years, claiming rent at the rate of 25 cents per acre. Essley claimed that the United States was entitled to rent at the rate of 25 cents per year for each tract leased.

PICKETT, CIRCUIT JUDGE.   It is well established in this circuit, and elsewhere, that in interpreting a written contract, the court should, as far as possible, place itself in the position of the parties at the time of its execution, and then, from a consideration of the instrument itself, its purposes and the circumstances surrounding its execution, ascertain the intention of the parties. The intention of the parties is not to be deduced from any specific provision or fragmentary part of the instrument, but from its entire context.

Section 17 of the Mineral Leasing Act of 1920, as amended, provided that "such leases shall be conditioned upon the payment by the lessee . . . in advance of the rental to be fixed in the lease of not less than 25 cents per acre per annum. . . ." The Regulations adopted by the Secretary of the Interior provided that the first year's rental should be 50 cents per acre, and the rental for succeeding years should be 25 cents per acre, with the second and third years' payments waived. The authorities are in agreement that unless the contract discloses a contrary intention, an existing statute will be read into it to the same effect as an express provision.

The statute and the regulations were also made part of the leases by specific reference. The leases recited that they were entered into under, pursuant and subject to the terms and provisions of the Mineral Leasing Act "which is made a part hereof." The lessee agreed to abide by and conform to any and all reasonable regulations of the Secretary of the Interior then or thereinafter in force, "all of which regulations are made a part of this lease; Provided, that such regulations are not inconsistent with any express and specific provision hereof. . . ."

The first sentence of the rental section of the leases provided that the first year's rental should be 50 cents per acre, and also fixed the payments to be paid for subsequent years. It would be wholly unrealistic to hold that the rentals for subsequent years provided for in the same sentence were limited to a total payment of 25 cents per lease because the term "per acre" was not included there. To hold otherwise would, except for the first year, require the same rental on leases irrespective of the amount of land leased. Furthermore, the Secretary of the Interior was without authority to lease for less than 25 cents per acre. Considering the leases as a whole, together with the Mineral Leasing Act of 1920, as amended, and the Regulations adopted pursuant thereto, is too clear for any doubt that the parties intended the rentals for the 4th and 5th years to be 25 cents per acre, and not 25 cents per tract of land.

Parol Evidence

Scope and Purpose of Parol Evidence Rule. Under the parol evidence rule, oral or extrinsic evidence is not admissible to add to, alter, or vary the terms of a written contract. The purpose of the parol evidence rule is to lend stability to written agreements by excluding from consideration any evidence of facts tending to show that the parties intended something different from that set out in the written contract. When the parties have expressed their contract or agreement in a writing free from ambiguity, such writing is the best evidence of their intent; all preliminary negotiations are merged in the writing.

The parol evidence rule has been made a part of the law of sales in those states which have enacted the Uniform Commercial Code. (2–202.)

Admissible Parol Evidence. Parol evidence is admissible if it is offered to prove that the writing is not a valid contract because it was induced by misrepresentation, fraud, duress, or undue influence, or to prove that the contract is illegal. In all such instances, oral evidence is offered to prove that the contract is voidable or is based on an illegal bargain, and not to add to, alter, or vary the terms of the contract. Parol evidence is also admissible to prove that a writing was executed on the condition that it was not to be operative unless or until an agreed, uncertain future event happened.

Subsequent Contracts. An oral contract, entered into subsequent to the making of the written contract, may be proved by oral evidence even though the terms of the oral contract are such that they cancel, subtract from, or add to the obligations of the prior written contract. Such parol evidence is not offered to alter, vary, or add to the written contract but is offered to prove the existence of a valid oral contract entered into subsequent to the making of the written contract.

Partial Writings. If a writing is incomplete and such fact is apparent from a reading of the writing in the light of the relation of the parties, the subject matter of the contract, and the surrounding circumstances, parol evidence is admissible to fill in the gaps. However, the parol evidence admitted must not tend to alter, vary, or contradict the written terms of the contract.

Ambiguous Contracts. Parol evidence is admissible to clear up ambiguities in a written contract or agreement. Such evidence is limited to testimony of facts and circumstances surrounding the making of a contract which will aid the court in interpreting the contract. Likewise, if there is nothing in the writing which indicates that the parties did not intend to contract in accordance with an existing usage, oral evidence of a business usage is admissible.

Summary

The parol evidence rule is a rule of substantive law. Under the parol evidence rule, oral evidence is not admissible to add to, alter, or vary the terms of a written contract. Oral evidence is admissible to prove the writing is voidable or illegal; to prove that at the time it was executed it was agreed that it would not be operative unless a specified future, uncertain event happened; to prove a subsequent contract; or to clear up an ambiguity in the contract.

From a practical standpoint a person should read a proposed writing carefully before he signs it and be certain that all the terms of the agreement are expressed in clear, concise language. If there are any provisions or words in the writing which he does not understand, he should demand an explanation of their meaning before he signs; after he signs, it is too late to ask for changes.

Leveridge Motors Co. v. Notaras
433 P.2d 935 (Sup. Ct. Okla. 1967)

This was an action brought by Notaras (plaintiff) against Leveridge Motors (defendant) to recover $1,450 paid for a used car. Judgment for Notaras and Leveridge Motors appealed. Affirmed.

At the time the transaction occurred, a written document entitled "SALES ORDER AGREEMENT" was signed both by Notaras, and by one "Rusty" Eidson, as salesman, for Leveridge Motors. In the printed portion of the agreement was the following recital:

I agree to pay the balance of the purchase price upon delivery of car or to give such security for payment as you may require. It is understood that *I have examined said motor car and accept it in its present condition and agree that there are no warranties or representations, expressed or implied, not specified herein, respecting the goods hereby ordered.* This order is not binding upon you until accepted and signed by your Retail Manager and approved by your Credit Department. Delivery will be accepted and signed by your Retail Manager and approved by your Credit Department. This order shall not be assignable except with your written consent. Delivery will be accepted by me at your place of business.

On the blank portion of the printed form, the salesman, Mr. Eidson, wrote the following, among other things, in his own handwriting:

"30 day warranty
Repair clutch as needed
not too exceed $100.00
date no later then Sat.
Feb. 24, 1963. . . ."

A week after purchasing the car, Notaras returned with it and had the Leveridge make some minor repairs and replacements on it. A little more than two weeks thereafter, or on March 9, 1963, Notaras again returned with it and had the Leveridge do other work, evidenced by work order whose items totaled $70.50. To pay this sum, Notaras delivered his personal check on a Stillwater bank, made payable in the amount of $70.50, to "Leveridge Motor" but thereafter he stopped payment on said check.

A few days later, Notaras drove the car on a trip from Stillwater to Tulsa, and while in Tulsa, took it to an establishment referred to as "Gobles Imported Cars," and had it inspected there. Upon completion of the inspection, Notaras unsuccessfully attempted, by long distance telephone from Tulsa, to prevail upon Leveridge Motor Company to go there and get the car, and returned to his home in Stillwater by bus. Later, however, on about March 18th and 19th, 1963, upon his promise to pay Leveridge Motors for bringing the car from Tulsa to Oklahoma City, Leveridge Motors did this.

BLACKBIRD, JUDGE. . . . The substance of one of these contentions is that the trial court erred in allowing Notaras, over Leveridge's objection, "to attempt to vary" a part of the hereinbefore quoted printed portion of the Sales Order Agreement by parol evidence. This refers to Notaras' testimony to the effect that the hereinbefore quoted words "30 day warranty" (handwritten into the blank part of the printed form of Sales Order Agreement by the salesman, Rusty Eidson, before it was signed) evidences an oral warranty Notaras was given on the car for that period. If Notaras was given a warranty against latent mechnical defects in the car that might appear, or be discovered, within 30 days after its purchase, such a warranty would be in obvious conflict with the idea that Notaras accepted the car "in its present condition" (on the date of the sale), which Leveridge takes the position that he did, by placing his signature below the hereinbefore quoted printed portion of the Sales Order Agreement. It is our opinion that admission of this testimony violated none of the rules against the introduction of parol evidence, because said instrument, or document, was rendered ambiguous, and subject to explanation and clarification through parol evidence, by the obvious conflict in connotation between the handwritten words on it, and its printed portion. Without evidence to explain the meaning of the expression "30 day warranty," revealing what sort of a warranty it referred to, said written memorandum of the parties' agreement was also incomplete. . . .

Green Chevrolet Co. v. Kemp
406 S.W.2d 142 (Sup. Ct. Ark. 1966)

Green Chevrolet Co. (plaintiff) brought this action against Kemp (defendant) to recover payments due on a contract whereby Kemp purchased a car. Kemp filed a cross-complaint for damages for breach of express and implied warranty. The trial court granted a judgment for Green Chevrolet on its claims and also allowed Kemp $1,000 on his cross-complaint. Green Chevrolet appealed. Reversed as to Kemp's cross-complaint.

BLAND, JUSTICE. Over the objection of Green Chevrolet, the trial court allowed Kemp to show that a Mr. Freeman, seller's agent, had made oral guarantees of the mechanical parts of the car for a period of one year. Both Kemp and his wife testified, over objections, that Green's agent had told them that the car was guaranteed for a year and that if they were not satisfied with the car to bring it back and the seller would make adjustments. The seller admitted signing the conditional sales contract which provided, among other things, that the buyer accepts the car, having first examined and tested same and found it in sound and first-class condition. It further provided that the contract covers all conditions and agreements between the parties. Kemp brought the car back and minor adjustments were made by Green. Kemp kept the car from June 25, 1964 until January 2, 1965, driving it in excess of 3,000 miles, at which time he refused to make any further payments on the car because Green would not pay a bill he had incurred while attending the Cotton Bowl Game at Dallas, Texas wherein it became necessary to repair the power steering, brakes and fuel pump.

The court was in error in admitting the testimony of Kemp and his wife with reference to representations made by Green's agent as to these warranties. This testimony was contradictory and inconsistent with the terms of the conditional sales contract. Under the Uniform Commercial Code the parol evidence rule is not changed. Under the circumstances of the instant case this evidence was inadmissible. . . .

Problem Cases

1. Troup Brothers, Inc., was prime contractor on a road project. Dunlap furnished marl for the job. He leased from Meadows Southern Construction Co., Inc. (Lessor), a dragline and bulldozer, which he used to remove marl from the marl pit, and

then failed to pay the rent for the equipment. Lessor brought suit against Troup Brothers, Inc. (Troup) claiming that their supervisor made an oral promise to pay the rent on the equipment leased to Dunlap. Troup set up the statute of frauds as a defense. Is this a good defense?

2. Gore and Williams contracted with H. V. Middleton, Inc. (Middleton) for the drilling of an oil well. At the time Middleton started operations, Gore and Williams gave him a $20,000 five-day draft as an advance and partial payment of Middleton's costs. The draft was dishonored and Middleton ceased operations. The Abrahams owned extensive mineral interests on land adjacent to the tract on which the well was to be drilled and they thereby stood to gain substantially if the well should prove to be a producing well. Oscar Abraham orally promised Middleton that if he would proceed to drill the well the Abrahams would pay for the drilling if Gore and Williams did not pay. Middleton completed the drilling of the well and Gore and Williams failed to pay. The Abrahams refused to pay and when sued set up the statute of frauds as a defense. Is this a good defense?

3. Aubrey had purchased from Workman a house which was in Workman's Park Row addition. He had executed a first lien note to J. E. Foster Company and a second lien note for $5,850 to Workman. Aubrey later experienced financial difficulties and defaulted on his payments. He claimed that he told Workman that he planned to rent the house and that Workman told him that a rental house would have an adverse effect on the sale of the unsold houses in the addition and that if he would not rent the house he (Workman) would release the second lien on the house and discharge the note. Aubrey abandoned the house and the first lien was foreclosed. Workman never released the second lien or surrendered the note to Aubrey. When sued on the note Aubrey set up as a defense Workman's oral promise to release the lien and discharge the note. Workman claimed that the oral promise was unenforceable under the statute of frauds. Is the statute of frauds a good defense?

4. On May 30, 1960, Sinclair entered into an oral contract with Sullivan Chevrolet Company (Sullivan) whereby he was employed as sales manager for a one-year period starting June 6, 1960, at a salary of $1,200 per month. Sinclair claimed that Sullivan promised him a bonus which would give him a minimum salary of $20,000 for the year, and that Sullivan was to pay Sinclair's moving expenses. He also claimed that the employment agreement was to be reduced to writing. As part of his case Sinclair alleged that Sullivan intentionally misrepresented his intention as to reducing the agreement to writing and as to paying the bonus. Sinclair asked damages of $12,527. Sullivan denied making the alleged misrepresentations and set up the statute of frauds as a defense. Is the statute of frauds a good defense?

5. Hughson owned and operated a milk bar, known as "Forsgate Milk Bar." On March 16, 1957, he entered into an oral contract to sell the business and the real estate on which it was located to Kufta for $65,000, payable $12,000 down and $53,000 by mortgage, payable in monthly installments over a 15-year period. Kufta paid $100 "as a binder to show our good faith." Mrs. Hughson typed the following memorandum:

> Selling to Andrew J. Kufta one hundred fifty (150) feet on Morris Avenue, one hundred twenty five (125) feet on Lehigh Avenue, ground, building, lock, stock and barrel. Price Sixty-five thousand (65,000) dollars, down payment twelve (sic) thousand (12,000) dollars, balance to be paid in fifteen years or

less at five per cent (5%) interest, payable monthly plus monthly payment on taxes.

Date for settlement, March 30, 1957.

Life insurance to cover mortgage.

> Myles Morrison
> > 7 West Grand Street
> > Elizabeth, N.J.
> Douglas Baker
> > 1172 Raymond Blvd.
> > Newark, N.J.

Messrs. Morrison and Baker were to be the attorneys for the parties.

This memorandum was not signed by either party.

On March 18, 1957, Kufta gave notice to his employer that he would quit on March 22, 1957. On March 20, 1957, Hughson returned the $100 check given him by Kufta and told Kufta that he (Hughson) had received a better offer and that he would not sell to Kufta. Kufta brought suit asking specific performance of the contract, and Hughson set up the statute of frauds as a defense. Can Kufta get specific performance?

6. Lambdin entered into a contract with Przyborowski to purchase a piece of real estate owned by Przyborowski. The contract provided,

> The balance of Twenty-one Thousand Dollars ($21,000) to be financed through a lending institution for a period of twenty years (20) at the buyer's expense. Settlement to be within ninety days (90) from the date first mentioned above at which time possession shall be given. In the event that this loan cannot be arranged, then all monies of the deposit shall be refunded to the buyers; and this contract shall become null and void.

Lambkin could not get a loan according to the terms of the contract. Przyborowski alleged that a new oral contract was made covering the terms of the loan, and that the requirements of the statute of frauds were met concerning this oral contract because, while under oath Lambdin testified that such a contract may have been made, sued for specific performance. Have the requirements for the statute of frauds been met?

7. The United Mine Workers of America (Union) through activities of violence, shooting, etc., in an effort to unionize mines, induced Osborne Mining Company to breach its contract with Love and Amos Coal Company (Love and Amos). The Union set up as a defense that the contract between Osborne Mining Company and Love and Amos could not be performed within a year of the making thereof and that it was oral and was therefore unenforceable under the statute of frauds. Is this a valid defense against a tort suit brought for having induced breach of contract?

8. Coan entered an oral contract with Orsinger in presence of witnesses to act as manager of Tyler Garden Apartments in return for $75 per week and a rent-free apartment. This agreement was to continue until Coan completed his law studies *in three years or was obliged to discontinue these studies.* Coan assumed his duties, but after one month received a letter terminating this contract. Coan sued Orsinger for breach of contract and Orsinger set the statute of frauds as his defense? Is this defense good?

9. Erving Paper manufactured and sold paper napkins in reusable polyethylene bags. Erving decided to purchase a special packaging machine from Sharp Machine Co.

in order to meet the increase demand for these napkins. Through oral negotiations with Sharp a price of $11,000 per machine was accepted by Erving. Erving placed a written order, specifying the exact package sizes the machine had to be able to wrap, the exact production rate (per minute) desired, and that the machine be equipped with change parts required to fit a second size of wrapping. A few days before the promised delivery date, Sharp informed Erving by letter that their Engineering Dept. was unable to design a machine that would meet the special requirements of the packaging job. Erving Paper sued for damages for breach of contract and Sharp set up the statute of frauds. Is this a good defense?

10. Langelier, area supervisor for Tidewater Oil, orally told Corkin that if Corkin would purchase certain real estate, Tidewater would lease the land and build a service station on it. Langelier sent Corkin the following signed letter:

> As per our discussion of August 31st I am sending today under separate cover a set of our Type 'C' specifications which call for construction of a two bay modern service station.
>
> It will be appreciated if you will secure construction costs and advise me when same are available so that we can then get together to arrive at a mutually agreeable rental agreement.

Tidewater later refused to go through with the deal and Corkin sued alleging breach of contract on the part of Tidewater. Tidewater set up the statute of frauds as a defense to the contract. Is the letter sufficient to prove a contract?

11. Arcuri and Weiss were negotiating for the purchase and sale of a restaurant. In the course of the negotiations Arcuri gave Weiss a check, payable to Weiss for $500. Printed on the left side of the check was the following: "Tentative deposit on tentative purchase of 115 City Line Ave., Phila. Restaurant, Fixtures, Equipment, Goodwill." Arcuri decided not to purchase the restaurant and demanded the return of the check. Weiss refused to return the check and when Arcuri brought suit against Weiss to recover a judgment for the amount of the check, Weiss set up that a contract of sale had been negotiated and offered the check, with the notation thereon, as a note or memorandum sufficient to satisfy the requirements of the statute of frauds. The trial court held that the notation was not sufficient and Weiss appealed. Should the case be reversed?

12. Mrs. Miletich delivered goods to Glascoe, who was in the moving and storage business, for shipment to Ottumwa, Iowa. At the time the goods were delivered to Glascoe, a written bill of lading was issued to Mrs. Miletich; and Glascoe promised orally to hold the goods and not ship them until notified by Mrs. Miletich. The bill of lading acknowledged receipt of the goods from Mrs. Miletich and provided that the carrier agreed to carry them to the destination indicated below which was written in as "Ottumwa, Iowa." The bill of lading contained no provision concerning when shipment would be made or when the goods would be delivered to their destination except that in the printed terms and conditions on the reverse side of the bill of lading there was the provision that the carrier was not bound to transfer the goods to any particular schedule or otherwise than "with reasonable dispatch." Glascoe did not hold the goods until notified by Mrs. Miletich but shipped them out as soon as they were received. Mrs. Miletich brought suit and offered oral evidence to prove that Glascoe agreed to hold the goods until notified to ship them. The oral evidence was objected to on the ground that it was not admissible under the parol evidence rule. Is the oral evidence admissible?

13. Continental Gin Company (Gin Co.) brought suit on a contract in writing to sell described machinery to Freeman. Freeman offered evidence of oral agreements

with Gin Co. by which it promised to install the machinery and to assume other obligations, and then failed to do so. Gin Co. objected to the admission of the evidence on the ground that its admission would violate the parol evidence rule. The court found that all of the matters offered were discussed prior to the execution of the written contract and that the writing was clear and complete and refused to admit the offered oral evidence. Should the evidence be admitted?

chapter 13. Rights of Third Parties

Assignment of Contracts

Introduction. In many early systems of the law the obligation of a debtor was personal in a literal sense, in that the body of the debtor could be taken by his creditors. In England, if a debtor did not fulfill his obligations, he could be imprisoned for debt. The accepted attitude toward one who did not pay his honest debts was that he was in effect a thief. This general attitude, together with the right of a creditor to have his debtor imprisoned if he failed to pay his debt, emphasized the personal nature of debt. At this time the courts held that a contract was personal to the parties and that neither party could assign his rights under the contract to a third person.

As trade developed, the need for credit increased, and with this development the treatment of the unfortunate debtor became less harsh. There was little change in the law in England until 1670, however, and the legislation enacted by parliament at that time proved to be ineffective. Later, some reforms were inaugurated, but imprisonment for debt was not abolished in England until after the United States gained its independence. Imprisonment for debt was abandoned early in the United States.

The negotiation of bills of exchange and their assignment were recognized in the 16th century. Promissory notes were not recognized as commercial instruments and were not negotiable or assignable until parliament made them negotiable by statute in 1704. At this time, certain types of contracts were assignable by operation of law.

With the development of trade and the attainment of higher standards of commercial morality, the practice of extending credit, especially in the area of commercial transactions, became common. The needs of merchants demanded procedural reforms in the courts in relation to commercial cases. The courts began to recognize the right to assign contract rights, yet any suit on the contract had to be brought in the name of the party to the contract and not in the name of the assignee. By gradual development the rules of law regarding the assignment of contracts became more liberal, and now we recognize the assignability of contracts which are not personal to the parties. Under the procedural statutes now in force in most states, the assignee of a contract may bring suit in his own name to enforce the contract.

Contracts Not Assignable.   An assignment is a transfer, to the assignee, of the rights which the assignor has under a contract. The assignee has the right to have the performance of the contract rendered to him. From the beginning of the law of contracts, we have recognized that the promisee cannot demand of the promisor a performance which differs in any material respects from that promised; consequently, if the duties of the promisor will be altered in any material respect by the assignment of the contract, the contract is not assignable. Only those contracts can be assigned, the performance of which can be rendered by the promisor to the assignee without materially altering or increasing the burdens of performance.

Any contract which is personal in nature cannot be assigned, since the nature of the contract is limited by the personality of the original promisee and the substitution of the assignee changes the nature of the performance required by the promisor.

Any contract the performance of which involves personal skill, judgment, or character is not assignable. A contract to support for life cannot be assigned. A property insurance policy cannot be assigned before the loss of the material insured because such policies are based in part on the character of the insured. A sharecrop lease is not assignable, since the rent received depends directly on the skill, ability, and honesty of the tenant.

If a contract contains a provision expressly prohibiting the assignment of the contract, the courts will hold that the contract is not assignable. The modification of this rule under the U.C.C. is discussed subsequently.

Contracts Which Are Assignable.   The typical example of an assignable contract is one in which a promisor has obligated himself to pay money to a promisee. In such a contract the promisor's duty to pay is fixed, the burden of performance is not increased by requiring payment to the assignee instead of to the promisee, and a minimum of personal relationship is involved. As a general rule a contract to sell and deliver goods or to sell land is assignable. However, if the contract to sell goods is what is known as a "needs" or "output" contract, such a contract is, as a general rule, held not to be assignable, since the assignee's "needs" or ability to produce may vary materially from that of the promisee.

Contracts not to compete with the buyer of a business or with an employer have been held by the majority of the courts to be assignable. The purpose of such a restraint clause is to protect the goodwill of a business. The goodwill is an asset which may be sold with the business; consequently, the courts have held that a contract not to compete can be assigned as an incident of the sale of the business to be protected.

The Delegation of Duties. The courts have held that the duties under a contract cannot be assigned but under some circumstances may be delegated. For instance, the courts have recognized the validity of the delegation of the duty to do building or engineering work, if the work is of such a nature that it may be performed by many persons, and if its performance does not depend on the skill, training, or character of an individual or group of individuals. The promisor cannot, however, relieve himself from his obligation under a contract by delegating his duties to some third party. He can still be held liable for breach of the contract if the party to whom the duties are delegated fails to perform.

The right to delegate the duties created by a contract to sell goods is expanded by Section 2–210 of the Code.

Summary

In the early period of the development of our law, if a debt was not paid, the debtor could be imprisoned. Under the law the contractual relation was held to be highly personal, and no contract was assignable. As the country developed and trade expanded, the extension of credit became a common practice, especially in connection with commercial transactions. By gradual development the right to assign contracts was recognized, and today a contract is assignable if it does not involve the performance of personal services or the skill or character of the promisor, and if the duties of the promisor will not be materially altered by the assignment. A contract to receive money is a typical example of an assignable contract. Duties under a contract cannot be assigned, but they can be delegated if they are wholly impersonal in character. The promisor cannot relieve himself from his obligations under a contract by the delegation of his duties.

Although the basic principles of law relative to the assignment of contracts are not changed under the provisions of the Code, some aspects of the law are simplified and made more flexible and more practical.

Berger v. Paalzow
289 S.W.2d 861 (Ct. App. Tenn. 1956)

This was an action by Seymour A. Berger and others (plaintiffs) against Mary L. Paalzow and others (defendants) asking for specific performance of a contract to lease an office building. Judgment for Paalzow, and Berger appealed. Judgment affirmed.

Mary L. Paalzow and her children owned the James Building, a large office building, in Chattanooga, Tennessee, which Jerome Berger and Seymour A. Berger wished to lease. After extensive negotiations and correspondence and after Paalzow had investigated the Bergers and learned that they were experienced and efficient managers of office buildings and that each was a millionaire in his own right, Paalzow contracted to lease the James Building to them. The Bergers assigned the contract to their niece, Halina Berger. A lease drafted in accordance with the contract and naming Halina Berger as lessee was submitted to Paalzow for execution, and Paalzow refused to execute it. When suit for specific performance was brought, Paalzow set up as a defense that the contract to lease was not assignable.

HOWARD, JUDGE. It seems to be the rule generally that rights arising out of a contract cannot be transferred if they are coupled with liabilities, or if they involve a relationship of personal credit and confidence.

In *Arkansas Valley Smelting Co.* v. *Belden Min. Co.,* a contract for the sale and delivery of lead ore by a mining company to persons conducting a smelter, the ore to be assayed after delivery, and the price to be ascertained and paid according to the results of the assay, no security being given for payment except the character and solvency of the parties to whom the ore was to be delivered, was held not assignable by the latter, the Court saying:

At the present day, no doubt, an agreement to pay money, or to deliver goods, may be assigned by the person to whom the money is to be paid or the goods are to be delivered, if there is nothing in the terms of the contract, whether by requiring something to be afterwards done by him, or by some other stipulation, which manifests the intention of the parties that it shall not be assignable. But everyone has a right to select and determine with whom he will contract, and cannot have another person thrust upon him without his consent. In the familiar phrase of Lord Denman, 'You have the right to the benefit you anticipate from the character, credit, and substance of the party with whom you contract.' The rule upon this subject, as applicable to the case at bar, is well expressed in a recent English treatise: 'Rights arising out of contract cannot be transferred if they are coupled with liabilities, or if they involve a relation of personal confidence such that the party whose agreement conferred those rights must have intended them to be exercised only by him in whom he actually confided.'

In *Crane Ice Cream Co.* v. *Terminal Freezing & Heating Co.,* the Court said:

A contract to pay money may doubtless be assigned by the person to whom the money is payable, if there is nothing in the terms of the contract which manifests the intention of the parties to it that it shall not be assignable. But when rights arising out of contract are coupled with obligations to be performed by the contractor, and involve such a relation of personal confidence that it must have been intended that the rights should be exercised, and the obligations performed by him alone, the contract, including both his rights and his obligations, cannot be assigned without the consent of the other party to the original contract.

Accordingly, we are of the opinion as was the Chancellor, that the Bergers' bill has no merit, and the decree dismissing the bill will be affirmed.

Rights Acquired by Assignee

General Rule. An assignment of a contract is in legal effect a sale to an assignee of an assignor's rights under a contract. The assignee takes the place of the assignor and is entitled to all the rights of the assignor. He can, however, acquire no greater rights than the assignor has at the time of the assignment, that is, he takes the contract subject to all the defenses that the promisor has to the contract.

Notice of Assignment. If the assignee wishes to protect the rights he has acquired by the assignment, he, or someone acting in his behalf, must give the promisor notice of the assignment. If the promisor is not given notice of the assignment and he renders performance to the original promisee, the promisor will have discharged his duty and will not be liable to the assignee under the contract. In such a situation the original promisee, having accepted performance of the assigned contract, is liable to the assignee for the value of the performance received by him. When notice is given to the promisor, he becomes liable at this time to render to the assignee any performance due the promisee.

Successive Assignments. If a promisee assigns his rights to one assignee and at a later date wrongfully assigns the same rights to a second assignee, who takes for value and without notice or knowledge of the prior assignment, the question then arises as to which of the respective assignees has the better right. There are two views on this point.

Under the rule known as the "American rule," the courts have held that the first assignee has the better right. This view is based on the rule of property law that a person cannot transfer greater rights in property than he has. Under the rule known as the "English rule," the assignee who first gives notice of the assignment of the contract has the greater right. Under this rule, the giving of notice is considered equivalent to the taking of possession of tangible property. Under the law of sales, if the same item of property is sold to two different innocent purchasers for value, the first to take possession has the better right.

All the courts hold that if the application of a rule will bring about unjust results, such rule will not be followed, in which case the contract will be awarded to the assignee who, in justice and fair dealing, is entitled to it.

Assignment of Wages. Under the common law an assignment of future wages was void unless the assignor had a contract of employment. This rule has been relaxed, and now, as a general rule, if the assignor is regularly employed, the courts will enforce an assignment of the future wages of such employee.

However, substantially all the states have enacted statutes regulating the assignment of future wages. These statutes range from those which make all assignments of future wages void to those which are rather elaborate and complex.

Summary ,

The assignee of a contract can acquire by the assignment no greater rights than those had by the assignor at the time of the assignment. If the assignee wishes to protect the rights acquired by the assignment, notice of the assignment must be given to the promisor. The rights acquired by the assignment will be such rights as the assignor had against the promisor at the time notice of the assignment was given to the promisor. In most states the assignment of future wages is regulated by statute.

General Factors, Inc. v. Beck

402 P.2d 221 (Ct. App. Ariz. 1965)

This action was brought by General Factors (plaintiffs) as assignees of a claim for construction materials sold by Tempe Gravel Co. to A. Deal Beck (defendant). Judgment for Beck and General Factors appealed. Affirmed.

In early October, Beck purchased from Tempe Company certain materials for use by Beck in his construction business. Invoices representing these purchases were then sent to General Factors, Inc., under an alleged assignment and factoring account. General Factors paid for these invoices, between the 10th and 31st of October, and mailed these invoices to Beck at his place of business.

The invoices bearing the name of Tempe had at the bottom the following statement:

"Accounts due and payable 15th of month following purchase."

General Factors affixed a sticker to each invoice which read as follows:

"Pay only to General Factors, Inc., 3500 North Central Avenue, Phoenix, Arizona. This account and the merchandise covered hereby is assigned and payable only to said corporation, to which notice must be given of any merchandise returns or claims of any kind."

And also stamped to the invoice was the following:

"To facilitate our accounts receivable bookkeeping, this invoice has been factored with General Factors, Inc., 3500 North Central Building, Suite 332 in Phoenix, Arizona. Make payment directly to factor."

Invoices were received by Beck's bookkeepeer and the bookkeeper merely opened the letters and checked the amounts on the invoices to determine any set-offs or "charge-backs". The bookkeeper did not have the authority to draw checks for payment of the invoices or any other accounts. These invoices were not handed to Beck until sometime between the 7th and 15th of November, 1960.

In the meantime, Tempe was experiencing financial difficulties and Beck paid off this account with Tempe.

CAMERON, JUDGE. The primary question before us concerns the question of notice of an assignment under the statutes and laws of the State of Arizona. The Arizona Revised Statutes provide as follows, at § 44–805:

"A. If a debtor, *without actual notice* that an assignment of his account has been made, makes full or partial payment of his debt to the assignor, his debt shall thereby be extinguished or reduced." (Emphasis supplied.)

It would thus appear that where the debtor has paid the creditor, as in the instant case, that his debt is thereby extinguished or reduced unless he has received "actual notice" before said payment was made. Our Supreme Court had discussed notice as follows:

"[T]hat where a statute does not specify the manner in which a notice is to be given, 'personal notice' is required.

"The rule has been laid down that in the absence of custom, statute, or express contract, a notice sought to be served by mail is not effective until it comes into the hands of the one sought to be served."

The testimony below does not show that notification of the factoring agreement by the bookkeepeer to Beck was within the scope of the authority of the bookkeeper. The bookkeeper merely opened the letters, checked the amounts to make sure that Beck was not being overcharged, computed any set-offs or charge-backs, and then presented the invoices to Beck for the purpose of paying accounts. The testimony is sufficient to find that Beck did not see any of these invoices with the notices attached thereto until he had made the payments to Tempe. . . .[1]

Nassau Discount Corp. v. Allen
255 N.Y.S.2d 608 (Sup. Ct. N.Y. 1965)

This was an action brought by Nassau Discount Corp. (plaintiff), as an assignee of book purchase contract, against Allen (defendant). Judgment for Allen.

In April 1963, a salesman representing Educational Guild went to Allen's house and convinced her that she was required to buy certain books for use by her school-age child. He did this by falsely representing that he was connected with the Board of Education.

Allen signed an installment purchase contract which stated on its reverse side:

Buyer will settle all mechanical, service and other claims of whatsover character with respect to the sale evidenced hereby, directly with Seller (and not with any such Assignee) and will not set up any such claim(s) as a defense or counterclaim to any action for payment or possession which may be brought by an Assignee who acquires this Contract in good faith and for value. . . .

On April 30, 1963, Discount Corp., took an assignment of the contract for value. On May 5, 1963, Discount mailed to Allen a Notice of Assignment requesting Allen

---

[1] It can be argued that Beck should not be allowed to deny the authority of his bookkeeper to receive notices of this kind. In any event, the case underlines the importance of giving actual notice by registered mail or personal contact where important matters are involved.

to notify Discount in writing within ten days from the date of the mailing of the notice of any defense that she might have arising out of the sale or otherwise be barred from asserting such defense in an action by Discount. Discount received no written response to its Notice of Assignment. However, Allen upon receipt of the notice immediately returned Discount's coupon payment book by mail. Allen refused to pay any installments of the contract.

HELLER, JUDGE.   The broad issue presented for determination by this court is whether Allen is barred by the waiver of defenses clause contained within the contract from asserting her defenses of fraud and non-delivery against plaintiff assignee. Subsidiary to the determination of this broad issue is whether the fraud alleged is fraud in factum, the real defense of fraud, or fraud in the inducement, and furthermore, whether Discount Corp. takes subject to the real defense of fraud.

Fraud in factum exists where one is induced to sign an instrument of a different nature or character than that he was led to believe was before him. In the present case Allen does not assert that she was deceived as to the nature of the paper she was signing but rather that she was *induced* to sign the contract through the fraudulent misrepresentations of the salesman. Therefore, the fraud involved in this case is fraud in the inducement of the contract and we need not decide whether plaintiff takes subject to the real defense of fraud.

More accurately phrased, the issue is whether Allen has waived her defenses of fraud in the inducement of the contracts and non-delivery. The controlling statute in the resolution of this issue is Section 403, subdivision 3(a) of the Personal Property Law which provides in substance that no contract shall contain any provision whereby the buyer agrees not to assert against an assignee a claim or defense arising out of the sale, but it *may* contain such a provision as to an assignee who acquires the contract in good faith and for value and to whom the buyer has not mailed written notice of the facts giving rise to a claim or defense within ten days after the assignee has mailed notice of the assignment to the buyer. Subdivision 3(a) further provides stringent requirements for the contents of the notice of assignment, all of which have been complied with by plaintiff.

Good faith necessarily requires that the assignee be "not so identified with the seller, to an extent that it could fairly be said that the dealings of one are inextricably interwoven with that of the other." *Public National Bank and Trust Co. of New York* v. *Fernandez*. The court further stated:

"Certain unmistakable indicia point inevitably that this plaintiff, far from being a bona fide assignee of a chose in action, was in fact a principal in the transaction . . ." It was pointed out that the contract provided that all installments be paid to the plaintiff assignee; that the title to the merchandise was to be retained by the holder, who was defined as either the seller or the assignee; that the assignment was made even before the goods were delivered to the buyer and that the sale and assignment were physically encompassed within the same document. The court concluded: "From all the above it would appear that the bank, rather than being a bona fide purchaser of the contract in question, was to all intents and purposes a party to the original agreement."

When contracts are supplied by an assignee, complete with the assignee's name printed thereon, it is obvious that the assignee is a specific assignee, vitally interested in the sale, so closely related that it is almost as if the assignee were "looking over the parties' shoulders when the sale was consummated." Form contracts supplied by a specific assignee containing waiver of defenses clauses inescapably point to the conclusion of a pre-formed intention upon the part of the assignee to defeat the rights of the buyer so as to negate the requirement of good faith.

It can fairly be said that Allen and Discount in the circumstances of this case were so inextricably intertwined as to impugn Discount's good faith status. This court, therefore, finds as an ultimate fact that an implied agency existed under the terms of the contract that Discount is subject to the defenses of fraud in the inducement and nondelivery.

Assignor's Liability to Assignee

Implied Warranties. When an assignor assigns a claim for value to an assignee, the assignor impliedly warrants to his immediate transferee that the claim is a valid claim, that is, that the parties have capacity to contract, that the claim is not void for illegality, and that it has not been discharged prior to the assignment or rendered unenforceable for any reasons known to the assignor. He also impliedly warrants that he has good title to the claim and that he has passed good title to the assignee.

If the claim is represented by a written instrument, the assignor impliedly warrants that the instrument is genuine and is in all respects what it purports to be. He also impliedly agrees to do nothing which will defeat or impair the value of the assignment. The assignment does not warrant the solvency of the promisor. These implied warranties may be limited or enlarged by the express agreement of the parties.

General Liability. If, after the assignment of a contract, payment is made to and received by the assignor, he holds the money as trustee for the assignee and is liable to the assignee for the money collected. If the assignor makes successive assignments of the same claim to two or more assignees, he is liable to the assignee or assignees who acquire no right against the promisor for the damages such assignee or assignees may have suffered as a result of the fraud.

Summary

An assignor impliedly warrants that the claim he assigns is a valid, subsisting claim and that he will do nothing to defeat or impair the value of the assignment. He does not warrant the solvency of the promisor.

If the assignor collects the assigned claim, he is liable to the assignee for all moneys collected. If he makes successive assignments of the same claim, he is liable to the defrauded assignees for the damages they have suffered.

Third-Party Beneficiary

Classes of Third-Party Beneficiary Contracts. Where the performance of the promise in a contract will benefit some person other than the promisee, the party benefited is a third-party beneficiary. As a general rule a person who is not a party to a contract has no rights in the contract, even though he may derive some advantage from its performance. However, if the parties to the contract enter into the contract with the intent of benefiting a third party, the beneficiary under the contract may enforce it by court action. Third-party beneficiaries have been divided into three classes: (1) donee beneficiaries, (2) creditor beneficiaries, and (3) incidental beneficiaries.

Donee Beneficiaries. If the primary purpose of the promisee, in contracting for performance to be rendered to the third person, is to make a gift of the performance to the third person, the third person is a donee beneficiary. In a donee beneficiary contract the promisee furnishes the consideration, and the promise of the promisor is made to the promisee, but the promise of the promisor is to confer a stipulated benefit on the beneficiary, who must be named or indicated with reasonable certainty. If the promisor does not perform his promise, both the promisee and the beneficiary have a cause of action against him. The beneficiary can recover a judgment for the value of the promised performance. The promisee can recover a judgment for any damage he can prove he suffered as a result of the promisor's failure to render performance to the beneficiary. As a general rule the promisee can recover only nominal damages.

A life insurance contract whereby the insurance company, in consideration of premiums paid, contracts to pay to the named beneficiary the amount of the policy on the happening of a stipulated event, usually the death of the insured, is a common form of the donee beneficiary contract. If the insurance company does not pay on the happening of the contingency, the beneficiary can bring suit in his own name and recover a judgment.

Creditor Beneficiaries. A person is a creditor beneficiary if the performance of the promise will satisfy an actual or supposed legal duty of the promisee to the beneficiary. Such a benefit is not intended as a gift. The primary distinction between a donee beneficiary and a creditor beneficiary is that the benefits conferred on one, the donee beneficiary, are a gift, whereas the performance of the promise in the case of the creditor beneficiary is intended to discharge a duty or supposed duty by the promisee. The duty need not be the payment of money but may be any type of obligation.

Incidental Beneficiaries. An incidental beneficiary is one who will benefit in some way from the performance of a contract which has been entered into by the promisee for his own benefit and without any intent of benefiting a third person. The purpose of the contract is to obtain the benefits for the promisee, not for a third person. An incidental beneficiary has no rights in the contract and cannot recover damages in a suit for breach of contract.

For example, suppose Adams contracts with Ball to dig a ditch which will drain a low place on Adams' farm. The low place extends over onto Clark's farm, and the drainage ditch will be of benefit to Clark also.

If Ball then breaches his contract with Adams and does not dig the ditch, Clark will not be allowed to recover damages in an action against Ball for breach of the contract. Although Clark would have benefited from the performance of the contract, he was not a party to the contract, nor was the contract entered into with the intent of benefiting Clark. Clark is an incidental beneficiary and has no rights under the contract.

Municipal or Governmental Contracts. As a general rule the members of the public are incidental beneficiaries of contracts entered into in the regular course of the carrying-on of the functions of the municipality or governmental unit. A member of the public cannot recover a judgment in a suit against the promisor, even though as a taxpayer he will suffer some injury from nonperformance. However, a municipality or governmental unit may enter into contracts which have as their objective the protection of the individual members of the public. If a member of the public is injured by breach of such a contract, he can recover damages in a suit brought in his own name.

Summary

A contract may expressly provide that performance shall be rendered to a named third person who is not a party to the contract, or a third person who is not a party to the contract may be benefited by the performance of the contract without being named. Such persons fall into three groups: (1) donee beneficiary, (2) creditor beneficiary, and (3) incidental beneficiary.

If the purpose of the promisee is to make a gift to a named third person of part or all of the performance of the promisor, such third person is a donee beneficiary. If the purpose of the promisee is to impose on the promisor an obligation to pay a debt owed to a third person by the promisee, such third person is a creditor beneficiary. Both donee beneficiary and creditor beneficiary have the right to bring suit on the contract. If a third person will benefit from the performance of the contract without any intent on the part of the promisee to confer such benefits, such person is an incidental beneficiary and has no rights in the contract.

Shillman v. Hobstetter
241 A.2d 570 (Ct. App. Md. 1968)

This was an action to recover home purchase deposits brought by Charles Hobstetter and other people (plaintiffs) who purchased homes from Maryland Corporation, a subdivision developer. The action was brought against Howe Shillman, an officer of Maryland Corp. and others who were creditors of Maryland Corporation (defendants). From a judgment for Hobstetter, Shillman and the other defendants appealed. Affirmed.

Maryland Corp. ran into financing difficulties and sought additional loan insurance commitments from the FHA. The FHA agreed to give these additional commitments provided that Shillman and the other defendants agreed in writing to guarantee the refund of all deposits received from home purchasers where Maryland Corp. failed to complete the homes on which the deposits had been made. Maryland Corp. failed to complete the homes of Hobstetter and the other plaintiffs.

BARNES, JUDGE.   Since the establishment of the doctrine of third-party beneficiaries in the landmark decision of the Court of Appeals of New York in *Lawrence* v. *Fox* (1859), substantially all state courts of last resort, including this Court, have adopted and applied the doctrine. It is a developing doctrine of law and its limits in particular cases are still being established.

In determining the intention of the parties, the language of the instrument is the primary source for that determination. The language of the contract of May 27, 1964, clearly identifies the class of persons to whom deposits would be refunded and provides that the defendants would guarantee that refund. This is the primary and indeed the only purpose of the contract and, *prima facie,* those contract purchasers are donee beneficiaries. The surrounding circumstances confirm that this was the intention of the parties. Borcherding [the FHA director] testified, without objection, that it was intended that the purchasers of homes in Sections 9, 10 and 11 were intended to be recognized as the primary parties in interest. This testimony, accepted by the trial court as correct, is entitled to substantial weight as representing the intention of the FHA. . . .

In the present case, the FHA clearly indicated its intent that the contract purchasers should be the donee beneficiaries, while Shillman and the other defendants had possibly other motivations, such as the need to obtain FHA conditional commitments on Section 12 in order to keep the developer functioning and to benefit subcontractors and possibly others. The face of the contract, however, indicates that the primary and direct benefit was intended for the contract purchasers. It is, in our opinion, a clear—if not a classic—case of a donee beneficiary contract. . . .

Burns v. *Washington Savings*
171 So.2d 322 (Sup. Ct. Miss. 1965)

This was an action by Lee Burns (plaintiff) against Washington Savings and Great Southern Savings & Loan Association (defendants) to recover, as third-party beneficiary, for the breach of contracts to make loans. Judgment for Washington Savings and Great Southern Savings and Loan Association and Burns appealed. Judgment affirmed.

Burns was a building contractor. Certain individuals entered into contracts with him to build separate residences upon land owned by them. These homeowners desired to obtain loans and Burns directed them to Washington Savings. The home-owners filed applications for loans and Burns aided them in obtaining such loans by furnishing surveys, credit reports, title insurance and plans and specifications which were filed with Washington Savings. Washington Savings gave written com-mitments to each homeowner and wrote Burns a letter informing him that it had done so. Washington Savings then refused to make the loans. As a result the home-owners defaulted on their payments to Burns and he took over the residences he had built and sold them at a loss. Burns contended that he was a third-party beneficiary of the loan commitment contracts and brought suit to recover damages for their breach.

ROGERS, JUSTICE.   It is a general rule of the law of contracts that in order to maintain an action to enforce the breach of a contract, or to recover damages grow-ing out of the breach, or for failure to carry out the terms of the contract, it is ordinarily a necessary prerequisite that the relationship of privity of contract exist between the party damaged and the party sought to be held liable for the breach of the contract.

An exception has been engrafted on this rule and stated succinctly, it is as fol-lows: A third person may sue on a contract made for his benefit between others to the consideration of which he is a stranger. Or stated differently, a third person may in his own right and name, enforce a promise made for his benefit even though he is a stranger both to the contract and the consideration.

The early cases establishing the rule in the United States appear to have arisen in New York where the doctrine was broadly established; that where one person makes a promise to another for the benefit of a third person, the third person may maintain an action on such promise. This principle of law has been recognized by most of the states of the United States, although some states have modified the rule.

The historical development of the rule giving the third-party beneficiary the right to maintain an action for the breach of the contract has not been entirely satis-factory to the courts so they have repeatedly declared that the rule is to be confined to its original limits. Thus, it has been established that an incidental benefit to a third party is not a sufficient legal ground to give him a right of action upon a con-tract. It is said:

The principle that one not a party or privy to a contract but who is the beneficiary thereof is entitled to maintain an action for its breach is not so far extended as to give to a third person who is only indirectly and incidentally benefited by the contract the right to sue upon it. A mere incidental, collateral, or consequential benefit which may accrue to a third person by reason of the performance of the contract, or the mere fact that he has been injured by the breach thereof, is not sufficient to enable him to maintain an action on the contract. Where the contract is primarily for the benefit of the parties thereto, the mere fact that a third person would be incidentally benefited does not give him a right to sue for its breach.

In order for the third-person beneficiary to have a cause of action, the contracts between the original parties must have been entered into for his benefit, or at least such benefit must be the direct result of the performance within the contemplation of the parties as shown by its terms. There must have been a legal obligation or duty on the part of the promisee to such third-person beneficiary. This obligation must have been a legal duty which connects the beneficiary with the contract. In other words, the right of the third-party beneficiary to maintain an action on the contract must spring from the terms of the contract itself.

In the Sideboard case, this Court said:

> The difficulty is to determine when a particular case comes within the rule. There are hundreds of cases on the subject. . . . Taking the leading among those cases, as, for instance *Smyth* v. *City of New York,* and searching through them for a more definite or a more tangible statement of the rule, we think it will be found that the best considered of these cases reason the matter down to this: (1) When the terms of the contract are expressly broad enough to include the third party either by name or as one of a specified class, and (2) the said third party was evidently within the intent of the term so used, the said third party will be within its benefits, if (3) the promisee had, in fact, a substantial and articulate interest in the welfare of the said third party in respect to the subject of the contract.

We find no expression or words in the alleged contract *expressly* including Burns, either by *name* or as one of the *specified class*. We find no *terms used* in the contract showing the *intent* of the parties to include Burns as a beneficiary. We find no substantial and articulate interest of the promisee in the welfare of Burns.

Assignment under the Uniform Commercial Code

Scope of Application.   Article 9 of the Code applies to any sale of accounts, contract rights or chattel paper. (Section 9–102.) [2] It does not apply, however, to a sale of accounts, contract rights, or chattel paper as a part of a sale of the business out of which they arose, or an assignment of accounts, contract rights, or chattel paper which is for collection only, or a transfer of a contract right to an assignee who is also to do the performance under the contract. (9–104[f].) The assignment of accounts, contract rights and chattel paper are treated primarily from the standpoint of secured transactions. Under the provisions of the Code, the basic principles of the assignment of contracts are retained. The primary purpose of the Code is to clarify, simplify, and make more practical the law relative to the sale or assignment of accounts, contract rights, and chattel paper. The provisions of the Code affecting assignment and sale of accounts, contract rights, and chattel paper will be discussed in greater detail in Chapter 31, "Secured Transactions."

Assignment.   The main provisions relative to the assignment of contracts for the sale of goods are to be found in Section 2–210 of the Code. This section provides that duties may be delegated unless the other party has a "sub-

---

[2] The numbers in the parentheses refer to the sections of the Uniform Commercial Code, 1962.

stantial interest" in having the original party perform or control the acts required in the sales contract. All rights are assignable except where the assignment would "materially" change the duties of the obligor or "materially" increase his risks. A right to damages for breach of a sales contract may be assigned despite an agreement prohibiting any assignment. Unless the circumstances indicate a contrary intent, a clause prohibiting assignment of a contract will be construed as barring only the delegation of duties. An assignment of "all of my rights" normally will operate as a delegation of duties. The other party may treat any assignment which also delegates duties as grounds for demanding assurances from the assignor. Section 9–206 applies to sale of goods contracts where the seller has retained a security interest.

Summary

In general, contract rights are assignable under the U.C.C. A right to damages for breach of a sales contract may be assigned despite terms in the contract prohibiting any assignment. Rights cannot be assigned where such assignment materially changes the duties of the obligor or materially increases his risks. Duties may be delegated in some contracts but the person delegating the duties remains liable on the contract.

First National Bank of Elgin v. Husted
205 N.E.2d 780 (Ct. App. Ill. 1965)

This was an action brought by First National Bank (plaintiff) against Husted (defendant) to recover payments due on a car purchase installment contract which Husted had entered with Reed Motors. Reed Motors assigned the contract to First National Bank.

The contract provided: "Buyer agrees to settle all claims against Seller directly with Seller and will not set up any such claims against Seller as defense, counterclaim, set off, cross-complaint or otherwise in any action for the purchase price or possession brought by any assignee of this contract."

DAVIS, JUSTICE.   The Uniform Commercial Code provides:

(1) Subject to any statute or decision which establishes a different rule for buyers of consumer goods, an agreement by a buyer that he will not assert against an assignee any claim or defense which he may have against the seller is enforceable by an assignee who takes his assignment for value, in good faith and without notice of a claim or defense, except as to defenses of a type which may be asserted against a holder in due course of a negotiable instrument under the Article on Commercial Paper. (Article 3.) A buyer who as part of one transaction signs both a negotiable instrument and a security agreement makes such an agreement.

(2) When a seller retains a purchase money security interest in goods the Article on Sales (Article 2) governs the sale and any disclaimer, limitation or modification of the seller's warranties." (9–206)

The first sentence of this subsection permits a contractual waiver of certain defenses by the buyer, and it is in accord with prior Illinois case law. While this section provides that either the legislature or the courts may establish a different rule, we view this as a legislative function, the exercise of will rather than judgment, and we are reluctant to change the prior decisional law.

The defenses which may be asserted against a holder in due course are:

(a) infancy, to the extent that it is a defense to a simple contract; and

(b) such other incapacity, or duress, or illegality of the transaction, as renders the obligation of the party a nullity; and

(c) such misrepresentation as has induced the party to sign the instrument with neither knowledge nor reasonable knowledge nor reasonable opportunity to obtain knowledge of its character or its essential terms; and

(d) discharge in insolvency proceedings; and

(e) any other discharge of which the holder has notice when he takes the instrument (3–305[2])

Thus, a buyer may contractually waive, as against an assignee, any defenses except those enumerated in articles [Sections] 3–305(2) and 9–206(2). In absence of allegation in Husted's affidavit that First National Bank did not take the assignment for value, in good faith, and without notice of claim or defense, and in view of the date of the contract and assignment, we believe that First National Bank is an assignee for value, in good faith, and without notice of claim or defense.

The buyers' defenses of failure of consideration, and subsequent promise and failure to repair the car were waived, as against First National Bank, under article [Section] 9–206 of the Uniform Commercial Code.

Problem Cases

1. Davis owned a tract of land which contained deposits of pumicite and vesicular basalt. He was experimenting with the development of a formula for the making of a lightweight plaster mix, and pumicite and vesicular basalt were the base materials being used in his formula. Davis sold the tract of land to Basalt Rock Co., which manufactured building block materials. In connection with the sale of the land, and as part of the consideration for the conveyance of the land to it, Basalt Rock Co. agreed that over a period of 60 years it would sell to Davis "as he may require, such amounts of pumicite and vesicular basalt of any size for plastering purposes" at an agreed price of $2.50 per ton in the bulk at Basalt Rock Co."s processing plant. The contract further provided that "the price is based on a blend of pumicite and vesicular basalt in accordance with the formula attached." The contract gave Davis the right to change the formula from time to time as he perfected his formula for the production of his lightweight plaster mix and also provided for price adjustments to compensate for the changes in the formula. Davis assigned the contract to Soule. Basalt Rock Co. refused to recognize the assignment and refused to make deliveries to Soule. Soule sued Basalt Rock Co. for damages for breach of contract, and Basalt Rock Co. set up as a defense that the contract was not an assignable contract. Is the contract assignable?

2. Newman contracted to sell all of the eggs produced to Sunrise Eggs Co. Newman then gave Crosby a written assignment of the proceeds of this contract. Sunrise knew of this assignment, but ignored it and made payments to Crosby only when Newman told Sunrise to do so, making all other payments directly to Newman. Newman failed to pay $17,000 of the assigned proceeds delivered by Sunrise. Crosby sued Sunrise for this amount. Can Crosby collect?

3. Dean Anderson, Inc. (Anderson), was a promoter of financial campaigns. Admiral Farragut Academy (Academy) was a boys' preparatory school. Anderson entered into a contract with Academy whereby Anderson was to put on a money-raising campaign for Academy. The contract provided for the payment of a fixed fee to Anderson of $11,750, payable in 51 payments of $225 each and 1 payment of $275. The campaign was to start December 5, 1946, and was to continue for a period of 52 weeks from that date.

    On April 30, 1947, Anderson borrowed $5,000 from Newton Title & Trust Company (Trust Company) and assigned the unpaid balance of the fixed fee to Trust Company as security for the loan. At this time, the unpaid balance was $7,500. At the time the assignment was made, Academy signed a written acknowledgment of the assignment, admitted notice of the assignment, admitted that the unpaid balance of the fixed fee was $7,500, and agreed to make all payments due on the fixed fee to Trust Company. Two payments were made to Trust Company, one of $225 on May 12, 1947, and one of $450 on May 26, 1947. No further payments were made by Academy because Anderson did not complete performance of the contract. Trust Company claimed that since Academy acknowledged the assignment and acknowledged the unpaid balance of the fixed fee, Academy was liable for the full amount of the unpaid balance of the fixed fee. Is Trust Co. correct?

4. The sheriff, by court order, sold certain property under a mortgage foreclosure sale. After payment of the mortgage debt, interest, and costs, there was a balance to be paid to Massie, the mortgagor. The court ordered the sheriff to hold this money until it (the court) gave a further order. On April 22, 1950, Smith sued Massie on a note, and on May 15, 1950, Smith attached the funds in the hands of the sheriff. On May 4, 1950, Massie had assigned the funds in the hands of the sheriff to Byttner by written assignment, and on May 13, 1950, Byttner had given the sheriff written notice of the assignment. Smith claims that she has first claim on the funds because she filed her suit before the assignment. Byttner claims he has first claim because he gave notice of the assignment before the funds were attached. Does Byttner have first claim?

5. Clancy owned a building which he leased to ABC Corporation. ABC was in reality owned and its stock controlled by Arnold Corporation. Rental payments were made to Clancy by ABC, and Clancy was not aware of the ABC-Arnold relationship. Clancy did not keep the building in proper repair as required by the lease agreement. Arnold Corporation sued Clancy for damages, on the theory that Arnold Corporation was a third-party beneficiary to the lease agreement. May Arnold Corporation maintain the action?

6. Auto-Lite Co. entered into a collective bargaining agreement with Metal Polishers Union. According to this agreement: (1) 8 consecutive hours except for lunch constituted a "normal" work day and 40 hours of 5 consecutive days (Monday-Friday) constituted a "normal" work week; (2) when a reduction in the work force becomes necessary, probationary employees were to be laid off first followed by others according to seniority to maintain "normal" work days and weeks.

Auto-Lite's chief customer cut its orders severely; and, as a result, the company decided to cut production to a four-day week without a reduction in work force. Wesley, third man in seniority in the Union was laid off for seven consecutive Fridays as was the rest of the work force. Wesley sued for wages lost in violation of the bargaining agreements. Can Wesley collect?

7. The government of Iraq entered into three separate agreements with the L. A. Parts Company for the purchase of surplus military parts and equipment. The first two agreements merely provided that "inspection certificates" accompany the goods. The content or form of such "inspection certificates" was not defined nor specified. The third agreement provided that Iraq would communicate with Hunt Company, "to whom we shall address an order to do the inspection work on our behalf."

Soon after the execution of the first agreement, the *sellers* (L. A. Parts Company) orally engaged Hunt Co. to make a visual inspection of the goods, and verify the quantity, ordnance part number and description of military truck parts. Similar oral orders were given by L. A. Parts to Hunt Company after the execution of the other two agreements between Iraq and L. A. Parts.

On each of the five occasions that Hunt Co. made an "inspection," it submitted a report of its findings to L. A. Parts. In each report the following clause appeared:

This report is only for our Client's use and represents our opinion on the date of examination only. The conclusions reached by our inspectors are matters of opinion, the accuracy of which we do not guarantee, and shall not be responsible for damages or loss of any kind which may be connected in any way with this report.

The parts were defective and Iraq sued Hunt Co. contending that Iraq is a third-party beneficiary to the contract between L. A. Parts and Hunt Co. Can Iraq collect under the contract?

chapter 14. Performance and Remedies

Conditions

Introduction. We have discussed the requirements essential to the making of a valid and enforceable contract and the rules followed by the courts in determining the rights and duties of the parties to the contract. The next step is to determine what action is required by the promisor if he is to perform the duties imposed on him by the contract.

In determining whether or not a contract has been performed, the court is faced with an exceedingly complex problem. The relation between the parties, standard practices in the trade, usage in the community, business, or trade, prior dealings between the parties, and a multitude of other possible relations and circumstances must be analyzed and weighed.

Nature of Conditions. As a general rule the duty of performance arises at the time the contract is entered into although the time of the performance of the duty does not arise until some future date. The parties may provide in their contract that no duty to perform shall arise until the happening of some future, uncertain event. Such a provision is a condition precedent. Likewise, the parties may provide in their contract that on the happening of some future, uncertain event the party on whom is imposed the duty of performance will be relieved of that duty. Such a provision is a condition subsequent.

In some contracts the terms of the contract and the accompanying circumstances are such that the courts will imply a provision that the parties will perform simultaneously. Such an implied provision is a concurrent condition.

Creation of Conditions. A condition in a contract is, as a general rule, created by an express provision in the contract. Although no particular language need be used to create a condition, a conditional clause will, as a general rule, be introduced by words such as "provided that," "on condition that," "if," "when," "while," "after," or "as soon as."

Conditions may also be implied from the nature of the performance promised. If a person contracts to unload the cargo of a ship which is at sea, there is an implied condition that the ship will arrive in port.

Concurrent conditions are usually implied by law. In a contract to sell for cash, the law implies concurrent conditions, that is, the seller's duty to deliver the goods is conditioned on the buyer's tender of the purchase price, and the buyer's duty to pay the purchase price is conditioned on the seller's tendering delivery of the goods. If neither party makes a tender within a reasonable time, both are discharged from their duty under the contract.

Independent Promises. In many contracts the promises are independent; that is, the duty of one of the parties to perform is not conditioned on the happening of any event or on the other party's tender of performance. In all contract situations, if one of the parties is guilty of a material breach of the contract, the injured party will be discharged from his duty to perform. The effect of a breach of contract will be discussed under "Performance and Breach."

Summary

The determination of the nature and scope of a promisor's duty under a contract requires the analysis of many complex situations.

A condition in a contract is a stipulation that on the happening of some future, uncertain event the promisor will owe a duty of performance—a condition precedent—or will be relieved from an existing duty—a condition subsequent. A concurrent condition requires simultaneous performance by the parties. Conditions may be created by express promises or by implication, or may be implied by law.

Ross v. Harding
391 P.2d 526 (Sup. Ct. Wash. 1964)

This was an action by Thomas B. Ross and Mildred H. Ross, husband and wife (plaintiffs), against Charlotte M. Harding and Max E. Lieb and Sophie P. Lieb, husband and wife (defendants), to recover a judgment for the unpaid balance on a conditional sales contract and to foreclose a mortgage. Judgment for Ross against Harding and dismissal of case against the Liebs.

Ross owned a grocery business which he sold to Harding on conditional sales contract and Harding gave Ross a real estate mortgage on certain real estate as additional security. The grocery store was located in a building at 4221 East 11th Street, Tacoma, Washington. On October 21, 1958, Harding signed a five-year lease with right of a five-year renewal on the premises. The lease provided that it could not be assigned without the written consent of the lessor. The lease was executed by Henry A. Keil as administrator. On October 9, 1959, Harding contracted to sell the grocery business to the Liebs. The Liebs paid Harding $1,500 for the business and assumed and agreed to pay the unpaid balance owing to Ross on the conditional sales contract and to pay the rent on the premises. The contract of sale to the Liebs contained the following provision: "It is specifically understood and agreed that this offer is made subject to the written consent of the lessor of said building to the assignment and/or renewal of the existing lease." Henry H. Kiel, as administrator, gave his consent to the assignment, but he had been discharged as administrator on July 29, 1957, and consequently, had no authority to lease the property or to give his consent to the assignment of the lease. Ross sued Harding and the Liebs and Harding asked for a judgment over against the Liebs. The Liebs set up as a defense the condition precedent in the contract and the failure to fulfill it.

JAMES, JUDGE.   The first question to be determined is whether or not the provision in question constitutes a "promise" or a "condition precedent."

A "condition" whether it be "precedent" or "subsequent" may be either express, implied in fact, or constructive.

"Conditions precedent" are those facts and events, occurring subsequently to the making of a valid contract, that must exist or occur before there is a right to immediate performance, before there is a breach of contract duty, before the usual judicial remedies are available. A breach of a "promise" subjects the promissor to liability in damages, but does not necessarily excuse performance on the other side. Nonperformance or nonoccurrence of a "condition" prevents the promisee from acquiring a right, or deprives him of one, but subjects him to no liability. Where it is doubtful whether words create a "promise" or an "express condition," they are interpreted as creating a "promise."

Whether a provision in a contract is a condition, the fulfillment of which excuses performance, depends upon the intent of the parties, to be ascertained from a fair and reasonable construction of the language used in the light of all the surrounding circumstances.

Any words which express, when properly interpreted, the idea that the performance of a promise is dependent on some other event will create a condition. Phrases and words such as "on condition," "provided that," "so that," "when," "while," "after," or "as soon as" are often used.

It would be difficult to choose words to more precisely express an intention to create a condition precedent than those used in the contract here to be construed: "It is specifically understood and agreed that this offer is made *subject* to the written consent. . . ." This language leaves no room for interpretation. We hold that the procuring of the written consent of the lessor to the assignment or renewal of a valid lease of the premises occupied by the grocery store was a condition precedent to the Hardings' right to specific performance against the Liebs.

Architects' and Engineers' Certificates

Requirement of Certificate.   The building or construction contracts in common use usually contain a clause making the payments provided for in the contract conditional on the production of the certificate of a named architect or engineer. The courts enforce such a provision and will deny the contractor the right to recover in a suit on the contract unless he produces the certificate or can excuse his failure to produce it.

When Failure to Produce Certificate Is Excused. Failure to produce the certificate is excused by showing that the named architect or engineer is dead, insane, or otherwise incapacitated and cannot issue the certificate, or that the certificate is fraudulently, collusively, or arbitrarily withheld; and in some instances the courts have excused the production of the certificate if it can be shown that the withholding is unreasonable. As a general rule, if the architect or engineer is acting honestly and has some reason for withholding the certificate, the courts will not allow a recovery unless it is produced. The parties have contracted for the expert judgment of the named architect or engineer, and if he has exercised that judgment honestly, the courts will not substitute their judgment for that of the architect or engineer and hold that the architect or engineer is mistaken or that his decision is incorrect. If a mistake has been made in computation, the courts will correct it.

Summary

When a contract makes the production of an architect's or engineer's certificate a condition precedent to payment, the certificate must be produced before a duty of immediate payment arises. However, the death or incapacitating illness of a named architect or the fraudulent or unjustified withholding of the certificate will excuse the failure to produce the certificate.

Performance and Breach

Duty of Performance. A promisor is obligated to perform as promised; however, his performance may range from perfection to no performance at all. In attempting to solve the problems relative to the performance of contractual obligations, the courts have attempted to set up practical, workable standards. As a general rule, they recognize three degrees of performance: (1) complete or satisfactory performance, (2) substantial performance, and (3) material breach.

Complete or Satisfactory Performance. Some types of contractual obligations can be completely performed; others cannot. Such obligations as the payment of money, delivery of a deed, and, in some instances, the delivery of goods can be performed either exactly or to a high degree of perfection, whereas such obligations as the erection of a building, the construction of a road, the cultivation of a crop, and many similar obligations cannot be performed without some slight deviation from perfection, due to the limitations of human ability.

The standard set up by the courts as a measure of the degree of perfection of performance to which the promisee is entitled is the test of "reasonable expectation." The promisee is entitled to that degree of perfection which is standard for the type of obligation owed by the promisor. If the promisor owes the promisee $10, the promisee is justified in expecting the obligation to be discharged by the payment of $10. The payment of $9.99 will not satisfy the requirement of "reasonable expectation." However, if the promisor's obligation is to erect a building of several stories according to plans and specifications, the promisee is not justified in expecting a building which deviates in no degree from the plans and specifications. All the promisee is justified in expecting is a building which is built in a "good and workmanlike manner"—that is, one which comes up to the accepted standards of the degree of perfection attained in the erection of that type of building.

Substantial Performance. Substantial performance is a degree of perfection of performance which is slightly below that of complete or satisfactory performance. If the promisor has made an honest effort to perform but, due to lack of ability or other reasons beyond his control, has deviated in some slight degree from accepted standards, and if, in addition, the consideration given to the promisee is such that it cannot be returned to the promisor, the courts will hold that the promisor has substantially performed his contract. He will, as a general rule, be entitled to the contract price less any damage the promisee has suffered as a result of the defective performance. Each case involving substantial performance must be decided on the basis of the facts of that individual case.

Material Breach. The promisor will be guilty of a material breach of his contract if his performance or tendered performance fails to reach that degree of perfection which the promisee is justified in expecting under the circumstances. If the promisor has materially breached his contract, he has no right of action on the contract, unless the promisee has accepted the defective performance without objection. If defective performance is tendered, and the circumstances are such that the promisee can reject the tender, he has a right to do so. If performance is defective to such a degree that it amounts to a material breach but the circumstances are such that it is impractical for the promisee to reject the defective performance, the promisor may be able to recover for benefits conferred on the promisee in an action in quasi contract.

Prevention of Performance. The promisor assumes all the risks incident to the performance of the contract. However, if the circumstances are such that a condition precedent will be implied, the promisor will owe no duty of performance until the condition is fulfilled, and in some situations the promisor may be discharged completely from his duty of performance on the ground of impossibility.[1]

---

[1] Impossibility is discussed in a later section.

The promisee owes a duty to cooperate with the promisor in the performance of the contract. The extent of the promisee's duty to cooperate will depend on the subject matter of the contract and the surrounding circumstances. If the promisee fails to fulfill his duty of cooperation, or if he is guilty of affirmative acts which materially hinder or delay performance on the part of the promisor, the promisee will be guilty of a material breach of the contract, and the promisor will be relieved of a duty of further performance.

Time Is of the Essence.   The time within which the promisor is to complete his performance may or may not be expressly stated in the contract. If no time for performance is expressly stated or implied in the contract, the courts will hold that performance must be completed within a reasonable time. What is a reasonable time is a question of fact and must be determined from all the surrounding circumstances. If the time for performance is stated or implied in the contract, the promisor's failure to perform within the allotted time is a breach of the contract.

Under some circumstances a failure to perform on time will be held to be a material breach on the part of the promisor, and such breach will relieve the promisee of his duty of reciprocal performance. If failure to perform on time is a material breach of the contract, then "time is of the essence" of the contract. The contract may expressly stipulate that time is of the essence of the contract, in which case the courts will enforce the provision, unless its enforcement would impose on the promisor an unjust and burdensome penalty. If the circumstances are such that the promisee will derive little or no benefit from late performance, the courts will hold that time is of the essence of the contract even though the contract does not expressly so provide.

If time is not of the essence of the contract, the promisee will be required to accept late performance, provided performance is completed within a reasonable time after that stipulated in the contract. If the promisee has suffered an injury as the result of a delay in performance, he is entitled to set off against the contract price the loss he has suffered.

Performance to Personal Satisfaction.   The promisor may obligate himself to perform to the personal satisfaction of the promisee. Such contracts fall into two categories: (1) those situations in which personal taste and comfort are involved, and (2) those situations in which mechanical fitness or suitability for a particular purpose is involved.

If personal taste and comfort are involved, the promisee has the right to reject the performance without liability to the promisor, if he (the promisee) is honestly dissatisfied with the performance rendered or tendered.

If mechanical fitness or suitability is involved, the court will apply the "reasonable man" test; and if the court holds that a reasonable person would be satisfied with the performance rendered or tendered, the promisee must accept the performance and pay the contract price.

Summary

A promisor is obligated to perform as promised. Since performance may range from perfection to no performance at all, the courts recognize three stages of perfection of performance: (1) complete or satisfactory performance, (2) substantial performance, and (3) material breach. Complete or satisfactory performance is performance up to accepted standards; substantial performance falls short of complete performance only in minor respects, and the promisee is not deprived of a material part of the consideration bargained for. The promisor is guilty of material breach if his performance is defective in some major respect.

If the performance is complete or satisfactory, the promisor is entitled to the contract price; if substantial, he is entitled to the contract price less damage resulting from defects. If he is guilty of a material breach, he cannot recover on the contract but may be entitled to some recovery in a suit in quasi contract.

The promisor may be relieved from his duty of performance by an implied condition precedent, by impossibility, or by interference on the part of the promisee.

If time is of the essence of a contract, failure to perform within the permitted time is a material breach of the contract, and such breach will relieve the promisee from his obligations under the contract. If time is not of the essence, the promisee must accept late performance, if completed within a reasonable time, in which event he will be compensated in damages for injury suffered.

If personal taste and comfort of the promisee are involved, the promisee need not accept performance if he is honestly dissatisfied. If fitness or utility is involved, the "reasonable man" test is applied.

Lowy v. *United Pacific Insurance Co.*
429 P.2d 577 (Sup. Ct. Calif. 1967)

This was an action for damages for breach of an excavation and grading contract brought by Lowy and others (plaintiffs) against Wolpin and others (defendants). Wolpin filed a cross complaint for payments due. Judgment for Wolpin and Lowy appealed. Affirmed.

Lowy entered into a contract with Wolpin, a licensed contractor, for certain excavation and grading work on lots and streets, together with street improvement work. After Wolpin had performed 98 percent of the contracted excavation and grading work, a dispute arose between the parties regarding payment of $7,200 for additional work, consisting of importing dirt for fills, necessitated by changes made by Lowy in the plans.

Wolpin ceased performance and Lowy immediately employed others to do street improvement work called for by the contract and thereafter sued Wolpin and his bonding company for breach of contract.

McComb, Associate Justice.   Lowy agreed to pay Wolpin for the excavation and grading work (including street grading work) the sum of $73,500, as set forth in Exhibit "A" of the contract and they agreed to pay Wolpin for the paving of the streets and the installation of curbs and gutters (all commonly called "street improvement work") pursuant to the unit prices set forth in Exhibit "B" of the contract.

Accordingly, since the consideration was apportioned, the contract was a severable or divisible one.

Under the circumstances, the fact that Wolpin did not perform the second phase of the contract does not prevent his recovering for work done under the first phase.

Wolpin did not entirely perform under the first phase of the contract. However, the doctrine of substantial performance, ordinarily applied to building contracts, is here applicable, since the evidence shows that Wolpin completed 98 percent of the work under the first phase and was prevented from completing the balance through the fault of Lowy.

Where a person agrees to do a thing for another for a specified sum of money, to be paid on full performance, he is not entitled to any part of the sum until he has himself done the thing he agreed to do, unless full performance has been excused, prevented, or delayed by the act of the other party.

In *Thomas Haverty Co.* v. *Jones,* we held that in the case of a building contract where the owner has taken possession of the building and is enjoying the fruits of the contractor's work in the performance of the contract, if there has been a substantial performance thereof by the contractor in good faith, if the failure to make full performance can be compensated in damages to be deducted from the price or allowed as a counterclaim, and if the omissions and deviations were not wilful or fraudulent and do not substantially affect the usefulness of the building or the purpose for which it was intended, the contractor may, in an action upon the contract, recover the amount of the contract price remaining unpaid, less the amount allowed as damages for the failure of strict performance.

Appleton State Bank v. *Lee*

148 N.W.2d 1 (Sup. Ct. Wisc. 1967)

This was an action by Appleton State Bank (plaintiff) as assignee of an installment sales contract under which Mr. & Mrs. Lee (defendants) agreed to buy a vacuum cleaner. Judgment for Mr. and Mrs. Lee and Appleton State Bank appealed. Reversed.

Mr. and Mrs. Lee entered into a conditional sales contract with the Kirby Company in which they agreed in writing to purchase a Kirby vacuum cleaner and attachments for $269 plus the costs of finance and sales tax. As an inducement for this purchase, Kirby included a "New Home" Sewing Machine for $200 and took in trade Mr. and Mrs. Lee's used vacuum cleaner for $200. At the time of the sale, the Kirby salesman left with Mr. and Mrs. Lee a new Kirby vacuum cleaner with attachments and a "Modernaire" Sewing Machine and took their trade-in vacuum cleaner. The conditional sales contract was assigned to the Appleton State Bank.

The day after the sales contract was entered into, the Lees discovered that the sewing machine left by the Kirby salesman was not a "New Home" but rather a "Modernaire." When this fact was brought to the attention of the Kirby Company, it offered immediately to exchange the "Modernaire" for a "New Home" model but the Lees refused and requested that the contract be cancelled. Other attempts by the Kirby Company to supply the Lees with a "New Home" Sewing Machine met with similar refusals and requests of cancellation. Mr. and Mrs. Lee attempted to return the Kirby vacuum cleaner but the tender was not accepted. Appleton State Bank brought suit as assignee to recover the contract price.

HANLEY, JUSTICE. The Lees argue that the failure of Kirby Company to deliver the brand name sewing machine as specified in the conditional sales contract was a material breach of the contract.

The question here is whether there has been a substantial breach of the agreement so as to warrant rescission by the Lees.

In order to establish a breach sufficient to constitute repudiation of the entire agreement the nonperformance or breach must be substantial.

". . . a breach which goes to only a part of the consideration, which is incidental and subordinate to the main purpose of the contract, and which may be compensated in damages does not warrant a rescission of the contract; . . ."

Before a party not in default may be entitled to the relief of rescission there must be so serious a breach of the contract by the other party as to destroy the essential objects of the contract.

Here the contract was entered into on a Thursday. The Lees sought to cancel on Friday and on Saturday. They were offered a sewing machine of the exact kind called for in the conditional sales contract but refused to accept it. The testimony indicates that the Modernaire sewing machine was left with the Lees through an innocent error. The salesman removed the machine from the container in the presence of the Lees. There is no contention of deceit. There was also uncontradicted testimony that the Modernaire and New Home sewing machines are exactly the same thing.

Whether the alleged breach would justify rescission would depend upon whether time were of the essence of the contract. Time is not of the essence of a contract unless it is clear that the parties intended to make it so.

The trial court's reasoning that since the Lees bought the vacuum cleaner mainly due to their need of a sewing machine and since a New Home sewing machine, serial number 171, had been bargained for and not received there was a substantial breach of the contract by the Kirby Company is not supported by the evidence.

The testimony shows that Mr. Lee knew nothing about a New Home sewing machine and so far as he was concerned there was really nothing special about a New Home machine except its purported value of $200. The purported value of $200 was never disproven by the Lees.

We conclude that the real bargain in addition to the vacuum cleaner was for a $200 sewing machine, that the testimony reveals that the sewing machine delivered is of the same value as the New Home machine described in the sales contract and that the Lees never established that the sewing machine delivered was of a value less than $200.

We further conclude that the trial court was not correct in finding a substantial breach of the contract when time was not of the essence and the Kirby Company immediately attempted to rectify the error of delivery.

Impossibility of Performance

Nature of Impossibility. The common-law legal concept of impossibility is narrower than the popular concept. Impossibility means: "It cannot be done," not "I cannot do it." If a person contracts to perform an obligation, inability to perform or intervening hardship will not discharge his obligation. If he fails to perform, he will be liable to the promisee for any injury resulting from such failure.

The courts recognize three situations in which the promisor will be discharged from his failure to perform on the ground of impossibility: (1) incapacitating illness or death of the promisor, (2) intervening illegality, and (3) destruction of the subject matter essential to performance. Some courts have recognized a fourth ground for discharging the promisor from his obligation, that of commercial frustration.

The Uniform Commercial Code (2–615) [2] adopts less rigorous standards for excusing nonperformance of sales of goods contracts. Nonperformance is excused if the performance as agreed has been made "impracticable by the occurrence of a contingency the non-occurrence of which was a basic assumption on which the contract was made or by compliance in good faith with any applicable foreign or domestic governmental regulation or order." The Code further provides, however, that if the contingency affects only a part of the seller's capacity to perform, he must allocate production and deliveries among his customers in a "fair and reasonable" manner. The seller is also required to give buyers reasonable notice of any delay and of any limited allocation of the goods.

Illness or Death of Promisor. The promisor is discharged from his obligation to perform on the ground of impossibility only if the contract is personal in nature. If the obligations under the contract are such that they can, under the law of assignment of contracts, be delegated, the incapacitating illness or death of the promisor does not discharge the contract. It can be performed by the agents or personal representatives of the promisor.

---

[2] The numbers in the parentheses refer to the sections of the Uniform Commercial Code, 1962.

An incapacitating illness is one that renders the party incapable of performing his ordinary duties. Whether the illness of the promisor is of such nature as will justify him in terminating the contract will depend on all the facts and circumstances of the case, such as, for instance, the nature of the work to be done, the urgency of the work, the probable duration of the illness, etc.

A promisor may be relieved from his liability on the grounds of impossibility if he has contracted to have a named person perform special services and that person is prevented from performing due to his death or illness. For example, in one case in which a booking agency had contracted to furnish the services of a certain entertainer who was well known and the entertainer became ill and was unable to perform, the court held that the booking agency was discharged of its obligation.

Performance Declared Illegal. In some instances, parties may enter into a contract the performance of which is legal when entered into but may be declared illegal by an intervening statute or official order before performance is due. In such a case, performance is not impossible, but since it is illegal, the promisor is excused from his duty to perform. The increased powers of regulating business granted to the federal government during World War I and World War II have given rise to many cases involving the application of this rule. As a general rule, if a regulatory statute or rules and regulations promulgated under a regulatory statute prevent the performance of the contract, the promisor is excused from his duty to perform; but if the performance of the contract is merely rendered more difficult or less profitable, the promisor is not excused from his duty to perform.

Destruction of Subject Matter. If the performance of the act required by the contract to be performed is necessarily dependent on the continued existence of a specified thing, the destruction of such thing before performance of the required act without the fault of the promisor will excuse the nonperformance of the contract. For example, the destruction of a warehouse after a contract to reroof it is entered into but before the contract is performed would excuse the nonperformance of the contract. If a contract is partially performed at the time the subject matter essential to the performance of the contract is destroyed, the recipient of the benefits of the partial performance must pay, as a general rule, on a pro rata basis for the part performance. Neither party is liable in damages for the nonperformance of the contract.

Commercial Frustration. Some courts have extended the scope of impossibility to include those cases in which performance by the promisor would be impractical due to unforeseen developments having made performance of no value to the promisee. And some courts have included in the scope of impossibility cases in which the cost of performance to the promisor would be great, due to some extreme or unreasonable difficulty, expense, injury, or loss, and the benefits to the promisee would be of little or no value.

Summary

Impossibility of performance should be distinguished from inability to perform. The impossibility must arise after the contract is entered into, and it must be due to the nature of the thing to be done. Impossibility of performance arises in three situations: (1) incapacitating illness or death of promisor if contract requires performance of personal service, (2) intervening statutes or governmental regulation making performance illegal, and (3) destruction of subject matter essential to the performance of the contract without fault of either party. The U.C.C. adopts less rigorous standards for excusing nonperformance of sales of goods contracts.

Death always terminates a contract for personal service. Whether illness will justify termination of the contract will depend on the nature of the work, the term of the employment, the seriousness of the illness, and the duration or probable duration of the illness.

Before a statute or governmental regulation can be used to excuse nonperformance, it must be such that the performance of the contract will be illegal. A statute or governmental regulation which makes performance more difficult or less profitable will not excuse the promisor from performance on the ground of impossibility.

Destruction of the subject matter which is essential to the performance of the contract will excuse the promisor from performance. Destruction of subject matter which the promisor expects to make use of in the performance of the contract but which is not essential to the performance of the contract will not be an excuse for nonperformance.

In some recent cases the promisor has been discharged from his obligation to perform on the ground of commercial frustration.

Transatlantic Financing Corp. v. *United States*
363 F.2d 312 (D.C. Cir. 1966)

This was an action by Transatlantic Financing Corp. (plaintiff) to recover for costs incurred by diversion of a ship operated by Transatlantic because of the closing of the Suez Canal. Transatlantic appealed from a judgment in favor of the United States (defendant). Affirmed.

Transatlantic had a contract with the United States to deliver a cargo of wheat to Iran. The closing of the Suez Canal required that the delivery be made around the Cape of Good Hope.

WRIGHT, CIRCUIT JUDGE. The doctrine of impossibility of performance has gradually been freed from the earlier fictional and unrealistic strictures of such tests as the "implied term" and the parties' "contemplation." It is now recognized that " 'A thing is impossible in legal contemplation when it is not practicable; and a thing is impracticable when it can only be done at an excessive and unreasonable cost.' " The doctrine ultimately represents the evershifting line, drawn by courts hopefully responsive to commercial practices and mores, at which the community's interest in having contracts enforced according to their terms is outweighed by the commercial senselessness of requiring performance. When the issue is raised, the court is asked to construct a condition of performance based on the changed circumstances, a process which involves at least three reasonably definable steps. First, a contingency—something unexpected—must have occurred. Second, the risk of the unexpected occurrence must not have been allocated either by agreement or by custom. Finally, occurrence of the contingency must have rendered performance commercially impracticable. Unless the court finds these three requirements satisfied, the plea of impossibility must fail.

The first requirement was met here. It seems reasonable, where no route is mentioned in a contract, to assume the parties expected performance by the usual and customary route at the time of contract. Since the usual and customary route from Texas to Iran at the time of contract was through Suez, closure of the Canal made impossible the expected method of performance. But this unexpected development raises rather than resolves the impossibility issue, which turns additionally on whether the risk of the contingency's occurrence had been allocated and, if not, whether performance by alternative routes was rendered impracticable.

Proof that the risk of a contingency's occurrence has been allocated may be expressed in or implied from the agreement. Such proof may also be found in the surrounding circumstances, including custom and usages of the trade. The contract in this case does not expressly condition performance upon availability of the Suez route. Nor does it specify "via Suez" or, on the other hand, "via Suez or Cape of Good Hope." Nor are there provisions in the contract from which we may properly imply that the continued availability of Suez was a condition of performance. Nor is there anything in custom or trade usage, or in the surrounding circumstances generally, which would support our constructing a condition of performance. The numerous cases requiring performance around the Cape when Suez was closed, indicate that the Cape route is generally regarded as an alternative means of performance. So the implied expectation that the route would be via Suez is hardly adequate proof of an allocation to the promisee of the risk of closure. The doctrine of deviation supports our assumption that parties normally expect performance by the usual and customary route, but it adds nothing beyond this that is probative of an allocation of the risk.

If anything, the circumstances surrounding this contract indicate that the risk of the Canal's closure may be deemed to have been allocated to Transatlantic. We know or may safely assume that the parties were aware, as were most commercial men with interests affected by the Suez situation, that the Canal might become a dangerous area. No doubt the tension affected freight rates, and it is arguable that the risk of closure became part of the dickered terms. We do not deem the risk of closure so allocated, however. Foreseeability or even recognition of a risk does not necessarily prove its allocation. Parties to a contract are not always able to provide for all the possibilities of which they are aware, sometimes because they cannot agree, often simply because they are too busy. Moreover, that some abnormal risk was contemplated is probative but does not necessarily establish an allocation of the risk of the contingency which actually occurs. In this case, for example, nationalization by Egypt of the Canal Corporation and formation of the Suez Users Group did not necessarily indicate that the Canal would be blocked even if a confrontation resulted. The surrounding circumstances do indicate, however, a willingness by Transatlantic to assume abnormal risks, and this fact should legitimately cause us to judge the impracticability of performance by an alternative route in stricter terms than we would were the contingency unforeseen.

We turn then to the question whether occurrence of the contingency rendered performance commercially impracticable under the circumstances of this case. The goods shipped were not subject to harm from the longer, less temperate Southern route. The vessel and crew were fit to proceed around the Cape. Transatlantic was no less able than the United States to purchase insurance to cover the contingency's occurrence. If anything, it is more reasonable to expect owner-operators of vessels to insure against the hazards of war. They are in the best position to calculate the cost of performance by alternative routes (and therefore to estimate the amount of insurance required), and are undoubtedly sensitive to international troubles which uniquely affect the demand for and cost of their services. The only factor operating here in Transatlantic's favor is the added expense, allegedly $43,972.00 above and beyond the contract price of $305,842.92, of extending a 10,000 mile voyage by approximately 3,000 miles. While it may be an overstatement to say that increased cost and difficulty of performance never constitute impracticability, to justify relief there must be more of a variation between expected cost and the cost of performing by an available alternative than is present in this case, where the promisor can legitimately be presumed to have accepted some degree of abnormal risk, and where impracticability is urged on the basis of added expense alone.

We conclude, therefore, as have most other courts considering related issues arising out of the Suez closure, that performance of this contract was not rendered legally impossible. Even if we agreed with Transatlantic, its theory of relief seems untenable. If the contract is a nullity, Transatlantic's theory of relief should have been *quantum meruit* for the entire trip, rather than only for the extra expense. Transatlantic attempts to take its profit on the contract, and then force the Government to absorb the cost of the additional voyage. There is no interest in casting the entire burden of commercial disaster on one party in order to preserve the other's profit.

Discharge

Nature of Discharge. A contract is discharged where the parties to the contract are released from all obligations of the contract, and in the majority of contractual transactions this is brought about by complete performance by the parties to the contract.

Earlier in this chapter, we discussed the discharge of a contract by the occurrence or nonoccurrence of a condition precedent or subsequent, by material breach, and by impossibility of performance. A contract may also be discharged by agreement. The agreement may be in the form of a mutual agreement to cancel, a rescission, an agreement to forgo rights, a substitute contract, a novation, or a waiver. Under some circumstances a contract may be discharged or the right of action to enforce the contract may be barred by operation of law.

Discharge by Agreement.   A contract is created by the mutual agreement of the parties, and it may be discharged in like manner, unless rights of third parties will be involved. Any agreement to discharge a party to a contract from his obligations under the contract must be supported by consideration if such agreement is to effect a discharge. Mutual promises to rescind an executory contract will make the rescission valid since such an agreement is supported by consideration, in that both parties surrender their rights under the contract.

If a contract which has been performed either fully or partly is rescinded by the agreement of the parties, each party returns to the other the consideration he has received; consequently, such an agreement is supported by consideration. If one party has performed and the other has not, an agreement by the party who has performed to forgo his right to the return performance is not enforceable, since it lacks consideration. However, the party who has performed may make a gift of the return performance to the party who has not performed.

A contract or parts of it may be discharged by a substitute contract. If, subsequent to the making of a contract, the parties mutually agree on new terms which are inconsistent with terms of the old contract, the inconsistent terms of the old contract will be discharged. Likewise, if the parties enter into a new contract which covers the same subject matter as did the old contract but with which it is wholly inconsistent, the old contract will be discharged. Discharge by novation was discussed earlier.

Waiver.   A party to a contract may voluntarily relinquish a right which he has under the contract. Such a relinquishment is known as a "waiver." If one party tenders an incomplete performance and the other party accepts such defective performance without objection, knowing that the defects will not be remedied, he will have waived his right to strict performance. If he wishes to insist on strict performance, he should object to the incomplete or defective performance. In any instance in which performance is defective, notice should be given within a reasonable time that the defects must be remedied or damages will be claimed. If failure to give notice will justify a belief that strict performance will not be claimed, failure to give notice will amount to a waiver.

Suppose, for instance, that Arnett sells goods to Baker, agreeing to deliver them to Baker on June 15 but does not do so until June 17, and Baker then accepts the goods without objection. Baker will have waived his right to have the goods delivered on time. Suppose Arnett delivers to Baker goods which are not in compliance with the contract, and Baker inspects the goods and knows of their defects, but accepts them and makes no objection. Baker will have waived any rights he might have claimed as a result of the defects in the goods. If Baker wishes to protect his rights, he must give notice to Arnett. Whether or not one's conduct results in a waiver of rights depends on the circumstances.

Discharge by Alteration. If a party to a written instrument intentionally alters it in any material respect, the other party to the instrument is discharged from all his duties. If the instrument is altered by one not a party to it and without the knowledge and consent of either of the contracting parties, the alteration does not affect the rights of the parties. If an alteration is made by one of the contracting parties with the consent of the other conracting party, or if the other contracting party consents to the alteration after he learns of it, the party consenting to the alteration is not discharged from his duties.

Discharge by Statute of Limitations. From the earliest times the courts have refused to grant a remedy to one who has delayed an unreasonable time in bringing suit. In modern times the various states have by statute declared that an action must be brought within a stated time after the action accrues. Such statutes are known as "statutes of limitations."

The time limit for bringing suit for breach of contracts differs in the various states, and in many states the statutes distinguish between oral contracts and written contracts; for example, in Indiana the time limit for bringing suit on an oral contract is 6 years, whereas on a contract in writing it is 10 years. In Illinois the time limit is 5 years on oral contracts and 10 on written contracts. The time is computed from the time the cause of action accrues.

If one is incapacitated or beyond the jurisdiction of the court, the time during which the incapacity continues or the time during which one is beyond the jurisdiction of the court is not, by the terms of many statutes, counted in computing the statutory time for bringing suit.

Uniform Commercial Code. The Code provides "any claim or right arising out of an alleged breach can be discharged in whole or in part without consideration by a written waiver or renunciation signed and delivered by the aggrieved party." (Section 1–107.)

Sec. 2–309 (2) (3) are the only parts of the Code which specifically treat termination rights and liabilities. *Subsec.* (2) states that where a contract "provides for successive performances but is indefinite in duration it is valid for a reasonable time but unless otherwise agreed may be terminated at any time by either party." *Subsec.* (3) "provides termination of a contract by one party except on the happening of an agreed event requires that reasonable notification be received by the other party and any agreement dispensing with notification is invalid if its operation would be unconscionable."

Comment 7 to Subsec. (2) by the editorial board which drafted the Code states that when an arrangement has been carried on over many years the reasonable time "can continue indefinitely and the contract will not terminate until notice." Comment 8 to Subsec. (3) states that this subsection:

. . . recognizes that the application of principles of good faith and sound commercial practice normally call for such notification of the termination of a going contract relationship as will give the other party reasonable time to seek a substitute arrangement. An agreement dispensing with notification or limiting the time for the seeking of a substitute arrangement is, of course, valid under this subsection unless the results of putting it into operation would be the creation of an unconscionable state of affairs.

Comment 10 states: ". . . The requirement of notification is dispensed with where the contract provides for termination on the happening of an 'agreed event.' 'Event' is a term chosen here to contrast with 'option' or the like."

The Code (2–725) stipulates a four-year statute of limitations for contracts involving the sale of goods.

Summary

A contract is discharged when the parties to a contract are released from their obligations under the contract. A contract is generally discharged by performance. The promisor is generally discharged from his duty to perform by a material breach of the contract, by the failure of the event to occur, which event has been stipulated in a condition precedent, by the occurrence of the event stipulated in a condition subsequent, or by impossibility. A contract may be discharged by mutual agreement, rescission, substitute contract, novation, or waiver. Under some circumstances a contract may be discharged by operation of law.

The Code requires that reasonable notification be given where sales of goods contracts provide for successive performances but are of indefinite duration. Any agreement dispensing with notification is invalid if its operation would be unconscionable.

Sinkoff Beverage Co., Inc. v. Jos. Schlitz Brewing Co.
273 N.Y.S.2d 364 (Sup. Ct. N.Y. 1966)

This was an action brought by Sinkoff Beverage Co. (plaintiff) against Joseph Schlitz Brewing Co. (defendant) to enjoin Schlitz from selling to others in Suffolk County. Held preliminary injunction denied.

In 1960 the parties contracted in writing regarding Sinkoff's wholesale purchase of beer from Schlitz. The agreement specifically provided that it might be terminated at any time without cause or notice by either party. No exclusive rights were granted, but Sinkoff is nevertheless claiming the existence of an "understanding" making it Schlitz's exclusive Suffolk County distributor from the time of the 1960 agreement to date. As a practical matter, for six years Sinkoff was actually Schlitz's exclusive distributor in Suffolk County. However, on June 8, 1966, Schlitz notified Sinkoff that it was discontinuing its sales and deliveries to Sinkoff, in ten days.

STANISLAW, JUDGE.   Sinkoff devotes considerable of its facilities just to the handling of the business the result of six years of exclusive distribution of Schlitz's products. It claims the privilege, nowhere to be found in the agreement with Schlitz, of a year's notice of termination of the relationship. First, the diminution of its gross sales and net profit is alleged to be serious enough to raise a question of its ability to continue in business altogether. Then too, Sinkoff believes itself entitled to more than the ten days' notice of termination it received based upon the continuing, exclusive-in-fact relationship. Sinkoff argues that reasonable notice is required in these circumstances, and that a reasonable period would be one year.

Schlitz responds not only by pointing to the terms of the 1960 agreement but also by showing that it had expressed dissatisfaction with Sinkoff's wholesaling of its product in November, 1965, and several more times until it finally terminated the relationship. Furthermore, Schlitz denies the existence of any parol understanding or arrangement between the parties. In addition, Schlitz notes that the contract refutes any such possibility as either emanating from it or available at all other than in writing.

As to the extra-contractual, verbal franchise Sinkoff relies upon we find ourselves, and even more particularly Sinkoff, bound by the writing which expresses no such exclusivity and in fact acknowledges the complete absence of such status. In the face of these terms Sinkoff has not shown enough to extricate itself by properly establishing other than a simple distributorship.

The auxiliary issue presented is apparently one of first impression. Relying on section 2–309(3) of the Uniform Commercial Code, Sinkoff argues that it is entitled to "reasonable notification" of the termination of the contract. The cited section so provides, "except on the happening of an agreed event . . . an agreement dispensing with notification is invalid if its operation would be unconscionable." The court has the power to determine the issue of unconscionability and may limit the application of a clause found to be so in order to avoid an unconscionable result (Uniform Commercial Code, section 2–302). A hearing may be directed to aid the making of such determination (Uniform Commercial Code, section 2–302). The official comment for this section of the Code advises that "The basic test is whether, in the light of the general commercial background and the commercial needs of the particular trade or case, the clauses involved are so one-sided as to be unconscionable under the circumstances existing at the time of the making of the contract." Further on, the comment visualizes the power extended the courts as directed against one-sided, oppressive and unfairly surprising contracts, but not against the consequences of uneven bargaining positions or even simple old-fashioned bad bargains.

It seems too, that the hearing called for is mandatory rather than discretionary once the court has initially accepted a possibility of unconscionability (see 1 *Anderson's Uniform Commercial Code,* section 2–302:5). Therefore, the precise question must at first be whether we can see a specter of oppression in the termination clause of the instant contract *as of the time the contract was made.*

Applying the required limitation of time to the question we may not take into consideration the volume increase in Sinkoff's business and Sinkoff's subsequent expansion and development of facilities and expense due to and in reliance upon its continued relationship with Schlitz. For all that appears the mere creation of any relationship between Sinkoff and Schlitz was, at that first point in time, of great benefit to both and perhaps even particularly favorable (and thus especially inoppressive) to Sinkoff.

We find no basis for a reasonable belief that the termination clause of the contract might have been unconscionable. The motion for a preliminary injunction is denied, without prejudice (noting the absence of any data relevant to conditions existing when the contract was executed in 1960).

Nature of Remedies

Objective in Granting Remedy. When a party has failed to perform his obligations under a contract and the other party to the contract has suffered a resulting injury, the injured party is entitled to be put, as nearly as is practical, in the same position as that he would have occupied had the contract been performed. The majority of business contracts are entered into with the expectation of acquiring something of economic value or of making a profit. With few exceptions, if the injured party is granted a money judgment for the value of the thing he contracted to acquire or for the profit which he would have realized had the contract been performed, he will be in substantially the same position he would have held had the contract been performed. Consequently, the remedy usually granted is the legal remedy of damages.

If the circumstances are such that the legal remedy of damages is inadequate, the court may grant the injured party an appropriate equitable remedy. The equitable remedy of specific performance of the contract is the one most frequently granted for breach of a contract. However, under some circumstances the injured party may be granted the remedy of rescission, and under others the remedy of injunctive relief.

Enforcement of Remedy. When a money judgment has been granted, the creditor is entitled to the aid of the court in the enforcement of the judgment if the debtor does not pay it. In the enforcement of the judgment the clerk of the court will issue either a writ of execution or a writ of garnishment.

A writ of execution directs the sheriff to take into his possession and sell so much of the judgment debtor's property which is not exempt from execution as is necessary to satisfy the judgment. All states have exemption laws, although they vary widely, which provide that certain property or property of a stated value shall be exempt from levy of execution. The procedure to be followed in the levy of an execution and the sale of the property levied on is set out by the statutes of the state in which the levy is made.

Garnishment is also statutory and is supplemental to the execution. In general, it is used to reach property or credits of the judgment debtor which are in the hands of a third person, and the procedure varies with the different states. As a general rule, garnishments are used to reach bank accounts, wages due, or accounts receivable; however, under some statutes, one can reach goods in storage, the redemption value of pawned goods, and other similar assets.

Under some circumstances the plaintiff may have the sheriff seize property of the defendant at the time suit is started. This procedure is called an "attachment." The grounds for attachment are generally set out by statute and are not uniform throughout the United States. Generally, if the debtor is a nonresident and has property within the jurisdiction of the court, the property may be attached at the time suit is started. The remedy of attachment is usually available in tort cases, especially those involving fraud. If the debtor is about to remove or dispose of his property for the purpose of defeating, defrauding, or delaying his creditors, a creditor may start suit by attachment. As a general rule, one starting suit by attachment must give bond to protect the defendant in the event the plaintiff is unable to obtain a judgment and the defendant is injured as a result of the attachment.

If one of the equitable remedies has been granted and the party fails or refuses to comply with the order of the court, he will be in contempt of court. The judge may fine or imprison the recalcitrant party for contempt of court or punish him in some other appropriate manner. If the order is to execute a deed, mortgage, or other document, the decree of the court may be so drafted that it will serve as a substitute for the document.

Uniform Commercial Code.   The remedies available to the parties to a contract which comes within the scope of the provisions of the Code are set out as follows:

(1) The remedies provided by this Act shall be liberally administered to the end that the aggrieved party may be put in as good a position as if the other party had fully performed but neither consequential or special nor penal damages may be had except as specifically provided in this Act or by other rule of law.

(2) Any right or obligation declared by this Act is enforceable by action unless the provision declaring it specifies a different or limited effect. (Section 1–106.)

The remedies of both the buyer and the seller in the event of a breach of the sales contract are set out in detail in Part 7 of Article 2, "Sales." Special remedies available to the parties are set out in the other articles of the Code.

In general, the remedies available under the Code are in keeping with the general principles of the law of remedies and are, with few exceptions, set out specifically and in considerable detail.

Summary

The remedy usually granted for breach of contract is a judgment for damages, but if the remedy at law is inadequate, an equitable remedy may be granted.

A judgment is enforced by levy of execution, garnishment, or attachment.

Remedies available for breach of those contracts which come within the scope of the Code are, for the most part, defined in the Code.

Classification of Damages

Introduction. The different classes of damages awarded by the court as a remedy for injury resulting from breach of contract are known as (1) compensatory, (2) consequential or special, (3) liquidated, and (4) nominal.

Compensatory damages are damages which can be compensated for by the payment of a sum of money which will make good or replace the loss caused by the wrong or injury. They are the damages which would normally and usually result from the breach of a contract such as that into which the parties have entered.

Consequential or special damages are those damages which do not flow directly or immediately from the breach of the contract but only from some of the special or unusual circumstances of the particular contractual relation of the parties.

Liquidated damages is the term applicable when a specific sum of money has been expressly stipulated by the parties as the amount of damages to be recovered by the injured party in the event the contract is breached.

Nominal damages are those damages awarded to the injured party where there is a technical breach of the contract but still no actual loss suffered as a result of the breach.

Basis for Awarding Damages. Before the plaintiff is entitled to a judgment for damages, he must prove that he has suffered a loss as the direct result of the breach of the contract; and in addition, he must prove with a reasonable degree of certainty the amount of the loss. Damages are awarded on the basis of an assumption-of-risk theory.

The promisor, in making the promise, is presumed to have intended to assume only the risks which are normally incident to the performance of the contract, and therefore should be required to pay only the damages which normally result from the breach of the contract. Under this theory of damages, if the promisor has been given notice of facts or should know from the circumstances that a greater loss is probable than would usually follow a breach of such a contract, he will be presumed to have assumed the risks of such unusual loss and will be liable for the special loss resulting from his breach of the contract, that is, he will be liable for consequential damages.

Measure of Damages. The measure of the amount of compensatory damages, in case of default, to be awarded the injured party is generally the value of the unfulfilled promise less the cost to the injured party of fulfilling his promise to the defaulting party. For example, if Allman contracts to remodel a house for Burch according to plans and specifications for $5,000 and Allman abandons the work and Burch sues Allman to recover a judgment for damages the measure of damages would be the total cost to Burch of having the work completed less the $5,000 he contracted to pay for the job.

No formula has been adopted for the determination of consequential (special) damages. In determining the amount to be awarded as consequential (special) damages, the court will take into consideration all the facts and circumstances and will award the injured party a sum which will reimburse him for the loss he has actually suffered.

Loss of profits is an allowable element of damages, provided the amount of profits lost can be established with a reasonable degree of certainty. If the plaintiff has been in business for a reasonable period of time and has a fair set of books, he should be able to show loss of profits in most instances. However, if the contract is a new or speculative venture, he will be unable, in most instances, to establish such loss.

Mitigation of Damages. If the defendant has breached the contract, the plaintiff owes a duty to the defendant to make a reasonable effort to avoid damage. If the plaintiff can avoid or minimize the damages he will suffer as a result of the defendant's breach without undue risk, expense, or humiliation, he owes a duty to the defendant to avoid the damage.

In employment contracts, if the employer wrongfully discharges an employee before the end of the term of the employment, the employee is entitled to recover his wages for the remainder of the term. However, he owes a duty to make a reasonable effort to obtain similar employment elsewhere and minimize the damages. If the employee is employed as a skilled plumber, he would not be expected or required to accept employment such as digging sewers to minimize the damages, but he would be required to make a reasonable effort to obtain other employment as a skilled plumber in the same locality.

Liquidated Damages. The courts will not enforce a provision in a contract for liquidated damages unless (1) the damages to be anticipated are uncertain in amount or difficult to prove, (2) the parties intended to liquidate the damages in advance, and (3) the amount stipulated is a reasonable one, that is, not greatly disproportionate to the presumable loss or injury. If the amount stipulated to be paid in the event of the breach of a contract is disproportionate to the loss or injury suffered, the courts will declare it to be a penalty and refuse to enforce it.

Frequently, in contracts for the sale of property, where the buyer is paying the purchase price in installments, a provision will provide that, in the event the buyer defaults in the making of a payment, the seller may repossess the property and may retain all payments made by the buyer as rent for the use of the property and as liquidated damages. If the circumstances are such that the enforcement of the damage provision of the contract would impose a forfeiture on the buyer, the court will not enforce such a provision.

If a liquidated damage provision in a contract is declared to be a provision for a penalty or a forfeiture and therefore unenforceable, the injured party will be granted compensatory damages, provided he can prove that he suffered a loss as the direct result of the breach of the contract and can prove with reasonable certainty the amount of the resulting loss.

Nominal Damages. The courts have held that failure to perform a contractual duty is, in itself, a legal wrong. As a result a wronged party who is unable to prove actual damages will not be denied a judgment on the ground that the law will not be concerned with trifles. He will be granted a judgment for nominal damages, which may be an amount ranging from 1 cent to $1, depending on the policy of the courts trying the case. In some jurisdictions or under some circumstances, if a party recovers a judgment for nominal damages, the party against whom the judgment is granted will be obligated to pay the taxable costs of the suit. However, in most jurisdictions, unless a party recovers a judgment for a minimum amount, say $50, for example, he will have to pay his own costs, and the taxable costs will be adjudged against him. Frequently, an action may be brought as a "test case" for the purpose of establishing the law relative to the transaction involved. In such a situation the recovering of a judgment for nominal damages will establish the rights of the parties.

Summary

Damages awarded for the breach of a contract may be (1) compensatory, (2) consequential (special), (3) liquidated, or (4) nominal. Damages are awarded on the basis of the reasonable contemplation of the parties at the time the contract is entered into. The measure of compensatory damages is the value of the unfulfilled promise less the cost to the injured party of fulfilling the promise. The measure of consequential (special) damages is the loss suffered by the injured party as the direct result of the default. Loss of profit may be allowable as an element of damages if such loss can be established with reasonable certainty. In all instances the injured party owes a duty to make a reasonable effort to minimize the damages he suffers by reason of a default. The measure of liquidated damages is the amount stipulated by the parties, and they are allowed by the court unless the amount stipulated is unreasonable, that is, for instance, a penalty. Nominal damages is a token amount awarded for the breach of a contract in those cases when the injured party establishes the breach of the contract but cannot prove with reasonable certainty that he suffered a loss as the direct result of the breach.

Clark v. Ferro Corp.
237 F.Supp. 230 (E.D. Tenn. 1964)

This was an action by William F. Clark, Trustee in bankruptcy for Hood Ceramic Corporation (plaintiff), against Ferro Corporation (defendant) to recover a judgment for damages for breach of contract. Judgment for Clark.

Hood Ceramic Corporation (Hood) contracted with Ferro Corporation (Ferro) for the designing and construction of a tunnel kiln. The kiln was designed and constructed and was completed on January 10, 1958. Ferro supervised the operation of the kiln, making the necessary adjustments for its proper operation. It was not until December, 1958, that the last of the Ferro personnel departed, leaving the further operation of the kiln to Hood. The kiln did not operate properly and this suit was brought. Hood claimed as damages (1) the difference in the contract price of the kiln designed and constructed by Ferro and the value of the kiln as actually constructed; (2) the expenditures made by Hood in attempting to modify the kiln in order to make it operate in accordance with the specifications of the contract; and (3) Hood's business losses and loss of profits resulting from the failure of the kiln to perform in accordance with the contract specifications.

WILSON, DISTRICT JUDGE.   Compensation, and not reward or penalty, is the primary aim in measuring damages for breach of contract. The general purpose of the law is to place the plaintiff in the position he would have been in had the contract been fulfilled in accordance with its terms. At one time in the development of the law this general statement of the rule of damages in breach of contract cases was about all the law there was to guide the finder of fact, except for a few special rules for particular types of agreements which are not here significant. However, in 1854 the English Court of Exchequer handed down an opinion in the case of *Hadley v. Baxendale,* that has since furnished the generally accepted standard for determining the measure of damages for breach of contract. A claim was there made against a carrier for breach of contract by delay in delivery of a shipment. The damage claimed was for loss occasioned by the enforced idleness of a mill due to a delay in the shipment of a grist mill shaft. The Court, in denying recovery for such loss on the ground that they were not in the contemplation of the parties at the time the shipment contract was made, laid down the rule that damages recoverable for breach of contract are (1) such as may fairly and reasonably be considered as arising in the usual course of events from the breach of the contract itself, or (2) such as may reasonably be supposed to have been in the contemplation of the parties at the time they made the contract. Thus the rule was established that while direct and usual damages could be recovered irrespective of whether such damages were shown to be in the contemplation of the parties at the time the contract was made, losses of an unusual kind, sometimes termed "consequential" or "special" damages, can only be recovered where they are shown to have been in the contemplation of the parties at the time they made the contract. 15 Am. Jur., Damages, Sec. 52.

The rule has likewise been adopted by the *Restatement of Contracts,* and is set forth in Section 330 as follows:

In awarding damages, compensation is given for only those injuries that the defendant had reason to foresee as a probable result of his breach when the contract was made. If the injury is one that follows the breach in the usual course of events, there is sufficient reason for the defendant to foresee it; otherwise it must be shown specifically that the defendant had reason to know the facts and to foresee the injury.

In the case of *Chisolm & Moore Mfg. Co.* v. *United States Canopy Co.,* involving a claim for loss of profits due to breach of contract by the defendant in furnishing defective parts for use by the plaintiff in manufacturing canopies, the Tennessee Court expressly relying upon *Hadley* v. *Baxendale,* stated:

It is true, in general, that the measure of damages for breach of an executory contract of sale of personalty is the difference between the contract price and the market value of the goods at the time and place of delivery. It is also true that, in general, profits cannot be allowed as damages, for the reason that they are usually uncertain; depending, as they do, upon the dangers and hazards of business. But it cannot be said that there are no exceptions to the rule.

The reasons underlying the general rule, and also a succinct statement of the grounds of the exceptions recognized to the rule, may be found in the following excerpt from *Howard* v. *Stillwell & B. Mfg. Co.,* which we adopt as a sound statement of the law, viz:

The grounds upon which the general rule of excluding profits in estimating damages rests are (1) that in the greater number of cases such expected profits are too dependent upon numerous uncertain and dangerous contingencies to constitute a definite and trustworthy measure of actual damages; (2) because such loss of profits is ordinarily remote, and not, as a matter of course, the direct and immediate result of a nonfulfillment of the contract; (3) and because most frequently an engagement to pay such loss of profits in case of default in the performance is not a part of the contract itself, nor can it be implied from its nature and terms. But it is equally well settled that the profits which would have been realized, had the contract been performed, and which have been prevented by its breach, are included in the damages to be recovered in every case where such profits are not open to the objection of uncertainty or of remoteness, and where, from the expressed or implied terms of the contract itself, or the special circumstances under which it was made, it may be reasonably presumed that they were within the intent and mutual understanding of both parties at the time it was entered into.

With regard to Hood's right to recover business losses and loss of profits, the Court is of the opinion that Hood has not established any right to such damages both as a matter of law and by reason of the terms of the contract and by reason of the speculative and uncertain nature of the evidence relating to such losses.

The Court is of the opinion that while expenditures made in an effort to bring the kiln up to contract specifications would be such a direct, usual and foreseeable loss as to be subject to recovery, alleged business losses and loss of profits would not be such a direct, usual and foreseeable loss, but rather would be an indirect or consequential loss. In the absence of a showing that damages for business losses and loss of profits were in the contemplation of the parties at the time they made the contract, the Court is of the opinion that such damages would not be recoverable under the rule of *Hadley* v. *Baxendale,* and *Chisolm & Moore Mfg. Co.* v. *United States Canopy Co.* Upon the contrary, the parties here expressly contracted against liability for consequential damages. Paragraph IX expressly provides that:

> The engineer assumes no liability for consequential damages of any kiln and the purchaser by the signing of this agreement will assume all liability for the consequences of its use or misuse.

Otinger v. Water Works and Sanitary Sewer Board
177 So.2d 320 (Sup. Ct. Ala. 1965)

This was an action brought by S. J. Otinger Construction Company (plaintiff) against the Water Works and Sanitary Sewer Board of the City of Montgomery, Alamaba (defendant), for work and labor done. The Board filed its answer denying any indebtedness to Otinger, and also by way of counterclaim sought recovery of $2,627.55, it had allegedly overpaid Otinger. The trial court ruled neither claimant could recover and Otinger appealed. Affirmed.

Otinger required 250 days to complete the job although the contract contained the following provision:

> It is mutually agreed between the parties hereto that time is the essence of this contract, and in the event the construction of the work is not completed within the time herein specified, it is agreed that from the compensation otherwise to be paid to the Contractor, the second party may retain the sum of $50.00 per day for each day thereafter, Sunday and holidays included, that the work remains uncompleted, which sum shall represent the actual damages which the Owner will have sustained per day by failure of the Contractor to complete the work within the time stipulated, and this sum is not a penalty, being the stipulated damage the second party will have sustained in the event of such default by the first party.

HARWOOD, JUSTICE.   It has been consistently held that when a contract is entered into, and the nature and amount of damages resulting from a breach thereof are conjectural and uncertain, the parties have a right to fix the same by contract, and having employed language showing an intention to fix the damages for a breach of contract and if reasonable, the courts are not authorized to abrogate such provision by declaring it a penalty.

The total amount to be paid for the work by the Board under the contract was $118,648.75. The damages to the Board if the contract was not completed in time were uncertain and conjectural. The amount fixed as liquidated damages in relation to the amount involved under the contract does not appear unreasonable. The fact that Sundays and holidays were included in the limitation fixed in which the contract was to be completed, cannot be deemed to change the amounts fixed as liquidated damages into a penalty. The parties were legally competent to contract. Their intent was clear. If the provision including Sundays and holidays in the limitation was hard or improvident, courts are unauthorized to grant relief merely on such basis. We find no basis for disturbing the lower court's conclusion that the provision of the contract relating to liquidated damages was a valid and enforceable provision.

Otinger further contends that the facts presented below show that the Board by its action waived the time limit provided for in the contract.

This argument is based upon correspondence between Otinger and the Board. By letter dated 19 February 1962, addressed to the Board, Otinger stated he "would like to request at this time that the City Water and Sanitary Board give every consideration that they possibly can to our request for an extension of time to complete the project we are engaged in on the Catoma Creek Outfall and Pump Station."

To this the Board replied:

The Board considered your letter in the regular monthly meeting, Tuesday, February 20th, noting that the request made no specific mention of the number of days you were requesting.

I was directed to write you that since the completion date (Feb. 4, 1962) has passed, that you proceed with the unfinished work with reasonable and continual progress until the project has been completed and approved by the Consulting Engineers, J. B. Converse and Company.

At that time the Board will be glad to have you appear for a review of the delay and to assure you of its full consideration of those circumstances.

As we read the above letter from the Board, it is a denial of the request for a waiver of the time limit, though a statement that such matter would be considered upon completion of the contract. This the Board apparently did, and instead of withholding from Otinger the full amount of the liquidated damages, it withheld only the additional engineer fees it had incurred as a result of the delay.

Where a contract fixes the time for completion of work and makes time of the essence, the obligee does not waive nonperformance within the specified time by merely allowing the work to go on to completion after expiration of the time limit. A waiver must operate by way of an estoppel or be supported by a valuable consideration to be binding.

It is next contended by Otinger that he was excused from performance within the time limit of the contract by an act of God, i.e., the flood conditions of Catoma Creek during the progress of the work.

Where an obligation is imposed by law, such as the obligation of a common carrier, the law will excuse a failure to perform resulting from an act of God. On the other hand, where one by his contract creates an absolute obligation in which the obligation rests on himself, he is bound to perform within the terms of the contract, or answer in damages despite an act of God, unexpected difficulty, hardship, or inevitable accident, since he should have provided against such contingencies by his contract.

Particularly is this doctrine applicable where the contingency could reasonably have been foreseen and guarded against. The senior engineer for J. B. Converse and Company, consulting engineers for the Board, testified flood conditions were not unusual at Catoma Creek, and further, that "it is a known fact that here in Montgomery during the winter months that Catoma Creek does get up and spread out." No merit attaches to the contention of Otinger that the flood conditions of Catoma Creek furnished to him an excuse for non-performance within the time limits fixed by the contract.

Equitable Remedies

Specific Performance.   The granting of the equitable remedy of specific performance rests in the sound discretion of the court. The court will not grant specific performance of a contract if a money judgment, the remedy at law, is adequate. Since the remedy is equitable, the court has the power to withhold it when the ends of the law will thus be best served.

As a general rule the court will grant specific performance of a contract to sell and convey land. Since no two tracts of land are alike, a money judgment is not a fair substitute for the land bargained for; consequently, a money judgment is not an adequate remedy. The remedy of specific performance will, as a general rule, be granted as the remedy for breach of a contract to sell and deliver a work of art, a rare jewel, or some other object which has a sentimental value or esthetic interest which cannot be measured in money.

Under the provision of the Uniform Commercial Code a buyer's remedy of specific performance has been liberalized in several respects.[3]

Specific performance of a contract for personal service will not be decreed, since it is against the policy of the law to require persons to continue personal relations which are distasteful to them. Also, the courts will not grant the remedy of specific performance of a contract the performance of which would require prolonged and detailed supervision by the court, such as a contract to build a large office building; nor will they grant specific performance of a contract the performance of which would cause undue hardship.

Injunction.   The injunction is an equitable remedy designed to protect property or other rights from irreparable injury by commanding acts to be done or prohibiting their commission. It is used in a multitude of situations and affords the court of equity a flexible remedy which may be resorted to in an unlimited variety of situations.

It may be used to prevent hardship and oppression in contract cases; however, it is a remedy which is used sparingly in contract situations, because it is only in the exceptional case that some other adequate remedy is not available. The court may grant an injunction enjoining the negotiation of a nego-

---

[3] Uniform Commercial Code, Section 2–716. This section will be discussed in greater detail in Part VII, "Sales."

tiable instrument, the transfer of property essential to the performance of a contract, or the violation of a building restriction. If one sells his business and contracts not to enter into business in competition with the purchaser, the courts may enforce such a provision by injunction. If one having exceptional skills contracts to employ those skills exclusively for a party and then threatens, in violation of the contract, to employ those skills for others, the court may enjoin the use of such skills for anyone except the one with whom he contracted.

Summary

If the remedy at law, a judgment for damages, is inadequate, the injured party may be entitled to one of the remedies in equity. The remedy of specific performance may be granted if it is very difficult to determine the effect of the breach of the contract or if it is difficult to estimate the damages. Courts will, as a general rule, grant a decree of specific performance of a contract to sell land. They will not grant a decree of specific performance of a contract to sell personal property unless the property contracted for has a sentimental value or unless it is very difficult or impossible to obtain a duplicate elsewhere.

The courts will not grant a decree of specific performance of a contract for personal services or of a contract the performance of which involves much detailed work. The court will deny a decree of specific performance if the ends of justice will thus be best served.

The injunction is issued to prevent hardship. As a general rule, it is in the form of a court order ordering a party threatening to breach a contract to refrain from his threatened course of action.

Madsen v. Chrysler Corp.
261 F.Supp. 488 (N.D. Ill. 1966)

This was an action by Clarence Madsen (plaintiff) against Chrysler Corporation (defendant) for an injunction restraining termination of Madsen's franchise and for damages under the Automobile Dealers' Day in Court Act (15 U.S.C. §1221–1225). Judgment for Madsen. (Note: The facts are exceedingly long and complicated and will not be repeated because it is believed that the major points in the decision can be learned from the parts of the opinion quoted. In substance, however, Chrysler established a sales quota, called minimum sales responsibility (MSR), for each dealer. In Madsen's situation this formula was used in inconsistent ways by various Chrysler officials until Chrysler used it as a basis for terminating Madsen.)

WILL, DISTRICT JUDGE. It must be observed that Chrysler's conduct between March 1964, and even after notice of termination was served, is hardly consistent with the contention it now advances, i.e., that Madsen had clearly defaulted on its contractual obligations and that therefore Chrysler had the unqualified right to terminate the dealership agreement at any time. The evidence set out above leads to but one conclusion: That Chrysler wanted to terminate Madsen's dealership because it believed that a large, new, modern corporate-financed dealership in the combined Wheaton-Glen Ellyn sales area would have substantially better results than any private dealer or dealers could obtain. . . . The fact that Chrysler thought that another type of operation would produce better results obviously does not create the right to terminate an existing dealership on a forced basis. While it might give Chrysler a good faith reason to fail to renew an agreement, Chrysler has chosen to give its dealers continuing agreements terminable only for the causes stated. Conversely, the fact that Chrysler's main purpose in terminating Madsen was as indicated above does not mean that it cannot terminate an agreement if cause in fact exists. . . .

We conclude that MSR [Minimum Sales Responsibility] calculated simply as provided in the Chrysler dealership agreements without adjustment for the various factors herein discussed and which results at all times in a substantial number of dealers being in technical default is an arbitrary, coercive and unfair provision since it would enable Chrysler to terminate roughly one-third to one-half of all its dealerships at any time. We conclude also that Chrysler has waived failure to achieve MSR as a default in Madsen's dealership agreements by treating it as a performance goal rather than as a condition of those agreements. Moreover, to permit Chrysler to terminate in reliance on Madsen's failure to achieve MSR would be particularly unfair here where, at Chrysler's urging, Madsen invested substantial funds in new sales and service facilities for the purpose of increasing sales and service volume. Before the remodeling of the new facilities was completed Chrysler representatives notified plaintiffs of the intention to terminate their franchises so that a cloud has hung over the expanded operation from the start and no measure of normal performance has been possible.

Chrysler's termination of Madsen's franchises, therefore, constitutes a breach of the dealership agreements and a violation of the Dealers' Day in Court Act.

. . . Madsen seeks a permanent injunction against termination of the franchise agreements without valid cause under such agreements. Chrysler, while denying that their asserted termination was invalid urge that, even if the Court finds their action to be a breach of those agreements, no permanent injunction should be granted since, they allege, Madsen has an adequate remedy at law, i.e., money damages.

Two elemental propositions of law are here involved, first, that courts will not enjoin a breach of contract if money damages can adequately compensate the injured party; second, that a court of equity has power to enjoin such a breach if money damages will be impossible to calculate or will not constitute adequate compensation. The applicable criterion then is: can money damages which would adequately compensate plaintiffs be here computed?

It must first be noted that automobile dealer franchises are not available on the open market. The record is clear that Madsen would not be able to use any money damages he might recover to secure a replacement automobile dealer franchise in the Wheaton-Glen Ellyn area in which he has worked his entire life. If he is to continue as an automobile retailer, it will necessarily be in a community new to him, will require an investment not now determinable and the economic success or failure of which is likewise incalculable at present. It will, therefore, be impossible to calculate the amount of money necessary to enable Madsen to restore the status quo.

Nor will it be possible to calculate with any degree of certainty the monetary damages Madsen will sustain by virtue of Chrysler's breach. . . .

It seems apparent from the foregoing that money damages which will adequately compensate Madsen for Chrysler's breach of the franchise agreements are not calculable. Under these circumstances an injunction against wrongful termination is the only appropriate relief.

[*Author's NOTE: It is doubtful that the logic of this case would be followed by a majority of the courts. It is entirely possible, however, that this case may establish some of the guidelines for the future development of law in this area.*]

Lanners v. *Whitney*
428 P.2d 398 (Sup. Ct. Ore. 1967)

This was an action by Alice Lanners (plaintiff) against Whitney (defendant) to rescind a contract and recover damages on the ground of innocent misrepresentation. Judgment for Whitney and Lanners appealed. Reversed.

Whitney sold Lanners an airplane making certain representations concerning its airworthiness and the fact that it had been inspected. Unknown to Whitney, these representations were false.

REDDINGS, JUDGE. The trial court denied Lanners the remedy of rescission, concluding that Lanners failed to prove certain allegations of his complaint and that Lanners had an adequate remedy at law. . . . A thorough review of the record has convinced us that Lanners established by the preponderance of the evidence a material misrepresentation was made by Whitney, which induced him to enter into the contract. In denying rescission, or more appropriately "cancellation" as the U.C.C. terms it, the availability of an adequate remedy at law is wholly irrelevant to Lanners' right to elect to proceed in equity for cancellation.

Under Sec. 2–711, both cancellation and damages are available concurrently and not in the alternative as was the case prior to the adoption of the U.C.C. Since the legal remedy of damages and the equitable remedy of cancellation are available concurrently, the availability of, or the adequacy of remedy at law, is not the criterion for the denial of cancellation. We hold that plaintiff Lanners is entitled to the remedies outlined in Sec. 2–711, afforded a buyer who properly revokes acceptance insofar as they are warranted by the evidence.

Lanners is entitled to cancellation of the contract and the recovery of so much of the price as has been paid, including $6,200 representing the values of the Cessna airplane given to Whitney as part of the price.

In addition, Lanners may recover for incidental damages as provided in Sec. 2–711 and Sec. 2–715 for expenses reasonably incurred as a result of seller's breach, including those incurred in the care and custody of the goods. Comment 2 to 2–711 tells us that such expenses are measured by their cost. We find that Lanners is entitled to recover the amounts spent in repair on the aircraft on the Chicago trip, amounts spent to preserve the craft after the Chicago trip, including cost of removal of the radio and battery, installation of storage oil, ground insurance and storage charges. Lanners is further entitled to a judgment for interest on the entire purchase price paid at the rate of six percent from October 6, 1964, the date of cancellation and demand.

Problem Cases

1. Haugen, a contractor, entered into a contract with Raupach whereby Haugen contracted to build a house for Raupach according to plans and specifications prepared by an architect selected by Raupach. Payments were to be made to Haugen, as the work progressed, and on production of the architect's certificate. Final payment was to be made on the production of the architect's certificate certifying that the work was completed according to the plans and specifications.

   From the inception of the performance of the contract, Haugen was harassed by Raupach with objections and demands that were trivial, unreasonable, and capricious. When the house was completed the architect was of the opinion that there had been a substantial performance of the contract but at the instance of Raupach he made written objections to the work and no certificate of completion was issued. Haugen demanded payment of the balance due on the contract and payment was refused. Haugen brought suit and Raupach set up failure to produce the architect's certificate of completion as a defense. Is this a good defense?

2. Drew contracted to haul for Goodhue all the pulpwood that should be cut upon a certain tract and was to be paid therefore 85 cents per cord, of which 25 cents per cord was to be held back until completion of the contract.

   The whole number of cords cut was 8,345. Goodhue refused to pay Drew the 25 cents per cord withheld, claiming that he had not completed the contract, and Drew brought this suit to recover the sum withheld. After the suit was brought, Drew went over the tract and found 7½ cords which had been concealed by snow and had been overlooked. This amounted to about one stick in 1,170 which had been overlooked. Can Drew recover the full contract price?

3. Thomas Haverty Co. entered into a contract with Jones for the construction of the plumbing, steam-heating and ventilating plant in a four-story building erected by Jones. Jones refused to pay the balance of the contract price and when sued set up that the work was defective in several respects. In the trial the court found that the cost of remedying the defects plus the damage to the building due to defective workmanship was $2,930.87, and that the unpaid balance on the contract was $10,775.64. It therefore rendered a judgment for the difference, $7,844.77. Should this judgment be affirmed on appeal?

4. Haislmaier owned a house which he contracted to sell to Zache for $32,500. Zache paid $500 on July 18, 1961, at the time of the signing of the contract and was to

give his note for $2,000, payable September 1, 1961. He was to pay the balance at the time of the closing of the transaction which was to be on or before September 1, 1961, or at such other time as might be designated by the parties in writing. Zache made application for a loan and the loaning institution required that Zache furnish an abstract of title two weeks before the closing of the loan. Haislmaier had not furnished an abstract and on August 23, 1961, Zache engaged an attorney who wrote Haislmaier giving him notice of cancellation of the contract and demanding the return of the $500 down payment. On August 24 or 25, Haislmaier furnished Zache an abstract brought down to August 18, 1961. Zache did not pay the $2,000 note when due and Haislmaier sued. Zache had, on October 1, 1961, purchased and moved into another house. He defended on the ground that time was of the essence and Haislmaier's delay was a material breach of the contract. Is this a good defense?

5. This was an action by Wasserman Theatrical Enterprise, Inc. (plaintiff), against Jed Harris (defendant) to recover damages for breach of contract for production of theatrical performance. Judgment for Harris, and Wasserman Theatrical Enterprise, Inc., appealed. Judgment affirmed.

   On October 30, 1946, Wasserman Theatrical Enterprises, Inc. (Wasserman), entered into a contract with Jed Harris whereby Harris agreed to present Walter Huston in a theatrical performance entitled *The Apple of His Eye* at Worcester, Massachusetts, on the night of December 16, 1946. On December 12, 1946, Harris canceled the performance due to Huston's illness. Prior to that time Wasserman had spent considerable money in advertising the performance and in preparing the theater for the performance. Wasserman brought this suit to recover for money expended in preparation for the show and for loss of profits. Harris set up as a defense that Huston was the chief artist and essential performer in the production, and that by reason of his illness performance of the contract on December 16, 1946, was rendered impossible. Is Huston liable for breach of contract?

6. Kennedy entered into a contract with Reese whereby Kennedy was to drill a 12-inch well to an estimated depth of 400 feet and case it with 6-inch casing, with bottom half perforated and gravel packed. Kennedy selected the site on Reese's land and drilled to a depth of 130 feet where he struck rock. Reese obtained permission for Kennedy to drill on neighboring land at a site selected by Kennedy. Kennedy drilled to a depth of 270 feet and again struck rock whereupon he abandoned without the permission of Reese. Evidence offered at the trial of the case to the effect that the rock encountered was brittle and that it could be drilled through. Kennedy sued to recover for labor performed and set up impossibility as a defense to the counterclaim filed by Reese. Is this a good defense to the counterclaim?

7. Bailey entered into a contract with the Martins whereby he agreed to furnish all the materials and perform all the work for the construction of a residence on property owned by the Martins, such work to be done in accordance with certain drawings and specifications. The total cost was $11,927.62. The contract provided that no deviation from the drawings and specifications or changes or substitution of material, "shall be made without prior written approval of the owner (the Martins)."

   During the course of the construction of the residence, the Martins orally ordered several additions and changes, and Bailey carried out these orders. The costs required in making the additions and changes was $751.77. The Martins refused to pay for these extras and when sued set up that since they were not ordered in writing as stipulated in the contract they were not liable. Bailey claimed that the original contract was altered by mutual agreement. Had the original contract been altered?

8. Crawford entered into a contract with Publishing Company whereby Crawford engaged to write for publication in Publishing Company's newspaper not less than two columns a week on the progress of the world and other appropriate subjects at a compensation of $50 a week. Crawford was to be employed for a period of two years "provided Crawford's services shall be satisfactory to Publishing Company, and in case they are not, Publishing Company has the right to discharge Crawford on one week's notice." Before the expiration of the two-year period, Publishing Company discharged Crawford, claiming that his work was unsatisfactory. Crawford contended that his writings were of the highest literary quality, and he sued Publishing Company to recover a judgment for breach of contract. Is Crawford entitled to a judgment?

9. Sechrest Plywood Company sued Forest Furniture Company for $10,267.52, a sum due for plywood drawer bottoms manufactured according to Forest's specifications. As a defense, Forest asserted the doctrine of "frustration of purpose," in substance: "(1) the defendant's manufacturing plant was housed in one building which was completely destroyed by fire on April 25, 1963, necessitating the complete abandonment of all its manufacturing activities; (2) the parties contemplated that the drawer bottoms would be used by the defendant in its manufacturing operations; (3) the fire occurred without fault on the part of the defendant." Is this a legitimate defense for breach of contract and did defendant, above, apply the doctrine correctly?

10. Jurovaty purchased a television from Tuckel who was in the business of selling radio and television sets; the full purchase price was $340. Jurovaty paid $85 as a down payment, promising to pay the remainder within 30 days. At the end of the 30-day period the purchaser paid an additional $85 in cash and enclosed a check for $170, drawn to the order of the purchaser by Joseph Irving.

    Tuckel's agent accepted the check and marked the bill paid in full. The check was not honored by the bank because of insufficient funds. Jurovaty contends the acceptance and marking of the bill as paid discharges his obligation. Is this a valid defense?

11. Morristown Lincoln-Mercury, Inc. (Mercury, Inc.), and Roy N. Lotspeich Publishing Company (Publishing Co.) entered into a contract in writing whereby Publishing Co. contracted to publish in its newspaper for three days an advertisement by Mercury, Inc., of a special sale of new and used Mercury automobiles. A competitor of Mercury, Inc., who was a regular advertiser of Publishing Co., objected to the publication of such advertisement, and Publishing Co. canceled it. Mercury, Inc., claims that it had ordered 30 new Mercury automobiles in preparation for the advertised sale and that when the advertisement was rejected it had to cancel its order for 20 automobiles. It further claims that the profit it would have realized on the sale of the 20 automobiles would have been $300 for each automobile, or $6,000. Can Mercury collect $6,000 damages?

12. Worley deposited $4,000 with McCarty in connection with a preliminary sales agreement to purchase a hotel. The agreement provided that the seller would furnish an abstract of title and tax history showing a marketable title in the seller or in lieu thereof a Title Company Policy of Title Insurance. It further provided that ". . . If the deposit money is forfeited for nonperformance by purchaser, the Seller agrees that one-half of such deposit shall be paid the Broker . . . for services rendered." It was further agreed that the purchaser (Worley) would timely complete the purchase "or forfeit to the Seller the deposit made as liquidated damages." Is this a valid liquidated damage clause?

13. G. C. Davis and wife, Ruth Davis, contracted in writing to sell real estate which they owned to A. J. Saunders, Jr. The contract was signed on Sunday, and G. C. Davis was drunk at the time he signed it. The contract was signed again on Monday morning. The price to be paid for the property was only about one half of its fair value. Davis and wife refused to convey the property to Saunders, and Saunders brought this suit asking specific performance of the contract. Will the court grant specific performance?

14. Gordon ordered a Studebaker car from Wade & Dunton on August 16, 1946, a time when private passenger cars were still in short supply due to cutbacks in production caused by the war which had recently ended. The car arrived 20 months later and Gordon had signed a contract requiring him not to sell or transfer title to the automobile for a period of six months without having first offered it to Wade & Dunton at a price discounted for depreciation. There was a provision obligating the buyer to pay Wade & Dunton $400 as liquidated damages for breach of this provision. Gordon disregarded it and sold the car immediately upon receiving it from Wade & Dunton. Wade & Dunton sued Gordon. Is the liquidated damages clause valid? Is the provision relating to the car's resale valid?

15. Rubin ordered goods from Consolidated for resale to customers; however, Consolidated breached the contract by failing to deliver the ordered items. Rubin sued, claiming that loss of goodwill was a compensable and legitimate item of damages for which recovery should be granted in his favor. Does section 2–715 of the Uniform Commercial Code give him any support?

16. Hogan entered into a contract with the owner of Norfleet Gas and Appliance whereby Hogan acquired an option to purchase the business at a future date. The sales price agreed upon in the contract included the purchase of all of the business' assets along with goodwill and the exclusive franchise (the franchise covered a particular territory) under which the business was operated. When Hogan decided to exercise his option the owner refused to convey the business to him. Hogan sued for specific performance. The owner contends specific performance is not an appropriate remedy because this contract is for the sale of personal property. Which party will prevail?

PART IV *Agency*

chapter 15. Creation of Relation and Authority

Introduction

Nature of Relation. An agency relationship is a means whereby an individual can utilize the services of others to accomplish more than he could alone. It is a personal relation created by the mutual consent of the parties; there must be consent but not necessarily a contract. The existence of the relation does not depend upon the subjective intent of the parties but is determined by their acts. If the factual relation between them is such that one party is acting for and under the control of the other, the relation of agency exists. The agency may be gratuitous. When it is created, it brings into play a developed body of law which defines the rights and liability of the parties in their relation to each other and also in their relation to third persons. Since the relation is personal, parties cannot be forced into it against their will nor, generally, can they be forced to continue it.

Early Development. The forerunner of agency was the relation of owner and slave. Since the slave was a mere chattel without legal rights, it was logical to hold the owner legally liable for the acts of the slave, especially if the acts were done at the direction of the owner. It was during this era that the concept of *respondeat superior*—the responsibility of a principal for the acts of his servant or agent—had its origin. This concept is basic in modern agency law. It was not until a later date, when both parties to the relation were free men, that agency law emerged.

English Law. As is true of most areas of the law, the law of agency developed in response to the needs of the time. In England the relation of master and servant was first recognized. Social and economic relations were such that there was little or no reason for one person to delegate the transaction of business to another. In fact, most of the trade of the times was carried on by merchants in the fair cities, and the law which the merchants applied to their transactions and to the controversies arising therefrom was, with few exceptions, determined in the merchants' courts. However, in early England the king empowered men to act for him, for example, by issuing letters of credit enabling agents to borrow money and promise repayment in his name. High churchmen also carried on business through agents.

By the latter part of the 17th century the broker and the factor were well known and played a prominent role in commerce. The brokerage business was regulated by act of parliament late in the 17th century;[1] however, the courts treated brokers, factors, and agents as servants. They did not recognize the distinction between the relation of principal and agent, and that of master and servant, until industry and commerce began to develop during the 18th century.

Scope of Agency. In its narrowest sense the term "agency" includes only the relationship of a principal and agent in which the agent's authority is confined to the power to alter the contractual liability of the principal to third persons. As the term is used in the law, however, it includes not only the relation of principal and agent but also that of master and servant. In general, it connotes any relation in which one person is acting for the benefit and under the control of another. Agency includes all degrees of such a relationship existing between two persons from that where one is engaged by the other to perform the most menial of physical services to that which arises when one person is engaged by the other to transact business which involves great responsibility. The terms "agent" and "agency" are sometimes used to refer to relationships which do not come within the law of agency. For example, a merchant who has a franchise to sell the products of the Ford Motor Company is often referred to as a Ford agent, and his business is referred to as a Ford agency; but the merchant is not an agent of the Ford Motor Company, and the relationship between the Ford Motor Company and the merchant is not that of agency. Such a person is an independent merchant dealing in Ford Motor Company products.

Summary

Agency is a personal relationship which exists between two parties when one consents to act for the benefit and under the control of the other. The relation is created by the mutual consent of the parties, and when it is created, it brings into play a body of developed law.

The forerunner of the relation of agency was the relation of master and slave, and it is from this early relation that we inherit the concept of the liability of the master or principal for the acts of the servant or agent. In

---

[1] 9 William III C.32, ¶14.

England, since slavery did not exist, the relation of master and servant re-placed that of master and slave. Social and economic relations were such that there was little or no reason for one person to delegate the transaction of business to another.

By the latter part of the 17th century the factor and broker began to play an important role, and with the development of industry and commerce during the 18th century the relationship of principal and agent was recognized by the courts.

The term "agency," as used in the law, includes both the relation of master and servant and that of principal and agent.

Classification

Introduction. Since agency is broad in its scope, it is desirable, from the standpoint of practical considerations, to subdivide the area into classes, the classification being based on the nature of the services performed. The two classes of relationships generally recognized are master and servant, or em-ployer and employee, and principal and agent. A third relationship, termed "independent contractor," has many of the characteristics of these two classes. The distinctions between these classes are based on the nature of the services rendered and the degree of control which is retained over the representative.

Master and Servant. The term "master and servant" was used in the early law, and its use still predominates; but outside the field of law the term "em-ployer and employee" is more commonly used. The major feature of the master and servant relationship is that the physical conduct of the servant (employee) is subject to the control of the master (employer). The factory employee who performs physical labor under the direct or indirect supervision of the employer is a clear-cut example of this class. At the next level in the factory organization classification is more difficult. Although the foreman is an employee, control over him is less with respect to his physical activities than his conduct as a representative of the employer, and this is even more true as one approaches top management.

It is not uncommon for an employee to be directed to do work for another employer, with the original employer being paid for the services of his em-ployee. The question arises as to which employer (master) is liable for a tort committed by an employee (servant) in this situation. The inference is that the "loaned servant" remains the employee of his original employer, who will be liable to him for his pay and will remain his employer under most statutes, such as social security, unemployment and workmen's compensation. However, if the primary right of control is shifted to the special employer, under the "loaned servant doctrine," he becomes liable for the employee's torts. Which employer has the right of control is frequently a difficult question of fact.

Principal and Agent. A principal also has control over the conduct of an agent but, in contrast to the master-servant relationship, the control is with respect to business activities or other acts which may alter the legal relations between the principal and third persons. Buying and selling, borrowing and lending money, and managing a business are examples of acts that agents may perform for their principals. It might be said that an agent deals primarily with persons while a servant deals primarily with things, and that a servant is paid for his time and an agent for his results.

A professional agent is a person who is in business for himself, and his business is that of acting as an agent for others. Attorneys, brokers, factors, and auctioneers fall into this category. The professional agent usually acts as agent for many different principals. His business is so operated that he is subject to the control of the principal in regard to the particular business he is transacting for him, but he is not under his control in regard to his physical acts.

General and Special Agents. Agents are often further classified as general or special agents. A general agent is a person who acts for the principal on a number of transactions over a period of time. He may be given authority to act for the principal in a rather wide range of matters, such as the manager of a business unit, or he may be authorized to handle all transactions of a certain class for the principal, such as a general purchasing agent. A special agent, on the other hand, is one who is authorized to act either in a single transaction or a limited series of transactions. A stockbroker typically acts as a special agent. The distinction between general and special agent, however, is no more clear-cut than between agent and servant.

Independent Contractor. The distinction between a servant or employee and an independent contractor is based upon the degree of control retained over the physical conduct of the person performing the service. Whether a particular person or group is acting as an independent contractor is often a difficult question of fact. If Archer needs a new machine, he may build it in his own shops, in which case those persons who build the machine will be Archer's employees. Archer may submit the specifications for the machine to Burch, who will contract to build the machine according to the specifications and for an agreed price. In this case, Burch will not be an employee of Archer, since Burch has contracted to produce a result and is free to proceed by whatever method he may wish in producing that result. Burch's physical conduct is not under the control of Archer. Burch is an independent contractor. The employee is subject to the direction of his employer; the independent contractor obligates himself to produce a result and is free to pursue his own methods in the performance of the work.

Summary

Within the scope of the law of agency are two major classes of relationship, the employer and employee (master and servant) and the principal and agent. In the former the employer has the right to control the physical activities of the employee while in the latter the principal has control over the acts of the agent which may affect the legal relations between the principal and third persons.

Closely related to the employer and employee relationship is that of employer and independent contractor. The primary basis for the distinction is the control of the employer over the physical conduct of the worker. The independent contractor's duty is to produce a stipulated result and he, rather than the employer, has the right to determine the methods used. Similarly the professional agent is employed to produce a stipulated business result without control from the principal as to his physical conduct. A general agent acts for the principal in a number of transactions over a period of time and is considered to have broader authority than a special agent who is employed for a single or limited series of transactions.

New York Central Railroad Co. v.
Northern Indiana Public Service Co.

221 N.E.2d 442 (App. Ct. Ind. 1966)

This was an action by New York Central Railroad Company (plaintiff) against Northern Indiana Public Service Company (defendant) for reimbursement pursuant to a contract of indemnity entered into between the parties. Judgment for Nipsco and NYC appealed. Judgment affirmed.

NYC owned a set of tracks over which Nipso desired to extend its power lines. The written licensing agreement by which Nipsco obtained right-of-way over the tracks provided that Nipsco would indemnify NYC for all losses sustained directly or indirectly as a result of the power lines *"except* such as may be caused by the sole negligence of NYC, its agents or employees." Some time later NYC rented a crane to unload replacement rails for track repairs just below the power lines. The crane was maintained by an operator and an oiler employed by the rental company. While the crane operator was unloading sections of track with the help and direction of NYC employees, the boom struck one of the power lines. As a result, a NYC laborer was electrocuted while working in the gondola car. A claim was instituted by the widow of the employee and was settled by NYC for $30,000. NYC now sues Nipsco to recover that amount pursuant to the indemnity clause in the licensing agreement. Nipsco claims that under the borrowed servant doctrine the crane operator was acting as an employee or agent of NYC and thus the loss falls within the exception to the indemnity clause.

HUNTER, JUDGE. Both parties seem to agree that the determining question placed before this court involves the borrowed servant doctrine which states that an employee while generally employed by one party, may be loaned to another in such a manner that the special employer may be responsible for the acts of the employee under the doctrine of *respondeat superior*.

There can be found three leading theories used to analyze the borrowed servant situation. First, is the "whose business" test. This test attempts to discern whether the operator was furthering the business of the special or general employer. It would seem to be an accurate statement to say that in the borderline cases, the liability will be placed on that employer's business which the court or the jury under the facts chooses to emphasize. Second is the "control test" which is normally used in conjunction with the "whose business" test. This test attempts to analyze the borrowed servant question by finding which employer had the right to control the specific act in question. The third test, "the scope of business" was developed to cure the ambiguities and confusion that resulted from the application of the "whole business" and "control" tests. This test attempts to incorporate the scope of employment terminology and application as used in the normal *respondeat superior* situation; that is, if the work being done by the servant is within the scope of business of the special employer, then the liability for such acts lies with the special employer.

Indiana has adopted the "control" and "whose business" tests in attempting to discern which employer had the right to control the specific act in question.

In the facts at bar the general employer had the right to hire and fire the servant. It paid the servant's wages and was in charge of the care and maintenance of the machine. Additionally the general employer was in the business of renting similar machines and the operator was a semi-skilled employee. In some respects these uncontroverted facts would indicate that the general employer had a right to control the specific act in question.

However, other facts indicate the contrary. The appellant in leasing the machine did not indicate what work was to be done. When the operator and oiler arrived at the job, the foreman asked them if they were the crew that was to work for him. He explained the method of operation required as to where to lay the rails upon being unloaded from the gondola car. He had directed the placement of the gondola below the high tension wires. The crane was working in close contact with the other employees of the railroad. The crane operator could not see into the gondola car where the men were working and attaching the tongs to the rails. The operator was looking for some signals from the foreman at the moment the boom hit the overhead wires. There had been some directions given by the foreman previously. In addition the general employer had no idea of the nature of the work. The lease was to continue for an indeterminate period at the option of NYC. Also the nature of the work was well within the scope of business of the railroad, that of unloading a car of rails, and there is testimony in the record to the effect that the foreman was an experienced crane operator. From all of these facts the court could have concluded that the special employer (NYC) had the right to control the operator in the operation of the crane as to the act in question, and that the work being done was within the scope of the appellant's business.

Certainly we have present a case where reasonable men might differ as to which employer had the right to control the operator in the movements and operation of the crane and as to whether the operator was within the scope of business of the special employer. However, we believe that all of the facts outlined above were properly considered and the findings and conclusions of law are supported by sufficient evidence.

Flick v. Crouch

434 P.2d 256 (Sup. Ct. Okla. 1967)

This was an action by Mrs. Flick (plaintiff) against Elmer Crouch (defendant) for the wrongful death of her husband while employed by Crouch. Crouch's motion to dismiss was sustained and Flick appealed. Reversed.

Mrs. Flick's husband was killed at a well site when a derrick suddenly collapsed. She claims the collapse was due to faulty welds at the base of the derrick. The welders who did the work had been procured by Crouch.

Crouch would not be subject to suit if he were an employee of the Parker Drilling Co., as he claimed, since he would be immune under the Workmen's Compensation Act. Mrs. Flick argued that Crouch was an independent contractor.

Crouch owned a truck and welding equipment and supplied his own welding rods and arc. He operated under the trade name of Crouch Welding Company, and had been in the welding business for 15 years. All of the work he did was for Parker Drilling Co., and he had stopped doing work for others because Parker kept him "busy." Crouch maintained his own insurance coverage. He billed Parker monthly at the rate of $7.00 per hour, keeping his own time records. He was not required to work regular hours. Crouch had signed the invoices submitted by the other welders who were employed for the job on the derrick. Crouch was not told by Parker how to use his equipment or what kind of equipment to use but was given a sketch from which the size of the steel to be used to reinforce the derrick could be determined.

McINERNEY, JUSTICE. According to the widow's contention, these welders were independent contractors. The widow complains that under the evidence . . . the status of the welders in relation to Parker presented a jury question. She asserts error in treating that issue as one of law.

As is a general rule the line of demarcation between an independent contractor and a servant is not clearly drawn. The question of such relationship must be determined from the facts peculiar to each case. The various elements to be considered, as set forth in *Page* v. *Hardy* are:

(a) the nature of the contract between the parties, whether written or oral; (b) the degree of control which, by the agreement, the employer may exercise on the details of the work or the independence enjoyed by the contractor or agent; (c) whether or not the one employed is engaged in a distinct occupation or business and whether he carries on such occupation or business for others; (d) the kind of occupation with reference to whether, in the locality, the work is usually done under the direction of the employer or by a specialist without supervision; (e) the skill required in the particular occupation; (f) whether the employer or the workman supplies the instrumentalities, tools and the place of work for the person doing the work; (g) the length of time for which the person is employed; (h) the method of payment, whether by the time or by the job; (i) whether or not the work is a part of the regular business of the employer; (j) whether or not the parties believe they are creating the relationship of master and servant; and (k) the right of either to terminate the relationship without liability.

An independent contractor is one who engages to perform a certain service for another, according to his own method and manner, free from control and direction of his employer in all matters connected with the performance of the service, except as to the result thereof. Those who render service but retain control over the manner of doing it are not servants. Where the defendant's status forms a material issue in the case and the facts bearing on that issue are disputed, or *where there is room for reasonable difference of opinion as to the proper inference to be drawn from the known facts,* the issue is for the jury under proper instructions by the court. [Emphasis added by court.]

Burriss v. Texaco, Inc.
361 F.2d 169 (4th Cir. 1966)

This was an action by Robert E. Burriss, Jr. (plaintiff) against Texaco, Inc. (defendant) to recover for fire damage to Burriss' feed mill located in Anderson, South Carolina. Judgment for Burriss and Texaco appealed. Judgment affirmed.

For more than thirty years Texaco held a lease on certain lands in the vicinity of Burriss' feed mill. It built storage facilities there, and they were used for the distribution of gasoline to Texaco service stations in the area through a "consignment agreement" with Joe Crudup, Jr.

During the unloading of gasoline from a Texaco railroad car approximately 100 gallons were spilled and entered a drainage ditch which discharged under Burriss' feed mill. Fire broke out in the ditch and spread to Burriss' mill. A city fire ordinance required the maintenance of a separation box to prevent the entrance of flammable liquids into public drainage ditches, and under South Carolina law failure to comply with a safety ordinance constitutes negligence *per se.* Texaco contended that the consignment agreement made Crudup an independent contractor and immunized it from liability for responsibility for noncompliance with the ordinance.

SOBELOFF, CIRCUIT JUDGE.   Under South Carolina law, the terms of a consignment agreement are not conclusive on the question of independent contractor, where there is evidence *dehors* the contract which establishes a true agency relationship. The test as developed in South Carolina and other jurisdictions is whether or not the purported principal has the right to control the conduct of his alleged agent. A review of the facts, undisputed on this record, shows that Texaco retained the right to control the detailed operation of the enterprise, and actively exercised it, so that Crudup was in fact merely Texaco's Anderson agent.

Texaco owned the storage tanks, pipe lines and other equipment used for unloading and storage of gasoline delivered in tank cars owned by Texaco. The land on which these tanks were built, held by Texaco on lease from the railroad, was not sub-leased to Crudup. The consignment agreement provided that Texaco would deliver to Crudup quantities of gasoline for sale in the Anderson area, to be sold at prices not less than Texaco's prescribed minimum. Under the distributorship agreement, Crudup was required to purchase annually no less than 284,000 gallons of gasoline, and he could not take more than 340,000 gallons.

There are some 35 Texaco service stations in the Anderson area. Each has a contract directly with Texaco, not Crudup, for the annual purchase of specified quantities of gasoline. Texaco consigned the gasoline needed to Crudup, who in turn delivered to individual retailers. Title to the gasoline remained in Texaco until delivery by Crudup to the stations. Sales of this gasoline to the dealers were required to be strictly for cash, except where authorized by Texaco. All invoices to the local dealers were on Texaco, Inc., billheads and Texaco maintained a separate bank account in its name in Anderson for deposit of payments made to Crudup by the retailers. Crudup was required to account promptly to Texaco for all moneys in his possession, and he kept daily records of his operations on forms supplied by Texaco. The telephone was listed in Texaco's name, and the Texaco trademark was painted on one of the storage tanks and the warehouse. Although the Anderson license for the operation of a bulk storage plant was in Crudup's name, Texaco paid all taxes on merchandise, stock and equipment of the consignor.

Texaco furnished Crudup a manual entitled "Successful Bulk Station Operation Suggestions for Consignees," which stated in its preface that the consignee should promptly report to the company any dangerous or defective conditions in order that the company could make needed repairs and replacements. The body of the "Suggestions" lays down procedures for maintenance and operation of the distributorship, the forms and reports to be used, and the manner of extending credit and making collections on sales to Texaco service stations. Every step in the handling, storage, and unloading of gasoline was prescribed in most minute detail, even to the location of receptacles for discarded cigarettes. In view of Texaco's power to terminate the contract on five days' notice, and to make thrice-monthly inspections, Crudup's testimony that he followed all the "suggestions" to the letter is not surprising.

Crudup was simply Texaco's local distributing agent in Anderson. This is not a case in which a manufacturer in search of an outlet for his product commissions a local businessman to handle a line of goods, leaving him free to operate his business as he sees fit. By the very nature of the business and the dangerous character of the product sold, Texaco retained a high degree of control over the distribution. The relationship was exactly the same as if Texaco had retained Crudup on its payroll—although on a commission basis—and assigned him to operate its Anderson plant. The relationship was not altered by merely clothing him in the garment labelled "independent contractor."

Creation of Relation

Requirement to Create Agency. As a general rule, no formality is required to create the relationship of master and servant or principal and agent. Whether or not such a relationship exists is a question of fact, and if, from the circumstances, it appears that one person is acting for the benefit and under the control of another, the courts will hold that an agency exists. The relation may be created without either party being aware of its existence and even though the parties have expressly stated that they do not intend to create it.

In by far the majority of instances the relationship of master and servant, and that of principal and agent, is created by contract. However, the fact that an agent is acting gratuitously and that no enforceable contract of agency has been entered into between the principal and agent will in no way affect the validity of the contracts negotiated in the name of the principal by the agent. The gratuitous agent owes to his principal a fiduciary duty and is responsible to him for any failure to exercise due care in the transaction of the principal's business entrusted to him. The gratuitious agent may terminate the relationship at any time without incurring liability.

Statutory Requirements.   In many states the authority of an agent to sell and convey, to mortgage, or to create a trust in real property is required by statute to be in writing. In a few states an agent must be authorized in writing to execute, in behalf of his principal, any contract which, to be enforceable, is required to be evidenced by a writing. At common law an agent's authority to execute a contract under seal was required to be under seal. This rule still prevails in the states where the efficacy of the seal is recognized, but in most states the distinction between contracts under seal and unsealed contracts has been abolished by statute.

Summary

As a general rule, no formality is required to create the relation of employer and employee or principal and agent; it may be created by the mutual consent of the parties, or it may be implied from their conduct. However, the fact that an agent is acting gratuitiously does not affect his power to bind his principal, nor does it relieve him from the fiduciary duty an agent owes to his principal. Under the statutes of some states, written evidence of the agent's authority is required.

Capacity of Parties

Infants and Insane Persons as Principals.   Since the relation of principal and agent is not contractual, it is not necessary that the principal have, when he appoints an agent, the capacity to contract. However, agency is a consensual relation; consequently, the principal must have sufficient legal capacity to give the consent essential to the creation of the relation.

A person of limited capacity cannot enlarge his legal capacity by appointing an agent and acting through the agent. The infant or insane person is bound by the acts of a person whom he has appointed and authorized to act as his agent only to the extent that he (the infant or insane person) would be bound had he acted in person.

Unincorporated Associations as Principals. Under the common-law rule an unincorporated association is not recognized as an entity having legal capacity. It cannot, as a general rule sue, be sued, own property, or enter into a contract. Under special statutes, however, such associations have been made subject to suit and their assets are subject to execution. This is especially true of labor unions. If an unincorporated association is not liable to suit under the provisions of a statute, its members who have legal capacity may be held liable. If a person is appointed an agent for an unincorporated association, such person may be the agent of all of its members or of only certain ones of them. If the one appointing and authorizing the agent to act has been authorized by all of the members of the association to act in their behalf, he is agent for the members and can bind them if he acts within the scope of his authority. A class action, or action against a representative group of the members on behalf of all members, is the means to enforce the liability of all the members for the acts of an agent acting within his authority. A judgment in such an action is good against the assets of the association. Whether one is acting for the entire membership of the unincorporated association or for only a group of the members will depend on the circumstances of the particular case.

Capacity to Act as Agent. A person may have capacity to act as an agent even though he does not have the capacity to contract. In the transaction of business through an agent the principal is the party to the transaction, not the agent. The agent's capacity is immaterial so long as he has sufficient ability to carry out his instructions. A partnership, as a general rule, can act as an agent. Whether or not a corporation can act as an agent will depend on the scope of its charter powers. A husband or wife may act as the agent of the spouse but there is no agency merely by virtue of the marital relationship. The liability of a husband for the necessities purchased by his wife is an aspect of the marital relationship itself and does not constitute the wife an agent for her husband.

Business Organizations as Principals. Business organizations, such as corporations, partnerships, and business trusts, which have the power to contract have the capacity to appoint agents. All the business of a corporation is, in fact, transacted through its agents. And although the partnership is not recognized as an entity, each partner acts as the agent of his copartners in the transaction of partnership business. One who has been appointed the agent of a partnership by a member of the partnership who is authorized so to act is the agent of all the partners.

The extent to which a business trust may act through an agent will depend on the terms of the trust agreement creating the trust.

Summary

An infant, insane person, or other persons may appoint agents and act through such agents to the same extent as they might act in person, but they cannot enlarge their legal capacity by acting through agents. The courts have held infants liable for the torts of their agents provided the agent's acts have been directed by the infant.

As a general rule an unincorporated association has no capacity to contract and cannot appoint an agent. Its members, however, may act through an agent.

A married woman may appoint her husband her agent, and a husband may appoint his wife his agent, but neither is the agent of the other by virtue of the marital relationship.

A business organization which has the power to contract has the capacity to appoint an agent.

A person who does not have full capacity to contract may act as an agent.

Authority to Bind Principal

Authorization.   An agent is authorized to act for a principal when the principal has by his acts or conduct made it manifest to the agent that he (the principal) intends the agent to act on his (the principal's) account. The authority of the agent to bind the principal is based on the conduct of the principal. In general, the authority to act on the account of the principal may be conferred on the agent by written or spoken words or by other conduct of the principal which, reasonably interpreted, causes the agent to believe that the principal intends the agent so to act on the principal's account.

In analyzing the power of an agent to bind the principal, the courts and writers have not been consistent in the terms used. In our analysis, we shall follow a three-part classification: (1) express authority, (2) implied authority (also referred to as incidental authority), and (3) apparent authority (also referred to as ostensible authority and similar to "authority by estoppel").

Express Authority.   Express authority is that authority which is explicitly conferred on the agent by the principal. It may be conferred either orally or in writing, but in either event the principal must express to the agent the exact acts he wishes the agent to perform. For example, if the principal instructs his agent, either orally or in writing, to draw a check payable to Tucker for a stated sum and to sign the check in the principal's name and deliver it to Tucker, the agent will have express authority to draw, sign, and deliver the check.

Implied Authority.   In almost all situations the agent will have authority to perform some acts not included in his express authority. Expressly to include every act which an agent is to perform in the carrying-out of his mission would be almost impossible. An agent is appointed by the principal to accomplish an objective. If the agent is a special agent—that is, if he is appointed to conduct a single transaction or to conduct a number of transactions which do not involve continuity of services—the express authority may include the majority of acts the agent is authorized to perform. If an agent is authorized to sell a piece of real property or several pieces of real property and his authority is in writing, the express authority may be sufficiently detailed to include most of the acts to be performed by the agent. However, it will not include every detail of the transaction authorized. If the agent is a general agent—that is, if he is appointed to conduct a series of transactions involving a continuity of services—the express authority, even though carefully worded to cover the agent's duties in detail, cannot include more than the major acts the agent is to perform. In carrying out the objective of the agency, the agent will be authorized to do many acts not detailed in the express authority.

Unless the principal limits the authority of the agent by express instructions or by clear implication, the authority to negotiate a transaction includes the authority to do those acts which are usually or customarily done in conducting transactions such as the agent is authorized to transact or to do those acts which are reasonably necessary to accomplish the objective of the agency. Such authority is generally termed "implied authority" or "incidental authority."

In determining the scope of the agent's express and implied authority, the measure used is the justified belief of the agent. The same principles apply to the interpretation of an agent's authority as apply in interpreting an offer to contract. The nature of the agency, whether special or general, usages of trade, prior relations between the principal and agent, and such other facts and circumstances which are material in the particular case are weighed in determining what authority the agent is justified in believing the principal intended to confer on him. The problem of determining the scope of the agent's authority is closely related to the problem of the relation of the principal to the third person which is discussed in Chapter 16.

Apparent Authority.   Whereas the scope of an agent's express or implied authority is determined by analyzing the relation between the principal and the agent, an agent's apparent authority is determined by analyzing the relation between the principal and a third person. An agent's apparent authority may be less than, coextensive with, or greater than his express or implied authority. An agent's apparent authority, sometimes termed ostensible authority, is the authority which the principal by his conduct has led the third person, acting as a reasonable and prudent person, justifiably to believe is conferred on the agent by the principal.

Apparent authority is created by the same method as that by which express or implied authority is created except that the manifestations of the principal must be made to the third person rather than to the agent. In holding the principal liable on the ground of the apparent authority of the agent, the third person must prove that the principal was responsible for the information which justified the third person in believing that the agent was authorized to act. The information on which the third person justifies his belief may come directly from the words or conduct of the principal; it may be based on standard practices of trade; or it may result from the principal entrusting certain documents to the agent or from the appointment of the agent to a position which carries with it the implication of authority. Also, apparent authority may be established by showing that the agent has been conducting similar transactions or doing similar acts to the knowledge of the principal and without his objecting thereto.

Summary

The authority of an agent to act for his principal is based on the manifestation of the principal. Authority may be conferred by written or spoken words, or by other conduct of the principal. The authority of the agent may be express, implied, or apparent. The agent has the express and implied authority which he, as a reasonable person familiar with the business to be transacted, is justified in believing the principal intended to confer on him. Express authority is the authority expressly conferred on the agent by the principal; implied authority is the authority to do those acts which are reasonably necessary to accomplish the objective of the agency.

Apparent authority is determined by analyzing the relation between the agent and the third person. The agent has such apparent authority as the principal, by his conduct, has led the third person, acting as a reasonable person familiar with the business to be transacted, justifiably to believe has been conferred on the agent.

Jennings v. *Pittsburgh Mercantile Co.*
202 A.2d 51 (Sup. Ct. Pa. 1964)

This was an action by Dan R. Jennings, a real estate broker, and his associate, Daniel B. Cantor (plaintiffs), against Pittsburgh Mercantile Company (defendant) to recover a real estate brokerage commission for the alleged consummation of a sale and leaseback of all of Mercantile's real property. Judgment for Jennings and Cantor, and Mercantile appealed. Judgment reversed.

In April, 1958, Egmore, Mercantile's Vice-President and Treasurer-Comptroller, and Stern, its financial consultant, met with Jennings, explained Mercantile's desire to raise cash for store modernization, and provided Jennings with financial information. At the meeting Egmore represented that the Executive Committee, of which he was a member, controlled Mercantile, that this committee would determine whether the company would accept any offers produced by Jennings, and that subsequent Board of Directors approval would be automatic. Egmore outlined preliminary terms of an acceptable offer, and promised payment of a commission if Jennings produced an offer acceptable to the Executive Committee.

In July and August, 1958, Jennings brought Egmore three offers, none of which met the originally specified terms. The first two were quickly rejected, but the third came close to the original terms. On November 4, 1958, Jennings was informed by Stern that the Executive Committee had "agreed to the deal." However, within a week Egmore informed Jennings that the third offer had been rejected. Mercantile refused to pay Jenning's bill for commission of $32,000 and suit was instituted. Mercantile claimed that Egmore and Stern had no authority to accept the offer for sale and leaseback thereby binding it to payment of the brokerage commission.

COHEN, JUSTICE.   At the outset, we note that for Mercantile this proposed sale and leaseback was not a transaction in the ordinary course of business. Rather, it was unusual and unprecedented. The transaction envisaged Mercantile's relinquishment of ownership of all its real property, worth approximately $1.5 million, for a period of 30 years. Hence, the apparent authority which Jennings seeks to establish is the apparent authority to accept an offer for an extraordinary transaction.

Apparent authority is defined as that authority which, although not actually granted, the principal (1) knowingly permits the agent to exercise or (2) holds him out as possessing.

Jennings strongly contends that Egmore's representations gave rise to the apparent authority asserted. We do not agree. Without regard to the extraordinary nature of a transaction, a disclosed or partially disclosed principal cannot be bound on the doctrine of apparent authority by virtue of the extrajudicial representations of an agent as to the existence or extent of his authority or the facts upon which it depends. An agent cannot, simply by his own words, invest himself with apparent authority. Such authority emanates from the actions of the principal and not the agent. Therefore, the representations upon which Jennings relies so heavily do not support his contention.

Jennings further argues that apparent authority arose by virtue of (1) certain prior dealings of Egmore and (2) the corporate offices held by Egmore. However, the evidence advanced in support of this argument is insufficient to permit a reasonable inference of the existence of apparent authority in Egmore to accept Jennings' offer.

Focusing on the first of these factors, in order for a reasonable inference of the existence of apparent authority to be drawn from prior dealings, these dealings must have (1) a measure of similarity to the act for which the principal is sought to be bound, and, granting this similarity, (2) a degree of repetitiveness. Although the required degree of repetitiveness might have been present here, the prior acts relied upon consisted solely of Egmore's provision of financial information to Jennings and other brokers with regard to the sale and leaseback, and Egmore's solicitation of offers through them. The dissimilarities between these acts and the act of accepting the offer in issue are self-evident, and apparently authority to do the latter act cannot be inferred from the doing of the former.

As to the second of the above factors, the corporate offices of Vice-President and Treasurer-Comptroller, which Egmore held, do not provide the basis for a reasonable inference that Mercantile held out Egmore as having the apparent authority to accept the offers produced by Jennings. [Cases cited.] Each of these cases involved a suit against a corporation for a brokerage commission for securing a purchaser for all of the corporation's realty. The principal issue in each was the apparent authority possessed *virtute officii* to consummate an extraordinary transaction. On facts stronger than those present here, the claims of apparent authority were rejected. We hold likewise on the present facts, for any other conclusion would improperly extend the usual scope of authority which attaches to the holding of various corporate offices, and would greatly undercut the proper role of the Board of Directors in corporate decision-making by thrusting upon them determinations on critical matters which they have never had the opportunity to consider.

Finally, the extraordinary nature of this transaction placed Jennings on notice to inquire as to Egmore's actual authority, particularly since the appellees were an experienced real estate broker and investment counselor-attorney team. Had inquiry been made Jennings would have discovered that the Board never considered any of the proposals and obviously did not delegate actual authority to accept offers.

Lux Art Van Service, Inc. v. Pollard
344 F.2d 883 (9th Cir. 1965)

This was an action by Art Pollard (plaintiff) against Lux Art Van Service, Inc. (defendant) to recover damages resulting from the death of a brood mare which died while being transported by Lux Art. Judgment for Pollard and Lux Art appealed. Judgment affirmed.

Chinchilla was an outstanding brood mare. In January, 1962, Pollard took her from his ranch to the stud farm operated by Vessels Ranch, Inc. near Los Alamitos, a small town in Southern California. He had taken other mares there to be bred and it was his regular practice to transport them both ways, using his own equipment and personnel. During their stay, which varied from three to six months, the mares were in the care and under the exclusive control of Vessels. When they were well in foal, Vessels so advised Pollard who then fetched them himself. However, in this instance, Vessels did not notify Pollard, but instead made arrangements with Lux to return Chinchilla.

While being transported by Lux employees, in the center stall of a large van across the near desert area of southwest California, Chinchilla collapsed and died from heat exhaustion. In defense to Pollard's claim of negligence, Lux took the position that Pollard had constituted Vessels Ranch as his agent, and that Lux's liability was limited to the $150.00 value declared by Vessels Ranch in the Bill of Lading. The cost of transportation was based upon that figure, and it appeared that Vessels had not requested that the horse be hauled at any of the higher rates available to shippers desiring greater protection.

KOELSCH, JUDGE. Lux does not contend that Pollard had expressly requested Vessels Ranch to return Chinchilla to him or have her returned by someone else. Indeed, it appears that Pollard was entirely unaware of Vessels' action. Nor does the evidence require the conclusion that such authority existed because of a past course of dealing between Pollard and Vessels, or some general practice commonly followed by those engaged in the business of breeding horses. Rather, as Lux states in brief:

"What defendant does contend is that plaintiff, by placing his mare temporarily in the exclusive control of Vessels Ranch, necessarily vested his bailee with apparent authority to return the mare to its owner and, for the purpose of effecting such shipment, to enter into a contract binding upon the owner."

Accurately speaking, "apparent authority" is not authority at all, but is merely a power to affect the principal's affairs. It arises not by authorization in the consensual sense, but from the principal's negligent omission or his acquiescence in the agent's activities. The law gives to the latter the effect of a representation to the party dealing with the "agent" that the "principal consents to have the act done on his behalf." To apply the rule of apparent authority, there must therefore be some basis for what may be loosely termed an estoppel against the principal. And this "estoppel" depends upon manifestations by the principal to the third party and not to the agent. *Restatement (Second) Agency* § 49(b) indicates that "if there is a latent ambiguity in the manifestations of the principal for which he is not at fault, the interpretation of the apparent authority is based on the facts known to the principal."

In this case the sole basis of an "estoppel" against Pollard must rest upon the fact of Vessels' possession. The rule is of long standing, however, that possession of a chattel, standing alone, does not authorize an agent to affect the principal's interest. The reason is plain: mere possession carries no indication of any right to engage in transactions of serious consequence to the owner of the chattel. Possession is as consistent with tortious acquisition as with full ownership and provides no basis for an assumption that the possessor may deal with the chattel as he pleases.

We think the circumstances of this case preclude a finding that the Vessels Ranch had apparent authority to ship the mare. Here we had an obviously valuable horse to be shipped on a long and arduous journey across one of the hottest areas of the United States. The numerous risks attendant such trip convince us that an owner must do some act of greater significance than to merely relinquish possession before being deemed to have undertaken the risks of this shipment.

Ratification

Nature of Ratification. Ratification in the law of agency is the subsequent adoption and affirmance by one person of an act which another, without authority, has previously assumed to do for him while purporting to act as his agent. Ratification is equivalent to a previous authorization and relates back to the time when the act ratified was done, except where intervening rights of third parties are concerned. Any act which the principal could have authorized at the time the act was done may be ratified.

Requirements for Ratification.   To have a valid ratification, the following conditions must be satisfied: (1) The person ratifying must have had the present ability to do the act himself or authorize it to be done, (2) the person for whom the act was done must have been identified or the circumstances must have been such that he was capable of identification, (3) the person acting must have acted as agent of his principal or the person represented to be his principal, (4) the principal or person represented to be the principal must have been in existence at the time the act was done and must have been competent to do or authorize the act done, (5) the principal or person represented to be the principal must have had knowledge of all the material facts at the time he ratified, (6) the third party must not have canceled the transaction, and (7) the circumstances must have been such that the intervening rights of third persons were not cut off by the ratification.

There are no formal requirements for ratification. It may be expressed or implied from the acts of the principal. Usually, acceptance of benefits or failure to repudiate within a reasonable time will be convincing evidence of intent to ratify, provided the principal, at the time, has knowledge of all the material facts.

What Acts May Be Ratified.   As a general rule, any act which the principal could have done or authorized at the time the act was done or authorized may be ratified. The principal may ratify an illegal act of his agent. If the act ratified is both a tort and a crime, ratification by the principal will make the principal liable for the tort, but it will not make him liable for the crime. Ratification by the principal of an agent's illegal act will not relieve the agent from his individual tort or criminal liability.

Since ratification relates back to the time the act was done, and since the principal must have been in existence at that time, it naturally follows that a proposed but nonexistent corporation, when it comes into existence (receives its charter), cannot ratify the acts done by the promoters in the name of the proposed but nonexistent corporation. It may, however, as discussed in Chapter 24, adopt such acts when it comes into existence.

Effect of Ratification.   When a principal ratifies the unauthorized acts of his agent, the principal then accepts and receives all responsibility for such acts from the time they were done. When the principal has effectively ratified the acts of his agent, he cannot at a later time repudiate the ratification.

Ratification releases the agent from liability to both his principal and third persons for having exceeded his authority. It also gives the agent the same rights against the principal as to compensation that he would have been given had the acts been previously authorized. In return the principal is entitled to receive from the agent everything to which he would have been entitled had the act been originally authorized.

Under the rule generally followed in the United States, the third person has the right to cancel or withdraw from the unauthorized transaction at any time before the principal ratifies it, but not afterward.

Ratification Must Be Entire.   If the principal wishes to ratify, he must ratify the entire transaction. He cannot ratify those portions of the contract which are beneficial and repudiate those parts which are detrimental. On ratification the principal will be bound in the same manner and to the same extent as he would have been if the agent had had full authority in the first instance.

Summary

Ratification is the subsequent adoption of an act which was unauthorized originally. In order to make the ratification valid, the existing and identifiable principal, with knowledge of the material facts, must indicate his intention to be bound by the agent's unauthorized acts done in the name of the principal. All that is necessary for ratification is that the principal, either expressly or impliedly, indicate his intention to be bound by the originally unauthorized act of his agent. Any act which could have been done or authorized by the principal may be ratified. The principal must have been in existence at the time the act was done.

A ratification is retroactive and supplies the authority lacking at the time of the commission of the act. Unless third parties have acquired rights which would be cut off by ratification, the effect of ratification is to place all involved parties in the position they would have held had the act been authorized at the time it was done. If the principal wishes to ratify, he must ratify the transaction in its entirety.

Wilks v. Stone

339 S.W.2d 590 (Ct. App. Mo. 1960)

This was an action by Hazel Wilks (plaintiff) against Bill Stone (defendant) to replevin an automobile. Judgment for Wilks and Stone appealed. Judgment reversed and remanded.

Larry Wilks, son of Hazel Wilks, traded a Plymouth automobile to Stone in part payment for a Chevrolet convertible. Hazel Wilks claimed that she was the owner of the Plymouth automobile and that Larry had no right to trade it to Stone and that Stone acquired no ownership in the Plymouth. On the trial, Stone offered in evidence testimony to prove that Larry gave a check for $1,695, representing the balance of the purchase price, which was returned marked "no account" and that Higgins, salesman for Stone, discussed the returned check with Hazel Wilks in which discussion she stated that she knew of the exchange and that "the matter would be straightened out and consummated." Further testimony was offered to prove that Larry sold the Chevrolet with the knowledge and consent of Hazel Wilks. The trial judge refused to admit this evidence. Refusal to admit evidence to prove that Larry Wilks represented that he acted as Hazel Wilks's agent in negotiation and that Hazel Wilks ratified his acts was set up as ground for reversing the judgment of the trial court.

RUARK, JUDGE.   As relates to agency, "ratification" is an express or implied adoption or confirmation, with knowledge of all material matters, by one person of an act performed in his behalf by another who at that time assumed to act as his agent but lacked authority to do so. Ratification relates back and is the equivalent of authority at the commencement of the act. It is the affirmance of a contract already made. The existence of agency and the authority of the agent can be and often is implied by proof of facts, circumstances, words, acts, and conduct of the party to be charged. As applied to the agency or authority which is created or related back by means of ratification, it may be implied by any facts and circumstances from which it can be reasonably inferred that the party to be charged (with knowledge of the facts) acquiesced in and accepted the transaction as his own, or which are inconsistent with any other intention. The intent to ratify may be implied from the circumstances, and this implication may be made even though the person to be charged as principal may have had an intention not to ratify.

As to what facts, circumstances, and conduct will justify the inference of agency, no fixed rule can be stated. There is no particular mode by which it must be established. It depends upon the situation in each individual case. One of the circumstances to be considered is the relationship of the parties. Although the bare relationship of parent and child is not, in and of itself, sufficient to justify the inference, such relationship is a factor of "considerable weight" to be considered along with all other circumstances as tending to establish the fact. The prior conduct of the parties is also a factor to be taken into account if such conduct is a part of the "chain of circumstances" surrounding the transaction. Under some conditions the mere silence and inaction of the party to be charged, a failure to dissent or speak up when ordinary human conduct and fair play would normally call for some negative assertion within a reasonable time, tends to justify the inference that the principal acquiesced in the course of events and accepted the contract as his own.

Probably the most certain evidence of implied ratification is the acceptance and retention of the fruits of the contract with full knowledge of the material facts of the transaction. Although this ratification by acceptance of the fruits does not necessarily apply where the benefits went to the assumed agent or some third party, nevertheless we think the party to be charged as principal should not be permitted to escape if she, with full knowledge of the facts, knowingly channels the benefits into the hands of another, or assists, aids, and abets the benefited party in making away with the fruits of the transaction so that the *status quo* cannot be restored. Such conduct is inconsistent with a good faith claim of no authority at the outset.

We think these facts and circumstances, some of which were denied by Wilks, had they been permitted in evidence, would have permitted a finding by the trier of the fact that Mrs. Wilks ratified the sale or exchange of her automobile, and that consequently the trial court was in error in excluding such evidence.

Problem Cases

1. Boman-Chase, a construction company, was employed by Phillips Petroleum Co. to dismantle a cooling tower at its refinery. Phillips asked Robinson to furnish a truck and driver to haul the dismantled materials to a designated location. In the process of unloading a welding shed from the truck. Wigart, one of the Boman-Chase employees helping to unload the shed was killed. Boman-Chase employees helping on the unloading had indicated where the shed was to be placed and had given signals to the driver from time to time. Wigart and Britain, the Robinson driver, agreed that the method to use was "shaking off" the shed, which involved unwinding the truck's winch 2 or 3 feet, backing the truck, then braking quickly so that the momentum caused the shed to slide backwards a little each time. The shed fell when Britain left some slack in the winch line. The jury found Britain to be negligent and that he was not a loaned employee of Boman-Chase, and judgment was entered against Robinson. Was Britain a loaned employee of Boman-Chase?

2. McIlroy, a forest ranger, engaged Humphreys to clean out a well being used by the U.S. Forest Service. Humphreys was given complete charge of cleaning out the well, was hired for that specific job alone, and and did not normally work for the Forest Service. The government supplied him with a rope and pulley, and Humphreys was to obtain any other equipment he needed on his own. In cleaning out the well, Humphreys was asphyxiated by poisonous gas. Humphreys' wife sues for wrongful death under the Federal Tort Claims Act. The act provides for recovery by employees of the government but not by independent contractors. Can Humphreys' wife recover for his death?

3. Raasch was injured in an automobile accident caused by the negligence of an employee of Dulany, who was in the automobile-leasing business as a licensee of Avis. Raasch seeks to recover from Avis, claiming Dulany was Avis' agent. Under his contract with Avis, Dulany was limited in his business to a particular geographic area and was required to submit monthly reports on Avis' forms and to purchase liability insurance protecting Avis. Rate setting was controlled by Avis, and he was required to conduct the business in accordance with the methods, rules and regulations of Avis. Avis could terminate the contract at any time for cause, cause being defined as failure of Dulany to meet reasonable standards prescribed by Avis. Avis moved for summary judgment, claiming Dulany was not its agent. Should the motion be granted?

4. Smith and her grandmother hailed a taxicab to take them from an Atlanta railroad station to the bus station. The cab they rode in had "Checker Cab" lettered on the sides. On the way to the station the cab collided with the rear of another vehicle at a street intersection and Smith was injured. The cab driver gave her a card bearing his name, the cab number and the telephone number of a firm known as Veterans Cab Co. The driver also admitted that the collision was his fault. Smith had no further conversation with the driver. Veterans Cab Co. admitted that it did business

under the name "Checker Cab." Smith claims that this evidence alone is sufficient proof to hold Veterans Cab Co. liable for her injuries. Is Veterans Cab Co. liable?

5. Petersen financed Coffield's purchase of a tavern. Coffield defaulted on her debt and Petersen threatened to foreclose. Coffield advertised the tavern for sale and Turnbull responded. In discussing the purchase of the tavern in Petersen's home and in his presence, Coffield misrepresented to Turnbull the volume of business done by the tavern. Turnbull purchased the tavern, issuing her note and mortgage directly to Petersen. Turnbull defaulted and Petersen brought a foreclosure action. The court denied recovery, holding that Petersen had made Coffield his agent and so was bound by Coffield's false representations. Was Coffield Petersen's agent?

6. Bereni, an 18-year-old student, went to Hogan for the purpose of obtaining automobile liability insurance for his car. Hogan was known to be an insurance agent and he prepared an application which Bereni signed. Bereni paid the premium and Hogan delivered the policy on which he was designated as agent by Badger Ins. Co. Later Bereni returned to Hogan to transfer the insurance to a second automobile. Hogan handled the details and Badger issued an endorsement. Later Bereni asked Hogan to transfer the insurance to a third automobile. A provision in the policy permitted this if the company were notified within 30 days. Hogan failed to notify Badger. The third auto was involved in an accident in which Harris was injured. Badger denies liability. Is it liable on the policy?

7. Studley, a real estate broker, was asked by Burkhiser, manager of the building services department of Gulf Oil, to prepare a report on office space in New York City which might meet Gulf's needs. Burkhiser had been instructed by Gulf's president to review Gulf's New York office situation. Studley was told that the matter was confidential and should not be disclosed to Gulf's employees in New York. Studley showed Burkhiser the Sperry Rand and other buildings, and there were subsequent phone calls and letters between Studley and Burkhiser. When Cadman, the senior executive of Gulf in New York, learned of plans to consolidate several scattered offices in New York into one in a different building than the one in which he had been located, he contacted Cushman & Wakefield and was shown several buildings including Sperry Rand. Cadman later notified Burkhiser that all future negotiations regarding the Sperry Rand building were to be conducted by Cushman & Wakefield. Gulf leased the Sperry Rand space and Rock-Uris, the owner of the building, paid a commission to Cushman & Wakefield who Cadman advised was Gulf's broker. Studley admits he had no agreement with Gulf that Gulf would pay him a commission. However, he claims that there was an agreement that if he found a suitable lease Gulf would enter into it and that he would be the broker in the transaction and entitled to the owner's commission. Can Studley recover a commission from Gulf?

8. Close was a lawyer with banking experience who was employed by the principal promoter of a proposed national bank to perform the legal work involved in obtaining its charter. In a news story he was mentioned as "attorney for the group of incorporators." Erickson saw the article and, knowing Close, indicated to him an interest in investing in the venture. Erickson paid Close $3,150 and received a "receipt and agreement" signed by Close indicating that Erickson would be issued 100 shares of stock upon authorization by the U.S. Comptroller of Currency. Prior to this time an application had been filed with the Comptroller which recited the capital stock of the proposed bank and showed all shares to have been fully subscribed, but Erickson

was unaware of this. After the bank was chartered Erickson demanded that it issue him 100 shares of its capital stock. Is Erickson entitled to the stock?

9. Farmers Elevator Co. entered into a contract with Scraper to construct on its premises two grain storage bins for $9,000, paying 10 percent down. Scraper ordered the bins from Columbian Co. Farmers Elevator agreed with Scraper that it would pick up the equipment at Columbian's place of business, which it did. Columbian sent Farmers Elevator the bill for the bins. Farmers Elevator paid this amount, approximately $6,000, to Scraper under its agreement to pay for material as delivered to the job site. At the end of the month Columbian sent Farmers Elevator another statement for the price of the bins, which Farmers Elevator returned with a note on it that the amount had been paid to Scraper. Scraper did not pay Columbian and Columbian sued Farmers Elevator on the theory that Scraper had acted as agent for Farmers Elevator and that it had ratified his act. Is Farmers Elevator liable to Columbian?

chapter 16. Relation of Principal and Third Person

Disclosed or Partially Disclosed Principal

Liability of Agent of Disclosed Principal. A principal is disclosed when both the existence of the agency and the identity of the principal are known to the third person. If the agent is acting for a disclosed principal, the third person will, as a general rule, intend to contract with the principal, not the agent. For that reason the principal is bound by all contracts which are negotiated by the agent in the name of the principal, provided the agent has acted within the scope of his authority, express, implied, or apparent, or if the principal has ratified the acts of the agent. The third person does not intend to contract with the agent, and the agent is in no way bound by such a contract.

An agent may make a contract in his own name, in which event he is one of the contracting parties and is liable on the contract; he may join the principal as joint obligor in the making of the contract, in which case he is jointly liable with the principal; or he may guarantee the performance of the contract by the principal, in which event he is liable as surety. The mere fact that an agent, in negotiating a contract, uses such expressions as "I will sell' or "I will build," when it is clearly understood that he is acting for and in the name of his principal, will not make the agent a party to the contract or a surety for the principal.

Liability of Agent of Partially Disclosed Principal. A principal is partially disclosed when the existence of the agency is known to the third person but the identity of the principal is not known to him. The agent for the partially disclosed principal will, in the usual situation, be a party to the transaction he is negotiating. Since the identity of the principal is unknown to the third person, such third person will not, as a general rule, be willing to rely wholly on the credit and integrity of an unknown party. He will desire the promise of the agent either as a guarantor or as a copromisor. In such a situation, both the principal and the agent will be liable to the third person. The agreement may, however, expressly state that the agent is not liable and that the third person will look solely to the principal for performance.

Execution of Writings. An agent for a disclosed or partially disclosed principal need not sign an informal writing in any particular manner in order to make the writing binding on his principal. In the event the writing is drafted and signed in such a manner that it is not clear who the parties to the contract are, the courts will admit parol evidence to clear up the ambiguity. Good business practices, however, dictate that the principal should be named in the body of the writing as the party to be bound by the writing, and the agent should sign it in such a way as clearly to indicate that he is executing the writing for the principal in a representative capacity. For example, the following would clearly indicate the relations of the parties:

> I, Peters, hereby * * *.
> (Signed) PETERS
> By ARCHER, his agent

In the execution of a formal writing—an instrument under seal or a negotiable instrument—more care must be exercised in the drafting and signing of the instrument if the agent does not intend to become a party to the instrument. Only persons whose names appear on a formal instrument can be held as parties to the instrument. Since the identity of a partially disclosed principal is not known to third persons, the principal's name would not appear on the formal instrument, and he would consequently not be bound by it. In jurisdictions in which a seal on an instrument is superfluous or an unsealed instrument is binding on the parties, the rule relative to informal writings applies, but if the seal is essential to the validity of the instrument, or if the writing is a negotiable instrument, the principal whose name does not appear on the instrument cannot be held liable. If the principal's name is omitted through mistake, inadvertance, oversight, or fraud of the agent, a court of equity, on a proper showing, may reform the instrument and hold the principal liable.

Summary

A principal is disclosed when the existence of the agency and the identity of the principal are known to the third person; he is partially disclosed when the existence of the agency is known to the third person, but not the identity of the principal. In the usual situation the agent of a disclosed principal will not be a party to the transaction, provided he is acting within the scope of his authority, expressed, implied, or apparent. The agent may, by express agreement, make himself a party to a transaction he is negotiating for his principal. The agent of the partially disclosed principal is, together with his principal, a party to the transaction he is negotiating unless it is understood that he is not to be liable.

An agent should draw written instruments in the name of the principal and sign them in the name of the principal, followed by the name of the agent, indicating that he is signing as agent. However, if the instrument is other than a sealed instrument or a negotiable instrument, and there is any indication that the party signing is acting as agent, the parties to the instrument may be established by oral evidence. A principal cannot be bound by a sealed instrument or a negotiable instrument unless his identity is disclosed in the instrument.

Undisclosed Principal

Nature of Relation. A principal is undisclosed if both the existence of the agency and the identity of the principal are unknown to the third person. In such a situation, if the common-law rules of contract law were followed, the principal, since he is not a party to the contract, could not be held liable on it. However, under the law of agency, the undisclosed principal is held liable as though he were a party to the contract, provided the agent intends, in negotiating the transaction, to act for the undisclosed principal and has acted within the scope of his powers. The liability of the undisclosed principal is imposed on him by operation of law.

Rights of the Third Person. Since, in the case of an undisclosed principal, the agent is the contracting party, he is liable on the contract. If the third person discovers that an agency exists and learns the identity of the principal, he has the right to recognize the agency and hold the principal liable or to pursue his rights on the contract against the agent. He must make an election to hold either the principal or the agent liable; he cannot hold both. The undisclosed principal and the agent are not joint or joint and several promisors.[1]

Just when the third person has made his election as to whether he will pursue his rights under the contract and hold the agent liable or recognize the agency and hold the undisclosed principal liable will depend, primarily, on the circumstances of each case. Obviously, the third person cannot make his election until he learns of the existence of the agency and knows the identity of the principal. If the agent or the principal has fully performed the contract, the third person will have no occasion to make an election. If the contract is not fully performed, the third person may, under the majority rule, proceed against the principal.

Some courts have held that if the third person has brought suit against the agent and obtained a judgment against him before he learns of the agency, he

---

[1] Pennsylvania does not follow this rule. *Joseph Melnick Building & Loan Ass'n. Melnick,* 64 A.2d 773 (Sup. Ct. Pa. 1949).

may elect to abandon his judgment against the agent and bring suit against the principal. If the third person knows of the agency and the identity of the principal at the time he brings suit against the agent, the bringing of the suit against the agent is strong evidence of the third party's intent to elect to hold the agent.

There is a conflict in the decisions as to the third person's rights against an undisclosed principal who has settled accounts with his agent. The rule that the principal is not liable if he has settled accounts with his agent is supported by the argument that the third person bargained for the obligation of the agent and that the right against the principal is in the nature of a bonus, and that if the principal has, in good faith, settled with the agent, it is inequitable to impose on him liability to the third person. This view imposes the major burden of the risk of the agent's dishonesty on the third person.

The rule generally followed is that the undisclosed principal remains liable to the third person regardless of the fact that he has settled accounts with his agent, unless the third person, after learning of the existence of the agency and the identity of the principal, follows a course of action which justifies the principal in believing that such person intends to pursue his rights against the agent, and the principal then, in reliance on such course of action, settles with the agent. This rule is supported by the argument that the agent of an undisclosed principal can have the appearance of prosperity without owning the assets entrusted to him and that the principal stands to benefit from the transaction, and further that the principal selected the agent and has an opportunity to protect himself through bonding or other devices not open to the third person. It is argued that under these circumstances the major risk of the agent's dishonesty should be imposed on the principal.

Scope of Liability of Undisclosed Principal. The liability of an undisclosed principal for the acts of his agent is the same as that of a disclosed principal where the acts are authorized. However, the liability of an undisclosed principal for the acts of his agent may exceed that of a disclosed principal where the acts are unauthorized. Since the third person does not know of the existence of the agency, he cannot be put on notice of limitations on the authority of the agent.

The undisclosed principal is liable for the unauthorized acts done on his account by his agent, provided the acts are usual or necessary in a transaction such as that entrusted to the agent. For example, an undisclosed principal who entrusts the management of his business to an agent will be liable to third persons on all transactions entered into by the agent on the principal's account if such transactions are usual in the business, even when the agent acts in disregard of the instructions of his principal. If an undisclosed principal entrusts the operation of a retail store to his agent, who operates the store in his (the agent's) name, the principal will be liable for goods purchased on credit for resale in the regular course of the operation of the business, even though the principal has instructed the agent not to buy on credit or has instructed him not to stock that particular brand of goods.

An undisclosed principal will not be liable on sealed instruments, if the seal is essential to the validity of the instrument, or on negotiable instruments executed or issued in transacting the business of the undisclosed principal, since his name will not appear on the instrument.

Rights of Undisclosed Principal. The undisclosed principal is given substantially the same rights in a transaction negotiated by his agent as is given an assignee or beneficiary of a contract. He takes the rights subject to all the outstanding equities as they exist at the time the third person learns of the existence of the agency and the identity of the principal. That is, he takes the transaction subject to all defenses, such as setoff, counterclaims, and payment, which the third person would have against the agent had the agent brought suit on the contract at the time the third person learned of the agency and the identity of the principal.

Under some circumstances the terms of the contract or the nature of the acts to be performed may be such that the undisclosed principal cannot claim the rights under the contract.

Summary

A principal is undisclosed if both the existence of the agency and the identity of the principal are unknown to the third person. In an undisclosed principal transaction, the transaction, of necessity, is negotiated in the name of the agent. If the third person discovers the existence of the agency and learns the identity of the principal, he has the right, when he learns of the existence of the agency, to hold the agent on the contract or to recognize the agency and hold the principal. He cannot, under the majority rule, hold both. The third person may make his election by indicating either by his words or by his conduct which party he intends to hold.

There is some conflict as to the liability of an undisclosed principal who has settled accounts with his agent. Under one view, he is not liable to the third person; and under the other view, he is liable unless the third person by his conduct, justifiably relied upon, has led the principal to believe that the third person intends to pursue his rights against the agent.

In general, the undisclosed principal is liable to the third person on all authorized acts of his agent and on unauthorized acts, provided such acts are done on the account of the principal and are usual or necessary in the carrying-out of the transaction entrusted to the agent. The undisclosed principal is not liable on a sealed instrument, if the seal is essential to the validity of the instrument, or on negotiable instruments issued in the name of the agent, even though executed or issued in the course of a transaction carried out in behalf of the principal.

As a general rule the principal has the right to take over and claim the benefits of all business transacted by his agent. However, in taking over a transaction, the principal must accept it in its entirety and subject to all the rights of the third person against the agent.

Howell v. *Smith*

134 S.E.2d 381 (Sup. Ct. N.C. 1964)

This was an action by Hubert M. Howell (plaintiff) against Herbert Smith (defendant) to recover a judgment for petroleum products sold. Smith set up as a defense that the petroleum products were sold to the Atlantic Building Block Company, Inc. Judgment for Howell and Smith appealed. Judgment affirmed.

Howell sold petroleum to A. J. Marlow, trading as Atlantic Building Block Company. Marlow sold the business to Smith, who was introduced to Howell as the purchaser of the business, and Howell continued to sell petroleum products to Smith. Smith incorporated the business but Howell was not notified that it had been incorporated and he continued to carry the account in the name of Atlantic Building Block Company and to make out invoices in that name. Several checks given in payment of invoices were signed "Atlantic Building Block Company, Inc.," and were signed by Smith, but he did not indicate that he was signing the checks in a representative capacity. When sued, Smith set up as his defense that he was acting as agent for Atlantic Building Block Company, Inc., and that this was known to Howell.

SHARP, JUSTICE. An agent who makes a contract for an undisclosed principal is personally liable as a party to it unless the other party had actual knowledge of the agency and of the principal's identity. The disclosure of the agency is not complete so as to relieve the agent of personal liability unless it embraces the name of the principal. The duty is on the agent to make this disclosure and not upon the third person with whom he is dealing to discover it. It will not relieve the agent from personal liability that the person with whom he dealt had means of discovering that the agent was acting as such. "Actual knowledge brought by the agent, or, what is the same thing, that which to a reasonable man is equivalent to knowledge, is the criterion of the law." *Conant Co.* v. *Lavin.* Mere suspicion and means of knowledge do not amount to actual knowledge. "It is not sufficient that the seller may have the means of ascertaining the name of the principal. If so the neglect to inquire might be deemed sufficient. He must have actual knowledge. There is no hardship in the rule of liability against agents. They always have it in their own power to relieve themselves, and when they do not, it must be presumed that they intend to be liable." *Cobb* v. *Knapp.* The cases are in substantial accord that the use of a trade name is not as a matter of law a sufficient disclosure of the identity of the principal and the fact of agency.

The liability of the agent is not exclusive. When the principal becomes known, the other party to the contract may elect whether he will resort to him or to the agent with whom he dealt unless the contract is under seal, a negotiable instrument, or expressly excludes him. Ordinarily, however, it is an alternative liability. The principal and agent are not jointly liable unless the agent has, by contract or by his conduct, added his own liability to that of the principal. It is competent for an agent, although fully authorized to bind his principal, to pledge his own personal responsibility instead. The aggrieved party seeking damages must elect whether he will hold the principal or the agent liable; he cannot hold both.

The right of the third party to sue the agent is not impaired by a discovery of the identity of the principal after the contract was made. The disclosure of the principal comes too late to discharge the agent after the third party has extended credit, performed services, or entered upon the performance of an indivisible contract. To protect himself, the agent must disclose the fact that he is acting for a designated principal in time for the third party to determine beforehand whether he will accept the responsibility of the principal in the transaction. Knowledge of the identity of a principal acquired after the performance of the contract, cannot release the obligated agent to whom credit was extended and substitute a stranger to the transaction.

Liability on Special Transactions

Basis of Liability.   In all transactions negotiated by an agent, the basis of the principal's liability is the authority of the agent. It is sometimes difficult to determine the scope of this authority, even though it is set out in writing. The nature of the business entrusted to the agent, standard practices of business, and the circumstances surrounding the transaction will be considered in determining the scope of an agent's authority, both implied and apparent. The third person is bound by notice or knowledge of limitations on the agent's authority and has the burden of proving that the agent had authority to bind his principal.

Presumptions as to an agent's authority or lack of authority in relation to certain common types of transactions have been developed by the courts. Such presumptions apply only in the absence of credible evidence as to the agent's actual authority or lack of authority.

Liability for Agent's Representations.   In the ordinary course of transacting business, statements and representations relative to the business at hand will be made by the negotiators. An agent has implied authority to make such statements and representations as are reasonably necessary to accomplish the objective of the agency, and has apparent authority to make such statements and representations as are usual and customary in the transaction of the business entrusted to the agent. If the principal has instructed the agent not to make certain statements and representations, or has informed him of defects in goods entrusted to him for sale, but the agent, in violation of his instructions or in violation of his duty not to misrepresent, makes the statements and representations he has been instructed not to make, or represents the goods as free from defects, the principal will be bound if the statements and representations are within the scope of the agent's apparent authority, and if the third person has no notice or knowledge of the limitations on the agent's authority or of the violation by the agent of his instructions.

In order to avoid being bound on misrepresentations of salesmen, businessmen frequently adopt the practice of limiting their salesmen to soliciting written offers on a preprinted form which must be accepted by the businessman to complete the contract. A clause included in the offer form specifically states that the salesman has no authority to make oral representations and that only representations appearing in writing on the offer form will be binding. Courts are not in accord as to the effect of such exculpatory clauses. The better view is that the third party has the right to rescind the contract if the agent has made false representations and the third party has signed the offer in justifiable reliance upon such representation. A few recent cases have even permitted the buyer to recover damages for fraudulent representations of the agent despite such an exculpatory clause.

A third person has the right to rescind a contract into which he has entered in reliance on false representations made by the agent. This right is absolute and can be exercised even though the principal is in no way connected with the making of the false representations and even though the representations are in excess of the agent's authority. This rule is based on the plainest dictates of justice. It would be unjust and inequitable to permit the principal to enjoy the benefits of the misrepresentations of his agent and yet disclaim the responsibility therefor.

Liability for Agent's Warranties. The liability of the principal for warranties made by the agent in a sale of goods depends on many factors. In the absence of special circumstances the principal will be bound by a warranty such as is customarily made in the market in which the goods are being sold. The principal will also be bound if the warranties made by the agent are no more extensive than those implied in law. At the other extreme the principal is not liable on an unauthorized warranty made by his agent if the warranty is unusual and extraordinary in nature.

Between these two extremes the courts are not in complete accord. The test generally applied is whether or not it is customary to make similar warranties in the sale of such goods in the market in which the goods are sold. In effect, the test is one of usage of trade. If it is customary, in the market in which the goods are sold, to make the warranty made by the agent, the principal will be bound by it; otherwise, he will not. The third person will be bound by such limitations or instructions if he has notice or knowledge of them.

Liability for Payment to Agent. The fact that an agent has negotiated a transaction does not, as a matter of law, confer on the agent the authority to collect. Such authority arises when it is the usual and reasonable incident of the business to be transacted. As in other cases, it may be shown that the agent has express, implied, or apparent authority to collect; but as a general rule, authority to sell does not confer on the agent authority to collect or receive payment. A sales agent who has authority to solicit orders for future delivery does not thereby have the authority to collect the purchase price of the goods. However, it is generally held that if the selling agent has possession of the goods, he has implied authority to collect the purchase price of goods sold. Also, it is generally held that an agent making over-the-counter sales has authority to collect. Usage of trade, course of dealing, or the acts of the principal may confer on the agent authority to collect.

Possession of an instrument evidencing the debt is strong, yet not conclusive, evidence of authority to collect. If the agent has negotiated a loan, sold property, or transacted other similar business for the principal and has received from the third person a negotiable instrument payable to the principal, the agent has apparent authority to receive payment and discharge the instrument if the principal permits the agent to retain possession of the instrument. However, in several cases the courts have held that payment to the agent before the due date does not discharge the debt. The authority to collect on the due date does not necessarily include authority to collect before the due date. If a person wishes to make payment to an agent before the due date, he should make careful inquiry as to the agent's authority to collect.

If the agent has not been permitted to retain the instrument evidencing an indebtedness, the third person is put on notice that the agent does not have authority to collect.

Liability for Credit Contracted by Agent. The agent, in the absence of express authority, will not have authority to purchase on the principal's credit. This rule is not absolute. If the agency is general, and if, in order to carry out the purpose of the agency, it becomes necessary for the agent to borrow money or purchase goods on the principal's credit, the principal will be bound. If the principal has held the agent out as having authority to borrow money or purchase goods on his credit or has knowingly permitted the agent to borrow money or purchase goods on his credit, the principal will be bound.

If the agent is authorized to purchase goods and is furnished money by the principal with which to make the purchase, and if the third person accepts the personal check of the agent in payment of the goods, the third person cannot recover from the principal if the check is not honored. If the agent is authorized to purchase goods but is not furnished the money with which to pay for the goods, the agent will have implied authority to purchase on the credit of the principal.

Liability on Negotiable Instruments. The negotiable instrument is given a separate and distinct place in the business world. The nature of the negotiable instrument and the liability of the parties to it are such that the authority to sign, or to endorse and negotiate, or to cash such instruments is sparingly conferred on an agent, unless the agent represents a corporation.

Express authority to sign or endorse negotiable instruments is strictly construed and will not be enlarged by interpretation. The authority to sign or endorse negotiable instruments will not be implied unless the nature of the business entrusted to the agent is such that it cannot be effectively carried on without the signing or endorsing of negotiable instruments. An authorization "to transact any and all business" does not expressly or impliedly authorize the agent to sign or endorse negotiable instruments unless such acts are essential to the carrying-on of the business entrusted to him.

Only in exceptional cases will the courts hold that an agent has apparent authority to sign or endorse negotiable instruments. The fact that an agent is given a special title, such as president, secretary, treasurer, general manager, or cashier of a corporation, does not as a general rule give him apparent authority to sign or endorse negotiable instruments in the name of the corporation. A member of a partnership has the authority, under partnership law, to sign or endorse negotiable instruments in the partnership name, unless such authority is withheld by the terms of the partnership agreement.

Summary

A principal's liability for the acts of his agent in the negotiation of business transactions is based on the established principles of agency law. Rules of law have been developed which apply in common types of business transactions unless special circumstances exist.

As a general rule the principal is liable for the representations of his agent made in the regular course of the transaction. If the agent has made misrepresentations on which the third person has justifiably relied, the third person has the right to rescind the transaction, even though the representations were unauthorized or expressly forbidden by the principal.

The principal is bound by the warranties made by a selling agent, provided they are of the nature usually made in the trade, but he is not liable for unusual warranties made by the agent.

Authority to sell does not confer on the agent authority to collect the purchase price. Authority to make a loan does not imply authority to accept payment and discharge the debt when the loan falls due. If negotiable paper is left in the hands of the agent, it is evidence of authority to accept payment on the due date, but it is not evidence of authority to accept payment before the due date.

As a general rule an agent does not have authority to pledge his principal's credit. Such authority is not implied unless there is a clear necessity for such action.

Authority to sign or endorse negotiable instruments in the principal's name is granted with caution. The agent will not have authority to sign or endorse negotiable instruments in the principal's name unless the authority is express or unless the nature of the business entrusted to the agent is such that it is absolutely necessary to sign or endorse negotiable instruments in order to transact the business. The strongest of evidence is necessary to establish apparent authority to sign or endorse negotiable instruments.

Harnischfeger Sales Corp. v. *Coats*
48 P.2d 662 (Sup. Ct. Calif. 1935)

This was an action by Harnischfeger Sales Corporation (plaintiff) against E. C. Coats (defendant) to recover the balance due on a conditional sales contract. Judgment for Harnischfeger Sales Corporation and Coats appealed. Judgment reversed.

Coats entered into a conditional sale contract for the purchase of a power shovel from Harnischfeger Sales Corporation (Harnischfeger). The contract was negotiated by an agent of Harnischfeger and contained the following provision: "This agreement shall not be considered as executed, and shall not become effective until accepted by the vendee, and executed and approved by the president, or vice-president or secretary of the vendor, and it is hereby further declared, agreed and understood that there are no prior writings, verbal negotiations, understandings, representations or agreements between the parties, not herein expressed." Coats, when sued, set up that the agent induced him to execute the contract by making fraudulent representations, and he counterclaimed for tort damages for the fraud. The jury brought in a verdict in favor of Coats on his counterclaim for $2,500. The court set the verdict aside and gave judgment for Harnischfeger for the full amount of its claim.

Langdon, Justice.   It seems clear that this stipulation limits the authority of the agent to make representations, and purports to absolve the principal from all responsibility therefor. The question is whether such a stipulation may be given effect.

This problem was the subject of conflicting decisions in California until recently, when this court, in *Speck* v. *Wiley* announced the governing rule. It was there held that an innocent principal might by such a stipulation protect himself from liability in a tort action for damages for fraud and deceit, but that the third party would nevertheless be entitled to rescind the contract. This is the rule declared in the *Restatement of the Law of Agency,* §§ 2 9 and 260. The distinction between the two situations is a sound one. The principal would normally be liable in tort for misrepresentations by an agent acting within the scope of his actual or ostensible authority, and by stipulating in the contract that the agent has no such authority, the principal has done all that is reasonably possible to give notice thereof to the third party. Under such circumstance the innocent principal may justly be relieved of liability for the agent's wrong. But where the principal sues to recover on the contract, he is seeking to benefit through the agent's fraud. This he cannot be permitted to do. His personal liability may be avoided, but the fraudulently procured contract is subject to rescission.

In the instant case, the counterclaim, which seeks the affirmative relief of damages, is objectionable for the same reason that an independent tort action would be. However, the principle followed in *Speck* v. *Wylie,* supra, warrants relief for fraud whether the injured party sets it up in an affirmative action for rescission, or as defensive relief in an action by the other party to enforce the contract; that is to say, the right of the aggrieved buyer to rescission exists regardless of which party initiates the proceeding on the contract. That the buyer may set up a claim for rescission in the seller's action has recently been held by the District Court of Appeal. The defensive relief must not be such as to subject the plaintiff to affirmative liability for damages; nor would it be proper, under the rule just discussed, to permit an award of damages to offset liability for the balance of the purchase price. Coats's relief is limited to rescission of the contract. Hence the affirmative verdict in favor of Coats on his counterclaim for damages is improper; but Coats may be entitled, because of the fraud, to be placed in *statu quo,* by restoration of the consideration or its equivalent by both parties.

Brunswick Corp. v. *Sittason*
167 So.2d 126 (Sup. Ct. Ala. 1964)

This was an action in deceit by Sittason (plaintiff) against Brunswick Corporation (defendant). Judgment in the amount of $30,000 for Sittason and Brunswick appealed. Affirmed.

Sittason wished to establish a bowling alley in a small town. He negotiated with Grauer, the area salesman for Brunswick, signed an order and gave a down payment after being told that Brunswick would accept only one order in the town. The salesman indicated to Sittason over several weeks that his order would be accepted and encouraged him to start building. In the meantime the salesman was dealing with Nelson for a similar bowling establishment in the same town. Sittason's lawyer was assured by the office manager of Brunswick's regional office that Sittason "has a contract" and that Brunswick would stand behind it. After Sittason had expended about $14,000 for a lot, for architectural and legal services and had started building, he was informed that Nelson's order was being accepted and his rejected. Brunswick's order form contained an exculpatory clause to the effect that no representations had been made other than those contained in the order, that no one had authority to alter the conditions of the order and that it could be accepted only by an authorized officer in Brunswick's headquarters office.

SIMPSON, JUSTICE. There is only one way to do business with a corporation and that is through its agents, servants and employees. We have the anomalous situation of a mere salesman (who knew his company would deal with only one group) taking two orders of no validity until accepted by the home office—and yet telling the two buyers that the only order to be accepted would be that of the group first commencing its building.

Was this the action of a mere soliciting agent or the furtherance of a stated policy of the Brunswick Corporation? There is no denial by Brunswick that it was untrue or that Brunswick would not and did not accept the fruits of such a policy.

From the foregoing review of the evidence, certainly it would strain the conscience of the average juror or businessman to say that Brunswick's home office, through its agents and employees, did not, in fact, know of the circumstances in this particular case.

The end result, namely the acceptance of the "Nelson" order and the rejection of the "Sittason" order upon the sole ground that "It would be improper to honor your order as construction has already started on another installation which makes your proposed operation a poor business risk; we, therefore are arranging cancellation of your order and full return of your deposit," is nothing more or less than an express confirmation of the statements and action of Grauer. Such a course of conduct is sufficient acknowledgment that the Brunswick Corporation was, indeed, well aware of the activities of the agent Grauer and therefore, a participant in the fraud and deceit being practiced upon the "Sittason" group.

The Brunswick Corporation, according to the testimony, does many millions of dollars of business each year and certainly is in a position to approve or disapprove an order within a reasonable time. It should not be allowed through its silence, delay, and reassurances of soliciting agents to lull its prospective customers into a sense of false security, have them expend money, time and effort and then hide behind its corporate structure and soliciting agents and in this manner rake (sic) financial damages to its would-be customers.

It is well to keep in mind that this is not a suit on a contract. There is no contention on the part of the appellees that the order in this case ever ripened into a contract. The action sounds in deceit and fraud and it is appellee's contention that the Brunswick Corporation ratified, affirmed, or should be estopped by its silence, inaction, and delay from contending that the actions of the agent were limited by the written terms of the order. We would affirm on the theory that a jury could find that the Brunswick Corporation through its silence, undue delay, the rejection of the "Sittason" order, coupled with the late entry and approval of the "Nelson" order, together with the activity of its soliciting agent being ratified by the Memphis office and its silence and inaction during a period of some six weeks, was tantamount to an acquiescence and participation in the fraud of its agent.

Notice to or Knowledge of Agent

Effect of Notice to Agent. Notice of any fact given to an agent or acquired by him which relates to business that the agent is transacting for the principal is binding on the principal, or, in other words, notice to the agent is notice to the principal. The earlier courts based this rule on the concept of the identity of the principal and the agent. The modern courts base the rule on the fact that the agent owes a duty to communicate to the principal all matters coming to the agent's notice if these matters are material to the principal for his protection or guidance.

The rule is also supported by public policy. The principal has selected the agent and has placed his confidence in the agent. If the agent fails to perform his duties, the principal, not the innocent third person, should bear any resulting loss.

When Notice Is Not Binding on Principal.   Notice given to the agent of matters which are not within the scope of the agency are not binding on the principal unless the agent communicates the notice to the principal and unless the notice comes from a reliable source. The agent is not required to communicate to his principal every rumor and detailed fact which comes to his notice, even though such rumor or detailed fact might be of some importance to his principal.

Knowledge of Agent.   Knowledge of the agent includes those things of which he has been given notice during the course of the negotiation of a transaction and those things which, by the exercise of reasonable prudence, he would have learned. Whether or not knowledge gained by the agent in prior transactions not transacted for the principal will be imputed to the principal depends entirely on the circumstances of the case. If it appears that knowledge of certain material facts, learned during the transaction of earlier unrelated business, was present in the mind of the agent and was used to the advantage of the principal, the principal will be bound by such knowledge.

Substantially the same rule applies to knowledge gained in earlier business transacted for the principal. If the agency is a continuous agency, such as, for example, the manager of a store, knowledge of the agent gained in earlier transactions will be imputed to the principal if under the circumstances the agent should have such knowledge in mind at a later time when he negotiates business for his principal. Knowledge gained by an agent after the agency has been terminated is not imputed to the principal unless the agency is a continuing agency. In such a case the principal will be bound by notice given to the agent by a third person who has customarily dealt with the agent and who, at the time of giving the notice, had no notice or knowledge of the termination of the agency.

Limitations on the Rule.   The rule does not apply in those situations in which it is clear that the agent would not communicate the knowledge to his principal. The courts have held that if the agent's interests conflict with the interests of the principal and the agent's interests will be furthered by not communicating a fact to the principal, the principal will not be bound by the knowledge of the agent. If, however, an innocent third person will be injured if the principal is not bound by the uncommunicated knowledge of the agent, the courts will hold that the principal is bound. If the agent and the third person collusively or fraudulently withhold knowledge from the principal, the principal will not be bound.

Under this rule the knowledge of the agent is imputed to the principal; hence the principal's knowledge is constructive, not actual. The principal cannot be held criminally liable where knowledge is an essential element of the crime if the agent has not communicated such knowledge to the principal and the principal does not have actual knowledge.

Summary

Notice of facts given to the agent regarding business being transacted by the agent for the principal is binding on the principal. Notice of facts given to the agent regarding matters unconnected with the business entrusted to the agent is not binding on the principal unless communicated to him.

Knowledge of the agent, present in his mind at the time he is transacting business for the principal, will be imputed to the principal. Whether or not knowledge was present in the mind of the agent is a matter of fact to be established in each case.

If the agent's personal interests conflict with the duties he owes to his principal, or if the agent and third person are in collusion to defraud the principal, the knowledge of the agent will not be imputed to the principal.

In criminal law, knowledge means actual knowledge, not imputed knowledge. Therefore a principal cannot be held criminally liable for an act of his agent if knowledge is an essential element of the crime, even though the agent has knowledge but has not actually communicated that knowledge to the principal.

Southern Farm Bureau Casualty Insurance Co. v. Allen
388 F.2d 126 (5th Cir. 1967)

This was an action by Southern Farm Bureau Casualty Insurance Company (plaintiff) against Betty Allen (defendant) for a declaratory judgment that an automobile liability policy issued by it was void and that it had no liability under it. Judgment for Allen and Southern appealed. Reversed and remanded.

Southern had rejected the application for a policy by Joe Jezisek, a minor who had a record of a previous accident and two "moving violations." Jezisek then arranged to transfer the title of the automobile to his brother who was carrying insurance with Southern. The registration slip which was shown to a secretary in the office of the insurance agent showed that title had been transferred for insurance purposes. The insurance application showed that the auto would be kept in the town where Joe lived rather than where his brother lived several hundred miles away. There was testimony that the insurance agent, Wattenbarger, had suggested or at least approved the suggestion of the change of title.

The policy was issued to Joe's brother and then forwarded to Joe, who paid the premiums. Three months later Joe was involved in an accident with the auto which resulted in the death of Cecil Allen. The trial court found that the insurance agent was aware of the transaction between the Jeziseks and that this knowledge was imputed to Southern.

WISDOM, CIRCUIT JUDGE.   The general rule in insurance cases and other cases, of course, is that "notice to the agent is notice to the principal." Two conditions are necessary for the application of this rule, however: (1) The agent must be acting within the scope of his authority and in reference to a matter over which his authority extends; and (2) the insured (or applicant) must not be involved with the agent, even informally, in perpetrating a fraud against the insurer.

The authorities are uniform to the effect that a principal is not affected by notice to an agent who is acting adversely to the interests of his principal, and either for his own benefit or for the benefit of a third party.

If a person colludes with an agent to cheat the principal, the latter is not responsible for the acts or knowledge of the agent. The rule which charges the principal with what the agent knows is for the protection of innocent third persons, and not those who use the agent, to further their own frauds upon the principal.

The defendants (Allen) in the trial below argued, and the trial court found, that Wattenbarger actively participated in the scheme whereby paper title to the Chevrolet was transferred to George Jezisek for insurance purposes, with the insurance policy to be listed in his name, knowing that Joe Jezisek was to be the actual owner and sole operator of the vehicle. In the least, Wattenbarger is "placed in the light of having assisted in bringing about the consummation of the fraudulent transaction. . . . Such action is sufficient to constitute collusion." We therefore find Southern Farm not estopped to avoid the policy on account of its agent's knowledge.

Liability for Acts of Subagents

Appointments of Subagents.   The liability of a principal for the acts of a subagent or employee (servant) will depend on the relation between the appointing agent and his principal. The agent may be authorized to appoint agents or employees for his principal, or he may have apparent authority to make such appointments. The circumstances may be such that the agent will be authorized to delegate to subagents or employees certain acts which he is authorized to perform for his principal. For example, the personnel officer of a corporation is authorized to appoint agents and employees for his principal, the corporation. Such persons are the agents and employees of the corporation, not of the personnel officer. The agent of an insurance company who operates his own insurance business may appoint agents and employees to whom he may delegate certain functions. Such agents and employees are answerable to the agent and are not the agents or employees of the insurance company.

Liability of Principal for Acts of Subagents.   If an agent is authorized to appoint agents or employees for his principal, the persons appointed, provided the agent has acted within the scope of his authority, are the agents and employees of the principal and are under his direct control; consequently, the principal is liable for the acts of such agents and employees to the same extent as he would have been had he made the appointments himself. In this situation the appointing agent is not liable for the acts of the appointed agents or employees unless he has failed to exercise reasonable care and skill in selecting the appointees, in which case his liability is based on his failure to exercise care and skill, and is not a direct liability for the acts of the appointees. Suppose, for instance, Parker is engaged in the business of selling merchandise door to door and he appoints Alexander as his agent and authorizes him to hire and supervise crews of door-to-door salesmen in the name of Parker. Such salesmen hired by Alexander will be the agents of Parker and will be subject to his control.

The circumstances may be such that the agent will be authorized to delegate to agents and employees of his selection certain acts required in the performance of his duties to his principal. Such appointees are the agents and employees of the original agent and as such are under his control, and he is liable for their acts. However, the original principal is liable indirectly for their acts which are done at the direction of or are delegated to them by the original agent, provided such acts are within the scope of the authority of the original agent. For example, suppose Albert is the agent of Perfect Insurance Company and he appoints Bates as his agent, authorizing him to prepare and execute insurance policies of Perfect Insurance Company in fulfillment of applications for insurance which Albert has approved. If Bates prepares and delivers a policy of insurance in the name of Perfect Insurance Company which is issued within the scope of Albert's authority, Perfect Insurance Company will be liable on the policy. But suppose Bates, when on his way to deliver the policy, operates his automobile in a negligent manner and injures a pedestrian. Perfect Insurance Company will not be liable to the injured pedestrian.

If the principal, in appointing an agent, makes the appointment in reliance on the discretion, judgment, skill, or character of the appointee, such agent cannot delegate his authority to a subagent or to a third person and any attempt to delegate such authority is a nullity. Acts which involve no discretion but which are ministerial in nature may, as a general rule, be delegated.

Summary

The variation in the authority to appoint subagents and employees is so great that no specific rules can be formulated. The authority to make such appointments will depend on the circumstances of the particular case. The agent may be authorized to make appointments in behalf of the principal, in which event such appointees will be under the control of the principal and will be his agents or employees. The agent may be authorized to perform portions of his duties to his principal by delegating certain functions to others. In such a situation the appointees will be the agents and employees of the original agent, and the original principal will be liable indirectly for the acts of such appointees only to the extent that they are performing delegated acts which the original agent is authorized to delegate.

An agent cannot delegate his authority if the principal has selected the agent on the basis of judgment, discretion, skill, or character. As a general rule, ministerial acts may be delegated.

Liability for Torts of Agent

General Rule. The doctrine of *respondeat superior*—let the master answer —is a very old legal rule making the employer liable, without fault on his part, for torts committed by his employee (servant) while acting within the scope and in the course of his employment. The principal cannot escape liability by proving that he exercised the greatest of care in the selection of the employee, that he trained him in safety measures, and that he gave him specific instructions not to do the things he did nor make the representations which were tortious.

Most agents are employees and thus the principal is liable for their torts under the doctrine of *respondeat superior*. However, as will be discussed subsequently in this section, the liability of a principal for an agent who is not an employee, such as a professional agent, is somewhat more limited.

Scope and Course of Employment. Whether or not a tort committed by an agent or employee (servant) was committed within the scope and in the course of the employment is primarily a question of fact. Generally, an employee is held to be engaged in the employment of the employer from the time he starts his work in the morning until he completes his work for the day. If he leaves his work for a lunch period and is free to go wherever he wishes and do whatever he may desire, he is not engaged in the employer's employment during such period.

The act must be within the scope of the employment, and it will be held to be within the scope of the employment if it is incidental to or aids in the accomplishment of the objective of the employment. The tests applied in determining the scope of the employment are similar to those applied in determining the scope of an agent's authority.

If an employee abandons his employment temporarily, the employer, as a general rule, is not liable for the torts committed by him during the time he has abandoned his employer's business. The courts have made a distinction between abandonment of the employment and deviation in the course of the performance of the work. The employer is liable if the tort is committed by the employee while he is merely deviating from the course of the employment. The distinction between deviation and abandonment is one of degree of digression.

For example, suppose a truck driver does not follow the most direct route in making a delivery because he wishes to stop at the home of a friend and make arrangements for a fishing trip. If, after he has left the direct route and before he has returned to it, he drives the truck negligently and injures a pedestrian, is the principal liable to the pedestrian?

The courts have, as a general rule, held that if the deviation is minor in nature, the employer will be liable; but if the deviation is substantial, or if it is clear that the employee has abandoned the employment, the employer is not liable. If the truck driver had driven to his friend's house where the friend joined him and they had then started in another direction to go fishing, and while on the fishing trip the truck driver had injured the pedestrian, the employer would not be liable. The employer will be liable for the torts of his employee who has abandoned his employment as soon as the employee returns to his employment. There is considerable diversity in the cases as to when an employee has returned to his employment. In the above example, some courts would hold that the truck driver had returned to his employment when he started to return to his delivery route, whereas others would hold that he had not returned to his employment until he had reached the route or until he had reached a point near the route.

Liability for Torts of Professional Agent.   The professional agent is an independent contractor in respect to his physical acts and an agent in respect to the negotiations he is carrying on for the principal. The principal is not liable for the torts of the professional agent which result from misconduct in respect to physical acts, but he is liable for his torts committed in the course of the negotiation of the principal's business to the same extent as he is liable for similar torts of other agents. A principal is not liable for harm caused by negligent physical acts of an agent who is not an employee nor is he generally liable for an intentional physical act unless he authorized the act. For example, suppose Peters lists a house and lot for sale with Ames, a real estate broker. Ames, while taking Talbott, a prospective purchaser of the house, to inspect the house, operates his automobile negligently and injures Talbott. Peters is not liable to Talbott in tort for his injuries. If Ames makes fraudulent representations to Talbott and these representations induce Talbott to purchase the house, Peters' liability to Talbott for Ames's deceit will be determined by the application of the general principles which apply in determining the liability of a principal for the fraudulent misrepresentations of his agent.

Liability for Deceit of Agent.   Whether or not the principal can be held liable in damages in a tort action of deceit for the misrepresentations of the agent depends on the facts and circumstances of the case. The courts are not in accord in their holdings; however, if the principal has participated in the fraudulent representations, it is clear that he is liable in a tort action. To bind the principal, it must appear that the fraudulent acts of the agent were done during the existence of the agency in the course of the transaction and within the scope of the agent's actual or apparent authority, or the principal must have ratified the acts of the agent. If the principal ratifies an unauthorized transaction in which a tortious act occurred, the principal will be liable for the tort. Some courts have held the principal liable in deceit if there is something in the business being transacted or in the terms of the employment or in the authority conferred on the agent which includes the making of representations, and if under the circumstances the principal, in justice and good morals, should be bound.[2]

Tort Liability Is Joint and Several. The principal or employer and the agent or employee are jointly and severally liable for the torts of the agent or employee. That is, the principal and agent or employee may be joined in the same action, or they may each be sued in a separate action. However, the injured party is entitled to only one satisfaction. When the injured party has been compensated for his injuries, whether he recovers from the principal or from the agent or employee, he has no further right of action.

Summary

The employer is liable for the torts of his employees (servants) if the tort is committed within the scope and in the course of the employment. The employer's liability is absolute and does not depend on the authority conferred on the employee or on the fault of the employer. If a tortious act is committed by the employee while he is engaged in the performance of his duties and the act is directly connected with the business or task assigned to him by his employer, it will be held that such act was committed within the scope and in the course of employment.

The courts are not in accord as to the tort liability of a principal for the fraudulent representations of his agent. If the principal has falsely instructed his agent or has colluded with the agent or has ratified the acts of the agent, the principal may be held liable in an action of deceit. Some courts have held that the principal is not liable in deceit if he has properly instructed the agent and the agent has willfully violated his instructions in making the fraudulent representations.

The principal is not liable for the tortious physical acts of a professional agent employed by the principal, but he may be held liable for torts committed in the actual transaction of the business.

The liability of the principal or employer for the torts of the agent or employee is joint and several.

---

[2] See opinions above in *Harnischfeger Sales Corporation* v. *Coats* and *Brunswick Corporation* v. *Sittason*.

Swanson v. Domning
86 N.W.2d 716 (Sup. Ct. Minn. 1957)

This was an action by Joanne E. Swanson (plaintiff) against Leonard Domning and Ruth Domning, his wife, and others (defendants). Judgment for Domning, and Swanson appealed. Judgment reversed.

Lee was a real estate broker and through business relations he became well acquainted with Swanson. Domning had listed with Lee a seventeen-acre tract of land with a house thereon. Lee interested Swanson in the property and showed her the house, but the bathroom was closed and she was unable to inspect it. Lee told her, however, that the bathroom was complete and that the fixtures were of good quality. Lee told Swanson that after some repairs had been made on the house it could be sold with two acres of land for more than the total cost of the property to her and that the remainder, when platted into lots, would bring $1,000 an acre. Swanson contracted to purchase the property for $11,000 and paid $3,000 down at the time she signed the contract to purchase the property.

Soon after Swanson contracted to purchase the property, she learned that there were no fixtures in the bathroom, that the property was worth less than she paid for it, and that the lots, after the land was platted, would not sell for enough to pay for the platting and what she had paid for the land. Swanson gave notice of rescission of the contract and brought suit to recover a judgment for the down payment. Domning set up as a defense that he did not authorize Lee to make the fraudulent statements made by him and that he had no knowledge that false statements had been made by Lee.

KNUTSON, JUSTICE.   There is no dispute that the Domnings received and still retain the down payment of $3,000. Under these circumstances, if liability were established against Lee, the Domnings would be liable as a matter of law, and the requested instruction, or one similar in substance, should have been given. Where, after learning of the fraud, a principal retains the benefits of a transaction consummated for him by an agent as the result of a fraudulent representation, he takes the benefits subject to the taints under which they were obtained. The principal may not retain the benefits of a transaction obtained by a fraudulent representation and at the same time escape liability for the fraud by which the benefits were obtained. The rule is stated in 1 *Dunnell, Dig.* (3 ed.) § 184, as follows:

. . . When a principal retains the benefits of a contract obtained for him by his agent, he cannot repudiate the acts of the agent which induced the other party to the contract to enter into it on the ground that such acts were unauthorized. By accepting the contract he takes it with whatever taint attached to its origin, and by retaining the fruits of the unauthorized acts he assumes the same responsibility therefor as though they had been done with his authority. *One who accepts a sale of property negotiated through the medium of another is bound by the representations made to accomplish the sale.* [Italics supplied.]

In *Ablitz* v. *Minneapolis & P. Ry. Co.,* we said:

The defendant is not in position to deny the authority of its agent to make the representations. It cannot retain the benefits of the transaction, and repudiate the remainder. If it accepted and retained the contract, it must take it with whatever taint attached to its origin.

This statement has been cited frequently and has been followed since the decision in that case.

Sandman v. Hagan
154 N.W.2d 113 (Sup. Ct. Iowa 1967)

This was an action by Jerry Sandman (plaintiff) against William Hagan and Charles Striegel d/b/a Beane Plumbing and Heating Co. and Andrew Montagne (defendants) for injuries inflicted on Sandman by Montagne. Sandman appealed from a judgment for Hagan and Striegel notwithstanding a jury verdict against them. Affirmed.

Beane Plumbing and Heating Co. was engaged in making a hookup to the city water system in Sioux City, Iowa. Sandman, an employee of the city water works, came to the job site to inspect the refilling of the excavation under the water main. He jumped down into the excavation to show Brunssen, one of Beane's employees, that the refilling had been improperly done. An argument developed and Sandman hit Brunssen. Montagne, another of Beane's employees, who had been shoveling dirt into the hole then struck Sandman on the head with his shovel, causing injury.

LARSON, JUSTICE. The sole issue presented on appeal by appellant Sandman is whether at the time in question employee Montagne was acting within the scope of his apparent authority so as to make Striegel liable and sustain the jury determination on that issue.

The trial court concluded there was no evidence to sustain a finding that Montagne's authority extended beyond that of putting in water lines and refilling excavations, or that his duties contemplated conflict with others, or that the assault was done in the furtherance of the employer's business or interests within the scope of his employment. We must agree.

It is well established in Iowa that under the common law the master and servant may each and both be liable for a servant's torts committed within the course of employment.

The difficulty encountered by various courts in cases of willful torts committed by servants has resulted in irreconcilable decisions, and unless carefully scrutinized, the authorities seem to be in hopeless confusion. The difficulty is in defining and applying the concept of acts within the course of employment or the scope of the servant's authority.

It has been said an act is "within the scope of the servant's employment" where such act is necessary to accomplish the purpose of the employment and is intended for such purpose, although in excess of the powers actually conferred on the servant by the master.

It is safe to say that "within the scope of the employment" requires that the conduct complained of must be of the same general nature as that authorized or incidental to the conduct authorized.

Generally speaking, an employer is responsible to third persons for his servant's tortious acts if committed while the servant is engaged in furthering the employer's business or interests within the scope of his employment, but absent nondelegable duty, such as that imposed by the relationship of carrier and passenger or hotel and guest, the servant's battery does not make the employer liable unless the employment is of such nature that it is likely to bring the servant into conflict with others.

The case at bar obviously does not fall within the class of carrier and passengers or hotels and guests. There is no dispute as to the duties of the employee Montagne or his authority over others. He testified his duties were to "put in water lines, dig and fill ditches." He worked on the outside crew as a laborer and was under the supervision of a foreman. He had done this work for about seven years. There was no evidence that he exercised any authority over others, and there was nothing shown to indicate that the nature of this employment was likely to bring him into conflict with others.

As we have pointed out, a deviation from the employer's business or interest to pursue the employee's own business or interest must be *substantial in nature* to relieve the employer from liability. Here, the employer contends the assault was clearly a deviation substantial in nature, for under no theory advanced would the duty of installing water lines and digging ditches include the exercise of force upon others. It is difficult to see how his employer's business or interest would ever be furthered by such an employee attack, especially on an inspector. The trial court found nothing was shown to sustain a finding that the act of defendant Montagne was anything his employment contemplated or was something which, if he would do lawfully, he might do in his employer's name. We agree.

Although the question of whether an act is within the scope of employment is ordinarily a jury question, depending on the surrounding facts and circumstances, the question as to whether the act departs markedly from the employer's business is still within the scope of employment may well be for the court.

We are aware of the so-called modern trend to find liability in this class of cases on the basis that such wrongs are committed by the employee only because of the employment situation, and that since the employer has the benefit of the enterprise as between two innocent third parties, he is better able to bear the risk of loss. If he cannot altogether avoid such wrongs, he can at least minimize them. In those cases it is argued that a general sense of fairness requires that the employer, as the person interested and benefited by the business, rather than the persons who have no concern in or control over it, should bear the burden of such wrongs as incidental to such business.

If employer liability is to be extended this far, we believe it should come from the legislature, and do not find that this concept has substantial support in judicial decisions.

We are satisfied here that the employee Montagne's assault on Inspector Sandman was a substantial deviation from his duties, that his act was substantially different in nature from that authorized by the employer, and that at the time thereof he was acting outside the scope of his employment.

Problem Cases

1. Smith contracted to serve Anderson as an architect. Anderson did not disclose to Smith at the time the contract was entered into that he was acting, not as an individual, but as agent for Anderson, Inc. Smith received partial payment for his services through checks signed by the corporation, but when he was not paid in full, he sued Anderson as an individual for the balance. Anderson maintains that as a mere agent he cannot be sued, and that Smith was put on notice of the agency by the checks signed by the corporation. Is Anderson liable as an individual?

2. Blackshaw, as agent for Big Bear Co., sold two city lots to Eamoe. Blackshaw showed the lots to Eamoe and executed in the name of the principal a preliminary contract of sale. In the preliminary contract and in the contract of sale executed by the principal the lots were described as "Lots 2 and 3 of Tract 164." Eamoe started to build a house on one of the lots and was stopped by Teal, who claimed to own the lot. On investigation, Eamoe discovered that the lots shown to him by Blackshaw were Lots 2 and 3 of Tract 159 and that Big Bear Co. did not own these lots. Eamoe removed his house from Lots 2 and 3 of Tract 164 to Lots 2 and 3 of Tract 159 and accepted a deed from Big Bear Co. to Lots 2 and 3 of Tract 159. He then brought suit to recover damages on the ground that Blackshaw fraudulently represented the lots and that the principal, Big Bear Co., was liable for the representations of Blackshaw. Is Big Bear liable?

3. Stewart, a salesman for Harring, sold Skaggs a safe and warranted it to be fire- and burglarproof. Burglars stole money and other valuables from the safe. The locks on the safe were found to be inadequate, and the safe could be burglarized with little difficulty. Skaggs sued Harring to recover damages for breach of warranty. Harring set up as a defense that Stewart had no authority to warrant the safe. Is Harring liable?

4. Westfall authorized Townsend to purchase lumber for him. He supplied Townsend with funds with which to buy the lumber and instructed Townsend to pay cash for all lumber purchased. Townsend purchased lumber from Brittain on credit. The lumber was delivered to and accepted by Westfall, who had no notice or knowledge that it had not been paid for. Townsend absconded with the money furnished him for the purpose of purchasing lumber. Brittain sued Westfall to recover the purchase price of the lumber. Westfall set up as a defense Townsend's lack of authority. Is Westfall liable for the purchase price of the lumber?

5. On June 18, 1951, an industrial life insurance policy for the sum of $400 was issued on the life of Roney D. Boykin without medical examination. In the application, materially false statements regarding the health of Boykin were made. Boykin died on September 29, 1951; the insurance company refused to pay the amount of the policy, and suit was brought. The insurance company set up the misrepresentation as a defense. The beneficiary proved that the insured gave the correct information regarding his health to the agent of the insurance company, but the agent filled in

incorrect answers. The insured signed the application and knew what answers had been filled in. The beneficiary contends that since the agent of the insurance company knew the true state of the insured's health, such knowledge would be imputed to the insurance company, and the defense of misrepresentation is not available to it. Is the insurance company liable on the policy?

6. A barbershop singing quartet calling themselves the "Discords" were auditioned by WMMN, a radio station. It agreed to permit them to tape recordings in its studio at mutually convenient times to be broadcast, solely at WMMN's discretion, at a specified time each week. No remuneration was paid the Discords but the arrangement continued for about a year. Immediately after making a tape, one of the quartet, McKinney, who weighed 328 pounds, used a WMMN restroom. In raising himself from the toilet seat, McKinney rested his weight on the washbasin, pulling it from the wall and breaking the water pipe. The water damaged Levin's premises below and he sued WMMN for his loss. The jury found McKinney was an employee of WMMN and that he was acting within the scope of his employment. Should these findings be overruled?

7. Fisher, a Negro mathematician employed by the National Aeronautics and Space Agency (NASA), attended a business meeting at the Carrousel Motor Hotel. A buffet luncheon for the group was prepared in the Brass Ring Club, a part of the hotel. As Fisher was standing in line about to be served, Floyd, the manager of the club and an employee of the hotel, snatched the plate out of Fisher's hand and shouted that he could not be served. Fisher sued both the manager and Carrousel for actual and punitive damages. Carrousel argued that as principal it could not be liable for punitive damages. Is it correct?

8. Lathrop was employed by Toren as a trainee in his photography studio. Lathrop was on the way home late at night, after taking photographs for Toren at a wedding and reception, when his automobile collided with another due to his negligence and Bajdek was killed. Bajdek's administrator joined Torens as a defendant in his suit. Torens argued that Lathrop was not in the course of his employment since he was not required to return the camera equipment that night. The administrator argued that he was in the course of his employment because he was required to safeguard the equipment and film. Can Torens be held liable?

9. Paur had been employed as a salesman by Rose City Dodge. He was discharged by the general manager, Green, because he had advised a friend not to agree to a deal which had been offered her by another salesman. Green told Moss, employed as a lot boy, "If Mr. Paur comes back throw him out." After Green had gone, Paur returned the keys of a car at which time the sales manager, who had been present at the time of discharge, told Moss to throw him out. As Paur was leaving Moss attacked him from behind. The jury awarded $5,000 general and $15,000 punitive damages against Rose City Dodge as well as against Moss, Green, and the sales manager individually. Can Rose City Dodge be liable for the assault and battery?

10. Cash was an electrician for D & F Electric Co. He had no authority to contract wiring jobs for D & F but so contracted with Higgins. While Cash was performing the agreed upon work, Higgins was electrocuted under circumstances which would have made D & F liable had Cash been authorized. Higgins' executrix claims D & F ratified Cash's acts when, knowing the facts, it applied to qualify the job for a $100 payment under Georgia Power Co.'s Residential Rewiring Program and applied for a permit for the job from the country electrical inspector. Is D & F liable for Higgins' death?

chapter 17. Relation of Agent to Third Person

Liability on Authorized Contracts

Disclosed Principal. An agent who is acting for a disclosed principal and who acts within the scope of his authority and in the name of the principal is not a party to the contract he negotiates unless he expressly or impliedly makes himself a party thereto or unless he contracts to act as surety for his principal. The fact that the agent, in the negotiation of the contract, uses such expressions as "I will sell' or "We will buy" in negotiating a contract for his principal will not make the agent a party to the contract.

Contracts in Writing. The liability of the principal and the agent on a written contract will depend on whether the contract is formal or informal, on its terms, and on the form of signing. This was discussed under the heading "Execution of Writings" in the preceding chapter.

Partially Disclosed Principal. If the principal is partially disclosed—that is, the existence of the agency is known to the third person but the identity of the principal is unknown—the agent is, of necessity, a party to the contract and, as a general rule, is liable on the contract. If the agent wishes to escape liability, he must give such complete information concerning the principal's identity that the principal can be easily identified, and the agreement with the third person must clearly indicate that the agent is not to be bound.

Undisclosed Principal. If the principal is undisclosed, the contract will have to be a contract between the agent and the third person. Since the third person does not know of the existence of the agency, it is clear that he intended to contract with the agent, and the agent is liable on the contract. On the discovery of the existence of the agency and the identity of the principle, the third person may elect to hold the principal.

Agent as Party to Contract. An agent may, by express agreement, make himself a party to a contract he is negotiating for his principal. He may become a copromisor with the principal and become jointly liable with the principal, or he may guarantee the performance of his principal. The nature of the agent's liability will depend on the promises made by the agent.

Summary

The agent of a disclosed principal is not liable to the third person unless he makes himself a party to the transaction. An agent will be liable on sealed contracts and negotiable instruments unless the name of the principal appears in the instrument.

An agent is a party to a contract negotiated for a partially disclosed or an undisclosed principal. If the agent and the third party agree that the agent of a partially disclosed principal shall not be liable on the contract and the identity of the principal is indicated in such a way that he may become known, the agent is not liable.

By express agreement the agent may make himself a party to the contract. The extent of the agent's liability will be determined by the terms of the contract.

Savoy Record Company, Inc. v. *Cardinal Export Corp.*
203 N.E.2d 206 (Ct. App. N.Y. 1964)

This was an action by Savoy Record Company, Inc. (plaintiff), against Cardinal Export Corp. (defendant) to recover a judgment for unpaid royalties. The trial court denied a motion of Cardinal Export Corp. to dismiss the action, and it appealed. The Supreme Court, Appellate Division, affirmed the holding and permission was granted for an appeal to the Court of Appeals. The order was reversed and complaint dismissed.

Savoy Record Company, Inc. (Savoy), contracted with Armonia E. Ritmo of Italy (Armonia) to grant to Armonia the exclusive right to manufacture and market its records in Italy for a period of two years, and in return Armonia was to pay a royalty of $8,000 a year. The letters incorporating the contract were lengthy and profuse in detail and contained the following paragraph.

"You [Armonia] represent and warrant that Cardinal Export Corp., New York, New York, is authorized to sign this agreement in your behalf, and Cardinal Export Corp. for $1.00 and other good and valuable consideration agrees by its signature to guarantee the payment of all moneys payable to Savoy Record Company, Inc., by you under this contract. If the foregoing meets your approval please so indicate in the space provided below."

After the "Very truly yours" came the signature:

> "Savoy Record Co., Inc.
> "By: /s/ Herman Liebensky, Pres."

and to the left, a space or two below, and at the margin, there appeared:

"Accepted and Approved
"Cardinal Export Corp., As Agent
"on Behalf of ARMONIA E. RITMO
"By /s/ Arthur Lerner"

Armonia did not pay royalties due and Savoy sued Cardinal Export Corp. (Cardinal) as guarantor. It defended that it signed as agent for a disclosed principal and was not liable on the contract.

FULD, JUDGE.   Any proper consideration of the question of Cardinal's responsibility under the agreement must proceed from the precedent, settled for this court in *Mencher* v. *Weiss* that an agent for a disclosed principal "will not be personally bound unless there is clear and explicit evidence of the agent's intention to substitute or superadd his personal liability for, or to, that of his principal." If such an intention can be ascribed to Cardinal at all, it must, by virtue of the requirements of the Statute of Frauds, be gathered from the language, set forth above, of Savoy's letters. The difficulty we encounter at the outset, in seeking "clear and explicit evidence" of the agent's intention to be personally bound, lies in the anomalous character of the writing upon which Cardinal's responsibility as a guarantor must depend. If liability is to be imposed, it must have been the intention of all the parties—Armonia and Cardinal in addition to Savoy—that the signature of Cardinal perform, at once, a threefold function: (a) to bind the principal (Armonia) to the agreement; (b) to support the very agency (of Cardinal) itself, since by a peculiar "bootstrap device" the principal is to "represent and warrant" the authority of the very agent whose signature is to bind it to the agreement; and (c) to bind the agent (Cardinal) as a guarantor of its principal's obligation.

The writing states that Cardinal is to signify its agreement to be personally bound "by its signature." It may well have been Savoy's intention, as Special Term noted, that Cardinal's act of signing once, solely as agent for Armonia, would likewise bind it as guarantor. However, in determining whether there has been compliance with the Statute of Frauds in such a case, Savoy's intent or belief is beside the point. What is of crucial importance, as our recent decision in *Salzman Sign Co.* v. *Beck* demonstrates, is the intention of the agent, the party to be charged—in this case, Cardinal —to be personally bound. In this context, the writing must be viewed, as it relates to Cardinal, only as an *offer* to the agent to enter into a binding personal commitment as guarantor and the courts cannot, without more, convert a signature by Cardinal "As Agent on Behalf of Armonia" into a binding *acceptance* of such an offer.

Agent's Liability on Unauthorized Contracts

General Rule.   When a third person is negotiating with an agent of a disclosed principal, he expects and is entitled to an obligation binding on the principal. If the agent exceeds his authority, or if no agency exists, the principal will not be bound, in which event the third person will be injured to the extent that he does not get the benefit of an obligation binding on the principal.

If the third person has acted in good faith, without notice or knowledge of the lack of authority and in justifiable reliance on the misrepresentation of authority, and if the principal has not ratified the transaction, the agent will be liable for any resulting loss.

Three forms of remedy have been recognized by the courts as available to the other party to the contract, each being based upon a distinction in the nature of the liability: (1) an action against the agent upon the contract, as principal in the contract; (2) an action against the agent for damages for breach of his warranty of authority to execute the contract; and (3) an action for deceit where the agent has acted in bad faith in his assumption of authority.

Agent's Liability on the Contract.   Some of the older cases held that the agent was liable on the contract as principal. The decisions in these cases were based on the theory that it must be the intent of the parties to bind someone and since the principal was not bound the agent should be. Most of the cases have repudiated this doctrine.

Agent's Liability on Implied Warranty of Authority.   If a person purports to act as agent for a legally competent party whom he has no authority to represent, that party will not be bound on the contract. The person representing himself to be an agent will be liable to the third person upon an implied warranty of authority, unless the parties have agreed that the agent does not warrant his authority or unless the third party knows that the agent's acts are not authorized. Even though the agent acts honestly in the mistaken belief that he has been authorized to act as agent for the person whom he represents to be his principal and that he is not exceeding his authority, such belief will not relieve him from liability to the injured third party who has innocently and justifiably relied on the representations.

Agent's Liability for Deceit.   If the existence of an agency or the scope of an agent's authority is knowingly and intentionally misrepresented by a person or agent, and a third person, in justifiable reliance thereon, enters into a transaction involving the agency, such person or agent will be liable to the third person in the tort of deceit for any resulting injury. In such a case the third person will have the right to elect either to sue in tort or to waive the tort and sue on the implied warranty.

Some courts have held that if the agent, in making the misrepresentations, intends no wrong but honestly and justifiably expects the principal to ratify his acts, he will not be held liable in tort but instead will be liable for breach of implied warranty of authority.

Ratification or Knowledge of Third Person.   Since ratification by the principal relates back to the time the transaction was negotiated, the relation of the parties after ratification is the same as it would have been had the agent had full authority to bind his principal at the time the transaction was negotiated. Since the principal is bound, the agent is not liable to the third person either in tort or on the theory of implied warranty.

The agent's liability to the third person is based on misrepresentation of authority by the agent, justifiably relied on by the third person. If the third person knows or, in the exercise of ordinary prudence, should know that the agent is not authorized to negotiate the transaction in behalf of his principal, the agent will not be liable to the third person, since such third person is not justified in relying on the agent's misrepresentation.

If the agent is uncertain as to the scope of his authority and makes a full disclosure to the third person—for instance, shows his contract of employment or power of attorney to the third person, and the third person then, after having such knowledge, decides that the agent has authority to bind his principal, when as a matter of fact he does not have such authority, the agent is not liable to the third person, since he has made no misrepresentation as to the scope of his authority.

Transactions Not Binding on Principal. The courts have also held that if the principal will not be bound, even if the agent is authorized to negotiate the contract, the agent cannot be held liable. Suppose Allen, acting without authority, enters into an oral contract in the name of Plum as principal to purchase a tract of land from Turner. Turner cannot hold Allen liable if Plum refuses to carry out the contract. The contract is unenforceable under the statute of frauds because there is no note or memorandum of the agreement; and even if Allen had had authority to purchase for Plum, Plum would not have been bound.

Summary

If a person purports to act as agent for a party when he has no power to bind such party, he will become liable to the third person thereto upon an implied warranty of authority. If he tortiously misrepresents the existence of the agency or the scope of his authority, he will be liable in tort for his deceit.

If the third person knows that the agent does not have authority, or if the agent informs the third person that he is uncertain as to the scope of his authority or reveals the facts and circumstances of his authorization, the agent will not be liable to the third person for misrepresentation of his authority or for breach of implied warranty of authority.

If the principal will not be bound by a contract which the agent has authority to negotiate, the agent will not be liable to the third person.

Killinger v. Iest

428 P.2d 490 (Sup. Ct. Idaho 1967)

Action by Gale Killinger (plaintiff) against Case Iest and A. W. Tadlock (defendants) to recover for furnishing and installing an irrigation pump. Motion for dismissal granted and Killinger appealed. Affirmed as to Iest, reversed and remanded as to Tadlock.

Iest owned a farm near Twin Falls, Idaho, and Tadlock was his tenant under an oral lease. Tadlock telephoned Killinger, who operated an electric appliance repair shop, to repair a malfunctioning irrigation pump used on the farm. The pump was taken to his shop by Killinger. The next day Tadlock went to inspect the pump which needed extensive repairs. Believing that it would take a long time to repair the pump, he decided that a new, more efficient pump should be installed immediately. At this time he informed Killinger that he was Iest's tenant but asserted that he had authority to repair the pump or to purchase a pump and that Iest would pay the agreed price.

A few days later Killinger installed a new pump and sent the bill for $2,048 to Iest. This was Iest's first knowledge of the new pump. He refused to pay and denied that Tadlock had authority to bind him on the purchase. A major expenditure for a concrete pipeline earlier installed had been ordered personally by Iest. Tadlock once had a broken shaft repaired on Iest's tractor, but Tadlock himself paid the bill without consulting Iest.

SMITH, JUSTICE.   Killinger first contends that the trial court erroneously ruled that Tadlock's declarations as to the existence and scope of his authority would not be binding on Iest, the alleged principal. That ruling was proper. The declarations of an alleged agent, standing alone, are insufficient to prove the grant of power exercised by him and to bind his principal to third parties.

The statements by the alleged agent, as to the scope of his authority, are admissible if, at the time the statements are offered in evidence, the existence of the agency has been proven by independent evidence.

Killinger adopted the position at trial that, even if Tadlock originally lacked authority to act as Iest's agent in purchasing the pump, Iest subsequently ratified the transaction by accepting and retaining benefits resulting from Tadlock's use of the pump. Killinger established that Tadlock irrigated the 1963 crops with the new pump, but Killinger nevertheless failed to prove that Iest in any way benefited from Tadlock's use of the pump. The benefits must accrue directly to the principal as the proximate result of the unauthorized transaction in order to constitute ratification by the principal.

Although the dismissal of Killinger's action against Iest was proper, the dismissal of the action against Tadlock stands upon different grounds. Killinger's evidence, particularly his own testimony, established that Tadlock had represented he had authority as Iest's agent "to make this extensive repair and improvement," "to repair the pump or purchase a pump," and to bind Iest for the agreed purchase price. The testimony of Ralph Taylor, Killinger's assistant, corroborated appellant's testimony, and this evidence remained uncontradicted through the examination of Iest and Tadlock.

A party entering into a contract in his self-assumed capacity as agent, with no actual authority from the purported principal, or in excess of an existing authority, is personally liable to the other contracting party who acted in good faith and in reliance on the false representations. The liability terminates only if the purported principal is estopped to deny the authority or subsequently ratifies the transaction.

Lack or Limitation of Capacity of Principal

Nonexistent Principal. If an agent purports to act for a nonexistent principal, such agent will be personally liable on the contract. However, if the understanding of the parties is that the agent is in no event to be held liable, this rule does not apply, unless the understanding is induced by misrepresentations made by the purported agent. The basis for the rule is the inference that the party dealing with the agent intends to contract with an existing person, and if there is no principal in existence, the agent should be held as the other party to the contract.

A common example of an agent acting for a nonexistent principal is afforded in the case of a promoter of a corporation contracting in the name of the corporation prior to the time it receives its charter. As a general rule the promoter is personally liable on such contracts; however, his liability will depend on the knowledge of the third person as to the fact that the corporation is in contemplation and not in existence, and as to the terms of the contract. The extent of a promoter's liability will be discussed in more detail as a part of our discussion of the law of corporations in Chapter 24.

Incompetent Principal. The liability of an agent who purports to act for a person who is wholly incompetent, for instance, a person who has been officially adjudged insane and whose estate is being administered by a conservator, is substantially the same as that of an agent acting for a nonexistent principal. The agent is liable as a party to the contract.

Principal Lacking Full Capacity. An agent acting for a person who does not have full capacity to contract, as in the case of an infant, is not liable to the third person on the contract. The agent will be held liable to the third person if the agent misrepresents or conceals the status of his principal's capacity. However, if the identity of the principal is disclosed and the agent has no reason to think that the third person does not know of the principal's lack of full capacity to contract, the agent will not be liable. Under some circumstances, if the agent knows that the third person is unaware of the principal's lack of full capacity to contract, the agent's failure to inform the third person of such lack of capacity may amount to concealment.

Defenses Available to Agent. The defenses available to an agent who is a party to a contract will depend on the terms of the contract and the relation of the parties. In general, the agent will have all the defenses which arise out of the transaction itself, such as fraud, misrepresentation, nonperformance, payment, accord and satisfaction, infancy, and setoff, together with illegality if the third person is a party to a collusive agreement or other plan which requires or permits the agent to violate his fiduciary duty to his principal. In addition, the agent will have the defenses which are personal in nature and which exist between the agent and the third person.

If the agent is a party to a contract as surety for his principal, the rules of law relative to a surety's rights and duties apply in determining the agent's defenses against the third person.

Summary

A person who purports to act for a nonexistent or wholly incompetent principal is personally liable to the third person in a transaction involving such principal unless it is the understanding of the parties that the agent is not to be held liable.

If the principal lacks full capacity to contract, the agent is not liable on the contract he negotiates for the principal and is not liable to the third person on the contract unless he (the agent) misrepresents the capacity of his principal or conceals the fact that his principal does not have full capacity. Failure to disclose the fact that the principal does not have full capacity to contract may, under some circumstances, amount to concealment.

As a general rule, all defenses which arise out of a transaction and all defenses, personal in nature, which exist between the agent and third person are available to the agent if he is sued on the contract. If the agent is a party to a contract as surety, the laws of suretyship apply in determining his liability to the third person.

Dixie Drive It Yourself System v. *Lewis*
50 S.E.2d 843 (Ct. App. Ga. 1948)

This was an action by Dixie Drive It Yourself System (plaintiff) against John G. Lewis (defendant) to recover a judgment for the damage to a rented station wagon. Judgment for Lewis and Dixie Drive It Yourself System appealed. Judgment reversed.

John G. Lewis, principal of Hapeville High School rented two station wagons from Dixie Drive It Yourself System to be used in transporting students engaged in athletic activities. The rental contract was signed "Hapeville High School, John G. Lewis, Principal." One of the terms of the contract was that the customer would pay for any damage which might occur to the vehicle while in his possession. During the rental of these two station wagons, a wreck occurred and damaged one of them to the extent of $400. Dixie Drive It Yourself System sued Lewis and he set up as a defense that he signed the contract as agent for Hapeville High School. The trial court held that Lewis was not liable and Dixie Drive It Yourself System appealed.

GARDNER, J. The only question presented here for decision is whether the contract in question is the individual undertaking of Lewis. It is clear that both parties to the contract knew that the Hapeville High School had no legal entity. It could not sue or be sued. So neither Dixie Drive It Yourself System nor Lewis were misled. They were both bound by this knowledge. This is true, even though the Hapeville High School is a unit of the Fulton County school system. Therefore, as a legal entity the Hapeville High School was non-existent. The question before us was discussed at length in *Hagan* v. *Asa G. Candler Inc.* The court in that case said: "One who professes to contract as agent for another, when his purported principal is actually non-existent, may be held personally liable on the contract, unless the other contracting party agrees to look to some other person for performance." In a similar case, *Wells* v. *Fay & Egan Co.,* the Supreme Court said: "If one contracts as agent, when in fact he has no principal, he will be personally liable." This court, in *Harris* v. *Stribling,* said: "The note sued on is signed 'Harris-Stribling Sales Company, L.S., by J. D. Stribling, L.S.' It is alleged that at the time of the execution of the note there was no such person, corporation, or other legal entity as 'Harris-Stribling Sales Company,' and that J. D. Stribling is personally liable on the note. The note, on its face, purports to have been signed by J. D. Stribling. He signed it 'Harris-Stribling Sales Company,' by himself, 'J. D. Stribling.' If 'Harris-Stribling Sales Company' is not a person or corporation or other legal entity, it is a purely fictitious name, and the note being signed by J. D. Stribling as such constitutes his individual obligation." We do not think that the decision sustains the contentions of Lewis. Upon reading the other cases relied on by Lewis, it will be found that in each of those cases there was an existing principal and legal entity. Not so in the instant case. That is the distinction. A non-existent legal entity can have no agent. This principle was ruled very clearly in *Hagan* v. *Asa G. Candler Inc.,* where the Supreme Court said: "At the time the contract was executed and at the time the suit was filed, no such corporation as Food Shops Inc. was in existence, but this fact was unknown to the plaintiff. By reason of these facts, the contract was one between Asa G. Candler Inc. and H. G. Hagan, individually." In that case H. G. Hagan represented that the Food Shops Inc. was a corporation and that he had a right to sign the contract "Food Shops Inc., by H. G. Hagan." Under those circumstances, this court held that this was an individual undertaking of H. G. Hagan, and on *certiorari* the Supreme Court affirmed the judgment of the Court of Appeals. In view of the authorities cited and the record in the instant case, the contract was the individual undertaking of Lewis.

Agent's Liability for Tort

General Rule. As a general rule the fact that an agent is acting within the scope of his authority or on the instruction of his principal or at the direction of the principal does not relieve him from personal liability for his tortious acts. An agent may escape liability where he is exercising a privilege of the principal or a privilege held by the agent for the protection of the principal. For example, if the principal has an easement of right-of-way over the land of another, the agent would not be liable to the owner of the land if he uses the right-of-way in carrying on the business of his principal, provided he does not exceed, in his use of the right-of-way, the principal's rights thereunder. Since the tort liability of a principal and agent is joint and several, the fact that the principal may be held liable for the agent's tort does not relieve the agent from his personal liability for his torts.

Liability for Deceit and Duress. An agent is liable to an injured third person if the agent knowingly makes misrepresentations in the transaction of his principal's business or knowingly assists his principal or other agents of the principal in defrauding the third person. However, if the agent is innocent and does not know, and in the exercise of reasonable prudence would not know, that the representations he makes are false, the agent is not personally liable. For example, suppose Parker authorizes Arnold to sell his house. He tells Arnold that the house is fully insulated with rock wool when it is not. Arnold does not know that the house is not insulated, and he would not discover such fact on an ordinary inspection. If Arnold, in making a sale of the house to Thomas, tells Thomas that the house is fully insulated with rock wool, Arnold will not be liable to Thomas in an action of deceit.

In making a sale, an agent may use sales talk and puff his principal's goods in the same manner and to the same extent as may the principal, in which case the agent will not render himself liable to the third person for deceit.

The same general rules which apply regarding an agent's liability for deceit apply in determining the agent's liability for duress.

Liability for Conversion. An agent is personally liable for the conversion of another's goods, and this is true even though at the time the agent takes possession of the goods he has reason to believe that his principal is entitled to the possession of the goods. For example, suppose Parker has loaned his plow to Thomas' tool shed and gets a plow which he believes is Parker's plow but which really belongs to Thomas. Arnold is liable to Thomas for the conversion of the plow.

If a principal delivers to his agent for safekeeping goods which the principal has wrongfully taken from a third person, and later the agent, without knowledge of his principal's wrongdoing, redelivers the goods to the principal, the agent is not liable to the third person for the conversion of the goods. However, if the third person gives the agent notice of his right to the goods and demands the return of the goods and thereafter the agent returns the goods to the principal, the agent is liable to the third person for the conversion of the goods.

Liability for Negligence. An agent is liable to a third person for any injury the third person may suffer as a result of the negligence of the agent. If the principal furnishes the agent a defective instrument and the agent does not know and by the exercise of reasonable care would not know of the defects in the instrument, and owes no duty to third persons to discover such defects, the agent will not be liable to third persons for injuries resulting from the defects in the instrument.

Liability to Third Persons for Breach of Duty to Principal. Under established rules of contract law a person who is not a party to a contract has no right of action for breach of the contract, unless he is a donee or creditor beneficiary under the contract. The relation of principal and agent is, as a general rule, a personal relation, and a third person would have no right of action against an agent for breach, by the agent, of his duty to exercise care and skill in the performance of the duties he owes to his principal. However, as stated above, if an agent has defrauded a third person or has colluded with his principal to defraud a third person, or through his negligence has injured a third person, the agent is liable in tort for the injury suffered by such third person.

The courts have been confronted with cases which do not fall clearly within the scope of either the contract rule or the tort rule. Suppose, for example, a principal engages an accountant to audit his books and prepare a balance sheet, and the accountant is negligent in making the audit and prepares a balance sheet which does not reflect the true financial condition of the business. If a third person then, in reliance of the balance sheet, transacts business with the principal, who believes the balance sheet to be accurate, and thereby suffers a loss, will such third person be able to hold the accountant liable for such loss?

Courts generally have held that an accountant or other individual who renders professional service is not liable to a third person even though his lack of skill and care has caused the third person to suffer loss. However, where he has been grossly negligent in his work, professional agents have been held liable without privity of contract on the theory of constructive fraud. Of course, if the injured party can be viewed as a third-party beneficiary to the contract, he can recover for the agent's negligence. A few courts have gone further and have held the professional agent liable for his negligence to anyone relying on his work who is in the class of persons or is the person for whose benefit or guidance the work was prepared. Accountants may also be held liable to third parties for failure to disclose information under Section 10b of the Securities and Exchange Act of 1934.[1]

Summary

An agent is liable to third persons for his torts, and the fact that the principal also may be liable does not relieve the agent of his liability.

The agent is liable in tort in an action of deceit if he knowingly makes false

---

[1] *Fischer* v. *Kletz,* 266 F.Supp. 180 (S.D. N.Y. 1967), see Chapter 27.

representations even though he does not profit personally therefrom. He is not personally liable for making statements which he has no reason to know are false and which are based on statements made to him by his principal.

An agent is liable for conversion even though the agent is following the instructions of the principal in the wrongful taking or conversion of the goods and does not know that his acts are wrongful.

An agent is liable for injury resulting from his own negligent conduct, but he cannot be held liable for injury resulting from the negligence of his principal or fellow agent if he himself has not been negligent.

An agent, as a general rule, is not liable to a third person for injury resulting from the agent's failure to perform a duty owed to the principal. However, professional agents such as accountants have in some instances been held liable to third persons who might be expected to and do rely on their work.

Rusch Factors, Inc. v. Levin
284 F.Supp. 85 (D. R.I. 1968)

This was an action by Rusch Factors, Inc. (plaintiff) against Leonard Levin (defendant), an accountant, to recover damages sustained as a result of alleged negligence in the preparation of financial statements. Motion to dismiss for failure to state a cause of action (and other grounds not here considered) denied.

In late 1963 and early 1964, a Rhode Island corporation sought financing from Rusch. Rusch requested certified financial statements to determine the financial condition of the company. The corporation employed Levin to prepare the statements. They represented the corporation to be solvent by a substantial amount. In fact, the corporation was insolvent. Relying on the certified statements, Rusch loaned the corporation $337,000. Subsequently, the corporation went into receivership, resulting in a loss to Rusch of $121,000.

PETTINE, DISTRICT JUDGE.   No appellate court, English or American has ever held an accountant liable in negligence to reliant parties not in privity. The reluctance of the courts to hold the accounting profession to an obligation of care which extends to all reasonably foreseeable reliant parties is predicated upon the social utility rationale first articulated by Judge Cardozo in the *Ultamares* case. In that case the defendant accountants were employed by a company to perform the company's yearly audit. The defendants negligently overvalued the company's assets in the balance sheet upon which the plaintiffs, creditors of the company, subsequently relied. In holding the defendant accountants free from liability for their negligence, Judge Cardozo stated:

If liability for negligence exists, a thoughtless slip or blunder, the failure to detect a theft or forgery beneath the cover of deceptive entries, may expose accountants to a liability in an indeterminate amount for an indeterminate time to an indeterminate class. The hazards of a business conducted on these terms are so extreme as to enkindle doubt whether a flaw may not exist in the implication of a duty that exposes one to these consequences.

The wisdom of the decision in *Ultramares* has been doubted. Why should an innocent reliant party be forced to carry the weighty burden of an accountant's professional malpractice? Isn't the risk of loss more easily distributed and fairly spread by imposing it on the accounting profession, which can pass the cost of insuring against the risk onto its customers, who can in turn pass the cost onto the entire consuming public? Finally, wouldn't a rule of foreseeability elevate the cautionary techniques of the accounting profession?

This Court need not, however, hold that the Rhode Island Supreme Court would overrule the *Ultramares* decision, if presented the opportunity, for the case at bar is qualitatively distinguishable from *Ultramares*. There, the plaintiff was a member of an undefined, unlimited class of remote lenders and potential equity holders not actually foreseen but only foreseeable. Here the plaintiff is a single party whose reliance was actually foreseen by the defendant. The case at bar is, in fact, far more akin to the case of *Glanzer* v. *Shephard*, another Cardozo opinion and the first case to extend to persons not in privity, liability for negligent misrepresentation causing pecuniary loss. In *Glanzer* a professional weigher contracted with a bean seller to weigh a shipment of beans and certify the weight to the bean buyer. The plaintiff bean buyer paid his seller for the beans in accordance with their weight as represented by the defendant's certificate. When it turned out that the weigher had overweighed, and hence that the buyer had overpaid, the Court allowed the buyer to recover the difference from the misrepresenting weigher. In fact, the *Glanzer* principle has been applied to accountants. The tentative drafts of the *Restatement* (*Second*) *of Torts* § 552 states the rule of law as follows:

(1) One who, in the course of his business, profession or employment, or in a transaction in which he has a pecuniary interest, supplies false information for the guidance of others in their business transactions, is subject to liability for pecuniary loss caused to them by their justifiable reliance upon the information, if he fails to exercise reasonable care or competence in obtaining or communicating the information.

(2) Except as stated in subsection (3), the liability stated in subsection (1) is limited to loss suffered

(a) by the person or one of the persons for whose benefit and guidance he intends to supply the information, or knows that the recipient intends to supply it; and

(b) through reliance upon it in a transaction which he intends the information to influence, or knows that the recipient so intends, or in a substantially similar transaction.

(3) The liability of one who is under a public duty to give the information extends to loss suffered by any of the class of persons for whose benefit the duty is created, in any of the transactions in which it is intended to protect them.

With respect, then to the plaintiff's negligence theory, this Court holds that an accountant should be liable in negligence for careless financial misrepresentations relied upon by actually foreseen and limited classes of persons. According to the plaintiff's complaint in the instant case, the defendant knew that his certification was to be used, for and had as its very aim and purpose, the reliance of potential financiers of the Rhode Island corporation. The defendant's motion is, therefore, denied.

The Court does not rule upon, but leaves open for reconsideration in the light of trial development, the question of whether an accountant's liability for negligent misrepresentation ought to extend to the full limits of foreseeability.

Third Person's Liability to Agent

Agent's Right of Action on Contract. An agent who is acting for a disclosed principal and who has negotiated a contract within the scope of his authority and in the name of the principal has no right to bring an action in his own name against the third party to the contract to recover a judgment for breach of such contract. This rule applies even though the principal has authorized the agent to bring the action in the name of the agent. Since the agent is not a party to the contract, he has no right, under the rules of procedural law, to bring an action on the contract in his own name. The principal may assign an informal contract or negotiate a negotiable instrument to his agent and thereby make him the owner of the right, in which case the agent may, under the laws of most states, bring the action in his own name.

If the agent is a party to the contract, other than as a surety for his principal, he will be a party in interest and as such may bring an action in his own name to recover for a breach of the contract.

An agent acting for an undisclosed or partially disclosed principal will be a party to the contract and may bring an action on the contract in his own name. However, if the undisclosed or partially disclosed principal wishes to bring the action in his name, he has the right to do so. If an action is brought in the name of the principal, the agent will not have the right to bring a second action in his (the agent's) name. One suit exhausts the remedies for breach of a contract.

Agent with Property Interest in Contract. If the agent has negotiated a contract in the name of his principal and the agent has a special interest or property in the contract, the agent may bring a suit in his own name for damages suffered as a result of a breach of the contract.

Professional Agents. An auctioneer or commission merchant (factor) who has sold goods for his principal may bring suit in his own name to collect the purchase price of the goods. It is customary for auctioneers and commission merchants (factors) to make sales, extend credit, and bring suits in their own names.

Agent's Right of Action for Possession. If a principal entrusts goods to his agent and a third person tortiously interferes with the agent's possession, the agent may bring an action in his own name to recover a judgment for the unlawful interference with his possession. Likewise, if a third person has the possession of goods owned by the principal when the agent is entitled to their possession, the agent has the right to bring an action in his own name to recover possession of the goods. In both of these situations the agent is basing the action on his personal right to possession.

Agent's Action for Tort. If a third person has wrongfully injured an agent, the agent may bring suit to recover damages for his personal injuries.

Summary

An agent acting within the scope of his authority and contracting in the name of his principal cannot bring an action in his own name to recover for the breach of the contract. An agent who is acting for an undisclosed or partially disclosed principal, or who is acting for a disclosed principal but at the same time is a party to the contract other than as surety for his principal, may bring an action in his own name for breach of the contract. However, if an undisclosed or disclosed principal elects to bring the action, the agent's right to bring suit is cut off. An auctioneer or factor, as a general rule, may bring an action in his own name. An agent may bring an action in his own name against a person who has interfered with his possession of his principal's goods. An agent has a right of action against third persons who have wrongfully injured the agent.

Problem Cases

1. Bowman, a broker, negotiated the sale of the fixtures and equipment of a restaurant as agent for Macris. The purchaser, Priolette, gave Bowman a $1,000 down payment, which Bowman turned over to Macris. Macris refused to perform the contract, and Priolette sued Macris and Bowman to recover the $1,000 down payment and damages for breach of the contract. Is Bowman liable?

2. Konodi hired Stockholm to make certain repairs on the S.S. *Providencia,* an Italian ship docked at Albany, N.Y. Konodi was on board the ship and gave instructions to Stockholm's men. Konodi was acting merely as an agent for the owner of the ship in odering the repairs. Earlier Stockholm had worked on the same ship and had been paid by Konodi's own check. Stockholm again billed Konodi and brought suit when he refused to pay. Konodi's defense was that he was only an agent. Is he liable?

3. Fink obtained in his own name a lease on some parking facilities from the City of Denver and formed a corporation named Den-Park Co. Prior to obtaining the lease and prior to the formation of Den-Park, Fink received a letter from Elevator Co. offering to negotiate for servicing of the garage elevators should Fink be awarded the lease. After the lease was signed, negotiations for a service and repair contract were entered into between Elevator Co. represented by its agent and Den-Park represented by Fink. The service contract was signed in the name of Den-Park Co. by Victor L. Fink; it was then signed by the agent representing Elevator Co. The work on the elevators commenced and it was discovered that much more extensive repairs were needed than had originally been anticipated. Periodic invoices were sent by

Elevator Service to Den-Park and several were paid by City-Park checks. When the total of the billings greatly exceeded the amount agreed upon in the contract, City-Park refused to make further payments. Elevator Service claims that it dealt with Fink as an individual and Fink is personally liable on the contract. Is Fink liable to Elevator Service?

4. Anderson, assuming to act for the owner of real estate, listed it for sale with Brawley, who found a buyer ready, willing and able to buy the property at the price fixed by Anderson. Anderson was not authorized to act for the owner of the property and instead of submitting the purchaser's offer to the owner of the property returned it to Brawley. Brawley sued Anderson to recover the commission he would have earned had Anderson been authorized to list the property. Will he recover?

5. Zuspan owned a farm which she rented to Byers. Her son, Newell Zuspan, negotiated with Byers for the sale of the farm to him, representing that he was his mother's agent. An agreement was reached to sell the farm to Byers. In reliance on the agreement, Byers made improvements on the farm. Later Newell Zuspan told Byers that his mother would not sell the farm and that he had no authority to sell it. There was no writing executed by Zuspan which would satisfy the statute of frauds. Byers sued Newell Zuspan to recover damages for his failure to get the farm. Will he recover?

6. Graham, the head of an unincorporated association, engaged Comfort as attorney to represent the interests of the association. The association did not pay Comfort for his services, and Comfort sued Graham on the contract of employment to recover a judgment for the amount due him for services rendered to the association. Is Graham liable on the contract of employment?

7. Investment Corp. contracted to buy a large block of stock in Belcher-Young Company. The agreement was subject to the condition that Belcher-Young would furnish Investment Corp. a certified financial statement, and if the statement disclosed an adverse change in Belcher-Young's financial position in the three months since a previous statement, Investment Corp. could rescind the contract. Buchman was employed by Belcher-Young to prepare the statement, which it did negligently. Investment Corp. purchased the stock but within a year Belcher-Young became bankrupt. May Investment Corp. recover its loss from Buchman, the accountant?

8. Glenn stole some cattle from Caviness and sold them to Preston. Preston delivered the cattle to Walker, a livestock commission merchant, who sold the cattle and paid the proceeds of the sale to Preston. Caviness sued Preston and Walker in tort to recover a judgment for the conversion of the cattle. Walker set up as a defense that he sold the cattle as agent for Preston and therefore was not liable. Is Walker liable for the conversion of the cattle?

9. Scott, as agent for Coal Co., contracted in the name of his principal to sell Railroad Co. 34,500 tons of coal. The contract with Coal Co. was in writing, and was drawn and signed in the name of Coal Co. by Scott, its agent. Under Coal Co.'s contract with Scott, it was obligated to pay Scott a commission of 10 cents a ton for all coal sold by him, provided the buyer accepted delivery and paid for the coal ordered. Railroad Co. refused to accept and pay for 22,210 tons of the coal contracted for. Scott sued Railroad Co. to recover a judgment for the commission he would have received had Railroad Co. accepted and paid for the coal in fulfillment of the contract. Is Scott entitled to a judgment against Railroad Co. for the claimed commissions?

chapter 18. Relation of Principal and Agent

Agent's Duty of Loyalty

Duty in General. In a majority of situations the relation of principal and agent will be created by contract, and the court, in determining the duties owed by the agent to his principal, will interpret the contract and will enforce its provisions, provided they are not illegal as tested by contract law. The agent may, by the terms of the contract of employment, relieve himself, within limits, of the duties he would normally owe to his principal, or he may, by agreement, assume added burdens. Since an agent owes a fiduciary duty to his principal, his duties extend beyond those set out in the contract of employment. The duties of a gratuitous agent are, with some degree of variation within this area, the same as those of a compensated agent.

As a fiduciary the agent owes a duty of honesty and undivided loyalty to his principal. He must use his best efforts to further his principal's interests and will not be permitted to put himself in a position where his individual interests conflict with the duty he owes to his principal. Since the principal must disclose his business to his agent in order to enable the agent to perform his duties, it is essential that the agent treat such disclosures as confidential and that he not be permitted to use confidential information, acquired either directly or indirectly as a result of the relationship, for his own profit to the detriment of his principal.

Secret Communications. If, in the course of the employment, the principal reveals to the agent secret formulas or processes, the agent owes a duty not to disclose such information to third persons. The agent also owes a duty to his principal not to use such secret information for his own benefit to the detriment of the principal. The same rule applies to customer lists, special methods of doing business, or any other confidential matters.

397

The agent is permitted to use the general information acquired during the course of his employment. In transacting his principal's business, the agent, as a general rule, will acquire a general knowledge of the business in which his principal is engaged. He will learn the general usages of the business, will develop his judgment, and will acquire an efficiency in the particular type of business. If the employment is terminated, the agent is privileged to acquire similar employment and thereby benefit by his knowledge in that particular field of business.

Duty Not to Buy from or Sell to Self. An agent who is authorized to buy or sell property for his principal will not be permitted to buy from or sell to himself unless he makes a full disclosure of all the material facts to the principal and the principal consents to the transaction.

If an agent does buy from or sell to himself, either directly or indirectly, without the consent of the principal, the principal has the right to have the transaction set aside, irrespective of the fact that the price was the best obtainable, that the transaction was free from fraud, and that the agent honestly believed that he was pursuing a course which would be most beneficial to his principal. The courts hold that to permit an agent to buy from or sell to himself would encourage sharp dealing, and they will not enforce such transactions against the wishes of the principal. Such contracts are voidable at the election of the principal; they are not void.

A contract is voidable at the election of the principal if the agent uses some third person as a cover-up for his interest in the transaction. For example, if the agent sells to his wife or other relative with the understanding that they will sell the property to the agent at a later date, or if he sells to a corporation in which he is the principal stockholder, or to a partnership in which he is a member, the court will set the transaction aside at the request of the principal.

Duty to Act for Only One Party to Transaction. As a general rule an agent will not be permitted to act as agent for both parties to a transaction. The generally accepted principle that "no man can serve two masters" is applied by the courts to the relation of principal and agent. However, if the agent is acting as a middleman, and his duty is to bring the parties together and they then negotiate their own transaction, the agent may represent both parties, provided both parties have been fully informed regarding the agent's dual role and have consented to it.

If the agent is acting for both parties without the knowledge and consent of both, he is not entitled to compensation. If only one of the parties knows of and consents to the agent's acting for both parties to the transaction, the party having knowledge and giving his consent is bound, but the other party may elect to have the transaction set aside. In such a situation the agent is not entitled to compensation from either party. The agent has breached his duty to the party not consenting, and the agreement between the agent and the party consenting is a fraud on the other party, is against public policy, and is illegal.

A similar situation arises if a third person agrees to pay an agent a secret commission, make him a gift, or compensate him in any way. A promise on the part of a third person to benefit an agent in any respect is a fraud on the principal and is illegal. Any benefits given the agent by the third person may be claimed by the principal, whether the benefits are in the form of a secret commission or a gift.

Summary

The agent owes a duty of undivided loyalty to his principal. He must not put himself in a position where his individual interests conflict with his duties to his principal.

An agent owes a duty to his principal not to disclose any confidential information gained in the transaction of his principal's business, and not to reveal any secret formulas, processes, secret business methods, customer lists, or other similar information with which he is entrusted by his principal.

An agent authorized to buy or sell for his principal must not buy from or sell to himself unless he makes a full disclosure of all the facts to the principal and the principal consents to the transaction.

As a general rule the agent will not be permitted to act as agent for both parties to a transaction. However, if the agent is acting as a middleman and both parties to the contract consent, the agent may act for both parties.

Rushing v. *Stephanus*

303 P.2d 281 (Sup. Ct. Wash. 1964)

This was an action by Eugene Rushing and wife (plaintiffs) against Paul Stephanus (defendant) alleging negligence, fraud, and breach of Stephanus' fiduciary duty as an agent, and seeking recovery of commissions and excessive loan expenses. Judgment for Rushing and Stephanus appealed. Judgment affirmed.

Rushing was a sewer contractor with a fifth-grade education. He wanted to borrow $1,800 for use in his business, and he and his wife went to Stephanus, doing a mortgage loan brokerage business as the Prudential Mortgage Co. Stephanus indicated that he could secure a first mortgage loan for them at 8% interest which would refinance the pre-existing $3,200 mortgage on Rushing's home and provide $1,800 in cash. He asked Rushing and his wife to sign a stack of papers, representing that the loan application, which was on top, was in several copies. In this manner the Rushings signed blank forms not only for a loan application but a note, a mortgage and a hold harmless agreement. Stephanus filled in the application to show the loan amount as $6,600.

Although the proposed loan was marketable, Stephanus did not place it promptly. After a month, the Rushings expressed concern and were told that there was a problem with the title to the home, and Stephanus suggested an interim loan of $1,000. The Rushings again signed another stack of papers in blank. On this loan Stephanus received a commission of $160. Finally, a month later a savings and loan association accepted the original loan. Stephanus advised the association prior to the closing that he held a recorded mortgage on the premises (one of the papers Rushings signed) which had an unpaid balance of $660. This was actually his $660 commission, and it was paid in the closing transactions. By the use of this device, Stephanus' commissions were not noticed by the Rushings.

As a result of all of these transactions the Rushings received $1,560 and increased their debt on their house from $3,200 to $6,600 and Stephanus received $820 in commissions plus $85 in closing fees, appraisal and other fees. The Rushings recovered in the trial court the $905 which had gone to Stephanus plus $480 in expenses on the interim loan.

FINLEY, JUDGE.   The entire $905 received by Stephanus as agent is forfeit, including the commissions and the $85 in "fees," only a few dollars of which were ever shown to have been passed on to third parties. The record is ample to support the findings of fraud and breach of an agent's fiduciary duty. The obtaining of signatures by trickery, misrepresentation and concealment of mortgages and fees, which appear staggering from the standpoint of amount alone, are all elements found by the trial court on substantial evidence. The broker must fully reveal the nature and extent of his fees to the client for whom he acts, and the failure to do so will render him liable. Where there has been a breach of the fiduciary relationship in addition to the partial concealment of fees, the rule is stated as follows in the *Restatement, Agency* (2d), § 469:

"An agent is entitled to no compensation for conduct which is disobedient or which is a breach of his duty of loyalty; if such conduct constitutes a wilful and deliberate breach of his contract of service, he is not entitled to compensation even for properly performed services for which no compensation is apportioned."

Stephanus is likewise liable, as a loan broker, for the expenses imposed upon his clients as a result of his failure to exercise due diligence or care. The item of $840 represents the loss caused when Stephanus failed to exercise reasonable diligence in obtaining the first mortgage as agreed, but also affirmatively acted to secure an expensive interim loan which the trial court found was totally unnecessary. This interim loan was arranged at a 20 per cent discount, a 10 per cent interest rate, and a penalty for a pay-off prior to maturity, despite the fact that Stephanus knew it was to be paid off with the proceeds of the $6,600 loan as soon as possible. Reviewing the above evidence, we cannot say that there was insufficient evidence of negligence to support the finding of the trial court.

Spratlin, Harrington & Thomas, Inc. v. *Hawn*
156 S.E.2d 402 (Ct. App. Ga. 1967)

This was an action by Spratlin, Harrington & Thomas, Inc. (plaintiff), against W. R. Hawn and others (defendants) to recover a fee for obtaining a loan commitment to Hawn. Judgment for Hawn appealed. Affirmed.

Hawn and others d/b/a Greenbriar Shopping Center sought a commitment for a loan of $10,000,000 for construction of a shopping center in Atlanta. Greenbriar requested the services of the commercial loan department of Spratlin, Harrington & Thomas (S. H. & T.), a mortgage banking concern, to advise it and to obtain a loan commitment. It agreed to pay S. H. & T. a fee of $50,000 (½%) upon acceptance of a commitment in line with the loan application which S. H. & T. prepared. S. H. & T. obtained a commitment from American National Insurance Co., and during the year and one half of construction it worked with American National and Greenbriar preparing for the closing of the loan, which included the analysis of all leases to see that they met the standards of the commitment.

Unknown to Greenbriar, S. H. & T. had an agreement with American National to pay it a $10,000 finders fee plus ¹⁄₁₆% ($6,250) for servicing, although Greenbriar did know that S. H. & T. regularly submitted loan applications to American National and another lender. Prior to the expiration of American National's commitment, Greenbriar obtained financing elsewhere and advised that it would not close the loan. When S. H. & T. sued for its fee, Greenbriar set up dual agency as its defense.

QUILLIAN, JUDGE.   The Georgia courts have held: "Contracts of dual agency are not void per se, but only so when the fact that the agent represented both parties was not known to each." *Red Cypress Lumber Co.* v. *Perry.* Therefore, the question here involved is whether knowledge of and consent to the dual agency within the meaning of the cited cases is simply knowing that one represented a lender as a correspondent or encompasses at least an understanding of the material aspects of the agency. We agree with counsel for the appellant that the amount the agent might receive is immaterial.

The first duty of an agent is that of loyalty to his trust. He must not put himself in relations which are antagonistic to that of his principal. His duty and interest must not be allowed to conflict. He cannot deal in the business within the scope of his agency for his own benefit . . . ; nor is he permitted to compromise himself by attempting to serve two masters having a contrary interest, unless it be that such contracts of dual agency are known to each of the principals. *Arthur* v. *Georgia Cotton Co.* It is of the essence of the contract of the agent that he will use his best skill and judgment to promote the interest of his employer. . . . To represent both parties as their agent is to undertake inconsistent duties. . . . An agent cannot use his best skill and judgment to promote the interest of his employer where he acts for two persons whose interests are essentially adverse. Such a situation places the agent under a temptation to deal unjustly with one or both of his principals. . . . He thus commits a fraud on his principals in undertaking, without their consent or knowledge, to act as their mutual agent. . . . The law of agency is, that the principal bargains for the exercise of "the disinterested skill, diligence, and zeal of the agent for his exclusive benefit." He can have no interest and do no act adverse to the interest of his employer, or incompatible with the application of his best skill, zeal, and diligence to the promotion of that interest. *Napier* v. *Adams.*

The facts that no actual fraud has been practiced, no damage has resulted, and no bad faith has been exercised, in a transaction in which the agent has acted in a dual capacity, do not make the contract valid, in the absence of knowledge on the part of the principal, of all the material facts. Anno. 48 *A.L.R.* 917, 925. Requirements of good faith demand that, in the principal's interest, it is the agent's duty to make known to the principal all material facts which concern the transactions and subject matter of his agency. *Lichten-stein Co.* v. *Nebraska.*

Under the circumstances of this case the S. H. & T. failed to reveal to Greenbriar a pertinent and possibly vital fact that they were going to receive a fee from the lender. This failure to disclose was a violation of a fundamental tenet of the agency relation. Without such disclosure we cannot hold that the evidence demands a finding that Greenbriar "knew" of the dual agency so as to, in effect, waive the protection of the "dual agency" rule.

S. H. & T. contend they were mere middlemen with no discretionary authority and thus the rule is applicable:

Another exception to the doctrine generally forbidding dual agencies is that the agent may represent both parties, provided that the acts in which he is to represent the one in no wise conflict with the full exercise of his duty to the other. An agent may perform mere ministerial acts, involving no discretion, for one of the parties to the contract, though he is agent for the other party. He is forbidden to act for both only when there is opportunity that the skill and judgment which he should exercise for the one may conflict with the skill and judgment he should exercise for the other. *Todd* v. *German American Insurance Co.*

It is urged that a broker is not an agent in a true sense because a broker merely serves as a conduit to bring the parties together and afterwards they do all the negotiating and reach a final agreement without the broker's aid. S. H. & T. contend the "middleman" rule is therefore especially applicable under these facts where Greenbriar had already determined and prescribed the amount of loan and its basic requirements.

Furthermore, here the evidence and pleading reveal that: S. H. & T. undertook to assist Greenbriar in obtaining a loan on the most favorable terms possible; that pursuant to this aim S. H. & T.'s agents received from Greenbriar confidential information as to their plans for the development of the shopping center they proposed to construct; that S. H. & T. gave Greenbriar advice with respect to the amount and terms of the loan that they might expect to obtain, the interest rate they should seek, and the amount of "standby fee" they should pay for a loan commitment; that S. H. & T. actually negotiated a loan commitment from American National Insurance Company on behalf of Greenbriar. Hence, the rule would be applicable: "A broker is simply a middleman, within the meaning of this exception, when he has no duty to perform but to bring the parties together, leaving them to negotiate and to come to an agreement themselves without any aid from him. If he takes, or contracts to take, any part in the negotiations, however, he cannot be regarded as a mere middleman, no matter how slight a part it may be. . . ." *Jensen* v. *Bowen.*

Agent's Duty to Obey Instructions and to Use Care and Skill

Duty to Obey Instructions. The agent owes a duty to follow faithfully all legitimate instructions given him by his principal. The agent is engaged to transact business or perform services for his principal, and the principal has the right, within the limits of legality, to have the business transacted or the services performed as he wishes. If the agent, even though it be a gratuitous agency, fails or refuses to follow the legitimate instructions of the principal, he will be liable to the principal for any damages suffered by the principal as the result of the agent's failure to act as instructed. In addition, the agent's failure or refusal to follow instructions will, as a general rule, justify the principal's termination of the agency.

There are some situations in which the agent may be justified in not following instructions. If an emergency arises and the agent cannot consult with his principal, he may be justified in using his own judgment, especially if following instructions would clearly result in injury to the principal; but if no emergency has arisen, the agent must follow instructions, even though he deems the course of action designated by the principal to be clearly injurious to the principal. If the principal instructs the agent to do an illegal or criminal act, the agent is not bound to follow instructions. If the agency is general in its nature and the principal has not given the agent detailed instructions, the agent must use his own judgment and follow that course of action which in his judgment will best further his principal's interests.

Standard of Care and Skill. In the absence of an agreement imposing on the agent a duty of a greater or lesser degree, the agent owes a duty to act with standard care and skill. That is, the agent must possess and exercise the care and skill which is standard in the locality for the kind of work he is employed to perform. If the agent is acting gratuitously, this fact may be taken into consideration in determining whether he has acted with reasonable care and skill. In all instances the paid agent owes a duty to exercise at least the skill he represents himself as having. The agent may warrant that his undertakings will be successful or that his performance will be satisfactory to his principal, but in the absence of such a warranty, he does not assume the risk of the success or satisfaction of his performance.

Duty to Communicate Notice or Knowledge. Since the principal is bound by notice given to the agent or knowledge acquired by him during the transaction of the principal's business, the agent owes a duty to communicate to his principal all notice which is given to him in the course of the transaction of his principal's business and to disclose all facts within his knowledge which are material to the matters entrusted to him by his principal. Failure to communicate notice or to disclose knowledge is a breach of duty and will render the agent liable to his principal for any resulting injury.

Duty in Making Collections. If an agent is authorized to collect money due his principal, he is negligent if he accepts payment in anything other than money, unless he is given authority to do so. The agent owes a duty to follow instructions as to the method used in remitting money, and if no special instructions are given, he owes a duty to use ordinary means of remittance. If the agent uses a hazardous means of remitting and as a result the funds are lost, he will be liable to his principal for the loss. If the agent is authorized to collect on negotiable paper, he must present the instrument, and if it is not paid, he must give notice to endorsers or other persons secondarily liable on the paper if such is necessary to preserve its value.

Duty in Extending Credit. An agent authorized to sell property on credit owes a duty to use ordinary care in checking the credit standing of the buyer. Likewise, an agent authorized to make loans for his principal must investigate the credit standing of the borrower, and if it is customary to require security, it is the duty of the agent to demand that the borrower give adequate security. The agent is not an insurer of the loans made, but he must exercise ordinary care in selecting the borrowers and in investigating the security given.

Duties of Professional Agent. The agent may contract to perform duties requiring special skills, in which case he must possess and exercise that degree of special skill which is possessed and exercised by persons in the community performing such skilled services. For instance, if Peters engages Archer, a certified public accountant, to make an audit, Archer must possess and exercise that degree of skill which is possessed and exercised by certified public accountants practicing in that locality. If Archer does not and, as a result, Peters is injured, Archer will be liable. A professional agent does not insure his work—that is, he is not liable for honest errors in judgment, but he must bring to the job and exercise the trained judgment usually possessed and exercised by those practicing the same profession.

Summary

An agent owes a duty to follow and obey the instructions of his principal, provided the principal does not instruct the agent to do a criminal or illegal act. In an emergency an agent may be justified in not following instructions if doing so would result in injury to the principal.

An agent owes a duty to communicate to the principal all notices received in the course of the transaction of the principal's business. He also owes a duty to disclose all material facts which come to his knowledge during the performance of his duties.

An agent authorized to collect money for his principal must not accept payment in anything other than money unless he is given authority to do so.

An agent authorized to sell on credit owes a duty to investigate the credit standing of the buyer. If the agent is authorized to make loans for the principal, the agent must investigate the credit standing of the borrower, and if customary to demand security, he must do so.

A professional agent must possess and exercise the degree of care and skill possessed and exercised by agents performing such skilled services in the locality.

Fall Lumber Co. v. *Heman*
181 N.E.2d 713 (Ct. App. Ohio 1961)

This was an action by Fall Lumber Co. (plaintiff) against Stanley A. Heman and Doris L. Heman, his wife (defendants), for the foreclosure of a mechanic's lien in which the Hemans filed a cross-petition in an action against North Akron Savings Association. Judgment for the Hemans against North Akron Savings Association and it appealed. Judgment affirmed.

The Hemans entered into a contract with M. W. DeWitt Construction Company for the erection of a house on a lot owned by them for the sum of $17,500. The Hemans borrowed $11,000 from North Akron Savings Association (Bank). Bank retained the money and the Hemans secured and deposited in escrow with Bank an additional $5,500. The Hemans gave Bank a construction mortgage on the lot and house to be built to secure the payment of the $11,000 loan. Bank orally promised to act as agent in the payment of labor and material bills incurred in the construction of the house. Bank paid out money to the construction company without requiring any compliance with the terms of the statute concerning construction mortgages and without requiring the construction company to submit releases under the mechanic's lien law of Ohio. The funds in the hands of Bank were paid out to the construction company, and mechanics' liens for a total of $5,500 were filed against the house. The Hemans claimed that the loss was the result of Bank's failure to exercise due care and skill in the handling of the funds as agent and asked a judgment against Bank for the amount of the resulting loss.

HUNSICKER, JUDGE.   It certainly is reasonable to conclude that one who undertakes to act for another in the disbursing of funds is answerable for failure to do so with due care. An agent owes to his principal the use of such skills as may be required to accomplish the object of his employment.

Thus, in *Bank* v. *Bank,* the court determined that if, by reason of the neglect of an agent to take proper action in the matters for which he was employed, a principal suffers loss, the agent becomes liable to his principal for the resulting damages.

In *Ott* v. *Schneiter* the court said:

"The law is clearly established that a sub-agent who negligently performs his duties, thus injuring the rights of the principal, is liable to the principal to the extent of the injury suffered by him."

The duty of the Bank, in the instant case, with reference to the money belonging to Mr. and Mrs. Heman, was much like that of a trustee engaged to hold and disburse funds of the trust estate. Just as a trustee who has failed to properly administer a trust, thereby causing a loss to the trust, may be charged with such loss, so should an agent be held liable to his principal for a loss due to the neglect of the agent to properly conduct the business undertaken for his principal.

We therefore conclude that, when the Bank undertook to disburse money for Mr. and Mrs. Heman, for the construction of the home being built for them by the M. W. DeWitt Construction Company, it was required to use reasonable care to see that mechanics and materialmen were paid by the contractor, and to that end it was obliged to use ordinary care to protect Mr. and Mrs. Heman from having mechanics' liens placed against their home. The failure to exercise ordinary care in the discharge of its duty subjected the Bank to an action of tort for the loss so sustained.

Agent's Duty to Account

Duty to Account for Money and Property. An agent owes a duty to account to his principal for any money or property coming into his possession in the course of the transaction of his principal's business. The principal may demand an accounting at any time he wishes, and the agent owes a duty to make such an accounting. If the nature of the business entrusted to the agent involves collections, receipts, expenditures, and similar transactions, the agent owes a duty to keep accurate accounts and to render such accounts to his principal.

Duty to Keep Principal's Property Separate. An agent owes a duty not to commingle the property of his principal with his own property, and if he does, he will be liable to the principal for any resulting loss. If the commingled property cannot be separated, the agent must satisfy every legitimate claim of the principal. If it is necessary to grant the entire mass of the commingled property to the principal in order to protect his interest, the court will do so.

An agent owes a duty not to deposit in his own name or in his own personal bank account his principal's money, and if he does, the agent will be liable to the principal for any loss resulting from the defalcation of the depository.

Unless the agent has been given instructions as to the disposition to be made of the principal's money which comes into his hands, he may deposit it in a bank. If the agent deposits his principal's money in a bank, he must use ordinary care in selecting the bank and must deposit the money in the principal's name or under some designation which will clearly indicate that he is depositing his principal's money and not his own. For example, he may deposit it in his own name as trustee for the principal, in which case the deposit, if made by Ames for Peters, would be entitled "Ames in trust for Peters," or some similar designation.

Liability for Use of Principal's Property. If an agent uses his principal's property with the intent of depriving the principal of it, the agent will be guilty of the crime of embezzlement. If the agent has used his principal's property or failed to keep it separate, the principal may claim his property if he can identify it, or he may hold the agent liable for the value of the property in the tort action of conversion.

If the agent has used his principal's money for his own purposes, the principal is entitled to a judgment against him for the amount of the money used, or if the agent has purchased property with the money or has invested it in securities which he still has, the principal may, at his election, claim such property or securities, even though they have increased in value since the agent acquired them. For example, suppose Alden, acting as agent for Pape, collects $5,000 for Pape and, instead of remitting the money to him, purchases corporate stock with it. Pape, if he can prove that Alden purchased the stock with his money, may claim the stock even though it has increased in value since Alden purchased it, or he may hold Alden accountable for the money collected.

Summary

An agent owes a duty to keep a true and accurate account of all property and money of his principal coming into his possession. He owes a duty not to commingle his principal's property or money with his own.

If the agent commingles his principal's property with his own, deposits his principal's money in his own name, or uses his principal's money or property for his own use and benefit, the agent is liable for any and all resulting loss.

Bain v. Pulley
111 S.E.2d 287 (Sup. Ct. Va. 1959)

This was an action by Marion T. Bain and Harry L. Bain (plaintiffs) against Douglas H. Pulley (defendant) asking for an accounting. Judgment for Pulley and the Bains appealed. Judgment reversed and remanded.

The Bains were trustees of the Thomas L. Bain, deceased, estate, which was composed of a business and farms. The Bains as trustees employed Pulley as agent to operate and manage the business and farms. Pulley continued in the employ of the Bains from June, 1936, to January 1, 1956. During this time Pulley kept and maintained books and records pertaining to the estate business and properties. The books and records were kept entirely in Pulley's handwriting. Over the years, substantial profits from the operation were paid to the beneficiaries of the estate.

From January, 1952, and continuing through January, 1956, Pulley rendered an annual income report. These reports were not verified or checked with the records by the accountants or the trustees or the beneficiaries. No audit of Pulley's accounts was made between 1943 and 1956, when Pulley resigned as agent and manager of the estate. This action was brought asking for an accounting. Pulley contended that since he had rendered an annual report the Bains were not entitled to an accounting.

EGGLESTON, CHIEF JUSTICE.   The general duty of an agent who is required to handle money is thus laid down in *Restatement of the Law of Agency,* 2d, Vol. 2, § 382, p. 185:

Unless otherwise agreed, an agent is subject to a duty to keep, and render to his principal, an account of money or other things which he has received or paid out on behalf of the principal.

Where such fiduciary relation exists the principal may invoke the aid of a court of equity in requiring an accounting by his agent.

In an action for an accounting, the agent has the burden of proving that he paid to the principal or otherwise properly disposed of the money or other thing which he is proved to have received from the principal.

We do not agree that the acceptance by the beneficiaries of the income reports for the years 1951 to 1955, both inclusive, was a valid and sufficient reason for denying the prayer for an accounting. Clearly, these reports did not constitute an annual accounting between the parties and a settlement of their transactions. As has been said, the reports merely showed a list of items of income and disbursements and the amount of cash in bank for the respective years. There was no showing that the stated amount of cash had been reconciled with the records of the estate or those of the bank. Nor was there any evidence that the trustees, beneficiaries and Pulley agreed or considered that they were final accountings for the respective years.

But even if the furnishing and acceptance of these reports be considered an account stated for the respective years, it does not constitute an estoppel but is subject to impeachment for mistake or error clearly proved.

Neither do we agree with the trial court's holding that since the beneficiaries knew of and acquiesced in Pulley's "method of bookkeeping and the method in which the business was conducted," they are estopped to demand an accounting of him. There is no showing that his method of keeping his books and conducting the business were improper. Indeed, he insists in his brief that these were proper and that his records correctly show his transactions. Nor is there any evidence that the beneficiaries had actual or implied knowledge of, or acquiesced in, the discrepancies disclosed by the evidence, or the lack of records and vouchers which might have explained and accounted for such discrepancies. Not until they received the auditors' preliminary report in August, 1956, did the beneficiaries know of these alleged discrepancies and lack of adequate records. Within a few months thereafter the present suit was brought. Hence, there is no showing that the beneficiaries were guilty of laches which would preclude their right to require an accounting of Pulley for the recent period in controversy, from 1951 to 1955, both inclusive.

Principal's Duties to Agent

Duty to Compensate Agent. As a general rule the relation of principal and agent is created by contract, and the contract creating the agency will stipulate the compensation the agent is to receive for his services. In such cases, if a controversy arises as to the compensation due the agent, the rights of the agent will be determined by interpreting the contract. If there is no express agreement creating the agency or if the agreement creating the agency does not stipulate the amount of compensation to be paid to the agent, whether or not he is to be compensated will be determined from the relation of the parties and the surrounding circumstances. In such cases, if the agent is to be compensated, he is entitled to the reasonable value of the services rendered.

The courts have held that the agent is not entitled to compensation (1) if he is also representing interests adverse to those of the principal without the knowledge or consent of the principal, (2) if he is guilty of fraud or misrepresentation, (3) if he is negligent in the performance of his duties and his negligence results in material injury to his principal, or (4) if he is transacting business which is illegal.

Duty If Compensation Is Contingent.   Frequently, the agent's compensation is contingent on his accomplishment of a stipulated result. In such cases, he is not entitled to compensation until he has accomplished the result, regardless of how much effort he expends in attempting to do so. If the agent is to be paid on a contingent basis, the principal must cooperate with him in the accomplishment of the result and must not do anything which will prevent him from earning his compensation. If the principal by his acts prevents the agent from accomplishing the stipulated result, he (the agent) will be entitled to the designated compensation.

When the agent has accomplished the stipulated result, he is entitled to his compensation even though the principal is not benefited by the agent's performance. For example, suppose a salesman is to be paid a commission on all orders accepted and approved by his principal. The principal has accepted and approved orders taken by the salesman but, as the result of a shortage of materials, is unable to produce and ship the goods. The principal must pay the agent the agreed commission on the orders taken and approved. On the other hand, no matter how hard the salesman works, if he obtains no orders, he is entitled to no compensation.

Compensating Professional Agents.   The services rendered by professional agents are of such a nature that the compensation for such services is frequently a combination of a retainer and a contingent fee. As a general rule, the duties of the agent, the conditions which must be fulfilled, and the amount of his compensation are established by usage. However, the contract of employment usually will be in writing, and it will include provisions covering these points. The statutes of some states provide that contracts of employment of defined types of professional agents must be in writing, and if they are not, the agent is not entitled to recover compensation.

Brokers are usually paid a commission on business transacted for the principal. For example, the commission paid a real estate broker is commonly 6 percent of the sale price of the property sold, and the commission is earned when the broker finds a buyer "ready, willing, and able" to buy on terms acceptable to the principal. The commission of stockbrokers is standardized throughout, and their relation to their customers is also standardized. Generally, factors or commission merchants are paid a percentage of the amount received for property sold. The *del credere* agent, since he guarantees the credit of the purchaser, is paid on the basis of money actually collected. However, if the *del credere* agent extends credit and fails to collect, he must bear the loss.

Auctioneers are usually paid a percentage of the amount received for property sold.

An attorney may be paid a fee, or he may be paid on a contingent basis. In handling claims, such as collections and claims for damages for negligent injury to property or person, the attorney may take the case on a contingent basis. He will be paid a percentage of money actually collected.

Reimbursement for Expenditures.   If the agent has made advancements in behalf of the principal in the transaction of the principal's business and within the scope of the agent's authority, the agent is entitled to reimbursement for all such advancements. Also, if the agent has suffered losses in the conduct of the principal's business, the principal is legally bound to indemnify the agent for such losses, provided the agent has acted within the scope of his authority.

Summary

The principal owes a duty to pay the agent any compensation due him by the terms of the contract of employment. If there is no agreement as to the compensation to be paid to the agent and it is clear that the agency is not gratuitous, the principal must pay the reasonable value of the agent's services.

If the agent's compensation is made contingent on his accomplishing a stipulated result, the principal must cooperate with the agent in its accomplishment and must pay him when he has accomplished the result.

Professional agents may be compensated on a fee basis or on a contingent basis. Performance required and commission charged by certain types of professional agents are standardized.

The principal must reimburse the agent for all money advanced and expenditures made in the course of the performance of his duties, if the advances or expenditures are expressly or impliedly authorized.

Axilbund v. *McAllister*

180 A.2d 244 (Sup. Ct. Pa. 1962)

Action by Jacob Axilbund and partners (plaintiffs) against McAllister and 917 Filbert Street Corp. (defendants) to recover a commission on the sale of the Filbert building. The trial gave judgment to Filbert (McAllister had died) notwithstanding a verdict for Axilbund. Reversed and new trial directed.

Axilbund learned that Filbert wished to sell its building and McAllister, president of Filbert, promised Axilbund that "if they produced a purchaser for the premises for $300,000 net, the usual brokerage commission would be paid." Axilbund told

McAllister that he had a client named Gross who could use the building. He showed Gross the building, informed him it was available at $315,000, and provided him with additional information. He talked to Gross on the telephone several times over several months, even after Gross told him he was not interested in the building. Unknown to Axilbund, Gross purchased the building directly from McAllister for $295,000.

Filbert's defense to Axilbund's claim to the commission was (1) that the sale was induced by direct contact between Gross and McAllister and (2) that if there was any contract between Axilbund and Filbert it was a "special contract," i.e., that Axilbund was retained on a non-exclusive basis to sell the building for not less than $300,000 net and that Axilbund had not performed that condition of the contract.

JONES, JUSTICE.   In this area of the law certain principles are well established: (1) a broker cannot recover a commission, even though he brought the seller and buyer together, unless he can prove a contract of employment, express or implied, oral or written, between himself and the buyer (or seller) or an acceptance and ratification of his acts by the buyer (or seller); in the absence of an exclusive agency, if the actions of a broker constitute the efficient cause of the production of a buyer (or seller), he is generally entitled to his commission even though the sale was finally concluded and completed by the seller (or buyer) himself, or another broker; (3) the mere fact that the broker has carried on negotiations with a prospective buyer (or seller) does not entitle the broker to a commission unless his efforts constituted "the efficient procuring cause of the sale"; (4) where the prospective buyer (or seller) and the seller (or buyer) or the broker-agent fail to reach an agreement and there is a *break in their negotiations,* and, at a later date, the property is sold to (or bought by) the same prospective buyer, the original broker is not entitled to a commission.

. . . Filbert contends that this oral contract was a "special contract," which constitues an exception to the principles usually applied in this area of the law.

Section 447 of the *Restatement of the Law, Agency,* recognizes this exception: "An agent whose compensation is conditional upon procuring a transaction on specified terms is not entitled to such compensation if, as a result of his efforts, a transaction is effected on different or modified terms, although the principal thereby benefits." Comment a, Section 447 states: ". . . a clearly expressed condition that the principal will pay a commission only if the agent's services result in a transaction with another on specified terms is binding, and the agent is not entitled to a commission if the principal, acting in good faith, . . . enters into a transaction with another procured by the agent, but with terms less favorable to the principal." *Restatement of Law 2d, Agency,* §447, p. 354.

There is adequate evidence on this record that Axilbund brought Gross and Filbert together but there is no evidence that Gross was ready and willing to pay such price for the building as would *net* Filbert $300,000 *and* yield a commission to Axilbund. Therefore, Axilbund did not perform in accordance with the terms of the contract. Under such circumstances, the sale by Filbert to Gross of this building for $295,000 *net* would not entitle Axilbund to a commission *unless Filbert had acted fraudulently or in bad faith.* Whether Filbert acted fraudulently or in bad faith was never submitted to nor passed on by the jury in the court below.

Termination of Agent's Powers

General Rules. Since an agent's authority is derived from the will of the principal, such authority terminates when the agent knows, or the circumstances are such that he should know, that the principal does not wish him to continue to exercise the authority vested in him. An agent's authority to represent the principal may be terminated, yet the agent may continue to have the power to bind the principal if dealing with persons who have dealt with him before and who have had no notice or knowledge of the termination of his authority. Even though the agency is terminated, the agent may still have apparent authority to bind the principal.

Termination by Will of Parties. The agency relation may be terminated at the will of either the principal or the agent, and no formalities are necessary for such termination. All that is needed is that the principal indicate that he does not wish the agent to represent him or that the agent indicate that he does not intend to represent the principal. This may be brought about by the mutual consent of the parties or in violation of an existing contract of employment. If either party, in terminating the agency relation, breaches the contract of employment, he is liable in damages to the injured party.

Termination by Contract Provisions. If the contract of agency provides that the agency is to continue for a specified time, it will terminate on the expiration of the time stipulated, and if no time is stipulated, it terminates on the expiration of a reasonable time. If the agent is appointed to accomplish a specific result, the agency terminates on the accomplishment of the desired result. If the agency contract provides that the agency shall terminate on the happening of a specified event, it will then terminate when such event happens.

Termination by Change of Circumstances. Certain changes or happenings may cause the termination of the agency. The courts have held that, as a general rule, the agency is terminated by (1) the death of either the principal or the agent, (2) the insanity of the principal (to continue the period of insanity), (3) the bankruptcy of the principal (as to matters affected by the bankruptcy), (4) the bankruptcy of the agent (under limited circumstances), (5) the objective of the agency becoming illegal, (6) impossibility of performance, (7) the disqualification of principal or agent (loss of license when license is required), (8) loss or destruction of subject matter of agency, or (9) changes in values or in business conditions.

In general, the basis for holding that the agency is terminated on the happening of the events listed above is that it is reasonable to believe that the principal, if he knew the circumstances, would not wish the agent to act according to his original intent, or that the event is such that the accomplishment of the objective is rendered impossible or illegal. In most of the situations mentioned, there may be circumstances which justify the courts in holding that the general rule does not apply.

Termination of Powers Given as Security. A power given as security is, in the older cases and texts, referred to as an agency coupled with an interest. The relation arises when a party has a property interest in the subject matter of the agency and the power is granted for the purpose of protecting such interest. The commonest example of such an agency is a security transaction in which the party secured or some person acting for his protection is authorized to sell the property pledged as security in the event of default. For instance, suppose Allen loans Peters $1,000, and Peters pledges his diamond ring as security for the repayment of the loan. Under the terms of the pledge agreement, Allen is authorized, as Peters' agent, to sell the ring at public or private sale in the event that Peters defaults in the repayment of the money loaned. Allen has a power given as security. Such a power is irrevocable by the party granting the power and is not terminated by the death or incapacity of the grantor of the power.

A power given as security is terminated by the discharge of the obligation secured. In the above example, if Peters repays the $1,000 before default or before Allen exercises the power, Allen's power is terminated. Also, the power holder, if he be of full capacity, or likewise the beneficiary of the power, may surrender the power, or it may be terminated by its exercise becoming illegal.

Notice to Third Persons. An agent may have apparent authority to bind his principal after the termination of the agency. If the agency is general, third persons who have transacted business with the principal through the agent are justified in believing that the agent still has authority to represent the principal unless they have notice or knowledge of the termination of the agency. If the principal wishes to protect himself against the results of the acts of a former agent, he must give third persons, who have dealt with him through the agent, notice of the termination of the agency. Good business practice dictates that personal notice be given to such third persons. As to all other persons, notice by publication is usually sufficient.

If the agency is terminated by the death of the principal, the agent will not have the power to bind the estate of his deceased principal; and as a general rule, any act of the agent after the death of the principal will not bind the deceased principal's estate even though at the time of the transaction neither the agent nor the third person had notice of the principal's death.

This rule places a heavy burden on innocent agents and third persons who act without notice or knowledge of the principal's death. In some states the rule has been relaxed by statute. In general, the rule is not applied to banks that pay checks which have been issued prior to the drawer's death but presented for payment after his death and before the bank has notice of his death, and checks which are in the process of being collected at the time of the drawer's death. (Uniform Commercial Code, Section 4–405.)

Summary

The relationship of principal and agent may be terminated at the will of either the principal or the agent. If the termination of the agency is a breach of the contract of employment, the injured party is entitled to a judgment for the resulting damage. The agency may be terminated by the terms of the appointment, the accomplishment of its objective, the death of the principal or agent, the illegality of the objective, the loss or destruction of the subject matter of the agency, or the happening of events which would make it reasonably clear that the principal would not wish the authority of the agent to continue.

A power given as security is created when the power is granted for the protection of the power holder or third person. It is not revocable by the grantor of the power or affected by his death or incapacity.

If notice of the termination of the agency is not given to third persons who have been dealing with the agent, and they have no knowledge of the termination, the principal will be bound by the acts of the agent. At common law, this rule did not apply if the agency was terminated by the death of the principal, and the common-law rule applies today with some exceptions, especially as to the payment of checks.

Problem Cases

1. Hoggan and Hall operated an incorporated advertising agency for 10 years. They then accepted Higgins as a third stockholder and director. Three months later it lost its biggest account. When the subsequent month's results showed a loss, Higgins called a meeting and suggested that Hoggan's salary be eliminated. Hoggan said he would take any cut in salary the others would take. Higgins then said he would leave the company. The following week Hall and Higgins contacted most of the accounts they had been serving to ask them to go with them into a new firm, Hall and Higgins. Four accounts did shift. They had been with Hoggan and Hall for 10, 8, and 6 years respectively. Hoggan, Hall and Higgins, Inc. sued for damages for loss of business on grounds that Hall and Higgins violated their fiduciary duty as employees of the corporation. Are Hall and Higgins liable?

2. Merkley employed MacPherson, a realtor, to find a buyer for Merkley's apartments. MacPherson located a buyer and presented a purchase agreement to Merkely, which Merkley signed. The agreement stated that MacPherson had received from the buyers and was holding earnest money in the form of a demand note for $2,700, and it provided that upon forfeiture by the buyers the earnest money should be divided equally between Merkley and MacPherson. The buyers refused to complete the sale, forfeiting

the earnest money under the agreement. However, MacPherson was unable to produce the note upon the demand of Merkely, having negligently failed to procure it from the buyers. Merkley sues MacPherson for the amount of the note. Is he entitled to all or any part of this amount?

3. Baskin asked Dam, a realtor, to find a lot for him in a certain area. There was no agreement either on the price of the lot or on the amount of the commission. Dam looked for a lot and told several people in the area that Baskin was looking for a lot to buy. Dam located a lot, showed it to Baskin. Dam represented that he owned it, and agreed to sell it to Baskin for $6,400. Dam then bought it for $5,000. However, instead of carrying out his agreement with Baskin, he sold it at a higher price to another buyer. Baskin seeks to recover Dam's profit because of breach of duty as his agent. Is Dam Baskin's agent and is he entitled to the $1,400?

4. Mrs. Moon had a stroke and subsequently suffered from mental depression. Her physician prescribed drugs and gave psychotherapy. He found that the farm she owned was the source of several unhappy comments and produced little income. He advised her to sell it, recommending his father-in-law, Phipps, as the only realtor he knew that he could trust. Phipps took Mrs. Moon to the farm, and then while his wife gave her refreshments, he got her to sign what she thought was a listing agreement. Later she discovered that it was an agreement giving Phipps an option to purchase the farm on installments for $12,500. The farm had a value of $25,000. Can Mrs. Moon rescind the option agreement?

5. Josefsberg was given a five-year appointment as U.S. sales representative by Fricke & Son, a small manufacturer of dies and molds used in fabricating plastic products. Josefsberg sold the molds to three companies in which he had financial interests. Fricke & Son was aware of his interest in two of these companies, but not in Dale Co. None of his associates in these companies knew of his commission arrangement with Fricke & Son. Fricke & Son, learning of Josefsberg's interest in Dale Co., refused to pay commissions on his sales. Can Josefsberg recover the agreed upon commissions on his sales to Dale Co.?

6. Jarrell furnished McQueen certain appliances to be built into a new house McQueen was constructing for sale. Dallas Title Co. was financing the project, and its authorized agent promised Jarrell that Dallas Title Co. would withhold and pay over to Jarrell, when the house was sold, the amount due Jarrell for the appliances furnished by him for the house. The house was sold, but Dallas Title Co. did not withhold and pay to Jarrell the amount of his claim. Jarrell was unable to collect for the appliances and sued Dallas Title Co. to recover the amount of his loss. Dallas Title Co. set up as a defense that its promise to collect was a promise to act as a gratuitous agent and that it was not liable for the loss. Is Dallas Title Co. liable to Jarrell for the loss?

7. Mitton, as agent for Granite Insurance Co., issued an insurance policy to Construction Co. on its heavy machinery. The policy contained landslide and flood coverage. Granite Insurance Co. ordered Jones, its state agent, to instruct Mitton to cancel the landslide and flood provisions of the policy. After some delay, Mitton canceled the landslide coverage but did not cancel the flood coverage. The machinery covered by the policy was damaged by flood, and Granite Insurance Co. had to pay Construction Co. $11,612.23. Granite Insurance Co. sued Mitton to recover the $11,612.23 it had paid out on the flood coverage. Is Granite Insurance Co. entitled to a judgment?

8. Collection Agency entered into an agreement with Wanamaker whereby Wanamaker submitted its delinquent accounts to Agency for collection. The agreement provided that Agency would be paid a fee for collection based and contingent upon the accounts

it successfully collected. The arrangement continued with Agency being paid for the accounts it collected until Wanamaker notified Agency that its services were no longer desired. Agency then sued Wanamaker alleging that it was entitled to a fee based on all the accounts referred to it, both collected and uncollected, because Wanamaker had not shown "just cause" in terminating Agency relationship. Must Wanamaker pay for the uncollected accounts?

9. Hoffman was a free-lance salesman in the Pittsburgh area for Lomma Enterprises, which manufactured miniature golf courses and related equipment. It was agreed that Hoffman would be paid a commission on any sale he made. The percentage varied with the price of the product sold, but was 12 percent for sales amounting to more than $9,900. Lomma directed Hoffman to contact a prospect named Castellucci, but when it appeared that he was considering a number of pieces of equipment, Hoffman was told to stay out and that Lomma's officers would negotiate directly. A sale amounting to $37,500 was concluded but no commission was paid. Lomma argued that Hoffman was authorized only to sell small prefabricated installations and that there was a break in the negotiations when Castellucci executed a contract with a. competitor. Neither Lomma nor Hoffman was aware of this contract when it was made and it was never executed. Is Hoffman entitled to a commission on the sale?

PART V *Partnerships*

chapter 19. Creation of Partnership

Introduction

Historical Background. The basic concept of a partnership, two or more people joining forces to attain benefits for their common welfare, was practiced in prehistoric times. The Babylonians, a commercial and agricultural people, were familiar with the partnership, and provisions of the Code of Hammurabi—2300 B.C.—included provisions regulating partnerships. Under Hebrew law the Jews, who were a pastoral people, held land jointly from the earliest time in a crude form of partnership. At a later date, when Jewish commerce was carried on by the caravans, men would join their capital and labor and organize the caravans, and would share the profits and losses of such undertakings. These early partnerships were organized to undertake a single venture and were in many respects similar to our modern joint venture.

The partnership concept was highly developed in Roman law, and the definition of partnership in the Justinian Code does not differ materially from that in our Uniform Partnership Act. The partnership was likewise known in the Asiatic countries. The Chinese law of partnerships, although it differs in many respects from the law of Western nations, includes many rules which are similar to English partnership law.

During the Middle Ages, much of the trade between nations was carried on by partnerships, and partnership law became a well-developed part of the law merchant. When the law merchant was adopted by the English courts as part of the common law, the mercantile law of partnerships, with some modifications, became the partnership law of England. When the United States became an independent nation, it adopted the English common law insofar as it was suitable to social and economic conditions in the United States; consequently, we in effect adopted the English law of partnerships.

419

Uniform Partnership Act.   The Commissioners on Uniform State Laws drafted a Uniform Partnership Act which has been adopted by 40 states. Dr. Samuel Williston stated the purpose of the uniform laws as follows:

(1) To produce uniformity of law. (2) To state the law in a compendious form in which it will be susceptible to easier reference and more exact determination than if sought from decisions. (3) To settle uncertain questions of law without litigation. Legislation is cheaper than litigation as a means of fixing the law in these particulars. . . . (4) To harmonize into a more consistent whole a body of doctrines, many of which have grown up, if not haphazardly, at least without particular reference to one another.

The Uniform Partnership Act was not intended to include every phase of partnership law, nor was it intended to reform the law. It does cover the basic law. As to what may be termed the fringes of the law, the act provides: "Section 5. Rules for Cases Not Provided for in This Act. In any case not provided for in this act the rules of law and equity, including the law merchant, shall apply."

Nature of Partnership.   A partnership is an organization created for the purpose of carrying on a business for profit. In our economy the partnership holds a place midway between a single proprietorship and a corporation. A partnership is defined in the Uniform Partnership Act (6) [1] as an association of two or more persons to carry on as co-owners a business for profit. This definition excludes those associations organized to accomplish other objectives.

Many unincorporated associations, such as church groups, classes in schools and colleges, clubs, and political groups, may transact a substantial volume of business in the carrying-out of their objectives, and they may realize a profit from the business carried on, but since the profits are used in furthering some objective of the association and are not distributed to the members, such associations are not partnerships. In discussing the partnership, we shall confine ourselves to the partnership as defined in the Uniform Partnership Act.

Partnership Not an Entity.   In its basic organization a partnership is not a legal entity, that is, it does not have a legal existence separate and apart from the persons associated together to create it; it is not a legal person. However, businessmen, in carrying on a partnership business, treat the partnership as an entity, and in several situations the courts treat it as such.

A partnership is treated as an entity for the purpose of keeping partnership accounts. The capital contributed to the partnership, generally referred to as the "firm," is treated as a debt owed by the firm to the contributing partners. On the books of the partnership, all transactions are entered as firm transactions, and profits are distributed to the partners as a distribution of firm profits.

The separateness of the firm and the individual partners is recognized by the federal income tax statutes and by the Federal Bankruptcy Act. At com-

---

[1] The numbers in the parentheses refer to the sections of the Uniform Partnership Act.

mon law a suit by a partnership or against a partnership had to be brought in the name of the individual partners. Such a case would usually be titled "John Adams and William Blair, Copartners, doing business as Adams and Blair Company." A number of states have statutes permitting suit to be brought against the partnership in the partnership name, but such statutes are generally held not to be mandatory. However, in Lousiana, which follows the civil law, a commercial partnership is held to be an entity, and suit must be brought in the partnership name.

The English concept that a partnership is not an entity is reflected in the lack of formal requirements for the organization of a partnership and in the absence of special statutes regulating the business of a partnership. A partnership may be formed to operate any legitimate business by the mutual agreement of the partners. They do not have to obtain permission of the state to carry on a business as partners. In fact, a partnership may be organized without even a formal agreement between the partners. It may arise out of the conduct of the parties. The right of the partnership to carry on intrastate business in states other than the state of domicile of the partners is the same as that of a natural person.

Partnership versus Corporation. The partnership and the corporation each have their place in our economy. The ease with which a partnership may be organized, the lack of special regulation of the partnership with the accompanying freedom from filing reports, and the freedom from special taxes make the partnership a desirable form of organization for small businesses and for business ventures which will be of relatively short duration. It may prove a desirable form of organization until a business is established as a going concern, at which time the parties may wish to incorporate. They may not wish to incur the expense of incorporating until they are reasonably certain that their business venture will be a success.

The corporation has several advantages over the partnership. The principal advantage is that of limited liability of the shareholders. A shareholder risks only his initial investment, while a partner is personally liable for all the obligations of the partnership. However, the limited liability of the shareholders of small corporations may be defeated by creditors insisting that the shareholders guarantee the obligations of the corporation. Two other important advantages are the continuous life of the corporation and the transferability of the shareholder's interest in the corporation. A partnership is dissolved by the death or withdrawal of a partner. The existence of a corporation is not affected by the death of a shareholder or by a shareholder's sale of his stock.

A corporation has other advantages over a partnership. As a general rule a corporation can acquire needed capital with less difficulty than can a partnership. Limited liability encourages small investors to buy corporate stock. Also, as a general rule the centralized management of a corporation has proven to be more efficient than the management of a partnership, especially if the organization is composed of many persons.

Summary

The partnership was known from the earliest times in Asia, the Middle East and Europe. The partnership concepts of the Romans were highly developed and one type of partnership recognized by them was quite similar to ours today.

Mercantile partnerships were common in the Middle Ages in Europe and when the law merchant became a part of the common law of England, its rules on partnership became English partnership law. This became the basis for American partnership law. The Uniform Partnership Act has been adopted by most jurisdictions in the United States.

A partnership is not considered as an entity having an existence separate and apart from the persons who have associated together to form it. However, in the carrying-on of the business of the partnership, the partners treat it as an entity.

Under some circumstances a partnership may have some advantages over a corporation, while under other circumstances the corporation is the more desirable form of business organization. The partnership may be organized without complying with any set formalities. It is almost free from special regulations, and its right to transact intrastate business in states other than the state of domicile of the partners is the same as that of an individual. The corporation has the advantage of limited liability of the shareholders, continuous life, and the right of a shareholder to transfer his interest in the corporation without affecting the existence of the corporation.

Creation of Partnership

No Formalities Required. A partnership may be organized without the necessity of complying with statutory formalities. Persons have, from the earliest times, been free to combine their capital and skill in the operation of a business, and an agreement to operate a business as partners has never been considered as an illegal restraint of trade, even though such an association does tend to reduce competition. If two or more persons enter into an agreement to form a partnership, or if they do those acts which are characteristic of a partnership, the relation arises.

Intent of Parties. In the early English and American cases the courts held that if the parties divided the profits of a venture, they were liable to third persons as partners. This rule was both impractical and illogical, but it was applied by the courts until modern times. Today, in the United States, the courts apply, with few if any exceptions, the intent rule in determining the existence of a partnership. That is, they pose the question: "Did the parties intend to form a partnership?" In answering this question, the subjective intent of the parties is immaterial. Intent is determined by the words and acts of the parties, interpreted in the light of surrounding circumstances.

If the parties have drafted and signed written articles of partnership, the judge will interpret the writing and determine whether or not a partnership exists. If the parties declare in their agreement that they are partners, their declaration will be given weight by the judge in interpreting the agreement, but it will not be accepted as conclusive evidence of the existence of a partnership. Likewise, if the parties expressly state that they did not intend to form a partnership, this declaration is not conclusive. What the parties have done, not their declaration of their intentions, is controlling. In the absence of written articles of partnership, it is often difficult to determine whether or not a partnership exists. The existence of the partnership is a question of fact to be determined by the jury, or by the judge in a nonjury case.

Tests of Existence of Partnership. Since the intention of the parties to organize a partnership is determined objectively, the courts analyze the facts surrounding the relation, and if certain combinations of elements exist, they will hold that the parties are partners. No element standing alone is conclusive proof of the existence of a partnership. The sharing of the profits and losses of the enterprise is prima facie evidence of the existence of a partnership, and unless there is substantial evidence which disproves such existence, proof of the sharing of profits and losses will justify the court in holding that a partnership exists.

The sharing of profits without the sharing of losses is evidence of the existence of a partnership. However, the Uniform Partnership Act expressly provides (7 [4]) that no inference that a party is a member of a partnership shall be drawn solely because he receives a share of the profits (1) as payment of a debt, (2) as wages or as rent, (3) as an annuity to a deceased partner's widow or others, (4) as interest on a loan, or (5) as consideration for the sale of goods.

The courts have held that the division of the gross proceeds of a business is not a sharing of profits. For example, the typical crop-share lease, where the crop produced is divided between the landowner and the tenant, does not make the landowner and the tenant partners in the operation of the farm.

Another element which is considered in determining the existence of a partnership is community of interest. The definition of a partnership in the Uniform Partnership Act includes the requirement of community of interest, in that it provides for the operation of the business "as co-owners." This does not make all co-owners of property partners. Persons may own property as joint tenants, tenants in common, or tenants by the entirety and as such share the net income from the property and not be partners. On the other hand, a person may be a member of a partnership and have no property interest in the property used by the partnership in the operation of its business. The courts have held that a business, separate and apart from the assets used in the operation of the business, is property. Under the provisions of the Uniform Partnership Act, it is the business which is co-owned by the partners. The community of interest is in the profits of the business and like rights.

A voice in the management of the business standing alone is not conclusive proof of the existence of a partnership. However, as a general rule the sharing of profits and a voice in the management of the business will be sufficient to justify the court in holding that the person is a partner. For example, if a landlord, an employee, or a person loaning the partnership money is to receive in return a share of the profits as rent, wages, or interest, and is also given a voice in the management of the business, he will be held to be a partner.

Summary

No formalities need be complied with in forming a partnership; the intent of the partners is controlling, not the subjective or undisclosed intent but the intent as evidenced by the agreements and acts of the parties.

There is no simple test for the existence of a partnership. However, sharing in profits and losses, community of property, and voice in the management are the principal tests of the existence of a partnership. Sharing of profits and losses is prima facie evidence of the existence of a partnership, and sharing of profits and losses and having a voice in the management of the business have been held to be conclusive evidence of the existence of a partnership.

Rosenberger v. Herbst
232 A.2d 634 (Sup. Ct. Pa. 1967)

This was an action by Rosenberger d/b/a Clover Leaf Mill (plaintiff) against Herbst (defendant) on account for grain, feed and fertilizer. Judgment for Clover Leaf Mill and Herbst appealed. Reversed.

Clover Leaf Mill had sold farm supplies to Parzych who operated a farm owned by Herbst. Parzych operated the farm under an agreement which gave him use and occupancy of the farm and acknowledged his indebtness to Herbst in the amount of $6,000, repayable with 5% interest per annum. Herbst and Parzych were to equally share net profits and losses and the actual farming operation was to be "under the full control of Parzych." The agreement further recited that "the parties do not intend by this agreement to establish a partnership of any kind or type, but rather (a relation) of Debtor and Creditor and Landlord and Tenant." Parzych failed to pay for farm supplies purchased from Clover Leaf and Clover Leaf demanded payment for these debts from Herbst.

HOFFMAN, JUDGE. The Uniform Partnership Act, § 12(4), specifically provides:

The receipt by a person of a share of the profits of a business is prima facie evidence that he is a partner in the business, *but no such inference shall be drawn if such profits were received in payment:* (a) As a debt by installments or otherwise, (b) As . . . rent to a landlord . . . (d) As interest on a loan, though the amount of payment vary with the profits of the business . . . [Emphasis supplied.]

As previously noted, Parzych's indebtedness to Herbst was to be repaid from the proceeds of the farming operation. Furthermore, the agreement specifically provided that Herbst's remuneration was to be considered rental payments. Accordingly, no inference of partnership may be drawn from Herbst's receipt of a fractional share of the proceeds of the farming operation.

The construction of this contract must, ultimately, be determined by reference to the intent of the parties. Our Supreme Court has held: "[W]here [the parties expressly declare that they are not partners this settles the question, for, whatever their obligations may be as to third persons, the law permits them to agree upon their legal status and relations [as between themselves]." In light of the parties' express statement of intention, coupled with the inconclusive nature of the remainder of the agreement, we hold that defendant Herbst and Eugene Parzych were not partners *inter se.*

There is testimony in the record that Parzych represented himself as Herbst's partner to Clover Leaf, at some unspecified date, and that Clover Leaf allegedly relied on Herbst's credit, for some unspecified period of time. There is nothing in the record, however, to suggest that Herbst, himself, by words spoken or written or by conduct, ever made or consented to such a representation. Parzych's unauthorized statement, without more, cannot give rise to an estoppel against Herbst.

Capacity to Be a Partner

Infants and Insane Persons. In general, any natural person who has capacity to own property and to contract may become a member of a partnership. An infant may become a member of a partnership, but since an infant's contracts are voidable, the infant has the right to disaffirm the contract of partnership and withdraw at any time. Courts are divided as to whether the infant, upon disaffirmance, can recover from his adult partners the full amount of his investment or must bear his proportionate share of losses up to, but not exceeding, the amount of his investment. The fact that a member of the partnership is an infant does not make the contracts of the partnership voidable. In most jurisdictions a person officially adjudged insane cannot become a member of a partnership, and the Uniform Partnership Act (32) provides that upon the application of or for any partner, dissolution of a partnership shall be decreed if a partner has been adjudged insane. An insane person not officially declared insane stands in the same position as an infant.

Corporations.   For many years courts tended to hold that corporations had no implied power to enter partnerships and many secretaries of state refused to accept proposed articles of incorporation which expressly conferred such power. It was argued that the corporate directors could not surrender a portion of their control of the corporation to the other members of the partnership. However, courts and administrative officials recently have become increasingly willing to permit corporations to join partnerships if their articles expressly grant the power. The Uniform Partnership Act (2 and 6 [1]) includes corporations as persons who may form partnerships. The Model Business Corporation Act (4g) permits corporations to join partnerships. Courts have long permitted corporations to become a limited partner and have acquiesced in their participation in joint ventures.

Summary

Any natural person having the capacity to own property and to contract has the capacity to become a member of a partnership. An infant may disaffirm his contract of partnership and withdraw but courts differ as to whether he must bear losses up to the amount of his investment. There is a trend toward permitting corporations to become members of partnerships if their articles expressly so provide.

Carrying on a Business

Requirements for Carrying on a Business.   The carrying on of a business involves a continuity of business transactions pursued for an appreciable period of time with the objective of making a profit. Engaging in a single venture has been held not to be carrying on a business, even though the venture may involve several transactions. For example, the opening of a mine, the drilling for oil and gas, and the selling of an issue of corporate stock through a syndicate lack that continuity of business transactions usually associated with the carrying-on of a business.

Co-owners of a Business.   To have a partnership, two or more persons must carry on as co-owners a business for profit. The co-ownership of the partners may be limited to that of the partnership business, and it does not necessarily involve tangible property. For example, suppose Allen, a doctor, has an established practice and a fully equipped office. Allen enters into a partnership with Beech, a young doctor, to engage in the practice of medicine. Beech has no equipment. It is agreed that all the office equipment, etc., shall remain the individual property of Allen. Allen and Beech are co-owners of the business—practice of medicine—but the partnership of Allen and Beech owns no tangible property.

Co-owners Who Are Not Partners.   Persons may be co-owners of property and not be partners. Frequently, two or more persons will own property as tenants in common. For example, Allen, Beech, and Carter may own an apartment building as tenants in common and not be partners. They may rent the building as a unit and divide the net proceeds, or they may rent each apartment separately and divide the net proceeds and not be held to be partners. The renting of the apartment building or the separate apartments is not operating a business for profit. The owner of a farm and his tenant who own stock and equipment as tenants in common and who divide the proceeds of the farm are not, as a general rule, partners. Neither are farmers who organize an association to purchase a threshing machine for their several uses. The same would be true of business or professional men who organize an association to further or protect their common interests and purchase property for the use of the association. In each instance the parties are co-owners of property, but they are not carrying on a business and are not partners.

Business Must Be Carried on for Profit. The carrying on of a business for the purpose of making a profit to be distributed to the owners of the business is an essential element of a partnership. If an association of persons is carrying on a business for purposes other than the making of a profit for the owners, the association is not a partnership. Many charitable associations engage in business transactions with the expectation of making a profit, but any profits realized are to be used to further the objectives of the association and will not be distributed to its members. The undertakings of such associations are not classed as a carrying on of a business for profit, and the members of such associations are not partners.

Summary

The carrying on of a business involves a continuity of business transactions pursued for an appreciable period of time.

To have a partnership, the partners must carry on a business as co-owners. The required co-ownership of a business need not include co-ownership of the tangible property used in the business.

Co-ownership of property may be as joint tenants or as tenants in common, and the tenants will not be partners even though an income is realized from the property.

If the business carried on by an association of persons is not carried on for a profit, the members of the association are not partners.

Borum v. Deese
26 S.E.2d 538 (Sup. Ct. Ga. 1943)

This was an action by H. B. Deese and others (plaintiffs) against V. B. Borum and others (defendants) asking a decree partitioning certain real estate. Judgment for Deese and Borum appealed. Judgment affirmed.

Charlie Borum owned in his lifetime a lot with a residence thereon. Under the terms of his will this property was devised to his wife for life, the remainder to his four children. Charlie Borum died in 1929. The wife and four children occupied the premises as their home until the death of the wife after which the children continued to live together in the house. They agreed among themselves to occupy the residence as a home and to share equally the paying of taxes, insurance, repairs, improvements, and other expenses. In addition, they agreed to share jointly in their living expenses, including food and necessaries of life with the exception of clothing. The arrangement continued for several years.

H. B. Deese, claiming to have contributed $1,200 more than the others toward these purposes, brought this action asking that the property be sold and that out of the proceeds he be reimbursed for the $1,200 and that the balance be divided among the parties. Borum defended on the ground that the parties were partners and that the proper action was dissolution and winding-up of the partnership.

REID, CHIEF JUSTICE.   With reference to partnership our Code, ¶ 75–101, declares: "A partnership may be created either by written or parol contract, or it may arise from a joint ownership, use and enjoyment of the profits of undivided property, real or personal." The theory urged by Borum is that since the four remaindermen who were cotenants of the premises agreed to occupy them jointly and to maintain a home thereon, the expenses of which were to be equally shared by them, the relation thus created constituted such a partnership as must be first dissolved as provided by the Code, ¶ 75–106, which is that where there is a partnership at will, it "may be dissolved at any time by any partner on his giving three-months notice to his partners." In addition to what has been quoted from our Code on the subject, many definitions may be found as to what constitutes a partnership in the ordinary sense in which that term is used. We are not here involved with such inquiries as have often grown out of dealings between members of alleged partnerships and others. Our inquiry relates merely to the relationship between the alleged partners, i.e., the cotenants, who jointly owned the premises, no interest of third persons being involved, as was the case in *Butler* v. *Frank,* where Judge Powell pointed out from decisions of this court, and from other sources, various instances where a partnership relation would be declared. To constitute a partnership as between members there must ordinarily be more than mere common ownership or interest. So it is found that the term is used with reference to some business enterprise, or the joint pursuit of some objective, profit at least having some connection with it. This is not to be understood as an exact or embracing definition of a partnership, or even as a definition at all; but it is intended merely to point out what we generally have in mind when a partnership is referred to. Definitions may be found in 31 Words and Phrases as indexed on page 166, where it is pointed out at page 217 that "Partnership is the relation which subsists between persons carrying on a business in common with a view of profit. It is necessary to note the significance of the words 'carrying on a business,' which implies a relation entirely different from the enforced relation of tenants in common, as the owners of a ship or of a house, who must either let the property lie idle or keep it in some way occupied or used, deriving a return from such occupation or use." It is further said that a partnership is a legal entity distinct from its members. Many cases are there cited to support this view. Our own court has held, in *Drucker* v. *Wellhouse,* that "Though a firm or partnership is not a person, it is a legal entity, and for some purposes is recognized as a quasi person having powers and functions exercisable by one of the partners severally or all of them jointly." Likewise the distinction between the relation of cotenancy and that of partnership has been pointed out in 40 Am. Jur. 129, ¶ 5, in the following language: "While partnership property has many characteristics of an estate in common and of joint tenancy or cotenancy, the interest of the partners therein is neither that of joint tenants, tenants in common, nor cotenants. Their interest in the firm property is *sui generis.* Each is possessed of a joint interest in the whole, but does not own any separate part, and each has an undivided interest in the property of the partnership only after the debts are paid. A mere tenancy in common does not create a partnership, and a partnership will not be implied from the joint ownership or joint purchase of land, even when accompanied by an agreement to share the profits and losses of selling it; yet tenants in common may become partners, like other persons, where they agree to assume that relation towards each other." It will be noted that the language of our Code on the subject speaks of a partnership which may arise "from a joint ownership, use, and enjoyment of the profits of undivided property." In the present case, that these joint owners agreed to be equally responsible for taxes and upkeep of the property added nothing to the relation which already obtained between them, they being joint owners in equal parts. The only additional undertaking on their part as between themselves, appearing from Borum's petition, was that they would share living expenses. This, it seems to us, to be purely incidental to the other relation, and had no connection with the ownership of the land itself, and as such constituted no burden upon the land. Certainly no profit was contemplated by any agreement or facts which appear. The foregoing has been stated without reference to the question as to whether or not, if elements of a partnership appeared, the one here claimed would be valid as being sufficiently definite as to time.

Persons Represented to Be Partners

Effect of Holding out as Partner. Some of the earlier cases held that a person could become a member of a partnership by being held out as a partner, even though he never consented to becoming a partner and never actually participated in the affairs of the partnership. This theory of ostensible partnership has been abandoned. The Uniform Partnership Act (7 [1]) provides: "(1) . . . persons who are not partners as to each other are not partners as to third persons." However, a person not a partner may, by holding himself out or permitting himself to be held out as a partner, incur liability to a third person who has dealt to his injury with the partnership in reliance on such holding out. The liability is based on the theory of estoppel, not on the theory that the party is a member of the partnership. Before a person can recover, he must prove (1) that the party held himself out to him or permitted himself to be held out to him as a partner, (2) that in justifiable reliance on the holding out, he dealt with the partnership, and (3) to his injury. The only person who can hold a party liable as a partner is that person who knows of the holding out and in justifiable reliance thereon has dealt with the partnership to his injury.

Holding out or Consenting to Holding out.   The cases are not in accord as to what acts on the part of a person who has been held out to be a partner will amount to permission. Some of the earlier cases have held that if one is held out to be a partner and is aware of that fact, and yet does not take affirmative action to stop it, and also takes no action to notify the public that he is not a partner, he will have permitted himself to be held out as a partner. The later cases and the Uniform Partnership Act take the view that to be held liable as a partner, one must consent to the holding out. Under this view, knowledge that one is being held out as a partner, without other facts, will not amount to consent. For example, suppose that, although no partnership exists, Adams advertises in the local newspaper that he and Book are operating a garage as partners. Book will not have to run a notice in the local newspaper denying that he is Adams' partner in the garage business in order to protect himself from liability as Adams' partner.

Summary

Persons who are not partners as to each other are not partners as to third persons. However, if a person holds himself out as a partner or permits himself to be held out as a partner, he will be liable to a party who in justifiable reliance on the holding out has dealt with the partnership to his injury.

Unless the party being held out as a partner acquiesces in the holding out, thereby contributing to the creation of the appearance that he is a partner, he cannot be held liable as a partner.

Wisconsin Telephone Co. v. *Lehmann*
80 N.W.2d 267 (Sup. Ct. Wisc. 1957)

This was an action by Wisconsin Telephone Company (plaintiff) against Walter R. Lehmann (defendant) to recover a judgment for the unpaid balance of a telephone bill. Judgment for Wisconsin Telephone Company, and Walter R. Lehmann appealed. Judgment reversed and judgment entered for Walter R. Lehmann.

Walter R. Lehmann had been in business with his son, Wayne R. Lehmann. They were doing business under the name of W. R. Lehmann and Son but by February, 1952, Wayne had withdrawn and gone into business for himself as a dealer in calves.

Wayne lived across the road from his father, Walter R. Lehmann, and had his business headquarters in a building on his father's farm over which was a sign, "W. R. Lehmann & Son—Dairy Cattle." Telephone No. 196W was located in that building.

Commencing in February, 1952, Wisconsin Telephone Company (Telephone Co.) carried telephone No. 196W in the name of Wayne R. Lehmann. The bills were sent to and paid by Wayne. In May, 1953, Wayne requested Telephone Co. to list telephone 196W under the name of W. R. Lehmann & Son. The change was made, and thereafter bills were sent to W. R. Lehmann & Son, R. R. 4, Watertown (which was also Wayne's address), and were paid by check signed by Wayne. The bill for December, 1954, in the amount of $1,261.16, was not paid, and Telephone Co. sued Walter R. Lehmann to recover a judgment for this bill. There was no showing that Walter R. Lehmann knew that Wayne was going to list telephone No. 196W in the name of W. R. Lehmann & Son or that he consented thereto. Telephone Co. never billed Walter R. Lehmann for the service of telephone No. 196W until Wayne failed to pay the December bill.

WINGERT, JUSTICE. The general principle applicable to cases of this kind is stated by a leading authority as follows:

A person who is not actually a partner may render himself liable as though he were one, by so conducting himself as to reasonably induce third persons to believe that he is a partner and to act upon that belief. This rule is based upon the same principle as that which has been discovered in the law of Agency,—that a person may become liable for the acts of another who was not really his agent, if he has so conducted himself as to lead others reasonably to believe that such person was his agent. It is a case in which the principle of estoppel applies.

The principle has been codified in the Uniform Partnership Act, under the heading "Partnership by estoppel."

(1) When a person, by words spoken or written or by conduct, represents himself, or consents to another representing him to any one, as a partner in an existing partnership or with one or more persons not actual partners, he is liable to any such person to whom such representation has been made, who has, *on the faith of such representation, given credit to the actual or apparent partnership,* and if he has made such representation or consented to its being made in a public manner he is liable to such person, whether the representation has or has not been made or communicated to such person so giving credit. . . .

(2) When a person has been thus represented to be a partner in an existing partnership . . . he is an agent of the persons consenting to such representation to bind them . . . with respect to persons who *rely upon the representation.* . . .

The liability of the nonpartner being based on estoppel, it is essential to the cause of action that the party asserting liability must have been induced by the misleading appearance to change his position to his detriment.

It (partnership by estoppel) involves some express or implied representation by the person in question that he is a partner, in reasonable and bona fide reliance upon which the person now seeking to hold him liable as such has extended a credit, or otherwise changed his position, in such a manner that he will now be prejudiced if the representation be denied. . . . The party seeking to hold him liable as a partner must, in the exercise of reasonable prudence and good faith, have relied upon such condition or thing and been misled by it.

Estoppel *in pais* is an equitable doctrine, and in general does not operate against one unless his conduct has induced another to change his position to his prejudice.

Application of this principle to the evidence in the present case leads to the conclusion that there was no basis on which the jury could find for Telephone Co. There is no evidence in the record that Telephone Co. did anything it would not have done or refrained from doing anything that it otherwise would have done, had it known the true facts relative to the relationship between Walter R. Lehmann and Wayne. There is no evidence that Telephone Co. would not have furnished the service to telephone No. 196W or would have cut it off sooner if it had known that Wayne Lehmann was not a partner or authorized agent of Walter R. Lehmann. The service had theretofore been rendered when the telephone was listed in Wayne's name, and there is no showing that Telephone Co. would not have continued to render the service as long as the bills were paid, had it known that only Wayne would be responsible for payment. There is nothing to show that in changing the listing from Wayne's name to that of W. R. Lehmann & Son, Telephone Co. relied in any way on Walter R. Lehmann's credit.

Since Telephone Co. was seeking to hold Walter R. Lehmann liable by estoppel it had the burden of proving the elements of estoppel. Having failed to offer any proof of change of position to its prejudice in reliance on the misleading appearance Telephone Co. failed to make a *prima facie* case for the jury. Therefore, Walter R. Lehmann's motion for nonsuit should have been granted.

Joint Venture

Nature of Joint Venture. Courts have distinguished joint ventures (or joint adventures) from partnerships but the distinction is not clear cut. A joint venture (sometimes called a syndicate or pool or joint enterprise) is limited to a particular venture or transaction and it is intended that the relationship will dissolve when the venture is completed although this may require a number of years. Joint ventures are common in real estate transactions. Corporate promoters prior to incorporation and groups underwriting a corporate securities issue may also be treated as joint venturers. The relations between joint venturers are governed by practically the same rules of law as those that govern partnerships. However, the power of one member of the joint venture to bind the others is more limited.

Two or more corporations frequently join together to form a corporation to conduct some business in which both are interested. These are frequently referred to as joint ventures, but since incorporated they fall under the rules of corporation rather than partnership law.

Limited Partnership

Nature of Limited Partnership. A limited partnership is composed of one or more limited partners and one or more general partners. The liability of the limited partner or partners is limited to his or their contribution to the capital of the limited partnership. The liability of the general partner or partners for the obligations of the partnership is unlimited. It is the same as the liability of a partner in a general partnership.

Necessity for Enabling Statute. A limited partnership may not be organized unless such a partnership is permitted by the statutes of the state. A Uniform Limited Partnership Act was drafted, and this act has been adopted by 42 states. These statutes set out the requirements for the creation of a limited partnership and the rights and liabilities of the parties. They are similar in many respects to the general corporation-for-profit statutes.

Requirements for Creation of Limited Partnership. Two or more persons may organize a limited partnership. Under the provisions of the Uniform Limited Partnership Act the persons desiring to organize a limited partnership must sign, swear to, and file, with the county recorder or some other designated official, a certificate which states the name of the partnership, the character of its business, the location of its principal place of business, the term for which the partnership exists, the capitalization of the partnership, the contribution of the limited partner, and other general information regarding the rights of the partners between themselves.

Any business which may be carried on by a partnership may be carried on by a limited partnership. In general, the surname of the limited partner may not be used as part of the name of the limited partnership. The limited partner may not take part in the control of the business, and if he does, he is liable to creditors of the partnership as a general partner.

Summary

A limited partnership is composed of one or more limited partners and one or more general partners. The liability of the limited partner is limited to his contribution to the capital of the partnership. A limited partnership may not be organized unless its organization is authorized by the statutes of the state. To organize a limited partnership, the parties must sign, swear to, and file, with the designated official, a certificate which complies with the requirements of the statute.

Davis v. Davis

429 P.2d 808 (Sup. Ct. Ore. 1967)

This was an action by Robert Davis (plaintiff) against James Davis (defendant, who is no relation to Robert) seeking dissolution of a partnership and equal distribution of its assets. Judgment for Robert and James appealed. Judgment affirmed.

Robert and James were engaged in a trucking business. They had signed a certificate of limited partnership but did not file this certificate with the county clerk as required by statute. Throughout the years, Robert and James had assumed equal liability on debts of the partnership and had shared equally in the profits of the growing firm. During the last two years, Robert devoted more time to the actual running of the business than did James; however, during the middle period of the business relationship both partners had devoted equal time to its affairs. James elected to terminate the partnership and insisted that Robert was only a limited partner and entitled only to return of his original investment and his undistributed share of partnership profits. Robert claimed to be a general partner and sued for an equal distribution of the partnership assets.

GOODWIN, JUSTICE.   James relies primarily upon two facts in seeking to reverse the trial court's decision. First, it is conceded that in all the banking and other business transactions of the enterprise, the name "Davis Company, Oreg. Ltd." was used. Although this name is some evidence of the type of association intended, it is not conclusive. A name, if it does not reflect the true facts, cannot be used to the prejudice of the rights of third parties. In a case of an intramural dispute between the partners themselves, we believe that an inconsistency between the name of the enterprise and the method of doing business is even less significant that it would be if strangers were involved.

In addition to using a business name suggesting a limited partnership, the parties had, as noted, executed a certificate of limited partnership. The certificate was not filed with the county clerk as required by statute, however, and this failure to file tends to cast doubt on the effect the parties intended the certificate to have. Further, the certificate is merely a document required by statute for the effective formation of a limited partnership. Its purpose is to give notice to third parties dealing with the business. It does not purport to embody the entire business arrangement between the parties. Therefore, it is not as persuasive as evidence of intent as a comprehensive agreement would be.

When the evidence shows that the parties for many years conducted the business in every respect as a general partnership, and at no time as a limited partnership, any inference created by the certificate is quickly overcome. Whatever may have been the intention of the parties when they started the enterprise, their conduct proved beyond doubt that the parties were general partners from and after 1957.

Problem Cases

1. Buck and Aldridge commenced operation of a hay mill. Shortly thereafter they entered into written agreement which stated that Buck was leasing a barn and milling equipment to Aldridge in return for one third of the net profits of the mill.

    Buck devoted part of his time and Aldridge all of his time to operating the mill. Partnership tax returns had been filed. Buck had signed a contract which identified the mill business as a partnership and the signing parties as general partners. Goodpasture sued Buck as partner to collect an account against the hay mill. Buck denied being a partner and claimed to be a lessor. Is Buck a partner?

2. Johnson and McNaughton jointly leased a parcel of ground on which Johnson erected a store building at his own expense. McNaughton operated a package liquor store in the building under an agreement whereby McNaughton was to receive $60 per week in salary and was to pay 50 percent of the balance of the net profits to Johnson. Johnson loaned McNaughton the funds used for stocking the store but this was repaid. McNaughton carried on the business in his own name and performed all financial and management functions. The business ran into financial difficulty, and Escoe, alleging a partnership, sued Johnson as well as McNaughton to recover on dishonored checks. Did a partnership exist?

3. W. H. Teague, Mary J. Evans, and Sallie Mullins, brother and sisters, owned, in their own right, tracts of land which adjoined lands of their father, Lewis Teague, and of J. J. Evans and G. W. Fortner. On September 1, 1925, these persons executed what is called a "pool agreement" by which they conveyed to W. H. Teague all the unmined coal on their respective properties. W. H. Teague, as trustee, was to lease the land for coal-mining purposes. The accruing royalties were to be paid to the grantors according to the acreage owned by them. The right to mine coal on this land was granted to Tennessee Jellico Coal Company for a period of 50 years. Mary J. Evans died, and her husband, J. J. Evans, claimed her share of the royalties on the ground that she had only an interest in a mining partnership which under the statutes of the state descended as personalty to him as surviving husband. The heirs of Mary J. Evans deny the existence of a partnership and claim that the royalties are real estate and descend to them. Were the parties partners in a mining partnership?

4. The seven children of C. H. Sternberg inherited his farm. They entered into a detailed agreement making William, one of the heirs, manager of the farm with broad authority. He was paid an agreed compensation and was to distribute profits to the heirs when he deemed it advisable and could call on the heirs pro rata for money to operate the farm. He contracted with Sternberg Dredging Co. for dredging to be done on the farm and gave a promissory note signed by William as agent for the heirs. The note was not paid and at his death was filed as a claim against William's estate. His executor argues that the note is a partnership obligation, and the heirs deny the existence of a partnership. Was there a partnership?

5. Albina supplied scaffolding and cables to Safway under a contract which named Safway as "agent and representative" of Albina for sale, rental, and servicing of the equipment under terms, conditions, and prices prescribed by Albina. Title to all rental equipment remained in Albina, and Albina was entitled to 50 percent of its "suggested rental schedule" on all rentals of its equipment, regardless of the rental Safway actu-

ally received. Safway used its own rental forms, assumed all credit risks, and serviced all equipment. Abel was injured when a scaffold collapsed as a result of Safway's failure to repair damaged cables. Abel sues Albina and Safway as joint adventurers. Albina claims Safway was an independent contractor with reference to the equipment rental. Should Albina be held liable as a joint adventurer in the rental enterprise?

6. Blomquist Electric Company operated under a "Certificate of Formation of Limited Partnership" which designated Blomquist and Preston as general partners and Lowe as a limited partner. Preston left the partnership early in 1962. Blomquist and Lowe operated the business on this basis until September 3, 1963, when they filed a new partnership agreement which made no mention of Lowe remaining a limited partner.

Sometime after Preston's withdrawal, Power and Light extended credit to Blomquist Electric. In a suit to collect money due on that account, Preston claimed that he made a valid withdrawal prior to the extension of credit and Lowe maintained that the limited partnership certificate protected him from liability on the partnership debt. Can either Preston or Lowe be held liable on the partnership debt?

chapter 20. Relation of Partners between Themselves

Introduction

Nature of Relation. Partners bear toward each other a fiduciary relation of the highest order. It is one of mutual trust and confidence and is based on mutual good faith. The basic principles of agency law are applicable to the partnership. Each partner, in the carrying-on of the partnership business, acts as agent for the business and for the other members of the partnership. When a partnership is formed, the internal relationship, as well as that between the partnership and third persons, is defined by a body of developed law. The members of the partnership may, within certain limits, define the rights and duties owed to each other and may, by contract, alter in some respects the relation of the partners and the partnership to a contracting third person. In the absence of an agreement or contract, however, the rights and duties of the parties will be determined by the application of the rules and principles of partnership law.

Articles of Partnership. Formal articles of partnership are not essential to the creation of a partnership, but from the standpoint of good business practice, they are highly desirable. Although the partners cannot, by mutual agreement, relieve themselves of the fiduciary duty they owe each other or escape, without the consent of the third person, their unlimited liability on partnership obligations, there are many details of the relation which may be fixed by such agreement. If the parties execute carefully drafted articles of partnership which define in a fair degree of detail the important features of the partnership arrangement, the probability of future controversy is minimized.

Provisions of Articles of Partnership. Usually, the articles of partnership will give the name of the firm, the business to be carried on, the place at which the business is to be conducted, term of the partnership, capital investment of each partner, how the profits and losses will be shared, how the business will be managed, how books are to be kept, wages or drawing account of each partner, definition of the authority of the partners to bind the firm, provisions for withdrawal of partners, provision for dissolution and winding-up of the business, and often provisions for continuing the business after the death of one of the partners. Even in the most carefully drawn articles of partnership, it is impossible to anticipate all the contingencies which may arise in conducting the business. In the event a situation is not provided for in the articles of partnership, general partnership law will apply.

Summary

The partnership relation imposes on the members of the partnership certain ties. These duties are similar in many respects to the duties arising in the principal-agent relationship. A body of law has been developed which applies to the relationship.

The partners may, in a partnership agreement, define, within certain limits, their relationship to each other. They cannot, however, relieve themselves of the fiduciary duty they owe each other.

The partners should draw up articles of the partnership which will define the nature of the partnership business and the powers of the partners and will set out the basic organization of the partnership business.

Partnership Property

What Is Partnership Property?   The Uniform Partnership Act provides that (1) all property originally brought into the partnership stock or subsequently acquired by purchase or otherwise, on account of the partnership, is partnership property, and (2) unless the contrary intention appears, property acquired with partnership funds is partnership property. In determining whether or not an item is partnership property, one must determine whether the property was "originally brought into the partnership stock," whether it was subsequently acquired "on account of the partnership," or whether the property was acquired with partnership funds and was intended by the partners to be partnership property. The fact that an item of property is being used by the partnership in the operation of the partnership business does not necessarily indicate that it is partnership property. In the final analysis, it is the intention of the partners which is controlling.

The business will be partnership property, but all the tangible and intangible property, other than the business, may be individually owned by the members of the partnership, or may be rented by the partnership. In many respects, it is immaterial whether property used by a partnership in the operation of its business is partnership property or the property of the individual partners, since each partner is individually liable for all the obligations of the partnership. But if the partnership and the partners are insolvent, the ownership of property becomes important, since partnership creditors have first claim on partnership property and individual creditors have first claim on individual property.

Usually, a partnership commences business with capital contributed to it by the partners. However, the partnership, as such, may own no property other than the business. In the operation of the business the partnership may use property which is owned by the individual partners or which is loaned or rented to the partnership. As a general rule, money used by a partnership as working capital will be partnership property, and in the absence of strong evidence that such money was a loan to the partnership, it will be so held.

Property purchased with partnership funds and used for partnership purposes will be held to be partnership property, unless the intention of the partners to own such property as individual property is shown by clear and convincing evidence. And even then, if holding such property to be the individual property of the partners would result in defeating the rights of partnership creditors, the courts will refuse to rule it to be individual property irrespective of the intentions of the partners.

The goodwill of a partnership may be a valuable asset of the business; however, it is an intangible element of value which cannot be separated from the business as such and dealt with as a separate asset of the business. The courts have recognized the partnership name as a partnership asset and under some circumstances have granted to certain of the partners, on the dissolution of the partnership, the right to use the partnership name. Usually, the use of the partnership name will carry with it a portion of the goodwill of the business which formerly used the name.

Title to Partnership Property. The title to the personal property owned by a partnership may be held in the name of the partnership. At common law the courts held that since a partnership had no existence separate and apart from the members, real property could not be held in the name of the partnership but had to be held in the name of a member or in the names of the members of the partnership. The Uniform Partnership Act [8(3)] [1] provides: "Any estate in real property may be acquired in the partnership name. Title so acquired can be conveyed only in the partnership name."

Some of the states which have not adopted the Uniform Partnership Act have enacted statutes which enable partnerships to acquire and convey real property in the partnership name. In those states which have not enacted enabling statutes, the common-law rule is generally still followed.

---

[1] The numbers in the parentheses refer to the sections of the Uniform Partnership Act.

If real estate is deeded to the members of a partnership in their individual names as tenants in common or as joint tenants, or is deeded to one of the partners in his name, there is a strong presumption that it is the individual property of the parties or party named in the need, but this presumption may be overcome by evidence showing that it was acquired with the intent that it become partnership property.

If partnership real property has been conveyed to an individual partner or to the partners as tenants in common or as joint tenants, innocent third-party purchasers may acquire rights in the property superior to the rights of the partnership or to the rights of partnership creditors by virtue of the operation of the recording statutes.

Possession of Partnership Property.   Each partner has the right of possession of partnership property for partnership purposes. If a partner takes possession of partnership property for his own purposes without the consent of his partners and to their exclusion, he will have violated his duties as a partner, and his wrongful acts may be ground for the dissolution of the partnership. Although a partner has wrongfully deprived the partnership and his partners of the possession of partnership property, his partners cannot maintain a possessory action, such as replevin, against him, since the only remedy available to partners for breach of partnership duties is the remedy of dissolution and accounting.

Incidents of Partnership Ownership.   The partnership owns the partnership property as a unit; and the partners, as individuals, do not own proportional interests in separate items of partnership property. Under the Uniform Partnership Act (25), partnership property is owned by the partners as tenants in partnership.

The individual partner, as a tenant in partnership, has the right to possess partnership property and to have it used for partnership purposes. He cannot assign any interest in separate items of partnership property, and such separate items are not subject to levy of execution or attachment by the creditors of an individual partner. If partnership property is levied on or attached for partnership obligations, the individual partner has no right to claim such property as exempt under homestead or exemption laws.

Creditors of Individual Partner.   The nature of the interest of the individual partner in the partnership property is the basis of the rights of the individual partner's creditors against the partnership property. It is well settled that the creditor of a partner can acquire no greater rights in the partnership property than the debtor partner has. The problem has been: By what manner of process can the partner's interest be reached so that it may be applied to the discharge of his individual debts? Prior to the adoption of the Uniform Partnership Act, there was almost no consistency in the holdings of the courts.

In some jurisdictions the interest of a partner in the partnership property could not be reached by legal process. In other jurisdictions the theory of community of ownership of partnership property was recognized; and the courts held that levy could not be made on particular items of partnership property in satisfaction of a judgment against an individual partner but that the sheriff could levy on the entire assets of the partnership, take possession of them, and sell the debtor partner's interest in the assets. Technically, this procedure was in accord with the prevailing theory of the individual partner's interest in partnership assets, but the procedure was objectionable from a practical standpoint because of the interference with the operation of the partnership business during the period the partnership assets were in the possession of the sheriff. Also, one wishing to purchase the debtor partner's interest would have no way of determining the value of the interest. In several states, statutes have been passed defining the rights and duties of the parties. The objective of this legislation is to provide a procedure whereby the interest of the debtor partner can be reached by his creditors with a minimum of injury to the other partners. This objective is substantially accomplished under the provisions of the Uniform Partnership Act (28), which provides for the obtaining of a charging order by a judgment creditor of an individual partner. Under the charging order a receiver of the partner's interest in partnership profits may be appointed and the court may ultimately order the partner's interest in the partnership sold. Provision is made for the payment of the judgment by the other members of the partnership, thereby relieving the partnership from the charging order.

Summary

Only that property is partnership property which is intended by the partners to be such. As a general rule, property purchased with partnership funds for partnership purposes will be held to be partnership property. The name and the goodwill of a partnership are partnership property.

At common law, partnership real property could not be held in the name of the partnership; it had to be held in the names of the individual partners or in the name of a partner. However, under the Uniform Partnership Act and similar statutes, real property may be held and conveyed in the name of the partnership.

Each partner has the right to possess partnership property and to have it used for partnership purposes. Partnership property is owned by the partners as tenants in partnership, a type of unit ownership.

The individual creditors of a partner may reach the partner's interest in the partnership by legal process. At common law, the judgment creditor levied on all the assets of the partnership and sold the debtor partner's interest. Under the Uniform Partnership Act a judgment creditor of an individual partner may maintain a charging order and thereby obtain satisfaction of the judgment out of the debtor partner's interest in the partnership.

Pendleton v. Strange
381 S.W.2d 617 (Sup. Ct. Ky. 1964)

This was an action for the settlement of the affairs of a partnership. The court held that a 568-acre farm was the individual property of Strange, and Pendleton appealed. Judgment affirmed.

Malcolm E. Strange and Dwight L. Pendleton were partners in the practice of law and the operation of farms. There were no written articles of partnership. A 568-acre farm was conveyed by Strange to his brother, and in 1952 the brother conveyed the farm back to Strange but the deed was not recorded. In 1958 an identical deed was executed by the brother to Strange and this deed was recorded. The consideration for the conveyance was $2,500 and the assumption of a $7,000 lien on the farm. In 1955 Strange and Pendleton executed a note payable to Rowland, the holder of the $7,000 note secured by the lien on the farm, in the sum of $9,793.50, which included the $7,000 note. Other real estate owned by the partnership was deeded to Strange and Pendleton. The partnership granted an easement over the farm to a utility company, granted a prospecting and mining rights lease to the farm, paid the taxes out of partnership funds, and collected rents from the farm. Furthermore the ASC office assigned a single number to all the farms, and agricultural conservation payments were made to Strange and Pendleton. The trial court held that this evidence of partnership ownership of the farm was not sufficient to overcome the presumption of individual ownership created by the deed to Strange as an individual.

WILLIAMS, JUDGE.   The Uniform Partnership Act, which became effective in 1954, does not appear to change the common-law partnership principles applicable to this case. The intention of the parties evidenced by their conduct governs what constitutes partnership property. Evidence given considerable weight by courts in determining partnership intent, where title is held by one partner, includes use of partnership funds to improve the property, treatment of farm accounts as a partnership asset, use of partnership property to pay claims and expenses, declarations or admissions by the partner with title that the property is a partnership asset, and receipt of income by partnership.

The evidence heretofore recited is persuasive of a finding that the farm was partnership property. However, on the evidence as a whole, there is a doubt whether the property was intended to be a partnership asset. This Court has often said that considerable weight should be given the findings of the chancellor and his judgment will not be disturbed where, on all the evidence, the matter is left in doubt. There is a presumption against including as a partnership asset real estate owned by a partner which can be rebutted only by a clear manifestation of partnership intent.

The evidence most favorable to the heirs established that Strange was the sole owner of record of the property at his death. That fact, plus the fact that he had conveyed a one-half interest in other property to Pendleton but had not done so with this property, is sufficient to sustain the findings of the trial court.

Management of Business

Right to Voice in Management. In the absence of an agreement as to the organization and management of a partnership, each partner has an equal voice in the management of the business. In a partnership, in the absence of an agreement, there is no relation between participation in the management of the business and the partner's contribution to the capital of the partnership.

Agreements as to Management. The partners may by agreement grant the authority to manage the business to one or more of the partners, or they may set up an organization in which the authority to manage certain defined divisions of the business is given to one or more of the partners. In partnerships having several partners, an organization similar to that of a corporation may be set up, giving the authority to manage the business to a small group or committee of partners. Irrespective of the organization of the partnership business, each partner has the right of free access to the books of the partnership, and each partner owes a duty of full disclosure of his knowledge of the affairs of the business to all of the other partners. The exclusion of a partner from a voice in the management of the business has been held to be ground for the dissolution of the partnership.

Voting Rights. Each partner in a partnership has one vote regardless of the proportion of the capital invested by him in the enterprise. In regard to decisions relative to the everyday operation of the business, the vote of the majority of the partners controls. In the event there is an even number of partners and the vote results in a deadlock, their only course, if they cannot reach an agreement, is to dissolve and wind up the partnership. Before any change may be made in the nature of the partnership or in its location which would materially alter the risks of the business, all the partners must agree to such change. In entering into the business, each partner has agreed to assume the risks incident to its operation, and he cannot be forced, without his consent, to assume different risks.

Right to Resort to Courts. As a general rule the partners cannot resort to the courts for the settlement of disputes arising in the course of the operation of the business. The partnership relation is a personal one, and the success of the business depends on the cooperative action of the partners. If they cannot agree on matters of business policy, their course is to dissolve the partnership and wind up the business. In some instances a court of equity has granted an equitable remedy and decreed the continuation of the partnership business, but before a partner is entitled to this extraordinary remedy, he must show that the only way his interests can be protected is by the continuation of the partnership. The usual action in case of disagreement is to petition for an accounting, for the appointment of a receiver, and for a winding-up of the partnership business.

Summary

In the absence of an agreement to the contrary, all partners in a partnership have a right to an equal voice in the management of the business. The partners may, by agreement, grant authority to one or more of the partners to manage the business or a division of it, but a partner cannot be denied all participation in the management of the business.

Each partner has one vote, and a majority of the partners have the right to make decisions regarding the everyday operation of the business. However, all the partners must consent to the making of fundamental changes.

If the partners get into a dispute regarding partnership affairs, they cannot resort to the courts for the settlement of the dispute; their only course of action, if they cannot settle their dispute, is a dissolution and winding-up of the business.

Hauke v. Frey
93 N.W.2d 183 (Sup. Ct. Neb. 1958)

This was an action by Albert P. Hauke (plaintiff) against John H. Frey (defendant) asking that Frey be enjoined from taking possession of assets claimed by Hauke to be his individual property. Judgment for Frey and Hauke appealed. Judgment affirmed.

Hauke owned a certain lot on which he constructed a building in which bowling alleys were installed. A business known as Bowl Arena was operated in the building by Frey and Hauke. Frey managed the business and received a salary of $425 a month and Hauke received $500 as rent for the building and equipment. The parties planned to organize a corporation to operate the business but this plan was never carried out. Hauke claimed that he was sole owner of the business and that Frey was his employee. Hauke gave Frey notice that he was discharged and brought this action asking that Frey be enjoined from taking possession of the assets of the business or in any manner interfering with the management or operation of the business. The court held that Hauke and Frey were partners in the operation of the business and denied the injunction.

YEAGER, JUSTICE. The conclusion reached is that here was a partnership although there is not in evidence an agreement containing either complete details of organization or of functions after organization. This court said in *Bard v. Hanson,* "The scope of a partnership may be evidenced by written or oral agreement, or implied from the conduct of the parties and what was done by them." The acts of the parties and what was done, as disclosed by the testimony of Hauke, indicated a partnership which was to continue until plans could be worked out and a corporation organized to take its place.

This being a partnership Hauke could not by injunction deprive Frey of his possession of the partnership property and his rights in the management of the partnership business.

Section 67–318(*e*), R.R.S. 1943, (UPA Sec. 18[e]) provides: "All partners have equal rights in the management and conduct of the partnership business."

The general rule is that one partner may not maintain an action against his copartner on account of a partnership transaction where there has been no settlement of the partnership accounts and business.

Profits and Losses

Rights and Liabilities of Partner. In the absence of an agreement defining the partner's rights in the profits of the partnership business, profits are distributed equally, irrespective of the capital contributions of the partners. Likewise, each partner is liable for an equal share of any losses suffered by the partnership.

If the partnership agreement sets out the distributional proportions by which the profits of the business will be divided among the partners but is silent as to the way the liability for losses will be divided, each partner will be liable for losses according to the proportion in which he shares in the profits.

Relation between Partners

Nature of Duty Partner Owes to Partner. Parties engaging as partners in a business venture owe to each other the highest degree of good faith in all partnership matters. Lack of good faith is, in effect, a fraud on one's partners and is treated as such. It is a duty imposed by law and need not be provided for in the partnership agreement, and a partner cannot relieve himself of this duty by contract. The partnership relation is one of trust and confidence, and the members of the firm sustain a trust relation toward each other with reference to partnership matters.

A partner may deal with the firm or the individual members of the firm provided he deals in good faith and makes a full disclosure of all matters which affect the transaction and which he should know are not known to the other party. A partner is not allowed to gain an advantage over a copartner by fraud, misrepresentation, or concealment. And a partner who profits by his misrepresentations in connection with a partnership transaction must account to his copartners for the profit. In dealing with the partnership, the partner will not be permitted to retain profits made on the transaction.

If a partner, in contemplation of the organization of the partnership, acquires property which will be needed by the partnership when organized, he will not be permitted to sell the property to the partnership at a profit. It has been held, however, that a partner, having acquired property prior to his entering the partnership and not in contemplation of the partnership's need of the property, may sell the property to the partnership for more than he paid for it.

A partner is liable to his copartners if he uses partnership property for his individual purposes, misappropriates partnership funds, makes a secret profit out of the transaction of partnership business, engages in a competing business without the knowledge and consent of his copartners, accepts a secret commission on partnership business, or uses information gained as a partner to the detriment of the partnership.

Duty in Transacting Partnership Business. In transacting partnership business, each partner owes a duty to use reasonable care and skill and not to exceed the authority granted him by the partnership agreement. A partner is not liable to his partner or partners for losses resulting from honest errors in judgment, but he is liable for losses resulting from his negligence or lack of care and skill in the transaction of partnership business, and for losses resulting from unauthorized transactions negotiated in the name of the partnership. For example, suppose Arnold, Bond, and Cline are partners and the partnership agreement provides that no partner shall accept in the partnership name any draft for the accommodation of a third person. Suppose Arnold then accepts a draft in the name of the partnership for the accommodation of Thomas and the partnership has to pay the draft, thereby suffering a loss. Arnold will have to bear the loss.

Books of Partnership. The Uniform Partnership Act (19) provides for the keeping of partnership books, and further provides that such books shall be kept at the principal place of business and that "every partner shall at all times have access to and may inspect and copy them." The books to be kept are determined by the agreement of the partners. Each partner owes a duty to keep a reasonable record of all business transacted by him for the partnership and to make such records available to the person keeping the partnership books. Under some circumstances a partner may be entitled to a formal accounting.

Disclosure of Information. Each partner owes a duty to disclose to his partner or partners all information material to the partnership business. He owes a duty to inform his partner or partners of notices he has received which affect the rights of the partnership. Partners are presumed to have knowledge of matters appearing on the books of the partnership, and failure to inform a partner of such matters is not a breach of duty.

If one partner is selling his interest in the partnership to a copartner, he owes a duty to disclose to the buying partner all the facts having a bearing on the value of the interest in the partnership which are not open to the buying partner. Likewise, the buying partner owes the same duty of full disclosure to the selling partner. Neither the buying nor the selling partner owes a duty to disclose facts appearing on the books or in the records of the partnership.

Right to Wages. In the absence of an agreement each partner owes a duty to devote his entire time and energy to the partnership business. This does not mean that a partner cannot have outside interests, but it does mean that the partner must not engage in outside activities which will interfere with the performance of the duties he owes to his partner or partners. He must not engage in activities which are in competition with the partnership business or which will be injurious to it.

A partner is not entitled to wages, irrespective of the relative proportion of time spent by the partners in the carrying-on of the partnership business, unless there is an agreement to pay wages. A partner's compensation is presumed to be his share in the profits of the business.

Right to Sue Partner. Partners cannot sue each other or the partnership on partnership claims, nor can the partnership sue the individual partners on partnership claims. If any partner has a claim against a copartner or against the partnership growing out of the transaction of the partnership business, or if the partnership has a claim against an individual partner, the claims must be adjusted in the course of an accounting of the partnership affairs, and no judicial remedy is available other than the dissolution, accounting, and winding-up of the partnership affairs.

Summary

Each partner owes a duty of undivided loyalty to the partnership and to his copartners. The duty of loyalty of a partner is the same as the duty of loyalty of an agent to his principal.

In transacting partnership business, a partner is not liable to his partner or partners for losses resulting from honest errors of judgment, but he is liable for losses resulting from his negligence or his lack of care or skill. He is also liable for losses resulting from unauthorized transactions.

Each partner has free access to all the books and records of the partnership. A partner owes a duty to disclose to his partner or partners all matters affecting the partnership business which are not disclosed by the books and records of the partnership.

In the absence of an agreement to pay wages, a partner is not entitled to wages for services rendered to the partnership.

Partners cannot sue each other or the partnership to enforce claims growing out of the internal affairs of the partnership. The only remedy available is the dissolution, accounting, and winding-up of the partnership affairs.

Alford v. Lehman
86 N.W.2d 330 (Sup. Ct. Mich. 1957)

This was an action by Dr. S. E. Alford (plaintiff) against Albert Lehman (defendant) for the dissolution of a partnership and an accounting. Lehman's claim for salary was not allowed and Lehman appealed. Judgment as to salary was affirmed.

On November 15, 1945, Alford and Lehman executed a partnership agreement whereby they were to manufacture a small tractor on which Lehman was to obtain a patent by virtue of his having invented certain parts which went into the tractor. Dr. Alford was to pay into the venture $20,000, and Lehman was to contribute his patents, when obtained, and the use of his machine shop, equipment, and tools. Lehman was to have complete management of the business and was to devote his full time to the partnership business. The agreement, relative to Lehman's salary, contained the following: ". . . in consideration of such services, the party of the first part (Lehman) shall be allowed an annual salary in an amount or amounts to be agreed upon by the parties hereto."

The venture was a complete failure and the $20,000 investment of Dr. Alford was a total loss. Lehman never devoted his entire time and facilities to the partnership business but continued to do work for Great Lakes Steel Corporation. On the dissolution of the partnership in February, 1950, Lehman claimed that he was entitled to a credit of $17,500 as salary. The parties never agreed on an amount of salary to be paid to Lehman and he drew no salary during the operation of the business. Dr. Alford claimed that Lehman was to have no salary unless the business made a profit.

EDWARDS, JUSTICE.   Lehman's claim for salary must be founded upon the express terms of the agreement itself since, under Michigan statute and case law, partners are not generally entitled to compensation for services.

We note Lehman's reliance upon the rule cited in *Arthur v. McCallum:*

In the absence of agreement, one partner cannot collect pay for services performed for the copartnership; each partner is presumed to devote his time, skill, and endeavor to the partnership business and this without compensation, other than his share of the profits. But it does not follow that the court is precluded from taking into consideration all the surrounding facts and circumstances of the case, the course of dealing between the partners, the reasonableness or unreasonableness of the claim made, the probabilities arising out of the conduct of the business, in determining whether such agreement exists.

Among the circumstances in the *Arthur* case was the fact of a prosperous business. The circumstances in the cause we have currently before us include a venture which was financially catastrophic and a material violation of the partnership agreement as to full time endeavor on the part of the partner who now claims a right to salary. The express terms of this agreement pertaining to salary for Lehman were never complied with. We agree with the chancellor that under all the circumstances no liability therefor may be found.

Liggett v. Lester

390 P.2d. 351 (Sup. Ct. Ore. 1964)

This was an action by George H. Liggett (plaintiff) against his former partner, Odell Lester (defendant) for dissolution of the partnership and recovery of additional profits made by Lester on partnership purchases. Judgment for Liggett and Lester appealed. Judgment affirmed.

Liggett and Lester entered into a written partnership agreement on January 3, 1957, for the purpose of conducting a service station business in Dallas, Oregon. The partners operated the business until April 26, 1958, when the station was closed because of a disagreement over certain billing practices employed by Lester.

Prior to the formation of the partnership, Lester had obtained a "distributorship" classification from an oil company which permitted Lester to buy petroleum products at a discount. The partners contemplated that Lester's ability to purchase at favorable prices would be an advantage in their business. Liggett entrusted Lester with payment of the firm's bills as this was deemed necessary in order to take advantage of Lester's status as a distributor. Shortly after formation of the partnership, Lester acquired a bulk plant in Dallas and arranged with the oil company to receive an additional discount of up to one and a half cents per gallon as a "jobber." Liggett was unaware of this discount arrangement and the discount was not passed on to the partnership.

This dispute arose when Liggett discovered the secret profit taking. Lester argues that he is not accountable to the partnership for these profits because the partnership was not deprived of its customary discount of three cents per gallon, the additional price concession to him personally represented a reasonable return upon his investment in the bulk plant, and the partnership could not have financed the bulk plant operation necessary in order to obtain the extra discount.

GOODWIN, JUSTICE.   The conduct of Lester in concealing his additional profit on purchases made for the partnership constituted a breach of a fiduciary duty one partner owes another. Lester's profits on such purchases amounted to secret commissions wrongfully, withheld from his partner. It was Lester's duty to obtain petroleum products for the partnership at the best price possible. It matters not that the partnership paid no more for its merchandise than it would have had to pay on the open market for the same purchases. The breach of duty was the failure to disclose the existence of the extra discount so that the partners could decide, as partners, how it should be treated.

It is true, as Lester argues, that a partner may engage in enterprises in his own behalf while he is a member of a partnership, provided that he acts in good faith toward the other partners. This qualified right to engage in other business, however, is further qualified and limited where the separate business is of the same nature as that engaged in by the partnership. In such a case, the consent of the other partners must be obtained before one partner may engage in a competitive enterprise.

Problem Cases

1. Wise, Sr. and Wise, Jr. were doing business as a general partnership under the trade name of "Nu-Tone Products Company." Wise, Sr. and his son purchased a $10,000 life insurance policy with Wise, Jr. the named insured, Wise, Sr. the primary beneficiary, and Nu-Tone Products as beneficiary if Wise, Sr. should predecease the insured. Premiums were paid by the partnership. Wise, Sr. died on October 12, 1954, and under his will Nu-Tone Products was reorganized as a limited partnership with Wise, Jr. the general partner, and his three sisters as limited partners. On February 25, 1960, Wise, Jr. sold his interest in the partnership to his sisters for $100,000. Thereafter the sisters incorporated the business and assigned their interests to the corporation. The corporation subsequently sued Wise, Jr. to recover the cash value of the life insurance policy which Wise, Jr. has refused to deliver. Wise, Jr. contends that the life insurance policy is his personal property and at no time was a partnership asset which he would be required to deliver under the sales agreement. Is Wise, Jr.'s argument correct?

2. Dean and Clemmer, partners in the operation of a restaurant, wanted new quarters for the restaurant. Dean conveyed to Clemmer an undivided half interest in a lot he owned. A building for the restaurant was constructed on the lot and used by the partnership. The cost of erecting the building, the taxes and insurance for the building were paid out of partnership funds. Rents from a part of the building not used by the partnership were paid to and used by the partnership. Upon Dean's death the lot and building were sold as partnership property. Rockingham Bank, a creditor of Dean, seeks to have the sale set aside and the property declared to be held by Dean and Clemmer as tenants in common. Is this contention correct?

3. Four brothers owned and operated a dairy farm under the firm name of Bender Bros. Two of the brothers had mortgaged specific items of partnership property to Klein as security for the repayment of money loaned to the two brothers as individuals. Windom Bank obtained a judgment against the two brothers and, in conformity with the provisions of the Uniform Partnership Act, had a receiver appointed over the interest of the brothers in the partnership. Windom Bank contends that the mortgage given to Klein is void. Is the mortgage given to Klein void?

4. Kovacik, a building contractor, and Reed, a job superintendent and estimator, entered into a joint venture for kitchen remodeling work in the San Francisco area. Kovacik agreed to invest $10,000 in the venture if Reed would supervise and estimate the jobs. Profits were to be shared on a 50-50 basis. Reed's only contribution was his own labor and Kovacik provided all financing throughout the venture. After about nine months, Kovacik determined that the venture was unprofitable, terminated the venture, and demanded that Reed share the loss estimated at $8,680. Reed refused to contribute or pay any loss. Can Kovacik recover 50 percent of the loss from Reed?

5. Sims and Alexander had been partners in the retail jewelry business. Sims became ill and underwent surgery. The operation disclosed cancer in an advanced stage, but this

was not made known to Sims. Learning of Sims's condition, Alexander had a new partnership agreement prepared which provided that upon the death of one partner all of the partnership assets should become the sole property of the surviving partner. Sims signed the agreement while in the hospital. The following day Sims learned of her condition. A few months later she asked for a copy of the partnership agreement and then executed a will in which she expressly bequeathed her interest in the partnership to her parents. After Sims's death her executor brought an action to recover the value of her interest in the partnership. Did Sims's interest in the partnership pass to Alexander upon her death?

6. On September 1, 1953, Mousseau and John and James Walker commenced a partnership business under the name of "Sanitation Service." Mousseau conducted the business personally for almost seven months until the Walkers came to work full time. Several disagreements arose as to the division of responsibilities between the partners and in December, 1954, the Walkers forcibly ejected Mousseau from the premises and declared the partnership at an end. Mousseau had no desire to sell his interest and after dissolution the Walkers used his assets to continue the business. In 1956, Mousseau filed suit to dissolve the partnership and for an accounting, including his share of the 1955 net profits. The Walkers admit a net profit of $8,387 during 1955, but claim that this amount is subject to deduction for wages for themselves in the amount of $6,240. Were the Walkers entitled to compensation for their services following Mousseau's departure from the business?

7. Hargett procured an option on a piece of property upon which he desired to erect a motel. He cleaned off the property and poured the footings for the building, but being financially unable to exercise the option or erect the building, he formed a partnership with Miller. Bank financing was arranged and Miller agreed to pay $825 monthly on the indebtedness until the motel was in operation and funds available to make the payments. Hargett was to manage the motel and reimburse Miller from partnership profits. The motel was unsuccessful and was sold. A balance remained after payment of partnership obligations (including Miller's reimbursement). Hargett contends that prior to division of surplus he is entitled to reimbursement for his expenditures prior to formation of the partnership. Should Hargett recover?

8. Lichtman and Sasson were partners in the operation of a business. Lichtman presented false invoices and, on the basis of the false invoices, withdrew funds from the partnership. When Sasson discovered that Lichtman had fraudulently withdrawn funds from the partnership, Sasson brought an action at law to recover a judgment against Lichtman for the amount of the funds fraudulently withdrawn. Is Sasson entitled to a judgment against Lichtman?

9. Hensley was one of eight partners in the firm of Mary Gail Coal Company. The partnership operated a coal mine and had a fleet of 30 or more trucks which were regularly serviced at a filling station owned and operated by the company. Hensley personally owned one truck which was "hired" by the company to haul coal. On June 10, 1958, this truck was destroyed as a result of a fire at the company gasoline station. Hensley sued the partnership and the individual partners (including himself) claiming that negligence of partnership employees, in permitting spilled gasoline to remain exposed on the ground, caused the fire. Can such a suit be maintained?

chapter 21. Relation of Partners to Third Persons

Partner as Agent of Partnership

General Powers of Partner. The relations of the partnership to third persons, and the power of a partner to bind the partnership and his copartners, are set out in Sections 9–14 of the Uniform Partnership Act. Every partner is the agent of the partnership for the purpose of its business. Consequently, the partnership is bound by all transactions negotiated by a partner, if such transactions come within the usual course of the partnership business, unless the third person has notice or knowledge of limitations on the authority of the partner to bind the partnership. This general authority includes "the execution in the partnership name of any instrument, for apparently carrying on in the usual way the business of the partnership." This would authorize a partner to issue negotiable instruments in the name of the partnership, endorse in the name of the partnership negotiable instruments payable to it as payee or endorsed to it, issue bills of sale, sign contracts, or execute in the name of the partnership any instrument which would customarily be issued or used in the carrying-on of a business such as that in which the partnership is engaged. In determining the scope of a partner's power to bind the partnership, the principles of the law of agency apply. The scope of a business is a matter of fact. As a general rule the scope of a business will be determined by the customs of the locality in which the business is being carried on.

Relation of Third Persons to Partnership. The duties owed by third persons to a partnership principal are substantially the same as those owed by third persons to any principal. The rules of agency law apply. The third persons cannot, with safety, blindly assume that a partner has unlimited authority to bind the partnership. The third person must ascertain whether or not a partnership exists, and he must take notice of apparent limitations on the partner's authority. Unless the third person has notice or knowledge of limitations on the partner's authority, he may safely assume that the partner has the authority of a general agent.

The courts have made a distinction between a trading partnership and a nontrading partnership, but such a distinction is not recognized by the Uniform Partnership Act. A partnership engaged in a business, such as retailing, wholesaling, general construction, or exporting and importing, would be classed as a trading partnership. A partnership engaged in providing a service, such as the practice of law, medicine, or dentistry, would be classed as a nontrading partnership. The scope of the business of a nontrading partnership is more limited than that of a trading partnership; consequently, the authority of a partner of a nontrading partnership to bind the partnership is more limited than the authority of a partner of a trading partnership.

As a general rule, if the partnership is a trading partnership, a partner will have the power to borrow money and pledge or mortgage partnership assets to secure the indebtedness, issue or endorse negotiable instruments, execute contracts, make sales, purchase goods, receive payments, pay debts, bring suits, engage attorneys, engage agents and employees, and perform all other acts customarily performed in the carrying-on of a business such as that in which the partnership is engaged.

Partner's Power to Convey Partnership Real Property. Since each state, by statute, requires certain formalities for the conveyance of real property located within its borders, the power of a partner to convey partnership real property and the manner in which the instrument of conveyance must be signed will be affected by such statutory requirements. To bind the partnership, the conveyance must be made in the regular course of the partnership business, or, in other words, it must be within the scope of the general power of the partner. Under the Uniform Partnership Act (10) [1] if the real property has been conveyed to the partnership in the partnership name, it may be conveyed by a conveyance executed in the name of the partnership by a partner. If title to the real property is in the name of the partnership, a conveyance signed by a partner in his name will pass the equitable interest of the partnership in the property. If title to the real property is in the name of one or more but not all of the partners and the record does not disclose the partnership's rights in the property, a conveyance signed by the partners in whose name the property stands will pass good title to an innocent purchaser for value. If the purchaser, however, has notice or knowledge of the partnership's interest in the property, he will take subject to such interest. In the same situation a conveyance executed by one of the partners in the partnership name or in his own name passes the equitable interest of the partnership.

---

[1] The numbers in the parentheses refer to the sections of the Uniform Partnership Act.

The same rule applies if the real property is held in the name of a third person in trust for the partnership. If the title to the real property is held in the name of all the partners and the conveyance is executed by all the partners, the conveyance passes all their rights in such property.

Special Situations.   The partnership is bound by admissions or representations made by a partner concerning partnership affairs which are within the scope of his authority. Likewise, notice to or the knowledge of a partner relating to partnership affairs is binding on the partnership to the same extent and in a like manner as notice to or the knowledge of an agent is binding on his principal.

General Limitations on a Partner's Power.   The Uniform Partnership Act [9(2) and (3)] sets out the limitations on a partner's power. It provides generally that acts which are not apparently for the carrying-on of the partnership business in the usual way do not bind the partnership. The act also sets out specific acts of partners which, in the absence of the authorization of all the partners, will not bind the partnership. Assignments for the benefit of creditors, disposal of the goodwill of the business, acts which would make it impossible to carry on the partnership business in the usual way, confession of judgments, or submission of a claim or liability to arbitration or reference will not bind the partnership. Also, if the partners have, by agreement, limited the authority of a partner to bind the partnership, the partnership will not be liable for the partner's unauthorized acts if the third party has notice or knowledge of the limitations. Although not specifically set out in the Uniform Partnership Act, the courts have generally held that a partner does not have authority to bind the partnership as guarantor or surety for a third person unless such undertaking is in the furtherance of the interests of the partnership.

Summary

In the absence of an agreement limiting the authority of a partner, each partner has the power to bind the partnerships by acts which are ordinarily done in the carrying on of a business such as that in which the partnership is engaged. The authority of the partners or a partner to bind the firm may be limited by the agreement of the partners.

Partnership real property, title to which is in the partnership name, may be conveyed by a conveyance executed by a partner in the name of the partnership. If title to the real property is in the name of one or more but not all of the partners, or is held in trust in the name of a third person, a conveyance executed by a partner in the name of the partnership or in his own name will convey the equity of the partnership, provided the partner has acted within the scope of his power. If the title to the real property is in the name of all partners and the conveyance is executed by all the partners, such conveyance passes all of their rights in the property. In general, agency rules apply to admissions, to representations of a partner, and to notice to or knowledge of a partner.

A third person is not justified in assuming that a partner has unlimited authority to bind the partnership. The third person must take notice of apparent limitations on a partner's authority, and he is bound by notice or knowledge of such limitations.

As a general rule a partner does not have the authority to do acts which will defeat the purposes of the partnership or impose unreasonable burdens on the partnership, such as selling all the partnership assets or obligating the partnership as surety or guarantor for third persons.

Borrowing on Partnership's Credit

Partner's General Power to Borrow Money. Whether or not a partner will have the power to borrow money on the firm's credit will depend on the nature of the business being carried on by the partnership. If, in the locality in which the partnership business is being operated, it is customary for persons carrying on such businesses to borrow money to finance their operations, a partner will, as a general rule, have the power to borrow money on the firm's credit. The fact that the partnership has not borrowed money in the past will not be controlling.

If the partnership is engaged in manufacturing, contracting, or retailing, or in a similar business, a partner would have the power to borrow money on the firm's credit, since such businesses are usually financed in part with borrowed money. However, if the partnership is engaged exclusively in the performance of services, such as, for example, the practice of law or medicine or any professional service, a partner would not have the power to borrow money on the firm's credit, since such businesses are not, as a rule, financed with borrowed money.

Partner's Power to Pledge Firm Assets. Closely related to the power to borrow money on the firm's credit is the partner's power to pledge the firm's assets. If the circumstances are such that a partner would have the power to borrow money on the firm's credit and it is customary to give security for the repayment of money borrowed, the partner would, as a general rule, have the power to pledge firm assets as security for the repayment of money borrowed.

Partner's Power to Bind Firm on Negotiable Instruments. Negotiable instruments play such an important role in the carrying-on of a business that a partnership will, regardless of the nature of its business, use negotiable instruments to some extent. If the partnership has a commercial account with a bank, a partner will have the power to endorse for deposit in the partnership bank account checks drawn payable to the partnership. As a general rule a partner will have the power to endorse and cash checks drawn payable to the order of the partnership, and will likewise have the power to endorse drafts and notes payable to the order of the partnership and discount them.

Whether or not a partner will have the power to issue drafts and notes in the partnership name will depend on the nature of the partnership business and its methods of operation. If the partner would have the power to borrow money on the firm's credit, he would have, as a general rule, the power to issue a negotiable instrument for the money borrowed. Likewise, if a partner has the authority to buy materials on the firm's credit, he would have the power to issue negotiable instruments in payment for materials purchased on credit, if it were customary to do so.

If the partnership has a checking account, only those partners whose names are on the signature card on file with the bank will have power to sign checks. However, a partner whose name is not on the signature card may bind the partnership on a check signed in the partnership name, if such check is issued to a third person who has no knowledge of the limitation on the partner's authority.

Whether or not the partnership will be liable on a negotiable instrument signed or endorsed by a partner for the accommodation of a third person will depend on the circumstances of the case. As a general rule, if the party to whom the accommodation instrument is delivered knows that it has been signed or endorsed for the accommodation of a third person, the firm will not be bound unless all of the partners have consented to such signing. However, if the holder of the instrument has paid value for it and has taken it in the regular course of business before it is overdue and without notice or knowledge that it was signed or endorsed for the accommodation of a third person, the partnership will be liable.

Partnership's Liability for Money Borrowed. If a partner, having power to borrow money on the firm's credit, borrows money in the firm's name, the partnership will be liable for the money borrowed, even though the money borrowed is converted by the partner borrowing it to his own use. If a partner borrows money in his own name and on his individual credit, without in any way joining the partnership, the partnership cannot be held liable, even though the borrowed money is used for partnership purposes.

Summary

A partner's power to borrow money on the firm's credit will depend primarily on the nature of the partnership's business and whether or not it is standard practice in such business to use borrowed money to aid in financing its operation.

As a general rule the power to borrow money on the firm's credit will carry with it the power to pledge firm assets to secure the repayment of the borrowed money.

A partner has the power, ordinarily, to endorse for deposit or for discount negotiable instruments drawn payable to the order of the partnership. A partner's power to issue negotiable instruments in the name of the partnership is closely related to his power to borrow money on the firm's credit.

A partnership's liability on negotiable instruments issued or endorsed in the name of the partnership for the accommodation of third parties will depend on the circumstances of each case.

In general, a partnership is liable for money borrowed in its name, even though it is converted by a partner to his own use; and the partnership is not liable for money borrowed by a partner in his own name, even though it is used for partnership purposes.

Reid v. *Linder*
251 Pac. 157 (Sup. Ct. Mont. 1926)

This was an action by Edgar P. Reid as receiver of the Bank of Twin Bridges (plaintiff) against A. A. Linder, James P. Darnutzer, Carl Darnutzer and A. J. Wilcomb, partners, doing business as Trout Creek Land Company (defendants), to recover a judgment on partnership notes. Judgment for Reid, and A. A. Linder, James P. Darnutzer and Carl Darnutzer appealed. [Wilcomb did not join in the appeal.] Judgment affirmed.

The Trout Creek Land Company, a partnership, was organized by A. J. Wilcomb, A. A. Linder, James P. Darnutzer, and Carl Darnutzer and at various times during its existence had rented land and raised wheat, purchased land and raised cattle, and speculated on the wheat market. The firm had no capital but borrowed money from the bank to finance its operations. It seems that substantially all of its undertakings resulted in losses which were absorbed by the bank. A. J. Wilcomb was cashier of the bank and handled the finances of the firm. In June, 1921, Wilcomb borrowed a total of $16,828.26 from the bank upon four promissory notes signed "Trout Creek Land Company by A. J. Wilcomb." The money was used by Wilcomb to speculate in the grain market and was lost. The bank was declared insolvent and ceased business on May 28, 1923, and this suit was brought by the receiver on the four notes. The partners, except Wilcomb, appeared and set up as a defense (1) that the firm was a nontrading partnership and that the making of the notes was not within the scope of the firm's business and not necessary to the transaction of such business, (2) that the power to borrow money and execute notes was vested only in the members acting together and that no one member had authority to execute a note in the firm name, (3) that no one of the defendants nor the firm received anything of value paid for the notes, and (4) that the bank had knowledge of the limitations on the authority of a partner to act for the firm because Wilcomb was cashier of the bank and a member of its board of directors.

MATTHEWS, JUSTICE. The evidence does not establish a custom of the firm known to the bank, requiring that all notes of the firm be signed by all of the members, for the record discloses notes, acknowledged as firm notes and paid or renewed as such, signed only by one or more members of the firm or signed as were the notes in question and endorsed on the back by the individuals constituting the firm.

It is contended that the firm was a nontrading co-partnership. The question is important, as in such a partnership a partner has no implied power to borrow money and give firm mercantile paper therefor.

"The test of the character of the partnership is buying and selling. If it buys and sells, it is commercial or trading; if it does not buy or sell, it is one of employment or occupation." *Lee* v. *Bank.*

"The partnership must be in a trade or concern to which the issuing or transfer of bills is necessary or usual." *Chitty on Bills.*

And although a firm may ordinarily come within the definition of a nontrading partnership, where the partnership engages in trading requiring capital and the use of credit, the rule as to nontrading partnerships does not apply.

Here no question of fact arises; the facts are undisputed. They show that the firm engaged in buying and selling cattle, as well as in farming and selling grain, and that it required capital and the use of credit; in fact, it operated from the beginning on credit alone and established a custom within itself long prior to the issuance of the notes in question. Whether the firm was a trading or nontrading partnership was but a question of law for the court. It appears that the issuance of negotiable paper was justified by custom and necessity of the firm as well as by the fact that the firm engaged in trading.

As the notes were traced back on the books of the bank as renewals of notes, the proceeds of which were credited to the checking account of the firm, it is apparent that the bald statement made by Linder *et al.,* that neither as individuals nor as members of the firm did they receive any consideration for the notes, presents no issue requiring determination by the jury.

As the firm was a trading partnership, each member of the firm was the agent for the partnership in the transaction of its business and had authority to do whatever was necessary to carry on such business in the ordinary manner and for that purpose could bind the partnership by an agreement in writing; and notes executed by one of the partners for the benefit of the firm became partnership obligations, binding upon all of the members of the firm, in the absence of bad faith on the part of the contracting partner and knowledge thereof on the part of the payee.

But it is contended that Wilcomb used the firm credit for the purpose of playing the wheat market, without authority from the other members of the firm and, in this, acted with bad faith toward his co-partners. Even though this be admitted to be true, the borrowing was ostensibly authorized; and, if the bank was a bona fide lender, it was entitled to recover on the notes, even though the partner borrowing was actually obtaining the money for his own use.

It is contended, however, that the bank was not a bona fide lender, as Wilcomb had full knowledge of all the facts regarding the notes and their purpose and that, as Wilcomb acted as agent for the bank in the transaction, his knowledge was imputed to the bank. In passing, it may be said that the record clearly discloses that Wilcomb was superseded as managing agent of the bank three days before the notes were given; but, as the notes were renewals of other notes issued as far back as 1919, this fact may be disregarded.

It is the general rule that knowledge obtained by an officer of a bank while acting for the bank is imputed to the bank but that knowledge obtained by such officer while acting not on behalf of the corporation but for himself, or in a manner antagonistic to the corporation, is not imputable to it.

Partner's Individual Liability

Nature of Liability for Torts.   The standards and principles of agency law are applied in determining the liability of the partnership and of the other partners for the wrongful acts of a partner. If the wrongful act is committed within the scope and in the course of the transaction of partnership business or is a breach of trust as defined in the Uniform Partnership Act (14), the Uniform Partnership Act (15) provides that the partnership and the partners will be jointly and severally liable. Whether or not the tort was within the scope and was committed in the course of the transaction of partnership business is a question of fact.

Partner's Crimes.   If a partner commits a crime in the course of the transaction of partnership business, his partners are not criminally liable unless they have participated in the criminal act. The partnership itself, since it is not a legal entity, cannot be held to be criminally liable for the crimes of its partners.

Suing the Partnership.   The partners are liable jointly on contracts of the partnership. At common law, it was generally necessary, in order to recover on a joint obligation, to get personal service on each of the joint obligors. This was frequently impossible. Most states have changed this by statute, but the statutes are not uniform. Some statutes make all joint obligations joint and several, that is, suit may be brought against the partners jointly or against each individual partner. Common name statutes permit the complainant to proceed to judgment if he serves one or more of the partners even though he does not gain service over all. The judgment, when obtained, is enforceable against the joint assets of the partnership and against the individual assets of the parties served with process. If all partners are served with process, a judgment may be enforced against the partnership property or against their individual property. Since partners are individually, as well as jointly, liable for torts chargeable to the partnership, the problem discussed above does not exist, and recovery can be had from any one or more of the partners who can be served with process.

Summary

The rules of agency law are applied in determining when the tort of a partner becomes the act of the partnership. Since a partnership is not an entity it is not liable for the crimes of the partners.

Partners are jointly liable on contracts of the partnership and jointly and severally liable for torts chargeable to the partnership. At common law all partners had to be served in a suit against the partnership on joint obligations. Most states have changed this by statute. Usually these statutes make it possible to reach partnership property if any individual partner can be served and to reach the individual property of all partners personally served with process.

Vrabel v. *Acri*

103 N.E.2d 564 (Sup. Ct. Ohio 1952)

This was an action by Stephen J. Vrabel (plaintiff) against Florence Acri (defendant) to recover damages for personal injuries. Judgment for Vrabel, and Acri appealed. Judgment reversed and judgment entered for Acri.   ———

Florence Acri and Michael Acri owned and operated a cafe as partners. They had had domestic difficulties and Florence had sued Michael for divorce. At times Florence had helped in the cafe, but following their domestic troubles, Michael was in complete control of the management of the cafe.

On February 17, 1947, Vrabel and a companion went into the cafe to buy drinks of alcoholic beverages. While Vrabel and his companion were sitting at the bar drinking, Michael, without provocation, shot and killed Vrabel's companion and assaulted and seriously injured Vrabel. Michael was convicted of murder and sentenced to life in the state prison.

Vrabel brought this suit against Florence Acri to recover damages for his injuries on the ground that Florence, as a partner of Michael, was liable for the tort of Michael.

ZIMMERMAN, JUDGE.   The authorities are in agreement that whether a tort is committed by a partner or a joint adventurer, the principles of law governing the situation are the same. So, where a partnership or a joint enterprise is shown to exist, each member of such project acts both as principal and agent of the others as to those things done within the apparent scope of the business of the project and for its benefit.

The Uniform Partnership Act provides: "Where, by any wrongful act or omission of any partner acting in the ordinary course of the business of the partnership or with the authority of his co-partners, loss or injury is caused to any person, not being a partner in the partnership, or any penalty is incurred, the partnership is liable therefor to the same extent as the partner so acting or omitting to act."

Such section, although enacted after the cause of action in the instant case arose, corresponds with the general law on the subject.

However, it is equally true that where one member of a partnership or joint enterprise commits a wrongful and malicious tort not within the actual or apparent scope of the agency or the common business of the particular venture, to which the other members have not assented, and which has not been concurred in or ratified by them, they are not liable for the harm thereby caused.

We cannot escape the conclusion, therefore, that the above rules, relating to the nonliability of a partner or joint adventurer for wrongful and malicious torts committed by an associate outside the purpose and scope of the business, must be applied in the instant case. The willful and malicious attack by Michael Acri upon Vrabel in the Acri Cafe cannot reasonably be said to have come within the scope of the business of operating the cafe, so as to have rendered the absent defendant accountable.

Since the liability of one partner or of one engaged in a joint enterprise for the acts of his associates is founded upon the principles of agency, the statement is in point that an intentional and willful attack committed by an agent or employee, to vent his own spleen or malevolence against the injured person, is a clear departure from his employment and his principal or employer is not responsible therefor.

Horn's Crane Service v. Prior

152 N.W.2d 421 (Sup. Ct. Neb. 1967)

This was an action by Horn's Crane Service (plaintiff) against Wendell Prior and Orie Cook (defendants) to recover sums due under a written contract and for supplies and services furnished a partnership comprised of Prior, Cook, and C. E. Piper. Piper was not joined in the action. Dismissed for failure to state a cause of action and Horn's Crane Service appealed. Affirmed.

The substance of Horn's theory of recovery was that Prior and Cook were members of a partnership and on that basis individually and jointly liable for the partnership debts. Horn's did not bring suit against the partnership itself and did not allege that the partnership property was insufficient to satisfy the debt.

WHITE, CHIEF JUSTICE.   In an action seeking a personal judgment against the individual members of a partnership or a joint adventure the petition does not state a cause of action if it fails to state that there is no partnership property or that it is insufficient to satisfy the debts of the partnership or joint adventure. There are several reasons for the rule. One of the most obvious is that credit having been extended to the partnership or firm, the members ought to have a right to insist that the partnership property be exhausted first. And to permit a firm creditor to by-pass the partnership property and exhaust the assets of an individual member leaving the partnership property extant, would be an obvious injustice, permit the other partners to profit at his expense, and place him in an adverse position with relation to his co-partners.

Problem Cases

1. Petrikis and Ellis owned and operated the Chariot Bar as partners. Petrikis and Ellis signed the following agreement: "We hereby agree to sell our interest in the Chariot Bar. If and when the sale takes place and after all bills are accounted for, the remainder of the money is to be divided according to the share each partner now attains in the said business." Thereafter, Petrikis negotiated a sale of the business to Hanges. Hanges' attorney drew up a contract of sale, and Hanges deposited with the attorney in escrow a cashier's check for $17,500—the agreed sale price of the business. Hanges took immediate possession of the Chariot Bar, and the stock was inventoried. Petrikis and Hanges signed the contract of sale, Petrikis signing in the name of the partnership and in his own name. When the contract of sale was presented to Ellis for his signature, Ellis objected to certain restrictive clauses in the contract. Two days later and before Ellis had signed the contract, Hanges gave notice of the withdrawal of his offer to purchase the business and returned the possession of the Chariot Bar back to Petrikis and Ellis. Petrikis and Ellis contend that the "contract of purchase" signed by Petrikis in the partnership name and by Hanges was a binding contract, and they brought suit to recover damages for breach of the contract. Is Hanges liable for breach of the contract?

2. Lowe was a member of the firm of Robinson & Co., a partnership dealing in real estate. Lowe sold land belonging to the partnership to Daughtry, giving him a deed signed in the name of Robinson & Co. Robinson, the other member of the partnership, brought an action, claiming that the deed conveyed only Lowe's interest in the land. Is Robinson's claim correct?

3. Wheeler & Co. was a partnership engaged in the plumbing contract business. It did not maintain a retail store but purchased from jobbers and manufacturers plumbing supplies used in the fulfillment of its contracts, and it also hired laborers to do the work necessary in performing the contracts. Marsh, a partner, executed in the partnership name and issued certain promissory notes. The notes were not paid, and suit was brought against the partnership on the notes. The partnership set up the defense that Marsh had no authority to issue the notes. Is the defense good?

4. Dr. Pearson and Marjory Pearson were partners operating under the name of Casa Blanca. They exchanged properties with the Nortons. Dr. Pearson died and Marjory Pearson brought an action seeking damages for deceit against the Nortons. The Nortons then filed a cross-complaint against Pearson and the partnership for deceit in the same transaction. Judgment was given the Nortons by the trial court. Marjory Pearson appeals claiming that, since she was not a party to the deceit, it was error to grant a judgment against her individually. Is she correct?

5. Alice was a passenger in an automobile owned by Eule Motor Sales and operated by her husband, a partner in the Eule firm. As a result of her husband's negligence, a collision occurred and Alice was injured. She brought an action against Eule, as a partnership, to recover for injuries sustained. Eule argued that the action was in effect a forbidden suit against the husband because each partner individually rather than the partnership "entity" could be liable for the tort. Should Alice be allowed to maintain the action?

6. Gran-Wood Co., a partnership, joined Gaither & Boe, also a partnership, in acquiring and developing certain real estate. The agreement between them had the effect of

establishing a partnership. One of its provisions declared, "Neither of the contracting parties herein shall be liable to any third person, firm, or corporation for the debt, default or undertaking, contract or tort of the other contracting party, but shall be answerable only for its own acts or omissions." Construction was undertaken on several dwellings but was halted due to defective foundations and walls. A number of sub-contractors and suppliers filed mechanics' liens against the property and claimed that both Gaither & Boe and Gran-Wood were individually liable. Can Gran-Wood escape liability on the basis of the above-quoted contract provision?

7. Olson sued a partnership of which Puntervold was a member under a New York statute permitting suit in the partnership name. Puntervold was not served with process. Judgment against the partnership was obtained by Olson who then brought action on the judgment against Puntervold individually in Florida. Will Puntervold's motion to dismiss be granted?

chapter 22. Dissolution and Winding Up

Dissolution

Definition and Effect of Dissolution. Dissolution is defined in the Uniform Partnership Act (29) [1] as follows: "The dissolution of a partnership is the change in the relation of the partners caused by any partner ceasing to be associated in the carrying on as distinguished from winding up the business." Under this definition, it is possible for a partnership to be dissolved without the dissolution having any effect on the combined operation of the business. The business of the dissolved partnership may be carried on without interruption by a new partnership, a surviving partner, or a purchaser, or the partnership business may be incorporated and continued as the business of the corporation. The Uniform Partnership Act (30) expressly provides that on dissolution the partnership is not terminated, but continues until the winding-up of the partnership affairs is completed. The closing out of a partnership business is a three-step process: (1) dissolution, (2) winding-up, and (3) termination.

A partnership may be dissolved without any violation of the partnership agreement; it may be dissolved in violation of the partnership agreement; or it may be dissolved by operation of law.

Dissolution without Violation of Agreement. The dissolution of a partnership is caused, without any violation of the partnership agreement, by the expiration of the term of the partnership agreement or by the accomplishment of its objectives. If the partnership agreement states no definite terms or special undertaking, any partner has the right to cause the dissolution of the partnership at any time he wishes.

If the partner has assigned his interest in the partnership and no charging order has been issued against a partner's interest, the partners may cause the

---

[1] The numbers in parentheses refer to the sections of the Uniform Partnership Act.

dissolution of the partnership at any time by mutual agreement. Also, if one or more of the partners have violated the partnership agreement, the copartner or copartners have the right to cause the dissolution of the partnership by the expulsion of the guilty partner or partners.

Dissolution in Violation of Agreement. A partnership will be dissolved by the withdrawal of a partner irrespective of the terms of the partnership agreement. The partnership relation is personal, and unless the circumstances are very unusual, the courts will not decree a continuation of the partnership against the will of a partner. In withdrawing from the partnership, the withdrawing partner may be guilty of breach of the partnership agreement, in which case he will be liable in damages to his copartners for any injury they may suffer as the result of his withdrawal.

Dissolution by Operation of Law or Court Decree. The dissolution of the partnership may also be caused, irrespective of the provisions of the partnership agreement, by the business of the partnership becoming illegal, by the death of a partner, by the bankruptcy of a partner, or by a court decree.

A court will not decree the dissolution of a partnership unless the facts and circumstances of the case demand such action. In general, the court will decree a dissolution if a partner becomes insane or incapable of performing his duties, if a partner persists in conduct which is detrimental to the partnership or is guilty of material violation of the partnership agreement, if the business can be carried on only at a loss, or if a judgment creditor has obtained a charging order and is entitled to have the partnership dissolved under the order.

Summary

Any change in the membership of a partnership causes its dissolution. Dissolution should be distinguished from the winding-up and termination of the partnership.

Dissolution, without violation of the partnership agreement, may be caused by the expiration of the term or by the accomplishment of the objective of the partnership, or if no term or objective is stated, at the will of any partner, or if third-party interests are not involved, by the mutual agreement of the partners.

Irrespective of the provisions of the partnership agreement, a partnership may be dissolved by the withdrawal of a partner. The withdrawing partner may be liable to his copartners in damages for breach of the partnership agreement.

A partnership may be dissolved by the death of a partner or by the bankruptcy of a partner, or it may be dissolved by a court decree. The court will not decree the dissolution of a partnership unless the facts and circumstances demand such action.

Cox v. Jones
412 S.W.2d 143 (Sup. Ct. Mo. 1966)

This was an action by Dr. William L. Cox (plaintiff) against his former partner, Dr. Charles E. Jones (defendant), seeking an accounting and a share of remaining accounts receivable. Judgment for Dr. Cox and Dr. Jones appealed. Judgment reversed in part (affirmed on issues not here discussed).

Dr. Cox and Dr. Jones were partners in a medical practice. The written partnership agreement provided that a withdrawing partner's capital investment would be purchased by the remaining partner at book value and that for six months following withdrawal all accounts receivable collections would be divided per the existing percentage formula. At the end of this period, all accounts receivable were to become the property of the remaining partner. Following a series of disagreements, Dr. Jones orally informed Dr. Cox that he was leaving as of October 1, 1963. Dr. Cox thereafter sought another doctor to join the practice, but prior to October 1, Dr. Jones gave notice that he had changed his mind and was not leaving. Dr. Jones refused to set a definite termination date and on November 9, 1963, Dr. Cox wrote to Dr. Jones requesting his withdrawal as of December 31, 1963. The letter stated that if Dr. Jones refused to withdraw, Dr. Cox would withdraw as of February 15, 1964. Dr. Jones took no further action, and on February 15, Dr. Cox left the practice. Dr. Cox claimed that he was entitled to the accounts receivable as the remaining partner by reason of Dr. Jones's oral notice of withdrawal as of October 1, 1963.

PER CURIAM.   The letter of November 9, 1963, from Dr. Cox to Dr. Jones, has no legal significance except as a *written* notice of partnership termination by Dr. Cox effective February 15, 1964. It is clear that as of the date of the letter the partnership had not been dissolved by Dr. Jones's acts or conduct as of October 1, 1963. The record shows only that he withdrew his oral notice of dissolution before it was acted upon (accepted) by Dr. Cox. That Dr. Jones could do this is elementary in contract law. Dr. Cox testified that Dr. Jones told him he had changed his mind *before* the oral termination date of October 1, 1963. It thus appears from all the evidence that Dr. Jones was not the withdrawing partner as of October 1, 1963. Dr. Cox's letter of November 9 could not have the effect of forcing Dr. Jones to give a notice and become a withdrawing partner and thus work a forfeiture of his interest in the accounts receivable, in accordance with paragraph 11 of the April 1, 1962 partnership agreement. On this record we can conclude only that by the November 9, 1963 letter, Dr. Cox became the withdrawing partner as of his own termination date, February 15, 1964. The result which we reach is that Dr. Jones does not forfeit his interest in the accounts receivable, but under the terms of these parties' agreement, each partner must share equally in all the accounts receivable for six months after February 15, 1964, after which the remaining accounts and collections thereon are the property of Dr. Jones.

Change in Membership

Effect of Change in Membership. The Uniform Partnership Act (29) provides that a partnership is dissolved by "the change in the relation of the partners caused by any partner ceasing to be associated in the carrying on as distinguished from the winding-up of the business." The effect of the addition of a partner to a going partnership without the withdrawal of a partner is not specifically stated in the Uniform Partnership Act. The courts have, however, generally held that the admission of a new partner into an existing partnership has the effect of dissolving the existing partnership by the mutual agreement of the partners. Consequently, under existing law any change in the membership of a partnership causes the dissolution of the partnership. The business of the dissolved partnership may be carried on without interruption. However, the dissolution of a partnership by a change in its membership and the continuation of the business does result in some important changes in the legal relations of the parties involved.

Acquisition of Partner's Interest by Copartners. If a partner withdraws, dies, or is adjudged bankrupt, and his partner or partners acquire his interest in the partnership and continue the partnership business, there will be no change in the liabilities of the parties as to existing partnership creditors. All of the parties will be personally liable for existing partnership liabilities. Under the provisions of the Uniform Partnership Act (4[1]) the creditors of the dissolved partnership are also creditors of the person or partnership continuing the business.

The withdrawal, death, or bankruptcy of a partner dissolves the partnership. The estate of a deceased partner or the trustee in bankruptcy of a bankrupt partner is not liable for the debts of a partner or partners who continue the business. However, a withdrawing partner will be liable unless the person extending credit to the continued business has notice or knowledge of the dissolution of the partnership. Notice of dissolution resulting from the death of a partner is not required, and notice of bankruptcy of a person is given to his creditors by the bankruptcy court.

A Partner Transfers His Interest to a Third Person. A partner may, with the consent of his copartners, transfer his interest in the parnership to a third person. In such a case the old partnership is dissolved, and a new one is created which continues the business and is liable for the obligations of the old partnership. The withdrawing partner remains liable for the obligations of the old partnership and will be liable for the obligations of the new partnership unless he gives the required notice of his withdrawal or unless the party dealing with the new partnership has knowledge of the dissolution. The new partner will be liable to the creditors of the old partnership only to the extent of the assets of the old partnership acquired by the new partnership unless he assumes and agrees to pay their claims, in which case such creditors will be third-party creditor beneficiaries of the contract between the transferor partner and the new transferee partner.

An agreement by the new partner to assume the obligations of the old partnership will not relieve the withdrawing partner from liability for the obligations of the old partnership, unless the creditors of the old partnership, in consideration of the new partner's promise to perform such obligations, agree to release the withdrawing partner from them. Such an agreement is known as a novation.

Addition of a Partner.   If an existing partnership takes in a new partner, the old partnership is dissolved, and a new partnership is created. As to the liability of the new partners the Uniform Partnership Act (17) provides that a person admitted as a partner into an existing partnership is liable for all the obligations of the partnership arising before his admission as though he had been a partner when such obligations were incurred, except that this liability shall be satisfied only out of partnership property. The incoming partner may, by express agreement, assume unlimited liability for existing partnership obligations.

The Common-Law Rule.   At common law a new partnership created under the circumstances discussed above was not held liable for the obligations of the old partnership, and the creditors of the old partnership had to look to the partners of the old partnership for the satisfaction of their claims. The provisions of the Uniform Partnership Act (17 and 41), however, impose on the new partnership liability for the obligations of the old partnership.

Summary

Any change in the membership of a partnership dissolves a partnership, but it does not make it necessary to wind up and terminate the business.

If a partner's interest in a partnership is purchased by his copartners, the new partnership is liable for the obligations of the old partnership. The withdrawing partner or his estate continues to be liable for the obligations of the partnership. A selling partner is liable for the debts of the new partnership unless proper notice is given.

In the event a partner sells his interest in the partnership to a third person, the new partnership is liable for the obligations of the old partnership, and the withdrawing partner continues to be liable unless there is a novation. The new partner is not liable for the obligations of the old partnership unless, as part of the purchase agreement, he assumes such obligations. The withdrawing partner is liable for the obligations of the new partnership unless proper notice is given.

If a new partner is added, he is liable for the obligations of the old partnership. Such liability must, however, be satisfied out of partnership property only, unless it is increased by express agreement.

At common law a new partnership acquiring the assets of an old partnership and continuing its business was not liable for the obligations of the old partnership.

White v. *Brown*

292 F.2d 725 (D.C. Cir. 1961)

This was an action by William A. Brown (plaintiff) against John J. White, Jr. (defendant) to recover a judgment on a partnership obligation. The District Court judge directed a verdict for Brown and White appealed. The judgment was reversed and a trial ordered.

White was a member of a partnership, a firm of architects. He withdrew from the partnership in January, 1957, under an agreement with the two continuing partners whereby the continuing partners agreed to assume all responsibility for partnership debts and to indemnify White for all liability for partnership obligations. At the time of White's withdrawal, the partnership owed Brown $20,695.27 for services as consulting engineer to the partnership. Brown was given notice in April, 1957, of White's withdrawal from the partnership and the terms of the withdrawal agreement. In September, 1957, Brown accepted a series of twelve promissory notes executed by the continuing partners, one of the series payable each month in the principal sum of $2,000 with interest at six per cent. None of the notes was paid and the partnership became insolvent within a year. Brown sued White on the partnership debt, and White maintained that Brown discharged him by accepting the liability of the continuing partners in lieu of that of the original partnership.

FAHY, CIRCUIT JUDGE. While the indemnity agreement could not in itself alter the rights of creditors, yet, whether or not the creditor is a party to the agreement, it constitutes a promise made for his benefit and one of which he is at liberty to take advantage. *Byvesky* v. *Agains*. If Brown assented to the arrangement and adopted the remaining partners as his debtors, then the liability of White is at an end. White was discharged from his liability if there was an agreement to that effect between himself, the remaining partners and Brown; and such agreement may be inferred from the course of dealing between the remaining partners and the creditor who has knowledge of the dissolution agreement.

We do not adopt the "slight evidence" criterion set out in *Regester* v. *Dodge,* which is not generally approved, but that aside there is enough evidence in this case to go to the jury on the issue of discharge by agreement. The evidence tends to show more than a continued dealing by Brown with the remaining partners. That alone is not enough. *Tuckerman* v. *Mearns.* But we do not find the *Tuckerman* case or others cited by Brown, to bear sufficient factual similarity to the case at bar to militate against the position we take. Brown not only continued for some time to deal with the new partnership with respect to the matters now in suit but also took the notes of the remaining partners, construable as extending for a definite period the time for payment of the indebtedness. And there was evidence that Brown acted with knowledge of White's withdrawal and the assumption of the debt by the remaining partners. That this conduct continued over a relatively brief period of time is a factor to be considered. But the gist of the matter is that the evidence was sufficient to be submitted to the jury for its determination whether an agreement to discharge White's liability should be inferred.

We come to White's further contention that he became a surety for the indebtedness to Brown, and that the latter's conduct brought about White's discharge from his obligation as surety.

Where a partner withdraws from a partnership under an agreement with his former partners who continue the business that they assume the partnership obligations and will indemnify him, and notice of these arrangements is given a creditor, who acquiesces in the situation, the rule derived from a majority of the decisions appears to be that the withdrawing partner becomes a surety for the payment of the obligation. This occurs by operation of law, that is, by equitable implication, rather than by express agreement between the creditor and the withdrawing partner.

Notice of Dissolution

Necessity of Notice. As a general rule, third persons dealing with a partnership are justified in assuming that it will continue in business, and unless such persons have notice or knowledge that the partnership has been dissolved, they are justified in continuing to deal with it in the accustomed manner. For this reason, in the event of dissolution of a partnership, the partners must, if they wish to protect themselves against continued liability as partners, give notice of its dissolution to third persons who have dealt with the partnership or who have known of its existence.

If dissolution is brought about by the death or bankruptcy of a partner, no formal notice is required, since such matters are considered matters of general public knowledge; otherwise, notice must be given.

Who Is Entitled to Notice. Under the provisions of the Uniform Partnership Act (35), if a third person has extended credit to the partnership, he must be given actual notice. If notice is mailed, properly addressed, and postage prepaid, the presumption is that it will be received; but if it is not received, the third person is not bound. As to others not having extended credit to the partnership but knowing of it, notice published in a paper having a general circulation in the community or communities where the partnership carried on its business is sufficient. If one has knowledge of the dissolution, it is equivalent to actual notice.

Summary

Third persons are justified in assuming that a partnership will continue in business, and if proper notice is not given in the event that the partnership is dissolved, the partners will continue to be liable as partners. If the partnership is dissolved by the death or bankruptcy of a partner, no formal notice is required.

Third persons who have extended credit to a partnership are entitled to actual notice of voluntary dissolution. To third persons knowing of the partnership but not having extended credit to it, notice may be given by an advertisement in a paper having general circulation in the community.

Credit Bureaus of Merced County, Inc. v. *Shipman*
334 P.2d 1036 (Sup. Ct. Cal. 1959)

This was an action by Credit Bureaus of Merced County, Inc., assignee (plaintiff) against Russell C. Shipman and Donald E. Davis *et al.* (defendants) to recover a judgment for partnership debts. Judgment for Credit Bureaus of Merced County, Inc., and Davis appealed. Judgment affirmed.

Donald Davis and Russell Shipman formed a partnership in 1954 under the name of Shipman & Davis Lumber Company. On September 20, 1955, the partnership was dissolved by written agreement. A notice of dissolution was published in a newspaper of general circulation in the county where the business was conducted but no actual notice of dissolution was given to the firms which had extended credit to the partnership at the time of dissolution.

Under the terms of the dissolution agreement Shipman was to continue the business and was to assume and pay all partnership debts. After the dissolution several firms which had previously extended credit to the partnership continued to extend credit to the continued business. Their claims were not paid. Several claimants assigned their claims to Credit Bureaus of Merced County, Inc., and it brought suit against Shipman and Davis. Davis claimed that he was not liable for goods sold or services rendered after the date of dissolution.

SCHOTTKY, JUSTICE. Davis argues first that at the time of the suit he was not liable for the debts sued upon. He contends that no liability exists as to Laird Welding & Manufacturing Works because the amount which was due at the time of dissolution was subsequently paid, and, therefore, no liability existed at the time of suit. As to the repair item incurred on November 3, 1955, which was after the date of the dissolution, Davis would not be liable therefor if Laird Welding & Manufacturing Works had notice of the dissolution. While the evidence is conflicting as to whether the Welding Works had notice of the dissolution at the time the repairs were made, it is sufficient to support the finding of the court that the company did not have notice. The burden is on a defendant relying on dissolution to prove notice of dissolution. Davis cannot rely on the provisions of section 15035.5 of the Corporation Code (U.P.A. Sec. 35) to show actual knowledge. This section provides for publication of notice of dissolution of a partnership. However, as to firms having prior credit dealings with the partnership, actual notice of dissolution is necessary. While publication may be evidence from which actual knowledge could be inferred, publication alone would not compel a finding of actual knowledge. A retiring partner is not justified in placing sole reliance upon the publication of notice of dissolution, but should assure himself that existing creditors who have extended credit to the partnership receive actual notice of such dissolution.

As to the Merced Hardware account it is clear that the debts for the items sued upon were all incurred after February, 1956. Davis contends that he is not liable for these items of debt because they were incurred after the dissolution of the partnership. Credit Bureaus in reply points out that section 15035 of the Corporation Code provides that after a dissolution a partner can bind the partnership "By any transaction which would bind the partnership if dissolution had not taken place, provided, the other party to the transaction: I. Had extended credit to the partnership prior to dissolution and had no knowledge or notice of the dissolution." Here again the evidence is conflicting as to whether Merced Hardware & Implement Company had notice of dissolution of the partnership, and we are bound by the court's finding that it did not. There is also evidence that Merced Hardware & Implement Company had previously extended credit to the partnership.

Winding up Partnership Business

Procedure in Winding Up. If a partnership business is to be terminated, the next step after the dissolution is the winding up of the partnership business. This involves the orderly liquidation of the assets of the business. The partnership continues to exist until the liquidation is completed and the proceeds are distributed. During this period the partners continue to owe a fiduciary duty to each other; however, the powers of a partner to bind the partnership are limited to those acts which are reasonably necessary to the winding up of the partnership affairs. The business of the partnership is not terminated until the assets of the partnership are liquidated, the partnership creditors are paid, and the remaining assets are distributed to the partners, or, in the event of the death or bankruptcy of a partner, to his estate.

Who Winds up Business. Under the provisions of the Uniform Partnership Act (37), if the dissolution of a partnership is brought about amicably and during the lifetime of the partners, they have the right to wind up the business. If the dissolution is due to the death or bankruptcy of a partner, the surviving partners, or partners not bankrupt, have the right to wind up the business. If the dissolution is by court decree, usually, although not necessarily, a receiver is appointed who winds up the business. If a partner sells his interest in the business to his partner or partners, or to a third person whom the other partners have agreed to accept as a partner, the business is continued; but the affairs of the old partnership are wound up usually in accordance with an agreement into which the parties entered at the time of the sale.

Partner's Power in Winding Up. The partner or partners who have charge of winding up the partnership business have the power to bind the partnership in any transaction necessary to the liquidation of the assets. They may collect on negotiable paper held by the partnership, collect moneys due, sell partnership property, sue to enforce partnership rights, and do such other acts as the nature of the business and the circumstances dictate. As a general rule a partner who is winding up a partnership business cannot borrow money in the name of the partnership. However, if by borrowing money and using it to pay partnership obligations he can preserve the assets of the partnership, he will have such power. The majority of jurisdictions hold that he has no power to make, renew, or endorse negotiable instruments. His power to bind the partnership on contracts will depend on the nature of the contract. If the contract is in furtherance of the orderly liquidation of the assets, he can bind the partnership; but if it is "new business," the partnership will not be bound.

Rights of Estate of Bankrupt or Deceased Partner. If the partnership is dissolved by the bankruptcy of a partner, the partner or partners not bankrupt have the right to wind up the partnership business. They must liquidate the assets, pay partnership creditors, and pay to the trustee of the bankrupt's estate any amount due to the bankrupt partner. If the partner or partners not bankrupt wish to continue the partnership, it is possible for the referee in bankruptcy to authorize the trustee of the bankrupt partner's estate to sell the bankrupt partner's interest to the partner or partners not bankrupt.

On the death of a partner the partnership is dissolved, and title to all partnership property, including real property owned by the partnership, vests in the surviving partner or partners. However, the surviving partner or partners hold the property in trust for the purpose of winding up the partnership business. They must, within a reasonable time, liquidate the partnership assets, pay partnership creditors, and turn over to the representative of the deceased partner's estate, in cash, the deceased's share of the partnership assets.

If the surviving partner or partners continue to operate the partnership business after the death of a partner without the consent of his representative, the estate of the deceased partner is entitled to the value of the deceased partner's interest in the partnership at the time of his death, plus either the interest on this sum from the time of dissolution until payment is made or the distributive share of the profits to which the deceased partner was entitled under the partnership agreement. The representative of the deceased partner has a right to make his election to take either the interest or the profits, after an accounting has been made which will reveal to him which will be most advantageous to the deceased partner's estate.

The surviving partner or partners and the representative of the deceased partner's estate may enter into an agreement to continue the operation of the partnership business. In such a situation a new partnership, composed of the surviving partner or partners and the estate of the deceased partner, will be organized to operate the business.

The partners may, in the partnership agreement, provide for the disposition of a deceased partner's interest in the partnership, and if properly drawn, such provisions are enforced by the courts. The agreement may provide that on the death of a partner his interest will pass to the surviving partner or partners. Such an agreement deprives the deceased partner's estate of all interest in the partnership. The agreement may give the surviving partner or partners the right to purchase, from the deceased partner's estate, the deceased partner's interest in the partnership for a fixed sum or at its book or appraisal value.

A fairly common arrangement is one in which the partnership carries insurance on the lives of the partners and provides that on the death of a partner the insurance money will be paid to the estate of the deceased partner in lieu of his interest in the partnership or to the surviving partner or partners, in which case the deceased partner's interest in the partnership is sold, usually to the surviving partner or partners, and the proceeds of the sale are paid to the deceased partner's estate.

Summary

If the partnership business is to be terminated after dissolution, the partnership relation will continue to exist until the assets of the partnership are liquidated, the partnership creditors are paid, and the remaining assets are distributed to the partners.

The partners have the right to wind up the business of the partnership. In the event the dissolution is caused by the death or bankruptcy of a partner, the surviving partners or those not bankrupt have the right to wind up the business. If the partners cannot agree, a receiver may be appointed to wind up the business.

After dissolution the partner or partners who are winding up the partnership business have the authority to do those acts which are reasonably necessary to wind up the business, but they do not have authority to engage in new business.

The estate of a bankrupt or deceased partner has the right to have the partnership business wound up within a reasonable time and to have the interest of the bankrupt or deceased partner paid over in cash to the trustee in bankruptcy or to the representative of the estate. In case of bankruptcy of one of the partners, if the rights of third persons are not affected, the partner or partners who are not bankrupt may purchase the bankrupt partner's interest from the trustee in bankruptcy and continue the business. In case of death of one of the partners the surviving partner or partners may organize a new partnership with the estate of the deceased partner, or they may purchase the deceased partner's interest and continue the business. The partnership agreement may provide for the continuing of the partnership business after the death of a partner.

State v. *Ed Cox and Son*

132 N.W.2d 282 (Sup. Ct. S.D. 1965)

This was an action by the State of South Dakota for the use of Farmers State Bank (plaintiff) against Ed Cox and Son and William B. Cox (defendant) to recover a judgment for money loaned. Judgment for Farmers State Bank; and Tennefos Construction Company and United Pacific Insurance Company, surety, and Ed Cox and Son appealed. Judgment affirmed.

Ed Cox and Son, a partnership consisting of Ed Cox and William B. Cox, entered into a contract with the State of South Dakota for the construction of a section of highway. Ed Cox and Son executed a performance bond with United Pacific Insurance Company (Pacific) as surety. Tennefos Construction Company was co-contractor with Ed Cox and Son. Ed Cox and Son, prior to June 1, 1956, borrowed money from Farmers State Bank (Bank). Between June 1, 1956, and August 16, 1956, Ed Cox borrowed from Bank further sums and after August 16, 1956, William B. Cox, as surviving partner (Ed Cox died on August 16, 1956), borrowed further sums. Ed Cox and Son owed Bank $108,492.42 at the time of suit. On June 1, 1956, Ed Cox and William B. Cox dissolved the partnership of Ed Cox and Son but Bank was not given notice of dissolution and had no knowledge of it. The money borrowed from Bank by William B. Cox as surviving partner was used to pay for labor and materials necessary to complete the construction contract. Pacific contends that it is not liable for moneys loaned to Ed Cox and Son by Bank after June 1, 1956.

RENTTO, JUDGE. The death of Ed Cox dissolved the partnership, but it did not terminate it. As declared in SDC 49.0602 the partnership continued until the winding up of its affairs was completed. The dissolution resulting from the death of Ed Cox terminated the authority of William Cox to act for the partnership "Except so far as may be necessary to wind up partnership affairs or to complete transactions begun but not then finished." This reiterated in SDC 49.0607 wherein it is provided that "After dissolution a partner can bind the partnership . . . (a) By any act appropriate for winding up partnership affairs or completing transactions unfinished at dissolution; . . .". Transactions unfinished at dissolution have been held to include road and other construction contracts. Funds advanced or furnished to the surviving partner for such purpose are legitimate expenses for which the partnership is liable.

Under SDC 49.0609 William Cox as a surviving partner had the right to wind up the affairs of the partnership. In fact it was his duty. He was so engaged when the notes in question were executed. In our view they are proper obligations of the partnership. Ed Cox and Pacific argue that because of the dissolution agreement of June 1st he was not a surviving partner when his father died. This dissolution was secret as far as the bank was concerned and the subsequent conduct of William Cox in his dealings with it was consistent with the partnership's continuation. As to the bank the partnership continued until the death of Ed Cox.

Distribution of Assets

Order of Distribution.   The order of distribution of the assets of a partnership is set out in the Uniform Partnership Act (40) as follows:

  I. Those owing to creditors other than partners,
  II. Those owing to partners other than for capital and profits,
  III. Those owing to partners in respect of capital,
  IV. Those owing to partners in respect of profits.

If the partnership has been operated without losses which impair the capital, few problems are presented in the distribution of the assets. Everyone having an interest in the partnership will be paid in full. If there is a disagreement as to the amount due any party in interest, the dispute will usually be resolved by an audit which will be ordered by the court and which will, as a general rule, settle the fact question of the amount due.

Distribution of Assets of Insolvent Partnership.   If the partnership is insolvent, the order of distribution set out above will be followed, but additional problems will be encountered. For example, the relative rights of partnership creditors and individual creditors, and the distribution of losses, will be involved. In final analysis the problem of the distribution of the assets of an insolvent partnership and the adjustment of the rights of partnership creditors against individual creditors is primarily one of accounting. When the accounts are accurately worked out, the application of the rules of law to the established facts presents few difficulties.

In adjusting the rights of partnership creditors and individual creditors, the rule that partnership creditors have first claim on partnership assets and individual creditors have first claim on individual assets is usually followed.

If a partner has, in addition to contributing capital, loaned money to the partnership, no distinction will be made, on dissolution, between the capital contributed and the money loaned as far as the rights of the partnership creditors are concerned. The only difference which might arise would be in adjusting the rights of the partners. After payment of creditors, a partner, under some circumstances, will be allowed interest on a loan, whereas no interest is allowed on capital contributed.

As an example of distribution of the assets of an insolvent partnership, suppose Alden, Bass, and Casey organize a partnership. Alden contributes $25,000, Bass contributes $15,000, and Casey contributes $10,000. After operating for several years, the firm suffers losses and is insolvent. The assets of the partnership, when liquidated, total $30,000. The partnership owes to partnership creditors $40,000. The accounts of the individual partners are as follows:

	Contributed to Capital of Partnership	Individual Assets	Individual Liabilities
Alden	$25,000	$75,000	$5,000
Bass	15,000	10,000	2,000
Casey	10,000	2,000	6,000

The $30,000 will be distributed to partnership creditors pro rata, leaving $10,000 of partnership debts unpaid. Alden's individual creditors will be paid in full, leaving a $70,000 balance in Alden's individual estate. Bass's individual creditors will be paid in full, leaving an $8,000 balance in Bass's individual estate. Casey is insolvent; his creditors will receive 33⅓ percent of their claims.

The losses of the partnership total $60,000 (capital investment, $50,000, plus unpaid debts after distribution of assets, $10,000). In the absence of a provision in the partnership agreement as to distribution of profits and losses, they are distributed equally. Each partner would be liable for $20,000, one third of the loss.

	Capital	Loss	
Alden	$25,000	$20,000	+$ 5,000
Bass	15,000	20,000	− 5,000
Casey	10,000	20,000	− 10,000

In this case, Bass is legally liable to contribute $5,000 and Casey, $10,000. This sum would be distributed $10,000 to partnership creditors and $5,000 to Alden. In our illustration, Casey is insolvent and can contribute nothing; consequently, his share of losses over and above his capital investment will be redistributed between the solvent partners. However, Bass has only $3,000 in his estate, and the final result will be that Bass will pay $3,000 of this loss and Alden will pay $7,000. Bass will have a claim against Casey for the $3,000 he pays, and Alden will have a claim against Casey for $7,000. If one of the partners is an infant, that fact will alter the distribution of the assets accordingly.

Summary

If a partnership has been operated without a loss, the order of distribution of assets is unimportant, since everyone will be paid in full.

If the partnership is insolvent, the order of distribution is important. Partnership creditors have first claim on partnership assets, and individual creditors have first claim on the individual assets of their debtor. The order of distribution is set out in Section 40 of the Uniform Partnership Act.

Jackson v. Caldwell
415 P.2d 667 (Sup. Ct. Utah 1966)

This was an action by A. R. Jackson (plaintiff) against Grant R. Caldwell (defendant) for an accounting of good will at the time of dissolution of the partnership agreement between the parties. Judgment for Caldwell and Jackson appealed. Judgment affirmed.

Jackson and Caldwell were partners in the public accounting firm of Messina, Jackson, Caldwell & Company. Messina died in August, 1959. Subsequent to the death of Messina discontent arose among the partners and employees regarding management of the firm. Beginning in January 1961, meetings were held in an effort to solve the problems, but to no avail. Caldwell advised Jackson that with respect to the partnership he (Jackson) could have any account, and employee, and the office space then under lease. Jackson rejected these offers and gradually withdrew from active partnership participation. Caldwell gave formal notice of termination of the partnership as of March 31, 1962, and the parties agreed that clients and accounts were to be allowed to follow the accountants of their choice without solicitation by either party. Immediately upon termination of the partnership Caldwell and Jackson agreed upon a division of the assets, and both proceeded to establish new firms to service the old accounts.

Jackson makes no claim of undue solicitation by Caldwell but seeks an accounting for purposes of obtaining his share of the good will of the partnership. Good will had not been mentioned in either the partnership or dissolution agreements.

NELSON, DISTRICT JUDGE. It appears that the substantial weight of authority in this country is to the effect that no value can be attached to the good will of a professional partnership, although there are cases to the contrary based upon particular facts and circumstances.

We subscribe to the general rule as stated in 40 *Am. Jur. Partnership,* Section 271:

"The general rule is that a professional partnership the reputation of which depends on the individual skill of the members, such as partnerships of attorneys or physicians has no 'good will' to distribute as a firm asset on its dissolution."

We are of the opinion, and so hold, the same rule applies in a partnership of public accountants, unless the parties have in their partnership agreements provided otherwise, or the facts and circumstances of the particular case would require a modification of the general rule.

Where the partners had concurred in the practice of not carrying good will as an asset on the partnership books and had determined the assets upon dissolution without reference to good will; and where there has been insufficient showing that the partnership agreement contemplated that it should be included in computing book value as in this case it is proper to exclude good will as an item requiring an accounting of one party to another.

Problem Cases

1. Clark, Allen, and Truhan formed a partnership to establish and operate a radio station. The written partnership agreement contained the following provision, "Upon voluntary dissolution of the partnership by any partner . . . the remaining parties shall have the first right to purchase the interest of such partner in the business, assets and goodwill, by paying the value of such interest as determined by current accounting and inventory. . . ." There were numerous complications resulting in a six months' delay in getting the station into operation. Clark was critical of Allen's efforts and was uncooperative during this period and even after the business became profitable. Clark filed an action for dissolution and an accounting, contending that Allen had breached the partnership agreement. Allen and Truhan claim the right to purchase Clark's interest, contending that Clark's action was a voluntary dissolution. Is the contention of Allen and Truhan correct?

2. Bessie Straus, Samuel Straus, J. Louis Straus, and Harry Straus, partners, were doing business under the firm name of Straus Knitting Mill. The partnership agreement provided that the partnership should be for a period of two years from December 31, 1949, and from year to year thereafter. It further provided that any partner could terminate the partnership by giving notice 60 days prior to the end of the calendar year. Harry gave notice of termination in May 6, 1957, and in November, 1957, brought suit, asking the appointment of a receiver and the winding up of the partnership business. The partnership is solvent, and the copartners have not violated the partnership agreement. (a) Does Harry have the power to dissolve the partnership prior to the end of the calendar year? (b) Should the court appoint a receiver?

3. In 1956, Audrey Kelly entered into a written partnership agreement with Nancy Kelly to conduct a beauty parlor to be known as "Kelly and Kelly Salon of Beauty." The parties operated the business under this agreement until August, 1965, when Audrey sold all of her interest in the partnership to Beverly McMillon for the sum of $5,000. Nancy, as required by the partnership agreement, consented to the sale. Audrey contends that the written partnership agreement provides for an accounting upon dissolution of the partnership and that she is therefore entitled to $2,440 as her share of the partnership assets. Can she recover?

4. Mrs. Ingrao and Mrs. Karsten operated, as partners, the Venetian Dining Room. On January 3, 1947, the partnership was dissolved, but no notice of the dissolution was given, either actual or by advertising. On January 25, 1957, Mrs. Karsten borrowed $2,400 from Miss Falzone, and executed and delivered to Miss Falzone a promissory note payable to Miss Falzone and signed in the name of the partnership by Mrs. Karsten. The note was negotiated to Vogler. The note was not paid when due, and Vogler sued Mrs. Ingrao and Mrs. Karsten. Mrs. Ingrao set up as a defense the dissolution of the partnership prior to the giving of the note. Vogler claims that the defense is not valid because of failure to give notice of dissolution. Is Mrs. Ingrao liable on the note?

5. Three brothers, W. S., King, and A. J. Murphy, had operated a mercantile and farming business as a partnership for many years. A. J. became the sole survivor and continued to operate the business. The executors of the estates of W. S. and King brought an action asking for an accounting and the appointment of a receiver three years after the second brother had died. They allege that A. J. is not keeping accurate records,

that he is not making reports or accounting to them and that he is insolvent. Is it error for the trial court to dismiss the action?

6. Fielder and his partner borrowed $6,600 from First Bank. They both signed the note but the partnership name did not appear on it. The proceeds were deposited in the partnership account and were used for partnership purposes. Fielder died and both his personal estate and the partnership estate were insufficient to meet the claims of their respective creditors. First Bank claims that the note was a personal obligation of Fielder and that it has the right to participate in the distribution of his estate. It further claims that the rule of marshalling of assets does not apply to this case. Is First Bank correct?

7. Claude and Ben formed a partnership for the purpose of "raising and selling eggs, turkeys, cattle, sheep, hogs, and feed." Ben furnished his farm and the equipment "that was out there." Claude was to do all the work and occupy the farmhouse rent free; any profits were to be divided equally. The partners were subsequently unable to cooperate and the partnership was dissolved. In the action for an accounting Claude objects to an allowance of $748.08 to Ben for "inventory used" and to a charge of $821.80 against himself for the full amount of partnership funds retained. He claims the allowance should not have been made because there was no express agreement that the inventory should be replaced and that he should only be charged with one half of the partnership funds retained. Should Claude's objections be allowed?

8. Settle, a radiology specialist, had engaged in practice since 1946. In 1958, he entered into a partnership agreement with Berg, who had been employed as an assistant, whereby Berg agreed to purchase a 45 percent interest in the business for $40,500. Thus for the purpose of this agreement the business was valued at $90,000. In 1960, pursuant to the entry of a third partner into the practice, a valuation formula was derived whereby the total partnership business was valued at $100,000. This transaction was never carried to completion. In 1962, Berg withdrew from the partnership and Settle continued operation of the business. Berg sues for an accounting to determine his rightful share upon dissolution. Is Berg entitled to a proportionate share based on a fair market value of approximately $100,000 or to a much smaller share based on the book value of $40,000?

PART VI *Corporations*

chapter 23. Nature of Corporation and Incorporation

Historical Background

Early History. The general idea that a corporation is a fictitious legal person distinct from the actual persons who compose it is very old. The Romans recognized the corporation, and in England the corporate form was used extensively even before A.D. 1600.

Although the business corporation was known in England prior to 1600, it did not play an outstanding role in the economy until after that date. The colonization of America, however, and the general increase in economic activity, not only in England but throughout Europe, gave great impetus to the organization of business corporations. Between the years 1600 and 1700, charters which gave corporations the right to trade and colonize in the New World were granted by the king or by parliament. The Hudson's Bay Company, which was granted a charter by the king in the year 1670, still exists and is engaged in trade in Canada.

During this period, charters were also granted to municipal, educational, ecclesiastical, and charitable or eleemosynary corporations. The church used the "corporation sole" as a device for the holding of title to land to avoid the complications which arose in regard to the descent of land on the death of the holder of the title. Usually, the bishop was the owner of the corporation, and the ownership passed to the successor in office, thus providing continuous existence.

The trading corporations of this period usually were organized to exercise monopolistic privileges and were quasi-governmental in nature. As a general rule, in addition to being given a monopoly of the trade in an area, they were given the power to colonize, to govern the colony, and to exercise other functions of a governmental nature.

483

Development in the United States. Business was developing rapidly in the American colonies by the time they won their independence from England. There were many business opportunities available, but the risks incident to such ventures were relatively great. Persons in England and on the Continent who had investment capital were willing to risk it by investing in New World ventures, but they were unwilling to assume unlimited liability for the outcome of the undertakings. Attempts were made to form associations which would give the investor the desirable limited liability. The joint-stock company and the Massachusetts trust (a business trust) were used, but the corporation for profit proved to be the most satisfactory form of association. It gave the investor limited liability and also a voice in the management of the business.

At first, in the United States, a corporation was granted its charter by the state legislature. The early corporations were organized to operate toll roads, toll bridges, and other types of businesses which were of a public nature and which were basically monopolistic in character. In granting corporate charters, the legislature was careful to limit the powers of the corporation to the needs of the business to be undertaken. The idea of special privilege was still dominant in corporate organization; and in the United States at that time, special privileges were not freely granted.

In 1811, New York state enacted the first general corporation-for-profit statute. Under the provisions of this statute, any group of persons who complied with the procedure set out in the statute would be granted a corporate charter. Today the procedure to be followed in obtaining a corporate charter is the same in most of the basic aspects as that set out in this early New York statute. The early general corporation statutes placed many restrictions on the corporations. They set out the types of business which could be operated by a corporation, the maximum capital the corporation could have, and other similar restrictions. Other states followed the lead of New York, but the corporation for profit, as a business association, did not come into prominence until after the Civil War.

These statutes have been liberalized and broadened, and have been made more detailed in their provisions. In all the states, businesses have been classified, and corporations which are to operate businesses of special public interest, such as banks, insurance companies, building and loan associations, marketing cooperatives, and public utilities, must be incorporated under special statutes which are more restrictive in their provisions than are the general corporation statutes.

Summary

The general idea of a corporation as a fictitious legal person, distinct from the actual persons who compose it, is very old. Several types of corporations were known and used in England prior to 1600.

The early English trading corporation was organized to exercise monopolistic trade privileges. It also had the power to colonize and to govern the colony.

At first, in the United States, corporations were chartered by acts of the state legislatures. In 1811 the first general corporation statute was enacted by the state of New York. Other states followed the lead of New York, and today every state has general statutes providing for the incorporation of businesses.

Nature of Corporation

Principal Characteristics.   Basically, a corporation is an institution which enlists the energies of men in the service of legitimate, social purposes which further the general welfare of all members of society. In its early form it often was a governmental unit such as a chartered town. This idea of the granting of a franchise by a ruler is today reflected in the necessity of obtaining a charter from the state as an indispensable condition of corporateness. Unincorporated associations, such as partnerships and business trusts, may have many of the characteristics usually attributed to corporations, but none will have all of them.

Under varying circumstances, unincorporated associations may be treated as having a legal existence separate and apart from the persons who compose it, yet the existence of the corporation as a separate and distinct legal person is generally considered as one of the outstanding characteristics of the corporation. As a legal person, it has the power to own property, to contract, to sue and be sued, and to do such other acts as are necessary to carry on a business. The corporation is the owner of the assets of the business and is liable for its obligations. Although the shareholders own the corporation as such, they do not have title to the assets of the corporation and are not individually liable for its obligations.

The existence of the corporation is not affected by the death or bankruptcy of a shareholder or by the transfer of its shares. It has a continuous existence during the period for which it is chartered, which may be indefinite, or until it surrenders or forfeits its charter. The corporation has a centralized management, but the shareholders elect those who manage it and control its affairs. Other business associations have some of these characteristics, but none has all of them.

Corporation versus Partnership.   A partnership is not given the standing of a legal person, although it is treated as an entity in some respects. Under the Uniform Partnership Act a partnership may hold and convey real property in the partnership name, and under the statutes of some states, it may sue and be sued in the name of the firm. Although a partnership does not have continuous existence and is dissolved by the death or bankruptcy of a partner, the continued existence and operation of the partnership business may be provided for by including appropriate provisions in the articles of the partnership.

It is difficult for partners to escape the burden of unlimited liability for partnership obligation. They may attempt to do so by including in partnership contracts a provision relieving the partners from personal liability, but a party contracting with the partnership may refuse to accept such a provision. A partnership may set up a type of centralized management, but unless the partnership is composed of a large number of partners, such a plan is not feasible.

Since the partnership is an association of individuals, it has many of the privileges of a natural person not enjoyed by a corporation. It has the right to carry on its business without obtaining a charter, does not have to file the many reports required by corporations, and may have certain tax advantages. Recent legislation, however, has given the closely held corporation most of the tax advantages of a partnership.

Corporation versus Limited Partnership. In a limited partnership a limited partner's liability is similar to that of a shareholder in a corporation. He is not individually liable for the obligations of the partnership. Also, a limited partnership cannot be organized by mutual agreement of the parties but, like the corporation, is dependent for its existence on a state statute under which it may be organized. All states have limited partnership acts. In other respects the limited partnership is the same as the general partnership.

Corporation versus Business Trust. The business trust or Massachusetts trust is a business association based on the principles of the common-law trust. Through this type of association the members are able to obtain limited liability for the obligations of the association. Each member of the association contributes capital to the venture and is issued a trust certificate which entitles him to participate in the profits of the venture and share in the distribution of the assets on the termination of the trust. Title to all the trust property is vested in the trustees, and they are authorized to manage the trust property in accordance with the provisions of the trust agreement. The trust agreement sets out the nature of the business to be conducted by the trustees and contains such grants of power and such limitations on the power of the trustees as the drafters of the trust deem expedient.

Under the law of trusts the beneficiaries of the trust (the certificate holders) are not liable on the contracts entered into by the trustee in the management of the trust, nor are they liable for the torts of the trustee which he commits in the course of the performance of his duties as trustee. The trustee is personally liable for both his contracts and his torts, but in his trust accounting, he is entitled to reimbursement from the trust fund, provided the obligation is incurred within the scope of his duties as trustee.

Some states refuse to recognize the business trust as a legitimate trust but hold the association to be a partnership and hold the trustees and certificate holders liable as partners. In those states which recognize the validity of the business trust, the courts are not in accord as to the extent of the control which the certificate holders, through the election of trustees, may exercise over the management of the business. Some states hold that if the certificate holders retain any control over the management, even to the extent of the election of a trustee to fill a vacancy caused by the death or resignation of a trustee, the association is a partnership. Other states permit such an election, and a few states permit the annual election of trustees by the certificate holders. In no state, however, are the certificate holders permitted to control the trustees in the management of the business.

The business trust has continuous existence, centralized management, and limited liability of the certificate holders. The certificate holder has little or no control of the management of the business, and his position is uncertain in many respects. The business trust is considered an undesirable type of business association in most states. Under state and federal tax laws a business trust is subject, with few exceptions, to the same taxes as are corporations.

Classification of Corporations. Corporations may, under existing statutes, be divided into three classes: (1) corporations for profit, (2) corporations not for profit, and (3) governmental corporations.

A corporation for profit is a corporation operated for the purpose of making a profit which may be distributed in dividends to the stockholders. In the United States today, corporations for profit which operate a business affecting the public interest, such as railroads, banks, insurance companies, building and loan associations, farm marketing cooperatives, are incorporated under special statutes which impose on such corporations higher standards and more stringent regulations than are imposed on the ordinary business corporation which is incorporated under the general corporation-for-profit statutes.

Incorporated churches, lodges, fraternities, schools (not incorporated for the profit of the stockholders), etc., are corporations not for profit. The object of corporations not for profit is generally charitable, social, or educational. Most states have enacted a special statute under which corporations not for profit are incorporated.

Governmental corporations are corporations organized for governmental purposes. Incorporated municipalities, the Tennessee Valley Authority and the Reconstruction Finance Corporation, are examples of governmental corporations.

We shall confine our discussion, with few exceptions, to the corporation for profit.

Summary

In England and the United States, certain unincorporated associations have many of the characteristics usually attributed to corporations. In general, persons who wish to organize a corporation must comply with certain requirements set up by the state in which they wish to incorporate. Characteristics usually attributed to corporations are existence as a legal person with the power to sue and be sued, and to own and convey property; perpetual existence; centralized management; limited liability of shareholders; and in general, the power to do all acts necessary to carry on a legal business.

The partnership enjoys many of the privileges of a natural person and is free from special regulations and taxes which are imposed on corporations.

In a limited partnership the limited partners enjoy limited liability but have no voice in the management of the business. The position of the general partners in a limited partnership is substantially the same as that of the partners in an ordinary partnership.

The business trust or Massachusetts trust has continuous existence and centralized management, and the certificate holders have limited liability, but the certificate holder has little or no control over the management of the business. The organization is cumbersome in some respects, and some states hold the trustees and certificate holders of a business trust to be partners and liable as such.

Corporations may be classified as (1) corporations for profit, (2) corporations not for profit, and (3) governmental corporations.

Corporation as Legal Person

Distinction between Corporation and Shareholder.   The right to carry on a business as a corporation is a privilege granted by the state. It is no longer a special privilege, since the right to transact business as a corporation is granted to any association of persons who can and do comply with the requirements of the statute under which such a corporation may be organized.

A corporation is a legal person which has an existence separate and apart from the shareholders. As an artificial person a corporation is considered to have its domicile in the state where it is incorporated and the place where it has its registered office in that state. Where it is a different place, the site of its principal office is sometimes said to be its "commercial domicile."

Generally, there is held to be no fiduciary duty between the shareholders and the artificial person which is the corporation.[1] No fiduciary relation exists

---

[1] However, controlling shareholders do owe fiduciary duties, at least when selling control of the corporation, *Perlman* v. *Feldman* 219 F.2d 173 (2d Cir. 1955).

between the shareholders and the corporation. The shareholders may deal with the corporation in the same manner and to the same extent as would any other person. The shareholder is not an agent or representative of the corporation by virtue of his stock ownership. The courts recognize the separateness of the corporation and its shareholders even though all the shares of the corporation are owned by one man.

Disregarding Separateness of Corporation and Shareholder. Achievement of limited liability by the shareholders is generally considered a legitimate purpose of incorporation. However, the separateness between corporation and shareholder may be disregarded if the corporate form is adopted to promote fraud, to evade the law, or to accomplish purposes detrimental to society. This problem arises most frequently in the "close" corporation—a corporation in which there is only one or a few closely knit shareholders. If the shareholders' personal transactions are intermingled with those of the corporation and corporate formalities are not observed, if the corporation is established with so little capital as to be unable to meet normal business obligations or if the corporation is otherwise formed to defraud or to evade existing obligations, courts will disregard the corporate entity or, as it is often phrased, will "pierce the corporate veil." They will hold the shareholders liable on the same basis as if no effort had been made to incorporate. Generally, this means the active shareholders will be held liable as if they were general partners.

Similar principles are followed by the courts in dealing with suits brought against corporations which operate a segment of their business through a subsidiary corporation whose stock is controlled or fully owned by the parent corporation. If, in fact, the two corporations have no separateness except their individual charters or the subsidiary is formed as a shield for a "shady" purpose, the parent corporation will be held responsible for the acts and debts of its subsidiary.

Summary

The courts recognize the corporation as a legal person having an existence separate and apart from the shareholders who own it. The shareholders generally do not owe a fiduciary duty to the corporation and may deal with it in the same manner as would persons having no ownership in it.

If the shareholders use the corporation as a means of accomplishing ends which are detrimental to society, the courts will deny the stockholders the advantage of limited liability.

A corporation may own the controlling stock in a subsidiary corporation and not be liable for its obligations. However, if the parent corporation uses the subsidiary as a screen behind which it is attempting to gain some unfair advantage, the parent corporation will be held responsible for the acts and debts of the subsidiary.

Consolidated Sun Ray, Inc. v. *Oppenstein*
335 F.2d 801 (8th Cir. 1964)

This was an action by Michael Oppenstein (plaintiff) against Berkson Brothers, Inc., and Consolidated Sun Ray, Inc. (defendants), to recover a judgment for rent. Judgment for Oppenstein and Berkson Brothers, Inc., and Consolidated Sun Ray, Inc., appealed. Judgment affirmed.

All of the capital stock of Berkson Brothers, Inc. (Berkson), was owned by Consolidated Sun Ray, Inc. (Consolidated). The District Court found the facts of the case to be as follows:

That on December 4, 1939, Oppenstein leased certain property to Berkson for a term of 26 years and 11 months ending June 30, 1967; that prior to June or July, 1955 Berkson was the sole obligor as lessee under the lease; that after June or July, 1955, Consolidated made certain changes in its dealings with its wholly owned subsidiary Berkson, such as (a) eliminated Berkson's control of money received from its retail store which was operated at the leased premises and reserved to Consolidated alone the right to issue checks on the bank account deposited in the Commerce Trust Company in Kansas City; (b) in 1959 closed the bank account, opening a new one in Consolidated's name so that thereafter Berkson operated without an account in its own name; (c) pledged Berkson's accounts receivable as security for a loan Consolidated negotiated for itself from Walter Heller and Company; (d) took from Berkson its former independent buying discretion and merchandising policies, buying merchandise for Berkson in New York and warehousing it in its own building in New York and directed complete retail price details; (e) changed fire and liability insurance on the leased premises from the name of Berkson to Consolidated; (f) prepared in New York and completely controlled all advertising; (g) arranged so that the directors and officers of Berkson were persons employed by Consolidated and were the same persons who were directors or officers of Consolidated, and no director or officer of Berkson lived in the Kansas City, Missouri, trade area, and the local store manager was not a director or officer of Berkson; (h) charged against Berkson a share of the cost of Consolidated's accounting and warehousing operations; (i) in 1956, just after the changeover, Consolidated entered into a Chapter XI, Reorganization Plan under the Bankruptcy Laws. At the same time Berkson's operating costs increased despite reductions in personnel; (j) in 1956 Berkson's sales dropped $224,000 and its merchandise cost for inventory was reduced by Consolidated in the amount of $220,000; (k) many of the corporate minutes of Berkson were printed forms apparently used by Consolidated for all of its subsidiaries, with the name "Berkson's" typed in; (l) all correspondence pertaining to the business of the lessee under the lease, whether written to the lessor, to third parties or to agents of Consolidated, was on Consolidated's letterhead and was for the most part signed "Consolidated Retail Stores by"; in such correspondence Consolidated referred to the lease, the leasehold estate and the demised premises as "its lease," "its property," and "its rent"; (m) Consolidated employed a realty firm and in letters exchanged between the two companies and third parties, efforts were made for Consolidated to sell the leasehold estate for a consideration to be paid to Consolidated; (n) in October, 1961, the retail store on the leased premises was closed and the inventory was sold to Macy's; the consideration therefor was paid to and kept by Consolidated, no part being made available to apply on the rent due Oppenstein for November, 1961, or thereafter; (o) Consolidated operated Berkson the same as if it were one of the division stores of Consolidated rather than a wholly owned subsidiary; (p) Consolidated did maintain substantially all the legal formalities required of Berkson as a separate corporation, such as filing necessary papers, reports and corporate tax returns.

VOGEL, CIRCUIT JUDGE.   From the evidence in this case there can be no reasonable doubt but that Consolidated did completely control and use Berkson as a mere conduit, instrumentality or adjunct of Consolidated itself. The ultimate fact question for determination, then, was what was Consolidated's purpose in so doing. If that purpose was unlawful or improper or for some illegitimate purpose which might result in damage to Oppenstein, then the court has the power to look behind Berkson, the alter ego, and hold Consolidated liable for Berkson's obligations. This necessitates a determination by the trier of the facts. Here the court, with the aid of an advisory jury, found against Consolidated on that issue. The law of Missouri is that, where the subsidiary is a mere conduit, instrumentality, or adjunct through which the parent corporation achieves some improper end, its own corporate entity will be disregarded.

Both parties quote from and rely on *May Department Stores Co.* v. *Union Electric Light & Power Co.,* as being the leading case in Missouri on the question of piercing the corporate veil. In May, the parent owned the subsidiary, as in the instant case; both companies had the same offices and the same manager, as herein; the parent corporation paid the payroll of the subsidiary and all other expenses, as in the present case; the parent paid the subsidiary's plant rent, as in the instant case; all receipts by the subsidiary were turned over to the parent, as was the fact herein; intercompany accounts recorded credits and debits from the moneys taken in and expended as between the two, as in the instant case; the subsidiary maintained its apparent separate identity for customer relation purposes, as in the instant case; and, as is true herein, all corporate reports were made in the name of the subsidiary in order to preserve its paper identity. In finding an improper purpose had been established in that case, the Supreme Court of Missouri said at page 55 of 107 S.W.2d:

. . . It does seem, however, that the determination of whether there is a case for equitable relief could and should be decided by the test of whether or not the arrangement involved is being used for a proper purpose. Should not all these other suggested tests be used only as aids for determining the true purpose of the arrangement? *Making a corporation a supplemental part of an economic unit and operating it without sufficient funds to meet obligations to those who must deal with it would be circumstantial evidence tending to show either an improper purpose or reckless disregard of the rights of others.* Equity sets aside legally sufficient conveyances if their purpose is to defraud creditors. If any intercorporate affiliation is devised for or is being used to accomplish an improper or unlawful purpose, certainly equity does have the authority to tear down technical legal barriers and reach beyond them to impose liability or grant proper relief. If the purpose is lawful, and fair and equitable to those with whom it is intended to deal, legal forms and relationships should be observed. Men have the right to use legal forms which they believe to be helpful in accomplishing proper purposes. (Emphasis supplied.)

In *Osler* v. *Joplin Life Insurance Co.,* the Supreme Court of Missouri said:

. . . The affairs of the corporations named were completely managed and controlled by those named, including the appellant corporation. The corporations were used as instrumentalities to achieve the purpose of the persons above named. There is no merit in appellant's points. 18 C.J.S. 376 to 385, Corporations, §§ 6, 7. At page 382 we find the following: "The rule followed in many cases is that the legal fiction of distinct corporate existence may be disregarded where a corporation is so organized and controlled, and its affairs are so conducted, as to make it merely an instrumentality or adjunct of another corporation. The courts will ignore separate corporate entities in order to defeat a fraud, wrong, or injustice, at least where the rights of third persons are concerned."

In *Darling Stores Corporation* v. *Young Realty Co.,* suit was brought against Darling Shops, Inc., and Darling Stores Corporation, charging that Darling Shops, Inc., was the mere adjunct, agent and instrumentality of Darling Stores Corporation; that the latter wholly dominated, directed, and controlled the former and was directly liable to the appellee realty company on the lease assumed by Darling Shops, Inc. This court affirmed the judgment of the District Court, holding Darling Stores Corporation liable on the lease, saying:

The findings of the trial court, abundantly supported by the evidence, identify the partnership and its corporation successor as constituting the same business entity. Darling Shops, Inc., existed only to serve the parent organizations—the partnership first, and Darling Stores Corporation subsequently. . . . In such case it is well settled law, as stated by this court in *Chicago Mill & Lumber Co.* v. *Boatmen's Bank,* 8 Cir., 234 F. 41, 45, that "when one corporation owns or controls the entire property of another, and operates its plant and conducts its business as a department of its own business, or as its alter ego, it is responsible for its obligations incurred in so doing."

The only apparent distinction between Darling and the instant case is that in Darling the subsidiary never operated the business in question, but served only the function of making the lease. In the present case, from and after June, 1955 Berkson never actually operated the business, but served as the nominal lessee. In both cases, the subsidiary ended up serving completely the interests of the dominant corporation.

Corporation and State

State's Right to Charter Corporations. At the time the Constitution of the United States was being drafted, a proposal to include in it a provision delegating to Congress the authority to charter corporations was defeated, and as a result this authority was left with the several states. The power to charter corporations is vested in the legislative bodies of the individual states. It is not an unrestricted power, since its exercise is limited by general provisions of the federal Constitution and is further limited in various respects by the constitutions of the states. Today, each state has enacted general corporation acts under which the various types of corporations may be incorporated.

General corporations for profit may be incorporated by complying with the provisions of the general corporation-for-profit act. In many states, persons wishing to incorporate defined types of public or quasi-public corporations must first obtain a certificate of "convenience and necessity" from a designated official or board as a prerequisite to incorporation. The corporation statutes of the states are not uniform in their provisions. There is a substantial degree of uniformity, however, as to the basic requirements for incorporating.

Under our governmental organization, one state cannot grant to its citizens privileges which are to be exercised in some other state. However, all the states permit a foreign corporation (a corporation chartered by another state or country) to transact intrastate business, provided it first obtains a license permitting it to do business within the state as a foreign corporation. Since interstate commerce is regulated by the federal government, corporations have the right to transact interstate commerce in any state.[2]

State Regulation of Corporations. The state's right to charter corporations carries with it the right to regulate the corporations it charters. In many respects the statute under which the corporation is incorporated is regulatory in nature. It places certain restrictions on the powers the corporation may exercise, it sets up certain requirements as to incorporation and management, and it sets out the rights and liabilities of shareholders.

In all states, in addition to the general limitations placed on a corporation by the general corporation statutes, special regulatory statutes have been enacted. In a majority of states, corporations are required to file annual reports, to pay special taxes and fees, and to qualify their securities with a special commission before they can be offered for sale to the public.

The state's power to regulate corporations is not without limitation, however. Any statute enacted by a state which would impair the obligation of contracts between the corporation and its shareholders or between the corporation and its creditors, or which would result in the taking of corporate property without due process of law, would be declared to be unconstitutional and void. Under existing general corporation statutes or provisions of state constitutions, the state may reserve the right to repeal, alter, or amend the corporate charter; but such power cannot be exercised in an arbitrary, unreasonable, or oppressive manner.

Federal Regulation of Corporations. The federal government has the right to regulate some phases of corporate activity if the corporation is engaged in interstate commerce. It may also impose special taxes on corporations. The Federal Securities Act of 1933 regulates the sale of corporate securities in interstate commerce, and the Federal Securities and Exchange Act of

---

[2] See Chapter 28.

1934 regulates the securities exchanges and securities dealers as well as also imposing specific duties upon corporations, their officers, directors and controlling shareholders. These two acts are administered by the Securities Exchange Commission.

Termination of Corporation. The existence of a corporation may be terminated (1) by voluntary dissolution, (2) by suit of minority shareholders, (3) by expiration of its charter, (4) by forfeiture of its charter, or (5) by merger or consolidation. In all cases the procedure to be followed in the dissolution of the corporation and in the winding-up and termination of its business will be set out by the statutes of the state of incorporation.

If the shareholders and directors of a corporation wish to terminate the corporation by voluntary dissolution, they may do so without court action by complying with all the provisions of the statute of the state of incorporation.

If the minority shareholders wish a termination of the corporation, they may petition the court to appoint a receiver and to authorize him to terminate the corporation. This is an equitable action, and the courts have broad discretionary powers. However, courts are reluctant to order an involuntary dissolution. Cases where courts have exercised this power tend to fall into one of three classes: (1) where corporate functions have been abandoned, (2) where the main purposes of the corporation are no longer attainable, and (3) where there is a deadlock among shareholders so that the corporation cannot operate effectively.

If a corporation is chartered for a stated number of years, as was the case with some of the older corporations, the existence of the corporation terminates on the expiration of the charter. However, a new charter may be obtained, and the business of the corporation may be continued without interruption.

If a corporation has been guilty of serious violation of its privileges, the state may bring a special proceeding in *quo warranto* to forfeit the charter of the corporation. Frequently, the state statutes will provide that a corporation's right to transact business will be suspended on the corporation's failure to pay franchise fees or to file its annual report, but such statutes do not work a forfeiture of the corporation's charter.

When two corporations are merged, one of the corporations surrenders its charter and is merged with the other corporation. When two corporations are consolidated, the corporations surrender their charters and are consolidated into a new corporation. The procedures for merger and consolidation are statutory.

Summary

The right to charter a corporation is vested in the state. The right to charter a corporation carries with it the right to regulate it. However, there is a limit on the restrictions a state may place on a corporation. Any statute which will result in the impairment of a contract or take corporate property without due process of law will be declared unconstitutional.

The federal government has enacted regulatory statutes which regulate the sale of corporate securities in interstate commerce and impose certain duties on corporations, their officers, directors, and controlling shareholders.

The existence of a corporation may be terminated (1) by voluntary dissolution, (2) by suit of minority shareholders, (3) by expiration of its charter, (4) by forfeiture of its charter, or (5) by merger or consolidation.

Levant v. Kowal
86 N.W.2d 336 (Sup. Ct. Mich. 1957)

This was an action by J. Phillip Levant and others (plaintiffs) against Isadore Kowal and others (defendants) for a dissolution of a corporation and the distribution of its assets. Judgment for Levant *et al.,* and Kowal *et al.* appealed. Judgment affirmed.

The Keywell family owned one half of the capital stock of the Barlum Hotel, Inc., and the Kowal family owned the other half. The bylaws of the corporation provided: All of the stock is required to constitute a quorum for a stockholders' meeting and all of the directors (12 in number) must be present in order to constitute a quorum for the transaction of business. A bitter dissension arose between the two families which grew to such intensity that they were quarreling almost constantly. The arguments were frequently carried on in the lobby of the hotel in the presence of guests. As a result of the dissension no stockholders' or directors' meeting was held from 1950 up to the time of starting suit (November 30, 1954). No profits had been withdrawn since 1949 and a $13,000 loss was suffered for the 1954 fiscal year. An opportunity to sell the hotel for approximately one million dollars was rejected because of personal enmity between members of the respective families. One conference in the latter part of September, 1950, ended in actual fisticuffs. This suit was brought, asking for the appointment of a receiver, the dissolution of the corporation and the sale and distribution of its assets.

SMITH, JUSTICE. Under these circumstances may equity decree dissolution? The question from an historical point of view is not without difficulty. At an earlier time, corporations received their charters from the legislatures through special acts thereof. Under such circumstances it was frequently held that the sovereign grant could only be revoked by the sovereign power. "The state gave, and the state only can take away, that life." *Capital City Water Company v. State ex rel. MacDonald.* The validity and applicability of such reasoning today, when the corporate charter is obtained simply through administrative process prescribed in broad statutory terms is doubtful. Moreover, a change in the customs of the business community played a significant part in the erosion of the sovereign doctrine. As the corporate device became employed for the transaction of business with increasing frequency, courts of equity were increasingly called upon, in the exercise of their traditional powers, to correct abuses in corporate management. The relief requested varied with the circumstances of the case, from the appointment of temporary receivers to the dissolution of the corporation itself. There is a noticeable trend, in cases decided since the turn of the century, toward recognizing the inherent power of a court of equity to grant relief in proper cases. The reasons therefor were well expressed by Judge Lamm of the Missouri court in the case of *Cantwell* v. *Columbia Lead Company:*

> But when all this has been said, it may further be said that this court has never denied power in a chancellor to prevent a scheme of irreparable injury and wrong merely because the movers in that scheme speak and act in a corporate capacity rather than in an individual capacity. That solvent corporations are wrecked for purely selfish and illegal purposes, that minority interests are 'frozen out,' that business immorality has run amuck under the assumption that courts are powerless, is too true. But the assumption is wrong. Judicial hesitancy does not mean judicial atrophy or paralysis. The board of directors of a corporation are but trustees of an estate for all the stockholders and may not only be amenable to the law, personally, for a breach of trust, but their corporate power under color of office to effectuate a contemplated wrong may be taken from them when, by fraud, conspiracy, or covinous conduct, or extreme mismanagement, the rights of minority stockholders are put in imminent peril, and the underlying, original, corporate *entente cordiale* is unfairly destroyed. It would be a sad commentary on the law if, when the trustee of a corporate estate is making an improper disposition of it, or has shown improper partiality towards one of its conflicting parties, or has put the estate in a fix where it is liable and likely to be either wasted or destroyed, or mercilessly taken from all and given to a part, a court could not reach out its arm, and preserve and administer the estate. We have never so declared the law.

Moreover, it will not be forgotten that the State has and retains an interest in the proper functioning of a corporation. As it has been expressed in an oft-quoted statement, "The charter (of a corporation) is a contract between the State and the corporation; second, it is a contract between the corporation and the stockholders; third, it is a contract between the stockholders and the State." These duties of a corporation in respect of its compact with the state in the exercise of its charter privilege were well expressed by Cowen, J., in the early case of *People* v. *Bristol and Rensselaerville Turnpike Company*. It was there held that a corporation "must come up to all the substantial objects for which it was instituted. If it depart from any one of these, it is guilty of a breach of trust. It was made a political body on the implied condition that it should demean itself faithfully and honestly in the use of all its franchises."

Incorporation

Where to Incorporate. When persons are contemplating the organization of a corporation, they must first decide in which state they wish to incorporate. If the business of such corporation is to be primarily intrastate, it will ordinarily be most advantageous to incorporate in the state in which the business is to be carried on. However, if the business is to be primarily interstate, the promoters of the corporation will wish to incorporate in the state which has corporate statutes that best serve the purpose of the proposed corporation.

Comparative taxes are, of course, an important factor. There is a considerable range among states with respect to the imposition of or amount of organization taxes, annual taxes such as franchise and income taxes, and taxes on the issuance and transfer of shares in the corporation, a few states impose a "cessation" or dissolution tax. Of equal or greater concern may be the limitations placed upon the operation of the corporation. The statutes and court decisions in some states, especially Delaware, give promoters and management much greater freedom than do some other states. Such liberality, however, may not always be in the interest of minority shareholders. Furthermore, in choosing the state of incorporation, it must be remembered that a state may amend its corporation statutes at will and its courts may overrule prior precedents or shift their viewpoint as new issues come before them, so that desired advantages may be lost subsequent to incorporation.

Model Business Corporation Act. More than half of the states have substantially adopted the Model Business Corporation Act as their general incorporation act. At least a half dozen additional states have followed the Model Act in amending their acts. These do not include such major industrial and commercial states as New York, Delaware, Massachusetts, California, and Texas. However, it has influenced the statutes and court decisions in these and other nonadopting states. The Model Act was drafted and is updated periodically by the Committee on Corporate Laws, a part of the American Bar Association's Corporation, Banking and Business Law Section. The committee was and is composed of leading corporate lawyers and scholars. The first draft, which was patterned largely on the Illinois statute, was prepared in 1946. It has been revised and amended several times since, but it assumed substantially its present form in 1950.

The Model Business Corporation Act follows the policy of granting broad discretion to the incorporators. It is drafted so as to permit them, by adoption of appropriate articles and bylaws, to adapt the corporation to their interests whether the corporation be a "close corporation," that is one whose stock is held by one or a few closely knit shareholders, or a large publicly held corporation. For example, although Section 30 provides that normally a quorum for taking action at a meeting of shareholders shall be 50 percent of the shares, it permits the corporation in its articles to set the quorum as low as one third of the shares or as high as 100 percent. Section 136 permits the corporation to establish a requirement of a higher proportion of shares voting in favor of any corporate action than provided for in the act by so declaring in its articles, thus presumably giving notice to its shareholders.

Steps in Incorporation. The steps prescribed by the incorporation statutes of the different states vary but they generally include the following, which appear in the Model Act: (1) preparation of articles or incorporation; (2) signing and authenticating the articles by one or more persons or a domestic or foreign corporation; [3] (3) filing of the articles, accompanied by the specified fees, with the Secretary of State; (4) issuance of a certificate of incorporation by the Secretary; (5) payment to the corporation of a prescribed minimum amount of capital ($1,000 in the Model Act) by shareholders; and (6) holding an organization meeting of the board of directors named in the articles for the purpose of adopting bylaws, electing officers, and transacting other business.

In addition, in many states copies of the articles must be filed with a county official in the county where the registered office of the corporation is located and in some states the articles must be published in a newspaper. Furthermore, qualification or registration of the corporation's stock under the Federal Securities Act of 1933 and/or a state securities law may be required.

Articles of Incorporation. The statutes of various states also vary somewhat with respect to what must be included in the articles of incorporation, but in general the requirements are similar to the following which appear in the Model Act (48) [4]: (1) name of the corporation; (2) its duration; (3) its purposes; (4) number and classes of shares; (5) if appropriate, designation of classes and relative rights; (6) if appropriate, designation of relative rights between series; (7) statement of consideration for shares to be paid before commencing business; (8) if desired, a provision limiting or denying preemptive rights; (9) any additional provisions desired, not inconsistent with law, for the regulation of the internal affairs of the corporation; (10) registered office and registered agent; (11) number of and names and addresses of initial directors; and (12) the name and address of each incorporator.

Name and Seal. The incorporators must give the corporation a name, and it is customary, but not required, that it adopt a seal. Under the Model Act (7), the name must contain the word "corporation," "incorporated," or "limited," or an abbreviation of one of these words. It may not be the same as or deceptively similar to the name of any other corporation incorporated in or authorized to transact business in the state. The Model Act also prohibits the use of a word in the name which indicates that the corporation is organized for any purpose other than those stated in its articles. A number of corporation statutes specifically prohibit the use of a word denoting an activity, such

---

[3] Many states require that three natural adult persons serve as incorporators—as did the Model Act prior to amendment in 1962. Some states require that the incorporators be subscribers.

[4] The numbers in the parentheses refer to sections of the Model Business Corporation Act.

as "bank" or "trust" or "insurance," which would indicate that it has been incorporated under a special more restrictive statute rather than the general corporation statute.

To facilitate the selection of a name unlike those of preexisting corporations, the Model Act (8) provides for advance application to the Secretary of State for a desired name. If he finds the name to be available, it may be reserved for a period of 120 days while the corporation is being formed.

Many states require the signing on behalf of the corporation of documents pertaining to real estate, such as deeds and mortgages, to be authenticated by a "seal." If the corporation does not adopt a seal it may be asked to furnish a certificate to that effect when executing such documents. Therefore, it is advisable to adopt a simple seal, which is customarily held in the custody of the corporate secretary and affixed to documents by him.

Duration and Purposes. Most states and the Model Act permit corporations to have perpetual existence although a few states provide a limit as low as 25 years.[5] However, the articles of incorporation may provide for a short period even when state law permits perpetual life.

All jurisdictions require that the corporate purpose or purposes be set forth in the articles, although in a few states it is sufficient to state, alone or together with specific purposes, that the corporation may engage in any lawful activity. Other statutes require corporations to list specific purposes or limit a corporation to a single purpose. Most general corporation statutes, including the Model Act (3), exclude types of activity which require incorporation under special statutes. Otherwise, the limitations as to scope of business placed upon the corporation are self-imposed, and they are stated in the articles for the protection of stockholders.

Financial Structure. The Model Act gives wide latitude to the incorporators in establishing the capital structure of the corporation. Various classes of shares may be established with or without par value and with or without voting rights (except in the case of certain extraordinary transactions). Certain classes may be subject to redemption by the corporation or may be given convertibility at the option of the holder into a different class of share. Under the Model Act the board of directors may be given authority by the articles to divide the classes of shares into series and establish the different rights and preferences for the various series. Some state statutes are more restrictive and a few do not permit a corporation to limit voting rights of common shares or do not allow no par or convertible shares or liquidation preferences for shares designated as common stock. Some states require that shares designated as preferred stock have some preferential features.

---

[5] Arizona 25 years, Michigan (Constitution) 30 years, and Georgia 35 years.

Management. The Model Act states (33), "The business and affairs of a corporation shall be managed by a board of directors." It requires (34) a minimum of three directors, but it does not require that directors be shareholders of the corporation, adults or residents of the state of incorporation, or even U.S. citizens. The articles need only state the number of initial directors and their names and addresses. These directors hold office until the first annual meeting of shareholders. Subsequently, the number is to be specified in the bylaws and may be increased or decreased by amendment of the bylaws. Some statutes reserve the power to change the number of directors to the shareholders. Directors must be elected at each annual shareholders' meeting, but the Model Act permits dividing the directors into two or three classes when they number nine or more. When classes are established, one class is to be elected at each annual meeting.

The bylaws are, in effect, private legislation for the structuring and operation of the corporation. Under the Model Act (25) the initial bylaws are to be adopted by the board of directors, and the power to alter them or to adopt new bylaws is vested in the board unless reserved to the shareholders by the articles of incorporation. Bylaws, of course, must be consistent with law and the articles of incorporation.

Regulation of the calling of, conduct of, and voting at shareholders and directors meetings is also generally specified in the bylaws. Most state corporation laws and the Model Act (27, 39) contain provisions in this respect designed to ensure minimum standards of fairness. The Model Act (44) specifies that there "shall be a president, one or more vice presidents as may be prescribed in the bylaws, a secretary, and a treasurer." It provides that the board of directors may elect or appoint such other officers and assistant officers and agents as may be prescribed in the bylaws and that their duties shall be provided in the bylaws or by resolution of the board of directors. The Model Act permits the same person to hold any two or more offices except those of president and secretary. A few states permit the same person to hold any two offices, but some of these states provide that no officer may act in more than one capacity in executing or acknowledging corporate instruments which require the action of two or more officers.

Domicile of Corporation. Although a corporation is an artificial person and cannot vote, get married, commit a common-law crime, or enjoy those special privileges reserved to natural persons, it does have legal rights and is under legal duties which require that it have a domicile—a home. Some confusion has resulted from the attempt to apply the legal concept of domicile to the corporation; but at the same time, certain basic principles have been developed which aid in clarifying the situation.

The state in which the corporation is incorporated is the state of domicile, and the place where it has its principal office is its domicile in the state. A federal corporation which has been organized by special act of Congress has no domicile unless the incorporating act assigns a domicile to it.

Summary

The incorporators of a business must first decide in which state they wish to incorporate. Since the corporation law of the states are not uniform, there may be some advantage to be gained by incorporating under the laws of a particular state. A majority of the states, but excluding some of those in which the largest number of businesses have incorporated, have adopted substantially all of the Model Business Corporation Act, which follows the policy of granting broad discretion to the incorporator or incorporators. A number of states require three natural persons as incorporators.

The corporation statutes will set out the framework within which the business may be incorporated and the steps to be followed. The articles of incorporation and the bylaws define the basic structure of the corporation and, in very general terms, the procedures for its management.

A name which is not confusingly similar to that used by another corporation doing business in the state must be selected, and usually the word "corporation" or some variant of it must be included in the name.

The purpose or purposes of the corporation must be stated in the articles of incorporation but most states permit this to be very general. Corporations to operate special types of businesses, such as banking, railroads, insurance, and building and loan associations, must be incorporated under special statutes.

The domicile of the corporation is the state of its incorporation, and within the state its domicile is, as a general rule, the county within which its principal place of business is located.

Corporations *De Jure* and *De Facto*

The *De Facto* Doctrine. Since the process of incorporation involves a series of steps, courts have frequently been faced with the question of how to classify a business association which holds itself out to be a corporation but which has not completed all of the steps required by statute. For example, are the persons acting as a corporation to be held as partners or protected from loss beyond their investment?

Over the years the courts developed a tripartite classification system: (1) *de jure* corporation, (2) *de facto* corporations, and (3) no corporation.

If the incorporators comply essentially with all of the mandatory provisions of the corporate statute and fulfill in a substantial manner all the required prerequisites for the organization of the corporation, they will create a *de jure* corporation. The validity of a *de jure* corporation is not subject to attack even in a direct action brought by the state even though its organization may not be perfect. Failure to comply with statutory provisions which are considered only directive, not mandatory, will not prevent the organization of a *de jure* corporation.

De Facto Corporation. If the incorporators fail in some material respect to comply with the mandatory provisions of the corporate statutes, they will not have organized a *de jure* corporation. The courts have held, on the basis of public policy, that a *de facto* corporation is formed when: (1) there is a valid statute under which the corporation could be organized, (2) the parties have made an honest effort to organize under the statute, and (3) they have done business as a corporation. The corporate existence of a *de facto* corporation cannot be collaterally attacked. That is, in a suit by or against the corporation, neither the corporation nor the other party to the suit will be permitted to defend on the ground of the defects in the corporation's organization. However, the state may attack its claim of corporate status in a direct action brought for that purpose (*quo warranto*). A corporation whose charter has expired is usually treated as a *de facto* corporation during the interval before it is renewed. Courts have not been consistent in their treatment of cases when no attempt is made to reinstate the charter.

Estoppel to Deny Corporate Existence. If persons hold themselves out as doing business as a corporation and induce third persons to deal with them as such, they will not be permitted to set up their lack of incorporation as a defense against the third persons. Likewise, if a third person has dealt with an association of persons as a corporation, such third person will not be permitted to escape liability by setting up the lack of corporate existence as a defense. Having dealt with the persons as a corporation, the third person has impliedly agreed that his rights and liabilities will be determined on the basis that such persons are transacting business as a corporation.

This theory of estoppel to deny corporate existence is an extension of the theory of *de facto* corporate existence. However, the theory of estoppel to deny corporate existence applies only in determining the rights and liabilities of the parties in particular transactions, whereas the *de facto* corporation is recognized as having a corporate existence for all corporate purposes.

Statutory Effect on *De Facto* Doctrine. Under the Model Act (50), issuance of a certificate of incorporation by the Secretary of State is conclusive evidence of incorporation except against the state, which is permitted to bring an action challenging corporate status. Since it is unlikely that failure to complete steps in the procedure short of the issuance of the certificate would be held to constitute the enterprise a *de facto* corporation, this would appear to eliminate the distinction between a *de facto* and a *de jure* corporation.

Liability on Failure to Organize Corporation. If persons attempt to organize a corporation but their efforts are so defective that not even a *de facto* corporation comes into existence, or if they carry on a business for profit representing that they have incorporated the business when they have made no effort to do so, the courts have generally held such persons to be partners and liable as such.

The courts are not in accord as to the liability of a person who purchases stock in a corporation which is so defectively organized that it does not have even the status of a *de facto* corporation. Some courts have held that such a person is a co-owner of the business and as such is liable as a partner. Other courts have held that one who justifiably believes that he is purchasing stock in a validly organized corporation will not be held liable as a partner. These courts impose the unlimited liability of a partner on only those stockholders who are actively engaged in the management of the business or who are at fault for the defects in the organization of the corporation.

A third person may be estopped from denying the existence of the corporation and may be denied the right to recover from the stockholders as partners.

Summary

If the organizers of a corporation have substantially complied with the mandatory provisions of the corporation statutes and have fulfilled all the required prerequisites for incorporation, they will have organized a *de jure* corporation. The organization of a *de jure* corporation is not subject to direct attack by the state.

If a statute exists under which a corporation may be incorporated and persons make an honest effort to incorporate under the statute and do business as a corporation but do not comply with all the mandatory provisions, a *de facto* corporation will have been created. Any attack on a *de facto* corporation must be made by the state in a direct proceeding brought for that purpose.

If persons have held themselves out as doing business as a corporation but either have made no attempt to comply with the corporation statutes or have complied so defectively that they have not formed even a *de facto* corporation, they will be estopped, under some circumstances, from denying their existence as a corporation. Likewise, a third person dealing with such an association of persons will be denied the right to escape liability by setting up the lack of corporate existence of the association.

As a general rule, if persons purport to carry on a business for profit as a corporation but have made no attempt to incorporate or have made an attempt which was so defective that even a *de facto* corporation was not brought into existence, such persons will be liable as partners.

By statute in many states the distinction between *de jure* and *de facto* corporations has been eliminated.

Robertson v. Levy
197 A.2d 443 (D.C. Ct. App. 1964)

This was an action by Martin G. Robertson (plaintiff) against Eugene M. Levy (defendant) to recover the balance due on a note signed by Levy as president of Penn Ave. Record Shack, Inc., which had not been incorporated at the time the note was executed. Judgment for Levy and Robertson appealed. Judgment reversed.

Levy agreed with Robertson to form a corporation to purchase Robertson's record store business. An agreement assigning Robertson's lease was made to Penn Ave. Record Shack, Inc., and signed by Levy as president on December 22, 1961. Levy submitted articles of incorporation to the Superintendent of Corporations on December 27. On January 2, 1962, Levy began to operate the business as Penn Ave. Record Shack, Inc. On this same day he received notification that his articles of incorporation were rejected. On January 8, Robertson executed a bill of sale of his assets to the "corporation" and received a note signed in the name of the corporation by Levy as president. A certificate of incorporation of Penn Ave. Record Shack, Inc., was issued on January 17. One payment was made on the note. In June, 1962, the corporation ceased doing business and no assets remained.

Hood, Chief Judge.   The Business Corporation Act of the District of Columbia is patterned after the Model Business Corporation Act which is largely based on the Illinois Business Corporation Act of 1933. On this appeal, we are concerned with an interpretation of sections 29–921c and 29–950 of our act. Several states have substantially enacted the Model Act, but only a few have enacted both sections similar to those under consideration. A search of the case law in each of these jurisdictions, as well as in our own jurisdiction, convinces us that these particular sections of the corporation acts have never been the subject of a reported decision.

For a full understanding of the problems raised, some historical grounding is not only illuminative but necessary. In early common law times private corporations were looked upon with distrust and disfavor. This distrust of the corporate form for private enterprise was eventually overcome by the enactment of statutes which set forth certain prerequisites before the status was achieved, and by court decisions which eliminated other stumbling blocks. Problems soon arose, however, where there was substantial compliance with the prerequisites of the statute, but not complete formal compliance. Thus the concepts of *de jure* corporations, *de facto* corporations, and of "corporations by estoppel" came into being.

Taking each of these in turn, a *de jure* corporation results when there has been conformity with the mandatory conditions precedent (as opposed to merely directive conditions) established by the statute. A *de jure* corporation is not subject to direct or collateral attack either by the state in a *quo warranto* proceeding or by any other person.

A *de facto* corporation is one which has been defectively incorporated and thus is not *de jure*. The Supreme Court has stated that the requisites for a corporation *de facto* are: (1) A valid law under which such a corporation can be lawfully organized; (2) An attempt to organize thereunder; (3) Actual user of the corporate franchise. Good faith in claiming to be and in doing business as a corporation is often added as a further condition. A *de facto* corporation is recognized for all purposes except where there is a direct attack by the state in a *quo warranto* proceeding. The concept of *de facto* corporation has been roundly criticized.

Cases continued to arise, however, where the corporation was not *de jure,* where it was not *de facto* because of failure to comply with one of the four requirements above, but where the courts, lacking some clear standard or guideline, were willing to decide on the equities of the case. Thus another concept arose, the so-called "corporation by estoppel." This term was a complete misnomer. There was no corporation, the acts of the associates having failed even to colorably fulfill the statutory requirements; there was no estoppel in the pure sense of the word because generally there was no holding out followed by reliance on the part of the other party. Apparently estoppel can arise whether or not a *de facto* corporation has come into existence. Estoppel problems arose where the certificate of incorporation had been issued as well as where it had not been issued.

One of the reasons for enacting modern corporation statutes was to eliminate problems inherent in the *de jure, de facto* and estoppel concepts. Thus sections 29–921c and 950 were enacted as follows:

§29–921c. (§50 of Model Act) Effect of issuance of incorporation.

Upon the issuance of the certificate of incorporation, the corporate existence shall begin, and such certificate of incorporation shall be conclusive evidence that all conditions precedent required to be performed by the incorporators have been complied with and that the corporation has been incorporated under this chapter, except as against the District of Columbia in a proceeding to cancel or revoke the certificate of incorporation."

"§29–950. (§139 of Model Act) Unauthorized assumption of corporate powers.

"All persons who assume to act as a corporation without authority so to do shall be jointly and severally liable for all debts and liabilities incurred or arising as a result thereof."

. . . . .

The authorities which have considered the problem are unanimous in their belief that section 29–921c and section 29–950 have put to rest *de facto* corporations and corporations by estoppel. Thus the Comment to section 50 of the Model Act, after noting that *de jure* incorporation is complete when the certificate is issued, states that:

"Since it is unlikely that any steps short of securing a certificate of incorporation would be held to constitute apparent compliance, the possibility that a *de facto* corporation could exist under such a provision is remote."

. . . . .

The portion of §29–921c which states that the certificate of incorporation will be "conclusive evidence" that all conditions precedent have been performed eliminates the problems of estoppel and *de facto* corporations once the certificate has been issued. The existence of the corporation is conclusive evidence against all who deal with it. Under §29–950, if an individual or group of individuals assumes to act as a corporation before the certificate of incorporation has been issued, joint and several liability attaches. We hold, therefore, that the impact of these sections, when considered together, is to eliminate the concepts of estoppel and *de facto* corporateness under the Business Corporation Act of the District of Columbia. It is immaterial whether the third person believed he was dealing with a corporation or whether he intended to deal with a corporation. The certificate of incorporation provides the cutoff point; before it is issued, the individuals, and not the corporation, are liable.

Turning to the facts of this case, Penn Ave. Record Shack, Inc., was not a corporation when the original agreement was entered into, when the lease was assigned, when Levy took over Robertson's business, when operations began under the Penn Ave. Record Shack, Inc., name, or when the bill of sale was executed. Only on January 17 did Penn Ave. Record Shack, Inc., become a corporation. Levy is subject to personal liability because, before this date, he assumed to act as a corporation without any authority so to do. Nor is Robertson estopped from denying the existence of the corporation because after the certificate was issued he accepted one payment on the note. An individual who incurs statutory liability on an obligation under section 29–950 because he has acted without authority, is not relieved of that liability where, at a later time, the corporation does come into existence by complying with section 29–921c. Subsequent partial payment by the corporation does not remove this liability.

Problem Cases

1. Olson was a real estate operator who, with members of his family, owned the stock of and controlled several corporations. Olson and all of the corporations maintained an office at the same address and employed the same bookkeeper. Olson engaged Zaist to clear and grade parcels of land in three cities for shopping centers and instructed him to send the bills, which eventually totaled nearly $200,000, to East Haven, one of his corporations, which had operated as a general contractor. East Haven maintained a separate checking account, separate corporate and financial records and had a number of employees. None of the parcels was held in the name of East Haven but were owned by and transferred between Olson and several of the other corporations as became convenient in financing Olson's real estate operations. Title came to rest in Olson personally and in Olson, Inc., but as Olson's operations became financially unsound, the stock of Olson, Inc., was sold, as was his personal interest in the lands in question. East Haven became insolvent leaving $23,000 due Zaist.

   Zaist sues Olson for the balance claiming that East Haven was his instrumentality and the benefit of the services went to him. Is Olson personally liable?

2. Carlton organized and was a principal shareholder in 10 corporations each owning and operating two taxicabs in New York City. Each corporation carried a $10,000 liability insurance policy, the minimum required by state statute. The vehicles, the only assets of each corporation, were mortgaged. The 10 corporations were operated more or less as a unit with respect to supplies, repairs, employees, etc. Walkovszky was severely injured when run down by one of the taxicabs and sues Carlton person-

ally, alleging that the multiple corporate structure amounts to fraud upon those who might be injured by the taxicabs.

Should the court "pierce the corporate veil" to reach Carlton individually?

3. Jones owned and operated an outdoor movie theater. He and members of his family also owned the stock of Jumping Jills, Inc., which offered to the public the use of pieces of gymnastic equipment known as "trampolines." The corporation leased land from Jones adjacent to the theater. A fence separated the two businesses and separate admission prices were charged at different entrances. Advertising was placed separately and separate books of account were maintained. Banks was injured while using the equipment through negligence attributable to the corporation. The corporation was properly dissolved before suit was brought and the insurer of the corporation had become bankrupt.

Banks's mother seeks to recover from Jones personally on the ground that the corporate entity was a fiction. Will she recover?

4. Heuskinkveld operated a business in which he bought and sold grain and mineral supplements and operated a number of semitrailers which were used for delivery of such materials. The deliveries were such an important part of the total business as to constitute illegal carriage for hire. The business was incorporated in 1963 with Heuskinkveld as sole shareholder and the method of doing business was changed. Later the ICC entered a cease and desist order against the corporation as well as Heuskinkveld as an individual on the basis of testimony as to illegal carriage by the business prior to incorporation.

Should the cease and desist order have been issued against the corporation?

5. Galloway owned all of the capital stock of Hardware Company, Inc., which he sold and transferred to McLendon for $10,000. McLendon paid Galloway $4,000 at the time of the transfer and gave him his note for the $6,000 balance. McLendon did not pay the note when due, and Galloway brought suit against him on the note. McLendon claims as a defense that Galloway owed a past-due debt of $12,163.57 to Hardware Company, Inc. Is the defense good?

6. Marks was sole owner of the outstanding shares of Sa-Rey-Mar, Inc., whose assets were largely intangible property. The corporation paid the state intangibles tax on this property but Marks did not report his stock in Sa-Rey-Mar on his intangibles tax return and refuses to do so when ordered by the tax authorities on the grounds that it would duplicate the tax already paid on the same property by the corporation. Is Marks liable for the tax?

7. The State Liquor Commission issued off-sale permits to several corporations which were owned by the same small group of shareholders. The state law provided, "No person shall directly or indirectly hold more than two off-sale permits at one time." The Wholesale Beverage Association seeks to have the permits revoked, and the Commission defends on the grounds that a corporation is a "person." Was the Commission action justified?

8. McGinnis, Inc., brought suit against Video Theatres for alleged violations of the federal antitrust laws. Video's defense was that McGinnis had no capacity to sue under a statute which provided that after a corporation's right to do business has been forfeited "it shall be denied the right to sue or defend in any court in this state." McGinnis was incorporated in Oklahoma in 1958. On April 26, 1962, it was notified by the Oklahoma Tax Commission that under the franchise tax statute its charter was suspended for nonpayment of the tax. The law provided for lifting the suspension if

the delinquent tax were paid within one year, but if not, it directed the Secretary of State to "revoke and cancel the articles of incorporation" after giving notice 30 days prior to the expiration of the one-year period. McGinnis did not pay and the notice was given. However, on January 29, 1965, after the suit against Video was brought, the Tax Commission found that the delinquent taxes were paid and ordered that the corporate rights of McGinnis be reinstated. Is McGinnis entitled to bring the suit?

chapter 24. Organizing and Financing the Corporation's Business

Promoters

Function of Promoters. The function of a promoter is to bring about the incorporation and organization of a corporation. It is a most vital activity in a free enterprise system and it is unfortunate that a few unscrupulous individuals have given the term a stigma. The promoter initiates the business; finds persons who are willing to finance the project; negotiates all contracts, leases, purchases, etc., necessary for the operation of the proposed venture; incorporates the business; and gets it started as a going concern.

In its broadest sense the term "promoter" applies to anyone who assumes the task of organizing and starting a corporation. If a member of a going partnership is instrumental in forming a corporation to which the assets of the partnership are transferred in exchange for stock in the corporation, such a person would be a promoter. However, the term is generally applied to one who causes the formation of a corporation for the purpose of carrying on a new business.

Relation of Promoter and Corporation. The relation of a promoter to the corporation and the persons whom he interests in the venture is unique. He is not an agent, since he is self-appointed. Technically, he cannot be the agent of the proposed corporation, since it is not in existence. He is not the agent of the persons interested in the venture, since they did not appoint him and he is not subject to their direction and control in regard to the promotion of the proposed corporation. A few courts have attempted to draw an analogy between the relation of a promoter and the corporation and that of a trustee and the beneficiary, but important elements of a common-law trust are missing.

The promoter owes the duty of a fiduciary to the corporation he is promoting and to the persons interested therein. In general, the relation of the promoter to the corporation and others interested in the project is analogous to that of the trustee or any other person occupying a trust position. In his dealings he owes a duty of perfect candor, full disclosure, the utmost of good faith, and absolute honesty. The courts have held that he will be liable to the corporation, subscribers or others injured if he takes a secret profit at their expense, and will allow them to recover in a direct suit brought against the promoter.

For example, if the promoter takes an option on property or purchases property in contemplation of selling it to the corporation after its incorporation and he misrepresents to the corporation the option or purchase price of the property, thereby making a secret profit, the corporation may recover a judgment against the promoter for the secret profit. However, if the promoter makes a full disclosure to an independent board of directors who purchase at the increased price, the corporation would have no right of action against the promoter. If the board of directors is under the control of and is manipulated by the promoter, the corporation may rescind the transaction or recover damages.

If the misrepresentations are made to the persons interested in the corporation and they, in behalf of the corporation, take up the option or purchase the property, paying the promoter a secret profit, a majority of the courts have permitted the corporation, when it is incorporated, to bring an action to rescind or recover damages. A few courts have held that only the persons who purchased from the promoter have a right of action.

A more confused situation is one in which property is conveyed to the corporation at a greatly inflated value in payment for shares of stock of the corporation, with the knowledge and consent of all persons interested in the corporation, and then the issued stock is sold to the public at a price substantially in excess of its true value. The federal courts have held that in such a situation the corporation has no right of action against the promoters of the corporation who have engineered the deal.[1] In such a case brought in the Massachusetts courts, the judge held that the corporation could recover.[2] The Massachusetts court reasoned that when the stock was issued with the intent to sell it to the public, thus bringing in new shareholders, the bringing-in of these new shareholders was the equivalent of creating a new corporation with the same rights as though the promoters had sold to the corporation making a secret profit on the transaction. In a later U.S. Supreme Court case, in which bonds were issued in payment for property purchased at a greatly inflated value, thereby rendering the corporation insolvent from its inception, the court permitted the receiver of the corporation to recover, for the benefit

---

[1] *Old Dominion Copper Mining & Smelting Co.* v. *Lewisohn,* 210 U.S. 206 (1908).
[2] *Old Dominion Copper Mining & Smelting Co.* v. *Biglow,* 203 Mass. 159, 89 N.E. 193 (1905).

of creditors, a judgment against the promoters for the secret profit.[3] The opportunities for illegal manipulation by promoters has been greatly lessened by the adoption of the Securities Act of 1933 and by the Securities Exchange Act of 1934.

Corporation's Liability on Promoter's Contracts. The corporation, when it comes into existence, is not liable upon contracts made in its behalf by the promoter. It cannot be held liable, since it was not in existence at the time the contracts were made, and therefore cannot be held as principal. Several theories whereby the corporation can be held liable on promoter's contracts made in its behalf have been advanced. All require some action by the corporation after it is formed, if only acceptance of the benefits of the contract. The most common ones are: (1) adoption, (2) ratification, (3) novation and (4) continuing offer. The adoption and novation theories both appear to depend upon the fourth, that is, that the third party with whom the promoter dealt impliedly made a continuing offer to the corporation to adopt the contract, or in the case of novation, for the corporation to be substituted for the promoter. The ratification theory is based upon the agency concept permitting a principal to ratify the unauthorized acts of the agent, although it is a dubious extension because no principal was in existence when the act was done. Massachusetts, like England, does not accept any of these theories, including implied novation, and requires an express agreement between the three parties after the corporation is formed.[4]

Regardless of which one of these theories the state follows as the basis for finding the corporation liable on promoter's contracts, the corporation will not be held liable if the promoter's contract is illegal, fraudulent, not supported by consideration or is beyond the powers of the corporation. For the corporation to adopt or ratify a promoter's contract, the contract must be a valid, subsisting contract which is within the powers of the corporation. The corporation must accept the contract in its entirety, and the officers or agents who purport to adopt or ratify the promoter's contract must have authority to bind the corporation to such a contract.

Liability of Promoter. Contracts made by promoters on behalf of proposed corporations have generally been held to bind the promoters. If the corporation is not formed or fails to adopt or ratify the agreement, the promoter remains liable on it. Obviously, the promoter alone is liable if the contract is made by him without reference to a proposed corporation but with the intent to assign it to the corporation later.

The effect on the liability of the promoter differs under the adoption and ratification theories. Under the adoption theory the promoter remains liable. He would not, of course, under the implied novation theory. No agreement

---

[3] *McCandless* v. *Furlaud*, 296 U.S. 140 (1935).
[4] *Abbott* v. *Hapgood*, 22 N.E. 907 (1889); *Henshaw* v. *McBride*, 2 N.E.2d 445 (1936).

between the corporation and the promoter will relieve the promoter of his liability unless the third party consents to it, thus establishing a novation. Courts have held in a few cases that neither the third party nor the promoter intended to bind the promoter. Such an arrangement would be only a "gentleman's agreement" rather than a contract and would not bind the third party either.

Summary

The function of a promoter is to bring about the incorporation and organization of the corporation and to do those things necessary to get it operating as a going business.

The relation of the promoter to the corporation is unique. He is neither agent nor trustee, yet he owes a fiduciary duty to the corporation and the persons interested in the venture. He will not be permitted to make a secret profit at the expense of the corporation or of the persons interested in the venture. The courts are not in accord as to a corporation's rights against the promoter who conveys property to the corporation at an inflated value in payment of stock issued, with all the parties interested in the corporation having full knowledge of the transaction, the deal being entered into with the intent of selling the issued stock to the public at a price greatly in excess of its true value. Under the federal rule the corporation cannot recover, but under the rule laid down by the Massachusetts courts, it can.

The corporation is not liable on the promoter's contracts, but it may, by its actions, make itself liable. Ratification, adoption, continuing offer, and novation are theories used to support liability.

The promoter continues liable on preincorporation contracts unless there is a novation. He is not relieved from the liability by the adoption of the contract by the corporation.

Killeen v. Parent

127 N.W.2d 38 (Sup. Ct. Wis. 1964)

This was an action by Thomas W. Killeen (plaintiff) against Gaile M. Parent and Raymond E. Flanders (defendants) to recover a judgment for damages resulting from their deceit as promoters of a new corporation. Judgment for Killeen and Parent appealed. [Flanders did not join in the appeal.] Judgment affirmed.

The facts in the case were in dispute but the jury found that Parent, Flanders and Priebusch contracted to purchase all of the assets of a lumberyard for $45,000. A corporation was organized to make the purchase and operate the business. Parent, Flanders and Priebusch each purchased 100 shares of the $100 par value stock. Each paid $2,000 in cash and the three borrowed, as individuals, $4,000 from a bank. The $10,000 was paid as a down payment on the purchase price of the business.

The balance was financed by borrowing from the bank. (A $21,000 mortgage on the assets was given the bank to secure the $4,000 borrowed by Parent, Flanders and Priebusch and $17,000 paid on the purchase price of the business.) An $18,000 second mortgage was given to the sellers of the business to secure the unpaid balance of the purchase price.

Killeen was induced to purchase 100 shares of the stock for $10,000. Parent and Flanders represented to Killeen that the business was of the value of $65,000 (Killeen claimed that he was told that $65,000 was the purchase price of the business) and that he would be a one-fourth owner of the corporation. Parent and Flanders intimated that they had each paid $10,000 for their stock. This transaction took place in December, 1958. In January, 1962, when the business was adjudged bankrupt, Killeen first learned that the business was purchased for $45,000 and that Parent and Flanders had paid only $2,000 for their 100 shares of stock. This suit was brought against Parent and Flanders to recover for their deceit as promoters of the corporation.

GORDON, JUSTICE.   Evaluating such testimony, the jury concluded that there was a relationship of trust between Killeen and Parent and Flanders and that the latter had used bad faith in failing to inform Killeen of all the facts. They determined that the stock for which Killeen paid $10,000 was in fact worth only $4,000 at that time.

It is reasonably clear that the defendants were promoters. That is a term applied to those who actively assist in promoting, projecting and organizing a corporation.

The trial court granted judgment on the theory that Parent and Flanders as promoters had a fiduciary responsibility to disclose material facts and that they violated this obligation in failing to disclose material facts to Killeen. This resulted in an unfair advantage to Parent and Flanders and a loss to Killeen. The fiduciary burden of a promoter is recited in a number of Wisconsin cases.

Since a fiduciary relationship existed, it was not necessary that the representations were of such a character as to have influenced the conduct of an ordinarily prudent person.

Parent and Flanders urges that the reason for Killeen's loss was the bankruptcy of the corporation, which in turn resulted from the lack of adequate capital. Even if this were accepted as an explanation of the ultimate failure of the company, it would not exculpate Parent and Flanders from their misrepresentations. However, it is to be noted that the jury answered affirmatively to the following portion of question No. 12:

Was there a direct relationship of cause and effect between any loss sustained by the plaintiff, Thomas W. Killeen, and

. . .

(b) the failure to disclose the details of defendants' transactions in relation to the assets of the yard business?

Even though the promoters expended their own time and money, the failure of the venture does not relieve them from liability for deceitful inducements to those who subscribed for stock.

There was conflicting evidence presented to the jury as to the existence of deceit. The promoters had special knowledge of the financial structure of the new corporation which they did not fully disclose to Killeen, although it was their fiduciary duty to do so. Whether the misrepresentations were affirmatively made or resulted from nondisclosure, these were factual issues which the jury was obliged to resolve. The verdict is supported by credible evidence which was "clear and satisfactory," and it cannot be disturbed. The trial court was warranted in granting judgment upon the verdict.

Completing Corporate Organization

Organization Meeting.   After the charter has been granted, the Model Act (52) [5] requires an organization meeting of the board of directors, who are to be named in the articles. Many statutes specify that the organization meeting shall be held by the incorporators. Even where the statute does not specifically require one, it is customary to hold an organization meeting although the incorporators, or even, in some cases, the directors, are "dummies" who are associates and employees of the lawyer handling the incorporation. The use of dummies may facilitate completion of the routine business of incorporation, the substitutes then resigning in favor of the operating directors. The organization meeting requires a proper notice. The Model Act requires a call by the majority of incorporators and the giving of three days' notice by mail to the directors.

Business of Organization Meeting.   The business to be transacted at an organization meeting will depend on the nature of the business to be carried on by the corporation, on the laws of the state of incorporation, and on the provisions of the articles of incorporation. The Model Act specifies only that bylaws shall be adopted and officers elected. Where the meeting is held by the incorporators, election of directors would be necessary unless they are named in the articles. Other matters usually included would be adoption of a corporate seal, approval of the form of stock certificates, acceptance of stock subscriptions, authorization of issue of stock, adoption of promoters' contracts, authorization of payment of or reimbursement for incorporation expenses and fixing the salaries of officers. Action on other matters which are appropriate to get the corporation into operation may also be taken at this time.

Bylaws of Corporation.   The power to adopt the initial bylaws is given to various groups in different jurisdictions. While the Model Act (25) gives it to the initial directors named in the articles, some states give it to the incorporators and others to the shareholders or subscribers. The Model Act also gives the power of amendment, repeal, and adoption of new bylaws to the directors

---

[5] The numbers in the parentheses refer to the sections of the Model Business Corporation Act.

unless this power is reserved to the shareholders by the articles of incorporation. Again, there is wide variation among the states. It is, therefore, necessary to examine the articles of incorporation as well as the statutes of the state of incorporation to determine where the power lies in any specific corporation. If, as is true in some states, the statute is silent as to who may make and amend bylaws, this power rests with the shareholders but may be delegated by them to the directors.

Although normally the procedures outlined in the bylaws for their amendment must be adhered to, if a different practice is customarily followed with the implied consent of those who could amend it, the courts will treat the bylaw as amended or repealed "by custom and usage."

To be valid bylaws must be consistent with state law and with the articles of incorporation. They must also be "reasonable" and related to a corporate purpose. Since usually a bare majority may make and amend bylaws, the latter requirement provides the minority with some protection against oppression by the majority.

Provisions of Bylaws. Since the purpose of the bylaws is to regulate the conduct and define the duties of the members toward the corporation and among themselves, they will include provisions setting out the authority of the officers and directors and such other provisions as are deemed desirable for the guidance of the operation of the corporate business. The bylaws will usually state the time and place at which the annual shareholders' meeting shall be held, set forth how special meetings of shareholders may be called, define a quorum, state how shareholders' meetings shall be organized, and regulate how the voting shall be carried on and how elections shall be conducted. They will also provide for the organization of the board of directors, state the place and time for the regular meetings of the board of directors, set forth how special meetings shall be called, state the officers to be elected or appointed and the duties of the officers, and also state who shall be authorized to sign contracts, etc., in behalf of the corporation. The bylaws may make provision for special committees, defining the scope of their activities and the membership of such committees. They will set up the machinery for the transfer of shares of stock, for the keeping of stock records, etc., and will also make provision for the declaring and the paying of dividends.

Persons Bound by Bylaws. Shareholders are bound by all valid bylaws properly adopted, whether they approve of them or not. It is not necessary that a shareholder have notice or knowledge of a bylaw to be bound by it. As a general rule a bylaw which would deprive a shareholder of voting rights or other contractual rights arising out of his membership in the corporation is not valid; however, such a bylaw may be valid if it is adopted by the unanimous consent of the shareholders and does not violate the laws of the state or the express provisions of the articles of incorporation.

Third persons are not bound by the bylaws except as to those provisions which are expressly authorized by the articles of incorporation or those provisions of which they have notice or knowledge. Shareholders are bound by the bylaws in respect to their rights as shareholders; but in respect to general contracts entered into with the corporation, the shareholder is considered a stranger to the corporation, and his rights are the same as the rights of any third person dealing with the corporation.

Summary

An organization meeting is held after the corporation has been granted its charter. Under the Model Act the initial board of directors are the participants in this meeting. Some statutes specify that the incorporators conduct the meeting. The business to be transacted at the meeting depends upon the laws of the state of incorporation and also the nature of the business and the provisions of its articles of incorporation.

Under the Model Act the initial bylaws and amendments are adopted by the board of directors unless the articles of incorporation give the power of amendment and repeal to the shareholders. Some statutes specify that the incorporators will adopt initial bylaws.

The bylaws usually include provisions regarding annual meetings of shareholders, meetings of the directors, the duties of the officers of the corporation, where the bank account will be kept, and who shall sign checks. They will set up the machinery for the transfer of stock and such other details as the nature of the corporate business warrants.

The bylaws are binding on the shareholders, but a bylaw cannot deprive a shareholder of rights granted him by the articles of incorporation. Third persons, as a general rule, are not bound by any provision of the bylaws of the corporation unless they have notice or knowledge of it.

Keating v. *K.C.K Corp.*
383 S.W.2d 69 (Tex. Civ. App. 1964)

This was an action by Leonard M. Keating and wife (plaintiffs) against K-C-K Corporation and others (defendants) involving a contest for the management of a close corporation. The trial court enjoined the Keatings from performing their duties as officers of the corporation and they appealed. The judgment was reversed, the injunction dissolved, and the case remanded to the trial court.

The corporation was organized under the laws of Texas. The Texas corporation statute provides that the initial bylaws of a corporation shall be adopted by the board of directors and that the power to alter, amend or repeal bylaws is vested in the shareholders but such power may be delegated by the shareholders to the board of directors.

The corporate charter provides that the number of directors may be fixed by the bylaws but shall not be less than three. Article IX of the charter provides: "The board of directors is expressly authorized to make, alter or amend the by-laws of this Corporation or to adopt by-laws."

However, Article VII of the original bylaws reserved to the shareholders the right to alter, amend or repeal bylaws and required a vote of three-fourths of the total number of shares issued to exercise this reserved power.

In 1957 and 1958 three directors were elected. In 1959, 1960, 1961 and 1962 four directors were elected. The bylaws were never formally amended. In 1963 a motion was made to elect three directors but it failed to obtain a favorable vote of three-fourths of the shareholders. In all shareholder meetings 100% of the issued stock was present and voting.

COLEMAN, JUSTICE. Article IX of the Corporate Charter is inconsistent with the Article 2.23 of the Business Corporation Act, and must be considered surplusage, since the power to delegate to the board of directors authority to alter or amend the by-laws is given to the shareholders by the Act, and the Corporate Charter may not contain any provision inconsistent with the provisions of the Business Corporation Act.

The question arises, therefore, whether the board of directors, in the exercise of their statutory power to enact the initial by-laws, may restrict the power of the shareholders to amend these by-laws by requiring a greater vote than a simple majority.

Art. 2.28 of the Business Corporation Act answers this question. A by-law requiring more than a simple majority for stockholder action is clearly authorized. The by-law with which we are concerned is not inconsistent with the law of this State.

It is the Keatings' contention that the by-law under discussion has been amended, so that the number of directors is now four, by acts and conduct of the shareholders and directors. The minutes of the stockholders' meetings, as well as the undisputed testimony of witnesses, establish that for the four years preceding the meeting in question four directors were elected.

Either all of them were directors or none of them were. The minutes reflect that the directors were elected in 1959 by a "motion, duly made and seconded." The minutes also reflect that all of the stockholders were present. The minutes of the meetings held in 1960, 1961 and 1962 reflect that the owners of 100% of the stock outstanding were present at the meetings; that four persons were nominated as directors and that "all votes cast were for said nominees, and they were declared duly elected."

Art. 2.32 of the Business Corporation Act requires that the number of directors be fixed by the by-laws of the corporation and that the number may be increased or decreased from time to time by amendment of the by-laws. The action of the stockholders in electing four directors must be viewed with this provision of the law in mind. It is also significant that all of the stockholders were directors and active in the management of the Corporation prior to 1959 and thereafter, and that there is no evidence that anyone objected to the election of a four-member board of directors prior to the present controversy.

Where by statute, or by charter provision, certain formal procedures are prescribed for the enactment, or amendment, of by-laws they must be substantially followed, but since both the charter and the Texas Business Corporation Act are silent as to the formalities to be observed, no particular mode of enactment or formality is necessary. Under such circumstances, it is a general rule that by-laws may be adopted, or amended, orally or by acts evidenced by a uniform course of proceeding, or usage and acquiescence.

Financing the Corporation

Obtaining Capital. The capital of a corporation is obtained by issuing stock. The shareholders are the owners of the corporation, and they must contribute to the corporation the assets with which it begins business. The original capital may be contributed in the form of money, property, or services performed. Since the shareholders are not liable for the obligations of the corporation, the credit standing of the new corporation is determined on the basis of the true value of the assets contributed by the shareholders. The Model Act (51) requires that $1,000 be paid in on shares before the corporation transacts business or incurs indebtedness. The purpose of most of the state securities statutes (blue-sky laws) and the Federal Securities Acts is to assure the investing public that the true financial condition of the issuing corporation is revealed, not that the corporation has adequate capital with which to carry on its business or that the stock of the corporation is a wise investment.

Stock may be issued for money, for property—tangible or intangible, or for labor actually performed or services actually rendered. If stock is issued for money, the corporation statutes usually provide that promissory notes or uncertified checks shall not be accepted in payment. If stock is issued for property or services, the price placed on the stock is of relatively little importance. From the standpoint of investors and persons extending credit to the corporation, the important thing is the true value of the property exchanged, the labor performed, or the services rendered in payment for the stock.

Most statutes permit corporations to issue either par or no-par stock. If a par value is established, it is done so in the articles. However, par is not always the price at which the corporation will sell par value shares.

Price of Par Value Stock. The Model Act (17) provides that the price of par value stock is to be established from time to time by the directors, but it cannot be less than the value stated in the articles of incorporation except for treasury stock. If sold for more than par, the overage becomes "capital surplus." Some states permit corporations to issue stock for less than par value in certain circumstances.

Price of No-Par Value Stock. The Model Act (17) provides that shares of stock without par value may be issued for such consideration, expressed in dollars, as may be fixed from time to time by the directors unless the articles of incorporation reserve this power to the shareholders, who may act by majority vote of all shares entitled to vote. Generally the directors have the power unless the articles reserve the right to the shareholders. In some states no-par stock may be issued in payment of promoters' services or for property without placing a definite value on it, and it may be issued in connection with the sale of bonds or preferred stock. However, it has been held in some states that it is illegal to include no-par stock as a bonus with the purchase of par value stock on the theory that the effect is to make an illegal gift or to sell the par value security below par. In fixing the price of no-par stock, the board of directors must observe the general equitable limitations on the discretion of directors and fix a price which is not fraudulent or discriminatory.

The directors may allocate part of the price of the no-par stock to capital surplus. The Model Act (19) specifies that this must be done within 60 days after issuance or the entire consideration received must be treated as stated capital.

Qualifying Stock for Sale to Public. If stock is to be issued to the general public, it may be necessary to qualify the stock with the state securities commission or with some other state body. The blue-sky laws of the states are not uniform in their requirements, and the laws of the state in which the issue is to be sold will have to be consulted to determine whether or not the stock is exempt from the provisions of the law and, if not, what procedure is necessary to qualify the shares. If the stock is to be sold interstate or through the mails, the Federal Securities Act must be complied with.

Borrowing Money. A corporation has the power to borrow money for the purpose of carrying on its operations. The courts have held that it is permissible for the organizers of a corporation to pay in the minimum amount of capital required by statute to be paid in before the corporation begins business and then to loan to the corporation such additional funds as it may need to start its operations.

If a corporation wishes to finance its operations by issuing bonds secured by a lien on part or all of its assets, the question then arises as to who has the power to authorize such an issue. The bond issue, to be valid, may require shareholder action, or the board of directors may have the power to authorize it.

In deciding who has the authority to authorize the bond issue, it will be necessary first to analyze the issue and determine the nature of the obligations imposed on the corporation. Then the statutes of the state of incorporation and the articles and bylaws of the corporation must be examined. On the basis of this analysis the question of authority will then be decided. No formula can be set up which will serve as a test of the authority to authorize or of the validity of a bond issue.

Under the provisions of the Uniform Commercial Code corporate bonds are classed as investment securities (Section 8–102) and are declared to be negotiable (8–105).

The corporation, as a general rule, has the power to borrow money needed for its everyday operations and to issue negotiable instruments—notes, drafts, trade acceptances, checks and like instruments—to evidence the indebtedness.

Summary

The capital of a corporation is obtained by issuing stock. The credit standing of the corporation will be determined on the true value of the assets contributed by the shareholders.

Stock may be issued for money, property or past services rendered. The par value of shares is established in the articles of incorporation, but the directors may establish a higher issuing price. The stated value of no-par stock is established by the directors. If the price at which the shares are actually sold by the corporation is above par for par value shares or stated value for no-par shares, the excess becomes capital surplus.

If stock is to be issued to the general public, it must be qualified under the blue-sky laws of the state, and if sold interstate, the provisions of the Federal Securities Act of 1933 must be complied with.

One of the powers of a business corporation is the power to borrow money. Part of the money needed to operate the corporate business may be borrowed. If the bonds are to be issued, the bonds must be authorized in accordance with the statutes of the state and the articles of incorporation of the corporation.

Problem Cases

1. Dunnet and associates acquired two royalty contracts for $18,000 and $2,500, respectively, which amounts they borrowed from a bank. They formed a corporation and transferred the royalty interests to it in exchange for the entire authorized capital stock of 200,000 shares. Dunnet then donated back 80,000 of the shares to the corporation, which had no other assets than the royalty contracts at the time. Arn bought some of this stock from the corporation at $3.50 per share. The corporation paid off notes of Dunnet and his associates with proceeds of stock sold. The price of oil dropped, the corporation became financially embarrassed and Arn seeks to have canceled the stock retained by Dunnet and his group. Should the court cancel the stock?

2. The founders of Pipelife Corporation, as partners, took without paying any cash consideration, a nonexclusive license to use a patented process for extending the life of installed pipes in 44 of the then 48 states. The license provided for royalty payments of 5 percent of the licensee's gross income from use of the process. They then organized a corporation and by action of the board of directors, four out of five of whom were the partners, transferred the license to it in return for 367,000 shares of $1 par stock, divided among the partners according to their partnership interests.

To raise operating capital the corporation then sold 100,000 additional shares, using part of the proceeds to purchase about $50,000 worth of equipment to apply the process. Approval for this sale was obtained from the Texas Securities Commission on the basis of an appraised valuation for the license of $400,000 made by the president of the corporation which granted the license. This appraisal was made after the issuance of shares to the founders. The company was unsuccessful, and new management took over. It brings suit, on behalf of the corporation, to cancel the shares issued to the founders on grounds that they were issued without consideration. Is the corporation entitled to the requested relief?

3. McCrillis was employed by Lord to be general manager of a group of root beer drive-ins to be taken over by a corporation to be formed by Lord, who would hold the office of chairman of the board. The term of employment was to be five years and McCrillis was given an option to buy at a fixed price 2 percent of the stock each year for five years. The corporation later received its charter. McCrillis was employed for 18 months and then discharged on the ground that his services were no longer required. The corporation defends McCrillis' action on the contract on the ground that the contract was made before the corporation was formed. Is this a good defense?

4. Richard L. Chartrand and Barney E. O'Malia agreed to form a corporation. The agreement provided that they would contribute $80,000 each to a proposed corporation, Barney's Club, Inc., and both would receive 255 shares or 25½ percent of the outstanding stock. The corporation was formed with O'Malia acting as president and director. The other two directors of Barney's Club, Inc., were O'Malia's wife and son, so for all intents and purposes O'Malia ran the corporation. After incorporation and acceptance by the corporation of Chartrand's $80,000, the board of directors issued 240 shares to Chartrand, 240 shares to O'Malia, 15 shares to O'Malia's son, and 15 shares to O'Malia's wife. Chartrand sues to compel the corporation to issue him 15 additional shares of stock. Can the corporation be compelled to issue the stock even though Chartrand and O'Malia's agreement was entered into before incorporation?

5. Mr. and Mrs. Dooley owned real estate which they leased to the Akel Corporation. At the time the lease was entered into the Akel Corporation had not been incorporated, although incorporation was completed prior to the start of the leasehold term. Can the Dooleys hold Mr. and Mrs. Akel, owners and officers of the corporation who executed the lease, personally liable on it if the Dooleys were unaware at the time of executing the lease that the corporation was nonexistent?

6. Prior to the formation of Water Heater Company, two of the promoters and Burns another promoter, signed a contract reciting that Burns was to be employed as secretary-treasurer and general manager of Water Heater Co. when incorporated. Burns performed duties and received his salary following incorporation but was discharged without the 60-day notice provided in the agreement. He brings suit seeking to hold the other promoters liable on the contract. Are they personally liable?

7. Quaker Hill negotiated with Parr and Presba, principal officers of Denver Memorial Gardens, a corporation which had recently been formed to operate a cemetery, for the sale of a large quantity of nursery stock. Quaker Hill suggested that a separate corporation be formed to consummate the order. An agreement providing for a down payment of $1,000 with the balance, $13,500, due one year later and guaranteeing replacement of stock that might die was signed, "Denver Memorial Nursery, Inc., E. D. Parr, Pres., James P. Presba, Sec'y.-Treas."

Because of name confusion, Denver Memorial Nursery was never formed but articles for Mountain View Nurseries, Inc., were properly filed about a week after the purchase was made. Then at the suggestion of Quaker Hill a new contract in the name of Mountain View Nurseries was prepared and signed by the same individuals. Neither Denver Memorial nor Mountain View ever functioned as a going concern nor had any assets. The nursery stock died prior to the due date of the balance. Can Quaker Hill hold Parr and Presba personally for the balance?

8. Charles Baum signed a contract for the purchase of real estate in the name of Ruth Realty Corporation, a corporation represented by him as then in the process of formation. Ruth Realty Corporation was never formed and the purchase never carried out. The sellers now seek to hold Baum as the real vendee, demanding judgment against him that he specifically perform the contract. Should specific performance against Baum be granted?

9. Coos Bay Lumber & Coal Company at the time of incorporation adopted a bylaw which provided "that no salary or compensation for services of any nature shall be allowed to any officer, director, agent or employee of said corporation, unless consent to such salary or compensation be first given by the owners of at least three-fourths of the trust certificates to be issued. . . ." Boutin was elected president and later treasurer. He paid himself $100 per month out of corporate funds for his services as an officer of the corporation for many years and for seven years he drew salary at a rate of $250 per month.

   The corporation seeks to recover the salary payments as paid in violation of the bylaw. Boutin defends on the grounds that the bylaw was invalid because it was inconsistent with and repugnant to the provision in the Wisconsin corporation statutes stating that "the stock, property, affairs and business of every such stock corporation shall be under the care of and be managed by a board of directors." Is Boutin entitled to keep the payments?

10. The Coleman Realty Company had 6,000 shares of stock outstanding, 4,000 of which were held by Garvin. The bylaws of the corporation contained the following restriction which was printed on the face of each certificate: "Section 4. No stock shall be sold or transferred by any stockholder to any person not already a stockholder until an offer has first been given to the corporation or the remaining stockholders in proportion to their interest in the corporation to purchase said stock at its book value as appearing on the books of the company, except that stock may be transferred by any stockholder to an employee in recognition of his services and ability in behalf of the corporation." The bylaws also provided that they could be amended by a majority of the outstanding stock. When Garvin died, Ludgate purchased his stock from his estate, and at the next shareholders meeting, Section 4 of the bylaws was repealed by the vote of Ludgate's shares against those of the minority stockholders. The minority shareholders brought an action to declare invalid the repeal of the bylaw. Was the repeal effective?

11. The Belle Isle Corporation seeks to cancel 75,000 shares of its stock issued to MacBean for past services by action of the board of directors at a meeting attended by four directors on grounds that a quorum was not present. In order to provide representation on the board to a special group under an agreement involving the company's stock, the corporation bylaws had been amended in 1939 to increase the number of directors from 7 to 10.

   This agreement expired without having been carried out and the group was never represented on the board. Between 1939 and June, 1944, no directors' or shareholders' meetings were held. In a meeting in 1945, MacBean advised the directors that three directors should be elected to fill the three current vacancies.

MacBean argued that the bylaw had been amended by custom so that, in effect, the size of the board was seven at the time the stock was issued. Was a quorum present under Delaware law which specifies that a majority of the directors constitute a quorum?

chapter 25. Operating the Corporate Business

Scope of Business and Corporate Powers

Statutory Limitations. A corporation obtains its powers from the state, and it cannot have powers that exceed those conferred by the constitution and statutes of the state of its incorporation. However, there are certain inherent or traditional powers of corporations which all corporations have. They include: (1) existence independent of its members and unaffected by their death; (2) right to sue and be sued in the corporate name; (3) right to acquire, hold and convey property for corporate purposes in the corporate name; (4) to have a seal; and (5) to make bylaws. In addition a corporation will have the powers specifically granted by the statute under which it is incorporated. Corporations which must be formed under special statutes, such as banks, insurance companies, and railroads usually have fewer powers and are put under special restrictions and supervision for the protection of the public.

Some states limit or prohibit the acquisition of agricultural land by corporations. Corporations have, in the past, been denied the privilege altogether of engaging in some of the professions such as, for instance, that of law, medicine, or dentistry. However, a number of states have recently enacted statutes which permit physicians and other professionals to incorporate in order to take advantage of federal tax laws encouraging establishment of retirement plans by corporations. Some of these statutes expressly provide that individual liability is not limited.

Powers Granted by the Model Act. The trend has been to broaden, both through court decision and statute, the powers of general business corporations. For example, the Model Act (4)[1] specifically grants the following powers in addition to the five above numerated: (1) to lend money to its employees other than its officers and directors; (2) to buy, hold and sell stock, interests

---

[1] The numbers in the parentheses refer to the sections of the Model Business Corporation Act.

524

in or obligations of other domestic corporations, foreign corporations, associations, partnerships and individuals; (3) to make contracts and guarantees, borrow money and give security; (4) to lend money for corporate purposes; (5) to carry on its business and have offices in any state, territory or foreign country; (6) to elect or appoint officers and agents; (7) to make donations for charitable, scientific, or educational purposes; (8) in time of war to transact any lawful business in aid of the United States in the prosecution of the war; (9) to indemnify directors and officers for expenses in defending suits against them growing out of performance of their duty to the corporation, unless they are adjudged liable for negligence or misconduct; (10) to pay pensions and to establish pension plans, profit sharing, stock option and other incentive plans for any of its directors, officers and employees; (11) to cease its corporate activities and surrender its franchise; and (12) to exercise all powers necessary and convenient to its corporate purposes.

In addition, Section 5 expressly grants corporations the power to purchase or otherwise acquire, hold and dispose of its own shares.

Some of the corporate actions specifically authorized by the Model Act are those for which corporate power was once in doubt, such as the power of a corporation to participate in a partnership, to acquire shares in other corporations, to make gifts to charitable and educational organizations, to indemnify directors, and to purchase its own shares of stock.

Limitations in Articles of Incorporation. Under the Model Corporation Act (48) and some other statutes not derived from it, an explicit statement of corporate powers is not required in the articles of incorporation. Under such statutes a corporation will have all of the powers enumerated in the statute without the necessity of repeating them in the articles. Nor can the corporation through its articles expand its powers beyond those expressly given it by the statute under which it is incorporated and those powers incidental to or implied by the express powers.

All jurisdictions require that the articles set forth the corporate purposes. This may be as broad as permitted by the statute, which under the Model Act (3) may be "any lawful purpose or purposes, except for the purpose of banking or insurance." It is common for statements of purpose to be drafted to take full advantage of this freedom. Indeed, many corporations state their purpose with an all-inclusive phrase such as, "To engage in commercial, industrial, real estate and service enterprises to the extent permitted under the laws of the State of _____." However, the incorporators may desire to use the statement of purpose as a self-imposed limitation. The statement becomes then a promise on the part of the corporation to its shareholders that it will confine the business risks taken by the corporation to those normally incident to the operation of a business such as that defined in the purpose section of the articles of incorporation.

The articles of incorporation and the bylaws are considered as a contract between the corporation and its shareholders. As a general rule the courts will give a liberal interpretation to the statement of the purpose of the corporation, but in case of doubt the courts will give that construction to the language used which will be most favorable to the interests of the public.

Summary

The powers of a corporation are limited to those conferred by the constitution and statutes of the state of its incorporation, although certain traditional powers are considered inherent in the corporate form of organization. The trend of modern corporation statutes, including the Model Act, is to broaden the powers of general business corporations.

The articles of incorporation are required to set forth the purpose(s) of the corporation, which may be as broad as permitted by the statute. However, a more restricted statement of purpose acts as a self-imposed limitation for the benefit of the shareholders. Some statutes, including the Model Act, do not require a specific statement of corporate powers in the articles, and the corporation will then have all those powers granted by the statute under which it is formed.

Kavanagh v. Capitol Service, Inc.
94 N.W.2d 814 (Sup. Ct. Mich. 1959)

This was an action by Thomas M. Kavanagh, Attorney General (plaintiff), against Capitol Service, Inc. (defendant), in the nature of *quo warranto* for the ouster of Capitol Service, Inc., from its corporate franchise. The Supreme Court of Michigan held that Capitol Service, Inc., was exercising power in excess of its chartered power, warranting ouster of the corporation from its charter.

Capitol Service, Inc., was incorporated under the general corporation for profit statute of the state. The attorney general contended that it was an educational corporation and should have been incorporated under a special statute which required it to obtain a license from the State Board of Education as a private trade school, business school or institute.

The purpose of Capitol Service, Inc., was stated in its articles of incorporation as follows: "To aid, assist, advise and counsel persons seeking employment with governmental agencies, to provide information, pamphlets and data relating to employment with governmental agencies, to print, publish, sell and distribute periodicals, pamphlets, papers, brochures, cards and letters relating to employment with governmental agencies, to manufacture, sell and deal in books, maps, charts, examination papers, stationery, models, casts, drawings, engravings, instruments and school supplies of every class and description.

"To make, perform, and carry out contracts of every kind and description pertaining to the purpose of this corporation and for any lawful purposes necessary and expedient thereto with any person, firm, association or corporation."

Capitol Service, Inc., was in the business of preparing persons to take the civil service examination. It had prepared a two-year course of study which included furnishing course outlines and materials, having the trainee prepare and submit lessons, giving and grading examinations and giving further coaching if necessary. The trainees were given grades during and on the completion of the course. The attorney general contended that it was operating an educational institution which was in excess of its power.

DETHMERS, CHIEF JUSTICE. Capitol Service, Inc., counters by asserting that its use of labels and terminology describing its merchandise for sale as a "course of training" or "lessons" and its customers as "students," undoubtedly lending itself admirably to consumption by gullible prospects for that type of education, ought not to beguile this Court into believing that it is engaged in teaching, educating or educational activities because its conduct in fact, does not amount to that, but only to the business of selling materials. While labels are not controlling, so long as Capitol Service, Inc., sticks to them, it ought not to complain of being stuck with them. All nomenclature aside, however, we think that Capitol Service, Inc.'s, course of action does constitute an educational activity, in excess of the power conferred by its corporate franchise, and is, therefore, *ultra vires*. Section 170 of the act provides for incorporation of an "institution of learning where preparatory subjects or the arts, sciences, professions, special occupations and higher learning may be taught." There can be no doubt that the furnishing to a student, for valuable consideration, of educational materials, the submitting of examination questions to him, the correction, grading and returning of the same to him for his information, and subsequent forwarding to him of further lessons and assignments in logical order, giving him a complete review of his training for a period of two years and preparing him for civil service examinations does amount to teaching. Capitol Service, Inc., is engaged in teaching subjects. It therefore fits the language of the statute and, as such, should be incorporated thereunder and subject itself to the requirements of the statute and of the State Board of Education and superintendent of public instruction as by law provided. For Capitol Service, Inc., to proceed otherwise, as it has done, is contrary to public policy as declared by the legislature and violative of the law.

The *Ultra Vires* Doctrine

Nature of the *Ultra Vires* Doctrine. The original conception of a corporation was an artificial person created by and given limited powers by governmental authority. From this came the view that any act by a corporation which is beyond the authority given it by the state or by its articles of incorporation which are consistent with that grant by the state is illegal and void as being *ultra vires*. Under the *ultra vires* doctrine, want of capacity by the corporation could be urged by either the corporation or the other party in defense of a suit on the contract alleged to be *ultra vires*. Oftentimes it was merely a convenient justification for reneging on an agreement no longer considered desirable.

The Model Business Corporation Act (6) and some statutes not based upon it have eliminated such collateral attacks on the capacity of the corporation. The trend in business corporation statutes toward granting corporations very broad powers and for draftsmen of articles of incorporation to use very broad statements of purpose have also diminished the vitality of the *ultra vires* doctrine in the states which have not abolished it.

Under Section 6 direct attacks upon *ultra vires* actions are still permitted. Shareholders may seek an injunction to restrain the corporation from carrying out a proposed action which is beyond its powers, thus seeking to prevent a breach of his membership contract with the corporation. The corporation itself, or through a legal representative such as a receiver or shareholder in a representative suit, may bring an action against its officers or directors for damages resulting from *ultra vires* actions taken by them. Also under Section 6, the state's attorney general may enjoin the corporation from transacting unauthorized business. Under Section 87, he may, if it continually exceeds or abuses its power, bring an action to dissolve the corporation.

Liability under the Doctrine.   One reason for the strong trend toward abolishing the doctrine is that there had been much confusion and uncertainty in the holdings of the courts in regard to *ultra vires* contracts. Courts have generally refused to enforce contracts which are wholly executory but have been unwilling to strike down contracts which are fully executed by both parties even when viewed as being beyond the corporate capacity. The partially executed contracts have been the source of confusion and disagreement. The older rule was that the partially executed contract would not be enforced although a quasi-contractual remedy might be appropriate. A majority of courts have held that the contract is enforceable if one of the parties has received a benefit.

Summary

Under the *ultra vires* doctrine any act of a corporation which is beyond the powers given to it by the state or its articles of incorporation is void, and either the corporation or the other party to a contract may allege as a defense that the making of the contract is beyond the powers of the corporation. The Model Act and some other modern statutes have eliminated this defense, but they permit shareholders or the state attorney general to enjoin an *ultra vires* act and the corporation may bring an action against its officers or directors for damages resulting from actions taken beyond the corporation's power.

A major reason for the trend toward abolishing the *ultra vires* doctrine is the confusion in the law regarding the enforceability of *ultra vires* contracts. Courts have generally refused to enforce wholly executory contracts and have not interfered with fully executed contracts. However, partially executed contracts have been a source of confusion and disagreement.

Rio Refrigeration Co. v. Thermal Supply of Harlingen, Inc.
368 S.W.2d 128 (Tex. Civ. App. 1963)

This was an action by Thermal Supply of Harlingen, Inc. (plaintiff), against Rio Refrigeration Company (defendant) to recover a judgment for an account receivable. Judgment for Thermal Supply of Harlingen, Inc., and Rio Refrigeration Company appealed. Judgment affirmed.

Rio Refrigeration Company (Rio) and Coastal Refrigeration Service, a partnership, were competitors in the refrigeration and air-conditioning business. Rio purchased the business, parts and assets of Coastal Refrigeration Service and as part of the transaction contracted to pay the account owed by Coastal Refrigeration Service to Thermal Supply of Harlingen, Inc. (Thermal Supply) in the amount of $2,161.35. Rio then refused to pay Thermal Supply and it brought suit. Rio set up as a defense that the contract was a guaranty of the debt of a third person and was *ultra vires* and did not bind it.

BARROW, JUSTICE.   Rio Refrigeration was incorporated in 1948, for the purpose of buying and selling goods, wares and merchandise of any description by wholesale and retail. It has never adopted the Texas Business Corporation Act enacted in 1955, which by Art. 2.04, *Vernon's Ann. Civ. St.* abolished the defense of *ultra vires*. It is our opinion however, that this defense is here without merit. It is not ordinarily necessary for the conduct of a corporation's business that it lend its credit to another business, and in the absence of an express charter power, a corporation has no right to stand as surety or guarantor for the debt of another. Here the contract was of direct and material benefit to Rio, in that it eliminated a competitor and purchased parts, supplies and equipment used in Rio's business. The law is well settled that in all grants of corporate powers there exist not only the powers expressly granted, but also such implied powers as are necessary or reasonably appropriate to the exercise of those powers expressly granted. It is our view that the powers granted Rio would include the power to assume payment of Coastal's account with Thermal Supply as partial consideration for the assets purchased from Coastal.

In any event, Rio is estopped to assert the defense of *ultra vires* in that it had operated under and attained the benefits of the contract.

Management of the Corporation

Authority.   The shareholders are the owners of the corporation and have the ultimate power to determine the course of the business. However, they do not have, by virtue of ownership, the right and duty of management. The law gives these to the directors, who are elected by the shareholders. Shareholders' approval is required for certain extraordinary corporate matters such as changes in the articles of incorporation, sale of assets not in the regular course of business, merger and dissolution. Other major questions and policies are determined by the directors, who also elect the officers and delegate to them the authority to manage the everyday operations of the business.

This right and duty of the directors to manage the corporation exists under the corporation statutes of all states even when one man owns all of the stock of the corporation and holds the office of president and chief executive or general manager (the latter is an older term which today is used more frequently by small than large corporations). As has been frequently pointed out by students and critics of corporations, even in large, publicly held corporations the chief executive may choose the board members and/or make all policy decisions for the corporation with the board of directors acting merely as a rubber stamp. Even what may be the directors' most important duty, to choose the chief executive's successor, may effectively have been usurped by the training opportunities given to possible candidates within the organization. However, in the long run, acceptance of a rubber stamp role by the board is likely to lead to corporate stagnation and decay, and it may lead to the personal liability of board members for default in carrying out their duties.

Directors

Duties and Powers of Directors. Since directors are given by statute the broad, general duty of "management of the corporation," they have the power to make all decisions for the corporation except those reserved by statute to the shareholders. Under the Model Act as well as other statutes, certain corporate actions can be taken only by authorization of the board. These include: authorizing a change in the registered office or registered agent of the corporation (12); establishing the time of payment of stock subscriptions (16); establishing the price for sale by the corporation of shares of stock, except when the power to establish the price of no-par stock is reserved in the articles to the shareholders (17); establishing the value of noncash consideration received for shares (18); increasing stated capital by transfer of surplus (18); adopting initial bylaws and, unless this power is reserved to the shareholders in the articles, amendment or repeal of bylaws (25); establishing record dates for dividend and shareholder meeting purposes (28); filling a vacancy on the board of directors (36); declaring dividends (40); electing officers and assigning duties to them not inconsistent with the bylaws (44); removing officers (45); and selling, leasing or mortgaging assets of the corporation in the normal course of its business (71).

Directors are required under the Model Act to initiate and propose to the shareholders certain major changes affecting the corporation which can be accomplished only with approval of the shareholders. These include: amendments to or restatements of the articles of incorporation (54 and 57); reduction in stated capital (63); merger or consolidation (65 and 66); a sale, lease, or mortgage of substantially all assets of the corporation other than in the normal course of business (72); and a voluntary dissolution of the corporation (77).

Unless the directors are full-time officers of the corporation, they cannot possibly make all management decisions nor if they were full-time would it be feasible to make them all in group meeting. Therefore, actions other than the ones which must be taken by the directors, as listed above, are often delegated to the officers and many of those are redelegated to employees of the corporation.

Important financial transactions of the corporation are usually approved by the directors. In addition to declaration of dividends, issuance of securities, and any pledge of assets for loans (which actions are required to be taken by directors), this would include approval of large capital expenditures and various budgets. In large publicly held corporations only a few of the most basic policy decisions are likely to be discussed and voted upon by the directors except in connection with financial transactions. However, it is not uncommon for directors to undertake to approve broad policies in the area of product pricing and labor relations as well as to define the business of the corporation in terms of products and markets.

The National Industrial Conference Board, in summarizing its latest survey of directorship practices, stated that it found wide variations in the functions of directors but seven areas appeared to have general acceptance. They are: (1) to establish the basic objectives and broad policies of the corporation; (2) to elect the corporate officers, advise them, approve their actions, and audit their performance; (3) to safeguard, and to approve changes in, the corporate assets; (4) to approve important financial decisions and actions and to see that proper reports are made to shareholders; (5) to delegate special powers to officers and employees to sign contracts, open bank accounts, sign checks, borrow money, and perform other such activities; (6) to maintain, revise, and enforce the corporate charter and bylaws; and (7) to assure maintenance of a sound board through selection of the management slate at regular elections and filling interim vacancies.[2]

An individual director has no management function or power except as he may be appointed an agent of the corporation. He does, however, have the right to inspect corporate books and records, since information concerning the corporation and its affairs is essential for him to perform his duties. Although often said to be an absolute right, in contrast to the qualified right of

---

[2] National Industrial Conference Board, *Corporate Directorship Practices,* Studies in Business Policy #125 (New York, 1967), pp. 93–94.

a shareholder, the director's right of inspection has been denied in a few cases where the director clearly had an interest adverse to the corporation.

Number and Qualifications of Directors. The Model Act (34) specifies that there shall be at least three directors but otherwise leaves the number to be fixed in the bylaws except that the size of the initial board is to be fixed in the articles. A few but growing number of states permit a corporation to have only one director. Some states require that directors be shareholders in the corporation. The Model Act does not make such a requirement but permits it to be established, if desired by the incorporators, in the articles or bylaws. The Model Act has no requirement with respect to the citizenship of directors, but some states require that a certain number of directors be residents of the state of incorporation and/or that directors be citizens of the United States.

Most publicly held corporations and not a few close corporations have both "inside" and "outside" directors. The term "inside" director is applied to one who is an officer of the corporation or an affiliated corporation and devotes substantially his full time to it. The term is also often applied to controlling shareholders who are not officers. There has been a trend toward having more "outside" members on corporate boards.[3] Even the preeminent example of the "inside" board, Standard Oil Company of New Jersey, added outside directors in 1966. However, many leading corporations have few or no "outside" directors.

Election and Removal of Directors. Directors are elected by the shareholders at their annual meeting and normally hold office until the succeeding annual meeting or until a successor has been elected and qualified. However, most statutes, including the Model Act, permit a corporation to provide in its articles for staggered terms for directors. Under the Model Act a corporation having a board of nine or more members may establish either two or three approximately equal classes of directors with only one class of directors coming up for election at each annual meeting.

Vacancies occurring on the board of directors can be filled only by the shareholders, absent a provision in the statute, articles or bylaws. Most statutes permit the directors to fill vacancies at least until the next shareholders' meeting. The Model Act (36) provides that a majority vote of the remaining directors, even though less than a quorum, is sufficient to elect persons to serve out unexpired terms. It also explicitly deals with the troublesome ques-

---

[3] The National Industrial Conference Board has been making studies of the directorship practices of a broad sample of corporations since 1938. These show a slow but steady increase in firms with a majority of outside directors. In the 1967 report, outside directors predominated on the boards of 63 percent of the manufacturing companies in the sample. Almost all of the banks, utilities, insurance, mining, and transportation companies in the study had a majority of outside directors while only a 39 percent of the merchandising firms did. National Industrial Conference Board, *op. cit.,* pp. 6, 7.

tion whether if directors have the power to increase the size of board, they may, without a vote by the shareholders, also fill the "vacancy" created. The Model Act provides that such a created "vacancy" must be filled by the election of shareholders.

Unless there is authorization for such shareholder action in the statute or in articles or bylaws adopted prior to his election, a director may not be removed without cause, that is without misconduct or action contrary to the interests of the corporation.

Shareholders, but not directors, have inherent power to remove directors for cause and may do so even if the articles or bylaws give this power to the directors and despite a shareholder agreement. Bylaw provisions establishing the proportion of vote required are upheld, however. A shareholder agreement to elect and maintain in office certain persons as directors would prevent removal without cause by such shareholders. Before removal for cause, the director must be given adequate notice and an opportunity for a hearing.

An optional section of the Model Act (36A) permits shareholders by a majority vote to remove directors or the entire board with or without cause. The rationale of this section is that as owners the shareholders should have the power to judge the fitness of directors at any time. If less than the entire board is to be removed and cumulative voting [4] is in effect, then a removal action fails if the votes cast against the removal of a director would have been sufficient to have elected him initially.

Directors' Meetings. Traditionally, directors can act only when properly convened as a board and cannot vote by proxy or informally, as by a telephone poll. This rule is based upon belief in the value of consultation and collective judgment. Obviously, agreement with a proposal by the chairman is more likely if he talks to each director individually and there is no opportunity to consider the doubts or opposition expressed by a potential dissenter. However, where the statute is silent some courts have upheld action in casual meetings not properly called but attended by all directors and also action taken which has been consented to by all directors without a meeting.

Today the corporation laws of a majority of states specifically permit action by the directors without a meeting if all directors consent in writing. Although subject to possible abuse, such authorization is useful for routine matters or when formal action is required by a third party and the underlying policy decision has been previously made after full discussion. Close corporations are likely to take advantage of such a method of action more often than large public corporations holding monthly meetings of the board. Section 39A was only recently added as an optional provision of the Model Act to permit corporations to authorize such informality in their articles or bylaws.

---

[4] For discussion of cumulative voting, see Chapter 27.

Meetings need not be held within the state of incorporation even under older statutes.

Reasonable notice, including the purpose, is required of special but not of regular meetings. Actual attendance at a meeting by all directors, unless for the limited purpose of raising an objection to the lack of notice, is generally held to cure defects in the notice. Also, directors may waive notice, and it is normal practice for corporate secretaries to obtain signed waivers when notice is defective. To be effective under common law, a waiver of notice must be signed by all directors either before or during the meeting. However, the Model Act (137) makes waivers of notice signed after the meeting equally effective.

Directors each have one vote regardless of their stock holdings. In order for the directors to act, a quorum must be present. The Model Act (37) provides that a quorum shall be a majority of the number of directors fixed by the bylaws. If none is so fixed, then a majority of the number stated in the articles constitutes a quorum. If there is a quorum, the act of the majority of directors present is the act of the board. However, the Model Act permits the corporation to require a greater number for a quorum by a provision in the articles or bylaws.

Committees of the Board.   The bylaws of most large corporations establish an executive committee of the board which is given full authority to act for the board when the entire board is not in session, although this is frequently limited to matters not already acted upon by the board. The executive committee is usually composed of board members who reside near the corporate headquarters or who can be easily summoned to a meeting on short notice. Thus, the executive committee is available to give a timely formal authorization such as approval of a routine sale of property or a bank transaction. It may also serve as a screening committee for preliminary consideration of complicated or weighty matters prior to presentation to the full board. Other common board committees are salary and bonus, stock option, audit and finance committees.

The Model Act (38) provides that the directors may by resolution establish an executive committee and other committees which may exercise all the authority of the board within the limits established in the resolution or in the articles or bylaws, except that committees shall not have authority to act in connection with extraordinary corporate matters such as amendment of articles, merger, disposition of substantially all of the assets not in the normal course of business or a voluntary dissolution.

Compensation of Directors.   The traditional view is that directors are presumed to perform their ordinary duties as director without compensation and that they have no power to fix their own salaries. The Model Act (33) and other modern statutes permit the directors to fix their compensation unless the articles forbid this. In the NICB study only 2 or 3 percent of the companies reported that outside directors served without compensation in 1967.[5]

Summary

Since corporation statutes generally provide that directors have the duty of "management of the corporation" they have the power to make all decisions for the corporation not reserved to the shareholders. The statutes specifically require directors to authorize certain actions. However, generally most other management decisions are delegated to the officers or employees. An individual director as such has no management function or power, although he may be appointed an agent of the corporation.

Although a director is said to have an absolute right of inspection of corporate books and records, a few cases have denied inspection where the director clearly had an interest adverse to the corporation.

Some statutes permit a corporation to have only one director but the Model Act and most states require at least three, and some states have other requirements, e.g., that they be shareholders in the corporation and citizens of the United States.

Directors are normally elected by the shareholders at their annual meeting and hold office until the next annual meeting. Most statutes and the Model Act permit staggered terms. Vacancies are filled by shareholders unless, as is usually the case, the statute, articles or bylaws give this power to the directors to fill the vacancy until the next shareholders' meeting.

Shareholders have inherent power to remove a director for cause but not without cause unless this power is specifically given in the statute, articles or bylaws prior to his election.

Generally, directors take action only in a properly convened meeting, but many statutes today specifically permit action without a meeting if all directors consent in writing. Reasonable notice is required for a special meeting but not for a regular meeting of the directors. A majority of the board is usually required to constitute a quorum but many statutes permit the articles or bylaws to establish a higher number for a quorum.

Although traditionally directors serve without compensation, modern statutes permit directors to fix their own compensation unless the articles forbid this, and most outside directors are today paid for their service as a director.

Essential Enterprises Corp. v. *Automatic Steel Products, Inc.*
159 A.2d 288 (Ch. Del. 1960)

This was an action by Essential Enterprises Corp. (plaintiff) against Automatic Steel Products, Inc., and three of its directors (defendants), to determine the validity

---

[5] National Industrial Conference Board, *op. cit.*, p. 29.

of the removal of the directors and the removal of one of them as chairman of the board. The court held that removal of the directors was invalid but removal of the chairman by a later enlarged board was valid.

A shareholders' meeting was called for June 2, 1959, for the purpose of voting for the removal of three of the six directors of Automatic Steel Products, Inc., and a majority of the shares voted for their removal. The parties agreed that the removal was without legal cause. The certificate of incorporation provided for staggered terms with three classes of directors, each director to hold office for three years or until his death or resignation. A bylaw provided that a director could be removed, either with or without cause, at any time by the affirmative vote of the majority in interest of shareholders.

Following the removal action the shareholders elected three new directors. Later the same date the "new board" removed one of the old directors as chairman of the board. On July 21, 1959, the stockholders held another special meeting and amended the bylaws to increase the directors from six to nine and filled these directorships. The enlarged board then adopted and ratified all actions taken in the meeting of June 2. Also, at the next annual meeting of stockholders the removal of the chairman at the June 2 meeting was ratified. There was no challenge to the legality of enlarging the board.

SEITZ, CHANCELLOR.   We start from the premise that a bylaw which is in conflict with a provision in a certificate of incorporation is invalid. Of course, every reasonable effort should be made to reconcile the two, particularly where, as here, both were adopted at the same time.

Essential Enterprises argues that the stockholders should be permitted as a matter of policy to remove directors without cause, claiming that they have no "vested" interest in the office as against the "owners" of the corporation. This may be so but "there are ways" to do things and expediency is a poor substitute for reasonable predictability in our business society. After all, the stockholders adopted the staggered term provision with its dispersion of board responsiveness to the wishes of its stockholders.

The bylaw here involved, at least as to its removal without cause provision, is inconsistent with the provision of the certificate calling for staggered three year terms for its directors. This is so because it would permit the removal of directors without cause in a manner which would frustrate the plan and purpose behind the provision for staggered terms and because it is incompatible with the pertinent language of the statute and the certificate. Thus, three directors were here purportedly removed at one time although under the certificate and statute only two could be replaced by stockholder vote in any one year.

I conclude that the individual defendants were not validly removed as directors because Automatic Steel Products' bylaw at least in its "without cause" aspect is invalid. It follows that the three persons purportedly elected as their successors were not validly elected and are not directors.

In view of my decision that the individual defendants were not validly removed by the stockholders at the June 2, 1959, meeting, it follows that the action of the board on the same date in removing Johnston as chairman was also invalid. This is so because it was not done by the vote of a majority of a quorum of the board. But Essential Enterprises says this decision was ratified by the action of the enlarged board in its meeting of July 21, 1969, in approving, adopting, ratifying, and confirming the action taken at the June 2, 1959, meeting in removing Johnston. Under the bylaws the board is given the power to remove the chairman.

At least as of July 21, 1959, Johnston was validly removed as chairman. I say this because at its meeting on that date the board, through the action of a majority of an admitted quorum, voted such removal by adopting the action taken at the June 2, 1959, meeting in that respect.

Hill Dredging Corp. v. *Risley*
114 A.2d 697 (Sup. Ct. N.J. 1955)

This was a suit by Hill Dredging Corp. (plaintiff) against Elton Risley (defendant), its former president and majority shareholder, to set aside sale to Risley of stock formerly owned by Dredging Corp. in a bridge company and for an accounting of dividends received by Risley on the stock. The Chancery Court entered judgment for Dredging Corp. and Risley appealed. Affirmed.

Elton Risley, while president, director and majority shareholder of Dredging Corp., purchased from the corporation 365 shares, which constituted effective control of Margate Bridge Company at a price of $100 per share. Risley called, without a prior notice, a meeting of the directors of Dredging Corp. to approve the sale. One of the three directors, Harry Kaupp, was in Florida on corporate business and did not attend. Carl Risley and Elton Risley attended, both signing a waiver of notice. Kaupp later signed a waiver of notice and statement approving the transaction. Carl Risley claimed he did not favor the sale but merely replied, "What can I do?" when asked in the meeting how he voted. The minutes, signed by Carl Risley as corporate secretary, however, showed a unanimous vote in favor of the sale. The Bridge Co. owned a toll road with several bridges and was profitable. Expert witnesses differed widely in their appraisals of the value of the Bridge Co.'s stock, Dredging Corp.'s witnesses making estimates of from $300 to $800 per share and Elton Risley's witnesses estimating approximately $90 per share.

PER CURIAM.   The judgment is affirmed for the reasons expressed in the opinion of Judge Ewart in the court below. (Judge Ewart's opinion was made a part of the report of the case and included the following excerpts.)

". . . there was no legal convocation of the directors at the meeting of July 19, 1951. Elton Risley and Carl Risley were actually present at the meeting so that they, of course, needed no notice of the meeting. Harry Kaupp, however, neither received notice of the meeting nor was he present. Every director is entitled to an opportunity to be present and participate in the deliberations of the board and to express his opinion with respect to any proposed action. A special meeting such as was the meeting of July 19, 1951, held without notice to one of the three directors, is not a legally convened meeting and the action purported to be taken at such meeting is not the act of the corporation nor binding upon it.

"Nor can the fact that Harry Kaupp, upon his return from Florida and under date of July 31, 1951, signed a waiver of notice of the meeting of July 19, 1951 and an express approval of the action taken, serve to make the meeting legal or to validate the action purported to have been taken.

" '. . . consent given subsequent to the meeting looking to ratification of what was done is without force to validate the action taken.'

"Director Kaupp had no notice of the meeting of July 19, 1951, nor was he present. Elton Risley, by reason of his interest adverse to the corporation of which he was a director, was disqualified from voting as a director at said meeting and could not be counted to make a quorum. Hence there was no quorum at the meeting of July 19, 1951. For these reasons, that meeting was a nullity and the purported action of the board authorizing the sale of the bridge company stock to Elton Risley at a price of $100 per share was null and void and was not binding upon the dredging company."

Officers and Employees

Officers of the Corporation.   The Model Act (44) provides that the officers of a corporation shall be the president, one or more vice presidents, a secretary, and a treasurer. Some statutes require fewer officers and most allow more if desired. It is increasingly common for a corporation to establish the office of chairman of the board. Under the Model Act any two or more offices may be held by the same person except the offices of president and secretary.

The officers are agents of the corporation, and as such, they will have the express authority which is conferred upon them in the bylaws or by the board of directors. In addition, they will have implied authority to do those things reasonably necessary to accomplish the functions delegated to them. Like any agent they may be held accountable by the corporation for exceeding such actual authority. However, like any agent they also may bind the corporation on the basis of apparent authority, when acting beyond their actual authority.

In addition, courts have held that certain officers may have authority by virtue of their office. The cases are difficult to reconcile, but such *ex officio* powers are much more restricted than laymen are likely to expect. Even the president traditionally had no power to bind the corporation by virtue of his office, but merely served as presiding officer in shareholder and director meetings. However, if he acts as general manager or chief executive—that is, he is given general supervision and control of the business—he has the broad implied authority to make such contracts and do such other acts as are appropriate in the ordinary business of the corporation.

A vice president has no authority by virtue of that office, but if he is vice president of sales or some other department of the business, he will have the authority of a manager of the specified department to transact the normal business of the corporation which falls within his departmental functions.

The secretary, or clerk as he is called in some states, usually keeps the minutes of director and shareholder meetings and other corporate records and has custody of the corporate seal. He has no authority to bind the corporation by virtue of his office but there is a presumption that a document to which he affixes the seal has been duly authorized.

The treasurer has custody of the funds of the corporation and is the proper officer to receive payments to the corporation and to disburse corporate funds for authorized purposes. He can bind the corporation by his receipts, checks and endorsements but does not by virtue of his office have authority to borrow money or issue negotiable instruments.

Like any principal, the corporation may ratify the unauthorized acts of its officers. This may be accomplished through a resolution of the board of directors or of the shareholders.

Employees of the Corporation. Employees of the corporation who are not officers may also be delegated authority to act as agents for the corporation and the usual rules of agency will apply both to their relationship to the corporation and to third parties. Both officers and other agents can best protect themselves from personal liability by having their authority for conducting out-of-the-ordinary transactions for the corporation stated in writing, either in a bylaw or a specific resolution of the board of directors and then making it clear in signing as agent for the corporation that they do not intend to join individually. The proper form is, of course:

"THE WIDGET CORPORATION
By JOHN DOE, *President*."

Those dealing with a corporation in out-of-the-ordinary transactions likewise are well advised to assure themselves that the agent with whom they deal is authorized.

Summary

The Model Act specifies that the officers of a corporation shall be the president, one or more vice presidents, a secretary and a treasurer and that two or more offices may be held by one person except the offices of president and secretary. Officers are agents of the corporation and have express, implied and apparent authority like any agent.

Ex officio powers are limited even for the president. Only if he acts as general manager does he have broad implied authority to make contracts and conduct the ordinary business of the corporation. A vice president has only such authority as he may be given as manager of some division of the corporation's business. The secretary's function is to keep minutes and other records, and he has no implied authority except to affix the corporate seal. The treasurer can bind the corporation by his receipts, checks and endorsements but does not, by virtue of his office, have authority to borrow money.

Employees of the corporation other than officers may be delegated to act as agents for the corporation.

Parks v. Midland Ford Tractor Co.
416 S.W.2d 22 (Ct. App. St. Louis, Mo. 1967)

This was an action by Parks (plaintiff) against Midland Tractor Co. (defendant) for breach of an alleged oral contract to pay a certain bonus. Judgment for Midland and Parks appealed. Affirmed.

Parks was employed by oral agreement with the president of Midland as vice-president and general manager of the corporation. Parks claimed that the agreement not only provided for a salary and a bonus based upon gross sales of the company but also a bonus graduated upwards from $10,000 if net profits before taxes exceeded $200,000. The employment was later terminated owing to differences of opinion about policy and instructions. Parks then brought suit when Midland refused to pay a bonus based on profits in accordance with the alleged agreement. One of Midland's defenses was that even if the bonus had been promised, the president had no authority to make such a promise and it could not bind Midland.

Midland was incorporated in Minnesota. The pertinent statute declared, "All officers shall, respectively, have such authority and perform such duties . . . as may be prescribed in the bylaws." Midland's bylaws provided:

"The president shall be chief executive officer. . . . He shall have general charge, supervision and control of the business and affairs of the corporation subject, however, to the control of the board of directors."

TOWNSEND, COMMISSIONER. The power of a corporate officer, like that of any other agent, to bind his corporation in contract rests either upon his actual authority or upon his apparent authority. His actual authority derives, on the one hand, from statute or from the articles and by-laws of the corporation or on the other hand from his exercise of functions on behalf of the corporation, long tacitly acquiesced in by those in legal control of the corporation, the directors. . . . In contrast, apparent authority is brought into existence by the principal's creation of an appearance of affairs which would cause a reasonable person to believe that the officer had actual authority to do a particular act, upon which appearance a third person relies.

While Parks introduced no direct evidence to show that Woods had the actual authority to make the alleged promise, it is established without question that Woods was the president of Midland at the time asserted. The question then suggests itself: What actual authority can be implied from the fact an officer—here the president—

occupied a named office and possessed a particular title? Or as the question is some-times put: What power inheres in the very fact that one occupies the presidency?

Out of a welter of decided cases, Fletcher on *Corporations* (Vol. 2, Sections 559, 592) arrives at the following conclusions:

"In view of the fact that presidents of corporations are often given general supervision and control over their management the liberal and modern rule seems to be that con-tracts or acts made or done by the president of a corporation in the course of its ordinary business will be presumed to have been within his authority unless the contrary appears, or else it is expressly stated that the president has no such powers.

. . . Even if the president be deemed to have power to act in behalf of the corpora-tion, or there is a presumption in fact of his authority, the power does not extend to acts outside the ordinary course of business nor to acts merely for his own benefit. In other words, if the terms of a contract entered into on behalf of a corporation by its officers are extraordinary or unusual, such as are not ordinarily made by the president or other officer in the ordinary course of the transaction of the current business of the corporation, the party contracting with the officer is put upon inquiry as to his authority."

Thus if there be inherent authority in a president resulting from the mere fact that he occupies the office, then even under what Fletcher has found to be the "liberal and modern rule" such inherent power is limited to the doing of acts—or the making of contracts, described sometimes as routine, sometimes as ordinary or usual, or—"in the course of its ordinary business" or "of an ordinary nature" or "in the usual course of business."

It could not be maintained with any degree of plausibility that making a contract to install a third person as overall general manager of a corporation's business was a routine transaction in the ordinary course of the corporation's business. Such a con-tract was not "of an ordinary nature" and the necessity therefore did not arise "in the usual course of business." The same must be said regarding any contract for the sharing of the corporation's profits. The latter is so extraordinary that it must be excluded from any concept of the usual course of business. It must be held that there was no inherent power in Woods to enter into the contract here in question arising from the mere fact that Woods occupied the position of president.

Liability for Torts and Crimes

Torts. The view in the early cases was that torts committed by a corpora-tion's agents were *ultra vires* and, therefore, the corporation was not responsi-ble. Today, as is clear from the cases in Chapter 3, the rule of *respondeat superior* applies to corporations, and the only issue is whether the agent was acting within the scope of his authority. The corporation may be liable even though it had expressly instructed its employees to avoid the act. Where the agent's acts are willful, wanton, or malicious and punitive damages would be appropriate, however, there is split of authority as to whether the corporation will be held liable for punitive damages in the absence of authorization or ratification.

Since neither the directors nor the officers are the principal they are not personally liable unless they have authorized or participated in the tort.

Crimes. Although corporations cannot be imprisoned, courts no longer find difficulty in holding them guilty even of crimes requiring intent. Corporations have been found guilty of most crimes except rape and bigamy and some statutes specifically provide punishment for crimes such as improper dividends or illegal purchase of its own shares which could be committed only by a corporation. Other laws such as tax laws and securities laws impose duties on corporations to file reports or perform other acts and impose criminal liability for failure to do so.

Criminal liability of the corporation is also imposed where the commission of the offense was authorized by, requested or performed by the board of directors, or an officer or agent having responsibility for formulating corporate policy or by a high-level administrator having supervisory responsibility over the subject matter of the offense and acting within the scope of his employment. The law is not as well settled with respect to acts committed by lower level employees but a number of cases have imposed liability on the corporation, although there was no actual authority and no actual benefit to the corporation, and even where there was an express prohibition against the criminal act performed. The trend is to impose vicarious criminal liability on the same basis as tort liability, liberally applying only the general test whether the act was performed by the agent while he was acting within the scope of his authority and in the course of his employment. Directors and officers may be found guilty of criminal acts when the corporation is acquitted if they act outside the scope of their authority.

An officer or director who requests or authorizes the commission of a crime by an employee of the corporation is, of course, equally guilty of that crime. He alone may be convicted if he commits a crime held to be outside his employment.

Summary

The general agency rules concerning torts and crimes apply to corporations. A corporation is liable for the torts of its employees done within the scope and in the course of the employment even when it expressly instructs the employee to avoid the act. Corporations may also be found guilty of crimes, including those requiring intent, if the offense is authorized or performed by policy-making managers or high-level administrators acting within the scope and in the course of employment. Although the law is not well settled, a number of cases have found corporations guilty of crimes committed by lower level employees, and the trend is to impose criminal liability on the same basis as tort liability.

McGlynn v. *Schultz*
231 A.2d 386 (Super. Ct. App. Div. N.J. 1967)

This was an action by the receiver of Neptune Center Associates (N.C.A.), a partnership, to recover damages from Schultz and other officer-directors of Office Buildings of America (O.B.A.) for their participation in the corporation's conversion of trust funds belonging to N.C.A. The officer-directors appealed from a judgment for $388,900 in favor of the receiver. Affirmed.

O.B.A. was engaged in the real estate syndication business. Its practice was to acquire a contract to purchase an income-producing property which it would then convey, or assign at a profit to a limited partnership. It would then take back a "net" lease from the partnership, the rental usually guaranteed to return 9 percent of the partners' investment.

O.B.A. contracted to purchase the Neptune City Shopping Center for $400,000 cash plus assumption of mortgages of about $1,850,000 and through a subsidiary organized N.C.A. and sold limited partnership shares in it to the public, using a prospectus which indicated that the purchase price to N.C.A. would be $720,000 over and above the mortgages. The N.C.A. limited partnership agreement expressly provided for a separate bank account but none was opened and the $414,900 collected from the limited partners was deposited in O.B.A.'s account.

Before title to the shopping center, which had been in serious financial condition at the time N.C.A. was organized, could be closed, O.B.A. was declared bankrupt.

KILKENNY, JUDGE.   As we said in *Sensale* v. *Applikon Dyeing & Printing Corp.*:

"A director or officer of a corporation does not incur personal liability for its torts merely by reason of his official character, but a director or officer who commits the tort or who directs the tortious act to be done, or participates or cooperates therein, is liable to third persons injured thereby, even though liability may also attach to the corporation for tort."

In brief, any officer or director who aids, instigates or assists in a conversion by his corporation becomes personally liable. It does not matter that the conversion was for the benefit of the corporation and that the individual directors did not personally receive any of the misappropriated monies.

The directors assert that they relied upon the advice of counsel for the corporation that it was not necessary to escrow or segregate these investors' funds. Several of the directors testified that he told the executive committee there was no legal or statutory requirement to escrow. The attorney categorically denied that he gave any such advice at that time. Apparently, at a subsequent special meeting of the full board of directors the attorney advised the board that there was "no statute" in New Jersey requiring that such monies be held in escrow, but a statute requiring escrow had been proposed, but not yet enacted. Such a statute has since been adopted.

Judge Mintz found it unnecessary to determine whether or not the directors in good faith relied upon the advice of counsel. He concluded that since good faith is not a defense to an action for conversion, it follows that "good faith in reliance upon advice of counsel is likewise no defense." We agree. Liability for a conversion is not necessarily precluded by the fact that the defendants acted in good faith. . . .

. . . Defendant directors knew of the corporation's "dire cash position," as the trial court found, and took the chance of using these trust funds in the hope that new monies would come in to replace them. Unfortunately for them, their expectations were not realized and they have made themselves personally liable for knowingly acquiescing in and ratifying the misappropriations by their corporation.

Fiduciary Duties of Directors, Officers, and Others

General. Directors as such are not agents of the corporation but hold a position which is *sui generis*. Nevertheless, they and corporate officers are treated as having fiduciary, or at least quasi-fiduciary, duties to the corporation which are essentially similar to the duties to his principal of any agent. They may generally be stated as (1) to act within one's authority and within the powers given to the corporation, (2) to act diligently and with due care in conducting the affairs of the corporation, and (3) to act in loyalty and good faith for the benefit of the corporation.

The trend of statutory and case law, and especially of the regulatory activity of the Securities and Exchange Commission, has been to raise the standard of conduct required of directors and officers and to extend some of the prohibitions to employees who are not officers and even to controlling shareholders. There also appears to be a trend toward more suits against directors, usually by shareholders in the name of the corporation, for breach of their duties to the corporation.

Acting within Authority. Like any agent, officers have a duty to act within the authority conferred upon them by the articles and bylaws of the corporation and by the directors. Directors must act within authority given to the corporation and to them by statute and by the articles and bylaws, as discussed above in the section on *ultra vires*. Either an officer or director may be liable to the corporation if it is damaged by an act exceeding his or the corporation's authority.

If directors honestly believe that a transaction approved by them is within the scope of the corporate business, and they are justified in that belief, they will not be held personally liable for injury to the corporation resulting from the transaction, even if the transaction is held to be *ultra vires*. Also, if the transaction is not illegal and is later ratified by the shareholders, the directors will be relieved of personal liability to the corporation.

Due Care and Diligence. Directors and officers are liable for losses to the corporation resulting from their negligence or lack of attention to their responsibilities. The Model Act does not define the standard of care but the New York statute defines it in a manner similar to that declared by some courts. It states: "Directors and officers shall discharge the duties of their respective positions in good faith and with that degree of diligence, care and skill which ordinarily prudent men would exercise under similar circumstances in like positions." [6] They may reasonably rely upon others—directors upon officers, both directors and officers upon accountants and lawyers, but lack of knowledge of the actual state of affairs of the corporation is not an adequate defense if the knowledge was obtainable through reasonable diligence.

The cases are in conflict as to whether a person's lack of capacity as a director will save him from liability. Certainly the failure to attend directors' meetings or the fact that a director receives no compensation does not permit him to escape liability, although if a director receives no compensation, is engaged full time in another business and lives at a distance from the corporation these are circumstances that would affect the degree of care and diligence expected. Directors and officers are not liable for mere errors of judgment if they act with care and diligence and in good faith. This rule is known as the "business judgment rule." However, they are liable for negligence both in taking action and in failing to take appropriate action. This would include liability for negligence in the selection and supervision of officers and employees of the corporation.

Loyalty and Good Faith. [7] Cardozo in a much quoted opinion well stated the duty to act in loyalty and good faith. He declared that a director:

owes loyalty and allegiance to the corporation—a loyalty that is undivided and an allegiance that is influenced by no consideration other than the welfare of the corporation. Any adverse interest of a director will be subjected to a scrutiny rigid and uncompromising. He may not profit at the expense of his corporation and in conflict with its rights; he may not for personal gain divert unto himself the opportunities which in equity and fairness belong to his corporation. He is required to use his independent judgment. . . . He must, of course, act honestly and in good faith. . . .[8]

The requirement of loyalty and good faith is general and is as broad as the inventiveness of avaricious humans to which it is addressed. Only four kinds of situations where questions of the good faith of directors or officers have been adjudicated will be discussed. They are: (1) transactions with the corporation, (2) usurpation of a corporate opportunity, (3) transactions in the corporation's stock, and (4) oppression of minority shareholders.

Transactions with the Corporation. Fiduciaries are generally not permitted any type of self-dealing, and earlier decisions held that any transaction

---

[6] McKinney's N.Y. Bus. Corp. Law, § 717.
[7] See also "Defense of Good Faith," later in this Chapter.
[8] *Meinhard* v. *Salmon*, 164 N.E. 545, 546 (1928).

with the corporation in which a director was involved directly or indirectly was voidable at the discretion of the corporation. However, transactions in which a director or officer, or another business organization in which he has an interest, supplies facilities, products or services to or is served by the corporation may clearly benefit the corporation. So more recently the majority of courts have held that such a transaction is voidable only if unfair to the corporation. If the director or officer represents the corporation as well as himself in the transaction or if his presence is necessary for a quorum or his vote for the approval of the transaction, then a court is less likely to enforce the contract. Failure to disclose fully his interest in the transaction is more important and is likely to be fatal to the director's attempt to enforce the contract even if its terms are fair to the corporation.

The most frequently arising self-dealing situation is the setting of salaries of officers who are also directors. Generally courts have viewed director action on officer-director salaries voidable if unfair unless the vote of none of the interested directors is essential to the action. The Model Act (33) authorizes the directors to fix their own compensation unless the articles provide otherwise, thus clarifying an uncertainty in the law. Section 18A (an optional section) requires any stock option plan which is to issue options to directors, officers, or employees of the corporation to be approved by a majority of the stock but the directors' judgment as to the adequacy of the consideration for the options is declared to be conclusive in the absence of fraud.

Usurpation of a Corporate Opportunity.   Directors and officers may not take for themselves business opportunities which come to them in their corporate capacity and which fall within the normal scope of the corporation's business and which it is able to undertake. They may not, for example, buy up land that the corporation could use and then resell it to the corporation at a profit nor may they personally buy the rights to manufacture a product which would fit into the corporation's line. If the corporation is unable to finance the opportunity or accepting it would be *ultra vires* or a noninterested majority of directors vote against accepting it, then the director or officer is free to exploit it personally unless it would result in harmful competition to the corporation.

Transactions in the Corporation's Stock.   Directors and officers have access to information affecting the value of the corporation's securities unavailable to other securities holders. Are they entitled to make a profit from knowledge by buying and selling the corporation's stock or other securities without disclosing this information to the other party in the transaction? In the early cases courts concluded that directors and officers had no fiduciary duty to existing or potential shareholders but only to the corporation. Therefore, they were accountable for their trading profits neither to the corporation, which suffered no loss, nor to the individuals from whom they bought or to whom they sold stock. However, in this century there has been a trend in the court decisions toward finding a duty on the part of the director or officer, and even an employee or controlling shareholder, to disclose his knowledge as a condition to his right to buy or sell. Under this view the other party to the transaction may recover the difference between the stock's value had the information been known and the actual trading price. As will be discussed, this is already the law under the Securities Exchange Act, but it remains only a minority rule in suits not brought under that act.

Some relatively recent decisions have held that controlling shareholders are liable to their fellow shareholders for breach of a duty to exercise due care to guard their interests against potential looters of the corporate assets and also have permitted them to recover the premium over and above the inherent value of the stock paid the controlling shareholders for sale of control of the corporation.

Oppression of Minority Shareholders. Directors and officers owe a duty to the corporation to exercise their management functions in the best interests of the corporation as a whole. Although this duty is generally recognized, so also is the right of the majority to manage the corporation with considerable discretion through the "business judgment" rule. Courts are frequently faced with suits, usually involving close corporations, which allege oppression of minority shareholders or attempts to "freeze" them out of the corporation which require balancing these two principles. The means of oppression complained of are many. They include dividend withholding, siphoning off profits in high salaries to controlling shareholders in management, mergers or reorganizations or merely charter amendments which alter the rights and preferences of a certain class or classes of stock and sale or lease of major corporate assets to or from controlling shareholders for an unfair consideration. Generally minority shareholders have been successful in obtaining an injunction or recovering damages only where the acts of directors have been clearly in bad faith, arbitrary or clearly abuse the discretion allowed them under the "business judgment" rule.

Federal Securities Laws Limitations on "Insiders." The Securities Exchange Act contains two provisions dealing with stock trading by "insiders." Section 16 requires directors, officers, and owners of 10 percent or more of any class equity security of a corporation which has one or more classes of such securities listed on a stock exchange or total assets exceeding $1,000,000 or any class of stock held by 500 or more persons, to report monthly on any change in their stock holdings. It further provides that any so-called "short-swing" profit (a profit made upon a purchase and sale or sale and purchase made within six months of each other) can be recovered by the corporation. This can be accomplished by a shareholder suit if the corporation itself fails to exercise its right.

Section 10(b) prohibits deceptive practices in the sale of any security in interstate commerce. The Securities Exchange Commission in its rules and in its policing function has taken the position that this includes the failure to state any material fact. In the much discussed *Texas Gulf Sulphur* case,[9] the SEC received the support of the Circuit Court of Appeals for its position that anyone in possession of material confidential information about the corporation is an "insider" and unable to trade in the stock until the knowledge is generally available to the investing community. The SEC's view is that a fact is material if its disclosure would reasonably be expected to affect the market price of the stock or would materially affect the decision of a prospective buyer or seller whether to buy, sell, or delay. Certainly such matters as proposed mergers, tender offers for the corporation's stock, plans to introduce an important new product or indications of an abrupt change in the profit expectations of the company are examples of what would be considered material facts. More difficult is the question how early in the development of the plan or trend disclosure or abstention from buying or selling is required.

Other Statutory Liabilities of Directors.   The federal securities laws also impose liabilities on directors, signing officers and controlling shareholders to injured persons for false statements or omissions in the required registration statements and prospectuses (discussed in Chapter 26) and for failing to file required reports. Criminal liabilities are also imposed.

The Model Corporation Act (43) imposes personal civil liability to the corporation upon directors for certain acts taken in conducting the internal affairs of the corporation. These acts include: (1) assenting to the payment of a dividend or a distribution of assets in violation of the statute or the articles; (2) assent to the purchase of its own shares by the corporation contrary to Section 5; (3) assent to the distribution of assets during liquidation without providing for the payment of all known debts; (4) assent to making a loan to an officer or director of the corporation; and (5) assent to commencement of business by the corporation before it has received at least $1,000 for the issuance of stock. To protect himself if the board takes any of these illegal actions, a director who attends the meeting at which the action is taken must have his dissent recorded in the minutes or if he did not vote in favor of the motion he may file a written dissent with the secretary of the corporation immediately after adjournment of the meeting.

Defense of Good Faith.   The Model Act protects the director in the first three situations if he acts in good faith upon financial statements represented to him to be correct by the president or the officer of the corporation having charge of its books of account or on a written report by an independent public accountant. This appears merely to codify the "business judgment" rule. In a number of cases the courts have held that good faith reliance by an officer

---

[9] *S.E.C.* v. *Texas Gulf Sulphur Co., 401 F.2d 833 (2d Cir. 1968) infra.*

or director upon the opinion of counsel is a defense to personal liability, but this defense has perhaps more frequently been rejected and the cases probably cannot be reconciled.

Summary

Although directors are not agents of the corporation, they and corporate officers are treated as having fiduciary duties to the corporation.

The trend of the law is toward raising the standard of conduct required of directors and officers and there appears to be an increase in suits brought against them, usually by stockholders, for breach of their duties to the corporation.

They must act within their authority and within the powers given to the corporation. They are liable to the corporation for losses due to their negligence or lack of attention to their responsibilities but not for mere errors in judgment. They also owe a duty of loyalty and good faith to the corporation and must put its welfare above their own.

A director or officer may transact business with the corporation but he must disclose to the corporation any conflict of interest he may have and the corporation may avoid a contract with him which is unfair to the corporation. He may not usurp a corporate opportunity by taking for his personal advantage some opportunity coming to him in his corporate capacity or which may have the effect of putting him in competition with the corporation.

There is a trend in the case law towards holding that directors and officers may not use information not generally available to the investing public to personally buy and sell the corporation's shares. This is now clearly the law under the Securities Exchange Act.

The duty of good faith is to act for the best interests of the corporation as a whole and if the actions of the directors or officers are taken primarily for the purpose of oppressing minority shareholders or "freezing" them out of the corporation, the minority may be able to obtain injunctive relief or damages.

Directors and officers may also be civilly, and in some instances even criminally, liable for making false statements and omissions in registration statements for the sale of securities and in required reports and in taking certain illegal actions.

Graham v. Allis-Chalmers Manufacturing Co.
188 A.2d 125 (Sup. Ct. Del. 1963)

This was a derivative action by Graham and other shareholders (plaintiffs) on behalf of Allis-Chalmers Manufacturing Company against its directors (defendants) for damages sustained by the corporation as a result of antitrust violations. The Court of Chancery dismissed the complaint. Affirmed.

Allis-Chalmers manufactured electrical equipment and other machinery. It employed over 31,000 persons and had sales greater than $500,000,000 annually. The company management was organized into two groups headed by senior vice presidents. The Industries Group was divided into five divisions, one of which produced electrical equipment. It was in connection with the sale of the products of this division that the corporation was indicted and pleaded guilty to price-fixing violations of the antitrust laws.

The company policy was to delegate authority to the lowest possible management level. Prices for standard products were set by the department manager while prices for large or special equipment would be established in consultation with the division manager. Annually the board of directors reviewed group and departmental profit goal budgets but did not participate in fixing the prices of particular products.

The board of directors was composed of 14 members, 4 of whom were officers. They met monthly, usually for several hours, and decided matters of the general business policy of the company. None of the director-officers were indicted in the price-fixing cases.

WOLCOTT, JUSTICE.   From the *Briggs* case and others cited by the plaintiffs . . . it appears that directors of a corporation in managing the corporate affairs are bound to use that amount of care which ordinarily careful and prudent men would use in similar circumstances. Their duties are those of control, and whether or not by neglect they have made themselves liable for failure to exercise proper control depends on the circumstances and facts of the particular case.

The precise charge made against these director defendants is that, even though they had no knowledge of any suspicion of wrongdoing on the part of the company's employees, they still should have put into effect a system of watchfulness which would have brought such misconduct to their attention in ample time to have brought it to an end. . . . On the contrary, it appears the directors are entitled to rely on the honesty and integrity of their subordinates until something occurs to put them on suspicion that something is wrong. If such occurs and goes unheeded, then liability of the directors might well follow, but absent cause for suspicion there is no duty upon the directors to install and operate a corporate system of espionage to ferret out wrongdoing which they have no reason to suspect exists.

The duties of the Allis-Chalmers directors were fixed by the nature of the enterprise which employed in excess of 30,000 persons, and extended over a large geographical area. By force of necessity, the company's directors could not know personally all the company's employees. The very magnitude of the enterprise required them to confine their control to the broad policy decisions. That they did this is clear from the record. At the meetings of the board in which all directors participated, these questions were considered and decided on the basis of summaries, reports and corporate records. These they were entitled to rely on, not only, we think, under general principles of the common law, but by reason of 8 Del.C. § 141(f) as well, which in terms fully protects a director who relies on such in the performance of his duties.

In the last analysis, the question of whether a corporate director has become liable for losses to the corporation through neglect of duty is determined by the circumstances. If he has recklessly reposed confidence in an obviously untrustworthy employee, has refused or neglected cavalierly to perform his duty as a director, or has ignored either willfully or through inattention obvious danger signs of employee wrongdoing, the law will cast the burden of liability upon him. This is not the case at bar, however, for as soon as it became evident that there were grounds for suspicion, the board acted promptly to end it and prevent its recurrence.

Robinson v. Brier
194 A.2d 204 (Sup. Ct. Pa. 1963)

This was a derivative stockholder's suit brought by Phillip and Henry Robinson (plaintiffs) to recover for the Mado Manufacturing Corporation, profits made by Brier (defendant), its manager who was also one of its four directors, in transactions with the corporation. The court denied recovery. Affirmed.

The Robinsons and Brier bought all of the stock of Leeds Travelwear Corporation, of which Mado was a subsidiary. Brier individually owned two other luggage companies. Brier was put in charge of Mado, which assembled the soft luggage sold by Leeds and undertook a cost reduction program. In reviewing the cost of supplies he went to Washington Woodcraft, the only known supplier of the wooden frames that gave the luggage rigidity. He secured price reductions on certain sizes, but after making a cost analysis of producing the required frames in one of his own companies, Saberly, he arranged for Mado to buy Saberly's entire output of frames at prices substantially below the quotations from Washington. Brier's interest in Saberly and Saberly's sales to Mado were common knowledge to all of the directors of Mado including the Robinsons. Brier made no statement that he was making a profit on the sales.

COHEN, JUSTICE.   Robinson's first contention is that Brier usurped a corporate opportunity by permitting Saberly to manufacture the wooden frames instead of having Mado perform the work itself.

Where the corporation is *unable* to avail itself of the business opportunity, there can be no usurpation of a corporate opportunity. . . .

The record discloses that all of Mado's available space was being utilized for the assembling and storage of soft luggage. Moreover, since Mado was already behind in filling the orders of large customers such as Sears-Roebuck and Macy, any allocation of space to frame manufacturing would have resulted in a further delay in production. Because of the pressure of back orders and this critical space situation, it was correctly decided that Mado should devote its energies to assembling and storing luggage instead of becoming involved in the manufacture of wooden frames. . . .

Accordingly, there was no usurpation of a corporate opportunity.

Robinson next contends that Brier breached his fiduciary duty by selling the wooden frames to Mado without (1) explicitly stating that he was making a profit and (2) without revealing the amount of the profit.

Transactions between a corporation and its directors are not prohibited but rather are governed by a strict standard of "fairness." While the interested director has the heavy burden of demonstrating the fairness of the transaction, we conclude that Brier has satisfactorily sustained that burden under the facts presented in this case.

The record discloses that Brier made diligent efforts to locate the lowest source of frames and that Saberly's prices were below those of any other competitor, thereby resulting in substantial savings to Mado, that Brier's dealings with Mado were open and scrupulously honest, with Brier never representing that he was not making a profit; and that Braverman, a non-interested director, testified that he expected Brier to make a profit. These circumstances indicate that Brier's dealings with Mado were eminently fair and we conclude that he was entitled to retain any profits resulting therefrom.

The mere fact that Brier did not affirmatively state that he was making a profit did not render the dealings unfair. The other directors as reasonable businessmen should have known and, indeed, must have been aware, as Braverman was, that Brier would not invest capital and energy into a venture from which he did not expect to profit. . . .

. . . Having charged Mado a price substantially lower than that quoted by others, and having revealed his interest in the transactions, it was not necessary for Brier to state the amount of profit he was earning. . . . If Robinson's theory were to prevail, corporations would be deprived of the goods and services of highly competent individuals and organizations because of the natural unwillingness of businessmen to reveal the financial details of their business affairs. . . .

Guth v. *Loft, Inc.*
5 A.2d 503 (Sup. Ct. Del. 1939)

This was a bill in Chancery by Loft, Inc. (plaintiff), against Charles G. Guth, Grace Company and Pepsi-Cola Company (defendants) seeking to impress a trust in favor of Loft upon all of the capital stock of Pepsi-Cola. The Chancellor found for Loft. Affirmed.

Loft manufactured and sold candies, syrups, beverages and foodstuffs in 115 retail stores on the Middle Atlantic seaboard and its wholesale activities amounted to sales of $800,000. It dispensed Coca-Cola at all of its stores. Guth, a man of long experience in the candy and soft drink business joined Loft in 1929 and became president and general manager in 1930. In 1931 he tried to persuade Coca-Cola to give Loft a jobber's discount in view of its very large purchases. Coca-Cola refused and Guth learned that Pepsi-Cola syrup could be purchased for about two-thirds the price of Coca-Cola. While this was under consideration, the corporation owning the secret formula and trademark for Pepsi-Cola was adjudicated a bankrupt and the man controlling it sought Guth's help in forming a new corporation. This was done with approximately half of the stock going to Grace, a corporation owned by Guth's family which made syrups for soft drinks and which sold one of its syrups to Loft. Most of the rest of the stock came to be owned by Guth through subsequent transactions with the man previously controlling Pepsi-Cola. During this period Guth was very heavily indebted to Loft and was in serious financial straits and Grace was insolvent.

Guth used Loft's working capital, its credit, its plant and equipment and its executives and employees in producing Pepsi-Cola, although Loft was subsequently reimbursed for wages paid to workers. Loft was Pepsi-Cola's chief customer. It suffered diminution of profits in its retail stores estimated at $300,000 due to discarding Coca-Cola, despite advertising expenditures of $20,000 to promote Pepsi-Cola, which was relatively unknown.

Guth claimed he offered the Loft directors the opportunity to take over Pepsi-Cola but they declined because they did not wish to compete with Coca-Cola, that it was not in line with Loft's business, and that it involved too great a financial risk. However, he also claimed that later the directors authorized the use of Loft facilities and resources upon Guth's guarantee of all advances. No record of either action appeared in the corporate minutes of Loft, and the Chancellor found that the directors were without knowledge of the use of Loft's money, credit, facilities and personnel in furthering the Pepsi-Cola venture.

LAYTON, CHIEF JUSTICE.   Corporate officers and directors are not permitted to use their position of trust and confidence to further their private interests. While technically not trustees, they stand in fiduciary relation to the corporation and its stockholders. A public policy, existing through the years, and derived from a profound knowledge of human characteristics and motives, has established a rule that demands of a corporate officer or director, peremptorily and inexorably, the most scrupulous observance of his duty, not only affirmatively to protect the interests of the corporation committed to his charge, but also to refrain from doing anything that would work injury to the corporation, or to deprive it of profit or advantage which his skill and ability might properly bring to it, or to enable it to make in the reasonable and lawful exercise of its powers. The rule that requires an undivided and unselfish loyalty to the corporation demands that there shall be no conflict between duty and self-interest. The occasions for the determination of honesty, good faith and loyal conduct are many and varied, and no hard and fast rule can be formulated. The standard of loyalty is measured by no fixed scale.

If an officer or director of a corporation, in violation of his duty as such, acquires gain or advantage for himself, the law charges the interest so acquired with a trust for the benefit of the corporation, at its election, while it denies to the betrayer all benefit and profit. The rule, inveterate and uncompromising in its rigidity, does not rest upon the narrow ground of injury or damage to the corporation resulting from a betrayal of confidence, but upon a broader foundation of a wise public policy that, for the purpose of removing all temptation, extinguishes all possibility of profit flowing from a breach of the confidence imposed by the fiduciary relation. Given the relation between the parties, a certain result follows; and a constructive trust is the remedial device through which precedence of self is compelled to give way to the stern demands of loyalty.

The rule, referred to briefly as the rule of corporate opportunity, is merely one of the manifestations of the general rule that demands of an officer or director the utmost good faith in his relation to the corporation which he represents.

It is true that when a business opportunity comes to a corporate officer or director in his individual capacity rather than in his official capacity, and the opportunity is one which, because of the nature of the enterprise, is not essential to his corporation, and is one in which it has no interest or expectancy, the officer or director is entitled to treat the opportunity as his own, and the corporation has no interest in it, if, of course, the officer or director has not wrongfully embarked the corporation's resources therein.

Although the facts and circumstances disclosed by the voluminous record clearly show gross violations of legal and moral duties by Guth in his dealings with Loft, Guth makes bold to say that no duty was cast upon him, hence he was guilty of no disloyalty. The fiduciary relation demands something more than the morals of the marketplace. Guth's abstractions of Loft's money and materials are complacently referred to as borrowings. Whether his acts are to be deemed properly cognizable in a civil court at all, we need not inquire, but certain it is that borrowing is not descriptive of them. A borrower presumes a lender acting freely. Guth took without limit or stint from a helpless corporation, in violation of a statute enacted for the protection of corporations against such abuses, and without the knowledge or authority of the corporation's Board of Directors. Cunning and craft supplanted sincerity. Frankness gave way to concealment. He did not offer the Pepsi-Cola opportunity to Loft, but captured it for himself. He invested little or no money of his own in the venture, but commandeered for his own benefit and advantage the money, resources and facilities of his corporation and the services of his officials. He thrust upon Loft the hazard, while he reaped the benefit. His time was paid for by Loft. The use of the Grace plant was not essential to the enterprise. In such manner he acquired for himself and Grace ninety-one percent of the capital stock of Pepsi-Cola, now worth many millions. A genius in his line he may be, but the law makes no distinction between the wrong-doing genius and the one less endowed.

Jacobson v. Yaschik
155 S.E. 2d 601 (Sup. Ct. S.C. 1967)

This was an action by Jacobson (plaintiff) against Yaschik (defendant) seeking to recover the difference between the price at which Jacobson bought Yaschik's stock and his selling price. Yaschik appealed from the trial court's action in overruling his demurrer. Judgment affirmed.

Yaschik owned 150 shares and was president and general manager of a corporation which owned as its only asset 82 acres of land along a highway. Jacobson owned the other 50 shares outstanding. After negotiations Jacobson agreed on May 8 to sell her stock to Yaschik for $30,000. Unknown to Jacobson, Yaschik had agreed on May 8 to sell to a third party all of the capital stock for $144,000, the equivalent of $36,000 for Jacobson's interest in the corporation.

MOSS, CHIEF JUSTICE.   The issue involved in this case is whether, under the circumstances above set forth, it was the duty of Yaschik, acting in good faith, to disclose to Jacobson the facts bearing upon or which might affect the value of her stock. Yaschik argues that no cause of action is stated in the complaint because a corporate officer owes no fiduciary duty to a stockholder before purchasing the stock of such stockholder for himself. The question of the obligation of an officer of a company to disclose all information that he may have as to the value of the corporate stock before purchasing the stock of a fellow stockholder for himself has been the subject of some conflict of authority.

The majority rule is that an officer or director of a corporation does not stand in a fiduciary relation with a stockholder with respect to his stock and in the absence of circumstances from which fraud or unfair dealings may be inferred, an officer or director of a close corporation is under no duty to volunteer information to a stockholder from whom he purchases stock. An exception or limitation to this general or majority rule is that where a director or officer has knowledge of special facts by virtue of which the value of the stock had been enhanced, but which special facts are not known to the minority stockholder, the officer or director is required to make a full disclosure of such facts. The failure of such officer or director to make a full disclosure may amount to actual fraud or deceit so as to entitle the minority stockholder to relief. The minority rule is that an officer or director of a corporation stands in a fiduciary relationship to the individual stockholders and irrespective of any special facts an officer or director of a corporation acts in a fiduciary capacity and in every instance must make a full disclosure of all relevant facts when purchasing shares of stock from a stockholder.

We think that the holding in the *Black* case commits this court to the minority rule above stated, that officers and directors of a corporation stand in a fiduciary relationship to the individual stockholders and in every instance must make a full disclosure of all relevant facts when purchasing shares of stock from a stockholder. Having reached this conclusion, it was the duty of Yaschik to disclose to Jacobson the price at which he was selling all of the stock in the corporation to Southern Mortgage Company.

S.E.C. v. *Texas Gulf Sulphur Co.*
401 F.2d 833 (2d Cir. 1968)

This was an action by the Securities Exchange Commission (plaintiff) against the Texas Gulf Sulphur Co. (TGS) and thirteen of its officers, directors and employees (defendants) alleging violations of Section 10(b) of the Securities Exchange Act of 1934. The District Court found that two of the individuals, Clayton and Crawford, had violated the act but otherwise dismissed the complaint. On appeal the judgment was affirmed as to Clayton and Crawford and reversed as to all other parties but one, Murray, who was held not to have committed a violation. The case was remanded to determine whether TGS had violated the act and to determine remedies.

TGS had for several years made serial geophysical surveys in Eastern Canada followed by drilling exploratory cores into geological formations that looked promising. On November 12, 1963, the core from the first drilling on a parcel of land near Timmins, Ontario, was fabulously high in copper content as well as in zinc and silver. Diversionary holes were then drilled elsewhere until the balance of the land covered by the formation could be acquired by TGS. The land acquisition program had progressed far enough for TGS to resume drilling in the area on March 31, 1964. The next two cores also showed substantial quantities of the same minerals and additional rigs were put to work drilling more holes beginning on April 8. Meanwhile, rumors of a major ore strike were circulating in Canada and on Saturday, April 11, two major New York papers printed reports of TGS activity and appeared to infer a rich strike from the fact that the drill cores were being flown to the United States.

Following this publication on Saturday, Stephens, the president of TGS, and Fogarty, the executive vice president, were concerned by the publicized rumors and talked with Mollison, the TGS vice president who was in charge of the operations near Timmins. He had left the drilling on Friday and was at his home near New York City for the weekend. As a result on Sunday a news release was distributed for use on Monday, April 14. The release stated that most of the drilling in eastern Canada had shown nothing of value with a few holes indicating small or marginal ore bodies. It said that shipment of the cores to the United States was routine. It then added:

Recent drilling on one property near Timmins has led to preliminary indications that more drilling would be required for proper evaluation of this prospect. The drilling done to date has not been conclusive, but the statements made by many outside quarters are unreliable and include information and figures that are not available to TGS.

The work done to date has not been sufficient to reach definite conclusions and any statement as to size and grade of ore would be premature and possibly misleading. When we have progressed to the point where reasonable and logical conclusions can be made, TGS will issue a definitive statement to its stockholders and to the public in order to clarify the Timmins project.

On April 16 at 10:00 A.M. TGS held a conference for the financial press and disclosed that the ore body would run to at least 25,000,000 tons of ore. This information was published on the Dow-Jones tape at 10:45 A.M.

Some of the individual defendants had purchased stock or calls upon stock in TGS between the time the results were known to them of the first core drilled on the site and the appearance of the second release on the Dow-Jones tape. Others, including Stephens and Fogarty, had accepted options to buy TGS stock from the corporation's stock option committee of the board of directors which was unaware of the find. The market price of TGS stock rose from approximately $18 per share on November 12, 1963, to $58 on May 15, 1964. In addition to alleging a violation of the Securities Exchange Act by the individuals, the S.E.C. claimed that the first press release of TGS, issued April 12, was deceptive and misleading in violation of the Act.

WATERMAN, CIRCUIT JUDGE.

I. The Individual Defendants

Rule 10b-5, 17 CFR 240, 10b-5, on which this action is predicated, provides:

It shall be unlawful for any person, directly or indirectly, by the use of any means or instrumentality of interstate commerce, or of the mails, or of any facility of any national securities exchange,

(1) to employ any device, scheme, or artifice to defraud,

(2) to make any untrue statement of a material fact or to omit to state a material fact necessary in order to make the statements made, in the light of the circumstances under which they were made, not misleading, or

(3) to engage in any act, practice, or course of business which operates or would operate as a fraud or deceit upon any person, in connection with the purchase or sale of any security.

. . . The essense of the Rule is that anyone who, trading for his own account in the securities of a corporation has "access, directly or indirectly, to information intended to be available only for a corporate purpose and not for the personal benefit of anyone" may not take "advantage of such information knowing it is unavailable to those with whom he is dealing," i.e., the investing public.

Insiders, as directors or management officers are, of course, by this Rule, precluded from so unfairly dealing, but the Rule is also applicable to one possessing that information who may not be strictly termed an "insider" within the meaning of Sec. 16(b) of the Act.

Thus, anyone in possession of material inside information must either disclose it to the investing public, or if he is disabled from disclosing it in order to protect a corporate confidence, or he chooses not to do so, must abstain from trading in or recommending the securities concerned while such inside information remains undisclosed. So, it is here no justification for insider activity that disclosure was forbidden by the legitimate corporate objective of acquiring options to purchase the land surrounding the exploration site: if the information was, as the SEC contends, material, its possessors should have kept out of the market until disclosure was accomplished. . . . Material facts include not only information disclosing the earnings and distributions of a company, but also those facts which affect the desire of investors to buy, sell, or hold the company's securities.

.　.　.　.　.

In each case, then, whether facts are material within Rule 10b-5 when the facts relate to a particular event and are undisclosed by those persons who are knowledgeable thereof will depend at any given time upon a balancing of both the indicated probability that the event will occur and the anticipated magnitude of the event in light of the totality of the company activity.

Here, notwithstanding the trial court's conclusion that the results of the first drill core, K-55-1, were "too 'remote' . . . to have had any significant impact on the market, i.e., to be deemed material, knowledge of the possibility, which surely was more than marginal, of the existence of a mine of the vast magnitude indicated by the remarkably rich drill core located rather close to the surface (suggesting mine-ability by the less expensive open-pit method) within the confines of a large anomaly (suggesting an extensive region of mineralization) might well have affected the price of TGS stock and would certainly have been an important fact to a reasonable, if speculative, investor in deciding whether he should buy, sell or hold.

We hold, therefore, that all transactions in TGS stock or calls by individuals apprised of the drilling results of K-55-1 were made in violation of Rule 10b-5.

· · · · ·

Appellant Crawford, who ordered the purchase of TGS stock shortly before the TGS April 16 official announcement, and defendant Coates, who placed orders with and communicated the news to his broker immediately after the official announce-ment was read at the TGS-called press conference, concede that they were in pos-session of material information. They contend, however, that their purchases were not proscribed purchases for the news had already been effectively disclosed. We disagree. . . . Before insiders may act upon material information, such information must have been effectively disclosed in a manner sufficient to insure its availability to the investing public. Particularly here, where a formal announcement to the entire financial news media has been promised in a prior official release known to the media, all insider activity must await dissemination of the promised official announce-ment.

Assuming that the contents of the official release could instantaneously be acted upon, at the minimum Coates should have waited until the news could reasonably have been expected to appear over the media of widest circulation, the Dow-Jones broad-tape, rather than hastening to insure an advantage to himself and his broker son-in-law.

· · · · ·

Contrary to the belief of the trial court that Kline had no duty to disclose his knowledge of the Kidd project before accepting the stock option offered him, we believe that he, a vice president, who had become the general counsel of TGS in January, 1964, but who had been secretary of the corporation since January, 1961, and was present in that capacity when the options were granted, and who was in charge of the mechanics of issuance and acceptance of the options, was a member of top management and under a duty before accepting his option to disclose any material information he may have possesed, and, as he did not disclose such infor-mation to the Option Committee we direct rescission of the option he received.

· · · · ·

II. The Corporate Defendant

[I]t seems clear from the broad legislative purpose Congress expressed in the Act, and the legislative history of Section 10(b) that Congress when it used the phrase "in connection with the purchase or sale of any security" intended only that the device employed, whatever it might be, be of a sort that would cause reasonable investors to rely thereon, and, in connection therewith, so relying, cause them to purchase or sell a corporation's securities. There is no indication that Congress intended that the corporations or persons responsible for the issuance of a misleading statement would not violate the section unless they engaged in related securities transactions or otherwise acted with wrongful motives; indeed, the obvious purposes of the Act to protect the investing public and to secure fair dealing in the securities markets would be seriously undermined by applying such a gloss onto the legislative language.

Absent a securities transaction by an insider it is almost impossible to prove that a wrongful purpose motivated the issuance of the misleading statement. The mere fact that an insider did not engage in securities transactions does not negate the possibility of wrongful purpose; perhaps the market did not react to the misleading statement as much as was anticipated or perhaps the wrongful purpose was something other than the desire to buy at a low price or sell at a high price. Of even greater relevance to the Congressional purpose of investor protection is the fact that the investing public may be injured as much by one's misleading statement containing inaccuracies caused by negligence as by a misleading statement published intentionally to further a wrongful purpose.

. . . . .

To render the Congressional purpose ineffective by inserting into the statutory words the need of proving, not only that the public may have been misled by the release, but also that those responsible were actuated by a wrongful purpose when they issued the release, is to handicap unreasonably the Commission in its work.

. . . . .

[T]he investing public is hurt by exposure to false or deceptive statements irrespective of the purpose underlying their issuance. It does not appear to be unfair to impose upon corporate management a duty to ascertain the truth of any statements the corporation releases to its shareholders or to the investing public at large.

Accordingly, we hold that Rule 10b-5 is violated whenever assertions are made, as here, in a manner reasonably calculated to influence the investing public, e.g., by means of the financial media, if such assertions are false or misleading or are so incomplete as to mislead irrespective of whether the issuance of the release was motivated by corporate officials for ulterior purposes. It seems clear, however, that if corporate management demonstrates that it was diligent in ascertaining that the information it published was the whole truth and that such diligently obtained information was disseminated in good faith, Rule 10b-5 would not have been violated.

. . . . .

In the event that it is found that the statement was misleading to the reasonable investor it will then become necessary to determine whether its issuance resulted from a lack of due diligence. The only remedy the Commission seeks against the corporation is an injunction, and therefore we do not find it necessary to decide whether a lack of due diligence on the part of TGS alone, absent a showing of bad faith, would subject the corporation to any liability for damages. . . . .

We hold only that, in an action for injunctive relief, the district court has the discretionary power under Rule 10b-5 and Section 10(b) to issue an injunction, if the misleading statement resulted from a lack of due diligence on the part of TGS. The trial court did not find it necessary to decide whether TGS exercised such diligence and has not yet attempted to resolve this issue. . . .

It is not altogether certain from the present record that the draftsmen could, as the SEC suggests, have readily obtained current reports of the drilling progress over the weekend of April 10-12, but they certainly should have obtained them if at all possible for them to do so.

However, even if it were not possible to evaluate and transmit current data in time to prepare the release on April 12, it would seem that TGS could have delayed the preparation a bit until an accurate report of a rapidly changing situation was possible.

At the very least, if TGS felt compelled to respond to the spreading rumors of a spectacular discovery, it would have been more accurate to have stated that the situation was in flux and that the release was prepared as of April 10 information rather than purporting to report the progress "to date." Moreover, it would have obviously been better to have specifically described the known drilling progress as of April 10 by stating the basic facts. Such an explicit disclosure would have permitted the investing public to evaluate the "prospect" of a mine at Timmins without having to read between the lines to understand that preliminary indications were favorable—in itself an understatement.

The choice of an ambiguous general statement rather than a summary of the specific facts cannot reasonably be justified by any claimed urgency. The avoidance of liability for misrepresentation in the event that the Timmins project failed, a highly unlikely event as of April 12 or April 13, did not forbid the accurate and truthful divulgence of detailed results which need not, of course, have been accompanied by conclusory assertions of success.

. . . . .

We conclude, then, that, having established that the release was issued in a manner reasonably calculated to affect the market price of TGS stock and to influence the investing public, we must remand to the district court to decide whether the release was misleading to the reasonable investor and if found to be misleading, whether the court in its discretion should issue the injunction the SEC seeks.

Problem Cases

1. A corporation which had gained control of and subsequently liquidated several companies made a tender offer for 80 percent of the shares of LaClede-Christy Corp. stock at a price approximating current assets per share. This came after a meeting of the board in which it voted unanimously not to entertain any offer to buy the company. LaClede-Christy's president then called a special board meeting and announced his opposition to the tender offer. He subsequently used company funds to purchase for the company 2,900 shares of the company stock and to employ proxy-soliciting specialists, lawyers, and consultants to assist in fighting the offer. The corporate minutes recorded no approval of these actions. The company making the offer succeeded in gaining control, and after replacing the board and discharging the president, brings suit against the latter for violating his fiduciary duties and acting without board authority in expending corporate funds to prevent it from gaining control. Is the corporation entitled to reimbursement for the monies expended?

2. The bylaws of Arien, Inc., provided for five directors and that a quorum should consist of three directors. Two of the directors resigned. At a board meeting held after proper notice but not attended by Weiss, the third director, new directors were elected to fill one of the vacancies and subsequently Weiss was removed as president. Weiss claims the removal is illegal and attempts to continue to act as president. Is he correct?

3. To quiet rumors that the corporation was for sale, the directors entered into a five-year contract with Streett, who was then holding the office of president. The contract provided that the corporation would employ Streett as "general manager and chief operating officer." The agreement recited that it was the expectation of the parties that he would continue to act as chief operating officer and that "the present board of directors, insofar as it can bind succeeding boards, hereby employs Streett as president for five years." Ownership of the corporation changed, the board was replaced and Streett fired four months later.

    Streett sues for breach of contract. The corporation's defense is that the contract was void because it attempted to bind future boards of directors. Is the defense good?

4. Asher Company owned coal-bearing lands which it leased to mining companies. It had previously leased to Har-Bel by an instrument signed by Robert Asher, president, and Asher's secretary. Har-Bel entered negotiations for a different property with Robert Asher and, on the strength of an oral agreement moved in equipment and began mining. A few days later an attorney was asked to prepare a written lease and subsequently a third draft was signed by Robert Asher. The president of Har-Bel called upon the secretary of Asher Company but he would not sign. The Asher directors refuse to approve the lease. Can Har-Bel enforce the lease signed by Robert Asher?

5. The stock of Fox Hill, Inc., is owned as follows: Baker, 425 shares; Sarner, 325 shares; and a third party 100 shares. Baker is general manager and the board of directors is composed of Baker, his wife and his attorney. At a directors' meeting the directors, with Baker abstaining, voted to compensate Baker for his management services by transferring him 100 shares of treasury stock which it valued at $145 per share and an option to purchase up to 250 additional shares at $120 per share, of which Baker purchased 50 shares. The bylaws require a majority of the directors for a quorum and a majority of those present are required to take action. May a complaining shareholder void the stock transaction?

6. The Horns were engaged in the produce business in New York City and held all of the stock of three corporations, each owning a low-rental apartment building. They encouraged Mrs. Burg to join them in a similar investment and Darand Realty Corporation was organized with the two Horns and Mrs. Burg each furnishing one third of the capital and each serving as a director with the Horns serving as managers and Mr. Burg as accountant. During the following 10 years, the Horns purchased nine similar low-rent properties individually or through wholly owned corporations. Loans from Darand Realty totaling $800 and from Mrs. Burg totaling $6,250 were used in the purchase of a few of these properties. The Burgs moved to California and thereafter disagreements arose between them and the Horns respecting the accounting for rent receipts to Darand Realty. Mrs. Burg also seeks an accounting from the Horns for appropriating corporate opportunities in purchasing the nine additional properties. Is Darand Realty entitled to these properties?

7. Carroll, Pape, and Luegering, who were president, vice president and secretary, respectively, of the Lackner Custom Sign Service Co., together owned a majority of

Lackner stock and constituted a majority of its directors. Most of Lackner's business was in plastic signs. A competing company, Plastisign, was offered for sale to Carroll as president of Lackner. When the proposition was discussed by Carroll with Lackner's sales manager, he strongly recommended acquisition as necessary to Lackner's business and because he thought it would be profitable. The three directors and the sales manager purchased all the stock of Plastisign as individuals.

Hubbard, a minority stockholder in Lackner, learns of the operation of the competing business by the officers of Lackner and seeks an accounting of profits from Plastisign and transfer of ownership to Lackner. Is Lackner entitled to Plastisign?

8. At a special stockholders' meeting, the president of a close corporation in which there had been considerable dissension insisted that he would either sell his stock to the other stockholders or buy theirs. He also falsely represented that the financial condition of the corporation was extremely weak and prospects for the future dismal. After this portrayal of the corporation's status, the stockholders agreed to sell to the president at his named price unless another stockholder offered more by an agreed upon date. There is no other offer but the selling stockholders refuse to convey the stock. Is the president entitled to specific performance of the agreement?

9. Steiner and Westphal, sons-in-law of Lank, established a corporation which served as a commission distributor for Socony Oil Company in which each of the three owned equal shares, although only the sons-in-law were active. After several years the relationship between Steiner and Westphal became strained and Lank, then more than 80 years old, tended to side with Steiner, who with his wife had been very attentive to Lank. They kept him in their home while he convalesced from an illness and ran errands for him. Lank offered to sell his stock to Steiner so that Westphal would not get any of it. Steiner was unable to make the purchase but did take an option to buy it within 10 years at the book value to be computed as of the date exercised. When Lank asked the current value, Steiner accurately told him $270 per share. However, he did not mention that an offer of $600 per share had been made for the assets of the corporation, an offer which had been discussed in a stockholder's meeting in which Lank had actively participated.

Lank died and Westphal seeks to have the option declared invalid on the ground that Steiner breached his fiduciary duty in responding to Lank's question by not explaining that the true value of the stock was $600 rather than book value. Did Steiner breach this duty?

10. Leon and William Slavin and Morris and Eugene Kardon each owned one fourth of the capital stock of Western Board and Paper Co., and each was an officer and together constituted the board of directors. Leon Slavin agreed on behalf of the corporation to sell its plant and equipment to National Gypsum for $1,500,000 plus a favorable contract to buy one third of the output of the plant for three years. Shortly thereafter the Slavins purchased all of the Kardons' stock in the corporation for $504,000. The Kardons had no knowledge of the agreement with National Gypsum and at the meeting when the sale of the stock was consummated Leon Slavin responded in the negative to a question by the Kardons' attorney as to whether Slavin had made any agreement to sell the stock.

Are the Kardons entitled to an accounting for profits from the Slavins under Section 10(b) of the Securities and Exchange Act of 1934?

chapter 26. Corporate Securities

Introduction

Sources of Funds. The initial funds and property for a corporation usually come from the promoters and from other investors. They furnish money and property or settle claims for services rendered in exchange for securities of the corporation, which may be one or more types of stock and possibly bonds as well. However, sometimes a potentially large supplier or customer or a bank may provide money on notes of the corporation, perhaps cosigned by the promoters.

Once the corporation is operating profitably, it may rely heavily on retained earnings for increasing the funds available to the business. In addition it may use accounts receivable financing, inventory financing, and other means for increasing its available funds. Dollars charged off to depreciation which are not actually spent for replacement, renewal, or additions to plant and equipment also become additional available funds.

Securities. There are two main types of securities: equity securities and debt securities. Each type has many variants, and there have been some securities which are hybrids.

The equity securities constitute the "capital stock" of the corporation. Because of much confusion in terminology and definition with respect to "capital" and "stock," the Model Act uses the term "stated capital." Whatever the term, the value of the capital stock, which may be divided into two or more classes of differing amounts and stated values, is fixed at the time the stock is issued. That value will be the par value or, in case of stock without par value, the value determined by the directors to be the stated value (17 and 19).[1] If the stock is sold for more than the par or stated value, the excess will

---

[1] The numbers in the parentheses refer to the sections of the Model Business Corporation Act.

become capital surplus. The value on the books of the corporation of the capital stock will not be affected by changes in the value of the corporation's assets or the market price of its stock. It can be changed only by amending the articles of incorporation (53).

Debt securities give the holder the status of a creditor of the corporation. Corporations are generally considered to have implied power to borrow money and the Model Act (4h) as well as other statutes expressly grant this power. Equity securities create an ownership relation between the holder and the corporation, and the holder is called a stockholder or shareholder. However, a shareholder has no property rights in the assets of the corporation, since title to them is vested in the corporation.

Traditionally, shareholders are viewed as having a threefold proportionate interest in the corporation: in its earnings, in its net assets, and in its control. However, modern statutes permit corporations to issue more than one class of stock and to vary the preferences, limitations and rights of the various classes. Most statutes even permit voting rights to be restricted or denied. The Model Act (55, 67, 72 and 77) provides, however, that the articles cannot eliminate the right to vote of any class of stock on certain extraordinary transactions including merger, dissolution, sale of assets not in the normal course of business and certain amendments to the articles.

Every business corporation must issue some stock. Certificates are issued to represent the shares of stock, but they are not the stock. Indeed, as the volume of trading in stocks became so heavy as to overload the facilities of brokerage houses in 1968, proposals were made to eliminate stock certificates. However, presently under the Uniform Commercial Code (8–105 [1]) all types of corporate securities, including stocks, stock warrants and bonds are declared to be negotiable instruments but Article 8 rather than Article 3 of the Code applies.

Summary

The initial funds and property for a corporation usually come from the promoters and from other investors in exchange for one or more types of stock and possibly bonds.

The two major types of securities, equity securities and debt securities, have many forms. Every business corporation must issue some equity securities or stock and may issue two or more classes and vary their preferences, limitations and rights so that shareholders do not have their traditional threefold proportionate interest in the corporation: in its earnings, in its net assets and in its control.

Certificates are issued to represent shares but they are not the stock itself.

Kinds of Corporate Securities

Common Stock. If a corporation has only one class of stock it is, in effect, common stock. Its holders share the voting rights proportionately, are entitled proportionately to any distributions from earnings and, in case of liquidation, to the net assets remaining.

When there is more than one class of stock the common shareholders generally bear the major risks of the venture and stand to profit most if it is successful. Therefore, ordinarily no special contract rights or preferences are granted to common shareholders. They receive what is left over after the preferences of other classes have been satisfied, both with respect to net earnings payable in dividends and net assets upon liquidation. To balance this, they generally have control or the predominant voice in management.

However, there is under the Model Act and most statutes no limit on the ingenuity of promoters and their financial advisors in apportioning preferences, rights, and limitations to suit their interests and those of prospective buyers of the securities. As a result, the distinction between common and preferred stock is frequently blurred. It is not unusual to have one class of common shares with voting rights, perhaps designated "Class A," and another without voting rights except in case of the extraordinary transactions referred to above which might be referred to as "Class B" shares.

Preferred Stock. Classes of stock which have rights or preferences over other classes of stock are called preferred stock. Preferred shareholders are customarily given preferences as to dividends and distribution of assets on the dissolution of the corporation. In regard to dividends the preferences granted may vary greatly. The stock may be cumulative or noncumulative, and participating or nonparticipating. Dividends on cumulative preferred, if not paid in any year, will be payable later if funds are available for payment of dividends, whereas dividends on noncumulative preferred not earned and paid in any one year are not payable at a later date. Participating preferred has priority as to a stated amount or percentage of the dividends, and after a prescribed dividend is paid to common shareholders, the preferred shareholders participate with the common shareholders in additional dividends paid. Various combinations, such as cumulative participating or noncumulative participating, may be issued. If funds are not available for the payment of dividends, no dividends will be paid on preferred stock regardless of the type of stock. Under the Model Act (40) and the laws of substantially all states, it is unlawful to pay dividends out of capital.

Preferred stock may be made redeemable, and provision may be made for the setting-up of a sinking fund for the redemption of such stock. It may be convertible, in which case provision will be made whereby it may be converted into common stock or into other securities of the corporation. Preferred stock may be given voting rights, especially in the event of default in the payment of dividends.

The preferences granted will usually be set out in the articles of incorporation. The Model Act (14 and 15) provides that the preferences of the various classes, if more than one, must be stated in the articles of incorporation but permits the articles to authorize the directors to issue any preferred class of stock in series and to establish variations between the different series with respect to: (1) the rate of dividend; (2) whether the stock may be redeemed, and if so, the price and terms of redemption; (3) the amount payable upon the stock in liquidation; (4) sinking-fund provisions, if any, for redemption of the stock; and (5) the terms and conditions, if any, on which the stock may be converted.

Warrants and Rights. Options to purchase stock of a corporation which are evidenced by a certificate are known as warrants. They give the holder the right to buy a specified number of shares of the stock (usually common) at a specified price and they generally have a termination date. Although customarily issued in combination with another security, warrants may be bought and sold alone and may be listed on the American Stock Exchange. Although out of favor after the 1920's, warrants have been used rather extensively in recent years both as a "sweetener" in public and private debt placement and as a separate security usually issued as part of a "package" in connection with a merger or acquisition offer.

Rights are also options to purchase shares but the term is usually applied to short-term and often nonnegotiable options. They are a device used to give a present security holder the right to subscribe to some proportional quantity of the same or a different security in his corporation, often pursuant to preemptive rights requirements.

Bonds. The general term for debt securities of corporations is "bonds." However, short-term debt securities may be designated "notes," and evidences of debt which is unsecured may be called "debentures." Debenture holders participate on a pro rata basis with general creditors in the event of insolvency while the holder of a mortgage bond will have priority over general creditors as to the assets covered by the mortgage.

The possible variations in the terms of bonds are endless. The rights of the bondholder depends upon the provisions of the contract which constitutes the bond.

By the terms of the bond issue the corporation may be obligated to pay a fixed rate of interest on the bonds, or it may be obligated to pay interest only in case the corporate income is sufficient to cover the interest on the bonds.

Instead of being entitled to a fixed rate of interest, the bondholders may be paid a proportional percentage of the net profits of the corporation. The bondholders, as a general rule, do not have voting rights but may be given voting rights if the interest on the bonds is not paid when due or is not paid for a stated period of time. Also, a bond may be convertible, that is, the holder of the bond may be given the right to take common or preferred stock in payment of the bond on terms stated in the bond. A sinking fund may be provided. The bonds may be issued for a special purpose such as the purchase of certain equipment. In such a case the bond may provide that interest is to be paid only out of the proceeds from the use of the equipment.

Summary

If a corporation has only one class of stock it is common stock. If there is more than one class, the common shareholders generally bear the major risks of the venture, stand to gain the most and have control of the corporation.

Preferred shareholders are usually given preferences over one or more other classes of stock as to dividends and distribution of assets in case of liquidation. Preferences are stated in the articles of incorporation. The shares may be cumulative or noncumulative as to dividends. Preferred stock may be redeemable either with or without a sinking fund.

Warrants and rights are options to purchase shares.

Bonds represent obligations of the corporations, and the bondholders are creditors of the corporation. If the bonds are secured, in the event of the insolvency of the corporation, the bondholders have priority over general creditors as to the assets pledged as security. Interest may be a fixed obligation, or it may be payable out of profits. In general, bondholders have priority over all classes of stockholders.

Jones Valley Finance Co. v. *Tennille*
115 So.2d 495 (Ct. App. Ala. 1959)

This was an action by Tennille (plaintiff) against Jones Valley Finance Co. (defendant) to recover accrued interest on Finance Co.'s securities. Judgment for Tennille and Finance Co. appealed. Reversed and remanded.

Tennille bought securities issued by Finance Co. The certificate stated that he was the owner of 40 shares of preferred stock and it stated that Finance Co. "hereby guarantees the payment of interest, accumulated, on said shares at the rate of 4%, payable semi-annually." The articles of incorporation authorized Finance Co. to issue both common and preferred shares. The securities in question were issued pursuant to a resolution of the board of directors, ratified by the shareholders, which read:

"That the holders of the Preferred Stock would be entitled to receive, when and as declared by the Board of Directors, Dividends from the surplus or net profits of the corporation at the rate of 4% per annum, payable semi-annually on the 1st day of July and the 1st day of January of each year. Dividends on Preferred Stock would be cumulated from the date of issue and would be paid or set apart for payment before any dividend on any other stock of the corporation would be paid or set apart."

Alabama corporations were authorized by statute to create varied classes of stock "including debenture stock and preferred stock of one or more classes." (Debenture stock is a security more common in England than the United States which is similar to a bond secured by a mortgage on corporate property except that it has no maturity date and hence resembles an annuity. Interest in arrears may be recovered by an action against the company.)

CATES, JUDGE.   Our Legislature, in having provided the power in corporations to issue debenture stock, has thereby indicated that the law (on this matter) should put no impediment to corporate ingenuity which may be employed in the bargaining leading up to business financing, nor in the expression of the parties' bargain.

We are satisfied the power to make such a guaranty as was used here exists. The remaining question is solvable by the familiar—and often invisible—rule of ascertaining the intent of the parties to the agreement.

We consider that the instant certificates evidence the ownership of preferred stock as distinguished from a certificate of indebtedness and also do not include a promise to pay interest. Our reasons for this include (1) the legend employed on the certificate itself, using "preferred stock" (words of statutory connotation), coupled with the similar indication found on one of the panels on the reverse of the certificate; (2) the resolution of January 18, 1946, which, by law, is always available for the plaintiff's inspection at convenient hours at the company office; (3) the filing of the statutory certificate (of charter amendment) in the office of the judge of probate making the statement of the recapitalization a matter of public record; and (4) the absence of any compulsory redemption date of the preferred shares.

The expression "guarantees the payment of interest" fitted into the remainder of the text is but a provision calling for a cumulative dividend, which, of course, would mean that the payment would not be available, except upon declaration by the board of directors unless otherwise required under the rule of *Holcomb* v. *Forsyth:* this because a dividend as distinguished from an absolute promise to pay interest is the normal thing to expect as an incident of the ownership of preferred stock.

Stock Subscriptions, Issuance, Transfer and Redemption

Nature of Stock Subscription. In the absence of statutes most courts have held that preincorporation subscriptions to stock are merely offers which continue open until the corporation is chartered and that the subscriber may revoke his offer at any time before the occurrence of that event. Other courts have held that the subscription is a mutual agreement between the subscribers and enforceable unless all subscribers agree to release each other.

With only one exception the state incorporation statutes have provisions governing preincorporation subscriptions. The Model Act (16) does not require that a subscription be in writing but makes the subscription irrevocable for six months unless otherwise provided in the subscription or unless all subscribers agree to a revocation. A number of states require subscriptions to be in writing [2] and many provide for irrevocability, although the periods specified vary from three months to one year. Several statutes provide either that the subscription becomes binding upon filing of the articles or upon the issuance of the certificate of incorporation.

The subscription may provide for payment of the price of the stock on a specified day or in installments or it may be payable upon call of the board of directors. The Model Act (16) requires that calls for payment must be uniform as to all shares of the same class or series. It also requires (51) that at least $1,000 be paid in on stock before the corporation transacts any business.

If a subscription is made for the unissued shares of stock of an existing corporation, the generally accepted view is that the subscription is an offer to purchase which ripens into a contract on acceptance by the corporation. On acceptance the subscriber immediately becomes a stockholder, even though the delivery of the stock certificates is postponed until the purchase price of the stock is paid. An existing corporation may, in soliciting subscriptions for its unissued stock, so word its subscription agreement that it amounts to an offer to sell which is accepted when the subscriber agrees to purchase.

Issuing Shares of Stock. When a person has subscribed for stock in a proposed or existing corporation and his subscription has been accepted, the making of the contract between the subscriber and the corporation is generally termed "issuing stock." If the subscription agreement is a preincorporation agreement and more stock is subscribed than the corporation is authorized to issue, the corporation will, as a general rule, issue stock to the subscribers on a pro rata basis. Under the general rule, stock subscribed for by preincorporation agreement is issued when the corporation is chartered.

Although one can be a shareholder without having been issued a stock certificate and before he has fully paid for his shares, the Model Act (21) provides that no certificate shall be issued until the shares are fully paid, but it also provides (23) that an assignee or transferee of shares or a subscriber in good faith and without notice will not be personally liable to the corporation or its creditors for any unpaid portion of the consideration for the shares. This is consistent with Article 8 of the Uniform Commercial Code, which makes stock certificates negotiable.

---

[2] A preincorporation subscription is not considered a sale of goods covered by the statute of frauds so need not be in writing.

Liability of Issuer under U.C.C.   A corporation has a duty not to issue more than its authorized shares and often employs a bank or trust company as a registrar to prevent overissue through error in the issuance or transfer of its stock. Overissued shares are void. However, the Uniform Commercial Code (8–104) requires the issuer to obtain identical stock, if reasonably available, and to deliver it to the holder or, if unavailable, to reimburse him for the value paid plus interest. Under the U.C.C. (8–202 and 8–205), the issuer is not liable for a security which is not genuine, but it is liable to a purchaser for value and without notice if an unauthoried signature or a forgery is placed on the security by someone, such as an employee or transfer agent, to whom the security has been entrusted by the issuer.

Transfer of Corporate Stock.   Stock certificates have the effect of making the stock registered investment securities under Article 8, since they specifically name the owner or owners. Most stock certificates have an assignment form printed on the back, and this is endorsed by the registered owner to effect a transfer. However, a separate document, often referred to as a "stock power," may be used for assignment. If an assignment of a stock certificate is made without naming a transferee, it becomes transferable by delivery and is called a "street certificate."

Bonds are also covered by Article 8 as investment securities. They may be either registered or bearer bonds. A registered bond is transferred in the same manner as a stock certificate while a bearer bond is transferred by delivery. Interest is paid on the latter upon the presentation to the issuer or its agent of an interest coupon attached to the bond which is due and payable.

Restrictions on Transfer.   In the absence of a valid restriction investment securities are freely transferable. In close corporations, however, the shareholders often wish not only to select carefully their original business associates but to control the future disposition of the stock so that they can choose competent and compatible associates or keep control in the remaining members. Any restriction which would in effect make the stock nontransferable would be against public policy and void. Therefore, the validity of a restriction will turn on whether it is reasonable in objective and degree. Keeping outsiders from becoming shareholders and maintaining the proportionate interests between shareholders are usually held proper. The most common restriction requires the shareholder to offer his stock to the corporation and/or proportionately to other shareholders before transferring it to an outsider. The restriction may be imposed in the bylaws or by agreement between the shareholder and the corporation, but it appears from the cases that where there is doubt the restriction is more likely to be enforced if it is stated in the articles of incorporation. To be effective the restriction must be noted conspicuously on the certificate (U.C.C. 8–204).

Corporation's Duty to Transfer.   A corporation owes a duty to register the transfer of any registered security presented to it for registration, provided the security has been properly endorsed and other legal formalities have been complied with. (8–401). If the corporation refuses to make the transfer, it is liable to the transferee. The nature of the corporation's liability will depend on the laws of the state having jurisdiction of the case and the surrounding circumstances. In some cases the transferee has been able to recover the value of the stock in a suit in conversion, and in other cases he has been granted the remedy of specific performance by a court of equity.

The corporation has the right to make reasonable inquiry and investigation before it transfers stock or registered bonds. It will not be liable for any delay which is reasonably necessary to make whatever investigation the circumstances of the case warrant. If the corporation has a lien on the stock for an obligation owed to the corporation by the shareholder, it has the right to refuse to register a transfer until the obligation is satisfied. However, any lien in favor of the corporation, if it is to be valid against a purchaser of the security, must be noted conspicuously on the security. (8–103.)

If the owner of corporate stock or bonds dies, the ownership of such security passes to his estate, and his administrator or executor has the right to transfer the security. The procedure followed will depend on the probate laws of the state of his domicile. If the corporate security is held by one acting as trustee, the trustee is the legal owner of the stock, but such trustee may not have the authority to sell. The rights and obligations of the corporation regarding the transfer of registered corporate securities by a trustee are set out in Section 8–403 and 8–404 of the Uniform Commercial Code. The procedure to be followed in obtaining a new registered security or the transfer of a lost, destroyed, or stolen security is set out in Section 8–405.

Redemption and Purchase of Stock by Corporation. It is quite common for corporations to issue preferred stock subject to call or redemption. Redemption is an involuntary sale by the shareholder at a fixed price. Under the Model Act (14) the right of the corporation to redeem a preferred stock issue and the redemption price must be stated in the articles of incorporation. Redemption is not permitted when the corporation is or would become insolvent or when the prior claim of other shareholders upon its assets would be impaired (60). In a few jurisdictions the statutes are silent on redemption. It has been held that preferred shares may be redeemed in the absence of statute if the articles so provide. The New York statute permits redeemable common shares provided that the corporation has outstanding another class of common shares not subject to redemption. Redemption is usually at the discretion of the corporation but even if mandatory it is still subject to the solvency requirement. Some articles permit a partial redemption of a class of preferred shares.

A corporation may purchase its own common as well as preferred shares from a shareholder willing to sell without specific authorization in its articles.

In the Model Act (5) and most other statutes the restrictions safeguarding creditors and other shareholders are more confining than in the case of redemption. The Model Act permits such purchases only out of unrestricted earned surplus or, upon two-thirds vote of shareholders, unrestricted capital surplus may be used. When redeemable shares are reacquired by the corporation, the Model Act (61) requires their cancellation but purchased shares may be held as treasury shares and resold or they may be canceled (5).

Summary

A stock subscription is an agreement to purchase a stated number of shares of stock when issued. Most of the courts hold that a preincorporation subscription agreement is an offer which is accepted when the corporation is chartered.

A subscription to purchase the unissued stock of an existing corporation is an offer to buy stock, and a contract is completed when the corporation accepts the offer. Immediately on acceptance the subscriber becomes a stockholder, irrespective of when the stock certificate evidencing the shares of stock is executed and delivered.

Stock in a corporation is issued when the contract to purchase stock is completed. If a corporation issues stock in excess of the amount which it has the power to issue, it will be required to obtain and deliver, if available, identical stock, or it will be liable in damages for the amount which was paid for the stock or for its fair value.

The liability of an issuing corporation on the corporate securities issued by it is set out in the Uniform Commercial Code, Article 8, Part 2.

Under the Uniform Commercial Code, Article 8, Investment Securities, all investment securities, including corporate bonds, are given the characteristics of a negotiable instrument insofar as they are applicable.

Corporate stock and registered bonds are transferred by endorsement and delivery. A stock certificate may be endorsed in blank, and thereafter it may be transferred by delivery. A bearer bond is transferred by delivery.

The rights of the issuing corporation are not affected by the transfer of a corporate security until the security is duly presented to the corporation or its transfer agent for registration.

Reasonable restrictions, such as a requirement that stock for sale must first be offered to the corporation or its stockholders, have been held to be valid. A restriction which makes the stock nontransferable is void.

A corporation owes a duty to register the transfer of any registered security presented to it for registration, provided the security has been properly endorsed and other legal formalities have been complied with. A corporation is liable to the transferee if it wrongly refuses to transfer a registered security.

Preferred stock may, by provision in the articles, be issued subject to involuntary redemption. No authorization in the articles is required for the corporation to purchase outstanding securities.

Van Noy v. *Gibbs*
318 P.2d 351 (Sup. Ct. Utah 1957)

This was an action by Spencer Van Noy (plaintiff) against Richard Gibbs (defendant) for the balance due on a stock subscription. Judgment for Van Noy and Gibbs appealed. Affirmed with modification not here pertinent.

Van Noy and Gibbs formed a corporation known as Valley Amusement Enterprises. Each owned 1,950 shares of stock. A short time after the corporation was formed a dispute over the management of the business arose between them and each offered to buy the other's interest. Van Noys assigned his shares to Gibbs for $2,000, of which Gibbs paid $750 down. When Gibbs refused to pay the balance, Van Noy filed this action and Gibbs filed a counterclaim seeking to recover thé down payment.

At the time the contract between them was made, both parties believed the corporation owned a leasehold interest in the premises it occupied as an amusement center, but it was subsequently discovered that it did not have a valid lease. The corporation had other assets and the articles of incorporation set a value of $6,900 on the property taken into the corporation. The value placed on the leasehold was $3,100.

Gibbs claimed that he was not liable on the contract and was entitled to a return of his down payment because of a mutual mistake of fact as to the existence of the leasehold interest as an asset of the corporation.

TUCKETT, DISTRICT JUDGE.   One who buys stock in a corporation of necessity enters into a contract of a speculative nature and he will not ordinarily be permitted to rescind because the stock turns out to be of less value than the buyer and seller supposed it to be worth. Gibbs received all of Van Noy's interest in the corporation and that is what he bargained for.

Holmes v. *Birtman Electric Co.*
165 N.E.2d 261 (Sup. Ct. Ill. 1960)

This was an action by Helen M. Holmes (plaintiff) against Birtman Electric Company and its transfer agent, First National Bank of Chicago, executor of the estate of Charles Hansel (defendants), to recover a judgment for damages for the refusal to transfer corporate stock. Judgment for Holmes, and Birtman Electric Company and First National Bank of Chicago appealed to the Appellate Court which reversed the judgment. Holmes then appealed to the Supreme Court which reversed the judgment of the Appellate Court and affirmed the judgment of the trial court in part and remanded the cause to the Appellate Court with directions.

Charles Hansel, in his lifetime, owned 2,697 shares of the common stock of Birtman. About two years before his death he had the stock transferred to himself and his daughter, Helen M. Holmes, as joint tenants with right of survivorship. Hansel died on April 4, 1955, and on September 15, 1955, Marion Lenox, Helen

Holmes's sister, brought suit against Holmes and First National Bank of Chicago (the Bank) asking that the Bank and Holmes be restrained from transferring the Birtman stock and that the stock be held in trust for Lenox and Holmes. A temporary injunction enjoining the Bank from transferring the stock was denied. On September 10, 1955, an order was entered referring the question of the issuance of the injunction to the master in chancery and he was ordered to file his report on or before October 19, 1955. Lenox, in her complaint, charged that Holmes and her husband had by fraud, false representation and undue influence, schemed to cause Hansel, at a time when he was mentally incompetent, to transfer the shares into the names of himself and Holmes as joint tenants, with right of survivorship.

On September 23, 1955, Holmes, by her attorney, made personal demand upon the Bank to cause the shares to be transferred or reissued in the name of Helen Holmes. This demand was refused on the ground of the pending *Lenox* v. *Holmes* suit. A second demand was made and the Bank refused to make the transfer until the pending litigation was decided. The suit was decided in favor of Holmes on February 16, 1956, and the Bank made the transfer on February 20, 1956. On September 23, 1955, Birtman stock was selling for $24.50 per share and on February 20, 1956, it was selling for $16.50 per share. The stock held by Holmes was not salable until it was transferred into her name.

DAILEY, JUSTICE.   Where, as here, a daughter and her father hold stock as joint tenants with a right of survivorship, upon the father's death the daughter will be treated as a transferee of the stock and, hence, entitled to have the stock transferred to her individual name upon the corporate records. If a corporation wrongfully refuses to recognize a valid transfer of stock and permit a transfer on its books, the transferee can treat the wrongful refusal to allow a transfer as a conversion of the shares as of the time of the conversion, namely, the time of demand and refusal. The important words in the foregoing rule are "wrongfully refused," for conduct by the corporation or its transfer agent that might be considered as a wrongful refusal in one situation will not be so considered in another given fact situation.

In *Mundt* v. *Commercial National Bank of Ogden,* the court said: "The corporation should at all times guard its own interests, as well as those of its stockholders in making transfers, and it must exercise ordinary care in doing so. It is liable for negligence in making transfers; and hence it may always refuse to make a transfer when it has reasonable grounds for so doing; but it must act in good faith, and present some adequate reason for refusing to make a transfer, and support it by some evidence."

From the foregoing discussion it is apparent that the key words are "qualified refusal," "conflicting claims," "reasonable doubt," "delay registry," and "reasonable time." Thus, a corporation confronted by conflicting claims as to its stock may make a qualified refusal to transfer or register the shares, where there is a reasonable doubt as to the merits of the adverse claims, and the delay in transferring or registering the stock is for such temporary or reasonable time as to resolve the conflict. However, the law does not require or permit the officers or agents of a corporation to arrogate to themselves the functions of a court, and, by their decision, forever conclude the rights of the contending claimants.

Under the facts of the instant case, Birtman Electric Company and the Bank relied upon mere allegations, unsupported by proof. These allegations were insufficient to support a reasonable doubt as to the merits of the conflicting claims. The Bank, by its written refusal to reissue the stock to Holmes individually, a refusal which could have remained in effect a great length of time, assumed the role of a court in litigating the parties' rights. The Bank's actions were analogous to those of a volunteer, and the law does not protect volunteers.

First American National Bank v. *Christian Foundation Life Insurance Co.*
420 S.W.2d 912 (Sup. Ct. Ark. 1967)

This was an action brought by Christian Foundation Life Insurance Co. (plaintiff) for a declaratory judgment with respect to the validity of certain duplicate bearer bonds issued by the First Methodist Church of Mena, Arkansas. The Chancellor found that the bonds held by Christian Foundation Life and Charles Richard were valid and those held by First American National Bank (First Bank) were void. Reversed and remanded.

First Methodist employed Institutional Finance Company to sell $90,000 in bonds for the construction of a new church, and the church treasurer put her signature on a blank sheet of paper in the presence of the pastor and a trustee of the church and gave it to an officer of Institutional Finance to use as a facsimile signature upon the bonds. The printed bonds contained the facsimile signatures of the church treasurer and an officer of Institutional Finance but had no provision for an authenticating manual signature. Members of the church purchased $45,000 of the bonds but Institutional Finance had difficulty finding buyers for the remainder.

Hayes, the president of Institutional Finance, pledged $28,800 of the bonds to First Bank as collateral for a personal loan. He had been a previous borrower and the bank had no knowledge of his relationship to Institutional Finance or basis for suspicion that he did not own the bonds. Duplicates of these bonds and others were later ordered printed by Hayes and they were sold to Christian Foundation Life and Richard. Hayes's dishonesty became known when duplicate interest coupons were presented to the Mena bank for payment, and the bank refused to honor them until their validity had been established.

SMITH, JUSTICE. We find no merit in First Bank's insistence that its adversaries were not purchasers in good faith because they bought the bonds at discounts of 10 and 15 percent . . . there is no proof in this record to indicate that the discounts offered to Christian Foundation Life were so great as to arouse suspicion. Nor is there evidence to sustain the appellant's argument that the purchasers of the duplicates should have been put upon inquiry by the church's apparent inability to market the entire bond issue within a period of about a year.

We think the chancellor should have found all bonds held by bona fide purchasers to be binding obligations of the church. It is plain enough that the church was careless in entrusting its treasurer's facsimile signature to Institutional Finance and in failing to take the precaution of requiring authentication of the bonds by a manual signature. By contrast, the holders of the bonds acquired them in the ordinary course of business and in circumstances entitling them to the protection afforded to bona fide purchaser.

The case is controlled by the pertinent provisions of the Uniform Commercial Code. Before the adoption of the Code the church might have been held liable by contract to one purchaser and in damages to the other, but the draftsmen of the Code point out in their Comment to our §85-8-202 that the Code simply validates most defective securities in the hands of innocent purchasers, refusing to prefer one such purchaser over another.

Specifically, this controversy falls within §85-8-205, which provides that an unauthorized signature is effective in favor of an innocent purchaser when the signing is done either by a person entrusted by the issuer with the signing of the security or by an employee of such person or of the issuer itself. By resolution the church employed Institutional Finance as its fiscal agent to handle the sale of the bonds. The first line of the printed prospectus for the bond issue identified that concern as the issuer's fiscal agent. There can hardly be any serious contention that Hayes's wrongful use of the treasurer's facsimile signature did not fall within the purview of the Code.

It is too early at this state of the litigation to reach a final conclusion about the exact remedies of the bondholders. The church's refusal to pay interest was not absolute, being conditioned upon its uncertainty about the validity of the outstanding bonds. Under the Code it is liable to all bondholders who bought in good faith. It does not follow, however, that all bondholders stand in parity if it becomes necessary for them to foreclose the lien against the church property. First Bank's priority in time entitles it, as against the holders of duplicate bonds, to priority of lien, under the equitable maxim that as between equal equities the first in time must prevail. If the law were otherwise the security interest held by bona fide purchasers of a bond issue could be diluted by the later wrongful sale of duplicate bonds. . . .

Federal and State Securities Legislation

Securities Act of 1933.   This federal statute requires corporations preparing to offer an issue of securities to investors through the mails or in interstate or foreign commerce to register the issue with the Securities Exchange Commission and to furnish purchasers with a prospectus. The registration statement must contain a large amount of prescribed information concerning the business of the corporation, its management and control, its capitalization, its financial condition, the planned use of the proceeds from the issue, expenses of the issue, amounts paid within the past two years to promoters, and other matters which might affect the value of the securities. Most of this information must be included in the prospectus.

Private placement, such as to a small number of insurance companies or other institutional investors, is exempt from the registration requirement. So also are securities exchanged by an issuing corporation with its existing security holders if no commissions are paid for soliciting the exchange. Also exempt are securities which are part of an issue offered and sold only to persons resident of the state in which the issuer is incorporated. In addition the SEC may exempt securities involved in small offerings or those offered to a limited group if the aggregate amount of the issue offered to the public does not exceed $300,000.

The act also forbids the use of the mails or interstate commerce in the employment of any fraudulent scheme and any transaction which would deceive the purchaser. Criminal penalties are provided. In addition civil liability is imposed upon directors and underwriters and anyone who signs an untrue or misleading registration statement. Potential liability is also imposed upon accountants, engineers, and others who prepare or certify to any part of the registration statement. Purchasers of securities may also recover for misleading statements in a prospectus or made orally in communications with respect to the sale of a security.

Securities Exchange Act of 1934. While the 1933 act deals mainly with primary distribution of securities, the Securities Exchange Act of 1934 applies to subsequent trading in the securities. It requires issuers of registered securities to file periodic reports of financial and other information with the SEC and with the stock exchange or exchanges with which it is listed. The act also requires filing proxies in advance with the SEC, which prescribes rules for their form. The 1964 amendments extended jurisdiction to over-the-counter securities. As discussed in Chapter 25, Section 10b of the Act prohibits the use of manipulative and deceptive devices in the purchase and sale of securities. This has been used as the basis of many private actions against issuers, officers and directors, and even professionals such as accountants and lawyers who assist in the preparation of registration statements and reports required to be filed with the SEC. Section 16a requires directors, officers and principal shareholders to report to the SEC all purchases and sales of the corporation's shares that are registered. Section 16b provides for the recovery by the corporation of "short-swing" profits (those resulting from offsetting purchases and sales within a six months' period) of such persons. In addition it has a number of provisions applying to security exchanges and brokers.

State "Blue-Sky" Laws. State securities laws are frequently referred to as "blue-sky" laws, since the early statutes were designed to protect investors from promoters and security salesmen who offered stock in companies organized to pursue visionary schemes or to exploit uncertain resources. They are of several types. Some merely prohibit fraud in the sale of securities and make suit easier or provide stronger sanctions than the common law. Other statutes require the registration of and provide some regulation of the activities of brokers and securities dealers. Others, like the Securities Act of 1933, require registration of securities and seek to require sufficient disclosure to permit investors to protect themselves. Other registration statutes require approval by an official before the security can be offered for sale. Some statutes contain two or more of these types of provisions. The Securities Act of 1933 specifically permits concurrent jurisdiction by state agencies. However, a number of the states with registration statutes exempt securities which have been registered with the SEC. The Uniform Securities Act has been adopted in part by several states. It contains antifraud provisions, broker-dealer registration provisions and also provisions requiring the registration of securities.

Summary

The Securities Act of 1933 requires corporations preparing to issue securities to provide the SEC and prospective investors with a great deal of information. The act forbids certain types of deceptive and misleading statements. It establishes both civil and criminal penalties and gives a right of recovery to purchasers harmed by false and misleading statements.

The Securities Exchange Act of 1934, although dealing primarily with trading in securities, gives the SEC authority to prescribe rules for proxy statements, prohibits manipulative and deceptive devices in both the purchase and sale of securities, requires periodic reports by directors and officers of their trading in the corporation's shares and provides for the recovery of "short-swing" profits.

State securities laws vary greatly. Many exempt from their coverage securities which are registered with the SEC.

United States v. Custer Channel Wing Corp.
376 F.2d 675 (4th Cir. 1967)

This was a criminal contempt action by the United States (plaintiff) against Custer Channel Wing Corp. and Willard R. Custer (defendants) for violation of a District Court injunction prohibiting use of interstate commerce and mails to promote sales of unregistered securities. Custer was convicted and appealed. Affirmed.

In May, 1962, the District Court had issued an injunction against Custer and Channel Wing Corp. prohibiting them from engaging in practices in violation of Section 5 of the Securities Act of 1933 which forbids the use of interstate commerce or mails to sell or offer securities without having first filed a registration statement with the Securities and Exchange Commission. "Transactions by an issuer, not involving any public offering" are exempt from the registration requirement.

Subsequent to the injunction, 1,579,590 shares of Custer stock were sold via interstate commerce to 155 "associates" and individuals. Custer and the corporation contend that in view of the limited number of transfers, a resale restriction imposed on each transfer, and an acknowledgment by each prospective purchaser that he knew the stock was unregistered, the transactions were not a public offering and, therefore, were exempt from the registration requirements.

SOBELOFF, CIRCUIT JUDGE.   Since "public offering" is not defined in the Securities Act, the Supreme Court (in *S.E.C.* v. *Ralston Purina Co.*) looked to the purpose of the Act, which it declared was "to protect investors by promoting full disclosure of information thought necessary to informed investment decisions." Interpreting the exemption in the light of this statutory purpose, therefore, the court expressed the view that a transaction is exempt when the particular class of offerees had "access to the same kind of information that the act would make available in the form of a registration statement."

The District Court found, with full support of the record, that most of the individual purchases "were not furnished, nor did they have, anything more than the vaguest information about the financial affairs of Channel Wing." Even the few purchasers shown by the evidence to have gained access to the pertinent information when they later became directors of the corporation, lacked such access at the time they purchased most of their stock. The resale restriction and purchaser acknowledgment are not sufficient to constitute the Channel Wing offering a private one in the absence of proof that the purchasers actually had access to the kind of information that a registration statement would have disclosed. The contention that the number of transferees must be considered in determining whether an offering is public or private is refuted by the court's opinion in *Ralston Purina,* which declared that "the statute would seem to apply to a 'public offering' *whether to few or many.*"

Fischer v. *Kletz*

266 F.Supp. 180 (S.D. N.Y. 1967)

This was an action by about 150 shareholders of Yale Express System, Inc. (plaintiffs), against Peat, Marwick, Mitchell & Co. (PMM), public accountants (defendants), seeking damages for deceit and for violation of Section 10b of the Securities Exchange Act of 1934. PMM moved to dismiss the complaint as insufficient. Motion denied.

Early in 1964, Peat, Marwick, Mitchell & Co., acting as independent public accountants, undertook the job of auditing Yale, Inc.'s financial statements for 1963. On April 9, the annual report, containing the certification was issued to Yale's shareholders. Subsequently, a required Securities and Exchange Commission report was filed containing the same financial statements.

Shortly after completion of the audit, Yale engaged PMM to conduct "special studies" of Yale's past and current income and expenses. In the course of this special assignment, PMM discovered that the figures in the annual report were substantially false and misleading. Not until six months later, however, did PMM disclose this finding to the SEC or the general public.

Yale shareholders seek damages from PMM claiming that the firm has a duty under both common law and Rule 10b-5 of the Securities Exchange Commission to alert the public in some way to the fact that the financial statements were false and inaccurate.

TYLER, DISTRICT JUDGE. I find no sound reasons to justify barring the shareholders from an opportunity to prove a common-law action of deceit against PMM. The common law has long required that a person who has made a representation must correct that representation if it becomes false and if he knows people are relying on it. This duty to disclose is imposed regardless of the interest of defendant in the representation and subsequent nondisclosure. Plaintiffs have sufficiently alleged the elements of undisclosure . . . and must be given an opportunity to prove these allegations.

To conclude this is not to ignore the manifold difficulties that a final determination of liability on the part of public accountants for nondisclosure would create for professional firms and other business entities similarly situated. . . . How long, for instance, does the duty to disclose after-acquired information last? To whom and how should disclosure be made? Does liability exist if the after-acquired knowledge is obtained from a source other than the original supplier of information? Is there a duty to disclose if an associate or employee of the accounting firm discovers that the financial statements are false but fails to report it to the firm members?

These and similar questions briefly indicate the potentially significant impact upon accountants, lawyers, and business entities in the event that a precise rule or rules of liability for nondisclosure are fashioned and recognized in the law. On the other side of the coin, however, investors in publicly-held companies have a strong interest in being afforded some degree of protection by and from these professional and business persons whose representations are relied upon for decisional purposes.

A private remedy exists for defrauded investors under Section 10b and Rule 10b-5. Moreover, the statute and rule both state that they may be invoked against "any person" who indulges in fraudulent practices in connection with the purchase or sale of securities. In practice, however, defendants have fallen into four general categories: (1) insiders, (2) broker-dealers, (3) corporations whose stock is purchased or sold by plaintiffs, and (4) those who "aid and abet" one of the first three parties. PMM seemingly does not fit any of the four groupings.

From the foregoing discussion (of issues regarding PMM's gain, inside information, aiding and abetting, privity, and connection between the misrepresentations and stock purchases), it can be seen that PMM's motion to dismiss any claims based on Section 10b and Rule 10b-5 raises novel and difficult issues. Because of the importance of the questions involved and the need for further factual and legal development of them by the parties and the SEC, I deem it best to deny this branch of PMM's motion without prejudice to renewal at trial.

Myzel v. *Fields*
386 F.2d 718 (8th Cir. 1967)

Separate actions by Harry Fields, Samuel King, Rita Vertelney and Gordon Cohen (plaintiffs) seeking damages for violation of Section 10b of the Securities Exchange

Act of 1934 against Benjamin Myzel, the Levines and others (defendants) were consolidated for trial before a jury. Verdicts totalling $411,000 were returned in favor of Fields, King, Vertelney and Cohen. Affirmed.

Fields and King each purchased 30 shares at $50 per share in Lakeside Plastics and Engraving Co. (LPE), a close corporation, of Duluth, Minnesota, when it was founded in 1946. Vertelney purchased 100 shares and Cohen 40 shares. They had made the investment upon the advice of their close friend, Benn Myzel, who was also a relative of Zelman Levine, one of the founders of the company. Myzel was an early director of the company, going off the board in 1949 but returning to it in 1954. At all times relevant to the case he served the corporation as a financial advisor. The company made advertising signs, and from 1946 to 1951 it struggled for sales, made little profit and paid the shareholders nothing on their investment. The shareholders were discouraged and in the 1949 shareholders' meeting Fields made a motion for dissolution. In 1952 sales increased substantially but not to a record level and a profit of $7,500 was made, after which the company still showed a $43,000 deficit. The company secured a large contract with Blatz Brewing Company and in the first four months of 1953 the company earned a profit of $30,000 but this interim financial statement was not disclosed at the June shareholders' meeting.

Myzel and his brother, who acted as his undisclosed agent, using the telephone and personal solicitation, bought the shares of Fields, King, Vertelney and Cohen toward the end of 1953 and in early 1954 at prices from $6.67 to $45.00 per share. In each instance the Myzels made representations that the stock was not worth anything, that the company was not making money and that Benn Myzel was "going to get out of the company" or suggested that the company was on the verge of bankruptcy.

Myzel later sold the shares at a substantial profit to the Levines who came to own all of the shares of the company. In addition, he received other substantial amounts from the Levines for his service in buying the stock. After 1953 the sales of LPE increased very greatly and large profits came shortly thereafter.

LAY, CIRCUIT JUDGE.   Both Section 10 of the Act and Rule 10b-5 require as a jurisdictional basis "the use of *any means or instrumentality of interstate commerce or of the mails,* or any facility of any national securities exchange." The evidence is undisputed that the telephone was used only on an intrastate basis in the solicitation or purchase of (the) stock. . . . We hold . . . that intrastate use of the telephone comes within prohibition of the Act.

Proof of affirmative misrepresentation, generally an essential element of common-law fraud, is not required in actions brought under Rule 10b-5, since the rule expressly prohibits material omissions as well. Several undisclosed facts in the present case assume relevance when coupled with the factual statements and reckless opinions offered by the Myzels. Among facts the jury could find not disclosed in the purchases were (1) the increased sales in 1953, (2) the April 1953 interim financial statements showing the successful Blatz contract and $30,000 profit, (3) the potential of 1954 sales or at least Zelman Levine's (President of LPE) optimism over prospects for the future and (4) the identity of the controlling purchasers.

These nondisclosures assume materiality when considered in the context of the affirmative representations made severally to Fields, King, Vertelney and Cohen. Phil Myzel's statement to Vertelney that Benn was "going to get out" of the company could be considered actionable as a misstatement of another's intent or state of mind. Benn's statements to King that he himself had sold his stock, that it was worthless and that the company wasn't making any money were misleading. Phil's statements to Fields that the company was on the "verge of bankruptcy" or "in bad shape" were material in view of the nondisclosures. And Benn's statements to Cohen that "he was not getting any money from the company" become significant with the discovery of Benn's commissions commencing in August 1953.

Proof of "scienter," i.e., knowledge of the falseness of the impression produced by the statements or omissions made, is not required under Section 10(b) of the Act.

Under the circumstances we conclude, although not without great difficulty, that all of the appellees presented sufficient proof of an "assortment" of nondisclosures and positive misrepresentations to carry their respective cases to the jury.

Problem Cases

1. Boston Holding Co. was in arrears on the dividends payable on its "public preferred" shares which had been issued under the provisions of a special statute which said, "The holders of such preferred stock shall, in preference and priority over all other stock of the corporation, be entitled, upon dissolution of the corporation or in liquidation of its affairs, or in case of a default in the payment of any stipulated dividend on said preferred stock, to payment of the par value thereof and accrued dividends thereon." The statute further provided that the preferred stock and accrued dividends should be a lien upon the shares in a railroad which were the only assets of the corporation. Hurley is an owner of some of the shares. Is she correct in her contention that she is a creditor?

2. Two members of the Kaneb family, Beton and Rachel, operated an oil business as a partnership. A family conference was held in which it was agreed to form a corporation and to transfer the assets of the partnership to it. It was agreed by Beton and Rachel that they would give 20 shares to their brother Albert, a recent law graduate who did the legal work in forming the corporation, and his name was listed as a subscriber. He died suddenly the day after incorporation. No certificates were issued until 11 years later. Was he a shareholder at the time of his death so that his heirs have a claim on his shares?

3. Traylor subscribed for $50,000 worth of shares in Broadcasting Co. At the time he subscribed Broadcasting Co. intended to make application to the FCC for a permit to build a very high-frequency television station but later it changed this to an application for an ultrahigh-frequency channel, for which permission was granted. Traylor paid 5 percent of the amount of the subscription. The subscription agreement provided that in the event a construction permit for a "television station" was not granted, the subscription would be canceled but shares would be issued for the 5 percent. Broadcasting Co. seeks to recover on the subscription. Is Traylor correct in claiming the changes of plan relieves him of his agreement to buy the additional shares?

4. Wagoner purchased 10 shares of Service, Inc., stock and surrendered the properly endorsed stock certificates for reissue in his name. Service refused to issue the stock certificate as requested and has declined to recognize Wagoner's rights as a shareholder to inspect corporate records and participate in shareholders' meetings. Can Wagoner maintain an action against Service to recover the face value of the stock certificates?

5. Carlson and others, seeking control of County Telephone Co., purchased 203 of the 356 outstanding shares. The stock certificates, together with assignments and proxies for voting purposes, were delivered to County Telephone officers with a request for transfer. The officers and directors were upset by the prospect of losing control and refused to transfer the shares because of a bylaw giving the directors the right to determine to whom shares might be transferred. Can the Carlson interests compel transfer of the stock?

6. Moseley inherited shares of stock in Wade-Corry Co. from his mother who had purchased the shares from a registered owner. Subsequent to the death of Moseley's mother the original holder sent a "stop-transfer" order to Wade-Corry. Moseley, thereafter, tendered the stock certificate in question to Wade-Corry with a request that it be transferred to his name. Wade-Corry refused this request. Can Moseley compel the transfer regardless of the "stop-transfer" order?

7. Perugino presented certificates for 500 shares of the common stock of Samson Land & Development Co. to the corporation's treasurer for transfer. They were properly endorsed and federal transfer tax stamps had been affixed. The treasurer refused to transfer the shares on the ground that there was a shareholder agreement forbidding the assignment of shares without a prior offer of them to other shareholders and that no offer had been made. No notation of the limitation appeared upon certificates. Is Perugino entitled to an injunction directing transfer?

8. The articles of incorporation of Memco, Inc., provided that the corporation could redeem all but not less than all of its preferred shares at $100 plus any accrued dividends in arrears. There were 1,000 shares of preferred stock outstanding. The corporation purchased 50 shares at $99.50 in three separate transactions and 902 shares at $99.75 in two additional transactions a year and a half later. Another owner of the preferred stock sues for the redemption price for his shares on the theory that the corporation violated its agreement not to redeem less than all outstanding shares. Will he win?

9. Janigan was the president and general manager of Besco, a special order steel foundry which had an old plant and was in poor financial condition. Taylor and his associates, several of whom were directors, owned most of the outstanding shares of the company, but left the management almost exclusively to Janigan, relying on his reports which were generally pessimistic. The directors called a shareholders' meeting to consider a sale or liquidation of the company. A month later Janigan himself made an offer to purchase the shares owned by Taylor and his associates for $40,000, and in response to one of the directors' questions said that there was no change in the affairs of the company. In fact, there was an increased backlog of orders at better prices. Two years later Janigan sold his stock for $700,000. Taylor and his associates seek to recover this profit, alleging a violation of Rule 10b-5 of the SEC. Are they entitled to judgment?

10. A group of shareholders in Susquehanna Corporation agreed if they were elected directors to sell 435,000 shares of the corporation's stock, which amounted to control of the corporation, to Korholz for $6,525,000, which was $1,740,000 in excess of

the market value of the shares. Part of the agreement was that they would then resign as directors in favor of appointees of Korholz, that Gypsum Corp. would acquire the Susquehanna shares from Korholz, borrowing $6,450,000 for this purpose, that Susquehanna and Gypsum would be merged and that the liability on Gypsum's loan would then be assumed by Susquehanna. The purchase price of the shares and the other details of the plan were disclosed in the proxy statement issued in connection with the meeting for the election of the directors. Other shareholders of Susquehanna sue on behalf of the corporation asserting that the sale of shares to Korholz was fraudulent and in violation of Section 10b of the Securities Exchange Act of 1934. Is the sale or the merger a violation of Section 10b?

11. Former officers of United Corporation who had resigned when it appeared that assets of the corporation would have to be written down by $7,000,000 promoted the organization of and actively supported the United Corporation Stockholders' Protective Committee. The committee was conducting a proxy contest to elect its slate of directors instead of the one proposed by management. The committee was formed by a law firm retained by the former officers. The proxy solicitation material sent to the 15,000 United shareholders by the committee did not disclose that the former officers had anything to do with the committee. The SEC seeks, under Section 14 of the Securities Exchange Act of 1934, to enjoin the holding of the shareholders' meeting for 60 days and to require the committee to disclose that the former officers were directly or indirectly instrumental in initiating the committee. Is it entitled to such a decree?

12. Gamble-Skogmo, Inc., had for six months been owner of more than 10 percent of the outstanding common stock of Western Missouri. On January 21, 1960, Gamble-Skogmo purchased 32,000 additional shares of Western Missouri stock at $32.35 per share. These shares were purchased for the purpose of making a mandatory annual contribution to a company trust fund. The contribution was not required to be in stock, but on January 28, Gamble-Skogmo transferred 25,942 shares of Western Missouri stock to the fund. On July 11, 1960, less than six months after purchase of the 32,000 shares, Gamble-Skogmo sold its entire holding of 1,262,102 shares of Western Missouri stock at $36 per share.

   Western Delaware Company, after acquisition of all assets formerly held by Western Missouri, demanded an accounting for profits which Gamble-Skogmo received as an "insider" from the "short-swing sale" of 32,000 shares of Western Missouri stock. Gamble-Skogmo paid the difference between cost and selling price on 6,058 shares, but refuses payment for profits on the 25,942 shares which were transferred to and remained in the trust fund. Is Western Delaware entitled to recover profits on the entire 32,000 shares?

13. Taormina and his wife paid, after talking with two officers and directors of the corporation, $3,500 and received a receipt signed by the president of the corporation "for payment in full for five percent of Antelope Mining Corp. stock to be authorized by the Corporation Commissioner." A week later they received a note for $3,500 signed on behalf of the corporation containing a notation, "This note to be secured by stock when authorized by the California Corporation Commissioner." The corporation in the previous year had been authorized by the Commissioner to issue 20,000 shares to the promoters with the provision that the certificates be held in escrow and that the owners of the shares should not sell any interest in them or receive any consideration for them until given written consent by the Commissioner. No consent had been given. Are the Taorminas entitled to recover their investment from the officers and directors?

chapter 27. Shareholders' Rights and Liabilities

Introduction

General. The relation between a corporation and its shareholders is contractual. The articles and bylaws of the corporation and provisions in the share certificates as well as applicable statutes constitute parts of the contract and establish the shareholder rights and duties with respect to the corporation.

A subscriber becomes a shareholder when the subscription is accepted. However, an agreement to subscribe is merely a contract, and the purchaser does not become a shareholder until the transaction is closed. Determining the nature of any particular agreement may be quite difficult.[1]

Shares of stock are subject to the same kinds of co-ownership as other kinds of personal property and may also be subject to split ownership by which record ownership is separated from beneficial ownership. For example, in a trust the trustee is the record owner but the beneficiary of the trust is the beneficial owner and is entitled to the fruits of the ownership.

Babbitt v. *Pacco Investors Corp.*
425 P.2d 489 (Sup. Ct. Ore. 1967)

This was an action by Ray Babbitt (plaintiff) against Pacco Investors Corp. (defendant) to recover statutory penalty for refusal to permit Babbitt, as a shareholder of record, to examine the books and records of the corporation. Judgment for Babbitt and Pacco Corp. appealed. Affirmed.

Babbitt was one of the organizers, and original subscribers (30 out of 500 authorized shares) of Pacco Corporation and was elected at the organization meeting

---

[1] See discussion in Chapter 26.

of subscribers to serve as a director until the first meeting of shareholders. He was also elected first vice president at the organization meeting. He attending the first meeting of shareholders and was again elected a director. Later, the corporation acquired land and Babbitt was employed to supervise the construction of an apartment house. The corporation was dissatisfied with the performance of his duties and dismissed him. A few weeks later Babbitt, through an attorney, citing his statutory right, notified the corporation that the attorney would appear on a certain date to examine and take abstracts from the books and records of the corporation. In reply the corporation stated that the records did not show Babbitt as a shareholder and the attorney was refused access to the records.

Lusk, Justice.   The contention that Babbitt was not a shareholder of record has two parts, one, that he was not a shareholder at all, and the other, that even so he was not a shareholder "of record." As to the first part, it is stated in Pacco's brief:

. . . The stock admittedly was not paid for, and the typed certificate to be issued to plaintiff was still held in the stockbook, unexecuted by the corporate officers. Therefore, plaintiff was not a stockholder, merely a subscriber, and was not entitled to make this demand.

No authority is cited for this proposition and it is contrary to our decisions. As stated in *Balfour* v. *Baker City Gas Co.:*

From an extended examination of the authorities we take the law to be that when the proposed corporation is formed as contemplated in the preliminary subscription, and within a reasonable time thereafter, the subscription, unless revoked in the manner authorized by law, becomes irrevocable; the subscriber becomes a shareholder, and liable as such, without any further act on his part.

That the plaintiff has not paid for his shares is immaterial. *Schwartz* v. *Manufacturers' Casualty Ins. Co.,* holds that payment is essential where the subscription is for shares of an existing corporation, but the opinion expressly recognizes that the rule is otherwise in the case of an original subscription for shares in a corporation to be formed. Neither is it necessary, in order for one to become a shareholder, that a certificate of stock, which is only evidence of ownership of an interest in the assets of the corporation, shall have been issued.

Not only was Babbitt's subscription never revoked in any manner recognized by law, but, as heretofore shown, with the consent of the other shareholders, he voted his shares in the organizational and first meetings of the shareholders and was elected an officer and director.

With respect to the second part of the question, we think that any record kept by the corporation which enables it to determine whether a person seeking examination of its books is a shareholder should be deemed sufficient. The statute does not prescribe any particular form in which the record must be kept, nor any particular book. The minutes of a corporation are a part of its records. Certainly, the failure to record the addresses of the stockholders would not be such a defect as to warrant a court in sustaining refusal of a shareholder's right to examine the books.

We hold that there was sufficient evidence that Babbitt was a shareholder of record.

Shareholder Meetings

Exercise of Shareholder Functions.   Shareholders generally can exercise their few functions only by voting in shareholder meetings, although the Model Act (138) and the statutes of many states permit shareholders to act without a meeting if consent to the action in writing is signed by all shareholders, which, of course, is practicable only in closed corporations. These shareholder functions include: the election and removal of directors (34, 36A), the adoption, amendment and repeal of bylaws under some statutes but generally not under the Model Act (25), approval of extraordinary corporate matters such as merger or consolidation (67), sale or mortgage of assets not in the normal course of business (72), reduction of stated capital (63), and amendment of the corporate articles (54).[2] As will be discussed later in this section, certain classes of shares may be denied voting rights except in some of the extraordinary corporate transactions.

Annual Meetings.   The general corporation statutes of most states and the Model Act (26) provide that an annual meeting of shareholders shall be held at the time specified in the bylaws. However, a failure to hold an annual meeting does not work a forfeiture or dissolution of the corporation. Some statutes provide that if the directors do not call an annual shareholders' meeting within a stipulated period of time, such as 18 months, any stockholder or some stipulated percentage of shareholders may call a meeting.

Usually, the most important business at the annual shareholders' meeting is the election of directors, but amendments to or repeal of bylaws or the amendment of the articles of incorporation, ratification of management's selection of auditors and resolutions introduced by management or shareholders are other matters which may be voted on. It is also customary for one or more members of the top management to give reports with regard to the operation and prospects of the corporation.

Only a few states require that shareholders' meetings be held within the state of incorporation. Some publicly held corporations, apparently to discourage actual attendance by shareholders, hold their meetings in their state of incorporation, such as Delaware or Maine which do not require local meetings, even though few shareholders live nearby. Other corporations, however, hire large halls in convenient locations to encourage shareholders to attend. A few rotate their meetings around to the major cities of the country.

Special Meetings.   Special shareholder meetings may be held whenever corporate matters arise which require shareholder action. Under the Model

---

[2] The numbers in the parentheses refer to the sections of the Model Business Corporations Act.

Act a special shareholder meeting may be called by the president, the board of directors or the holders of not less than one tenth of the shares entitled to vote at the meeting. The Model Act permits the corporation, in its articles of incorporation or bylaws, to specify that other officers or persons may call a special meeting.

Notice of Meetings.   The Model Act (27) and the statutes of most states set forth the requirements for notice of annual and special meetings of shareholders. The Model Act states that written notice giving the place, day, and hour of the meeting and, for special meetings, the purpose(s) of the meeting must be delivered not less than 10 nor more than 50 days before the date of the meeting to all shareholders entitled to vote at the meeting. For extraordinary changes such as merger, dissolution, or sale or mortgage of assets out of the regular course of business, specific notice of the proposal must be given all shareholders (67, 72, 77). Specific notice must be also given shareholders entitled to vote thereon when a reduction in stated capital (63), or an amendment to the articles of incorporation (54), is proposed. Those entitled to notice are the shareholders of the class or classes of shares entitled to vote who are "of record," that is, those whose names appear on the stock transfer book of the corporation. In jurisdictions where the statutes are silent as to notice, notice of a regular meeting is not required if the articles or bylaws specify the place, date, and hour.

If the prescribed notice is not given, any action taken at the meeting is a nullity, unless notice is waived in writing either before or after the meeting (137) or the action taken is later ratified in a properly called meeting. Actual attendance at a meeting, unless merely to object to the transaction of business, constitutes a waiver. Waiver is effective only if all shareholders either attend or waive in writing. Some statutes require written waiver by all shareholders.

Quorum.   The Model Act (30) permits the corporation to establish in the articles of incorporation the number of shares which must be represented in person or proxy at a meeting in order for the shareholders to transact business, except that it establishes one third of the shares entitled to vote as a minimum quorum. The statutes of the various states vary widely. Where there is no statutory requirement and none is specified in the articles or bylaws, those shareholders present, even though a minority, constitute a quorum. The statutes of a number of states provide that once a quorum is present at a meeting, later withdrawal by shareholders will not affect the validity of action taken by those remaining. This is also the rule in the absence of statute.

Conduct of the Meeting.   The articles or bylaws may state who shall preside at shareholders' meetings, and this is usually the chairman of the board, if there is such an office, or the president. If there is no such provision, then any shareholder may call the meeting to order and preside while a meeting chairman is elected. In publicly held corporations it is customary to provide inspectors of election whose responsibility it is to determine whether or not a person claiming to be a shareholder is entitled to vote. A few states have statutory provisions dealing with inspectors of election. It is customary and desirable, though not required by statute in most states, to keep minutes of shareholders' meetings, and they are usually recorded and kept by the secretary of the corporation.

Summary

Shareholders generally have few functions. They elect and remove directors, amend the articles of incorporation and vote on extraordinary corporate transactions such as merger and sale of the assets.

Annual meetings of shareholders are held at a time specified in the bylaws. All shareholders "of record" of classes entitled to vote are entitled to notice of special meetings and regular meetings if the specific time and place is not established in the bylaws.

The Model Act establishes as a quorum one third of the shares to be represented in person or by proxy at the meeting but permits the corporation to establish a higher quorum. Who is to preside at the meeting is usually established by the bylaws.

Camp v. Shannon
348 S.W.2d 517 (Sup. Ct. Tex. 1961)

This was an action by Emery E. Shannon (plaintiff) against Jesse R. Camp and others (defendants) to enjoin Camp from removing Shannon as president of Tank Cleaners, Inc. Judgment for Shannon, and Camp appealed to Court of Civil Appeals which affirmed the judgment and Camp appealed to the Supreme Court. Judgment reversed and injunction dissolved.

Shannon was a director, president and general manager of Tank Cleaners, Inc. The bylaws of the corporation provided that the meeting of stockholders for the election of directors be held on the 27th day of October each year. They also provided that notice of the meeting be mailed by the secretary-treasurer to the shareholders "ten days prior thereto."

A meeting for the election of directors was called for October 8, 1960, and notice of the meeting was mailed on September 30, 1960. Shannon ordered the meeting called and presided at the meeting. By the action of the stockholders at the meeting, Shannon was replaced as a director, and at a meeting of the directors held immediately after the stockholders' meeting he was replaced as president and manager of Tank Cleaners, Inc. Shannon brought this action to have the meeting declared illegal because it was held at a date other than that set by the bylaws and because "ten days' notice" of the meeting was not given. All of the stockholders were present at the meeting either in person or by proxy.

CALVERT, CHIEF JUSTICE.   The provision for ten days' notice, found in both the bylaws of Tank Cleaners, Inc. and in Art. 2.25 of the Business Corporation Act, is for the benefit of the stockholders. They may waive notice by written instrument as provided in Art. 9.09, Texas Business Corporation Act, or by voluntarily attending and participating in the meeting without protest. If they may waive notice altogether, it follows that they may likewise waive irregularities in the notice. Moreover, when a stockholder, without objecting, appears at and participates in a stockholders' meeting, he will not be heard to complain of lack of notice of the meeting or of irregularities in the notice.

We are also of the opinion, largely for the same reasons, that the election of directors was not illegal because the stockholders' meeting was held on October 8th instead of October 27th. That the election of directors on a date other than that fixed in the bylaws can be a legal election is illustrated by those cases in which directors have been compelled by judicial action to call and hold a meeting of stockholders for the election of directors after the date therefor fixed in the bylaws has passed. There is no evidence here that the meeting was called for October 8th in order to perpetrate a fraud on the stockholders. All stockholders were present or represented by proxy and agreed to and participated in the election of petitioners. Here, again, Shannon is estopped by his conduct from questioning the legality of the meeting and of the election of petitioners.

There is testimony in the record that on the day following the displacement of Shannon one of the stockholders who had voted his stock for each of the petitioners "felt it was a little harsh perhaps. He thought that Mr. Shannon should have stayed on the board." A harried or contrite conscience cannot be grounds, in law, for nullifying the election of those for whom the stockholder voted.

Voting Rights

Shareholders Entitled to Vote.   Whether a shareholder is entitled to vote at a shareholders' meeting depends upon statutory provisions and the articles and bylaws of the corporation. The Model Act (14, 31) permits the issuance of a class or classes of nonvoting stock if so provided in the articles. However, such nonvoting classes are entitled to vote on extraordinary corporate transactions (55, 67, 72, 77). The person who has legal title to the stock is the one generally entitled to vote, but it is common in publicly held corporations for the directors to establish a "record date." Those entitled to vote will be those appearing on a voting list prepared as of that date or the directors may close the transfer books for a period of from 10 to 50 days prior to a meeting. A title owner who is not the owner of record may obtain a proxy from the record holder. The Model Act (28) also provides that if none is established, the record date shall be the date of mailing of notice of the meeting.

A corporation may not vote its treasury shares (those once issued and then reacquired) if any, and, of course, unissued stock has no vote. Shares held by a subsidiary in a parent corporation may not be voted since the effect would be the same as the vote of the treasury shares, and this device could be used to perpetuate management. The Model Act (31), following a rule adopted by the courts, so provides.

The fact that a shareholder has a personal interest in the matter being voted will not disqualify him from voting or affect the validity of the action taken, since ordinarily shareholders have no fiduciary duty to the corporation. However, controlling shareholders will not be permitted to manipulate the corporate affairs in fraud of the rights of the other shareholders.[3]

Cumulative Voting. Although most corporations conduct the election of directors on the basis that each share is entitled to one vote for each vacancy, many corporations give shareholders the option to cumulate their votes by giving one candidate as many votes as the number of directors to be elected multiplied by his number of shares. The option to cumulate votes is given to all shareholders by constitutional provisions or statute in almost half of the states. Most of the rest of them permit corporations to provide for cumulative voting in their articles. A few statutes are silent, in which case some courts have permitted cumulative voting if so provided in articles or bylaws. The Model Act (31) offers mandatory and permissive cumulative voting as alternative provisions.

The purpose of cumulative voting is to give minority shareholders an opportunity to be represented on the board of directors. Whether this is desirable is a highly controversial issue. Its opponents argue that unity and stability of management will increase the likelihood of success of the corporation. Few large publicly held corporations are domiciled in states with mandatory cumulative voting, and promoters tend to avoid incorporation in these states.

The formula for determining the minimum number of shares required to elect one director is:

$$X = \frac{S}{D+1} + 1$$

where S is the number of shares voting and D is the total number of directors to be elected. Obviously, the fewer the number of directors to be elected the larger the minority interest must be to enable a shareholder to elect a director. One device for reducing the effect of cumulative voting is to provide for electing directors by classes, each class to remain in office for three years, the maximum permitted by the Model Act (35).

Proxy Voting. All state statutes permit shareholders to appoint an agent, known as a proxy, to vote for them. The Model Act (31) requires that the authority to vote as a proxy must be given in writing, but some states permit

---

[3] See Chapter 25.

oral proxies. Both the writing and the person designated to vote for the shareholder are called a proxy. Usually proxies are general, permitting the agent to vote on all matters properly coming before a shareholders' meeting, but they may be limited to a particular matter. Most states put a limit on the duration of a proxy. The Model Act limits it to 11 months from the date of execution unless the writing itself provides otherwise. Generally, proxies are revocable at any time by the shareholder. Exceptions are those "coupled with an interest," such as where the proxy is given to a pledgee of the shares or to a purchaser of the shares under an executory contract. Otherwise, irrevocability is considered against public policy. A proxy is automatically revoked when another proxy is given subsequently.

The Securities Exchange Commission is given rule-making power over solicitation of proxies by the Securities Exchange Act of 1934. Proxy solicitation in corporations under the jurisdiction of the act must be in accordance with its rules, which specify the information that must be given the shareholder, require giving the shareholder a "two-way" choice on matters to be acted upon, and provide for dating the proxy. If the proxy is to be used in an annual meeting at which directors are to be elected, the SEC further requires that an annual report either accompany or precede the management's solicitation of proxies. If misleading statements are made in the proxy solicitation, a court may enjoin the holding of the meeting or void the action taken. This statutory remedy is in addition to the common-law remedy for breach of fiduciary duty to shareholders.

Voting Trust. The Model Act (32) and most state statutes permit shareholders to establish voting trusts. The purpose of a voting trust is to concentrate shareholder power in one or a few persons who can control the corporation through the election of directors. One frequent use of the device is to give control of the corporation to creditors during corporate reorganization after bankruptcy.[4] Although courts earlier tended to hold voting trusts illegal as against public policy, the modern cases tend to uphold them even in the absence of statute unless the purpose for which the voting trust is formed is illegal, such as to gain a monopoly as in the case of the Standard Oil trust and others near the end of the 19th century, or to defraud minority shareholders.

The Model Act and most statutes require that the voting trust be created by an agreement in writing among the participating shareholders and that they transfer their shares to the trustee or trustees. The agreement, which states the purpose(s) of the trust and how the stock shall be voted by the trustee(s) or how the voting shall be determined, must, under the Model Act, be filed with the corporation and must be available to inspection by the beneficial owners of the shares in the trust. The Model Act also prescribes a maximum life of the

---

[4] The most notable recent voting trust was established in 1960 at the insistence of Trans World Airlines' creditors to vote the 78 percent of TWA shares owned by Hughes Tool Co.

trust agreement of 10 years. It is common for voting trust certificates to be given the shareholder in exchange for his share in the corporation and they entitle the holder to his ratable share of dividends and distributions paid by the corporation.

Summary

The voting rights of the shareholder are based on the statutes of the state of incorporation and on the articles and bylaws of the corporation. Nonvoting classes of stock are entitled to vote on certain extraordinary corporate transactions. Shareholders listed on the books of the company on the record date are those who are entitled to vote.

A corporation cannot vote unissued or treasury stock. The personal interest of a shareholder in a matter being voted on does not disqualify him.

Many states require corporations formed under their statutes to grant cumulative voting and most of the rest permit this system of voting, which is designed to give representation to minority shareholders, if provided for in the articles. Proxy voting is generally permitted and the SEC has rule-making power over the solicitation of proxies. Voting trusts are permitted if they have a legitimate purpose and a reasonable length of life.

Schott v. Climax Molybdenum Co.

154 A.2d 221 (Del. Ch. 1959)

This was an action by Alice F. Schott and other stockholders (plaintiffs) against Climax Molybdenum Company (defendant) to have its merger and consolidation with another corporation declared void. Motion for summary judgment denied.

Schott and other stockholders of Climax Molybdenum Company (Climax) brought this action asking that the merger and consolidation of Climax with American Metal Company Limited (American) be declared to be null and void. The merger was attacked on the ground that it was not approved by two-thirds of the outstanding common stock of Climax as required by statute. Of the 2,580,000 shares of Climax issued and outstanding, 1,720,000 shares (two-thirds) were required to vote for the merger to make it effective under the statute. The inspectors of election reported that 1,781,564 shares voted in favor of the merger. It has since been conceded by Climax, however, that 2,424 shares were incorrectly counted for the merger. Nevertheless, the defendant contends that 1,779,130 shares were properly voted for the merger, being 59,130 more shares than the required two-thirds. Schott *et al.* contend on several grounds that more than 59,130 shares were incorrectly counted for the merger.

Schott *et al.* contend that 62,834 proxies voted in favor of the merger were not signed by the registered owner but rather were rubber-stamped with the registered owner's name and were void and should not have been counted; that more than

59,130 shares were voted by pledgees rather than pledgors, contrary to the Delaware Corporation Law; and that a series of proxies was given by a single broker and that the entire series was counted rather than only the last proxy.

SEITZ, CHANCELLOR.   I think the use of the stamped facsimile signature is at least sufficient in the corporate proxy-voting field to cloak such signatures (of the registered owners) with the presumption of authenticity. I say this because the proxy material is generally sent to the registered owner and it must be presumed that he receives it. It is therefore not unreasonable to assume that he executed or authorized the execution of the returned stamped signature proxy. In the cases of brokerage houses, where the problem most frequently arises, it is evident that the stamped form is an accepted practice.

Considering the practicalities of corporate life, at least in the field of proxy voting, and realizing that the rubber-stamped signature gives rise only to a presumption of authority, I conclude that the proxies here involved were signed and therefore properly counted by the inspectors.

Schott *et al.* next contend that certain proxies were counted which should have been considered revoked by later proxies. The result would presumably be changed if Schott *et al.*'s contention has merit.

Some brokers gave a series of proxies, all of which were voted except in those cases where explicit instructions to the contrary appeared on the face of a subsequent proxy or where the series exceeded the total number of shares held by the broker, in which cases only the final proxy was counted.

Schott *et al.* say that only the last proxy should have been counted. Their theory is that a later proxy revokes an earlier proxy although such instructions are not given in the proxy and although the number of shares covered by the various proxies does not exceed the total number of shares registered in the proxy-giver's name. This raises what I believe to be a novel question in this court.

Clearly a later proxy revokes an earlier one when such instructions appear on the face of the later proxy. And there is no question but that a later proxy revokes an earlier one where the total number of shares registered in the name of the person giving the proxies is included in each proxy. But is the rule that a later proxy revokes an earlier one applied indiscriminately?

As noted, the various proxies in each series were not, in toto, in excess of the total registered in the particular stockholder's name. Nor were any instructions contained on the proxies. Thus, there is nothing on the face of the proxies which rendered the counting of all of such shares inconsistent. Although not the case here, such a later proxy might be intended to revoke an earlier one. Since it is not necessarily so, I believe the inspectors of election properly resolved the doubt in favor of counting both.

Finally, Schott *et al.* contend that the merger did not receive the approval of two-thirds of the common stock of Climax because brokers holding stock in margin accounts caused more than 59,130 shares of such stock to be voted in favor of the merger. They say that under 8 Delaware Code ¶ 217 such shares were not properly voted.

Since there was no challenge to the voting of such shares and since they were given by the unchallenged registered owners, the inspectors of election quite naturally counted the proxies here involved. The issue of their validity was raised for the first time in this action.

The shares involved were registered in the broker's name without qualification and with at least the tacit consent of the beneficial owner. As a practical matter, in a margin account, it is almost necessary that they be so registered to facilitate the right of the broker to borrow on them. I also take judicial notice of the regulation of the stock exchange which imposes certain duties on such brokers with respect to consulting the voting desires of the beneficial owner. Thus there is no "policy" which is frustrated by construing the statute to permit a broker holding shares in a margin account to vote such shares. At least this is so where the corporate books do not show that they are qualifiedly held or when the pledgor does not attempt to vote them.

Levin v. Metro-Goldwyn-Mayer, Inc.
264 F.Supp. 797 (S.D. N.Y. 1967)

This was an action by Levin and other shareholders (plaintiffs) against Metro-Goldwyn-Mayer, Inc., and certain of its directors (defendants) seeking to enjoin methods used by management in soliciting proxies. Injunction denied.

Levin, a director of MGM, and his associates in this action owned 11% of the outstanding shares of MGM and were seeking to gain control of the corporation through a proxy contest. They charged the MGM management with wrongfully committing the corporation to pay for the services of attorneys, a public relations firm and a proxy soliciting organization to secure support from shareholders for the current management. They further claimed that the use of MGM employees and business contacts were improper. No charge was made that any false or fradulent statements have been made by the management group in connection with proxy solicitation.

RYAN, DISTRICT JUDGE. It is quite plain that the differences between "the O'Brien [management] group" and "the Levin group" are much more than mere personality conflicts. These might readily be resolved by reasoning and hard-headed, profit-minded businessmen. There are definite business policies advocated by each group, so divergent that reconciliation does not seem possible. They appear so evident from the papers before us that detailed analysis would be a waste of time. However, in such a situation the right of an independent stockholder to be fully informed is of supreme importance. The controlling question presented on this application is whether illegal or unfair means of communication, such as demand judicial intervention, are being employed by the present management. We find that they are not and conclude that the injunctive relief now sought should be denied.

. . . Contrary to the shareholders' unsupported statement that 9,000 MGM employees are at work soliciting proxies, MGM has stated that the total number of employees who on their own time have consented to telephone shareholders to vote is less than 150. We do not find this an unreasonable situation under the circumstances. . . .

The employment of two proxy solicitation firms and the fees agreed to be paid to them were fully disclosed in the MGM proxy statement. Georgeson & Co. is in charge of solicitation of proxies from stockholders directly; the Kissel-Blake Organization is directing its efforts to brokerage solicitation. Here again, MGM states without contradiction that "in every year since 1956, MGM has employed the firms of Georgeson & Co. and The Kissel-Blake Organization, Inc., to solicit proxies for its stockholders' meetings." We do not find basis for injunctive relief in their employment, nor in the employment of Dudley King & Co., as a consultant in connection with corporate matters and stockholder relations. . . .

There have been set forth in paid advertisements statements by·actors, directors, writers and exhibitors supporting and expressing confidence in the present management. MGM states these expressions have been unsolicited and spontaneous and have been published by these persons [and] . . . paid for completely out of their own pockets without any direct or indirect promise of repayment by MGM. There is no proof to challenge this. Certainly, MGM should not be expected to deny or contradict what they regard as well-deserved compliments graciously paid to them. Nor do we find the publication of such unsolicited individual advertisements a violation of the Act of 1934.

. . . MGM engaged the services of Thomas J. Deegan Co., Inc. Deegan is a recognized and reputable public relations firm. The engagement was long before the present proxy contest. The employment is neither unusual nor unreasonable. It does not afford ground for injunctive relief.

Dividends

Introduction.   The law assumes that the purpose of a business corporation is to make a profit. Shareholders usually invest in a corporation primarily to share in the expected profit through dividends, although it is not unusual for corporations to retain over long periods of time all earnings and to reinvest them in the business. Such a policy may be attractive to shareholders in the higher income tax brackets if the result is rapid appreciation of the market value of their shares or, in close corporations, when liquidation or sale of the corporation is anticipated so that the reinvested profits will receive a capital gains treatment in the hands of the shareholders. Dividends must be paid ratably on the shares of any class.

Types of Dividends.   Dividends are usually paid in cash but assets of the corporation, such as shares in another corporation, may be distributed as a dividend. Such dividends are referred to as "property dividends" or "dividends-in-kind." Distribution of assets, including cash, which amount to a partial liquidation are not included within the meaning of the term dividend as used in the Model Act. "Stock dividends" are distributions of shares in the corporation itself and are of a different nature than the other two types of dividends and will be discussed separately. An "extra dividend" is not a special kind of dividend but is usually so designated by the directors to indicate that it is given in addition to what they consider to be the normal or regular dividend that they expect to be able to maintain.

Funds Available for Payment of Dividends.   The corporation statutes of most states specify the sources from which dividends may be paid. The common-law rule was that payment of a dividend was illegal if it resulted in the impairment of the capital of the corporation. The ingenuity of corporate promoters and managers in designing various types of shares and methods of establishing their value has made it difficult for the courts and legislatures to accomplish their objective of maintaining the original capital of the corporation as a "trust fund" for the protection of creditors and to help assure stockholders that the corporation may be able to carry out its purposes.

Tests of Validity of Dividend Payments.   There are three principal tests of the validity of dividend payments. They are: (1) the surplus test, based upon the balance sheet, (2) the current earnings test, based upon the income statement, and (3) the noninsolvency test.

The Model Act (40) forbids dividends which would render a corporation insolvent, that is unable to pay its debts as they fall due. Such a dividend is probably illegal as an invasion of creditors' rights even though not specifically forbidden in a statute.

The surplus test would permit dividends so long as there is a surplus even if there are no earnings during the current year. A corporation has a surplus when its assets exceed its liabilities plus its stated capital. A surplus may arise from several kinds of corporate transactions. "Earned surplus" arises from net profits made in the operation of the business. "Paid-in surplus" arises out of the difference between the par value (or stated value in case of no-par shares) and the price the corporation receives when it sells the shares to investors. "Revaluation surplus" is created by an upward revaluation of assets of the corporation. "Reduction surplus" is created by reducing stated capital.

The Model Act (40a) limits dividends to "earned surplus," and it is available for dividends in all states. However, some states allow dividends to be paid from either earned or paid-in surplus and a few permit payment from any kind of surplus.

Some states permit the payment of a dividend out of current net profits regardless of a negative surplus. This is referred to as the "nimble dividend" rule because the dividend must be declared before such net profits are closed to the surplus account, that is charged against the accumulated deficit. A few statutes specifically forbid payment out of unrealized appreciation or require assets to be reduced by unrealized depreciation in computing the source of dividends.

Directors' Discretion in Payment of Dividends. Declaration of dividends is the responsibility of the directors under the Model Act and most statutes, although under some statutes the shareholders may retain this power by an appropriate provision in the articles. Declaration of dividends is discretionary and within the business judgment of the directors. This discretion applies even to shares with a dividend preference, although a clearly worded provision in the articles may make the payment of a dividend mandatory if one can legally be paid. However, dividends are not gratuities handed out to shareholders by a benevolent board of directors; they are the expected returns on capital investment. Although the burden of proof is on the complaining shareholder and courts are hesitant to substitute their judgment for that of the directors, shareholders have occasionally been able to get a court to decree the payment of a dividend when the directors have refused to do so through a flagrant abuse of their discretion.

The federal government imposes heavy punitive taxes upon improper accumulation of corporate earnings, which also limits the discretion of directors. On the other hand, it is very common for creditors to prohibit the payment of dividends or to limit them to funds defined more narrowly than the legal prohibitions.

Payment of Dividends on Preferred Stock. The preferred shareholder's right to dividends is based upon his shareholder contract, subject to the availability of funds from which dividends can be paid. Considerable confusion exists as to the dividend rights of preferred shareholders under varying conditions, and great care in drafting the contract is essential. Unless the contract is interpreted as making the declaration of a dividend upon a preferred class of shares mandatory, the directors may refuse to declare and pay a dividend even though funds are available from which a dividend could legally be paid if, in their honest judgment, the payment of the dividend would be detrimental to the corporation.

Four types of contractual provisions are found in preferred stock. (1) A mandatory dividend preference entitles the holder to the contractual dividend if payment is legally permissible, leaving no discretion to the directors (such contracts are very rare; in case of ambiguity courts avoid interpreting preferences as mandatory, and at least one court has held such a contract unenforceable [5]); (2) a cumulative dividend preference entitles the shareholder to unpaid dividends for all prior periods before any dividend or distribution may be paid upon shares which are subordinate with respect to dividend rights; (3) a cumulative-to-the-extent-earned preference entitles the shareholder to unpaid dividends for all prior periods in which there were funds legally available for such

---

[5] *Lindgrove* v. *Schulter & Co.*, 176 N.E. 832 (Ct. App. N.Y. 1931).

dividends before subordinate shareholders may receive dividends or distributions; (4) a noncumulative preference only gives the shareholder the right to dividends in a fiscal period before dividends or distributions are paid to other shareholders.

There is a divergence of authority as to whether the preference on noncumulative shares extends beyond the current fiscal year. Most jurisdictions hold that even though earnings are legally sufficient for a dividend on the preferred shares, directors may retain them for reinvestment in the business. New Jersey, on the other hand, applies the "dividend credit theory" which holds that preferred shareholders have an equity in such reinvested funds. The effect is to treat noncumulative shares as if they were cumulative-to-the-extent-earned. Under the majority rule directors retaining earnings for a number of years without paying dividends to preferred shareholders may, nevertheless, be subject to a court finding that they have abused their discretion and be ordered to declare dividends.

Whether holders of cumulative preferred shares are entitled to the arrearages in case of liquidation of the corporation depends upon the interpretation of the shareholders' contract. Most courts hold that arrearages must be paid upon liquidation, if assets are sufficient, even though there were insufficient earnings to pay them when due.

Stock Dividends and Stock Splits.   A stock dividend is a distribution to shareholders of additional shares in the corporation and is, in effect, a capitalization of surplus. The shares distributed may be either of the same class as those held or of a different class or series. Under the Model Act (40e) no dividend payable in shares shall be paid to holders of shares of any other class unless the articles of incorporation so provide or such payment is authorized by a majority of the outstanding shares of the class in which payment is to be made. This limitation, of course, is for the protection of the holders of the class of shares being distributed, since such a distribution would dilute their shares. A dividend payable in the same class of shares has no effect on the equity of the shareholders since their interest in the corporation remains proportionately the same. Nevertheless, the total market value of the shareholder's interest frequently increases and shareholders seem to value the additional piece of paper. If the dividend rate remains the same on a per share basis, of course, the effect will be to increase the dividend received by the shareholder.

The difference between a stock dividend and a stock split is that in the former case the par or stated value of the shares distributed must be transferred from the surplus to the capital account (unless treasury shares are distributed) while in the case of a stock split there is no change in the total capital account but only in the par value or stated value of the shares. Payment of a stock dividend in the same class of shares requires only director approval while approval of shareholders is required for the amendment of the articles of incorporation necessary to make a stock split (53i, 55f). A reverse stock split is a decrease in the number of shares of a class such that, for example, two shares become one share. The most common purpose of a stock split is to adjust the market price to fall within the popular $20 to $40 range. It may also mask rapid changes in earnings per share.

Distributions. The Model Act (41) distinguishes a dividend from what it designates as a distribution from capital surplus. Such distribution may be made from capital surplus as distinguished from earned surplus. However, distribution may not be made when the corporation is insolvent, and unless the articles provide for such a distribution, two thirds of the shares of each class of shares, whether regularly entitled to voting rights or not, must vote in favor of the distribution. If it is a distribution from capital surplus, that fact must be disclosed to the shareholders when it is received. Other limitations include a provision that no distribution may be made when cumulative dividends have accrued or when the remaining net assets of the corporation would be insufficient to pay off preferential shares in a voluntary liquidation.

In addition, the Model Act permits, without a shareholder vote or authorization in the articles, distributions from capital surplus to discharge cumulative dividend rights of preferred shareholders so long as insolvency is avoided.

Dividend Declaration. A dividend is declared by formal action of the board of directors. Once declared, a lawful cash dividend becomes a debt owing to the shareholders, although a Massachusetts case has held that the directors may rescind their action prior to the time the declaration has become known to shareholders.[6] Thereafter, should the corporation become insolvent, the shareholders may share in the assets with other creditors to the extent of the dividend. However, stock dividend declarations, since they do not actually change the shareholders' interest in the corporation, are held to be revocable. Dividends other than stock dividends may be paid in cash or property of the corporation, such as stock in another corporation.

Effect of Transfer on Right to Dividend. As between the corporation and the shareholder, the corporation may treat the shareholder of record as the person entitled to receive the dividend. As between the transferor and transferee, the right to the dividend will depend on the agreement between the parties. In the absence of agreement the transferor is entitled to the dividend if the sale was made after the record date. If the sale is made on a stock exchange, the transferee is entitled to the dividends unless he buys the stock after it is declared "ex dividend," which is five business days before the record date for the dividend.

---

[6] *Ford* v. *Easthampton Rubber Thread Co.,* 32 N.E. 1036 (Sup. Jud. Ct. 1893); cf. *Brown* v. *Luce Mfg. Co.,* 96 S.W.2d 1098 (K.C. Ct. App. Mo. 1936).

Summary

Shareholders usually expect to share in the profits of a corporation through dividends. These are usually paid in cash but may be paid in property, such as shares in another corporation. A distinction is drawn between a distribution in partial liquidation and a dividend.

Corporation statutes usually specify the sources from which dividends may be paid. Three principal tests of the validity of dividends are used: (1) the surplus test, (2) the current earnings test, and (3) the noninsolvency test. Under the Model Act a dividend must meet both the second and third tests.

Declaration of dividends is the responsibility of the directors and is subject to their business judgment even with respect to shares with a dividend preference, except in the rare case of a mandatory dividend. Three other types of dividend preferences are: cumulative, cumulative-to-the-extent-earned, and noncumulative. New Jersey treats noncumulative shares as being cumulative-to-the-extent-earned. Most courts hold that arrearages on cumulative shares must be paid upon liquidation of the corporation, if assets are sufficient, even though earnings were insufficient at the time the dividends were due.

A stock dividend is a distribution of additional shares in the corporation and is, in effect, a capitalization of surplus. A stock split does not change in the total capital account but only in the par or stated value of the shares.

Under the Model Act a distribution is distinguished from a dividend and may be made from capital surplus while a dividend must be charged against earned surplus. Distributions may be used to discharge cumulative dividend rights.

Once declared a cash dividend becomes a debt but a stock dividend declaration may be rescinded.

The corporation may treat the stockholder of record as entitled to the dividend. In the absence of an agreement the transferee of shares bought on a stock exchange is entitled to the dividend unless he buys after it is declared "ex dividend."

Dodge v. *Ford Motor Co.*

170 N.W. 668 (Sup. Ct. Mich. 1919)

This was an action by John F. Dodge and Horace E. Dodge (plaintiffs) against Ford Motor Company and others (defendants) to force the directors of Ford Motor Company to pay a special dividend. Judgment for Dodge, and Ford Motor Company appealed. Judgment affirmed in part and reversed in part.

Dodge *et al.* were stockholders in the Ford Motor Company. From the beginning in 1903 to July 31, 1916, the corporate business had been profitable. The capital stock had been increased from $150,000 in 1903 to $2,000,000 in 1908. A regular dividend of 5 per cent per month on its capital stock of $2,000,000 had been paid since 1911, and in addition thereto special dividends had been paid which ranged from $1,000,000 to $10,000,000 per year and which totaled $41,000,000 for the years 1911 to 1915 inclusive. In 1916 the directors decided to continue to pay the regular dividend of 5 per cent per month on the corporation's capital stock of $2,000,000 but to discontinue all special dividends. At this time the corporation had a surplus of $112,000,000; its yearly profits were $60,000,000; its total liabilities including capital stock were less than $20,000,000; it had cash on hand of $54,000,000; and all planned improvements would cost approximately $24,000,000. This action was brought to force the directors to pay a special dividend.

OSTRANDER, CHIEF JUSTICE.   The rule which will govern courts in deciding these questions is not in dispute. It is, of course, differently phrased by judges and by authors; and, as the phrasing in a particular instance may seem to lean for or against the exercise of the right of judicial interference with the actions of corporate directors, the context, or the facts before the court, must be considered. This court, in *Hunter* v. *Roberts, Throp & Co.,* recognized the rule in the following language:

It is a well-recognized principle of law that the directors of a corporation, and they alone, have the power to declare a dividend of the earnings of the corporation, and to determine its amount. Courts of equity will not interfere in the management of the directors unless it is clearly made to appear that they are guilty of fraud or misappropriation of the corporate funds, or refuse to declare a dividend when the corporation has a surplus of net profits which it can, without detriment to the business, divide among its stockholders, and when a refusal to do so would amount to such an abuse of discretion as would constitute a fraud, or breach of that good faith which they are bound to exercise towards the stockholders.

The record, and especially the testimony of Mr. Ford, convinces that he has to some extent the attitude towards shareholders of one who has dispensed and distributed to them large gains and that they should be content to take what he chooses to give. His testimony creates the impression, also, that he thinks the Ford Motor Company has made too much money, has had too large profits, and that, although large profits might be still earned, a sharing of them with the public, by reducing the price of the output of the company, ought to be undertaken. We have no doubt that certain sentiments, philanthropic and altruistic, creditable to Mr. Ford, had large influence in determining the policy to be pursued by the Ford Motor Company—the policy which has been herein referred to.

In discussing this proposition, counsel have referred to decisions such as *Hawes* v. *Oakland, Taunton* v. *Royal Ins. Co., Henderson* v. *Bank of Australia, Steinway* v. *Steinway & Sons, People* v. *Hotchkiss.* These cases, after all, like all others in which the subject is treated, turn finally upon the point, the question whether it appears that the directors were not acting for the best interests of the corporation. We do not draw in question, nor do counsel for the Dodges do so, the validity of the general proposition stated by counsel nor the soundness of the opinions delivered in the cases cited. The case presented here is not like any of them. The difference between an incidental humanitarian expenditure of corporate funds for the benefit of the employes, like the building of a hospital for their use and the employment of agencies for the betterment of their condition, and a general purpose and plan to benefit mankind at the expense of others, is obvious. There should be no confusion (of which there is evidence) of the duties which Mr. Ford conceives that he and the stockholders owe to the general public and the duties which in law he and his co-directors owe to protesting, minority stockholders. A business corporation is organized and carried on primarily for the profit of the stockholders. The powers of the directors are to be employed for that end. The discretion of directors is to be exercised, in the choice of means to attain that end and does not extend to a change in the end itself, to the reduction of profits or to the nondistribution of profits among stockholders in order to devote them to other purposes.

There is committed to the discretion of directors, a discretion to be exercised in good faith, the infinite details of business, including the wages which shall be paid to employes, the numbers of hours they shall work, the conditions under which labor shall be carried on, and the price for which products shall be offered to the public.

It is said by Ford Motor Company that the motives of the board members are not material and will not be inquired into by the court so long as their acts are within their lawful powers. As we have pointed out, and the proposition does not require argument to sustain it, it is not within the lawful powers of a board of directors to shape and conduct the affairs of a corporation for the merely incidental benefit of shareholders and for the primary purpose of benefiting others, and no one will contend that, if the avowed purpose of the directors was to sacrifice the interests of shareholders, it would not be the duty of the courts to interfere.

The directors of Ford Motor Company say, and it is true, that a considerable cash balance must be at all times carried by such a concern. But, as has been stated, there was a large daily, weekly, monthly receipt of cash. The output was practically continuous and was continuously, and within a few days, turned into cash. Moreover, the contemplated expenditures were not to be immediately made. The large sum appropriated for the smelter plant was payable over a considerable period of time. So that, without going further, it would appear that, accepting and approving the plan of the directors, it was their duty to distribute on or near the 1st of August, 1916, a very large sum of money to stockholders.

Guttmann v. Illinois Central Railroad Co.

189 F.2d 927 (2d Cir. 1951)

This was an action by Alexander Guttmann (plaintiff) against the Illinois Central Railroad Co. (defendant) for a judgment decreeing that dividends on preferred stock for the years 1937 to 1947 were fully earned and should have been declared by the railroad's board of directors. Complaint dismissed and Guttmann appealed. Affirmed.

The railroad's net income in each of the years from 1937 to 1947, inclusive, exceeded the annual dividend on the non-cumulative preferred stock, but the directors did not declare such dividends and instead reduced the railroad's funded debt.

Dividends were paid on the preferred in 1948, 1949 and 1950 and in 1950 a dividend of $1.50 per share was paid on the common stock. Guttmann argued that a holding by the U.S. Supreme Court involving the Wabash Railway Co. applied only to the specific facts of that case. There the court held that non-cumulative preferred shareholders had no claim on the income when the railroad had invested it in capital improvements in the road and its equipment.

FRANK, CIRCUIT JUDGE.   (Guttmann) would have us treat the words "non-cumulative" as if they read "cumulative if earned except only when the earnings are paid out for capital additions." He argues that the Wabash ruling has no application when net earnings for a given year are legitimately retained for any one of a variety of other corporate purposes, and when in a subsequent year it develops that such retention was not necessary. We think the attempted distinction untenable. It ascribes to the Supreme Court a naïve over-estimation of the importance of tangibles (because they can be touched and seen) as contrasted with intangibles.

Here we are interpreting a contract into which uncoerced men entered. Nothing in the wording of that contract would suggest to an ordinary wayfaring person the existence of a contingent or inchoate right to arrears of dividends. The notion that such a right was promised is, rather, the invention of lawyers or other experts, a notion stemming from considerations of fairness, from a policy of protecting investors in those securities. But the preferred stockholders are not—like sailors or idiots or infants—wards of the judiciary. As courts on occasions have quoted or paraphrased ancient poets, it may not be inappropriate to paraphrase a modern poet, and to say that "a contract is a contract is a contract. . . ." But there are limits to the extent to which a court may go in so interpolating rights and obligations which were never in the parties' contemplation. In this case we consider those limits clear.

In sum, we hold that, since the directors did not "abuse" their discretion in withholding dividends on the non-cumulative preferred for any past years, (a) no right survived to have those dividends declared, and (b) the directors had no discretion whatever to declare those dividends subsequently.

Inspection of Books and Records

Common-Law Right to Inspect.   Disputes are frequent between corporations and shareholders who seek to examine records of the corporation. These arise when the corporation fears a use of the information which may be harmful to it or through a desire for secrecy. At common law shareholders have the right to inspect corporate books and records, including shareholders' list, books of account, minute books, and the properties of the corporation, so long as it is exercised for a proper purpose. However, even if his purpose were proper, the shareholder might suffer much delay and find it very expensive to obtain his remedy, which is usually a writ of mandamus.

The line between proper and improper purposes is not always clear, and in the earlier cases the courts put the heavy burden of proving a proper purpose upon the shareholder. Requests to inspect the books of account to determine the value of shares or the propriety of dividends and to inspect the stock ledger to identify fellow shareholders in order to communicate with them concerning corporate affairs are clearly proper purposes. On the other hand, to learn business secrets to aid a competitor or to get the names of shareholders for a "sucker list" or to obtain prospects for a personal business would clearly be improper purposes. Bare ownership of stock in a competing corporation would not, in itself, however, be sufficient grounds for denying access to the records. Mere curiosity or even a desire to be informed about corporate affairs has been held an insufficient purpose, especially where other means of gaining information, such as attendance at shareholder meetings, have not been fully utilized.

Statutory Inspection Rights. Statutes giving inspection rights usually aim to make it more difficult for a corporation to resist or delay proper requests by shareholders. Some give shareholders an absolute right of inspection, particularly with respect to the stock ledger or shareholder list.

The Model Act (29) gives an absolute right of inspection of the voting list, which must be maintained at the registered office of the corporation for 10 days prior to each meeting of shareholders. The Act (46) also provides that upon a written demand stating his purpose, any shareholder of record for at least the preceding six months or who holds 5 percent of the outstanding shares may examine in person or through an agent for any proper purpose the corporation's books of account, minutes, and record of shareholders and to make extracts of them. Any officer or agent who refuses to accede to a proper demand may be liable for a penalty of 10 percent of the value of the stockholders' shares plus any damages or other remedy afforded him by law unless within two years the person suing has offered for sale, or aided another in offering a list of shareholders of any corporation, or has improperly used information secured in any prior examination of the records of any corporation.

In addition, the act specifically recognizes the power of a court, upon proof of a proper purpose, to grant inspection rights without regard to the length of time the petitioner has been a shareholder. It also provides that upon written request the corporation must mail to a shareholder its most recent financial statements showing in reasonable detail its assets and liabilities and the results of its operations.

Summary

At common law shareholders have the right to inspect corporate books and records and the properties of the corporation so long as it is for a proper purpose. Statutes usually seek to make it more difficult for a corporation to resist or delay proper requests by shareholders and often give an absolute right to inspect the voting list of shareholders. The Model Act imposes penalties in addition to provable damages on corporate officers or agents who refuse proper requests.

G.S. & M. Co. v. *Dixon*
138 S.E.2d 662 (Sup. Ct. Ga. 1964)

This was an action by Robert Dixon, Administrator of the estate of Gaspore J. Nato (plaintiff) against G. S. & M. Company (defendant) to enforce his right to inspect the books and records of the company. The court held that petition was sufficient and permission was granted. G. S. & M. Company appealed. Holding was affirmed.

Dixon owned three fourths of a share of the capital stock of G. S. & M. Company. He requested the right to inspect the books of the corporation, including its bylaws, its minute books and its financial records. His counsel had been permitted a limited examination of its financial records, but the corporation had persistently refused to allow him to examine the minute books or bylaws. The court found that the examination was asked in good faith and for a specific and honest purpose and not to gratify speculative or vexatious purposes.

GRICE, JUSTICE.   That right is recognized in this State. A leading case declares: "A bona fide stockholder has the legal right to inspect the books and records of the company, where the examination is asked for in good faith for a specific and honest purpose, and not to gratify curiosity, or for speculating or for vexatious purposes, and provided, further, that the purpose of the stockholder desiring to make the examination is germane to his interest as a stockholder, proper and lawful in character, and not inimical to the interests of the corporation itself, and the inspection is made during reasonable business hours." In this State, the right of inspection stems from the common law. Furthermore, the rule is that "A stockholder may inspect the books of the corporation for the purpose of informing himself as to the manner and fidelity with which the corporate affairs are being conducted. . . . Inspection may also be required for the purpose of ascertaining the financial condition of the company, the value of its stock. . . ."

The basis of this right is simple and logical: "The basis of the right of stockholders to inspect the books and records is the ownership of the corporate property and assets through ownership of shares; as owners, they have the right to inform themselves as to the management of their property by the directors and officers who are their trustees in direct charge of the property."

This right is not dependent upon the amount of stock held. It is ". . . immaterial whether a stockholder asserting a right of inspection holds a few shares or many."

Preemptive Rights

General.   The shareholders' proportionate interests with respect to dividends, control, and assets are adversely affected by the nonproportionate issue of additional shares. A sale of additional shares at a price lower than book value would reduce the book value of existing shares and even a sale above book value may not necessarily result in earnings per share equal to the rate previously enjoyed. If there is but one class of shares these problems can be minimized if existing shareholders are given an opportunity to add proportionately to their holdings whenever new shares are to be sold by the corporation. The preemptive rights doctrine was evolved by the courts to accomplish this purpose, and many of the corporation statutes have codified the principal. Briefly stated, the doctrine gives the shareholder an option of subscribing to a new allotment of shares, in proportion to his holding of outstanding shares, before the newly alloted shares are offered to the public.

Application of Preemptive Rights. Generally, courts have held that preemptive rights do not apply to treasury shares, shares issued in connection with a merger or consolidation or issued for a noncash consideration. There is a conflict of authority with respect to shares which are unissued but which were authorized when the corporation was chartered. The rationale of courts holding that preemptive rights do not apply is that there was an implied agreement with original subscribers that these shares would be sold to raise capital for the business. If the sale of these shares is long postponed, the rationale breaks down and they are probably subject to preemptive rights. A common device used to give effect to preemptive rights is the issuance of short-term warrants or stock rights which entitle the holder to purchase a specified number of shares at a price fixed somewhat below the anticipated market price. The warrants are transferable and permit the shareholder to sell them if he does not wish to purchase the additional shares himself.

Preemptive Rights under the Model Act. The Model Act (24) contains alternative provisions permitting a legislature to choose the provisions which are consistent with its policy. One alternative recognizes no preemptive rights except to the extent provided in the articles of incorporation. The other gives preemptive rights but permits a corporation to limit or deny them in its articles. The latter alternative includes a provision designed to make employee stock option plans possible. It exempts from preemptive rights shares sold to officers and employees under terms which have been approved by holders of a majority of the shares. Even when shareholders are not entitled to preemptive rights courts will grant relief necessary to hold directors and majority shareholders to a high standard of reasonableness and fairness in issuing new shares. They will not be permitted to issue additional shares to themselves or to some favored group in order to gain an advantage over other shareholders.

Summary

A shareholder's preemptive right is the option of subscribing to a new allotment of shares, in proportion to his holding of outstanding shares. Preemptive right has generally been held not to apply to treasury shares, shares issued in connection with a merger or issued for a noncash consideration. There is a conflict of authority with respect to shares which are unissued but which were authorized when the corporation was chartered.

Many statutes permit a corporation to avoid the preemptive right.

Carlson v. Ringgold County Mutual Telephone Co.
108 N.W.2d 478 (Sup. Ct. Iowa 1961)

This was an action by Leroy T. Carlson and other stockholders (plaintiffs) against Ringgold County Mutual Telephone Company and its officers (defendants) to enforce preemptive rights. Judgment for Carlson and Mutual appealed. Judgment affirmed.

The authorized capital of Mutual was $10,000, represented by 1,000 shares with a par value of $10 each. In January, 1959, there were 356 shares outstanding, and the Carlson group purchased a majority interest of 203 shares at $200 per share. Shortly thereafter, the directors of Mutual voted to dispose of the 644 unsold shares "to such parties as the board of directors may approve at $40 per share, and upon the condition that before any such parties sell said stock they will first offer it to the corporation." Relatives, friends, and employees purchased 225 additional shares thereby divesting the Carlson group of majority interest.

The articles of incorporation provided, "When the outstanding capital is increased, additional stock shall be offered to existing stockholders in proportion to their then holdings. . . ." Mutual argues that the words "outstanding capital" and "capital shock" are used as the equivalent of each other and that preemptive rights guaranteed to stockholders are limited to situations where the authorized capital is increased.

SNELL, JUSTICE.   Defendants argue that the original authorized issue was for 1,000 shares and until these shares are issued there are no preemptive rights. . . .

While there are instances where the words "capital" and "capital stock" are used as the equivalent of each other, in a situation such as we have here the words should be clearly distinguished. The "capital" belongs to the corporation, and "capital stock" when issued belongs to the stockholders. "Capital" may be either real or personal property, but "capital stock" is always personal. The "capital" of a corporation is its property, while the "capital stock" of the corporation represents the interest of stockholders in the corporation, and is their property.

Here the net capital invested in the business was $68,778. This represented the actual value of the property invested in the business and belonging to the stockholders. These assets were owned by the owners of the 356 shares of stock outstanding.

To hold that additional stock over and above that outstanding, and up to the amount originally authorized, could be disposed of solely by action and in the sole discretion of the Board of Directors and without any preemptive rights, would place in the hands of the directors the power to practically destroy the property rights of stockholders by the arbitrary and capricious sale of stock to friends and relatives at far less than its actual value. In this case the directors did not have such arbitrary power.

Extraordinary Corporate Transactions

Introduction. At common law the corporate charter was considered as a contract between the state and the corporation, between the corporation and the shareholders and among the shareholders, and it could not be changed without the consent of all the parties, including unanimous consent of the shareholders. Modern corporation statutes [Model Act (142)] reserve the right to the legislature to change the statutes and regulations, thus changing the corporate charter, and to permit the corporation itself to change its articles and to make substantial changes in the nature of its business and the rights of its shareholders with approval of less than all of the shareholders. Thus the "vested rights" doctrine no longer is a bar to extraordinary corporate transactions, including amendment of articles, merger and consolidation, sale or mortgage of assets and dissolution.

Procedure for Amending Articles.   To amend the articles of incorporation, the procedure set out by the statutes of the state of incorporation must be complied with. The Model Act (54, 55) requires that a written notice setting forth the proposed amendment or a summary of the changes to be affected by it must be given to all shareholders entitled to vote and that the amendment be approved by at least two thirds of the shares. Certain kinds of amendments, which would substantially affect the rights of any class of shares, entitle the holders to a vote whether or not otherwise entitled to vote under the articles. Such changes include: changing the number of authorized shares of the class, changing the par value of those shares, changing the preferences or rights of the shares of the class, changing the shares into the different number of shares or a different class, creating a new class with preferences superior to an existing class, limiting or denying existing preemptive rights or canceled accrued dividends of that class of shares. In such cases a two-thirds vote of the shares of each class entitled to vote must be obtained to effectuate the amendment.

Other Extraordinary Transactions.   The statute of the state of incorporation must also be complied with in other extraordinary corporate transactions. In order to affect a merger or consolidation (65, 66, 67), sales or mortgage of assets other than in the regular course of business (72), or a voluntary dissolution of the corporation (77), the Model Act requires substantially the same procedure as for amendment of the articles. This includes approval of the board of directors, notice to shareholders and right to vote by all shareholders. Approval of two thirds of the shares is required to authorize the transaction.

Appraisal Right. A shareholder who disapproves of a proposed merger or consolidation or a sale or exchange of substantially all of the assets of the corporation otherwise than in the usual course of its business is entitled to payment of the value of his shares if he properly registers his dissent within 10 days (73, 74). If the transaction is completed, notice must be given by the corporation to the dissenting shareholders with an offer of a specific price for their shares. If any dissenting shareholder is unwilling to accept the offer, he may petition a court in the county where the corporation's registered office is located to determine the fair value of the shares. All dissenting shareholders, wherever they live, must be made parties to the suit and will be bound by the judgment. Costs of the action may be assessed against any or all dissenting shareholders if the corporation made an offer and the refusal was arbitrary or vexatious. However, if the corporation made no offer or one which was materially less than the judgment, the court is authorized to require it to pay the reasonable compensation of any expert employed by the dissenters in the proceedings. The act (5) exempts the purchase of shares from dissenters from the requirement that purchase of its own shares may be made only from unrestricted earned surplus.

Summary

The fundamental structure and purpose of the corporation may not be changed without the shareholders' consent. Corporation statutes today provide for amendment of the articles of incorporation with the approval of the owners of some proportion of the voting shares, usually two thirds. If the proposed amendment substantially affects the rights of a nonvoting class of shares, most states give that class a vote. Approval of voting shares is also usually required for extraordinary transactions such as merger, consolidation, sale of assets not in the normal course of business and for voluntary liquidation.

Dissenting shareholders are entitled to payment for the value of their shares in some of these situations. The Model Act gives the right of appraisal in case of merger or consolidation and in case of a sale of assets.

DuVall v. *Moore*
276 F.Supp. 674 (N.D. Iowa 1967)

This was an action by Thomas DuVall and others (plaintiffs) as minority shareholders against the majority shareholders, G. E. Moore, president, James Scherrman, secretary, and Midwest Limestone Co. (defendants) asking that an amendment to the articles of incorporation be set aside as illegal. The majority shareholders moved for summary judgment. Overruled.

Midwest was incorporated in Iowa in 1953 for 20 years and issued two types of common stock, Class A and Class B. Moore and Scherrman, individually, and as trustees of the corporation's profit sharing trust, owned a majority of both classes of stock. At the December, 1966, annual shareholders' meeting of the corporation, there was a vote on a proposal to amend the articles of incorporation to provide for perpetual existence for the corporation. As chairman of the meeting, Moore ruled, over the objection of the minority shareholders, that Class B shares were not entitled to vote on the amendment. A notice of dissent was filed by the minority shareholders.

The majority shareholders moved for summary judgment because Article V of the articles of incorporation provided that "The voting power shall be vested exclusively in Class A common stock . . ." and made no different provision for voting on amendments to the articles. The minority shareholders argued that if the articles were to be so interpreted they were invalid as in conflict with the Section 491.25 of the Iowa corporation act which grants appraisal rights to dissenting shareholders.

HANSON, DISTRICT JUDGE.   Plaintiffs place strong reliance upon the recent case of *Woodward* v. *Quigley*. . . . The court elaborated . . . that:

> . . . The original statute was similar to those enacted in most states to modify the common law rule which required unanimous consent of all the stockholders for a substantial change in the corporation structure. The increase in the number of corporations and stockholders made such a rule impracticable. The statute was enacted to permit a majority to vote to renew the corporate life and at the same time allow a dissenting minority to get out of the corporation with the "real value" of its stock. It prevented the minority from being squeezed out for a lesser price.

Since the *Woodward* case determined that Section 491.25 was enacted in order to negate the harsh common law rule of unanimous consent and provide for majority rule, plaintiffs were entitled to vote. The statute merely removed their dictatorial veto power.

In summary, the *Woodward* case decided that Section 491.25 was enacted to mitigate the unanimous consent rule on radical alterations in favor of a more practicable rule. Such a rule is rationally applicable to nonvoting stock.

Rath v. Rath Packing Co.
136 N.W.2d 410 (Sup. Ct. Iowa 1965)

This was an action by Howard G. Rath and other minority shareholders (plaintiffs) against Rath Packing Co. and certain of its officers and directors (defendants) to enjoin the carrying out of a "Plan and Agreement of Reorganization" with Needham Packing Co. The minority shareholders appealed from a judgment dismissing the case on the pleadings. Reversed and remanded.

The agreement between Rath Packing, an Iowa corporation with headquarters at Waterloo, Iowa, which processed mostly pork products, and Needham Packing Co., a Delaware corporation with headquarters at Sioux City, Iowa, which processed mostly beef products, called for a transfer of all of Needham's assets to Rath in exchange for 5.5 shares of Rath common stock and two shares of an 80-cent convertible preferred to be newly created and issued by Rath for each five shares of the

Needham stock outstanding and for Rath to change its name to Rath-Needham Corporation. This would result in Needham shareholders controlling 54 percent of the common shares of the Rath-Needham Corporation if the preferred shares were converted and the book value of Rath common shares would be reduced from $27.99 to $15.93 while Needham shareholders would have the book value of their holdings, assuming conversion of preferred shares, increased from $6.61 to $23.90.

The Iowa statutes required an affirmative vote of two-thirds of the shares to accomplish a merger but only a majority for an amendment to the articles, which could include change of corporate name, establishment of new classes of securities, etc. The Plan involved several amendments to Rath's articles but was not designated nor did it follow the statutory procedure for a merger. The affirmative vote on the proposed amendments to the articles by the Rath shareholders was 60.1 percent of the outstanding shares (77 percent of those voting). If the minority shareholders' view that the Plan was a merger were upheld, the affirmative vote was insufficient.

GARFIELD, CHIEF JUSTICE.   The principal point of law defendants asked to have adjudicated under rule 105, R.C.P., is that the provisions of [the corporation statute with respect to amending article] are legally independent of, and of equal dignity with, those relating to mergers and the validity of the action taken by defendants is not dependent upon compliance with the merger sections under which the same result might be attained. The trial court accepted this view.

We can agree all provisions of our chapter 496A are of equal dignity. But we cannot agree any provisions of the act are legally independent of others if this means that in arriving at the correct interpretation thereof and the legislative intent expressed therein we are not to consider the entire act and, so far as possible, construe its various provisions in the light of their relation to the whole act. . . .

We may also observe that the trial court

concluded the "safeguards" written into the codes of most states, including Iowa and Delaware, with respect to rights of dissenting shareholders in connection with mergers are based on outmoded concepts of economic realities, particularly in the case of an enterprise such as Rath which is regularly traded on the American Exchange and has a diversified stock ownership with over 4,000 shareholders. . . .

If the soundness of this view were admitted, the statutory safeguards should of course be removed by legislative, not judicial, action. Our 1959 legislature evidently had a purpose in enacting what we may call the merger sections of chapter 496A as well as those relating to amending articles and issuing stock. . . .

The "Plan and Agreement of Reorganization" clearly provide for what amounts to a merger of Rath and Needham under any definition of merger we know.

We have approved a statement that a merger exists were one corporation is continued and the other is merged with it, without the formation of a new corporation, from a sale of the property and franchises of one corporation to another. . . .

If, as we held, this agreement provides for what amounts to a merger of Rath and Needham, calling it a Plan and Agreement of Reorganization does not change its essential character. A fundamental maxim of equity, frequently applied, is that equity regards substance rather than form. . . .

The Power of a corporation to merge must be derived from the law of the state which created it. There must be some plain enactment authorizing the merger, for legislative authority is just as essential to a merger as to creation of the corporation in the first instance.

At common law no merger could take place without unanimous consent of the stockholders. However, statutes in all jurisdictions now authorize mergers upon a vote of less than all stockholders. A shareholder who dissents to a merger may obtain the value of his stock if the right thereto is provided by statute, if procedure is established therefor and is followed by him.

The Merger sections of chapter 496A clearly and expressly confer the necessary power to merge.

It is apparent that if the sections pertaining to amending articles and issuing stock are construed to authorize a merger by a majority vote of shareholders they conflict with the sections specifically dealing with the one matter of mergers which require a two-thirds vote of shareholders. The two sets of sections may be harmonized by holding, as we do, that the merger sections govern the matter of merger and must be regarded as an exception to the sections dealing with amending articles and issuing stock, which may or may not be involved in a merger.

The construction we give these sections is in accord with the cardinal rule that, if reasonably possible, effect will be given to every part of a statute.

Shareholders' Suits

Shareholders' Individual Suits. As a general rule a shareholder has no right to bring suit in his own name to recover a judgment for the impairment of his investment as a shareholder where such impairment resulted from a wrong to the corporation. When the suit is brought by the corporation, the interests of all the shareholders are protected in one suit, thereby avoiding a multiplicity of suits; and further, if individual shareholders were permitted to sue and collect damages, an asset of the corporation could be diverted from creditors to shareholders, thereby depriving creditors of their priority rights in corporate assets. Under the entity theory of corporations the person wronged is the corporation, and it is the only one who has a cause of action.

The courts have, however, recognized the shareholder's right to sue in his own name under some circumstances in which, although the wrong is based on corporate rights, the injury is primarily to the shareholder and rights of the creditors are not affected. For instance, where all but a small number of shareholders have participated in a misappropriation of funds, the nonparticipating shareholders have been allowed to recover a judgment sufficient to place them on a par with the participating shareholders.

A shareholder has a right to bring an action in his own name to redress or prevent the breach of the membership contract. A shareholder may bring an action in his own name to enforce his right to inspect the books, to recover a judgment for dividends declared but not paid when due, to enjoin the corporation from entering into *ultra vires* transactions, and to protect his preemptive rights and similar rights which are basically personal to the shareholder.

Shareholders' Derivative Suits.   Under some circumstances the courts recognize a shareholder's right to bring a derivative or class suit. A derivative suit is one brought by a shareholder to enforce a right of the corporation for the benefit of the corporation, its shareholders, and creditors. Any recovery usually goes to the corporate treasury for the protection and benefit of both shareholders and creditors. A class suit is one brought by one or more shareholders for the benefit of a class or group of shareholders having identical rights.

The typical situation in which the courts will allow a derivative suit is one in which the directors and managers of the corporation are also the controlling shareholders and in which they will benefit personally by not bringing suit to enforce the corporate right. The suit may be based upon wrongs committed by the insiders themselves or by outsiders.

Although the possibility of a derivative action may be a major deterrent to wrong doing on the part of officers and directors, it is also susceptible to abuse. "Strike suits" brought to gain an out of court settlement for the complaining shareholder personally or to earn large attorney's fees rather than a recovery for the corporation have not been uncommon. The U.S. Supreme Court long ago established several requirements for suits brought in federal courts to discourage abuse.[7] Under these rules the shareholder bringing the action must have held his shares or acquired them by operation of law (such as inheritance) from someone who held them at the time the alleged wrong was committed. He must also show that he has exhausted his intracorporate remedies by a prior demand upon the directors and, if appropriate, a demand on the shareholders. By statute many of the states have adopted these and additional safeguards. The Model Act (optional section 43a) contains the contemporaneous ownership requirement, and it also provides that the corporation may require the plaintiff(s) to post security for reasonable expenses and attorneys' fees which may be incurred by it and other defendants unless the plaintiff(s) own 5 percent of the outstanding shares or their shares have a market value in excess of $25,000. It also authorizes the court to assess the defendants' expenses and attorneys' fees whether or not security has previously been given, and whether or not it finds that the action was brought without reasonable cause. Statutes in a number of states, to prevent benefit only to the shareholder bringing the action, require court approval of any dismissal or settlement of the suit.

A shareholder who succeeds in gaining a benefit for the corporation in a derivative suit, whether or not the suit goes to final judgment, is entitled to be

---

[7] *Hawes* v. *Oakland,* 104 U.S. 450 (1882).

reimbursed by the corporation for his reasonable expenses including attorneys' fees. Otherwise, he could hardly afford to sue, since ordinarily the cost of the suit will far exceed the benefit to his shares alone. The result often is that the attorneys' fees and expenses of both plaintiffs and defendants are paid out of corporate funds should the suit be successful, and if the court thinks the suit is unreasonably brought, it may under Section 43a and similar statutes assess the costs of both parties to the unsuccessful shareholder complainant.

Occasionally, the officers or managers will refuse to defend a suit brought against a corporation. If a shareholder shows that the corporation has a good defense to the suit and that the refusal or failure of the directors or managers to defend is a breach of their fiduciary duty to the corporation, the courts will permit a shareholder to defend for the benefit of the corporation, its shareholders, and creditors.

Class suits are suits which are brought by one or more of the shareholders holding shares of a certain kind or class of stock against the corporation, its directors, or managers to protect the rights of all of the shareholders holding stock of the certain kind or class. For example, a person holding noncumulative preferred stock might bring suit in behalf of himself and all the other holders of the noncumulative preferred stock to prevent the directors of the corporation from omitting dividends on the noncumulative preferred stock when the corporation has made profits out of which the preferred dividend could be paid.

Minority Shareholders' Suits. The right to control the affairs of a corporation is vested in the holders of a majority of the shares. As has been previously discussed, approval of more than a bare majority is sometimes required by statute for the authorization of certain corporate acts. By provision in the articles even higher majorities or unanimous consent may be required for these or other acts.

However, the right of the holders of a majority of the shares to control the corporation is not an unrestricted right, as was stated in Chapter 25. The majority shareholders owe a duty to provide the corporation with a reasonably competent board of directors and to assure the operation of the corporation in a fair and impartial manner for the mutual benefit of all shareholders. If the majority shareholders pursue a course which will operate to deprive minority shareholders of their rights in the corporation, a court of equity will, on suit by minority shareholders, grant whatever relief the circumstances of the case demand. The courts are reluctant to interfere in the internal affairs of a corporation, and they will grant relief to minority shareholders only when the conduct of the majority shareholders amounts to a fraud on the minority shareholders.

Dissolution at Suit of a Minority Shareholder. Although there is authority to the contrary, in a number of cases courts have, upon the petition of a minority shareholder, appointed a receiver for the corporation and in a small number of cases have decreed dissolution without specific statutory authority. These cases have included situations where: (1) those in control of the corporation are benefitting themselves at the expense of the other shareholders in a cavalier manner or actually defrauding them; (2) corporate functions have been abandoned or the corporation has been inactive since organization; (3) the main purpose of the corporation can no longer be carried on without utter ruin or because the business has become illegal; and (4) there has been such a deadlock among directors and shareholders that corporate functions cannot be carried on. The Model Act (90a, 95) gives statutory authorization for liquidation and dissolution in all of these situations but the third. However, the power given is discretionary and would be exercised only if the court were convinced that liquidation and dissolution would benefit the shareholders as a whole.

Summary

As a general rule a shareholder has no right to bring a suit in his own name to recover damages for the impairment of his investment resulting from a wrong to the corporation. A shareholder may bring an action in his own name to redress or prevent a breach of his membership contract.

A shareholder may bring a derivative suit for the benefit of the corporation, its stockholders, and creditors if the directors and managers of the corporation have, in breach of their fiduciary duty, refused or failed to bring suit, and if their failure to bring suit will result in injury to the corporation.

Although courts are reluctant to interfere in the internal affairs of a corporation they will grant relief to minority shareholders if the conduct of the majority amounts to a fraud upon them. In a number of cases courts have appointed a receiver and decreed the dissolution of a corporation upon the suit of a minority shareholder, and some statutes specifically authorize dissolution in certain circumstances.

Saigh v. *Busch*
396 S.W.2d 9 (Ct. App. Mo. 1965)

This was a shareholders' derivative action brought by Fred and Elizabeth Saigh (plaintiffs) against August A. Busch, Jr., as an individual, and Anheuser-Busch, Inc. (defendants), seeking to require Busch to account to the corporation for salary and perquisites provided him in excess of the reasonable value of his services as president of the corporation. Motion to dismiss sustained, and Saigh appealed. Judgment affirmed.

The Saighs alleged that Busch had been given benefits in the form of salary, bonuses, stock purchase options, expense allowances not to be accounted for, personal club dues, life insurance, retirement annuity, yachts, private railroad cars, automobiles, residences, servants, etc., which far exceeded the reasonable value of his services.

Busch moved to dismiss on grounds that the complaint failed to state a cause of action because the Saighs failed to try to get other shareholders to take the action desired by them.

RUDDY, JUDGE.   As we have said, the primary authority to sue for corporate injuries is in the board of directors and managing officers. This is so because "[i]n the eyes of the law the injury is to the corporation (i.e., to the stockholders collectively) and not to the stockholders individually."

If it is necessary for a stockholder to bring a derivative action because the corporate management wrongfully refuses to do so, it is conducted by the stockholder as the representative of the corporation and in such action the corporation is the real party in interest and it is brought for the benefit of the corporation. If a money judgment is awarded, it must be paid to the corporation.

If a stockholder brings a derivative action in behalf of the corporation it is a settled principle of equity jurisprudence and, we add, a requirement of Civil Rule 52.08(b), that before a court will entertain such an action and inquire into wrongs complained of by the stockholder, the stockholder must show that he has no other avenue of recovery and this can be done only on a showing that he has exhausted all remedies and reasonable efforts within the corporation.

In order, therefore, to maintain the action, the individual stockholder must allege, and the proof show, either, that he has made demand upon the board of directors to take remedial action on behalf of the corporation and *that effort failing that he unsuccessfully sought action by the stockholders as a body, or a state of facts from which it appears that such demand or effort within the corporation and through corporate channels could have been futile and unavailing.* (Emphasis by court.)

While the rule stated above requires the stockholder who brings the derivative action to allege and show, if he failed with the directors, that he has made an honest effort to obtain action by the stockholders as a body and if this is not done, why it could not be done or that it was not reasonable to require it and would therefore be a futile act, the complaining stockholder need not make these allegations in his petition if his petition alleges that the officers and directors of the corporation violated the trust committed to them by perpetrating and doing *ultra vires,* illegal or fraudulent acts, because such acts cannot be ratified even by a majority of the stockholders. In such a situation equity will entertain an action for relief by a dissenting minority stockholder without first resorting or appealing to the stockholders as a body. Nor are allegations showing that a stockholder has made a demand upon the stockholders as a body necessary if the petition alleges a situation where the majority of the stockholders participated in the acts complained of, or, where the defendants sued are the holders of a majority of the shares, or other facts showing such a demand would be useless or futile. . . .

Applying the principles of law we have heretofore stated to the amended second amended petition of the Saighs, it is to be seen that the Saighs do not allege that they sought the action desired by them from stockholders, therefore, in order to maintain their action they must state facts sufficient to excuse their failure to obtain such action or show sufficient reasons for not making such effort. . . .

The petition does not allege that the directors or officers performed or perpetrated *ultra vires,* illegal or fraudulent acts.

The Saighs contend that since the action desired by them was the restitution of unreasonable compensation given to defendant Busch and since the setting of his compensation was within the management area of the board of directors and was beyond the statutory power of the stockholders, that they considered it not necessary to explain their failure to apply to the stockholders for redress. . . .

. . . Frequently officers and other stockholders submit to fellow stockholders proposals concerning the remuneration policy of the corporation. This is on the theory that every stockholder has a relationship to the management of the corporation. . . .

Paragraph 12(b)ii gives as the reason for the Saigh's inability to secure the election of a different board of directors that the present board and defendant Busch have access to funds for the purpose of soliciting proxies in behalf of themselves, and the Saighs further state that defendant Busch and the board thus effectively control the communications between the corporation and its very large number of and constantly changing list of shareholders. There is no allegation that defendant Busch or the board of directors have prevented the Saighs from securing proxies.

Blau v. Rayette-Faberge, Inc.
389 F.2d 469 (2d Cir. 1968)

This was an action by Blau, a stockholder, and Levy, his attorney (plaintiffs) against Rayette-Faberge, Inc. (defendant), to recover an attorney's fee for an investigation which resulted in the corporation's recovery under Section 16(b) of the Securities Exchange Act of 1934 of insider's profits in transactions in the corporation's securities. Blau and Levy appealed from a summary judgment for the corporation. Reversed and remanded.

Blau, acting in a derivative capacity for the corporation, employed Levy to investigate transactions in its securities by insiders of Rayette to discover whether the corporation was entitled to recover short swing profits under Section 16(b). Blau agreed to pay Levy a reasonable attorney's fee, contingent upon any benefit the corporation might derive from his efforts and upon reimbursement of Blau by the corporation for the amount of Levy's fee. Levy discovered that one of the officer-directors of the corporation had purchased and sold shares within six-months' periods and that the corporation might be able to recover his profits and that one claim was already barred by the two year statute of limitations and the other would be barred in six months.

Levy advised the corporation of the facts and its right of recovery and requested the corporation to file suit. He stated that Blau would sue after 60 days in the corporation's behalf if the profit had not been recovered or suit commenced. As they were about to bring suit, Levy was informed that the director-officer had paid the corporation $15,722 plus interest and that suit would be unnecessary. However, the corporation refused Blau's demand that it pay Levy for his services.

FEINBERG, CIRCUIT JUDGE.   In *Magida* v. *Continental Can Co.* we held that the possibility of champerty in violation of New York law would not justify setting aside recovery of over $57,000 in a section 16(b) suit, although a showing of misconduct would be relevant on a fee application. We pointed out that "the public policy of New York cannot nullify this federally created right, established for the effectuation of a broad federal policy." We realize that if investigatory work alone is compensable, there may be a greater incentive for abuse of professional conduct, but there will also be greater incentive to enforce the statute. Moreover, it is possible to achieve the latter without undue encouragement of the former. We do not suggest that counsel fees should be automatically awarded to overzealous attorneys; nor do we want lawyers poring over 16(a) reports as soon as they are made public to find a cause of action before the corporation does and thereby collect a fee. But there is a middle ground between that unattractive picture and denial of all compensation unless suit is brought: Reimbursement for information leading to corporate recovery will be allowed only if the corporation has done nothing for a substantial period of time after the suspect transactions and its inaction is likely to continue. In this way, not speed but careful investigation will be rewarded and the corporation will have adequate opportunity to enforce its rights without prodding from a stockholder. But if the corporation has been, and is likely to be, inattentive to its rights, a portion of any recovery should properly go to the stockholder for reimbursement of any reasonable legal expenses. Concededly, this standard is not precise, but rules of thumb in this field as elsewhere can be worked out on a case by case basis.

Bellevue Gardens, Inc. v. Hill
297 F.2d 185 (D.C. Cir. 1961)

This was an action by Hill and other minority shareholders (plaintiffs) against Bellevue Gardens, Inc., and controlling shareholders (defendants) to recover funds for the corporation allegedly improperly disbursed and for liquidation of the corporation. Liquidation was ordered and the controlling shareholders appealed. Affirmed.

Bellevue Gardens and another corporation involved in a similar suit were closely held corporations with the same ownership. They operated apartment projects valued at nearly two and a half million dollars. The controlling shareholders had engaged in a number of intercorporate transactions which resulted in what the trial court found to be wrongful diversion of $90,000 of corporate funds.

BURGE, CIRCUIT JUDGE.   The trial court found a pattern of conduct by the dominant stockholders, and a disposition on their part to continue the pattern, which was seriously prejudicial to the rights and interests of the minority. The court also found there was no readily available market for the stock of the minority. In these circumstances the cumulative effect of the challenged conduct of the majority and the resulting dissensions justified the drastic remedy the trial court applied. A "court of equity has inherent power to appoint a receiver to liquidate a corporation . . . where . . . abuse of trust is present whether or not insolvency is likewise present."

Shareholder Liability

Shareholder Liability on Shares. A shareholder is liable to the corporation on his share subscription contract, and a receiver or trustee of an insolvent corporation may recover the unpaid balance for the benefit of creditors. However, if he has paid the agreed price for nonassessable shares and that price is lawful, he is not liable to creditors' claims. The Model Act (23) makes all paid up shares nonassessable, that is not subject to further call for contribution, but at one time it was common for bank shares to be assessable. If the stock is "watered," that is, less than lawful consideration was given for it, then the shareholder is likely to be held liable either to the corporation or to creditors for the difference between what he paid and what would constitute lawful payment. In the absence of statute, courts apply several different theories which result in different conclusions in some situations.

Statutes also vary. The Model Act (18) recognizes neither promissory notes nor future services as payment for shares, but property and services actually performed are valid consideration. It makes the judgment of directors or shareholders as to the value of property or services received for shares conclusive in the absence of fraud.

The record holder of the shares is usually the one subject to shareholder liabilities. A transferee who in good faith believes that full consideration has been paid is not liable to the corporation or its creditors for any unpaid portion of the consideration (23).

Shareholder Liability on Illegal Dividends and Distributions. Dividends received by a shareholder with knowledge of their illegality may be recovered on behalf of the corporation even though he had no part in their declaration. However, despite lack of knowledge of the illegality, a shareholder is liable for a dividend received if the corporation were insolvent at the time the dividend was declared. Under the Model Act (43) primary liability is placed upon the directors who declared the dividend. However, any director against whom a claim is asserted for the wrongful payment of a dividend or distribution of assets of the corporation is entitled to contribution from shareholders who received a dividend or distribution knowing it was illegally declared.

Other Bases for Shareholder Liability. Four states impose personal liability on shareholders for wages due to corporate employees even though their shares are fully paid and nonassessable. They are Michigan,[8] New York,[9] Tennessee,[10] and Wisconsin.[11] Two other states recently rescinded such liability. Wisconsin limits liability to the par value of the stock or issue price for no-par stock. New York by a recent statutory change limits liability to the 10 largest shareholders and then only of corporations whose shares are not dealt in publicly. Michigan and Tennessee establish no limits on liability. In several states shareholders may be held liable for corporate debts if business is commenced before the required capital is paid in or the certificate of incorporation filed.

Summary

The shareholder remains liable to the corporation on any unpaid portion of his subscription and may become liable on "watered" stock. Creditors may enforce the right of the corporation.

Dividends received by a shareholder knowing of their illegality may be recovered on behalf of the corporation. Four states impose personal liability on shareholders for wages due to corporate employees even though their shares are fully paid.

United States v. *Seyler*

142 Fed.Supp. 408 (W.D. Pa. 1956)

This was an action by the United States (plaintiff) against Seyler and Beary (defendants) as shareholders to recover unpaid income taxes assessed against the Seekay Sales Engineering Company, Inc. Judgment for the United States.

Seyler and Beary were the principal shareholders of Seekay, Inc. During the year 1945 the corporation paid cash dividends of more than $55,000 which rendered the corporation insolvent. The income tax assessment on the corporation for its fiscal year ending June 30, 1945 exceeded $22,000.

MARSH, DISTRICT JUDGE. When a corporation is made insolvent by a transfer of assets to its stockholders, each stockholder is liable to creditors for the full extent of the amount received by him.

A subsequently assessed tax is a potential liability of a corporation of which stockholders may be charged with notice.

A transferee of assets of an insolvent corporation, charged with notice of a potential liability of the corporation, is liable for that potential liability to the full extent of the amount received by him.

---

[8] Michigan Comp. Laws 27 A.2908–2909.
[9] McKinney's N.Y. Bus. Corp. Law §§504(1), 628a.
[10] Tenn. Code Ann. §48–710.
[11] Wisc. Stat. Ann §180.40(6).

Problem Cases

1. Directors of a personal holding company on April 17 declared a dividend payable on May 10 to shareholders then of record. On May 9, the principal shareholders gave shares of the stock to their children and the dividends were paid to the children. The children reported and paid tax on the dividends as their income. The Commissioner of Internal Revenue assessed the parents for tax on the dividends as being their income. Is the Commissioner correct?

2. Five directors were to be elected at a shareholders' meeting of Standard Power & Light Corp., three by holders of $1 par value common stock and two by the holders of the Series B no-par common stock. A proxy fight developed with opposing slates of nominees for the two Series B directors. The vote was 40,828 votes each for the two management nominees and 42,519 each for the opposition nominees. There were 110,000 shares of Series B stock outstanding. The chairman of the meeting announced that a majority of the shares outstanding was required for election and since none of the candidates received a majority, the incumbents, who were also the management nominees, would remain in office. The articles of incorporation provided, "The holders of the Common Stock Series B shall have the right by the vote of a majority in number of shares of the Common Stock Series B issued and outstanding to elect a minority in number of the full board of directors of the corporation." Was the ruling of the chairman correct?

3. Copeland Corporation proposed a bylaw amendment which would substitute a classified board of directors, with three classes of three members each, for the existing nine-man board elected annually. At the annual meeting the amendment was approved and three board members elected for one year terms, three for two years, and three for three years. The amendment provided that at all subsequent annual elections, three directors would be elected for three-year terms.

   McDonough, representing the cumulative voting minority stockholders, sought to invalidate the amendment and maintain the minority voting power by claiming the protection of a Michigan statute which provided that "the number of directors of any corporation shall not be reduced in case the votes of a sufficient number of shares are recorded against such proposed reduction, which, if cumulatively voted, would elect one or more directors (but would be insufficient to elect the same number of directors on the reduced board)." Should summary judgment be granted Copeland on the basis of its argument that the number of directors has not been reduced?

4. Norton, a corporate director of Sweet Grass, and Port, a shareholder, solicited proxies for use at the annual meeting. The proxies were to be used in an attempt to prevent approval of a proposed corporate financing plan. In soliciting the proxies, Norton and Post made use of a leaflet quoting certain parts of a letter from the corporate counsel, Brussel, to the corporation president, in which he advised that the proposal seemed to be an unfair dilution of present shareholder's interests. Norton and Port deleted portions from this letter which advocated an alternative plan giving additional rights to current shareholders and concluded in the leaflet that Brussel "obviously had no stomach for this deal." In fact the plan had already been amended, prior to approval by the board of directors, to include the additional rights suggested by Brussel. The Norton-Port leaflet also stated that Brussel, acting as a director, "did not vote for" the proposal. In fact, Brussel was not present at the meeting when the proposal was

approved for submission to the shareholders. Should the court enjoin voting of the proxies based on the claim of other corporate directors that the proxies were obtained by fraud?

5. Camden Grocers Exchange was reorganized and operated on a cooperative plan in 1941. After the reorganization, the stock of the corporation, with the exception of a relatively small number of shares owned by the original shareholders, was owned by retail grocers. Under the cooperative plan, each shareholder who was also a customer of the company was refunded an amount equal to a certain percentage of his purchases. The directors determined the amount of the rebate. Some years it was 2 percent; other years the percentage was lower. Regular dividends of from $6 to $8 a share were paid on the stock from 1941 to the time of bringing suit. A surplus had also been built up, and the book value of the stock was 50 percent greater than in 1941. Klein claims that the giving of the rebate is a scheme to pay a larger dividend to certain holders of the same class of stock, and is illegal. Is Klein correct?

6. Keller Industries entered into an agreement with Fineberg and others to purchase all the issued common stock of Chemical Industries, Inc. In exchange, Fineberg was to receive 15,000 shares of Keller stock immediately and an additional number of shares in two years to be computed by an agreed upon formula using the original 15,000 shares as a base in computing the total number of shares due Fineberg. The agreement provided that the value of the first 15,000 shares received by Fineberg should not be diminished "by reason of any stock splits or reverse stock splits." Prior to the final settlement date, Keller declared a 20 percent stock dividend and 3,000 shares of Keller stock were thus distributed to Fineberg in addition to the original 15,000 shares. When the settlement date arrived, a dispute arose as to whether Keller was entitled to a credit against the purchase price for the 3,000 shares of stock dividend or whether the dividend was an incident of stock ownership completely independent of the purchase payment computations. Is Keller entitled to withhold the amount represented by the stock dividend?

7. Jones is a retired employee of Ralston Purina, a Missouri corporation, and owns a substantial number of shares of its capital stock. In the course of his employment, he had access to certain corporate documents which he now seeks to examine as a shareholder. The specific documents are known as "The Preliminary," "The Profit Analysis," and "The Balance Sheet." The documents are not final statements but are summarized work sheets reflecting operations within Purina's various divisions. The figures in the preliminary statements are unaudited, are subject to check, verification, and adjustment, and frequently must be changed from month to month. Purina considers the information so confidential that it is released only to each elected officer and director, who must then return the reviewed copies to the comptroller's office. A Missouri statute requires Purina to keep books open to each shareholder showing "records of account," stock ownership and transfer information," and "the amount of its assets and liabilities." Should the court require Purina to produce the requested documents for Jones' inspection?

8. Fuller and Krogh were, except for one share owned by Fuller's wife, the sole shareholders in Cormier Corp. The corporation was formed to furnish a building for a manufacturing corporation owned by the two men. Cormier Corp. was undercapitalized and the contractor quit because it was unable to pay him the monthly progress payments. Krogh took over the responsibility for completing the building in 1954. Prior to this time each of the parties had invested equal amounts and had been issued 218 shares of stock. Thereafter, Fuller was financially unable to pay his half of the

costs incurred on the building and Krogh accepted additional shares in lieu of cash payments for the materials, labor and supervision he furnished the corporation. As president of the corporation, Fuller signed the certificates issued to Krogh. By July, 1955, Fuller owned 244 shares and Krogh 527 shares. Fuller claims a preemptive right to purchase enough shares to equalize ownership. Is Fuller entitled to do so?

9. Marks was a shareholder of Universal Pictures, Inc., which had agreed to a short-form merger into Universal City Studios, Inc. A Delaware statute provides that notice of a short-form merger shall be sent to shareholders of the merging corporation. Thereafter, any dissatisfied shareholder, within 20 days after the date of notice, may object in writing to the merger, and may demand payment for his stock from the surviving corporation. If these conditions are met, the shareholder has established the necessary foundation for a right of appraisal.

   Marks sent a letter within the 20-day requirement, which stated: "It is our opinion that your tender offer of $75 per share is most unrealistic, and you may be certain that we will do everything in our power to prevent what we consider to be a confiscation of our property without due process of law." Marks later files a petition for appraisal of the stock. Should the court order an appraisal?

10. Lakeland Development Corporation owned 18 acres in the suburban area of Minneapolis suitable as a shopping center site. It engaged in no other activity. Real estate taxes amounted to approximately $800 per year and income from billboards was approximately $450. The corporation had also incurred legal expenses in connection with tax and condemnation proceedings. Stock in the corporation was owned by two brothers, James and David Anderson. James wished to sell and David to hold the land for further appreciation in value. As a result of disagreement no corporate meetings had been held and taxes had not been paid for the last three years. A professional appraiser estimated the value at from $125,000 to $150,000. However, an interested purchaser had refused to buy it at $125,000 but had offered to buy one half for $45,000. James petitioned the court for the appointment of a liquidating receiver under a Minnesota statute providing involuntary dissolution when "there is internal dissention and two or more factions of the shareholders in the corporation are so deadlocked that its business can no longer be conducted with advantage to its shareholders." David objects on grounds that two other brothers were entitled to buy equal amounts of the stock from the present owners and that their acquisition of this stock might break the deadlock and that the annual appreciation of the value of the land exceeded the real estate taxes and special assessments. Would the court appoint a liquidating receiver?

11. Lumber Co. suffered a fire which almost totally destroyed its plant and inventory. It moved its business to another city, certain citizens of which bought $73,000 of its preferred stock. However, the officers, who owned most of the common stock, were unable to borrow sufficient working capital and acute disagreements occurred between the officers and preferred shareholders. Operations were suspended and seven months later the preferred shareholders bring action against the corporation and its officers seeking appointment of a receiver and liquidation, alleging that the officers are mismanaging the corporation and by fraud and collusion are dissipating the corporation's assets. Would a court grant the petition?

12. Aiple brought a shareholder's derivative action against Twin City Barge Co. to prevent the management from increasing its capitalization by methods which the court found to be illegal. He then brings an action against the corporation to recover for his attorney's fees. Is he entitled to a summary judgment?

chapter 28. Foreign Corporations

Rights of Foreign Corporations

Introduction. A corporation is a "domestic corporation" in the state or country which has granted it its charter and is a "foreign corporation" in all other states, territories, countries, or subdivisions of countries. It may not be a "domestic corporation" in more than one state.

A corporation has no right to transact business except in interstate commerce in a state other than the one granting its charter. However, all states permit foreign corporations to become "authorized" (licensed or qualified) to do intrastate business within the state upon compliance with general statutes. They may impose in such statutes any reasonable condition upon foreign corporations seeking the privilege to do intrastate business.

Under the Commerce Clause of the Constitution the power to regulate interstate commerce is given to the federal government, and states have no power to exclude or to discriminate against foreign corporations which are engaged solely in interstate commerce. Nor can a state deny a foreign corporation due process of law or equal protection of the laws if it is admitted to do intrastate business. However, even if it is engaged only in interstate commerce, a foreign corporation is subject to nondiscriminatory regulations of business activities such as sanitary standards for food products, regulations on truck size and usury laws, and under recent Supreme Court decisions, it is subject to a suit in the state growing out of its activities and to taxation.

The Model Act. The provisions which apply to foreign corporations in the Model Business Corporation Act are set out in Sections 99 to 117. Similar to most such statutes, Section 103 requires the foreign corporation to apply for a certificate of authority from the Secretary of State, giving information similar to that required in an application for a charter from a domestic corporation and to file a copy of its articles.

The foreign corporation must maintain a registered office and a registered agent upon whom service of process upon the corporation may be served. The registered agent may be and frequently is a corporation which makes a business of providing such representation. The foreign corporation must also make an annual report.

A license fee, based upon the number of authorized shares of stock of the corporation apportioned according to the relative value of its property located in the state and outside and its gross income inside and outside of the state, must be paid at the time of filing for certificate of authority to do business in the state. An additional license fee is required when the articles are amended to authorize additional shares. In addition, a franchise tax is payable annually based upon the proportion of its property in and business done within the state.

If the taxes are not paid, if the reports are not submitted or other requirements are not met, the Secretary of State, under the Model Act and most state statutes, may revoke the certificate of authority of the foreign corporation to do business in the state. The penalties for failing to obtain a certificate of authority when required are discussed later in the chapter.

Summary

A corporation is a "domestic corporation" in the state which grants it its charter and a "foreign corporation" elsewhere. A corporation has a right to engage in intrastate business only in the state granting its charter, but it has a right under the Commerce Clause to conduct interstate business throughout the country.

To qualify to do intrastate business a foreign corporation must apply for a certificate of authority giving information similar to that required of a domestic corporation seeking a charter and must maintain a registered agent within the state. License and franchise fees must be paid to the state in which it is qualified.

"Doing Business"

Introduction.   The courts recognize three general types of "doing business" by foreign corporations. They are: (1) that which subjects the foreign corporation to suit in the state courts, (2) that which subjects the foreign corporation to taxation by the state, and (3) that which requires that the foreign corporation comply with statutes granting it permission to do intrastate business in the state. More business activity within a state is required to subject a corporation to admission (or qualification or license) as a foreign corporation than for either service of process or taxation, but it is difficult to say today that more activities are necessary to subject the foreign corporation to taxation than to subject it to service of process. Although there have been literally thousands of cases, clear standards have not been arrived at by the courts in any one of the three catetgories. What is "doing business" is a question of fact determined by all the circumstances in a particular case and apparently inconsistent decisions by the same court are not infrequent. The trend has been to require fewer local activities for any of the three types than in earlier times.

Subjecting Foreign Corporations to Suit. The leading case on the issue whether a foreign corporation can be hailed into court in the state is *International Shoe Company* v. *State of Washington*.[1] There the court rejected the traditional "doing business" test and held that an unlicensed foreign corporation could be subjected to suit if to do so would not offend traditional notions of fair play and substantial justice. Jurisdiction of the state court depends, under this decision, as much upon matters of convenience to the parties, location of witneseses and the expense of producing them within the state and the place where the events leading up to the suit took place as upon the extent of business activities within the state. Some local activity, or "minimum contacts" with the state, by the corporation are necessary, however, to give the state courts jurisdiction and then only with respect to a suit based upon or resulting from those contacts.

As a result of this decision, most states have passed so-called "long-arm" statutes to take advantage of the broadened jurisdictional power permitted in the *International Shoe* case. These give the local courts jurisdiction over unqualified foreign corporations when only a single contract has been entered into or a single tort committed. Usually, only residents of the state are permitted to sue under these expanded jurisdiction statutes. They generally provide for service of process upon the Secretary of State.

Taxing Foreign Corporations. A foreign corporation which is not required to apply for a certificate of authority to do business within the state may be subject to taxation by that state. There has never been any doubt that the property of the corporation stored in or otherwise located in the state is subject to taxation even though it is used in carrying on the corporation's interstate business.

More troublesome for the courts have been attempts by states to impose income taxes upon foreign corporations conducting only an interstate business and, therefore, not required to obtain a certificate of authority. The Supreme Court had tended toward permitting taxation with fewer and fewer activities within the state until its decision in *Northwestern States Portland Cement Co.* v. *Minnesota*.[2] In that case the court upheld the imposition by Minnesota of an apportioned, nondiscriminatory net income tax on a corporation engaged

---

[1] *International Shoe Co.* v. *State of Washington*, 326 U.S. 310 (1945).
[2] *Northwestern States Portland Cement Co.* v. *State of Minnesota*, 358 U.S. 450 (1959).

solely in interstate commerce in Minnesota and which had not qualified in Minnesota as a foreign corporation.

As a result of what it appeared to think was a too liberal decision by the court, Congress enacted the Federal Interstate Income Law [3] in 1959. It prohibits taxing bodies, state or local, from imposing net income taxes on income which is derived from interstate commerce in which the only activity in the taxing jurisdiction is the solicitation of orders to be accepted and shipped from another state. Also under the act a foreign corporation may employ an independent contractor who represents more than one principal as sales agent, even if he has an office in the state, without becoming subject to taxation.

Admission of a Foreign Corporation.   Subjection of the foreign corporation to the necessity of becoming domesticated (being admitted or qualifying) is dependent upon the wording of the statute, but so long as it limits its activities in the state to interstate commerce, it is protected by the Constitution from the necessity of obtaining a certificate of admission. The Supreme Court, of course, has the final determination of what constitutes interstate commerce.

The Model Act (99) [4] provides that "no foreign corporation shall have the right to transact business in this State until it shall have procured authority to do so. . . ." It then lists a number of activities which the foreign corporation may carry on which will not be considered transacting business for the purposes of the act. These activities include: bringing or defending suit, holding corporate meetings, maintaining bank accounts, soliciting sales through independent contractors, soliciting orders by mail or agents if the orders require acceptance outside of the state, collecting debts, conducting isolated transactions completed within 30 days if they are not in the course of a number of repeated transactions of like nature, as well as transacting business in interstate commerce.

It is difficult to state a general rule as to what activities constitute intrastate commerce. The following frequently quoted rule hardly seems to clarify the matter: "A foreign corporation is doing, transacting, carrying on, or engaging in business within a state when it transacts some substantial part of its ordinary business therein." [5] Generally, the maintenance of a stock of goods within a state even though the orders filled from the stock are accepted outside the state is treated as doing business. Even peddling goods from a truck sent in from outside the state or mere ownership of real estate have been held to require qualification. Statutory definitions such as Section 99 of the Model Act may not reach as far in requiring qualification as the Constitution has been interpreted to permit.

Penalty for Failure to Obtain Permission.   Generally, the states impose

---

[3] U.S.C. §§381–384.

[4] The numbers in parentheses refer to the sections of the Model Business Corporation Act.

[5] *Royal Insurance Co.* v. *All States Theatres,* 6 So.2d 494 (Sup. Ct. Ala. 1942).

by statute a penalty on foreign corporations which do intrastate business without first obtaining permission. They may, for instance, impose a fine on the corporation or on its agent in the state; they may hold the officers and stockholders liable as partners on all intrastate business; they may deny the corporation the right to bring suit in the state courts to enforce contracts entered into with residents of the state; or they may declare that intrastate contracts made by the corporation are void. Generally, if a corporation complies with the statute of the state after having transacted intrastate business without obtaining permission, such compliance will be retroactive and will cure the defect in such prior transactions.

In two states,[6] the nonqualifying corporation may not even defend a suit brought against it until it has qualified. The inability to bring a suit on a contract or tort in the particular jurisdiction may mean, practically, that the suit cannot be brought at all if jurisdiction over the defendant can be obtained only in that state.

Under the majority rule, if the intrastate contracts of a foreign corporation doing business in a state without having qualified are declared to be void by the state statute, such contracts are not enforceable by the corporation but may be enforced against it. These statutes are for the protection of the public; if the corporation were permitted to set up illegality as a defense to such contracts, it would be taking advantage of its own wrong, and the statutes would, in effect, penalize rather than protect the public.

Summary

The courts recognize three general types of "doing business" by foreign corporations: (1) that which subjects the foreign corporation to suit in the state courts, (2) that which subjects the foreign corporation to taxation by the state, and (3) that which requires qualification by the foreign corporation. More business activity is necessary to require the corporation to qualify to do intrastate business than for either service of process in a lawsuit or for taxation. There are no clear standards in any of the three situations but the trend has been toward requiring fewer local activities.

Under the most recent decisions of the U.S. Supreme Court, whether a foreign corporation can be subjected to suit within a state depends as much on matters of convenience to the parties as on the extent of the defendant corporation's business activities within the state. A single contract entered into within the state or a single tort committed within the course of the corporation's business within the state, even if the business is essentially interstate, will give jurisdiction to local courts.

The right of a state to take property of a foreign corporation located in the

---

[6] Nevada Rev. Stat., 80.210(1) and Wisconsin Stat. Ann., 180.847.

state even though used solely in carrying on its interstate business has long been upheld. Recent decisions, however, have permitted states to impose income taxes on foreign corporations doing only interstate business, although limitations on such taxation have been established by Congress.

States cannot require qualification by a foreign corporation which does only an interstate business in the state as defined by the Supreme Court in interpreting the Commerce Clause. States frequently penalize foreign corporations which fail to qualify when necessary by denying them the right to bring suit in state courts and/or by fines.

International Shoe Co. v. *State of Washington*
326 U.S. 310 (1945)

This was an action by the Office of Unemployment Compensation and Placement of the State of Washington (plaintiff) against International Shoe Co. (defendant) to recover money alleged due as contributions under the Unemployment Compensation Act. Shoe Co. appealed from a decision of the Washington Supreme Court affirming judgment for the State. Affirmed.

Shoe Co. maintained neither an office nor a stock of goods in Washington, and it made no deliveries in intrastate commerce there. During the years in question it employed eleven to thirteen salesmen in Washington who were under the direct supervision of sales managers located in its headquarters office in St. Louis. The salesmen occasionally rented rooms in hotels or other buildings in which they displayed samples of Shoe Company's merchandise. They solicited orders on terms fixed in St. Louis for acceptance or rejection there. When accepted the merchandise was shipped f.o.b. to the Washington customers from points outside Washington. The salesmen had no authority to make collections and merchandise was invoiced at the place of shipment.

Shoe Co. argued that its activities within the state were not sufficient to manifest its "presence" there and that in its absence the state courts were without jurisdiction, and, therefore, it was a denial of due process for the state to subject it to suit.

STONE, CHIEF JUSTICE.   Due process requires only that in order to subject a defendant to a judgment *in personam,* if he be not present within the territory of the forum, he have certain minimum contacts with it such that the maintenance of the suit does not offend "traditional notions of fair play and substantial justice."

Since the corporate personality is a fiction, although a fiction intended to be acted upon as though it were a fact, it is clear that unlike an individual, its "presence" without, as well as within, the state of its origin can be manifested only by activities carried on in its behalf by those who are authorized to act for it. To say that the corporation is so far "present" there as to satisfy due process requirements, for purposes of taxation or the maintenance of suits against it in the courts of the state, is to beg the question to be decided. For the terms "present" or "presence" are used merely to symbolize those activities of the corporation's agent within the state which courts will deem to be sufficient to satisfy the demands of due process. Those demands may be met by such contacts of the corporation with the state of the forum as to make it reasonable, in the context of our federal system of government, to require the corporation to defend the particular suit which is brought there. An "estimate of the inconveniences" which would result to the corporation from a trial away from its "home" or principal place of business is relevant in this connection.

Finally, although the commission of some single or occasional acts of the corporate agent in a state sufficient to impose an obligation or liability on the corporation has not been thought to confer upon the state authority to enforce it, other such acts, because of their nature and quality and the circumstances of their commission, may be deemed sufficient to render the corporation liable to suit.

Applying these standards, the activities carried on in behalf of International Shoe in the State of Washington were neither irregular nor casual. They were systematic and continuous throughout the years in question. They resulted in a large volume of interstate business, in the course of which International Shoe received the benefits and protection of the laws of the state, including the right to resort to the courts for the enforcement of its rights. The obligation which is here sued upon arose out of those very activities. It is evident that these operations establish sufficient contacts or ties with the state of the forum to make it reasonable and just according to our traditional conception of fair play and substantial justice to permit the state to enforce the obligations which International Shoe has incurred there. Hence we cannot say that the maintenance of the present suit in the State of Washington involves an unreasonable or undue procedure.

Di Giovanni v. *Gittelson*

181 So.2d 195 (D.C. App. Fla. 1966)

This action was brought by Di Giovanni (plaintiff) against Dr. Gittelson and Center Laboratories, Inc. (defendants), for injuries alleged to have resulted from a drug. Dismissal of the action against Center Laboratories for lack of jurisdiction appealed. Reversed and remanded.

Dr. Gittelson desired to use an anti-allergenic drug manufactured by Center Laboratories which was in the "investigative stage" of testing. He took instruction in its use from a physican in Boston and filled out "Investigator's Forms" and then was permitted to buy the drug on condition that he would record the clinical data required by the applicable federal law and forward it within certain time limits to Center Laboratories.

The drug was administered to Di Giovanni by Dr. Gittelson with resulting injurious effects. Center Laboratories was joined in the suit and service of process was accomplished on the Secretary of State of Florida under the provisions of Florida's "long-arm statute." Center Laboratories moved to dismiss on the grounds that it was a New York corporation and did no business in Florida. It had no sales personnel in nor did it advertise in Florida. It did not sell in Florida through brokers or wholesalers and owned or leased no property in Florida. Dr. Gittelson was in private practice and his patients were in no way connected with nor sent to him by Center Laboratories.

HENDRY, CHIEF JUSTICE.   . . . a foreign corporation is doing business in this state for the purpose of § 47.16 if it has some degree of control over the personal property in the hands of the "brokers, jobbers, wholesalers, or distributors," or has some degree of control over the "brokers, jobbers, wholesalers, or distributors" selling or distributing the personal property in this state. The application of this principle must be governed by the factual situation presented by a particular record.

In the *Fawcett* case, the court found that the appellant could exercise "not even a modicum of control" over those to whom it shipped its magazine, and therefore held that the facts were insufficient to justify the method of substituted service prescribed by §§ 47.16 and 47.30. In following cases the courts have denied the use of substituted service after finding "no control" and insufficient evidence to establish control or "even a modicum of control over its products"; however, the use of substituted service was affirmed when it was found that a "degree of control" was exercised.

The facts in this case reveal that Center Laboratories thoroughly examined Dr. Gittelson's qualifications prior to selling the drug to him. After furnishing the drug Center Laboratories required the physician to keep and report clinical data concerning the application and effects of the drug. Center Laboratories insisted that the data be transmitted within a specific time or else further shipment of the drug would be withheld.

We find from the facts presented that Center Laboratories did exercise control over the drug which it sold to Dr. Gittelson and which was subsequently administered to Di Giovanni. We hold that these facts are sufficient to justify the method of substituted service prescribed by §§ 47.16.

Northwestern States Portland Cement Co. v. *State of Minnesota*
358 U.S. 450 (1959)

This action was brought by the state of Minnesota (plaintiff) against Northwestern States Portland Cement Co. (defendant), a foreign corporation, to collect income taxes. Judgment for Minnesota affirmed.

Cement Co. was an Iowa corporation which regularly solicited orders in Minnesota for its products, each order being subject to acceptance, filling and delivery by it from its plant at Mason City, Iowa. It sold only to building material supply houses, contractors and ready-mix companies. Forty-eight percent of its total sales were made in Minnesota in this manner. It leased an office in Minneapolis and furnished it with its own furniture and fixtures. The office was occupied by an employee-salesman designated a "district manager" and two other salesmen and a secretary. Two additional salesmen were supervised from the office. It had not qualified to do business in Minnesota. Cement Co. had no bank account, owned no real estate and warehoused no merchandise in Minnesota but it did furnish two automobiles to its salesmen. It filed no tax returns.

Minnesota imposed a tax upon the taxable net income of four classes of persons, including domestic and foreign corporations whose business consisted "exclusively of foreign commerce, interstate commerce, or both." Ratios were used in determining the portion of net income taxable under the law: proportion of its total sales assignable to Minnesota, proportion of its total tangible property in the state, and proportion of its total payroll in the state.

Cement Co. argued that imposition of the income tax on purely interstate commerce violated the Commerce Clause of the Constitution and also the Due Process Clause of the Fourteenth Amendment.

CLARK, JUSTICE.   The taxes are not regulations in any sense of that term. Admittedly they do not discriminate against nor subject either corporation to an undue burden. While it is true that a State may not erect a wall around its borders preventing commerce an entry, it is axiomatic that the founders did not intend to immunize such commerce from carrying its fair share of the costs of the state government in return for the benefits it derives from within the State. The levies are not privilege taxes based on the right to carry on business in the taxing state. . . .

While the economic wisdom of state net income taxes is one of state policy not for our decision, one of the "realities" raised by the parties is the possibility of a multiple burden resulting from the exactions in question. The answer is that none is shown to exist here. This is not an unapportioned tax which by its very nature makes interstate commerce bear more than its fair share. . . . We cannot deal in abstractions. In this type of case the taxpayers must show that the formula places a burden upon interstate commerce in a constitutional sense. This they have failed to do.

Nor will the argument that the exactions contravene the Due Process Clause bear scrutiny. The taxes imposed are levied only on that portion of the taxpayer's net income which arises from its activities within the taxing State. These activities form a sufficient "nexus between such a tax and transactions within a state for which the tax is an exaction."

Eli Lilly and Company v. *Sav-On-Drugs, Inc.*

366 U.S. 276 (1961)

This was an action brought in New Jersey by Eli Lilly and Company (plaintiff) against Sav-On-Drugs, Inc. (defendant), to enjoin Sav-On, a retailer, from selling Lilly's products at prices lower than fixed under the New Jersey Fair Trade Act. Judgment for Sav-On because Lilly was doing business in New Jersey without being qualified and, therefore, had no standing to sue was affirmed by the New Jersey Supreme Court. Affirmed.

Lilly, an Indiana Corporation, sold its products in interstate commerce to certain selected wholesalers in New Jersey. The wholesalers in turn sold them in intrastate commerce to hospitals, retail drug stores and physicians. Lilly maintained an office in its name in Newark. Its district manager there supervised 18 "detail men" who were paid on a salary basis and whose function it was to visit retail pharmacists, physicians and hospitals to acquaint them with Lilly's products and to encourage them to purchase them from the wholesalers. They also made available to retail druggists, free of charge, advertising and promotional material.

Lilly sought to enjoin Sav-On from selling its products below the Fair Trade prices.

Lilly opposed Sav-On's motion to dismiss and urged that its business in New Jersey was entirely in interstate commerce and that to require it to obtain a certificate for its New Jersey business was forbidden by the Commerce Clause of the Federal Constitution.

BLACK, JUSTICE.   It is well established that New Jersey cannot require Lilly to get a certificate of authority to do business in the State if its participation in this trade is limited to its wholly interstate sales to New Jersey wholesalers. . . . On the other hand, it is equally well settled that if Lilly is engaged in intrastate as well as in interstate aspects of the New Jersey drug business, the State can require it to get a certificate of authority to do business. In such a situation, Lilly could not escape state regulation merely because it is also engaged in interstate commerce.

We agree with the trial court that "[t]o hold under the facts above recited that plaintiff [Lilly] is not doing business in New Jersey is to completely ignore reality." Eighteen "detailmen," working out of a big office in Newark, New Jersey, with Lilly's name on the door and in the lobby of the building, and with Lilly's district manager and secretary in charge, have been regularly engaged in work for Lilly which relates directly to the intrastate aspects of the sale of Lilly's products. These eighteen "detailmen" have been traveling throughout the State of New Jersey promoting the sales of Lilly's products, not to the wholesalers, Lilly's interstate customers, but to the physicians, hospitals and retailers who buy those products in intrastate commerce from the wholesalers. . . . And they sometimes even directly participate in the intrastate sales themselves by transmitting orders from the hospitals, physicians and drugstores they service to the New Jersey wholesalers.

Problem Cases

1. Bolger was Dial-A-Style's agent in promoting and selling its services and equipment to beauty parlors in Colorado. Bolger, as a result of false representations regarding his employment contract, filed suit against Dial-A-Style and its parent company, Beauty Industries, both New York companies. Thereafter, both Dial-A-Style and Beauty Industries appeared specially and moved to quash service of process on the basis that neither company transacted sufficient business in Colorado to render them subject to service in that state.

   The only direct contacts that the parent company, Beauty Industries, had in Colorado were an advertisement of Dial-A-Style franchises published in *The Wall Street*

Journal, one of Dial-A-Style billings to Bolger made on Beauty Industries stationery, and one written notice publicizing the beauty aid process in Colorado. If Dial-A-Style is found to be doing sufficient business to allow substituted service of process, is Beauty Industries, as parent corporation, also amenable to Colorado jurisdiction?

2. Nelson, Inc., manufactured electrical testing equipment at its plant in Iowa. This equipment was sold in Wisconsin through a dealer operating under an "Independent Dealer's Contract." The dealer, who resided permanently in Wisconsin, was required to pay cash for all merchandise ordered, devote full time to Nelson sales, report sales progress twice monthly to Nelson, maintain minimum sales requirements, validate company's customer guarantees, and establish service facilities for Nelson products.

    Mrs. Dettman had summons served on Nelson at the plant in Iowa to commence suit in the Wisconsin courts for the wrongful death of her husband, who was electrocuted while using a Nelson tester. Nelson appeared specially and made a motion to have summons quashed on the grounds that the dealer was an independent contractor, and, therefore, Nelson was not doing business in Wisconsin and could not be required to appear. Is this contention correct?

3. Jackson, a Wyoming resident, sued Joyner for breach of a contract to remodel a building in Wyoming. Joyner was president of Perma Shade, a Utah corporation not qualified to do business in Wyoming, which had entered into the remodeling contract with Jackson.

    The court awarded judgment to Jackson, and Joyner appealed claiming that the court should have dismissed the action because Perma Shade was not joined as a party. Was the lower court correct in not requiring joinder of Perma Shade and in holding Joyner personally liable for breach of the contract between Jackson and Perma Shade?

4. Virginia imposed a franchise tax laid on the intangible property of express companies operating within the state in lieu of taxes on its other intangible property and rolling stock. It was intended to tax their "going concern" value and was measured by gross receipts on business beginning or ending within the state and transportation through the state. Railway Express did its intrastate business in Virginia through a wholly owned domestic subsidiary so that the parent's business was exclusively interstate in nature. Railway Express claimed the tax violated both the Commerce Clause and the Due Process Clause of the 14th Amendment and was the same tax as a "privilege tax" declared unconstitutional earlier. Should Railway Express' contention be upheld?

5. Nebraska sought to impose its personal property tax on the airplanes of Mid-Continent Airlines (later merged with Braniff Airways). By its terms the tax applied only to regularly scheduled airlines and was apportioned using ratios relating activities in Nebraska to activities everywhere. The following three factors were used: the number of arrivals and departures during the year, revenue tons handled at airports, and originating revenue. The equipment was all used in interstate commerce and made 4 stops a day at Lincoln and 14 per day at Omaha. The stops lasted for periods of from 5 to 20 minutes each except for one plane which remained overnight in Nebraska. The carrier's overhaul base was in Minnesota and it was incorporated in Delaware.

    Is the tax unconstitutional as a burden on interstate commerce or as a violation of the due process clause of the 14th Amendment because of a lack of a "tax situs?"

6. Brown, a Kentucky distilling corporation, sued the Louisiana Collector of Revenue to recover state income taxes paid on Brown's earnings from activities in Louisiana. Brown maintained that it was engaged solely in interstate commerce, that it shipped goods to customers in Louisiana on orders submitted by "missionary men" who sent

orders to Louisville for acceptance or rejection, that the merchandise was shipped directly to the customers who remitted payment to Louisville, and that no warehouse or stock of goods was maintained in Louisiana. Is the income tax an unconstitutional burden on interstate commerce?

7. National is a mail-order house with its principal place of business in Missouri. It has neither outlets nor sales representatives in Illinois, but conducts business with Illinois customers via twice a year catalog mailings and supplemental flyers. Orders are mailed by customers to National in Missouri and are shipped direct from the plant by mail or common carrier.

   Under an Illinois statute, National is classified as a retailer maintaining a place of business within the state by reason of "engaging in soliciting orders within this state from users by means of catalogs or other advertising, whether such orders are received or accepted within or without this state." The statute requires collection and payment to Illinois of a use tax imposed upon customers who purchase goods for use within the state. Can Illinois require National to collect the tax?

8. Electromelt, a foreign corporation, brought action against City Glass for breach of contract in connection with its installation of a "booster melting system" in City's plant. City moved to dismiss on the ground that Electromelt, not having qualified to do business in West Virginia, was precluded from bringing action in that state.

   The applicable West Virginia statute provides: "No corporation chartered under the laws of any other state or jurisdiction shall hold any property or transact any business or bring or maintain any action, suit, or proceeding in this state without having complied with the requirements hereinbefore stated." Electromelt argued that its operation in the state consisted only of isolated or sporadic acts which did not constitute doing business in the state. Should the suit be dismissed?

9. Publishing Co., domiciled in New York, regularly sold its books in the State of Washington. The orders were taken by another corporation which sent them for acceptance to Publishing Co.'s home office in New York. The books were then shipped by mail from New York. Kuntz purchased some books and gave a promissory note in favor of Publishing Co. but defaulted after two payments. When Publishing Co. brought suit, Kuntz defended on the ground that Publishing Co. had failed to qualify and pay a license fee in the State of Washington. Can Publishing Co. maintain the suit?

10. On December 1, 1959, Neiderhiser entered into a franchise agreement with Henry's, an Illinois corporation, for the operation of a drive-in restaurant in Arizona. Henry's had previously leased the land for the restaurant and the contract provided for a sublease of a completed restaurant to Neiderhiser. On December 14, 1959, Henry's qualified to do business in Arizona. The restaurant was completed on May 1, at which time Henry's gave Neiderhiser notice to perform the contract. Neiderhiser repudiated the contract and sued for the return of his deposit money.

    When sued on the contract, Neiderhiser claims that the contract is void because Henry's failed to qualify to do business in Arizona prior to signing the contract. The applicable statute provides, "A foreign corporation before entering upon, doing or transacting any business, conducting any enterprise, or engaging in any occupation in this state shall (file its articles of incorporation, etc.)." Is Neiderhiser's defense good?

PART VII *Property*

PART VII

chapter 29. Personal Property

Nature and Classification

Nature of Property. Property or ownership may be defined as the exclusive right to possess, enjoy, and dispose of objects or rights having economic value. Property, in its legal sense, has a variety of meanings. It may refer to an object having a physical existence; it may refer to legal rights connected with and growing out of an object having physical existence; or it may refer to legal rights which are of economic value but not connected with a physical object.

A tract of land is property. If the owner leases the land, the lease is also property. The lease grants to the lessee the right to use the land, a right connected with and growing out of the physical object of land. A patent right is property; yet the patent right does not refer to or grow out of a physical object.

In the United States the legal concept of property is synonymous with ownership. To have property in the legal sense, it is necessary to have an organized society which has developed some concepts and some laws relative to property and ownership. A careful analysis of our concepts of property and ownership reveals that property or ownership is based on a bundle of legal rights recognized and enforced by society. We commonly refer to the physical object or to the specific right as the property, but from a legal sense, property is the right to the physical object or the right to enjoy the benefits flowing from the exercise of the specific right.

For example, we say that the house is John's property. From a legal standpoint the physical object is not property. The property is really the legal right which John has to use, enjoy, sell, mortgage, or rent the physical object, the house. Likewise, we say the patent is John's property. A patent has no physical existence. It is a bundle of rights which protects one in the enjoyment of the benefits flowing from the exclusive right to reproduce the patented object. The owner of the patent may sell the patent, he may license others to produce the patented article, or he may produce it himself. The total of these rights is the patent.

Under our free competitive society, private ownership of property is of primary importance. This concept is written into the Constitution of the United States. The 14th Amendment provides that no state shall "deprive any person of life, liberty or property without due process of law." We recognize and protect the individual in his right to acquire, enjoy, and dispose of property; yet we do not grant anyone unlimited property rights. Under the philosophy of a free competitive society the individual is encouraged to use his best efforts to produce; and our laws are framed to secure the fruits of his labors to one who has produced something beneficial to society. We also recognize that if each individual is to reap the greatest reward for his efforts, restrictions are necessary; consequently, one must pursue a course which does not deprive other individuals in society of their right of freedom of action. Our property laws have developed out of this philosophy of a free competitive society.

Possession.   The importance of possession in the law of property is indicated in the old saying, "Possession is nine points of the law." In any primitive society, possession is the equivalent of ownership. In the development of our law the courts have held that in a case of violation of property rights, the right violated is the right of peaceful possession, not the right of ownership. For example, the action of replevin is an action to recover possession of personal property. Ownership is important only as evidence of the right to the possession of the property. Today the courts recognize the importance of possession. In both the law of personal property and the law of real property, a person who buys property acquires ownership "subject to the rights of the party in possession." Possession indicates to all the world that the possessor has some property rights in the thing he possesses.

In our modern society, possession is used with such a variety of meanings that it is futile to attempt to define it in precise terms. In its simplest sense, possession signifies that a person has manual control over a physical object; however, in law this simple concept is inadequate. In connection with possession of personal property, two elements are of general importance: (1) manual control and (2) intent to claim property rights. The courts recognize legal possession, which is the legal right to control the physical object; manual control is not an essential element of legal possession. If a person is wearing his watch, he has both legal and manual control of the watch. He has possession of the watch in the popular sense of the word, and he also has legal possession. If he leaves his watch in his house while he is on vacation, he does not have manual control of the watch but does have legal control. He has legal possession, and anyone taking the watch from his house without his consent has invaded his right of possession.

A servant or an agent may have manual control of his employer's or principal's property yet not have legal possession of the property. The servant or agent has only custody of the property; the employer or principal has legal possession. For example, if a storekeeper gives a clerk the day's receipts to count in the storekeeper's presence, the clerk has custody of the receipts, but the storekeeper has legal possession.

The term "possession," when used in the abstract, includes such a multiplicity of situations that it loses its significance. Possession may indicate one factual and legal situation when we say that "to have a valid levy of execution, the sheriff must take possession of the property," another when we say that "to create a bailment of property, possession must be delivered to the bailee," and still another when we say that "the crime of larceny involves the felonious taking possession and carrying away of another's property."

Real and Personal Property. Because of the breadth of the subject of property and the varied incidents of ownership, property has been divided into various classes. These classes are not mutually exclusive; the same piece of property may, owing to its various characteristics, fall into more than one classification.

The most important classification is that of "real" and "personal" property. The earth's crust and all things firmly attached thereto are real property, while all other objects and rights capable of ownership are personal property; or, in other words, immovables are real property, and movables are personal property. This classification is both historical and logical. Property which can accompany the person of the owner and is consumable is naturally distinguished from property which is fixed and which continues for generation after generation.

Although the distinction as stated is simple, the problems arising are frequently complex because that which is real property can be converted into personal property by severance and that which is personal property can be converted into real property by attachment. Stone in the ground is real property, but when quarried, it becomes personal property; and if it is used in the construction of a building, it will again become real property. Perennial products, such as trees, grass, and fruit trees which need not be seeded each year, are, as a general rule, treated as part of the land. Crops resulting from annual labor, such as potatoes, corn, oats, and annual vegetables are in many cases treated as personal property, although generally they pass with the land. If perennial products are severed from the land, they become personal property. Some courts have held that an intent to sever and a dealing with the product as though severed is a legal severance and converts a product otherwise real property into personal property.

Tangible and Intangible Property. Property may be classed as "tangible" or "intangible"—sometimes termed "corporeal" or "incorporeal." The basis for classifying property as tangible or intangible is the physical nature of the property. Property which has a physical existence, such as land, buildings, and furniture is tangible; and property which has no physical existence, such as patent rights, easements, and bonds is intangible. This distinction is important in determining the right to tax, in the probating of estates, and in similar situations. As a general rule, tangible property is subject to taxation by the state in which it is located, whereas intangible property is taxable at the domicile (home) of the owner.

Public and Private Property.   Property is also classed as "public" or "private." The classification of property into public and private is based on the ownership of the property. If the property is owned by the government or a political division thereof, it is classed as public property; but if the property is owned by an individual, a group of individuals, a corporation, or some other business organization, it is classed as private property. The fact that property privately owned is devoted to a public use or is used to benefit a large class of persons does not change its nature so as to convert it into public property. Property owned by a municipal corporation, such as a city park, city hall, or municipal auditorium, is public property.

Summary

Property, or more specifically ownership, is the exclusive right to possess, enjoy, and dispose of objects or rights having economic value. In law, property is a bundle of legal rights to things having economic value, which rights are recognized and protected by society.

The concept of possession is of outstanding importance in our society; however, possession is used with such a variety of meanings that it is futile to attempt to define it in precise terms. Basically, it is the right to control things having physical existence.

Property is classified according to its various characteristics. The earth's crust and all things firmly attached thereto are classed as real property; all other objects and rights subject to ownership are classed as personal property.

Those things which have a physical existence are classed as tangible or corporeal property. Rights which have economic value but which are not related to things having a physical existence and rest solely in contemplation of law are classed as intangible or incorporeal property.

Property owned by the government or a government unit is classed as public property, whereas property owned by any person or association, even though used exclusively for public purposes, is classed as private property.

Acquisition of Personal Property

Production or Purchase.   A person owns the product of his own labors unless he has agreed to perform labor for another, in which event the employer is the owner of the product of the labors. This rule of law is so well-established and so generally accepted in the United States that it is almost never the subject of litigation.

The commonest means of acquiring ownership of personal property, other than by production, is by purchase. A special body of law regarding the purchase and sale of personal property has been developed which is treated under the heading of "Sales."

Taking Possession. Ownership of personal property was acquired, in the very early times, by taking possession of property which was unowned. This right to acquire ownership of unowned property by taking possession thereof is recognized today; however, it is of relatively little importance in modern society. Wildlife and abandoned property are classed as unowned property, and the first person to take possession of such property becomes the owner thereof. For example, a person who catches a wild animal becomes the owner thereof.

To acquire ownership of a wild animal by taking possession thereof, a person must attain such a degree of control over it as will deprive it of its freedom. Manual control is not necessary. For instance, the courts have held that a mortally wounded animal becomes the property of the person wounding it, even though he has not as yet obtained manual control of it. Animals in a trap or fish in a net have been held to be the property of the person who set the trap or net.

If a captured animal escapes and is again caught by another person, that person becomes the owner unless he knows that the animal is an escaped animal and that the prior owner is pursuing it with the intent of recapturing it. The courts have held that if an escaped animal is not native to the area, a person who captures it does not acquire ownership.

If property is abandoned by the owner, it then becomes unowned property, and the first person who takes possession of it with the intention of claiming ownership thereof becomes the owner of it. For example, if Abbott discards a clock on the public dump and Birge takes it from the dump and claims ownership of it, the clock then becomes the property of Birge.

Gift. A gift is a voluntary transfer of property by one person to another without any consideration being given for the transfer. To make a valid gift, the donor must presently deliver the property to the donee or to some third person, who holds the property for the donee, and this delivery must be unconditional and must be made with the intent of vesting ownership in the donee. Delivery is the transfer of possession from one person to another, and, as a general rule, there can be no gift without delivery. If the delivery is to a third person, who holds for the donee, the delivery must be made with the intent of divesting the donor of all rights in the property. After the delivery the third person must hold the property as trustee for the donee. If the donor reserves rights in the property, the third person will be held to hold as agent for the donor, and a valid gift will not result.

If the donee is already in possession of the property, a clear declaration by the donor that he gives the property to the donee is sufficient to make the gift valid. In some instances the courts have recognized symbolic delivery. For example, the delivery of the keys to a strongbox is symbolic delivery of the contents of the strongbox.

A gift of intangible property requires the execution and delivery of a certificate of gift. If the intangible property is evidenced by a stock certificate or a negotiable instrument, the delivery of the stock certificate or the negotiable instrument properly endorsed, if endorsement is required, is sufficient delivery.

Two types of gifts are recognized: gifts *inter vivos,* and gifts *causa mortis.* A gift *inter vivos* is a gift between living persons; a gift *causa mortis* is a gift in contemplation of death. A gift *causa mortis* has some of the elements of a testamentary disposition of property.

If a gift *causa mortis* is to be valid, the donor must make the gift in contemplation of death in the immediate future, and he must comply with all the requirements for a valid *inter vivos* gift. However, the gift *causa mortis* is a conditional gift and is subject to three conditions implied by law, the occurrence of any one of which will defeat the gift: (1) recovery of the donor from the peril or sickness under fear of which the gift was made, (2) revocation of the gift by the donee before his death, and (3) death of the donee before the donor. When one of these events takes place, title and the right to possession are immediately revested in the donor.

Lost Property.   Lost property becomes the property of the finder as against all persons except the original owner. If Abbott loses his ring and Birge finds it, and later Birge loses the ring and Crum finds it, Birge may claim the ring from Crum; but Abbott, the original owner, has the superior right to the ring and may claim it from either Birge or Crum.

If the finder of lost property knows the identity of the person who lost it yet appropriates it to his own use, he is guilty of larceny. If he does not know the identity of the owner and does not have reasonable means of discovering his identity and appropriates the property to his own use, he will be liable to the owner in conversion for the value of the property if the owner later proves his right to it. Some states have enacted statutes which permit the finder of lost property to clear his title thereto by complying with the statutory procedure.

The courts have made a distinction between lost property and mislaid property. If Abbott, while in Birge's store, drops his wallet in the aisle, the wallet will generally be classed as lost property; but if he lays it on the counter and, forgetting it, leaves the store, it will be classed as mislaid property. If the wallet is mislaid, Birge will become bailee thereof. If Crum finds the wallet in the aisle, he will have the right to take possession of it; but if Crum discovers the wallet on the counter, Birge will have the right to take possession of it. The distinction between lost and mislaid property was developed to increase the chance the property would be returned to its real owner where he knowingly placed it down but had forgotten to pick it up and might well be expected to remember later where he had left it and return for it. It is very difficult to distinguish between lost property and misplaced property; consequently, the cases on the subject are not in accord.

Confusion.   Title to personal property may be acquired by confusion or by accession. Confusion of goods is the inseparable intermixture of goods belonging to different owners. For example, suppose crude oil belonging to several persons is mixed in one tank. If the mixing is by common consent or inevitable accident, each party will be deemed the owner of a proportionate part of the mass. If the mixing is by willful, tortious act, the innocent party will be protected, and the entire mass will become the property of the innocent party if such action is necessary to protect his interest. In case of accidental confusion, if one of the owners is guilty of negligence, he will have to bear any loss resulting from the confusion.

Accession.   Literally, "accession" means that something has been added, and as applied to property, it means that new value has been added to existing property by labor or by the addition of other property or by a combination of both. As a general rule the owner of the original property will become the owner of the improvements. If Birge repairs Abbott's automobile by adding some new parts, Abbott will be the owner of the automobile when repaired and will also be the owner of the new parts which Birge has added.

Difficulty arises where one person improves the property of another by labor or by the addition of materials, or both, when the owner has not contracted for or consented to the improvement. The decisions of the courts in regard to the rights of the parties in such a situation are not in accord, and in many respects they are confusing. As a general rule, if one person has tortiously taken property of another and, by his labor or the addition of his materials, or both, improved the property, the owner of the original property may recover it in its improved state and will not be obligated to compensate the tort-feasor for his labor or materials. In developing this rule, the courts have applied the two following familiar principles of law: (1) One may not benefit from his own wrong, and (2) a person who is not guilty of a wrong may not be made a debtor unless he consents thereto. In a few decisions the courts have refused to follow this rule to its logical conclusion and have held that if the value of the improved property is so out of proportion to the value of the original property that to allow the owner to claim it in its improved state would shock the conscience of men, recovery of the property will be denied.

If the person making the improvement honestly but mistakenly believes that he is the owner of the property at the time he makes the improvement, the courts will, as a general rule, permit recovery for the benefits conferred on the true owner of the property as a result of the improvement. If the owner of the property wishes, he may sue the wrongdoer in tort for conversion of his property and recover a judgment for the value of the unimproved property. Whether the property itself can be recovered, after payment of due compensation to the improver for his improvements, will depend on: (1) the relative increase in value, (2) whether the form or identity of the property has been changed, and (3) whether the improvements can be separated from the original property.

Summary

Ownership of personal property may be acquired by (1) production, (2) purchase, (3) taking possession, (4) gift, (5) finding, (6) confusion, and (7) accession.

A person owns property produced by his own labor or by the labor of persons whom he hires to work for him.

The owner of personal property may sell or barter his property to another, and the purchaser then becomes the owner of the property.

The person who first reduces unowned property—wildlife or abandoned property—to possession with the intent of claiming ownership of the property acquires ownership thereof.

A gift is the transfer of the ownership of property from the donor to the donee without any consideration being given by the donee. To have a valid gift, the donor must deliver the possession of the property to the donee or to some third person with the intent of vesting ownership in the donee.

The finder of lost property acquires ownership of the property against everyone except the original owner. A distinction, which is not clear-cut, is made between lost property and mislaid property.

If a person confuses his property with that of another, the other party may acquire ownership of the entire mass.

If property is improved by the labor and addition of materials by another without the owner's consent, the owner of the original property becomes the owner of the property in its improved state.

Bunt v. Fairbanks

134 N.W.2d 1 (Sup. Ct. S.D. 1965)

This was an action by Rachel H. Bunt (plaintiff) against Marlys Bunt Fairbanks (defendant) to quiet title in herself to shares of corporate stock. Judgment for Fairbanks and Bunt appealed. Judgment affirmed.

Richard H. Bunt and his wife, Rachel, in his lifetime had a joint checking account. Rachel claims to have deposited in the account upwards of $3,500 of her separate funds. On October 28, 1965, Mr. Bunt, without his wife's knowledge, withdrew $8,000 for the purchase of National Securities Series stock. Immediately before the withdrawal the balance in the account was $$1,699.46. The stock certificate was issued to "Richard H. Bunt & Marlys Fairbanks as Jt Wr of Surv & not as Tenants in Common." Until his death Mr. Bunt received and retained the dividends therefrom. Marlys claims the stock as donee by right of survivorship.

FORSHEIM, CIRCUIT JUDGE. Rachel H. Bunt, the widow of Richard H. Bunt, deceased, and the mother of the defendant Marlys B. Fairbanks, seeks in this action to quiet title in herself to one thousand shares of National Securities Series stock and the dividends issued thereon. The defendant Fairbanks denies Mrs. Bunt has any interest in such personal property, and by counterclaim demands judgment for possession of the securities, and for the amount of dividends and distributions received by Mrs. Bunt from such stock.

Mrs. Bunt next contends the stock purchase was not a valid gift *inter vivos*. The essential elements of a gift *inter vivos* include intention, delivery, and acceptance.

Counsel for Mrs. Bunt stressed in argument that the evidence and findings are wanting as to donative intent. The second finding of fact adopted by the trial court reads: "By such purchase, issuance and delivery, the said Richard H. Bunt intended to and did make a gift of such interest as a joint tenant to the said Marlys B. Fairbanks." In our opinion the finding is adequate and is supported by evidence.

A gift is without consideration; and for that reason fails as a contract until executed. Delivery is the adrenaline that makes it a contract executed.

That this stock certificate was issued to joint tenants is a distinguishing fact. Our joint tenancy statute reads in part: "A joint tenancy interest is one owned by several persons in equal shares, by a title created by a single . . . transfer, when expressly declared in the transfer to be a joint tenancy. . . . Any . . . transfer . . . of . . . personal property to two or more grantees . . . which, by the method of describing such grantees or by the language of the granting habendum clause therein evinces an intent to create a joint tenancy in grantees shall be held and construed to create such joint tenancy." In South Dakota survivorship is an established incident of a joint tenancy.

Although donor retained possession of the certificate, he surrendered his exclusive dominion and control thereof when he had ownership placed in Mrs. Fairbanks and himself. Nothing more remained to be done to make the gift complete and absolute. It was irrevocable. Each co-owner had an equal right to possession of the certificate and since they could not both have manual possession at the same time, possession by one cotenant is, in contemplation of law, possession for both.

The delivery of a gift may be either actual or constructive, depending upon the circumstances under which the gift is made. The impossibility of both joint tenants holding possession at the same time made a constructive delivery according to the manner in which this particular stock certificate was susceptible of being delivered sufficient. Since the possession of joint tenants is in common and each has the right to the enjoyment of the whole property to the extent of his interest, if only one of them holds the property, he must be considered as possessing, not only for himself, but also for the benefit of his cotenant, although there is no contract between them. Retention of the dividends by deceased under these circumstances did not invalidate the gift.

Regarding the element of acceptance, it appears to be the rule that, in the absence of renunciation, acceptance of a gift will be presumed when it is unaccompanied by any condition to be performed by the donee, especially where the gift is from parent to child and it operates entirely to the donee's benefit.

Dolitsky v. Dollar Savings Bank
118 N.Y.S.2d 65 (City of N.Y. Mun. Ct. 1952)

This was an action by Betty Dolitsky (plaintiff) against Dollar Savings Bank (defendant) to recover $100 allegedly found by Dolitsky. Judgment for Dollar Savings Bank.

Betty Dolitsky rented a safe-deposit box from Dollar Savings Bank. The safe-deposit vault of the bank is in the basement and the vault area is walled off from all other parts of the bank. Only box renters and officers and employees of the bank are admitted to this area. To gain access to the area a box renter must obtain an admission slip, fill in his box number and sign the slip, have the box number and signature checked by an employee against the records of the bank, and then present the slip to a guard who admits the renter to the safe-deposit vault area.

On November 7, 1951, Dolitsky requested access to her box and the procedure as outlined was followed. While Dolitsky was in the booth she was looking through an advertising folder which had been placed there by the bank and found a $100 bill which she turned over to the attendant. Dolitsky waited one year and during that time the rightful owner of the $100 bill made no claim for it. Dolitsky then demanded that the bank surrender the bill to her claiming that she was entitled to the bill as finder. The bank claims the bill is mislaid property and that they owe a duty to keep the bill for the rightful owner.

TRIMARCO, JUSTICE.   At common law property was lost when possession had been casually and involuntarily parted with, so that the mind had no impress of and could have no knowledge of the parting. Mislaid property was that which the owner had voluntarily and intentionally placed and then forgotten.

Property in someone's possession cannot *be found in the sense of common law lost property*. If the article is in the custody of the owner of the place when it is discovered it is not lost in the legal sense; instead it is mislaid. Thus, if a chattel is discovered anywhere in a private place where only a limited class of people have a right to be and they are customers of the owner of the premises, who has the duty of preserving the property of his customers, it is in the possession of the owner of the premises.

In the case of mislaid property discovered on the premises of another, the common law rule is that the proprietor of the premises is held to have the better right to hold the same for the owner, or the proprietor has custody for the benefit of the owner; or the proprietor is the gratuitous bailee of the owner. The effect of the cases, despite their different description of the relationship, is that the proprietor is the bailee of the owner. Thus, the discoverer of mislaid property has the duty to leave it with the proprietor of the premises, and the latter has the duty to hold it for the owner. New York statutory requirements do not change this rule.

The bank is a gratuitous bailee of mislaid property once it has knowledge of the property. As such the bank has the duty to exercise ordinary care in the custody of the articles with a duty to redeliver to the owner.

The recent case of *Manufacturers Savings Deposit Co.* v. *Cohen,* which held that property found on the floor of a booth located in an outer room used by a safe-deposit company in conjunction with a bank, access thereto not being limited to box holders or officials of the safe-deposit company, was lost property and as such should have been turned over to the property clerk of the Police Department, can be distinguished from the present case. In the *Cohen* case the court found that the booth on the floor of which the money was found was not located within the safe-deposit vault but rather in an outer room adjoining said vault and in a part of the bank which was accessible to the ordinary customer of the bank for the purchase of bonds and the opening of new accounts; as such the court considers the room in which the booth was located a public place which was not restricted to safe-deposit officials and persons having safe-deposit boxes in the vault. The case is further distinguished from the present case since its facts disclose that the money was found on the floor of the booth which indicated to the court that the money was not mislaid. The court points out that the testimony shows the money to have been found on the floor of the booth and not on any table or other normal resting place.

Nature and Creation of Bailment

Essential Elements. Normally, in a bailment the title of personal property is in one person, the bailor, and the right of possession is in another person, the bailee. Not all transactions in which there is a division of title and possession are bailments. These essential elements must be present in order to have a bailment: (1) the title to the property or a superior right to possession must be in the bailor, (2) the bailee must have lawful possession without title, and (3) the bailee must owe a duty to return the property to the bailor or dispose of it as directed by him. The bailment is a common transaction, and frequently a bailment exists when the parties to the transaction are not aware of its existence. For instance, if you loan your lawn mower to your neighbor, a bailment arises. Rentals of personal property and the pledging of personal property as security for a loan involve bailments. However, there are borderline situations in which it is difficult to determine whether the transaction is a bailment or should be classified under some other heading. In such cases the courts endeavor to determine the intent of the parties and to carry out that intent.

Creation of Relation.   As a general rule a bailment is created by a contract entered into by the parties to the bailment. Whether or not a bailment exists must be determined from all the facts and circumstances of the case. The test generally applied is whether possession has been delivered and whether the person into whose possession the article has been delivered intended to assume costody and control over the object and has expressly or impliedly promised to return the article to the owner or to dispose of it as directed by the owner. Usually, if one goes into a restaurant or barber shop or like place and hangs his hat and coat on a rack provided for that purpose, no bailment will arise; but if the circumstances are such that it can be established that the owner of the establishment either expressly or impliedly assumes control over the hat and coat, the existence of a bailment may be established. If a checkroom is provided and the hat and coat are checked with the attendant in charge, a bailment will arise.

The courts have held that if a person parks his automobile in a parking lot, retaining the keys to his automobile and having the privilege of getting it himself whenever he wishes, the transaction is a lease and not a bailment. However, if a person takes his automobile to a parking garage and surrenders it to an attendant who parks it and returns it to the owner when the owner calls for it, a bailment is created. Some parking lots are so operated that it is difficult to determine the nature of the relation which exists between the owner of the automobile and the operator of the lot. Such cases must be decided on the basis of the facts of each case.

Custody of Servant or Agent.   The distinction between custody and possession of personal property is technical and is based on the law of master and servant. If a master entrusts his property to his servant, the master technically retains the legal possession of the property and the servant has the custody. For instance, a clerk working in a store has custody of the goods entrusted to him for sale, but the master (employer) has possession of the goods. In such a situation, no bailment exists since, in contemplation of law, there is no surrender of the possession of the goods.

The relationship of principal and agent is similar in most respects to that of master and servant. As a general rule the circumstances of the case will determine whether or not the court will hold that an agent has custody or has possession of his principal's goods. If the agent has custody of the goods, the rights of the parties will be determined by the application of the law of agency; if the agent has possession, such rights will be determined by the law of bailments.

Summary

A bailment is created when the owner of personal property, the bailor, delivers the possession of the property to another, the bailee, who is obligated to return the property to the bailor or to dispose of it as directed by him.

A bailment is created by contract, expressed or implied. Whether or not a bailment is created will depend on the facts and circumstances of the case.

Delivery of goods by a master to his servant does not, as a general rule, create a bailment. The servant has custody of the goods, not possession.

Kuchinsky v. Empire Lounge, Inc.
134 N.W.2d 436 (Sup. Ct. Wis. 1965)

This was an action by Kuchinsky (plaintiff) against Empire Lounge (defendant) to recover for the loss of Kuchinsky's coat. The trial court dismissed the complaint and Kuchinsky appealed. Affirmed.

Kuchinsky entered the Empire Lounge as a customer and hung his coat on a clothes tree near his table. His coat was stolen while he ate.

CURRIE, CIRCUIT JUDGE. A case very much in point is *Montgomery* v. *Ladjing.* There the plaintiff entered the restaurant kept by the defendant with a party of friends; he removed his overcoat and hung it on a hook affixed to a post near the table at which he seated himself; the attention of neither the defendant nor of any of his employees was called to the coat in any way; and fifteen minutes later the coat was missing. The court held that the plaintiff had wholly failed to show failure on the part of the defendant to exercise ordinary care, and declared:

The rule to be deduced from all these cases therefore is that, before a restaurant keeper will be held liable for the loss of an overcoat of a customer while such customer takes a meal or refreshments, it must appear either that the overcoat was placed in the physical custody of the keeper of the restaurant or his servants, in which cases there is an actual bailment, or that the overcoat was necessarily laid aside under circumstances showing, at least, notice of the fact and of such necessity to the keeper of the restaurant, or his servants, in which case there is an implied bailment or constructive custody, that the loss occurred by reason of the insufficiency of the general supervision exercised by the keeper of the restaurant for the protection of customers temporarily laid aside.

In *National Fire Insurance Co.* v. *Commodore Hotel,* the plaintiff was a guest at a luncheon held at the defendant's hotel. She hung her mink jacket in an unattended cloakroom on the main floor across from the lobby desk. After the luncheon and ensuing party the plaintiff went to the cloakroom to retrieve her jacket and discovered it was gone. The court held that no negligence had been established against the defendant and stated:

. . . In any event, we do not feel that it is incumbent upon a hotel or restaurant owner to keep an attendant in charge of a free cloakroom for luncheon or dinner guests or otherwise face liability for loss of articles placed therein. The maintenance of such rooms without attendants is a common practice, and where the proprietor had not accepted control and custody of articles placed therein, no duty rests upon him to exercise any special degree of care with respect thereto.

Likewise, failure to post a warning disclaiming responsibility would not seem to constitute negligence when, as here, a guest is aware that a cloakroom is unattended, adjacent to the lobby, and accessible to anyone; and has used it under similar circumstances on many prior occasions. The absence of such warning signs does not appear to have been material in a number of decisions absolving proprietors from liability although when posted they appear to be regarded as an added factor in establishing such nonliability.

Weinberg v. Wayco Petroleum Co.
402 S.W.2d 597 (Ct. App. Mo. 1966)

This was an action by Weinberg (plaintiff) against Wayco Petroleum Company (defendant) for the theft of personal property which occurred while Weinberg's car was parked in Wayco's parking garage. The circuit court awarded Weinberg, a $500 judgment. Reversed on appeal.

Weinberg was the holder of a "Parkard" issued by Wayco for which he paid $10.50 per month and which entitled him to park his automobile at Wayco's garage located in St. Louis. This garage had five stories and entrance was gained by inserting the "Parkard" into a slot causing the entrance gate to open. This was so-called "self-park garage" and there were no attendants on duty at the time Weinberg parked his automobile at about 11:30 P.M. on September 25, 1962. After securing admission to the garage with the Parkard, Weinberg parked his own car, locked it, and took the keys with him. When he returned to his automobile in the evening of September 27th, he found it had been broken into and certain personal property stolen from it. The automobile had not been moved.

The "Parkard" stated: "This card licenses the holder to park one automobile in this area at holder's risk. Lock your car. Licensor hereby declares himself not responsible for fire, theft or damage to or loss of such automobile or any article left therein. Only a license is granted hereby, and no bailment is created." Weinberg testified that prior to this occurrence he had read this language on the card and knew what it said.

BRADY, COMMISSIONER. With respect to cases involving automobiles and the contents thereof when loss occurs after the automobile is left in a parking lot, the relationship between the parties is usually one of bailment or license, and whether it is one or the other depends upon the circumstances of the particular case and especially upon the manner in which the parking lot in question is being operated and with whom control of the allegedly bailed article or articles is vested.

A "bailment" in its ordinary legal sense imports the delivery of personal property by the bailor to the bailee who keeps the property in trust for a specific purpose, with a contract, express or implied, that the trust shall be faithfully executed, and the property returned or duly accounted for when the special purpose is accomplished or that the property shall be kept until the bailor reclaims it. This court has said that ". . . the term 'bailment' . . . signifies a contract resulting from the delivery of goods by bailor to bailee on condition that they be restored to the bailor, according to his directions, so soon as the purposes for which they were bailed are answered."

It is obvious from the facts in the instant case that there was no delivery to Wayco sufficient to create the relationship of bailee and bailor between the parties here involved. Cases of the nature here involved are to be distinguished from those where the parking operation is such that the attendants collect a fee and assume authority or control of the automobile by parking it and/or retaining the keys so that the car can be moved about to permit the entrance or exist of other automobiles and where the tickets that are given to the owner of the automobile are issued for the purpose of identifying the automobile for redelivery. In such instances a bailment relationship is almost invariably held to exist. In the instant case Wayco never secured control or authority over Weinberg's automobile. No agent or employee of Wayco parked it or kept the keys to it or issued any ticket whereby the automobile could be identified by comparison of a portion of the ticket left with the automobile when it was parked. Weinberg parked his own automobile, locked it, and took the keys with him. Certainly Wayco, the alleged bailee, did not have the right under these circumstances to exclude the purposes of the owner or even of anyone else who might have had the keys. In the instant case Weinberg never made a delivery, actual or constructive, of the automobile to Wayco under circumstances leading to the creation of a bailee-bailor relationship between them.

Rights and Liabilities of Parties

Bailee's Duty of Care. In determining the liability of the bailee for damage to or loss of the bailed property, bailments have been divided into three classes: (1) mutual benefit bailments, (2) bailments for the sole benefit of the bailor, and (3) bailments for the sole benefit of the bailee.

All commercial bailments are mutual benefit bailments, that is, both the bailee and the bailor receive benefits from the relation. For example, if goods are stored in a warehouse, the warehouseman (the bailee) is compensated for his services, and the owner of the goods (the bailor) has his goods cared for during the period of storage. The mutual benefit bailee owes a duty of ordinary care and is liable for damage to or loss of the goods only if such damage or loss is the result of his negligence. Ordinary care has been defined as that care which a man of ordinary prudence would take of his goods of like nature under the same or similar circumstances.

A bailment for the sole benefit of the bailor is one in which the bailee renders some service in respect to the bailed property without receiving a return benefit. For instance, if you permit your neighbor to put his automobile in your garage while he is away on a trip, and he pays you nothing for the privilege, the bailment is for the sole benefit of the bailor. In such a bailment the bailee owes a duty of slight care. The bailee will be liable for damage to or loss of the bailed goods only if he does little or nothing to protect them when it is apparent that they will be damaged or lost and when the bailee could prevent the damage or loss without any substantial cost or sacrifice on his part.

A bailment for the sole benefit of the bailee arises when the owner of goods permits another to use his goods free of charge. For instance, if you loan your lawn mower to your neighbor, the bailment is for the sole benefit of the bailee. In such a bailment the bailee owes a duty of great care. If the bailee is negligent in any respect in his use or care of the bailed goods and as the result of such negligence the goods are damaged or lost, the bailee is liable.

Recently some courts have moved away from the three classes of bailments with their distinctions as to degree of care which sound fine in theory but are often difficult to apply in practice. Instead, these courts require a reasonable amount of care on the part of all bailees. What is reasonable care in any given situation depends on: (1) the nature and value of the bailed property, (2) who the bailee is—for example, whether he is a professional bailee, and (3) whether the bailment was paid for or whether it was gratuitous.

A bailee is never liable for damage to or loss of the bailed goods unless the damage or loss is the result of some degree of negligence on the part of the bailee; the bailee, in the absence of a special agreement, is not an insurer of the safety of the bailed goods.

Whether or not the bailee had the right to use the bailed property will depend on the facts and circumstances of each case. As a general rule, the bailee does not, in the absence of an agreement permitting him to do so, have the right to use the bailed property. If the bailee's use of the bailed property would benefit the bailor, the court would be justified in holding that the bailee had such right.

Alteration of Liability by Contract.   The liability of the bailee may be either increased or decreased by the contract of the parties. The extent to which a bailee may relieve himself from his liability for his own negligence is limited to some extent. Under the law of contracts, a contract whereby a person relieves himself of liability for his own negligence may be against public policy and void. The courts have, as a general rule, enforced provisions in contracts of bailment whereby the bailee is relieved from specific perils; but the courts have been reluctant to enforce provisions in such contracts whereby the bailee is relieved from all liability for his negligent acts.

The effect of the posting of notices, the printing of terms on a check or receipt given to the bailor, or the doing of other similar acts by the bailee in an attempt to limit his liability was discussed in Chapter 6, "Offer." The question is primarily one of communication of the terms of the contract. The knowledge of the bailor of the facilities of the bailee or of his method of doing business or the nature of prior dealings may give rise to an implied agreement as to the duties of the bailee. The bailee may, if he wishes, assume all the risks incident to the bailment and contract to return the bailed property undamaged or to pay any damage to or loss of the property.

Bailee's Duty to Return Property.   On the termination of the bailment, the bailee owes a duty to return the bailed property in an undamaged condition to the bailor or to dispose of it as directed by the bailor. If the bailee cannot return the property to the bailor in an undamaged condition, he may excuse his failure by showing that the goods were damaged or destroyed without negligence on his part. If the bailed property is taken from the bailee by legal process, the bailee should notify the bailor and must take whatever action is necessary to protect the bailor's interest.

If a third person claims to have, in the bailed property, rights which are superior to the rights of the bailor and demands possession of the bailed property, the bailee is in a dilemma. If the bailee refuses to deliver the bailed property to the third-person claimant and the third-person claimant is entitled to the possession of it, the bailee will be liable to such claimant. If the bailee delivers the bailed property to the third-person claimant and the third-person claimant is not entitled to possession, the bailee is liable to the bailor. The circumstances may be such that the conflicting claims of the bailor and the third-person claimant can be determined only by judicial decision. In some cases the bailee may protect himself by bringing a bill of interpleader, but this remedy is not available in all cases. The bailee cannot set up a claim to the bailed property which is adverse to the rights of the bailor if the claim is based on rights which existed at the time the property was bailed. By accepting the property as bailee, the bailee is estopped from denying the bailor's title to the bailed property.

Bailee's Right to Compensation. The bailee's right to compensation will depend entirely on the agreement or understanding of the parties. If the bailment is a gratuitous bailment, the bailee will be entitled to no compensation even though the bailment is for the sole benefit of the bailor. If the bailment is created by the rental of personal property, the bailee will be obligated to pay the agreed rent. If the bailment is for the storage or repair of property, the bailee will be entitled to the contract price for his services. If there is no agreement as to compensation, the bailee will be entitled to recover the reasonable value of the services rendered. In many situations the bailee, if he is entitled to compensation, will have a lien on the bailed property for the reasonable value of his services.

Bailor's Liability for Defects in Bailed Property. If personal property is rented or loaned to a bailee, the bailor impliedly warrants that there are no defects in the property which will make it unsafe for use.

If the bailment is a mutual benefit bailment, that is, if the property is rented to the bailee, the bailor must use reasonable care in inspecting the property and in seeing that it is in a safe condition for use for the purpose for which it is rented. The bailor is liable to the bailee or an employee of the bailee for damages resulting from the use of the defective property if the bailee should have, in the exercise of due care, discovered the defect.

If the bailment is for the sole benefit of the bailee, as is the case when the bailor loans property to the bailee, the bailor is liable for injuries resulting from defects in the bailed property only if the bailor has knowledge of the defects and fails to give the bailee notice of the defects.

Summary

The bailee owes a duty of due care to prevent loss of or damage to the bailed property. In determining whether or not due care has been exercised by the bailee, the nature of the bailment is of outstanding importance.

The parties within the limits of the legality of their contract, may, by agreement, increase or decrease the scope of the liability of the bailee.

On the termination of the bailment the bailee must return the bailed property to the bailor or dispose of it according to the direction of the bailor. If a third person having a right of possession superior to that of the bailor demands the surrender of the property to him, the bailee is obligated to deliver the property to such third person.

The bailee is entitled to reasonable compensation for services rendered in the care of the property. If the contract of bailment stipulates the compensation, the bailee is entitled to the stipulated compensation.

If the bailor rents property to the bailee, he (the bailor) owes a duty to inspect the property to see that it is free from dangerous defects. If the bailor loans the property to the bailee, he owes a duty to warn the bailee of any known dangerous defects in the property.

Allen v. Southern Pacific Co.
213 P.2d 667 (Sup. Ct. Utah 1950)

This was an action by Frank J. Allen (plaintiff) against Southern Pacific Company (defendant) to recover a judgment for $2,190, the value of a traveling bag and contents. Judgment for Allen for $25 and Allen appealed. Judgment reversed.

Allen checked his traveling bag with its contents at the parcel checking room of Southern Pacific Company (Pacific) in the Union Station at Portland, Oregon. When he presented his claim check and asked for its return, it could not be found. At the time the bag was checked Pacific gave Allen a parcel check or receipt which had printed on one side the following:

"Notice—Liability for loss of, damage or delay to any parcel limited to not to exceed $25.00 unless at time of deposit value is declared and paid for at the rate of 10 cents for each $25.00 or fraction thereof for thirty days or less. No parcel valued in excess of $250.00 will be accepted." On the reverse side was printed:

"Date and time of delivery"

"For Excess Liability See Notice on Opposite Side."

There was also posted a sign at this parcel room to the same effect as the printing on the check.

At the time Allen checked his bag his attention was not called to the provisions printed on the claim check or to the sign, and he did not read either. Pacific claims that its liability is limited to $25. Allen claims that, since his attention was not called to the provisions limiting liability and since he had no knowledge of them at the time he checked his bag, he is not bound by them.

WADE, JUSTICE.   The sole question before this court is: Was the court correct in holding that respondent's liability was limited by contract?

Ordinarily, a bailee for hire is responsible for the value of the goods entrusted to him if they are lost or destroyed. However, the parties may enter into a valid agreement to modify the obligations which would otherwise arise from the relationship of bailor and bailee if it

". . . does not violate the law or contravene public policy, and so long as it is actually a part of the contract of bailment and is expressed in clear and unmistakable language . . ." 6 Am. Jur. Bailments, Sec. 174, page 268.

The great weight of authority is that a bailee cannot entirely exempt himself by contract from liability due to his negligence and contracts limiting his liability for negligence during the course of a general business with the public are usually regarded as being against public policy. But even where such contracts are not against public policy there must be actual assent to the conditions modifying the bailee's liability growing out of the contract of bailment.

In the instant case the court, as the trier of the facts, found that Allen did not see or read the notice posted at the parcel room, nor did he read the check, that he had no actual knowledge of the limitations contained therein, nor were such limitations or conditions called to his attention. Under such a state of facts, it cannot be said that Allen actually assented to the limitations contained in the notice and check.

Pacific contends that the rules that a bailee may not exempt himself from liability for loss due to his negligence because such a contract is against public policy and that he may not limit his liability unless the contract is fairly and freely made and the bailee has actual knowledge of such limitations do not apply to the type of contract made herein where the limitations of liability varies in amount in direct proportion to the value declared and the charge paid by the bailor. In support of this argument it cites a number of United States Supreme Court cases. We have carefully read each of these cases and find that they deal with baggage or other personal property involved in a contract of carriage in interstate commerce and which are subject to the rules and regulations of the Interstate Commerce Commission and applicable laws of Congress. Under these rules the railroads have to file schedules giving the rates, charges and fares for transportation between different points and these cannot be changed by contract. These cases and the reasoning therein are distinguishable from the cases where the railroad company acts as a warehouseman, where the baggage is left for care and not for transportation. As stated by the court in *Boston & M. R. R.* v. *Hooker,* in holding that where baggage is in interstate commerce it is subject to published rates and even though the shipper was not aware of the fact that there were different rates for different valuations of the property, the common carrier's liability was limited to the amount actually provided by the different scheduled rates:

It is to be borne in mind that the action as tried and decided in the state court was not for negligence of the railroad company as a warehouseman for the loss of the baggage after its delivery at Sunapee Lake station, but was solely upon the contract of carriage in interstate commerce.

A checkroom business is no part of the business of a common carrier and when it acts in in that capacity it is acting as a warehouseman.

In the instant case the court found as facts that Allen did not actually know of the printed conditions and that such conditions were not called to his attention by Pacific's agent. Under such a state of the facts the court erred in concluding that as a matter of law a contract was entered into limiting liability to $25.

Edward Hines Lumber Co. v. Purvine Logging Co., Inc.
399 P.2d 893 (Sup. Ct. Ore. 1965)

This was an action by Edward Hines Lumber Co. (plaintiff) against Purvine Logging Co., Inc. (defendant), to recover a judgment for the value of a donkey engine destroyed by fire. Judgment for Purvine Logging Co., Inc., and Edward Hines Lumber Co. appealed. Judgment affirmed.

Edward Hines Lumber Co. (Hines) was the owner of a donkey engine. Purvine Logging Co., Inc. (Purvine), was a logger engaged in the performance of a logging contract for Hines. Hines delivered the donkey engine to Purvine to be used in the performance of the logging contract. The written agreement entered into by the parties provided in part that the "equipment (donkey engine) shall be kept in good operating condition maintained by contractor (Purvine) and . . . redelivered . . . in as good condition as of this date, reasonable wear and tear excepted, . . ." The donkey engine was destroyed by fire of unknown origin.

HOLMAN, JUSTICE.   The trial court in the case at bar correctly applied the common law rule. A contract to return in good condition, reasonable wear and tear excepted, does not make the bailee an insurer of the goods. The parties may by contract place the risk of loss as they see fit, but in the absence of an agreement to the contrary, the common law rule applied. An agreement to return in good order, fair wear and tear excepted, is not an agreement to shift the risk of loss.

Hines argues further that, even if the bailee is not to be held liable without fault, a doctrine akin to that of *res ipsa loquitur* applies the necessary inference of negligence and shifts to the bailee the duty of explaining the fire in a manner consistent with the exercise of due care on the part of the bailee. This question was probed in detail in *National Fire Ins. Co.* v. *Mogan et al.* We held that, after it had been shown that the goods had not been returned, the burden of going forward with the evidence shifted to the bailee. We also observed, in passing, that if the bailee could explain why the goods were not returned, as by showing that a fire occurred without fault on the bailee's part, such a showing would absolve the bailee from liability. We adhere to the view expressed in *National Fire Ins. Co.* v. *Morgan et al.*

In the case at bar, the trial court correctly concluded that the bailee had gone forward with a sufficient explanation of the fire to show that it had occurred under circumstances which were fully consistent with the exercise of due care by the bailee. The fire started on a weekend when woods operations were shut down. The logging site was near a public highway, and the area was accessible to fishermen, picnickers, and the like. The trial court believed that the fire was of an unknown, and unknowable, cause and that under the circumstances any inference of negligence that might arise initially under *National Fire Ins. Co.* v. *Mogan et al.* was overcome by the bailee's evidence that due care had been exercised. The ultimate burden of proof of negligence remained on Hines, and the trial court found that negligence had not been proven.

Moore v. *Ellis*

385 S.W.2d 261 (Ct. Civ. App. Tex. 1964)

This was an action by Harold Ellis (plaintiff) against John J. Moore and H. R. Wardlaw (defendants) to recover a judgment for personal injuries. Judgment for Ellis, and Moore and Wardlaw appealed. Judgment reversed and judgment entered for Moore and Wardlaw.

Moore and Wardlaw furnished a tractor and disk to Harper for use in disking land. The hydraulic cylinder lift used to raise and lower the disk was not operating properly. The disk could be raised by the three point hitch lift. However, if the disk was overloaded with dirt when lifted with the three point lift, it would cause the front end of the tractor to raise up. Upon disengaging the clutch or releasing the gas throttle, the front of the tractor would then come down. Moore informed Harper that the hydraulic cylinder lift was inoperative. Harper hired Harold Ellis to operate the tractor and disk. The ground being disked at the time was wet and this wet condition was causing the disk to become overloaded. Twice on the day before the accident the front of the tractor reared up. Ellis was told and he knew that the hydraulic cylinder lift (which was safe to use if in working order) was defective and would not work. The fourth time the tractor reared up when Ellis lifted the disk it flipped over, pinning Ellis underneath and injuring him seriously.

DUNAGAN, CHIEF JUSTICE. In the case of *Nesmith* v. *Magnolia Petroleum Co.*, the court said:

One who supplies directly or through a third person a chattel for another to use, is subject to liability to those whom the supplier should expect to use the chattel with the consent of the other or to be in the vicinity of its probable use, for bodily harm caused by the use of the chattel in the manner for which and by a person for whose use it is supplied, if the supplier (a) knows, or from facts known to him should realize, that the chattel is or is likely to be dangerous for the use for which it is supplied; (b) and has no reason to believe that those for whose use the chattel is supplied will realize its dangerous condition; and (c) fails to exercise reasonable care to *inform* them of its dangerous condition or of the facts which make it likely to be so. These general principles apply alike to donors, lenders, and lessors of chattels. . . .

Therefore, all three of the above elements must exist concurrently before liability can be assessed against Moore and Wardlaw.

In the case at bar it is undisputed that Harold Ellis knew of the inoperable cylinder lift, and it is further undisputed that McCrary told Harold Ellis about the inoperable cylinder lift. Furthermore, the jury found that at the time and on the occasion in question, Harold Ellis knew that the cylinder lift was not in operating condition. Therefore, elements (b) and (c) did not exist, but, rather, the evidence showed that the duty imposed was fulfilled and not breached.

Special Bailment Situations

Bailment of Fungible Goods. As a general rule the bailee is required to return to the bailor the identical goods he deposited. If the parties enter into a contract whereby the party to whom the goods are delivered has the right to surrender other goods, though of the same kind and value, the transaction is a sale, not a bailment. This rule has not been applied to the storage of grain and other fungible goods. The courts hold that if grain of several persons is stored in a common mass in an elevator and the operator of the elevator contracts to return to the depositor an equal quantity of grain of the same kind and quality, the transaction is a bailment.

The courts are not in complete accord as to the nature of the transaction if the storage contract permits the payment of the purchase price of the grain in lieu of delivery. They are in accord in holding that the transaction is a bailment if the depositor has the absolute right to demand the return of grain of the same kind and quality or to demand the payment of the market price at the time he makes his demand in lieu of accepting delivery of the grain. But most of the courts hold that the transaction is a sale if the depositary (the elevator) has the right, at the time the demand is made, to pay the market price of the grain in lieu of delivery of the grain. Some courts hold that if the depositary is given an option to purchase at the market price at the time the depositor returns his receipt and demands delivery, the transaction is a bailment until such time as a demand is made and the option to purchase is exercised, at which time it becomes a sale.

Safe-Deposit Boxes. In the operation of a safe-deposit box, the box and the property in the box are in the manual possession of the bank. However, neither the bank nor the renter can gain access to the contents of the box without the consent and cooperation of the other. To open the box, two keys are used. One of the keys is kept by the bank and the other by the renter. The bank need have no knowledge of the nature, amount, or value of the property in the safe-deposit box. Although there has been some diversity of opinion as to the nature of the relation, some courts have held that the renter is a bailor and the bank is a bailee.

Involuntary Bailments. Sometimes a person finds himself in possession of the personal property of another without having consented to accept such possession. For instance, the personal property of one person may be deposited on the premises of another by storm or flood, or the animals of one person may stray onto the premises of another. In such cases a few courts have held that no bailment arises, whereas other courts have held that an involuntary bailment arises.

There are no well-established rules as to the rights and duties of the involuntary bailee. He does not have a right to destroy the property willfully, convert it to his own use, or refuse to redeliver it to the owner. The affirmative duties of the involuntary bailee are uncertain and, in many instances, do not require him to assume control over the goods. Under the circumstances of some cases the duties imposed are those of the bailee in a bailment for the sole benefit of the bailor. Each case must be decided according to the facts of the case.

Common Carrier. A person is a common carrier if he holds himself out to carry, for hire, the property of any person who chooses to employ him. A person is a private carrier if he carries the property only for those whom he selects. Both common carriers and private carriers are bailees. The common carrier is held to a standard of responsibility higher than of the private carrier. This distinction is historical and is based on the social conditions which existed in England during an early period. To prevent collusion between the carrier and highwaymen, the carrier was held to be the insurer of the property he carried. This imposed an absolute liability on the carrier for the damage or loss of property he carried.

This rule is in force in the United States today; however, there are several exceptions to the general rule. The common carrier is not liable if the damage or loss is the result of an act of God, an act of the public enemy, an act of the state, or an act of the shipper, or if the damage or loss is caused by the nature of the goods.

Innkeepers. The hotel owner or innkeeper is one who holds himself out to provide food and lodging to transients. He is obligated to serve the public; and like the common carrier, he is held to a responsibility greater than that of the ordinary bailee. The hotel owner or innkeeper is not a bailee in the strict sense of the word, since the guest does not surrender the exclusive possession of his property to the hotel owner or innkeeper; but the hotel owner or innkeeper is the insurer of his guest's property. Losses resulting from acts of God or acts of public enemies, and losses suffered by guests resulting from the acts of members of their own parties, are exceptions to this strict liability. Some courts have held that a hotel owner or innkeeper is not liable for loss or damage to his guest's property by fire, provided the fire is not caused by the negligence of the hotel owner or innkeeper. Many states have enacted statutes which relieve the hotel owner or innkeeper from this strict liability or, in other words, limit his liability.

Summary

The courts have held a transaction to be a bailment if fungible goods of several persons are stored in a common mass and the depositary is to return an equal quantity of goods of the same kind and quality. Most of the courts have held the transaction to be a sale if the depositary has the right, at the time demand for return of the goods is made, to pay the market price in lieu of returning the goods.

The courts are not in accord as to the relation between the bank and the renter of a safe-deposit box. Some courts have held the relation to be that of bailor and bailee.

A person may become an involuntary bailee if the goods of another are deposited on his land by storm or flood or by the acts of third persons, or if the domestic animals of another stray onto his land. Such a bailee owes a minimum of duty. He cannot willfully destroy the property or convert it to his own use.

A common carrier is the insurer of the goods he carries against loss or damage unless such loss or damage is caused by an act of God, an act of the public enemy, an act of the state, or an act of the shipper, or by the nature of the goods.

An innkeeper is an insurer of the goods of his guests. Many states have statutes permitting innkeepers to limit their liability.

Problem Cases

1. Liesner shot and mortally wounded a previously wounded wolf. Before Liesner could reach the wolf, Warnie, with his gun pointed within 3 feet of the wolf, fired the finishing shot. Liesner had the wolf in such condition that escape was improbable if not impossible. Who owned the wolf, Liesner or Warnie?

2. Henry Blandy desired to make some provisions for the maintenance and support of his daughter, Amanda Flanders. He purchased and set apart as a "gift" to her $2,000 worth of U.S. bonds. The bonds were never delivered to Amanda who lived some distance away and she never had manual possession of them. Rather, by her request and assent they were left under the dominion and control of her father for safekeeping. Each year he collected and sent to her the interest that had accrued on the bonds. Blandy became interested in the cashmere goat business and decided that such an investment would be more profitable to his daughter. So he sold the bonds and invested the money in that business. He then wrote Amanda, telling her if she did not accept the new investment, he would pay to her, in place of the bonds, $2,000 plus interest. Blandy dies and Amanda claims she is entitled to $2,000 because her father had made a valid gift to her of the bonds. Did he make a valid gift?

3. While the *Olympia,* a passenger ship, was moored at a pier in New York City and receiving passengers for an imminent sailing, Kalyvakis, who was a steward on the ship, found $2,010 in U.S. currency on the floor of a public men's room on the

upper deck. The room was accessible to all passengers, their guests and the ship's personnel; the money was found shortly before visitors and guests were required to leave the ship. Kalyvakis deposited the money with the chief steward to be held for the true owner should he make any claim for it. No claim has been made for the money for three years, and Kalyvakis asks that the money be returned to him. His employer contends the money belongs to it, the owner of the ship. Who is entitled to the money?

4. Roberts employed Danielson to clean the rubbish out of an old hen house. While so engaged, Danielson dug out of the rubbish a can of gold coins. The premises had been owned by several persons, and no one knew who had placed the can of gold coins in the hen house. Who has the best right to the gold coins, Roberts or Danielson?

5. Faulke, a passenger on Railroad Company's train, saw on the seat opposite him a package which had been left by a passenger who had alighted. Faulke picked up the package, examined it, found no name or mark on it, and took the package with him when he disembarked. Was the package lost property?

6. Ochoa's Studebaker automobile was stolen. Eleven months later the automobile through some unaccountable means found its way into the hands of the U.S. government which sold it at a "junk" auction for $85 to Rogers. At the time it was purchased by Rogers no part of the car was intact. It had no top except a part of the frame; its steering rod was without a wheel; it had no tires, nor rims, no cushions, no battery; the motor was out of the car, but included in the junk, as was also the radiator; one headlight was entirely gone, the other was useless; part of the gears were out and one wheel was gone, as was one axle; the fenders were partly gone, and had to be entirely replaced; the differential was beyond repair, and the frame, or chassis, was there, but broken. It was no longer an automobile but a pile of broken and dismantled parts of what was once Ochoa's car. Having purchased these parts, Rogers used them in the construction of a delivery truck, at an expense of approximately $800. When the truck was completed, he put it in use in his furniture business. Several months later, Ochoa, passing Rogers' place of business recognized the machine from a mark on the hood and another on the radiator and discovered that the serial and engine numbers matched those on the car he had owned. Ochoa demanded the car from Rogers, who refused to surrender it. Ochoa brought suit to recover possession of the property, or, in the alternative, for the value thereof at the time of the suit, which he alleged to be $1,000, and for the value of the use of the car at the rate of $5 per day from the time Rogers purchased it from the government. Can Ochoa recover?

7. Plaintiff, a permanent resident of defendant's hotel, had her son take two diamond rings from her apartment and deposit them with the hotel clerk for safekeeping. In accordance with customary practice in performing the service, the rings were exhibited to the clerk and placed in a sealed "safety deposit envelope" used by the hotel for depositing valuables belonging to guests. Plaintiff's son received a depositor's check stub which bore a number corresponding to the one on the envelope and signed his name on the envelope. The stub and his signature were both necessary for the return of the envelope. The envelope was kept in a safe located in the hotel's front office, 4 or 5 feet behind the registration desk. The safe was used not only to keep valuables of guests, but also cash for use in the hotel's cafe, bar, and coffee shop. Although the safe was equipped with a combination lock, during the 16 years that defendant operated the hotel the safe door, while customarily closed, was never locked. A clerk was on duty at the registration desk at all times. Subsequently, the hotel was robbed by two armed men at 3:30 A.M. and the rings taken from the safe.

Plaintiff sues for value of rings. The hotel claims the robbery was a supervening cause, relieving it of any liability. Can plaintiff recover?

8. Pond owned and operated a parking lot. Rehling parked his automobile on Pond's lot, which was near Crosley Field, and proceeded with others to a night baseball game. Rehling paid $1 to the parking lot attendant, for which he received a "claim check." Before leaving his automobile, Rehling turned the ignition switch to neutral, rolled up the windows, locked the doors, and took the keys with him. When he returned after the ball game to get his automobile, it was gone. The parking lot attendants testified that at about the third inning of the ball game, they saw a person walk directly to Rehling's automobile, get in, back up, and drive away.

There was no showing that the claim check was ever used for anything but identification in case a patron was unable to find his automobile on the lot. Is Pond liable as bailee for the loss of the automobile?

9. Alderman delivered his automobile containing some personal property to Welding Shop to have it equipped with a hitch and agreed to pay Welding Shop for its work. When the automobile was returned, it was in a damaged condition, and the personal property which was in the automobile when it was delivered to the shop was missing. Alderman sued Welding Shop to recover damages, stating in his declaration only the facts relative to the delivery of the automobile and personal property, and the damage and loss. Welding Shop made no defense but claimed that since Alderman did not allege acts of negligence on its part resulting in the damage and loss, it was not liable. Is Welding Shop's contention correct?

10. Wells rented a trailer from Brown and agreed to return the trailer clean and in the same condition as when rented. The trailer was damaged when a tree was blown across it during a violent windstorm. The damage was caused solely by the violence of the storm and without any negligence of fault on the part of Wells. Brown sues Wells to recover for the damage done to the trailer. Can he recover?

chapter 30. Real Property

Fixtures

Nature of Fixture.   From a technical, legal standpoint a fixture is a personal property which is so attached to or used with real estate that it is considered to be a part of that real estate. The term *fixture* is also used to designate personal property, such as, for instance, a store fixture, which may appear to be a part of the real estate but is not attached thereto and is removable. A wide variety of fact situations have been before the courts in controversies which arise when one person claims that an article of personal property has become a fixture and another claims that the article continues as personal property. The cases involving such controversies appear to be in conflict, but a careful analysis reveals that the courts have developed standards for determining issues regarding fixtures and have consistently applied these standards.

In the modern cases the courts apply the reasonable-man standard, which is: Would a reasonable man familiar with the community and with the facts and circumstances of the case be justified in assuming that the person attaching or using the personal property with the real estate intended it to become a fixture? The intention of the parties, determined by the application of this objective test, is controlling in all the cases. In applying this standard, all the facts of the case, such as the time, place, usage, relation of the parties, mode of attachment, and adaptability for use with the particular premises, must be considered, and the case must be decided by a commonsense application of this accepted standard.

Express Agreement.   Since intention of the parties is controlling, if the parties have, by express agreement, indicated their intention as to whether or not an article of personal property shall or shall not become a fixture, the courts will, within limits, enforce the agreement of the parties. Parties cannot, however, by their agreement convert into personal property such property as a city lot or a farm, nor can they convert into a fixture an article which is in no way attached to or used with real property. The courts have held that if articles of personal property, such as brick, stone, beams, and girders, are permanently built into a building so that they become an integral part of the building, they become a part of the real property, irrespective of any express agreement by the parties to the contrary.

Mode of Attachment.   In some of the early cases the courts held that attachment was the sole test for determining whether or not an article of personal property had become a fixture. Today, attachment is of outstanding importance, but it is not conclusive in determining the intention of the parties.

As already noted, if an article of personal property is built into a building so that it becomes an integral part of the building, it loses its character as personal property and becomes real property, irrespective of any declared intention of the parties. If an article of personal property is firmly attached to the real property in such a manner that its removal will substantially destroy the article and will also injure the real property to which it is attached, the court will consider such attachment as very strong evidence that the parties intended the article to become a fixture. If attachment is slight and the article can be removed without injury to the article or to the real property, such attachment is of little importance as evidence.

An article which is attached to the land only by gravity may become a fixture. For example, a building set on blocks on top of the ground and a statue weighing several tons set on a cement foundation, but not attached to the foundation, have in some cases been held to be fixtures.

Use with Real Property.   The appropriateness of the use of the article of personal property with the real property is important as evidence of the intention of the parties. As a general rule, some degree of attachment is considered as necessary to indicate an intention that an article is to become a fixture, but in some cases the courts have held certain articles to be fixtures, even though the articles are not attached to the real property, if such articles would be of little or no value except as used with that particular property. Such articles as keys to doors, storm windows, and screens for windows have been held to be fixtures although not attached to the real property.

In one case, in-a-door beds, refrigerators, stoves, cabinets, and similar items, which were installed in an apartment house, were held to be fixtures even though they were so attached to the real property that they could be easily removed. In such a case the appropriateness of the use of the article with the real property is given great weight in determining the intentions of the parties.

Additions by Owner.   The relation of the parties is also of outstanding importance. If the owner of real property improves it by the addition of personal property, there is an all but conclusive presumption that he intended the improvement to become a part of the real property; and if he sells or mortgages the real property without reservation, the courts have held that the additions are fixtures and pass as real property to the purchaser or mortgagee.

If the owner of real estate purchases personal property, the seller retaining a security interest in such property as security for the payment of the purchase price, and attaches the personal property to his real estate, the seller's security interest in the attached property will, under the provisions of the Uniform Commercial Code, have priority over all persons having an interest in the real estate, provided the seller's security interest has been perfected. On default, the seller may remove the personal property but he will be liable to third parties, such as prior real estate mortgagors, for damage to the real estate caused by its removal.[1]

Additions by Tenants. As between landlord and tenant, the earliest cases held that any improvement made by a tenant became a part of real property; but the courts soon began to make a distinction between attachments made by tenants of business property for trade purposes and those made by tenants of other kinds of real property. This distinction is important today. The courts have generally held that personal property brought onto premises leased for business purposes, for use in the carrying-on of the business for which the premises are leased, remains personal property irrespective of the mode of attachment. Such property is known as trade fixtures. However, if the personal property is so built into the real property that its removal will weaken the structure, the courts have held that it becomes a part of the real property.

In cases involving domestic and agricultural tenancies, the general rule of intention has been applied. However, the presumption that the property which is attached to the real property is to remain personal property is usually not so strong in the case of domestic and agricultural tenancies as in the case of business tenancies.

In all cases in which a tenant has added trade, domestic, or agricultural fixtures, if the tenancy is for a definite period, the tenant must remove the article before the expiration of his term, and if he does not, the article becomes the property of the landlord. This rule had its origin in the early English land law and has been recognized by the courts ever since. Two reasons for the rule have been given: (1) that the failure to remove is conclusive indication of an intention to abandon the article and (2) that after the expiration of the term the tenant would be a trespasser if he entered the land to remove the article.

If the tenancy is for an indefinite period, such as a tenancy for life or a tenancy at will, the tenant will have a reasonable time after the termination of the tenancy to remove such property. The courts have held that if there is an express agreement that articles attached by the tenant shall remain personal prop-

---

[1] Uniform Commercial Code, Article 9, Section 9–313.

erty and may be removed by him, he will have a reasonable time after the expiration of his term in which to remove the articles.

Summary

A fixture is personal property which by attachment to or association in use with land is regarded as real property. The reasonable-man standard is applied by the courts in determining whether or not an article of personal property has become a fixture. The objective intent of the parties is the basic test.

Within reasonable limits the courts enforce the agreement of the parties relative to whether an article of personal property shall or shall not become a fixture.

Mode of attachment is important as evidence to be considered in determining the intention of the parties. If there is no attachment, that fact is prima facie evidence that the article of personal property is not a fixture.

The appropriateness of use with the real property is a fact which is always considered in determining the intention of the parties. In exceptional cases, appropriateness of use with the real property, without attachment, may be sufficient to justify holding that the article is a fixture.

The relation of the parties is always of outstanding importance. If an owner attaches his own personal property to his real property for the purpose of improving the real property, the article becomes a fixture.

Under the provisions of the Uniform Commercial Code if one sells personal property to be attached to real estate, retaining a security interest in such property, his lien will have priority over rights of third persons provided it is perfected.

Tenants who have added to the leased premises articles of personal property which are classed as trade, domestic, or agricultural fixtures may remove the articles on the termination of the lease. If the lease is for a definite term, the articles must be removed before the expiration of the term; if the lease is for an indefinite term, the articles must be removed within a reasonable time after the expiration of the lease.

Sherburne Corp. v. *Town of Sherburne*

207 A.2d 125 (Sup. Ct. Vt. 1965)

This was an action by Sherburne Corporation (plaintiff) against the Town of Sherburne (defendant) to determine whether a ski lift was personal property or real estate. The lower court held it was personal property and Sherburne Corporation appealed. Holding was reversed.

Sherburne Corporation erected a ski lift on land leased from the state. The Town of Sherburne taxed the ski lift as personal property and Sherburne Corporation brought an action asking that the ski lift be declared a fixture and not subject to tax by the Town of Sherburne. Additional facts are stated in the judge's opinion.

BARNEY, JUSTICE. The resolution of this case depends upon he classification of the lift facilities as either real property or personal property. This decision is necessarily peremptory, because the facilities are perhaps truly neither, or a little of both. The requirements of such classification have presented such an acute problem in the law, that a special sub-grouping has accumulated its own identity as a device to determine which side of the arbitrary boundary between chattels and real estate the nature of a given object places it. This is the law of fixtures. Fixtures are usually classed as real estate; trade fixtures, an exception to the rule, are usually classed as personal property.

When a scheme of classification is used to serve more than one purpose, internal conflicts frequently develop. The object of classification is to define categories so that like objects invariably fall into the same class. But "likeness" may vary as the purpose for classification varies. The incentive to class an object as either real estate or chattel for tax purposes may call for a result contrary to that arrived at when done in the context of a bailment.

However, in *First National Bank* v. *Nativi,* certain tests for resolving the classification of things as real or personal property have been set out as general rules: (1) the annexation, actual or constructive, of the article to the real estate; (2) its adaptation to the use of the realty to which it is annexed; and (3) whether or not the annexation has been made with the intention to make it a permanent accession to the freehold. By applying these tests in the first instance, we can decide what the character of the property at issue is under the law generally, without the pressures brought to that determination by possible tax consequences or the identity of the parties.

The characteristics of the lift installations appear from the findings. The lifts, including towers, cables, chairs, railings and platforms, are integrated devices for providing uphill transportation. Each one is a substantial structure, the longest lift being 6,300-feet long. The towers are designed according to the topography of the line of the particular lift, and each tower is embedded in a heavy cement base. They cannot be removed without permanent damage to the real estate. Over half of the cost of the lifts was for installation, amounting, in one case, to more than $120,000. These lifts could not be moved without a loss of a substantial portion of the installation investment. The buildings associated with the lifts are uniquely adapted to the land upon which they are located, are set upon heavy cement foundations and also cannot be moved without substantial damage to the real estate.

From the established facts already stated, annexation to the real estate and adaptation to the use of the real estate to which the property is annexed are amply evidenced. This satisfies the first two criteria previously set out. The remaining issue concerns intention to make the property a part of the real estate. This is crucial, since if the intention to make it a permanent accession is doubtful, it remains a chattel.

It is also clear from the findings that these lifts are items used in the trade or business conducted on the premises by the lessee. This is a characteristic typical of trade fixtures, which retain the nature of chattels, and may be removed at the end of a lease. As such, they are an exception to the rule pertaining to fixtures generally.

However, when we use this sort of test to arrive at an article's classification, we are ascertaining the intention of the parties by inference. Declarations in the documents representing the transaction may be useful to shed light on equivocal situations, or to directly contradict inferred intentions.

Here we have a lease. Sherburne Corp. lays great emphasis on the provision which states that the lift facilities shall be deemed to be real estate and the property of the State upon erection. Town, on the other hand, stresses the provisions that require the State to pay for the lifts in the future. From this Town argues that the provision "deeming" the facilities real estate is without real substance and a mere tax evasion device.

A reading of the lease does not bear out Town's view. The statement that the lift facilities be deemed real estate on construction is reinforced by the balance of the lease. The basic ingredient necessary to make such property trade fixtures is a right to remove them at the expiration of the lease. The entire contemplation of this lease is that the lifts cannot be removed by the lessee in any event.

Rights and Interests in Real Property

Fee Simple.   The basic land ownership interest in the United States is the fee simple which entitles the owner to the entire property for an unlimited duration of time with the unconditional power to dispose of it during his life or upon his death and which will descend to his heirs if he dies without making a will. The holder of a fee simple may grant many rights to others without changing the nature of his interest. For example, Archer, who owns land in fee simple, may give Burch a mortgage on the land, grant Clark an easement of right-of-way over the land, and lease the land to Fox for a period of years. Archer has granted rights to Burch, Clark, and Fox; but Archer still owns the land in fee simple. On the termination of the rights of Burch, Clark, and Fox, such rights revert to the owner of the fee and merge into the fee, and may again be granted by the owner.

Life Estate.   A life estate is an interest in land which is limited in time to the life or lives of persons in being. A life estate may be for the life of the holder or for the life or lives of another or others. The life tenant has the right to use the property, but he does not have a right to do acts which will result in permanent injury to the property.

Leasehold.   A leasehold gives the lessee the right to occupy and possess a given piece of real property. This right may be for a fixed period of time, such as a month or a year, or for what is known as a "tenancy at will" where the time period is not fixed in advance and either the lessor or the lessee can terminate the leasehold after giving notice to the other party of his intention to do so. The law of landlord and tenant is discussed later in this chapter.

Easements.   An easement is the nonpossessory right to use or enjoy the land of another person. It may be an easement appurtenant or an easement in gross. An easement appurtenant is the right which the owner of a particular parcel of land has, by reason of such ownership, to use the land of another for a specific purpose. The land benefited by the easement is known as the "dominant tenement," and the land subject to the easement is known as the "servient tenement." For instance, if the owner or occupier of land, tract A, has an easement of right-of-way over the land, tract B, tract A is the dominant tenement, and tract B is the servient tenement.

An easement may be created which is not accessory to adjoining land. Such an easement is known as an "easement in gross." If the easement in gross is granted to an individual, it will, as a general rule, be held to be personal to him and not assignable, transferable, or inheritable, although in a few cases such an easement has been held to be transferable. Easements to utility companies are usually easements in gross. For instance, an easement granted to a railroad company to run its tracks across the land of others or to a telephone company to string its lines across the land of others is an easement in gross.

An easement may be an affirmative or a negative easement. An affirmative easement is the right to make certain uses of the land of another. The right to drive across, to run a sewer across, or to drill for gas and oil on the land of another are affirmative easements. A negative easement is the right to have an adjoining landowner refrain from making certain uses of his land. The right to have an adjoining landowner refrain from erecting a structure on his premises which would cut off light and air from your buildings is a negative easement.

An easement may be acquired by an express grant, by a reservation in a grant, by implication, by estoppel, by necessity, or by prescription (adverse possession). Since an easement is an interest in land, it is within the purview of the statute of frauds and usually must be evidenced by a writing if it is to be enforceable. Under the statutes of most states, the grant of an easement must be executed with the same formalities as is the grant of a fee simple in real property. However, nonexpressly granted easements such as those by implication, necessity, estoppel or prescription are enforceable even though they are not in writing.

Licenses.   A license is similar in some respects to an easement; however, it is not an interest in land and may be created orally and, unless coupled with an interest, may be revoked at the will of the licensor. Permission to cross the land of another or to hunt or fish on the other's land is a license. A person entering on the land of another for the purpose of transacting business is a licensee. If a person purchases from another trees which are to be cut and hauled away, the purchaser would have an irrevocable license to go onto the land for the purpose of cutting and hauling the logs. There are innumerable situations in which one person has a license to go onto the land of another. A license, as a general rule, creates a temporary right to use another's land in a limited and specific manner.

Summary

Ownership in fee simple is the highest estate a person can hold in land. It is the original source of all rights in land and is not limited in time.

A life estate is a freehold estate for the life or lives of persons in being.

A leasehold is the right to occupy and possess real property and is limited in time.

An easement is a nonpossessory right in the land of another. An easement in gross is an easement which is not accessory to adjoining land and an easement appurtenant is accessory to adjoining land. An affirmative easement gives the owner of the easement the right to make certain uses of another's property, and a negative easement gives the owner of the easement the right to have another refrain from making certain use of his land.

An easement may be acquired by an express grant, by a reservation in a grant, by implication, by estoppel, by necessity, or by prescription. It is an interest in land, and to be enforceable, it usually must be evidenced by a writing.

A license creates a temporary privilege to make some specific use of another's land, and it is not an interest in land.

Helton v. *Jones*

402 S.W.2d 694 (Ct. App. Ky. 1966)

This was an action by Jones (plaintiff) to enjoin Helton (defendant) from interfering with a passway easement Jones claimed to have over Helton's land. Judgment for Jones. Affirmed on appeal.

Prior to 1929 Tom Noe owned a single tract of ground bounded on two sides by parallel highways. Across Noe's land was a roadway approximately 125 feet in length connecting the two highways and which for more than fifty years had been used for access to the principal parallel highway. In 1929 Noe died and his land was divided into two tracts. Since that time the owners and occupants of the tract now owned by Jones have continued to use the roadway over the other tract now owned by Helton. Prior to the time Jones acquired the property in 1943, a gate was put up across the road. Sometimes this gate was locked by Helton but Jones was given a key to it. Then in 1964 Helton put a new lock on the gate and did not give Jones a key. Jones sued Helton to enjoin him from blocking the road.

CLAY, COMMISSIONER. Helton's contention is that the use of this passway (for a period of fifty years) has always been *permissive* and therefore the use of it never ripened into an easement. Jones contends that when the lands were originally divided an easement was created, but in any event, the long-continued use matured into an absolute right.

The facts in this case are almost identical with those in *Delong* v. *Cline*. It was therein held that upon a division of a tract of land under the same circumstances we have here, an easement will pass by implication "as if he had a deed thereto" to the party who acquired the parcel whose enjoyment required the use of a pre-existing passway over another parcel.

This principle amply supports the Chancellor's finding of the existence of an easement although his finding appears to have been based on his conclusion that appellee had acquired his rights by prescription or adverse possession. Such alternate ground of the decision is also amply supported by the record. The circumstances would justify no other conclusion but that appellee had a permanent easement as a matter of right. The existence of the gate may have restricted the scope of the easement but certainly did not destroy it.

Co-ownership of Real Property

Nature of Co-ownership. Co-ownership of real property exists when two or more persons own an undivided interest in such property. The co-owners do not have separate rights in any portion of the real property; each has a share in the whole property.

There are five kinds of co-ownership of real property recognized in the United States today: (1) tenancy in common, (2) joint tenancy, (3) tenancy by the entirety, (4) community property, and (5) tenancy in partnership. No one state recognizes all five kinds of co-ownership.

Tenancy in Common. A tenancy in common is created when real property is deeded to two or more persons as tenants in common or when two or more persons inherit real property. In most states, if real property is conveyed to two or more persons and the instrument of conveyance does not state how they shall hold the property, they will hold as tenants in common.

The interest which the tenants in common hold in the property is known as an estate of inheritance, that is, each tenant holds his interest as his individual property, and on his death his interest will descend to his heirs or devisees. He may sell or encumber his interest in the property, and it is subject to levy of execution by a judgment creditor. The shares of tenants in common need not be equal, that is, one tenant may own a two-thirds interest in the property and his cotenant may own the remaining one-third.

The only common right of tenants in common is the right of possession. Each tenant has the right to possess and use the common property, but he has no right to exclude his cotenants from equal rights of possession and use. If the property is rented, the cotenants share ratably in the income from the property and must make a ratable contribution to the taxes, repairs, and upkeep.

A tenant in common may petition the court to divide the property. In such an action the property will be physically divided if it is practical, and each tenant will receive his proportionate share in kind. If this is not practical, however, the court will order the property sold, and the proceeds from the sale will be divided according to the share of each tenant. The tenants may divide the property by mutual agreement.

Joint Tenancy. A joint tenancy is created when equal interests in real property are conveyed to two or more persons by one instrument which expressly states that the persons take as joint tenants. The outstanding characteristic of the joint tenancy is the right of survivorship; that is, on the death of one of the joint tenants, his interest passes to the surviving joint tenant or tenants. The interest of a joint tenant cannot be devised by will.

The interest of a joint tenant is subject to levy by his creditors, and the jointure may be destroyed by a conveyance by one of the joint tenants. If a joint tenant conveys his interest, the conveyee holds as a tenant in common with the other joint tenant or tenants.

The right of use, possession, contribution, and partition of joint tenants is the same as that of tenants in common.

The joint tenancy with right of survivorship has been abolished in some states and is not recognized in community property states.

Tenancy by the Entirety. Tenants by the entirety must be husband and wife. This is fundamentally a joint tenancy with rights of survivorship. It can be treated only by a conveyance to persons who are husband and wife at the time of the conveyance. A tenancy by the entirety cannot be destroyed by the acts of either party. Real property owned by the entirety cannot be sold under execution issued on a judgment rendered against either the husband or the wife individually, but it may be sold on execution issued on a judgment rendered against them on a joint obligation. Neither can convey the real property by deed unless the other joins, and neither can dispose of the property by will. Tenancies by the entirety are not recognized in all states.

Community Property. In some states, what is known as the "system of community property" prevails. The principal characteristic of the system is that whatever property is acquired by the efforts of either the husband or the wife during marriage becomes a common fund or, as it is called, "community property." Either the husband or the wife may own, in addition to his or her interest in the community property, "separate property." Generally, separate property includes that property owned prior to marriage or acquired after marriage by gift, devise, or descent, or in exchange for property owned as separate property. The details of the system are set out by the statutes of each of the community property states.

Tenancy in Partnership. Tenancy in partnership was discussed in Chapter 20. The incidents of the tenancy in partnership are set out in Section 25 of the Uniform Partnership Act.

Summary

Five types of co-ownership of real property are recognized: (1) tenancy in common, (2) joint tenancy, (3) tenancy by the entirety, (4) community property, and (5) tenancy in partnership.

Tenants in common need not hold equal shares. On the death of a tenant in common, if he dies intestate, his interest passes to his heirs. He may devise his interest by will. Tenants in common have the right to possess and use the property, and each is entitled to his proportionate share of the income. Each must contribute to taxes, repairs, and upkeep in proportion to his share or interest.

Joint tenants hold equal interests which must be created by the same instrument at the same time. They have the right of survivorship. In other respects, their rights are substantially the same as the rights of tenants in common.

Tenants by the entirety must be husband and wife. On the death of either, his or her interest passes by the right of survivorship to the other. Neither party can destroy the tenancy by his individual acts, and the property is not subject to the individual debts of either.

Community property is a type of ownership by husband and wife. The rights are created by statute, and the details of the system are set out by the statutes of the state.

Acquisition of Real Property

Origin of Title to Real Property. Original title to land in the United States was acquired either by grant from the federal government or by grant from a country which held the land prior to its acquisition by the United States. The land which was within the boundaries of the original 13 states was land which had, for the most part, been granted by the king of England to the colonies or to certain individuals. The Northwest Territory was ceded by the states to the federal government. Original title to this land was a patent from the federal government signed by the president. Most of the land in Florida and sections of land in the Southwest were held by Spain, and the ownership of this land is based on Spanish grants.

Acquisition by Purchase. One of the rights of ownership is the right to sell (the right of alienation). Under our law any agreement or restriction which deprives the owner of land of his right to alienate his land is against public policy and is void. Most persons who own real property today have acquired their title by purchasing the property from a prior owner. Each state has the right to regulate the formal requirements for the transfer of the ownership of the lands within the state. We shall discuss these formalities under the heading "Transfer by Deed."

Acquisition by Gift. Ownership in real property may be acquired by gift. The donor of such property must deliver to the donee, or to some third person for the benefit of the donee, a deed which complies with all the statutory requirements of the state in which the property is located. It is not necessary for the donee, or some third person acting for the donee, to take actual physical possession of the property. The essential element of the gift is the delivery of the deed. If the donor makes deeds to real property and leaves them in his safe-deposit box to be delivered to the named donee after the death of the donor, the gift will fail for lack of delivery.

Acquisition by Adverse Possession. Title to real property may be acquired by adverse possession. The statutory law of the states provides that no action shall be brought for the recovery of the possession of land after a stated number of years, which varies from 5 to 20 years. If a person holds land by open, continuous, and adverse possession for the statutory period, he can acquire title to the land by complying with certain statutory requirements. In order to acquire title by adverse possession, there must be (1) actual occupancy, (2) which is hostile to the owner's title, (3) with open claim to title, (4) continuously for the statutory period. In some states the claimant must, in addition to the four requisites set out above, pay the taxes. The same person need not occupy the land for the entire period, but the adverse possession must be continuous. Suppose, for instance, Bixby takes possession of land owned by Altman and claims title to the land and remains in possession for four years, at which time Bixby sells his interest to Clay, who immediately takes possession and remains in possession for six years. If the statutory period is 10 years, Clay can acquire title to the land at the end of his 6-year occupancy. He acquired Bixby's rights which, added to his rights, satisfy the statutory requirement.

Acquisition by Tax Sale. If the taxes assessed on real property are not paid, they become, as a general rule, a lien which is prior to the claims of all persons having an interest in the property. After a stated period of time, if the taxes remain unpaid, the state will sell the property at a tax sale, and the purchaser at such sale will acquire title to the property. The entire procedure is statutory, and there is no uniformity in the tax laws of the several states.

Acquisition by Will or Descent. The owner of real property has the right, subject to some restrictions which will be discussed in a later section, to dispose of his real property by will. The will, to be effective, must be drawn and executed in accordance with the statutory requirements of the state in which the real property is located. If the owner of real property dies without having made a will, the land will descend to his heirs according to the laws of the state in which the real property is located.

The formal requirements for transfer by will are discussed under the heading "Disposition on Death of Owner."

Summary

Original title to all lands in the United States was acquired either by grant from the federal government or by grant from a government which held the land prior to its acquisition by the United States.

Real property is usually acquired by purchase. The formal requirements for the transfer of real property are determined by the statutes of the state in which it is located.

Real property may be acquired by gift. To have a valid gift, the donor must deliver to the donee, or to some third person for the benefit of the donee, a deed which complies with the statutory requirements of the state in which the property is located.

To acquire ownership of real property by adverse possession, the claimant must have had open, adverse, and continuous possession of the property for the statutory period.

If the taxes on real property are not paid, the property, under the laws of most states, will be sold for taxes, and the purchaser at the tax sale will be given a tax deed which, if valid, cuts off all prior claims to the real property.

The owner of real property may dispose of such property on his death by will. If the owner leaves no will, the ownership descends according to the statutes of the state in which it is located.

Converse v. Kenyon

132 N.W.2d 334 (Sup. Ct. Neb. 1965)

This was an action by George N. Converse and others (plaintiffs) against Guy E. Kenyon and others (defendants) to establish the boundaries of land. Kenyon claimed that he had acquired title to approximately twenty acres of the land by adverse possession. Judgment for Kenyon and Converse appealed. Judgment affirmed.

Kenyon and Converse owned adjoining tracts of land. Kenyon owned the east half of the section of land and Converse owned the west half. Converse claimed that the line fence dividing their land had been moved to the west and that the true line should be established, whereas Kenyon claimed that the fence had been in the same location for over 21 years and claimed the land east of the fence by adverse possession. Converse claimed that he had paid the taxes on the entire southwest quarter of the section, which included the land in dispute. In 1962 Kenyon wrote Converse that he would move the fence but that he did not know when he could get it done.

Kenyon had farmed the east half of the section including the disputed tract from 1934 until 1956 when he leased the land to his son who has farmed it since that date.

BROWER, JUSTICE. "What is sufficient to meet the requirements for actual possession depends upon the character of the land and all of the circumstances of the case.

Acts of dominion over land must, to be effective against a true owner, be so open, notorious, and hostile as to put an ordinarily prudent person on notice of the fact that his lands are in the adverse possession of another. . . .

Where one, by mistake as to the boundary line, constructs upon and takes possession of land of another, claiming it as his own to a definite and certain boundary by an actual, open, exclusive, and continuous possession thereof under such claim for 10 years or more, he acquires title thereto by adverse possession.

The fact that one claiming title by adverse possession never intended to claim more land than is called for in his deed is not a controlling factor. It is the intent with which possession is held, rather than the intention to hold in accordance with the deed, that is controlling. The claim of adverse possession is founded upon the intent with which the occupant has held possession, and this intent is ordinarily determined by what he has done in respect thereto.

In 3 Am. Jur. 2d, Adverse Possession, s. 240, p. 339, it is said:

After the running of the statute, the adverse possessor has an indefeasible title which can only be divested by his conveyance of the land to another, or by a subsequent disseisin for the statutory limitation period. It cannot be lost by a mere abandonment, or by a cessation of occupancy, or by an expression of willingness to vacate the land, or by the acknowledgment or recognition of title in another, or by subsequent legislation, or by survey.

In *Martin* v. *Martin,* this court held: "One who has acquired absolute title to land by adverse possession for the statutory period does not impair his title by thereafter paying rent to the owner of the paper title." In the opinion of the cited case it was stated: "The law is well settled that recognition of title in the former owner by one claiming adversely after he has acquired a perfect title by adverse possession will not divest him of title."

Transfer by Deed

Formalities of Transfer. Since the states have the power to regulate the conveyance of land within their borders, each state has enacted statutes which set out the formalities with which the parties should comply in such conveyance. As a general rule the conveyance of land is accomplished by the execution and delivery of a deed; and in the law of real property a deed is an instrument in writing whereby the owner of land (the grantor) conveys to another (the grantee) some right, title, or interest in real property.

Quitclaim and Warranty Deeds. Two types of deeds are in general use in the United States: the quitclaim and the warranty deed. When the grantor conveys by a quitclaim deed, he conveys to the grantee whatever title he has at the time he executes the deed, but he does not, by the form of the deed, claim to have good title or, in fact, any title; and if the title proves to be defective, or if the grantor has no title, the grantee has no action against him under the deed. Quitclaim deeds are frequently used to cure a technical defect in the chain of title to property. In such a case the grantor may claim no right, title, or interest in the property.

A warranty deed may be a deed of general warranty or of special warranty. A warranty deed contains covenants of warranty; that is, the grantor, in addition to conveying title to the property, binds himself to make good any defects in the title he has conveyed. In a general warranty deed the grantor warrants against all defects in the title and all encumbrances, whereas in a special warranty deed the grantor warrants against only those defects in the title or those encumbrances which arose after he acquired the property. If the property conveyed is mortgaged or subject to some other encumbrance, such as an easement or long-term lease, it is a common practice to give a general warranty deed which contains a provision excepting from the warranty specific encumbrances.

Form and Execution of Deed.   Some states have enacted statutes setting out the form of deed which may be used in that state. These statutes have been held to be directive, not mandatory; that is, a deed may be valid even though it does not follow the statutory form. The statutory requirements of the different states for the execution of deeds are not uniform, but they do follow a similar pattern. As a general rule a deed states the name of the grantee, contains a recitation of consideration and a description of the property conveyed, and is executed by the grantor. In most states the deed, to be eligible for recording, must be acknowledged by the grantor before a notary public or other officer authorized to take acknowledgment.

Deeds executed by corporations must, as a general rule, be sealed, and in some states the statutes require all deeds to be "signed, sealed, and delivered." In a few states the statutes provide, in addition to the above, that the deed must be witnessed by one or two witnesses. The failure to comply with such requirements does not affect the validity of the deed, but it does render the deed ineligible for recording. In all states the deed, before it becomes operative, must be delivered.

Some courts have held that a deed, in order to be valid, must be complete in all material respects at the time it is executed and acknowledged by the grantor. Under the holdings of these courts, if the name of the grantee is not stated in the deed at the time of its execution but is filled in later, the deed is a nullity. However, this is a minority holding, and under the majority rule such a deed is valid when it is completed and delivered. An agent's authority to fill in blanks left in an executed deed need not be in writing.

No technical words of conveyance are necessary; any language is sufficient which indicates with reasonable certainty an intent to transfer the ownership of the property. The phrase "give, grant, bargain, and sell" and the phrase "convey and warrant" are in common use.

A consideration is recited in a deed for historical reasons. At an early time in England, if the deed did not recite a consideration, the presumption was that the grantee held the land in trust for the heirs of the grantor, and for that reason it became standard practice to recite a consideration in the deed. The consideration recited is not necessarily the purchasee price of the real property; it may be "one dollar and other valuable consideration."

The property conveyed must be described in such a manner that it can be identified. In urban areas, descriptions are as a general rule by lot, block, and plat. In rural areas the land, if it has been surveyed by the government, is usually described by reference to the government survey; otherwise, it is described by metes and bounds. However, a description, such as my farm, Green Acres in Cook County, Illinois, would be sufficient description unless the grantor owned more than one farm called Green Acres located in Cook County, Illinois.

As a general rule a deed is required by statute to be acknowledged by the grantor, but failure to acknowledge it does not make it a nullity. If the deed is not acknowledged by the grantor, the courts have generally held that title to the property passes to the grantee, but under the recording statutes generally in force the deed is not eligible for recording. In order to cure this defect in the chain of title, the party in interest may obtain from the grantor a properly executed quitclaim deed, or he may bring an action to quiet title, in which case the court will enter an appropriate decree.

Delivery is essential to the validity of a deed. Whether or not a deed has been delivered is, in cases of dispute, a question of fact to be decided by the jury, or by the judge in a nonjury case. If a person executes deeds to his real property and puts them in his safe-deposit box together with a note directing that the deeds be delivered to named persons after his death, the deeds are inoperative and pass no title by delivery after the death of the grantor. A deed, to be valid, must be delivered in the lifetime of the grantor.

Recording Deeds.   In the United States the several states have recording statutes which establish a system for the recording of all transactions affecting the ownership of real property. The statutes are not uniform in their provisions; but in general, they provide for the recording of all deeds, mortgages, and other such documents, and further provide an unrecorded transfer is void as against an innocent purchaser or mortgagee for value. Under this system, it is customary in some states for the seller to give the buyer an abstract of title certified to date. The abstract is a history of the title of the real property according to the records and is not a guarantee of title. The buyer, for his own protection, should have the abstract examined by a competent attorney who will render an opinion as to the title held by the grantor. The opinion will state whether or not the grantor has a merchantable title to the property; and if the title is defective, the nature of the defects will be stated.

Several of the states have adopted the "Torrens system." Under this system the person who owns the land in fee will obtain, through the procedure set up by the statute, a certificate of title from the designated official; and when the real property is sold, the grantor will deliver a deed and his certificate of title to the grantee, who delivers the deed and certificate of title to the designated official and receives a new certificate of title. All liens and encumbrances against the property will be noted on the certificate of title, and the purchaser is assured that his title is good except as to liens and encumbrances noted thereon. In some states, some encumbrances, such as liens for taxes, short-term leases, and highway rights, are good against the purchaser even though they do not appear on the certificate.

Summary

Any agreement affecting an interest in land and a conveyance of real property is required to be in writing.

Two forms of deed are in general use in the United States: the quitclaim deed and the warranty deed. In a quitclaim deed the grantor conveys his interest, whatever it may be. In a warranty deed the grantor conveys his interest and, in addition, warrants his title to be free from all defects except those stated in the deed.

A deed, to be valid, must comply with certain formal requirements. These requirements are not uniform, but as a general rule the deed must name the grantee, contain words of conveyance, recite a consideration, describe the property, and be executed by the grantor. It will usually be acknowledged, may be sealed and witnessed, and must be delivered.

Disposition on Death of Owner

Statutes of Descent and Distribution. If a person does not make a will, his property, on his death, will be distributed according to the statutes known as statutes of descent and distribution. His real property will be distributed according to the statutes of the state in which it is located, and his personal property will be distributed according to the statutes of the state in which he is domiciled. A person dies intestate if he dies without leaving a will. In the event a person dies intestate and leaves no heir or next of kin who can take under the statutes of descent and distribution, his property will escheat to the state, that is, the state will become the owner of the property.

Right of Disposition by Will. The right to dispose of property by will is statutory. Under the feudal system of land tenure in England the king was the title owner of all the land, and the lords and knights held only a life estate in the land. On the death of a landholder, his rights in the land which he held terminated, and no rights in the land descended to his heirs. In 1215 the king granted to the nobility the right to pass their interest in the land which they held to their heirs.

Today, in the United States, we recognize the theory of basic ownership by the state, and on the basis of this theory the courts have upheld the right of the state and the federal government to tax the estate of a deceased person and to tax an inheritance. Also, the right of the state to prescribe the formalities which must be complied with in the devising of property by will has been firmly established.

Execution of Will.   Although the statutes concerning wills are not uniform in the different states, they are similar in their basic requirements. The courts have been strict in interpreting these statutes, and they will declare a will to be void unless all the requirements of the statute have been complied with in the execution of the will, in which case the property of the deceased will be distributed according to the statutes of descent and distribution.

As a general rule, only persons of sound mind and of full age are permitted to dispose of property by will. In some states the age at which a person may make a valid will is stated in the statute and is as low as 18 years. The required formalities vary with the different states, and the laws of the states which may affect the will should be consulted before the will is executed. Formalities which are required by many states are: (1) The will must be in writing; (2) it must be witnessed by two or three witnesses; (3) it must be signed and sealed by the testator; (4) it must be published by the testator—as a general rule, all that is required for publication is a declaration by the testator, at the time of signing, that the instrument is his will; and (5) the testator must sign in the presence and in the sight of the witnesses, and the witnesses must sign in the presence and in the sight of the testator and in the presence and in the sight of each other. If the statutory formalities are not all complied with, the will is not valid. As a general rule an attestation clause, stating the formalities which have been followed in the execution of the will, is written following the testator's signature.

Some states recognize the validity of holographic wills, and some recognize the validity of nuncupative wills. A holographic will is one which is wholly written, signed, and sealed in the testator's or testatrix's own hand. The statutes of a few states recognize these wills as valid without formal execution or attestation. A nuncupative will is an oral will. In many states the oral wills made by sailors at sea or by soldiers in actual service are recognized as valid for the purpose of disposing of the personal estate in the actual possession of the testator at the time of the making of the will.

Limitations on Disposition by Will.   A person who takes property by will takes it subject to all outstanding claims against the property, both legal and equitable. Also, the rights of creditors are superior to the rights of a beneficiary under a will. If the deceased person is insolvent, persons named as beneficiary take nothing by virtue of the will.

Under the laws of most states the widow or widower of the deceased has statutory rights in the property of the deceased spouse which cannot be defeated by will. As a general rule a widow is given the right to claim certain personal property of the deceased husband, is given the right to the use of the home for a stated period, usually a year, and is given a portion of his real estate or a life estate in a portion of his real estate. In many states the widow's share in the husband's real property is a one-third interest or a life estate in one third of his real property. In some states the husband of a deceased wife is given an interest in her property, and this right cannot be defeated by will. In the community property states, each spouse has a one-half interest in the community property, and the rights of the surviving spouse cannot be defeated by will.

Revocation of Will. One distinguishing feature of a will is that it conveys no interest in the maker's property until his death. All wills are revocable at the option of the maker; and a will, at the time it is executed, does not confer any present rights in the property devised or bequeathed. A person may revoke his will by destroying or canceling it or by making a later will, duly executed, in which he expressly states that he thereby revokes all former wills executed by him. Under the statutes of the state, certain changes in relationship may operate as a revocation of a will. In some states the marriage of a man or a woman will revoke a will made by such person while single. The birth of a child after the execution of the will may, under the laws of some states, revoke a will or operate as a partial revocation of a will.

Summary

If a person dies intestate, that is, dies without having made a will, his property will be distributed according to the statutes of descent and distribution. His personal property will be distributed according to the statutes of the state of the deceased's domicile, and his real property according to the statute of the state in which it is located.

If a person disposes of real property by will, the statutory requirements of the state in which the real property is located must be complied with if the will is to be valid; and if a person disposes of personal property by will, the statutory requirements of the state of the domicile of the testator must be complied with.

There are statutory limitations on a husband's and a wife's right to dispose of their property by will.

A will transfers no interest in property until the death of the maker, and the maker may revoke his will at any time. A will may be revoked by operation of law as the result of the change in the status of the maker.

Landlord and Tenant

Nature of Lease. A leasehold is an interest in land and is created by a lease which, as a general rule, need not be executed with the same formalities as are followed in the execution of a deed. Although, technically, a lease is a conveyance of an interest in real property, the term "lease" is commonly used in a broader sense and includes not only the conveyance but also the contractual obligations created by the covenants usually included as a part of the agreement between the lessor and lessee.

In some respects a leasehold interest in real property is treated as personal property. In probating an estate after the death of a lessee, any leasehold interest which the lessee held at the time of his death is treated as personal property. Also, in some states the courts treat the breach of a lease as a breach of contract and assess damages accordingly.

Execution of Lease. A lease, to be valid, need not conform to any specific formal requirements. Basically, a lease is a contract, and in most states, if the lease is for a term of more than one year from the making thereof, it must, under the statute of frauds, be evidenced by a writing if it is to be enforceable. In some states, however, the statute of frauds expressly provides that leases for a term of three years or less need not be evidenced by a writing to be enforceable.

The statutes of many states provide for the recording of long-term leases— 5 or 10 years, or longer—and further provide that such leases, to be eligible for recording, must be executed with the same formalities as are used in the execution of a deed. The failure to execute a long-term lease with the formalities set out in the statute does not render it a nullity; the only effect of such failure is to render the lease ineligible for recordation.

In the leasing of real estate, good business practice demands that the parties execute a carefully drafted lease which defines their respective rights. Such a lease will contain covenants covering such essential matters as the use permitted by the tenant, who shall make repairs, the landlord's right to enter the premises and the purposes for which he may enter, the rent to be paid, warranties as to the condition of the premises, and whether or not the lease may be assigned or the premises sublet.

Rights, Duties and Liabilities of the Landlord. The rights, duties, and liabilities of the landlord, as well as of the tenant, must be considered in three different situations: (1) where there is no applicable and enforceable lease clause, (2) where there is an applicable and enforceable lease clause, and (3) where there is an applicable statute. The discussion in this section of the text relates primarily to the law which applies in the absence of a lease clause or statute, and it should be kept in mind that a lease clause or statute may supercede the common-law rule in any given situation.

When a landlord leases his premises, he impliedly warrants that he will give the tenant possession of the premises, or at least that the tenant will have the right to possession, and that the tenant's possession shall not be interfered with as the result of any act or omission on the part of the landlord or as a result of any defects in the landlord's title. In the absence of covenants in the lease to the contrary, the landlord has no right to enter onto the premises during the term of the lease, and if he does, he is a trespasser.

The landlord does not warrant the condition of the premises, nor does he warrant that the premises are suitable for the purposes of the tenant. The tenant takes the premises as he finds them. Since the landlord has no duty as to the condition of the premises, he is not liable to the tenant or his family for injuries or property damage due to obvious defects or failure to repair. To this general rule, there are some very important exceptions: (1) The landlord remains liable to use due care for those common areas of a building in which he retains control; (2) the landlord must disclose concealed defects known to him and not discoverable on a reasonable inspection by the tenant and is liable for those defects not disclosed that cause injury; (3) the landlord remains liable for the consequences of any negligently made repairs, even though he was not obligated to make them; (4) the landlord who rents a fully furnished dwelling for a short period impliedly warrants that the premises are safe and habitable.

Where the lease obligates the landlord to make repairs and he does not do so within a reasonable time, the tenant's best course of action in many cases is to have the repair made and deduct the reasonable expense of doing so from the rent. If the tenant does not do so and suffers injury or damage due to the landlord's failure to repair, the landlord may or may not be liable. In some states, the tenant is denied recovery under the rule of "avoidable consequences."

The emergence of substantial housing problems in large cities has led many cities and states to pass statutes imposing the duty to repair residential properties on the landlord. Failure to make the repairs may result in landlord liability for injuries or give the tenant the right to withhold rent until the repairs are made or to move out.

The landlord is entitled to the agreed rent, and at the expiration of the term of the lease, has the right to the surrender of the premises in as good condition as when leased, normal wear and destruction by the elements excepted.

Rights and Duties of the Tenant. The tenant may use the leased premises for any lawful purpose which is reasonable and appropriate, unless the purpose for which they may be used is expressly set out in the lease. Under the common-law rule the tenant has the exclusive right to the possession and use of the premises during the term of the lease, and if the landlord comes onto the premises without the consent of the tenant, he will be guilty of trespass. The tenant is fully responsible for the care and upkeep of the premises and owes a duty to make all ordinary repairs so that the premises will be returned in the same condition as rented except for normal wear and tear. The tenant has no duty to make major repairs except where he was negligent, but he must take steps to prevent further damage from the elements as when a window breaks or a roof leaks. If buildings are destroyed by fire or by the elements, the tenant owes no duty to rebuild them unless their destruction is the result of negligence on his part. However, the destruction of buildings does not release the tenant from his obligation to pay the entire amount of rent. This common-law rule has been changed by statutes in several states.

The tenant is normally liable to persons injured or property damaged because of the tenant's negligence on that part of the property over which he has control.

The tenant has in the leased premises a property interest which he may transfer to another by the assignment of the lease unless the lease expressly provides that it shall not be assigned. If the tenant assigns the lease, he does not relieve himself from any of his contractual obligations under the lease, but he does divest himself of his property interest in the leased premises. The tenant may sublease the premises or a part thereof. If he subleases the premises or a part thereof, he does not divest himself of his property interest therein, and he remains liable to the landlord on all the covenants in the lease. His relation to his sublessee is that of landlord. He cannot grant to a sublessee greater rights than he has under the original lease, and if the original lease contains a provision denying the tenant the right to sublease the premises or any part thereof, such provision is enforceable.

Termination of the Lease. Normally, a lease is ended by "surrender" of the premises by the tenant to the landlord and "acceptance" of the premises by the landlord. However, sometimes the tenant may be forced out by the landlord prior to the end of the lease period or the tenant may vacate the premises before the end of the lease period.

If the premises become uninhabitable because of the acts of the landlord, then under the doctrine of "construction eviction" the tenant may, after giving the landlord a reasonable opportunity to correct the defect, move out and incur no further liability for rent. The tenant must move out within a reasonable amount of time. For example, if the furnace breaks down in the middle of the winter and the apartment is without heat for February and March, the tenant cannot use this as an excuse for breaking the lease in August.

If the tenant abandons the premises before the end of the lease, the consequences vary from state to state. In some states the landlord is under an obligation to mitigate damages and must attempt to rerent or will lose any claim for further rent against the original tenant. In other states, the landlord may continue to collect rent from the tenant without rerenting, but loses the right if he does rerent. As a result, many leases contain a clause maintaining the landlord's right to the rent whether or not he tries to rerent and continuing the tenant's liability for any difference in rents if the landlord does rerent.

Summary

As a general rule, no formalities are required for the execution of short-term leases—one to three years—but leases for a longer period of time are required by the statute of frauds to be in writing. Long-term leases—5 to 10 years or longer—are required by the statutes of some states to be recorded, and such leases must be executed with the same formalities as are used in the execution of deeds to real property.

A landlord, in leasing premises, impliedly warrants that the tenant will have possession and quiet enjoyment of the premises. He does not warrant the condition of the premises or their suitability for the tenant's purposes. Unless the landlord agrees to make ordinary repairs he has no duty to do so; however, some statutes now require landlords to keep residential property in repair.

In the absence of covenants in the lease to the contrary, the tenant has the exclusive right to the possession of the premises and is responsible for the repair and upkeep of the same. The tenant has the right to make any lawful use of the premises he wishes, provided the use does not result in permanent injury to them.

Normally a lease is terminated by surrender by the tenant and acceptance by the landlord at the end of the lease term. However, if the premises become uninhabitable through the acts of the landlord the tenant may move out within a reasonable time after giving the landlord notice to remedy the defects. If the tenant abandons the premises prior to the end of the lease he may remain liable for the rent.

Brown v. Southall Realty Co.

237 A.2d 834 (Ct. App. D.C. 1968)

This was an action brought by Southall Realty (plaintiff) to evict Mrs. Brown (defendant) for nonpayment of rent. Mrs. Brown contended that no rent was due under the lease because it was an illegal contract. The trial court held for the landlord, Southall Realty. Judgment reversed on appeal, holding that no rent was owed by the tenant.

QUINN, JUDGE. The evidence developed, at the trial, revealed that prior to the signing of the lease agreement, Southall was on notice that certain Housing Code violations existed on the premises in question. An inspector for the District of Columbia Housing Division of the Department of Licenses and Inspections testified that the violations, an obstructed commode, a broken railing and insufficient ceiling height in the basement, existed at least some months prior to the lease agreement and had not been abated at the time of trial. He also stated that the basement violations prohibited the use of the entire basement as a dwelling place. Counsel for Southall Realty at the trial below elicted an admission from Brown that "he told the defendant after the lease had been signed that the back room of the basement was habitable despite the Housing Code Violations."

This evidence having been established and uncontroverted, Mrs. Brown contends that the lease should have been declared unenforceable because it was entered into in contravention to the District of Columbia Housing Regulations, and knowingly so.

Section 2304 of the District of Columbia Housing Regulations reads as follows:

No persons shall rent or offer to rent any habitation, or the furnishings thereof, unless such habitation and its furnishings are in a clean, safe and sanitary condition in repair, and free from rodents or vermin.

Section 2501 of these same Regulations, states:

Every premises accommodating one or more habitations shall be maintained and kept in repair so as to provide decent living accommodations for the occupants. This part of the Code contemplates more than mere basic repairs, and maintenance to keep out the elements; its purpose is to include repairs and maintenance designed to make a premises or neighborhood healthy and safe.

It appears that the violations known by appellee to be existing on the leasehold at the time of the signing of the lease agreement were of a nature to make the "habitation" unsafe and unsanitary. Neither had the premises been maintained or repaired to the degree contemplated by the regulations, i.e., "designed to make a premises . . . healthy and safe." The lease contract was, therefore, entered into in violation of the Housing Regulations requiring that they be safe and sanitary and that they be properly maintained.

In the case of *Hartman* v. *Lubar,* the court stated that, "the general rule is that an illegal contract, made in violation of the statutory prohibition designed for police or regulatory purposes, is void and confers no right upon the wrongdoer."

". . . To this general rule, however, the courts have found exceptions. For the exception, resort must be had to the intent of the legislature, as well as the subject matter of the legislation."

A reading of Sections 2304 and 2501 infers that the Commissioners of the District of Columbia, in promulgating these Housing Regulations, were endeavoring to regulate the rental of housing in the District and to insure for the prospective tenants that these rental units would be "habitable" and maintained as such. . . . To uphold the validity of this lease agreement, in light of the defects known to be existing on the leasehold prior to the agreement (i.e., obstructed commode, broken railing, and insufficient ceiling height in the basement), would be to flout the evident purposes for which Sections 2304 and 2501 were enacted. The more reasonable view is, therefore, that where such conditions exist on a leasehold prior to an agreement to lease, the letting of such premises constitutes a violation of Sections 2304 and 2501 of the

Housing Regulations, and that these Sections do indeed "imply a prohibition" so as "to render the prohibited act void."

[*The result reached in this case is not typical of the attitude many courts would presently take. It is, however, becoming an increasingly common result in large cities where courts and legislative bodies are attempting to deal with "slum" housing.*]

The Automobile Supply Co. v. The Scene-in-Action Corp.

172 N.E. 35 (Sup. Ct. Ill. 1930)

This was an action by Scene-in-Action Corporation (plaintiff) to vacate a confession judgment that Automobile Supply Company (defendant) had obtained for $1,750 rent for the last five months under a lease ending September 28, 1928. The trial court denied Scene-in-Action's motion to vacate the judgment, the Appellate Court affirmed this decision, and Scene-in-Action appealed to the Supreme Court. Affirmed.

Scene-in-Action moved to vacate the judgment on the grounds that it had been constructively evicted by the breach of the landlord's convenant to furnish steam heat during the ordinary business hours of the heating season. Scene-in-Action alleged that on a number of days in November, December, February, March, and April the premises were either without heat or that the temperature was below 50° so as to seriously interfere with or prevent its employees from carrying on their normal duties of making and selling advertising display signs. It further alleged that it gave notice in February to Automobile Supply Company that unless the terms of the lease were complied with, it would terminate the lease and vacate the premises on April 30. Scene-in-Action vacated the premises on April 30, delivered the keys to the lessor's agent, and did not thereafter occupy the premises.

DUNN, CHIEF JUSTICE. The eviction of a tenant from the possession or enjoyment of the demised premises, or any part thereof, by the landlord releases the tenant from the further payment of rent. Rent is the return made to the lessor by the lessee for his use of the land, and the landlord's claim for rent therefore depends upon the tenant's enjoyment of the land for the term of his contract. It follows that if the tenant is deprived of the premises by any agency of the landlord the obligation to pay rent ceases, because such obligation has force only from the consideration of the enjoyment of the premises. The eviction which will discharge the liability of the tenant to pay rent is not necessarily an actual physical expulsion from the premises or some part of them, but any act of the landlord which renders the lease unavailing to the tenant or deprives him of the beneficial enjoyment of the premises constitutes a constructive eviction of the tenant, which exonerates him from the terms and conditions of the lease and he may abandon it.

Not every act of a landlord in violation of his covenants or of the tenant's enjoyment of the premises under the lease will amount to a constructive eviction. Some acts of interference may be mere acts of trespass to which the term "eviction" is not applicable. To constitute an eviction there must be something of a grave and permanent character done by the landlord clearly indicating the intention of the landlord to deprive the tenant of the longer beneficial enjoyment of the premises in accordance with the terms of the lease. . . . The failure of a landlord to furnish heat for the demised premises in accordance with the terms of his covenant in the lease justifies the tenant in removing from the premises, and if he does so he is discharged from the payment of rent thereafter. . . . These facts constitute a constructive eviction. There can be no constructive eviction, however, without the vacating of the premises. Where a tenant fails to surrender possession after the landlord's commission of acts justifying the abandonment of the premises the liability for rent will continue so long as possession of the premises is continued. . . . Whether the acts of the landlord amount to a constructive eviction is ordinarily a question of fact for the decision of a jury, depending upon the circumstances of the particular case. . . .

The affidavit in support of the motion to vacate the judgment did not show a defense to the claim for rent under the principles stated. Conceding, without deciding, that the affidavit stated with sufficient definiteness and particularity conditions in regard to the furnishing of heat which would have justified the vacating of the premises in December, on February 20 and on April 9, yet the defendant did not vacate them. . . .

Where a landlord is guilty of such a breach of his duty to his tenant under the terms of the lease that the tenant would be justified in vacating the premises, he is not obliged to vacate immediately but is entitled to a reasonable time in which to do so. What is such reasonable time is usually a question of fact, though under the circumstances of a particular case it may become a question of law. . . . If the plaintiff in error on account of the failure of the defendant in error to furnish heat in December, as it had agreed, would then have been entitled to vacate the premises, it does not appear that it did so within a reasonable time, and it must therefore be regarded as having waived the defendant in error's breach of its covenant. Neither does it appear that the plaintiff in error vacated the premises within a reasonable time after February 20. If it had a right on that date to vacate the premises within a reasonable time for the previous breach of the defendant in error it did not have the right to declare a termination of the lease to take effect two months later. And the same thing is true of the breach of April 9. The affidavit shows no cause of complaint subsequent to April 9. The burden of showing a vacation of the premises on account of the landlord's breach of his duty to the tenant under the lease within a reasonable time after such breach is upon the tenant.

· · · · ·

The affidavit alleges an abandonment of the premises, but not an abandonment justified by the fault of the landlord, within a reasonable time after the occurrence of such fault, and the acceptance of the keys or entry of the landlord after such abandonment was not an acceptance of the abandonment as a surrender of the premises. . . .

Public Controls on the Use of Land

While the owner of an interest in real property may generally make such use of his property as he desires, he does not have an unlimited right to do so.

Society places a number of restraints on the property owner: (1) The owner cannot use his property in such a way as to unduly injure others; (2) through the use of the "police power," governmental units have the right to impose reasonable regulations on the use of property; and (3) society retains the right to divest ownership through the eminent domain power. As the population of the United States increases and the country becomes more urbanized, there is a tendency to make an increased use of these societal restraints on real property ownership.

Nuisance Control. When different uses are made of separate parcels of land, those uses may come into conflict and one or more of the users may become very unhappy. For example, the owner of a grove of orange trees finds that the dust from a nearby cement mill is forming a crust on his oranges, or the owner of a drive-in movie finds that the spotlights at a nearby auto racetrack are interfering with his patrons' enjoyment of the movies, or a housewife finds the noise from a nearby airport is interfering with her peace of mind. In some cases the courts have granted damages and injunctive relief to such aggrieved persons on the grounds that the use on the other property constitutes a nuisance which interferes substantially with the enjoyment of the property of the aggrieved person. The law of nuisance is discussed in Chapter 4.

Zoning and Subdivision Ordinances. State legislatures commonly delegate to political subdivisions the police power to impose reasonable regulations designed to promote the public health, safety, morals, and the general welfare of the community. Zoning ordinances are an exercise of such a power to regulate. Normally, zoning ordinances divide the political subdivision into a number of districts, specify or limit the use to which property in those districts can be put, and restrict improvements and use on the land.

Such restrictions and controls may be of four basic types:

1. Control of Use.   Regulation of the activity on the land such as single family dwellings, multi-family dwellings, commercial, light industry or heavy industry.
2. Control of Height and Bulk.   Control of the height of buildings, the setback from front, side and rear lot lines, and the portion of a lot that can be covered by a building.
3. Control of Population Density.   Control over the amount of living space that must be provided for each person and specification of the maximum number of persons who can be housed in a given area.
4. Control of Aesthetics.   Commonly used to control billboards, but also may be used to enforce similarity or dissimilarity of buildings as well as to preserve historical areas or communities.

When zoning ordinances are passed they have only a prospective effect so that already existing uses and buildings are permitted to continue. However, the ordinance may provide for the gradual passing out of such uses and buildings that do not conform to the general zoning plan. If a property owner later wants to use his property other than is permitted by the zoning ordinance, he must try to have it amended by showing his proposed changes are in accordance with the overall plan or by obtaining a variance on the ground the ordinance creates an undue hardship on him by depriving him of the opportunity to make a reasonable use of his land. Such attempts to obtain amendments or variances often conflict with the interests of other nearby property owners who have a vested interest in the zoning status quo and produce heated battles before the zoning authorities.

Many local governments also have ordinances dealing with proposed subdivisions. The ordinances often require that the developer meet certain requirements as to lot size, street and sidewalk layout, and provision for sanitary facilities, and that the city approve the proposed development. In addition, the ordinance may in some cases require the developer to dedicate land to the city for streets, parks, and schools. The purpose of such ordinances is to protect the would-be purchasers in the subdivision as well as the city population as a whole by ensuring that minimum standards are met by the developer.

Eminent Domain. The U.S. Constitution provides that private property shall not be taken for public use without just compensation. Implicit in this statement is the power of the state to take property for public use by paying "just compensation" to the owner of the property. This power of eminent domain makes possible our highways, water control projects, municipal and civic centers, public housing, and urban renewal.

Currently, there are several major problems inherent in the use of the eminent domain power. The first is what is meant by "just compensation." A property owner now receives the "fair market value" of his property; but some people feel that this falls short of reimbursing the owner for what he has lost since it does not cover the lost "goodwill" of a business or the emotional attachment a person may have to his home. Thus, some persons argue that the public at large does not pay for the benefit it is receiving and the person whose property has been taken has had an unfair burden placed on him.

A second problem is deciding when a "taking" has occurred. The answer is easy where the owner is completely dispossessed by a governmental unit. It is much more difficult where (1) the zoning power has been utilized to restrict the permissible use of a given piece of property only for a narrow and publicly beneficial use, such as a parking lot, or (2) where the government uses nearby land in such a way as to almost completely destroy the usefulness of adjoining, privately owned land as sometimes occurs in the case of municipal airports.

A third problem is determining when the eminent domain power can be properly exercised. Clearly where the governmental unit itself uses the property, as in the case of a municipal building or a public highway, the use of the power is proper. However, where as in the case of urban renewal, the condemned property may be resold to a private developer or the condemned property is not substandard, the use of the power is not so clearly justified. While the courts have approved these practices in some cases, the final legislative and judicial results on this point are not yet certain.

Summary

Society places a number of restraints on the ownership of real property. First, a person may not create a nuisance on his property such that it unreasonably interferes with another person's enjoyment of his own land. Second, legislative bodies may use the constitutionally provided police power to impose reasonable regulations on property designed to promote the public health, safety, morals and general welfare. Third, the government through the eminent domain power may divest ownership entirely of property it desires to use for public purposes by paying just compensation to the private owner.

Ferguson v. City of Keene

238 A.2d 1 (Sup. Ct. N.H. 1968)

This was an action by Ferguson (plaintiff) to recover for injury to her property from the noise and vibration emanating from the airport owned by the City of Keene (defendant). The trial court refused to hold as a matter of law that Ferguson had no cause of action in "inverse condemnation." The Supreme Court reversed, holding that no claim of inverse condemnation was stated, but that Ferguson had stated a cause of action in nuisance.

The airport had been established in 1942 and Ferguson acquired her property in 1947. In 1956 the airport was enlarged and part of Ferguson's property was taken for this purpose. Ferguson alleged that the use of a "warm up apron" located opposite her house resulted in such noise and vibration as to cause windows to break, to make conversation or sleep in the house impossible, and life generally unbearable. She further alleged that this use of the airport constituted a taking of her property for which she was required to be compensated.

DUNCAN, JUSTICE. It is the settled law of this jurisdiction that a municipality, like any property owner, is bound to use its property in a reasonable manner, and is liable if its use results in a private nuisance. The City of Keene contends, however, that no taking of Ferguson's property can properly be alleged, since she admits that the flight path of aircraft does not cross it, and damage alone without an actual taking requires no compensation. The City further argues that its use of the airport is "proper," and that subjection of airports to liability for claims such as this would unduly impede the progress of air transportation in the state. Ferguson asserts that the allegations of its writ include all of the classic elements of nuisance, and also that the defendant's conduct of the airport gives rise to a cause of action for "inverse condemnation," even though no overflights occur.

Inverse condemnation is a term used to describe "a cause of action against a governmental defendant to recover the value of property which has been taken in fact by the governmental defendant, even though no formal exercise of the power of eminent domain has been attempted by the taking agency."

Pertinent cases decided by the United States Supreme Court have not gone beyond the point of holding that there may be recovery in inverse condemnation for damages occasioned by direct flights of aircraft over a claimant's property. *U.S.* v. *Causby.* As was pointed out in Dunham, *Griggs* v. *Allegheny County* in *Perspective: Thirty Years of Supreme Court Expropriation Law:* "The question whether those (claimants) adjacent to airports, but not in any flight path, should be compensated thus remains an open one so far as the Supreme Court decisions are concerned. But the logic of *Causby* and its idea of fairness would seem to require compensation even where planes do not fly directly over the objector's land." However, in *Batten* v. *United States,* the Court of Appeals declined to extend the doctrine to a case where overflights did not occur, relying upon the proposition that the Federal Constitution requires compensation for a "taking" only. . . .

"Since there is hardly a government act which could not cause someone substantial damage, an arbitrary boundary line must be drawn between compensable and non-compensable injury." Under the federal Constitution, the line has been drawn at compensation for a taking of property. "The Fifth Amendment . . . requires just compensation where private property is taken for public use . . . (but) does not undertake . . . to socialize all losses. . . ."

A genuine distinction may reasonably be thought to exist between the nature of the injury suffered by the owner whose land is subjected to direct overflight, and that suffered by his neighbor whose land is not beneath the flight path. Only the former has lost the use of the airspace above his land, and he is subjected to risks of physical damage and injury not shared by the latter.

To what extent the nuisance of which Ferguson complains is essential to the public use of the City's airport is a question which is not determinable at this stage of this litigation. The question whether a defendant in circumstances such as these should be compelled by inverse condemnation to acquire an "easement" and compensate Ferguson therefore presents issues of social policy which might well be the subject of legislative study and appropriate enactment.

GRIMES, JUSTICE (dissenting).   Ferguson's writ alleges that

the noise from the planes "warming up" for take off, make such a great amount of noise that it is impossible for the people in the house to converse or talk on the telephone, the house vibrates and the glass in the windows shake and that more than 20 panes of glass have been broken by said vibration in the winter of 1963-1964, that it is often times impossible to sleep and there is no peace or quiet in their home and that life has become unbearable because of said noise.

The majority of the court says this declaration does not set forth a cause of action based on inverse condemnation. I disagree.

Our court long ago decided that in our state at least, the term "property" refers to "the right of any person to possess, use, enjoy and dispose of a thing" and is not limited to the thing itself, and that a person's property is "taken" for public use so as to entitle him to "just compensation" under our constitution when a physical interference substantially subverts one of these rights even though the thing itself is not taken.

I am unimpressed with the rationale of those cases which confine inverse condemnation to overflights. A person's property rights can be damaged as greatly by sound waves traveling horizontally as by those traveling vertically, and to draw a distinction is to ignore reality.

We are dealing here with an important and fundamental individual right, the roots of which reach back to Magna Carta. It is one which deserves to be stoutly defended and liberally construed. It is one which we should not deny to Ferguson because the means by which her property was taken was neither known to nor foreseen by the Barons of England or the Framers of our Constitution.

The court while denying the constitutional right has at least recognized that Ferguson has set forth a cause of action based on nuisance. This I think is a poor substitute from the standpoint of both parties.

Problem Cases

1. Dykes owned a ranch which he sold to Gomez. At the time of the sale, a trailer house, owned by an employee of Dykes, was parked near the permanent employee's house and was temporarily attached to it by pieces of tin held in place by placing cement blocks on them. There were no electrical, water, or gas connections of any kind made to the trailer house. The trailer house was set up on cement blocks which were not permanently annexed to the ground. No mention of the trailer house was made in the contract of sale or in the deed to the ranch. Gomez claims that the trailer house is a fixture and that he acquired ownership of it as part of the real estate. Is Gomez entitled to the trailer house?

2. Wolff rented a house from Realty Company. Realty Company gave Wolff written permission to install an oil-burning unit in the furnace, the oil burner to remain the property of Wolff with the right to remove it when he surrendered possession of the house. Realty Company sold the house to Sarafin. When Wolff moved he moved the oil burner and restored the furnace to its original condition. Sarafin sued Wolff to recover the value of the oil burner on the ground that it was a fixture and was his property. Is Sarafin entitled to a judgment?

3. Plaintiff and defendant own adjoining lots, and a strip of land 11 to 12 feet wide separates the houses on the lots. The distance from the plaintiff's house to the boundary is 7½ feet. Plaintiff's predecessor in title, Mrs. Brewer, and her husband owned automobiles from 1927 to 1949 and drove them on the strip, including the portion owned by their neighbors, because it could not be avoided and because it was impossible to tell where the lot line was. Plaintiff purchased the property from the Brewers in 1949 and continued to drive across the strip. Defendant purchased the other lot in 1948, began protesting the plaintiff's driving on his land in 1952, and in 1954 erected a chain link fence on the lot line which effectively prevented the plaintiff from driving his car across the strip to get to his garage. Plaintiff seeks an injunction ordering the defendants to remove the fence and other obstructions in the driveway and to enjoin

them from placing obstructions in the future. Should the injunction be granted? If so, on what grounds? If not, why not?

4. Sewell and Reilly owned adjoining lots. They entered into a written agreement whereby each agreed to allow the other to use the south 10 feet of his lot for alley purposes "for so long as the alley" over the other party's lot remained open. Did this agreement create an easement or a license?

5. Lee Waller, a widow, and her daughter, Blanche Bell, owned a house and lot as joint tenants. On October 9, 1958, Lee Waller and Blanche Bell joined in executing a contract whereby they contracted to sell the property to Edwin Hughes for $21,000. After the execution of the contract but before the purchase price was paid in full and a deed executed and delivered to Hughes, Blanche Bell died, leaving her husband surviving her. Under the laws of descent and distribution of the state a surviving husband is entitled to one third of the real estate of which a deceased wife owns at her death. Blanche's husband claims a one-third interest in the Hughes contract of sale. Lee Waller claims that she is the sole owner of the contract interest by right of survivorship. What are the rights of Lee Waller and Blanche's husband in the Hughes contract?

6. In 1935, the state purchased a tract of land for park purposes. It developed the tract to the edge of a cliff along the Columbia River. It fenced the property and built shelter houses and cared for it generally. No improvements were made from 1945 to 1947 but the park was open to the public. In 1947, Stockdale purchased an adjoining tract of land and at this time it was discovered that the portion of the state park along the cliff was included in the deed to the tract purchased by Stockdale. The statute of limitations is 10 years. The state claims the land along the cliff by right of adverse possession. Is the state the owner of the disputed tract?

7. Ellery owned a lot in Wilmington, and Howard owned a lot in San Diego. Ellery and Howard agreed that each would execute a quitclaim deed of his property in favor of the other for the sole purpose of avoiding proceedings in probate. The deeds were executed on November 9, 1950, and were placed by Howard in a safe-deposit box to which only he and his wife had access. In June, 1954, the agreement was canceled by mutual consent, and Howard sold his San Diego property. Later, at the request of Ellery, Howard returned Ellery's deed, and Ellery tore it into pieces, twice lengthwise and twice crosswise. Ellery died on August 19, 1956. Ellery left a will devising all his real estate to nephews and a niece. Two days after Ellery's death, Howard taped the pieces of the torn-up deed together and caused the document to be placed on record on August 21, 1956. Howard claimed that Ellery had stated to him that the deed was torn up accidentally and that Ellery gave the pieces of the deed to Howard.

Howard and his wife took possession of the Wilmington property and have lived here ever since. Is Howard the owner of the Wilmington property?

8. Winslow rented an apartment from Landlord and signed a lease which provided, in part, that "Landlord or landlord's agents shall not be responsible for the presence of bugs, vermin, or insects, if any, in the premises, nor shall their presence affect this lease." Some mice appeared in Winslow's apartment and despite efforts to get rid of them, they continued their presence in the apartment. Winslow moves out, claiming construction eviction, and cites §227 of the Real Property Law of New York which provides: "Where any building, which is leased or occupied, is destroyed or so injured by the elements or any other cause as to be untenable, and unfit for occupancy, and no express agreement to the contrary has been made in writing, the

lessee or occupant may if the destruction or injury occurred without his fault or neglect, quit and surrender possession of the leasehold premises. . . . and he is not liable to pay to the lessor or owner, rent for the time subsequent to the surrender." Landlord sues Winslow for rent for the unexpired portion of the lease. As judge, would you decide for Winslow or Landlord? Why?

9. Anna had leased a third-floor tenement apartment from Santo for about 15 years. Under Connecticut law, Santo was required to keep all public halls in the tenement lighted, but Anna had found it necessary to complain frequently about the adequacy of the lighting. One night Anna returned from work to the apartment house about 1:30 A.M. All of the hall lights were out. The light in the lower hall was turned on by a wall switch. The lights in the upper halls were operated by pull chains. None of the lights lighted the stairs adequately. She turned on the light in the lower hall and ascended the stairs. While reaching for the pull chain to turn on the light in the upper hall, she lost her balance and fell down the entire flight of stairs. Anna brought suit to recover damages for the personal injuries suffered. Santo claims that there was no breach of duty on his part and that Anna should also be precluded from recovering because she was contributorily negligent or had assumed the risk. Should Anna recover?

10. In 1951, Buyer acquired a piece of property in the City of Mount Vernon. While the property was surrounded completely by business buildings, it had been zoned for residential use in 1927 and the parking of automobiles allowed as a nonconforming use since that time. In 1952, the city council amended the zoning ordinance and placed Buyer's property in a zoning category known as "Designated Parking District" which prohibited all uses for the property except the parking and storage of automobiles. Buyer wants to erect a retail shopping center on the property. He claims that the effect of the zoning ordinance is to destroy the greater part of the value of his property and amounts to a taking of private property without just compensation. On these grounds he sues the city to have the ordinance declared unconstitutional. The city claims that the zoning ordinance limiting Buyer's property to the parking of automobiles is necessary because of parking and traffic congestion in the community. Should Buyer's argument prevail?

chapter 31. Secured Transactions

Introduction

Nature of Security. In the United States today a substantial portion of the business transacted involves the extension of credit. The term "credit" has many meanings. We shall use it, however, as designating a transaction in which goods are sold and delivered, services are rendered, or money is loaned in exchange for the recipient's promise to pay at some future date.

Unsecured Credit. A multitude of transactions are made which are based on unsecured credit. A common example of such credit is the monthly charge account at the local department store, where goods are sold and delivered to the customer, who promises to pay for them at a later date. Such a transaction is usually called an open-book account. The use of the open-book account or other types of unsecured credit is not confined to consumer transactions but is used extensively by jobbers, suppliers of raw materials, and manufacturers.

This type of credit transaction involves the maximum of risk from the standpoint of the creditor. When goods are delivered, services rendered, or money loaned on unsecured credit, the creditor loses all rights in the goods, services, or money and in return has only a claim against the debtor for the agreed price or for whatever he may have promised in return. If the promise is not fulfilled, the creditor's only course of action is to bring a suit and obtain a judgment. He then may have the sheriff levy an execution on any property subject to the execution, or he may garnish wages or other credits due the debtor which may be subject to garnishment. A person may be execution proof; that is, he may not have any property subject to execution, and at the same time he may not have a steady job or credits due him, in which case garnishment would be of no aid in collecting the judgment. A businessman may obtain credit insurance and thereby stabilize his credit risk, even though such action does not reduce it. The credit losses of a business extending unsecured credit is reflected in the price the consumer pays for the goods or services, or in the rate of interest paid by a borrower from such businesses.

Secured Credit. If the creditor wishes to minimize his credit risk, he can contract for security; that is, he may require his debtor to convey to him a security interest in property, or he may ask that some person promise to be liable in the event the debtor defaults. If a security interest in property is conveyed to the creditor and the debtor defaults in his payments, the creditor will have the right to sell the property and pay the debt out of the proceeds. If the proceeds are not sufficient to pay the debt, he will have, in the absence of a special agreement, an unsecured claim for the unpaid balance.

Development of Security. Various types of security devices have been developed as social and economic need for such arose. The rights and liabilities of the parties to a secured transaction depend on the nature of the security, that is, whether the security pledged is the promise of another to pay if the debtor does not or whether a security interest in goods, intangibles or real estate is conveyed as security for the payment of a debt or obligation.

If personal credit is pledged, the party may guarantee the payment of the debt, that is, become guarantor, or he may join the debtor in his promise to pay in which case he would become surety for the debt.

The use of personal property (goods and intangibles) as security has had an unorganized development. Under pre-Code law the rights and liabilities of the parties involved were determined, for the most part, on the satisfaction of formal requirements.

The oldest and simplest security device was the pledge. Some historians suggest that it had its origin in the tribal custom of giving hostages to assure the keeping of the peace. To have a pledge valid against third-person claimants it was necessary that the property used as security be delivered to the pledgee or a pledge holder. On default by the pledgor the pledgee had the right to sell the property and apply the proceeds to the payment of the debt.

Situations arose in which it was desirable to leave the property used as security in the possession of the debtor. To accomplish this objective the debtor would give the creditor a bill of sale to the property, thus passing title to the creditor. The bill of sale would include a defeasance clause, that is, it would provide that if the debtor performed his promise the bill of sale would become null and void, thus revesting title to the property in the debtor. By this device a secret lien on the goods was created and the early courts held that such a transaction was a fraud on third-party claimants and void as to them. Statutes were enacted providing for the recording or filing of the bill of sale which was later designated as a chattel mortgage. These statutes were not uniform in their provisions. Most of them set up formal requirements for the execution of the chattel mortgage and also stated the effect of recording or filing on the rights of third-party claimants.

To avoid the requirements for the execution and filing of the chattel mortgage, sellers of goods would sell the goods on a contract by the terms of which the seller retained the title to the goods until the purchase price of the goods was paid in full. On default by the buyer the seller could (*a*) repossess the goods or (*b*) pass title and recover a judgment for the unpaid balance of the purchase price. Abuses of this security device gave rise to some regulatory statutes. About one half of the states enacted statutes which provided that the conditional sales contract was void as to third parties unless it was filed or recorded.

No satisfactory device whereby inventory could be used as security was developed. Under the pledge, field warehousing was used and the after-acquired property clause in a chattel mortgage on a stock of goods held for resale partially fulfilled this need. One of the devices which was used was the trust receipt. It was a short-time marketing security arrangement and had its origin in the export-import trade. It was later used extensively as a means of financing retailers of high-unit value consumer goods.

Another method of using inventory as security was that of factoring. The goods involved were delivered to the factor for sale. As a general rule the factor sold the goods in his own name and guaranteed any credit he extended. The factor usually advanced money on the goods, and he had a lien on them for the money advanced and for his charges. Several states enacted factor acts defining the rights and liabilities of the parties involved.

Uniform Commercial Code.   The Uniform Commercial Code, Article 9, Secured Transactions, represents the first comprehensive scheme for the regulation of security interests in personal property and fixtures. It does not include security interests in real estate, nor does it replace existing statutory liens such as the Ship Mortgage Act of 1920, landlords' liens, artisans' liens, equipment trusts covering railroad rolling stock, and other listed special liens. (9–104.) [1] Furthermore, the Uniform Commercial Code makes no change in specific statutes such as those on usury, requirements for disclosure of finance charges, small-loan laws, pawnbrokers' laws, and the like. (9–201.)

One of the objectives of the Uniform Commercial Code is to abolish formal distinctions between security devices and to make distinctions where distinctions are necessary along functional rather than formal lines. The state, on adopting the Uniform Commercial Code, repeals its existing statutes regulating security interests in personal property and fixtures. The Code applies to all types of security interests created by contract and includes all of the familiar

---

[1] The numbers in the parentheses refer to the sections of the Uniform Commercial Code, 1962.

devices such as the pledge, chattel mortgages, conditional sales contracts, trust receipts, and such, regardless of form.

The general effect of the Code is expressed by Professor Coogan as follows:

Article 9 represents neither more nor less than a merger of the previously separate streams of chattel security law—those of pledge, chattel mortgages, conditional sale, assignment of accounts receivable, trust receipt, factor lien acts and the like. The merger has produced a more nearly rational set of rules under which the parties can create, perfect and enforce any of these different kinds of security interests produced under the pre-merger law, ranging from the solid pledge to something little removed, if at all, from a state-created priority. Any lawyer can easily trace practically every important concept, and even every important mechanical device, either to one or more of the pre-Code bodies of chattel security law of his own state or of a contiguous state. The bringing together of these rules into one statute is the Code's basic contribution to a more orderly chattel security system. Contrary to the impression created by the Official Comments, only minor differences in rules are based on the nature of the collateral.[2]

In discussing security interests in personal property and fixtures, we shall, with few exceptions, be dealing with old friends parading under new names. The drafters of Article 9 of the Code have put old wine into new bottles.

Security Interests in Real Estate. Three types of contractual security devices have been developed by which real estate may be used as security: (1) the real estate mortgage, (2) trust deed, and (3) land contract. In addition to these contract security devices all of the states have enacted statutes granting the right to mechanics' liens on real estate. The real estate mortgage is comparable to the chattel mortgage and the land contract is comparable to the conditional sales contract. The trust deed is used to avoid the expense and delay usually accompanying the foreclosure of a mortgage. When it is used the real estate is deeded to a trustee who is empowered to sell it if the debtor does not pay the debt and to apply the proceeds of the sale on the payment of the debt. Under the statutes of some states the trust deed is treated as a real estate mortgage and must be foreclosed as such.

Summary

Credit is a transaction in which goods are sold and delivered, services are rendered, or money is loaned in exchange for the recipient's promise to pay at some future date. When such credit is given on the recipient's unsupported promise to pay, such as, for instance, an open-book account, the credit is unsecured credit. When the credit is supported by the transfer of an interest in property or the supporting promise of a third person to which the creditor can resort for payment if his debtor does not pay, such credit is secured credit.

Various types of security devices have been developed to serve the needs of

---

[2] Peter F. Coogan, "The Lay Lawyer's Guide to Secured Transactions under the Code," 60 *Michigan Law Review* 685 (April, 1962).

our economy. The development in this area has been unorganized and the available security devices have been inadequate in many respects. The pledge is the oldest and simplest device. The chattel mortgage was used when it was desirable to leave the goods posted as security in the possession of the debtor. The conditional sales contract could be used only as security for the unpaid balance of the purchase price of the goods. The trust receipt was a short-time marketing device in which high-unit cost goods held as inventory are used as security. Factoring was an inventory security device in which the factor finances the inventory, sells it and repays the money advanced plus his commissions. The Uniform Commercial Code has provided a unified system of using personal property as security.

Real estate may be posted as security. The real estate mortgage is comparable to the chattel mortgage, and the land contract is comparable to the conditional sales contract. The deed of trust is used in a limited number of states in lieu of the real estate mortgage.

Common-Law and Statutory Liens on Personal Property

Persons Entitled to Common-Law Liens.   At common law, artisans, innkeepers, and common carriers were entitled to liens to secure the payment of the reasonable value of the services they performed. An artisan, it was reasoned, improved the property of another by his labor and by the addition of his materials, and that improvement became a part of the principal property by accession, and the title of the improved property vested in the owner of the principal property. Therefore the artisan who had enhanced the value of the property was allowed to claim a lien on the property for his reasonable charges.

The innkeeper and the common carrier were bound by law to serve the public. The innkeeper was allowed to claim a lien on his guest's effects for his reasonable charges for food and lodging, and the common carrier was allowed to claim a lien on the goods carried for his reasonable charges for the service. The giving of the common-law lien to the innkeeper and common carrier was justified on the ground that since they were obligated to serve the public, they were entitled to the protection of a lien. These common-law liens are generally recognized throughout the United States today. Several of the states have incorporated the concept of the common-law lien in their statutory liens on personal property, and other states have by statute modified the rights of the common-law lienholder.

Characteristics of a Common-Law Lien.   The common-law lien is a possessory lien; it gives the lienholder the right to retain possession of the debtor's property until the debt has been discharged. An artisan is not entitled to a common-law lien for his services unless possession of the property has been given to him. For example, if you take your chair to an upholsterer's shop and he upholsters it for you, he will be entitled to a lien on the chair for his reasonable charges. But if he brings his tools and materials and does the work in your house, he will not be entitled to such a lien.

Two essential elements of a common-law lien are possession and a debt created by the improvement of the property on which the lien is claimed. If the lien claimant surrenders possession to the debtor voluntarily, the lien is lost, but if the debtor obtains possession by artifice or fraud, the lien is not extinguished. If the debt is paid, the lien is discharged, since the foundation of the right to the lien is the existence of a debt without which a lien right cannot exist. However, the discharge of the lien before the debt is paid does not affect the right to recover on the debt.

Statutory Liens on Personal Property. Statutory liens on personal property are liens created by statutory enactment. Many of these statutes are little more than a codification of existing common-law liens. However, these statutes have created many additional liens and, at the same time, have provided a procedure for the foreclosure of the lien. To determine the scope of statutory liens, one must consult the statutes of the several states. Each state has its own lien statutes creating such liens as the needs of the people in the state suggest to the legislators. Carriers' liens and warehousemen's liens are provided for in Article 7, Documents of Title, of the Code.

If the lien created by statute is not recognized at common law, the statute creating the lien is said to be in derrogation of the common law The same is true of a statute providing for a lien which is recognized at common law but which gives to one of the parties rights not recognized under the common-law lien. The courts have developed a rule of statutory construction which is generally applied in interpreting and applying such statutes. If the statute is in derogation of the common law, it will be strictly construed; that is, all the provisions of the statute must be complied with before the party can claim benefits under the statute, and the courts will not enlarge the scope of the statute by implications. If one claims a lien on property when he is not entitled to a lien and refuses to surrender possession when demand is made by the owner, he will be liable to the owner either for the conversion of the property or for damages for the unlawful detention.

Foreclosure of Lien. The right of possession of the holder of a common-law lien does not give the lienholder the right to sell or claim ownership of the property if his charges are not paid. In the absence of statutes providing for the foreclosure of the lien, the lienholder must bring suit and obtain a judgment for his charges, have the sheriff levy execution on the property, and have the property on which he has a lien sold at execution sale.

Most states have enacted statutes which provide for the sale of the property, after it has been held for a designated period of time, on the giving of notice and on the advertising of the sale by posting or publishing notices of the sale.

Summary

Artisans, innkeepers, and common carriers are entitled to common-law liens for their reasonable charges. The common-law lien is a possessory lien. An artisan is not entitled to a common-law lien on property unless possession of the property on which work is to be done is surrendered to him. The two essential elements of a common-law lien are (1) the debt and (2) possession.

Most states have enacted statutes defining the rights to liens on personal property. Many of these statutes are little more than a codification of existing common-law liens. However, all states have enlarged, to some extent, the scope of liens on personal property by statutory enactment.

A common law lien gives the lienholder the right of possession of the goods, but if he wishes to foreclose the lien, he must sue the debtor, obtain a judgment, have an execution issued on the judgment and levied on the goods, and have the goods sold at a sheriff's sale. In most states a simplified foreclosure procedure has been provided for by statute.

Beck v. Nutrodynamics, Inc.

186 A.2d 715 (Super. Ct. N.J. 1962)

This was an action in which James S. P. Beck (plaintiff) brought an action in attachment against Nutrodynamics, Inc. (defendant), and attached a quantity of pills. Ivers-Lee intervened, claiming a common-law lien on the pills. The court held that the common-law lien had priority over the attachment and Beck appealed. The Superior Court affirmed the holding.

Prior to the time Beck commenced his suit and attached the pills, Nutrodynamics, Inc., delivered to Ivers-Lee a drug product in completed pill form. Ivers-Lee was to place the pills in foil packages and then in shipping containers suitable for delivery to customers of Nutrodynamics, Inc. The packaged pills were in the possession of Ivers-Lee when Beck instituted his suit by attachment. Approximately 193 cartons of the packaged pills were levied upon and taken into possession by the sheriff. Ivers-Lee claimed an artisan's lien to the goods by virtue of materials, labor and services rendered which had priority over Beck's attachment.

YANCY, JUDGE.   A common law lien is the right to retain the possession of personal property until some debt due on or secured by such property is paid or satisfied. This lien is one that arises by implication of law and not from express contract. It is founded on the immemorial recognition of the common law of a right to it in particular cases, or it may result from the established usage of a particular trade or from the mode of dealing between the parties.

The right to this common law lien applies to a bailee, to whom goods have been delivered. To entitle a bailee to a lien on the article bailed, more is necessary than the mere existence of the bailment relationship. The bailee must, by his labor and skill, contribute to the improvement of the article bailed. The bailee having thus performed, the well-settled rule of the common law is that a bailee (artisan) who receives in bailment personal property under an express or implied contract to improve, better, manufacture or repair it for remuneration, and enhances the value of such property by his skill, labor, or materials employed in such undertaking, has a specific lien on such property. This lien may be enforced against the bailor while the property remains in the bailee's possession, and until the reasonable value of his labor, skill, and expenses is paid.

The first question before the court, therefore, is whether the kind of work done by Ivers-Lee is such as to support its assertion to an artisan's lien. The undisputed facts set forth are that Nutrodynamics, Inc. delivered to the claimant a huge quantity of loose, unpackaged capsules so that the same could be rendered salable by having the claimant prepare, mark and package the capsules and place the packages in cardboard mailing containers suitable for delivery to the customers of Nutrodynamics, Inc. The claimant, Ivers-Lee, agreed to render the service and labor and to supply the materials necessary to accomplish the foregoing. The claimant did in fact supply such labor and packaging materials. This work and materials have become assimilated into the final product, and have enhanced the value of the heretofore loose unpackaged pills.

The case of *O'Brien* v. *Buston* dealt with a lien on goods for personal services rendered and for repairs to the goods. The court stated at page 878, 156 A. 17 at page 18:

A workman who by his skill and labor has enhanced the value of a chattel, under an employment . . . has a lien on the chattel for his reasonable charge. . . .

The lien arises from the rendering of the service, and if such service be not paid for, there is a right to detain. The court further stated:

. . . It is the natural outcome of the transaction wherein one takes his chattel to another with whom he contracts for the performance by the latter of some service upon it for its betterment.

It is to be concluded from the foregoing that the work done by Ivers-Lee did enhance the value of the product.

Security Interests in Personal Property

The Uniform Commercial Code—in Article 9—covers secured transactions involving personal property and fixtures. Basic to a discussion of secured transactions is the term "security interest" which is broadly defined by the Code to mean "an interest in personal property or fixtures which secures payment or performance of an obligation." [1–201(37.)] While it is normal to think of various types of goods as being used for collateral, the Code actually covers secured interests in a much broader grouping of personal property. The Code breaks personal property down into a number of different classifications which are of importance in determining how a creditor goes about getting an enforceable security interest in a particular type of collateral. These Code classifications are:

1. *Instruments.* This category includes checks, notes, drafts, stocks, bonds, and other investment securities.
2. *Documents of Title.* This category includes bills of lading, dock warrants, dock receipts, and warehouse receipts.
3. *Accounts Receivable.* This category includes rights to payment for goods sold or leased or for services rendered that are not evidenced by instruments or chattel paper but rather are carried on open account.
4. *Contract Rights.* This category includes rights to payment under a contract which have not yet been earned by performance and which are not evidenced by an instrument or chattel paper.
5. *Chattel Paper.* This category refers to writings that evidence both a monetary obligation and a security interest in specific goods and includes what is often referred to as a conditional sales contract.
6. *General Intangibles.* This is a catchall category which includes, among other things, patents, copyrights, literary royalty rights, and franchises.
7. *Goods.* Goods are divided into several classes; the same item of collateral may fall into different classes at different times, depending on its use.
   (a) *Consumer Goods.* Goods used or bought for use primarily for personal, family or household use such as automobiles, furniture, and appliances.
   (b) *Equipment.* Goods used or bought for use primarily in business, including farming or a profession.
   (c) *Farm Products.* Crops, livestock or supplies used or produced in farming operations as long as they are still in the possession of a debtor engaged in farming.
   (d) *Inventory.* Goods held for sale or lease or to be used under contracts of service as well as raw materials, work in process, or materials used or consumed in a business.
   (e) *Fixtures.* Goods which will be so affixed to real property so as to be considered a part of the real property.

Obtaining an Enforceable Security Interest. Once a creditor determines that the particular collateral offered by a debtor is included within the coverage of the Uniform Commercial Code, the creditor's next task is to secure a security interest that will be enforceable against the debtor, other creditors of the debtor, and, in some cases, purchasers of the collateral from the debtor.

In general, the obtaining of an enforceable security interest is a two-step process consisting of attachment and perfection.

Summary

A security interest is an interest in personal property or fixtures which secures payment or performance of an obligation. The Code sets out rules for obtaining secured interests in instruments, documents of title, accounts receivable, contract rights, chattel paper, general intangibles, and goods. Goods may be consumer goods, equipment, inventory, farm products, or fixtures. To obtain the maximum protection for his security interest the creditor must attach and perfect his security interest.

Attachment of the Security Interest

A security interest is not enforceable until it attaches to the collateral. In order that it attach there must be an agreement between the debtor and the secured party that it attach, value must be given to the debtor (unless there is a debt there can be no secured interest), and the debtor must have rights in the collateral. (9–204.)

The Security Agreement. As a general rule, the secured party will require that the agreement whereby the debtor grants him a secured interest in the collateral be in writing and signed by the debtor. Such a written agreement is required in all cases except where the collateral is in the possession of the secured party. (9–203.) The security agreement must describe the collateral with reasonable certainty so as to enable it to be identified.

The security agreement usually goes on to spell out the terms of the arrangement between the parties. Thus it will normally contain a promise by the debtor to pay certain amounts of money in a certain way or to perform other obligations and will specify what events will constitute a default. In addition it may contain provisions the secured party deems necessary to protect his interest in the collateral such as requiring the debtor to procure insurance or to periodically report sales of secured inventory goods.

SAMPLE SECURITY AGREEMENT

Mr. and Mrs.
Mrs.

BUYER   Miss—————————————————————

ADDRESS —————————————————————

CITY ————————————————— TEL. NO. —————

DELIVER TO: —————————————————————

Account No.

Date

SECURITY AGREEMENT
(NAME OF SELLER)

THIS AGREEMENT, executed between (name of Seller), as Secured Party ("Seller"), and Buyer named above, as Debtor ("Buyer"):

Seller agrees to sell and Buyer agrees to purchase, subject to the terms, conditions and agreements herein stated, the goods described below (hereinafter referred to as the "Collateral"), Seller reserving and Buyer granting a purchase money security interest in the Collateral to secure the payment of the balance owed (Item 7) and all other present and future obligations of Buyer to Seller.

DESCRIPTION OF COLLATERAL				TERMS
Quan.	Article	Unit Price	Total	
				(1) Cash Price
				(2) Down Payment
				Trade-in
				(3) Unpaid Principal Balance Owed
				(4) Finance Charge
				(5) Time Balance Owed
				(6) Sales Tax
				(7) Balance Owed

Buyer agrees to pay Seller, without relief from valuation and appraisement laws, the balance owed (Item 7) of $_____ in _____ successive weekly/monthly installments of $_____ each and a final installment of $_____, commencing on _____ _____, 19__, and continuing thereafter on the same day of each week/month, until paid, together with all delinquent charges, costs of repossession, collection, disposition, maintenance and other like charges, allowed by law, and reasonable attorneys' fees.

This sale is made subject to the terms, conditions and agreements stated above and on the reverse side hereof. Buyer hereby represents that the correct name and address of Buyer is as stated above, and that all statements made by Buyer as to financial condition and credit information are true.

Buyer hereby acknowledges delivery by Seller or Buyer of a copy of this agreement.

Buyer warrants and represents that the Collateral will be kept at Buyer's address unless otherwise specified as follows:_____; and will be used or is purchased for use primarily for: (check one) family or household purposes □; business use □; farming operations □. The Collateral will not be affixed to real estate unless checked here □. If the Collateral is to be affixed to real estate, a description of the real estate is as follows: _____

and the name of the record owner is _____

IN WITNESS WHEREOF, the parties hereto have executed this agreement on this _____ day of _____, 19__.

BUYER'S SIGNATURE   (NAME OF SELLER) Seller, (as Secured Party), Seller's address

_____ By_____

(as Debtor)

TERMS, CONDITIONS AND AGREEMENTS

1. The security interest of Seller shall extend to all replacements, proceeds (including tort claims and insurance), and accessories, and shall continue until full performance by Buyer of all conditions and obligations hereunder.

2. Buyer shall maintain the Collateral in good repair, pay all taxes and other charges levied upon the Collateral when due, and shall defend the Collateral against any claims. Buyer shall not permit the Collateral to be removed from the place where kept without the prior written consent of Seller. Buyer shall give prompt written notice to Seller of any transfer, pledge, assignment, or any other process or action taken or pending, voluntary or involuntary, whereby a third party is to obtain or is attempting to obtain possession of or any interest in the Collateral. Seller shall have the right to inspect the Collateral at all reasonable times. At its option, but without obligation to Buyer and without relieving Buyer from any default, Seller may discharge any taxes, liens or other encumbrances levied or placed upon the Collateral for which Buyer agrees to reimburse Seller upon demand.

3. If the Collateral is damaged or destroyed in any manner, the entire balance remaining unpaid under this agreement (hereinafter referred to as the "Agreement Balance") shall immediately become due and payable and Buyer shall first apply any insurance or other receipts compensating for such loss to the Agreement Balance. Buyer shall fully insure the Collateral, for the benefit of both Seller and Buyer, against loss by fire, theft and other casualties by comprehensive extended coverage insurance in an amount equal to the balance owed hereunder.

4. Buyer shall pay all amounts payable hereunder when due at the store of Seller from which this sale is made or at Seller's principal office in _____, Indiana, and upon default shall pay the maximum delinquent charges permitted by law. Upon prepayment of the Agreement Balance, Seller shall allow the minimum discount permitted by law.

5. Time is of the essence of this agreement. Buyer agrees that the following shall constitute an event of default under this Security Agreement: (a) the failure of Buyer to perform any condition or obligation contained herein; (b) when any statement, representation or warranty made herein by Buyer shall be found to have been untrue in any material respect when made; or (c) if Seller in good faith believes that the prospect of payment or performance is impaired. Upon a default, Seller, at its option and without notice or demand to Buyer, shall be entitled to declare the Agreement Balance immediately due and payable and, take immediate possession of the Collateral and enter the premises at which the Collateral is located for such purpose or to render the Collateral unusable. Upon request, Buyer shall assemble and make the Collateral available to Seller at a place to be designated by Seller which is reasonably convenient to both parties. Upon repossession, Seller may retain or dispose of any or all of the Collateral in the manner prescribed by the Indiana Uniform Commercial Code and the proceeds of any such disposition shall be first applied in the following order: (a) to the reasonable expenses of retaking, holding, preparing for sale, selling and the like; (b) to the reasonable attorneys' fees and legal expenses incurred by Seller; and (c) to the satisfaction of the indebtedness secured by this security interest. Buyer covenants to release and hold harmless Seller from any and all claims arising out of the repossession of the Collateral. No waiver of any default or any failure or delay to exercise any right or remedy by Seller shall operate as a waiver of any other default or of the same default in the future or as a waiver of any right or remedy with respect to the same or any other occurrence.

6. All rights and remedies of Seller herein specified are cumulative and are in addition to, and shall not exclude, any rights and remedies Seller may have by law.

7. Seller shall not be liable for any damages, including special or consequential damages, for failure to deliver the Collateral or for any delay in delivery of the Collateral to Buyer.

8. Buyer agrees that Seller may carry this agreement, together with any other agreements and accounts, with Buyer in one account upon its records and unless otherwise instructed in writing by Buyer, any payment of less than all amounts then due on all agreements and accounts shall be applied to any accrued delinquent charges, costs of collection and maintenance, and to the balances owing under all agreements or accounts in such order as Seller in its discretion shall determine.

9. Buyer authorizes Seller to execute and file financing statements signed only by Seller covering the Collateral described.

10. Any notice required by this agreement shall be deemed sufficient when mailed to Seller (state Seller's address), or to Buyer at the address at which the Collateral is kept.

11. Buyer shall have the benefit of manufacturers' warranties, if any; however, Seller makes no express warranties (except a warranty of title) and no implied warranties, including any warranty of MERCHANTABILITY or FITNESS. Buyer agrees that there are no promises or agreements between the parties not contained herein. Any modification or rescission of this agreement shall be ineffective unless in writing and signed by both Seller and Buyer.

(Name of Retailer)

Future Advances.   Under the provisions of the Code a security agreement may include a provision covering future advances. However, the security interest does not attach until value is given. (9–204[1].)

After-Acquired Property.   Under the provisions of the Code a security interest in after-acquired property may be created by a properly worded security agreement. However, the security interest in the after-acquired property cannot attach until the debtor acquires an interest in the collateral. (9–204.) A security interest in after-acquired property may be defeated if the debtor acquires some or all of his new property subject to a purchase money security agreement. Also, the rights of the secured party to property acquired by the debtor within four months of the adjudication of the debtor as a bankrupt are uncertain. Amendment of the Federal Bankruptcy Law is needed to clarify the rights of the secured party to after-acquired property in the event the debtor is adjudged bankrupt.

Proceeds.   The security agreement may provide that the security interest will cover not only the collateral described therein but will attach to the proceeds on the disposal of the collateral by the debtor. To create a security interest in proceeds all that is necessary is to add the word "proceeds" to the description of the collateral in the security agreement. (9–203 [1] [b].) The rights of the secured party in proceeds are set out in detail in Section 9–306 of the Code. If the security interest in the collateral is perfected, it continues, as a general rule, in any identifiable proceeds. If the original security agreement does not include proceeds, the secured party has 10 days in which to perfect his security interest in the proceeds. If the debtor becomes insolvent, the secured party with a perfected security interest in proceeds may claim cash proceeds (money, checks and the like) received by the debtor within 10 days of the insolvency subject to the limitations set out in Section 9–306 (4) (b) (c) (d). Subsection 5 of Section 9–306 sets out the rights of the secured party in collateral sold by the debtor and returned to him.

Summary

A security interest is not enforceable until it has been attached to the collateral. To effect this attachment there must be an agreement between the debtor and the secured party that the security interest attach, value must be given to the debtor, and the debtor must have rights in the collateral. A security agreement may cover future advances to be made by the creditor to the debtor. A security agreement may create a security interest in proceeds of the collateral and in after-acquired property of the debtor.

Perfecting the Security Interest

Along with the attachment of the security interest, the secured party is also concerned with obtaining the maximum protection available for the type of collateral involved. This protection against other creditors of the debtor and purchasers of the collateral is obtained through the process of perfecting the security interest. There are three main means of perfection under the Code:

1. *Public filing* of notice of the security interest;
2. The secured party's taking *possession* of the collateral;
3. Perfection by mere *attachment* of the security interest in certain special situations or for certain limited times.

Public Filing.   By far the most common method of perfecting a security interest is by filing a financing statement in a public office which then serves as constructive notice to the world that the secured party claims a security interest in collateral belonging to a certain named debtor. The financing statement will usually consist of a multicopy form available from the secretary of state's office although the security agreement may be filed as a financial statement if it contains the required items of information.

The financing statement, to be sufficient, must be signed by the debtor and the secured party, must give an address of the secured party from which information concerning the security interest may be obtained, must give a mailing address of the debtor, and must contain a statement indicating the types or describing the items of collateral. If the financing statement covers crops growing or to be grown or goods which are to become fixtures, the statement must also contain a description of the real estate concerned. (9–402.) The financing statement may be broad in its scope and include all of the debtor's personal property, accounts, contract rights and chattel paper which he owns at the time of its execution or may acquire in the future or it may include a class of property or a few items, or a single item of property.

The requirement as to the place of filing the financing statement is determined by the statutes of the individual state. In all states a security interest in fixtures must be filed in the office where a mortgage on the real estate concerned would be filed or recorded. (9–401 [1] [a].) Since no definition of a fixture is given in the Code (9–313), the determination of the character of the collateral is a matter of state law. The secured party acquiring a security interest in property which is a fixture or is to become a fixture, should, in order to obtain maximum security, double file, that is, file as a fixture and as a nonfixture.

In regard to collateral other than fixtures the state may require only central filing, usually in the office of the secretary of state. However, most states require local filing of those transactions which are local in nature, such as when the collateral is equipment used in farming operations, or is farm products, or accounts, contract rights or general intangibles arising from or relating to the sale of farm products by a farmer or consumer goods. (9–401.)

If no maturity date is stated in the financing statement or if the debt is payable on demand the filing is valid for five years. If a maturity date is stated in

```
UNIFORM COMMERCIAL CODE              STATE OF INDIANA                    FORM UCC-1
                                   FINANCING STATEMENT
  INSTRUCTIONS
     1. Please type this form. Fold only along perforation for mailing.
     2. Remove Secured Party and Debtor copies and send other three copies with interleaved carbon paper to the filing officer. Enclose filing fee of $1.00
        (plus $ .50 if collateral is or is to become a fixture).
     3. When filing is to be with more than one office, Form UCC-2 may be placed over this set to avoid double typing.
     4. If the space provided for any item(s) is inadequate, the item(s) may be continued on additional sheets, preferably 5"x 8" or sizes convenient to
        secured party in case of long schedules, indentures, etc. Only one sheet is required. Extra names of debtors may be continued below box "1" in
        space for description of property.
     5. If the collateral is crops or goods which are or are to become fixtures, describe the goods and also the real estate with the name of the record owner
        if he is other than the debtor.
     6. Persons filing a security agreement (as distinguished from a financing statement) are urged to complete this form with or without signature and seal
        with security agreement.
     7. If collateral is goods which are or are to become fixtures, use Form UCC-1a over this Form to avoid double typing, and enclose regular fee plus $ .50.
     8. The filing officer will return the third page of this Form as an acknowledgment. Secured party at a later time may use third page as a Termination
        Statement by dating and signing the termination legend on that page.
--------------------------------------------------------------------------------------------------------------------
     This Financing Statement is presented to Filing Officer for filing pursuant to the UCC:            3  Maturity Date (if any):
  1  Debtor(s) (Last Name First) and Address(es)     2  Secured Party(ies) and Address(es)    For Filing Officer (Date, Time, Number, and
                                                                                              Filing Office)



  4  This financing statement covers the following types (or items) of property (also describe realty
     where collateral is crops or fixtures):

                                                     This statement is filed without the debtor's signature to perfect a security interest in collateral
          Assignee of Secured Party                  (check [X] if so)

                                                      [ ]  under a security agreement signed by debtor authorizing secured party to file this statement, or
                                                      [ ]  already subject to a security interest in another jurisdiction when it was brought into this state, or
                                                      [ ]  which is proceeds of the following described original collateral which was perfected:

      Check [X] if covered:    [ ] Proceeds of Collateral are also covered.    [ ] Products of Collateral are also covered.  No. of additional Sheets presented:

      Filed with:   [ ] Secretary of State          [ ] Recorder of_____County


  By:_____            By:_____
            Signature(s) of Debtor(s)                         Signature(s) of Secured Party(ies)

  (1) Filing Officer Copy—Alphabetical               Approved by: Charles O. Hendricks
      FORM UCC-1—INDIANA UNIFORM COMMERCIAL CODE                            Secretary of State
```

the financing statement the filing is valid for the stated period plus 60 days but for a period not to exceed 5 years (9–403 [2].)

A continuation statement may be filed within 6 months before and 60 days after a stated maturity date of 5 years or less, and otherwise within 6 months prior to the 5-year expiration date. The continuation statement must be signed by the secured party, identify the original statement by file number, and state that the original statement is still effective. Successive continuation statements may be filed. (9–403 [3].)

When all debts and obligations of the debtor secured by a financing statement are completely fulfilled he is entitled to a termination statement signed by the secured party or an assignee of record. Failure to furnish a termination statement after proper demand subjects the affected secured party to a fine of $100 plus damages for any loss caused to the debtor by such failure. (9–404.)

Possession by the Secured Party as Public Notice. Secret liens have been suspect from the earliest times, and in the United States the validity of a lien on personal property left in the possession of the debtor was questionable. The holding of the courts led to the enactment of filing or recording statutes whereby public notice of the lien was given, thereby removing the stigma of a secret lien from the transaction. From the beginning the courts upheld the validity of the lien against the creditors of the debtor if the collateral was delivered to the lender or one who held possession for him.

Under the Code, change of possession of the collateral perfects the security interest of the secured party. (9–302 [1] [a].) Except for the 21-day temporary perfection permitted by 9–304(4) and (5), possession by the secured party is the only means of perfecting a security interest in instruments. Possession is an alternative and often the most satisfactory means of perfecting a security interest in chattel paper and negotiable documents of title.

Possession is also a possible means for perfecting a security interest in inventory. This is sometimes done through a field warehousing arrangement whereby part of the debtor's inventory is fenced off and withdrawals from it permitted only on the approval of the secured party or his on-the-scene representative.

Possession is usually not a practical means for perfecting a security interest in equipment, farm products, and consumer goods and, of course, is not possible at all with accounts receivable, contract rights or general intangibles.

The person to whom the collateral is delivered holds it as bailee and, as was the law under the pre-Code pledge, he owes the duties of a bailee to the parties in interest. (9–207.)

Perfection by Attachment. Perfection by mere attachment of the security interest, sometimes known as automatic perfection, is the only form of perfection that occurs without the giving of public notice. It occurs automatically when all the requirements of attachment are complete. This form of perfection is limited to certain classes of collateral and in addition may be only a temporary perfection in some situations.

Permanent perfection by attachment of the security interest alone is valid only with respect to purchase money security interests (see 9–107) in consumer goods or in farm equipment having a purchase price not in excess of $2,500. Thus, the retailer who sells a television set on a conditional sales contract to a consumer does not have to file a financing statement but is considered to have perfected his security interest just by virtue of its attachment to the television set now in the hands of the consumer.

There are, however, several important exceptions to this permanent perfection by attachment principle. First, it does not apply to those consumer goods which are or will become fixtures or to motor vehicles if they are required to have a certificate of title under state law. (9–302.) Second, although the retailer who relies on attachment for perfection of his security interest in consumer goods will prevail against other creditors of the debtor, he will not prevail over a buyer from the debtor if the buyer buys the collateral without knowledge of the security interest, for value, and for his own personal, family, or household use. To be protected against such a purchaser from the debtor, the secured party must file a financing statement rather than relying on attachment for perfection. (9–307 [2].)

Temporary perfection without filing or possession is automatically obtained for 21 days after attachment of the security interest in instruments and negotiable documents. (9–304.) To get protection beyond the 21-day period, the secured party must perfect by filing or possession. However, during the 21-day period of temporary perfection, any holder in due course of commercial paper or bona fide purchaser of a security or negotiated document will prevail over the secured party relying on temporary perfection. (9–309.)

Summary

To protect his security interest against other creditors of the debtor and purchasers of the collateral, the secured party must perfect his security interest. Under the Code there are three means of perfection: public filing of a financing statement; the secured party's taking possession of the collateral; and, in some limited cases, mere attachment of the security interest.

A financing statement is filed at either the secretary of state's office or the local recorder's office, depending on the type of collateral it secures. If no maturity date is stated, the filing is good for five years and may be extended for additional five-year periods by filing a continuation statement. A debtor who has fulfilled his obligations is entitled to a termination statement which removes the financing statement from the records.

Industrial Packaging Products Co. v. *Fort Pitt Packaging International, Inc.*
161 A.2d 19 (Sup. Ct. Pa. 1960)

This was a petition of Robert Mellin, receiver of Fort Pitt Packaging International, Inc. (plaintiff), against Industrial Packaging Products Co. (defendant) to show cause why an assignment made to Industrial Packaging Products Co. should not be declared null and void. The court held that the assignment was valid and Mellin appealed. Judgment affirmed.

JONES, JUSTICE.   The Provident Trust Company of Pittsburgh, pursuant to Sec. 9–403 of the Uniform Commercial Code filed the following financing statement in the office of the Prothonotary of Allegheny County on August 18, 1955:

15110 of 1955
Financing Statement
This financing statement is presented to a filing officer for filing pursuant to the Uniform Commercial Code.
1. Debtor (or assignor)—Fort Pitt Packaging Co., Inc., 5615 Butler Street, Pittsburgh 1, Pa.

2. Secured Party (or assignee)—Provident Trust Co., 900 East Ohio St., Pittsburgh 1, Pa.

3. Maturity date of obligation ————————.

4. The financing statement covers the following types of property: All present and future accounts receivable submitted.

Fort Pitt Packaging Co., Inc.
Leo A. Levy, Treas.
Provident Trust Company
A. W. Charlton
Executive Vice-Pres.

Under Sec. 9–403 of the Code such a statement remains effective for a period of five years. On August 19, 1955, Provident Trust Company filed a similar statement in the office of the Secretary of the Commonwealth in Harrisburg.

On February 4, 1957, Fort Pitt Packaging International, Inc., entered into a written contract with the United States Government for the maintenance, repair and overhaul of vehicles. On March 26, 1957, Fort Pitt entered into a contract with Empire Commercial Corporation wherein Empire agreed to lend Fort Pitt $140,000 and Fort Pitt agreed to assign to the Provident Trust Company as Empire's agent its contract with the United States Government and any and all payments due or to become due thereunder. On the same day, March 26, Fort Pitt sold and assigned to the Provident Trust Company, the payments due or which may become due under the governmental contract. Notice of the assignment was given to the Contracting Officer of the Department of the Army.

One year later, on March 27, 1958, Fort Pitt was placed in receivership and on May 27, 1958, upon petition of creditors (Industrial was a creditor), Robert Mellin, Esquire, was appointed receiver. On June 10, 1958, the said receiver petitioned the Court of Common Pleas of Allegheny County for a rule upon Empire to show cause why the assignments of the proceeds for Fort Pitt's services performed under the government contracts should not be declared null, void and ineffective as against the receiver. After hearing held and argument, the court below dismissed the receiver's petition. From that order this appeal was taken.

Mellin contends that the filing of the financing statement in 1955 was not sufficient to secure the amounts due under Fort Pitt's contract with the United States Government which was executed in 1957. The filing of the financing statement pursuant to Sec. 9–403 was entirely proper. The Uniform Commercial Code does not require that the secured party as listed in such statement be a principal creditor and not an agent. The purpose of filing this financing statement is to give notice to potential future creditors of the debtor or purchasers of the collateral. It makes no difference as far as such notice is concerned whether the secured party listed in the filing statement is a principal or an agent, and no provision in the Uniform Commercial Code draws such a distinction.

The financing statement covered "all present and future accounts receivable submitted." Section 9–110 of the Uniform Commercial Code provides that "for the purposes of this Article any description is sufficient whether or not it is specific if it reasonably identifies the thing described." There is no doubt that the description in the financing statement reasonably identifies the collateral security. It is difficult under the circumstances to imagine how the description could be more complete without filing new and amended descriptions each time a new account receivable falls within the purview of the financing statement. Nowhere in the Uniform Commercial Code is such a requirement set forth.

Section 9–204 (3) provides that "except as provided in subsection (4) [which deals with crops and consumer goods] *a security agreement may provide that collateral, whenever acquired, shall secure any* advances made or other *value given at any time* pursuant to the security agreement."

In the 1957 agreement between Fort Pitt and Empire, Fort Pitt agreed to assign to Provident Trust Company all payments to be received as they became due from the United States Government under Fort Pitt's contract on February 4, 1957 with the Government. These amounts due fell within the clause "future accounts receivable submitted" contained in the 1955 financing statement filed by Provident Trust Company. Comment 2 to Sec. 9–303 of the Code states that the "secured party is entitled to have his security interest recognized in insolvency proceedings instituted against the debtor." Therefore, the interest of the secured party, Provident Trust Company, is superior to that of the receiver in bankruptcy and any funds which have been placed in the hands of Provident Trust Company pursuant to the assignment by Fort Pitt need not be turned over to the receiver. These funds are properly being held by the Provident Trust Company for the benefit of its principal, Empire Commercial Corporation.

In Re Midas Coin Co., Inc.
264 F.Supp. 193 (D.C. Mo. 1967)

This was a bankruptcy proceeding against the Midas Coin Company. St. John's Community Bank filed a petition to foreclose a collateral note which the Bankruptcy Trustee opposed on the grounds the bank had not filed a financing statement and was required to do so in order to protect its security interest. The Bankruptcy Referee refused to allow the foreclosure petition and St. John's Community Bank appealed. Reversed on appeal with directions to approve the foreclosure petition.

Midas Coin was in the business of buying and selling coins and stamps for profit. On January 14, 1966, Midas executed a promissory note to St. John's Bank for $9,637.58 and pledged as collateral security coins from its inventory having a face value of $9,750.50. The security agreement provided that the collateral was to secure payment of all other liabilities owed to St. John's Bank as well as the note. At the date of bankruptcy, February 7, 1966, St. John's Bank had coins of a face value of $6,432.50 in its possession and was owed some $9,700 by Midas Coin. St. John's Bank claimed it had a perfected security interest in the coins and the trustee claimed that the security interest was unperfected because no financing statement had been filed.

REGAN, DISTRICT JUDGE. The Referee held that the instant transaction was governed by Article 9 of the Code which pertains to secured transactions. Section 9–102 provides that except as otherwise provided in two designated sections not here involved, Article 9 applies to any transaction which is intended to create a security interest in personal property, "including goods, documents, instruments, general intangibles, chattel paper, accounts or contract rights."

Section 9–302(1)(a) of Article 9 provides that a financing statement must be filed to perfect all security interests, except a security interest in collateral in possession of the secured party under § 9–305. The latter section authorizes the secured party to perfect a security interest in goods, instruments, negotiable documents or chattel paper (as well as letters of credit and advices of credit) by taking possession of the collateral. It is the Bank's position that having taken possession of the collateral, its security interest has thereby been perfected, so that no financing statement was required to be filed.

The trustee contends, and the Referee held, that § 9–305 is not here applicable, upon the theory that coins are money, and that since money is not one of the kinds of property enumerated in that section, the only method of perfecting a security interest therein is by filing a financing statement.

The trustee does not suggest any possible legislative purpose which would be served by differentiating between the transfer of physical possession of coins (or other money of numismatic value) and any other tangible personal property susceptible to such physical possession. If the coins in question are excluded as subject to pledge simply because they fit the statutory definition of "money," in spite of the fact they constitute part of inventory and in any realistic sense are a commodity, the result would be that without any rhyme or reason they would be the only species of tangible personal property in which a security interest could not be perfected without filing a financing statement. We do not believe such was the legislative intent.

Money as such does not customarily serve as commercial collateral. The coins are so in this case solely because of the numismatic value. We hold, therefore, that the coins which were pledged to the Bank under the security agreement constitute "goods," and therefore, the Bank was not required to file a financing statement in order to perfect its security interest.

In Re Nicolosi

4 U.C.C. Rep. 111 (S.D. Ohio 1966)

A trustee in bankruptcy filed a petition to sell a diamond ring in his possession free of liens. Rike-Kumber Company claimed it had enforceable lien on the ring. The court held that Rike-Kumber held a perfected security interest in the ring.

Nicolosi purchased the diamond ring from Rike-Kumber on July 7, 1964, as an engagement present for his financée. He executed a purchase money security agreement that was not filed; nor was any financing statement filed.

ANDERSON, REFEREE. If the diamond ring, purchased as an engagement ring by the bankrupt, cannot be categorized as consumer goods, and therefore exempted from the notice filing requirements of the Uniform Commercial Code as adopted in Ohio, a perfected security interest does not exist. See U.C.C. § 9-302.

No judicial precedents have been cited in the briefs.

Under the commercial code, collateral is divided into tangible, intangible, and documentary categories. Certainly, a diamond ring falls into the tangible category. The classes of tangible goods are distinguished by the primary use intended. Under U.C.C. § 9-109, the four classes are "consumer goods," "equipment," "farm products" and "inventory."

The difficulty is that the code provisions use terms arising in commercial circles which have different semantic values from legal precedents. Does the fact that the purchaser bought the goods as a special gift to another person signify that it was not for his own "personal, family or household purposes"? The trustee urges that these special facts control under the express provisions of the commercial code.

By a process of exclusion, a diamond engagement ring purchased for one's fiancée is not "equipment" bought or used in business, "farm products" used in farming operations, or "inventory" held for sale, lease or service contracts. When the bankrupt purchased the ring, therefore, it could only have been "consumer goods" bought for use "primarily for personal use." There could be no judicial purpose to create a special class of property in derogation of the statutory principles.

Another problem is implicit, although not covered by the briefs.

By the foregoing summary analysis, it is apparent that the diamond ring, when the interest of the bankrupt attached, was consumer goods since it could have been no other class of goods. Unless the fiancée had a special status under the code provision protecting a bona fide buyer, without knowledge, for value, of consumer goods, the failure to file a financing statement is not crucial. No evidence has been adduced pertinent to the scienter question.

Is a promise, as valid contractual consideration, included under the term "value"? In other words, was the ring given to his betrothed in consideration of marriage (promise for a promise)? If so, and "value" has been given, the transferee is a "buyer" under traditional concepts.

The Uniform Commercial Code definition of "value" (because of the code purpose of being so broad as to not derogate from the ideal ubiquitous secured creditor), very definitely covers a promise for a promise. The definition reads that "a person gives 'value' for rights if he acquires them . . . (4) generally, in return for any consideration sufficient to support a simple contract."

It would seem unrealistic, nevertheless, to apply contract law concepts historically developed into the law of marriage relations in the context of new concepts developed for uniform commercial practices. They are not, in reality, the same juristic manifold. The purpose of uniformity of the code should not be defeated by the obsessions of the code drafters to be all inclusive for secured creditors.

Even if the trustee, in behalf of the unsecured creditors, would feel inclined to insert love, romance and morals into commercial law, he is appearing in the wrong era, and possibly the wrong court.

Ordered, that the Rike-Kumler Company holds a perfected security interest in the diamond engagement ring, and the security interest attached to the proceeds realized from the sale of the goods by the trustee in bankruptcy.

Priorities

Because several secured parties may claim an interest in the same collateral of the debtor, the Code establishes a set of rules for determining which of the conflicting security interests has priority. If both security interests are perfected by filing, the first to be filed has priority, whether the security interest attached before or after filing (9–312 [5] [a]); if both have not been perfected by filing, the first to perfect has priority, regardless of which security interest attached first, and, in the case of a filed security interest, whether it attached before or after filing (9–312 [5] [b]); and, if neither has been perfected, then the first security interest to attach has priority. (9–312 [5] [c].)

Thus, if Bank A filed a financing statement covering Retailer's inventory on February 1, 1969, and Bank B filed such a financing statement on March 1, 1969, covering that same inventory, Bank A would have priority over Bank B even though Bank B might have made its loan and attached its security interest to the inventory prior to the time Bank A did so. If Bank A neglected to perfect its security interest, then Bank B as the only perfected security interest in the inventory would prevail. And if both neglected to perfect their security interest, then the first security interest that attached would have priority. In connection with the last situation, it is important to note that unperfected secured creditors do not enjoy a preferred position in bankruptcy proceedings, thus giving additional impetus to the desirability of filing or otherwise perfecting a security interest.

To these general rules there are several very important exceptions which are best discussed in the context of hypothetical situations. First, assume that Bank A takes and perfects a security interest in all present and after-acquired inventory of Debtor. Then Debtor acquires some additional inventory from Wholesaler who retains a security interest in the inventory until Debtor pays for it and then Wholesaler perfects this security interest. Wholesaler has a purchase money security interest in inventory goods and will have priority over the prior secured creditor (Bank A) if Wholesaler has perfected the security interest by the time the collateral reaches the Debtor and if Wholsaler sends notice of his purchase money security interest to Bank A. (9–312[3].)

Second, assume that Bank B takes and perfects a security interest in all the present and after-acquired equipment belonging to Debtor. Then Supplier sells some equipment to Debtor reserving a security interest in the equipment until it is paid for. If Supplier perfects the security interest by filing within 10 days of its attachment he will have priority over Bank B because a purchase money security interest in noninventory collateral prevails over a prior perfected security interest if the purchase money security interest is perfected within 10 days of its attachment. (9–312 [4].)

Finally, a buyer in the ordinary course of business other than a person buying farm products from a person engaged in farming operations takes free from a security interest created by his seller even though the security interest is perfected and even though the buyer knows of its existence. (9–307 [1].) In addition, certain liens arising by operation of law (such as artisan's liens) are given priority over a perfected security interest in the collateral. (9–310.)

Security Interest in Fixtures.   Special treatment for fixtures is provided for under the Code. A security interest which attaches to goods before they become a fixture and which has been perfected takes priority as to the goods over the claims of all persons who have an interest in the real estate. A security interest in goods before they become fixtures where such security interest has attached but has not been perfected and a security interest in goods after they become fixtures do not take priority over a subsequent purchaser for value of an interest in the real estate; or over a creditor with a lien on the real estate subsequently obtained by judicial proceedings; or over a creditor with a prior encumbrance of record on the real estate to the extent he makes subsequent advances.

On default the secured party has the right to remove the collateral from the real estate but he must reimburse any encumbrancer or owner of the real estate who is not the debtor and who has not otherwise agreed for the costs of repairs of any physical injury to the real estate. (9–313.)

National Cash Register Co. v. Firestone & Co., Inc.
191 N.E.2d 471 (Sup. Jud. Ct. Mass. 1963)

This was an action by National Cash Register Company (plaintiff) against Firestone & Co., Inc. (defendant), to recover a tort judgment for conversion of a cash register. Judgment for National Cash Register Company and Firestone Co., Inc., appealed. Judgment reversed.

On November 18, 1960, Firestone Co., Inc., (Firestone) made a loan to Edmund Carroll doing business as Kozy Kitchen. To secure the loan a security agreement was executed which listed the items of property included and concluded as follows: "together with all property and articles now, and which may hereafter be, used or mixed with, added or attached to, and/or substituted for any of the described property." A financing statement which included all of the items listed in the security agreement was filed with the town clerk on November 18, 1960, and with the Secretary of State on November 22, 1960. There was no reference to a cash register in either the security agreement or the financing statement and there was no after-acquired property provision in the financing statement. On November 25, 1960, National Cash Register Company (National) delivered a cash register to Carroll, on a conditional sales contract. National filed a financing statement on the cash register with the town clerk on December 20, and with the Secretary of State on December

21, 1960. Carroll defaulted in his payments to both Firestone and National. Firestone repossessed all of Carroll's fixtures and equipment covered by its security agreement, including the cash register and sold the same. National claimed that it was the title owner of the cash register and brought suit for its conversion.

WILKINS, CHIEF JUSTICE. Under the Uniform Commercial Code, after-acquired property, such as this cash register, might become subject to Firestone's security agreement when delivered, and likewise its delivery under a conditional sale agreement with retention of title in National would not, in and of itself, affect the rights of Firestone. Although National could have completely protected itself by perfecting its interest before or within ten days of the delivery of the cash register to Carroll, it did not try to do so until more than ten days after delivery. Thus the principal issue is whether Firestone's earlier security interest effectively covers the cash register.

The trial judge gave no reasons for his ruling. The Appellate Division rested its decision upon the mere statement of the omission of Firestone's financing statement to refer to after-acquired property or to the cash register specifically. The Massachusetts Commissioners on Uniform State Laws in their brief as *amici curiae* argue that there need be no reference to after-acquired property in the financing statement. Before we reach that question, however, we must consider several matters raised by National.

First, National argues that the debtor could not have intended to grant security interest to Firestone because the purchase was five months earlier, delivery was about to be made, and the cash register could be repossessed by National for default within the period of twenty-one months provided for instalment payments. It is also urged that, without the cash register, Firestone was well secured for its loan, a fact which cannot be inferred and which, in any event, would not be conclusive. The debtor's intent must be judged by the language of the security agreement.

In § 9–110, it is provided: "For the purposes of this Article any description of personal property or real estate is sufficient whether or not it is specific if it reasonably identifies what is described." In § 9-203 it is provided: (1) . . . a security interest is not enforceable against the debtor or third parties unless . . . (b) the debtor has signed a security agreement which contains a description of the collateral. . . ."

Contrary to National contention, we are of opinion that the security agreement is broad enough to include the cash register, which concededly did not have to be specifically described. The agreement covers "All contents of luncheonette including equipment such as," which we think covers all those contents and does not mean "equipment, to wit." There is a reference to "all property and articles now, and which may hereafter be, used . . . with, [or] added . . . to . . . any of the foregoing described property." We infer that the cash register was used with some of the other equipment even though the case stated does not expressly state that the luncheonette was operated.

The framers of the Uniform Commercial Code, by adopting the "notice filing" system, had the purpose to recommend a method of protecting security interests which at the same time would give subsequent potential creditors and other interested persons information and procedures adequate to enable the ascertainment of the facts they needed to know. In this respect the completed Code reflects a decision of policy reached after several years' study and discussion by experts. We conceive our duty to be the making of an interpretation which will carry out the intention of the framers of uniform legislation which already has been enacted in twenty-five States. That the result of their policy decision may be asserted to favor certain types of creditors as against others or that a different policy could have been decided upon is quite beside the point.

Sterling Acceptance Co. v. Grimes

168 A.2d 600 (Super. Ct. Pa. 1961)

This was an action in replevin by Sterling Acceptance Co. (plaintiff) against Patrick Grimes (defendant) to recover possession of an automobile. Judgment for Grimes and Sterling Acceptance Co. appealed. Judgment affirmed.

Grimes purchased a new Dodge automobile from Homish, a franchised Dodge dealer. The sale was made in the ordinary course of Homish's business and Grimes paid to Homish the purchase price of the automobile at the time of the sale. Homish had borrowed money from Sterling Acceptance Co. (Sterling) and had given it a perfected security interest in all his inventory and in addition had given Sterling a trust receipt covering the Dodge automobile sold to Grimes. A dealer's certificate of title showing the lien in favor of Sterling was issued and was in the possession of Sterling. Homish did not pay Sterling and it replevined the automobile from Grimes.

WOODSIDE, JUDGE. Article 9 of the Uniform Commercial Code deals with secured transactions including liens on personal property intended to be sold in the ordinary course of business. Section 9–307, provided:

(1) In the case of inventory, and in the case of other goods as to which the secured party files a financing statement in which he claims a security interest in proceeds, a buyer in ordinary course of business takes free of a security interest even though perfected and even though the buyer knows of the terms of the security agreement.

Section 2–403 provides, *inter alia:*

... (2) Any entrusting of possession of goods to a merchant who deals in goods of that kind gives him power to transfer all rights of the entruster to a buyer in ordinary course of business. (3) 'Entrusting' includes any delivery and any acquiescence in retention of possession regardless of any condition expressed between the parties to the delivery or acquiescence and regardless of whether the procurement of the entrusting or the possessor's disposition of the goods have been such as to be larcenous under the criminal law.

In the Comment on this section it is said:

The many particular situations in which a buyer in ordinary course of business from a dealer has been protected against reservation of property or other hidden interest are gathered by subsections (2)–(4) into a single principle protecting persons who buy in ordinary course out of inventory. Consignors have no reason to complain, nor have lenders who hold a security interest in the inventory, since the very purpose of goods in inventory is to be turned into cash by sale.

In the recent case of *Weisel* vs. *McBride,* we had occasion to review a sale from inventory of an automobile for which the purchaser was unable to obtain a certificate of title, because the dealer had fraudulently used the certificate to obtain additional financing. Judge Hirt, speaking for this Court: "The instant case presents one of 'the many situations' in which the Commercial Code intends to protect 'persons who buy in ordinary course out of inventory'. . . ."

According to the comment on § 9–307 (Purposes of Changes 2) of the Uniform Commercial Code, "The theory is that when goods are inventory or when proceeds are claimed the secured party contemplates that his debtor will make sales, and so the debtor has effective power to do so, even though his buyers know the goods they buy were subject to the security interest."

Under the provisions of the Uniform Commercial Code, Sterling must look to Homish for repayment of the loan it made to him, and not to the automobile in the possession of Grimes, who paid the full purchase price to Homish.

National Shawmut Bank of Boston v. *Jones*

236 A.2d 484 (Sup. Ct. N.H. 1967)

This was an action of replevin by National Shawmut Bank of Boston (plaintiffs) against Jones (defendant) to recover possession of a 1964 Dart automobile on which National Shawmut claimed to have an enforceable security interest. The case was transferred to the Supreme Court to have several questions of law answered. The questions were answered and the case was remanded.

On February 15, 1965, Robert Wever purchased the Dart from Wentworth Motor Company on a conditional sales contract for personal, family or household use. Wever executed a "Retail Sales Contract" which was assigned by Wentworth to National Shawmut Bank and which was filed with the town clerk pursuant to 9–401. Without National Shawmut's permission Wever sold the automobile to Hanson-Rock, an automobile dealer in the business of selling new and used cars to the public. Then Jones purchased the car from Hanson-Rock on April 8, 1966, for consideration, in good faith and without any actual knowledge of National Shawmut's security interest. Wever did not complete the payments under the installment plan and National Shawmut sought to foreclose its security interest in the automobile.

GRIMES, JUDGE. Since Wever purchased for personal, family or household purposes, the Dart is classified as consumer goods. (9–109.) National Shawmut's security interest was perfected by filing the financing statement with the town clerk of Hampton where Wever resided (9–401 (1) (a)), and continues when the collateral is sold without its consent as was the case here unless Article 9 provided otherwise. (9–306 (2).) In the case of buyers of goods, Article 9–307 (1) does provide otherwise in certain instances, as follows:

A buyer in ordinary course of business (subsection (9) of Section 1–201) other than a person buying farm products from a person engaged in farming operations takes free of a security interest created by his seller even though the security interest is perfected and even though the buyer knows of its existence

Since Jones purchased in good faith without knowledge that the sale to him was in violation of the security interest of another and bought in the ordinary course from a person in the business of selling automobiles, he was a "buyer in the ordinary course of business." (1–201 (9).) However, § 9–307 (1) permits him to take free only of "a security interest created by his seller." The security interest of National Shawmut was not created by Hanson-Rock, Inc., Jones's seller, but by Wentworth Motor Co., Inc. Jones, therefore, does not take free of National Shawmut's security interest under this section. Neither does he take free of the security interest by reason of the provisions of § 9–307 (2) relating to consumer goods even if he purchased for his own personal, family or household purposes (a fact not agreed upon) because "prior to the purchase, the secured party . . . filed a financing statement. . . ."These are the only two provisions of Article 9 under which a buyer of goods can claim to take free of a security interest where a sale, exchange or other disposition of the collateral was without the consent of the secured party. Jones does not benefit from either one. Article 9–306 (2) gives the court no leeway to create any other exceptions to its dictates and no custom, usage or agreement has been brought to our attention which would permit us to do so. (1–102 (2).)

Corbin Deposit Bank v. *King*
384 S.W.2d 302 (Ct. App. Ky. 1964)

This was an action by Corbin Deposit Bank (plaintiff) against Thomas L. King (defendant) to determine the rights in the proceeds of the sale of an automobile. Judgment for King and Corbin Deposit Bank appealed. Judgment affirmed.

Corbin Deposit Bank (Bank) had an enforceable security interest in a motor vehicle owned by Floyd Foreman. Foreman, while the Bank's security interest was in full force, had the motor vehicle repaired by King, who was engaged in the business of selling, repairing and furnishing accessories or supplies for motor vehicles. Foreman defaulted on his debt to the Bank and he did not pay King for the repairs. King had possession of the motor vehicle and claimed a lien for repairs which had priority over the security interest of the Bank. The Bank repossessed the motor vehicle under court order and it was sold in accordance with the applicable statute.

DAVIS, COMMISSIONER.   The narrow question is whether the first rights to the proceeds insure to the Bank under its perfected security interest or to King under its subsequently acquired statutory lien for services and materials furnished to repair Foreman's vehicle.

Determination of the question requires examination of 9–310, which is as follows:

When a person in the ordinary course of his business furnishes services or materials with respect to goods subject to a security interest, a lien upon goods in the possession of such person given by statute or rule of law for such materials or services takes priority over a perfected security interest unless the lien is statutory and the staute expressly provides otherwise.

In the 1958 text of the Uniform Commercial Code as published by National Conference of Commissioners on Uniform State Laws, American Law Institute, one of the purposes of the just quoted section is said to be:

(1): To provide that liens securing claims arising from work intended to enhance or preserve the value of the collateral take priority over an earlier security interest even though perfected.

It is recognized by the parties that prior to the effective date of Kentucky's Uniform Commercial Code in similar circumstances, this court had adhered to the rule allowing priority to a properly recorded chattel mortgage. The inquiry here is whether the pertinent sections of the Uniform Commercial Code require an opposite result. The trial court found that the provisions of the Commercial Code demand the opposite result, and we agree.

The course for construction of the Uniform Commercial Code was charted in *Lincoln Bank & Trust Co.* v. *Queenan, Ky.,* in which this court said:

The Code represents an entirely new approach in several areas of commercial law, and especially as to security transactions. Its adoption in this state signifies a legislative policy to join with other states in achieving uniformity. Code 1–102(2) (c). The realization of this purpose demands that so far as possible the meaning of the law be gathered from the instrument itself, unfettered by anachronisms indigenous to the respective jurisdictions in which it is in force. Cf. 50 Am.Jr. 480 (Statutes, 465). Accepting that principle, we adopt as a rule of construction that the Code is plenary and exclusive except where the legislature has clearly indicated otherwise.

It is patent that KRS 376.270 contains no provision which may be said to subordinate its statutory lien to an earlier security interest as prescribed in 9–310. Therefore, by the terms of the latter section, the lien of the security interest yields to the statutory mechanic's lien of KRS 376.270, despite the line of cases which had afforded priority to chattel mortgages in similar circumstances.

Default and Foreclosure

Contract Provisions. Within stated limitations the parties may agree as to the rights of the secured party in the event of default on the part of the debtor. In general, an agreement which deprives the debtor of his right to any surplus after sale of the collateral, his right to redeem before sale, his right to notice of the time and place of sale, his right to hold the secured party liable for breach of his duty, or any other basic right vested in the debtor, will not be enforced. (9–501.) The secured party may, if he so elects, reduce his claim to judgment in which event he will not surrender his right in the collateral and the foreclosure will proceed according to the procedure in judicial sales. The secured party may bid at the sale. (9–501 [5].)

Right to Possession.   On default the secured party is entitled to possession of the collateral. If the collateral is in the possession of the debtor and cannot be repossessed without breach of peace he can institute the possessory court action available under the procedural statutes of the state. He may, if the collateral is bulky and difficult to remove, have it rendered useless and sell it on the debtor's premises. (9–503.) If the collateral is intangible, such as, for instance, accounts, contract rights, chattel paper, instruments or documents, and performance has been rendered to the debtor, the secured party may give notice and have payments made or performance rendered to him. (9–502.)

Sale of Collateral.   The secured party may dispose of the collateral by sale or lease or in any manner calculated to produce the greatest benefit to all parties concerned; however, the method of disposal must be commercially reasonable. (9–504.) Notice of the time and place of a public sale must be given to the debtor and to others who have a perfected security interest in the collateral or who have an interest known to the secured party. Also, notice must be given of a private sale. The purchaser at a sale is protected against defects in the sale. (9–504 [4].)

Distribution of Proceeds.   Disposition of the proceeds from the liquidation of the collateral follows the standard pattern: expenses of retaking, holding, preparing for sale and the like, and reasonable attorney fees; satisfaction of indebtedness; junior security interests, if written notice fo demand is given before distribution; and surplus, if any, to debtor. (9–504 [1].) In the event the amount received on the liquidation is insufficient to satisfy the obligation, the secured party, in the absence of an agreement to the contrary, is entitled to a deficiency judgment. (9–504 [2].)

Consumer Goods.   If the security interest is in consumer goods, the secured party must sell if 60 percent of the purchase price or debt has been paid. If less than 60 percent has been paid or if the security interest is in collateral other than consumer goods, the secured party in possession may propose to retain the collateral in satisfaction of the obligation. If no written objection is made to the proposal within 30 days after written notice of the election to retain the collateral is given, the secured party may retain the collateral in satisfaction of the obligation. (9–505.)

Duties of Secured Party.   The debtor has an absolute right to redeem the collateral at any time before its disposal. (9–506.)

The secured party is liable to injured parties if, in his foreclosure and sale, he has not complied with the provisions of Article 9. (9–507.)

A sale will not be set aside solely on the ground that a better price might have been obtained had the sale been made at a different time or place, or if a different procedure had been followed. (9–507 [2].)

Summary

Within stated limitations the parties may agree as to the rights of the secured party if the debtor defaults. Unless otherwise agreed the secured party has the right to possess the collateral. If it is bulky or hard to remove he may render it useless and sell it where located. He may sell the collateral at public or private sale and he may buy the collateral but he must act in good faith and the sale must be commercially reasonable. The proceeds of the sale are distributed as follows: expenses, reasonable attorney fees, satisfaction of indebtedness, junior creditors, if any, and balance to debtor. If the security interest is in consumer goods the secured party must sell if 60 percent of the debt has been paid. If less than 60 percent has been paid, the secured party may, by agreement, keep the collateral and cancel the debt.

Fort Knox National Bank v. Gustafson

385 S.W.2d 196 (Ct. App. Ky. 1964)

This was an action by Edith M. Gustafson (plaintiff) against Fort Knox National Bank (defendant) to recover a judgment for damages for abuse of process arising out of an action to recover possession of a mobile diner in which the Bank had a security interest. Judgment for Gustafson and Fort Knox National Bank appealed. Judgment reversed.

On October 12, 1960, Arthur and Edith Gustafson borrowed from Fort Knox National Bank (Bank) the sum of $7,380. Arthur and Edith executed their joint promissory note secured by the transfer to the Bank of a security interest in a mobile diner and a lease of the lot on which the diner was located. At first Arthur and Edith operated the restaurant together. In October, 1961, Edith went to Texas to nurse her sick father. In June, 1962, Arthur abandoned the restaurant and went to New York. Edith returned from Texas and attempted to operate the restaurant. On her return she learned that the rent on the lot was $800 in arrears. Arthur was in financial difficulty on other enterprises in which he was engaged. In September, 1962, due to a disturbance and the default in rent payments, the lessor of the lot ordered Edith to remove the diner by October 1, 1962. Edith negotiated with the Bank for a settlement of her financial affairs but no solution was worked out. The Bank brought an action to repossess the mobile diner and Edith refused to surrender possession. There was a technical defect in the repossession bond filed by the Bank in its action. The note included an acceleration provision. The trial court granted Edith a judgment against the Bank of $20,500 actual damages and $15,000 punitive damages.

DAVIS, COMMISSIONER. The note contained an acceleration clause, authorizing the holder to precipitate the maturity date in the event the makers defaulted in any monthly payment. The acceleration clause also provided that the holder of the note could declare it due before maturity if the holder felt insecure. This type of acceleration is permitted by the U.C.C.

Since the acceleration clause was properly invoked, the bank had a right to obtain possession of the collateral by the terms of the security agreement. This right of possession is specifically assured by 9–503, which provides that the secured party may proceed to obtain such possession without judicial process, if this can be accomplished without breach of peace—or by judicial action. Here it is agreed that repossession could not be had peaceably. Thus, we are left to consider whether the judicial action was so defective as to expose appellant bank to the damage claims here asserted.

Upon the authority of *General Motors Acceptance Corp.* v. *Curry,* we hold that any technical flaw (if indeed there was one sufficient to invalidate the process) in the claim and delivery action did not afford a cause of action to Gustafson for the taking of the diner. We think *Stoll Oil Refining Co.* v. *Pierce* is compatible with the decision in the *Curry* case, and with our present holding. Although it is true that we approved an award for nominal damages in *Stoll Oil Refining Co.* v. *Pierce,* we conclude that 9–507(1) expresses the statutory policy and view of the Uniform Commercial Code that the debtor is confined to recovery of "any loss caused by a failure to comply." In this sense, we construe "loss" to relate to actual compensatory damages—not nominal damages. We think this same concept is implicit in 1–106.

As we have concluded that the bank acted in "good faith," it follows that no issue as to punitive damages was shown. Punitive damages do not flow from "good faith" conduct.

It was incumbent on the bank to comply with the requirements of 9–504(3), which requires that repossessed collateral be sold or disposed of by the secured party in a commercially reasonable manner. The record before us is voluminous, but it does not contain an adequate account of the disposition of the diner by the bank. The issue as to whether the sale was commercially reasonable was not developed in evidence, nor was it submitted to the jury. Upon another trial, details as to the sale and whether it was commercially reasonable will be developed in evidence, and any appropriate issues reflected in the evidence will be submitted to the jury.

In this connection, it must be noted that 9–507(1, 2) relate to the measure of damages applicable here. The debtor is entitled to recoup any "loss" caused by failure of the secured party to comply with the Uniform Commercial Code. However, the mere fact that a better price could have been obtained by sale at a different time, or different place or manner is not of itself sufficient to establish that the sale was not commercially reasonable.

Gustafson is not entitled to recover any damage for asserted loss as to the business. We have said that the bank was entitled to the possession of the diner under the terms of the security agreement. Manifestly, taking the diner into possession presupposes terminating the restaurant business conducted in it by the Gustafsons. The consequent disruption of the restaurant business incident to the legal repossession of the diner was a result which the Gustafsons impliedly consented to in the security agreement.

Real Estate Mortgages

Historical Development. The real estate mortgage, as a form of security, was used in England as early as the middle of the 12th century, but our present-day mortgage law developed from the common-law mortgage of the 15th century. The common-law mortgage was a deed which conveyed the land to the mortgagee, the title to the land to revest in the mortgagor on payment of the debt secured. The mortgagee was given possession of the land during the term of the mortgage, and if the mortgagor defaulted, the mortgagee's title to the land became absolute. The land was forfeited as a penalty for breach of condition, and the forfeiture did not discharge the debt. The mortgagee could sue on the debt, recover a judgment, and collect the debt, in addition to keeping the land.

The early equity courts did not favor the imposition of penalties and would relieve from such forfeitures, provided the mortgagor's default was minor in nature and was due to causes beyond his control. By gradual stages the courts became more lenient in permitting redemptions and allowed the mortgagor to redeem if he tendered performance without unreasonable delay, that is, if he was not guilty of laches. Finally, the courts of equity recognized the mortgagor's right to redeem as an absolute right which would continue until the mortgagee asked the court of equity to decree that the mortgagor's right to redeem be foreclosed and cut off. Our present law relative to the foreclosure of mortgage developed from this practice.

Form, Execution, and Recording. The early real estate mortgage was a deed containing a defeasance clause. In some states the deed with a defeasance clause is still used, but in other states a statutory form of mortgage is used. As a general rule the statutory form of mortgage does not contain words of conveyance but uses "mortgages and warrants" or similar language.

The real estate mortgage is generally recognized as conveying an interest in real property, and it must be executed with the same formality as is a deed. Unless a mortgage is executed as required by the statutes of the state in which the land is located, it is not eligible for recording.

An unrecorded mortgage is not valid against bona fide purchasers or mortgagees for value who have no notice or knowledge of the mortgage, nor is it valid against creditors who acquire a lien on the property. As between the parties the validity of the mortgage does not depend on the fulfillment of the formal requirements. If the transaction is intended as a loan and security for the payment of the loan, the courts will declare it a mortgage, irrespective of the form of the conveyance. The courts jealously guard the mortgagor's right to redeem and will not enforce any contract or agreement cutting off this right.

Even though the conveyance is in the form of a warranty deed, the courts will declare it a mortgage if it was given as security.

However, if a deed is given as security for the payment of a loan and the real property is sold by the owner of record (the mortgagee) to an innocent purchaser for value, the innocent purchaser for value acquires good title. The mortgagee will be liable to the mortgagor for any damages the mortgagor has suffered as a result of the sale of the property.

Rights and Liabilities of Mortgagor and Purchasers. The owner (the mortgagor) may sell the property without the consent of the mortgagee, but such a sale in no way affects the mortgagee's interest in the property or his claim against the mortgagor on the debt. In case there is a default, the mortgagee may foreclose the mortgage and have the mortgaged property sold. If, on foreclosure, sale of the property does not bring enough to pay the costs, interest, and principal, the mortgagee is entitled to a deficiency judgment against the original debtor, the mortgagor, although some courts show great reluctance to allow deficiency judgments where real property was used as security for a debt. If the property should sell for more than enough to pay the costs, interest, and principal, the surplus will go to the mortgagor or one who has purchased from him.

The purchaser may buy the mortgaged property "subject to the mortgage," or he may "assume" the mortgage. If he purchases subject to the mortgage and a default and a foreclosure follow, he is not liable for a deficiency; if he assumes the mortgage, he is liable for any deficiency. The property is always liable and may be sold to pay the mortgage debt; and the mortgagor, since he cannot assign his liability, is liable to the mortgagee on the mortgage debt. If the mortgagor sells the mortgaged property to a purchaser who "assumes and agrees to pay the mortgage debt," such purchaser is liable to the mortgagee for the amount of the mortgage debt. In most jurisdictions the mortgagor's liability is that of a surety. If there is a default followed by a foreclosure, the mortgagee in the event of a deficiency may obtain a deficiency judgment against both the mortgagor and the purchaser; and if the mortgagor pays the deficiency, he is entitled to recover the amount paid from the purchaser.

Mortgagee's Right to Assign Mortgage. The mortgagee may assign his interest in the mortgaged property. To do this, he must assign the debt. If the debt is evidenced by a negotiable note, the assignment is usually made by the negotiation of the note plus an assignment of the mortgage; however, in most jurisdictions the negotiation of the note carries with it the right to the security, and the holder of the note is entitled to the benefits of the mortgage.

Foreclosure of Real Estate Mortgage. Foreclosure is the process by which all further rights existing in the mortgagor or persons who have acquired the rights of the mortgagor to redeem the mortgaged real property are defeated and lost. Foreclosure proceedings are usually regulated by the statutes of the state in which the real property is located; and in many states, two or more alternative methods of foreclosure are available to the mortgagee or his assignee. The methods in common use today are (1) strict foreclosure, (2) action and sale, and (3) power of sale.

Under a strict foreclosure, all rights of the mortgagor are cut off by the foreclosure proceedings, and title to the mortgaged property is vested in the mortgagee. There is no sale of the property. Strict foreclosure is used extensively in only a few states, and in those states the right to strict foreclosure is generally confined to those cases wherein the debt is equal to or exceeds the value of the security, or where the mortgagor or a person who has acquired a right under the mortgagor has only a technical interest in the mortgaged property.

Foreclosure by action and sale is permitted in all states and is the only method of foreclosure permitted in some states. Although the state statutes are not uniform, they are alike in their basic requirements. In a foreclosure by action and sale, suit is brought in a court having jurisdiction. Any party having a property interest which would be cut off by the foreclosure must be made a party defendant, and if any such party has a defense, he must enter his appearance and set up his defense. The case must be tried in accordance with the established trial procedure of the state, after which a judgment is entered and a sale of the property ordered. The proceeds of the sale are applied to the payment of the mortgage debt, and any surplus is paid over to the mortgagor or such other person or persons who would be entitled thereto. If there is a deficiency, a deficiency judgment is, as a general rule, entered against the mortgagor and such other persons as would be liable on the debt.

The right to foreclose under a power of sale must be expressly conferred on the mortgagee by the terms of the mortgage. If the procedure for the exercise of the power is set out in the mortgage, such procedure must be followed. Several states have enacted statutes which set out the procedure to be followed in the exercise of a power of sale. No court action is required. As a general rule, notice of the sale must be given to the mortgagor, and the sale must be advertised. The sale must be at auction and must be conducted fairly, and an effort must be made to sell the property at the highest price obtainable. The proceeds of the sale are applied to the payment of costs, interest, and the principal of the debt. Any surplus must be paid to the mortgagor or such other persons as may be entitled thereto. If there is a deficiency and the mortgagee wishes to recover a judgment for the deficiency, he must bring suit on the debt.

Right of Redemption. At common law and under existing statutes the mortgagor or an assignee of the mortgagor has an equity of redemption in the mortgaged real estate; that is, he has the absolute right to discharge the mortgage when due and have title to the mortgaged property restored free and clear of the mortgage debt. Under the statutes of all states the mortgagor or any party having in the mortgaged property an interest which will be cut off by the foreclosure may redeem the property after default and before the mortgagee forecloses the mortgage. In several states by statute the mortgagor or any other party in interest is given what is known as a redemption period (usually of six months or one year and either after the foreclosure proceedings are started or after a foreclosure sale of the mortgaged property is made) in which to pay the mortgaged debt, costs and interest and redeem the property.

As a general rule, if a party in interest wishes to redeem, he must, if the redemption period runs after the foreclosure sale, pay to the purchaser at the foreclosure sale the amount the purchaser has paid plus interest up to the time of redemption. If the redemption period runs before the sale, the party in interest must pay the amount of the debt plus the costs and interest. The person who wishes to redeem from a mortgage foreclosure sale must redeem the entire mortgage interest; he cannot redeem a partial interest by paying a proportionate amount of the debt or by paying a proportionate amount of the price bid at the foreclosure sale.

Summary

At common law the mortgaged property was deeded to the mortgagee who took possession of the property. On default by the mortgagor the mortgaged property was forfeited to the mortgagee as a penalty for the default.

At an early date the courts of equity began to relieve from forfeiture immediately on default, and by gradual evolution the time in which the mortgagor had a right to redeem after default was extended until foreclosure of the mortgage.

Mortgages are executed with the same formalities as are deeds and must be recorded to be valid against third persons. Irrespective of the form of a conveyance, if it is made to secure a debt, the courts will declare it to be a mortgage and will permit the mortgagor the right to redeem.

The mortgagor may convey his interest in the mortgaged property, but the purchaser acquires no greater rights than the mortgagor has. Whether or not the purchaser becomes liable to the mortgagee for the payment of the mortgage debt depends on whether the purchaser has assumed and agreed to pay the mortgage debt as part of the purchase price of the property. The mortgagee may assign the mortgage debt and mortgage.

On default by the mortgagor the mortgagee must foreclose the mortgage to cut off the mortgagor's rights in the property. In foreclosing the mortgage, the statutory procedure of the state in which the land is located must be followed.

In most states the mortgagor and other parties in interest are given a period, usually one year, in which to redeem the property from the foreclosure.

Boysun v. *Boysun*

368 P.2d 439 (Sup. Ct. Mont. 1962)

This was an action by Mike E. Boysun (plaintiff) against John C. Boysun and Tillie Boysun, his wife (defendants), to quiet title to certain land. Judgment for Mike E. Boysun, and John C. and Tillie Boysun appealed. Judgment affirmed.

John C. and Tillie Boysun owned a farm which was mortgaged for $4,400. They were in default on their payments and delinquent in the payment of their taxes, and the mortgagee was threatening to foreclose.

John was unable to borrow money to pay the mortgage. Mike offered to purchase the land subject to the encumbrances. He stated at the time that it was worth no more than the encumbrances. John and Tillie executed a quitclaim deed conveying the farm to Mike. Mike orally agreed to reconvey the farm to John or to convey it to a purchaser if John found one. Thereafter John and his family moved to another state. Mike worked the farm in 1953 and 1954 and paid the taxes from 1951 through 1958.

In the early part of 1954 John told Mike that he had a purchaser who would pay $11,000 for the farm but Mike wished to keep the farm. Thereafter, Mike sent money to John, and the amount sent plus the amount Mike paid to discharge the encumbrances on the farm amounted to $11,000. John and Tillie claim that the quitclaim deed was to secure a loan and asked the court to hold it to be a mortgage. John claimed that the money Mike sent him was a loan.

HARRISON, CHIEF JUSTICE.   The ultimate question of whether a transaction was intended by the parties to be a mortgage or a sale rests on the intention of the parties at the time of the execution of the instrument, and to establish this intention the courts will examine the surrounding circumstances.

It has been repeatedly held that the evidence to prove that a deed, absolute on its face, was intended to be a mortgage must be clear and convincing. However, this rule is subject to some modification in situations where there is an option to repurchase or a conditional sale. The general rule is that if there is doubt whether a sale or a mortgage was intended, the court will be inclined to resolve the doubt in favor of the mortgage.

John and Tillie in this action rely heavily on the *Murray case*. In that case this court listed a number of facts and circumstances which, if present, tend to confirm the view that the transaction was a mortgage and not a sale. These factors are as follows:

(*a*) The transaction in its inception had for its purpose a loan, not a sale.

(*b*) The grantor was in financial distress at the time of the transaction.

(*c*) The price which the grantee claims he paid for the property appears to have been grossly inadequate.

(*d*) According to grantee's own theory, the transaction did not amount to an absolute sale, but to a conditional sale; that is, a sale with an option to grantor to repurchase.

John and Tillie list the four factors and allege that they are all present in the instant case. We have some difficulty with this assertion. The third principle relied on in the *Murray* case is based on the inadequacy of the price the vendor received for his property. The adequacy of consideration must be tested by conditions existing at the time of the transaction.

In *Titus* v. *Wallick,* the court held that in order for evidence of a disparity between the consideration for a deed and the value of the land to be of weight, it is essential that there be a satisfactory showing of such disparity.

There is no evidence in the record to support John and Tillie's allegation of a disparity between the purchase price and the value of the land at the time of sale. The only statement as to the value of the land at the time the deed was executed was the testimony of Mike Boysun. He stated the reason he would not loan money against the property was because it was not worth any more than what was against it.

In addition to the above-stated facts here are two elements present in the instant case which were not present in the *Murray* case. A deed, though absolute on its face, will be construed as a mortgage whenever it is shown that the instrument was intended to secure a debt. However, a debt must be shown to exist between the parties, as a mortgage is a mere incident of the debt.

In the *Murray* case there was testimony in the record that the parties intended the money paid to be a loan and that a debt was created between the parties. In the instant case, Mike Boysun testified that the agreement between the parties was that any time John paid the money spent by Mike on the property he was to get the property back. John's testimony supports this theory that he received an option to repurchase. His testimony indicates that he felt no obligation to pay any money back to Mike, but rather he had an option to do so if desired.

John and Tillie place considerable emphasis on the fact that Mike Boysun while testifying stated that John had a year or two to redeem the property. They cite this to show that a mortgage was intended. We feel little weight should be given to such statements made by a layman, especially in a situation such as the present wherein it is evident from the legal tangle of the parties that they knew little, if anything, about the law.

The second factor which is present in the instant case, which is absent from the *Murray* case, is the preponderant and inescapable fact that the option to repurchase was exercised. The testimony of two disinterested witnesses established the fact that in the Spring of 1954, John Boysun exercised his option to repurchase. In addition to exercising his option the testimony in the record establishes that he received his option price.

Trust Deeds and Land Contracts

Trust Deeds.   There are three parties to a trust deed transaction: the trustor, who borrows the money; the trustee, who holds legal title to the real property put up as security; and the lender, who is beneficiary of the trust. The purpose of a trust deed transaction is to facilitate the liquidation of the security in the event of default. Most of the states have declared a trust deed to be a mortgage and have required court foreclosure, thereby defeating the purpose of the arrangement.

In a deed-of-trust transaction the borrower deeds to the trustee the real property which is to be put up as security. If the borrower fails to make the required payments on the debt, the trustee is usually given, by the terms of the trust agreement, the power to foreclose or to sell the property. Usually, the trustee does not sell the property until the beneficiary (the lender or his assignee) notifies the trustee that the debtor is in default and demands that the property be sold. The trustee sells the property, usually at public sale, and applies the proceeds to the payment of costs, interest, and principal. If there is a surplus, it is paid over to the trustor. If there is a deficiency and the lender wishes to force collection, he will have to sue on the debt and recover a judgment.

Land Contracts. The land contract, as a security device, is limited in its use to the securing of the payment of the balance of the purchase price of real property. The seller of the property agrees to sell, and the buyer agrees to buy and pay the stipulated purchase price set out in the contract. Usually, the purchaser takes possession of the property, pays all taxes and assessments, keeps the property insured, and assumes all other obligations of an owner. In fact, the purchaser is the equitable owner, but the seller holds the legal title and does not deed the property to the buyer until the purchase price is paid in full. In the event the buyer defaults, the seller has the right to declare a forfeiture and take possession of the property, thereby cutting off all the buyer's rights in the property. The laws of the states vary in regard to the rights of the parties to a land contract.

As a general rule the procedure for declaration of forfeiting and recovery of property sold on land contract is simpler and less time-consuming than the foreclosure of a real estate mortgage by court action. In some states the procedure to be followed in the event of default on a land contract has been set out by statute. In other states the courts of equity have developed the procedure to be followed in the event of default and forfeiture. If the buyer, after default, voluntarily surrenders possession to the seller, no court procedure is necessary; the seller's title will become absolute, and the buyer's equity will be cut off.

Summary

A trust deed may be used in some states in lieu of a mortgage. In the trust deed transaction the borrower (the trustor) conveys the property to a trustee who, after the default of the trustor and at the request of the lender, sells the property and from the proceeds pays the debt.

The owner of real property may sell on land contract. The seller retains title to the property until the purchase price is paid in full. If the buyer defaults, the seller has the right to reclaim the property.

Mechanic's Lien on Real Estate

Nature of Mechanic's Lien on Real Estate. All rights to a mechanic's lien on real estate must be created by statutory enactment, since the courts have never recognized a common-law lien on real property. Consequently, all of the states have enacted statutes pertaining to mechanics' liens on real estate, but the requirements in the various states for obtaining such liens differ so widely and in so many particulars that space does not permit a discussion of these statutes in detail.

Persons Entitled to a Lien. Some statutes set out in detail the classes of persons who are entitled to a mechanic's lien, whereas others set them out in broad general terms. In general, any person whose labor or material has contributed to the improvement of real estate is entitled to a mechanic's lien.

Rights of Subcontractors and Materialmen. A general contractor is a person who has contracted with the owner to build, remodel, or improve real property. A subcontractor is a person who has contracted with the general contractor to perform a stipulated portion of the general contract. A materialman is a person who has contracted to furnish certain materials needed to perform a designated general contract.

Two distinct systems are followed by the several states in allowing mechanics' liens on real estate to subcontractors and materialmen: the New York system and the Pennsylvania system.

The New York system is based on the theory of subrogation, and the subcontractors or materialmen cannot recover more than is owing the contractor at the time they file a lien or give notice of a lien to the owner. Under the Pennsylvania system the subcontractors or materialmen have direct liens and are entitled to liens for the value of labor and material furnished, irrespective of the amount due from the owner to the contractor. Under the New York system the failure of the general contractor to perform his contract or his abandonment of the work has a direct effect on the lien rights of subcontractors and materialmen, whereas under the Pennsylvania system, such breach or abandonment by the general contractor does not directly affect the lien rights of subcontractors and materialmen.

Basis for Mechanic's Lien on Real Estate. In some states, statutes provide that no lien shall be claimed unless the contract for the improvement is in writing and embodies a description of the land on which the improvement is to take place, and of the work to be done, and a statement of the materials to be furnished. Other states permit the contract to be oral, but in no state is a licensee or volunteer entitled to a lien.

No lien can be claimed unless the work is done or the materials are furnished in the performance of a contract to improve specific real property. A sale of materials without reference to the improvement of specific real property does not entitle the person furnishing the material to a lien upon real property which is, in fact, improved by the use of the materials at some time after the sale. Unless the state statute specifically includes submaterialmen, they are not entitled to a lien. For example, if a lumber dealer contracts to furnish the lumber for the erection of a specific building and orders from a sawmill a carload of lumber needed to fulfill the contract, the sawmill will not be entitled to a lien on the building in which the lumber is used unless the state statute expressly provides that submaterialmen are entitled to a lien.

At times the question has arisen as to whether or not materials have been furnished. Some courts have held that the materialmen must prove that the material furnished was actually incorporated into the structure. Under this ruling, if material delivered on the job is diverted by the general contractor or others and not incorporated into the structure, the materialmen will not be entitled to a lien. Other courts have held that the materialman is entitled to a lien if he can furnish proof that the material was delivered on the job under a contract to furnish the material.

Requirements for Obtaining Lien. The requirements for obtaining a mechanic's lien must be complied with strictly. Although there is no uniformity in the statutes as to the requirements for obtaining a lien, they generally require the filing of a notice of lien with a county official, such as the register of deeds or county clerk, which notice sets forth the amount claimed, the name of the owner, the name of the contractor and claimant, and a description of the property. Frequently, the notice of lien must be verified by an affidavit of the claimant. In some states a copy of the notice must be served on the owner or posted on the property.

The notice of lien must be filed within a stipulated time. The time varies from 30 to 90 days, but the favored time is 60 days after the last work is done or after the last materials are furnished. Some statutes distinguish between labor claims, materialmen's claims, and claims of general contractors as to time of filing. The lien, when filed, must be foreclosed within a specified time, which varies from six months to two years.

Priorities and Foreclosure. The provisions for priorities vary widely, but most of the statutes provide that a mechanic's lien has priority over all liens attaching after the first work is performed or after the first materials are furnished. This provision in the statute creates a hidden lien on the property, in that a mechanic's lien, filed within the allotted period of time after completion of the work, attaches as of the time the first work is done or the first material is furnished, but no notice of lien need be filed during this period, and if no notice of lien is filed during this period, third persons would have no means of knowing of the existence of a lien. There are no priorities among lien claimants under the majority of statutes.

The procedure followed in the foreclosure of a mechanic's lien on real estate follows closely the procedure followed in a court foreclosure of a real estate mortgage. The rights acquired by the filing of a lien and the extent of property covered by such lien are set out in some of the mechanic's lien statutes. In general, the lien attaches only to the interest the person has in the property which has been improved at the time the notice is filed. Some statutes provide that the lien attaches to the building and city lot on which the building stands, or if the improvement is to farm property, the lien attaches to a specified amount of land.

Waiver of Lien.   The question often arises as to the effect of an express provision in a contract for the improvement of real estate that no lien shall attach to the property for the cost of the improvement. In some states, there are statutes requiring the recording or filing of the contract and making such provision ineffective if the statute is not complied with. In some jurisdictions, it has been held that such a provision is effective against everyone; in other jurisdictions the provision has been held ineffective against all except the contractor; while in still other jurisdictions, such provisions have been held ineffective as to subcontractors, materialmen, and laborers. Whether or not parties have notice of the waiver-of-lien provision plays an important part in several jurisdictions in determining their right to a lien.

Summary

The right to a mechanic's lien on real estate is statutory. The basis of a lien is the improvement of the real estate of one person by the addition of the labor and materials of another.

The persons who are entitled to mechanics' liens on real estate are set out in the statutes, and in this regard the provisions of the statutes vary widely. Under one type of statute the right of a subcontractor or materialman to a mechanic's lien is based on the right of the general contractor, and the total of their claims cannot exceed the amount due the general contractor. Under the other type of statute the subcontractor or materialman is entitled to a direct lien on the improved property for the full value of the work and material furnished. The work and materials must be furnished for the improvement of a particular premise or building. A person is not entitled to a lien for materials sold generally which are not until later incorporated into a building.

To obtain a lien, the lien claimant must comply strictly with the statutory requirements as to the form, content, and time of giving notice of lien, and any other requirements for the obtaining of a lien. As a general rule a lien dates from the time the first labor or materials are furnished and has priority over all subsequent lien claimants.

A lien is foreclosed in the same manner as that followed in a court foreclosure of a real estate mortgage. It attaches to the interest which the person having the improvement made has in the improved property. Under the provisions of some statutes the right to a mechanic's lien may be waived by the insertion of a waiver provision in the contract for the improvement.

Manpower, Inc. v. Phillips
179 N.E.2d 922 (Sup. Ct. Ohio 1962)

This was an action by Manpower, Inc. (plaintiff), against Phillips and Oakley Drive-In Theaters, Inc., and others (defendants) asking for a judgment for labor furnished and the granting of a mechanic's lien. Judgment for Manpower, Inc., and Oakley Drive-In Theaters, Inc., appealed to appellate court where the judgment granting a mechanic's lien was affirmed. Oakley Drive-In Theaters, Inc., appealed to the Supreme Court. Judgment reversed as to mechanic's lien.

Oakely Drive-In Theaters, Inc. (Oakley) engaged Phillips as a general contractor for the construction of an addition to the concession building of Oakley.

Manpower, Inc., had a contract with Phillips to furnish him laborers from time to time. Manpower, Inc., at the request of Phillips, furnished him laborers who worked on the Oakley job and paid the laborers a total of $1,955.45, but Phillips did not pay Manpower, Inc. The trial court granted a judgment against Phillips for $1,955.45 and no appeal was taken from this judgment. It also granted a mechanic's lien on the Oakley building and this appeal was taken from that holding.

GRIFFITH, JUDGE. The question presented in this appeal is whether, under Section 1311.02, Revised Code, a corporation which furnishes laborers to a contractor is entitled to a lien on the property of the owner of real property for labor and work rendered by such laborers, employees of the corporation, in the improvement of such property.

The precise question has never been decided by the courts of this state.

So far as pertinent, Section 1311.02, Revised Code, reads:

Every person or corporation who does work or labor upon, or furnishes machinery, material, or fuel for constructing, altering . . . repairing, or removing a house . . . or other building . . . by virtue of a contract, express or implied, with the owner, part owner, or lessee of any interest in real estate, or his authorized agent, and every person who as a subcontractor, laborer, or materialman, performs any labor, or furnishes machinery, material or fuel, to an original or principal contractor, or any subcontractor, in carrying forward, performing, or completing any such contract, has a lien to secure the payment thereof. . . .

The first part of that section deals with mechanics' liens for persons who deal directly with the owner or the lessee of the real estate; and the second part deals with those persons at least once removed from the owner or lessee who deal with the contractor or subcontractor.

Clearly, Manpower, Inc., did not have any contract, express or implied, with either the lessee or the fee holder.

The next question presented is: Was Manpower, Inc., a "subcontractor" as that term is used in the statute?

"A subcontractor agrees to do something for another, but it is not controlled or subject to the control of the other in the manner or method of accomplishing the result contracted for."

Suretyship and Guarantee

Surety and Guarantor.   A surety, in the broad sense, is a person who is liable for the payment of another person's debt or for the performance of another's person duty. A surety joins the principal in making the promise. Both parties make primary promises to the obligee; however, the relation between the promisors is such that if the surety is required to perform, he will be entitled to reimbursement from his principal for any resulting loss.

A guarantor does not join in making a promise. The guarantor's liability arises on the happening of a stipulated event, such as the failure of the principal to perform his obligation, or the insolvency or bankruptcy of the principal. The guarantor's promise is collateral to the primary promise and is unenforceable, under the statute of frauds, unless evidenced by a writing signed by the guarantor or his duly authorized agent.

The rights and liabilities of a surety and of a guarantor are substantially the same, and we shall not attempt to distinguish between the two in our discussion unless the distinction is of basic importance.

Creation of Relation.   The relationship of principal and surety or that of principal and guarantor is created by contract. The rules of contract law apply in determining the existence and nature of the relationship, and the rights and duties of the parties.

In some states the married women's statutes are so drafted that a married woman does not have the capacity to bind herself as surety. As a general rule a corporation does not have the power to bind itself as surety for third persons unless such power is granted to it in its articles of incorporation.

Defenses of Surety.   If the principal has a defense which goes to the merits of the primary contract, the defense is available to the surety. Defenses such as lack or failure of consideration, inducement of the contract by fraud or duress, or material breach on the part of the obligee are available to the surety. Defenses such as infancy, insanity, or bankruptcy of the principal, and other defenses which do not go to the merits of the contract but which are personal to the principal are not available to the surety.

The surety contracts to be responsible for the performance of his principal's obligation. If the principal and the creditor by mutual agreement alter the terms of the primary contract and the surety does not consent thereto, the alteration will operate to relieve the surety of his liability. The surety undertakes to assume the risks incident to the performance of a particular contract, and his obligation cannot be altered without his consent.

Under this rule, if a principal and a creditor enter into an agreement whereby the principal is given an extension of time for the performance of the contract, the surety will be released from his obligation unless he consents thereto. However, mere indulgence on the part of the creditor does not release the surety. If the creditor merely promises the principal that he may have additional time in which to perform, such a promise will not release the surety from his obligation, since it is not a valid agreement to extend the time of performance. The promise to extend the time of performance, if it is to be valid, must be supported by consideration.

Creditor's Duties to Surety. The creditor owes certain duties to the surety in regard to the risk the surety assumes. If he induces the surety to assume the risk by fraudulent representations as to the nature of the risk, or if he has knowledge of facts which would materially increase the risk and does not disclose such facts to the surety, the surety will be released from liability. If an employer (creditor) knows when he makes application for the bonding of an employee (principal) that such employee has been guilty of fraudulent or criminal misconduct, the employer must disclose this information to the surety. If an employer, after a bonded employee has been guilty of a defalcation covered by the bond, agrees to give the employee another chance and does not report the defalcation to the bonding company (surety), such action will release the bonding company from liability for further defalcations. If the principal has posted security for the performance of his obligation and the creditor surrenders such security without the consent of the surety, the surety will, as a general rule, be released to the extent of the value of the security surrendered. Some states have held, under such circumstances, that the surety is completely discharged.

Subrogation and Contribution. If the surety is compelled to perform the obligation of his principal, the surety acquires, by operation of law, all the rights the creditor had against the principal. This is known as the surety's "right of subrogation." If Arnold borrows $1,000 from Barber and Colby signs the contract as surety, and Arnold defaults and Colby pays Barber, Colby will acquire all the rights Barber had against Arnold. If Arnold had given Barber a security interest in stocks and bonds or physical personal property, Colby would be entitled to such security interest when he paid Barber. A surety's right of subrogation does not arise until the creditor has been paid in full.

If two or more persons become sureties for the same principal on the same obligation and one surety, on the principal's default, pays the obligation in full or pays more than his share of the obligation, he is entitled to reimbursement from his cosureties for the amount paid over and above his share. This is known as a surety's "right of contribution." If one or more of the cosureties is insolvent, the loss will be distributed equally among the solvent sureties. If a surety discharges the obligation for an amount less than the principal sum due, he is entitled to contribution only of the amount actually paid. Cosureties may enter into an express agreement which provides that the risks of the suretyship shall be distributed in unequal portions.

Summary

A surety, in the broad sense, is a person who is liable for the payment of another person's debt. Technically, a surety joins the principal in making the promise to the promisee, whereas a guarantor makes a collateral promise, promising to perform the principal's promise on the happening of a condition precedent.

The relation of surety is created by contract, and the general rules of contract law apply in determining the existence of a contract and in determining the rights and liabilities of the parties. As a general rule, any defense the principal has which goes to the merits of the case is available to the surety. Also, any agreement between the principal and creditor which alters the risks involved in the primary contract will discharge the surety unless he consents thereto or ratifies the agreement, or unless the rights against the surety are reserved.

The creditor owes a duty to use reasonable care in his dealings and not to increase unnecessarily the burden of risk assumed by a surety. If a surety pays his principal's debt, the surety is entitled to all the rights the creditor had against the principal. If there are cosureties and one surety pays more than his share of his principal's debt, he is entitled to contribution from his cosureties.

Problem Cases

1. O'Brien owned an iceboat which Buxton, as sailing master, sailed for O'Brien. O'Brien did not pay Buxton for his services as sailing master, and Buxton, who had possession of the iceboat, claimed a common-law lien on the iceboat for his services. Is Buxton entitled to a common-law lien on the iceboat?

2. Maxwell owned the timber on a certain tract of land. He hired Fitzgerald to cut the timber into logs and to put the logs in Maxwell's mill pond. Fitzgerald had the logs

cut and put on the bank of the mill pond where they were levied on by a judgment creditor of Maxwell's. Fitzgerald claimed a common-law lien on the logs for his labor in cutting and hauling them. Is Fitzgerald entitled to a common-law lien on the logs?

3. The United States held a perfected security interest in Antenna Systems' "present and future inventory (including supplies, raw materials, work in process and furnished goods)" and "all furniture, fixtures and equipment now owned and hereafter acquired." Antenna went into bankruptcy and a controversy arose between the bankruptcy trustee and the United States over rights to certain of Antenna's assets. These assets include (1) engineering blueprints, (2) bids, proposals and cost estimates compiled by company engineers in the process of bidding on numerous projects, (3) jigs, fixtures, patterns and core boxes used to manufacture products sold by Antenna, and (4) standard component parts of antenna systems which had been manufactured by and were on hand in various departments of Antenna. Which of the assets can the United States rightfully assert are covered by its security interest?

4. Park Plaza took a security interest in the inventory and equipment of a beauty shop to secure the beauty shop's obligations under a lease it had with Park Plaza. A financing statement was filed but it was signed only by the secured party, Park Plaza. However, a copy of the lease agreement granting the lien and signed by the debtor was attached to the financing statement and incorporated by reference. The beauty shop went into bankruptcy and the bankruptcy trustee claims Park Plaza does not have a perfected security interest because §9–402 provides that both parties must sign the financing statement. Did Park Plaza have a perfected security interest?

5. Ohio law provides that financing statements covering consumer goods are to be filed in the office of the county recorder in the county of the debtor's residence and that financing statements covering equipment are to be filed with the secretary of state. Associate Finance Company financed some refrigerators, gas ranges, washing machines, and household furniture for Bonnema which Bonnema installed in furnished apartments in order to produce a higher rental. Associate obtained a security agreement from Bonnema and filed a financing statement at the county recorder's office. The Trustee in Bankruptcy for Bonnema now claims that Associate does not have a perfected security interest in the refrigerators, etc. Is he correct? Why or why not?

6. Pennington sold some equipment to Gunderson and took a security interest in the equipment which he neglected to file. Then Consolidated Foods, which knew about Pennington's unperfected security interest, took a security interest of its own on the equipment and perfected it by filing a financing statement. Now Consolidated claims it is entitled to reclaim the equipment from Gunderson's Trustee in Bankruptcy in order to foreclose its lien. The Trustee argues that Consolidated's interest should not be deemed perfected because it knew of Pennington's claim and that therefore he as Trustee has a better right to the equipment than Consolidated. Who is entitled to the equipment? Why?

7. Acceptance Company had a blanket security interest, attached and perfected, on all of the stock, new and used vehicles, of Homer, an automobile dealer. In addition Homer had obtained a dealer's certificate of title to a Dodge automobile and had endorsed thereon a notice of lien in favor of Acceptance Company. Homer sold the Dodge automobile to Gregory who paid Homer the full purchase price. Homer did not deliver to Gregory a certificate of title to the automobile. Homer did not pay Acceptance Company and it repossessed the automobile from Gregory. Is Acceptance Company entitled to the automobile?

8. North Side Savings Bank took and filed a security interest in some plumbing fixtures prior to the time they were installed in a building on which Denis held a mortgage that he had recorded. The owner of the building defaulted to both North Side and Denis. North Side claims it is entitled to remove the plumbing; Denis claims it became a permanent part of the building and that North Side has no claim to it. Who is correct?

9. Root bought a tractor and accessories from Anderson Sales. He signed a conditional sales contract agreeing to make monthly payments and granting Anderson a security interest in the tractor and accessories. The contract also contained a warranty by Anderson that the equipment was "to be free from defects in material or workmanship," and an agreement by Root that:

"I will settle all claims of any kind against *SELLER* directly with *SELLER*, and if *SELLER* assigns this note I will not use any such claim as a defense, setoff or counterclaim against any effort by the holder to enforce this instrument."

Anderson assigned the contract to John Deere. Root defaulted in his payments; Deere repossessed the equipment, sold them, and sued Root for the deficiency. Root claims the tractor was defective and that he can assert the breach of warranty against Deere because it has only the assignee's rights on a contract. Deere points to Section 9–206(1). Would Root or Deere prevail?

10. Hiller owned a farm on which Oakdale Bank held a mortgage. He was in default on his payments and Oakdale Bank was threatening foreclosure. Hiller and Stamberg entered into an agreement whereby Stamberg was to pay Oakdale Bank the amount of the mortgage debt and the farm was to be deeded to Stamberg by absolute deed, and Stamberg was to lease the farm to Hiller for a period of two years with an option to purchase it. This agreement was carried out. Hiller did not exercise his option to purchase the farm within the two-year period, and Stamberg brought an action to recover possession of the farm. Hiller contended that the transaction was a mortgage and that since Stamberg had not foreclosed the mortgage, he was not entitled to possession. Should Stamberg's deed be held to be a mortgage?

11. Field was building a house, and Higginbotham had furnished materials which were used in the construction of the house. On May 18, 1948, Tomlinson loaned Field $2,500 and took a mortgage on the house as security. At this time the house was not completed, and this was known to Tomlinson, who had inspected the house before making the loan and knew that men were working on the house at the time. Field gave Tomlinson an affidavit to the effect that all indebtedness against the house had been paid. No notice of lien was filed against the house at the time the loan was made. Higginbotham was not paid for materials purchased, and within the statutory period, he filed the required notice and affidavit of lien. Tomlinson claims that his mortgage lien is superior to Higginbotham's mechanic's lien. The relevant state statute provides that a person who takes a lien in good faith for a valuable consideration without notice or knowledge of mechanics' liens will be given priority. Is Tomlinson's claim correct?

PART VIII Sales

chapter 32. Terms of Sales Contract

Introduction

Nature of Sales and the Law of Sales. A sale, as the term is used in the law of sales, consists of the transferring of the ownership of personal property, for a consideration, from one person to another. Modern courts do not attempt to distinguish between a sale and a contract to sell since the technical sale is preceded or accompanied by an agreement, which is supported by consideration, to transfer the ownership of the goods.

A majority of the rules and standards of law relating to the sale of goods deal with the formation, terms, obligations, performance and remedies of the sales contract. The law of sales is based on the fundamental principles of contract and personal property law. However, the vast variety of transactions involved in the marketing of goods has necessitated the development of special rules and standards which apply primarily to sales transactions. The developments in the law of sales have kept pace with the practices of merchants. Many of the technical requirements recognized and enforced in contract and property law serve no purpose in the marketplace and have been replaced with rules which assure to the merchant a more just and equitable result.

Uniform Commercial Code—Sales. Article 2 of the Uniform Commercial Code—Sales—does not follow the organization of the Uniform Sales Act nor does it adhere to its philosophy. The objective of the drafters of Article 2 of the Code was to clarify the law of sales and to recognize the developments which had taken place during the 50 years the Uniform Sales Act had been in force. The law of sales was not revolutionized by the adoption of the Code but some important changes were made.

Under the Uniform Sales Act the rules of general contract law were applied in determining whether or not an enforceable contract to sell had been nego-

747

tiated. It will be recalled from the chapters treating the principles of contract law that special Code rules are set out for the formation of contracts involving sale of goods, and these rules provide less rigid standards for testing the existence of an enforceable contract. Many of the provisions of the Code apply only to merchants or to transactions between merchants. Actions are measured by such concepts as "good faith" and what is "commercially reasonable," and the court is expressly given the right to refuse to enforce an unconscionable contract or an unconscionable clause in a contract.

Some of the important changes the Code makes in contract law include the following with references given to the pages in this text where these changes are discussed.

1. Firm Offers (see p. 110).
2. Statute of Frauds (see p. 259).
3. Unconscionable Contracts (see p. 235).
4. Additional Terms in Acceptances (see p. 127).
5. Modification (see p. 186).

Epstein v. Giannattasio
197 A.2d 342 (Super. Ct. Conn. 1963)

This was an action by Betty Epstein (plaintiff) against Marie Giannattasio, Sales Affiliates, Inc., and Clairol, Inc. (defendants), to recover a judgment for negligence and breach of warranty. A demurrer was filed to the claim for damages for breach of warranty. The court sustained the demurrer.

On or about October 5, 1962, Epstein visited a beauty parlor, conducted by Giannattasio, for the purpose of receiving a beauty treatment. During the course of that treatment, Giannattasio used a product called "Zotos 30-day Color," manufactured by Sales Affiliates, Inc., and a prebleach manufactured by Clairol, Inc. Epstein claims that as a result of the treatment she suffered acute dermatitis, disfigurement resulting from loss of hair, and other injuries and damages.

Giannattasio, Sales Affiliates, Inc., and Clairol, Inc., demurred to the claim for damages for breach of warranty on the ground that the transaction did not amount to a sale of goods.

LUGG, JUDGE. As to the remaining three grounds of demurrer, the applicable statutory law is the Uniform Commercial Code, adopted by this state as title 42a of the General Statutes. The issue reduces itself to the simple one of whether or not the use of the products involved in the course of the beauty treatment amounts to a sale or a contract for sale of goods under the pertinent sections of the code. Section 2–102 provides: "(T)his article (Sales) applies to transactions in goods. . . ." The word "transaction" is not defined in the act, "Goods" is defined in § 2–105 as follows: " 'Goods' means all things, including specially manufactured goods, which are movable at the time of identification to the contract for sale. . . ." Section 2–106 limits the words "contract" and "agreement," as used in the article, to the present or future sale of goods. "Contract for sale" includes a present sale of goods. (§ 2–106.) "A 'sale' consists in the passing of title from the seller to the buyer for a price as provided by section 2–401." (§ 2–106.)

As the complaint alleges, Epstein asked Giannattasio for a beauty treatment, and not for the purchase of goods. From such language, it could not be inferred that it was the intention of either party that the transaction be a transaction in goods within the meaning of the Code. This claim of Epstein is hence distinguished more by the ingenuity of its conception than by the strength of its persuasion.

There is another line of cases which involves blood transfusions received by patients in the course of medical care and treatment in hospitals. These concern the claim that injuries caused by such tranfusions are ground for a recovery under the Sales Act. This claim has been universally rejected. "Such a contract is clearly one for services, and, just as clearly, it is not divisible. . . . It has long been recognized that, when service predominates, and transfer of personal property is but an incidental feature of the transaction, the transaction is not deemed a sale within the Sales Act." To the same effect are *Dibblee* v. *Dr. W. H. Groves and Latter-Day Saints Hospital.*

There are other cases, involving differing facts, which have decided that "when service is the predominant, and transfer of title to personal property the incidental, feature of a transaction, the transaction is not a sale of goods within the application of statutes relating to sales."

Building and construction transactions which include materials to be incorporated into the structure are not agreements of sale.

The language in the second count against Giannattasio allegés that "(t)he Defendant #1, in recommending and applying said products to Epstein thereby warranted. . . ." This amounts to a claim of implied warranty. The fourth and sixth counts aver implied warranty in terms. When this plaintiff made her arrangement with the beauty parlor, she did so as the complaint sets forth: ". . . for the purpose of receiving a beauty treatment." Obviously, the subject of the contract was not a sale of goods but the rendition of services. The materials used in the performance of those services were patently incidental to that subject, which was a treatment and not the purchase of an article.

[*A few recent decisions have broken from the* Epstein *line of cases and found there was an identifiable sale of goods when a hospital patient was given a blood transfusion. See* Jackson *v.* Muhlenberg Hospital, *232 A.2d 879 (Sup. Ct. N.J. 1967).*]

Terms of the Contract

General Terms. Within broad limits the parties to a contract to sell goods may include any terms, not illegal, upon which they agree. In the everyday transactions of business many practices have become common, and the courts have ruled that in the absence of a provision in the contract stating the parties agreement on the particular matter the presumption is that the parties intended the established practice to control. In the Code the rights of the parties when certain terms are used are set out in some detail, and those terms apply unless the parties agree otherwise. If a contract includes an open-price clause or if nothing is said about price, the price would be what would be considered reasonable at the time of delivery. If the price is to be fixed by either the buyer or seller, such party, in fixing the price, must act in good faith. If a price is to be fixed otherwise than by agreement of the parties and one of the parties, through his acts, prevents the fixing of the price, the other party may, at his option, treat the contract as canceled or fix a reasonable price. If it is clear from their negotiations that the parties do not intend to be bound unless they agree on a price and the price is not agreed or fixed, no contract results. (2–305 [4].) [1]

Certain risks incident to a sale are allocated by the provisions of the Code. However, where such provision states the party who shall bear the risk "unless otherwise agreed," the parties may, by an appropriate clause in the sales contract, allocate or divide the risk as they may agree. (2–303.)

Terms in a sales contract which measure the quantity of goods sold on the basis of output or need are enforceable. In determining the quantity, the rule of good faith applies. Also, if the parties have entered into a lawful contract for exclusive dealing in certain goods, the seller is obligated to use his best efforts to supply the goods to the buyer and the buyer is obligated to use his best efforts to promote their sale. (2–306.)

If no time for performance is stated in the sales contract, the time for performance shall be a reasonable time. Where the contract provides for successive performances for an indefinite period of time the contract is valid for a reasonable time but unless otherwise agreed it may be terminated at any time by either party. Reasonable notice is required to terminate a contract in which the time is for an indefinite period. A clause in such a contract dispensing with notice is declared by the Code to be unconscionable and invalid. (2–309.)

Delivery and Payment Terms. Standardized shipping terms which through mercantile practice have come to have a specific meaning are customarily used in sales contracts. The Code includes provisions setting out these terms and their legal effect on the rights and duties of the parties when included in a sales contract.

The terms F.O.B. (free on board) and F.A.S. (free alongside) are basic delivery terms. If the delivery term of the contract is F.O.B. or F.A.S., the seller is obligated to deliver to the carrier goods which conform to the contract and which are properly prepared for shipment to the buyer and he must make a reasonable contract of carriage on behalf of the buyer. Under such delivery

---

[1] The numbers in the parentheses refer to the sections of the Uniform Commercial Code, 1962.

terms, the goods are at the risk of the buyer during transit. If the term is F.O.B. destination, the seller must deliver the goods to the designated destination and they are at the seller's risk during transit.

Unless otherwise agreed the buyer must give any needed instructions for shipment. (2–319.)

C.I.F. and C. & F. contracts are shipment contracts. The term "C.I.F." means that the price includes in a lump sum the cost of the goods and the insurance and freight to the named destinations. If the term is C.I.F., the seller is obligated to (1) deliver to the carrier conforming goods, properly packed for shipment, (2) make a reasonable contract for the carriage of the goods to destination, (3) prepay the freight, (4) insure, in the name of the buyer, the goods on such terms and against such hazards as is customary or as is stipulated in the sales contract, (5) prepare invoices and obtain shipping documents and such other documents as are necessary to effect shipment or to comply with the sales contract, and (6) forward these documents promptly to the buyer. The goods are at the risk of the buyer during transit provided the seller has fulfilled his obligations. The buyer must make payment on receipt of the required documents unless there is an agreement for extension of credit. (2–320.)

The term "C. & F." or "C.F." imposes the same duties on the seller and has the same effect as the term "C.I.F." with the exception that the seller is not obligated to obtain a policy of insurance. (2–320.)

Other terms may be added to a C.I.F. or C. & F. shipment. If the term "net landed weights" or comparable terms are added, the seller estimates the price and the buyer pays the estimated price on the delivery of the documents. The price is then adjusted on the arrival of the goods and the adjustment must be made with commercial promptness. The term "net landed weights" places on the seller the risk of shrinkage or ordinary deterioration but the goods are otherwise at the buyer's risk during transit. (2–301.)

When goods are shipped "payment on arrival" payment is due when the goods arrive at destination unless otherwise agreed, but the buyer is permitted to make such preliminary inspection as is feasible. If the goods are lost, delivery of the documents and payment are due when the goods should have arrived. (2–321.)

Unless otherwise agreed, a term for delivery of the goods "ex-ship" requires the seller to discharge all liens arising out of carriage and furnish the buyer with a direction which puts the carrier under a duty to deliver the goods to him. The risk of loss does not pass to the buyer until the goods leave the ship's tackle or are otherwise properly unloaded. (2–322.)

Where the contract contemplates overseas shipment and contains a term C.I.F. or C. & F. or F.O.B. vessel, the seller, unless otherwise agreed, must obtain a negotiable bill of lading stating that the goods have been loaded on board if the shipment is F.O.B. vessel and that the goods have been received for shipment if the term is C.I.F. or C. & F. The bill of lading must be issued and sent as required by established mercantile practices. (2–323.)

Under a term "no arrival, no sale" the seller must promptly ship conforming goods and if they arrive he must tender them on arrival to the buyer, but he is not liable for their nonarrival unless he causes it. Where without the fault of the seller the goods are lost or have so deteriorated as no longer to conform to the contract, the contract is voided if the loss is total; if the loss or deterioration is partial the buyer may inspect the goods which arrive and either accept or reject them. If he accepts the goods he is entitled to due allowance from the contract price. If the goods arrive after the contract time the buyer may accept or reject them. (2–324.)

If under the terms of the sales contract the buyer is to furnish a letter of credit, his failure to do so is a breach of the contract. If the buyer furnishes a letter of credit and it is dishonored, the seller may, after giving reasonable notice to the buyer, require payment directly from the buyer. Unless otherwise agreed, the term "letter of credit" or "banker's credit" in a contract for sale means an irrevocable credit issued by a financing agency of good repute, and where the shipment is overseas, of good international repute. The term "confirmed credit" means that the credit must also carry the direct obligation of such an agency which does business in the seller's financial market. (2–325.)

Summary

Standardized shipping terms have been adopted in mercantile circles. F.O.B. & F.A.S. obligates the seller to deliver conforming goods to the carrier and to make a reasonable contract for carriage. The goods are at the risk of the buyer during transit. If the term is C.I.F. the goods are at the risk of the buyer when the seller (1) delivers conforming goods to the carrier, (2) contracts for carriage, (3) prepays freight, (4) obtains insurance, (5) prepares invoices and other documents, and (6) forwards all documents to the buyer. C. & F. term imposes the same obligations on the seller except he does not insure the goods. If the term "net landed weight" is added to C.I.F. or C. & F. terms, the seller assumes the risk of ordinary deterioration, shrinkage and the like. An "ex-ship" term places the risk of loss or damage on the seller until the goods leave the ship's tackle. The seller must discharge all liens and put the carrier under a duty to deliver the goods to the buyer.

The Code sets out the requirements for an overseas shipment. Under a "no arrival, no sale" term, the goods are at the risk of the seller and the seller is not liable to the buyer if the goods are lost without fault on his part. If the buyer contracts to furnish a letter of credit, his failure to do so is a breach. If a letter of credit is dishonored, the seller may require the buyer to make payment directly to him.

Sales on Trial

Sale on Approval. If goods are delivered to a buyer under an agreement that he may test or use the goods for the purpose of determining whether or not he wishes to buy them, the sale is a sale on approval. (2–326.) In a sale on approval, unless otherwise agreed, the risk of loss and the title do not pass to the buyer until acceptance. The buyer may use the goods in a manner consistent with the purpose of the trial but an unwarranted exercise of ownership over the goods is an acceptance. Also, failure to notify the seller of election to return the goods is an acceptance; and if the goods conform to the contract, acceptance of any part is acceptance of the whole.

After due notification of election to return the goods, the return is at the seller's risk and expense but a merchant buyer must follow any reasonable instructions given by the seller for the return of the goods. Since the risk of loss and title remain with the seller, goods held on approval are not subject to the claims of the buyer's creditors until approval. (2–326 and 2–327.)

Sale or Return. If delivered goods may be returned by the buyer even though they conform to the contract, the sale is a sale or return where the goods are delivered primarily for sale. Under a sale or return, unless otherwise agreed, the risk of loss and title to the goods are in the buyer and are subject to the claims of the buyer's creditors while in his possession. The buyer's option to return extends to the whole or any commercial unit of the goods while substantially in their original condition, but such option must be exercised seasonably. The return of the goods is at the buyer's risk and expense. (2–326 and 2–327.)

If delivered goods may be returned by the buyer even though they conform to the sales contract, the transaction is "sale on approval" if the goods are delivered primarily for use. If the goods are delivered primarily for resale the transaction will be deemed sale or return.

Sale on Consignment or on Memorandum. Where goods are delivered to a person "on consignment" or "on memorandum" for resale and such person maintains a place of business at which he deals in goods of the kind involved, under a name other than the name of the person making delivery, then with respect to claims of creditors of the person conducting the business the goods are deemed to be on sale or return. For example: Jones operates a retail music store under the name of City Music Store. Baldwin Piano Company delivers to Jones a piano on consignment and no notices are posted indicating that it is so delivered. A judgment creditor could acquire a lien on the piano by levy of execution on it. However, the creditors of the person conducting the business may not so treat the goods if the person making delivery complies with an applicable law providing for a consignor's interest or the like to be evidenced by a sign, or establishes that the person conducting the business is generally known by his creditors to be substantially engaged in selling goods for others, or complies with the filing provisions of Article 9, Secured Transactions. (2–326.)

Summary

In a sale on approval the goods are delivered to the buyer for use or trial and the risk of loss and title remain in the seller. A sale or return is one where the goods are sold to the buyer for resale. The risk of loss and title is in the buyer and he may at his option return to the seller all or any commercial unit of the goods which is in substantially the same condition as when received. The return of the goods is at the buyer's risk and expense.

Goods delivered "on consignment" or "on memorandum" are subject to the claims of the creditors of the person to whom they are delivered if he operates a business selling like goods in a name other than that of the party delivering the goods. The person delivering the goods can protect his interest by posting notice as required by the state statute of filing under Article 9. Also, if the person to whom the goods are delivered is known to his creditors to be substantially engaged in selling goods for others the creditors cannot obtain an interest in the goods.

General Electric Co. v. Pettingell Supply Co.
199 N.E.2d 326 (Sup. Jud. Ct. Mass. 1964)

This was an action by General Electric Co. (plaintiff) against Pettingell Supply Co. and David S. Miller, assignee for the benefit of creditors (defendants), to replevin certain large lamps. Judgment for Pettingell Supply Co. and Miller, and General Electric Co. appealed. Judgment affirmed.

General Electric Co. delivered large lamps to Pettingell Supply Co. (Pettingell) as "agent to sell or distribute such lamps." Large lamps are "lamps used in commercial and industrial installations." Pettingell made an assignment to Miller for the benefit of creditors. Miller claimed the lamps for the benefit of the creditors of Pettingell. General Electric Co. replevined the lamps, claiming that the relation between it and Pettingell was that of principal and agent and that the lamps were its property.

WHITTEMORE, JUSTICE. We disagree with the contention that § 2–326 (3) of the Uniform Commercial Code is inapplicable. That subsection is by its terms concerned with certain transactions which, although they may not be sales under the definition of G.L. c. 106, § 2–106 (1), are nonetheless "deemed to be on sale or return" with respect to claims of creditors of the person conducting the business. . . ." The subsection specifically states that it is applicable even though the "agreement purports to reserve title to the person making delivery until payment or resale or uses such words as 'on consignment' or 'on memorandum.'" The agreement between General Electric Co. and Pettingell binds the former "to maintain on consignment in the custody of the agent, to be disposed of as herein provided, a stock of said General Electric large lamps."

General Electric Co. relies on the wording of the second sentence of § 2–326 (3) which states that the subsection applies even though there is a reservation of title "to the person making delivery until payment or resale." From this General Electric Co. argues that the subsection applies only where the manufacturer has sold the goods to the dealer because otherwise there could be no "resale." The second sentence gives examples of transactions to which the subsection applies and does not limit the plain meaning of the first sentence. The subsection is concerned with transactions "deemed" to be of "sale or return" and the first sentence is carefully drafted to apply to transactions which might not ordinarily be characterized as sales. Moreover, as a consignment the transaction falls within one of the examples stated in the second sentence. The Uniform Laws Comment on subsection (3) confirms our reading of that subsection.

The judge found that Pettingell maintained a place of business in which it dealt in goods of the kind involved, under a name other than the name of General Electric Co. General Electric Co.'s attack on this finding is based on the claimed absence of evidence that Pettingell sold any General Electric large lamps in its own name without disclosing its agency. We think the finding is supported by the evidence that Pettingell sold other electrical merchandise including other items from General Electric Co. The statute in referring to "goods of the kind involved" does not restrict the relevant business to dealings in the precise kind of electrical goods. Pettingell was a wholesaler "buying and selling electrical, hardware and housewares merchandise." Its gross annual business ranged from $300,000 to $400,000, and 25% of this business was in "the sale and distribution" of General Electric large lamps. This large lamp business was its only consignment business.

General Electric put in evidence forms supplied Pettingell for use by the latter in the sale of large lamps. These forms state they are "from" Pettingell as "serving agent for General Electric, consignor company." It is unnecessary for us to decide whether, if Pettingell sold and distributed large lamps only, these forms alone would show that Pettingell was not in business "under a name other than the name of the person making delivery" or whether, because of the concern of § 2–326 (3) with the rights of creditors, Miller need have only showed that "the consignee" did not completely identify "his business name with that of the consignor."

The issue under subsection (3) thus becomes the narrow one whether the "goods" were "delivered to" Pettingell "for sale."

Under the agency contract, Pettingell could sell directly to certain customers who bought for their own use or who bought in small volume for resale. Pettingell was also authorized to make deliveries under contracts of sale entered into between General Electric and purchasers and to "distribute" large lamps to other agents of General Electric. The latter were retailers under agency contracts with General Electric. The retail agents would procure the lamps from Pettingell, sell them as General Electric Co.'s agents and remit to Pettingell in accordance with the latter's invoices. The evidence showed that over a four-year period 74% of Pettingell's "sales" were to subagents and 20% were direct sales other than those which General Electric negotiated. Under the contract in suit Pettingell would not have title to the large lamps at any time.

We need not determine the ruling required if Pettingell's sole authority had been to distribute lamps to subagents. Since Pettingell, had authority to sell the lamps they were "delivered" to Pettingell "for sale." Section 2–326 (1) (b) does not, we think, require a different result. That section defines a "sale or return" as a sale where "goods are delivered primarily for resale." That subsection, read with § 2–326 (1) (a), might require us to determine in an appropriate case whether goods were delivered to a "consignee" primarily for his own use. It does not, however, exclude a consignment of goods to be sold or to be delivered to other agents as orders may require.

Bulk Transfers

Bulk transfer legislation was enacted in order to prevent fraud on creditors. The principal type of commercial fraud which this legislation is intended to prevent occurs most often where a merchant, owing debts, sells out his stock in trade for cash, pockets the proceeds, and then disappears, leaving his creditors unpaid. Although many states adopted bulk sales laws, there was no uniform bulk sales act ever drafted and adopted by the states. Article 6 of the Uniform Commercial Code—Bulk Transfers—attempts to simplify and make uniform the bulk sales laws of the states that adopt the Code.

This Article of the Code covers any transfer "in bulk" and not in the ordinary course of the transferor's business of a major part of the materials, supplies, merchandise or other inventory of an enterprise. A transfer of a substantial part of equipment is a bulk transfer if such transfer is part of a bulk transfer of inventory. The enterprises subject to this Article are all those whose principal business is the sale of merchandise from stock and those that manufacture and sell from stock their manufactured products such as, for instance, a retail bakery which makes and sells at retail its baked goods. (6–102.)

Transfer for security, assignments for the benefit of creditors, transfers in settlement of liens, transfers by executors, administrators, receivers, trustees in bankruptcy, and like persons acting under judicial process, transfers as part of a corporate reorganization and like transfers are excepted from the operation of this Article. (6–103.)

The general plan of the Article is to give creditors notice in advance of the transfer and provide a plan for their protection. The transferor is required to give the transferee a schedule of the property to be transferred and a sworn list of his creditors. The transferee is required to give the creditors on the list and any additional known creditors notice of the pending transfer at least 10 days before he takes possession of the goods.

A choice of plans is made available to the adopters of the Code. They may adopt the New York plan, under which the giving of notice is all that is required, or the Pennsylvania plan, under which the proceeds of the sale are distributed to the transferor's creditors. (6–106.) If the parties fail to comply with the requirements of this Article the transferee holds the goods in trust for the creditors of the transferor.

Special provision is made for the regulation of sales by auction. (6–108.)

A short statute of limitations provides that no action shall be brought or levy made more than six months after the date on which the transferee took possession of the goods unless the transfer has been concealed. (6–111.)

Problem Cases

1. Keonig, who was a patient in the hospital, was given, as part of his treatment, a transfusion of impure blood from which he was infected with hepatitis. The blood was furnished by the Milwaukee Blood Center, Inc., and the transfusion was given in Memorial Hospital. Keonig sued the Blood Center and Hospital to recover a judgment for damages for breach of warranty. Are the Blood Center and Hospital liable for damages for breach of warranty?

2. In October, 1964, Mincow and Finale entered into a written contract, by the terms of which Finale agreed to deliver to specified chain and department stores throughout the country such merchandise as Finale might see fit, for sale in those stores for the account of Mincow, as Finale's consignee. Title to the merchandise and the proceeds thereof was to be "always vested in Finale" and such merchandise was to be "at all times subject to and under the direction and control of Finale." Finale was to bear all risk of loss and Mincow was to remit sales proceeds, less commission, to Finale. The assignee for benefit of Mincow's creditors claims that he is entitled to the merchandise or proceeds thereof in preference to Finale's rights by reason of U.C.C. § 2–236. Should the goods be turned over to Mincow's assignee for the benefit of creditors?

3. Gantman brought a replevin action against Paul to recover three upholstered chairs, two game sets, and one area rug. Gantman claimed these articles had been purchased from Paul and later wrongfully repossessed by Paul. Gantman produced invoices showing dates of purchase, prices charged, and payments made on account. Paul's answer denied that Gantman was the owner of the goods, and averred that the goods had been placed in Gantman's home "on an approval basis . . . (and) were never finally approved." Should judgment be granted Gantman on the basis of his proof of purchasing and payments on account?

4. Trend House sold its business, including stock of merchandise on hand, to Erving's. Erving's failed to obtain a list of creditor's of Trend House and failed to give the prescribed notice of sale to the creditors. (U.C.C. § 6–107). The state in which the transfer was made had adopted the "Pennsylvania Plan" (U.C.C. § 6–106) under which the proceeds of the sale are required to be distributed to the transferor's creditors. Darby, as trustee in bankruptcy for Trend House brought an action against Erving's to recover the value of transferred merchandise. Can Erving's be held personally liable for the value of the property transferred in the bulk sale?

chapter 33. Title and Risk

Title

Introduction. At common law and under the Uniform Sales Act most of the problems relative to risks, insurable interests in goods, remedies and other similar rights and liabilities were determined on the basis of who was technical title owner at the particular moment the right or liability arose. After such determination the general rule of property law, that rights and liabilities relative to property followed ownership, was then applied. However, it frequently happened that although the parties to a sales contract had the right to agree as to the time title would pass, and such right was recognized, the parties seldom expressed any intention in regard to the passing of the title. Consequently, the courts, in such cases, were forced to develop and apply presumptions as to the time title would pass in the absence of an agreement on the part of the parties to the sales contract.

Under the Code the rights of the seller and buyer and of third persons do not depend on the technicality of who has title, and such rights are determined irrespective of such technicality unless the provision of the Code expressly refers to title. Under some circumstances who has title to the goods becomes important, for instance, a situation in which the rights of the seller's or the buyer's creditors in the goods must be determined. And, under some state statutes, the rights of the parties may be made to depend on who has title to the goods. (2–401.) [1]

Provisions for Passing of Title. Since, under some circumstances, the rights of the parties in goods will depend on who is title owner of the goods, rules as to the passing of title to goods are set out in the Code. Title to goods

---

[1] The numbers in the parentheses refer to the sections of the Uniform Commercial Code, 1962.

cannot pass from the seller to the buyer until the goods are identified to the contract. For example, if S agrees to sell B 50 chairs and S has 500 such chairs in his warehouse, title to 50 chairs will not pass from S to B until the 50 chairs which B has purchased are selected and identified as the chairs sold to B. The reservation by the seller of a security interest in the goods sold does not affect the passing of title. (2–401 [1].)

Unless otherwise specifically agreed, title passes from the seller to the buyer when the seller has completed his performance as to delivery of the goods. If the sales contract requires the seller to ship the goods, title passes when the seller delivers conforming goods to the carrier, but if the sales contract requires the seller to deliver the goods to the buyer, title does not pass until the goods are delivered and tendered to the buyer. (2–401 [2].) If the goods are in the possession of a third person as bailee and a negotiable document of title has been issued for the goods, title passes to the buyer on the endorsement, if endorsement is necessary, and delivery of the document of title to the buyer. If no negotiable document of title has been issued by the bailee and the goods at the time of contracting are already identified to the contract, title passes at the time and place of contracting. (2–401 [3].) If the buyer, whether justified or not, refuses to accept or retain the goods or if he justifiably revokes his acceptance, title revests, by operation of law, in the seller. (2–401 [4].)

Summary

Although under the provisions of the Code the "title" or "property" in goods sold does not have the significance it had under the common law or the Uniform Sales Act, there are situations in which the rights and duties of the parties will be determined on the basis of who has title to the goods.

Rules as to the passing of title are set out in the Code. Title cannot pass until goods are identified to the contract, and retention by the seller of a security interest in the goods does not affect the passing of title. Unless otherwise agreed, title passes when the seller has completed his performance. If he is to ship goods, title passes on delivery to the carrier; if he is to deliver the goods, title passes on delivery and tender. If the goods are in the possession of a bailee and a negotiable document of title has been issued, title passes on deilvery of the document of title. If no negotiable document of title has been issued and the goods are identified, title passes at the place and time of the making of the contract. Rejection of the goods by the buyer revests title in the seller.

Newhall v. Second Church and Society of Boston
209 N.E.2d 296 (Sup. Jud. Ct. Mass. 1965)

This was an action by Newhall (plaintiff) to enjoin the sale of five pieces of silver from Second Church and Society (defendant) to the Henry Francis duPont Winterthur Museum of Winterthur, Delaware, (defendant). The question before the court was whether for purposes of injunctive relief the Second Church and Society by special act effectively sold five silver vessels alleged to have been given to a predecessor unincorporated religious body, one piece in 1706 and four pieces in 1711. The trial judge held that title had not passed. Affirmed on this point on appeal.

The contract was completed by telephone and payment had been made by check. Terms as to delivery then negotiated did not appear in the contract. However, a letter from the curator of the Winterthur Museum tended to show that the contract included the obligation to deliver the silver pieces to the buyer's representative in Boston:

> Confirming our telephone conversation of this afternoon, I have made arrangements for Charles F. Hummel, associate curator of the Museum, to act on Mr. duPont's behalf in receiving from you the five pieces of silver. Mr. Hummel is of medium build and dark haired. He will meet you at the Shawmut Branch Bank, Beacon Street and Park Drive. I have asked him to bring a carbon copy of this letter with him and to have you sign a receipt form upon picking up the silver.

WHITTEMORE, JUSTICE.   On this record we think that the Uniform Commercial Code, § 2–401(2), is applicable. This provides: "(2) Unless otherwise explicitly agreed title passes to the buyer at the time and place at which the seller completes his performance with reference to the physical delivery of the goods, despite any reservation of a security interest and even though a document of title is to be delivered at a different time or place; and in particular despite any reservation of a security interest by the bill of lading. . . ." It follows that § 2–401(3) is *inapplicable:* "Unless otherwise explicitly agreed where delivery is to be made without moving the goods . . . (b) if the goods are at the time of contracting already identified and no documents are to be delivered, title passes at the time and place of contracting."

Rights of Third Parties

Introduction.   One of the fundamental rules of property law is that one cannot pass better title to goods than he has. There are, however, several exceptions to this rule, as is the case with most general rules, and three of the most generally accepted are: (1) one having a voidable title can pass good title to a bona fide purchaser for value, (2) one purchasing goods in the regular course of a retailer's business takes free from outstanding equities, and (3) one purchasing goods in the ordinary course of a dealer's business takes free from the claim of one who has entrusted his goods to such dealer. A corollary to the general rule is that a creditor cannot by legal process acquire greater rights in his debtor's goods than the debtor has.

Creditor's Rights.   If a seller, after he has sold goods or identified them to the contract, retains possession of them and the sale is, under any statute of the state, made for the purpose of delaying or defeating the rights of creditors, the sale or identification is void as to the seller's creditors. However, if possession of the goods is retained in good faith and for only a commercially reasonable time, the seller's creditors can acquire no rights in the goods. This rule applies to the seller's creditors and not to purchasers in the regular course of the seller's business. Also, if the sale or identification of the goods to the contract is bona fide, the buyer has the right to claim the goods.

A creditor having a perfected security interest in goods will have priority over a buyer and also over a buyer who takes goods in payment of a past due claim if the transfer is fraudulent or a voidable preference. (2–402.)

Transfer of Voidable Title. A seller having a voidable title has the power to pass good title to a good faith purchaser for value. A seller has a voidable title to goods if he has obtained his title through fraudulent representations. If a person has obtained goods by impersonating another, or if he has obtained the goods by giving a check or draft in payment for them and the check or draft is dishonored, or if he has obtained the goods without paying the agreed purchase price when it was agreed that the transaction was to be a "cash sale," such a person has a voidable title but can pass good title to a good faith purchaser for value. A buyer who takes goods in payment of a past obligation is not a purchaser for value. (2–403 [1].)

Buyer in Ordinary Course of Business. A "buyer in ordinary course of business" is defined in Section 1–201 (9) of the Code. The definition is broad in its scope and includes good faith purchasers from persons in the business of selling goods of the kind purchased, but it expressly eliminates purchases from pawnbrokers. Any person entrusting his goods to a merchant who deals in such goods confers on such merchant the power to pass good title to such goods to a buyer in the ordinary course of such merchant's business. For example, if O takes his watch to S, a retail jeweler, to have it repaired and S sells the watch to B, B would acquire good title to the watch. Since O entrusted his watch to S, who was a merchant dealing in such goods, O conferred on S the power to pass good title to B, a buyer in the ordinary course of S's business. However, a merchant seller cannot pass good title to stolen goods even though the buyer is a buyer in ordinary course of business. (2–403.)

Summary

A good faith buyer has priority over the creditors of a seller to goods identified to the sales contract even though the goods are left in the possession of the seller for a commercially reasonable time. A sale and identification of goods to a sales contract made for the purpose of delaying or defeating the rights of the seller's creditors is void as to such creditors.

One acquiring a voidable title to goods through false representations, giving a check or draft which is dishonored or on a "cash sale" without paying the agreed price can pass good title to a bona fide purchaser for value. A buyer in the ordinary course of business acquires good title to goods which have been entrusted to a merchant who deals in such goods.

Independent News Co. v. Williams
293 F.2d 510 (3rd Cir. 1961)

This was an action by the distributor, publisher and copyright owner of certain comic books (plaintiffs) to enjoin the sale of the comics by Williams (defendant). Judgment for Williams and the plaintiffs appealed. Affirmed.

The wholesaler of comic books, after receiving unsold comics back from retailers, was supposed to remove the covers from the unsold comics and return them to the distributor, Independent News, for credit. As to the remaining portion of the comics, the wholesaler was obligated by contract to see that they were mutilated so as not to be resold as publications but only as waste paper. The contract between the distributor and the wholesaler provided that:

"Title to all copies from which covers have been detached as above provided shall remain with the Company until the same are so destroyed or mutilated so as to be unusable for any purpose except waste. The use of such copies for any purpose other than waste is unauthorized and contravenes this agreement."

The wholesaler sold cover removed comics to a waste paper dealer who—rather than selling them as waste paper—sold them to Williams, a distributor of second-hand books and magazines.

McLAUGHLIN, CIRCUIT JUDGE. The first proposition upon which plaintiffs rely is conversion. They argue that after the covers of the comics are removed and returned to Independent for full credit, title to the insides of the magazines as "literary works" reverts to Independent. . . .

The district court rejected this argument and expressly found that the reservation of title in the contract had no effect upon the waste paper dealer who was a buyer in the ordinary course of business; the whole agreement between the parties was "at best, a sale or return transaction"; no agency relationship ever arose; and the waste paper dealer and in turn the defendant acquired the full complement of property rights in the comics.

Under the Uniform Commercial Code, adopted in Pennsylvania, Section 2–403(2), provides

"(2) Any entrusting of possession of goods to a merchant who deals in goods of that kind gives him power to transfer all rights of the entruster to a buyer in ordinary course of business."

That section of the Code has broadened the protection of buyers in the ordinary course of business and has changed prior Pennsylvania law.

In the case at bar, plaintiffs ". . . conceded that plaintiffs have 'entrusted' the magazines in question to the Wholesaler-Agent." However, they dispute the applicability of Section 2–403(2) stating:

"(a) Wholesaler-Agent is not a 'merchant who deals in goods of the kind . . .'" and "(b) neither the waste paper house nor the defendant is a 'buyer in the ordinary course of business' as defined by the Code."

The first assertion seeks to distinguish between the wholesaler ". . . selling new publications prior to or during the publication period," and the wholesaler selling the cover-removed magazines. The argument is specious. The wholesaler deals in comics, and the fact that the covers are present or not is irrelevant. His regular business is dealing with comics and as such he is a "merchant who deals in goods of that kind."

The interrelated second contention, namely, that neither the waste paper dealer nor the defendant are buyers in the ordinary course of business is equally without merit. In defining this concept, Section 1–201(9) of the Code provides:

"(9) 'Buyer in ordinary course of business' means a person who in good faith and without knowledge that the sale to him is in violation of the ownership rights or security interest of a third party in the goods buys in ordinary course from a person in the business of selling goods of that kind. . . ."

The district court's finding of fact forms a proper basis for the determination that the waste paper dealer is within that definition.

And there is no evidence in the record . . . that shows that the waste paper dealers had any notice of any restriction whatsoever on the cover-removed comics purchased from the wholesaler. It follows, that when the wholesaler sold these coverless comics to the waste paper dealer, the waste paper dealer, under Section 2–403(2) of the Code, obtained the totality of property rights in the comics which included the right to use or sell them as reading material.

Risks

Introduction. In the event that goods which are the subject matter of a sales contract are damaged or destroyed the question frequently arises as to which of the parties, the buyer or seller, must stand the loss. At common law and under the Uniform Sales Act the risk of loss was on the technical title owner of the goods unless the parties had indicated in their agreement a contrary intention. As a general rule, businessmen in negotiating a sale neither express nor indicate an intention as to when title to the goods is to pass. Rules of presumption as to the time of the passing of the title to the goods were developed by the courts and these rules were incorporated into the Uniform Sales Act. The basing of risks on title to the goods was unrealistic and the decisions of the courts were inconsistent in many respects. Under the provisions of the Code the parties may by their agreement shift the allocation of the risk or divide the risk (2–303) unless the provision in the agreement would be void as an unconscionable clause under Section 2–302.

Explicit Agreements. In some instances the parties to a contract may by the terms of their agreement indicate an intention as to which of the parties shall bear the burden of the risk. In other instances usage of trade or course of dealing may determine on which party the risk is to be placed. Under the Code title is relegated to a secondary position and the circumstances of the case are of primary importance. If the parties include delivery terms in their agreement such terms will indicate which party will bear the risk of loss while the goods are in transit. If delivery terms are F.O.B., F.A.S., C.I.F. or C. & F., the risks shift to the buyer on the delivery of the goods to the carrier and the making of a commercially reasonable contract of carriage. (2–319 and 2–320.) If the delivery terms are F.O.B. destination or delivery ex-ship the seller bears the risk. (2–319 [1] [b] and 2–322.) Other delivery terms and the accompanying risks are discussed in Chapter 32.

Identification and Insurable Interest. The general practice of insuring risks is recognized and provided for under the Code. Provision is made whereby the buyer may protect his interest in goods which are intended as the subject matter of a sales contract before the title to the goods vests in the buyer. The buyer obtains a special property and an insurable interest in existing goods when they are identified to the contract even though they are nonconforming. Identification of goods to a sales contract is the indication either by the agreement of the parties or, in the absence of an agreement, under the applicable provisions of the Code, that certain goods will be the subject matter of the contract. The goods may be nonconforming at the time of the identification and the seller may substitute other goods for those identified to the contract.

In the absence of an explicit agreement identifying the goods to the sales contract identification occurs when the contract is made if the goods are in existence and identified. If the goods are future goods, except growing crops or the young of animals, the goods are identified when they are shipped, marked or otherwise designated by the seller as the goods to which the contract refers. Crops are identified to the contract when planted, and the young of animals when conceived if the young are to be born within one year of the making of the contract or if the crops are to be harvested within one year or the next normal harvesting period. (2–501 [1].) The seller retains an insurable interest in goods so long as title or a security interest remains in him. (2–501 [2].)

A buyer who has paid for or has made a payment on identified goods which have not been shipped may, in the event of the insolvency of the seller within 10 days of the time payment was made, by making and keeping good a tender of the payment of any balance due, recover the goods identified to the contract. If the buyer has identified the goods to the contract he can recover the goods only if the goods identified to the contract conform to the sales contract. (2–502.)

Risks of Loss—General Rules. General rules relative to risks of loss are subject to the contrary agreement of the parties. In the absence of an agreement the risk of loss passes to the buyer on the delivery to the carrier of conforming goods unless the seller has agreed to deliver the goods at a particular destination, in which event the risk of loss passes to the buyer when the carrier so tenders the goods as to enable the buyer to take delivery. If the goods are in the possession of a bailee and are not to be moved, the risk of loss passes to the buyer on delivery to him of a negotiable document of title for the goods and if no negotiable document of title has been issued when the bailee acknowledges the buyer's right to the possession of the goods.

If the transaction is such that it does not fall within the situations discussed above, the risk of loss passes to the buyer on receipt of the goods if the seller is a merchant and if he is not a merchant on the tender of delivery of the goods. (2–509.)

When a seller tenders goods which do not conform to the contract and the buyer would have the right to reject the goods, the risk of loss remains with the seller until any defect is cured or until the buyer accepts the goods. Where the buyer rightfully revokes his acceptance, the risk of loss is with the seller from the beginning to the extent that the loss is not covered by the buyer's insurance. This rule gives the seller the benefit of any insurance carried by the buyer. Where a buyer repudiates a contract for conforming goods identified to the contract, the risk of loss, to the extent the loss is not covered by the seller's insurance, is on the buyer for a commercially reasonable time after the repudiation. (2–510 [3].)

Summary

Goods which are the subject matter of a sale may be damaged or destroyed and the question of which of the parties to the sales contract must bear the loss frequently arises. The parties to the sales contract may by explicit agreement designate who shall bear such loss or how the risk of loss shall be divided. The inclusion in the sales contract of delivery terms will indicate which of the parties shall bear the risk of loss during transit. The buyer acquires a property interest in goods identified to the sales contract and has an insurable interest in them even though they may be nonconforming.

If there is no explicit agreement identification occurs when the contract is made if the goods are in existence and identified, if they are future goods, then when they are shipped, marked or otherwise designated by the seller, if growing crops then when planted, and if young of animals, when conceived, provided the crops will be harvested or the young of animals will be born within one year.

A buyer who has made payment on goods identified to the contract may claim them if the seller becomes insolvent within 10 days of such payment. If transactions are not covered by the above rules and there is no agreement relative to who shall bear the risks of loss, such risk passes to the buyer on delivery of the goods to the carrier unless the seller has agreed to deliver the goods, then on delivery at destination. If goods are in the possession of a bailee and not to be moved, the risk passes to the buyer on delivery of a negotiable document of title and, if none, when the bailee acknowledges the buyer's rights. Nonconforming goods are at the risk of the seller. If the buyer repudiates the contract the goods are at the risk of the buyer for a commercially reasonable time. Insurance on the goods inures to the benefit of the party who must bear the loss.

Problem Cases

1. Witmer owned an automobile which he insured with State Farm Insurance Company. The policy provided that "Insured— . . . the unqualified word 'insured' includes (1) the named insured and also includes . . . (3) any other person while using the automobile, provided the actual use of the automobile is with the permission of the named insured." Witmer sold the automobile to Semple and delivered it to the place of Semple's employment late at night. At the time of delivery Witmer delivered the keys and the certificate of title to Semple. Witmer signed the certificate of title but it was not notarized as required by the state certificate of title statute. The parties agreed that the notarization of Witmer's signature would be obtained the next day. That night, while driving the automobile, Semple struck and injured Brown who sued Semple and was granted a judgment for $22,260. State Farm refused to pay the judgment and Semple sued State Farm, claiming that title to the automobile was in Witmer since a completed certificate of title had not been delivered to him and that he was driving the automobile with Witmer's consent and was, therefore, insured under Witmer's policy. State Farm contended that Semple was the owner of the automobile and that it was not liable to him on the policy. Is State Farm's contention correct?

2. Buyer sent a purchase order to Seller ordering 150 lawn mowers and instructing Seller to "Ship direct to 30th & Harcum Way, Pitts. Pa."—30th & Harcum Way being Buyer's address. The mowers were delivered to a carrier for shipment by Seller and were received and paid for by Buyer. At what point did title to the mowers pass to Buyer?

3. Chamberlin, a dealer in mobile homes in Popular Bluff, Missouri, sold Crowder a new camper unit for $1,757.74. Crowder gave Chamberlin a check in full payment. Crowder loaded the unit on a pickup truck that was too small to properly accommodate it and left Chamberlin's place of business without obtaining a bill of sale or title. Crowder drove to Jonesboro, Arkansas, where he sold the unit to Hollis, who was a dealer in used mobile homes. Hollis paid $500, knew the camper unit was new and worth at least $1,000, asked no questions about why the camper was affixed to the truck as it was, and asked for no title or bill of sale from Crowder except for requesting a bill of sale from Crowder to him. Crowder's check was dishonored and Chamberlin wants to recover the unit from Hollis. Can he do so?

4. Jacobson contracted to purchase from Kretz 1,500 sea-grass baskets at 85 cents per piece F.O.B. Hamburg and with cash to be paid on delivery. The invoice also contained the following provision: "Merchandise remains our property until full paid." The baskets were in good condition when delivered to the carrier in Hamburg, but were damaged in transit and were substantially valueless when they arrived in Miami. Under the circumstances of the case the carrier was not liable for the loss. Between Jacobson and Kretz, who must bear the loss?

5. Styli purchased a "diner" which had been the personal property of Conte and also leased some land from Conte on which the diner rested. Styli signed a conditional sales contract whereby he agreed to make monthly payments and both parties agreed that Conte was to retain title to the diner until it was paid for. The diner was destroyed by fire while Styli was using it but before he had made all the agreed payments. Between Styli and Conte, who had the risk of loss?

6. Regulator, a New York corporation having its offices and principal place of business in Connecticut, sold $45,000 worth of equipment to Extruder, a New Jersey corporation having no place of business in Connecticut and no certificate of authority to transact business in that state. Extruder refused to pay for the equipment and Regulator brought an action in Connecticut to recover the price. Under the long-arm statute [see Chapter 28, p. 627] whereby the Connecticut court could acquire jurisdiction over a foreign corporation, the mere making of the contract in Connecticut was not sufficient "contact" to satisfy jurisdictional requirements. Regulator sought to prove additional "contacts" by Extruder, claiming that since the contracts were F.O.B. Norwalk, Connecticut, risk of loss passed to Extruder upon delivery to the carrier in Norwalk. Extruder contended that Regulator was required to deliver the equipment to particular destinations outside the state because of "ship to" addresses on the purchase order forms. Therefore, they claimed, risk of loss didn't pass until delivery at the destination. At what point did risk of loss pass?

chapter 34. Warranty and Product Liability

Nature of Warranties

Representations. When a person is making an effort to sell goods, he usually makes some statements relative to the merits of the goods. Such statements are representations and may range in their legal effect from statements which are mere sales talk to statements which are fraudulent misrepresentations. In determining the legal effect of representations made by a seller, all of the facts and circumstances must be taken into consideration.

In the early period of the development of the law of sales, business was carried on in such a manner that the seller and the buyer negotiated face-to-face in the presence of the goods. Frequently, the seller was an itinerant merchant who would leave for parts unknown as soon as he had sold his wares. Also, the sale was quite often looked upon as a test of wits, the seller doing his best to drive a sharp bargain, and the buyer exercising all of the cunning at his command to get a good buy. Under such conditions, neither party placed much faith in the statements of the other. All representations made by a seller were accepted as sales talk and not binding on him unless he clearly and unequivocally assumed responsibility for the quality of the goods he was selling.

With the development of commerce, business methods changed, and there was a shift from the face-to-face sale in the presence of the goods to sales made by the seller's representative, who called on the customer and described or displayed samples of the goods the seller was offering for sale. Since the buyer, under this system of selling, could not examine the goods he was buying before he contracted to buy, he had to rely on the representations of the seller of his agent.

By gradual evolution, merchandising has progressed from a system in which the seller was not held responsible for representations made regarding the goods offered for sale to a system in which a high degree of responsibility is placed on a seller for such representations.

Under the law as it has developed, a seller is not responsible if he, in representing his goods, confines his statements to "sales talk" or "puffing," such as "It is a good buy," "These goods are high class," or "You should be happy with this." Also, the seller is not responsible if he merely expresses an opinion relative to the nature or quality of the goods. Whether a statement made by a seller will be interpreted as an opinion or a representation will depend, in many instances, on the relative experience and knowledge of the parties. If the seller is one who deals in goods such as he is selling, and the buyer does not deal in such goods and knows little about them, a statement relating to the quality or character of the goods might be interpreted as a warranty, whereas if the buyer is a dealer in such goods and has had experience and knowledge substantially equal to that of the seller, the same statements might be interpreted as statements of opinion.

Warranties—General. In its broadest sense a warranty is the assumption of responsibility, by the seller, for the quality, character, or suitability of goods sold. The seller may assume such responsibility by express agreement, in which case the warranty is created by contract and the rights and liabilities are contractual in nature. Such a warranty is called an express warranty.

If the seller has knowingly misrepresented the goods with intent to defraud and the buyer has justifiably relied on the representations to his injury, the seller will be liable to the buyer in damages in an action in tort for deceit. If the seller is guilty of deceit, the buyer may elect to pursue either his remedy for breach of warranty or his remedy for damages for deceit. If the seller's representations are confined within the limits of sales talk and expression of opinion, he will not be liable to the buyer on the ground of his representations.

Under some circumstances a degree of responsibility for goods sold is imposed on the seller by operation of law, in which case the nature and extent of the seller's responsibility will be determined by the nature of the transaction. Such responsibility is quasi-contractual in nature. The warranty is included in the sales agreement by operation of law, and such warranties are known as implied warranties.

Summary

As a result of the change in the method of doing business, we have developed rules of law under which a seller is held responsible for representations made to induce a buyer to purchase goods.

A warranty is the assumption by the seller of goods of the responsibility for the quality, character, and suitability of goods sold. A warranty may result from representations made by the seller, or it may be imposed on the seller by operation of law.

Express Warranties

Nature of Express Warranty.   An express warranty is based on contract and is the result of negotiation of the terms of the sales contract. It may be broad in its scope and include all phases of the quality, character, suitability and ownership of the goods involved or it may go to only one or more characteristics of the goods. When the seller has expressly warranted the goods, the courts have generally held that such warranty represents so clearly the intent of the parties that they will not interpret any language in the sales contract whereby the seller attempts to relieve himself from liability for the warranty as being effective if the language is general in its terms or is included in a form contract.

Creating an Express Warranty.   To create an express warranty it is not necessary that the seller use the words "warrant" or "guarantee," nor is it necessary that he intend to make a warranty. Any affirmation of fact or promise made by the seller to the buyer which relates to the goods and becomes a part of the bargain creates an express warranty that the goods shall conform to the affirmation or promise. An affirmation merely of the value of the goods or a statement purporting to be merely the seller's opinion or commendation of the goods does not create a warranty. Whether or not affirmations or statements made by a seller to a buyer in the negotiation of a sale are warranties or merely statements of opinion or commendation of the goods will depend to a large extent on the relation of the parties, their experience and knowledge, and all the facts and circumstances of the case.

In the negotiation of a sale the seller may use descriptive terms to convey to the buyer an idea of the quality or characteristics of the goods or he may use pictures, drawings, blueprints, or technical specifications. When a seller uses descriptive terms as the basis of the sales contract he will have expressly warranted that the goods delivered will conform to the description. If a sample or model is made a part of the basis of the bargain, the seller will have expressly warranted that the goods delivered will conform to the sample or model. If a sample is used, the court, in determining the scope of the seller's liability on the warranty, will take into consideration whether the sample is drawn from the bulk of the goods or is merely illustrative of the goods. (Section 2–313.) [1]

Summary

To expressly warrant goods such words as "warrant" or "guarantee" need not be used. Any affirmation of fact or promise, any description of the goods

---

[1] The numbers in the parentheses refer to the sections of the Uniform Commercial Code, 1962.

or a sample or model of the goods used as a basis of the bargain is an express warranty. An affirmation merely of the value of the goods or a statement purporting to be merely the seller's opinion or commendation of the goods does not create an express warranty.

Wat Henry Pontiac Co. v. Bradley
210 P.2d 348 (Sup. Ct. Okla. 1949)

This was an action to recover the sum of $324.56 damages for breach of an express oral warranty of a used car purchased by Mrs. Joe Bradley (plaintiff) from the Wat Henry Pontiac Co. (defendant). The trial resulted in a judgment against the Wat Henry Pontiac Co. in the sum of $279.56. Affirmed on appeal.

JOHNSON, JUSTICE. Mrs. Bradley testified that on October 22, 1944, she went to the Wat Henry Pontiac Company; that she contacted the manager of salesman in charge of the used cars; that she made a deal for the car; that she was with her brother; and that the brother was present during her negotiations for the purchase of the car; that she asked many questions about the car; that the seller assured her that the car was in good condition; that he had driven the car; that "this is a car we know; this is a car I can recommend"; that "it is in A-1 shape." She informed him that her husband was in Camp Shelby, Mississippi, and that her child was only seven months old; and that she wanted to be sure she was going to get there. Wat Henry further assured her that he knew the car, he knew the man who had brought it in, that it was "mechanically perfect" and that it would get her any place she wanted to go. That she asked to drive the car and try it out, but was told that gas rations were very short and they were not allowed to send cars out for trial, but that she had no cause to fear this car, that it was all right; that she could not see the connecting rod or crankshaft or rings; that she was not a mechanic, but was a trained nurse.

The salesman who sold the car testified in substance that he had been an auto mechanic for about twelve years before becoming a salesman; that he was engaged in demonstrating and selling cars; that he did not warrant the car, but explained to the buyer that the style was without a warranty, but did state that after the deal was closed that he told Bradley, "I would not be afraid to start, and I wouldn't have been afraid to start any place in the car, because it ran as nice as you would expect a car that age to run. There wasn't anything to indicate to me that there was anything wrong with the car, if there was anything wrong with it."

The rule is that to constitute an express warranty no particular form of words is necessary, and any affirmation of the quality or condition of the vehicle, not uttered as a matter of opinion or belief, made by a seller at the time of sale for the purpose of assuring the buyer of the truth of the fact and inducing the buyer to make the purchase, if so received and relied on by the buyer, is an express warranty.

This court in *International Harvester Co. v. Lawyer,* said:

" 'Warranty' is a matter of intention. A decisive test is whether the vendor assumes to assert a fact of which the buyer is ignorant, or merely states an opinion, or his judgment, upon a matter of which the vendor has no special knowledge, and on which the buyer may also be expected to have an opinion and to exercise his judgment. In the former case there is a warranty; in the latter case there is not.

"The buyer knew nothing about the capacity of the automobile purchased. The seller was an expert in the handling of automobiles, and was engaged in the business of demonstrating and selling the same. Held, a statement made by the seller that the automobile could be driven over the roads in a certain vicinity satisfactorily constituted a warranty and was not the expression of a mere opinion."

The facts in this case bring it squarely within the above well-settled principles of law, and the jury was justified in finding that there was an oral warranty.

Defendant argues that the facts in this case are governed by the rule that a seller is permitted to promote his wares so long as he does so in the bounds of reason, and cites *Smith* v. *Bolster* as his authority. The first paragraph of the syllabus reads: "Statements by a seller of an automobile, which had been used as a demonstrating car, and had been run about 1,500 miles, made to a buyer who knew the facts, that the car sold for less than 20 percent less than the price of a new car. . . , would go 11 miles to a gallon of gasoline on an average, were mere expressions of opinion, and did not constitute a warranty of the car."

Thus, it is obvious that in this case cited the buyer knew as much about the facts as the seller, and, of course, the buyer, knowing the facts, what the seller said was merely the expression of an opinion. The buyer here was ignorant of the facts, and the defects were hidden and not open to discovery by the buyer. The seller was an expert in handling automobiles, having served for a long period of time as an automobile mechanic before becoming a salesman; and his statements as to the condition of the car and where it could be driven constituted a warranty and not mere opinion.

Warranty of Title

Nature of Warranty of Title. A warranty of title differs from other warranties in that it protects the buyer in his ownership of the goods he has bought whereas other warranties go to the quality of the goods sold. Unless the buyer knows from the circumstances that the seller does not have title to the goods but is selling in an official capacity and purports to sell only such title as a third person has, a warranty of title attaches to the sale. A warranty of title may be excluded or modified but only by specific language. The courts have generally held that unless the language of a disclaimer of warranty clearly and unequivocally includes the warranty of title, the buyer is justified in believing that the intent is to disclaim warranties of quality and not warranties of title. (2–312 [2].)

Scope of Warranty of Title. In a contract for sale the seller warrants that the title conveyed shall be good, and its transfer rightful; and that the goods shall be delivered free from any security interest or other lien or encumbrance of which the buyer at the time of contracting has no knowledge. If the goods are encumbered by an outstanding secured interest or lien, the contract of sale may provide that the sale is subject to the encumbrance. If it does not so provide, the seller is obligated to discharge any outstanding encumbrance before time for the delivery of the goods. Although the warranty of title provision of the Code does not expressly warrant against disturbance of quiet possession, the language of the provision is such that a disturbance of quiet possession is a breach of the warranty of title. (2–312 [1].)

A seller who is a merchant regularly dealing in goods of the kind sold warrants that the goods shall be delivered free of the rightful claim of any third person by way of infringement or the like, unless such warranty is disclaimed by the contract. A buyer who contracts with a seller for the purchase of goods which comply with specifications furnished by him must hold the seller harmless against any claim of infringement or the like which arises out of compliance with the specifications. (2–312 [3].)

Summary

A warranty of title differs in some respects from other warranties. Unless the buyer knows that the seller is acting in an official capacity or does not have title or the warranty of title is excluded or modified in clear and unequivocal language, it attaches. In a sale the seller warrants that the title conveyed shall be good, that the goods when delivered shall be free from encumbrances of which the buyer has no knowledge, and, if the seller is a merchant dealing in goods of the kind, that the goods will be free from rightful claim of infringement. A buyer who furnishes specifications to a seller must hold the seller harmless from claims of infringement which arise out of compliance with the specifications.

Ivester v. E. B. Jones Motor Co.
311 S.W.2d 109 (App. Ct. Mo. 1958)

This was an action by Vernon L. Ivester and Madelyn E. Ivester (plaintiffs) against E. B. Jones Motor Company (defendant) to recover a judgment for damages arising out of breach of warranty of title to an automobile. Judgment for Ivester, and E. B. Jones Motor Company appealed. Judgment affirmed.

In March, 1951, the Ivesters purchased an automobile from E. B. Jones Motor Company (Jones). Jones told Ivester that he had purchased the automobile from Keepers who had an Ohio title to it. Jones filled out the necessary papers for a transfer of title to Ivester who then obtained a title to the automobile through the Missouri Department of Motor Vehicle Registration. In July, 1953, an agent for the Federal Bureau of Investigation called upon Ivester and questioned him about the automobile. Rent-A-Car Service, Inc., claimed to own the automobile. Ivester and the F.B.I. agent talked to Jones about the matter but he did nothing. In September,

1953, Rent-A-Car Service, Inc., filed a replevin suit, and Ivester informed Jones of the situation and requested that he defend the suit, which Jones refused to do. Ivester then filed a petition to have Jones made a party defendant to the replevin suit. This was done, but Rent-A-Car Service, Inc., refused to amend its pleadings so as to state a cause of action against Jones, and the third-party petition against Jones was dismissed. Rent-A-Car Service, Inc., recovered the automobile, and Ivester brought this suit against Jones to recover the value of the automobile.

WOLFE, COMMISSIONER.   It is contended that Ivester failed to make a submissible case. There appears to be no dispute about the general rule that there is an implied warranty of title when goods are in possession of a seller at the time of sale. No point is presented about the seller's warranty of title, but it is asserted that there was a failure to prove that Ivester surrendered the automobile to one having a superior title. This overlooks the conceded facts. The court files of the replevin suit were in evidence and no question was raised as to their authenticity or the verity of the matters recited in them. These show that Rent-A-Car Service, Inc., by that action did obtain the automobile.

It is stated by Jones that "Ivester proved through documentary evidence a chain of title originating in and continuing in the State of Texas. However, he also admitted that title was in Jones at the time of sale." This conclusion is predicated upon a statement made by Ivester that the Jones Company purchased the car from Keepers who had an Ohio title and that the Jones Company gave Ivester an application for title showing that it owned the car. The testimony was merely explanatory of the events that took place at the time of the sale and was not an admission that the real title and ownership was in the Jones Company as it would seek to construe it.

The general rule is that when a suit is brought by a third person against the purchaser, the seller may intervene and defend the title, and if he is duly notified he is bound to do so. When the seller is notified and fails to defend, he is bound by the results of such litigation. It must therefore be concluded that Ivester made a submissible case.

[*This case was not decided under the Code but the rules of law which were applied have not been changed by its adoption.*]

Implied Warranties

Nature of Implied Warranty.   Under present methods of merchandising and because of the complexity of goods sold, the buyer either has little or no opportunity to examine the goods or is not in a position to adequately test the goods to determine their quality. A merchant dealing in such goods is in a much better position than a buyer to make a thorough examination of the goods or to make tests to determine their quality. Therefore, in the interest of trade certain responsibilities are imposed on the seller, especially if he is a merchant dealing in such goods, relative to the quality, character and suitability of the goods sold. This responsibility is not assumed by the seller either by express promise or by the making of representations relative to the goods, but is imposed on him by operation of law. The responsibility imposed is the same, in its general nature, as that assumed by the seller when he expressly warrants goods. In fact the responsibility is a warranty implied in law.

This responsibility is not absolute. It attaches only under certain circumstances and the seller may contract against it. The courts, however, favor implied warranties, and if the seller wishes to relieve himself from the responsibility imposed on him by the implied warranties attaching to a sale, it must be clearly established that the parties to the sale did not intend it to attach.

There are two implied warranties of quality recognized under the Code: the implied warranty of merchantability and the implied warranty of fitness for a particular purpose. These two warranties overlap and under some circumstances the seller may be held liable for breach of warranty under either or both.

Implied Warranty of Merchantability. An implied warranty of merchantability attaches to a sale made by a merchant dealing in goods of the kind sold. The implied warranty may be excluded or modified by an appropriate agreement. (2–314 [1].) Under this section of the Code the serving for value of food or drink to be consumed either on the premises or elsewhere is a sale. This provision in the Code resolves the controversy as to whether or not the serving of food in a restaurant or hotel dining room is a sale. Under this provision of the Code it is a sale and the server, if the food or drink is unwholesome, may be held liable either for breach of implied warranty of merchantability or implied warranty of fitness for a particular purpose.

At common law and under the Uniform Sales Act the term "merchantable" was not clearly defined and there was little uniformity in the standards applied in determining whether or not goods were of merchantable quality. In an attempt to give more certainty to an uncertain situation six tests of merchantability are set out in the Code. Goods to be merchantable must be at least such as (1) pass in the trade under the contract description; (2) in the case of fungible goods, are of fair average quality within the description; (3) are fit for the ordinary purpose for which such goods are used; (4) run, within the variations permitted by the agreement, of even kind, quality and quantity within each unit and among all units involved; (5) are adequately contained, packaged, and labeled as the agreement may require; and (6) conform to promises or affirmations of fact made on the container or label if any. (2–314 [2].)

Implied Warranty of Fitness for Particular Purpose. To give rise to an implied warranty of fitness for a particular purpose the seller must at the time of contracting have reason to know the particular purpose for which the goods are required by the buyer and that the buyer is relying on the seller to select goods suitable for that purpose. To fulfill these requirements, the buyer need not bring home to the seller actual knowledge of that particular purpose for which the goods are intended or of his reliance on the seller's skill and judgment. All that is necessary is that the seller, under the circumstances, must have reason to know the particular purpose for which the buyer wants the goods and that the reliance exists.

If the buyer gives the seller technical specifications of the goods he wishes to buy or in some other manner clearly indicates the particular goods desired, there would be no evidence of reliance on the seller's judgment and no implied warranty of fitness for a particular purpose. An implied warranty of fitness for a particular purpose may arise whether or not the seller is a merchant. (2–315.)

Summary

There are two implied warranties of quality—that of merchantability and that of fitness for a particular purpose. The implied warranty, unless excluded or modified, becomes a part of the sales contract by operation of law.

Accompanying a sale by a merchant dealing in goods of the kind sold, there is, unless excluded or modified, an implied warranty of merchantability. The warranty imposes on the seller liability if the goods are not of fair average quality. Six tests of merchantability are set out in the Code. The serving for value of food or drink is a sale.

The implied warranty of fitness for a particular purpose is based on the seller's having reason to know the particular purpose for which the buyer wishes the goods and the buyer's reliance on the seller's skill and judgment in selecting the goods suitable for his purpose. The warranty may be excluded or modified. The seller need not be a merchant to have the warranty attach.

Hunt v. Ferguson-Paulus Enterprises
415 P.2d 13 (Sup. Ct. Ore. 1966)

This was an action by Hunt (plaintiff) against Ferguson-Paulus Enterprises (defendant) to recover damages for injury allegedly sustained through a breach of warranty. Judgment for Ferguson-Paulus and Hunt appealed. Judgment affirmed.

Hunt purchased a cherry pie from Ferguson-Paulus through a vending machine owned and maintained by them. On biting into the pie one of Hunt's teeth was broken when it encountered a cherry pit.

LUSK, JUSTICE.   If the cherry pie purchased by Hunt from Ferguson-Paulus was not reasonably fit for human consumption because of the presence of the cherry pit there was a breach of warranty and Hunt was entitled to recover his damages thereby caused.

In the consideration of similar cases some of the courts have drawn a distinction between injury caused by spoiled, impure, or contaminated food or food containing a foreign substance, and injury caused by a substance natural to the product sold. In the latter class of cases, these courts hold there is no liability on the part of the dispenser of the good. Thus in the leading case of *Mix* v. *Ingersoll Candy Co.,* the court held that a patron of a restaurant who ordered and paid for chicken pie, which contained a sharp sliver or fragment of chicken bone, and was injured as a result of swallowing the bone, had no cause of action against the restauranteur either for breach of warranty or negligence. Referring to cases in which recovery had been allowed the court said:

"All of the cases are instances in which the food was found not to be reasonably fit for human consumption, either by reason of the presence of a foreign substance, or an impure and noxious condition of the food itself, such as for example, glass, stones, wires or nails in the food served, or tainted, decayed, diseased, or infected meats or vegetables."

The court went on to say that:

". . . despite the fact that a chicken bone may occasionally be encountered in a chicken pie, such chicken pie, in the absence of some further defect, is reasonably fit for human consumption. Bones which are natural to the type of meat served cannot legitimately be called a foreign substance, and a consumer who eats meat dishes ought to anticipate and be on the guard against the presence of such bones."

Further the court said:

"Certainly no liability would attach to a restaurant keeper for the serving of a T-bone steak, or a beef stew, which contained a bone natural to the type of meat served, or if a fish dish should contain a fish bone, or if a cherry pie should contain a cherry stone—although it be admitted that an ideal cherry pie would be stoneless."

Other courts have rejected the so-called foreign-natural test in favor of what is known at the "reasonable expectation" test, among them the Supreme Court of Wisconsin, which, in *Betehia* v. *Cape Cod Corp.* held that a person who was injured by a chicken bone in a chicken sandwich served to him in a restaurant, could recover for his injury either for breach of an implied warranty or for negligence. "There is a distinction," the court said, "between what a consumer expects to find in a fish stick and in a baked or fried fish, or in a chicken sandwich made from sliced white meat and in roast chicken. The test should be what is reasonably expected by the consumer in the food as served, not what might be natural to the ingredients of that food prior to preparation. What is to be reasonably expected by the consumer is a jury question in most cases; at least, we cannot say as a matter of law that a patron of a restaurant must expect a bone in a chicken sandwich either because chicken bones are occasionally found there or are natural to chicken."

In view of the judgment for the defendant, we are not required in this case to make a choice between the two rules. Under the foreign-natural test the plaintiff would be barred from recovery as a matter of law. The reasonable expectation test calls for determination of a question of fact. The court has found the fact in favor of the defendant and this court has no power to disturb the finding.

Corneliuson v. *Arthur Drug Stores, Inc.*
214 A.2d 676 (Sup. Ct. Conn. 1965)

This was an action by Corneliuson (plaintiff) against Arthur Drug Stores, Inc. (defendant), for breach of an implied warranty of fitness of a home permanent waving lotion purchased by Corneliuson from Arthur. Corneliuson claimed that, as a result of her use of the lotion she sustained a severe dermatitis with concomitant physical and neurotic injuries. The jury returned a verdict for Corneliuson which the trial court refused to set aside. Reversed on appeal.

HOUSE, JUSTICE.   In *Crotty* v. *Shartenberg's-New Haven, Inc.,* we held that under our statute there may be an implied warranty that the goods sold shall be reasonably fit for a particular purpose, or that the goods shall be of merchantable quality and that the existence, nature and extent of either implied warranty depends on the circumstances of the case. We noted that some jurisdictions hold that if the article sold can be used by a normal person without injury, there is no breach of the implied warranty of reasonable fitness, while others adopt the theory that the seller is not absolved from liability under the implied warranty created by the statute by the mere fact that only a small proportion of those who use the product suffer injuries from its use. We concluded that the term "reasonable fitness" must, of necessity, be considered one of degree and that the term must be "related to the subject of the sale." Rejecting the rule limiting the application of the term "reasonable fitness" to a class or group designated as normal persons, we adopted the test of injurious effect to "an appreciable number of people." We held that not only the causal connection between the product and the injury must be established but also the plaintiff must be a member of a class who would be similarly affected by the product, identifying that class as an appreciable number of people.

In the course of the opinion we used the following language:

To establish a breach of the warranty, the plaintiff must show (1) that the product contains a substance or ingredient which has a tendency to affect injuriously an appreciable number of people, though fewer in number than the number of normal buyers, and (2) that he has, in fact, been injured or harmed by the use of the product. . . . The burden is on the plaintiff to establish these facts. Proof of the harmful propensities of the substance and that it can affect injuriously an appreciable number of persons is essential to his case. . . . If a buyer has knowledge, either actual or constructive, that he is allergic to a particular substance and purchases a product which he knows or reasonably should know contains that substance, he cannot recover damages for breach of an implied warranty. Nor can he recover if he suffers harm by reason of his own improper use of the article warranted. . . . When a manufacturer puts into a product to be sold for human use a substance which has deleterious qualities and a tendency to harm an appreciable number of its users, the manufacturer, and not the user, should shoulder the risk of injurious consequences. The same risk should be borne by the retailer who sells the article to a prospective user who, relying on the retailer, is entitled to believe that the article is reasonably fit for the purpose for which it is sold.

. . . Although there was evidence from which the jury could find that the Ogilvie Sisters lotion did cause injury to Corneliuson there was no evidence from which they could find that this lotion as compounded had a tendency to affect injuriously an appreciable number of people. Proof of both injury to Corneliuson and such injurious tendency are necessary for Corneliuson to prevail. Proof that all permanent waving lotions generally contain certain basic chemicals compounded in varying strengths in the different brands and that in the strength used in some of them the chemicals may injuriously affect some people is not alone a reasonable basis for a conclusion that any specific lotion, even though it contains in some form those same basic chemicals, has the injurious tendency requisite to establish liability and that that lotion is not "reasonably fit" or of "merchantable quality" as those terms are used in the statute on implied warranties. The basic test must be applied to the particular product as compounded, which necessarily includes any incorporated substance or ingredient in the strength and quantity used in the particular product, not in the strength and quantity which such substances or ingredients may be used in some other products.

McMeekin v. Gimbel Brothers, Inc.
223 F. Supp. 896 (W.D. Pa. 1963)

This was an action by Thomas O. McMeekin (plaintiff) against Gimbel Brothers, Inc. (defendants), to recover a judgment for damages for breach of implied warranty of fitness for a particular purpose in the sale of a lawn mower. Judgment for Gimbel Brothers, Inc.

McMeeken purchased a rotary-type lawn mower manufactured by the Eska Corporation from Gimbel Brothers, Inc. (Gimbel), on July 18, 1959. He used it for cutting his lawn throughout the remainder of the summer and fall of that year and in the spring of 1960 two or three times prior to May 28, 1960. On that day, while he was cutting the lawn some unknown object penetrated the eye of his 5-year-old son, destroying the sight of his eye. McMeeken's theory was that a small object was hurled through the grass chute at the right front of the mower with sufficient force to penetrate the eye of the child.

MARSH, DISTRICT JUDGE. As to McMeekin's contention that the defendant retailer is liable for breach of warranty, there was no proof of any express warranty. § 2–313.

Mr. McMeekin did not purchase the Eska mower for a purpose other than the general purpose of cutting grass, and he did not rely on defendant's skill and judgment in selecting the mower; hence, there was no implied warranty of fitness. § 2–315.

Finally, there was no proof of a breach of the implied warranty of merchantability or fitness for cutting grass. The McMeekins utterly failed to meet their burden of establishing that the mower was not of merchantable quality *when delivered on July 18, 1959.*

On the contrary, the evidence established that the mower operated effectively and satisfactorily upon delivery and during the summer of 1959 and the early spring of 1960 and was usable and fit for the general purpose for which it was purchased. It complied with the commercial standards applicable to other rotary mowers on the market.

There was no proof that the mower was a dangerous instrument when delivered. There was no proof of any specific defect when the mower was delivered or at any subsequent time. There was no proof that it was negligently designed, or was designed in a fashion materially different from other rotary mowers on the market.

Whether a breach existed at the time the mower was delivered cannot be based upon mere conjecture or guess arising from a freak accident occurring at a time remote from the date of purchase.

Exclusions, Modification, or Conflict of Warranties

Common-Law Rule. At common law the parties to a sales contract were free, by mutual agreement, to relieve the seller from all liability arising from warranties, either express or implied. The courts gave a narrow construction to exclusion clauses and held that a disclaimer of "all warranties stated herein" or similar language included in a sales contract did not exclude implied warranties. If the circumstances were such that it was clear that both parties were aware of the exclusion clause and agreed to it the court would enforce it. There were no general provisions in the Uniform Sales Act relating to exclusion or modification of warranty clauses in the sales contract. Section 15(3) of the Act did provide: "If the buyer has examined the goods there is no implied warranty as regards defects which such examination ought to reveal."

Exclusions or Modifications. The drafters of the Code recognized that the parties should, if they desired to do so, have the right to relieve the seller from all or any phase of his liability. Experience, however, demonstrated the need of protecting the buyer from the inclusion in a sales contract of an exclusion or modification clause unless the buyer was fully aware of the inclusion and freely consented thereto.

In framing the provisions of the Code relative to exclusion or modification of warranties, the drafters recognized the desirability of distinguishing between different types of warranties. An express warranty made in the negotiation of a sales contract or in the formal draft of it, and words or conduct tending to negate or limit the warranty shall be construed whenever reasonable as consistent with each other; but negation or limitation is inoperative to the extent that such construction is unreasonable. (2–316.) If a sales contract includes an express warranty and also includes a clause which seeks to exclude "all warranties, express or implied," such clause would be inoperative since it would be unreasonable. Also, if the sales contract is in writing, oral evidence of an agreement to exclude or modify warranties included in the written contract would not be admissible. (2–202.)

To exclude an implied warranty of merchantability or any part of it the language must mention merchantability and in case of a writing must be conspicuous. To exclude or modify an implied warranty of merchantability, where the sales contract is in writing, the exclusion clause would have to be printed or written into the contract in larger type or letters or in ink of a different color so that one reading the contract would not be likely to overlook it. If the seller wishes added protection he should have the buyer separately sign the exclusion clause. (2–316 [2].)

To exclude or modify an implied warranty of fitness for a particular purpose the exclusion must be in writing and conspicuous. Language to exclude all implied warranties of fitness is sufficient if it states, for example, that "There are no warranties which extend beyond the description on the face hereof." However, such clause in the contract, to be effective, would have to be printed or written in conspicuous type or letters. (2–316 [2].)

Unless circumstances indicate otherwise all implied warranties are excluded by expressions like "as is," "with all faults," or other language which in common understanding calls the buyer's attention to the exclusion of warranties and makes plain that there are no implied warranties. (2–316 [3] [a].)

When the buyer, before entering into the contract, has examined the goods or a sample or model as fully as he desires or has refused to examine the goods, there is no implied warranty with regards to defects which an examination ought in the circumstances to have revealed to him. If the seller merely makes the goods available to the buyer for examination and the buyer neglects to examine them, the seller would not be protected under this provision of the Code. The seller should not only make the goods available for examination but he should demand or follow a course equivalent to a demand that the buyer examine the goods. (2–316 [3] [b].)

An implied warranty can also be excluded or modified by course of dealings, or course of performance or usage of trade. (2–316 [3] [c].)

Conflict of Warranties. Frequently in a sales contract implied warranties supplement express warranties. The Code provides that warranties whether express or implied shall be construed as consistent with each other and as cumulative, but if such construction is unreasonable the intention of the parties shall determine which warranty is dominant. In case of conflict the court must determine from all the facts and circumstances which warranty was intended by the parties to be dominant. To aid the court in determining intention the Code provides: Exact or technical specifications displace an inconsistent sample or model or general language of description. A sample from an existing bulk displaces inconsistent general language of description. Express warranties displace inconsistent implied warranties other than an implied warranty of fitness for a particular purpose. (2–317.)

Summary

Language of a disclaimer in a sales contract is ineffective where such language is inconsistent with an express warranty included therein. To exclude or modify an implied warranty of merchantability, merchantability must be mentioned and in the case of a writing must be conspicuous. To exclude or modify an implied warranty of fitness for a particular purpose the exclusion must be in writing and conspicuous. Implied warranties are excluded by expressions like "as is" or "with all faults." If the buyer examines the goods or a sample or model or a demand is made that he examine them and he refuses, there is no implied warranty with regards to defects which the examination ought to reveal. An implied warranty can also be excluded or modified by course of dealing or course of performance or by usage of trade.

Express and implied warranties will be construed as consistent and cumulative unless such construction is unreasonable, and if unreasonable, the intention of the parties as to which warranty shall be dominant shall control.

Boeing Airplane Co. v. O'Malley
329 F.2d 585 (8th Cir. 1964)

This was an action by John A. O'Malley and V. J. Pedrizetti, Trustees in dissolution of Atlas Helicopter Service, Inc. (plaintiff), against Boeing Airplane Company (defendant) to recover a judgment for damages for breach of implied warranty. Judgment for O'Malley and Pedrizetti, and Boeing Airplane Company appealed. Judgment affirmed.

Boeing Airplane Company (Boeing) purchased The Vertol Aircraft Corporation (Vertol). Vertol had sold a helicopter to Atlas Helicopter Service, Inc. (Atlas), before Boeing purchased Vertol. Boeing on purchasing Vertol became liable for all of its obligations.

For some time representatives of Vertol had been negotiating with organizers of Atlas for the sale to them of a Vertol helicopter. Atlas was interested in acquiring the helicopter to be used in utility work such as the laying of heavy weights in construction. Vertol prepared a brochure for Atlas to be used in advertising its business. The brochure showed that the helicopter would lift 4,000 pounds of equipment, that it could be used in laying pipelines, in transporting up to 19 crew members or 2 tons of cargo, and in setting poles, and that it had a useful load of up to 5,360 pounds. The helicopter failed to perform as represented.

The contract included a disclaimer of warranty clause as follows: "(a) VERTOL warrants that it is the full legal and beneficial owner of the helicopter described in ARTICLE 1, and that it is not subject to any lien, charge or encumbrance.

"(b) The foregoing warranty is given and accepted in lieu of any and all warranties, express or implied arising out of the sale of the helicopter."

On the trial of the case Vertol set up this disclaimer of warranty as a defense.

VOGEL, CIRCUIT JUDGE.   The next step in the conclusion that an implied warranty existed as a matter of law, and in so instructing the jury, was for the District Court to hold that under the 1954 statute there was no modification or exclusion of the implied warranty. The statute provides that the exclusion or modification "must be in specific language" and if an ambiguity is created, it is to be resolved against the seller. This means that the disclaimer may not be merely by use of the clause disclaiming "all warranties express or implied," such as seems to have been attempted in the written agreement. An implied warranty under the statute must be disclaimed by the most precise terms; in other words, so clear, definite and specific as to leave no doubt as to the intent of the contracting parties. The disclaimer here fails as a matter of law to comply with the statute and accordingly we find that the District Court was correct in holding the attempted disclaimer inapplicable.

It should be pointed out here that even if it could be held that the 1959 amendment to the statute were applicable, it would make no difference in the result in this case because, while the implied warranty could under the 1959 statute be disclaimed by the form of language used in Article VI of the contract, the "writing must be conspicuous." Here it is not so. It is merely in the same color and size of other type used for the other provisions and under the statutory definition of "conspicuous" fails of its purpose. We accordingly must conclude that the District Court was entirely correct in holding as a matter of law that there was an implied warranty that the helicopter was fit for the purpose intended and that there was no effective disclaimer of such implied warranty.

Who Benefits from Warranty

General Rule.   The courts, in determining who is entitled to the benefit of a warranty, have considered the warranty as contractual. In many situations the seller expressly promises to assume responsibility for the failure of the goods to measure up to certain defined standards. Such a warranty is contractual. However, a warranty may arise as the result of representations which are not promissory in nature, and an implied warranty may attach by operation of law. Nevertheless, all suits for damages for breach of warranty are actions in contract, not in tort. Preceeding from the accepted theory that a warranty is contractual, the courts have applied the general rule of contract law, that one not a party to a contract has no right to enforce the contract. Traditionally, this has meant that a person who did not himself purchase the defective goods did not have a cause of action for breach of warranty and even the purchaser of defective goods could sue only his immediate seller and not the manufacturer with whom he was not in privity of contract.

Demise of the Privity Doctrine.   Today there is a growing tendency on the part of courts to allow recovery by an injured purchaser directly from the manufacturer or processor. In most cases the manufacturer or processor has control over the state of the product when it reaches the buyer's control and should be held liable for defects in it. The fact that the ultimate consumer may bring suit against the manufacturer or processor in no way relieves the retailer from his responsibility for the fitness or merchantability of the goods. In many states the buyer has been permitted to sue both the retailer and the manufacturer or processor in the same suit.

The manufacturers of many products give a manufacturer's warranty to the ultimate purchaser of their products in which they warrant their products against certain defined defects and in which they expressly limit their liability for breach of the express warranty. A manufacturer who has given such a warranty is liable on the warranty in a direct suit brought by the ultimate purchaser to whom the warranty is addressed.

Uniform Commercial Code.   The drafters of the Code took no position on whether an injured purchaser could directly sue the manufacturer; instead, they left the development of the law on this point open to the courts, which as indicated above tend to allow such direct actions.

The Code, in Section 2–318, does extend warranty protection to "any natural person who is in the family or household of his buyer or who is a guest in his house if it is reasonable to expect that such person may use, consume, or be affected by the goods and who is injured in person by breach of warranty." The Code further provides that the seller may not exclude or limit his liability to the members of the buyer's household or his guests for breach of warranty. (2–318).

Summary

Under the general rule a seller is liable for damages for breach of warranty to his immediate purchaser and to no one else.

The courts are now tending to hold manufacturers and processors liable to the ultimate consumer for damages for breach of warranty.

A manufacturer is liable to an ultimate purchaser for breach of a warranty directed to the ultimate consumer.

The Code extends the scope of a seller's warranty to include any natural person who is in the family or household of his buyer or is a guest, and further provides that the seller may not exclude or limit his liability to such persons.

Henningsen v. Bloomfield Motors

161 A.2d 69 (Sup. Ct. N.J. 1960)

This was an action for breach of warranty by Claus and Helen Henningsen (plaintiffs) against Chrysler Corporation and Bloomfield Motors (defendants). The trial court awarded damages to the Henningsens. Affirmed on appeal.

Claus Henningsen purchased a new 1955 Plymouth from Bloomfield Motors as a gift for his wife, Helen. At the time of purchase Claus signed a purchase order that included an express warranty against defects in material and workmanship but which limited Chrysler's obligation to replacing the defective parts. The "warranty clause" went on to say that this warranty was "expressly in lieu of all other warranties expressed or implied, and all other obligations or liabilities on its part." This statement was made in fine print on the reverse side of the purchase order as of the seventh of ten paragraphs. Shortly after the purchase and while Helen Henningsen was driving the car on a smooth dry pavement, she heard a loud noise as if something cracked, the steering wheel spun in her hands, and the car veered sharply to the right, crashing into a brick wall. This action was then initiated against Chrysler and Bloomfield Motors and the trial court awarded judgment to the Henningsens. The defendants appealed, arguing among other things (1) that no implied warranties ran from Chrysler to the Henningsens, (2) that there was an effective disclaimer of the implied warranties, and (3) that Helen Henningsen's lack of privity with the defendants barred a breach of warranty action against them.

FRANCIS, JUSTICE

I. The Claim of Implied Warranty against the Manufacturer.   Preliminarily, it may be said that the express warranty against defective parts and workmanship is not inconsistent with an implied warranty of merchantability. Such warranty cannot be excluded for that reason.

Chrysler points out that an implied warranty of merchantability is an incident of a contract of sale. It concedes, of course, the making of the original sale to Bloomfield Motors, Inc., but maintains that this transaction marked the terminal point of its contractual connection with the car. Then Chrysler urges that since it was not a party to the sale by the dealer to Henningsen, there is no privity of contract between it and the plaintiffs, and the absence of this privity eliminates any such implied warranty.

There is no doubt that under early common-law concepts of contractual liability only those persons who were parties to the bargain could sue for a breach of it. In more recent times a noticeable disposition has appeared in a number of jurisdictions to break through the narrow barrier of privity when dealing with sales of goods in order to give realistic recognition to a universally accepted fact. The fact is that the dealer and the ordinary buyer do not, and are not expected to, buy goods, whether they be foodstuffs or automobiles, exclusively for their own consumption or use. Makers and manufacturers know this and advertise and market their products on that assumption; witness, the "family" car, the baby foods, etc. The limitations of privity in contracts for the sale of goods developed their place in the law when marketing conditions were simple, when maker and buyer frequently met face to face on an equal bargaining plane and when many of the products were relatively uncomplicated and conducive to inspection by a buyer competent to evaluate their quality. With the advent of mass marketing, the manufacturer became remote from the purchaser, sales were accomplished through intermediaries, and the demand for the product was created by advertising media. In such an economy it became obvious that the consumer was the person being cultivated. Manifestly, the connotation of "consumer" was broader than that of "buyer." He signified such a person who, in the reasonable contemplation of the parties to the sale, might be expected to use the product.

As far back as 1932, in the well known case of *Baxter* v. *Ford Motor Co.,* the Supreme Court of Washington gave recognition to the impact of the existing commercial practices on the straitjacket of privity, saying:

"It would be unjust to recognize a rule that would permit manufacturers of goods to create a demand for their products by representing that they possess qualities which they, in fact, do not possess, and then, because there is no privity of contract existing between the consumer and the manufacturer, deny the consumer the right to recover if damages result from the absence of those qualities, when such absence is not readily noticeable."

Accordingly, we hold that under modern marketing conditions, when a manufacturer puts a new automobile in the stream of trade and promotes its purchase by the public, an implied warranty that it is reasonably suitable for use as such accompanies it into the hands of the ultimate purchaser. Absence of agency between the manufacturer and the dealer who makes the ultimate sale is immaterial.

II. The Effect of the Disclaimer and Limitation of Liability Clauses on the Implied Warranty of Merchantability.   What effect should be given to the express warranty in question which seeks to limit the manufacturer's liability to replacement of defective parts, and which disclaims all other warranties, express or implied? In assessing its significance we must keep in mind the general principle that, in the absence of fraud, one who does not choose to read a contract before signing it, cannot later relieve himself of its burdens. And in applying that principle, the basic tenet of freedom of competent parties to contract is a factor of importance. But in the framework of modern commercial life and business practices, such rules cannot be applied on a strict, doctrinal basis. The conflicting interests of the buyer and seller must be evaluated realistically and justly, giving due weight to the social policy evinced by the Uniform Sales Act, the progressive decisions of the courts engaged in administering it, the mass production methods of manufacture and distribution to the public, and the bargaining position occupied by the ordinary consumer in such an economy.

What influence should these circumstances have on the restrictive effect of Chrysler's express warranty in the framework of the purchase contract? As we have said, warranties originated in the law to safeguard the buyer and not to limit the liability of the seller or manufacturer. It seems obvious in this instance that the motive was to avoid the warranty obligations which are normally incidental to such sales. The language gave little and withdrew much. In return for the delusive remedy of replacement of defective parts at the factory, the buyer is said to have accepted the exclusion of the maker's liability for personal injuries arising from the breach of the warranty, and to have agreed to the elimination of any other express or implied warranty. An instinctively felt sense of justice cries out against such a sharp bargain. But does the doctrine that a person is bound by his signed agreement, in the absence of fraud, stand in the way of any relief?

The traditional contract is the result of free bargaining of parties who are brought together by the play of the market, and who meet each other on a footing of approximate economic equality. In such a society there is no danger that freedom of contract will be a threat to the social order as a whole. But in present-day commercial life the standardized mass contract has appeared. It is used primarily by enterprises with strong bargaining power and position. "The weaker party, in need of the goods or services, is frequently not in a position to shop around for better terms, either because the author of the standard contract has a monopoly (natural or artificial) or because all competitors use the same clauses. His contractual intention is but a subjection more or less voluntary to terms dictated by the stronger party, terms whose consequences are often understood in a vague way, if at all."

The warranty before us is a standardized form designed for mass use. It is imposed upon the automobile consumer. He takes it or leaves it, and he must take it to buy an automobile. No bargaining is engaged in with respect to it. In fact, the dealer through whom it comes to the buyer is without authority to alter it; his function is ministerial—simply to deliver it. The form warranty is not only standard with Chrysler but, as mentioned above, it is the uniform warranty of the Automobile Manufacturers Association.

The gross inequality of bargaining position occupied by the consumer in the automobile industry is thus apparent. There is no competition among the car makers in the area of the express warranty. Where can the buyer go to negotiate for better protection? Such control and limitation of his remedies are inimical to the public welfare and, at the very least, call for great care by the courts to avoid injustice through application of strict common-law principles of freedom of contract.

It is undisputed that the president of the dealer with whom Henningsen dealt did not specifically call attention to the warranty on the back of the purchase order. The form and the arrangement of its face, as described above, certainly would cause the minds of reasonable men to differ as to whether notice of a yielding of basic rights stemming from the relationship with the manufacturer was adequately given. The words "warranty" or "limited warranty" did not even appear in the fine print above the place for signature, and a jury might well find that the type of print itself was such as to promote lack of attention rather than sharp scrutiny.

Assuming that a jury might find that the fine print referred to reasonably served the objective of directing a buyer's attention to the warranty on the reverse side, and, therefore, that he should be charged with awareness of its language, can it be said that an ordinary layman would realize what he was relinquishing in return for what he was being granted? Under the law, breach of warranty against defective parts or workmanship which caused personal injuries would entitle a buyer to damages even if due care were used in the manufacturing process. Because of the great potential for harm if the vehicle was defective, that right is the most important and fundamental one arising from the relationship. Any ordinary layman of reasonable intelligence, looking at the phraseology, might well conclude that Chrysler was agreeing to replace defective parts and perhaps replace anything that went wrong because of defective workmanship during the first 90 days or 4,000 miles of operation, but that he would not be entitled to a new car. It is not unreasonable to believe that the entire scheme being conveyed was a proposed remedy for physical deficiencies in the car. In the context of this warranty, only the abandonment of all sense of justice would permit us to hold that, as a matter of law, the phrase "its obligation under this warranty being limited to making good at its factory any part or parts thereof" signifies to an ordinary reasonable person that he is relinquishing any personal injury claim that might flow from the use of a defective automobile. Such claims are nowhere mentioned. The draftsmanship is reflective of the care and skill of the Automobile Manufacturers Association in undertaking to avoid warranty obligations without drawing too much attention to its effort in that regard.

Public policy at a given time finds expression in the Constitution, the statutory law and in judicial decisions. In the area of sale of goods, the legislative will has imposed an implied warranty of merchantability as a general incident of sale of an automobile by description. The warranty does not depend upon the affirmative intention of the parties. It is a child of the law; it annexes itself to the contract because of the very nature of the transaction. The judicial process has recognized a right to recover damages for personal injuries arising from a breach of that warranty. The disclaimer of the implied warranty and exclusion of all obligations except those specifically assumed by the express warranty signify a studied effort to frustrate that protection. True, the Sales Act authorizes agreements between buyer and seller qualifying the warranty obligations. But quite obviously the Legislature contemplated lawful stipulations (which are determined by the circumstances of a particular case) arrived at freely by parties of relatively equal bargaining strength. The lawmakers did not authorize the automobile manufacturer to use its grossly disproportionate bargaining power to relieve itself from liability and to impose on the ordinary buyer, who in effect has no real freedom of choice, the grave danger of injury to himself and others that attends the sale of such a dangerous instrumentality as a defectively made automobile. In the framework of this case, illuminated as it is by the facts and the many decisions noted, we are of the opinion that Chrysler's attempted disclaimer of an implied warranty of merchantability and of the obligations arising therefrom is so inimical to the public good as to compel an adjudication of its invalidity.

. . . . .

V. The Defense of Lack of Privity against Mrs. Henningsen. Both defendants contend that since there was no privity of contract between them and Mrs. Henningsen, she cannot recover for breach of any warranty made by either of them. On the facts, as they were developed, we agree that she was not a party to the purchase agreement. Her right to maintain the action, therefore, depends upon whether she occupies such legal status thereunder as to permit her to take advantage of a breach of defendants' implied warranties.

In the present matter, the basic contractual relationship is between Claus Henningsen, Chrysler, and Bloomfield Motors, Inc. The precise issue presented is whether Mrs. Henningsen, who is not a party to their respective warranties, may claim under them. We are convinced that the cause of justice in this area of the law can be served only by recognizing that she is such a person who, in the reasonable contemplation of the parties to the warranty, might be expected to become a user of the automobile. Accordingly, her lack of privity does not stand in the way of prosecution of the injury suit against the defendant Chrysler.

It is our opinion that an implied warranty of merchantability chargeable to either an automobile manufacturer or a dealer extends to the purchaser of the car, members of his family, and to other persons occupying or using it with his consent. It would be wholly opposed to reality to say that use by such persons is not within the anticipation of parties to such a warranty of reasonable suitability of an automobile for ordinary highway operation. Those persons must be considered within the distributive chain.

Section 2–318 of the Uniform Commercial Code proposes that the warranty be extended to "any natural person who is in the family or household of his buyer or who is a guest in his home if it is reasonable to expect that such person may use, consume or be affected by the goods and who is injured in person by breach of the warranty." And the section provides also that "A seller may not exclude or limit the operation" of the extension. A footnote thereto says that beyond this provision "the section is neutral and is not intended to enlarge or restrict the developing case law on whether the seller's warranties, given to his buyer, who resells, extend to other persons in the distributive chain."

It is not necessary in this case to establish the outside limits of the warranty protection. For present purposes, with respect to automobiles, it suffices to promulgate the principle set forth above.

Product Liability

Liability of a manufacturer based on breach of warranty is only one theory of liability included in the area of product liability—the liability of a manufacturer of goods to the user of goods for personal injury or property damage resulting from the use of the goods. Product liability encompasses negligence and so-called strict liability in tort as well as warranty. The scope and nature of the liability of a manufacturer to the user of his product is in a stage of continual change and development. At the least, one should be aware of the movement in the direction of making the manufacturer the insurer of the safety of his product.

Negligence. The early rule was *caveat emptor,* that the buyer had to make his own inspection, rely on his own judgment and assume the risk of any defect in the goods he purchased. Gradually, American courts came to do away with this rule and to hold that a seller of goods is under a duty to exercise the care of a reasonable man to see that the goods do no harm to a buyer.

An important case in this line of cases was *McPherson* v. *Buick Motor Co.*[2] decided in 1916 by the New York Court of Appeals. In that case the manufacturer, Buick Motor Company, was held liable to a subpurchaser for injuries sustained when a wheel collapsed. The court found that Buick was negligent in its inspection of the wheel and was liable in tort on a negligence theory.

---

[2] 111 N.E. 1050 (Ct. App. N.Y. 1916).

Subsequent courts have found liability based on negligence not only where there was a failure to inspect but also for (1) misrepresentation as to the character of the goods or their fitness for a particular purpose, (2) failure to disclose known defects or to warn about known dangers, and (3) failure to use due care in designing and preparing the goods for sale.

In many cases, it would be extremely difficult for an injured person to show the circumstances in the seller's plant at the time a defective product was manufactured. At this point, the doctrine of *res ipsa loquitor* often comes to the injured person's aid. To invoke this doctrine he must show that the cause of the injury was something that lay within the responsibility of the defendant-manufacturer, thus putting the burden on the manufacturer to show it did exercise due care in the circumstances. The defendant-manufacturer can prevail against a suit based on negligence if it can show the defect was one that could not be discovered or avoided by the exercise of all reasonable care or that under the facts and circumstances all reasonable care was in fact exercised.

In the earliest cases the courts held that the manufacturer was liable only to the person with whom he contracted. Today a substantial number of courts allow an injured consumer to recover from the manufacturer in a direct suit. The requirement of privity is dispensed with and the decision have been, as a general rule, based on concepts of public policy or a conduit theory, that is, that the retailer is the conduit through which the product is distributed and that the manufacturer owes the duty of reasonable care directly to the consumer.

Strict Liability.   Once negligence became established as a basis for liability of sellers to the ultimate consumers, an effort was begun to carry the seller's responsibility even further and to hold the seller liable even though he had exercised reasonable care—in effect making him an insurer of the safety of his product. According to Prosser, the rationale for strict liability which has proved convincing to those courts which have accepted it consists of three main arguments: [3]

1. The public interest in human life and safety demands the maximum possible protection that the law can give against dangerous defects in products which consumers must buy, and against which they are helpless to protect themselves; and it justifies the imposition, upon all suppliers of such products, of full responsibility for the harm they cause, even though the supplier has done his best. This argument, which in the last analysis rests upon public sentiment, has had its greatest force in the cases of food, where there was once popular outcry against an evil industry, injuries and actions have multiplied, and public feeling is most obvious. It is now being advanced as to other products, such as automobiles.

2. The maker, by placing the goods upon the market, represents to the public that they are suitable and safe for use; and by packaging, advertising or otherwise, he does

---

[3] William L. Prosser, *Handbook of the Law of Torts* (3d ed.; St. Paul, Minn.: West Publishing Co.), pp. 673–74.

everything that he can to induce that belief. He intends and expects that the product will be purchased and used in reliance upon this assurance of safety; and it is in fact so purchased and used. The middleman is no more than a conduit, a mere mechanical device, through whom the thing sold is to reach the ultimate user. The supplier has invited and solicited the use; and when it leads to disaster, he should not be permitted to avoid the responsibility by saying that he has made no contract with the consumer.

3. It is already possible to enforce strict liability by resort to a series of actions, in which the retailer is first held liable on a warranty to his purchaser, and indemnity on a warranty is then sought successively from other supplier, until the manufacturer finally pays the damages, with the added costs of repeated litigation. This is an expensive, time-consuming, and wasteful process, and it may be interrupted by insolvency, lack of jurisdiction, disclaimers, or the statute of limitations, anywhere along the time.

The essential aspects of strict liability are expressed in Section 402A of the *Restatement of Torts* (Second):

§402A. Special Liability of Seller of Product for Physical Harm to User or Consumer.

(1) One who sells any product in a defective condition unreasonably dangerous to the user or consumer or to his property, is subject to liability for physical harm thereby caused to the ultimate user or consumer, or to his property, if

(a) the seller is engaged in the business of selling such a product, and

(b) it is expected to and does reach the user or consumer without substantial change in the condition in which it is sold.

(2) The rule stated in Subsection (1) applies although

(a) the seller has exercised all possible care in the preparation and sale of his product, and

(b) the user or consumer has not bought the product from or entered into any contractual relation with the seller.

As can be seen from the *Restatement,* the lack of privity of contract is not a defense available to the seller. The crucial elements of strict liability are a "defective condition" at the time the product leaves the seller's hands and which causes harm to a user and which is "unreasonably dangerous" to him or his property—that is, that it is more dangerous than the ordinary consumer would contemplate.

It is important to note that strict liability is not presently accepted by all states with regard to all types of products and all types of defects. Strict liability finds its most common acceptance with sales of food and drink, but is gradually being extended to a wide variety of products that can prove to be unreasonably dangerous because of defective manufacture. And, as presently applied, strict liability can be used against retailers as well as manufacturers of such defective products.

Summary

Product liability encompasses negligence and strict liability as well as warranties. A seller of goods is under a duty to use due care in the design, manufacture or preparation, inspection, and sale of goods; failure to do so may give rise to a cause of action for negligence by a person injured by a defective product.

Strict liability is imposed by some states on the sellers of some types of products. It arises when a product is sold in a defective condition unreasonably dangerous to a user or consumer or to his property and the defective product results in damage to the person or property. Neither lack of privity nor exercise of all possible due care are defenses to an action for strict liability.

Larsen v. General Motors
391 F.2d 495 (8th Cir. 1968)

This was an action by Erling David Larsen (plaintiff) against General Motors (defendant) to recover damages resulting from an alleged negligent design of the steering assembly of a Corvair automobile manufactured and sold by defendant. The District Court rendered summary judgment for General Motors and Larsen appealed. Reversed.

Larsen received severe bodily injuries while driving, with the consent of the owner, a 1963 Chevrolet Corvair. A head-on collision, with the impact occurring on the left front corner of the Corvair, caused a severe rearward thrust of the steering mechanism into Larsen's head.

Larsen did not contend that the design caused the accident but that because of the design he received injuries he would not have otherwise received or, in the alternative, his injuries would not have been as severe. The rearward displacement of the steering shaft on the left frontal impact was much greater on the Corvair than it would be in other cars that were designed to protect against such a rearward displacement. Larsen's complaint alleged (1) negligence in design of the steering assembly; (2) negligent failure to warn of the alleged latent or inherently dangerous condition to the user of the steering assembly placement; and (3) breach of express and implied warranties of merchantability of the vehicle's intended use. General Motors contended that it had no duty to design and manufacture a vehicle otherwise safe or safer to occupy during collision impacts.

GIBSON, CIRCUIT JUDGE.   General Motors contends that it has no duty to produce a vehicle in which it is safe to collide or which is accident-proof or incapable of injurious misuse. It views its duty as extending only to producing a vehicle that is reasonably fit for its intended use or for the purpose for which it was made and that is free from hidden defects; and that the intended use of a vehicle and the purpose for which it is manufactured do not include its participation in head-on collisions or any other type of impact, regardless of the manufacturer's ability to foresee that such collisions may occur.

Larsen maintains that General Motors' view of its duty is too narrow and restrictive and that an automobile manufacturer is under a duty to use reasonable care in the design of the automobile to make it safe to the user for its foreseeable use and that its intended use or purpose is for travel on the streets and highways, including the possibility of impact or collision with other vehicles or stationary objects.

There is a line of cases directly supporting General Motors' contention that negligent design of an automobile is not actionable, where the alleged defective design is not a causative factor in the accident. The latest leading case on this point is *Evans* v. *General Motors Corp.* A divided court there held that General Motors in designing a "X" body frame without perimeter support, instead of an allegedly more safe perimeter body frame, was not liable for the death of a user allegedly caused by the designed defect because the defendant's design could not have functioned to avoid the collision.

In *Shumard* v. *General Motors Corp.*, the United States District Court for the Southern District of Ohio held there was no liability where the alleged design defects in a 1962 Corvair automobile caused it to erupt into flames on impact, killing the plaintiff's decedent. That Court said: ". . . No duty exists to make an automobile fireproof, nor does a manufacturer have to make a product which is 'accident-proof' or 'fool-proof.' "

Generally, as noted in 76 A.L.R. 2d 93, Anno.: Products Liability—Duty As to Design, the manufacturer has a duty to use reasonable care under the circumstances in the design of a product but is not an insurer that his product is incapable of producing injury, and this duty of design is met when the article is safe for its intended use and when it will fairly meet any "emergency of use" which is foreseeable.

Accepting, therefore, the principle that a manufacturer's duty of design and construction extends to producing a product that is reasonably fit for its intended use and free of hidden defects that could render it unsafe for such use, the issue narrows on the proper interpretation of "intended use." Automobiles are made for use on the roads and highways in transporting persons and cargo to and from various points. This intended use cannot be carried out without encountering in varying degrees the statistically proved hazard of injury-producing impacts of various types. The manufacturer should not be heard to say that it does not intend its product to be involved in any accident when it can easily foresee and when it knows that the probability over the life of its product is high, that it will be involved in some type of injury-producing accident. O'Connell in his article "Taming the Automobile," 58 *Nw.U.L.Rev.* 299, 348 (1963) cites that between one-fourth to two-thirds of all automobiles during their use at some time are involved in an accident producing injury or death. Other statistics are available showing the frequency and certainty of fatal and injury-producing accidents. It should be recognized that the environment in which a product is used must be taken into consideration by the manufacturer.

We think the "intended use" construction urged by General Motors is much too narrow and unrealistic. Where the manufacturer's negligence in design causes an unreasonable risk to be imposed upon the user of its products, the manufacturer should be liable for the injury caused by its failure to exercise reasonable care in the design. These injuries are readily foreseeable as an incident to the normal and expected use of an automobile. While automobiles are not made for the purpose of colliding with each other, a frequent and inevitable contingency of normal automobile use will result in collisions and injury-producing impacts. No rational basis exists for limiting recovery to situations where the defect in design or manufacture was the causative factor of the accident, as the accident and the resulting injury, usually caused by the so-called "second collison" of the passenger with the interior part of the automobile, all are foreseeable. Where the injuries or enhanced injuries are due to the manufacturer's failure to use reasonable care to avoid subjecting the user of its products to an unreasonable risk of injury, general negligence principles should be applicable. The sole function of an automobile is not just to provide a means of transportation, it is to provide a means of safe transportation or as safe as is reasonably possible under the present state of the art.

Santor v. A and M Karagheusian, Inc.
207 A.2d 305 (Sup. Ct. N.J. 1965)

This was an action by Daniel Santor (plaintiff) against A and M Karagheusian, Inc. (defendant), to recover damages for defective carpeting. Judgment for Santor in trial court and A and M Karagheusian, Inc., appealed to the Superior Court, Appellate Division, which reversed the decision. An appeal to the Supreme Court was granted and it reversed the judgment of the Appellate Division and granted a new trial.

On September 6, 1957, Santor purchased for his home 96⅔ square yards of Gulistan carpeting from A. P. Davis Company, Inc., a retailer of A and M Karagheusian, Inc. (Karagheusian). Santor, immediately after the carpet was laid, noticed unusual lines in the carpet and telephoned the dealer who advised him it would wear away. The condition worsened and Santor complained of the condition to the dealer who assured him repeatedly that the condition would clear up.

Eight months after delivery Santor decided to "really have it out" with the dealer and drove to his place of business and found the place closed. Finally, sometime in 1960 Santor located the dealer in Maine, had correspondence with him and contacted him by telephone but the dealer refused to make any adjustment of the matter. Santor wrote Karagheusian in September in 1960 complaining about the carpeting and a factory representative examined it but no adjustment was made. Santor brought suit against Karagheusian and on the trial it contended that Santor, not being a privy to the contract between it and the dealer for sale of the carpeting, could not recover for breach of it.

Francis, Justice.   The manufacturer is the father of the transaction. He makes the article and puts it in the channels of trade for sale to the public. No one questions the justice of a rule which holds him liable for defects arising out of the design or manufacture, or other causes while the product is under his control. After completion the article may pass through a series of hands, such as distributor and wholesaler, before reaching the dealer at the point of ultimate intended sale. The dealer is simply a way station, a conduit on its trip from manufacturer to consumer. For these reasons in the recent past the courts of many jurisdictions, in an endeavor to achieve justice for the ultimate consumer, have imposed an implied warranty of reasonable fitness on the person responsible for the existence of the article and the origin of the marketing process. From the standpoint of principle, we perceive no sound reason why the implication of reasonable fitness should be attached to the transaction and be actionable against the manufacturer where the defectively made product has caused personal injury, and not actionable when an inadequate manufacturer has put a worthless article in the hands of an innocent purchaser who has paid the required price for it. In such situations considerations of justice require a court to interest itself in originating causes and to apply the principle of implied warranty on that basis, rather than to test its application by whether personal injury or simply loss of bargain resulted from the breach of the warranty. True, the rule of implied warranty had its gestative stirrings because of the greater appeal of the personal injury claim. But, once in existence, the field of operation of the remedy should not be fenced in by such a factor.

In this developing field of the law, courts have necessarily been proceeding step by step in their search for a stable principle which can stand on its own base as a permanent part of the substantive law. The quest has found sound expression, we believe, in the doctrine of strict liability in tort. Such doctrine stems from the reality of the relationship between manufacturers of products and the consuming public to whom the products are offered for sale. As we indicated in Henningsen, the great mass of the purchasing public has neither adequate knowledge nor sufficient opportunity to determine if articles bought or used are defective. Obviously they must rely upon the skill, care and reputation of the maker. It must be said, therefore, that when the manufacturer presents his goods to the public for sale he accompanies them with a representation that they are suitable and safe for the intended use. As the Supreme Court of California said, "such representation must be regarded as implicit in their presence on the market." *Greenman* v. *Yuba Power Products, Inc.* The obligation of the manufacturer thus becomes what in justice it ought to be—an enterprise liability, and one which should not depend upon the intricacies of the law of sales. The purpose of such liability is to insure that the cost of injuries or damage, either to the goods sold or to other property, resulting from defective products, is borne by the makers of the products who put them in the channels of trade, rather than by the injured or damaged persons who ordinarily are powerless to protect themselves. "Sales warranties," said the court, "serve this purpose fitfully at best."

This strict liability in tort is not conditioned upon advertising to promote sales. It arises from mere presence of the product on the market. In expressing this view, Chief Justice Traynor wrote in Yuba:

Under these circumstances [presence on the market], it should not be controlling whether plaintiff selected the machine because of the statements in the brochure, or because of the machine's own appearance of excellence that belied the defect lurking beneath the surface, or because he merely assumed that it would safely do the jobs it was built to do. It should not be controlling whether the details of the sales from manufacturer to retailer and from retailer to plaintiff's wife were such that one or more of the implied warranties of the sales act arose.

In *Goldberg* v. *Kollsman Instrument Corporation,* the New York Court of Appeals sanctioned a cause of action for breach of an implied warranty of fitness in favor of a passenger against the manufacturer of an airplane which crashed. It said that breach of the warranty was not only a violation of the sales contract out of which it arose, but was "a tortious wrong suable by a noncontracting party whose use of the warranted article is within the reasonable contemplation of the vendor or manufacturer." And, speaking of the Yuba case, Chief Judge Desmond remarked that the "strict tort liability" doctrine referred to there was "surely a more accurate phrase" than breach of implied warranty of suitability for use.

As we have indicated, the strict liability in tort formulation of the nature of the manufacturer's burden to expected consumers of his product represents a sound solution to an ever-growing problem, and we accept it as applicable in this jurisdiction. And, although the doctrine has been applied principally in connection with personal injuries sustained by expected users from products which are dangerous when defective, we reiterate our agreement with *Randy Knitwear, Inc.* v. *American Cyanamid Company,* that the responsibility of the maker should be no different where damage to the article sold or to other property of the consumer is involved. In this era of complex marketing practices and assembly line manufacturing conditions, restrictive notions of privity of contract between manufacturer and consumer must be put aside and the realistic view of strict tort liability adopted. As was done almost 50 years ago in *MacPherson* v. *Buick Motor Co.,* the source of liability must be put "where it ought to be." Its source must be put in the law.

Under the strict liability in tort doctrine, as in the case of express or implied warranty of fitness or merchantability, proof of the manufacturer's negligence in the making or handling of the article is not required. If the article is defective, i.e., not reasonably fit for the ordinary purposes for which such articles are sold and used, and the defect arose out of the design or manufacture or while the article was in the control of the manufacturer, and it proximately causes injury or damage to the ultimate purchaser of reasonably expected consumer, liability exists. Existence of the defect means violation of the representation implicit in the presence of the article in the stream of trade that it is suitable for the general purposes for which it is sold and for which such goods are generally appropriate. As we have said, this representation is found in the law. If it is not a fact—if the article is defective and the defect is chargeable to the manufacturer, his must be the responsibility for the consequent damage or injury. The liability does not depend on traditional requirements for proof of legal or equitable fraud. Considerations of good faith or innocence of the representation or wilfulness of the misrepresentation are immaterial to existence of the cause of action.

Problem Cases

1. Buyer acquired a 1955 Chevrolet Corvette from Seller for $2,800. Sometime later Buyer learns that a prior owner had placed a $3,600 lien on the automobile. Does Buyer have any recourse against Seller?

2. Morris Poultry Company was in the business of butchering and merchandising poultry, at wholesale, for kosher poultry markets. Morris decided to expand by acquiring additional automated equipment and a salesman for Gordon Johnson Company provided them with drawings showing how Johnson equipment would fit into the Morris operation. At the bottom of the drawings were the words "Kosher operation." Morris signed a contract to acquire the equipment; the contract contained a clause warrant-

ing the equipment to be free from defects in material and workmanship and agreeing to replace defective parts within 90 days. The warranty clause went on to say "This warranty to repair is the only warranty either express or implied, on which the Purchaser purchases the Seller's products. . . . All other warranties, implied, express or statutory, are expressly waived by the Buyer." The equipment proved unsatisfactory for a kosher operation and Morris claims there was a breach of the express warranty that the equipment would be satisfactory for kosher operation. Johnson claims this warranty was effectively disclaimed. Who prevails? Why?

3. Kepling purchased a frying pan for $2 to take hunting. It had a light metal cover clamped over the handle to decrease the transmission of heat to the hand of the user. Stamped on the handle were the words "Cold Handle." Mrs. Kepling grabbed the handle and attempted to carry the pan outside the house after grease in the pan caught fire. The handle burned her hand badly. She dropped the pan on the floor and the grease splashed up and burned her seriously. Kepling claims that the words "Cold Handle" constitute an express warranty by the manufacturer that the handle would stay cold. The manufacturer argues it is not liable because there was no reliance by Kepling since she testified she had not seen the words on the handle prior to the accident. Is Kepling entitled to a judgment?

4. Duckworth purchased a new Ford automobile from White on February 28, 1957. The steering mechanism did not function properly and this was mentioned when Duckworth returned the automobile for the 1,000-mile-checkup on March 28, 1957. On April 3, 1957, while driving the automobile, Duckworth attempted to steer it around a gradual turn in the road but, although he pulled on the steering wheel with all his strength, he was unable to turn it, and the car hit an 8 to 12-inch curb, jumped over it and struck a utility pole. The car was demolished and Duckworth was seriously injured. The steering failure resulted from the "locking" of the steering assembly caused when the adjusting screw on the steering assembly backed out and became wedged against the steering assembly cover plate. The locking nut which should have been put on the adjusting screw was omitted in assembling the steering mechanism. Duckworth sued Ford Motor Company for damages for breach of implied warranty of merchantability. Is Duckworth entitled to a judgment?

5. Webster, on April 25, was served a bowl of fish chowder by Blue Ship Tea Room in its restaurant in Boston. After eating three or four spoonfuls of the chowder she was aware that something had lodged in her throat because she couldn't swallow and couldn't clear her throat by gulping, and she could feel something in her throat. Webster had two esophagoscopies at the hospital, in the second of which, on April 27, a fish bone was found and removed. Webster then sued Blue Ship Tea Room for damages allegedly caused by a breach of the implied warranty of merchantability. Is Blue Ship Tea Room liable for breach of this implied warranty?

6. Deris ordered a banana split at a restaurant operated by Finest Foods. After Deris had eaten a portion of her banana split she bit into something hard. She swallowed a mouthful, assuming that what she had bitten into was a piece of ice or a piece of a nutshell. When she took another bite a substance scraped her tongue and she removed it and discovered a few small particles of glass. Deris called the waitress who had served her, who in turn summoned the manager of the restaurant. The manager came to the table and he suggested that Deris call her doctor. The doctor testified that a person may swallow small particles of glass without any direct physical harm resulting. Deris suffered no apparent physical harm but experienced a considerable

amount of mental and emotional anxiety as a result of the incident. Deris brought an action against Finest Foods for her injuries. Can she recover?

7. Vlases, a Greek immigrant, began building a chicken coop in 1958 and completed it in 1961 after working continuously on it during that time. Then he ordered 2,000 day-old chickens from Montgomery Ward. Several months after the chickens arrived it was discovered the flock had bird cancer and bumblefoot, causing the entire flock to die or to be destroyed. Vlases sued Montgomery Ward for breach of implied warranties. The court found the chickens were diseased when delivered but Montgomery Ward sought to defend on the ground the defect was not discoverable by it prior to delivery. Has it stated a good defense to a breach of warranty action?

8. Jackson received a blood transfusion from Hospital using blood supplied by Blood Bank. As a result of the transfusion, Jackson contracted hepatitis. Each bottle of blood furnished by Blood Bank bore in two places in two sizes of type the following disclaimer: "Despite the utmost care in the selection of donors, human blood may contain the virus of Homologous Serum Hepatitis. Therefore Eastern Blood Bank does not warrant against its presence in this blood."

   Jackson sued Hospital and Blood Bank, alleging breach of warranty. Hospital and Blood Bank contend there was no sale, hence no warranty, or, in the alternative, that there was an effective disclaimer of this particular defect. Evaluate these contentions.

9. Willman purchased a Chrysler automobile from Motor Sales Co. on February 28, 1959. On August 16, 1959, the automobile was destroyed by fire. The fire was caused by the malfunction of the power brakes. Willman sued Chrysler Corporation and Motor Sales Co. to recover damages for breach of implied warranty. Chrysler Corporation set up as a defense the following provision of its sales contract: "this warranty [Express Warranty] being expressly in lieu of all other warranties expressed or implied and all other obligations or liabilities on its part." Is this provision a sufficient disclaimer of liability on implied warranties of merchantability and fitness for a particular purpose?

10. The Siters purchased a quantity of tulip and hyacinth bulbs from Vandenberg to be shipped from Holland. The contract contained the following clause of warranty: "The seller warrants the goods to be sound and healthy at the time of shipment but does not otherwise warrant flowering or other planting, growing or forcing results. . . . All claims hereunder shall be deemed waived unless presented within eight (8) days after receipt of goods." An expert examined the bulbs more than eight days after arrival and testified that the bulbs were grown beyond their capacity in Holland and were not merchantable. The trial judge struck this testimony. The Siters contend that this was an error since the express warranty did not conflict with and exclude the implied warranty of merchantability. Vandenberg contends that the express warranty is exclusive. Who should prevail and why?

11. Vroman, age seven, was employed to cut the grass at a gas station owned by his uncle. Vroman pushed the power mower supplied by his uncle over a ball of copper wire and a piece of the wire entered Vroman's left eye causing permanent loss of sight in that eye. The mower had been purchased three years earlier from Sears by Vroman's grandfather. Prior to the accident, the grandfather gave the lawn mower to the uncle. Vroman sues Sears arguing that the company did not warn him of the dangerous potentialities of the mower and did not comply with published safety standards. Sears contends it is not liable because privity is absent. Is this a defense for Sears?

12. Corprew purchased some Atrazine-G for use on his corn crop from a retailer who had purchased the chemical from the manufacturer, Geigy Chemical. The Atrazine-G remained in the original Geigy container until it was opened and used. Corprew applied the chemical to his corn crop according to the directions supplied by Geigy and in reliance upon the representations made on the original container. The container indicated that Atrazine-G was recommended as a weed killer for use in the growing of corn and provided instructions for its use. The only warning given by Geigy was that it did not recommend a subsequent planting of corn within a year after application of the chemical. Corprew planted peanuts and soybeans on the land which had been treated the prior year with the chemical and followed accepted husbandry procedures. The crops harvested from the land which had been treated with Atrazine were lower in quantity and quality than those harvested from land which had not been treated. Geigy had attempted to take Atrazine-G off the market a year prior to Corprew's purchase because the chemical had produced injurious effects on succeeding crops. Corprew argues that Geigy was negligent and is liable for the damage to his crops. Is Geigy liable on this theory? In what ways might Geigy be found to have been negligent?

13. LaGorga, age five, was playing on the premises of a public school near a metal barrel in which refuse was burning. He was wearing a jacket which had been given to him as a Christmas present by his cousin. LaGorga and another child were poking sticks through holes in the barrel. A spark from the fire landed on LaGorga's coat and it burst into flames. The playmate tried to extinguish the burning coat by rubbing dirt on it but failed; she then tried to pull the zipper down but it stuck. LaGorga panicked and ran toward his home. He was noticed by an adult who threw him to the ground and extinguished the fire with considerable difficulty. LaGorga received burns covering 80 percent of his body, but he survived. The jacket was purchased at a Kroger Store. It was not packaged and was displayed on a table in the store with other similar unpackaged jackets. It was not labeled; there was no identity of the fabrics used in its outer shell, interlining or inner lining. There was no warning that it had not been treated with flame retardant. The jacket was designed with a cotton shell, interlining of mill waste comprised a 50 percent acrylic fibers and 50 percent unknown material interspersed with air pockets, and an acetate inner lining. It was established that synthetics of the type used in the jacket tend to melt rather than burn and produce high temperatures; also that when ignited and not immediately extinguished, severe and deep burns are inflicted. LaGorga contends that Kroger is liable for the injuries he received. Is Kroger liable and if so, on what ground?

14. Bailey, age 11, was playing with his brother's pogo stick when it came apart and struck him in the eye. Bailey's mother had seen the pogo stick advertised in the newspaper and she ordered it through the Montgomery Ward catalog as a Christmas gift for Bailey's younger brother. The pogo stick was obtained in a sealed box from Wards and was opened once by Bailey's father before Christmas. It was not opened again until Christmas morning when the younger brother opened it. The brother took the stick outside and used it several times and brought it back into the house. It remained there until Bailey took it outside and jumped on it a few times. He then came in bleeding from the eye saying that the pogo stick had injured him. Bailey contends that the product was defective and that Wards is liable for his injuries on a strict liability theory. Is Bailey correct?

15. Magrine was a patient of Krasnica, a dentist. Krasnica administered a local anesthetic by inserting a hypodermic needle into Magrine's jaw. The needle had been

assembled by Krasnica just before the injection and had been used approximately eight times for about three weeks prior to the accident. As the injection was being made the needle separated at the hub, leaving the 1⅝-inch length of the needle in Magrine's jaw. Krasnica did not know what caused the needle to break, but he believed there must have been a defect in it. He did not know from whom he purchased the needle. Magrine brought an action to recover for injuries sustained as a result of the accident. She makes no assertion that Krasnica was negligent. Magrine argues that strict liability is not confined to sales and that the basic policy considerations of the doctrine apply to the use of a needle by Krasnica even though he was not negligent. Krasnica contends policy considerations preclude the application of a strict liability theory under these circumstances. Should strict liability be applied?

chapter 35. Performance

Introduction

General Rules. The basic rules relative to the performance of a sales contract do not differ in any material respect from the rules of performance as applied to general contracts. In the event of a dispute it is the duty of the court to interpret the contract, determine the nature and scope of the obligations assumed by the parties, and decide whether such obligations have been fulfilled. Rules for the interpretation of sales contracts are set out in the Code. Where the contract of sale involves repeated occasions for performance by either party with knowledge of the performance and opportunity for objection to it by the other, any course of performance accepted or acquiesced in without objection shall be relevant to determine the meaning of the agreement. (2–208 [1].) [1]

Course of Dealing and Usage of Trade. In determining the obligations of the parties the express terms of the agreement and any course of performance, as well as any course of dealing and usage of trade, shall be construed whenever consistent with each other; but when such construction is unreasonable, express terms shall control course of performance, and course of performance shall control both course of dealing and usage of trade. (2–208 [2].)

Modification, Rescission, and Waiver. Under the general rules of contract law, the modification or rescission of a contract, to be effective, must be supported by consideration; a waiver need not be supported by consideration. Under the Code, consideration is not required to support a modification or rescission but a signed writing which excludes modification or rescission cannot be modified or rescinded except by a signed writing. Except as between

---

[1] The numbers in the parentheses refer to the sections of the Uniform Commercial Code, 1962.

merchants, a modification or rescission of a provision in a form supplied by the merchant must be separately signed by the other party. An inoperative agreement of modification or rescission can operate as a waiver. (2–209.)

A promisee who accepts, without objection, late payments on an installment contract for a substantial period of time will have waived his right to declare a forfeiture for failure of the promisor to make his payments when due. However, if the promisee gives the promisor reasonable notice that future payments must be made on time he may thereafter declare a forfeiture of the contract for late payment. This concept is made a rule under Section 2–209 (5) of the Code which provides that a party who has made a waiver affecting an executory portion of the contract may retract the waiver by reasonable notification received by the other party that strict performance will be required of any term waived, unless the retraction would be unjust in view of a material change of position in reliance on the waiver.

Assignment and Delegation.   The basic principles of the assignment of contracts are discussed in Chapter 13. Some of the rules of law and the standards developed under these basic principles, when applied to sales contracts, do not give desirable and realistic results. Under the Code the basic principles have been retained but there is a liberalization of their application to sales contracts, particularly in regard to the delegation of duties. The courts have generally recognized the right of the promisee in a sales contract to assign his rights but they have been reluctant to recognize the right of either party to delegate his duties.

Under the Code the right of the promisor to delegate his duties is recognized unless the parties agree that the duties shall not be delegated or unless the other party has a substantial interest in having his original promisor perform or control the acts required by the contract. In keeping with basic principles, the promisor cannot relieve himself from his responsibility for the performance of the contract by delegating his duties under it. (2–210 [1].) As an additional protection the promisee may, without prejudicing his rights against the promisor, demand assurance from the assignee. (2–210 [5].)

Unless the circumstances indicate the contrary, a prohibition of assignment of "the contract" is to be construed as barring only the delegation to the assignee of the assignor's performance. (2–210 [3].) An assignment of "the contract" or "of all my rights under the contract" includes a delegation of duties unless otherwise agreed or unless circumstances clearly indicate a contrary intent. (2–210 [4].)

Cooperation Respecting Performance.   The leaving of particulars of performance to be specified by one of the parties does not affect the validity of an otherwise enforceable contract. Also, specifications as to assortment of the goods may be left to the option of the buyer and, subject to some limitations, specifications relating to shipment are at the option of the seller. In the performance of a sales contract each party owes a duty to give to the other party reasonable cooperation in the performance and each must act in good faith and within the bounds of that which is commercially reasonable. (2–311.)

Summary

The basic rules of contract law relative to the performance of contracts apply to sales contracts. The conduct of the parties, course of dealing, and usage of trade are considered and weighed in determining the duties of performance of the parties to a sales contract. Under the provisions of the Code an agreement to modify or rescind a contract need not be supported by consideration to be valid. A waiver may be retracted if reasonable notice of retraction is given before the other party has changed his position in reliance on the waiver.

The rules relative to the assignment of rights and the delegation of duties under a sales contract have been liberalized by the Code provisions. An assignment of a sales contract, unless otherwise agreed, includes the delegation of duties, and a general prohibition of the assignment of a contract bars only the delegation of duties. The assignor does not relieve himself of his liability for the performance of the contract by the delegation of his duties.

Granting to the buyer and seller options as to performance of a sales contract does not affect the validity of a contract which is otherwise valid. Each party must act in good faith and within the scope of that which is commercially reasonable in exercising his options and must cooperate in a reasonable manner in the performance of the contract.

Associated Hardware Supply Co. v. The Big Wheel Distributing Co.

236 F.Supp. 879 (W.D. Pa. 1965)

This was an action by Associated Hardware Supply Co. (plaintiff) against The Big Wheel Distributing Co. (defendant) to recover a judgment for the unpaid balance of the purchase price of goods sold and delivered. Judgment for Associated Hardware Supply Co.

Associated Hardware Supply Co. (Supply Co.) on February 9, 1962, offered to sell to The Big Wheel Distributing Co. (Distributing Co.) merchandise, subject to a volume of $5,000 per week, at catalogue price which was based on a 20 percent markup less 11 percent discount. This offer was not formally accepted but dealings went ahead and between February, 1962, and May, 1964, Supply Co. shipped $800,000 worth of merchandise which Distributing Co. accepted and paid for at the invoice price of 11 percent discount from catalogue price. Distributing Co. refused to pay for $40,185.62 worth of merchandise which had been shipped by Supply Co. and accepted by Distributing Co. When sued for this unpaid balance Distributing Co. set up as a defense that the Supply Co. had agreed to sell it merchandise at cost plus 10 percent and that Supply Co. had been overpaid an amount in excess of the balance in suit, and Distributing Co. filed a counterclaim for over-payment.

DUMBAULT, DISTRICT JUDGE.   Section 1–205 (1) says: "A course of dealing is a sequence of previous conduct between the parties to a particular transaction which is in fact fairly to be regarded as establishing a common basis of understanding for interpreting their words and conduct."

Section 1–205 (3) provides: "The parties to a contract are bound by any course of dealing between them."

Section 1–205 (4) (a) declares that "Unless contrary to a mandatory rule of this Act: (a) A course of dealing . . . gives particular meaning to and supplements or qualifies terms of the agreement."

Section 2–208 provides: "Where the contract for sale involves repeated occasions for performance by either party with knowledge of the nature of the performance and opportunity for objection by the other, any course of performance accepted without objection shall be relevant to determine the meaning of the agreement or to show a waiver or modification of any term inconsistent with such course of performance."

Review of the foregoing Code provisions shows that the Code attaches great weight to the course of dealing of the parties, even in the absence of a written agreement with respect to every term of the contract. Weighing in the light of the Code the conduct of the parties here, it seems clear that the mode of calculating price set forth in Supply Company's letter of February 9, 1962, although not accepted formally by signature of a copy, was adhered to by both parties during an extensive course of dealing, during which Distributing Co. received, accepted, and paid for over $800,000 worth of merchandise. This course of dealing must be held applicable and governing with respect to the remaining merchandise which has been received and accepted but not paid for. Judgment should be rendered for Supply Co. for the amount due.

Delivery

General Rules.   Delivery terms F.O.B. and F.A.S. were discussed in Chapter 32. Unless otherwise agreed all of the goods called for by a sales contract must be tendered in a single delivery and the buyer owes a duty to accept and pay for the goods if they conform to the contract. Under some circumstances delivery in a single lot may not be practical, and if the circumstances are such that either party has the right to demand or make delivery in lots, the price of each lot may be demanded on delivery if the price can be proportioned and if there is no agreement for the extension of credit. (2–307.)

As to the place of delivery, the Code makes no material change in pre-Code law. Unless otherwise agreed the place of delivery is the seller's place of business, or if he has no place of business, then at his house. If the goods are identified and are known by the parties at the time of contracting to be in some place other than the seller's place of business or house, that place is the place of delivery. If the goods are represented by documents of title, such documents may be delivered through banking channels. (2–308.)

Seller's Duties of Delivery. A seller owes a duty to tender delivery of conforming goods in fulfillment of the sales contract. Tender of delivery requires the seller to put and hold conforming goods at the buyer's disposition and give him any notice reasonably necessary to enable him to take delivery. The tender must be made at a reasonable hour and the goods must be kept available for a time reasonably necessary to enable the buyer to take possession. The buyer, unless otherwise agreed, must furnish facilities reasonably suited for the receipt of the goods. (2–503 [1].) The seller's duties respecting shipment were discussed in Chapter 32.

Where the goods are in the possession of a bailee and the bailee has issued a negotiable warehouse receipt for the goods, the seller must endorse, if required for transfer, and deliver the warehouse receipt to the buyer. In other situations the seller must do that which is necessary to notify the bailee that the goods have been transferred to a buyer and obtain the bailee's consent to hold the goods for the buyer. The goods are at the risk of the seller until the bailee agrees to hold them for the buyer. If the seller is to deliver documents he must tender all necessary documents and they must be in correct form. Documents may be delivered through banking channels. (2–503.)

If the seller is to ship the goods, but not to deliver them at destination, he must put the goods in possession of the carrier, make a reasonable contract of carriage, obtain the usual documents in correct form, and promptly notify the buyer of the shipment. If material delay or loss results from the seller's failure to make a reasonable contract of carriage or to notify the buyer of the shipment, the buyer will have the right to reject the shipment. (2–504.)

If the seller is permitted, under the provisions of the sales contract, to retain a security interest in the goods until accepted and paid for, he may do so by shipping the goods on a negotiable bill of lading drawn to his own order or to the order of a financing agency or to the order of a nominee. A nonnegotiable bill of lading consigning the goods to the seller or his nominee reserves a security interest in the goods; if it consigns the goods to the buyer, it does not. The seller's shipment under reservation does not alter the relations of the buyer and seller in any respect other than as to the seller's security interest in the goods.

Shipment under reservation, where it is a breach of the sales contract, constitutes an improper contract of transportation but it impairs neither the rights given to the buyer by shipment and identification of the goods to the contract nor the seller's powers as a holder of a negotiable document. (2–505.)

When the seller tenders delivery of the goods to the buyer, he (the buyer) owes a duty to accept them and, unless otherwise agreed, to pay for them. The buyer's right to retain documents of title or goods is conditioned on his making the payment due. (2–507.)

If a seller tenders goods nonconforming and they are rejected he may, if time for delivery has not expired or if the seller had had reasonable grounds to believe they would be accepted, notify the buyer of his intention to cure the defect and may, within the time allowed for delivery or within a reasonable time, as the case may be, cure the defect by tendering conforming goods. (2–508.)

Summary

The seller owes a duty to tender conforming goods in fulfillment of the sales contract. Tender must be made at a reasonable time and the buyer must provide reasonable facilities for the acceptance of the goods. If the seller is to ship the goods he must deliver conforming goods to the carrier and make a reasonable contract of transportation. If the sales contract permits, the seller may ship the goods under reservation by shipping them on a negotiable bill of lading drawn to his order or to the order of a financing agency or to a nominee. If he ships the goods on a nonnegotiable bill of lading he can retain a security interest in them by consigning them to himself or a nominee. Where delivery of conforming goods is tendered, the buyer owes a duty to accept and make any payment due. If nonconforming goods are tendered and rejected the seller is given, under limitations stated, the right to cure the defective tender.

Inspection and Payment

Buyer's Right of Inspection.   Unless otherwise agreed, the buyer has the right to inspect the goods before he accepts or pays for them. The time and place of inspection may be determined by the agreement of the parties. In the absence of an agreement, if the seller is to send the goods the inspection may be made after arrival. In other situations the buyer may inspect the goods at any reasonable place and time and in any reasonable manner.

If the goods conform to the contract the buyer must pay the expenses of inspection but if the goods are nonconforming he may recover the expense of inspection from the seller. If the shipping terms are C.O.D. or payment against documents, the buyer must pay before inspection unless the goods are marked "inspection allowed." If the parties have agreed as to time, place, and method of inspection such agreement will control.

Where the contract requires payment before inspection, nonconformity of the goods does not excuse the buyer from payment unless the nonconformity is obvious without inspection. For example, if the contract called for the delivery of a horse and the seller tendered a cow, the buyer would be fully justified in rejecting the tender. Payment before inspection does not deprive the buyer of any of his remedies against the seller if the goods prove to be nonconforming. (2–512.)

Payment. The price of the goods may be paid in money, goods, realty, or otherwise. If all or part of the price is payable in realty the transfer of the goods and the seller's obligations in reference to them is subject to the law of sales but the transfer of the interest in the realty and transferor's obligations in connection therewith is subject to real estate law. (2–304.)

Unless the goods are sold on credit the buyer must pay on delivery or tender of the goods after he has inspected. If the goods are shipped under reservation the buyer must pay on arrival of the goods, after inspection. If the terms are C.O.D. or C.I.F. the buyer must pay on arrival of the documents. (2–310.) Unless otherwise agreed documents against which a draft is drawn are to be delivered to the drawee on acceptance of the draft if it is payable more than three days after presentment; otherwise, only on payment. (2–514.)

The buyer may make payment by personal check or any other means current in the ordinary course of business unless the seller demands payment in money and gives any extension of time reasonably necessary to procure it. Payment by check is conditional on the check being paid on presentment. (2–511.)

Summary

In general, the buyer has the right to inspect the goods before acceptance and payment. The place, time, and method of inspection may be fixed by the agreement of the parties. In the absence of agreement, if the goods are to be sent by the seller the place of inspection is the destination of the goods; otherwise at a time, place, and manner reasonable under the circumstances. If the goods are conforming the buyer pays the expense of inspection; if nonconforming, the seller pays the expense.

Unless there is an agreement for credit, payment must be made after inspection of the goods on tender or delivery of the goods or documents of title. Payment may be made by check or any manner current in the ordinary course of business unless the seller demands legal tender.

In re Lindenbaum's, Inc.

2 U.C.C. Rep. 495 (E.D. Pa. 1964)

This was an action to reclaim the value of goods shipped to Lindenbaum's, Inc., and in the hands of the trustee in the bankrupt estate of Lindenbaum's, Inc. The reclamation petition was granted.

On October 14, 1963, Modern Tufting Company (Modern) shipped from Dalton, Georgia, a C.O.D. shipment of carpeting for delivery to Lindenbaum's Inc., at Philadelphia, Pa. The carrier was authorized to accept Lindenbaum's check in payment.

The shipment was delivered to Lindenbaum's October 17, 1963. Upon delivery, Lindenbaum's gave to the carrier its check to the order of Modern in the sum of $382.34 drawn on the Central-Penn National Bank of Philadelphia. The check was received by Modern from the carrier about November 1, 1963, and immediately deposited in its account in the Bank of Dalton, Georgia. The check was returned by the bank because of the intervening bankruptcy of Lindenbaum's on October 28, 1963.

Both on October 17, 1963, and October 28, 1963, the balance in Lindenbaum's account in the Central-Penn National Bank was in excess of $382.34.

CURTIN, REFEREE IN BANKRUPTCY.   At the outset it must be recognized that the sale here was not a sale on credit. It was a cash sale under Section 2–507 (2) of the Uniform Commercial Code of Pennsylvania. Sec. 2–507 (2) providing:

"Where payment is due and demanded on delivery to the buyer of the goods . . . his right against the seller to retain or dispose of them is conditioned upon the making of the payment due."

Section 2–511 (3) of the Uniform Commercial Code provides:

"Sec. 2–511 Tender of Payment by Buyer; Payment by Check.

"(3) Subject to the provisions of this Act on the effect of an instrument on an obligation (Section 3–802), payment by check is conditional and is defeated as between the parties by dishonor of the check on due presentment."

The official comment to that subsection states:

"Subsection (3) is concerned with the rights and obligations as between the parties to a sales transaction where payment is made by check. This Article recognizes that the taking of a seemingly solvent party's check is commercially normal and proper and, if due diligence is exercised in collection, is not to be penalized in any way."

The delay in depositing, from October 17 to November 1, is not unreasonable.

The Petition directing the return of the sum in question is granted.

Acceptance; Revocation; Rejection

What Constitutes Acceptance. If a buyer, after he has inspected the goods purchased or has been given a reasonable opportunity to inspect them, signifies to the seller that he will take the goods as they are or fails to reject them, he will be held to have accepted them. Furthermore, if a buyer does any act inconsistent with the seller's ownership, such act will constitute an acceptance of the goods. He cannot, however, by such act deprive the seller of rights he has in the goods unless the seller ratifies the buyer's acts. The acceptance of a part of a commercial unit is acceptance of that entire unit. (2–606.)

Effect of Acceptance. If only a part of the goods purchased are accepted by the buyer he must pay for that part at the rate of the contract price. If the buyer accepts nonconforming goods he cannot at a later date reject them unless at the time he accepts them he has reason to believe that the nonconformity will be cured. A buyer does not, by acceptance, forfeit or waive his remedies against a seller for nonconformities in the goods but he must, if he wishes to hold the seller, give him seasonable notice that the goods were nonconforming. The burden is on the buyer to establish any breach with respect to goods accepted.

In the event the buyer is sued for infringement or for breach of warranty under conditions where he would have a right of action over against the seller, the buyer will be barred from such right unless he gives the seller notice of the suit thus providing him (the seller) an opportunity to defend. (2–607.)

Revocation of Acceptance. A buyer may revoke an acceptance of nonconforming goods if such nonconformity substantially impairs the value of the goods and if he has accepted them without discovering the nonconformity and his acceptance was induced either by the difficulty of discovery or by the assurance of the seller.

A buyer must exercise his right to revoke his acceptance within a reasonable time after he discovers or should have discovered the grounds for it and before there has been any substantial change in the goods. Such a revocation is not effective until the buyer notifies the seller. The buyer's rights, after he has revoked his acceptance, are the same as though he had rejected them when delivery was tendered. (2–608.)

Buyer's Rights on Improper Delivery. As a general rule, if goods tendered to the buyer do not conform to the contract he has an election: He may reject all of the goods, accept all, or accept any commercial unit or units and reject the rest, paying for the units accepted at the contract rate. He will not be permitted to accept part of a commercial unit and reject the rest. (2–601.)

However, if the contract is an installment contract in that it requires or authorizes delivery in separate lots to be separately accepted, the buyer's options are more limited. The buyer may reject a nonconforming installment if the nonconformity substantially impairs the value of that installment and cannot be cured; but if the nonconformity is not so great as to substantially impair the value of the whole contract and the seller gives assurance that the nonconformity will be cured, then the buyer must accept that installment. The official Comments to the Uniform Commercial Code provide that assurance of cure includes an allowance in price for the nonconformity. (2–612.)

Where the nonconformity or defect in one installment impairs the value of the whole contract, the buyer may treat it as a breach of the whole contract but must proceed carefully so as not to reinstate the remainder of the contract. (2–612.)

Manner of Rejection and Duties after Rejection. A buyer, if he elects to reject the goods, must act within a reasonable time after delivery or tender and must seasonably notify the seller of his rejection. If a buyer has paid part or all of the purchase price of rejected goods he will have a security interest in the rejected goods to the extent of payments made. (2–602.)

A merchant buyer, subject to any security interest he may have in the goods, when the seller has no place of business or agent at the market of rejection, is under a duty, if the goods are in his possession or under his control, to follow any reasonable instructions given by the seller as to the disposition of the goods. If the seller refuses or fails to give instructions and the goods are perishable or threaten to decline in value speedily the buyer owes a duty to make a reasonable effort to sell the goods for the benefit of the seller. The seller, if he gives instructions to the buyer, is bound, if demanded by the buyer, to give indemnity for expenses incurred in carrying out the instructions. (2–603 [1].)

If the buyer sells rejected goods under the circumstances set out above, he is entitled to reimbursement out of the proceeds for expenses incurred and to a commission as is usual in the trade. In making a sale the buyer must act in good faith. (2–603 [2] [3].)

If the rejected goods are not perishable or if there is no reason to believe they will decline in value speedily, the buyer may store the goods for the seller's account or reship them or resell them for the seller's account and reimburse himself for expenses plus a commission out of the proceeds. (2–604.)

After rejection and notice the buyer has no right to exercise ownership over the goods other than to fulfill his rights and duties as set out above. The buyer must exercise reasonable care in handling rejected goods in his possession and must hold them for a time sufficient to permit the seller to remove them. The buyer has no further obligations with regard to goods rightfully rejected. If the buyer wrongfully rejects goods he is liable to the seller for breach of the sales contract. (2–602 [2] [3].)

Failure to Particularize.   If the buyer, on rejection, fails to state in connection with his rejection a particular defect which is ascertainable by reasonable inspection, he will not be permitted to set up such defect to justify his rejection if the seller could have cured the defect had he been given reasonable notice of it. In a transaction taking place between merchants, the seller has, after rejection, a right to a written statement of all the defects in the goods on which the buyer bases his right to reject and the buyer will not be permitted to set up defects not listed in justification of his rejections. If payment against documents is made without reservation of rights, the buyer cannot recover the payments made if defects in the document are apparent on its face. (2–605.)

Summary

An acceptance of goods occurs when a buyer indicates to the seller, after he (the buyer) has inspected the goods or has had an opportunity to inspect them, that he will keep them in fulfillment of the seller's obligation or when he exercises acts of ownership over them inconsistent with the seller's ownership. Acceptance of any part of a commercial unit is acceptance of the entire unit. The buyer must pay for goods accepted at the contract rate. If the buyer accepts nonconforming goods, he must, if he wishes to hold the seller liable, give him seasonable notice that the goods are nonconforming. If the buyer is sued for infringement or breach of warranty and he has a right over against the seller, the buyer must give the seller notice that the suit has been brought and thus provide him (the seller) an opportunity to defend.

A buyer may revoke an acceptance where he has grounds for revocation if he acts within a reasonable time and if he gives the seller reasonable notice of his revocation.

The buyer, if the contract is an installment contract, has the right to reject any nonconforming installment if the non-conformity substantially impairs the value of the installment and cannot be cured. The seller may cure the defect, but if the defect impairs the value of the whole contract it is a breach of the whole contract.

If nonconforming goods are tendered, the buyer may reject all, accept all, or accept any commercial unit and reject the rest. The buyer has a security interest in rejected goods for any payment made. On rejection, if the goods are in the buyer's possession or control, he owes a duty to use reasonable care to protect the goods. He must hold them for a period sufficient to permit the seller to remove them; if the seller does not have a place of business or agent in the market, the buyer must follow the seller's instructions relative to disposition of the goods and if no instructions are given the buyer must, if the goods are perishable or subject to speedy change in value, sell them for the seller's account. If the goods are not perishable he may store, reship, or sell them for the seller's account. The buyer is entitled to reimbursement for the expenses plus commission. If the buyer wrongfully rejects goods he is liable to the seller for breach of contract.

Hudspeth Motors, Inc. v. *Wilkinson*
382 S.W.2d 191 (Sup. Ct. Ark. 1964)

This was an action by Hudspeth Motors, Inc. (plaintiff) against O. N. Wilkinson (defendant) to recover a judgment for the unpaid balance of the purchase price of a truck. Judgment for Wilkinson and Hudspeth Motors, Inc., appealed. Judgment reversed.

Wilkinson purchased a used truck from Hudspeth Motors, Inc. (Hudspeth), on February 13, 1962. Wilkinson claimed that the truck was represented to him to be in good repair, that it did not use oil, and that it was suitable for use on his milk route. He further claimed that on the first day he drove the truck on his route of from 80 to 85 miles, it used two quarts of oil. He also claimed that the two-speed mechanism did not work properly. He claimed that he attempted to report this but he never reported it to any official or agent of Hudspeth's. Wilkinson made two payments on the truck during a five-month period. He drove the truck daily for a period of several months. On June 19, 1962, the engine blew up and he hired a mechanic to dismantle the engine and see how badly it was damaged. There was no proof to indicate that the explosion was due to defects that existed at the time Wilkinson bought the truck. Wilkinson set up breach of warranty as a defense.

SMITH, JUSTICE.   Under the Code if the truck did not conform to the terms of the contract Wilkinson was required to reject it within a reasonable time, notifying the seller of his decision. §§ 2–601 and 2–602. His failure to make an effective rejection amounted to an acceptance. § 2–606. Although the buyer could have revoked his acceptance if it had been induced by the seller's assurances that the defects would be corrected, § 2–608, there is no such proof in this case. Wilkinson did not testify that anyone at Hudspeth Motors ever led him to believe that the vehicle could or would be put into good condition.

Rozmus v. Thompson's Lincoln-Mercury Co.

224 A.2d 782 (Super. Ct. Pa. 1966)

This was an action by Rozmus (plaintiff) against Thompson's Lincoln-Mercury (defendant) to recover the sales price of a used automobile that Rozmus had traded in on a new automobile. Judgment for Thompson's Lincoln-Mercury and Rozmus appealed. New trail ordered.

On Saturday, June 22, 1963, Rozmus signed an agreement to purchase a new Mercury. He paid $50 down, traded in the old car, and promised to pay the balance within five days. The contract contained a clause acknowledging Rozmus' acceptance of the new car in good order. While driving the automobile home that evening he noticed smoke coming from the exhaust and that the car made a loud, banging and thumping sound. Rozmus immediately called Thompson's salesman and, as it was Saturday, was told to bring the car in on Monday. In accordance with this request, Rozmus returned the car to Thompson's on Monday. Tuesday evening he called for it but upon driving it ascertained that the loud banging and thumping noise persisted. Rozmus immediately returned the car and sought out Stewart, Thompson's general manager, who confirmed the trouble in a test drive. Stewart and Rozmus then returned to the garage where Stewart instructed a mechanic to place the car upon a rack and to see what was causing the noise. Before the mechanic could correct the source of the trouble, which turned out to be two loose engine mounting bolts allowing a misalignment of the drive shaft to occur, Rozmus told Mr. Stewart he wanted another car or the return of the one he had traded in. His demands not being met, he left without taking the new automobile with him. The Mercury automobile was fully adjusted within a few minutes by Thompson's, but Rozmus never returned for it.

Soon after leaving the new automobile with Thompson's, Rozmus brought an action before a justice of the peace for the sale price of the traded Chevrolet car, $361.50. The question before the appeal court in this case was whether Rozmus had the right to revoke acceptance of the new automobile.

MONTGOMERY, JUSTICE. The law on the issue before us is found in § 2–608 which provides that a buyer may revoke his acceptance of goods received if its "nonconformity substantially impairs its value to him." There is no doubt that Rozmus accepted this new automobile. He executed the conditional sales contract which provided that he acknowledged the acceptance of the Mercury in good order, and he drove it from the showroom to his home. Section 2–606 provides that acceptance takes force when the buyer either signifies his acceptance to the seller or does an act inconsistent with the seller's ownership.

The reason why "a substantial impairment of value" must take place before a revocation under § 2–608 may take force is to preclude revocation for trivial defects or defects which may be easily corrected.

It seems clear from reading said § 2–608 that revocation of an acceptance of delivery is now permissible only if the nonconformity substantially impairs the value of the article which has been accepted either (a) on the reasonable assumption that its nonconformity would be cured and it has not been reasonably cured; or (b), without discovery of such nonconformity the acceptance was reasonably induced either by the difficulty of discovery before acceptance or by the seller's assurances. In the present case, Rozmus did not discover the nonconformity before he accepted the automobile as no opportunity to drive it before acceptance was afforded him, and he accepted on the basis of the usual warranties (assurances) which are part of new car sales.

If we review the evidence in the light most favorable to Thompson's, giving it the benefit of all reasonable inferences therefrom by reason of the original decision of Judge McCarthy being in its favor, we would be justified in concluding that the defect did not substantially impair the value of the automobile. . . . The only evidence in the case concerning the defect or nonconformity is that, due to an improper adjustment of the engine supports the drive shaft was moved out of line, which caused a bumping or thumping noise when the rear seat was fully occupied. When the cause was determined it was remedied within a few minutes by Thompson's mechanic. We find nothing in the record to justify a finding that Thompson's agreed to accept the return of the automobile. The evidence is to the contrary, and indicates that Rozmus abandoned the automobile when he left it in Thompson's repair shop.

Assurance, Repudiation, Breach, and Excuse

Assurance. If the circumstances are such that either party, tested by commercial standards, is justified in believing that the other party will be unable to perform his obligations under the contract, he may demand assurance of performance. Failure to provide assurance within 30 days after a justified demand is a repudiation of the contract. (6–609.)

Anticipatory Repudiation. If either party repudiates the contract the aggrieved party may await performance for a commercially reasonable time, or resort to any remedy for breach of the contract. The aggrieved party on repudiation of the contract may suspend further performance on his part or proceed to exercise his right to identify goods to the contract or to salvage unfinished goods. (2–610.)

If a party has repudiated his contract he may withdraw his repudiation provided he gives adequate notice to the aggrieved party and such party has not canceled the contract or materially changed his position. (2–611.)

Excuse. Under the Code excuse for the failure to perform a sales contract follows closely the general rules of contract law relative to impossibility. Commercial impracticability is substituted for impossibility in most situations. If goods required for the performance of the contract and identified to it are destroyed, the contract is avoided. If they are damaged or have deteriorated, the buyer at his option may either treat the contract as avoided or accept the goods with due allowance from the purchase price. (2–613.)

If the agreed means of transportation or of payment are not available at the time of performance but a commercially reasonable substitute transportation is available, it must be used and a substituted method of payment may be used provided the seller receives a substantial equivalent. (2–614.)

A seller is excused from delay in delivery or nondelivery in whole or in part if his failure to perform is the result of unforeseen or unforeseeable conditions which make performance impracticable. If only part of the seller's capacity to perform is affected he may allocate his production among his customers. In such a situation the seller owes a duty to notify the buyer seasonably of his allocation. (2–615.) The buyer, on receipt of the notice, may by written notification to the seller as to any delivery concerned, and where the prospective deficiency substantially impairs the value of the whole contract, terminate and discharge any unexecuted portion of the contract or agree to accept his available quota in substitution. If the buyer does not modify his contract within 30 days after receipt of notice from the seller the contract lapses with respect to any deliveries affected. (2–616.)

Summary

If either party to a sales contract deems himself insecure, as tested by commercial standards, he may demand assurance before he proceeds with his performance. If a party repudiates a sales contract the aggrieved party may wait or he may bring an action for breach of the contract. In event of repudiation the usual remedies for the breach of the sales contract are available to the aggrieved party. If the party who has repudiated a sales contract wishes to withdraw his repudiation he may do so by giving the aggrieved party notice of his withdrawal before such party has canceled the contract or materially changed his position in reliance on the repudiation.

A party to a sales contract is excused from performance if his performance, due to no fault on his part, becomes commercially impracticable. If the impracticability is as to means of transportation or means of payment, substituted means, if available, may be resorted to. If the impracticability causes delay or ability to perform only partially, the seller may allocate performances among his buyers. A buyer may accept his allotment or cancel the contract.

United States v. *Wegematic Corp.*

360 F.2d 674 (2nd Cir. 1966)

This was an action for breach of contract brought by the United States (plaintiff) against Wegematic Corporation (defendant). Judgment for the United States and Wegematic appealed. Affirmed.

In June 1956 the Federal Reserve Board invited electronics manufacturers to submit proposals for an intermediate-type, general purpose electronic digital computing system or systems; the invitation stressed the importance of early delivery as a consideration in determining the Board's choice. Wegematic, a relative newcomer in the field, submitted a proposal for the sale of a new computer designated as the ALWAC 800 which it characterized as "a truly revolutionary system utilizing all of the latest technical advances." In September the Board acted favorably on Wegematic's proposal ordering components of the ALWAC 800 with an aggregate cost of $231,800. Delivery was to be made on June 30, 1957, with liquidated damages of $100 per day for delay. The order also provided that in the event the defendant failed to comply "with any provision" of the agreement, "the Board may procure the services described in the contract from other sources and hold the Contractor responsible for any excess cost occasioned thereby."

After several requests for delays in the delivery time, Wegematic announced in mid-October, 1957, that "due to engineering difficulties it has become impracticable to deliver the ALWAC 800 Computing System at this time"; it requested cancellation of the contract without damages. The Board then procured comparable equipment from IBM and sued Wegematic for the excess cost of the new equipment and the delay costs under the liquidated damages clause. Wegematic sought to defend on the grounds of impossibility.

FRIENDLY, CIRCUIT JUDGE. The principal point of the defense, which is the sole ground of this appeal, is that delivery was made impossible by "basic engineering difficulties" whose correction would have taken between one and two years and would have cost a million to a million and a half dollars, with success likely but not certain. Although the record does not give an entirely clear notion what the difficulties were, two experts suggested that these may have stemmed from the magnetic cores, used instead of transistors to achieve a solid state machine, which did not have sufficient uniformity at this stage of their development. Wegematic contends that under federal law, which both parties concede to govern, the "practical impossibility" of completing the contract excused its defaults in performance.

We find persuasive Wegematic's suggestion of looking to the Uniform Commercial Code as a source for the "federal" law of sales. . . .

We see no basis for thinking that when an electronics system is promoted by its manufacturer as a revolutionary breakthrough, the risk of the revolution's occurrence falls on the purchaser; the reasonable supposition is that it has already occurred or, at least, that the manufacturer is assuring the purchaser that it will be found to have when the machine is assembled. As Judge Graven said: "The Board in its invitation for bids did not request invitations to conduct a development program for it. The Board requested invitations from manufacturers for the furnishing of a computer machine." Acceptance of Wegematic's argument would mean that though a purchaser makes his choice because of the attractiveness of a manufacturer's representation and will be bound by it, the manufacturer is free to express what are only aspirations and gamble on mere probabilities of fulfillment without any risk of liability. In fields of developing technology, the manufacturer would thus enjoy a wide degree of latitude with respect to performance while holding an option to compel the buyer to pay if the gamble should pan out. . . . We do not think this the common understanding—above all as to a contract where the manufacturer expressly agreed to liquidated damages for delay and authorized the purchaser to resort to other sources in the event of non-delivery. If a manufacturer wishes to be relieved of the risk that what looks good on paper may not prove so good in hardware, the appropriate exculpatory language is well known and often used.

Beyond this the evidence of true impracticability was far from compelling. The large sums predicted by Wegematic's witnesses must be appraised in relation not to the single computer ordered by the Federal Reserve Board, evidently for a bargain price, but to the entire ALWAC 800 program as originally contemplated. Although the record gives no idea what this was, even twenty-five machines would gross $10,000,000 if priced at the level of the comparable IBM equipment. While the unanticipated need for expending $1,000,000 or $1,500,000 on redesign might have made such a venture unattractive, as Wegematic's management evidently decided, the sums are thus not so clearly prohibitive as it would have them appear.

Problem Cases

1. Spada, an Oregon corporation, agreed to sell Belson, who operated a business in Chicago, Illinois, two carloads of potatoes at "4.40 per sack, F.O.B. Oregon shipping point." Spada had the potatoes put aboard the railroad cars; however, he did not have floor racks used in the cars under the potatoes as is customary during winter months. As a result there was no warm air circulating and the potatoes were frozen while in transit. Spada claims that his obligations ended with the delivery to the carrier and that the risk of loss was on Belson. What argument would you make for Belson?

2. Perilstein Company knew Mort Company was in financial difficulties so it agreed to sell Mort goods only on a C.O.D. basis. On October 25, 1961, Perilstein delivered the goods to Mort, and it gave its check in payment. On October 27, 1961, Mort was adjudged bankrupt, and the check was not paid because of the filing of the bankruptcy petition even though there were sufficient funds on deposit to pay the check. Perilstein claims this was a cash transaction and it should be entitled to recover the goods? Is this a good claim?

3. Scampoli purchased a new color television set for cash from Wilson. The sales ticket guaranteed 90 days' free service and replacement of any defective tube and parts for one year. Two days later the set was delivered and the picture had a reddish tinge to it. Wilson's service representative informed Scampoli that in order to eliminate the red cast from the picture he would have to remove the chassis from the cabinet and take it to the shop so as to determine the cause of the defective performance. Scampoli refused to allow the chassis to be removed, asserting he did not want a repaired set but that he was entitled to another brand new set or to have his money refunded for breach of warranty. Scampoli brings suit for revocation of acceptance and refund of the purchase price. Should the refund be given?

4. Pollack agreed to sell to Campbell the "contents of Magic Car Wash" for $8,000 and assured Campbell that everything within the four walls of the car wash building was included in the sale. Campbell removed some of the equipment from the premises and then discovered that under the terms of the lease of the building, the boiler, hot-air blowers and fluorescent lighting could not be removed because they belonged to the landlord. Campbell returned the equipment he had removed and notified Pollack he was rescinding the sale. Pollack claims that Campbell cannot revoke his acceptance because the noninclusion of the boiler, blowers and lighting does not constitute a "substantial breach" since they are worth only about $600. Is Pollack's argument valid?

5. On December 23, 1965, Casey purchased a used automobile from Auto Sales Company for $738 with a written, one-week guarantee that the car was in good condition. The car turned out to be something less than it appeared under the gleaming lights of Auto Sales' lot; the transmission and motor seal leaked, the turn signals and emergency brake did not work properly, a hole appeared in the tailpipe and the front motor mount did not hold up. The next day Casey took the car back to Auto Sales for repairs. Two weeks later it was redelivered to Casey in worse condition. Auto Sales then demanded Casey pay one half of the cost of repairs since the guarantee had expired. Based on the material in this chapter, what course of action would you recommend to Casey?

6. Government Hospital ordered 275 pounds of raw shrimp from Mazur Brothers. Mazur Brothers had the shrimp federally inspected, packed in ice, and delivered to the Hospital. The shrimp were kept refrigerated until the next day when they were put in steam kettles. The cook testified there appeared to be nothing wrong with the appearance of the shrimp in their raw state but after they had boiled for five minutes they had an unwholesome odor and were discolored. The shrimp were not served to patients and were kept refrigerated for four days pending reinspection by the Department of the Interior. Six days after delivery Hospital informs Mazur Brothers that it wants to reject the shrimp. Can it do so?

7. Alpirn contracted to purchase from Williams 40,000 feet of ½-inch new steel pipe, "the pipe not to be plugged." Shipment was C.O.D. When the pipe arrived Alpirn's foreman permitted the truck driver to unload about 50 pieces of pipe at which time he discovered that the pipe was plugged. Alpirn refused to accept the pipe. Williams contended that since the shipment was C.O.D. Alpirn was obligated to accept and pay for the pipe. Was Alpirn obligated to accept and pay for the pipe?

8. Whelan ordered fuel oil from Griffith to be delivered at his farm home which was located on a country road. The oil was to be delivered on an agreed C.O.D. basis. Griffith made two attempts to deliver the oil but each time no one was found at home. The morning after a night of heavy snowfall, the heaviest in over 20 years, Griffith equipped the truck with chains and made a third attempt to deliver oil but found on arrival at Whelan's house that the driveway was impassable due to snowdrifts approxi-

mately 6 feet high. When the driver drove past the house and attempted to turn around, the truck became stuck in the snow and had to be towed back to the main highway. Whelan ran out of oil and as a result of having no fuel the heating plant froze causing substantial damage to it. Whelan sued Griffith to recover a judgment for the damage to the heating plant claiming its breach of contract to deliver oil was the cause of the loss. Should Griffith be held in breach?

9. On April 15, 1959, Motter purchased farm machinery from Wrightstone on a conditional sales contract which provided: "the buyer is not bound to pay any specific amount each month, provided the total balance is paid within twenty-four months." Motter executed a judgment note for the balance which was renewed from time to time as payments were made. The last renewal was on May 5, 1960, in the amount of $590.40. On June 11, 1960, Wrightstone, Inc., repossessed the machinery and, on June 13, 1960, notified Motter that payment must be made in full of the balance. On June 28, 1960, Wrightstone advised Motter that the machinery had been sold and that he owed a balance of $205.90. Judgment was entered for this amount. Wrightstone based its right to repossess the machinery on the ground that it deemed itself insecure. Motter petitioned to have the judgment opened and the petition was granted. What should Wrightstone have done if it considered itself insecure?

chapter 36. Remedies for Breach

Sellers' Remedies

Recovery of Purchase Price. In the usual performance of a sales contract the seller delivers and the buyer accepts conforming goods and the seller is entitled to the agreed purchase price of the goods. If credit has been extended and the purchase price is not paid when due, the seller is entitled to a judgment for the purchase price of the goods. Also, the seller is entitled to the purchase price of conforming goods if the risk of loss has passed to the buyer and goods are lost or damaged within a commercially reasonable time after the risk of loss has passed to the buyer.

If the goods contracted for have been identified to the contract and the buyer refuses to accept and pay for them, the seller is entitled to the purchase price after he has made an honest effort to resell the goods and is unable to do so or if the circumstances reasonably indicate that the goods cannot be resold. If the seller has recovered a judgment for the purchase price of the goods he must hold them and deliver them to the buyer if he pays the judgment. If the seller has an opportunity, however, to sell the goods before the buyer pays the judgment he may do so and credit the amount received on the judgment. If the buyer has wrongfully rejected or revoked acceptance of the goods and the circumstances are such that the seller is not entitled to a judgment for the purchase price, he would be entitled to a judgment for damages. (2–709 [3].) [1]

Recovery of Damages for Breach. The objective of granting a judgment for damages for breach of a contract is to give the injured party a judgment for an amount which will compensate him for the loss suffered which results

---

[1] The numbers in the parentheses refer to the sections of the Uniform Commercial Code 1962.

directly from the breach. Under the common law the rules for determining damages in sales contracts do not always accomplish this objective. Under the provisions of the Code in the event the buyer breaches the contract by non-acceptance of the goods or by repudiating the contract, thus giving the seller a right to damages, the measure of damages is the difference between the market price at the time and place of tender and the unpaid contract price together with the incidental damages but less expenses saved in consequence of the buyer's breach. (2–708 [1].)

Incidental damages include any commercially reasonable charges such as expenses or commissions incurred in stopping delivery or in the transportation of the goods, and the expenses incurred in the care and custody of the goods after the buyer's breach. (2–710.) Expenses saved might be the cost of packaging the goods and of transportation which would be incurred in completing performance of the contract.

If these damages are inadequate to put the seller in as good a position as that he would have occupied had the contract been performed, he would be entitled to recover loss of profits as damages. For example, suppose the seller is a retail dealer in musical instruments and the buyer contracts to purchase a piano. The seller has or can obtain all the pianos needed to supply his customers. The buyer repudiates the contract and refuses to accept delivery of the piano. The seller would be entitled to a judgment for loss of profit on the piano including reasonable overhead and incidental damages. (2–708 [2].)

Resale as Measure of Damages.   In the event the buyer repudiates the sales contract the seller has the right to identify to the contract conforming goods which have not already been identified, if at the time of the breach they are in his possession or control, and to resell them. He may also treat as the subject of resale goods which have demonstrably been intended for the particular contract even though the goods are unfinished. If, at the time the buyer repudiates the contract, the goods are in process and have demonstrably been intended for the particular contract, the seller may, in the exercise of reasonable commercial judgment for the purpose of avoiding loss, either complete the manufacture of the goods and wholly identify the goods to the contract or cease manufacture and resell for scrap or salvage value, or he may proceed in any other reasonable manner. This rule permits the seller in such a situation to follow a reasonable course of action to mitigate damages and not be held responsible if the course followed is not as successful as some other course might have been. All that is required of the seller is that he act in good faith and exercise reasonable commercial judgment in determining the course of action to be followed. (2–704.)

On the buyer's breach of the sales contract the seller is not obligated to resell the goods but may bring an action to recover a judgment for damages. However, if the seller elects to resell the goods concerned or the undelivered balance of them, he is entitled to recover as damages the difference between the resale price and the contract price together with any incidental damages provided the resale is made in good faith and in a commercially reasonable manner.

For the protection of the seller rules have been promulgated which, if followed, will ensure the seller that he has made the sale in a "commercially reasonable manner." It does not follow, however, that if he pursues some other course of action he has not made the sale in good faith and in a "commercially reasonable manner." If the parties have agreed as to the manner in which the resale shall be made, the courts will enforce the agreement unless it would be found to be unconscionable. (2–302.) If the parties have not entered into an agreement relative to the resale of the goods, the sale may be at public or private sale but in all events it must be made in good faith and in a commercially reasonable manner. The resale must be reasonably identified as referring to the broken contract. If the goods are not in existence the resale may be in the form of a contract to sell future goods.

If the goods are resold at private sale the seller must give the buyer reasonable notification of his intention to resell. If the sale is a public sale, and a sale at auction is a public sale, only identified goods may be resold unless there is a future market for such goods. The seller must give the buyer notice of the time and place of the sale unless the goods are perishable or threaten to decline in value rapidly; the sale must be made at a usual place or market of public sales if one is reasonably available; if the goods are not within the view of those attending the sale the notification of the sale must state the place where the goods are located and provide for reasonable inspection by prospective bidders; and the seller may bid at a public sale. (2–706 [3] and [4].)

The purchaser at a public sale who buys in good faith takes free from any rights of the original buyer even though the seller has failed to conduct the sale in compliance with the rules set out in the Code. (2–706 [5].) On a resale the seller is not accountable to the buyer for any profit made on the resale. However, if the sale is in the nature of the foreclosure of a security interest in the goods, the buyer is entitled to any surplus over and above the debt, interest and expenses of the sale. (2–706 [6].)

Seller's Remedies on Discovery of Buyer's Insolvency. If the seller has not agreed to extend credit to the buyer for the purchase price of the goods, delivery of the goods and payment of the purchase price are concurrent. If the seller tenders delivery of the goods he may withhold delivery unless the agreed payment is made. Where the seller has agreed to extend credit to the buyer for the purchase price of the goods, but discovers before delivery that the buyer is insolvent, the seller may refuse delivery unless the buyer pays cash for the goods together with the unpaid balance for all goods theretofore delivered under the contract. (2–702 [1].)

At common law a seller has the right to rescind a sales contract induced by fraud and recover the goods unless they have been sold to a bona fide purchaser for value. Based on this general legal principle the Code provides that where the seller discovers that the buyer has received goods while insolvent, he may reclaim the goods upon demand made within 10 days after their receipt. This right granted to the seller is based on constructive deceit on the part of the buyer. The receiving of the goods while insolvent is equivalent to a false representation of solvency. To protect his rights all the seller is required to do is to make a demand within the 10-day period; he need not actually repossess the goods.

If the buyer has misrepresented his solvency to this particular seller in writing within three months before the delivery of the goods, the 10-day limitation on his right to reclaim the goods does not apply. However, the seller's right to reclaim the goods is subject to the prior rights of purchasers in the ordinary course of the buyer's business or other good faith purchasers for value or lien creditors. (2–702 [2] and [3].)

Seller's Right to Stop Delivery.   The seller's right to stop delivery of the goods is based either on the insolvency of the buyer or on the buyer's repudiation of the contract of his failure to make payment due before delivery. If the quantity of the goods is less than a carload, truckload, planeload or a large shipment of express or freight, the seller's right to stop delivery by the carrier is based on the insolvency of the buyer, but if the shipment is a carload, truckload, planeload or large express or freight shipment, the seller has the right to stop delivery if the buyer repudiates the sales contract or fails to make a payment due before delivery. (2–705 [1].)

The seller's right to stop delivery terminates when the buyer receives the goods, or when a bailee other than a carrier acknowledges to the buyer that he holds the goods for the buyer, or when the goods are reshipped or the carrier holds the goods for the buyer as a warehouseman, or when any negotiable document of title covering the goods has been negotiated to the buyer. (2–705 [2].)

To stop delivery the seller must notify the carrier or other bailee in time so that by the exercise of reasonable diligence he may prevent the delivery of the goods. After he receives notice to stop delivery the carrier or other bailee owes a duty to hold the goods and deliver them as directed by the seller. The seller is liable to the carrier or other bailee for any expenses incurred or damages resulting from complying with the seller's order to stop delivery. If a negotiable document of title has been issued for the goods, the carrier or other bailee owes no duty to obey a stop-delivery order unless the negotiable document of title is delivered to him. If a carrier has issued a nonnegotiable bill of lading he is not obliged to obey a stop-delivery order issued by any person other than the consignor. (2–705 [3].) Any person, however, in the position of the seller may stop delivery of the goods. A "person in the position of the seller" includes a financing agency which has acquired documents by honoring a letter of credit for the buyer or by discounting a draft issued by the buyer for the seller. (2–707.)

Summary

The seller is entitled to the purchase price of conforming goods delivered to and accepted by the buyer and of conforming goods where the risk of loss has passed to the buyer and the goods are thereafter damaged or destroyed. Also, if the goods have been identified to the contract and the buyer repudiates the sale, the seller is entitled to the purchase price of the goods that cannot, by a reasonable effort on the part of the seller, be resold for a fair price.

The seller is entitled to recover compensatory damages if the buyer breaches the contract and to special damages if such damages were reasonably within the contemplation of the parties. The seller on breach by the buyer is entitled to incidental damages. If necessary to put the seller in the position he would have held had the buyer performed, the seller may be granted loss of profits as damages. The seller is not obligated to resell on the buyer's refusal to accept the goods but if he does resell, in a commercially reasonable manner, he may recover as damages the difference between the sale price and the contract price. A purchaser at a public sale, if he buys in good faith, takes free from any rights of the original buyer.

On the buyer's insolvency the seller may reclaim the goods if he makes the demand within 10 days after receipt. If written misrepresentation of solvency has been made by the buyer to the particular seller within three months, the 10-day period does not apply.

On the buyer's insolvency the seller may stop delivery of the goods by a carrier or other bailee. Delivery of large lots may be stopped on the buyer's repudiation or failure to pay sum due before delivery. Reasonable notice to stop delivery must be given to the carrier or other bailee.

E-Z Roll Hardware Mfg. Co., Inc. v. H & H Products and Finishing Corp.

4 U.C.C. Rep. 1045 (N.Y. Sup. Ct., Nassau Cty., 1968)

This was an action for breach of contract by E-Z Roll Hardware (plaintiff) against H & H Products & Finishing Corporation (defendant). Judgment for E-Z Roll Hardware.

The contract, dated October 31, 1963, was in the form of a letter accepting a blanket order for 10,000 sets of "special folding door hardware." Prices were set forth as follows: 2 feet, 76 cents; 4 feet, $1.47; 5 feet, $1.54; 6 feet, $1.61; 8 feet, $1.75. There was to be a first shipment of 3,000 sets approximately December 15,

1963. The balance of 7,000 sets was to be shipped as needed by the buyer over a period of not later than nine months.

E-Z commenced shipments in January of 1964 which continued until April 7, 1964. A total of 3,010 sets were shipped for an aggregate price of $4,757.90. E-Z testified that on at least five occasions between June, 1964 and January, 1966, H & H was contacted about the balance of the order and each time received excuses for delay or promises that there would be larger orders. Finally, In January, 1966, H & H stated there would be no additional orders and this action was brought.

E-Z claimed as damages the sum of $11,101 on the theory that this figure represented the purchase price for the balance of the 7,000 sets computed by treating the price of 3,010 sets actually delivered ($4,757.90) as three-tenths of the full contract price. Judgment for E-Z for $4,002.40.

LYNDE, JUSTICE.   E-Z is entitled to relief, and the question becomes one of measure of damages. E-Z found itself with a large quantity of raw materials on hand which it could not use for any other purpose. Further work would have to be performed before H & H could use the merchandise: metal track would have to be cut to size; plating, assembly and boxing were required. A seller who is in the process of manufacturing goods for the buyer which are not readily saleable when finished and who elects to cease manufacture on repudiation by the buyer does not have an action for the purchase price as such. He does, however, retain his action for damages (U.C.C. § 2–709, sub (3)) which are measured by the difference between costs of performance and contract price and which include losses sustained, such as payments for labor and materials reasonably made in part performance of the contract to the extent that they are wasted if performance is abandoned.

The complicating factor here is that the buyer had the right to control the contract price. The buyer had five alternatives and had the right to demand delivery of the item bearing the lowest price. Its responsibility under the contract would have been fulfilled if it ordered that the balance of the sets (6,990) be delivered in two foot lengths. In such circumstances the return on the lowest price provides the standard for measuring damages. Assuming completion of the contract on this basis, E-Z would be entitled to $6,312.40 in addition to the amount of $4,757.90 previously received. In order to get that, however, it would have been required to expend an additional $810 in order to identify the material to the contract. H & H may have a credit for that amount plus a credit for $500, the salvage value of the material. The amount, therefore, which is due to E-Z is $4,002.40. This, of course, represents a loss to E-Z but it puts E-Z in the same position as though the contract had been completed. The court cannot remake the contract. Both parties apparently took a business risk when they entered into the agreement. H & H ordered special purpose equipment, hoping that it would have customers for the product and E-Z provided for a loss item in the contract, hoping it would not be a major factor in the entire order.

E-Z's claim for storage is rejected. To qualify for incidental damages as contemplated by U.C.C. § 2–710, there must be compliance with the statutory provisions (U.C.C. §§ 2–709, 2–706) designed to minimize damages. No such action was taken in this case.

In re Units, Inc.

3 U.C.C. Rep. 46 (D. Conn, 1965)

This was a reclamation petition filed by Northern Sash & Door Company (plaintiff) against the trustee in bankruptcy of Units, Inc. (defendant). Reclamation petition was denied.

On December 23, 1964, Units, which owed Northern $16,900 and which was legally insolvent at the time, sent a letter to Northern which read in part:

"Anticipating your anxiety over the status of our account with your company, we felt it wise to acquaint you with our situation at present.

"We are experiencing the typical year end 'receivable blues' this coupled with the fact our inventory is extremely heavy and unbalanced has put us in a temporary bind.

"Based on the above we are proposing the following payment schedule to help us through this period.

> December —$4,304.77 (check enclosed)
> January   —$4,304.77
> February —$3,856.61
> March   —$3,856.60"

At that time the bankrupt had an unfilled order for merchandise amounting to $8,149.09. On January 13, 1965, Northern's sales manager spoke with the bankrupt's treasurer and was allegedly told the January check would be sent if the merchandise was released. Northern sent the merchandise, but the check was never mailed. Northern made no effort to rescind or reclaim until after April 7, 1965, when the petition in bankruptcy was filed.

SEIDMAN, REFEREE.   Connecticut General Statutes § 42a-2-702 is controlling. It provides in part:

"(2) Where the seller discovers that the buyer has received goods on credit while insolvent he may reclaim the goods upon demand made within ten days after the receipt, but if misrepresentation of solvency has been made to the particular seller in writing within three months before delivery, the ten day limitation does not apply. . . .

"(3) The seller's right to reclaim under Subsection (2) is subject to the rights of a buyer in ordinary course . . . or lien creditor under §42a–2–403. . . ."

The reclamation petition alleged a fraudulent misrepresentation of solvency. The trustee pleaded that even if there was a fraudulent misrepresentation the petitioner is not now entitled to reclaim the property since a timely reclamation petition was not made. In reply the petitioner amended its petition by alleging that the bankrupt had made a written misrepresentation of solvency to the petitioner within three months before delivery.

Assuming that a promise that a check would be forthcoming was made, it would be a fraudulent representation that would give the seller a right to reclaim within ten days after delivery. This was not done in the instant case. If the reclaiming creditor is to prevail it is necessary therefore to find there was a misrepresentation of solvency in writing within three months before delivery.

The only evidence of the alleged misrepresentation of solvency is the letter dated December 23, 1964. A careful reading of that letter does not disclose any language which could reasonably be considered a representation of the solvency. The bankrupt in the letter admits that it is unable to pay its bills as they mature and refers to the anxiety which the creditor feels. The letter refers to an unbalanced inventory and a temporary bind. This language might put a reasonably prudent man on further inquiry as to whether or not the debtor is in fact insolvent.

It is impossible for the court to conceive of any reasonable interpretation of the letter of December 23, 1964, to construe it as being a written misrepresentation of solvency. But even assuming that the reclaiming creditor had received a written misrepresentation of solvency within three months before delivery, his right to reclaim is still subject to defeasance. Section 42a–2–703(3) provides the seller's right to reclaim under subsection (2) is subject to the rights of a lien creditor under § 42a–2–403. A lien creditor is defined in § 42a–9–301(3) as a creditor who has acquired a lien on the property involved by attachment, levy or the like and includes a trustee in bankruptcy from the date of the filing of the petition. In the instant case prior to the date of filing April 7, 1965, the creditor had made no effort to reclaim and his right would have been subject to the lien rights of the trustee in bankruptcy.

Buyers' Remedies

Right to Recover Goods. The buyer's right to recover the goods which are the subject matter of the sales contract is analogous in many respects to the seller's right to recover the purchase price of goods sold. The forms of action brought by a buyer to recover the goods are specific performance and replevin. The buyer is entitled to the remedy of specific performance only if his remedy at law is inadequate. If the goods are unique or of such a character that other goods of the same or similar characteristics would not be available, the courts will, as a general rule, grant the remedy of specific performance. The granting of this remedy, however, rests in the sound discretion of the court. In case a decree of specific performance is granted it may include such terms and conditions as to payment of the price, damages or other relief as the court may deem just. (2–716 [1] and [2].)

The buyer is entitled to the remedy of replevin if the goods have been identified to the contract and after reasonable effort he has been unable to obtain other goods of the same characteristics or the circumstances are such that it is reasonably apparent that a reasonable effort to obtain goods of the same characteristics would be unavailing. Also, if the goods have been shipped under reservation and the buyer has paid or tendered the amount necessary to satisfy the security interest in the goods he can recover the goods in an action of replevin. (2–716 [3].)

Buyer's Right to Damages for Nondelivery. In the event the seller fails or refuses to deliver the goods or repudiates the contract, the buyer is entitled to recover as damages the difference between the market price at the time the buyer learned of the breach and the contract price plus any incidental and consequential damages. The market price is to be determined as of the place for tender or, in case of rejection after arrival or revocation of acceptance, as of the place of arrival. A tender of delivery of nonconforming goods is a nondelivery as the term is used in the Code. (2–713.)

The buyer has the right to "cover"; that is, purchase in the market goods of the same characteristics as those contracted for. Any "cover" must be made in good faith and without unreasonable delay. If the buyer does purchase or contract to purchase substitute goods under his right to "cover," he can recover from the seller as damages the difference between the cost of cover plus incidental and consequential damages less expenses saved in consequence of the seller's breach. The buyer is not obligated to cover and his failure to do so will not bar him from any other remedy. (2–712.)

Incidental damages include the expenses reasonably incurred by the buyer in inspection, receipt, transportation, and the care and custody of goods rightfully rejected together with any commercially reasonable charges, expenses or commissions in connection with cover and other reasonable expenses incident to the delay or other breach. (2–715 [1].)

The buyer is entitled to recover consequential damages only if the seller at the time of entering into the contract knew or should have known that a failure to perform would result in special damages due to the buyer's general or special requirements or needs and if the damages could not have been prevented by cover. (2–715 [2] [a].)

The seller is liable in damages for injury to person or property resulting from any breach of warranty. (2–715 [2] [b].)

Damages for Defective Goods. If the buyer accepts defective goods and wishes to hold the seller liable in damages, he must give the seller notice of the breach within a reasonable time after he discovers or should have discovered the breach or he will be barred from any remedy. If the goods are not as warranted and the buyer has given the required notice, he can recover as damages the difference at the time and place of acceptance between the value of the goods accepted and the value they would have had if they had been as warranted, unless special circumstances show proximate damages of a different amount. The buyer may be entitled to incidental or consequential damages including damages to person or property. (2–714.)

The buyer may, on notifying the seller of his intention to do so, deduct all or any part of the damages resulting from any breach of the contract from any part of the price still due under the same contract. (2–717.)

On the buyer's rightful rejection or justifiable revocation of acceptance the buyer has a security interest in the goods in his possession or control for any payment made on their price and any expenses reasonably incurred in their inspection, receipt, transportation, care and custody and may retain possession of the goods until the seller returns the amount paid on the price plus the buyer's incidental expenses. If the seller does not pay the buyer the amount due him the buyer may sell the goods and deduct from the proceeds the amount due plus the reasonable expenses of the sale. Any surplus must be returned to the seller. (2–711 [3].)

Summary

The buyer is entitled to the remedy of specific performance if the goods which are the subject matter of the contract are unique or the circumstances warrant the granting of the remedy. The buyer may replevin the goods if they have been identified to the contract and he cannot, with reasonable effort, cover.

The buyer may recover as damages for nondelivery or repudiation on the part of the seller the difference between the market price of the goods and the contract price plus incidental, and under some circumstances consequential, damages. If the buyer covers, the measure of his compensatory damages is the difference between the cost of the cover and the contract price.

In the event the goods are defective and the buyer accepts them, he can, on giving the seller notice of the breach, recover as damages the difference between the value of the goods received and their value had they been conforming goods plus incidental, and under some circumstances consequential, damages.

If the buyer has paid part of the purchase price of the goods and he rejects them or revokes his acceptance, he may retain possession of the goods and claim a security interest in them for the amount paid on the purchase price plus incidental and consequential damages, if any.

Grandi v. *LeSage*

399 P.2d 285 (Sup. Ct. N.M. 1965)

This was an action by Henry Grandi and wife (plaintiffs) against R. S. LeSage and H. R. Claggett (defendants) to recover a judgment for damages for breach of a sales contract. Judgment for the Grandis, and LeSage and Claggett appealed. Judgment affirmed as to LeSage and reversed as to Claggett.

LeSage owned a four-year old gelding, Cur-Non, which was listed in the Sunland Park Race Track program as a horse (stallion). The price of the horse was listed as $3,500. Under the rules of the track a buyer could not inspect a listed entry before filing a claim on the entry. The Grandis filed a claim on Cur-Non intending to use him for breeding purposes. Cur-Non was sold to the Grandis and the Grandis shipped him to Phoenix, Arizona. Upon discovering that Cur-Non was a gelding they rescinded the contract. Claggett, agent of LeSage, had entered Cur-Non in the race and had conducted all of the negotiations for his sale.

CHAVEZ, JUSTICE. Sections 2–711 (1) (b), 713 and 715(1), give a buyer, who rightfully rejects or justifiably revokes acceptance of the goods, the right not only to rescind and recover back the purchase price paid, but, in addition, the right to recover incidental damages resulting from the seller's breach, including expenses reasonably incurred in the care and custody of such goods. While the Code permits recovery for such expenses, we see nothing therein evidencing an intent that an agent of the seller shall be held liable along with the seller under the circumstances here present and contrary to the rule as announced in the cases cited supra. The judgment against Claggett for such expenses must, therefore, be reversed.

By his point VI, appellant LeSage argues:

VI. That the plaintiffs accepted delivery of Cur-Non since after reasonable opportunity to inspect him:
(a) They did not reject Cur-Non within a reasonable time after they had taken delivery from the defendant LeSage; and
(b) They had him treated, removed from the State of New Mexico to the State of Arizona, and there caused him to be operated upon by a veterinarian, all said acts being inconsistent with the ownership of defendant LeSage."

Notwithstanding there may have been an acceptance within the meaning of § 2–606, under § 2–608, a buyer who justifiably revokes his acceptance has the same right to rescission as though he had rejected the goods in the first place. Such revocation is justifiable if he accepted them:

(b) without discovery of such nonconformity if his acceptance was reasonably induced either by the difficulty of discovery before acceptance or by the seller's assurances.
(2) Revocation of acceptance must occur within a reasonable time after the buyer discovers or should have discovered the ground for it and before any substantial change in condition of the goods which is not caused by their own defects. It is not effective until the buyer notifies the seller of it.

Even assuming an acceptance by the buyer, such acceptance was effectively revoked in accordance with § 2–608, supra.

Punitive damages were held to be properly awarded in an action for breach of contract accompanied by fraudulent acts, wanton in character and maliciously intentional, where compensatory damages had been granted. Since the Commercial Code, § 2–711, permits recovery of damages in an action for rescission, punitive damages may likewise be recovered in such action where the breach is accompanied by fraudulent acts which are wanton, malicious and intentional. We have examined the record and conclude that the trial court's finding, that appellant LeSage saw a Sunland Park program listing Cur-Non as a four-year-old colt when, in fact, he knew he was a gelding, and that he failed to advise the officials of such error, are sufficient evidence of ratification. It is apparent to us that LeSage had knowledge of the agent's unauthorized action and failed promptly to repudiate it and, that having received the benefits of the sale by his acceptance and retention of the consideration, he cannot now reject the burdens incident thereto. The award of punitive damages was not error.

Keystone Diesel Engine Co. v. Irwin
191 A.2d 376 (Sup. Ct. Pa. 1963)

This was an action by Keystone Diesel Engine Company (plaintiff) against Floyd T. Irwin (defendant) to recover a judgment for the cost of repairs to an engine and Irwin filed a counterclaim for damages for breach of warranty and loss of profits. Judgment for Keystone Diesel Engine Company and Irwin appealed. Judgment affirmed.

Keystone Diesel Engine Company (Keystone) was a dealer in diesel engines and Irwin operated tractor-trailers as a contract carrier. Keystone sold Irwin a diesel engine which was subsequently installed in a tractor. The engine did not function properly and Keystone performed certain modifications and repairs to it at its own expense. Subsequent repairs were required and Keystone performed the additional work allegedly based upon an oral contract with Irwin to pay Keystone for the additional work and Keystone brought suit. Irwin filed a counterclaim for loss of profits totalling $5,150.

EAGEN, JUSTICE.   The Uniform Commercial Code provisions which are appropriate in the instant case read as follows:

The measure of damages for breach of warranty is the difference at the time and the place of acceptance between the value of the goods accepted and the value they would have had if they had been as warranted, unless *special circumstances* show proximate damages of a different amount.

In a proper case any incidental and consequential damages under the next section may also be recovered.

Consequential damages *resulting from the seller's breach* include (a) any loss resulting from general or particular requirements and needs of which the seller at the time of contracting had reason to know and which could not reasonably be prevented by cover or otherwise.

"Special circumstances" entitling the buyer to damages in excess of the difference between the value as warranted and the value as accepted exist where the buyer has communicated to the seller at the time of entering into the contract sufficient facts to make it apparent that the damages subsequently claimed were within the reasonable contemplation of the parties. The language in *Globe Refining Co.* v. *Landa Cotton Oil Co.,* gives the rationale of the foregoing rule as follows: " '[O]ne of two contracting parties ought not to be allowed to obtain advantage which he has not paid for. . . . If [a liability for the full profits that might be made by machinery which the defendant was transporting . . .] had been presented to the mind of the ship owner at the time of making the contract, as the basis upon which he was contracting, he would at once have rejected it. . . . The knowledge must be brought home to the party sought to be charged, under such circumstances that he must know that the person he contracts with reasonably believes that he accepts the contract with the special condition attached to it.' "

In the case at bar, no facts are alleged that would put Keystone on guard to the fact that Irwin would hold Keystone responsible for any loss of profit arising from the inability to use the engine in question. Following Irwin's theory to its logical conclusion, whenever a motor vehicle is sold for use in a profit motivated enterprise and the seller warrants that the vehicle will function properly, the seller will be liable in damages for a breach of warranty to the extent of profits lost on completely unrelated business contracts, where those profits are lost due to the vehicle malfunctioning.

Anticipated profits are not recoverable unless within the contemplation of the parties when the contract was made: *Macchia* v. *Megow*. Clearly, the claim for loss of profits in the instant case was not within the contemplation of the parties to this contract.

General Rules

Buyer and Seller Agreements as to Damages. The courts will enforce an agreement entered into relative to the nature and amount of damages provided the agreement is not void as an unconscionable contract or clause or is not in violation of other provisions of the Code. (2–302.) An agreement for liquidated damages will be enforced provided the amount is reasonable, that is, not so excessive as to amount to a penalty or so small as to be unconscionable, and provided that in the event of a breach the amount of damages resulting would be difficult of proof and the obtaining of an adequate remedy otherwise would not be convenient or feasible.

If the seller has justifiably withheld delivery of the goods because of the buyer's breach, the buyer is entitled to recover any money or goods he has delivered to the seller over and above the agreed amount of liquidated damages, or if there is no such agreement, the seller will not be permitted to retain an amount in excess of twenty percent of the value of the total performance for which the buyer is obligated under the contract or $500, whichever is the smaller. This right of restitution is subject to the seller's right to recover damages under other provisions of the Code and to the amount of value of benefits received by the buyer directly or indirectly by reason of the contract. (2–718.)

The parties, by agreement, may provide for additional or substituted remedies other than those expressly provided in the Code. For example, the buyer's remedies may be limited to the return of the goods and the repayment of the price or to the replacement or repair of nonconforming goods or parts.

Resort to a remedy as provided is optional unless the agreement expressly states that the remedy is to be exclusive, in which case it will be the sole remedy. However, where the circumstances cause the limited or exclusive remedy to fail of its essential purpose, the parties are entitled to the remedies provided by the Code.

Consequential damages may be limited or excluded unless their limitation or exclusion would be unconscionable. Limitation of consequential damages for injury to the person in case of consumer goods is prima facie unconscionable but limitation of damages where the loss is commercial is not. (2–719.)

Unless a contrary intention appears, expressions of "cancellation" or "rescission" of the contract or the like shall not be construed as a renunciation or discharge of any claim in damages for an antecedent breach. (2–720.)

Proof of Market Price. Where the action based on anticipatory repudiation comes to trial before the time of performance with respect to some or all of the goods, any damage based on market price shall be determined according to the price of such goods prevailing at the time the aggrieved party learns of the repudiation. If such price is not available at the time and place, the court may receive evidence of the price of such goods at a commercially reasonable time before or after the aggrieved party learns of the repudiation and at any other place which in commercial judgment or usage of trade would seem as a reasonable substitute. If market price at any other time or place is to be offered in evidence, the other party must be given reasonable notice of such intent. (2–723.)

Reports of the prevailing price of the goods on an established market are admissible to prove market price. It does not have to be an organized market such as the New York Stock Market or the Chicago Board of Trade but must be a recognized market which issues quotations. (2–724.)

Statute of Limitations. The Code provides that any action for breach of a sales contract must be brought within four years after the cause of action accrues. The parties, by agreement, may shorten the period to one year but may not extend it. The cause of action accrues when the breach occurs, whether or not the aggrieved party knows of the breach. The cause of action for breach of warranty accrues when the goods are delivered unless the warranty is as to future performance in which case the cause of action accrues when the buyer should have discovered the breach.

Where suit begun within the four-year period has terminated so as to leave a remedy still available for the same breach, the aggrieved party has six months after the termination of the first action in which to bring another action, provided the first suit was not terminated by voluntary discontinuance or for failure to prosecute. This Code provision does not alter the law on tolling of the statute of limitations. (2–725.)

Summary

As a general rule the courts will enforce an agreement of the parties relative to the damages to which the parties will be entitled provided the agreement is not void as an unconscionable contract or clause. A liquidated damage provision in a contract is enforceable if the amount is reasonable and the damages for the injury suffered by the aggrieved party are not readily provable. The parties by agreement may provide for additional or supplemental damages, and consequential damages may be limited or excluded except damages for injury to the person in case of consumer goods.

In an action for damages for anticipatory breach, damages based on market price shall be determined according to the price of such goods prevailing at the time the aggrieved party learns of the repudiation. If such price is not available the price at a commercially reasonable time before or after the party learns of the repudiation may be used, and if a market price at the place of repudiation is not available a commercially reasonable place may be used. The reported price of the goods on an established market is admissible to prove market price.

The statute of limitations on sales contracts is four years from the time the cause of action accrues. The parties may, by agreement, limit the time to one year but they cannot extend it.

Denkin v. Sterner

1 U.C.C. Rep. 173 (Dist. Ct. Pa. 1956)

This was a petition by Denkin and his wife (plaintiffs) against Sterner (defendant) to open a judgment entered under a confession of judgment. Petition granted.

The Denkins contracted to purchase from Sterner certain refrigeration equipment for $35,500. The contract included a confession of judgment whereby, in the event of default by the Denkins, Sterner was given a power of attorney to enter judgment against the Denkins for the full purchase price, $35,500. The Denkins learned later that they could purchase the equipment at a lesser price from another dealer and they cancelled the contract with the Sterner who under their power of attorney, took a judgment against the Denkins for $35,500. The Denkins petitioned to have the judgment opened.

ANDERSON, JUSTICE. There is a paucity of decisions under the relatively new Uniform Commercial Code which will no doubt require considerable future court interpretation. We feel that the above sections must be read and interpreted together and as stated in the Comments to the above section, found in § 2–719. . . . "Thus any clause purporting to modify or limit the remedial provisions of this Article in an unconscionable manner is subject to deletion and in that event the remedies made available by this Article are applicable as if the stricken clause had never existed."

While under Section 2–709, we find the following:

The action for the price is now generally limited to those cases where resale of the goods is impracticable except where the buyer has accepted the goods or where they have been destroyed after risk of loss has passed to the buyer. . . . An action for the price under subsection (I) (b) can be sustained only after a 'reasonable effort to resell' the goods 'at reasonable price' has actually been made or where the circumstances 'reasonably indicate' that such an effort will be unavailing.

While there seems little doubt from the depositions taken under the rule issued in this case that Sterner is entitled to damages, for the Denkins admit that they canceled the agreement because they found out after checking that they could buy more equipment for less money elsewhere, yet it also seems evident under all the circumstances that to permit Sterner to recover the full amount of the purchase price without showing what goods, if any, have been identified to the contract, what goods were standard items and readily salable and what goods had actually been specially manufactured prior to the cancellation by the Denkins, as well as what goods have been or can be readily resold, would be in effect "unreasonably large liquidated damages" and, therefore, unconscionable and void.

Problem Cases

1. Seller contracted to sell Buyer a quantity of U.S. No. 1 onions for $2,920. However, the onions delivered to Buyer were not No. 1 grade because they contained a higher percentage of decay than that allowed under the U.S. Standards. The onions delivered were worth $340 less than No. 1 grade. Under the Perishable Agricultural Commodities Act, Buyer was bound to reject within 24 hours which he did not do and thus was deemed to have accepted them. However, Buyer later refunded them and Seller then made a commercially reasonable resale of the onions but incurred an out-of-pocket deficit of $120 in doing so. Seller now sues Buyer. To what measure of damages is Seller entitled?

2. On July 14, 1966, Donnkenny agreed to purchase from Jacobson 25,000 pounds of "skinny poor boy rib" knit at $1.72 per pound to be dyed according to Donnkenny's instructions. Jacobson shipped 14,000 pounds before receiving a letter in November from Donnkenny to hold up on deliveries. Then in March, Donnkenny refused without justification to accept any more deliveries. Jacobson now has 11,000 pounds of undyed "skinny poor boy knit" that is virtually worthless but has saved the 25½ cents a pound it would cost to have dyed the knit. What remedies are open to Jacobson?

3. In 1960 Hayward gave Textile Banking a security interest in his present and after-acquired inventory. This security interest was then perfected by filing a financing statement and a continuation statement was properly filed in 1965. In 1965, Hayward ordered inventory goods from a number of different suppliers. Within 10 days after the delivery of these goods, the suppliers found out Hayward was insolvent and made written demands for the return of the goods pursuant to Section 2–702. Textile Banking claims that its security interest prevails over the suppliers' right to reclamation, and cites Sections 2–702, 2–403(1) and 1–201 (32, 33, 44(b)). Is Textile's claim correct?

4. Phillips placed a verbal order with Union Motors for a demonstrator automobile with low mileage and to be as good as new. Phillips traded in two old cars, and Union Motors delivered a demonstrator car to him and warranted it to be in perfect condition and as good as new. After the purchase Phillips discovered that the automobile had been wrecked and imperfectly repaired and that Union Motors knew the car had

been wrecked and concealed this fact from him. Several witnesses testified that the wrecked car was worth 25 percent less than a car that had not been wrecked. The trial court found that there was a breach of warranty. What different types of relief might Phllips obtain?

5. Smith placed an order for seven AA-300-lb. steers and eight AA-400-lb. steers from American Hereford Farms. When the animals arrived, one was dead on arrival, another died shortly thereafter of a disease he had at delivery, and the remaining steers were substantially underweight, diseased, and not of the quality ordered. Smith kept the steers but incurred special veterinary expenses of $38, expenses for special medicines, feeds, and hired labor to treat the sick animals, and estimated he lost $300 by having his time diverted from his other business to care for the sick animals. In a suit for breach of warranty, to what measure of damages is Smith entitled? Which, if any, of the consequential damages should he be able to recover for?

6. On May 16, 1961, Augustine agreed to purchase a heating system from Perry. Assume that the heating system was installed during June of 1961 and the furnace was started in October of that year. In 1965, Perry filed suit to recover the contract price. On July 14, 1965, Augustine filed a counterclaim in which he alleged that Perry had given him a specific warranty that the heating system would "be able to heat at 75° inside at a −20° outside temperature," and further alleged that the furnace did not meet this guarantee as this was discovered after the furnace was started in October. Perry's attorney replied that the breach of warranty claim was barred by Section 2–725. Is the claim barred by Section 2–725? Why or why not?

PART IX Commercial Paper

chapter 37. Introduction

Background

Historical Background. History discloses that every civilization which engaged to an appreciable extent in commerce used some form of commercial paper. Probably the oldest type of commercial paper used in the carrying on of trade was the promissory note. Archeologists in their excavations found a promissory note of the approximate date 2100 B.C. made payable to bearer. The merchants of Europe used commercial paper, which under the law merchant was negotiable, in the 13th and 14th centuries. However, it appears that such paper was not used in England until about A.D. 1600. In 1896 a Uniform Negotiable Instruments Law was drafted.

Uniform Commercial Code—Commercial Paper. Today in the United States the law of commercial paper—drafts, checks, certificates of deposit, and promissory notes—is embodied in the Uniform Commercial Code's section on commercial paper. Other negotiable documents such as investment securities and documents of title are treated in other sections of the Code. Essentially, the Code makes no drastic changes in those basic rules of commercial paper which have been recognized for centuries, but it has adopted modern terminology and has coordinated, clarified, and simplified the law.

Forms of Commercial Money

Nature of Commercial Paper. All commercial paper is basically a simple promise to pay money. If the promise is in writing and is so drafted as to fulfill certain formal requirements, it is given the special characteristics which distinguish commercial paper from simple contracts. Other instruments given characteristics of negotiability by trade usage or by statute are not classed as commercial paper since they are not used currently in trade or are not payable in money. Such instruments as corporate stock, stock warrants, corporate bonds, negotiable bills of lading, and negotiable warehouse receipts are negotiable but are not commercial paper, and money, including bank notes and government notes, is treated as falling in a separate category. Commercial paper must be current in trade if it is to perform the function for which it is intended. Since the basic promise is a promise to pay money, it is a simple matter to determine whether or not the promise has been performed and under our concepts of the assignability of contracts a promise to pay money is generally held to be assignable. These characteristics make the simple contract to pay money peculiarly adaptable to its use to facilitate trade.

Traders need a simple "instrument which can be used in lieu of money." Commercial paper fulfills this need and its use also facilitates the use of credit. Through long usage, commercial paper has acquired certain characteristics not possessed by other types of contracts. A check, draft, certificate of deposit, or promissory note may be termed a contract in shorthand in that if it fulfills the formal requirements for negotiability and trade usage gives to it its full meaning. A signature on commercial paper may bind the signer to a contract composed of several distinct promises.

Thee are two major classes of commercial paper—orders to pay and promises. Drafts and checks are orders to pay, and certificates of deposit and notes are promises to pay.

Draft.   A draft is a three-party instrument. It is an order by a drawer addressed to a drawee ordering him to pay to a payee a sum certain in money. It has a variety of uses. If B owes A a past-due obligation, A may draw a draft for the amount of the debt naming B as drawee and himself or his bank as payee and send the draft to B's bank for presentment and collection. In freight shipments in which the terms are "cash on delivery" it is a common practice for the seller to ship the goods on an order bill of lading consigned to himself at the place of delivery to the buyer, endorse the bill of lading, attach a draft naming the buyer drawee, and then send them through banking channels to the buyer's bank where the draft is presented for payment and where on payment the bill of lading is delivered to the buyer. The result: the buyer gets the goods and the seller gets his money. If credit is extended, the same procedure is followed except a time draft is used, that is, a draft payable at some future time. In such a transaction the buyer will "accept" the draft instead of paying it. To accept the draft he writes his name across its face thereby making himself primarily liable on it, or in other words, he obligates himself to pay the amount of the draft when due. If the draft on its face states that it is drawn by the seller of goods on the buyer of goods for the purchase price of the goods, it is known as a "trade acceptance." A "trade acceptance" is given a preferential discount rate by the Federal Reserve Bank.

DRAFT

$ 133.47   July 15   19 70

On sight

the order of John Doe

One hundred thirty-three and 47/100

WITH EXCHANGE

Value received and charge the same to account of

To American National Bank

Chicago, Illinois 60606

Richard Thompson

Check. A check is a draft drawn on a bank and is payable on demand. It is the most widely used of the various forms of commercial paper, and is used in lieu of money. Neither drafts nor checks are drawn on drawees or banks unless there is some relation existing between the drawer and drawee which justifies the drawer in drawing the draft or check. The check plays such an important role in today's society that each state has enacted statutes making the drawing of a check on a bank a crime if the drawer has no credit balance or one insufficient to cover the check when presented for payment. No such statutes have been enacted in regard to drafts. However, the drawer of a draft should know that the drawee will not pay or accept the draft unless he (the drawer) has had business relations with the drawee which warrant the drawing of the draft.

CHECK

No. 1046

CHICAGO, July 15 19 70

PAY TO THE ORDER OF Harry J. Johnson $ 298.00

THE SUM **298** DOL'S **00** CTS   DOLLARS

THE TERMINAL NATIONAL BANK OF CHICAGO

Robert Clark

Certificate of Deposit. The certificate of deposit is a promise to pay. It is an acknowledgment by a bank of receipt of money with an engagement to repay it. Its use is confined to the issuing of the certificate of deposit as evidence of a time deposit with a bank. Usually, it is drawn for a period of six months or a year and draws interest if the money is left on deposit for the time stated.

CERTIFICATE OF DEPOSIT

CERTIFICATE OF DEPOSIT

BLOOMINGTON, IND. ___March 1___ 19 70 No. 1 8 8 6 6   71-227/712

THIS IS TO CERTIFY THAT___Albert Wells___   HAS DEPOSITED IN
8 Fee Lane
STREET OR R.F.D.   CITIZENS FIRST NATIONAL BANK
Spencer, Indiana   OF BLOOMINGTON $ 100.00
CITY & STATE   BLOOMINGTON, IND.
                                                47401
One hundred and no/100 Dollars

PAYABLE TO ___Albert Wells___   OR ORDER ___Six___ MONTHS
AFTER DATE WITH INTEREST THEREON AT THE RATE OF ___Three___ PER CENT PER ANNUM FROM DATE ON THE RETURN OF THIS CERTIFICATE PROPERLY INDORSED. NO INTEREST WILL BE PAID UPON THIS CERTIFICATE AFTER ITS MATURITY. THE BANK IS PROHIBITED BY FEDERAL LAW FROM PAYING THIS DEPOSIT IN WHOLE OR IN PART BEFORE ITS MATURITY AND FROM PAYING INTEREST AFTER MATURITY. THE RATE OF INTEREST PAYABLE HEREUNDER IS SUBJECT TO CHANGE BY THE BANK TO SUCH EXTENT AS MAY BE NECESSARY TO COMPLY WITH REQUIREMENTS OF THE FEDERAL RESERVE BOARD MADE FROM TIME TO TIME PURSUANT TO THE FEDERAL RESERVE ACT. THE BANK RESERVES THE RIGHT TO REQUIRE THIRTY DAYS NOTICE OF WITHDRAWAL IN WRITING.
DUE ___August 31, 1970___   Richard Roe
                                                                          CASHIER
NOT SUBJECT TO CHECK

Promissory Note. The promissory note is the simplest form of commercial paper and is very widely used. It is simply a promise to pay. The maker of the note promises to pay the named payee a stated sum of money on demand or at some future date. The note is primarily a credit instrument and is used in a variety of transactions in which credit is extended. If a person purchases an automobile or a home on time, the probability is that the seller will have the buyer execute a promissory note for the unpaid balance, secured by a security interest in the automobile, or by a real estate mortgage, deed of trust or land contract on the home.

The terms of payment of the note will correspond with the terms of payment stated in the sales contract on the automobile or the home. Money may

PROMISSORY NOTE

$ 460.00   July 15   19 70

Sixty days   *after date* I *promise to pay to*

the order of ___James Smith___

Four hundred sixty and no/100 _____*Dollars*

at ___American National Bank, Chicago, Illinois   60606___
Value received.
No. 143 ___Due 9/13/70___   Henry Jenkins

be loaned and an unsecured note given which evidences the amount of the loan and the terms of repayment.

A cognovit note is a combination of a promissory note and a confession of judgment. Such a note gives the holder the right to take judgment against the maker without trial if the maker fails to pay on the due date.[1]

Summary

Commercial paper is basically a simple promise to pay money. If the instrument satisfies certain formal requirements, it will be negotiable and will have certain characteristics which will distinguish it from simple contracts. To perform its intended function, commercial paper must be current in trade.

Through long usage commercial paper has acquired certain characteristics not possessed by other types of contracts. A signature on commercial paper may bind the signer to a contract composed of several distinct promises. Drafts and checks are orders to pay and certificates of deposit and notes are promises to pay.

A draft is an order by the drawer addressed to the drawee ordering him to pay the payee a sum certain in money at sight or at some future time. A check is a draft drawn on a bank and payable on demand. It is used in lieu of money to make all types of payments. A certificate of deposit is an acknowledgment by a bank of the receipt of money and an engagement to repay it. It is used by banks in connection with time deposits. The note is the simplest form of commercial paper. It is a promise by the maker to pay a sum certain in money to the payee on demand or at some future time. It is a credit instrument and has a wide variety of uses.

Benefits of Negotiability

Rights of Assignee of Contract. The assignee of a contract acquires no greater rights than his assignor has at the time of the assignment. The assignee cannot know with certainty the nature and scope of the defenses the obligor may have to the assigned contract; consequently, there are certain risks involved in acquiring contract rights as an assignee in addition to the credit risks incident to all contractual obligations. The assignment of contracts was discussed in Chapter 13.

Rights Acquired by Negotiation. The holder of a negotiable instrument acquires certain procedural advantages over the obligee or assignee of a contract. The holder of a negotiable instrument, if he brings suit on the instrument, need not allege and prove consideration. What other procedural advan-

---

[1] The confession of judgment in a cognovit note is not enforceable in many states.

tages he may have will depend upon the procedural statute of the state in which suit is brought.

If the negotiable instrument remains in the hands of the original parties, the advantages of having the promise negotiable in form are mostly procedural, since the original payee holds the instrument subject to all the defenses to the instrument. However, if a negotiable instrument is negotiated to a person who can qualify as a holder in due course,[2] such person takes the instrument free from all defenses to the instrument except defenses which go to the validity of the instrument in its inception.

For example, suppose Bell, by fraudulent representations, induces Albert to sign a nonnegotiable contract whereby Albert promises to pay Bell $100, and Bell then assigns the contract to Finch, who takes for value and without notice or knowledge of the fraud. When the $100 is due, Finch demands payment, and Albert refuses to pay and Finch brings suit. Albert can set up Bell's fraud as a defense, and the defense is good against Finch. Suppose Albert, instead of executing a nonnegotiable contract for the $100, issues to Bell his negotiable promissory note, and Bell negotiates the note to Finch, who takes it as a holder in due course. Albert then does not pay the note when due, and Finch sues on the note. The defense that Albert was induced to issue the note by Bell's fraudulent representations would not be a defense to the instrument in the hands of Finch.

If Bell should forge Albert's name to an instrument negotiable in form, and negotiate the instrument to a person who could qualify as a holder in due course, the defense of forgery would be available to Albert in a suit by such holder.

A person taking a negotiable instrument as a holder in due course takes it subject to only two major risks: (1) the ability of the holder to collect from the parties to the instrument and (2) the validity of the instrument in its inception. The assignee of a nonnegotiable contract takes it subject to all outstanding defenses between the parties.

Summary

The assignee of a contract acquires no greater rights than his assignor has.

The holder of a negotiable instrument, if he is an original party to the instrument, acquires technical procedural advantages to which the obligee or assignee of a nonnegotiable contract is not entitled.

If the holder of a negotiable instrument is a holder in due course, he holds the instrument free from personal defenses available to the original parties, but he does not hold the instrument free from real defenses, that is, defenses which go to the validity of the instrument in its inception.

---

[2] The requirements for a holder in due course are set out in Section 3–302 of the Uniform Commercial Code.

Problem Cases

1. Is the following instrument a note, a check, or a draft? Why? If it is not a check, how would you have to change it to make it a check?

   To: *Arthur Adams*   *January 1, 1969*
   Ten Days after Date Pay to the Order of: *Bernie Brown*
   the Sum of: *Ten and no/*100 Dollars.
                                                    Signed: *Carl Clark*

2. Jones sells Thomas $6,000 worth of goods. Thomas gives Jones his negotiable note for $3,000 payable in 30 days and Jones agrees to carry the $3,000 balance on open account payable in 30 days. Jones wishes to discount his receivables at the bank. Will the bank discount the negotiable note and the open account at the same discount rate? If not, why not?

chapter 38. Requirements for Negotiability

Formal Requirements

Basic Requirements. An instrument must satisfy certain formal requirements if it is to be negotiable. If the writing does not fulfill these requirements it is a nonnegotiable instrument; it will be a contract which lacks the characteristic of negotiability. The formal requirements for negotiability as set out in the Code—Commercial Paper may be stated briefly as follows: The instrument must be in writing and signed by the maker, if it is a certificate of deposit or a note, or by the drawer, if it is a draft or check. It must contain an unconditional promise, if it is a certificate of deposit or note, or an unconditional order, if it is a draft or check, to pay a sum certain in money, and no other promise, order, obligation or power given by the maker or drawer except as authorized by the provisions of the Code—Commercial Paper. It must be payable on demand or at a definite time and it must be payable to order or bearer. (3–104 [1].) [1]

The details necessary to fulfill the formal requirements are set out in other sections of Article 3 of the Code.

Commercial paper which fulfills the formal requirements for negotiability is a "draft" if it is an order; a "check" if it is a draft drawn on a bank and payable on demand; a "certificate of deposit" if it is an acknowledgment by a bank of receipt of money with an engagement to repay it; and a "note" if it is a promise other than a certificate of deposit. (3–104 [2].) The terms "draft," "check," "certificate of deposit" and "note" may be used to refer to instruments which are not negotiable. (3–104 [3].)

Importance of Form. Whether or not an instrument is so drafted that it

---

[1] The numbers in the parentheses refer to the sections of the Uniform Commercial Code, 1962.

satisfies these formal requirements is important for one and only one purpose, and that is for the purpose of determining whether the instrument is negotiable or nonnegotiable. Negotiability should not be confused with validity or collectibility. If the instrument is negotiable, the law of negotiable instruments will control in determining the rights and liabilities of the parties to the instrument. If the instrument is nonnegotiable, the general rules of contract law will control.

An instrument which fulfills all of the formal requirements is a negotiable instrument even though it is void, voidable, unenforceable, or uncollectible. Negotiability is a matter of form and nothing else. If a person gives an instrument in payment of a gambling debt in a state which has a statute declaring that any instrument or promise given in payment of a gambling debt is null and void and of no force and effect, the instrument is a negotiable instrument if it is negotiable in form even though it is absolutely void. Also, an instrument which is negotiable in form is a negotiable instrument even though signed by an infant. The fact that the infant may set up his infancy as a defense if suit is brought to enforce the instrument is immaterial. The instrument is voidable, but it is negotiable.

An instrument which is negotiable in form although void or voidable may give rise to liability on the part of a person who endorses and negotiates it or transfers it without endorsement whereas if it were nonnegotiable liability to the same extent would not be imposed on an assignor of the instrument.

Language of Negotiable Instrument. In determining the negotiable character of an instrument the language of the instrument must be carefully analyzed to determine whether or not it satisfies all the requirements for negotiability as set out in the Code—Commercial Paper. There are no technical words which must be used in drafting a negotiable instrument.

For example, the instrument

> I promise to pay Bearer one hundred dollars.
>
> (Signed) Albert Adams

is a negotiable instrument.

This does not follow the phraseology customarily used in the drafting of a promissory note, but it does satisfy all of the requirements of the Code for a negotiable note.

Summary

An instrument, in order to be negotiable, must comply with certain formal requirements which are set out in Section 3–104 of the Code.

The form of the instrument serves only in determining whether the law of negotiable commercial paper or general contract law will control in determining the rights and liabilities of the parties.

No particular technical terms need be used in drafting an instrument which is to be negotiable.

In Writing and Signed

Writing. Writing is defined in the Code as follows: "Written" or "in writing" includes printing, typewriting or any other intentional reduction to tangible form. (1–201 [46].)

Only something having tangible form can be used as a medium of exchange in the business world. Consequently, if a promise to pay is to be easily transferable, it must be given some tangible form, and a writing evidencing the promise is the most convenient way to satisfy the necessity for tangible form. No particular type of writing is required; no particular material is designated on which the writing shall appear; all that is required is that the instrument be in writing. A person could draw a valid negotiable instrument on a piece of wrapping paper in lead pencil. It would be poor business practice, but it would fulfill the statutory requirement that the instrument be in writing.

Signing. Signing is defined in Section 1–201 (39) of the Code as follows: "Signed" includes any symbol executed or adopted by a party with present intention to authenticate a writing. If an instrument is to be negotiable it must be signed by the maker or drawer. The common practice is for the maker or drawer to subscribe his name to the instrument but subscription is not required. A typed or rubber stamp signature is sufficient. From a technical standpoint any mark or design put on the instrument with the intent and for the purpose of authenticating the instrument is sufficient signing. However, from a practical standpoint the instrument should be so signed that the signer can be identified. Thus if Snuffy Smith signs his negotiable instrument with an X or other mark it is customary to write Snuffy's name on the instrument and indicate that the X is his signature.

As a general rule a commercial paper is signed in the lower, right-hand corner but it need not be signed in any particular place to be negotiable. Under some circumstances, however, the position of a signature on an instrument may be indicative of the capacity in which the person signed. The Code provides, Section 3–402, unless the instrument clearly indicates that a signature is made in some other capacity it is an endorsement.

A certificate of deposit or a note to be negotiable must be signed by the maker and a draft or check to be negotiable must be signed by the drawer. The nature of a certificate of deposit or note is such that there is almost no question as to whether such an instrument has been signed by a maker. However, since the draft or check is a three-party paper there may arise some question whether the instrument bears the signature of the drawer.

A time draft is customarily presented to the drawee for his acceptance. He accepts the draft by signing it on its face. If for some reason a draft should be presented to a drawee and he accepted it by signing his name across the front before it was signed by the drawer, the instrument in that form would not be negotiable since it would not be signed by the drawer.

Summary

To be negotiable, an instrument must be in writing. No particular form of writing is required.

The instrument must be signed by the maker if it is a note or a certificate of deposit or by the drawer if it is a draft or a check. Any mark made on the instrument with the intent of authenticating it is sufficient to satisfy the requirement that the instrument be signed.

Chrismer v. Chrismer

144 N.E.2d 494 (Ct. App. Ohio 1956)

This was an action by Vern Chrismer and Marie Chrismer (plaintiffs) against Estate of Francis M. Chrismer, deceased (defendant), to recover a judgment on a promissory note signed by Francis M. Chrismer as maker. Judgment for Estate of Francis M. Chrismer, deceased, and Vern and Marie Chrismer appealed. Judgment reversed and new trial ordered.

On April 17, 1951, Francis M. Chrismer, the father of Vern Chrismer, executed a promissory note in the sum of $6,000 payable to Vern or Marie Chrismer. Vern drafted the note and the father requested that the note be drafted in duplicate. Instead of drafting duplicate notes Vern put carbon paper between the two notes and made a carbon copy of the original. Francis M. Chrismer signed the original and a carbon copy of the signature was imprinted on the copy. Francis M. Chrismer kept the original and gave Vern the carbon copy. At the time this suit was brought Vern offered the carbon copy of the note in evidence and the suit was based on it. The trial court held that a proper foundation had not been laid for the admission of the carbon copy of the note as secondary evidence and that the signature on the carbon copy of the note was not a valid signature. The judgment was reversed for errors in the judge's ruling on a point in evidence. [This extract includes only that portion of the opinion relative to the signature on the carbon copy of the note.]

WISEMAN, JUDGE. First, is the instrument a negotiable instrument within the meaning of the Negotiable Instruments Act? We think it is not. Without question, the instrument is but a corbon copy of an original. The signature is made by imprint of the carbon paper. In our opinion the signature of the maker must be an original signature to be genuine and legal within the meaning of the Act. Section 8106, General Code, sets forth the requirements of a negotiable instrument, the first being that "it must be in writing and signed by the maker or drawer." Section 8123, General

Code, provides that no person shall be liable on an instrument whose "signature does not appear thereon." Section 8289. General Code, defines a negotiable promissory note, and one of the requirements is that it be "signed by the maker." In our opinion, a carbon copy of an instrument, which bears a carbon copy of what purports to be the signature of the maker, does not meet the requirements of the statute.

Finding no reported opinions on this proposition, it becomes a matter of first impression. In our opinion, the execution of a duplicate original negotiable promissory note is not contemplated by the Act, and, further, to do so would not be a sound trade practice or usage. We are cognizant of the fact that in modern trade practice carbon copies of negotiable promissory notes are made and retained for limited record purposes. However, in no sense can a carbon copy meet the statutory requirements of negotiability.

[*This is not a Code case. The result, however, would have been the same had the Code been in effect at the time of this transaction. Since the court found that the carbon copy signature was not affixed to the carbon copy of the note for the purpose of authenticating the writing it was not effective as a signature.* (1–201 [39].)

Unconditional Promise or Order

Requirement of Promise or Order. If an instrument is a draft or a check, it must contain an order to pay. The courts have held that a simple request to pay, as a favor, to the drawer of the instrument is not an order to pay; however, if the language used connotes a demand, even though framed in polite language, it is sufficient as an order to pay. For example, in an early case the court held that the following:

"Messrs. Songer, Please send Ten Pounds by the bearer, as I am so ill I cannot wait on you.

"Elizabeth Wery"

was only a request to pay, not an order. In another case the court held that the following:

"Mr. Strob: Please pay the bearer of these lines two hundred and thirty-six dollars and charge the same to my account.

"E. D. Wheatley"

was an unconditional order to pay.

Although these cases were decided at an early date the courts would apply the same standards of interpretation to the language used and would arrive at the same conclusion today. There is nothing in the Code which would justify a court in coming to a different conclusion in interpreting the same or similar language.

If an instrument is a note, or certificate of deposit, to be negotiable it must contain language which connotes an unconditional promise to pay. A mere acknowledgement of a debt is not sufficient, but an acknowledgment of a debt with words indicating that the debt is to be paid is a sufficient promise to pay. For example, "I owe you $100" has been held not to be a promise to pay, but "Due John Jones or order $100 payable December 1st" has been held to be a promise to pay.

Promise or Order Must Be Unconditional. If the promise does not bind the promisor to pay in all events, it is a conditional promise, and the instrument is nonnegotiable. Likewise, if the order does not demand the drawee to pay in all events, it is conditional, and the instrument is nonnegotiable. Whether or not a promise or order is unconditional must be determined from an interpretation of the language of the instrument. An instrument, to be negotiable, must be so drafted that, by reading it, the nature and extent of the parties' obligations can be determined. If an instrument is so drafted that it is necessary to read some other document, not a party of the instrument but referred to in it, in order to determine the obligations of the parties to the instrument, such instrument is not negotiable.

For example, an instrument which includes a statement such as "payment to be made subject to the terms of a mortgage of even date herewith" is nonnegotiable; but a statement in an instrument such as "This note is secured by a mortgage of even date herewith" does not affect the negotiable character of the instrument. In determining the rights of the parties to the first instrument, a person would have to read the instrument and the mortgage referred to in the instrument.

The reference to the mortgage in the second instrument merely states a fact—the instrument is secured by a mortgage—and the rights and duties of the parties to the instrument are in no way affected by the terms of the mortgage. In determining the rights of the parties, there would in such a case be no reason to refer to the terms of the mortgage.

Express Conditions. If the promise or order is expressly conditioned on the happening of some event, the instrument is nonnegotiable. For example, a promise to pay "if I am elected to Congress" is clearly conditional. If the instrument contains a stipulation which, under the accepted rules of contract law, would be interpreted as an express condition, the instrument is nonnegotiable.

Special Provisions of the Code. The Code sets out certain provisions which may be included in an instrument without affecting the instrument's negotiability. A provision in an instrument stating that it is given in payment for goods to be delivered at some future date does not render the instrument nonnegotiable. Some earlier decisions held that such a provision implied that the promise or order to pay was conditioned on the delivery of the goods. This view is rejected under the Code. (3–105 [1] [*a*].)

A statement of the consideration for which the instrument is given, whether such consideration has been performed or promised, or a statement of the transaction which gave rise to the instrument does not affect its negotiability. A notation on a check or other instrument stating that it was given in payment of last month's rent or next month's rent or a statement that the instrument is given in payment of the purchase price of goods will not render the instrument nonnegotiable. Likewise, a statement in an instrument that it is given for payment as per contract for the purchase of goods of even date, maturity being in conformity with the terms of such contract, does not affect the negotiable character of the instrument. Such a provision does not incorporate the contract by reference. (3–105 [1] [b].)

A statement that the instrument is drawn under a letter of credit or that it is secured, whether by mortgage, reservation of title or otherwise, is permissible, but a statement that the instrument is payable according to the terms of the mortgage or other security agreement would incorporate the terms of the security agreements and would render the instrument nonnegotiable. (3–105 [1] [d] and [e].) and 3–105 [2] [a].)

Where an instrument indicates a particular fund to be debited or any other fund or source from which reimbursement is expected, or where an instrument issued by a government or governmental agency or unit contains a provision stating that payment shall be made out of a particular fund or from the proceeds of a particular source, such an indication or provision does not render the instrument nonnegotiable. Such statements on instruments are interpreted as directions for record-keeping purposes and not as conditioning the promise or order. However, a promise or order to *pay out of a fund* will condition the promise or order since the instrument does not carry the general obligation of the maker or drawer; the obligation to pay is, in effect, conditioned on there being a sufficient balance in the fund to cover the instrument, and, since one would have to go outside the instrument to learn whether or not the balance was sufficient, an instrument containing such a provision would not be negotiable even though the fund would be sufficient. (3–105 [1] [f] and [g]) and (3–105 [2] [b].) As noted above, this latter rule does not apply to instruments issued by a government or governmental agency or unit. (3–105 [1] [g].)

Under pre-Code law the courts were not in accord as to the negotiable character of an instrument issued by a partnership or unincorporated association where such instrument obligated the partnership or unincorporated association to pay but did not bind the partners or members individually. Some courts held that since the partners or members were not bound individually the promise or order was conditional, and the instrument was not negotiable. The drafters of the Code resolved the controversy in favor of the negotiability of such an instrument. The Code provides that a promise or order otherwise unconditional is not made conditional by the fact that the instrument is limited to payment out of the entire assets of a partnership, unincorporated association, trust or estate by or on behalf of which the instrument is issued. (3–105 [1] [*h*].)

Summary

A draft or check, to be negotiable, must contain an order to pay and a certificate of deposit or note must contain a promise to pay. The promise or order must be unconditional. Whether a promise or order is or is not unconditional is a matter of the interpretation of the language used and it is the duty of the judge hearing the case to interpret the written instrument.

An instrument is not negotiable if the promise or order to pay is expressly conditioned. Provisions which may be included in an instrument without affecting its negotiable character are set out in the Code. Briefly, they are: implied or constructive conditions; notation of consideration given or the transaction giving rise to the instrument; reference to another agreement for rights of prepayment and acceleration; statement that it is drawn under a letter of credit or that it is secured; notation of account to be debited or out of which reimbursement is to be made; if issued by government or governmental agency or unit, fund out of which payment is to be made or procured; and duty to pay limited to entire assets of partnership, unincorporated association, trust or estate.

A promise or order governed by the terms of another instrument or a promise or order to pay out of a particular fund is not unconditional.

United States v. *Farrington*
172 F.Supp. 797 (D. Mass. 1959)

This was an action of the United States (plaintiff) against Phillips Farrington (defendant) to recover a judgment on a note. Judgment for the United States.

The note in litigation was given by Davis Aircraft Engineering, Inc., now bankrupt, to a bank as payee. The note contained the following: "having deposited with this obligation as Collateral Security assigned Government Contracts. This note evidences a borrowing made under and is subject to the terms of loan agreement dated Jan. 3, 1952, between the undersigned and the payee thereof and should the market value of the same, in the judgment of the holder or holders hereof decline we promise to furnish satisfactory additional collateral on demand." Farrington signed the note on the back. Farrington contended that the note was not negotiable and that therefore he was not liable on his endorsement. The court held the note was not negotiable but that Farrington was liable as a guarantor.

ALDRICH, DISTRICT JUDGE.   Farrington's position is that as a matter of law an instrument is conditional if it incorporates by reference a separate document making it impossible to know whether the obligation is certain or not until that document is examined. The Massachusetts cases upon which Farrington relies, with the possible exception of *Costelo* v. *Crowell,* all involved separate agreements that in fact imposed contingencies when read into the instrument. Whether the instrument becomes nonnegotiable because on its face it is subject to an agreement which may impose contingencies even though in actual fact it does not, is quite a different matter, leading to policy questions of large compass. Although this precise question is often left undiscussed by the cases, there is a considerable body of authority to the effect that if the instrument contains the phrase, "subject to" the terms of another document, or words to that effect, the reference is fatal to negotiability regardless of the actual provisions of the other document.

This principle has apparently been modified in some jurisdictions, particularly with regard to corporate bonds, to the extent of permitting the incorporation of terms of a mortgage or deed of trust designed to secure the obligation of the primary instrument. In such cases it is said that making the note of bond subject to the provisions of what is clearly an agreement regarding collateral security in no way "restricts, or burdens with conditions, the absolute promise to pay" contained in the instrument.

In the case at bar it could be argued from the placement of the handwritten words that the note was described as subject to the loan agreement for the purpose of indicating the circumstances under which it was executed, and setting forth more fully the undertaking with respect to collateral security, and not in order to limit the promise to pay. However, I believe this is not the only and necessary interpretation, and that the ambiguity can be resolved only by examination of the loan agreement. It is true that inspection of this agreement will resolve the ambiguity in favor of the United States, but I rule that that is not enough to make the instrument negotiable.

Sum Certain in Money

Sum Certain. The promise or order in an instrument must be to pay a sum certain in money. The sum is certain provided it is possible to compute from what is stated in the instrument the amount which will be required to discharge the instrument at any given time. The Code provides that the sum is certain even though it is to be paid with stated interest or in installments; or with different rates of interest before and after default or at a specified date; or with a stated discount or addition if paid before or after the date fixed for payment. A provision providing for the payment with exchange or less exchange, whether at a fixed rate or at the current rate, or a provision for the payment of the costs of collection or an attorney's fee or both on default does not render the instrument nonnegotiable. Although these charges or credits cannot be predetermined, business practice justifies the permission of their inclusion in the instrument without their making the sum payable uncertain. (3–106.)

Under pre-Code law where an instrument contained a provision which provided for the giving of a discount or an allowance if the party liable paid prior to the due date some courts would hold that such a provision made the sum payable uncertain and the instrument therefore nonnegotiable. Under the Code the inclusion of such a provision does not affect the negotiable character of the instrument. (3–106 [1] [c].)

Payable in Money. The requirement that, to be negotiable, the instrument must be payable in money distinguishes negotiable instruments from negotiable warehouse receipts, negotiable bills of lading, and similar instruments which have many characteristics of negotiability.

In some of the earlier cases the courts held that if an instrument was made payable in a foreign money not current at the place of payment, the instrument was not negotiable. Today, however, the courts hold the instrument to be negotiable if the money stipulated is issued by a government having a recognized standing in international trade.

If the holder has the option of accepting something other than money, the negotiability of the instrument is not affected, but if the party obligated to pay the instrument has the option of doing something other than paying money, the instrument is not negotiable.

The Code provides: An instrument is payable in money if the medium of exchange in which it is payable is money at the time the instrument is made. An instrument payable in "currency" or "current funds" is payable in money. (3–107 [1].)

The Code also provides that a promise or order to pay a sum stated in a foreign currency is for a sum certain in money and may be satisfied by payment of that number of dollars of the value of the foreign currency at the time of payment unless the instrument specified that it is payable in the foreign currency. (3–107 [2].)

Summary

Under the provisions of the Code a sum is a sum certain if the sum necessary to discharge the instrument at any specific time can be computed from the terms on the instrument. A provision for the payment of interest, payment in installments, payment of a different rate of interest before and after default or a specified date, or a discount or allowance for prepayment does not affect the negotiable character of the instrument. Provisions for the payment of exchange or collection costs or attorneys' fees are allowable.

An instrument is payable in money if the medium of exchange in which it is payable is money at the time the instrument is made. A stated sum payable in a foreign currency is a sum certain in money and may be paid in dollars of equal value unless otherwise agreed.

Olin of N.Y., Inc. v. Weintraub
1 U.C.C. Rep. 623 (N.Y. Sup. Ct., Nassau Cty. 1965)

This was an action by Olin of N.Y., Inc. (plaintiff), against Weintraub (defendant) on a promissory note in which a default judgment was entered and the case was before the court to open the default and stay all proceedings. The request was denied.

The note was payable in installments and Weintraub attempted to pay an installment with a certified check of a corporation. The check had been certified by the drawer. Olin of N.Y., Inc. refused to accept the check as payment.

LEVINE, JUDGE.   It is conceded by both parties that the judgment was entered upon a confession of judgment by reason of the fact that Weintraub attempted to pay an installment on a promissory note, payable in installments, by the check of a corporation, which was certified by the drawer. Such payment was rejected upon the ground that Olin of N.Y., Inc., was on notice that the corporate maker was unable to meet its obligations the extent of which is admittedly unknown to Olin of N.Y., Inc. The subject note contained an unconditional promise to pay a sum certain in money (Uniform Commercial Code section 3–104, section 3–107 [1]). Such an instrument can only be paid in legal tender in the absence of an agreement by the payee to accept some other medium of exchange. A certified check is not money within the meaning of the Uniform Commercial Code. (3–107 [1].) Since Olin of N.Y., Inc., was under no obligation to accept payment in any other medium of payment except money, it cannot be deemed to have entered judgment without legal sanction.

Payable on Demand or at Definite Time

Payable on Demand.   Instruments payable on demand include those payable at sight or on presentation and those in which no time for payment is stated. If the instrument is a note it is customary to state specifically that it is payable on demand. A draft usually states "on sight" or "on presentment" pay to, and so forth. Since no time of payment is stated in the standard form of a check it is payable on demand. (3–108.) A cause of action accrues on a demand instrument upon its date, or, if no date is stated, on the date of issue. (3–122 [1] [b].) Unless the instrument provides otherwise, interest runs on a demand instrument, in the case of a maker, acceptor or other party primarily liable, at the rate provided by law for a judgment, from the date of demand. (3–122 [4] [a].)

Definite Time.   From a commercial standpoint the time at which the payment of an instrument is due should be certain or readily ascertainable. The provisions in the Code relative to payment at a definite time are intended to provide for reasonable certainty as to such time. An instrument drawn payable on or before a stated date or at a fixed period after a stated date or at a fixed period after sight is payable at a definite time. (3–109 [1] [*a*] and [*b*].) If an instrument is payable at a fixed date, such as July 1, 1975, the obligor would have no right to pay and discharge his obligation before that date. To avoid this result an instrument may be made payable "on or before July 1, 1975." This gives the party primarily liable on the instrument the right to pay at an earlier date and thus stop the running of interest on an interest-bearing obligation.

It is a common practice to make an instrument payable at a specific time after date such as "30 days after date." If the instrument is dated it is payable at a fixed period after a stated date but in case it is not dated the instrument is not payable at a definite time and is not negotiable. The holder may cure this defect, however, by filling in the date before negotiating the instrument. (3–115.) A time draft may be payable at a fixed time after sight which is in effect a provision that it will be paid at a fixed time after the instrument is presented to the drawee for acceptance.

Under the Code provisions permission to accelerate or extend the time of payment of an instrument does not affect its negotiability. The instrument may, by its terms, give the holder the right to accelerate the time of payment at his option or if he deems himself insecure, or it may provide for automatic acceleration on the happening of a stated event. Also, the holder may be given the right to extend the time of payment at his option and the party primarily liable may be given the right to extend the time of payment to a further definite time, or the instrument may provide that the time of payment will be extended automatically upon or after a specified act or event. However, an instrument made payable only upon an act or event uncertain as to time of occurrence is not payable at a definite time even though the act or event has occurred. (3–109 [1] [*c*] and [*d*] and (3–109 [2].)

Summary

An instrument is payable on demand if it is stated to be so payable, or if it is payable at sight or on presentment, or if no time of payment is stated. An instrument is payable at a definite time if it is payable on or before a stated date or at a fixed time after a stated date or at a fixed period after sight. A provision in an instrument giving the parties the right to accelerate the time of payment, or giving the holder the right to extend the time of payment, or giving the party primarily obligated the right to extend the time of payment to a future fixed date does not affect its negotiability. An instrument payable only upon or after the happening of an act or event, the time of occurrence of which is uncertain, is not payable at a definite time.

Liberty Aluminum Products Co. v. *Cortis*
14 Pa. D. & C.2d 624 (1958)

This was an action by Liberty Aluminum Products Co. (plaintiff) against John Cortis and Julia Cortis (defendants) on a promissory note in which the Cortises petitioned to have a judgment entered against them set aside. Petition refused.

Liberty Aluminum Products Co. took a judgment on a promissory note in the amount of $3,400 against Cortis and wife. The Cortises made a motion to set the judgment aside basing their motion primarily on two alleged deficiencies: The lack of a maturity date of installments, and the failure to show a default prior to the entry of judgment.

CUMMINS, JUDGE.   The first alleged deficiency is the one which must be explored a little further. Cortises' motion to strike completely overlooks the Uniform Commercial Code § 3–108. This code states categorically that "instruments payable on demand include those payable at sight or on presentation and *those in which no time for payment is stated.*" Under the Commercial Code this instrument is a demand note by virtue of its tenor.

Even if this were not so, the logic of the situation compels this conclusion. The parties have the right to use a blank form and tailor it to their needs. And the failure to include installment payments simply and clearly means that none were intended.

The next question relates to the demand or default necessary prior to the entry of judgment on a demand note. The answer to that is simple: None. The entry of the note itself is sufficient demand for payment.

Payable to Order or Bearer

Necessity of Words of Negotiability.   A basic rule of contract law is that an obligation or risk will not be imposed on a party unless he has voluntarily assumed the obligation or risk. When a person issues a negotiable instrument he assumes obligations and risks which are greater than those assumed on a nonnegotiable instrument. By issuing a negotiable instrument the promisor gives the promisee the power to cut off, by negotiating the instrument to a holder in due course, all personal defenses he (the promisor) might have to the instrument, whereas if the instrument is not negotiable an assignee of the promisee takes subject to all outstanding defenses. The issuer of an instrument indicates that he intends the instrument to be negotiable by drawing it payable to bearer or to the order of a named payee.

"Bearer" and "order" are the words customarily used to indicate the issuer's intent that the instrument be negotiable. Other language, however, which clearly indicates such intent may be used. (3–104 [1] [*d*].)

Payable to Order. The general rule set out in the Code provides that an instrument is payable to order when by its terms it is payable to the order or assigns of any person therein specified with reasonable certainty, or to him or his order. For example: an instrument drawn payable "to the order of John Jones" or "to John Jones or order" or "to John Jones or assigns" would be payable to order. Also, an instrument is payable to order when it is conspicuously designated on its face as "exchange" or the like and names a payee. (3–110 [1].) However, an instrument containing words such as "payable upon return of this instrument properly endorsed" is not payable to order. (3–110 [2].)

An instrument may be payable to the order of the maker or drawer or to the drawee, or to a person who is not maker, drawer or drawee. If a note is drawn payable to the order of the maker, the maker is in effect promising to pay himself, and before the instrument could be put in the channels of trade the maker would have to endorse the instrument as payee and negotiate it. Drafts are frequently drawn payable to the order of the drawer. The standard form of a trade acceptance is drawn "pay to the order of ourselves," and an instrument so worded is payable to the order of the drawer.

If the customer of a bank owes the bank for money borrowed, he frequently draws a check on the bank as drawee payable to the order of the bank as payee. The effect of giving the bank such a check is to authorize the bank to pay itself out of the drawer's account with the bank. Usually an instrument is made payable to a payee who is not maker, drawer, or drawee. (3–110 [1] [*a*], [*b*], and [*c*].)

An instrument may be drawn payable to the order of two or more payees together or in the alternative. (3–110 [1] [*d*].) If the instrument is drawn payable to the order of two or more payees together—John Jones *and* Henry Smith—it is payable to all of the named payees and it may be negotiated, discharged or enforced only by all of them. (3–116 [*b*].) But if it is payable to the order of two or more payees in the alternative—John Jones *or* Henry Smith—it may be negotiated, discharged or enforced by any of them who possesses it. (3–116 [*a*].)

An instrument may be drawn payable to the order of an estate, trust or fund as, for example, "pay to the order of the estate of William Jones, deceased" or "pay to the order of the Wells Trust." In such case the instrument is payable to the representative of the estate or trust or to his successor. (3–110 [1] [*e*].)

An instrument may be drawn payable to the order of an office or to an officer by his title. An instrument drawn payable "to the order of the treasurer of Cook County" or "to the order of Henry Smith, treasurer of Cook County" is an order instrument. In case of the latter, the instrument is payable to Henry Smith as principal but the incumbent of the office or his successor may act as if he were the holder. (3–110 [1] [*f*].)

Under pre-Code law there existed an uncertainty as to the character of an instrument drawn payable to the order of a partnership or unincorporated association. Under the provisions of the Code such an instrument is an order instrument payable to the partnership or association and may be endorsed or transferred by any person authorized to act in behalf of the partnership or association. (3–110 [1] [g].) This provision of the Code is such that instruments drawn payable to the order of a partnership or unincorporated association are comparable in most respects to like instruments drawn payable to the order of a named corporation.

If an instrument is drawn payable both to order and to bearer it is payable to order unless the bearer words are handwritten or typewritten. (3–110 [3].) This rule clears up an ambiguity created when a form instrument is used and the issuer of the instrument fills in either "order" or "bearer" and neglects to cross out the printed "order" or "bearer" on the form with the result that it is drawn payable to both "order" and "bearer." The rule as stated is in keeping with the general rule that written words in a form take priority over printed words.

Payable to Bearer.   An instrument drawn "pay to bearer" or "pay to the order of bearer" or "pay to John Jones or bearer" is payable to bearer, but an instrument drawn "pay to bearer John Jones" is not bearer paper and is not a negotiable instrument. The term "pay to bearer John Jones" has been interpreted as authorizing payment to John Jones and no other person; consequently, the issuer of the instrument has indicated that he is not issuing negotiable paper. (3–111 [a] and [b]). An instrument drawn payable to "cash" or to the order of "cash" or any other indication which does not purport to designate a specific payee is bearer paper. Since the instrument is so worded that it indicates that the issuer intends it to be negotiable yet names no payee who can endorse and negotiate it, it is held to be bearer paper which is negotiable without endorsement. (3–111 [c].)

Summary

An instrument is payable to order when by its terms it is payable to the order or assigns of a payee specified therein with reasonable certainty or to him or to his order or when it is conspicuously designated on its face as "exchange" or the like and names a payee.

The instrument may be drawn payable to the order of the maker or drawer or drawee or to a person who is not maker, drawer, or drawee or to two or more payees together or in the alternative. It may be drawn payable to the order of an estate or trust in which case it is payable to the order of the representative of the estate or trust or his successor. An instrument payable to the order of an office or to the holder of an office or to a partnership or unincorporated association is an order instrument. An instrument payable both to order and bearer is an order instrument unless the word "bearer" is written or typewritten.

United States v. First National Bank of Boston

268 F.Supp. 298 (D. Mass. 1967)

This was an action by the United States (plaintiff) to recover payment it had made on a fraudulently issued postal money order to First National Bank (defendant), an endorsee of the postal money order. One question before the court in this case was whether the postal money order was a negotiable instrument within the meaning of the Uniform Commercial Code. The court held that it was not a negotiable instrument.

The face of a blank postal domestic money order, so far as relevant, shows a blank line following the words "PAY TO" to be filled in with the name of the person to whom the money order is payable; three blank lines following the word "FROM" to be filled in with the name and address of the purchaser; a blank for the "initial of issuing employee"; and a blank for the "issuing office stamp." On the back of such an order appears the following:

PAYEE MUST ENDORSE BELOW ON LINE MARKED 'PAYEE'. OWNERSHIP OF THIS ORDER MAY BE TRANSFERRED TO ANOTHER PERSON OR FIRM IF THE PAYEE WILL WRITE THE NAME OF SUCH PERSON OR FIRM ON THE LINE MARKED 'PAY TO' BEFORE WRITING HIS OWN NAME ON THE SECOND LINE. MORE THAN ONE ENDORSEMENT IS PROHIBITED BY LAW. BANK STAMPS ARE NOT REGARDED AS ENDORSEMENTS.
PAY TO _____

THIS ORDER BECOMES INVALID AFTER 20 YEARS. THEREAFTER NO CLAIM FOR PAYMENT WILL BE CONSIDERED.

WYZANSKI, CHIEF JUDGE. First National Bank's broadest contention is that today the postal domestic money order, unlike its pre-1951 prototype, is a negotiable instrument within the meaning of the Uniform Commercial Code and that it is therefore proper to apply to it § 3–418 of the Code which provides that "payment . . . of any instrument is final in favor of a holder in due course, or a person who has in good faith changed his position in reliance on the payment."

There is difficulty in sustaining this broad contention. To be a negotiable instrument within the Uniform Commercial Code and within the laws of the states which have adopted substantially all its provisions, a writing must "be payable to order or to bearer." § 3–104 (1)(d). "An instrument is payable to order when by its terms it is payable to the order or assigns of any person therein speciefid. . . ." § 3–110(1). We may assume, without deciding, that a money order though it does not use the word "order" uses equivalent language because the order, going beyond giving a direction to "PAY TO" a specified purchaser, states that "ownership of this order may be transferred to another person or firm if the person will write the name of such person or firm on the line marked 'pay to' before writing his own name on the second line." Compare Comment 5 to § 3–110. However, the money order adds that "More than one endorsement is prohibited by law." Such a restriction is contrary to § 3–301 of the Uniform Commercial Code which provides that "The holder of an instrument whether or not he is the owner may transfer and negotiate it," and is out of harmony with § 3–206(1) which provides that "No restrictive endorsement prevents further transfer or negotiation of the instrument." Thus it cannot be said that in all respects a postal domestic money order is like the ordinary negotiable instrument covered by modern codes and statutes.

Special Terms

Additional Terms and Omissions.   Businessmen and banks use many special forms of commercial paper drafted to serve their particular needs. Such forms may include terms which have no affect on the negotiability of the instrument. Likewise instruments are sometimes drafted which omit terms customarily included in standard forms of the instrument but their omission in no way affects the validity or negotiability of the instrument.

Standard forms of notes and drafts frequently include statements of consideration such as "for value received" or "in payment for goods sold and delivered." The omission of such statements of consideration, however, does not affect the negotiable character of the instrument.

It is also a common practice to state in the instrument the place where the instrument is drawn and/or where it is payable. The place where the instrument is drawn is usually stated together with the date of issue as, for example, Chicago, Ill., Sept. 26, 1970. And the place where it is to be paid is generally noted on the instrument by such a phrase as: "Payable at First Bank of Detroit, Mich." The negotiability of the instrument is not affected, however, by the omission of these details. (3–112 [1] [a].)

A statement that collateral has been given to secure obligations either on the instrument or otherwise of an obligor on the instrument, or that in case of default the holder may realize on or dispose of the collateral, or a promise or power to maintain or protect collateral or to give additional collateral does not render the instrument nonnegotiable. (3–112 [1] [b] and [c].) Under pre-Code law some courts held that such provisions were promises to do something other than pay money and that therefore the instrument was not negotiable.

A term authorizing the confession of judgment on the instrument when due or a term purporting to waive the benefit of any law intended for the advantage or protection of the obligor such as, for instance, appraisement and valuation laws or exemption laws, does not affect the negotiability of the instrument. However, a clause which authorizes confession of judgment prior to the due date of the note and a demand for payment has been held by a number of courts to render the note nonnegotiable.

The negotiability of a draft or check is not affected by a term providing that the payee by endorsing or cashing the draft or check acknowledges full satisfaction of an obligation of the drawer. Such a term is frequently included in a draft or check issued by an insurance company in payment of a loss claim. (3–112 [1] [*f*].)

A seal on an instrument does not affect the negotiable character of the instrument nor does it affect the character of the instrument insofar as the provisions of the Article on commercial paper are concerned. The seal may, however, have some effect on rights not covered in the Code. (3–113.)

The negotiability of an instrument is not affected by the fact that it is undated, antedated, or postdated. Where the instrument is antedated or postdated, the time when it is payable is determined by the stated date if the instrument is payable on demand or at a fixed period after date, and where the instrument or any signature thereon is dated, the date is presumed to be correct. (3–114.)

Ambiguous Terms.   The courts have been consistent in their interpretation of certain ambiguous terms sometimes found in commercial paper. Where there is doubt whether the instrument is a note or draft the holder may treat it as either except that a draft drawn on the drawer is treated as a note. In such an instrument the drawer is ordering himself as drawee to pay the draft.

The general rule of interpretation, that handwritten terms control typewritten and printed terms and typewritten terms control printed terms, applies to commercial paper.

If there is a conflict between the amount written on the instrument and the figures, the words control unless the words are ambiguous in which event the figures control.

If an instrument provides for the payment of interest but the rate is not stated, the rate payable is the judgment rate at the place of payment, and the interest is computed from the date of the instrument, or if it is undated from the date of issue.

If two or more persons sign an instrument as maker, acceptor or drawer or endorser as part of the same transaction, they are jointly and severally liable, unless the instrument specifies otherwise, even though the instrument contains such words as "I promise to pay." (3–118.)

Newman v. *Manufacturers National Bank*

152 N.W.2d 564 (Ct. App. Mich. 1967)

This was an action by Newman (plaintiff) against Manufacturers National Bank (defendant) on the grounds that Manufacturers had improperly paid two of Newman's checks totalling $1,200. Judgment for Manufacturers National Bank and Newman appealed. Affirmed.

In 1955, Newman drew the two checks payable to Belle Epstein but left them undated. There was a printed dateline on the checks which read "Detroit,

Mich. _____ 195____ "but Newman never filled it in. Newman claimed that over the next four years he had paid all but $400 of the $1,200 debt personally to Epstein and that she told him she had destroyed the two checks. Then on April 17, 1964, the checks were cashed under the endorsement of Belle Epstein. By that time someone had written in the date April 16, 1964 but the original printed figures "195____" remained clearly visible. Newman objected to having his account charged on the grounds the bank had not used ordinary care in paying checks that were stale and altered on their face.

HOLBROOK, JUDGE.   The two checks were dated April 16, 1964. It is true that the dates were completed in pen and ink subsequent to the date of issue. However, this was not known by Bank. Bank had a right to rely on the dates appearing on the checks as being correct. Section 3–114 provides in part as follows:

(1) The negotiability of an instrument is not affected by the fact that it is undated, antedated or postdated. . . .

(3) Where the instrument or any signature thereon is dated, the date is presumed to be correct."

Also (3–115) provides in part as follows:

The following rules apply to every instrument: . . .

"(b) Handwritten terms control typewritten and printed terms, and typewritten control printed.

. . . Without notice to the contrary, Bank was within its rights to assume that the dates were proper and filled in by Newman or someone authorized by him.

Newman admitted at trial that Bank acted in good faith in honoring the two checks of Newman's in question, and therefore Bank's good faith is not in issue.

· · · ·

In order to determine if defendant bank's action in honoring Newman's two checks under the facts present herein constituted an exercise of proper procedure, we turn to Article 4 of the U.C.C. Section 4–401 provides as follows:

(1) As against its customer, a bank may charge against his account any item which is otherwise properly payable from that account even though the charge creates an overdraft.

(2) A bank which in good faith makes payment to a holder may charge the indicated account of its customer according to

(a) the original tenor of his altered item; or

(b) the tenor of his completed item, even though the bank knows the item has been completed unless the bank has notice that the completion was improper.

Problem Cases

1. Invitations to bid for certain government contracts require bidders to make bid deposits in U.S. currency "or any other form of credit instruments, made payable . . . on demand including first party checks." Surplus Tire submitted a bid and enclosed its check for $500.50 payable to the United States Treasurer. On the face of the check was handprinted the following:

Bid deposit: DSSO Oakland.

Sale 44–8035—Notice: Do not deposit, cash or negotiate this check unless an award and contract is made pursuant to the bid submitted. Otherwise this check will be dishonored.

Surplus Tire's bid was rejected on the grounds the bid deposit was not a negotiable instrument and Surplus protests the decision. Is the Government or Surplus correct as to the negotiability of the check? Why?

2. Drawer drew eight checks which were negotiated from the payee to the current holder. Each check bore the printed words "This check is in payment of the following" followed by the written words "Subject to delivery (of a particular make and year of automobile) with title." Drawer alleges that the holder seeking payment of the checks, knew or should have known that the conditions had not been fulfilled, and did not become a holder in due course but only an assignee of the payee and subject to all defenses against the payee. Does Drawer have a winning argument?

3. An instrument otherwise negotiable contained the following provision: "This note is given in payment for merchandise and is to be liquidated by payments received on account of sale of such merchandise." Is this a negotiable instrument?

4. Is the following a negotiable instrument?

February 26, 1953

"Subject to Approval of Title
"Pay to the Order of Vernon Butterfield $1,997.90.
"The Culver Company
"By A. M. Culver"

5. Is the following a negotiable instrument?
"I.O.U. A. Gay, the sum of seventeen 5/100 dollars for value received.
"John R. Rooke"

6. Miller signed a promissory note for $15,000 payable on demand. The note also contained a clause stating that it was secured by a mortgage on real property. Would this be a negotiable note?

7. An instrument otherwise negotiable contained the following provision: "In case this note is collected by an attorney, either with or without suit, the maker agrees to pay a reasonable attorney's fee." Is the instrument negotiable?

8. An installment sales contract that otherwise would qualify as a negotiable instrument contains a clause stating that the holder of the contract can pay taxes, assessments, and insurance if the obligor does not and then recover what he pays from the obligor. Would this clause make the contract nonnegotiable? Why or why not?

9. Sylvia signed a note dated May 25, 1963, obligating him to pay to Ferri or to her order $3,000 "within ten (10) years after date." Is this a negotiable instrument?

10. O'Rourke sued the legal heirs of Frank J. Saltalamachia on the following instrument:

Pay to L. O'Rourke _____$1,000
F. J. Saltalamachia

The heirs contended that this is not a negotiable instrument. Was this contention correct?

11. A note dated January 20, 1966, and due on July 1, 1966, contained a clause that provided for confession of judgment at any time. Was the note negotiable?

chapter 39. Negotiation and Holder in Due Course

Negotiation

Nature of Negotiation. A negotiable instrument is intangible personal property and the basic rules of property law apply in determining the rights and liabilities of the parties to the transfer of such an instrument. In the previous chapter the requirements for negotiability were discussed. Certain special rules of law have been developed and these rules are applied in determining the rights acquired by the transferee where the property transferred is negotiable commercial paper.

A "holder" is a person who is in possession of a document of title, or an instrument, or an investment security, drawn, issued or endorsed to him, to his order, to bearer or in blank. (1–201 [20].) [1] Negotiation is the transfer of an instrument in such form that the transferee becomes a holder. The formal requirements for negotiation are very simple and are set out in the Code as follows: If the instrument is payable to order it is negotiated by delivery with any necessary endorsement; if it is payable to bearer it is negotiated by delivery. (3–202 [1].)

Nature of Endorsement. An endorsement of an instrument is made by the writing of the holder's name by him or on his behalf on the instrument or on a paper so firmly affixed thereto as to become a part thereof. (3–202 [2].) If the back of an instrument is written full of endorsements further endorsements should be made on a paper glued firmly to the instrument. Such a paper is called an "allonge."

To be effective as a negotiation an endorsement must convey the entire instrument or any unpaid residue. If it purports to be of less it operates only as a partial assignment. (3–202 [3].) This rule is based on consideration of

---

[1] The numbers in the parentheses refer to the sections of the Uniform Commercial Code, 1962.

practical business policy. One who has issued a negotiable instrument should not be required to make piecemeal payments to several persons. It is not an uncommon practice for a large obligation to be evidenced by a series of notes, thus enabling the holder to negotiate portions of the debt to different persons. Suppose, for instance, A borrows $10,000 from B. A might instead of giving B a $10,000 note, give him 10, $1,000 notes. B would then be in a position to negotiate a $1,000 note to each of 10 different persons.

Words of assignment, condition, waiver, guarantee, limitation or disclaimer of liability and the like accompanying an endorsement do not affect its character as an endorsement. (3–202 [4].) If holder A writes on the back of a negotiable instrument, "I hereby sell, assign and set over to B, without warranty, all my rights, title and interest in this instrument," and signs his name, this would operate as an endorsement and the instrument would thereby have been negotiated to B. However, the effect of the form of the endorsement on the rights of A and B is a matter separate and apart from that of endorsement and negotiation of the instrument. (3–119.)

Wrong or Misspelled Name. In endorsing an instrument the endorser should spell the name in the endorsement the same as it appears in the instrument. If the name is misspelled or is one other than his own the endorser may endorse in that name or his own, but a person who is paying or giving value for the instrument may require the endorser to sign both names. (3–203.)

Transfer of an Instrument. When an instrument is transferred the transferee has vested in him such rights as the transferor has therein. However, a transferee who has himself been a party to any fraud or illegality affecting the instrument or who as a prior holder has notice of a defense or claim against it cannot improve his position by taking from a later holder in due course. (3–201 [1].) For example, suppose Axe through fraudulent representations induces Bell to execute a negotiable note payable to Axe, and Axe then negotiates the instrument to Clark, who takes as a holder in due course. If Axe thereafter takes the instrument for value from Clark, Axe cannot acquire Clark's rights as a holder in due course. Axe was a party to the fraud which induced the instrument, and the holder of an instrument cannot improve his position by negotiating such instrument and then reacquiring it.

A transfer of a security interest in an instrument vests the rights of the transferor in the transferee to the extent of the interest transferred. Suppose, for example, Bell issues his negotiable note in the sum of $5,000 to Axe who then pledges it to First Bank to secure the payment of a $1,000 loan First Bank has made to Axe. First Bank takes as a holder in due course. Suppose then, before this loan which First Bank has made to Axe is due, First Bank is notified that Bell has a defense to the note. First Bank is a holder in due course only to the extent of its interest in the Bell note, that is, as security for the payment of the $1,000 obligation of Axe to First Bank.

Transfer of Order Instrument. If an order instrument is transferred without endorsement, the instrument has not been negotiated and the transferee does not become a holder in due course because he cannot qualify as a holder. However, unless the parties have otherwise agreed, any transfer for value of an instrument not payable to bearer gives the transferee the right to have the unqualified endorsement of the transferor, and should the transferor refuse to endorse the instrument with an unqualified endorsement the transferee would be entitled to a decree ordering the transferor to so endorse the instrument. The negotiation takes effect only when the endorsement is made and until that time there is no presumption that the transferee is the owner. If, subsequent to the transfer of the instrument to him but before he obtains the transferor's endorsement, the transferee learns that the obligor has a defense to the instrument or he learns of other matters which would prevent him from taking as a holder in due course, he could not qualify as a holder in due course. (3–201 [3].)

Summary

Negotiable commercial paper is intangible personal property. Such an instrument may be transferred or negotiated. Only a person to whom a negotiable instrument has been transferred can qualify as a holder in due course. If an instrument is payable to order it is negotiated by delivery with any necessary endorsement; if payable to bearer it is negotiated by delivery. An endorsement is made by the holder signing his name on the instrument or on a paper firmly affixed thereto. An instrument must be negotiated in its entirety. Words of assignment, condition or like accompanying an endorsement do not affect its character as an endorsement. In endorsing an instrument, if the holder's name is misspelled, the recommended practice is to endorse the name as it appears on the instrument followed by the correct name.

When an instrument is transferred the transferee acquires all the rights his transferor has in the instrument. A person cannot, however, improve his position by reacquiring an instrument. If one takes an instrument as security he acquires in the instrument only the value of his security. The transferee for value of an unendorsed order instrument has the right, unless otherwise agreed, to have the unqualified endorsement of his transferor. His position as a holder in due course is determined as of the time the transferor endorses the instrument.

Watertown Federal Savings & Loan Association v. *Spanks*

193 N.E.2d 333 (Sup. Jud. Ct. Mass. 1963)

This was an action by Watertown Federal Savings & Loan Association (plaintiff) against Robert W. Spanks and wife (defendants) to recover a judgment on a note.

Judgment for Watertown Federal Savings & Loan Association and the Spankses appealed. Judgment affirmed.

Spanks and wife executed a negotiable note payable to "Greenlaw & Sons Roofing & Siding Co." Greenlaw & Sons Roofing & Siding Co. indorsed the note "Greenlaw & Sons" and negotiated it to Colony Distributors, Inc., and Colony Distributors, Inc., negotiated the note to Watertown Federal Savings & Loan Association. Spanks refused to pay the note when due and set up defective work as a defense. Spanks and wife contended that the note was not properly indorsed and that Watertown Federal Savings & Loan Association is not a holder in due course.

CUTTER, JUSTICE. The trial judge correctly denied the Spanks' requested ruling as immaterial. It does not appear that Greenlaw & Sons and Greenlaw & Sons Roofing & Siding Co. are not the same company. The indorsement by Greenlaw was not shown to have been in a name other than his own nor is it shown that the name of the payee, as stated in the note, was not a name under which Greenlaw individually did business, identifiably repeated in the indorsement. Section 3–203 purports to give only an indorsee for value, and not the maker of a note, the power to require indorsement in both names in the circumstances stated in the section. No evidence was introduced with respect to the indorsement. It comes within § 3–307 (and see the official comments on that section), which reads in part, "(1) . . . When the effectiveness of a signature is put in issue (a) the burden of establishing it is on the party claiming under the signature; but (b) the signature is presumed to be genuine or authorized [with an exception not here pertinent]. (2) When signatures are . . . established, production of the instrument entitles a holder to recover on it unless the defendant establishes a defense." There was no evidence whatsoever to counter the presumption of the indorsement's regularity existing under § 3–307 (1) (b). Thus the signature of Greenlaw was established under § 3–307 (2), and the bank, as the holder of the note, see § 1–201 (20), is entitled to recover.

Jett v. Atlanta Federal Savings & Loan Association, Inc.

123 S.E.2d 27 (Ct. App. Ga. 1961)

This was an action by A. V. Jett (plaintiff) against Atlanta Federal Savings & Loan Association, Inc., and Mrs. Louise Obie (defendants). Judgment for Atlanta Federal Savings & Loan Association, Inc., and Mrs. Obie, and Jett appealed. Judgment reversed.

Atlanta Federal Savings & Loan Association, Inc. (Atlanta), drew a check in the amount of $2,000 on Fulton National Bank as drawee naming Mrs. Obie as payee. Mrs. Obie transferred the check, without indorsement and for consideration, to Jett. The drawee bank refused to pay the check on the ground that it was not indorsed by the payee. Jett sued Atlanta and Mrs. Obie on the check and Atlanta filed a demurrer which was sustained by the trial court.

TOWNSEND, PRESIDING JUDGE. Code § 14–420, which is § 49 of the Uniform Negotiable Instruments Law, provides in part: "Where the holder of an instrument payable to his order transfers it for value without indorsing it, the transfer vests in the transferee such title as the transferor had therein, and the transferee acquires, in addition, the right to have the indorsement of the transferor." Under this section it has been uniformly held that the common law or law merchant was changed to the extent that such a transferee receives all of the title of the transferor to a negotiable instrument and is entitled to sue thereon in his own name, but, without the indorsement, the instrument has not been negotiated and he takes subject to all the equities between the maker or drawer and the transferor. It is well settled in Georgia that such a transferee has title to and may maintain an action on a note purchased by him for a valuable consideration and in his possession without indorsement.

Atlanta contends, however, that as to checks, a form of bill of exchange, the rule should be different for the reason that Code § 14–102 defines a holder as "The payee or indorsee of a bill or note, who is in possession of it, or the bearer thereof," and under Code § 14–703 presentment for payment of a bill of exchange must be made by "the holder or by some person authorized to receive payment on his behalf," thus excluding a transferee who is not a payee or indorsee of order paper. It is obvious that as to a check, as well as to notes and other negotiable paper, title passes upon transfer and delivery for a valuable consideration. "A check may be transferred without written indorsement and such transfer vests in the transferee such title as the transferor had." Jett here has the legal title to the check and is entitled to enforce it, not in any capacity of a holder or a holder in due course, which he is not, but by virtue of his ownership.

[*This is not a Code case but the result would have been the same had the Code been in effect at the time of this transaction. Under Section 3–201, the transferee for value of an unendorsed order paper acquires ownership and the right to the transferor's endorsement.*]

Endorsements

Effect of Endorsement on Negotiation.   The effect of an endorsement on the further negotiation of the instrument will depend in part on whether it is an order instrument or a bearer instrument and in part on the form of the endorsement. It should be remembered that the form of an endorsement can have no effect on the negotiable character of the instrument; if an instrument is a negotiable instrument when issued, it continues to be a negotiable instrument, irrespective of the form of endorsement on the instrument. However, the form of the endorsement is important in determining the right of the holder to negotiate the instrument and in determining what the holder must do to negotiate the instrument.

A negotiable instrument may be endorsed for two distinct reasons. It may be endorsed because the endorsement is necessary to the negotiation of the instrument, or it may be endorsed for the purpose of adding the obligations of the endorser to those of the party primarily liable. When a person endorses a negotiable instrument, he thereby makes contractual promises to the endorsee and, with some exceptions, to subsequent holders of the instrument. The contractual liability of endorsers will be discussed in the next chapter. We shall confine our present discussion to the effect of the endorsement on the further negotiations of the instrument.

Kinds of Endorsements.   There are five kinds of endorsements recognized by the Code: (1) special, (2) in blank, (3) restrictive, (4) qualified, and (5) unqualified. Either of the first two kinds of endorsements may be combined with (4) and (5). If an instrument is endorsed with a special or in blank endorsement without the addition of qualifying words, the endorsement is unqualified. If an instrument is endorsed either with a special or in blank endorsement and qualifying words such as "without recourse" are added, the endorsement would be a qualified special or a qualified blank endorsement. Only the special, in blank and restrictive endorsements will, when used, have any effect on the further negotiation of the instrument. Whether an instrument is endorsed with a qualified or unqualified endorsement will affect only the contractual liability of the endorser.

Special Endorsement.   A special endorsement specifies the person to whom or to whose order it makes the instrument payable. Any instrument specially endorsed becomes payable to the order of the special endorsee and may be further negotiated only by his endorsement. (3–204 [1].) A special endorsement need not include words of negotiability; "Pay to Hall" is a special endorsement, "Pay any bank, banker or trust company," has been held to be a special endorsement. An order instrument endorsed with a special endorsement continues as an order instrument whereas a bearer instrument endorsed with a special endorsement is converted into an order instrument and must be endorsed by the endorsee before it is further negotiated.

Blank Endorsement.   An instrument endorsed in blank specifies no particular endorsee and may consist of a mere signature. An instrument payable to order and endorsed in blank becomes payable to bearer and may be negotiated by delivery alone until specially endorsed. (3–204 [2].) If an instrument drawn "Pay to the order of Brown" is endorsed "Brown," it is endorsed in blank. Such an instrument then becomes a bearer instrument and thereafter it can be negotiated by delivery alone until it is specially endorsed.

If an instrument is endorsed in blank and delivered to a holder, he may convert the blank endorsement into a special endorsement by writing over the signature of the endorser in blank any contract which will not in any way alter the obligation imposed by the blank endorsement. (3–204 [3].) If a negotiable instrument drawn "Pay to the order of Brown" is endorsed "Brown" and delivered to Finch as endorsee, Finch has the right to write over Brown's endorsement "Pay to Finch," thereby converting the bank endorsement into a special endorsement, and the instrument would then have to be endorsed by Finch before it could be further negotiated.

Restrictive Endorsement.   An endorsement is restrictive which either is conditional or purports to prohibit the further transfer of the instrument. (3–205 [a] and [b].) Such an endorsement as "pay to Clark if and only if he completes construction of house before November 1, 1966," is conditional, and an endorsement "Pay to Clark only" purports to prohibit the further transfer of the instrument.

Instruments deposited in banks by their customers are frequently endorsed with a restrictive endorsement. An endorsement which includes the words "for collection," "for deposit," "pay any bank," or like terms signifying a purpose of deposit or collection is a restrictive endorsement; and an endorsement which states that it is for the benefit or use of the endorser or of another person such as "Pay to Clark in trust for Drew" is also a restrictive endorsement. (3–205 [c] and [d].)

Effect of Restrictive Endorsement.   In regard to the effect of a restrictive endorsement a distinction is made between a bank as a restrictive endorsee and a nonbank restrictive endorsee. In general, no restrictive endorsement prevents further transfer or negotiation of the instrument. (3–206 [1].) Under this section of the Code a restrictive endorsement such as "Pay to Clark only," although recognized as a restrictive endorsement, would have no more effect on the further negotiation of the instrument than would on unrestricted endorsement.

In clearing checks and other collection items the standard practice is for the depository bank to send the item through "banking channels." Suppose, for instance, Clark endorses an item drawn on Y Bank or payable at Y Bank "for deposit" or "for collection" and deposits it at A Bank in which Clark has a commercial account. A Bank will credit the item to Clark's account and send it to M Bank which is a correspondent bank with which A Bank does business. M Bank in turn will send the item on to Y Bank for payment or collection. A Bank is the depository bank, M Bank the intermediary bank, and Y Bank the payor bank. M Bank and Y Bank in handling this item are neither given notice nor otherwise affected by the restrictive endorsement of Clark. (3–206 [2].)

Except for an intermediary bank, any transferee under an endorsement which is conditional or includes the words "for collection," "for deposit," "pay any bank," or like terms must pay or apply any value given by him for or on the security of the instrument consistently with the endorsement and to the extent that he does so he becomes a holder for value.

Suppose Clark endorses a check payable to his order "for deposit" and deposits it in A Bank in which Clark has a commercial account and A Bank credits Clark's account with the amount of the check. If the check is paid when presented to the drawee bank and remittance is made to A Bank, it will accept the money for the benefit of Clark. However, suppose A Bank permits Clark to withdraw part or all of the credit created by crediting his account with the amount of the check and the drawer of the check then stops payment on the check. The check will be returned to A Bank marked "payment stopped." A Bank is a holder for value for the amount of the credit created by the deposit of the check which A Bank has permitted Clark to withdraw, and, if it took the check before it was overdue and without notice or knowledge of defenses to it, A Bank can qualify as a holder in due course. (3–206 [3].)

The first taker of an instrument restrictively endorsed for the benefit of the endorser or another person must pay or apply any value given by him for or on the security of the instrument consistently with the endorsement and to the extent that he does so he becomes a holder for value. Suppose a negotiable instrument payable to the order of Clark is endorsed either "pay to Bell as trustee for Clark" or "Pay to Bell in trust for Drew." Bell, as trustee, owes a fiduciary duty to administer the trust instrument or its proceeds for the benefit of Clark or Drew as the case may be and to the extent he does so he is a holder of the instrument for value and if he can satisfy the additional requirements for a holder in due course he is a holder in due course to the extent he has given value. If Bell negotiates the instrument to Mack, Mack can take as a holder in due course unless at the time he (Mack) knows or should know that Bell is negotiating the instrument in breach of his duties as trustee. (3–206 [4].)

Grounds for Rescission of Endorsement. Negotiation is effective to transfer an instrument although the negotiation is made by an infant, a corporation exceeding its powers, or any other person without capacity; or it is obtained by fraud, duress or mistake of any kind; or is part of an illegal transaction; or is made in breach of duty. A negotiation made under the above circumstances is in an appropriate case subject to rescission, the declaration of a constructive trust or any other remedy permitted by law unless the instrument has subsequent to such endorsement been negotiated to a transferee who can qualify as a holder in due course. (3–207.) The situation discussed above is analogous to a sale of goods where the sale has been induced by fraud or misrepresentation. In such a case the seller may rescind the sale and recover the goods provided he acts before the goods are resold to a bona fide purchaser for value.

Reacquisition. Where an instrument is returned to or reacquired by a prior party he may cancel any endorsement which is not necessary to his title and reissue or further negotiate the instrument, but any intervening party is discharged as against the reacquiring party and subsequent holders not in due course and, if his endorsement has been canceled, is discharged as against subsequent holders in due course as well. For instance, suppose Axe as maker issues his negotiable note payable to the order of Clark. The note bears the following special endorsements: "Pay Drew, Clark," "Pay Evans, Drew," "Pay Finch, Evans," "Pay Gage, Finch," "Pay Drew, Gage." Drew has reacquired the instrument and may again negotiate it. When Drew reacquires the instrument he is relegated to the position he held when he first acquired the instrument. Consequently Evans, Finch, and Gage are not liable to Drew as prior endorsers and they would not be liable to a transferee of Drew who was not a holder in due course. If Drew, after reacquiring the instrument, canceled the endorsements of Evans, Finch, and Gage or any of them and then negotiated the instrument to a holder in due course, the endorser or endorsers whose endorsement was canceled would not be liable to a holder in due course. (3–208.)

Summary

Under the Code there are five kinds of endorsements: (1) special, (2) in blank, (3) restrictive, (4) qualified, and (5) unqualified. The first three have an effect on the negotiation of the instrument; the last two affect the liability of the parties only.

A special endorsement names a payee, and an instrument specially endorsed must be again endorsed before it is negotiated. A blank endorsement names no endorsee and may be the endorser's signature only. A blank endorsement converts the paper to a bearer instrument.

A restrictive endorsement does not prevent the further negotiation of the instrument but it does impose certain restrictions on the rights of the holder. Special rules relative to the rights of banks to instruments endorsed with words such as "for deposit" are set out in the Code.

If the instrument is endorsed by one not having contractual capacity or authority to endorse or the endorsement is obtained by fraud, duress or mistake, the endorsement is subject to rescission provided it is rescinded before the instrument is negotiated to a holder in due course.

One who reacquires an instrument does not improve his position. He may renegotiate it and his reacquisition discharges intervening endorsers from their liability to him.

McCullough v. *Stepp*

85 S.E.2d 159 (App. Ct. Ga. 1954)

This was an action by W. E. McCullough (plaintiff) against William C. Stepp (defendant) to recover a judgment on a promissory note. Judgment for Stepp, and McCullough appealed. Judgment reversed.

Floyd W. McBerry executed and delivered his negotiable promissory note payable to the order of William C. Stepp. Stepp indorsed the note as follows, "I hereby transfer my rights to this note over to W. E. McCullough. (signed) William C. Stepp," and negotiated it to McCullough. The note was not paid when due and McCullough sued Stepp as indorser of the note. Stepp set up as a defense that it was the intention of both Stepp and McCullough that Stepp was to transfer the note to McCullough "without recourse" and that he (Stepp) was not liable for the maker's default.

FELTON, CHIEF JUDGE. The indorsement in and of itself was not a qualified indorsement. N.I.L., sec. 38 provides:

A qualified indorsement constitutes the indorser a mere assignor of the title to the instrument. It may be made by adding to the indorser's signature the words, "without recourse," or any words of similar import. . . .

The words, "I hereby transfer my right to this note over to W. E. McCullough," are not words of similar import to "without recourse."

In Georgia, indorsements may be special, in blank, restrictive, qualified or conditional. (N.I.L., sec. 33.) A special indorsement specifies the person to whom, or to whose order, the instrument is to be payable, and the indorsement of such indorsee is necessary to the further negotiation of the instrument. An indorsement in blank specifies no indorsee, and an instrument indorsed in blank is payable to bearer and may be negotiated by delivery. (N.I.L., sec. 34.) In the instant case an indorsee was named and his indorsement was necessary to a further negotiation of the instrument. Therefore the indorsement here was a special indorsement. The indorsement being a special indorsement in full, Stepp could not contradict the terms thereof and show that the indorsement was intended to be a qualified one, in the absence of fraud or mistake. The only question presented in this case is the effect of the indorsement, and no questions of conditional delivery or the capacity of the indorser are involved.

The court erred in overruling the demurrer to the allegation in the answer set out above. Such error rendered all further proceedings in the case nugatory.

[*Although this is not a Code case the result would have been the same had the Code been in effect at the time of this transaction. The Code states that a purported assignment is an endorsement (3–202 [4]) and that if an endorsee is named the endorsement is a special endorsement. (3–204 [1].)*]

South End Bank and Trust Co. v. Nasin

158 A.2d 591 (Sup. Ct. Conn. 1960)

This was an action by South End Bank and Trust Company (plaintiff) against Joseph Nasin (defendant) for judgment for the amount of a check drawn by Nasin. Judgment for South End Bank and Trust Company and Nasin appealed. Judgment affirmed.

On December 26, 1956, Nasin drew a check for $10,000 on the Willimantic Trust Company to the order of Constructor's Inc. Constructor's Inc. endorsed the check "for deposit only, Constructor's Inc.," and deposited it on December 27, 1956, in its checking account in South End Bank and Trust Company (Bank). The deposit slip provided: (1) that the Bank was the depositor's agent for collection and assumed no responsibility beyond its exercise of due care, (2) that all items were credited subject to final payment, (3) that all checks were sent through regular banking channels for clearance, and (4) that the Bank had the right to charge back uncollectable items. The Bank credited the account of Constructor's Inc. with the $10,000 and permitted it to draw checks against the balance thus created. The credit was exhausted before the Bank received notice that payment had been stopped on the check. Nasin contends that since the check was endorsed with the restrictive endorsement, "For deposit only," the Bank cannot take as a holder in due course and that the defense of failure of consideration is available to him.

MELLITZ, ASSOCIATE JUSTICE.   The issue here is not determined solely by the character of the endorsement or by the statements on the deposit slip. We need not decide whether the endorsement is restrictive within the meaning of § 39–37 because the fact that an endorsement is restrictive does not necessarily prevent the endorsee from being a holder in due course. Irrespective of the language employed in the endorsement or on the deposit slip, Bank and Constructor's Inc. had a legal right to make their own contract with respect to the deposit, so long as the rights of third parties were not injuriously affected and the contract was not contrary to law or public policy. The legal effect of the deposit of the check, as well as the controlling factor determining the legal relationship of the parties, is to be found in their intent as disclosed by the circumstances of the transaction at the time the deposit was made. In accordance with the practice, which had prevailed on many prior occasions, of permitting Constructor's Inc. to draw against deposits of checks yet uncollected, the proceeds of the check were made immediately available for withdrawal upon the deposit of the check by Constructor's Inc. Under such circumstances, the presumption is that title to the check passed to the bank. It became a holder for value in due course. General Statutes, § 39–53. The facts and circumstances surrounding the making of the deposit indicated a clear intention by the parties that Constructor's Inc. might draw against the deposit immediately, and it did so. The relationship between the parties was fixed by these unchallenged acts rather than by what appeared in the endorsement or on the deposit slip. When it was delivered by Nasin to Constructor's Inc., the check was negotiable on its face. Constructor's Inc. had the power to deliver it to the Bank, and the Bank could accept it for collection, or for credit to the account of Constructor's Inc. with a right in the latter to draw against it immediately. It was competent for the Bank to waive the provision printed on its deposit slip to the effect that it was acting merely as collecting agent, and the Bank manifested by its conduct with relation to the deposit that it did so.

Nasin put the check into circulation. Prior to the receipt of notice that payment of it had been stopped, the Bank gave value and became the holder of the check in due course. The losses, if any, arising from a default by Constructor's Inc. in the performance of an obligation it owed Nasin must fall on him.

[*The basis for this decision has been codified by the Code —Section 3–206* [3] *and sections 4–203 and 4–204.*]

Holder in Due Course

General Requirements.   In order to be accorded the special position in negotiable instruments law known as a holder in due course, a person must first be a "holder." As was indicated earlier, a "holder" is a person who is in possession of an instrument drawn, issued or endorsed to him, to his order, to bearer or in blank. (1–201 [20].) It is important that all endorsements on the instrument at the time it was order paper be authorized endorsements. A forged endorsement is not effective and prevents anyone from becoming a holder unless and until he obtains a complete chain of authorized endorsements.

To qualify as a holder in due course, the holder must take the instrument (1) for value, (2) in good faith, and (3) without notice that it is overdue or has been dishonored or of any defense against or claim to it by any person. (3–302 [1].) If the holder cannot comply with all of these requirements, he is not a holder in due course.

A person who has purchased an instrument at a judicial sale, or has taken it by legal process, or has acquired it by taking over an estate, or has purchased it as part of a bulk transaction not in the regular course of the business of the transferor does not take as a holder in due course. (3–302 [3].) A person taking an instrument under the circumstances set out above has not taken the instrument in the regular course of trade.

Payee as Holder in Due Course. Section 3–302 (2) expressly provides that a payee *may* be a holder in due course. This provision clears up a conflict which existed under pre-Code law. To become a holder in due course the payee must comply with all the requirements for a holder in due course as set out in Section 3–302 (1) of the Code. Ordinarily, a payee will have notice or knowledge of defenses to the instrument and will know if it is overdue or has been dishonored; consequently, he cannot qualify as a holder in due course. But suppose, for example, Drew draws a check on First Bank as drawee, payable to the order of Parks but leaves the amount blank. Drew delivers the check to Axe, his agent, and instructs him to fill in $300 as the amount. Axe, instead of filling in $300, fills in $500 as the amount and Parks gives Axe $500 for the check. Axe gives Drew $300 and absconds with the extra $200. In such a case Parks, as payee, is a holder in due course of the check since he has taken it for value, in good faith and without notice of defenses.

Purchases of Limited Interest. The purchaser of a limited interest in an instrument can be a purchaser in due course only to the extent of the interest purchased. (3–302 [4].) For example, Wells agrees to purchase a note payable to the order of Parks. The note is for the sum of $5,000. Wells pays Parks $1,000 on the negotiation of the note to him (Wells) and agrees to pay the balance of $4,000 in 10 days. Before the payment is due Wells learns that Bell, the maker of the note, has a valid defense to it. Wells is a holder in due course for only $1,000.

Summary

To qualify as a holder in due course the holder must take the instrument for value, in good faith and without notice that it is overdue or has been dishonored or of any defense against or claim to it on the part of any other person. If the holder has not taken the instrument in the regular course of trade, he cannot qualify as a holder in due course. A payee may be a holder in due course.

One who purchases a limited interest in an instrument can be a holder in due course only to the extent of the interest purchased.

Stone & Webster Engineering Corp. v. The First National Bank & Trust Co. of Greenfield

184 N.E.2d 358 (Sup. Jud. Ct. Mass. 1962)

This was an action by Stone & Webster Engineering (plaintiff) against The First National Bank & Trust Company of Greenfield (defendant) to recover a judgment for money paid out on checks on which the payee's endorsement was forged. Stone & Webster had drawn three checks in the total amount of $64,755.44 on The First National Bank of Boston payable to the order of Westinghouse Electric Corporation. An employee of Stone & Webster obtained possession of the checks, forged Westinghouse's endorsement to them, cashed them at the First National Bank & Trust Company of Greenfield, and put the proceeds to his own use. The first two checks were endorsed in typewriting, "For Deposit Only: Westinghouse Electric Corporation By: Mr. O. D. Costine, Treasury Representative" followed by an ink signature "O. D. Costine." The third check was endorsed in typewriting, "Westinghouse Electric Corporation by: (Sgd.) O. D. Costine, Treasury Representative." When Stone & Webster sued the Greenfield Bank for conversion, one of the issues discussed by the court was the status of the Bank. That portion of the opinion follows.

WILKINS, CHIEF JUSTICE.   In the case at bar the forged endorsements were "wholly inoperative" as the signatures of the payee, Code § § 3–404(1), 1–201(43), and equally so both as to the restrictive endorsements for deposits, see § 3–205(c), and as to the endorsement in blank, see § 3–204(2). When the forger transferred the checks to the collecting bank, no negotiation under § 3–202(1) occurred, because there was lacking the necessary endorsement of the payee. For the same reason, the collecting bank could not become a "holder" as defined in § 1–201(20), and so could not become a holder in due course under § 3–202(1).

Waterbury Savings Bank v. Jaroszewski

238 A.2d 446 (Cir. Ct. Conn. 1967)

This was an action by Waterbury Savings Bank (plaintiff) against the Jaroszewskis (defendants) based on a promissory note in the sum of $1,850 payable in twenty-four installments. Judgment for Waterbury Savings Bank.

Execution of the note had been preceded by negotiations between the Jaroszewskis and Merit Food Corporation, a concern which specialized in the sale of food to homeowners on a contract basis and in periodic shipments. The final discussions took place at the home of the Jaroszewskis when two salesmen from Merit were present. At the time, the Jaroszewskis signed a "Purchase and Sales Agreement" covering three deliveries by Merit of frozen foods, for $2,000, and loan of a freezer. The agreement provided for payment of the balance over twenty-four months. At that time, the Merit salesmen exhibited to the Jaroszewskis a four-page form prominently displaying the name of plaintiff bank. The first page was captioned, "Request for personal loan." The second page was a promissory note form. The third page, containing many blanks was entitled "Credit Application." The fourth page provided for an authorization by the Jaroszewskis to Waterbury to pay the proceeds of the loan, $1,850, directly to Merit. Both Jaroszewskis signed the note, as well as the first page of the credit application, which contained details as to their financial status.

The Jaroszewskis contended that the note was signed as a result of fraudulent representations by employees of Merit to the effect that the note was merely a "credit application" and nothing more. The Jaroszewskis further alleged fraud of Merit in that they signed the documents when they were not fully completed, and that the Merit employees misrepresented what would be filled in. The Jaroszewskis attempted to impute knowledge to Waterbury of the claimed fraud, alleging that Waterbury knew, or should have known, of Merit's misconduct, as a result of prior similar transactions financed by Waterbury for Merit customers. Waterbury denied these allegations and relied upon a claim of status as a holder in due course.

LEVINE, JUDGE.   It is now established that Waterbury, as a payee, may be a holder in due course. The court finds, in the instant case, that Waterbury is, in fact, a holder in due course in that it took the note in good faith and under the validating conditions of 3–302. Initially, no representative of Waterbury was present at the meeting at the Jaroszewski home when the documents were signed and there was no testimony that any agent of the bank participated, in any way, in the negotiations leading to execution of the note and contract. There was nothing in the evidence to show that Waterbury was aware of any defenses at the time it discounted the note. The fact that, subsequent to said conference, and after Waterbury had issued its check to Merit, the Jaroszewskis complained to Waterbury regarding Merit's conduct and their status as comakers does not alter the basic conclusion. If Waterbury was a holder in due course at the time it took delivery of the Jaroszewskis' note, notice thereafter to it of Merit's claimed fraud or defective performance would not change its legal position. 3–304(6).

The evidence disclosed that Waterbury had engaged in about five to six hundred similar financing transactions with Merit and its customers and that complaints of defective food service, or related items, had been received by Waterbury in about three to four cases. The complaints, percentagewise, were quite minimal. In any event, it is settled that receipt by a lender of miscellaneous prior complaints regarding a vendor does not prevent the lender from qualifying as a holder in due course, so long as the lender had no notice of a complaint by the particular customer involved, at or before the time it accepted the customer's note. Hence, the Jaroszewskis' attack on Waterbury's status, based on the "prior experience" argument, is without merit.

Failure of Waterbury to inquire as to proper performance by Merit of its underlying contract with the Jaroszewskis does not show a lack of good faith or alter its status under 3–302, 3–304(4), (6).

It is undisputed that Waterbury supplied the forms used by Merit to secure the Jaroszewskis' signatures on the note and credit application. This fact, alone, however, falls short of creating a principal-agent relationship between Waterbury and Merit so as to impute knowledge to Waterbury of Merit's conduct, or make Waterbury responsible for Merit's acts or omissions.

For Value and in Good Faith

Value. A person, to qualify as a holder in due course of an instrument, must give value therefor. Value includes more than consideration. Under the provisions of the Code a holder takes the instrument for value to the extent that the agreed consideration has been performed or that he acquires a security interest in or a lien on the instrument otherwise than by legal process; or when he takes the instrument in payment of or as security for an antecedent claim against any person whether or not the claim is due; or when he gives a negotiable instrument for it or makes an irrevocable commitment to a third person. (3–303.)

A bank or any person who discounts an instrument in the regular course of trade has given value for it. Likewise, if a loan is made and an instrument is pledged as security for the repayment of the loan, the secured party has given value for the instrument to the extent of the amount of the loan. If Axe owes Bell a past-due debt and he endorses and delivers to Bell an instrument issued to him (Axe) in payment of the debt or as security for its repayment, Bell has given value for the instrument.

Suppose Axe borrows $1,000 from Bell. Axe gives Bell a note for that amount payable in 30 days and Bell endorses and delivers to Axe a check for $1,000 drawn by Clark and payable to Bell. Axe, in issuing his note for $1,000 to Bell, has given value for the Clark check. Also, suppose Bell and Clark enter into a contract whereby Clark obligates himself to deliver an automobile to Axe and Bell endorses an instrument issued by Drew and delivers it to Clark in payment for the automobile. Clark has given value for the Drew instrument.

Good Faith. Good faith is defined in the Code as follows: "Good faith" means honesty in fact in the conduct or transaction concerned. (1–201 [19].)

The requirement that to qualify as a holder in due course, a person must take the instrument in good faith introduces into the law of negotiable instruments an element of uncertainty. It is undesirable, as well as impractical, to reduce the requirement of good faith to an exact rule of law. Good faith implies commercial honesty. If negotiable instruments are to serve their purpose of facilitating the carrying-on of trade, they must pass freely in the channels of commerce, and a person must be permitted to take a negotiable instrument without first investigating its origin and the intervening transactions whereby the present holder acquired the instrument.

Good faith always involves a question of fact. The courts have held that the fact that a person takes an instrument under suspicious circumstances is not sufficient to prove bad faith. However, if a person acquires an instrument under circumstances which should have created an inevitable inference that an infirmity existed in the instrument, the person could not have taken such instrument in good faith.

Summary

Value includes the performance of an agreed consideration, the taking of an instrument as security, as payment or security for an antecedent claim whether due or not, or the giving of a negotiable instrument, or the assuming of an irrevocable obligation to a third person. Good faith is honesty in fact.

Korzenik v. Supreme Radio, Inc.

197 N.E.2d 702 (Sup. Jud. Ct. Mass. 1964)

This was an action by Armand A. Korzenik and another (plaintiffs) against Supreme Radio, Inc. (defendant), to recover a judgment on two trade acceptances. Judgment for Supreme Radio, Inc., and Korzenik appealed. Judgment affirmed.

Korzenik and his partner in law took two trade acceptances given by Supreme Radio, Inc. (Supreme), to Southern New England Distributing Corporation (Southern). The trade acceptances were transferred to Korzenik "as a retainer for services to be performed." The two trade acceptances had been obtained by fraud and Supreme set up the fraud as a defense. Korzenik claimed that he was a holder in due course. Korzenik and partner did some work but there was no testimony offered as to the value of the work. Korzenik did not know that the trade acceptances had been obtained by fraud.

WHITTEMORE, JUSTICE. Decisive of the case, as the Appellate Division held, is the correct ruling that Korzenik and partner are not holders in due course under § 3–302; they have not shown to what extent they took for value under § 3–303. That section provides:

A holder takes the instrument for value (a) to the extent that the agreed consideration has been performed or that he acquires a security interest in or a lien on the instrument otherwise than by legal process; or (b) when he takes the instrument in payment of or as security for an antecedent claim against any person whether or not the claim is due; or (c) when he gives a negotiable instrument for it or makes an irrovocable commitment to a third person.

Under clause (a) of § 3–303 the "agreed consideration" was the performance of legal services. It is often said that a lawyer is "retained" when he is engaged to perform services, and we hold that the judge spoke of "retainer" in this sense. The phrase that the judge used, "retainer *for services*"; shows his meaning as does the finding as to services already performed by Korzenik at the time of the assignments. Even if the retainer had been only a fee to insure the attorney's availability to perform future services, there is no basis in the record for determining the value of this commitment for one week.

The Uniform Laws Comment to § 3–303 points out that in this article "value is divorced from consideration" and that except as provided in paragraph (c) "[a]n executory promise to give value is not . . . value. . . . The underlying reason of policy is that when the purchaser learns of a defense . . . he is not required to enforce the instrument, but is free to rescind the transaction for breach of the transferor's warranty."

Section 3–307 (3), provides: "After it is shown that a defense exists a person claiming the rights of a holder in due course has the burden of establishing that he or some person under whom he claims is in all respects a holder in due course." The defense of fraud having been established this section puts the burden on Korzenik and partner and they have failed to show "the extent . . . [to which] the agreed consideration . . . [had] been performed."

The only other possible issue under § 3–303 is whether, because of or in connection with taking the assignments, Korzenik made "an irrevocable commitment to a third person." There is no evidence of such a commitment. The finding as to a payment to counsel shows only that some of the proceeds of other assigned items have been expended by Korzenik.

Pazol v. Citizens National Bank of Sandy Springs
138 S.E.2d 442 (Ct. App. Ga. 1964)

This was an action by Citizens National Bank of Sandy Springs (plaintiff) against Sidney Pazol (defendant). Judgment for Citizens National Bank of Sandy Springs and Pazol appealed. Judgment affirmed.

Pazol issued his check for $49,600 drawn on the National Bank of Atlanta and payable to the order of Edison and Seiden Construction Company, Inc. (Edison). Edison caused the check to be indorsed and deposited in its checking account with the Citizens National Bank of Sandy Springs (Bank). Bank allowed Edison to withdraw all of the credit created by the deposit of the check before it learned that there were defenses to it. When the check was presented for payment it was dishonored. Bank sued Pazol, the drawer of the check to recover a judgment for the amount of the check. Pazol defended on the ground that Bank was not a holder in due course of the check.

FULTON, CHIEF JUDGE.   An examination of the provisions of the U.C.C. and a comparison of it with the law prior to its passage reveal that the adoption of the U.C.C. has not changed the result under the present alleged factual situation. Bank is at least a holder, as defined by Code Ann. 1–201 (20), i.e., "a person who is in possession of a document of title or an instrument or an investment security drawn, *issued or indorsed* to him or to his order or to bearer or in blank." The petition alleges that the payee delivered the check to Bank and "caused the same to be endorsed for deposit." Even if this is construed to mean that the payee did not personally indorse the instrument, as indeed the copy of the check attached as an exhibit shows to be the case, it was issued to Bank. Code Ann. 3–202 (2) provides that "[a]n indorsement must be written by *or on behalf of* the holder," which holder may be the payee under Code Ann. 302 (2). Code Ann. 4–205 (1) provides as follows: "A depositary bank which has taken an item for collection may supply any indorsement of the customer which is necessary to title unless the item contains the words 'payee's indorsement required' or the like. In the absence of such a requirement a statement placed on the item by the depositary bank to the effect that the item was deposited by a customer or credited to his account is effective as the customer's indorsement." The comment of the National Conference of Commissioners on Uniform State Laws and the American Law Institute pertaining to this particular section explains that this subsection "is designed to speed up collections by eliminating any necessity to return to a *non-bank depositor* any items he may have failed to indorse." The phrase "non-bank depositor" means a depositor which is not a bank, rather than one depositing in something other than a bank, as is contended by Pazol. Under the provisions of Code Ann. 3–301, "[t]he holder of an instrument whether or not he is the owner may transfer or negotiate it and, except as otherwise provided in 3–603 on payment or satisfaction, discharge it or *enforce payment in his own name.*"

Furthermore, under the allegations of the petition, Bank was a holder in due course as defined by Code Ann. 3–302 (1), which requires that the holder take the instrument "(a) for value; and (b) in good faith; and (c) without notice that it is overdue or has been dishonored or of any defense against or claim to it on the part of any person." Regarding requirement (a), Code 4–209 provides as follows: "For purposes of determining its status as a holder in due course, the bank has given value *to the extent that it has a security interest in an item* provided that the bank otherwise complies with the requirements of 3–302 on what constitutes a holder in due course." Code Ann. 4–208 (1) provides that "[a] bank has a security interest in an item . . . (a) in case of an item deposited in an account to the extent to which credit given for the item has been withdrawn or applied." Code Ann. 3–303 also provides that a holder takes an instrument for value to the extent that he acquires a security interest in the instrument. Code Ann. 3–205 defines a restrictive indorsement as one which "(c) includes the words 'for collection,' 'for deposit,' 'pay any bank,' or *like terms signifying a purpose of deposit or collection.*" Code Ann. 3–206 (3) provides that the transferee of an instrument with such an indorsement ". . . must pay or apply any value given by him for or on the security of the instrument consistently with the indorsement and to the extent that he does so he becomes a *holder for value.* In addition such transferee is a *holder in due course* if he otherwise complies with the requirements of 3–302 on what constitutes a holder in due course." By causing the check to be indorsed 'for deposit,' as alleged, the payee signified its purpose of deposit and the plaintiff bank, by applying the value given consistently with this indorsement by crediting the payee-depositor's account with the amount of the check, became a holder for value.

Regarding requirement (b) of a holder in due course, Code Ann 3–302 (1), there is nothing on the face of the petition to indicate a lack of good faith on the part of the plaintiff in accepting the check. Good faith is presumed until questioned by appropriate pleadings.

Norman v. World Wide Distributors, Inc.
195 A.2d 115 (Super. Ct. Pa. 1963)

This was an action by Clarence W. Norman and wife (plaintiffs) against World Wide Distributors, Inc., and Peoples National Fund, Inc. (defendants), to have a judgment obtained on a note against Norman and wife declared void. Judgment for Norman and wife, and World Wide Distributors, Inc., and Peoples National Fund, Inc., appealed. Judgment affirmed.

Mancen, agent for World Wide Distributors, Inc. (World Wide), called upon the Normans and outlined to them "a program for direct advertising." He represented to them that if they purchased a breakfront, he would pay them $5 for each letter they wrote to a friend requesting an appointment for World Wide's agent to explain the details of a sound advertising program and $20 for each sale made to any such person. Each friend was to be given the same opportunity to supply names. He persuaded the Normans to sign, without reading, a purchase agreement, and attached judgment note in blank and an "Owners Participation Certificate."

After the note was signed and taken from the home of the Normans it was filled in for $1,079.40 and made payable to H. Waldran T/A State Wide Products at the office of Peoples National Fund (Peoples). The note was purchased by Peoples on January 25, 1961, for $831 and judgment was entered thereon February 7, 1961. World Wide was nowhere to be found. Within approximately a year its principals had operated first under the name of Carpet Industries, then under State Wide, and finally under World Wide Distributors. Peoples dealt with all three companies and its officers had knowledge of the referral plan. The referral plan was a fraudulent scheme based on an operation similar to the chain letter racket. Peoples claims that even though World Wide may have been guilty of fraud, it can collect on the note because it was a holder in due course.

WOODSIDE, JUDGE. "A holder in due course is a holder who takes the instrument (a) for value; and (b) in good faith; and (c) without notice that it is overdue or has been dishonored or of any defense against or claim to it on the part of any person." (3–302 [1].)

Section 1–201 (19) of the Code defines "good faith" as meaning "honesty in fact in the conduct or transaction concerned." Thus, to be a holder in due course Peoples must have acted in good faith.

The freedom from the defense of prior equities afforded to a holder in due course is an extraordinary protection, which, although having its origin in the law merchant, is closely akin to similar protection given in other types of cases by courts of equity; and running through all the authorities dealing with holders in due course we find the principle, not always stated, perhaps, that he who seeks the protection given one in that position must have dealt fairly and honestly in acquiring the instrument in controversy and in regard to the rights of all prior parties, this is, the kind of good faith which the law demands, and the principle is closely analogous to the equitable doctrine of clean hands.

He who seeks protection as a holder in due course must have dealt fairly and honestly in acquiring the instrument as to the rights of prior parties, and where circumstances are such as to justify the conclusion that the failure to make inquiry arose from a suspicion that inquiry would disclose a vice or defect in the title, the person is not a holder in due course.

When the defense of fraud appears to be meritorious as to the payee, the burden of showing it was a holder in due course is on the one claiming to be such.

Peoples here had knowledge of circumstances which should have caused it to inquire concerning the payee's method of obtaining the note. Peoples knew enough about the referral plan to require it to inquire further concerning it. The fact that Peoples' vice-president called the makers of the note and denied any connection with the referral plan, indicates his own suspicion concerning it. The frequency with which the principals changed the name under which they were operating—three times in approximately one year—should have added to his suspicion. Furthermore, the appellant paid $831 for a $1,079.40 note payable three days after date. Under all the circumstances, Peoples was bound to inquire further into the operation of the seller of these notes, and having made no inquiry, it is held as though it had knowledge of all that inquiry would have revealed.

Notice of Defenses

Nature of Notice. Notice is something less than knowledge and more than mere suspicion. It is knowledge of facts and circumstances which would prompt an honest person to make inquiry to learn the facts. Section 1–201 (25) provides: "A person has 'notice' of a fact when (a) he has actual knowledge of it; or (b) he has received a notice or notification of it; or (c) from all the facts and circumstances known to him at the time in question he has reason to know that it exists." In the cases involving an interpretation of Section 3–302 (1) (c) of the Code, "notice" usually involves notice as defined in Section 1–201 (25) (c).

Incomplete Paper. A person cannot take an instrument as a holder in due course if the instrument is, at the time he takes it, blank as to some material term. The courts have held that the fact that the instrument is incomplete in some material respect puts any person taking it on notice that the holder has limited authority to fill in the blanks, and charges the purchaser with knowledge of facts which a reasonable inquiry would disclose. If the instrument contains blanks, the party taking the instrument takes it subject to all defenses available to the original parties irrespective of whether or not there is any relation between the blank terms and the defense.

The courts have held that an instrument is incomplete if it is payable to order and the name of the payee is left blank. An instrument which was drawn payable "——— after date, etc." and one drawn "ten ——— after date, etc." were held to be incomplete. Failure to fill in a pronoun does not make the instrument incomplete, as "——— promise to pay." Likewise, the omission of connective words such as "pay to Brown order" does not make the instrument incomplete. To be material, the omitted term must be one which affects the legal obligations of the parties to the instrument.

Filling in Blanks. When a paper whose contents at the time of signing show that it is intended to become an instrument is signed while still incomplete in any necessary respect, it cannot be enforced until completed, but when it is completed in accordance with authority given it is effective as completed. (3–115.) Under this provision of the Code a person who takes an instrument which is incomplete in some material respect cannot take as a holder in due course. However, if an incomplete instrument is filled in, a person taking the instrument without notice or knowledge that it was incomplete when delivered or that it was not completed as authorized takes as a holder in due course and can enforce the instrument as completed. (3–407 [3].)

Irregular Paper. The wording of Section 3–304 (1) (*a*) of the Code does not change in any material respect the pre-Code law relative to irregular paper. Anything on the face of an instrument which would put a person on notice that there is something wrong with it makes the instrument irregular on its face. If the instrument is irregular, the person taking it cannot take as a holder in due course. A person taking an instrument which is irregular on its face takes subject to all defenses available to the parties to the instrument, whether or not there is any relation between the irregularity and the defense to the instrument. The existence of the irregularities puts the person taking the instrument on constructive notice of facts which a reasonable inquiry would disclose.

A person is put on notice if one of his experience and training should, in the exercise of reasonable prudence detect the irregularity. Any noticeable alteration makes an instrument irregular on its fact, but a clever alteration does not. However, an alteration might be such as would put a bank cashier on notice but might not put on notice a person who was not accustomed to handling negotiable instruments. The courts have held that the following do not make the instrument irregular on its face: (1) postdating, (2) omission of revenue stamps when revenue stamps are required by statute, (3) difference between the handwriting in the body of the instrument and that in the signature, (4) differences in the handwriting in the body of the instrument, and (5) statement of the amount in figures and not in writing. It has also been held that an instrument which is detached from a contract is not irregular paper.

An instrument which is stamped "Paid" or "Payment refused," or one made out to an officer of a corporation and signed by the same officer as agent of the corporation, or an instrument which provides for a usurious rate of interest has been held to be irregular paper. A draft, trade acceptance, or check does not have to be accepted by the drawee to be regular paper.

Summary

A person who takes an instrument which is, at the time he takes it, blank in some material respect, cannot take as a holder in due course.

If a person who can qualify as a holder in due course takes an instrument after the blanks have been filled in, he can enforce the instrument as it is filled in.

Anything on the face of the instrument which would put the holder on notice that there is something wrong with the instrument is an irregularity, and a person taking such an instrument cannot take as a holder in due course.

A. J. Cannon & Co. v. Collier

84 S.E.2d 482 (Ct. App. Ga. 1954)

This was an action by A. J. Cannon & Company (plaintiff) against Rosa Collier and Coleman Gravitt (defendants) to recover a judgment for the amount of a dishonored check. Judgment for Collier, and A. J. Cannon & Company appealed. Judgment affirmed.

FELTON, CHIEF JUDGE.   The evidence showed: that the signed check was delivered by the defendant Gravitt to Mrs. Moore, the payee, with the amount left blank; that Mrs. Moore took the blank check to A. J. Cannon & Company's (Cannon) place of business and there discussed her account with Cannon with one of its agents; that the agent saw that the check was blank as to the amount; that after discussion of Mrs. Moore's account with the agent, Mrs. Moore in the presence of the agent and with the agent looking on filled in the check in the amount of $1,275; that the agent did not make any inquiry as to Mrs. Moore's authority concerning what the amount should have been; that the check was not supposed to be filled in for the amount of $1,275. Section 14 of the U.N.I.L. provides:

Where the instrument is wanting in any material particular, the person in possession thereof has a prima facie authority to complete it by filling up the blanks therein. A signature on a blank paper delivered by the person making the signature in order that the paper may be converted into a negotiable instrument operates as a prima facie authority to fill it up as such for any amount. In order, however, that any such instrument when completed may be enforced against any person who became a party thereto prior to its completion it must be filled up strictly in accordance with the authority given and within a reasonable time. If any such instrument, after completion, is negotiated to a holder in due course, it is valid and effectual for all purposes in his hands, and he may enforce it as if it had been filled up strictly in accordance with the authority given and within a reasonable time.

Whatever may have been the law prior to the adoption of this section, the section puts a purchaser of blank paper on inquiry as to the authority given regarding the blanks. In the instant case when Mrs. Moore took the check to Cannon's place of business with the amount in blank and filled in the blank with Cannon's knowledge, it was put in the same position it would have been in had Mrs. Moore transferred the check to it in blank. In either event, Cannon would be put on inquiry as to Mrs. Moore's authority relative to the amount of the check, and when it took the check under the circumstances described, it took at its peril. The court did not err in awarding the nonsuit.

[*Section 3–304 (1) (a) provides, "The purchaser has notice of a claim or defense if the instrument is so incomplete . . . as to call into question its validity" and Section 3–115 provides, "One taking an order instrument in which the order payee's name is left blank could not take as a holder in due course."*]

Matathias v. Bell-Mar Laboratories
2 U.C.C. Rep. 1161 (Sup. Ct. N.Y. 1965)

This was an action by Matathias (plaintiff) against Bell-Mar Laboratories (defendant) on two checks on which Bell-Mar had stopped payment. Matathias moved for summary judgment and the motion was granted.

On September 28, 1964, Bell-Mar Laboratories made two checks for $9,500 payable to the order of J. H. Wember. It dated one of the checks December 29, 1964, and the other January 14, 1965. Prior to those dates Factors and Note Buyers Corporation acquired the checks. In October Factors discounted the checks to Matathias. Matathias duly presented the checks on their due dates but the drawee refused payment on the ground that payment had been stopped. Bell-Mar had stopped payment on November 5, 1964, when it returned the goods that had been sold it by Wember. Matathias then brought suit. Bell-Mar contended that it had a fraud defense that was good against Matathias. It claimed Matathias was not a holder in due course because the instrument was not negotiable and Matathias was on notice of an infirmity or defense since it discounted the checks.

MANGAN, JUSTICE.   Matathias asserts that he is an innocent third-party bona fide holder in due course of the checks and had become the holder, for value, and without notice of any defect or infirmity one month prior to the return of the merchandise November 5. Bell-Mar resists judgment, claiming that Matathias is not a holder in due course. In essence, Bell-Mar argues that the checks issued to Wember during September, 1964, were post-dated; that upon issuance, it was orally agreed that the checks would not be discounted or negotiated, but would be held until the due date by Wember. Moreover, Bell-Mar urges that the fact that the checks were post-dated, and that a discount was given thereon, was notice to Matathias of infirmities in the instrument. Post-dated checks are simply promissory notes,[2] and may be freely

---

[2] The judge appears to be in error on this point since a postdated check is a draft, not a note. This does not, however, affect the negotiability of the instrument.

negotiated. That subsequent to the negotiation of the instrument a difficulty arose between the parties to the instrument is not sufficient to deprive the holder of its status as a bona fide holder in due course. The fact that the notes were discounted establishes no more than suspicious circumstances as distinguished from facts bringing home to Matathias either knowledge or a duty to make further inquiry. Suspicious circumstances alone do not constitute notice of an infirmity or defect in the instrument sufficient to constitute bad faith and destroy the status of a holder in due course. The discount here does not appear to be so great under the circumstances as to support an inference that Matathias knew the notes had been dishonestly or improperly acquired. Other arguments which Bell-Mar seeks to raise, such as a fraud perpetrated on it by Wember, are not available against Matathias as a holder in due course. It does not appear—nor is it alleged—that Matathias was a party to or knew of the fraud. Accordingly, the motion for summary judgment is granted.

Voidable Paper and Fiduciaries

Voidable Paper. A holder cannot qualify as a holder in due course if he has notice or knowledge that the obligation of any party is voidable in whole or in part. Notice or knowledge that any signature on the paper was obtained by misrepresentation, fraud, or duress or that the paper was signed by mistake would prevent the holder from qualifying as a holder in due course. If an instrument is paid in full to the holder, all parties are discharged. However, if the party paying an instrument does not take it or have it marked "Paid" or "Canceled" so that it is apparent that it has been discharged, the holder can negotiate it, and any party taking such instrument having no notice can take it as a holder in due course. (3–304 [1] [b].)

Negotiation of Fiduciary. Whether or not a purchaser who takes an instrument which has been negotiated to him by a fiduciary takes as a holder in due course will depend on whether such purchaser has notice or knowledge that the fiduciary has negotiated the instrument in violation of his fiduciary duties. The Code provides: The purchaser has notice of a claim against the instrument when he has knowledge that a fiduciary has negotiated the instrument in payment of or as security for his own debt or in any transaction for his own benefit or otherwise in breach of duty. (3–304 [2].)

Summary

A holder cannot qualify as a holder in due course if, at the time he took the paper, he had notice or knowledge that the obligation of any party was voidable in whole or in part or that all parties had been discharged.

A purchaser from a fiduciary cannot take as a holder in due course when he has knowledge that the fiduciary has negotiated the paper for his own benefit or otherwise in breach of duty.

Maber, Inc. v. Factor Cab Corp.

244 N.Y.S.2d 768 (App. Div. N.Y. 1963)

This was an action by Maber, Inc. (plaintiff), against Factor Cab Corp. and others (defendants) to recover a judgment on a note. Judgment for Maber, Inc., for less than full amount of note and it appealed. Judgment affirmed.

Factor Cab Corp. issued a series of notes drawn payable to "the order of Donald E. Richel as attorney for Francisco Silvestry." Twenty-one of the notes were indorsed by Richel and his wife and sold to Maber, Inc. Maber, Inc., in purchasing the notes, made its check payable to Richel in his individual name, without qualification or restriction, in the amount of $5,796.24. In addition, it discharged by payment Richel's personal indebtedness to a bank in the amount of $3,903.75. Richel and his wife indorsed the notes as individuals.

Factor Cab Corp. paid some of Silvestry's hospital bills directly and thereby obtained a counter-claim against the notes. Maber, Inc., contended that it took the notes as a holder in due course and free from the counterclaim.

BREITEL, JUSTICE PRESIDING.   When Maber took the notes from the attorney, by reason of the descriptive qualification of the named payee (i.e., as attorney for Francisco Silvestry), the holder was on notice that the attorney had received the notes as an agent rather than as a principal, and that the funds might be subject to claims in the right of others. This did not mean that the attorney was not entitled to negotiate the notes. On the contrary, he could. (U.C.C. §§ 3–117, 3–207, 3–301, 3–304 [4] [e].) He was even empowered to negotiate them for cash, because it may have been within the fiduciary purpose to convert them into cash, provided, of course, there were no other circumstances to put the holder on notice that the instrument was being diverted from a fiduciary purpose. (U.C.C. § 3–304, Comment 5.)

But the case is entirely different when it appears, as it did here, that the notes were negotiated for the benefit or individual purpose of the agent. Under such circumstances the holder is charged with bad faith and notice of any defect or infirmity in the instrument, and is not a holder in due course (U.C.C. §§ 3–302 [1], 3–304 [2]). This includes the absence or failure of consideration whether in whole or in part. (U.C.C. § 3–408.)

Overdue and Dishonored Paper

Paper Payable at Definite Time.   A person must take an instrument before it is overdue if he wishes to take as a holder in due course. The courts have based this rule on the reasoning that as a general rule obligations are performed when performance is due, and if an instrument is not paid when due, the non-payment of the instrument is a circumstance sufficient to put the purchaser on notice that the party primarily liable has a defense to it, and a person taking an overdue instrument takes with notice of all defenses to such instrument.

The Code provides that the purchaser has notice that an instrument is overdue if he has reason to know that any part of the principal amount is overdue or that there is an uncured default in payment of another instrument of the same series. (3–304 [3] [*a*].) For example, suppose Axe borrows $1,000 from Bell and gives Bell 10 notes for $100 each, numbered from 1 to 10 and due serially 1, 2, 3, and so forth, months after date, the 10th note being due 10 months after date. Clark purchases note number five, and at the time he purchases it he has reason to know that notes two and three are past due and unpaid. Clark does not take note number five as a holder in due course.

An instrument payable at a definite date is overdue at the beginning of the day after the due date. An instrument payable at a definite time after date or after sight or presentment is overdue at the beginning of the day after the time stated has elapsed. In counting time, the day the instrument is issued is excluded, but the date of payment is included. For example, if an instrument dated January 2 is payable 30 days after date, January 3 is the first day counted, and the instrument is due on February 1 and overdue at the beginning of February 2. A person taking the instrument on February 2 or thereafter cannot take as a holder in due course. If the date of payment falls on a Sunday or a holiday the instrument is payable on the next succeeding business day.

Instruments Subject to Acceleration. If the holder has the right to accelerate the time of payment of an instrument, the purchaser has notice that the instrument is overdue if he has reason to know that acceleration of the instrument has been made. (3–304 [3] [*b*].)

Demand Paper. If an instrument is drawn payable on demand or on sight or presentment, a person taking the instrument an unreasonable time after its issue cannot take as a holder in due course. The Code provides in Section 1–204 (2): What is a reasonable time for taking any action depends on the nature, purpose, and circumstances of such action, and in Section 3–304 (3) (c): A reasonable time for a check drawn and payable within the states and territories of the United States and District of Columbia is presumed to be 30 days. It should be noted that this provision states *is presumed* to be 30 days, not *is* 30 days. The Code further states: "Presumption" or "presumed" means that the trier of fact must find the existence of the fact presumed unless and until evidence is introduced which would support a finding of its nonexistence. (1–201 [31].)

In determining whether a demand instrument is overdue usage of trade, business practices, the facts and circumstances of the particular case must be considered. In a farming community where the normal period for loans to farmers is six months, a demand note as a general rule can be outstanding a longer period of time before it becomes overdue than could a demand note issued in an industrial community, where the normal period of a loan is 30 to 60 days. In determining when an instrument is overdue, the nature of the transaction in which the instrument is used, the relation of the parties, and all other facts and circumstances must be taken into consideration.

Dishonored Instruments.   An instrument has been dishonored when it has been presented for payment or acceptance, and payment or acceptance has been refused. If a demand note has been presented to the maker for payment and payment has been refused, the note has been dishonored. Likewise, if a draft has been presented to the drawee for acceptance or payment, or if a check has been presented to the drawee bank for payment, and acceptance or payment has been refused, the draft or check has been dishonored. Any purchaser taking such note, draft, or check if he has reason to know it has been dishonored cannot take as a holder in due course.

Summary

An instrument payable at a definite time or at a stated time after date is overdue at the beginning of the day following the day on which it is payable. A person taking an instrument when it is overdue cannot take as a holder in due course. A purchaser has notice that an instrument is overdue if he has reason to know that any part of the principal amount is overdue, or that an uncured default exists in the payment of another instrument in the same series, or that the holder of an instrument subject to acceleration has been accelerated.

Demand paper is overdue if it is not paid within a reasonable time after issue, and a reasonable time for the payment of a check drawn and payable in the states or territories of the United States or the District of Columbia is presumed to be thirty days.

Demand paper is dishonored when it is presented for payment or acceptance and payment or acceptance is refused.

State & City Bank & Trust Co. v. *Hedrick*
151 S.E. 723 (Sup. Ct. N.C. 1930)

This was an action by State & City Bank & Trust Company (plaintiff) against M. N. Hedrick, G. C. Hobgood and another (defendants). Judgment for State & City Bank & Trust Company, and Hobgood and another appealed. Judgment reversed.

Suit was brought on a note dated September 23, 1919, and payable on demand. This note was negotiated to State & City Bank & Trust Company (Bank) on June 10, 1920. The Bank claims that it is a holder in due course of the note. The maker and indorsers claim that the Bank took the note after it was overdue and that it is not a holder in due course.

CONNOR, JUSTICE.   It is generally held, without regard to statutory provisions, that a negotiable instrument due and payable on demand is not overdue for the purpose of negotiation, until after the lapse of a reasonable time, and that what is a reasonable time depends upon the facts and circumstances of the particular case. These principles have been recognized as the law and are included in the Uniform Negotiable Instruments Act, which has been enacted as the law in this State. Where a negotiable instrument, payable on demand, is negotiated an unreasonable length of time after its issue, the holder is not deemed a holder in due course. Upon the facts found by the referee, in the instant case, and approved by the Court, we are of opinion that as a matter of law, the negotiation of the notes dated 23 September, 1919, and due on demand, to the Bank on 10 June, 1920, was after the lapse of a reasonable time, and that therefore it was error to hold that the Bank became and was the holder in due course of said notes. Even if it should be held that upon the facts of the instant case, the notes were not overdue until after 20 December, 1919, nearly six months had elapsed from said date before the notes were negotiated to the Bank on 10 June, 1920. This is an unreasonable time, and the Bank cannot be held a purchaser of the notes before maturity, which is essential to make it a holder in due course.

[*The pre-Code law in regard to when a demand note is overdue is not changed by the adoption of the Code.* (See 3–304 [3] [c].)]

Home Savings Bank v. Bentley

92 N.W.2d 377 (Sup. Ct. Wis. 1958)

This was an action by Home Savings Bank (plaintiff) against James W. Bentley *et al.* (defendants) to recover on a check. Motion for summary judgment by Home Savings Bank denied and it appealed. Judgment affirmed in part and reversed in part. [The holding on the point raised in this abstract was affirmed.]

Bentley issued a check dated July 18, 1957, payable to the order of R. B. General Trucking, Inc. The check was drawn on a bank other than Home Savings Bank. On July 26, 1957, R. B. General Trucking, Inc., indorsed the check and Home Savings Bank paid it $500, the face amount of the check. Bentley stopped payment on the check. Bentley claims that since Home Savings Bank took the check eight days after the date of issue, it took it an unreasonable length of time after issue and is not a holder in due course.

CURRIE, JUSTICE.   The applicable statutes are secs. 116.58, 118.62, and 116.01 (15), Wis. Stats. Under the provisions of sec. 116.01 (15), two of the determining factors are the nature of the instrument and the usage of trade of business. It is a matter of common knowledge of which this court may take judicial notice that banks and stores frequently cash checks which are more than eight days old. A severe burden would be placed on these businesses if they were to be denied the status of holders in due course every time they cashed a check, or accepted the same in payment of merchandise, which was a few days old.

In *Anderson* v. *Elem,* the plaintiff hotel keeper cashed a check for the payee on which the defendant was the drawer. Twenty-four days had elapsed between the date of issuance and such cashing. The defendant in the meantime had stopped payment on the check so that the drawee bank refused payment to the plaintiff. The same defense was made by the drawer in the plaintiff's action to recover the amount of the check as has been made by James W. Bentley in the instant action, viz., unreasonable delay in the presentment of the check. In holding that there was no merit to such defense, the Kansas Court declared:

It is perfectly true that a check is ordinarily to be regarded as an instrument for present use; but the Negotiable Instruments Act did not declare that a check is due at once, or that it must be presented, or put in course of collection, by close of business on the next business day after issue. A check is not overdue, for purpose of negotiation, unless there has been unreasonable delay in presenting it, and unreasonable delay must be interpreted to mean such delay as to make the check obviously stale.

The facts are all before the court. It is essential to uniformity that the court itself should determine questions of this character, and the court holds that the time elapsing between the issuing of the check and its negotiation did not deprive the plaintiff of the rights of a holder in due course.

[*In a state which has adopted the Code there would be no serious question as to the court's decision in a controversy such as existed in this case.* (See 3–304 [3] [c].)]

Facts Which Are Not Notice

Code Provisions. For the purpose of clarifying uncertainties in the law, situations are set out, knowledge of which does not, standing alone, give a purchaser notice of a defense or claim. Knowledge that an instrument is antedated or postdated or that it was issued or negotiated in return for an executory promise, or that it was accompanied by a separate agreement, does not give the purchaser notice of a defense or claim, unless the purchaser has notice that a defense or claim has arisen from the terms thereof. Also, knowledge that a party signed for accommodation or that an instrument was incomplete when delivered and has been completed, unless the purchaser has notice of an improper completion, or that the instrument was negotiated by a fiduciary or that there has been default in the payment of interest on the instrument or in payment of any other instrument, except one of the same series, does not give the purchaser notice of defenses or claims. (3–304 [4].)

If a purchaser of a negotiable instrument can otherwise qualify as a holder in due course, it is not necessary for him to examine the public records to determine whether there are outstanding defenses or claims to the instrument since the filing or recording of a document does not of itself constitute notice. (3–304 [5].)

Notice, to be effective, must be received at such time and in such manner as to give a reasonable opportunity to act on it. (3–304 [6].)

Rights of Holder in Due Course

Personal Defenses. The keystone of the law of negotiable commercial paper is the rule that a holder in due course of a negotiable instrument takes it free from "personal defenses" or claims which may exist between the original parties to the instrument. The holder in due course takes free of such defenses as lack or failure of consideration, misrepresentation or fraud in the inducement, setoff or counterclaim, breach of warranty of goods sold for which the instrument was issued, and all other defenses which would be available to a promisor in a suit on a simple contract. (3–305 [1].)

Real Defenses. From the standpoint of public policy there are certain defenses which do go to the validity of the instrument and which are good against a holder in due course of a negotiable instrument. These are the so-called "real defenses." In general a holder in due course takes the instrument free from all defenses of any party to the instrument with whom he has not dealt except the following: Infancy, to the extent that it is a defense to a simple contract; and such other incapacity, or duress, or illegality of the transaction, as renders the obligation of the party a nullity; and such misrepresentation as has induced the party to sign the instrument with neither knowledge nor reasonable opportunity to obtain knowledge of its character or its essential terms; and discharge in insolvency proceedings; and any other discharges of which the holder has notice at the time he takes the instrument. (3–305 [2].)

In regard to infants and others having limited capacity to contract it is basically a matter of social policy whether it is more desirable to protect a holder in due course and thereby facilitate trade or protect the inexperienced and weak from the results of their injudicious acts. As the law has developed the decision has been to protect infants and others having limited contractual capacity. The courts have held that promises made under extreme duress and, usually by statutory enactment, promises made in defined illegal transactions are held to be totally unenforceable. By logical deduction, if the promise in a negotiable instrument is a nullity it is unenforceable, even by a holder in due course of the instrument. The law also protects those persons who have been "tricked" into signing any paper if they have used a reasonable degree of care.

The objective of our bankruptcy laws and other insolvency laws is to relieve the debtor from his debts and give him a new start. In general, the discharge features of these laws are broad enough to discharge the debtor of all his commercial obligations, including debts owing on negotiable instruments held by holders in due course.

Persons Not Holders in Due Course. Negotiable commercial paper is basically a simple contract to pay money. If the holder of such paper is not a holder in due course his rights are no greater than are the rights of any promisee or assignee of a simple contract. Such a holder takes the paper subject to all valid claims on the part of any person and subject to all defenses of any party which would be available in an action on a simple contract. (3–306.)

Procedure. Unless specifically denied, the signatures on a negotiable instrument are admitted. If not admitted, the burden of establishing the signature is on the person claiming under the signature. The signature is presumed to be genuine or authorized except where the action is to enforce the obligation of a purported signer who has died or become incompetent before proof is required.

Production of the instrument entitles the holder to recover if signatures are admitted unless the defendant establishes a defense. For example, if suit is brought by a holder on a negotiable commercial paper and the defendant does appear and defend, all that would be required of the holder would be that he produce the instrument, offer it in evidence and give testimony as to the amount due.

If the party sued on negotiable commercial paper sets up a defense, a person claiming the rights of a holder in due course has the burden of establishing that he or some person under whom he claims is, in all respects, a holder in due course. (3–307.)

Summary

A holder in due course of negotiable commercial paper takes free from personal defenses existing between the parties but takes subject to the real defense of infancy, and other incapacities available as a defense to a simple contract; duress or illegality of the transaction which renders the obligation a nullity; promises induced by "trickery"; discharge in insolvency proceedings; and discharges of which he has notice.

A holder not a holder in due course takes negotiable commercial paper subject to all the defenses which would be available to a promisor on a simple contract to pay money.

Signatures on negotiable commercial paper are admitted unless specifically denied. If denied, the party claiming under the instrument has the burden of establishing it. Production of the instrument entitles the holder to recover unless a defense is established in which event the holder has the burden of proving he holds as a holder in due course.

Reading Trust Co. v. Hutchison

35 Pa. D. & C.2d 790 (Ct. of Common Pleas Pa. 1964)

This was an action by Reading Trust Company (plaintiff) to obtain judgment by confession on a note on which the Hutchisons (defendants) were the makers. Judgment was entered and the Hutchisons moved to open the judgment. Motion to open was denied.

On March 7, 1963, an agent of Gracious Living, Inc., called upon the Hutchisons and identified himself as a "demonstrator" of water softening equipment. It was alleged that upon completion of a demonstration the representative explained the cost of purchasing the equipment and indicated that Gracious Living, Inc., would install it on a four months' trial basis if the Hutchisons would give a list of their friends and neighbors and then permit a demonstration in the Hutchison home. The arrangement also provided for compensation to them if sales resulted from such lists. The Hutchisons maintained that the agent "asked the defendants to sign a form which he could show to his boss to prove that he had made the demonstration and also as a bond to cover the unit while it was on the property of the defendants and until they decided to keep it. Defendant signed both of these forms." The Hutchisons testified that it was not until they received an installment book from Reading on March 27, 1963 that they realized "that they had been tricked into signing a contract and a judgment note." The plaintiff Trust Company clarified that it was not a party to the transaction; that it took the note in the normal course of business and that it had no knowledge of the representations made by the agent of Gracious Living.

KOCH, PRESIDING JUDGE.   At the outset it must be said that the petitioners have not established that Reading Trust had any knowledge of fraudulent business practices. . . .

The Uniform Commercial Code . . . provides as follows:

(1) A holder in due course is a holder who takes the instrument
(a) for value; and
(b) in good faith including observance of the reasonable commercial standards of any business in which the holder may be engaged; and
(c) without notice that it is overdue or has been dishonored or of any defense against or claim to it on the part of any person.

The crux of petitioners' position is that even though the Hutchisons may have had no specific knowledge of the circumstances surrounding the execution of the note, Section 3–305(2)(c) defeats its rights as a holder in due course. This portion of the Code is as follows:

To the extent that a holder is a holder in due course he takes the instrument free from
(1) . . .
(2) All defenses of any party to the instrument with whom the holder has not dealt except
(c) Such misrepresentation as has induced the party to sign the instrument with neither knowledge nor reasonable opportunity to obtain knowledge of its character or its essential terms.

The Uniform Commercial Code Comment to the foregoing subsection follows:

Paragraph (c) of subsection (2) is new. It follows the great majority of the decisions under the original Act in recognizing the defense of 'real' or 'essential' fraud, sometimes called fraud in the essence or fraud in the factum, as effective against a holder in due course. The common illustration is that of the maker who is tricked into signing a note in the belief that it is merely a receipt or some other document. The theory of the defense is that his signature on the instrument is ineffective because he did not intend to sign such an instrument at all. Under this provision the defense extends to an instrument signed with knowledge that it is a negotiable instrument, but without knowledge of its essential terms.

The test of the defense here stated is that of excusable ignorance of the contents of the writing signed. The party must not only have been in ignorance, but must also have had no reasonable opportunity to obtain knowledge. In determining what is a reasonable opportunity all relevant factors are to be taken into account, including the age and sex of the party, his intelligence, education and business experience; his ability to read or to understand English, the representations made to him and his reason to rely on them or to have confidence in the person making them; the presence or absence of any third person who might read or explain the instrument to him, or any other possibility of obtaining independent information; and the apparent necessity, or lack of it, for acting without delay.

Unless the misrepresentation meets this test, the defense is cut off by a holder in due course.

We are in accord with the views expressed in this comment. . . . We do not agree with the petitioners' contention that this case presents the classic illustration of a maker who was "tricked" into signing a note in the belief that it was another document. While we do not condone some of the high pressure tactics which were used in this case, nevertheless, a reading of the depositions persuades us that upon taking into consideration the factors of excusable ignorance of the contents of the writing signed the judgment should not be opened.

An analysis of the factors shows that the husband petitioner, age 48, is a high school graduate and is employed as a clerk; the wife, age 51, completed her junior year in high school. In addition to their undoubted ability to read and write the English language and their high degree of intelligence as indicated by their depositions neither of them could establish any basis which would indicate that they had any reason to have confidence in the representations made by the agent for Gracious Living, Inc.

In further analyzing the factors we find that there was a third person present on the occasion of the signing, Mr. Albert Mitchell, an uncle of Mrs. Hutchison. He, too, is a high school graduate, and despite his presence, was not asked by the petitioners for advice.

Problem Cases

1. Program Aids accepted a number of drafts or trade acceptances payable to Bean. The drafts were given as payment in the sale by Bean to Program Aids of catalogs for physical training equipment. Bean negotiated the acceptances to Bank which took them as a holder in due course; the Bank later negotiated the acceptances back to Bean. Bean brought suit on the acceptances against Program Aids. Program Aids sought to defend on the grounds Bean had breached the sales contract by improperly preparing the catalogs. Bean claims he is not subject to the personal defense in this action because he is a transferee from a holder in due course and therefore has the rights of a holder in due course. Is Bean's claim a valid one?

2. A check was endorsed: "Pay to the order of any bank, banker, or trust company. All prior endorsements guaranteed." Was the endorsement a special endorsement?

3. Wilson signed a promissory note as maker that was payable to Citizens Bank. Citizens Bank endorsed the note to Stockbridge Investment Corporation. Stockbridge then endorsed the check to Finance Company as collateral for current and antecedent loans made by Finance Company to Stockbridge. Finance Company at that point qualified as a holder in due course. Stockbridge defaulted on the loans and Finance Company included the note in a judicial sale of the collateral it held on the Stockbridge loan. At the sale, Finance Company repurchased the note in its own name. Now Finance Company sues Wilson on the note and Wilson claims that under 3–302(3) Finance Company is not a holder in due course. Should this claim be sustained?

4. Maker made a promissory note payable to Payee who orally agreed not to transfer it until his contractual obligations to Maker were completed. However, Payee did negotiate the note to a bank which credited the note against an indebtedness owed by Payee to the bank. Now the bank seeks to collect the note from Maker. Maker contends (1) that the bank is not a holder in due course because it did not give value, and (2) that, in any event, Maker has a good defense based on Payee's promise not to transfer the instrument until he completed his obligations, which promise he had broken. Are Maker's contentions correct? Why or why not?

5. In April, 1963, there were presented to the Peoples Bank two checks drawn by Haar and payable to the order of Western Aircraft Leasing. Peoples Bank then cashed the $3,500 check for the payee and allowed him to deposit the $4,000 check in an account, giving him immediate credit on it. Haar had drawn these two checks and delivered them to the payee on April 3, 1963, as payment for some unspecified interest in Western Aircraft Leasing Company. He then became concerned that he would not receive the interest he bargained for and on the 3rd or 4th day of April, 1963, he requested each of the banks on which the checks were drawn to stop payment. In the regular channels of banking, Peoples Bank was advised payment had been stopped, and immediately froze the account to which the $4,000 check had been deposited. It applied the remaining funds in the account to cover the advance it had made on the $3,500 check, and the credit given on the $4,000 check. The amount was insufficient to reimburse the bank for these advances and credit and, after some payments were made by the payee, Peoples Bank was still due $2,299.40. It then filed an action against Haar alleging it was a holder in due course of the two checks. Can Peoples Bank qualify as a holder in due course?

6. Williams signed a contract with Peerless and Reynolds whereby Peerless agreed to make certain improvements on the Williams' home and to pay the balance remaining on their automobile. Williams promised to pay $3,200 in monthly installments. Subsequent to the execution of the contract Williams signed a promissory note payable to Reynolds in the amount of $6,399.60 representing principal and interest over a 10-year period. Reynolds negotiated the note to Financial Credit Corporation as part of a purchase of 480 notes. Financial paid $704 for the Williams' note. Financial later sued Williams on the note and Williams sought to impose a fraud defense, claiming that Financial was not a holder in due course. There was testimony at the trial that "every Marylander knew" from the newspapers about Reynold's fraudulent activities. Could Financial qualify as a holder in due course?

7. Greenwald brought suit as endorsee of a negotiable promissory note signed by Frank M. and Rose Manzon. The Manzons claimed that the note was incomplete and irregular on its face since the place of payment was not specified in the place provided therefor on the printed form and since the blanks on the printed form appeared to have been filled in by different persons using different colored inks. They also

claimed the instrument was irregular because the endorsements on the back were not in the same order as they were signed in. Are these valid claims?

8. Acceptance Corp. contracted to consolidate Distilling Co.'s obligations. As part of the contract, Distilling Co. executed and delivered its promissory note payable to the order of Acceptance Corp., leaving the amount blank. Acceptance Corp. filled in $800,000 as the amount and discounted the note at Peoples Bank. On the due date, Distilling Co. refused to pay the note, and, when sued on it by Peoples Bank, set up as a defense that the amount filled in by Acceptance Corp. was in excess of the amount authorized. Is the defense good?

9. Two notes were endorsed by the payee and negotiated to the bank as security for a loan before they were overdue. The endorsee was a regular depositor of the bank, and the loan was made to enable him to purchase a business. The bank made no inquiry regarding the origin of the notes and had no knowledge of the fact that the two notes had been given in payment for stock in an oil company and that the stock had never been delivered. Is the bank a holder in due course?

10. On March 17, 1966, McQueer purchased some equipment from Johnson's Garage and gave it a note for $10,698 dated March 17, 1966, payable "five days after date." Payee, Johnson's Garage, negotiated the note for value on March 28 to Unadilla National Bank. The bank claims that when it acquired the note, it was payable "forty-five days after date." On April 1, McQueer who was unaware that the note had been negotiated, paid Johnson's Garage the sum of $10,698. Now the bank seeks to collect on the note from McQueer, and he asserts that he has a personal defense of payment that is good against the bank. Can he assert the defense?

11. On March 2, 1960, Radio Sales drew a negotiable check payable to the order of Black. Black negotiated the check to Alexander, who deposited it in the Citizens Bank on March 10, 1960. The next day the check was presented to the drawee bank for collection, and payment was refused. Radio Sales had stopped payment on the check. Alexander sued Radio Sales on the check, and it set up lack of consideration as a defense. Radio Sales claims that since Alexander did not take the check until March 10, 1960, he is not a holder in due course because the check was overdue before he took it. Is Alexander a holder in due course of the check?

12. Holder in Due Course of some notes sued Luccarelli, the maker. Luccarelli claims that the notes were signed by him in blank and delivered to Weiss, an associate of his, at Weiss's request and in reliance on his good faith. He also claims that he, even though he knew the nature of the instruments, did not know that the notes would be negotiated. Luccarelli is not proficient in English but has been engaged in business for a number of years and knows the nature of negotiable instruments. Luccarelli seeks to use Section 3–305 (2)(c) as a defense against Holder in Due Course. On these facts, has he stated a good defense? Why or why not?

13. Blackburn acquired an automobile from Vanella and gave him a check in payment of it. Vanella endorsed the check and took it to Marine Midland Bank where the bank gave him cash and credit in his account for the check. Blackburn found out that Vanella had misrepresented to him that the automobile was free of liens, and so he stopped payment on the check. Now Marine Midland sues Blackburn as drawer of the check. Even though he admits Marine Midland is a holder in due course, Blackburn claims he has a defense of fraud good against even a holder in due course. Does he?

chapter 40. Liability of Parties and Discharge

Signed

Effect of Signing. The English and American courts have held from the earliest time that any party who has not signed a formal contract cannot be held liable on that contract. A negotiable instrument is classed as a formal contract and consequently this rule has been adopted and applied to negotiable commercial paper. The Code provides that no person is liable on an instrument unless his name appears thereon. (Section 3–401 [1].) [1]

When it is necessary to determine the capacity in which a person has signed an instrument, the position of his signature on such instrument is important but not conclusive. If a signature is placed on the lower right-hand corner of an instrument, the presumption is that he has signed as a maker or drawer. If the named drawee signs across the face of the instrument, it is a clear indication that he has accepted it but his signature on any part of the instrument, front or back, in the absence of credible evidence of an intent to sign in some other capacity, will be held to be an acceptance. A signature on the back of an instrument is presumed to be an endorsement. Unless the instrument clearly indicates that a signature is made in some other capacity it is an endorsement. (3–402.)

Signing by Representative. Negotiable commercial paper may be signed by an authorized agent and, if properly signed, the principal will be bound as he would be had he signed it himself. All negotiable paper issued by a corporation is signed by an agent of the corporation and such agent is usually an officer of the corporation who is authorized to sign negotiable instruments.

No particular form of appointment is necessary to establish the authority to sign negotiable paper as agent. (3–403 [1].)

---

[1] The numbers in the parentheses refer to the sections of the Uniform Commercial Code 1962.

Since the liability of the parties to a negotiable instrument is determined by what is on the instrument, and parol evidence is admissible only to clear up ambiguities, the manner of signing in a representative capacity is important. An authorized agent is personally liable if he signs the instrument in his own name and neither the name of the principal nor the fact that he is signing in a representative capacity is shown on the instrument. For instance, if Axe, authorized agent of Parks's, signs a negotiable instrument, "Axe," Axe will be individually liable on the instrument. (3–403 [2] [a].)

If an authorized representative signs a negotiable instrument in his own name and so signs that he indicates that he has signed in a representative capacity but does not name the person represented, parol evidence would be admissible, as between the immediate parties, to prove that the parties to the instrument intended that the party represented be liable and not the party signing in the representative capacity. For example, if a negotiable instrument is signed, "Axe, agent" and is not negotiated and the payee then sues Axe on the instrument, parol evidence would be admitted to prove that the payee knew that Axe was acting as agent for Parks, his principal, and that the parties intended Parks to be bound and not Axe. But if this instrument were negotiated to a holder in due course, Axe would be personally liable on the instrument. (3–403 [2] [b].)

If a negotiable instrument is signed in the name of an organization and the name of the organization is preceded or followed by the name and office of an authorized individual, the organization and not the officer who has signed the instrument in a representative capacity will be bound. (3–403 [3].)

The proper way for a person executing a negotiable instrument in a representative capacity is as follows:

> "Parks Corporation
> "By Axe, Treasurer." or
> "Paul Parks
> "By Leonard Axe, his Agent."

Unauthorized Signature. If the name of a person is signed to a negotiable instrument by a person who has no authority to so sign the instrument, the signature is wholly inoperative and does not bind the person whose name is signed. Such a signing is a forgery. If an agent signs the name of his principal to a negotiable instrument and indicates that he signs in a representative capacity when in fact he has no authority to sign negotiable instruments in his principal's name, the principal will not be bound. In either situation, the party whose name is signed to the instrument may ratify the act of the party signing and will thereby bind himself or he may act in such manner as will preclude him from denying the validity of the signature. For example, if an instrument signed "Paul Parks" is shown to Parks by a prospective purchaser of the instrument and Parks assures the person that the signature is genuine, and the party then, and in reliance on this assurance, purchases the instrument, Parks would be precluded from thereafter denying the validity of the signature. An unauthorized representative who has signed the name of another to a negotiable instrument is personally liable on the instrument. (3–404.)

Summary

Under the general rule relative to the liability of a party on a formal contract, no one can be held liable whose name does not appear on the contract. A person may use any name or symbol as his signature but if he signs in an ambiguous capacity, he will be presumed to have signed as an endorser.

Commercial paper may be signed by one acting in a representative capacity and no formal authorization is necessary. If one acting as an authorized representative signs only in his own name he is individually liable on the instrument. If the instrument names the person represented and the representative so signs that he indicates that he has signed in a representative capacity only the person represented will be bound. As between the immediate parties if the person represented is not named but the person signing indicates that he is signing in a representative capacity, parol evidence is admissible to prove the intent of the parties. If the instrument is negotiated to a holder in due course, the representative who has signed will be individually liable to the holder in due course. If an instrument is signed in the name of a corporation and the name of an authorized officer followed by an indication of his office, only the corporation will be bound.

Bell v. *Dornan*

201 A.2d 324 (Super. Ct. Pa. 1964)

This was an action by James G. Dornan (plaintiff) against Margaret S. Bell, executrix of the estate of William Bell, Jr. (defendant), to have a judgment taken on a judgment note set aside. Judgment for Dornan and Bell appealed. Judgment reversed and judgment reinstated.

In the lifetime of William Bell, Jr., a note signed as follows:

(Corporate Seal)	"Memma M. Good "Chet B. Earl Inc., (Seal) "James G. Dornan (Seal)"

and payable to him was issued. After the death of William Bell, Jr., the executrix of his estate took judgment on the note against James G. Dornan alone and individually.

MONTGOMERY, JUDGE. Under the Uniform Commercial Code § 3–403, it is provided: "(2) An authorized representative who signs his own name to an instrument is also personally obligated unless the instrument names the person represented and shows that the signature is made in a representative capacity. The name of an organization preceded or followed by the name *and office* of an authorized individual is a signature made in a representative capacity."

Mr. Dornan's signature follows the name of the organization but does not show his office. In fact, opposite his name is the word "(SEAL)" as printed on the form of note used, which is in addition to the formal corporate seal imprint which was placed on the note, presumably by the proper custodian. Therefore, we are constrained to hold that under the provision of the code previously set forth he is personally obligated on the instrument. The presence of the corporate seal does not alter our view. The note might very well have been an obligation of the corporation as well as of the appellee.

Pittsburgh National Bank v. *Kemilworth Restaurant Co.* is readily distinguishable. First, the lower court had admissible depositions and undenied allegations of the petition on which to base its order. In the present case there were neither depositions nor admitted facts. Second, there were allegations of mutual accident and mistake in that case, whereas in the present case the only allegation was that by inadvertence the office was omitted and there was no allegation of accident or mistake or that the inadvertence was mutual. In fact, in the *Pittsburgh National Bank* case both parties to the judgment contended that a mistake had been made in the execution of the instrument.

Pollin v. Mindy Mfg. Co., Inc.

236 A.2d 542 (Sup. Ct. Pa. 1967)

This was an action by Pollin (plaintiff) against Mindy Manufacturing Company and its president, Robert Apfelbaum (defendants), to recover on thirty-six checks drawn in the name of the Company and signed by Apfelbaum. Judgment for Pollin. Apfelbaum appealed. Judgment reversed as to Apfelbaum.

The checks in question had been boldly imprinted at the top with "Mindy Mfg. Co., Inc., 26th & Reed Streets, Philadelphia, Penn., 19146 _____ Payroll Check No. _____" and with "Mindy Mfg. Co., Inc." imprinted above two blank lines appearing at the lower right-hand corner. Under the imprinted name of the corporate defendant on the checks was the signature of Robert Apfelbaum without any designation of office or capacity. Pollin contended that Apfelbaum was liable on the checks since his signature was absolute and unqualified. Apfelbaum claimed he had signed in a representative capacity as president of Mindy Manufacturing and not in his individual capacity.

MONTGOMERY, JUSTICE.   Summary judgment against appellant was entered by the lower court on the authority of Section 3–403 of the Uniform Commercial Code which provides, "(2) An authorized representative who signs his (own) name to an instrument. . . . (b) except as otherwise established between the immediate parties, is personally obligated if the instrument names the person represented but does not show that the representative signed in a representative capacity. . . ," and our decisions thereunder.

The issue before us, therefore, is whether a third party to the original transaction, the endorsee in the present case, may recover against one who affixes his name to a check in the place where a maker usually signs without indicating he is signing in a representative capacity, without giving consideration to other parts of the instrument or extrinsic evidence. This appears to be a novel question under the Uniform Commercial Code.

If this were an action brought by the payee, parol evidence would be permitted to establish the capacity of the person affixing his signature under Section 3–403(b) previously recited and our decisions in *Bell* v. *Dornan* and *Pittsburgh National Bank* v. *Kemilworth Restaurant Co.*

However, since this is an action brought by a third party our initial inquiry must be for the purpose of determining whether the instrument indicates the capacity of appellant as a signer. Admittedly, the instrument fails to show the office held by appellant. However, we do not think this is a complete answer to our problem, since the Code imposes liability on the individual only ". . . if the instrument . . . does not show that the representative signed in a representative capacity . . ." This implies that the instrument must be considered in its entirety.

Although Section 3–401(2) of the Uniform Commercial Code provides that "A signature is made by use of any name, including any trade or assumed name, upon an instrument, or by any word or mark used in lieu of a written signature," which would be broad enough to include the printed name of a corporation, we do not believe that a check showing two lines under the imprinted corporate name indicating the signature of one or more corporate officers would be accepted by any reasonably prudent person as a fully executed check of the corporation. It is common to expect that a corporate name placed upon a negotiable instrument in order to bind the corporation as a maker, especially when printed on the instrument, will be accompanied by the signatures of officers authorized by the by-laws to sign the instrument. While we do not rule out the possibility of a printed name being established as an acceptable signature, we hold that such a situation is uncommon, and against a valid corporate signature. Corporations act through officers.

Next we must give consideration to the distinction between a check and a note. A check is an order of a depositor on a bank in the nature of a draft drawn on the bank and payable on demand. It is revokable until paid or accepted for payment. A note is an irrevocable promise to pay on the part of the maker. The maker of a check impliedly engages not only that it will be paid, but that he will have sufficient funds in the bank to meet it. In the present instance the checks clearly showed that they were payable from a special account set up by the corporate defendant for the purpose of paying its employees. This information disclosed by the instrument of itself would refute any contention that the appellant intended to make the instrument his own order on the named bank to pay money to the payee. The money was payable from the account of the corporation defendant over which appellant as an individual had no control.

Considering the instrument as a whole we conclude that it sufficiently discloses that appellant signed it in a representative capacity.

Acceptance

Acceptance by Drawee.   A drawee is not liable on a check or other draft until he accepts it. The drawing of a check or draft on a named drawee is not an assignment of funds in the drawee's hands but is instead an order by the drawer addressed to the drawee ordering him to pay to the payee the sum for which the instrument is drawn. Until the drawee accepts the instrument, there is no contractual relation between the holder of the instrument and the drawee. The drawee may, and usually does, owe a contractual duty to the drawer of the check or draft to pay or accept it and if he dishonors the instrument by his failure or refusal to accept or pay it, he will be liable to the drawer for breach of the drawer-drawee contract. (3–409.)

Nature of Acceptance.   An acceptance is the drawee's signed engagement to honor the draft as presented. The acceptance must be written on the draft and it may consist of the drawee's signature alone. The drawee may, however, if he wishes, in addition to his signature, name a particular bank or place in the United States where payment is to be made, unless the acceptance states that the draft is to be paid only at such bank or place. The drawee may accept a draft before it has been signed by the drawer, but such an instrument is not a negotiable instrument until signed by the drawer. (3–104 [1] [a].) Also, the drawee may accept a draft which is incomplete or is overdue or has been dishonored. If the drawee accepts a draft payable at a fixed period after sight and does not date his acceptance, the holder may complete it by supplying a date in good faith. (3–410.)

The holder of a draft has a right to the unqualified acceptance of the draft as drawn and if the drawee's proffered acceptance in any manner varies the draft as presented, the holder may refuse the acceptance and treat the draft as dishonored in which event the drawee, if he has signed the draft, is entitled to have his acceptance canceled. If the holder assents to an acceptance which varies the terms of the draft, each drawer and endorser who does not affirmatively consent is discharged. (3–412.)

Summary

A draft or check is not an assignment of funds in the hands of the drawee and the drawee is not liable on the instrument until he accepts it. The drawee may accept a draft by signing his name on the draft. An acceptance is an engagement to honor the draft as drawn, and the drawee may accept the draft before the drawer has signed it, or while it is incomplete or overdue or after it has been dishonored.

The holder is entitled to the unqualified acceptance of the drawee and if he proffers (offers) anything less the holder can treat the draft as dishonored. If the holder consents to a qualified acceptance, drawers and endorsers are discharged unless they affirmatively assent to the variation.

Merson v. Sun Insurance Co. of New York

253 N.Y.S.2d 51 (Civ. Ct. N.Y. 1964)

This was an action by Merson (plaintiff) against Sun Insurance Company of New York (defendant) to recover, as indorsee, on a draft drawn by Sun Insurance Company. Judgment for Merson.

Facts are stated in the opinion.

GREENFIELD, JUDGE.   The draft issued by the insurance company in this case was a fully negotiable bill of exchange. The words "upon acceptance" meant acceptance by the drawee bank. These words did not render the instrument conditional, since presentment for acceptance may be required for any check or bill of exchange. Uniform Commercial Code, § 3–410 (2). A trade acceptance has always been deemed a negotiable instrument; a banker's acceptance even more so. Nonacceptance may be signified by the drawee bank either because it does not have sufficient funds of the drawer, or because the drawer has instructed it not to pay—exactly as in the case of negotiable check or note.

Merson, to whom the instrument was endorsed by the payee, took without notice of any defect, and is a holder in due course. The drawee bank did not irrevocably accept the draft by notification or delivery, despite its tentative approval of it; hence the holder's right of recourse accrued against Sun Insurance Company, as the drawer. The defense of mistake in issuing the instrument is of no avail against Merson.

Parties to Commercial Paper

Primary and Secondary Liability. A party to a negotiable instrument may be either primarily or secondarily liable for the payment of the instrument. The person primarily liable on a negotiable instrument is the person who, by the terms of the instrument, is absolutely required to pay the instrument. For instance, the maker of a note is absolutely required to pay the note and is the person primarily liable.

No person is primarily liable on a draft until it has been accepted by the drawee, after which the drawee becomes the person primarily liable.

Usually, a check is paid when presented to the drawee bank, and no person becomes primarily liable on it. However, the drawee bank may, at the request of the drawer or holder, certify the check, in which case the certification of the check makes the certifying bank absolutely liable for the payment of the check.

All other persons who are liable for the payment of a negotiable instrument are secondarily liable. The drawer of a draft or check and the endorsers on any negotiable instrument are secondarily liable. That is, their liability is collateral, and they will not be required to pay the instrument unless the person primarily liable defaults or unless the instrument is dishonored on its presentment to the drawee.

Nature of Secondary Liability. The liability of the parties secondarily liable on negotiable commercial paper is comparable in most respects to that of the guarantor on a simple contract. His liability is a contingent liability and does not arise until the party who is primarily liable has defaulted in his performance. Since in the normal course of events a guarantor will not know that the party primarily liable has defaulted, the promisee, if he wishes to hold the guarantor liable, must give him notice of the default within a reasonable time thereafter. These basic rules apply in determining the liability of persons secondarily liable on negotiable commercial paper. However, the duties of the holder of defaulted paper are set out in detail in the Code.

Summary

Parties to negotiable commercial paper are either primarily or secondarily liable for payment of the instrument. Makers of notes and acceptors of drafts or checks are primarily liable; all other parties to such instruments are secondarily liable. In determining the nature and scope of the liability of secondary parties the basic rules relative to the liability of the guarantor of a simple contract apply with some modifications.

Presentment, Notice and Protest

Presentment. Presentment may be for acceptance or for payment. Presentment for acceptance is necessary to charge the drawer or endorsers of a draft in the following three situations: (1) where the draft provides that presentment for acceptance must be made, or (2) where the draft is payable at a place other than the residence or place of business of the drawee, or (3) where the draft is payable at a fixed time after presentment or sight. The holder need not present any other draft for acceptance but if the draft is payable at a stated date he may, at his option, present it for acceptance at any time before its due date. (3–501 [1].) Presentment for payment is necessary to charge any endorser. (3–501 [1] [b].)

Time of Presentment. The Code sets out rules as to the time for the presentment for acceptance or payment of an instrument. The basic rule recognizes that an instrument should be presented within a reasonable time. To lend a degree of certainty as to the time for presentment the Code provides that unless a different time for presentment is expressed in the instrument the time for any presentment is determined as follows.

Where an instrument is payable at, or a fixed period after, a stated date any presentment for acceptance must be made on or before the date it is payable. (3–503 [1] [a].) In the ordinary course of business if a time draft is not presented for acceptance before the due date any presentment made thereafter would be presentment for payment, not for acceptance.

Where the instrument is payable after sight it must either be presented for acceptance or negotiated within a reasonable time after date or issue whichever is later. (3–503 [1] [b].)

Where an instrument shows a date on which it is payable, presentment for payment is due on that date, and where an instrument is accelerated presentment for payment is due within a reasonable time after the acceleration. (3–503 [1] [c] [d].)

In respect to any instrument not included in the above categories, to charge parties secondarily liable presentment for acceptance or payment is due within a reasonable time after such party becomes liable thereon. (3–503 [1] [e].)

A reasonable time for presentment for acceptance or payment is determined by the nature of the instrument, by usage of banking or trade, and by the facts of the particular case.

In the event the instrument is an uncertified check which is drawn and payable in the United States and which is not a draft drawn by a bank, the following are *presumed* (1–201 [31]) to be reasonable periods within which to present for payment or to initiate bank collections: with respect to the liability of the drawer, 30 days after date or issue whichever is later; and with respect to the liability of an endorser, 7 days after his endorsement. (3–503 [2].) The purpose of these rules is to clear up an existing ambiguity. Making the time for holding the drawer liable longer than the time holding the endorser liable is justified on the ground that the drawer normally expects the amount of the check to be paid out of his account and should stand back of it longer than an endorsee who merely receives the check and passes it on without any expectation of having to pay it. If he will be required to pay it, he should know it soon after he negotiates the check.

If the date for presentment falls on a day which is not a full business day presentment is due the next succeeding day which is a full business day for both parties. (3–503 [3].)

Presentment to be sufficient must be made at a reasonable hour, and if presentment is to be made at a bank, during its banking hours. (3–503 [4].)

When presentment for acceptance is made, the drawee may defer acceptance without dishonoring the instrument until the close of the next business day. This gives the drawee an opportunity to check signatures or other matters relative to the instrument. The holder acting in good faith may, in order to obtain acceptance and without either dishonor of the instrument or discharge of secondary parties, allow postponement of acceptance for an additional business day. This allows a reasonable but not unlimited time to clear up any doubts relative to the validity of the instrument or the nature of the drawee's obligation to the drawer of the instrument.

The time allowed for investigation prior to the acceptance of documentary drafts drawn under a letter of credit is the close of business on the day of presentment. (3–506.)

How Presentment Made.   If an instrument is not payable by, through, or at a bank, the collecting bank may, unless otherwise instructed, present the instrument by sending to the party to accept or pay a written notice that the bank holds the instrument for acceptance or payment, as the case may be. The notice must be sent in time to be received on or before the day when presentment is due. If presentment is made by notice and neither honor nor a demand for exhibition of the instrument or for other rights of the party to whom presentment is made is received by the close of business on the day after maturity or, in the case of a demand instrument, by the close of business on the third banking day after notice was sent, the presenting bank may treat the instrument as dishonored and charge any secondary party by sending him notice of the facts. (4–210.)

Presentment of instruments not handled by a collecting bank may be made by mail, in which event the time of presentment is determined by the time of the receipt of the mail, or through a clearinghouse. (3–504 [2] [a] and [b].)

If a place of acceptance or payment is specified in the instrument, presentment should be made at that place; if no place of presentment is specified, presentment is made at the place of business or residence of the party to accept or pay. If neither the party to accept or pay nor anyone authorized to act for him is present or accessible at such place, presentment is excused. (3–504 [2] [c].) The acceptance may be made to any one of two or more makers, acceptors, drawees or other payors or to any person who has authority to make or refuse the acceptance or payment. A draft which has been accepted or a note made payable at a bank in the United States *must* be presented at such bank. (3–504 [3] and [4].)

Rights of Party to Whom Presentment Is Made.   The party to whom presentment is made may, without dishonoring the instrument, require the exhibition of the instrument and reasonable identification of the person making presentment and evidence of his authority to make it if he is making it for another. (3–505 [1] [a] and [b].)

Furthermore, the party to whom presentment is made may require that the instrument be produced for acceptance or payment at the place specified in it and, if no place is specified, at any place reasonable under the circumstances. If partial payment is made, the payor may require that a receipt for the payment be made on the instrument, and if payment in full is made, the payor may require the surrender of the instrument. (3–505 [1] [c] and [d].)

Failure to comply with any of the requirements set out above invalidates the presentment but a person presenting has a reasonable time in which to comply, and the time for acceptance or payment runs from the time of compliance. (3–505 [2].)

Effect of Unexcused Delay in Presentment. If presentment, without excuse, is delayed beyond the time it is due, any endorser is discharged from liability on the instrument and any drawer or acceptor of a draft payable at a bank or maker of a note payable at a bank who because the drawee or payor bank becomes insolvent during the delay is deprived of funds maintained with the drawee or payor bank to cover the instrument may discharge his liability by written assignment to the holder of his rights against the drawee or payor bank in respect of such funds, but such drawer, acceptor or maker is not otherwise discharged. (3–502 [1].) This provision applies, with some modification, to the pre-Code law relative to the discharge of the drawer of the check which the holder has not presented within the permitted time and the drawee bank has become insolvent during the delay. Under pre-Code law the drawer was discharged only to the extent of the loss suffered as the direct result of the drawee bank's insolvency. Under this provision of the Code, if the drawer or acceptor of a draft or the payor of a note payable at a bank has on deposit funds for the purpose of discharging his obligation on the instrument and the holder does not present it when due and thereafter the bank becomes insolvent, the drawer, acceptor or payor can discharge his liability on the instrument by making a written assignment of the funds on deposit for the purpose of discharging the instrument to the holder. This places the entire loss and delay resulting from the bank's insolvency on the holder whose negligence in presenting the instrument has caused the loss or delay.

Summary

Presentment for acceptance is necessary to charge the drawers and endorsers of a draft (1) if required by the draft, (2) if payable elsewhere than the place of business or residence of the drawee, or (3) if its date of payment depends on such presentment. The holder may at his option present any other draft. Presentment for payment is necessary to charge endorsers. Unless a different time is expressed in the instrument, presentment must be made within a reasonable time. It must be presented for acceptance, if payable at a fixed date, before date of payment; if payable after sight, within reasonable time after date or issue, whichever is later. Presentment for payment must be made on date payable, and if accelerated, within a reasonable time after acceleration.

A reasonable time to present a check to charge the drawer is presumed to be 30 days, and to charge an endorsee within 7 days of his endorsement. If due on a day that is not a business day, presentment is made the next day following which is a full business day for both parties.

Presentment may be made by mail or through a clearinghouse or at a place specified or, if none is specified, at the place of business or residence of the party to accept or pay. Presentment may be made to any one of two or more makers, acceptors, drawees or payors or to a person having authority to make or refuse the acceptance or payment. If payable at a bank in the United States, a draft accepted or a note made payable at a bank must be presented at such bank.

Exhibition of the instrument, identity and authority of the party presenting, receipt for payments, and surrender of the instrument on payment in full may be demanded. Failure to present the instrument when due without excuse discharges endorsers and permits the drawer, acceptor of a draft or payor of a note payable at a bank to shift, by assigning funds in writing to holder, any burden resulting from the intervening insolvency of the bank to the holder.

Dluge v. *Robinson*
204 A.2d 279 (Super. Ct. Pa. 1964)

This was an action by Ethel Dluge and Benjamin Rimm, Executors of the estate of Isaac Dluge, deceased (plaintiffs), against Joseph G. Robinson (defendant) to recover a judgment for the amount of a check. Judgment for Dluge and Robinson appealed. Judgment reversed and judgment for Robinson entered.

Robinson endorsed two checks and negotiated them to Isaac Dluge. When presented for payment the drawee bank refused payment because of insufficient funds. Evidence was offered to prove that the checks were returned to Robinson but there was no evidence offered to prove that a demand was made, and the trial court found that demand was not made until nearly seven months after the dishonor of the checks.

FLOOD, JUDGE.   If Dluge and Rimm were holders in due course, they would have to prove only (1) that Robinson endorsed the checks and delivered them to Dluge, and (2) that they had been presented to the endorser for payment within a reasonable time. Uniform Commercial Code, § 3–501 (1) (b). In the case of an uncertified check this is presumed to be within seven days after the endorsement. U.C.C., § 3–503 (1) (e), § 3–503 (2) (b).

"Presentment is a demand for acceptance or payment . . . by or on behalf of the holder." U.C.C., § 3–504 (1). The only evidence of any demand was the admission by Robinson that he received a letter from Dluge's attorney demanding payment. Robinson did not state when he received this letter. Dluge did not offer the letter in evidence and there is no way to determine from the record when it was sent except that it was presumably sent before the complaint was filed on September 12, 1960, seven months after the checks were dishonored by the drawee bank. Since Robinson denied any demand at the time the checks were returned to him, and the record is otherwise barren of any evidence of demand within seven days, or any reasonable time, after endorsement, the Dluges did not establish any right to recover even if they had been holders in due course.

Dluge's executors are not holders in due course. Dluge gave the checks to Robinson without any demand for payment, so far as the record shows, and was not in possession of them when the suit was brought. Therefore he was not the holder. " 'Holder' means a person who is in possession of a document of title or an instrument or an investment security drawn, issued or indorsed to him or to his order or to bearer or in blank." U.C.C., § 1–201 (20). *A fortiori,* he was not a holder in due course. U.C.C., § 3–302 (1).

Dishonor, Protest, Notice and Waiver

Dishonor. An instrument is dishonored when it has been duly presented and acceptance or payment cannot be obtained within the prescribed time, or in case of bank collection the instrument is not returned by the midnight deadline, or if presentment is excused and the instrument is not duly accepted or paid. (3–507 [1].)

When an instrument has been dishonored, the holder has an immediate right of recourse against the drawers and endorsers provided he has given any necessary notice of dishonor and protest. (3–507 [2].) The return of an instrument for lack of proper endorsement is not dishonor. (3–507 [3].) If a draft, by its terms or an endorsement thereon, allows a stated time for re-presentment where it is not accepted or paid when first presented, the holding of the draft and the re-presenting of it within the time allowed does not discharge parties secondarily liable. (3–507 [4].)

A purported protest, the purported stamp or writing of the drawee, payor bank or presenting bank on the instrument or accompanying it stating that acceptance or payment has been refused for reasons consistent with dishonor, or any book or record of the drawee, payor bank, or any collecting bank kept in the usual course of business which shows dishonor are admissible as evidence to create a presumption of dishonor. (3–510.)

Protest. Unless excused, protest of any dishonor is necessary to charge parties secondarily liable on any draft where the draft on its face appears to be drawn or payable outside the states or territories of the United States and the District of Columbia. A holder may at his option make protest of any dishonor. (3–501 [3].)

Protest is a certificate of dishonor made under the hand and seal of a person authorized to certify dishonor by the law of the place where dishonor occurs.

It may be made upon information satisfactory to such person. The certificate must identify the instrument, and certify that due presentment has been made and, if not, the reason why, and that the instrument has been dishonored. The certificate may also state that notice has been given to all parties or to specified parties. Protest is due by the time notice of dishonor is due, except where the instrument has been noted for protest in which case the protest may be made thereafter as of the date of noting. (3–509.)

Notice. Notice of dishonor or protest, unless waived, is necessary to charge any endorsers; and, as to any drawer, the acceptor of a draft payable at a bank or the maker of a note payable at bank, notice of any dishonor is necessary, but failure to give notice discharges such drawer, acceptor or maker only as discussed under the heading "Effect of Unexcused Delay in Presentment." (3–502 [2].)

Notice may be given in any reasonable manner. It may be given to any person who may be liable on the instrument by or on behalf of the holder or any party who has himself received notice, or any other party who may be compelled to pay the instrument. In addition an agent or bank in whose hands the instrument is dishonored may give notice to his principal or customer or to another agent or bank from which the instrument was received. Notice given by a bank must be given before its midnight deadline.

The notice must describe the instrument with reasonable certainty, and sending the instrument bearing a stamp, ticket or writing stating that acceptance or payment has been refused or sending a notice of debit with respect to the instrument is sufficient.

Written notice is given when sent although it is not received; notice to one partner is notice to each although the firm has been dissolved, and, in the event insolvency proceedings have been instituted after the issue of the instrument, notice may be given either to the party or to the representative of his estate. When any party is dead or incompetent notice may be sent to his last-known address or to his personal representatives. Notice, when sent, operates for the benefit of all parties who have rights on the instrument against the party notified. (3–508.)

Waiver or Excuse. Delay in presentment, protest or notice of dishonor is excused when the party is without notice that it is due as, for example, when the holder takes an instrument after the time of payment has been accelerated or takes a demand instrument after demand and he has no knowledge of such fact. Delay is excused if the holder makes an honest effort to make presentment and is unsuccessful because of circumstances beyond his control, but he must act with reasonable diligence after the cause of delay ceases. (3–511 [1].)

Presentment or notice or protest, as the case may be, is entirely excused when the party to be charged has waived it expressly or by implication before or after it is due. Where a waiver provision is embodied in the instrument, it binds all parties but where written above the signature of an endorser, it binds him only.

When the party himself has dishonored the instrument or countermanded payment or otherwise has no reason to expect or require that the instrument be accepted or paid, presentment or notice or protest is entirely excused. Such a situation occurs when the drawer of a check issues a stop-payment order to the drawee bank or has no account with the bank or insufficient credit to cover the check.

Presentment is also entirely excused when the maker, acceptor or drawee of any instrument except a documentary draft is dead or in insolvency proceedings instituted after the issue of the instrument, or when acceptance or payment is refused but not for want of presentment.

Where a draft has been dishonored by nonacceptance, a later presentment for payment and any notice of dishonor and protest for nonpayment are excused unless in the meantime the instrument has been accepted.

A waiver of protest includes a waiver of presentment and of notice of dishonor even though protest is not required. (3–511 [2], [3], [4], [5], and [6].)

Summary

An instrument has been dishonored when it has been duly presented and acceptance or payment cannot be obtained within the prescribed time. When an instrument is dishonored and required notices have been given, the holder has a right of recourse against the drawers and endorsers. The usual stamps on the instrument and the records of the dishonor of it are admissible as evidence of presumption of dishonor.

Protest is a certificate of dishonor made under the hand of a person authorized to certify dishonor. The certificate must identify the instrument and certify that due presentment has been made.

Notice of presentment and protest, unless waived, is necessary to charge any endorser. As to any drawer or acceptor of a draft or maker of a note payable at a bank, failure or delay in presentment or giving notice relieves the drawer, acceptor or maker of any liability only as to the loss he suffers as a result thereof. The notice must describe the instrument with reasonable certainty and written notice is effective when sent although not received. Due diligence must be exercised in the giving of notice.

Presentment may be waived by any party and is excused when the party is without notice that the instrument is due or when the party has himself dishonored the instrument or knows that it will not be accepted or paid or when the maker, drawer or drawee is dead or in insolvency proceedings. If dishonored by nonacceptance, it need not be presented for payment unless later accepted. Waiver of protest includes waiver of presentment and notice.

Contract of Parties

Contract in General. The terms of the contract of the parties to negotiable commercial paper are not set out on the face of the instrument but are instead written into the contract by operation of law and are as much a part of the contract as though written out in full. Parol evidence is not admissible to alter, subtract from or add to such terms. The terms of the contract of the party will depend on the capacity in which he signs the instrument. The terms of the contract of the several parties to the different types of negotiable commercial paper are set out in the Code.

Contract of the Maker, Acceptor, and Drawer. The maker of a note and the acceptor of a draft are primarily liable on the instrument. Each engages that he will pay the instrument according to its tenor at the time of his engagement or as completed if incomplete, provided it is completed in accordance with authority given. (3–413 [1].) When a drawee accepts a draft he becomes liable on the draft as it reads at the time of his acceptance, and in the hands of a holder in due course such defenses as the alteration of the instrument before he accepted it, forgery of the drawer's signature, lack of authority of the drawer or incapacity of the drawer are not available to him.

The drawer of a draft is secondarily liable on the draft, and he engages that upon dishonor of the draft and the necessary notice of dishonor or protest he will pay the amount of the draft to the holder or to any endorser who takes it up. Since the drawer is secondarily liable on the draft, he may disclaim this liability by drawing without recourse. (3–413 [2].)

By making, drawing or accepting an instrument the party admits as against all subsequent parties including the drawee the existence of the payee and his then capacity to endorse. (3–413 [3].) If an instrument when issued names as payee a nonexistent corporation or an infant or an incompetent person, such fact cannot be set up by the maker, drawer or acceptor of the instrument as a defense to his liability on the instrument.

Contract of Endorsers. All endorsers are secondarily liable. An endorser may avoid certain liability by qualifying his endorsement, that is, by endorsing without recourse. Unless the endorsement otherwise specifies, every endorser engages that upon dishonor and any necessary notice of dishonor and protest he will pay the instrument according to its tenor at the time of his endorsement to the holder or to any subsequent endorser who takes it up, even though the endorser who takes it up was not obligated to do so. (3–414 [1].)

An endorser who endorses "without recourse" or other qualifying language of similar import is not liable to the holder or endorsers for the nonpayment of the instrument by the party primarily liable. By so endorsing he relieves himself from the contractual liability as a guarantor of the instrument.

The endorsers are liable in the order in which their names appear on the instrument unless they have otherwise agreed. For example, if an instrument is endorsed A, B, C, D, and E each would be liable to all subsequent endorsers but not liable to prior endorsers. A is liable to B, C, D, and E, but E is liable to only the holder of the instrument.

Contract of Accommodation Party. The contract of an accommodation party will depend on the capacity in which he signs the instrument. He is one who signs the instrument in any capacity for the purpose of lending his name to another party to it. The accommodation party may sign as maker, drawer, acceptor or endorser. If Axe wishes to accommodate Parks he may execute a note payable to the order of Parks with the intention that Parks will discount the note at the bank. Axe will be liable to the discounting bank as maker, even though it knew at the time it took the note that Axe signed as accommodation maker. If Axe accepts or draws a draft or endorses an instrument for the accommodation of Parks, he will, in each instance, be liable to a holder who takes the instrument for value in accordance with the capacity in which he signed the instrument, even though the holder knows that Axe signed for the accommodation of Parks. (3–415 [2].)

As against a holder in due course and without notice of the accommodation, oral proof of the accommodation is not admissible to give the accommodation party the benefit of discharges dependent on his character as such, but in other cases the accommodation character may be shown by oral proof. (3–415 [3].) An endorsement which shows that it is not in the chain of title is notice of its accommodation character. (3–415 [4].)

An accommodation party is not liable to the party accommodated, and if he pays the instrument he has a right of recourse on the instrument against such party. (3–415 [5].) For example, if Axe signs a note as maker for the accommodation of Parks and Parks endorses the note and discounts it at First Bank and Parks then pays the note when due, he would have no recourse against Axe on the instrument since Parks is the accommodated party. However, if Axe pays the instrument he would have a right of action against Parks on the instrument.

Summary

The terms of the contract of the parties to negotiable commercial paper are written into the instrument by operation of law. The maker of a note and the acceptor of a draft contract to pay it according to the terms of the instrument. The drawer promises to pay the holder if the instrument is dishonored and he is given notice. Makers, acceptors and drawers admit the existence of the payee and his then capacity to endorse. Endorsers, who do not qualify their endorsements, contract to pay if the instrument, on presentment, is dishonored and they are given notice. Endorsers are presumed to be liable in the order in which they have endorsed.

An accommodation party is liable in the capacity in which he has signed the instrument.

Held v. Moore
2 U.C.C. Rep. 14 (Pa. Ct. of Com. Pleas,
Lancaster Cty. 1964)

This was an action by Held (plaintiff) against Herbert U. Moore and Lois Moore (defendants) to recover a judgment on a note. Judgment for Held.

Herbert U. Moore executed a note in the amount of $15,000 payable to Held. Lois Moore signed her name on the back of the note under the following indorsement: "For value received the undersigned and each of them hereby forever waive presentment, demand, protest, notice of protest and notice of dishonor of the within note, and the undersigned and each of them guarantees the payment of said note at maturity and consent without notice to any and all extensions of time or terms of payment made by holder of said note."

Presentment for payment was made to Herbert U. Moore and payment was refused. On July 18, 1963, presentment for payment was made to Lois Moore and payment was refused. When suit was brought on the note. Herbert U. Moore did not appear and defend. Lois Moore appeared and set up as a defense that she did not know in what capacity she signed the note or her reason for signing, and she also denied that the note was presented to her for payment.

JOHNSTONE, JUDGE.   Lois Moore's answer sets up none of the common defenses to an action of this kind, such as payment, release, failure of consideration, fraud, illegality, duress or the statute of limitations. She, in effect, says, I signed the note but I don't know why or in what capacity I signed it. Does this constitute a good defense or is it a valid reason for not entering judgment on the pleadings? We think not. The Uniform Commercial Code provides in § 3–414 that in the absence of a qualified indorsement, the indorser engages upon dishonor and any necessary notice of dishonor and protest to pay the instrument according to its tenor at the time of his indorsement. Lois Moore specifically guaranteed payment of the note at maturity by the indorsement on the back of the note. This makes her liable to the payee (Held) of the note if payment was not made by the maker. Section 3–416 of the Code provides, (1) Payment guaranteed or equivalent words added to a signature means that the signer engages that if the instrument is not paid when due, he will pay it according to its tenor without resort by the holder to any other party.

Warranties of Parties

Whether or not a person signs the instrument he may be liable on the basis of certain implied warranties. These warranties are of two types: (1) those imposed on persons who *transfer* instruments and (2) those imposed on persons who *present* instruments *for payment or acceptance.*

Transferor's Warranties. Any person who transfers an instrument and receives consideration makes five transferor's warranties to his transferee; in addition, if the transfer is by endorsement, they are made to any subsequent holder who takes the instrument in good faith. The five transferor's warranties are:

1. That the transferor has good title to the instrument or is authorized to obtain payment or acceptance on behalf of one who has a good title and that the transfer is otherwise rightful;
2. That all signatures are genuine or authorized;
3. That the instrument has not been materially altered;
4. That the transferor has no knowledge of any defense that is good against him; and
5. That the transferor has no knowledge of any insolvency proceedings instituted with respect to the maker or acceptor or the drawer of an unaccepted instrument. (3–417(2).)

A transferor who endorses with an unqualified endorsement warrants that no defense of any party is good against him, instead of merely warranting that he has no knowledge of defenses as in the case of the transferor without endorsement or the qualified endorser. (3–417 [2] and [3].)

While secondary liability often furnishes a sufficient basis for suing a transferor when the party primarily liable does not pay, warranties are still important. First, they do apply even where the transferor did not endorse. Second, unlike secondary liability, they do not depend on presentment, dishonor, and notice, but may be utilized before presentment has been made or after the time for giving notice has expired. Third, it may be easier to return the instrument to a transferor on the grounds of breach of warranty than to prove one's status as a holder in due course against a maker or drawer.

Presentment Warranties. Under commercial law, a distinction as to warranties is made between a person who transfers an instrument to another person and a person who presents the instrument for payment or acceptance to a maker or drawee. The person to whom an instrument is presented for acceptance or payment will not normally pay or accept unless he thinks he is legally obligated to pay or is legally entitled to credit or payment from a third party. As a general rule, when payment or acceptance of an instrument is made, it is final in favor of a holder in due course or a person who in good faith changed his position in reliance on the payment. (3–418.) Thus if a drawee bank pays a check without checking to see if the drawer's signature is valid, the drawee cannot later obtain repayment from a holder in due course who presented it for payment if the drawee finds the drawer's signature was forged; likewise, the drawee bank that pays a check out of an insufficient funds account cannot obtain repayment from a holder in due course.

However, the general rule of finality of payment or acceptance is subject to three exceptions which are embodied in the Uniform Commercial Code as warranties made by a party presenting an instrument for payment or acceptance and all prior transferors. These warranties, in general, are:

1. That the party has good title to the instrument or is authorized to obtain payment or acceptance on behalf of one who has a good title;
2. That the party has no knowledge that the signature of the maker or drawer in unauthorized;
3. That the instrument has not been materially altered. (3–417 [1].)

In certain exceptional cases these warranties do not apply when holders in due course are the presenting parties. For example, a drawer or maker should recognize his own signature and a maker or acceptor should recognize whether the instrument has been materially altered, so they do not get warranties covering these points from a holder in due course.

Summary

The transferor of an instrument warrants title, genuineness of signatures or the authority of one signing, that the instrument has not been materially altered, that no defenses of any party are good against him (if he qualifies his warranty he warrants he has no knowledge of defenses to the instrument) and that he has no knowledge of any insolvency proceedings instituted with respect to the maker or acceptor or the drawer of an unaccepted instrument.

Any person who obtains payment or acceptance and any prior transferor warrants to a person who in good faith accepts or pays the instrument that he has good title or is authorized to act for a person who has good title to the instrument and that the instrument has not been materially altered. A holder in due course acting in good faith does not warrant to a maker or drawer the genuineness of their signatures.

First National City Bank v. *Bankers Trust Co.*

4 U.C.C. Rep. 324 (N.Y. Sup. Ct., N.Y. Cty. 1967)

This was an action by First National City Bank (plaintiff) against Bankers Trust Company (defendant) to recover for breach of the transferor's warranty that all signatures on the instrument were genuine or authorized. First City National Bank moved for summary judgment and the motion was granted.

MARKEWICH, JUDGE. Plaintiff bank received from defendant bank a purported genuine draft for collection. It was timely presented for payment, which was refused because the instrument was forged, of which fact plaintiff immediately informed defendant, though it had in the interim provisionally settled for the draft's face amount. When the item was forwarded for collection, the signatures were warranted to be genuine or authorized (U.C.C. § 4–207(2)); this warranty was breached, and defendant is required to repay. The fact that there are other claimants interpleaded by defendant cannot interfere with plaintiff's clear right to recovery on this transaction.

[*The transferor's warranties made by a collecting bank under Section 4–207(2) are essentially the same as those made by an individual transferee under Section 3–417(2)*]

Conversion of Instruments

Conversion of Instrument. Conversion of an instrument is an unauthorized assumption and exercise of ownership over it. An instrument is converted by a drawee to whom it is delivered for acceptance if he refuses to return it on demand; or by a person to whom it is delivered for payment and who refuses on demand either to pay or to return it; or by a person who pays on a forged endorsement. (3–419 [1].)

The measure of a drawee's liability who has converted an instrument is the face amount of the instrument; in the other situations set out above, the measure of liability is presumed to be the face amount of the instrument. (3–419 [2].) A special rule applies to banks which handle instruments in the ordinary course of their banking business. (3–419 [3] and [4].)

Harry H. White Lumber Co., Inc., v. Crocker-Citizens National Bank
61 Cal. Rptr. 381 (Ct. App. Cal. 1967)

This was an action by Harry H. White Lumber Company (plaintiff) against Crocker-Citizens National Bank (defendant) to recover for the conversion of a check payable to White Lumber Co. that was paid by Crocker-Citizens Bank on a forged endorsement. White Lumber Company's action was dismissed by the trial court and it appealed. Judgment reversed.

Between December 10, 1964, and January 15, 1965, AIRE-TARE wrote four checks totalling about $4,700 payable to the order of Timberline Roofing Company and Harry H. White Lumber Company and delivered the checks to the joint payee, Timberline Roofing Company. Timberline endorsed its name and then forged the Harry H. White Lumber Company name to each of the checks. Timberline presented them to and received payment for them from Crocker-Citizens National Bank. Harry H. White Lumber claimed it had an interest in the checks, that it was damaged when the bank cashed them for Timberline, and that it was entitled to recover those damages from Crocker National.

McCoy, Judge.   The question posed by this appeal is: Does a joint payee of a check have a cause of action against a collecting bank which has paid a check made payable to joint payees bearing an endorsement effected by one joint payee signing his own name and forging that of his joint payee? We hold "yes" under both the Negotiable Instruments Law and the California Commercial Code—Commercial Paper provisions.

The relevant portion of the Commercial Code § 3116 provides: "An instrument payable to the order of two or more persons . . . (b) if not in the alternative is payable to all of them and may be negotiated, discharged or enforced only by all of them." By the express provisions of § 3116, subdivision (b) all the joint payees must join not only for negotiation, but also for discharge as well.

. . . . .

Other pertinent sections of the Commercial Code are: § 3404: "(1) Any unauthorized signature is wholly inoperative as that of the person whose name is signed unless he ratifies it or is precluded from denying it; but it operates as the signature of the unauthorized signer in favor of any person who in good faith pays the instrument or takes it for value. (2) Any unauthorized signature may be ratified for all purposes of this division. Such ratification does not of itself affect any rights of the person ratifying against the actual signer." Section 1201, subsection 43: " 'Unauthorized' signature or endorsement means one made without actual, implied or apparent authority and includes a forgery." Section 3306: "Unless he has the rights of a holder in due course any person takes the instrument subject to. . . . (d) The defense that he or a person through whom he holds the instrument acquired it by theft. . . ." Section 3419: "(1) An instrument is converted when . . . (c) It is paid on a forged endorsement."

The comments under § § 3404 and 3419 indicate that § 3419 changes the preexisting California law and now gives the payee of a forged check a cause of action for conversion against the drawee (payor) bank. But no change is indicated as to the preexisting California case law permitting the payee to recover from a collecting bank which has paid out on a forged endorsement.

Thus, the plaintiff has a cause of action against the defendant collecting bank on the check governed by the provisions of the Uniform Commercial Code. . . .

Discharge

Discharge by Payment or Tender.   Generally all parties to negotiable commercial paper are discharged when the party primarily liable on it pays the amount due in full to the bona fide holder at or after the due date. (3–601 [3].) The liability of any party is discharged to the extent of his payment or satisfaction to the holder. If a third party claims the instrument, payment or satisfaction to the holder will discharge the party making payment even though he is given notice or has knowledge of the claim unless the claimant either supplies indemnity deemed adequate by the party seeking the discharge or enjoins payment or satisfaction by order of a court of competent jurisdiction in an action in which the adverse claimant and the holder are parties. (3–603 [1].)

A party is not discharged who in bad faith pays or satisfies a holder who acquired the instrument by theft or who (unless having the rights of a holder in due course) holds through one who acquired it by theft. (3–603 [1] [a].) Also, a party is not discharged who pays or satisfies a holder of an instrument which has been restrictively endorsed in a manner not consistent with the terms of such restrictive endorsement unless the party paying is an intermediary bank or a payor bank which is not a depository bank. (3–603 [1] [b].)

Payment or satisfaction may be made with the consent of the holder by any person, including a stranger to the instrument. If the holder surrenders the instrument to such a person, it gives him the rights of a transferee of the instrument. (3–603 [2].)

A tender of payment does not discharge the liability of the party making the tender *in toto* but any party making tender of full payment to a holder when or after it is due is discharged to the extent of all subsequent liability for interest, costs and attorney fees. (3–604 [1].)

The holder's refusal of a tender wholly discharges any party who has a right of recourse against the party making the tender. (3–604 [2].) For example, suppose Axe is the maker of a note and Held is the holder, and the note is endorsed by Parks, the payee, and Irwin, endorsee. Axe, at or after the due date, tenders payment in full to Held who refuses the tender. Parks and Irwin will be wholly discharged of their liability as endorsers.

If the instrument is made payable at a bank or other place of payment and the maker or acceptor is able and ready to make payment at any and all such places specified in the instrument when it is due, it is equivalent to tender. (3–604 [3].)

Discharge by Cancellation or Renunciation. The holder of a negotiable instrument may discharge the instrument by cancellation. Any destruction or mutilation of a negotiable instrument is a cancellation if such destruction or mutilation is done with the intent that the instrument will not longer evidence an obligation. (3–605 [1] [a].) However, if such destruction or mutilation is by accident, the instrument will not be discharged. In the event the instrument is lost, destroyed, or mutilated, the original terms of the instrument may be established by parol or secondary evidence. (3–804.) An instrument may be discharged by marking it paid or canceled, or by marking it with appropriate words indicating an intent to cancel the instrument and delivering it to the principal debtor.

The holder of a negotiable instrument may discharge the instrument by expressly renouncing his rights against the principal debtor. The renunciation, to be effective, must be in writing and must be absolute and unconditional. A renunciation does not affect the rights of a holder in due course without notice. Neither a cancellation nor a renunciation, to be valid, need be supported by consideration. Either is, in effect, a gift of the instrument to the principal debtor. (3–605 [1] [b].) Neither cancellation nor renunciation without surrender of the instrument affects the title thereto. (3–605 [2].)

Discharge by Alteration. Any alteration of an instrument is material which changes the contract of any of the parties thereto in any respect. A change in the number or relation of the parties, or the completing of an incomplete instrument otherwise than as authorized, or the changing of the writing as signed by adding to it or removing any part of it is a material alteration. (3–407 [1].) A change which in no way affects the contract of the parties such as crossing a "t" or dotting an "i" or correcting the grammar in the instrument is not a material alteration.

Against any person other than a subsequent holder in due course, an alteration by the holder which is both fraudulent and material discharges any party whose contract is thereby changed unless the party consents to the change or is precluded from asserting the defense. (3–407 [2] [a].) No other alteration discharges any party and the instrument may be enforced according to its original tenor, or as to incomplete instruments according to the authority given. (3–407 [2] [b].)

A holder in due course who has taken the instrument after it has been altered can enforce it according to its original tenor, and when an incomplete instrument has been completed, he may enforce it as completed. (3–407 [3].)

Discharge by Impairment of Recourse. A holder who discharges any party to an instrument without reserving the rights of others against such party discharges such other persons from liability. For example, if the holder of a note which is signed by Axe as maker and is endorsed by Parks, Rick and Snell discharges Axe from his liability without reserving the rights of Parks, Rich, and Snell, they will be discharged from their liability on the note. If the holder expressly reserves rights against Park, Rich, or Snell or agrees not to sue Axe and one of the endorsers pays the amount of the instrument to the holder, such a one can proceed against Axe in the same manner as though the holder had not discharged or agreed not to sue Axe.

Also, if a party has posted collateral to secure his performance and a holder surrenders the collateral without the consent of parties who would benefit from the collateral, such parties are discharged. (3–606.)

Summary

Payment to a bona fide holder at or after the due date of negotiable commercial paper discharges all parties to the instrument. If a third party makes a claim to the instrument, payment to the holder discharges the party making payment unless the party making the claim supplies indemnity or enjoins payment in a suit in which the adverse claimant and the holder are parties. Payment in bad faith to a thief does not discharge the party.

Tender of full payment to the holder at or after the due date discharges any party who has recourse against the party making the tender and stops the running of interest and costs and attorney fees.

Cancellation must be destruction of the instrument with intent to discharge the parties or by marking it on the face in such a manner that the intent to cancel is apparent. A renunciation must be in writing.

Any material alteration of an instrument by the holder with fraudulent intent discharges any party whose contract is altered thereby, but it does not affect the rights of a holder in due course.

The release of any party or the surrender of collateral discharges any party who has recourse against the discharged party unless all rights are reserved.

Chenowith v. Bank of Dardanelle
419 S.W.2d 792 (Sup. Ct. Ark. 1967)

Action by Bank of Dardanelle (plaintiff) against Chenowith (defendant) to recover on two checks drawn by Chenowith. Judgment for Bank and Chenowith appealed. Reversed.

On January 13, 1966, Chenowith drew two checks in the amounts of $3,800 and $3,000 payable to Parham. Parham deposited the checks on the Bank of Dardenelle, where he had an account. Bank forwarded the checks for payment and then learned that payment had been stopped. It then placed a "hold" on $6,800 in Parham's account pending return of the checks. However, when the checks were returned to Bank, a clerk mistakenly sent them on to Parham. In the meantime another clerk had allowed a $6,800 check written by Parham to clear his account, despite the "hold" order and there were no funds left in the account. Parham and Chenowith, who had a continuing business relationship, settled among themselves for the two checks. Bank then brought suit against Chenowith to obtain payment for the two checks.

HARRIS, CHIEF JUSTICE.   This case is governed by the provisions of the Uniform Commercial Code. Section 3–603 provides as follows:

(1) The liability of any party is discharged to the extent of his payment or satisfaction to the holder even though it is made with knowledge of a claim of another person to the

instrument unless prior to such payment or satisfaction by the person making the claim either supplies indemnity deemed adequate by the party seeking the discharge or enjoins payment or satisfaction by order of a court of competent jurisdiction in an action in which the adverse claimant and the holder are parties. This subsection does not, however, result in the discharge of the liability.

(a) of a party who in bad faith pays or satisfies a holder who acquired the instrument by theft or who (unless having the rights of a holder in due course) holds through one who so acquired it;

. . . .

Appellant contended that his liability was discharged under the provisions of § 3–603 since he fully satisfied the amount of these checks with the holder (Parham). The Circuit Judge, however, denied the motion for directed verdict, because Chenowith was with Parham at the bank when Hamilton (bank's vice-president) advised that the checks were unpaid. This ruling was erroneous. It will be noted that the statute says that the liability of the party is discharged "even though it is made with knowledge of a claim of another person to the instrument," unless the claimant (the bank) supplies indemnity deemed adequate by the party seeking the discharge (Chenowith) or enjoins payment or satisfaction by court order in an action in which the adverse claimant (Chenowith) and the holder (Parham) are parties. No indemnity was supplied, nor did the bank, in filing its suit, seek an injunction as provided by the statute. It is also asserted by appellee that Chenowith and Parham were acting in bad faith, i.e., they knew the checks had not been paid at the time they made this settlement. Appellee, in its brief, asserts that Parham was nothing more than a bailee, and his conduct amounted to a conversion of the checks "to his own use or a larceny by bailee, and accepting them with knowledge of the circumstances, Chenowith participated in the conversion or larceny and was nothing more than an accessory thereto."

Under the statute, Chenowith would not have been discharged from liability if he paid or satisfied a holder "who acquired the instrument by theft or who holds through one who so acquired it," but the commissioners' comment with reference to Subsection (1) makes clear the question of good or bad faith has nothing to do with liability. That comment is as follows:

"Subsection (1) changes the law by eliminating the requirement of the original Section 88 that the payment be made in good faith and without notice that the title of the holder is defective."

Of course, Parham did not steal the check, and it might also be mentioned that the complaint does not charge Chenowith and Parham entered into a conspiracy to defraud the bank.

Appellee also argues, as a matter of supporting its judgment, that Chenowith and Parham had not completely settled their financial transactions with each other (this contention being made on the basis of Parham's testimony), and since they had not fully settled, Chenowith's liability had not been discharged. We disagree. Whether the entire indebtedness between the men had been settled is immaterial here, for it is admitted that the checks had been turned over to Chenowith by Parham, who had become the holder, having been sent the checks by the bank. Thus, Chenowith had settled *this* indebtedness with Parham.

Of course, the checks were sent back to Parham by the bank through error, but, under the quoted section of the Commercial Code, this is of no aid.

Exceptions to General Liability Rules

Normally, a check bearing a forged payee's endorsement is not properly chargeable to a drawer's account nor must a maker pay the note to the current possessor of a note bearing a forged payee's signature. Likewise, the maker or drawer is normally liable for an instrument only according to its tenor at the time he signed it. However, the Uniform Commercial Code makes several exceptions to these general rules of liability.

Imposter Rule. An imposter is a person who misrepresents his identity to another for the purpose of inducing such another to deal with him in the belief that he is the person he represents himself to be. If a negotiable instrument is drawn payable to the order of or is endorsed to the person whom the imposter represents himself to be or to his confederate, an endorsement of the instrument by any person in the name of such payee or endorsee is effective. (3–405 [1] [a].) For example, suppose Axe steals Parks's automobile. Axe finds the certificate of title in the automobile and then representing himself to be Parks sells the automobile to Berger Used Car Company and it draws its check payable to Parks for the agreed purchase price of the automobile and delivers the check to Axe. Any person can negotiate the check by endorsing it in the name of Parks.

Fictitious Payee Rule. Where the person signing as or on behalf of a maker or drawer intends the payee to have no interest in the instrument, or where an agent or employee of the maker or drawer has supplied him with the name of the payee intending the latter to have no interest in the instrument, any person can negotiate the instrument by endorsing it in the name of the named payee. For example, suppose Axe who is employed by the Moore Corporation as an accountant in charge of accounts payable prepares a false invoice naming Parks, Inc., a supplier of the Moore Corporation, as having supplied Moore Corporation with goods and draws a check payable to Parks, Inc., for the amount of the invoice. He then presents it to Temple, treasurer of Moore Corporation, together with other checks with invoices attached, for Temple's signature, all of which Temple signs and returns to Axe for mailing. Axe then withdraws the check payable to Parks, Inc. Anyone can negotiate the check by endorsing it in the name of Parks, Inc. In such a case an employee of the drawer has supplied the drawer with the name of a payee, intending the named payee to have no interest in the check. (3–405 [1] [b] [c].)

Negligence in Signing. If a person is so negligent in the drawing or signing of a negotiable instrument that he in effect invites the alteration or unauthorized signing, such negligent person will be precluded from asserting the alteration or lack of authority against a holder in due course or against a drawee or other payor who pays the instrument in good faith and in accordance with the reasonable commercial standards of the drawee's or payor's business. (3–406.) If a business uses an automatic signing device and leaves this device and blank checks unguarded where they are available to office employees generally, and an employee who is not authorized to issue checks prepares a check and when he has an opportunity signs the check with the signing device, the drawee bank would be protected in cashing the check. Also, if a check or other instrument is drawn for "one dollar" ($1) in such a manner as would easily permit one to alter it to read One Hundred—one Dollar ($101) and it is altered and a person who can qualify as a holder in due course takes the check for $101, the drawer will be held liable for the amount of $101 if under the circumstances the court finds that the negligent manner in which the check was drawn contributed to its alteration.

Summary

Where an imposter has induced a person to issue a negotiable instrument to a named payee whom he intends to have no interest in it, such instrument can be negotiated by an endorsement in the name of the payee made by any person. If the drawer or a person authorized to sign for the drawer makes out a check to a named payee and does not intend that the named payee have any interest in the check, then under the fictitious payee rule any person may sign the name of the named payee and the endorsement will be effective to negotiate the instrument. The drawer of an instrument which is so negligently drawn that it invites alteration or an unauthorized signature and is altered or a forged signature added may be precluded from asserting the alteration or forgery.

Philadelphia Title Insurance Co. v. Fidelity-Philadelphia Trust Co.
212 A.2d 222 (Sup. Ct. Pa. 1965)

This was an action by Philadelphia Title Insurance Company (plaintiff), the drawer of a check, against Fidelity-Philadelphia Trust Company (defendant), the drawee on the check, to have its account recredited. Philadelphia Title argued that one of the payees' signature had been forged so that the check was not properly payable by Fidelity-Philadelphia. Judgment for Fidelity-Philadelphia. Affirmed on appeal.

Mrs. Jezemski was separated from her husband and decided to obtain some money from him by having a mortgage placed on some property her husband held as administrator and heir of his mother's estate and taking the proceeds herself. She went to a lawyer with a gentleman whom she introduced as her husband, and they made out a bond and mortgage on her husband's land. Then she went to a title insurance company which under Philadelphia custom takes care of placing mortgages on property and paying the proceeds to the mortgagor. She told Philadelphia Title's representatives that her husband was too busy to come in that day, but that her husband's signature on the mortgage had been witnessed by the lawyer. Philadelphia Title then placed a mortgage on the property and gave Mrs. Jezemski a check made payable to Edmund and Paula Jezemski and Edmund Jezemski as administrator for his mother's estate. Mrs. Jezemski then forged her husband's signature to the check and negotiated it to a bank. Eventually the check was paid by Fidelity-Philadelphia which then charged the check to Philadelphia Title's account.

COHEN, JUSTICE. The parties do not dispute the proposition that as between payor bank (Fidelity-Philadelphia) and its customer (Title Company), ordinarily, the former must bear the loss occasioned by the forgery of a payee's endorsement (Edmund Jezemski) upon a check drawn by its customer and paid by it, 3–414. The latter provides, inter alia, that "(1) Any unauthorized signature [Edmund Jezemski's] is wholly inoperative as that of the person whose name is signed unless he ratifies it or is precluded from denying it. . . ."

However, the banks argue that this case falls within an exception to the above rule, making the forged indorsement of Edmund Jezemski's name effective so that Fidelity-Philadelphia was entitled to charge the account of its customer, the Title Company, who was the drawer of the check. The exception asserted by the banks is found in § 3–405(1)(a) of the Uniform Commercial Code—Commercial Paper which provides:

"An indorsement by any person in the name of a named payee is effective if (a) an imposter by the use of the mails or otherwise has induced the maker or drawer to issue the instrument to him or his confederate in the name of the payee; . . ."

The lower court found and the Title Company does not dispute that an imposter appeared before McAllister (attorney) and DiBenefetto (realtor) impersonated Mr. Jezemski, and, in their presence, signed Mr. Jezemski's name to the deed, bond and mortgage; that Mrs. Jezemski was a confederate of the imposter; that the drawer, Title Company, issued the check to Mrs. Jezemski naming her and Mrs. Jezemski as payees; and that some person other than Mr. Jezemski indorsed his name on the check. In effect, the only argument made by the Title Company to prevent the applicability of Section 3–405(1)(a) is that the imposter, who admittedly played a part in the swindle, *did not "by the mails or otherwise" induce the Title Company* to issue the check within the meaning of Section 3–405(1)(a). The argument must fail.

. . . . .

Both the words of Section 3–405(1)(a) and the official Comment thereto leave no doubt that the imposter can induce the drawer to issue him or his confederate a check within the meaning of the section even though he does not carry out his impersonation before the very eyes of the drawer. Section 3–405(1)(a) says the inducement might be by "the mails or otherwise." The Comment elaborates:

"2. Subsection (1)(a) is new. It rejects decisions which distinguish between face-to-face imposture and imposture by mail and hold that where the parties deal by mail the dominant intent of the drawer is to deal with the name rather than with the person so that the resulting instrument may be negotiated only by indorsement of the payee whose name had been taken in vain. The result of the distinction has been under some prior law to throw the loss in the mail imposture forward to a subsequent holder or to the drawee. Since the drawer believes the two to be one and the same, the two intentions cannot be separated, and the 'dominant intent' is a fiction. The position here taken is that the loss, regardless of the type of fraud which the particular imposter has committed, should fall upon the drawer.

Moreover, the Legislature's use of the word "otherwise" and the Comment, which suggests that results should not turn upon "the type of fraud which the particular imposter committed," indicates that the Legislature did not intend to limit the applicability of the section to cases where the imposter deals directly with the drawer (face-to-face, mails, telephone, etc.). Naturally, the legislature could not have predicted and expressly included all the ingenious schemes designed and carried out by imposters for the purpose of defrauding the makers or drawers of negotiable instruments. Something had to be left for the courts by way of statutory construction. For purposes of imposing the loss on one of two "innocent" parties, either the drawer who was defrauded or the drawee bank which payed out on a forged endorsement, we see no reason for distinguishing between the drawer who is duped by an impersonator communicating directly with him through the mails and a drawer who is duped by an impersonator communicating indirectly with him through third persons. Thus, both the language of the Code and common sense dictate that the drawer must suffer the loss in both instances.

May Department Stores Co. v. Pittsburgh National Bank
374 F.2d 109 (3rd Cir. 1967)

This was an action by May Department Stores Company (plaintiff) against Pittsburgh National Bank (defendant) for allegedly charging May Department Store's checking account with amounts paid on forged endorsements. Summary judgment for National Bank was affirmed on appeal.

An employee of the May Department Stores fraudulently caused it to draw some checks payable to fictitious suppliers. The wrongdoing employee then forged the endorsements of the fictitious payees, cashed the checks at National Bank, and converted the proceeds. The defendant drawee, National Bank, charged the checks paid against the May Department Store account. May Department Stores sued National Bank, claiming the checks were not properly chargeable to the account since they were paid on forged endorsements.

PER CURIAM.   . . . the district court properly concluded that the bank was protected by the following provision of the Uniform Commercial Code as in force in Pennsylvania.

"(1) An indorsement by any person in the name of a named payee is effective if . . .

(a) an agent or employee of the maker or drawer has supplied him with the name of the payee intending the latter to have no such interest." § 3–405(1)(c).

Park State Bank v. *Arena Auto Auction, Inc.*

207 N.E.2d 158 (App. Ct. Ill. 1956)

This was an action by Park State Bank (plaintiff) against Arena Auto Auction, Inc. (defendant), to recover a judgment on a check. Judgment for Park State Bank and Arena Auto Auction, Inc., appealed. Judgment affirmed.

Arena Auto Auction, Inc. (Arena), drew a check payable to the order of Tom Plunkett of Alabama and mailed it by mistake to Tom Plunkett at Rockford, Illinois. Arena had done business with Tom Plunkett of Rockford and had sent him at least one check in the past. Tom Plunkett of Rockford knew that Arena owed him nothing and that the check was not intended for him, but he indorsed it and cashed it at Park State Bank (Bank) with which he did business. Arena discovered the error and stopped payment on the check. It drew another check payable to Tom Plunkett and repeated the former error and again mailed the check to Tom Plunkett of Rockford. Tom Plunkett presented this check to Bank for payment but since payment was stopped on the first check, it refused to cash the second check. By this time Arena and Bank had discovered the error and Bank requested Tom Plunkett to return the money paid to him in error, but he refused. He had since left Rockford without leaving an address and his whereabouts were unknown. Bank sued Arena to recover the amount paid out on the check.

PETERSON, JUSTICE. Bank relies upon Section 3–406; which, being a new section of our Commercial Code, is as follows:

Any person who by his negligence substantially contributes to a material alteration of the instrument or to the making of an unauthorized signature is precluded from asserting the alteration or lack of authority against a holder in due course or against a drawee or other payor who pays the instrument in good faith in accordance with the reasonable commercial standards of the drawee's or payor's business.

Hence, we may have a case of first impression in construing the latter section of our statutory law.

Without repeating the various errors previously recited, it appears to this Court presumptuous on the part of Arena Auto Auction, Inc., to insist that they did nothing for which they should be held accountable. We point out the interval of lapsed time before they, in their fast-thinking, fast-operating business, decide first to stop payment.

Secondly, bearing in mind the erroneous sending of a second check to the same payee, and considering the custom of the trade as set forth by the testimony of the several gentlemen of the financial world as to the routine handling of checks in banking institutions, it is our considered conclusion that to require the recipient

Bank to stop and question persons known to that Bank and presenting checks in routine business and issued by makers likewise known to the Bank, would be placing cogs in the wheels of business, which, in turn, would bring those wheels of the banking business to an astounding and abrupt halt. This, as we see it, was neither the intent nor the purpose of our legislators in passing the section in our Commercial Code to which reference was made.

We, therefore and accordingly, do conclude that the Trial Court was correct in holding that Arena, by their own negligence, substantially assisted in making it possible that an unauthorized person's signature passed title to the funds represented by said check.

Leonard v. National Bank of West Virginia
145 S.E.2d 23 (Sup. Ct. W. Va. 1965)

This was an action by Leonard (plaintiff) against a drawee bank, National Bank of West Virginia (defendant), to recover money paid by Bank on an alleged forged check and charged to Leonard's account. The Supreme Court held that Bank was entitled to a directed verdict in its favor.

On August 3 1961, Leonard made out a check for $600, signed it as drawer, and also endorsed his signature on the back of the check. He did not date the check nor did he fill in the payee's name. Leonard claimed he gave the check to a man named Santo to whom he owed $600 and that he endorsed the check on the back so that Santo could cash it "at the track." When the check was returned to Leonard by National Bank after it had charged the check to his account, the word "thrity" had been written in front of the "six hundred," the name Martin Mattson had been entered as payee, and the endorsement of Martin Mattson appeared on the back of the check above Leonard's signature. Leonard then sued National Bank to have his account recredited for $3,600.

BERRY, JUSTICE.   The general rule with regard to altered or raised checks is that if a bank pays such checks it does so at its peril and can only debit the drawer's account for the amount of the check as originally drawn, but there is an exception in the case of altered or raised checks to the effect that if the altering or raising of the check is because of the carelessness of the maker or depositor, the bank cannot be held liable in such case. . . .

It is clear from the evidence in this case and from the check, which was introduced into evidence as an exhibit, that the name of the payee was left blank, that the amount of the check opposite the dollar sign was left blank and a one and one-half inch space to the left of the words "Six hundred" was left blank, and that Leonard's signature on the back of the check as an endorser left a blank space of one inch from the top of the check. As the check was drawn, the blank space for the payee's name could have been made to "cash," any amount could have been placed in the space for the figure opposite the dollar sign and more than enough room was left for words to be filled in before the words "six hundred" in order to alter or raise this check, and all of such blank spaces were filled up in such manner that they could not easily arouse the suspicions of a careful person. It has been repeatedly held in such cases that the drawer is barred from recovery.

The check in question was drawn in such manner that it could be readily raised or altered and such changes could not be detected by the use of ordinary care. In fact, the carelessness of the drawing of the check in question would amount to gross negligence and Leonard would be estopped from any recovery if his were the only negligence involved because such action on his part would amount to negligence as a matter of law.

However, it has been held that the negligence of a depositor in drawing a check which can be altered does not render him liable if the bank fails to exercise due care in paying such check, but if the maker's carelessness is the proximate cause of the payment of such altered check on the part of the bank, the bank is not liable.

The negligence which the plaintiff endeavors to charge the bank within connection with this transaction is almost entirely based on evidence introduced by the plaintiff to the effect that the bank was negligent in not having the person who presented the check to the defendant bank for payment identified as the named payee and endorser on the check, Martin Mattson. There is no evidence in this case that the person who presented the check was not Martin Mattson, the named payee and also the person who endorsed the check above the endorsement of the plaintiff. . . . It would therefore, appear that the question as to whether the bank was guilty of negligence in not having Martin Mattson identified would be immaterial in this case when it was not proved that the signature was a forgery and further the evidence indicated that the bank did perform some identification procedure in this instance. Leonard also contends that the bank was negligent in not having the person who presented the check endorse it after the endorsement of J. P. Leonard. The signature in question speaks for itself and the more than sufficient space for endorsement of a payee above the name of Leonard's signature on the back of the check would constitute negligence on the part of Leonard for having left such space above his endorsement, and the bank could not be charged with negligence in such instance. Leonard further stated that he endorsed the check on the back in order that it could be cashed at the track which would clearly show his intention that the check could be cashed without difficulty, and the fact that he did endorse the check in blank and it was the last endorsement on the back thus made the check easily cashed without difficulty on the part of any person who presented it because it made the check bearer check payable on delivery. . . .

The only other matter in which the defendant Bank could be charged with negligence in connection with the cashing of the check in question was the word evidently intended as thirty which appeared before the words "Six hundred" in a misspelled form as "Thrity." However, the writing is very similar to the words "Six hundred," which the jury found was in the handwriting of Leonard.

Problem Cases

1. Chiles, the president and chief stockholder of Chiles Planting Company, made a note payable to Mann & Mann and signed it "Chiles Planting Company, By E. B.

Chiles, Jr." Now Mann & Mann seek to hold Chiles personally liable on the note. Chiles wants to show he signed only in a representative capacity. Can he try to do so?

2. Two couples went together to purchase some real estate. The husband of one of the two women signed all four persons' names to the promissory note given in exchange for the property. On two later occasions a mortgage was executed on the property and all four persons signed their own names. All the persons shared in the benefits of owning the property. Leonzi, the man who had made the signatures on the note, died some eight years after the note was executed. The remaining persons, for the first time, then claimed they were not liable on the note because their signatures were forgeries. Are they liable on the note?

3. New Waterford Bank was a holder for value of a check that had been issued in the name of Morrison Buick on drawer by Zuzow, its treasurer. The check was a printed check carrying two signature lines under the printed name of Morrison Buick, one line being followed by the word "Pres." and the second by the word "Treas." On the check in question, the first line was blank and the second contained Zuzow's signature. New Waterford Bank brought suit to collect the check after Morrison Buick had stopped payment on it. In its defense Morrison Buick claims: (1) that New Waterford Bank should not be considered a holder in due course because the missing signature was such an irregularity or incompleteness to put it on notice of a defense; (2) that since it had filed a corporate resolution with the drawee stating that two authorized signatures were required, no one signature could constitute an authorized signature and it should not be liable on the check. Has Morrison Buick stated good defenses? Why or why not?

4. Payee Bank brought suit against Defendant as a result of Defendant's nonpayment of a promissory note. Defendant admitted that he executed and delivered the note, that value was given, but alleged as an affirmative defense that he was only an accommodation maker and that the Bank had orally agreed to look to a third person for payment. Can Defendant escape liability on this argument? Why or why not?

5. Murphy was the payee of a check drawn on drawee Bank of America. When Murphy presented the checks for payment, Bank of America refused to pay the checks on the ground the drawer had stopped payment. Murphy now sues to force the drawee to pay the checks. Does he have a good cause of action?

6. Payee on a check for $4,335 took the check to the Drawee Bank for payment but the Drawer's account contained insufficient funds. Payee left the check with Drawee for collection and took a receipt for it. Payee later talked by phone with Drawee and was informed that if Drawer made a contemplated $5,000 deposit, Drawee would pay the check. Drawer made the deposit but before it was used to cover Payee's check, a group of other checks written by Drawer were paid from the account and so several days later it again contained insufficient funds and payment of Payee's check was again refused. Payee contends that Drawee accepted the check over the phone and is therefore liable on it. Is this contention correct? Why or why not? If it is not, on what other basis might Payee claim Drawee is liable?

7. Holder sued the maker and endorser of a note. On the face of the note were the words "protest waived." The endorser defended on the ground the note was not presented for payment and was not protested for nonpayment, nor was notice of protest or nonpayment given to him. The holder moves to strike the defense on the grounds no valid defense is stated. Should the defense be stricken?

8. Holder of a promissory note brings suit against Endorser of the note on the note after Maker defaulted. The note contained a stipulation for payment of attorney's

fees or costs of collection, and Holder claims Endorser is liable for the face of the note plus $2,300 as reasonable attorney's fees for the collection of the promissory note. Endorser claims he is not bound by the provision as to attorney's fees where he did not expressly agree in the note to pay them. Is Endorser liable for the attorney's fees?

9. The U.S. Treasurer drew a check for $3,041 payable to Pearl Bartley. Someone forged Bartley's endorsement to the check and negotiated it to Corporation. Corporation deposited the check, without endorsing it, in its account in Bank and Bank credited Corporation's account. Bank then obtained payment of the check. Two years later the forgery was discovered and the United States obtained repayment from Bank. Bank then charged Corporation's account for the returned check over Corporation's objection. On what Code grounds is Bank entitled to charge the account?

10. Corporation executed a note in obtaining a bank loan and Accommodation Maker signed as an accommodation maker. When Corporation ran into financial difficulties, Bank requested Accommodation Maker pay the note which it did and the Bank assigned the note to him. Now Accommodation Maker sues Corporation on the note. Corporation claims it was discharged when the note was paid to the Bank by Accommodation Maker. Was the Corporation discharged of liability on the note?

11. Maker made a note payable to Payee. At the time he signed the note it contained a confession of judgment clause in favor of "payee." Payee assigned the note to Holder in Due Course. Sometime after Maker signed the note someone had added the words "or assignee" to the confession of judgment clause. Holder in Due Course had judgment entered on the note. Now Maker claims that the judgment should be opened and that he should bear no liability on the note because there was a "material alteration" in it under 3–407(1). Is the Maker's contention correct?

12. Drawer's agent made a check payable to a payee, intending the named payee to have no interest in the check. The payee's name was forged to the check and deposited in Collecting Bank. Collecting Bank forwarded the check to Drawee Bank which paid the check and charged it to Drawer's account. Now, Drawee sues Collecting Bank for breach of warranty of genuineness of signatures. As things stand now, can Drawee hold Collecting Bank liable for breach of warranty?

13. Hill, a claim adjuster for Liberty Mutual, submitted false claims, and Liberty Mutual, in payment of these claims, delivered checks to Hill drawn on First Bank and payable to the order of the fictitious claimants. Hill endorsed the checks in the names of the fictitious payees and cashed them. When presented to First Bank for payment, it paid the checks and charged the amount to the account of Liberty Mutual. Liberty Mutual claims that the checks were order checks, that the endorsements were forged, and that First Bank must stand the loss. Must First Bank stand the loss?

chapter 41. Checks and Documents of Title

Checks

Relation between Drawer and Drawee Bank. The use of checks as a method of making payments has become all but universal in the United States. The rights and liabilities of the parties to a check have been discussed in the preceding chapter. Much of the law regarding the rights and liabilities of banks in the handling of checks is not a part of the law of commercial paper. A dual relation exists between the bank and its commercial account customer who draws checks.

When the customer makes a deposit in a bank, the relation created between the customer and the bank is that of debtor and creditor, and if the deposit is a commercial account, the relation is also one of principal and agent. The customer is the principal and the bank is the agent. Under banking law as set out in the Code, the bank as agent owes a duty to the customer as principal to honor all checks properly drawn and payable, provided the customer has a credit balance sufficient to cover the amount of the check. A check is not an assignment of the account (Section 3–409)[1] but is an order to the bank to make payment.

Bank's Duty to Pay. If a bank dishonors a check when the customer has a credit balance in his account sufficient to cover the check, the bank is liable for damages proximately caused by the wrongful dishonor. If the dishonor occurs through a mistake on the part of the bank, its liability is limited to actual damages. However, consequential damages, such as damages for arrest or prosecution, may be recovered if the customer can prove such damages with reasonable certainty. (4–402.)

Bank's Right to Charge to Account. The bank has the right to charge any

---

[1] The numbers in parentheses refer to the sections of the Uniform Commercial Code, 1962.

item, properly payable, to a customer's account even though the charge creates an overdraft. If an overdraft is created, the customer becomes indebted to the bank for the amount of the overdraft, and the bank has the right to charge the next deposit the customer makes with the amount of the overdraft. (4–401 [1].)

If the bank in good faith pays an altered check, it may charge the customer's account with the amount of the check as originally drawn. Also, if an incomplete check of a customer gets into circulation and is completed and presented to the drawee bank for payment and the bank pays the check, it can charge the amount to the drawer—customer's account, even though the bank knows the check has been completed, unless it has notice that the completion was improper. (4–401 [2].)

Stop-Payment Orders.   Since the bank acts as agent of the drawer in the payment of checks, it must follow all reasonable orders of the drawer relative to payments to be made on his behalf. If the drawer draws a check and then before the check is presented for payment or certification requests the bank not to pay the check—issues a stop-payment order—the bank owes a duty to the drawer not to honor the check when presented. To be effective, the stop-payment order must be received by the bank at such time and in such manner as to afford the bank a reasonable opportunity to act on it prior to the time the bank has paid, certified, or committed itself on the check. (4–403 [1].)

The stop payment may be oral in which case it is binding on the bank for a period of only 14 days unless confirmed in writing within that time. When confirmed in writing, the writing is good for six months. The time may be extended, however, by renewing the stop-payment order before the expiration of the six-months. (4–403 [2].) The bank is under no obligation to a customer to pay a check, other than a certified check, which is presented more than six months after its date, but may charge its customer's account for payment made thereafter in good faith. (4–404.)

The Code does not cover a situation in which a written stop-payment order is given to the bank but is not renewed, and the check is then presented to and paid by the bank after the expiration of the six-month period. The bank has not violated the stop-payment order by paying the check but there is an unanswered question as to whether or not under such circumstances the bank would be liable on the ground that it had not paid the check in good faith.

Bank's Liability for Payment after Stop Payment.   The bank is liable to the drawer of a check which it pays while a stop-payment order is in effect for any loss he suffers by reason of such payment, but the drawer has the burden of establishing the amount of the loss. To show a loss the drawer must establish that if the drawee bank had honored the stop-payment order so that the holder of the instrument had to come after the drawer for payment, that the drawer had a valid defense to payment which could have been successfully asserted against that holder of the instrument. To the extent the drawer had such a defense, he has suffered a loss due to the drawer's failure to honor the stop-payment order of the drawer. The bank cannot by agreement disclaim its responsibility for its own lack of good faith or failure to exercise ordinary care nor can it limit the measure of damages for such lack or failure; but the parties may by agreement determine the standards by which such responsibility is to be measured if such standards are not manifestly unreasonable. (4–103 [1].)

If the bank pays a check after it is given a stop-payment order, it acquires the rights of a transferee of the item and acquires, by subrogation, all of the rights of the person to whom it made payment, including his rights based on the transaction on which the check was based. For example, if the party to whom payment was made held the check as a holder in due course, the bank could recover the amount of the check from the drawer, or if the check was given in payment of goods which were defective but which the buyer (the drawer of the check) kept, the bank could recover from the drawer an amount equal to the value of the goods, that is, the amount the seller (payee of the check) could recover if he brought suit. (4–407.)

Certified Check.   Certification of a check is an acceptance by the drawee bank. Unless otherwise agreed, the bank owes no obligation to certify a check. Under pre-Code law, the courts held that the certification of a check by an officer of a bank at any place other than at the bank did not bind the bank. Apparently this law has not been changed by the provisions of the Code. When the bank certifies a check, it debits the amount of the check to the drawer's account and credits the amount to the certified check account. This certified check account, however, is not a trust fund set up for the payment of such checks, and if the certifying bank becomes insolvent before the certified check is presented for payment, the holder is merely a creditor of the bank.

If a check is certified for the drawer, he is secondarily liable on the check, but if it is certified for a holder, the drawer and all prior endorsers are discharged. A bank may certify a check before returning it for lack of proper endorsement, but if it does so, the drawer is discharged. (3–411.)

Death or Incompetence of Customer.   Under the general principles of agency law, the authority of an agent to bind his principal is terminated on the death or incompetence of the principal. This rule has been modified by the provisions of the Code relative to a bank's right to honor check drawn prior to the death or incompetence of the drawer but presented to the drawee bank for payment thereafter. Under the provisions of the Code, the bank has authority to pay checks drawn by an incompetent customer unless the bank knows of the adjudication of incompetence. Neither death nor incompetence of a customer revokes the bank's authority to pay or certify a check until the bank knows of the fact of death or of an adjudication of incompetence and has a reasonable opportunity to act upon it. Even though the bank has knowledge of the death of the customer, it may, for a period of 10 days after the date of his death, if it elects to do so, pay or certify checks drawn by him on or prior to that date. However, any person claiming an interest in the deceased customer's estate may order the bank to stop payment. (4–405.)

Customer's Duty to Report Forgeries and Alterations. The canceled checks drawn by a customer together with a statement of account are usually returned by the bank to the customer once a month, or they may be held pursuant to a request or instructions of its customer, or otherwise in a reasonable manner made available to him. The customer, on receiving the checks and statement, owes a duty to examine them to discover if any of his signatures on the checks are forgeries or unauthorized or if any of the checks have been altered. (4–406 [1].)

If the customer fails to examine the checks and statement within a reasonable time, he cannot hold the bank responsible for the payment of checks on which there are forgeries, unauthorized signings or alterations. If a series of forgeries, unauthorized signings or alterations are made by the same wrongdoer on any checks paid in good faith by the bank after the first check which had been forged or signed without authority or altered was available to the customer for a reasonable period not exceeding 14 calendar days and before the bank received notification from the customer of any such forgery, unauthorized signature or alteration, the customer cannot hold the bank responsible for paying the check.

For example, suppose Axe employs Fell as an accountant and over a period of three months Fell forges Axe's signature to 10 checks and cashes them. One of the forged checks is included in the checks returned to Axe at the end of the first month and within 14 calendar days after the return of these checks Fell forges two more checks and cashes them. Axe does not examine the returned checks until a lapse of three months after the checks which included the first forged check were returned to him. The bank would be responsible for the first forged check and the two checks forged and cashed within the 14-day period after the return of the first statement and checks, but it would not be liable for the seven forged checks cashed after the expiration of the 14-day period. (4–406 [2].)

In other situations the bank will not be held responsible for the honoring of checks on which the customer's signature is forged or unauthorized or which are altered if the customer does not discover and report the forgery, unauthorized signature or alteration within one year from the time the statement and checks are made available or does not within three years of that time discover and report any unauthorized endorsement. (4–406 [4].)

Summary

The relation between a bank and a customer having a commercial account on which checks may be drawn is that of debtor and creditor and principal and agent. In drawing a check the customer as principal authorizes the bank as agent to honor the check. The customer as principal has the right to order the bank to stop payment on a check and if the order to stop payment is received by the bank at such a time and in such form as to give it a reasonable opportunity, the bank owes a duty to refuse payment on an uncertified check. If it pays a check in disregard of a stop-payment order, it is liable to the drawer for any resulting loss.

A bank is not obligated to certify a check, but on certification it becomes primarily liable on the check and, if certified at the request of the holder, the drawer and all prior endorsers are discharged.

A bank may pay checks drawn during a customer's lifetime or while competent and for a period of 10 days after death or adjudication of incompetence.

A customer owes a duty to report to the bank, within a reasonable time after a statement of account and canceled checks are made available, unauthorized signatures and alteration. Failure to do so relieves the bank from responsibility.

Malphrus v. Home Savings Bank of the City of Albany
254 N.Y.S.2d 980 (Albany Cty. Ct. N.Y. 1965)

This was an action by Jesse Malphrus (plaintiff) against Home Savings Bank of the City of Albany (defendant). Judgment for Malphrus.

Carol Kuebler purchased an automobile from Malphrus for $450. Kuebler, a depositor in Home Savings Bank of the City of Albany (Savings Bank), requested it to issue a teller's check in the amount of $450 payable to the order of Malphrus and to charge the amount to her account, and she delivered the check to Malphrus in payment for the automobile. The check was drawn on National Commercial Bank and Trust Company and when it was presented to the drawee bank payment was refused on the ground that Savings Bank had stopped payment. Malphrus sued Savings Bank on the check.

SCHENCK, JUDGE.   The point of law raised here appears to be novel. The rights of the parties are governed by the Uniform Commercial Code which became effective in this State September 27th, 1964, just a few days before the series of transactions referred to above. That a customer may (provided certain rules are followed) stop payment on a check is clearly covered Section 4–403 (1) of the Uniform Commercial Code. Furthermore, Section 4–104 (1) (e) specifically defines a "customer" as including "a bank carrying an account with another bank." The question presented is whether or not payment on a teller's check may be stopped by the issuing bank within the purview of the Uniform Commercial Code. It seems that one purpose of granting authority and providing procedure to stop payment of a check is to afford protection to a party who may have discovered fraud or engaged in a disagreement as to terms or consideration in connection with the underlying contract pursuant to which the check was issued. Here the transaction for the sale and purchase of the automobile was between Malphrus and Miss Kuebler. The defendant Savings Bank had no stake in that transaction whatsoever. The other purpose of prescribing procedure for payment stoppage is to protect the bank on which the check is drawn. The National Commercial Bank is clearly covered and protected by the Uniform Commercial Code so that it incurred no liability by refusing payment on its depositor's check. The question is: did the defendant Savings Bank have the authority to interject itself so as to defeat Malphrus' claim herein? I am of the opinion that it did not have such right.

By issuing a teller's check the defendant Savings Bank gave to its depositor an instrument upon which Malphrus relied in making the sale and delivery of an automobile. Malphrus did not rely on Miss Kuebler's credit but in good faith accepted the check of a savings bank. The underlying transaction, as indicated above, was between Malphrus and Miss Kuebler. Malphrus accepted a bank check as in the nature of cash. This is a procedure that is widely followed in business transactions of many varieties throughout this area and presumably elsewhere in the State of New York. A teller's check has generally been treated as "cash." As a business practice such checks have been used and regarded on the same basis as certified checks. There are, of course, legal distinctions between certified checks and teller's checks. Their respective legal effects may be different under different circumstances. Here, however, there is no basis upon which to make a determination that Malphrus should have considered the teller's check in any different light than he would have considered a certified check. This was a bank obligation which he received as consideration when he delivered his merchandise.

Although the foregoing conclusion is without precedent in this jurisdiction it receives support in other provisions of the Uniform Commercial Code. For example, subdivision (1) of Section 3–802 provides that ". . . where an instrument is taken for an underlying obligation

"(a) the obligation is *pro tanto* discharged if a bank is drawer, maker or acceptor of the instrument and there is no recourse on the instrument against the underlying obligor." It would seem from the foregoing that Malphrus has no recourse now against the defendant Savings Bank. If the defendant Savings Bank is not liable to Malphrus it would seem that he has no rights enforceable under the Uniform Commercial Code which was enacted to protect persons engaged in business transactions involving instruments for the payment of money including, of course, checks.

It seems to me that the defense urged by Savings Bank would be applicable only where the bank issuing the teller's check is an actual party to a transaction. For example, if the defendant Savings Bank were engaged in a contract for the purchase of property, equipment, etc., it would be regarded as the actual obligor in the transaction and could stop payment if it discovered fraud or a question arose as to the consideration, etc., in the same manner as any individual could stop payment. Here, however, the defendant Savings Bank, in effect, sold an instrument which was used exactly as one might use cash or a certified check. The defendant Savings Bank was in no sense a party to the transaction between Malphrus and Miss Kuebler. The arguments raised by Savings Bank in reliance on Sections 4–403 (1) and 4–104 (1) (e) are not applicable here, at least as far as the rights of Malphrus acting in good faith are concerned. The motion for summary judgment is granted with costs and interest.

Jackson v. First National Bank
403 S.W.2d 109 (Ct. App. Tenn. 1966)

This was an action by Jackson (plaintiff) on behalf of Greater St. Matthews Church of which he was senior Trustee against First National Bank (defendant) to have the Church's account recredited for 50 checks on which had been forged and charged to the Church's account. Judgment for Jackson was affirmed on appeal.

The Church had opened a checking account in First National Bank in August, 1963, and specified that two signatures, those of Jackson, the Trustee, and Cleve Jordan, the Financial Secretary, were required for withdrawals. The account specified that statements and cancelled checks were to be mailed to Cleve Jordan. The checks involved in this case were drawn between August, 1963, and August, 1964, were payable to Cleve Jordan, and had the signature of Jackson forged on them. The cancelled checks and monthly statements had been sent to Cleve Jordan. The Bank contended that the Church should not be able to recover because of its delay in reporting the forgeries and its negligence.

BEJACH, JUDGE.   Under the above quoted statutes (3–405 and 4–406) a drawee bank which pays the check on a forged signature is deemed to have made the payment out of its own funds and not the depositor's, provided the depositor has not been guilty of negligence or fault that misled the bank. In such situation, the burden is upon the bank to show that the loss was due to the negligence of the depositor, rather than to its failure to exercise its legal duty.

In the instant case, the negligence of the depositor relied on by the bank is its failure to examine the checks and report the forgery, thus preventing a repetition thereof. The fallacy of this argument is the checks were mailed to Cleve Jordan, Financial Secretary of the Church, who was the forger. He was an unfaithful servant, and obviously his knowledge and information on the subject would not be reported by him to the Church, nor imputed to it. He had been a faithful and trusted member of the Church and one of its officers for about twenty years, and, consequently, the Church cannot be held guilty of negligence in employing an unfaithful agent. The contention is made, however, that the church officials, other than Cleve Jordan, himself, should have called on Jordan for an accounting from time to time, and that the Church was negligent in its failure to perform this duty. The proof shows that the Church did from time to time call on Cleve Jordan for production of the checks and records of the Church, but that he made excuses, said he forgot to bring them, or made other excuses. Under these circumstances, in view of his previous good record and reputation, we cannot say that the Bank carried the burden of showing negligence on the part of the Church.

Under the Negotiable Instruments Law, no time limit establishing a reasonable period is fixed within which a depositor must examine the canceled checks returned to him, but under the provisions of the Uniform Commercial Code, such limit is fixed at fourteen days. Under the provisions of § 4–406, subsection 2(b), a depositor is precluded by failure to examine the checks within fourteen days from asserting liability against the bank on account of unauthorized signature or alteration of a check paid by the bank in good faith, but subsection (3) of the same Code section provides: "The preclusion under subsection (2) does not apply if the customer establishes lack of ordinary care on the part of the bank in paying the item(s)."

In *Farmers' and Merchants' Bank* v. *Bank of Rutherford,* the Supreme Court held that, "It is negligence in a drawee bank to pay a forged check drawn on it in the name of its customer, whose signature is well known to it, where the cashier does not examine the signature closely, but relies on the previous endorsements." It is argued on behalf of the Bank that such examination of the signature card, which admittedly was not made in the instant case, is not practical under modern banking methods. Such may be true as a practical matter, but, if so, the Bank, because of that fact, cannot escape the consequences and must, under that decision, be held guilty of negligence.

We think, however, that the Bank must be held to be guilty of negligence in another and much stronger aspect of the instant case. The Bank account here involved was that of a church, which obviously involved trust funds, and the counter signature of Milton Jackson, Trustee, whose signature has been forged, was required on all checks. In the case of *Fidelity and Deposit Co. of Maryland* v. *Hamilton Nat'l Bank* (1938) this court held that one who takes paper from a trustee importing upon its face its fiduciary character, is bound to inquire of the transferor the right to dispose of it. . . . Any adequate inquiry made in the instant case by the Bank would have disclosed the situation that Cleve Jordan was forging the name of Milton Jackson, Trustee, and would have prevented a repetition of such forgery.

There is another and a stronger reason why the Bank must be held guilty of negligence and held responsible for the result of the forgery here involved. All of the checks, recovery for which was granted in the instant case, were made payable to Cleve Jordan, personally; and many of them bear the endorsement of the Southland Racing Company, which is the corporation operating the dog racing track in Arkansas across the Mississippi River from Memphis. These circumstances, and especially the one that the checks were made payable to Cleve Jordan, personally, should have put the bank on inquiry as to whether or not the funds represented by these checks were being withdrawn for unauthorized purposes. Any inquiry would have disclosed the true situation and prevented further depletion of the Church's bank account. The bank account being a trust fund and the checks withdrawing same being made to one of the authorized signers of checks, was sufficient to put the Bank on notice that the funds were being improperly withdrawn, or should at least have required the bank to make inquiry as to whether or not the withdrawals involved were authorized.

Documents of Title

Introduction. The practice of storing or shipping goods and the giving of a warehouse receipt or bill of lading representing the goods and the transfer of such warehouse receipt or bill of lading as representing the goods is of ancient origin. The warehouseman or the common carrier is a bailee of the goods and he contracts to store or transport the goods and to deliver them to the owner, or to act in accordance with the lawful directions of the owners. The warehouse receipt or the bill of lading may be either negotiable or non-negotiable. To be negotiable, a warehouse receipt, bill of lading or other document of title must, by its terms, provide that the goods are to be delivered to bearer or to the order of a named person. (7–104 [1].) The primary difference between the law of negotiable commercial paper and that of negotiable documents of title is based on the difference between the obligation to pay money and the obligation to deliver specific goods.

Warehouse Receipts. A warehouse receipt, to be valid, need not be in any particular form, but if it does not embody within its written or printed form each of the following, the warehouseman is liable for damages caused by the omission to a person injured thereby: (*a*) the location of the warehouse where the goods are stored; (*b*) date of issue; (*c*) consecutive number of the receipt; (*d*) whether goods are to be delivered to bearer or to the order of a named person; (*e*) rate of storage and handling charges, except that where goods are stored under a field arrangement, a statement of that fact is sufficient on a nonnegotiable receipt; (*f*) description of the goods or the packages containing them; (*g*) the signature of the warehouseman, which may be made by his agent; (*h*) if the receipt is issued for goods of which the warehouseman is owner, either solely, jointly, or in common with others, such fact of ownership; and (*i*) statement of the amount of advances made and of liabilities incurred for which the warehouseman claims a lien or security interest. Other terms may be inserted. (7–202.)

A warehouseman is liable to a purchaser for value in good faith of a warehouse receipt for nonreceipt or misdescription of goods. The receipt may conspicuously qualify the description by a statement such as "contents, condition and quantity unknown." (7–203.)

Since a warehouseman is a bailee of the goods, he owes to the holder of the warehouse receipt the duties of a mutual benefit bailee. Such duties are set out in Section 7–204 of the Code. The warehouseman may terminate the relation by notification under the conditions and circumstances set out in Section 7–206 of the Code.

Where a blank in a negotiable warehouse receipt has been filled in without authority, a purchaser for value and without notice of the want of authority may treat the insertion as authorized. Any other unauthorized alteration leaves the receipt enforceable against the issuer according to its original tenor. (7–208.) Unless the warehouse receipt otherwise provides, the warehouseman must keep separate the goods covered by each receipt except that different lots of fungible goods may be mingled. (7–207.)

Bills of Lading. In many respects the right and liabilities of the parties to a negotiable bill of lading are the same as those of the parties to a negotiable warehouse receipt. The contract of the issuer of a bill of lading is to transport goods whereas the contract of the issuer of a warehouse receipt is to store goods. Like the issuer of a warehouse receipt, the issuer of a bill of lading is liable for nonreceipt or misdescription of the goods, but he may protect himself from liability where he does not know the contents of packages by marking the bill of lading "contents or condition of contents of packages unknown" or similar language. Such terms are ineffective when the goods are loaded by an issuer who is a common carrier unless the goods are concealed by packages. (7–301.)

A carrier who issues a bill of lading must exercise the same degree of care in relation to the goods as a reasonably careful man would exercise under like circumstances. A liability for damages not caused by the negligence of the carrier may be imposed on it by a special law or rule of law. Under tariff rules a common carrier may limit his liability to a shipper's declaration of value provided the rates are dependent on value. (7–309.)

Negotiation of Document Title. A negotiable document of title and a negotiable instrument are negotiated in substantially the same manner. If the document of title provides for the delivery of the goods to bearer, it may be negotiated by delivery. If it provides for delivery of the goods to the order of a named person, it must be endorsed by that person and delivered. If an order document of title is endorsed in blank, it may thereafter be negotiated by delivery unless it bears a special endorsement following the blank endorsement, in which event it must be endorsed by the special endorsee and delivered.

A person taking a negotiable document of title takes as a bona fide holder if he takes in good faith and in the regular course of business. The bona fide holder of a negotiable document of title has substantially the same advantages over a holder who is not a bona fide holder or over a holder of nonnegotiable document of title as a holder in due course of a negotiable instrument has over a holder who is not a holder in due course or over the holder of a non-negotiable instrument.

Rights Acquired by Negotiation. A negotiable document of title is "duly negotiated" when it is negotiated by delivery, if a bearer document, or by endorsement and delivery, if an order document, to a holder who purchases in good faith without notice of any defense against or claim to it on the part of any person and for value, unless it is established that the negotiation is not in the regular course of business or financing or involves receiving the document in settlement of a money obligation. (7–501 [4].) A person who acquires a negotiable document of title by due negotiation acquires (1) title to the document, (2) title to the goods, unless the goods are fungible, (3) the right to the goods delivered to the bailee after the issue of the document, and (4) the direct obligation of the issuer to hold or deliver the goods according to the terms of the document. (7–502[1].) As to fungible goods, a buyer in the ordinary course of business of fungible goods sold and delivered by a warehouseman who is also in the business of buying and selling such goods takes free of any claim under a warehouse receipt even though it has been duly negotiated. (7–205.)

Under the broad general principle that a person cannot transfer title to goods he does not own, a thief or the owner of goods subject to a valid outstanding in summary security interest cannot, by warehousing or shipping the goods on a negotiable document of title and then negotiating the document of title, transfer to the purchaser of the document of title a better title than such thief or owner has. Under the law of sales, however, if a person can transfer the ownership of goods to a bona fide purchaser for value, he can then warehouse or ship the goods on a negotiable document of title and by negotiating the document of title to a person who takes in due course confer on such person a good title to the goods. (7–503.)

Warranties of Transferor of Document of Title.   The transferor of a negotiable document of title warrants to his immediate transferee, in addition to any warranty of goods, only that the document is genuine and that he has no knowledge of any facts that would impair its validity or worth and that his negotiation or transfer is rightful and fully effective with respect to the title to the document and the goods it represents. (7–507.) A collecting bank or intermediary warrants only his good faith and authority. (7–508.)

Summary

The warehouseman or common carrier is a bailee of the goods and he contracts to store or transport them. The warehouse receipt or bill of lading may be either negotiable or nonnegotiable. If the warehouse receipt issued by the warehouseman omits in its written or printed terms the information required under the provisions of the Code, the warehouseman is liable to a purchaser in good faith of a warehouse receipt for failure to describe or for misdescription of the goods. He owes to the holder of a warehouse receipt the duties of a mutual benefit bailee. The common carrier's liability on a negotiable bill of lading is the same in most respects as that of the issuer of a negotiable warehouse receipt. His liability may be increased by special law or rule.

The rules of law relative to the negotiation of a negotiable document of title are the same in most respects as the law relative to the negotiation of negotiable commercial paper.

In general, a holder by due negotitaion of a negotiable document of title gets good title to the document and the goods and the contractual rights against the bailee. However, a thief or an owner of goods which are subject to a valid perfected security interest cannot, by warehousing or shipping the goods on a negotiable document of title and negotiating it, pass to such transferee greater rights in the goods than such thief or owner has.

A holder who transfers a negotiable document of title warrants to his immediate transferee that the document is genuine and that he has no knowledge of any facts that would impair its validity or worth and that his transfer is rightful and fully effective.

National Dairy Products Corp. v. *Lawrence American Field Warehousing Corp.*
255 N.Y.S.2d 788 (App. Div. N.Y. 1965)

This was an action by National Dairy Products Corporation (plaintiff) against Lawrence American Field Warehousing Corporation (defendant) to recover for failure to deliver goods on presentation of warehouse receipts. Summary judgment for National Dairy Products Corporation and Lawrence American Field Warehousing Corporation appealed. Judgment affirmed.

Quantities of soybean oil were delivered to Lawrence American Field Warehousing Corporation (Lawrence) for which nonnegotiable warehouse receipts were issued. National Dairy Products Corporation (National) held warehouse receipts for some of the soybean oil. On presentation of the receipts it was discovered that no soybean oil was in the storage tanks. No satisfactory explanation was given for the disappearance of the soybean oil—95,233,792 pounds. Either the oil had been stolen or the warehouse receipts had been issued without the receipt of soybean oil.

Breitel, Justice Presiding.   Section 7–207 (2) of the Uniform Commercial Code does in some situations change the prior law by giving to certain holders of "overissued" receipts for a portion of a fungible mass the rights of a holder who has made a delivery of existing goods to the warehouseman. Thus the holder of an overissued receipt may obtain a proprietary interest in bailed fungibles of another even though the receipt was not originally issued for the deposit of actual oil. If this provision be applicable, then the holders of overissued receipts for nonexisting oil would be owners of a pro rata share of existing oil and entitled to sue in conversion for the wrongful failure to deliver that share on demand. However, by its own terms this provision of section 7–207 (2) benefits only those holders to whom overissued receipts have been "duly negotiated," and therefore would not seem to apply to nonnegotiable receipts. (U.C.C., § 7–501.)

It is true, as defendants argue, that a bailee is not an insurer. Thus, if despite the exercise of due care, there is an inability to deliver, the bailee is not liable to the one entitled to possession of bailed goods. Consequently, the matter of due care requires consideration before the issues in these cases can be determined.

Thus far the legal issues have been discussed in the light of the applicable New York rules. In truth the rules in New Jersey and New York are the same, largely because the matters arise in a commercial context in which there is little or no diversity among the states. The parties have also briefed the legal issues on this presupposition. With respect to the warehouseman's duty of care there is no reason to depart from this approach. While undoubtedly New Jersey law is applicable to the bailments, the New York rules are not different. In New Jersey the Uniform Commercial Code was in effect at the time of the transactions in suit. In New York the Uniform Warehouse Receipts Act was in effect (General Business Law, art. 9, §§ 90–143). Since then, the Uniform Commercial Code was adopted in New York, effective September 27, 1964. For all practical purposes insofar as the issues in these cases are involved the result is the same.

With the foregoing prefatory comment it is appropriate to consider the obligation of the warehouseman to exercise care. He has not only the obligation to exercise care, but concededly he has the burden of explanation for any loss or disappearance of the property bailed. He is also liable for damages arising from the improper issuance of receipts or documents of title.

From Lawrence's point of view there has not been any showing of sufficient care or explanation to exculpate them from liability. It is not enough to assert that care was taken, describing the practices used, when the disappearance of the oil remains wholly unexplained. This situation is not at all like that of a bailee showing how carefully the property was secured and that nevertheless the thief broke in and removed the property, without fault on the part of the bailee by any reasonable standard. In showing care, the bailee must explain the loss or damage, and not simply point to a mystery for which it has no better explanation than the bailor.

Koreska v. *United Cargo Corp.*
258 N.Y.S.2d 432 (App. Div. N.Y. 1965)

This was an action by Koreska (plaintiff) against United Cargo Corporation (defendant) to recover a judgment for the value of goods delivered without taking up an order bill of lading. Summary judgment for Koreska granted.

United Cargo Corporation (United) issued a negotiable order bill of lading for goods consisting of four large packages. The goods were consigned to Koreska and the order bill of lading named as Koreska's collecting agent a New York bank. On arrival of the goods United delivered them to Park Whitney, Koreska's customer, without taking up the bill of lading by an oral waiver made by Koreska's agent and also by a binding trade custom or course of dealing. The court found that no agent authorized to act for Koreska had waived the taking up of the bill of lading and that no course of dealing was established.

PER CURIAM.   Even if a factual issue had been raised with respect to Allgemeine's agency, Koreska would be entitled to summary judgment. In the case of an order, or negotiable bill of lading, as opposed to a straight, or nonnegotiable bill, it is ordinarily the consignee or other holder of the negotiable bill, who alone is entitled to authorize a diversion or modification of the delivery term. Even if Allgemeine obtained possession of the bill after authorizing a waiver, as claimed by United, it was never a holder with power to divert, in the absence of an actual indorsement of the bill to it. Moreover the seller-shipper, Koreska, never became a consignee or holder, and therefore did not, under these rules, have the power to divert the goods without the cooperation of its collecting agent-consignee, the New York bank. It follows that its alleged agent, Allgemeine, similarly had no such power.

A further reason why United may not avail itself of the alleged waiver, is that the waiver was oral only, and would modify the express term of the bill that delivery was to be made at the order of the New York bank consignee. One of the conditions printed on the back of the bill provides:

"None of the terms of this bill of lading shall be deemed to have been waived by any person unless by express waiver signed by such person, or his duly authorized agent."

Ordinary prudence, moreover, would dictate that the carrier require that such instructions be noted on the bill itself.

For similar reasons evidence of the course of dealing or trade custom is also without significance. The express term, requiring delivery in accordance with the consignee's order, is controlling, whenever the course of dealing or trade custom is inconsistent with it. (U.C.C., § 1–205 [4].)

Problem Cases

1. Weaver drew a check for $32.68 to the order of J & E Tire Shop. Although Weaver had on deposit a sum sufficient to cover the check, the drawee, Bank of America, refused to pay the check and marked on the face of it "account closed." When J & E Tire Shop received the check, it swore out a warrant for Weaver's arrest. Weaver was arrested, charged with petty theft, and temporarily confined. Does Weaver have any recourse against Bank of America?

2. Geffner, a depositor in Savings Bank, requested Savings Bank to draw a cashier's check for $10,000 payable to Ruskin. Savings Bank drew the check on Commercial Bank. The check was delivered to Ruskin but Savings Bank, acting on Geffner's instructions, stopped payment on the check and Commercial Bank refused payment to Ruskin on the basis of the stop-payment order. Now Ruskin sues Savings Bank as drawer. Savings Bank says it stopped payment on the check because Geffner requested it do so, telling them that the check had been drawn for the purpose of starting a business with Sol Ruskin, but that she had lost confidence in him and had been hasty in actions and unclear in her mind due to the fact she had only recently been "widowed." Savings Bank claims it should be discharged as the mere "stakeholder" besieged by adverse claimants. Is this a good defense?

3. Keleher issued a check payable to the order of O'Keefe, who had the check certified. Later, Keleher issued a stop-payment order to the bank before the check was presented for payment. Keleher has a valid defense if sued on the check. Should the bank pay the check to O'Keefe?

4. Cook had issued a check payable to the order of Light. The next morning, before banking hours, Cook telephoned the bank, talked to the cashier, and ordered payment of the check stopped. Later in the day the bank certified the check and subsequently paid it. When sued, the bank set up as a defense (*a*) that the stop-payment order was not given during banking hours and (*b*) that the stop-payment order was not in writing. Is either of these defenses good?

5. Allen had a checking account with First National Bank. It was a rule of the bank to post the depositor's book about once a month and then render him a statement, showing the deposits and checks and balance. From about the 5th of September, 1960, to March 4, 1961, Tomlin, a clerk of Allen's, forged several checks which were paid by First Bank. Allen did not discover the forgeries until March 4, 1961. Allen claims that First National Bank is liable for the loss occasioned by all the forgeries. Is this claim correct?

6. Dovax had been shipping goods with Delivery Company for more than a year. On November 1, 1966, Dovax gave Delivery Company goods valued at $1,799.95 for delivery to three different consignees. Delivery Company kept the goods in one of its trucks overnight but the next morning the truck was discovered stolen along with the goods. On the bills of lading given to Dovax was the legend "Liability limited to $50 unless greater value is declared and paid for." Dovax claims he should recover $1,799.95 for the loss; Delivery Company wants to pay only $150. Who is correct?

7. Lippincott agreed to consign groceries to Groceries, Inc. Under the agreement, title to the groceries consigned was to remain in Lippincott, and Groceries, Inc., was to pay Lippincott for the groceries as it sold them. Groceries, Inc., placed the consigned groceries shipped to it by Lippincott in the warehouse of Warehouse Co., for which groceries a negotiable warehouse receipt was issued to Groceries, Inc. Groceries, Inc., pledged the negotiable warehouse receipt to Peoples Bank as security for a note owing to it. Groceries, Inc., defaulted in the payment of the note, and Peoples Bank seized the groceries represented by the negotiable warehouse receipt. Lippincott brought suit to recover the groceries, claiming that Grocries, Inc., had no title to them and that Peoples Bank acquired no rights in them through the negotiable warehouse receipt. Is Lippincott entitled to the groceries?

8. Canty entrusted some goods to Wyatt, a warehouseman, and they orally agreed on a bailment for hire. Wyatt was unable to return the goods to Canty due to a fire in Wyatt's warehouse which destroyed the goods. After showing these facts in court, Canty rested his case. Wyatt moved to dismiss the action on the grounds Canty had not shown the fire was due to Wyatt's negligence. Should Wyatt's motion be granted?

9. Christoffersen, a California turkey raiser, contracted to ship a truckload of turkeys to Murray. He consigned together with a sight draft drawn on Murray, to a New York bank for collection. Without paying the draft and without obtaining the bill of lading Murray obtained possession of the turkeys from the carrier's truck driver by telling him that payment had been taken care of. Then Murray sold the turkeys to Pride Wholesale Meat which in turn sold them to Castellano and Fort Meat Wholesalers. Now Christoffersen sues Pride, Castellano and Fort Meat for conversion of his turkeys. Is he entitled to a judgment?

10. On October 15, Young delivered 207 bags of rice to Atteberry's warehouse and received a nonnegotiable receipt. Young then transferred the receipt to Brock for a valuable consideration and on November 3 Brock notified Atteberry of the transfer. However, prior to November 3 Young had procured a negotiable receipt for the rice along with some other rice he had deposited with Atteberry. Now Brock presents his nonnegotiable receipt to Atteberry and demands delivery of the rice. Atteberry contends no rice is held there on Brock's account. Who is correct?

PART X Miscellaneous

chapter 42. Legal Problems Involving Consumer Credit

The Development of Our Credit Society

The early years of our American economy were characterized by a cash-and-carry business environment. Credit was not available to the 19th century wage earner because it could be more usefully employed in capital producing enterprises. Furthermore, consumer goods and services other than those required for general subsistence simply were not procurable by the average consumer; consequently there was no demand for consumer lending organizations. By the end of World War I tremendous increases in production made the widespread availability of durable consumer goods possible. What followed was a consumer credit phenomenon which has taken the American society by surprise. For example total consumer debt in 1923 was $7 billion; in June, 1969, that figure had increased to $116 billion. The annual charge to consumers for their debt in June, 1969 was $15.1 billion, more than twice the 1923 amount of total consumer credit. Equally significant is the growth of credit cards, which in 1968 accounted for over $50 billion of credit purchases.

Legal and Social Problems of Credit. Developments in the law of credit transactions have generally failed to keep pace with the growth of consumer credit itself. The merchants' courts centuries ago built up the law of negotiable instruments which today is embodied in Article 3 of the Uniform Commercial Code; of the 50 states it is now law in all except Louisiana. The courts and legislatures over many years also developed a body of law in each state covering credit transactions involving collateral. These are now covered by Article 9 of the Code. However, this law does not cover some important social and legal problems that have arisen in consumer credit transactions. For instance, purchasers tend to focus their attention only on the agreed upon monthly payment to the exclusion of the frequently very high charges for the credit extended. Another tendency is for merchants to encourage purchases on credit so that they may make an additional profit either through a kickback from the lender who actually extends the credit or by assuming the lending functions themselves, charging a higher rate than the money costs them. Many buyers on credit are unaware of the common add-ons which provide at a cost such services as insurance protection of the goods and health insurance for the debtor, and charges for official fees and for default or delinquency. A number of merchants have also been known to use credit to defraud the customer by not giving the proper credit for his payments and by keeping him in perpetual debt by making a series of sales, each secured by the goods involved in all previous purchases. These practices too often result in situations where the consumer is unable to pay his existing debts. Subsequently, there is garnishment of wages, usually leading to a loss of job and an ever deeper spiral of debt and inability to pay. Ultimately, this spiral can end only in bankruptcy, an undesirable by-product of credit transactions. The increase in number of personal bankruptcies from 18,000 in 1950 to 207,000 in 1967, reflects the severity of this problem.

Credit cards present additional problems, largely because this form of credit is so new and does not fit squarely within traditional legal categories such as contracts, letters of credit or negotiable instruments. The result has been that there are both many unanswered questions and inconsistent decisions on those problems which have been adjudicated.

Summary

Consumer debt has become a price characteristic of our American economy, and with its growth many social and legal problems have developed. Legislatures and courts have yet to solve some of the questions relating to consumer credit, including: hidden charges on loans, fraudulent practices of creditors, garnishment of wages and bankruptcy of debtors, and credit card transactions.

Federal Legislation: Truth in Lending

Introduction. The size of the consumer debt and its rate of growth indicate the magnitude of the savings that might be possible if there were price competition in the consumer credit industry. If, as a result of vigorous price competition, the average rate of interest on consumer debt could be reduced by only 1 percent, American consumers would save $1 billion a year. One recent study asked a sample of eight hundred families to estimate the rate of interest they were actually paying on their debts. The average estimate was 8.3 percent per year. The actual rate was nearly three times higher, or 23.2 percent.[1] In

---

[1] Justen and Shay, *Consumer Sensitivity to Finance Rates,* National Bureau of Economic Research, New York, 1964, p. 51.

1967, President Johnson observed in his Message to Congress on American Consumer Protection, that to understand the price of consumer credit, with all of its variations, including add-ons, discounts and other gimmicks, a consumer would have to be an actuary or mathematician in order to know exactly what he was paying for the use of money. It was in this contemporary setting that Congress passed the Consumer Credit Protection Act (The Truth in Lending Act) in 1968, believing that market competition could lower the average rate of interest on consumer debt and that government fiat as to interest rate ceilings was unnecessary. Therefore, the purpose of the CCPA is to require a seller of credit to inform a buyer of credit just what the price of his money is.

Disclosure Requirements. The basic provision of Title I of the Consumer Credit Protection Act, is that all persons who in the regular course of business extend or arrange to extend consumer credit, must inform the potential debtor of two items: (1) the amount of the finance charge in dollars and (2) the finance charge in annual percentage rate. Although there are certain exemptions from coverage such as business or government credit loans, there are generally three types of transactions which require disclosure: the open-end credit plans such as revolving credit card systems, the non open-end plan such as real estate transactions, and consumer loans such as the typical bank type loan. Thus, a bank making a 30 day, one payment loan at interest is covered as well as the department store with a revolving credit plan. A lumber yard that allows a 2 percent discount on goods sold if paid in 10 days, net 30 (since there is in fact a finance charge of 2 percent for 20 days) is also covered.

Title I also requires that the total finance charge as well as the annual percentage rate be printed on the contract or security agreement and placed on the face of the note. Included in the "finance charge," as specified in Regulation Z under the Act, are loan fees, service and carrying charges, discounts, interest, investigation fees, cost of guarantee and insurance. Likewise the Act and Regulation Z spell out the manner in which the annual percentage rate is determined, with reference to be made to tables provided by the federal government. Other items which require disclosure under the act are the cash price, the amount allowed as trade in or cash, the difference between the cash price and the down payment, amounts payable, and their time of payment, and any additional charges for delinquency or default.

Truth in Advertising. The CCPA also provides that any advertisement which states a rate of finance, must express that rate in annual percentage terms. If the ad includes mention of a down payment, the amount or number of installments, or the period of repayment, then it must also state the cash price and the rate of finance charge expressed as an annual percentage rate. Presumably, this provision will cover such advertisements as "No money down", "42 months to pay", and "As little as $5.13 per month".

Requirements on Real Estate. All transactions involving real estate loans are covered by the CCPA and proper disclosure is required. In addition, when a security interest is given in the debtor's home, the debtor has three business days in which to rescind the transaction. He must be told of his right of rescission and provided with a form for this purpose. It is provided that rescission becomes effective upon posting in the U.S. mail, thus placing the risk of failure of delivery upon the creditor and making uncertain the enforceability of the security agreement.

Limitations on Garnishment. As previously noted, the increased use of credit in our society had led to the not uncommon situation in which the consumer is unable to pay. A favorite ploy of creditors has been to garnish a debtors wages, often leading the debtor to job dismissal, and bankruptcy. Under Title III, wage garnishment may never exceed 25 percent of the debtors wages. The Act also provides that an amount 30 times the federal minimum hourly wage is exempt from garnishment. Finally no employer may dismiss any employee because of garnishment, for any one garnishment.

Enforcement of CCPA. Overall enforcement of the CCPA is left to the Federal Trade Commission, subject to specific areas reserved for other federal agencies. Heavy criminal penalties are provided for improper disclosure, and even negligent failure to make a proper disclosure is subject to civil liability of double the amount of the finance charge, with a minimum of $100 and a maximum of $1,000.

Other Legislation. Currently, the Uniform Consumer Credit Code is being considered for adoption in many states as another legislative inroad on consumer credit. Promulgated by the Commissioner on Uniform State Law, the U.C.C.C. is designed as an approach to substitute one coherent law for a host of separate state statutes which presently exist in the field of consumer credit. However, at the time of this writing, the U.C.C.C. is not yet law in any state. Consequently, one seeking to understand the law of consumer credit must read not only the contract involved, but also the Uniform Commercial Code, the CCPA, a state installment sales law, and Federal Trade Commission materials. If adopted, the U.C.C.C. might reduce these sources.

Summary

The Consumer Protection Act is an attempt to lower the cost of credit and to decrease the incidence of wage garnishment and bankruptcies. The act provides for disclosure of the finance charge in dollars and an annual percentage rate for restrictions on the collection device of garnishment, and for a rescission device in the sale of real estate. Although only time will tell whether the act accomplishes its purpose, the buyer now can be reasonably certain of the accuracy of the credit information he receives, and the creditor now knows what minimum duties he must fulfill.

The following is an example of a form for a loan from a bank containing all of the necessary disclosure requirements:

PROMISSORY NOTE

$5,000.00
Morgantown, West Virginia
July 29, 1969

For value received, we promise to pay to the order of the Farmers' and Merchants' Bank, a West Virginia Corporation, at 466 High Street, Morgantown, West Virginia, the full and just sum of Five Thousand ($5,000.00) Dollars, together with interest thereon at the rate of 6 percent per annum. This note shall be paid in equal, consecutive monthly installments of Ninety Six Dollars and Sixty Seven ($96.67) Cents each. The first payment shall be made on the 1st day of August, 1969, and a like payment shall be made on the same day of each month thereafter until the full principal sum plus interest is fully paid and satisfied.

Any unpaid balance may be paid at any time without penalty. In the event the makers default on any payment, a charge of $3.00 may be assessed. If such default continues for two (2) consecutive payments, then the owner and holder of this note, may at its option, declare the full balance due and payable.

This note is secured by Deed of Trust bearing even date herewith wherein certain real property in Monongalia County, West Virginia, was conveyed to John R. Goodwin, Trustee.

1. Proceeds	$ 5,000.00	
2. *None*	$ 0.00	
Other charges		
3. Amount financed	$ 5,000.00	
4. FINANCE CHARGE	$ 800.20	
5. Total of payments	$ 60	
6. ANNUAL PERCENTAGE RATE	$ 6	%

WITNESS the following signatures and seals:
Receipt of a copy if this
note is hereby acknowledged:

_____(SEAL)

_____   _____(SEAL)

The Credit Card

The Risk of Loss. When someone's credit card is lost or stolen and then used by some unauthorized person to make a purchase, that person usually cannot be found and the loss must fall on some relatively innocent party, i.e. the card-holder, the card-issuer, or the merchant-seller. Courts look first for some contractual apportionment of risk clause between the parties in the application for the card or in the literature that accompanied the issuance of the card. Such a clause might read to the effect that the card-holder is liable for purchases made with his card until written notice of loss or theft is received by the card-issuer. Where no such clause exists, the courts have used such contractual concepts as implied promises to pay, guarantee, and assignment or such tort concepts as due care and relative fault to resolve the question of loss. In the process of applying such concepts, the decisions reveal diametrically different end results with some card-holders being absolutely liable for card misuse while others bear no responsibility.

Where there is a risk apportionment clause, the courts may hold the card-holder strictly to the terms of the clause. However, all courts do not view the situation as being this simple and ask other questions which are common to present contract law. Such questions include: (1) is the risk apportionment clause unconscionable and against public policy; (2) was the clause stated in clear language, conspicuous, and likely to have been notice by the card-holder; (3) was the card solicited by the card-holder or did it arrive unsolicited through the mail? Even where there is an enforceable risk-allocation clause, the possibility remains that there might be circumstances present in a particular case to justify disregarding the clause. Primarily these circumstances would be the lack of exercise of due care on the part of the holder, issuer or merchant-seller.

Personal Defenses of Card Holder. Another problem area has to do with the assertion of defenses against payment, a problem that parallels the negotiable instrument area. As an example of the problem we might suppose that James Brown used his First National Bank credit card to purchase a television set from Sam's Appliance Store. Normally Sam would then send the charge slip to First National Bank and receive immediate payment or credit (less a discount which usually amounts to 3 to 6 percent); this process represents the primary advantage to the merchant, i.e. relieving him of the risks and costs that would accompany his making and carrying his own credit sales. Suppose that after receiving the television, Brown discovers that it is seriously defective but Sam refuses to remedy the defect. When First National Bank presses for payment on the credit card account, must Brown pay the bank or can he set up a defense of breach of warranty against payment? If Sam held the account, Brown could use this defense against full payment, but in the instant situation Brown generally must pay the bank and then bring a separate action against Sam for breach of warranty. In practical terms this may well mean that Brown has no meaningful way to enforce his rights since bringing a suit may be too expensive, inconvenient or time consuming to warrant bringing it. However, at the time of this writing, there is no authority on this problem of defense against payment, because no case has yet been adjudicated on an appellate level.

Summary

With the increase in use of credit cards have come the problems of allocating the loss due to unauthorized use and of asserting a defense for breach of warranty by the card holder against the card-issuer rather than the merchant-seller. Courts have generally divided lost-credit-card cases into two categories: (1) those in which the court, moved by special or peculiar circumstances, imposed certain duties upon the issuer and merchant which were not required in the credit card contract; and (2) those in which the holder who accepted the terms of the contract was strictly held to these terms. In categorizing the cases, courts have considered whether the holder was negligent in losing the card or notifying the issuer, whether the merchant was negligent in honoring the card, whether the contract was unconscionable, and whether the merchant, the seller, or the holder is best able to bear the risk of loss. The law relating to credit cards has had little opportunity to foster a solid, time tested body of law; modification and development of existing doctrines can be expected in future decisions.

Union Oil Company of California v. *Lull*
349 P.2d 243, (Sup.Ct.Ore, 1960)

This was an action by Union Oil Co. (plaintiff) against Lawrence Lull (defendant) to recover the amount if unauthorized purchases on Lull's lost or stolen credit card. Judgment for Lull and Union Oil appealed. Judgment reversed and remanded for new trial.

Union Oil invited Lull to make application for a credit card. Although the application form contained no reference to the card holder's liability for unauthorized use of the card, the credit card itself contained the following conditions, printed on the back of the card: "The customer to whom this card is issued guarantees payment . . . of products delivered or services rendered to anyone presenting this card, guarantee to continue until card is surrendered or written notice is received by the company that it is lost or stolen."

Unauthorized purchases totalling $1,454.25 were made between April 26, 1958 and May 26, 1958 through the use of defendant's lost or stolen card. Although Lull had no knowledge of the terms on the back of the card, the trial court held Lull bound by those conditions. However, the trial court also found that he would be excused from the performance of the conditions if he acted as a reasonable man in connection with possession and use of the card.

O'CONNELL, JUSTICE. In absence of proof that the terms of the contract were put in deceptive form which would mislead a reasonable person, and that the defendent was so misled, he is bound by the conditions of the contract whether or not he read them. Defendant would have us recast the terms of the contract by limiting the card holder's liability to cases in which he had authorized the use of the card or where, through his fault, the card was used by one not authorized to do so. There is nothing in the transaction between the plaintiff and defendant which would justify the modification of the conditions clearly expressed on the card . . . Therefore, it is our interpretation of the contract that the defendant was not absolved from liability by exercising care in the use and custody of his card and that it was error to instruct the jury as the trial court did.

(However), we think that the agreement in the instant case must be interpreted as subjecting defendent to liability for sales made through the unauthorized use of its credit cards only if due care is exercised by plaintiff . . . to ascertain the authority of the customer who presents the card. The burden of proving that reasonable inquiry was made is upon the plaintiff.

Problems

1. Assume you are the owner of the Ace Loan Company who advertises in the local paper as follows:

Borrow	Pay 12 mo.	Pay 24 mo.
$100	$ 9.74	$ 5.59
$300	$28.81	$16.31
$500	$47.06	$26.19

Now that the Consumer Credit Protection Act has become law; how would you change the ad to conform with the disclosure requirements?

2. Assuming that the minimum hourly wage is $1.60, under CCPA regulations, what portion of Dan Debtor's income may be garnished under the following conditions? He earns $50 per week. He earns $64 per week. He earns $100 per week.

3. Texaco Gas Co. sent Harold Goldstein a credit card which stated that the holder assumed full responsibility for all purchases made with the card, that written notice would be given to the issuer in case of loss or theft of the card, and that retention or use of the card constituted acceptance of its terms. Goldstein's card was stolen but he never reported the theft. Texaco sues Goldstein for value of the illegal purchases made with his card; Goldstein claims that he is not bound by the terms printed on the card since they were never brought to his attentions. Is this defense valid?

4. Whited had a Diners Club card which was nontransferable, i.e. restricted to use by the named holder only. A provision on the card stated that if the card was lost or stolen, holder would be liable for all purchases until the issuer was notified. Whited did not discover the loss of his card until $1,600 worth of purchases had been fraudulently charged against him. Can Diners Club collect this amount from Whited on grounds that Whited was absolutely liable on the contract?

chapter 43. Insurance

The Insurance Contract

Nature of Contract. All persons, in their everyday activities, are subjected to risks. For instance, there are risks involved in the ownership of property and in the use or possession of property. Consequently, a body of law has been developed by which it can be determined which person must bear these risks. As a general rule the risks of personal injury fall on the injured person, and the risks of loss, destruction, or damage to property must be borne by the owner. However, if the personal injury or the loss, destruction, or damage to property results from the negligence of another, the law imposes on the negligent person the liability for such injury or such loss, destruction, or damage to property. If a judgment against the negligent person is uncollectible, then the person suffering the harm must bear it. In some situations, we have statutes which shift risks from the allocation made at common law to a different allocation— for example, the "workmen's compensation acts."

The person on whom the risk of loss in any transaction is cast may shift such risk to another by a contractual arrangement. A seller's warranty of goods sold is an example of such an arrangement. Also, a person may, by entering into a contract of insurance, relieve himself, at least in part, from the burden of a risk which under the law is cast on him.

Basically, a contract of insurance is a risk-bearing contract. The insurer, for a consideration called the "premium," contracts to reimburse the insured for losses suffered on the happening of a stipulated event. In the case of property insurance the amount which can be recovered in the event of the loss is directly related to the value of the property insured, but in life insurance and in health and accident insurance the amount to be recovered in the event of death, sickness, or accident is usually a fixed amount. The business of insurance has for

963

its purpose the distribution of existing risks so that the losses resulting from the risks do not fall on one person or a small group of persons.

It is often difficult to distinguish between insurance contracts and other contracts of contingent obligations, such as contracts of guarantee or contracts for services to be rendered on the happening of some future, uncertain event. However, owing to the present regulation of insurers by the state, it is frequently important to distinguish insurance contracts from other contracts of contingent obligation.

Kinds of Insurance. The different kinds of insurance contracts written at the present time are as numerous and varied as the human undertakings which are subject to the risks of future events. For convenience, insurance contracts may be divided into two large classes: property and personal insurance. The property insurance contract is a contract of indemnity. Any contract of property insurance whereby the insured expects to gain by the happening of the event insured against is in the nature of a wagering contract and is not allowed. The purpose of property insurance is to indemnify a person against a loss actually suffered, not to wager on the happening of the event.

The ordinary life insurance contract is not an indemnity contract. It is an arrangement whereby the insured pays an annuity and the insurer agrees to pay a certain sum at an uncertain time. The amount to be paid is based on the amount of the periodic payments and not on the value of the insured's life. We do not attempt to put a monetary value on human life. The life insurance contract differs from the property insurance contract in another respect. The payment contracted for in the property insurance contract is conditioned on the happening of an uncertain future event, and the time within which the event is to happen is expressly limited; the payment contracted for in the life insurance contract is conditioned upon an event which is certain to happen, but the time at which it will happen is uncertain. The contract of insurance for either life or property, if it is to be valid, must possess the essential elements which are requisite to the validity of all contracts—offer, acceptance, consideration, parties having capacity to contract, and legality of the contract.

Summary

Each of us, in our everyday activities, is subject to risks. A body of law—common and statutory—has been developed by which it may be determined which person must bear a loss. The person who must bear a risk may shift the risk by a contractual arrangement, or he may, by a contract of insurance, relieve himself from the major burden of a risk.

Basically, a contract of insurance is a risk-bearing contract. It is not a wagering contract, since the risk insured is an existing risk and not one created for the purpose of bearing it.

Insurance contracts are generally classed as contracts of personal insurance

—life, health, and accident insurance—and contracts of property insurance— fire, theft, hail, and casualty insurance.

The State of Texas v. *Memorial Benevolent Society of Texas*
384 S.W.2d 776 (Ct. Civ. App. Tex. 1964)

This was an action by the State of Texas (plaintiff) against Memorial Benevolent Society of Texas (defendant) to forfeit the charter of the Society. Judgment for Memorial Benevolent Society of Texas and State of Texas appealed. Judgment reversed.

Memorial Benevolent Society of Texas (Society) was chartered in 1961. The membership was wholly voluntary, but it had a radio program every Sunday morning at which time it solicited membership. The Society had agreed that it would pay a stipulated sum on the death of a member in good standing for burial expenses or expenses of the last illness—$300 if death should occur within three months after joining the Society and $600 if death should not occur until after three months. Each of them was obligated to contribute two dollars on the death of each member but was not expected to contribute more than ten dollars a year. The initial membership fee ranged from eleven dollars to thirty-six dollars and a one-dollar renewal fee was charged each year. An audit of the books of the Society revealed that its liabilities exceeded its assets by a substantial amount.

PHILLIPS, JUSTICE. The society, although chartered as a nonprofit corporation calling its assessments "donations," is engaging in the business of insurance without a Certificate of Authority issued by the State Board of Insurance.

The case is very similar to *Farmer* v. *State* where the court allowed the State to forfeit corporate franchises of the "Masonic Mutual Benevolent Association of Texas" because it was acting as an insurance company without having incorporated in accordance with the insurance laws of the State. The court spoke as follows:

. . . The benefits received are not gratuitous. They are due to the member on account of the money he pays into the society. It takes the risk of his continued existence and good health. If it be benevolent to pay one money under such circumstances, then every mutual life insurance company is acting in a benevolent manner toward the family of an insured member when it pays the policy it had issued thereon for a moneyed consideration. It matters not what name the association may assume. The law looks to the real objects of the body, and not to the name indicative of benevolence which it may have assumed.

The court in Farmer defined an insurance contract as follows:

It is a contract by which one party, for a consideration, promises to make a certain payment of money upon the death of the other; and it is well settled that whatever may be the terms of the payment of the consideration by the assured, or the mode of estimating or securing payment of the insurance money, it is still a contract of insurance, no matter by what name it may be called.

In Article 12.02 Texas Insurance Code we find the following:

Any person or persons desiring to organize a local mutual aid association to be operated upon the assessment as needed or similar plan or a burial company, association or society as defined in Article 14.37, Chapter 14, of this code, shall be permitted to do so upon the terms and conditions hereinafter set forth and by complying with the provisions of this chapter. No person, firm or corporation shall hereafter operate in this State any sort of a local mutual aid society or association paying a death benefit or other benefits and providing its funds by assessments as needed, except under the provisions hereof, or under other specific provisions of the laws of this State.

This Court held that the Legislature was within its authority to regulate Local Mutual Aid Associations in *Phillips et al.* v. *Daniel et al.*

Society maintains that it is a "charitable organization"; however, it has in no way pointed out to this Court how it can accommodate itself to the provisions of the Code for charitable or fraternal societies. Upon reference to these provisions (Art. 10.38; 10.01 *et seq.*), we find that they are not applicable here. The mere fact that Society has made donations to certain cemeteries or churches found by the liquidator to be in the neighborhood of $300 will not in itself qualify it as a charitable organization. Nor are we impressed by the fact that neither a physical examination nor a statement regarding health is required. Such requirements are merely contractual and the fact that they are not present in this contract is of no significance.

Making the Contract

General Requirements. An insurance policy is a personal contract between the insurer and the insured. A contract of fire insurance is an agreement by the insurer to indemnify the insured against loss resulting from a fire and does not inure to the benefit of a purchaser of the insured property. Likewise, a policy of public liability insurance does not give the owner of damaged property or a person injured as the result of the negligence of the insured a right of action against the insurer.

In a contract of insurance, as in other contracts, there must be an offer made and accepted, the agreement must be supported by consideration, the parties must have capacity to enter into such a contract, and the objective of the contract must be legal.

In addition, the agreement, if it falls within the provisions of the statute of frauds, must be evidenced by a note or memorandum in writing. Under the statutes of some states, certain types of insurance contracts are required to be in writing; and under the statutes of a substantial number of states, contracts of property insurance must contain certain standard provisions, the terms of which are set out in the statute.

As a general rule the insurance contract, both property and personal, contains many provisions which define the scope of the risks insured and the rights and duties of the parties to the contract. Since a court will not make a contract for the parties and cannot enforce an agreement unless its terms are reasonably certain, it is necessary that the insurance contract be set out in some detail.

Many usages have, however, been established in the field of insurance, and these aid in filling in the gaps which may appear in the negotiations for insurance coverage. For example, in the area of property insurance, it is an established practice for an authorized insurance agent to contract to insure property on a "binding slip," or "binder," which may be oral or in writing. All that is necessary to make a valid binder is for the insured to give the insurer a general description of the property to be covered, the location of the property, and the amount of the coverage. By usage, it is understood that the property is insured under the terms of a standard insurance policy and that the insured will pay the established premium for the insurance. Many other standard practices are followed in the writing of insurance.

The Application (Offer). The established practice in the field of insurance is for the person seeking insurance to offer to enter into a contract for insurance with the insurer. There is no reason, however, from a legal standpoint, why the insurer should not make the offer. Most insurance is solicited by agents of the insurer, and such agents are not authorized to bind the insurer; their function is to induce the prospective insured to make an offer to "buy" insurance.

In the field of property insurance the agent may be authorized to issue standard policies of insurance if the risk to be insured is not exceptional in its nature. The usual procedure, however, is for the prospective insured to fill out and sign a printed application which has been prepared by the insurer. Such application will contain questions relative to the property to be insured. The questions will concern the value, location, type of construction, type of roof, and such other information as the insurer may deem important as the basis for evaluating the risk. In the event of high-value structures the insurer may, in addition, inspect the premises.

If the application is for personal insurance, the questions will concern the age, health, family history, etc., of the person for whom the insurance is to be issued. In addition, a doctor approved by the insurer will give the proposed insured a physical examination and report to the insurer. After the application is completed, it is sent, as a general rule, to the home office of the insurer, where it will be considered and accepted or rejected.

When Application Is Contract of Insurance. The application may be so drafted that the insurance becomes effective on the signing of the application. This is a commoner practice in the field of property insurance than in the field of personal insurance. When the insurance becomes effective on the signing of the application, the courts have generally held that the parties are bound by the terms of the general policy of insurance for which the application is made. The application may bind the insurer until the insurance is terminated by rejection of the application, or it may expressly limit the duration of the temporary insurance.

Acceptance of Offer in Application. An application which is a mere offer is not accepted by the delay of the insurer in rejecting it, and the fact that the insured has paid his first premium does not alter the rule. It has, however, been held by a few courts that retention for an unreasonable time of the premium paid with the application constitutes an acceptance. In some states, statutes have been passed requiring the insurer, in emergency insurance, such as hail, to give notice of rejection within a stated time or he will be bound.

Several courts have allowed a recovery in tort for the insurer's negligent delay in acting upon the application. Such holdings are based on the theory that an insurance company is licensed by the state and owes a duty to the public to insure those who are qualified, and that an unreasonable delay in acting on the application delays the party in obtaining protection. This theory has been accepted by several courts and appears to be growing in favor.

Summary

To have an enforceable contract of insurance, all of the essential elements of a binding contract must be present. The typical insurance contract includes many provisions defining the risk insured.

The standard practice of insurers is to have the prospective insured fill out and sign an application prepared by the insurer. Such application is so drafted that it is an offer to enter into a contract of insurance on terms stipulated by the insurer. In some situations, especially in the writing of property insurance, the application may be so worded that it is a temporary contract of insurance. As a general rule a contract of insurance does not result until the insurer notifies the prospective insured that his offer has been accepted. Under some exceptional circumstances, however, failure to reject an application for insurance within a reasonable time has been held to be an acceptance. Under some circumstances, several courts have allowed a recovery against an insurer for negligent delay in acting on an application.

Metropolitan Life Insurance Co. v. *Wood*

302 F.2d 802 (9th Cir. 1962)

This was an action by Constance C. Wood (plaintiff) against Metropolitan Life Insurance Company (defendant) to recover, as beneficiary, the proceeds of a life insurance policy. Judgment for Wood and Metropolitan Life Insurance Company appealed. Judgment affirmed.

On January 12, 1959, Jean L. Wood delivered an application for a life insurance policy and a check for the first premium to an agent of Metropolitan Life Insurance Company (Insurance Co.) His wife Constance C. Wood was designated on the application as beneficiary. On January 17, 1959, Wood was examined by Insurance Co.'s physician; later that day he died. Insurance Co. thereafter rejected the application and offered to return the premium.

PER CURIAM. The determination of this issue turns on the proper interpretation of the language of the application. The same language was before this Court in *Metropolitan Life Ins. Co.* v. *Grant.* Relying on *Ransom* v. *Penn Mutual Life Ins. Co.,* we there concluded that under the law of California, an applicant might reasonably construe the language to mean "pay the portion of the premium required in advance and in consideration thereof you will have protection until your application is accepted or rejected." We further concluded on the basis of Ransom that the Supreme Court of California would require any ambiguity in the language to be resolved against the insurance company which drafted it, and would therefore hold that "interim insurance was in force and effect from the time of the receipt by Insurance Co.'s agent of the application and check. . . ." Ransom, as applied in Grant, would appear to be dispositive of this case.

Insurance Co. argues, however, that the decedents in both Ransom and Grant were insurable at the time the applications and premium payments were submitted, whereas, in the present case Mr. Wood concededly was not. Insurance Co. suggests that the rule of Ransom should be limited to situations in which the applicant was insurable when the application was submitted. In Ransom the insurance company sought to avoid liability on the ground that the applicant in that case was in fact an unacceptable risk for the insurance plan for which he had applied when he filed his application. The Supreme Court of California rejected the argument, pointing out that at the time of the applicant's death, the insurance company had not finally determined the applicant was unacceptable. The California Court adopted the rule reflected in the line of cases holding "that the provision to the effect that the insurance shall be in force from the date of the application if the premium is paid gives rise to a contract of insurance immediately upon receipt of the application and payment of the premium, and that the proviso that the company shall be satisfied that the insured was acceptable at the date of the application creates only a right to terminate the contract if the company becomes dissatisfied with the risk before a policy is issued." Under the California rule as reflected in Ransom the insurability of the applicant at the time of application is irrelevant.

Finally, Insurance Co. suggests that neither Ransom nor Grant considered the applicability of Section 10115 of the California Insurance Code, and that this statute imposes liability upon the insurance company in cases such as this only when the insured is actually insurable at the time of application. We need not agree or disagree with Insurance Co.'s construction of Section 10115. The statute imposes liability upon an insurance company in the circumstances described in the statute, but concededly Insurance Co. remained free to assume a greater liability by contract if it wished to do so. The question is simply whether it did so in this case. Our reading of Ransom is that we must hold that it did.

Delivery of Policy

Importance of Delivery of Policy. The delivery of a policy is not a necessary prerequisite to a valid contract of insurance. Whether or not a contract of insurance is completed prior to the delivery of the policy or without the delivery of a policy will depend on the intention of the parties. In the absence of a statute requiring the contract of insurance to be in writing in order to be valid, an oral contract of insurance will be valid; and in such a situation, no policy will be issued, and none can be delivered. The courts have held that the insurance becomes effective when the terms of an unexecuted policy have been accepted by the insured. In some instances the parties may agree that the insurer or its agent will hold the policy until the insured calls for it, in which event the contract of insurance will be completed before delivery of the policy.

In the area of property insurance, when the insured makes application for a designated amount of insurance on specific property, the agent to distribute the risk among several insurers whom he represents, each company becomes liable as soon as the policy is signed, although it is not delivered. In a situation such as this the agent represents the insured in accepting the contract of insurance.

It is generally true, in the absence of an agreement or under special circumstances, that there is no contract of insurance until the delivery of the policy. A provision commonly found in an application for insurance is one that states that the insurance is not effective until the delivery of the policy. If the application contains such a provision, the courts hold that the delivery of the policy is essential to the completion of the contract of insurance. Under some exceptional circumstances the courts have refused to so hold.

When Policy Is Delivered. The courts are not in accord as to just what acts on the part of the insurer will amount to delivery. Most of the courts have held that when the insurer has executed and mailed the policy, it is delivered and that any loss suffered after the policy has been mailed is covered. Under some circumstances the courts have held that the policy is delivered and the insurance is operative when the policy has been completely executed, although it remains in the physical possession of the insurer. In some instances the insurer sends the policy to its local agent for delivery to the insured. If the agent is vested with some discretionary power in regard to delivery, the insurance, as a general rule, will not become operative until the agent has delivered the policy. However, in the field of life insurance, if the application provides that the insurance will not be operative unless the insured is in good health at the time of the delivery of the policy, the courts have held that the insurance becomes operative at the time of the mailing of the policy if the insured is in good health at that time, even though the policy has been mailed to the local agent for personal delivery to the insured. In these cases the courts have held that the agent's duty is merely to explain the policy to the insured and not to determine his "good health."

Summary

The delivery of a policy of insurance is not a necessary prerequisite of a valid contract of insurance.

The courts are not in accord as to when a policy of insurance has been delivered. It will depend, in many instances, on the wording of the application.

Liberty National Life Insurance Co. v. Patterson
175 So.2d 737 (Sup. Ct. Ala. 1965)

This was an action by Opal L. Patterson (plaintiff) against Liberty National Life Insurance Company (defendant) to recover a judgment on a life insurance policy. Judgment for Patterson and Liberty National Life Insurance Company appealed. Judgment affirmed.

On August 21, 1961, Milton C. Patterson made written application for a $10,000 policy to Hughes, agent of Liberty National Life Insurance Company (Insurance Co.). Patterson paid the premium and was given a receipt. The application provided that no insurance would take effect unless and until the policy had been manually delivered to and accepted by Patterson during his lifetime and good health. No medical examination was required. The policy was issued by the home office with the effective date of September 13 and transmitted to the district office. Later it was taken to the Russelville office out of which Hughes worked. Patterson died suddenly of a coronary occlusion on September 17, 1961, before the policy had been delivered to him. Both Insurance Co. and Patterson rely on the declarations in section (2) of the application, which read:

That no insurance shall take effect unless and until the policy has been manually delivered to and accepted by the Owner and the first premium paid during the lifetime and good health of the Proposed Insured (except as provided in the receipt bearing the same number as this application if the full first premium has been paid and acknowledged and such receipt issued).

Section 1 of the receipt provided:

Insurance under the terms of the policy applied for and subject to the limits specified below shall take effect as of: (a) the last date of any medical examination or tests required under the rules and practices of the Company, or (b) the date of this payment, whichever shall be later; provided that on such applicable date the Proposed Insured is in good health and in the opinion of the Company's authorized officers at its Home Office is insurable and acceptable under the rules and practices of the Company as a standard risk for the policy, in the amount and on the plan exactly as applied for.

The receipt did show full payment of the premium, and bore the same number as the application.

MERRILL, JUSTICE.   We have held that a policy that had a provision that it would not be effective until the first premium was paid and the policy delivered to the applicant during her lifetime and in good health was not enforceable when the policy was not delivered during applicant's lifetime, and that there can be no binding delivery of a policy after the death of the insured.

But there is more to the documents issued by Insurance Co. than a requirement of manual delivery. That requirement was subject to the receipt which provided that the "Insurance . . . shall take effect as of: . . . the date of this payment . . . provided that on such applicable date the Proposed Insured is in good health and in the opinion of the Company's authorized officers at its Home Office is insurable and acceptable under the rules and practices of the Company. . . ."

Here, the full premium was paid when the application for insurance was made, and the receipt signed by agent Hughes bore the same number as the application and the home office issued the policy in question and sent it to the district office to be delivered. All of these events occurred prior to the death of the insured.

Insurance Co. raises the point of the lack of authority of agent Hughes to bind the company prior to the manual delivery of the policy to the insured, but that point has been decided in *National Life & Accident Ins. Co.* v. *Claytor,* where it was held that even though there was no evidence of the authority of the soliciting agent to issue a receipt and binder, when the home office accepted the application and issued the policy, it ratified and approved the binder as a temporary contract. So here, when the policy was issued, the actions of agent Hughes had been ratified.

The application in the *Claytor* case contained a provision that "the proposed contract shall not be effective until the policy has been issued and the first premium actually paid and accepted by the company and the policy has been delivered to and accepted by me in my lifetime, and while in good health, . . ." There, the evidence was that the insured had cancer of the lung when the policy was delivered and that he died shortly thereafter, but there was no indication of such affliction when the application was made and the receipt and binder given. This court said:

> It results that the provision in the policy, which we have quoted, that it becomes effective after its delivery to the insured during his lifetime and in good health, must be considered in connection with the temporary binder as soon as the company accepted and approved the application. It was without power under the terms of the binder, after it was approved and accepted, to refuse to deliver the policy to the insured, although he may then be in a state of health which rendered him uninsurable, if at the time when the application was taken and the medical examination made, he was in a state of health then insurable under the contract and made no material false representations or warranties with actual intent to deceive or as to a matter which increased the risk of loss.

In a similar case, the Supreme Court of Georgia said: "As seen above, the provision in the application that the insurance shall become effective only after delivery of the policy and acceptance of the first premium while the insured is in good health is modified by the provisions of the binder receipt which are intended to supersede them to the extent of any conflict. . . ." And further, ". . . The application and receipt must be taken together, and if together they contain all the elements of a contract they are binding upon both parties. . . ."

We hold that the statement in the application that the policy must be delivered manually before the insurance became effective was modified by the reference to the receipt, which receipt made the insurance effective upon the issuance of the policy by the home office, subject to the condition that the insured was in good health when the policy was issued.

Representations and Warranties

Nature of Representations and Warranties. In the law of insurance a distinction is made between concealment, representations, misrepresentations, warranties, and conditions. There is a close relation between concealment, representations, and misrepresentations, and also between warranties and conditions. A concealment is the intentional withholding of any fact material to the risk which the insured, in honesty and good faith, should reveal. In marine insurance the insurer relies to a large degree on the insured's description of the risk, and for this reason any withholding of a fact material to the risk is a concealment and grounds for the avoidance of the contract of insurance.

Representations and misrepresentations have the same effect on the enforceability of an insurance contract as they have on contracts in general. A representation is a statement as to some fact or state of facts relative to the transaction under negotiation. The statement may be as to an existing or past fact, or it may be a promise as to future happenings.

Warranties are statements or promises which become a part of the insurance contract. They may be written in the contract, or they may be incorporated in the contract by reference. If a warranty statement is false, or if a warranty promise is unfulfilled, the contract of insurance is rendered voidable at the election of the insurer, irrespective of the materiality of the statement or promise, and regardless of whether or not the insurer has suffered injury as the result of the breach.

Effect of False Representations. It is the duty of an applicant for insurance to state to the insurer the nature of the risk he wishes to insure and to reveal all of the material facts concerning the risk so that the insurer may determine whether or not he wishes to accept the application and the terms on which he will accept in case he wishes to do so. In marine insurance the insurer generally relies on the statements of the applicant; but in other types of insurance, especially in the United States, the insurer makes an independent investigation; for example, if one wishes to insure his life, a doctor in the employ of the insurer will examine the applicant to determine whether or not he is an insurable risk. However, the applicant is required to describe the risk. This description of the risk may be an oral statement, a written application, or the filling-in of a blank form furnished by the insurer.

If the applicant for insurance conceals any facts which are material to the risk to be insured, or if he intentionally misrepresents a material fact, the concealment or misrepresentation will render the contract of insurance voidable at the election of the insurer. It is immaterial that a false representation is made in the honest belief that it is true. It is the duty of the applicant to give the insurer the information he requests concerning the risk. If this information is incorrect and the insurer accepts the risk in reliance on such incorrect information, the insurer's injury is as great as though the incorrect statement had been made fraudulently. If the statement is not a statement of a material fact, the misstatement will have no effect on the validity of the insurance contract.

If the insurer has prepared a written application form and requests the applicant to fill out such form, the presumption is that the application furnishes the insurer all of the information he desires regarding the risk, and the failure of the applicant to disclose additional facts will not render the contract of insurance voidable unless the applicant fraudulently conceals a material fact which he knows will affect the risks involved.

Effect of False Warranty.   Since a warranty is included in the contract, either as a part of the contract or incorporated by reference, it is generally agreed by the parties to the contract that the warranty is an essential provision of the insurance contract. The warranty is conclusively presumed to be material to the risk assumed by the insurer; and if the statement of warranty is not true in every respect, the insured cannot recover on the insurance contract in the event of a loss.

Construing Representations and Warranties.   In construing representations and warranties, the courts have favored the insured. If a representation is substantially true and there is no evidence of bad faith, the courts, as a general rule, will declare the insurance contract enforceable. In determining whether or not certain statements are warranties, the courts have held the statements to be representations unless it is clear that the parties intended them as warranties. The practice of inserting warranties in contracts of insurance often works hardship on the insured. For example, if the statement that one is of good health and free from disease is included in a life insurance contract as a warranty and it can be shown that the insured was not free from disease at the time the insurance contract was entered into, the insurer can escape liability even though the insured honestly thought he was free from disease and even though an ordinary medical examination would not have revealed the presence of the disease. To avoid such undesirable results, some courts have held that all the insured warranted was his good faith. Some states have remedied the situation by passing statutes which either abolish or modify the doctrine of warranties.

Summary

A representation is a statement made by an applicant for insurance to the insurer relative to the risk to be insured. A warranty is a statement or promise made by the insured and is a part of the insurance contract. If the applicant makes false representations of material facts which are relied on by the insurer, the insurance contract is voidable at the election of the insurer. If the insured makes false warranties, he cannot recover on the insurance contract in the event of a loss.

In construing representations and warranties, the courts have favored the insured. Some courts have held that where the applicant states in an application for life insurance that he is free from diseases listed in the application form, the applicant warrants only his good faith in answering the questions.

Allstate Insurance Co. v. *Meloni*

236 A.2d 402 (Super. Ct. N.J. 1967)

This was an action by Allstate Insurance Co. (plaintiff) against Mr. and Mrs. Vincent Meloni and others (defendants) to have its automobile liability policy declared void on grounds of material misrepresentations made in the application for the policy. The Melonis appealed from judgment for Allstate. Affirmed.

Mrs. Meloni applied to Allstate on April 2, 1965, for insurance on an automobile she had just purchased. On the written application she answered "no" to the question, "With respect to the applicant or any member of his household; . . . Has any license or permit to drive any automobile been revoked, suspended, or refused?" Actually, Mrs. Meloni's husband had had two previous suspensions of his driver's license, once for a point system violation in December, 1962, and the second for failure to maintain proof of financial responsibility in January, 1964. At the time she applied for insurance she told the Allstate representative that she would be the only driver and that her husband did not have a driver's license and would not be driving.

On February 25, 1965, Mr. Meloni was involved in an accident while driving the insured automobile which resulted in the death of a passenger of Meloni and injuries to the driver of the other automobile. While investigating the accident Allstate learned for the first time of the previous suspensions of Vincent Meloni's driver's license, and it then brought this suit to have the policy declared void.

LABRECQUE, JUDGE.   In general, a representation by the insured, whether contained in the policy itself or in the application for insurance, will support the forfeiture of the insured's rights under the policy if it is untruthful, material to the particular risk assumed by the insurer, and actually and reasonably relied upon by the insurer in the issuance of the policy.

Here the untruthfulness of Mrs. Meloni's representation is conceded, but it is contended that she was justified in assuming that the question referred to her driver's license only. The trial judge was not impressed with this contention—nor are we. The wording of the question was clear. It referred to the applicant *or any member of his household.*

The policy also contained a provision as follows:

"11. Effect of Policy Acceptance

"By acceptance of this policy the named insured agrees that the Declarations on the Supplement Page are his agreements and representations, and that this policy embodies all agreements, relating to this insurance, existing between himself and Allstate or any of its agents."

In the absence of proof of fraud or unconscionable conduct on the part of Allstate or its agents, defendants were chargeable with knowledge of the terms and contents of the policy.

The Melonis rely upon the fact that upon receipt of Mrs. Meloni's application, Allstate ordered an investigation by Service Review, Inc., a firm which made confidential investigations for insurance companies. The fact that such an investigation was ordered did not absolve her from speaking the truth nor did it lessen the right of the company to rely upon her statement, unless the investigation disclosed facts sufficient to expose the falsity of the representation made or was of such a nature as to place upon the company the duty of making further inquiry.

The Melonis argue that Service Review's investigation should have been extended to Mr. Meloni and that a copy of his driving record, obtainable from the Division of Motor Vehicles for a nominal fee, would have revealed the truth of the matter. But nothing in the contents of the application or in the subsequent report by Service Review pointed to Mr. Meloni as an actual, or even a potential driver of the insured vehicle. It is conceded that Mrs. Meloni told Froio in April that her husband did not and would not drive the car and had no interest in doing so. She assured Harwood, Service Review's investigator, that "she was the sole driver, . . . her husband had no license and was not interested in driving." Further, he made a "street" investigation which satisfied him that Meloni was not driving the car. We conclude that Allstate's omission to extend its inquiry to Meloni's driving record was not unreasonable in view of Mrs. Meloni's representations.

We are satisfied that the evidence fully supports the implied finding of the trial judge that Allstate reasonably relied upon the representation referred to, and that its right to do so was in no wise lessened by the investigation which was undertaken in its behalf.

Insurable Interest

Nature of Insurable Interest.   Under the laws of all of the states, wagering contracts are illegal. A contract whereby a person insures property in which he has no interest or takes out personal insurance on a person to whom he is in no way related has been held to be a wagering contract and therefore void.

In such a situation the insured does not have an "insurable interest" in the subject matter insured. A person has an insurable interest when he will suffer a loss on the happening of the event insured against. In discussing insurable interest, we must distinguish between property insurance and personal insurance. In the field of property insurance the purpose of the insurance is to indemnify against a loss which will be of such a nature that it can be expressed in terms of dollar values. In personal insurance, there is an element of indemnity, especially in health and accident insurance; but the indemnity element is of minor importance. We do not attempt to value human life. Life insurance is more of an investment than indemnification against loss. In the field of property insurance, if one has such an interest in the thing insured that he will suffer a loss if it is destroyed or injured, he can insure against the loss, the amount of the insurance being limited by the value of the interest to be protected.

Another important difference between property insurance and personal insurance concerns the time at which the insurable interest must exist. The insurable interest in property must exist at the time of the loss, whereas the insurable interest in personal insurance must exist at the time the insurance contract is entered into. This difference is due to the difference in the nature of the insurance. Property insurance is indemnity insurance; and if the insured has no interest in the property at the time of its injury or destruction, he has suffered no loss. Life insurance is an investment; the event, especially with regard to life insurance, is certain to happen, and so it is logical to determine the insurable interest at the time the contract of insurance is entered into.

Insurable Interest in Property Insurance. A person who has the legal title to property has an insurable interest in the property. It is not necessary that the title carry with it the right to present possession enjoyment. A person who has a reversionary interest in property has an insurable interest, but an heir who has only an expectancy does not have an insurable interest, irrespective of how certain it may be that he will not be cut off. A person who has an equitable title or a lien on property, such as a mortgage, a mechanic's lien, or an execution lien, has an insurable interest; but a general creditor does not. A bailee or one holding property in trust, or a sheriff who has levied execution on property and has it in his possession, has an insurable interest. It has been held that a mortgagor who has sold the mortgaged property to a purchaser who has assumed and agreed to pay the mortgage debt still has an insurable interest in the property because in the event the purchaser defaults and the property will not sell for the amount of the mortgage debt, the mortgagor will be personally liable. The property insured need not be in existence at the time the insurance contract is entered into, but the insurance will not be valid until the property is acquired. The insuring of stocks of goods for resale when the value of the stock fluctuates is a typical example of the insurance of goods not in existence at the time the insurance contract is entered into.

Losses of profits and interests closely akin to profits may be insured. Football games, fairs, etc., are insured against rain and similar hazards which affect the profits of the venture.

Insurable Interest in Personal Insurance.   Personal insurance such as health and accident insurance is, as a general rule, taken out by the insured and not by any other person. If A should take out accident insurance on B, making the proceeds of the policy payable to A, such an insurance contract would be against public policy and would therefore be void. An accident or health insurance contract entered into by an employer, the benefits of the policy being made payable to an employee, would, as a general rule, be enforceable, especially if the employee consented to the arrangement.

Life insurance contracts may be divided into two groups—those taken out by the insured on his own life for his own benefit or for the benefit of named beneficiary, and those taken out on the life of another. A person has an insurable interest in his own life, and the generally accepted rule is that the beneficiary need have no insurable interest in the life of the insured. With regard to an insurable interest in the life of another, one test is whether the party who takes out the insurance has a bona fide desire and interest that the life insured shall continue to its natural end. Under this test, pecuniary interest has played an important part. If the party who takes out the insurance is dependent on the insured for support and care, it is strong evidence of an insurable interest. Relationship is another test. Close blood relationship is held by some courts to be sufficient, while other courts have required some interest in addition to mere relationship. Relationship by marriage, except husband and wife, will not, standing alone, create an insurable interest.

A creditor may insure his debtor's life for the purpose of protecting his debt, the principal question in such cases being the amount of insurance allowable. No satisfactory test for determining such amount has been adopted, the courts being content with the rule that the amount of the insurance must not greatly exceed the amount of the debt. A corporation may insure the life of its officers, and a partner may insure the life of his partner. In these commercial cases the element of indemnity is more prominent, and the amount of the insurance must not greatly exceed the interest insured.

Summary

An accident or health insurance policy taken out by A on B, payable to A, is against public policy and void. Under some circumstances an employer, with the consent of the employees, may take out accident and health insurance on such employees if the benefits are payable to the employees.

A contract of insurance is void for illegality unless the insured has an insurable interest in the subject matter insured. In a contract of property insurance the insured must have such an interest in the property insured that he will suffer a loss on the happening of the event insured against. In a contract of personal insurance the insured must bear such a relation to the person insured that he will benefit by the continued existence of that person.

Atlantic Insurance Co. v. Massey
381 F.2d 520 (10th Cir. 1967)

This was an action by Bill Massey and Fireman's Fund Insurance Co. (plaintiffs) against Atlantic Insurance Co. Judgment for Massey and Fireman's Fund. Atlantic appealed. Affirmed as to Massey, reversed as to Fireman's Fund.

Massey contracted with a builder to build him a home for $26,000. The builder took out a builder's risk policy with Fireman's Fund which provided that "where any other valid and collectible insurance exists . . . this insurance shall not apply or contribute to the payment of any loss until the amount due from all such other insurance shall have been exhausted."

Prior to completion of the home, Massey got permission from the contractor to move in, and he was issued a homeowner's policy by Atlantic before he moved. Three days after Massey moved and while the house was still under construction, it was heavily damaged by an explosion and fire. Fireman's Fund paid the contractor $14,223, which amount was applied to the contract price due from Massey. Massey then purchased the remains of the structure from the contractor and had it rebuilt. Massey assigned to Fireman's Fund his claim against Atlantic for refusal to pay on the policy. The Masseys had done work on the house themselves and contended that they had suffered an additional loss of $1,250, for which they brought suit against Atlantic. Fireman's Fund, as assignee of the Masseys, sued Atlantic for the $14,223 it had paid on the loss, claiming that its policy, by its terms, was excess insurance and therefore it had no liability.

HILL, CIRCUIT JUDGE. Atlantic contends: That, as a matter of law, the insurable interest of a builder and the owner are separate and distinct; that it had no legal duty, under the facts presented, to reimburse Fireman's; that if an assignment from Masseys to Fireman's did take place, such assigned right could not exceed the Masseys' insurable interest; and that the granting of the summary judgment was error because a genuine issue as to the facts existed concerning the alleged assignment. We are compelled to agree generally with Atlantic.

The Masseys and the contractors each had an insurable interest in the property damaged by the explosion and fire and each had an insurance policy covering such insurable interest. Their policies could not, obviously, cover more than their respective insurable interests. In the agreement between the contractors and Masseys, it is specifically provided that title to the house shall remain in the contractors until it is completed. Fireman's Fund argues that the house was completed, but we certainly do not agree. We are thus forced to reach the inescapable conclusion that the contractors' insurable interest in the house at the time of the loss was the value of the labor and materials they had put into it. That interest suffered a loss of

$14,222.78. Masseys' interest was the amount they had put into the house during the process of construction, over and above the expenditures of the contractor. That interest suffered a loss of $1,182.05.

Atlantic issued a binding contract of insurance to Masseys which covered their insurable interest and the trial court rendered judgment in favor of Masseys and against Atlantic for the amount of loss to that interest. We think this part of the judgment was proper. The "excess coverage" clause of Fireman's policy cannot apply because the two policies did not cover the same insurable interest and were issued to different insureds. Firemen's Fund then seeks to ground their case against Atlantic on an alleged oral assignment from Masseys to Fireman's of Masseys' legal rights against Atlantic. We have pointed out that there is no evidence in this record to sustain a finding on this point under a motion for summary judgment. Even if such a finding could be upheld, it would not sustain the judgment rendered in favor of Fireman's. Masseys had no legal rights against Atlantic beyond the amount of loss to their insurable interest, which is now fully satisfied by a part of the judgment, and Masseys had nothing more to assign.

Notice and Proof of Loss

Notice of Loss. The insured is required to give the insurer notice of loss in order to afford him an opportunity to investigate and thus protect himself from fraud and imposition. The parties may stipulate in the insurance contract that notice of loss shall be given within a stated time after the loss occurs and that failure to give notice of loss within such time shall preclude recovery. The courts will enforce such a provision provided the time so fixed is not unreasonably short. A provision in a policy of health and accident insurance requiring the giving of notice of illness or injury within 10 days of its inception or occurrence was held to be reasonable. Some states have enacted statutes regulating the giving of notice and the furnishing of proof of loss.

Under the provisions of some insurance policies notice that is required to be given is expressed in such terms as "prompt," "immediate," "forthwith," or "as soon as possible." The courts have held that such provisions impose on the insured a duty to give notice within a reasonable time. In determining what is a reasonable time for giving notice the nature of the thing insured is important. In personal injury cases covered by automobile liability insurance, in theft of small, yet valuable articles and in similar cases, it is important that the insurer have prompt notice in order that he may seasonably take steps to protect his interests.

Proof of Death, Sickness, or Accident. The beneficiary under a life insurance policy must prove the death of the insured. Usually, the insurer, on notice of the death of the insured, will send the beneficiary a proof-of-death form to be filled out and returned. A certified copy of the death certificate filed in the office which keeps the records of vital statistics may be required.

Health and accident policies, if indemnity policies, usually provide that the insured shall send to the insurer the receipted bills of the attending physician and the hospital. Under the terms of some health and accident policies the attending physician and the hospital send their bills directly to the insurer.

In both life insurance and health and accident insurance, the failure to file proof of loss in substantial compliance with the terms of the policy and within a reasonable time will relieve the insurer from liability. The filing of proof is a condition, and the failure to comply with the condition terminates the insurer's obligation.

Proof of Loss Required in Property Insurance. The standard fire insurance policy provides that proof of loss must be made within 60 days of the giving of notice. It also sets out in detail the duties of the insured in regard to the proof of loss. Sworn statements of loss may be required. Under the terms of some policies the rendering of the proof of loss within the time stated is made a condition, and failure to comply with this condition will relieve the insurer from his obligation. Under the terms of other policies the failure to file the required proof of loss suspends the insurer's duty to pay until such time as proper proof of loss is filed.

In other types of property insurance the time for filing proof of loss and the nature of the proof required will be set out in the policy. To recover for the loss, the insured must substantially comply with the requirements of the policy.

Summary

The insurer requires notice of loss for his own protection. The time within which notice of loss must be given and the content of the notice are usually stated in the contract of insurance.

The insured bears the burden of proving that he has suffered a loss, and the death of the insured must be proven. The time within which proof of loss or death must be made and the type of proof required are usually set out in the contract of insurance.

In property insurance the requirements for proof of loss are usually set out in the policy. Sixty days is the standard time allowed for making proof of loss in fire insurance policies.

Lindus v. Northern Insurance Co. of New York

438 P.2d 311 (Sup. Ct. Ariz. 1968)

This is an action by Roger Lindus through his guardian (plaintiff) as judgment creditor of insured against Northern Insurance Company of New York and The Travelers Insurance Company (defendants). Judgment for the insurers and Lindus appealed. Reversed.

Roger Lindus, a 12-year old student at the Orme Ranch School, was seriously injured in an accident which resulted when another student was pouring gasoline into the carburetor of an automobile. William Nelson, a third student at the school switched on the ignition and attempted to start the engine. The engine backfired and the can of gasoline was ignited. The boy pouring the gasoline threw it away to avoid being burned and it struck and critically burned Lindus, who was walking nearby.

Lindus recovered a judgment for $92,500 against Nelson but Northern and The Travelers, Nelson's insurers, both refused to defend the suit or to pay the judgment. Their defense was lack of notice. Travelers was not notified of the accident for 17 months and Northern for two years after the accident.

BERNSTEIN, JUSTICE.   The issue for our determination is whether the insured's two-year delay in notifying Northern of the accident and his delay of seventeen months in notifying Travelers, his automobile liability insurer, is a good defense when notice is made an express condition precedent to liability under the policies. We have held in the past that an insurance company is not relieved of its contractual liability because of the insured's failure to give notice unless it can show that it has been prejudiced thereby. However, in that case the policy did not include a specific forfeiture clause.

The California court, on the other hand, in dealing with a similar case has held that an insurance company cannot prevail on its defense of lack of notice unless they can show prejudice even where notice is made an express condition precedent in the policy.

Moreover, the burden of proving prejudice is on the insurance company.

In the case at bar the trial court found that both Northern and Travelers had been prejudiced but the only fact relied on to reach that conclusion, as shown in the record, was the insured's delay in giving notice of the accident. The record indicates, however, that all of the investigative reports would have been made available to both insurers, and that Lindus was perfectly willing to aid them in any further investigation they wished to pursue. We conclude therefore, that in the instant case Northern and Travelers failed to show *actual* prejudice.

Moreover, we cannot assume that an eighteen-year-old boy would know that he was an additional insured under a family motor vehicle liability policy; that the automobile involved, although not the family car, was covered by this policy; and that he might be liable for negligence when Phillippi threw the gasoline can which injured Lindus. Under our holding in *Carpenter* v. *Superior Court,* the burden is on the insurer to either show that an additional insured knew of the policy and its conditions, or that they made a reasonable effort to apprise the insured of the extent and conditions of the policy. In the instant case the insurance companies failed to prove this fact.

Termination and Lapse

Nature of Termination and Lapse.   A contract of insurance is terminated when the insurer has the power to extinguish all rights under the policy and has exercised that power. A policy has lapsed when it is permitted to expire either by the running of the term of the policy, by the failure of the insured to pay premiums, or by some other similar default on the part of the insured. The ground on which one of the parties may terminate the policy or the circumstances under which a policy will lapse depend on whether the policy is one of personal insurance or property insurance.

Termination of Contract of Personal Insurance. The nature of life insurance is such that it cannot be terminated at the option of the insurer. If the insurer were permitted to terminate such insurance, he could do so at a time when the insured had become too old to acquire other insurance, or when the risk had increased materially, or when it had become obvious that a loss would have to be paid. Such action on the part of the insurer would amount to fraud of the insured.

A policy of health and accident insurance may be terminated by the insurer if the policy limits the coverage to a defined occupation and the insured accepts employment in an occupation which does not come within the scope of the defined occupation. Since some health and accident insurance policies are cancelable and some are not, the insurer's right to terminate such policies will depend on the terms of the policy. If the insurer has been induced to enter into an insurance contract in reliance on the misrepresentation of the insured, the insurer may terminate the policy if seasonable action is taken.

It is common practice of insurers in the field of life insurance to put an "incontestable clause" in the policy. Such a clause provides that the policy cannot be contested after a stated period of time except for nonpayment of premiums. The time within which an insurer may terminate a contract of life insurance for misrepresentation and fraud is fixed by statute in most states. These statutes differ from the usual statutes of limitation on actions in deceit in that the action to terminate the contract of life insurance must be brought within the stipulated time from the date of the issuance of the policy, whereas the usual statute of limitation provides that the action must be brought within the statutory period from the time the fraud is discovered or, in the exercise of due diligence, should have been discovered.

If the insured wishes, he may terminate life insurance at any time by surrendering the policy to the insurer. On the surrender of the policy the insured is entitled to the "cash surrender value" of his policy. As a general rule the insured has the privilege under the terms of his policy to take either paid-up insurance or extended insurance. If he takes paid-up insurance, he will be issued a paid-up policy of life insurance for such amount of insurance as the cash surrender value of his policy will purchase at his age. If he takes extended insurance, he will be issued a term policy for the original amount, the length of the term being determined by the cash surrender value of his policy.

Lapse of Contract of Personal Insurance. Contracts of personal insurance, with some exceptions, are not written for a stipulated period of time. This is particularly true of life insurance. The standard form of a personal insurance contract provides that the insurance shall continue in force as long as the insured pays a stipulated premium at designated times.

If the insured fails to pay the premiums on his policy, the policy will lapse. By statute, the insured is given 30 days after the premium falls due in which to pay. The mailing of a check for the premium on the 30th day after the due date has been held to be sufficient to satisfy the requirements. However, if the check is not honored when presented for payment, the policy will lapse. If the insured permits his policy to lapse for nonpayment of premiums, he will have the same privilege of election as when he surrenders his policy. He may elect to take either the cash surrender value, paid-up insurance, or extended insurance. As a general rule, life insurance policies provide that in the event the policy is permitted to lapse for nonpayment of premiums and the insured does not make an election within a stated time, the provision for extended insurance shall be effective.

Termination of Standard Property Insurance.   Contracts of property insurance insure a risk, the happening of which is uncertain, and are written for a definite period of time, and they terminate at the expiration of the time stipulated in the policy of insurance. It is customary to define the term of the policy with a high degree of definiteness, such as, for instance, at noon C.S.T., June 15, 1971. Either party may terminate a property or casualty policy by giving the other party notice. Under existing statutes, if the insurer elects to terminate a policy, he must give the insured five days' notice. Under the terms of the revised New York standard policy the notice must be in writing. If the insurer terminates the policy, he must return the unearned portion of the premium. The insured may terminate the policy at any time by surrendering his policy. If the insured terminates the policy, he is entitled to the return of premiums paid on the "short-rate" basis, that is, the premiums for the time the policy has been in force are computed at a rate slightly higher than for the full term of the policy, and the overplus is returned to the insured.

Termination by Increase of Risk.   A contract of property insurance will be terminated if the insured does anything which materially increases the risks insured. The policy of property insurance customarily provides that if the insured, by his acts, materially increases the risk, the insurer's liability shall terminate. The policy will, in addition to such general clause, contain clauses which will state specifically that certain acts on the part of the insured shall terminate the insurer's liability. Acts which are customarily prohibited by such clauses are generating illuminating gas on the premises, keeping on the premises explosives and inflammable substances, and allowing the premises to remain vacant or unoccupied for a stated period. Also, if any portion of the building collapses, the insurance terminates.

Special Provisions in Contracts of Property Insurance. If the property insured consists of a stock of goods for resale, the policy must contain an "iron safe clause" which provides that the insured must take an inventory once a year, that he must keep a set of books showing all sales, both cash and credit, and that the inventory and books must be kept in a fireproof safe or other place not exposed to danger. The courts are not in accord as to the effect of the violation of such a provision of the policy. Some of the courts hold that the violation of such a provision terminates the policy *in toto*. Most of the courts hold that the liability of the insurer is suspended during such time as the prohibited condition exists. For example, suppose Abbott insures his house against fire with the Bond Insurance Company. The policy provides that if the house is vacant or unoccupied beyond a period of 10 days, the insurer shall not be liable for loss occurring. Abbott's house is vacant and unoccupied for a period of 15 days. Thereafter, it is again occupied, and while occupied, it is damaged by fire. Under the minority rule, Abbott could not recover because the house had been vacant and unoccupied for a period in excess of that permitted by the policy, thus causing the policy to lapse. Under the majority rule the policy would be in effect during the first 10 days the house remained vacant and unoccupied, but would not be in effect during the succeeding 5 days. However the policy would again become effective as soon as the house was again occupied. In order to take care of such a situation, it is customary to attach a rider, known as a "vacancy rider," on a policy during the time a building is vacant. Any other provision of an insurance policy may be waived by the attachment of a rider or by any other act of the insurer which indicates his intention to relinquish his rights under the provision.

Summary

A contract of insurance is terminated when one of the parties cancels the contract. A contract of insurance is permitted to lapse when the insured fails to take some action necessary to keep the contract in force.

As a general rule the insurer cannot terminate a contract of personal insurance except for misrepresentation or fraud. The time within which the insurer has the right to terminate a contract of personal insurance for misrepresentation or fraud is limited either by the terms of the policy or by statute. The insured is usually given the right to terminate a contract of personal insurance at his election. If the insured fails to pay the premiums on personal insurance, the contract will lapse.

The standard contract of property insurance is written for a specific term, and it terminates on the expiration of the term. If the insured increases the risk insured by a contract of property insurance, the contract is either terminated or suspended. Usually, the provisions of the policy cover the rights of the parties in the event of increase of the risk. A contract of property insurance will, as a general rule, contain special provisions and will stipulate that the violation of these provisions will relieve the insurer from his liability on the policy.

American Mercury Insurance Co. v. Inland-Western Finance Co.
433 P.2d 60 (Ct. App. Ariz. 1967)

This was an action by Inland-Western Finance Company (plaintiff) against American Mercury Insurance Company (defendant) on a mortgage clause of a policy covering an aircraft destroyed by fire. Summary judgment for Inland-Western and American Mercury appealed. Affirmed.

Edwin Widmer purchased an airplane on a conditional sales contract which was assigned to Inland-Western with a balance of $16,300 owing. American Mercury later issued to Widmer an insurance policy on the airplane. The policy contained a breach of warranty endorsement, for which an additional premium had been paid, which provided that,

Coverage as to the interest therein of the mortgage ONLY, shall not be invalidated by any act, omission or neglect of the insured which will constitute a breach of warranty or policy condition; PROVIDED, that in the event the insured shall fail to pay any premium due, the mortgagee shall, on demand, pay the same. . . .

In the event of any material change in or cancellation of this policy ten (10) days written notice will be mailed to the above of such change or cancellation.

Widmer failed to pay the March 23, 1964 premium on time and American Mercury sent a cancellation notice to Widmer and a copy to Inland-Western. The notice said the policy would be cancelled on April 16 if the premium was not sent by that time. This premium was sent within the specified time but the next payment two weeks later was also delinquent. Similar notices were sent, and again the payment was made within the grace period. However, the next premium was also delinquent and it was never made. The notice, copy of which went to the mortgagee, Inland-Western, stated that the policy would be cancelled on May 30 unless payment was made prior to that date. In the notice was the statement: "If we have already received this payment, or if we receive it before the effective date of this cancellation, *your policy will be continued in force without any interruption of your protection.* If this cancellation takes effect, you can again have insurance by: . . ." On October 17, 1964, the aircraft was totally destroyed.

Upon refusal of American Mercury to pay any part of the loss Inland-Western brought suit.

STEVENS, JUDGE.   The issue presented to this Court is whether the copy of the notice to the insured of possible future cancellation of the insurance policy is a sufficient demand for payment upon the mortgagee named in the breach of warranty endorsement so that the insurance company, since no premium was received, could effectively cancel, without any further action, the breach of warranty endorsement as well as the underlying policy of insurance?

American Mercury contends that the copy of the notice of possible future cancellation sent to Inland-Western was a sufficient demand for payment and notice of cancellation under the terms of the breach of warranty endorsement. With this contention we do not agree.

This is not a case wherein there was no duty to inform because of a lack of contractual relationship. The breach of warranty endorsement, in the form of a standard union mortgage clause, constituted a separate contract between American Mercury and Inland-Western.

An insurer's right to cancel a policy containing a standard mortgagee clause on the mortgagee's failure, on demand, to pay premiums can be exercised only after strict compliance by the insurer with the terms of the agreement between the insurer and the mortgagee.

The notice of cancellation mailed out by American Mercury did not meet the requirement of strict compliance. The notice did not demand payment of the premium by Inland-Western. It was directed to Mr. Widmer with a notation that a copy was being sent to Inland-Western and it merely stated that the policy would be cancelled at a future date if the premium was not paid. Under the terms of the endorsement, Inland-Western was entitled to a specific demand for payment. Furthermore, there was a failure to comply with the provision of the endorsement entitling Inland-Western to 10 days' notice of cancellation of the policy. A notice of possible future cancellation in 10 days did not suffice as the endorsement clearly requires that 10 days' notice be given if the policy is cancelled. The wording of the endorsement requires after-the-fact notification, not before-the-fact notification.

Assignment of Contract of Insurance

Assignment of Personal Insurance. A contract is assignable only when its performance can be rendered by the promisor to the assignee without materially altering or increasing the burden of performance. Any contract which is personal in nature, however, cannot be assigned; and a contract is personal in nature if its performance involves the personal skill, judgment, or character of the promisor. Applying this test to contracts of personal insurance, the courts have held that the standard type of life insurance contract is assignable. By the terms of such a policy the insured pays a set premium and requires the insurer to pay a sum certain on the happening of an event which is certain to happen. The assignment of such a contract does not impose on the insurer any additional burden of performance. The parties to a contract, otherwise assignable, may by agreement, however, prevent or limit its assignment.

If a life insurance contract provides that the insurer will, on the happening of the stipulated event, pay the proceeds of the policy to a named beneficiary, the insured cannot change the name of the beneficiary or assign the policy unless he has reserved the right to change the name of the beneficiary, in which case he may assign the policy. And even though he has reserved the right to change the name of the beneficiary and to assign the policy, if the policy provides that the insurer will not be bound by any change in the named beneficiary or by any assignment of the policy unless the insured gives the insurer notice of such change or assignment by filling out and filing with the insurer a prescribed form of notice, any attempt to change the beneficiary or to make an assignment of the policy will be void, as against the beneficiary and the insurer, until the prescribed form of notice is filed with the insurer.

As a general rule, if a policy of personal insurance is assignable, it may be assigned to whomever the insured may wish to assign it. However, if the assignment is made to a person who has no insurable interest in the life of the insured, and if the assignment is not a bona fide transaction but is made for the purpose of accomplishing an illegal purpose, that is, of permitting the assignee of the policy to wager on the length of the life of the insured, the assignment will be void.

Assignment of Property Insurance.   One of the important risk elements in property insurance is the character of the person who is contracting for the insurance. This personal element in the contract relation between the insured and the insurer makes the contract of property insurance nonassignable. If the insured were permitted to assign a contract of property insurance without the consent of the insurer, the insured could materially alter the risks assumed by the insurer without his consent. If the owner of property on which a fire insurance policy has been issued sells the property, the purchaser acquires no interest in the policy. If the insurer is notified of the sale and consents to the transfer of the insurance policy to the purchaser, most of the courts treat the transaction as a novation, that is, a new contract results between the purchaser and the insurer.

After a loss has been suffered, the insured may assign the benefits accruing to him under the contract of insurance. It has been held that the insured may assign a fire insurance policy as security for a debt. Such an assignment gives the assignee the right to any money which may become due to the insured as the result of a loss suffered. The courts upholding such an assignment do so on the ground that there is no change in the ownership of the insured property and, consequently, no change in the risk. The same rule is generally applied when the insured property is mortgaged and the policy of property insurance is assigned to the mortgagee, as his interest may appear.

Summary

The rules of law relative to the assignment of contracts apply to the assignment of contracts of insurance. A contract of life insurance is assignable unless the contract contains provisions denying the insured the right to assign or limiting his right to assign. As a general rule a life insurance policy is so drafted that an assignment is not valid against the beneficiary or the insurer unless the beneficiary has consented to the assignment and the insurer has been given notice of the assignment on forms supplied by the insurer.

A contract of property insurance is not assignable without the consent of the insurer.

Problem Cases

1. Mutual Co. was soliciting membership in its association. Each member was to pay a $10 membership fee, $2 per year dues, and $1 on the death of a member of the division. The beneficiary of such member was to receive as many dollars as there were members in his division, not to exceed $5,000. Was Mutual Co. engaged in the insurance business?

2. Wright signed an application for a $10,000 life insurance policy with double indemnity for accidental death. Pilot Life's agent issued Wright a "conditional receipt" showing his advance premium payment. It stated that if the application were approved without restriction the insurance would be in effect "from the date of this application." The reverse side of the printed form of the receipt was for signature by those, unlike Wright, who did not pay an advance premium. It stated, "Although the agent has explained to me how I may make settlement under this application, thereby placing it immediately in full force and effect . . . provided that I am insurable, it is not my desire to take advantage of this opportunity." Within the period covered by the prepaid premium Wright was killed in an accident. Is Pilot Life liable on the risk?

3. Marshall signed an application and paid an initial premium on an accidental injury policy sold by an agent of Life and Casualty Co. The agent assured him that the coverage went into effect immediately and that there was no problem about the company accepting it because no physical examination was required. The application provided "Policy hereby applied for will not take effect until it is issued by the Company . . . and the Company is not bound by any knowledge of, or statements made by, or to any agent, unless set forth herein." It also stated, ". . . Accidents incurred before date of issue of the policy by the Company . . . ARE NOT INSURED." Marshall signed below a statement that he had read the application and that he understood the first statement, it having been read to him by the agent. Life and Casualty Co. refuses to pay benefits. Marshall claims that he has a valid agreement for temporary insurance. Is he correct?

4. Mrs. Hardy purchased an automobile on March 1, 1962 on an installment purchase contract and authorized application for credit life insurance to secure the balance due. The purchase was jointly in the names of Mr. Hardy, who was then a terminal cancer patient in a veterans' hospital, and Mrs. Hardy. Mr. Hardy was listed as the insured in the policy, which was to be effective until March 1, 1965. The top of the insurance certificate bore the following statement:

> "This certificate is null and void unless the insured is between the ages of 18 and 65 and in good health on the effective date hereof."

The automobile salesman, who also served as agent of the insurance company had sold the Hardys another auto a year earlier and at that time took the installment sales contract to the hospital for Mr. Hardy to sign. He did not inquire as to Mr. Hardy's health at the time of the 1962 purchase.

Mr. Hardy died on May 8, 1962 and the insurer refused payment, claiming that Hardy was not in good health when the policy was issued. Is the insurer liable on the policy?

5. Alderson purchased a mobile home and executed a security agreement on it to Credit Corp. to secure a note. The note was further secured by a life insurance policy on Alderson's life with Credit Corp. listed as beneficiary. Alderson sold the mobile home to Kincaid who agreed to pay the unpaid balance to Credit Corp. Alderson died and the insurer paid the balance of the note to Credit Corp. Kincaid claims that since the note has been paid, he is entitled to a bill of sale to the mobile home. Credit Corp. argues that it, but not Kincaid, has an insurable interest in Alderson's life. Is it correct?

6. Mrs. Dennison purchased from Liberty National a $1,500 life insurance policy on the life of the two-year-old daughter of her husband's sister. Mrs. Dennison was listed as beneficiary. A few months later the girl died from poisoning and Mrs. Dennison was convicted of murder. Weldon, the girl's father, sued Liberty National for negligence in issuing the policy to one who had no insurable interest. In the trial court judgment was given Weldon in the amount of $75,000. Liberty National appealed, claiming that Mrs. Dennison did have an insurable interest and that it had no duty to use care to avoid issuing the policy to one not having such an interest. Is Liberty National correct?

7. Radio Foods Corp. suffered a small fire which activated the sprinkler system causing water to seep through the floor to the premises of Salvage Shoe Co. below. Adjusters of Radio Foods' and Salvage Shoe's insurance carriers examined the premises. The day following the fire an attorney for an insurer of Salvage Shoe wrote a letter requesting Radio Foods not to move or affect the condition of a large refrigerator whose compressor had ignited at the time of the fire, but nothing was said in the letter or in various conversations between Salvage Shoe personnel or their insurers and Radio Foods managers suggesting that Radio Foods employees had been negligent. More than four months later the attorney wrote another letter, in which he did claim that the fire resulted from negligence. This letter was forwarded to the agent of the company carrying the fire insurance for Radio Foods, who returned it. A few days later a complaint was served on Radio Foods, which then promptly sent all papers to the agent of Consolidated Mutual, Radio Foods' liability insurer. The liability insurer denies liability because of failure to notify it "as soon as practicable." Is this defense good?

8. Mrs. Fleischer was riding with her friend, Mrs. Cooper, when contact occurred between the Cooper car and another which cut across the path of the Cooper car after weaving in and out of traffic. No damage was done to either car, but Mrs. Cooper phoned the police because of the way the other car had been operated. When the police inquired about injuries Mrs. Fleischer complained of nausea, a headache and said her ankle hurt. The two friends continued to see each other intermittently and Mrs. Fleischer made no further reference to an injury. Mrs. Cooper gave no notice to her insurer of the incident until she received notice to defend a lawsuit brought by Mrs. Fleischer nearly two years later. The insurer claimed coverage was forfeited by failure to give notice as required by the policy "as soon as practicable." Mrs. Cooper claims she gave notice as soon as practicable. Is Mrs. Cooper correct?

9. Duckworth owned a farm dwelling subject to a mortgage. He insured it with Peoples Insurance Co. The policy provided that Insurance Co. should not be liable for any loss or damage occurring while the building was vacant or unoccupied beyond 10 days without written endorsement attached to the policy. It further provided that the interest of the mortgagee should not be invalidated by the occupation of the premises for purposes more hazardous than permitted by the policy, but if Insurance Co. should be required to pay the mortgagee for a loss under the policy that it should be subrogated to all rights of the mortgagee.

   Duckworth's tenant moved out on May 30 and the house was destroyed by fire on July 7. Insurance Co. had not been notified nor had a vacancy endorsement been added to the policy. Insurance Co. paid the mortgagee but refused to pay Duckworth and claimed it was subrogated to the mortgagee's security rights. Can Duckworth recover from Insurance Co.?

10. Ewing's automobile was being driven by his daughter when it collided almost head-on with an automobile being driven by Pugh and it was seriously damaged. Ewing was insured with Equity Mutual and had $50 deductible collision coverage. The automobile was repaired and Ewing signed a release which stated the amount of settlement, ($1,229 less the $50 deductible) and which subrogated Equity Mutual to all rights and causes of action arising out of the damage to the automobile. After the car was repaired Ewing returned it a number of times to the repair shop which had done the work but was dissatisfied. One of his complaints was that the automobile could not be "lined up," resulting in excessive wear on the tires. Ewing sued Pugh, asserting damage of $2,300, pleading payment of $1,179 and assignment of that amount only to Equity Mutual, and asked for $1,150. Pugh defends on grounds that Equity Mutual rather than Ewing is the real party in interest. Is Pugh correct?

chapter 44. Bankruptcy

Background

Bankruptcy Laws in the United States. The framers of the Constitution of the United States gave the federal government the right to regulate and control bankruptcies. This power was first exercised in 1800, when Congress passed a bankruptcy act. Our present federal Bankruptcy Act is the act of 1898 as amended. The act has been amended many times since it was first enacted, but its general plan has not been changed by the amendments. In the United States, Congress has restudied our bankruptcy legislation following each major depression, and many new features have been added to the Bankruptcy Act of 1898 since the depression of 1929. The principal additions are the provisions for railroad reorganizations, corporate reorganizations, municipal debt readjustments, agricultural compositions and extensions, and compositions and extensions.

Purpose and Scope of Bankruptcy Act. The purpose of the Bankruptcy Act is (1) to protect creditors from one another, (2) to protect creditors from their debtors, and (3) to protect the honest debtor from his creditors. To accomplish these objectives, the debtor is required to make a full disclosure of all his property and to surrender it to the trustee. Provisions are made for examination of the debtor and for punishment of the debtor who refuses to make an honest disclosure and surrender of his property. The trustee of the bankrupt's estate administers, liquidates, and distributes the proceeds of the estate to the creditors. Provisions are made for the determination of creditors' rights, the recovery of preferential payments, and the disallowance of preferential liens and encumbrances. If the bankrupt has been honest in his business transactions and in his bankruptcy proceedings, he is granted a discharge.

Bankrupts

Voluntary Bankruptcy. Under the provisions of our federal Bankruptcy Act a debtor may be adjudged bankrupt on his own petition, in which case he is known as a voluntary bankrupt. Under the earlier bankruptcy statutes, there were no provisions which permitted a person to be adjudged a voluntary bankrupt. These earlier statutes permitted only persons engaged in business to be adjudged bankrupt and then only on the petition of their creditors.

Under the present Bankruptcy Act, any person, partnership, or corporation, with few exceptions, may be adjudged a voluntary bankrupt after filing a petition asking that such judgment be rendered. The person, partnership, or corporation asking to be adjudged bankrupt need not be insolvent at the time of the filing of the petition. Such action must, however, be taken in good faith and not for the purpose of using bankruptcy as a means of perpetrating a fraud. Municipal, railroad, insurance, and banking corporations and building and loan associations are excepted from the operation of the Bankruptcy Act, since other statutes have been enacted which provide for the handling of the affairs of such corporations and associations in the event of their insolvency.

Involuntary Bankrupts. A debtor may, if he has committed an act of bankruptcy, be adjudged an involuntary bankrupt on the petition of his creditors. Under the provisions of the Bankruptcy Act an involuntary petition may be filed against any natural person, except a wage earner or farmer, and any moneyed, business, or commercial corporation, except a building and loan association, a municipal, railroad, insurance, or banking corporation, owing debts amounting to $1,000 or more and having committed an act of bankruptcy within four months before the filing of the petition. The petition may be filed in the federal district court having jurisdiction over the party involved.

Acts of bankruptcy by a person shall consist of having (1) concealed, removed, or permitted to be concealed or removed any part of his property, with intent to hinder, delay or defraud his creditors or any of them, or made or suffered a transfer of any of his property, fraudulent under section 67 or 70 of this act; or (2) made or suffered a preferential transfer as defined in subdivision of section 60 of this act; or (3) suffered or permitted, while insolvent, any creditor to obtain a lien upon any of his property through legal proceedings or distraint and not having vacated or discharged such lien within 30 days from the date thereof or at least 5 days before the day set for any sale or other disposition of such property; or (4) made a general assignment for the benefit of his creditors; or (5) while insolvent or unable to pay his debts as they matured, procured, permitted, or suffered voluntarily, or involuntarily the appointment of a receiver or trustee to take charge of his property; or (6) admitted in writing his inability to pay his debts and his willingness to be adjudged bankrupt.

An involuntary petition in bankruptcy may be filed against a person by 3 or more creditors who have provable claims not contingent as to liability against a person, amounting in the aggregate to $500 in excess of the value of any security held by them, or, if all the creditors of a person are less than 12 in number, then 1 or more of the creditors, whose claim or claims equal that amount, may file a petition to have him adjudged bankrupt; but the claim or claims if unliquidated shall not be counted in computing the number and aggregate amount of the claims of the creditors joining in the petition, if the court determines that the claim or claims cannot be readily determined or estimated to be sufficient, together with the claims of the other creditors, to aggregate $500, without unduly delaying the decision upon the adjudication.

A creditor is not estopped to act as a petitioning creditor because he participated in a prior matter or judicial proceeding, as, for example, where he consented to a prior receivership proceeding or to a prior assignment for the benefit of creditors, or participated in such proceedings, or accepted dividends therein. However, the courts have held that if a party has brought an action asking for the appointment of a receiver or has participated actively in inducing a debtor to make an assignment for the benefit of creditors, he is estopped from acting as a petitioning creditor.

Summary

A person who is adjudged a bankrupt on his own petition is a voluntary bankrupt. Substantially any person, partnership, or corporation, except a municipal, railroad, insurance, or banking corporation or a building and loan association, may be adjudged a voluntary bankrupt.

Under certain circumstances a debtor may be adjudged bankrupt on the petition of his creditors. Such a debtor is known as an involuntary bankrupt. To be adjudged an involuntary bankrupt, the debtor must have, within four months from the filing of the petition and while insolvent, committed an act of bankruptcy. The Bankruptcy Act sets out what acts are acts of bankruptcy.

Administration of Bankrupt's Estate

Adjudication and Appointment of Trustee.   Petitions for both voluntary and involuntary bankruptcy are filed in the federal district court. After adjudication the estate of the bankrupt is referred to the referee for the purpose of administration.

The referee calls the first meeting of creditors not less than 10 days nor more than 30 days after the adjudication. At the first meeting of creditors the the judge or referee presides. The first step in the administration of the estate is the allowance of claims and the election of the trustee. The trustee is elected by a vote of the claims which have been allowed, and the person who receives the majority vote in number and amount is elected. In determining the number of claims voted, claims of $50 or less are not counted, but such claims are counted in computing the amount. The judge or referee is not bound to appoint the person elected by the creditors as trustee. If the person elected is not qualified or for some other reason would not be desirable as trustee, the judge or referee may appoint someone of his own selection.

Examination of Bankrupt. The next step is the public examination of the bankrupt. He is examined by the judge or referee who presides at the meeting and, in addition, may be examined by any creditor. This may be done by the creditor himself or by an attorney whom the creditor has employed to conduct the examination in his behalf. The purpose of the examination of the bankrupt is to bring out all the facts relating to his bankruptcy, to determine whether he has made a full and complete disclosure of all his property, to determine whether he has been guilty of any acts which would bar his discharge, and to clear up any questions arising as to claims, assets, or other matters affecting the bankrupt's estate.

Rights and Duties of Trustee. The trustee, as soon as he has qualified, takes possession of all the property of the bankrupt, inventories it, has it appraised, and sets aside the bankrupt's exemptions. He also examines the claims filed, and objects to any claims which are not allowable or which for any reason are improper. The trustee reduces the estate to money as expeditiously as is compatible with the best interests of the parties.

The trustee represents the creditors in the administration of the estate. Title to the bankrupt's property vests in the trustee, and he has all the rights in such property that the bankrupt had at the time of the adjudication. In addition, the trustee has all the rights against the bankrupt's property that a creditor holding an unsatisfied lien on the property of the bankrupt would have. For example, a creditor who has a security interest in certain property of the bankrupt, but whose security interest has not been perfected by compliance with the recording statutes of the state, has a lien on such property which is valid against a creditor with an unsatisfied execution. In such a situation a trustee in bankruptcy would have all the rights of the creditor with the unsatisfied execution.

To protect the interests of the creditors, the trustee in bankruptcy is given the right to bring suit in any court in which the bankrupt could have brought suit to enforce claims of the bankrupt's estate. Such suits are brought in the name of the trustee. All such suits are brought under the supervision of the court in which the bankruptcy proceedings are pending. Also, the trustee owes a duty to defend all suits brought against the bankrupt estate.

The trustee must keep an accurate account of all the property and money coming into his hands, deposit all money in the authorized depositories, pay by check or draft all dividends within 10 days after they are declared by the referee, and lay before the final meeting of the creditors a detailed statement of the administration of the estate.

Summary

The debtor is adjudged bankrupt by the judge of the federal district court. After adjudication the case is referred to the referee in bankruptcy where, at the first meeting of creditors, a trustee in bankruptcy is elected or appointed. After the election or appointment of the trustee the bankrupt is examined in regard to any matters material to the administration of the estate. The trustee takes possession of all the assets of the bankrupt, collects all claims, sets aside the bankrupt's exemptions, liquidates the assets, and distributes the proceeds among the creditors. Title to the bankrupt's estate vests in the trustee. The trustee must keep accurate accounts and make a final accounting of the administration of the estate.

Pacific Finance Corp. v. *Edwards*
304 F.2d 224 (9th Cir. 1962)

This was an action in a bankruptcy proceeding in which Pacific Finance Corporation claimed a valid lien on an automobile, and Eleanor Edwards, trustee in the matter of W. J. Myers, bankrupt, contended that the lien was void. The referee entered an order holding that the lien was void and the order was affirmed by the District Court. Pacific Finance Corporation appealed. The order was reversed.

On November 10, 1959, Strato Motors, Inc., sold W. J. Myers an automobile, and Myers executed a conditional sales contract to secure the unpaid balance of $2,616.40. By mistake the conditional sales contract was dated October 10, 1959. The conditional sales contract was assigned to Pacific Finance Corporation (Pacific) on November 12, 1959. Under the laws of the state, a conditional sales contract, to be valid against subsequent creditors, must be recorded within 10 days of its execution. There were no creditors having claims against Myers which were incurred after October 10, 1959. Edwards claimed that since the conditional sales contract was not recorded within ten days after October 10, 1959, it was void as to the creditors of Myers even though the obligations were incurred prior to October 10, 1959.

JERTBERG, CIRCUIT JUDGE.   Thus, the question presented to us for resolution may be stated as follows:

Does ¶ 70, sub. *c* vest a trustee as of the date of bankruptcy with all the rights, remedies, and powers of a creditor then holding a lien on the property of the bankrupt by legal or equitable proceedings, whether or not such a creditor actually exists, in the absence of a creditor of the bankrupt who could have obtained a lien on such property at the date of bankruptcy?

We have reached the conclusion that the answer to the question must be in the negative and that the order of the District Court confirming the Referee's order in the instant case must be reversed.

Under its plain language, ¶ 70, sub. *c* applies only where there is property, whether or not coming into the possession or control of the Court, "upon which a creditor of the bankrupt could have obtained a lien by legal or equitable proceedings at the date of bankruptcy, . . ." We believe that the word "creditor" in the foregoing quoted language means an actual creditor. Such construction is confirmed by the remainder of ¶ 70, sub. *c* which provides that the trustee "shall be deemed vested as of such date with all the rights, remedies, and powers of a creditor then holding a lien thereon by such proceedings, whether or not such a creditor actually exists." The clause "whether or not such a creditor actually exists" refers only to a "creditor then holding a lien thereon." Under our construction of ¶ 70, sub. *c* the Trustee is empowered to exercise the powers given him even if no actual creditor has obtained a lien, but he cannot do so if no actual creditor could have obtained a lien. In the instant case, as presented to us, there was in existence at the date of bankruptcy no actual subsequent creditor of the bankrupt who could have obtained a lien on the Cadillac automobile at the date of bankruptcy. For such reason, the Trustee could not acquire the hypothetical status of a creditor holding a lien because the existence of an actual creditor who could have obtained a lien is a condition to the acquisition by the Trustee of the status of a creditor holding a lien.

We are further convinced that the conclusion which we have reached is commended by the rationale, if not the holding, of the Supreme Court of the United States in *Lewis* v. *Manufacturers Nat. Bank*. The *Lewis* case arose in the State of Michigan. Prior to bankruptcy the bankrupt borrowed money from a bank, giving as security a chattel mortgage on an automobile. The Michigan statute had been construed to require the chattel mortgage to be filed immediately with the Register of Deeds, and unless so filed the chattel mortgage was void as against creditors who extended credit in the interim between the date of the instrument and its filing for record. The chattel mortgage was dated November 4, 1957, and filed for record on November 8, 1957. On April 18, 1958, the borrower filed a voluntary petition in bankruptcy and an adjudication of bankruptcy followed, petitioner being named trustee. There was no evidence that any creditor had extended credit to the bankrupt between November 4th and November 8th, 1957. The Referee held that the mortgage was void as against the trustee because the mortgage had not been immediately recorded. The District Court overruled the Referee, and the Court of Appeals affirmed the District Court. The Supreme Court affirmed, holding that the rights of creditors—whether existing or hypothetical—to which a trustee succeeds under ¶ 70, sub. *c* are to be ascertained as of the date of bankruptcy and not at an anterior point of time, stating:

. . . The rule pressed upon us would deprive a mortgagee of his rights in States like Michigan, if the mortgage had been executed months or even years previously and there had been a delay of a day or two in recording without any creditor having been injured during the period when the mortgage was unrecorded.

That is too great a wrench for us to give the bankruptcy system, absent a plain indication from Congress which is lacking here. *Lewis* v. *Manufacturers Nat. Bank*.

In the instant case, as in the *Lewis* case, there was no actual creditor of the bankrupt who extended credit after October 10, 1959, and prior to the date of bankruptcy. There was no creditor of the bankrupt who was injured.

Debts

Provable Debts. The debts of a bankrupt, for the purpose of the administration of his estate, are classified as "provable debts," "allowable debts," "debts having priority," and "dischargeable debts." If a debt is provable, it is the basis of its owner's right to share in the estate of the bankrupt.

Provable debts include those founded upon a fixed liability as evidenced by a judgment or an instrument in writing absolutely owing at the time of the filing of the petition by or against him, whether then payable or not, with accrued interest or any rebate of interest due; costs taxable against the bankrupt in a suit by him which the trustee declines to prosecute; taxable costs of creditor incurred in good faith by a creditor; an open account, or a contract express or implied; provable debts reduced to judgment after filing of the petition and before consideration of the bankrupt's discharge; workmen's compensation awards and like awards if the injury occurred prior to adjudication; the right to recover damages in any action for negligence instituted prior to and pending at the time of filing of the petition in bankruptcy; contingent debts and contingent contractual liability; and claims for anticipatory breach of contract, executory in whole or in part, including unexpired leases of personal property or leases not to exceed damages equivalent to one year's rent.

Allowable Debts. The fact that a debt is classed as a provable debt does not assure its owner's participation in the distribution of the assets. Before a creditor can participate in the bankruptcy proceedings, he must prove his claim, and the claim must be allowed. The proof of claim is a sworn statement of the amount of the claim, the consideration therefor, security held, and so forth; and if it is based on a written instrument, such instrument must be filed with the proof. Claims which are not filed within six months after the first date set for the first meeting of creditors will not be allowed. If the bankrupt has any defense to the debt, such defense will be set up by the trustee, and if established, the claim will not be allowed; or if the defense goes to only part of the claim, the amount of the claim will be reduced. All the defenses which would have been available to the bankrupt will be available to the trustee.

Debts Having Priority. Certain claims are declared by the Bankruptcy Act to have priority over other classes of claims and should not be confused with those secured. The following claims have priority: Costs and expenses of administration; costs of preserving the estate; filing fees; costs expended by a creditor in the recovery of property which has been transferred or concealed by the bankrupt provided it is recovered for the benefit of the estate; trustee's expenses in opposing the bankrupt's discharge or in his criminal prosecution for violation of the Bankruptcy Act; one reasonable attorney's fee and other professional expenses incurred in connection with a hearing on a voluntary or involuntary petition for the adjudication of bankruptcy if the court adjudges the debtor bankrupt; wages and commissions earned within three months before the commence of proceedings, due workmen, servants, clerks, or traveling or city salesmen not to exceed $600; and taxes legally owing by the bankrupt to the United States or any state or any subdivision thereof, not to exceed the value of the bankrupt's estate.

Dischargeable Debts. Certain debts are not affected by the bankrupt's discharge. Section 17 of the Bankruptcy Act provides that a discharge in bankruptcy shall release a bankrupt from all his provable debts, whether allowable in full or in part, except such as (1) are due as a tax levied by the United States, or any state, county, district, or municipality; or (2) are liabilities for obtaining money or property by false pretense or false representations, or for willful and malicious injuries to the person or property of another, or for alimony due or to become due, or for maintenance or support of wife or child, or for seduction of an unmarried female, or for breach of promise of marriage accompanied by seduction, or for criminal conversation; or (3) having not been duly scheduled in time for proof and an allowance, with the name of the creditor, if known to the bankrupt, unless such creditor had notice or actual knowledge of the proceedings in bankruptcy; or (4) were created by his fraud, embezzlement, misappropriation, or defalcation while acting as an officer or in any fiduciary capacity; or (5) are for wages which have been earned within three months before the date of commencement of the proceedings in bankruptcy due to workmen, servants, clerks, or traveling or city salesmen, on salary or commission basis, whole or part-time, whether or not selling exclusively for the bankrupt; or (6) are due for moneys of an employee received or retained by his employer to secure the faithful performance my such employee of the terms of a contract of employment.

These debts are provable debts, and the owner of such a debt has the right to participate in the distribution of the bankrupt's estate; but his right to recover the unpaid balance of the debt is not cut off by the bankrupt's discharge. All provable debts except those listed above are dischargeable debts, that is, the right to recover the unpaid balance is cut off by the bankrupt's discharge.

Summary

Provable debts include substantially all claims except unliquidated tort claims. Contingent claims arising on contracts are provable debts. If a debtor wishes to participate in the bankrupt's estate, he must file a proof of claim in the estate within six months of the first meeting of creditors. Certain debts are given priority by the provisions of the Bankruptcy Act. Certain debts, although provable, are not dischargeable.

Preferences, Liens, and Fraudulent Transfers

Preferential Payments. A preferential payment is a payment made by a debtor (1) while he is insolvent, (2) within four months of the filing of a petition in bankruptcy by or against the debtor, (3) which payment enables the creditor receiving the payment to obtain a greater percentage of his debt than other creditors in the same class, and (4) which creditor, when he received the payment, must have had reasonable grounds to believe that the debtor was insolvent. If a debtor makes a preferential payment, such act is an act of bankruptcy. If a debtor is adjudged bankrupt, the trustee in bankruptcy has the right to recover for the benefit of the estate all preferential payments that have been made by the bankrupt.

One of the purposes of the Bankruptcy Act is to ensure equal treatment for the creditors of an insolvent debtor and to prevent an insolvent debtor from distributing his assets to favored creditors to the detriment of his other creditors. Under the common law, the creditor who first attached or obtained a lien on his debtor's property or who was able to induce a debtor to pay his claim could retain the advantage he had gained, irrespective of the fact that such advantage might deplete the debtor's estate to such a degree that other creditors could recover nothing. Also, under the common law, if a debtor was solvent but for some reason was temporarily unable to meet his obligations as they matured, one creditor, by starting suit against such debtor, could cause other creditors to rush in and try to salvage as much of their claims as they could, with the result that all persons involved would suffer unnecessary loss due to costs of suit and the inability to realize the full value of assets which would be sold at forced sale. Under the Bankruptcy Act the rights of all persons can be protected.

Even though a debtor is insolvent, he can carry on his business without fear of being adjudged bankrupt if he does not commit an act of bankruptcy. Payments made in the regular course of a business are not preferential payments, and such payments are not acts of bankruptcy. For example, if an insolvent debtor purchases property, paying the purchase price on delivery, such a payment is not a preferential payment. The debtor's estate has been neither increased nor decreased if the property purchased is worth the price paid. Also, the courts have held that if the debtor has purchased goods on credit, the payment of the price of the goods when the account is due is not, under ordinary circumstances, a preferential payment. Such payments are not acts of bankruptcy, and if the debtor is adjudged bankrupt, the trustee in bankruptcy cannot recover such payments even though they have been made while the debtor is insolvent and within four months of the adjudication of bankruptcy.

Preferential Liens. A creditor may attempt to obtain a preference by obtaining a lien on the debtor's property. The lien may be obtained either by legal or equitable process or by contract with the debtor. Any lien which is obtained within four months of the filing of the petition is null and void if the lien is to secure a preexisting debt and if the debtor was insolvent at the time the lien was obtained. A lien which is given as security for present value received is valid against the trustee in bankruptcy.

If an insolvent debtor borrows money or purchases goods and gives a lien on his assets to secure the repayment of the money borrowed or the purchase price of the goods, his assets have not been diminished by the transaction, and the creditor has gained no advantage over existing creditors by the taking of the lien. Such liens are valid against a trustee in bankruptcy of the debtor.

Fraudulent Transfers. Transfers for the purpose of hindering, delaying, or defrauding creditors are null and void. This rule is applied generally throughout the United States. Transfers made by a debtor and every obligation incurred by him within one year of the filing of the petition in bankruptcy are void as to creditors, if made or incurred without fair consideration and while insolvent, or if the transfer or obligation will render him insolvent. If one makes a transfer of property or incurs obligations without fair consideration in contemplation of incurring debts beyond his ability to pay, the transaction is fraudulent to both existing and future creditors. In all the foregoing situations the transfer or obligation may be declared void if made within one year from the date of the filing of the petition in bankruptcy. A transfer made or an obligation incurred within four months of the filing of the petition is fraudulent as to existing and future creditors if made with the intent to use the consideration obtained to effect a preference which is voidable under the act.

In addition to the above, any transfer made or suffered or any obligation incurred by a debtor who has been adjudged a bankrupt, which under any federal or state law applicable thereto is voidable by any creditor having a provable claim, shall be void as against the trustee. Such property remains a part of the bankrupt's estate and passes to the trustee, and the trustee owes a duty to reclaim the property or collect its value for the benefit of the estate.

All these safeguards are set up to prevent the debtors from concealing or disposing of his property in fraud of his creditors or to prevent him from favoring one creditor at the expense of his other creditors; yet they are so framed that the honest but hard-pressed debtor is not unduly handicapped in continuing the operation of his business. If the debtor "plays fair," he is protected; if he does not, the creditors are protected.

Summary

A preferential payment is a payment made to a creditor by an insolvent debtor within four months of his adjudication as a bankrupt, which payment enables the creditor to realize a greater percentage of his claim than other creditors of the same class; such creditor must have reasonable grounds for believing that the debtor is insolvent. A lien given by an insolvent debtor within four months of his adjudication as a bankrupt, to secure a preexisting debt, is void. Any transfer made or obligation incurred without consideration within one year from the debtor's adjudication as a bankrupt is void as to creditors.

Kravetz v. *Joange Building Corp.*
341 F.2d 561 (2nd Cir. 1965)

This was an action in bankruptcy by Kravetz, trustee (plaintiff), against Joange Building Company (defendant) to set aside a transfer as a preference. Judgment for Kravetz and Joange Building Company appealed. Judgment affimed.

Joange Building Company (Joange) leased a building to M.F.C. Card, Inc. (Bankrupt), and loaned it $5,000, payable in installments, to enable Bankrupt to buy fixtures and inventory. Bankrupt was soon in default on nearly all notes due and in several monthly payments on rent. Bankrupt intended to discontinue the business and had surrendered the keys to Joange, apparently intending to leave all the fixtures on the premises. All this Joange knew before the execution sale. In December, 1962, Joange took a judgment against Bankrupt and had his assets sold on execution sale in January, 1963. On that day, Bankrupt was insolvent and was adjudged bankrupt within less than four months from that date.

MOORE, CIRCUIT JUDGE.   In his affidavit opposing summary judgment, Berfond, an officer of Joange, professed only ignorance of Bankrupt's insolvency and absence of reasonable cause to believe it. Although Bankrupt's President, Max Fraiden, stated that he had told Berfond that he was "having a difficult time" meeting his obligations to all his creditors, Berfond claimed that he "had no idea" and "did not know" whether Bankrupt had any business creditors or whether they were being paid. We would be surprised if any creditor-landlord of a small greeting-card store, whose notes and rent were in default, would not suspect that his debtor-tenant had some unpaid suppliers. Moreover, the test is not the subjective one of what Berfond believed but the objective one of what he had reasonable cause to believe.

Knowledge of insolvency is not necessary, nor even actual belief thereof; all that is required is a reasonable cause to believe that the debtor was insolvent at the time of the preferential transfer. A creditor has reasonable cause to believe that a debtor is insolvent when such a state of facts is brought to the creditor's notice, respecting the affairs and pecuniary condition of the debtor, as would lead a prudent business person to the conclusion that the debtor is insolvent.

Where the trustee alleges that the defendant had reasonable cause to believe that the debtor was insolvent, an averment by the defendant that he had no personal knowledge of the debtor's insolvency is insufficient. *Idem.* at sec. 60.61 (1).

The facts undisputedly known by Joange as of the date of the execution sale (January 3, 1963) more than meet the requirements of reasonable belief. As the facts related above demonstrate, this is not a case where the transferee merely knew that the bankrupt had failed to pay a debt when due, which, although a relevant fact, here it was not standing alone, there was the quitting of the business and the intention to leave the stock-in-trade and fixtures; nor has defendant suggested that a trial would develop new or different facts. The only question would concern the proper inferences to draw. Given all the facts indisputably known to Joange, the inference that a prudent man would have believed that the debtor was unable to meet its obligations as they arose was so compelling that the judge could properly draw it without the need of a trial.

Discharge

Basis for Granting Discharge. A bankrupt who has not been guilty of serious infractions of the code of business ethics and who has fulfilled his duties as a bankrupt is entitled to a discharge in bankruptcy. The adjudication of any person, except a corporation, shall operate as an application for a discharge. A bankrupt may, however, before the hearing on his application, file a written waiver of his right to discharge. A corporation may, within six months after its adjudication, file an application for a discharge in the court in which the proceedings are pending.

Filing Objections to Discharge. After the statutory filing fees have been paid in full, the court shall make an order fixing the time for filing objections to the bankrupt's discharge. The date fixed shall be not less than 30 days after the first date set for the first meeting of creditors. If the examination of the bankrupt has not been completed or will not be completed prior to the time fixed for filing objections, the court, on its own motion or on the motion of the receiver, trustee, creditor, or other party in interest, shall extend the time of filing objections. Notice of the time fixed for filing objections to the discharge is given to all interested parties. If objections have been filed within the time fixed or within any extension of time which may have been granted by the court, the court will hear proofs of the objections at such time as will give the parties a reasonable opportunity to be fully heard. If the court is satisfied that the bankrupt has not committed any of the acts which are a bar to his discharge, the discharge will be granted.

Acts Which Bar Discharge. The acts which are a bar to a bankrupt's discharge are set out in Section 14, Subsection *c,* of the Bankruptcy Act as follows:

The court shall grant the discharge unless satisfied that the bankrupt has (1) committed an offense punishable by imprisonment as provided under title 18, United States Code Section 152; or (2) destroyed, mutilated, falsified, concealed, or failed to keep or preserve books of account or records, from which his financial condition and business transactions might be ascertained, unless the court deems such acts or failure to have been justified under all the circumstances of the case; or (3) while engaged in business as sole proprietor, partnership or as executive of a corporation, obtained for such business money or property on credit or an extension or renewal of credit by making or publishing or causing to be made or published in any manner whatsoever a materially false statement in writing respecting his financial condition or the financial condition of such partnership or corporation; or (4) at any time subsequent to the first day of the twelve months immediately preceding the filing of the petition in bankruptcy, transferred, removed, destroyed, or concealed, or permitted to be removed, destroyed, or concealed, any of his property, with intent to hinder, delay, or defraud his creditors; or (5) in a proceeding under this Act commenced within six years prior to the date of filing the petition in bankruptcy been granted a discharge, or had a composition or arrangement by way of composition or a wage earner's plan by way of composition confirmed under this Act; or (6) in the course of a proceeding under this Act refused to obey any lawful order of, or to answer any material question approved by, the court; or (7) failed to explain satisfactorily any losses of assets or deficiency of assets to meet his liabilities: *Provided,* that if, upon the hearing of an objection to a discharge, the objector shall show to the satisfaction of the court that there are reasonable grounds for believing that the bankrupt has committed any of the acts which, under this subdivision *c,* would prevent his discharge in bankruptcy, then the burden of proving that he has not committed any of such acts shall be upon the bankrupt.

Who May File Objections.   The trustee, a creditor, the U.S. attorney, or such other attorney as the Attorney General may designate may file objections to and oppose the discharge of a bankrupt. When requested by the court, it is the duty of the U.S. attorney located in the judicial district in which the bankruptcy proceeding is pending to examine into the acts and conduct of the bankrupt. If satisfied that probable ground exists for the denial of a discharge and that public interest warrants the action, it is his duty to oppose the bankrupt's discharge. Also, if the bankrupt fails to appear at the hearing on his discharge or, having appeared, refuses to submit himself to examination at the first meeting of creditors or at any subsequent meeting called for his examination, he shall be deemed to have waived his right to a discharge.

Summary

A bankrupt is granted a discharge unless he has been guilty of serious infraction of the code of business ethics or has failed to fulfill his duties as a bankrupt. The time for filing the objections to a bankrupt's discharge is fixed at the first meeting of creditors or at a special meeting called for that purpose.

The grounds for denying a bankrupt's discharge are set out in the Bankruptcy Act. The trustee, a creditor, the United States attorney, or an attorney designated by the Attorney General may file objections to a bankrupt's discharge.

Charles Edward & Associates v. England
301 F.2d 572 (9th Cir. 1962)

This was an appeal by Charles P. Trafficante and Paul J. Trafficante from an order of the District Court which set aside the individual discharges in bankruptcy granted by the Referee. Judgment affirmed in part.

The Trafficantes filed individual voluntary petitions in bankruptcy and a short time later Charles Edward & Associates, a partnership composed of the two Trafficantes, was adjudged a bankrupt in an involuntary proceeding. The two individual estates and the partnership estate were consolidated for the purposes of administration. The trustee petitioned the Referee for an extension of time for filing objections to the discharge of the individual bankrupts but through error did not include the partnership. The order extending the time was limited to the individuals. The trustee filed objections to the discharge of both the partnership and the individual partners. The objections were based on the individual partners' failure to keep books, the partnership's transfer of property to the individual partners, in defraud of creditors and within one year of the filing of the bankruptcy petition, the individual partners' failure to explain losses in their individual assets amounting to $56,000, and the withdrawal of large amounts of cash within one year of the filing of the petition in bankruptcy and when the partnership was insolvent, with the intent to defraud creditors.

SOLOMON, DISTRICT JUDGE. The failure to keep or preserve books of account or records from which a bankrupt's financial condition and business transactions might be obtained is a ground for the denial of a discharge in bankruptcy under the Bankruptcy Act (Act), 11 U.S.C.A. ¶ 32, sub. *c* (2).

Specification 1 charges:

1. That said Bankrupt copartnership and each of the bankrupt individual members thereof failed to keep books or records from which the financial condition of said bankrupt copartnership might be ascertained in that they, and each of them, wholly failed and neglected at all times during the existence of said copartnership to maintain books or records relating to the accounts payable of said copartnership.

The Trafficantes contend that this specification charges misconduct against the partnership and not against the individual partners, and they claim that any other construction would disregard the entity theory of partnership.

Although the Bankruptcy Act of 1938 adopted the entity theory for some purposes and the aggregate theory for other purposes, the entity theory is specifically rejected in ¶ 5, sub. *j* of the Act, 11 U.S.C.A. ¶ 23, sub. *j*, which provides that the discharge of a partnership does not discharge the individual partners from partnership debts.

Under either theory, a partner who has engaged in conduct proscribed by the Act, either on behalf of the partnership or on his own behalf, is not entitled to a discharge.

In many cases, as in this one, substantially all of the debts of the individual partners were those of the partnership. The failure of a partner to keep partnership books and records may preclude a creditor or a trustee from ascertaining the true financial condition of a partner.

The Referee's ruling was clearly erroneous, and the District Court was correct in setting it aside.

The transfer of property with intent to hinder, delay or defraud creditors, within twelve months of the filing of a petition in bankruptcy, is also a ground for the denial of a discharge in bankruptcy. 11 U.S.C.A. ¶ 32, sub. *c* (4).

Specification 2 charges:

2. That at times subsequent to the first day of the twelve months immediately preceding the filing of the individual partners' petitions in bankruptcy, and also at items [*sic*] subsequent to the first day of the twelve months immediately preceding the filing of the petition in bankruptcy against the said bankrupt copartnership, the said partnership, while continually insolvent, the individual members thereof having full knowledge of such partnership insolvency and with intent to defraud the partnership creditors, transferred to the individual members thereof, property of said partnership, to wit, cash in the sum of $22,819.07 or thereabouts.

Specification 4 is similar to 2, but, in addition, charges that the individual partners made cash withdrawals from partnership funds in the amount of approximately $23,000 and that the partners transferred the money to themselves with intend to defraud partnership creditors.

These two specifications clearly allege improper conduct against the individual partners in personally withdrawing large sums from the partnership with intent to defraud partnership creditors. An individual discharge will be denied a partner who withdraws funds from a partnership with intent to defraud creditors.

Problem Cases

1. After making various assessments for back taxes, the United States obtained on August 20, 1965, a lien on property of Gaines. A number of Gaines's creditors then filed an involuntary petition in bankruptcy on August 27, 1965. The property was sold by the United States on September 8, 1965, to satisfy the lien. Thereafter, an amended petition was filed, alleging that Gaines, while insolvent, had permitted the government to obtain this lien through "distraint." Can Gaines argue that no act of bankruptcy was committed because the government's tax liens arose by statute on the various dates when the taxes were assessed, and not by "distraint" under the bankruptcy statute?

2. An involuntary petition in bankruptcy was filed against Camp Ganeden, Inc. The petition alleged that Camp Ganeden, Inc., was insolvent and that while insolvent and within four months of the filing of the petition it had entered into an agreement to transfer for $25,000 all of its assets, which were of the value of $65,000, to Camp Winslow, Inc. Is the petition sufficient to justify the court in adjudging Camp Ganeden, Inc., bankrupt?

3. Kane was the owner of an automobile under a mortgage or installment sales contract. In October, 1966, he filed a petition of voluntary bankruptcy and listed First

National Bank as a creditor in the amount of $1,945, secured by the automobile of the same value. Kane was not in default on his automobile payments at the time of filing the petition and the Bank filed proof of secured claim and a rejection of the bankruptcy plan. In December, having received no further payments and not expecting payments to be maintained under the circumstances, the Bank repossessed the car by removing it from a parking lot. Thereafter the trustee in bankruptcy filed a motion to require the Bank to return the car. Should the Bank be allowed to keep the car?

4. Cohen entered into a contract to serve as a high school teacher for "the school year 1966–1967." The contract provided that Cohen's services were to begin on August 30, 1966, and the school year was scheduled to end on June 13, 1967. Although the services under the contract were to be performed during the nine and one-half months of the school year, Cohen's salary was payable in 12 equal monthly installments. Cohen was declared a bankrupt as of February 24, 1967, and on May 5, 1967, the trustee filed an application for a turnover order for amounts due Cohen under the employment contract as of the date of bankruptcy. The trustee claims accrued earnings in the amount of $684 were due Cohen as of that date, based on a pro rata computation of payments to be made during the two and one-half months of summer vacation. Should the turnover order be granted?

5. Oil Co. was adjudged bankrupt. Schneider filed proof of claim with the trustee, claiming to be a creditor of the bankrupt Oil Co. Schneider was the owner of a certificate of Oil Co. stock denominated "preferred stock." The certificate provided: "The owners of this stock are entitled to receive and the company is bound to pay on January 1, 1939, the par value thereof, together with all accumulated and unpaid dividends." Should the claim of Schneider be allowed?

6. On March 30 and April 18, 1960, the District Director of Internal Revenue assessed and made demands upon Travis Body Works for withholding taxes for the fourth quarter of 1959 and the first quarter of 1960. Nature of such liens was filed on April 1 and April 22, 1960. In June of 1960, Travis filed past-due state sales tax returns for the third and fourth quarter of 1959 and the first quarter of 1960. The North Dakota Tax Commission then filed notice on June 6, 1960, of sales tax liens covering each of the three quarters. Travis filed a voluntary petition of bankruptcy and a bankruptcy adjudication was made on June 29, 1960. The Tax Commission claimed that the sales tax lien had priority over the lien of the United States for unpaid withholding tax because the North Dakota sales tax statutes provided that the sales tax become a lien against all property of Travis as of April 30, 1960. Should the sales tax lien have priority?

7. United Associates, Inc., was adjudged bankrupt on November 22, 1948. United Associates, Inc., transacted its banking business with State Bank and had borrowed money from State Bank. On October 13, 1948, notes in the amount of $8,441.45 fell due. These notes were secured by chattel mortgages. Between October 13, 1948, and October 26, 1948, State Bank and United Associates, Inc., had several conferences relative to the payment of the notes, but no agreement was reached. October 23, 1948, United Associates, Inc., deposited in its checking account $5,000 and on October 25, 1948, it deposited $15,000 in its checking account. These deposits were made in the regular course of business and not for the purpose of paying the notes. On October 27, 1948, State Bank charged the overdue notes against the checking account of United Associates, Inc. Was this a preferential payment?

8. International Marketing was engaged in buying and selling petroleum and gas products under the direction of sole stockholders Davis, Clark, and Wood. Cooper Petroleum was likewise engaged and the two companies were in the practice of conducting as much business as possible with each other. Fagan, who was a dominant figure in the management of Cooper Petroleum, acquired one fourth of International's stock, and subsequently transferred it to the members of his family who also occupied executive positions with Cooper Petroleum. Clark served as vice president and director of both companies. On June 2, 1964, an involuntary bankruptcy petition was filed against International. Records of the companies disclosed that during the four-month period preceeding bankruptcy, Cooper Petroleum delivered $45,000 worth of goods to International on a running open account and was paid a total of $40,154.94 on that account. Creditors of International sought to recover the $40,154.94 from Cooper Petroleum claiming that these were preferential payments. Can Cooper Petroleum avoid the preferential payment rule by claiming that since the payments did not exceed the value of goods delivered, the net estate of International was thereby enriched by the aggregate transaction and no prejudice resulted to other creditors?

9. Gomez acquired a parcel of land from Capital Building and Loan Association on October 10, 1961. Capital retained a vendor's lien and a mortgage on the lot to secure the purchase price of $15,500. On December 16, 1965, Gomez granted a second mortgage on the same land to secure a $5,400 note held by Second Mortgage Company, Inc. Gomez defaulted on both notes, and in a bankruptcy proceeding the property was seized and awarded to Capital as a result of its security interest under the first mortgage. Second Mortgage Company brought suit to recover the balance due on the second mortgage and Gomez pleaded the prior discharge of bankruptcy as a bar to the suit. Second Mortgage Company contended that Gomez's failure to make payments on the first mortgage, thus allowing foreclosure by the first mortgage holder, constituted a "willful and malicious injury to property" and under the bankruptcy statutes debts arising therefrom are not dischargeable. Can Second Mortgage Company collect?

10. On November 2, 1964, Shainman was adjudicated a bankrupt upon the filing of a voluntary petition. In October, 1963, Shear's of Affton had loaned Shainman $10,000 secured, at least in part, by inventory. Shear's objected to the discharge of Shainman on the grounds that Shainman had issued a false inventory statement as of January 31, 1964, wherein his inventory was valued at over $800,000 when actual value as established by a physical inventory was less than $175,000. Shear's alleged that this false statement had been relied upon by Receivables Finance Company in extending business loans to Shainman. Should the discharge be denied because of Shear's objections based on false financial statements issued to another creditor?

11. Johnstone had recovered a judgment against Gardner for property damage and personal injury suffered in an automobile accident. The court found that prior to the accident Gardner had had very little sleep and that as he approached the point where the accident occurred he dozed or blacked out, that he sideswiped Johnstone's automobile, and at that point he snapped out of his daze. Thereafter, Gardner was adjudged bankrupt, and the Johnstone judgment was properly scheduled. Gardner was granted a discharge. Johnstone contends that his judgment was not discharged because his damage was the result of the willful and malicious conduct of Gardner. Was Johnstone's judgment a dischargeable debt?

PART XI   *Economic Relations and the Law*

chapter 45. Competitive Torts and the Protection of Ideas

Introduction

Rights Protected. Tort law protecting economic relations from unreasonable interferences developed more recently than did tort law in other areas. However, rights and duties arising out of economic relations are now clearly established in three main categories.

First, business firms are protected against injurious falsehoods or other deceitful practices by competitors which result in diversion of their patronage or otherwise injures their goodwill. Second, protection is given to ideas by the law relating to trade secrets, patents, and copyrights. Third, protection is given against certain unjustifiable interferences with contracts or economic expectations. To an important extent, the rights in these areas now are governed by federal and state statutes creating special procedures, rules, and remedies.

Deceitful Diversion of Patronage

Disparagement. The torts of libel and slander, discussed in Chapter 3, afford remedies against competitors who publish defamatory falsehoods charging other businessmen with personal misconduct. If the falsehood relates to the quality of the product, to the seller's title, or to the type service provided, it is the tort of *disparagement* and proof of actual damage is essential. Although the tort of disparagement originated with cases protecting tangible property rights from injurious falsehoods, protection was later extended to intangible property rights including trademarks, patents, corporate shares, and copyrighted material.

Another form of deceitful diversion of patronage occurs where one firm "palms" its goods off as being those made by a competitor. Although "palming off" is a tort, nearly all actions of this type are now brought under the Lanham Act which affords very extensive protection for trademarks and other product and service identifying marks used by most business firms.

Trademarks and Other Marks.   A trademark is a distinctive mark, work, design, or picture which is affixed to goods so that purchasers may identify their origin. In general, a trademark must be fanciful, arbitrary, unique, and nondescriptive. Generic terms such as "car" or "ham" and descriptive terms such as "good" or "extra soft" may not be exclusively appropriated as a trademark.

A *trade name* is used as the name under which a firm operates. *Service marks* are used to identify services and need only to be registered. *Certification marks* are used by people who do not own the marks but who have a right to identify the product as being approved or authorized by the owner of the mark. The "Good Housekeeping Seal of Approval" is an example of a certification mark. A *collective mark* is employed by an association or group of people to identify the group as being the source of the product or service. Trade union or trade association marks fall into this category.

Since 1946 the Lanham Act (15 U.S.C. Sections 1050–1127) has greatly expanded the scope of registrability and the protection afforded to trademarks, trade names, service marks, certification marks, and collective marks. Such marks are protected against misuse or infringement by Section 1 of the act which states:

Any person who shall, in commerce, (a) use, without consent of registrant, any reproduction, counterfeit, copy or colorable imitation of any registered mark in connection with the sale, offering for sale, or advertising of any goods or services or in connection with which such use is likely to cause confusion or mistake or to deceive purchasers as to the source of such goods or services shall be. . . [liable for damages and subject to injunction].

Under the Lanham Act there is a Principal Register for the registration of "technical" trademarks (marks which distinguish the goods from those of others); and a Supplemental Register for "all marks capable of distinguishing applicant's goods or services and not registrable on the principal register, including marks which consist of surnames and geographical names but also packages and the configuration of goods.

Registration on the Principal Register carries important presumptions of validity and extends protection beyond that accorded to marks registered on the Supplemental Register. If a firm can establish that any mark has acquired a distinctive secondary meaning identifying its goods, such mark may be registered on the Principal Register. Proof of substantial exclusive continuous use for a period of five years preceding application for registration is prima facie evidence of acquired *secondary meaning.*

Summary

The tort of disparagement protects businessmen from injurious falsehoods relating to the quality of their products, their services, or the title to their property. The Lanham Act now gives extensive protection to registered trademarks, trade names, service marks, certification marks, and collective marks.

Testing Systems, Inc. v. Magnaflux Corp.

251 F.Supp. 286 (E.D. Pa. 1966)

This was an action for product disparagement brought by Testing Systems, Inc. (plaintiff), against Magnaflux Corp. (defendant). Judgment for Testing.

Testing and Magnaflux were competitors making equipment and chemical products. Testing Co. sued Magnaflux for damages for having orally and in writing disparaged Testing Co.'s products. This included statements to Testing Co.'s customers and prospective customers that Testing Co.'s products were "no good" and that the "government is throwing them out." It also included a written report falsely stating that the government had tested Testing Co.'s products and found them to be only 40% as effective as the products of Magnaflux.

LORD, DISTRICT JUDGE. The fine line that separates healthy competitive effort from underhanded business tactics is frequently difficult to determine. Apart from the tradesman's right of free speech, which must be vigorously safeguarded, the public has a genuine interest in learning the relative merits of particular products, however that may come about. To advance these interests the law of the marketplace gives the competitor a wide berth in the conduct of his business. As Mr. Justice Maxey of the Pennsylvania Supreme Court said in 1932,

> [H]e may send out circulars, or give information verbally, to customers of other men, knowing they are bound by contract for a definite term, although acting upon the expectation and with the purpose of getting the trade of such persons for himself.
>
> [H]e may use any mode of persuasion with such a customer . . . which appeals to his self-interest, reason, or even his prejudices.
>
> [H]e may descant upon the extent of his rival's facilities compared with his own, his rival's means, his insolvency, if it be a fact, and the benefits which will result to the customer in the future from coming to the solicitor rather than remaining where he is. . . . "the law of competition" . . . takes little note of the ordinary rules of good neighborhood or abstract morality.

Nonetheless, there is an outer perimeter to permissible conduct. The tradesman must be assured that his competitors will not be suffered to engage in conduct which falls below the minimum standard of fair dealing.

> [I]t is no answer that they can defend themselves by also resorting to disparagement. A self-respecting businessman will not voluntarily adopt, and should not be driven to adopt, a selling method which he regards as undignified, unfair, and repulsive. A competitor should not, by pursuing an unethical practice force his rival to choose between its adoption and the loss of his trade.

Magnaflux's comments in the case presently before this Court do not entitle it to the protection accorded to "unfavorable comparison." There is a readily observable difference between saying that one's product is, in general, better than another's . . . and asserting, as here, that such other's is only 40% as effective as one's own. The former, arguably, merely expresses an opinion, the truth or falsity of which is difficult or impossible of ascertainment. The latter, however, is an assertion of fact, not subject to the same frailties of proof, implying that the party making the statement is fortified with the substantive facts necessary to make it. This distinction has never been seriously questioned. Magnaflux in this case admittedly circulated to Testing's present and prospective customers false statements to the effect that the government had tested both products and found the Magnaflux to be 60% more effective than Testing's. This is not the sort of "comparison" that courts will protect.

Apart from this, there is at least one additional factor which withdraws Magnaflux's comments from the category of unfavorable comparison. Not content with making the admittedly false statements and allowing them to be evaluated independently of any extraneous influence, Magnaflux here gave added authenticity to its assertions by invoking the reputation of a third party, the United States Government. It is unnecessary to speculate on the additional force Magnaflux's remarks must have had when coupled with the purported approval of so highly credible a source. This, of course, is to say nothing of the statements to the effect that Testing had been "thrown out," which by no stretch of the imagination could be termed mere comparison.

Société Comptoir de L'Indus. v. *Alexander's Department Store*
299 F.2d 33 (2nd Cir. 1962)

This was an action by Comptoir (plaintiff) against Alexander's Department Store (defendant) for damages and an injunction in which Comptoir alleged that Alexander was guilty of certain unfair competitive practices. Judgment for Alexander's and Société appealed. Affirmed.

Société is a group of foreign and domestic corporations who do business under the names "Dior" and "Christian Dior," which names are registered as trademarks. Alexander is the owner of retail, discount type, department stores in a metropolitan area and is well known for its low cost retailing policies which are made possible by the use of self-service merchandising techniques and a high volume, low mark-up policy. Alexander used the name of "Dior" and "Christian Dior" extensively to promote the sale of garments copied from original creations designed by the house of Dior. Société sued Alexander asking for damages and an injunction against the use of the Dior name.

SMITH, CIRCUIT JUDGE.   Alexander's representation that the garments being sold by it were copies of Société's original creations was apparently truthful. We do not understand Société to claim that the garments were so poorly made or executed as not to constitute copies; but in any event they have certainly failed to establish that to be the case. The merchandise was so described in newspaper advertisements, on hang tags attached to the garments reading, "Original by Christian Dior—Alexander's Exclusive—Paris—Adaptation;" and on a television fashion show sponsored by Alexander which employed a singing commercial.

The District Court concluded that no attempt had been made to deceive the public and that no deception or confusion existed with respect to the garments being sold or as to sponsorship by Société. While it is possible that Société may be able to show some confusion in the public mind as to sponsorship, or origin of the goods, at a full trial, there is certainly nothing in the record before us to indicate that the factual finding that neither the hang tags, the newspaper advertisements nor the television show in fact deceived the public as to origin or sponsorship of the garments, was clearly erroneous.

Société urges that by virtue of its licensing arrangements with others the public is confused as to sponsorship of the garments. But if it be true that the public associates all dresses referred to as copies of "Dior Originals" with the Société, then Société, the licensor, must be prepared to show that control was maintained, not only of the manner and the price at which the dresses were retailed, but of the manufacture of the garments, for a bare license is a fraud upon the public and unlawful. But it is sufficient at this stage of the proceedings to say that neither of the District Judges concluded that a sufficient showing of confusion had been made and we are not persuaded this conclusion was clearly erroneous.

In any proceeding under the Lanham Act the gist of the proceeding is a "false description or representation," 15 U.S.C.A. § 1125 (a), or a use of the mark which "is likely to cause confusion or mistake or to deceive purchasers as to the source of origin of such goods or services," 15 U.S.C.A. § 1114 (1). The registering of a proper noun as a trademark does not withdraw it from the language, nor reduce it to the exclusive possession of the registrant which may be jealously guarding against any and all use by others. Registration bestows upon the owner of the mark the limited right to protect his good will from possible harm by those uses of another as may engender a belief in the mind of the public that the product identified by the infringing mark is made or sponsored by the owner of the mark. Lanham Act does not prohibit a commercial rival's truthfully denominating his goods a copy of a design in the public domain, though he uses the name of the designer to do so. Indeed it is difficult to see any other means that might be employed to inform the consuming public of the true origin of the design.

Those cases involving sponsorship, whether trademark infringment or unfair competition, protecting the owner of the mark, are based upon a finding that the defendant's goods are likely to be thought to have originated with, or to have been sponsored by, the true owner of the mark.

Common law unfair competition must be grounded in either deception or appropriation of the exclusive property of the plaintiff. . . .

In the case at bar it is conceded that the "pirating" of the design is lawful and proper. The only property right alleged to have been invaded is the good will embodied in the trademark. But the right of the complainant in his mark is limited to dilution which is brought about by confusion as to source or affiliation.

Involved in the instant case is a conflict of values which necessarily arises in an economy characterized by competition and private property. The courts have come to recognize the true nature of the considerations often involved in efforts to extend protection of common law trade names so as to create a shield against competition. The interest of the consumer here in competitive prices of garments using Dior designs without deception as to origin, is at least as great as the interest of Société in monopolizing the name.

Hobart Manufacturing Co. v. Kitchen Aid Service, Inc.
260 F.Supp. 559 (E.D. N.Y. 1966)

This was an action by Hobart Manufacturing Co. (plaintiff) against Harold Cohen (defendant) for unfair competition in misappropriating the use of Hobart's trade name. An injunction and damages were granted to Hobart.

Starting with its use on other articles in 1919, Hobart effected a series of registrations of KitchenAid shown always as written without a space between the component words. The registrations for dishwashers on the Principal Register, and the more recent service mark registration on the Principal Register, are in plain type but exhibit modest stylistic peculiarities. Cohen had been an "authorized" Kitchen-Aid dealer whose distributorship had been terminated. Soon afterward Cohen, who at all times since has conducted his business as a sole proprietorship, had a New York corporation formed with the name "Kitchen Aid Service, Inc." which performed no function whatever but Cohen used that corporate name for listings in the white pages of the local telephone directories. In the yellow pages he inserted a display advertisement that featured the Kitchen Aid name; "Kitchen Aid Service" was featured, too, on Cohen's panel truck and on the uniforms that Cohen and his men wore on service calls. The repair service Cohen performed fell far short of the standards expected by Hobart and its regional distributor of authorized dealers.

DOOLING, DISTRICT JUDGE.   There is no doubt that Cohen's course of conduct was calculated to and did mislead Kitchen Aid owners into engaging his services in the belief that he was identifiable with Hobart or had Hobart's sponsorship.

It is argued that Cohen did not use Hobart's trademark precisely, since they have varied the type-style and separated it into two words, and that, in any case, the trademark is too undistinguished in appearance and too wanting in requisite trademark fancifulness to warrant legal protection. If the argument might have force in other and innocent circumstances, on the facts it is altogether clear that Cohen here exactly and successfully trespassed on just that area of unmistaken identifications of the word "KitchenAid" with Hobart that did exist, and that Cohen capitalized on that identification intentionally by causing confusion between Cohen and those dealers properly identified as KitchenAid dealers through using a colorable imitation of the identifying word.

Cohen is not in competition with Hobart but with distributors and dealers in the area who extend a repair service. Cohen's practices hurt Hobart by denying to it (indirectly) a market for sales of replacement parts—for Cohen used rebuilt parts on many occasions and "authorized" dealers are expected to use factory-new parts. Cohen's practices also hurt Hobart by associating it with an inferior repair service that counteracted the goodwill generally attaching to Hobart and its product.

It is doubtful that the first element of harm is legally significant in the absence of evidence, not here reliably present, that Cohen "palmed off" their rebuilt parts as Hobart's KitchenAid factory-fresh parts.

The second kind of harm, that flowing from associating Hobart with an inferior repair service, furnishes the basis of relief, aided, perhaps by the consideration the Cohen simply may not fairly display in stolen plumage. Since Hobart has not been shown in this case to furnish a repair and maintenance service under the KitchenAid designation or otherwise, the registration of the word as a service mark is irrelevant. Nor is there any evidence that KitchenAid is entitled to protection as a collective or certification mark. But recognition that Cohen is not making infringing sales of a kind of service that Hobart sells under a service mark, and that Cohen is not making infringing sales of a kind of goods that Hobart sells under a trademark, does not end the matter. Hobart has a right to be free of the corrosive effect of Cohen's inferior service performance on the good will connected with Hobart's business and associated with the trademark KitchenAid that it uses on its products when, as here, it is made to appear that Cohen gains the chance to render the damagingly inferior service by the false pretense of a connection with Hobart, or of sponsorship by Hobart.

That the corporate name was "open" in New York, so that Cohen was able to occupy it, is quite beside the point. It emphasizes that Cohen's trespass is not on the corporate name of Hobart but on the good will associated with its trademarked products.

There remains the question of relief. Injunctive relief is, of course, proper and will forbid continued use of the corporate name of Kitchen Aid Service, Inc. and any conduct on Cohen's part that suggests a connection with or sponsorship, approval or authorization by Hobart. (The court also set up the procedures by which the plaintiff might obtain an accounting for the purpose of fixing damages.)

Trade Secrets, Patents, and Copyright

Trade Secrets. Society's interest in free competition is so strong that copying of competitor's product is lawful unless trademark, trade secret, patent, or copyright rights are infringed. Copying or product simulation is a widespread practice in American business.

A trade secret is any formula, pattern, device, or compilation of special information which gives the firm developing it a differential advantage over competitors. A firm claiming a trade secret must be able to show that the device or pattern was protected and treated as a secret within the firm. This usually means only a few people are allowed access to it and that it is never disclosed to anyone except on a confidential basis. Knowledge generally available in the trade cannot form the basis of trade secrets.

Trade secrets are given only limited protection by the law. It is only where competitors discover the secrets by bribery, theft, commercial espionage, or other wrongful means that injunctions and damages may be granted. If a trade secret is disclosed to someone on a confidential basis, any breach of this confidence will constitute a wrongful misappropriation.

Although a trade secret must confer some special competitive advantage, it need not embody the degree of inventiveness required for patentability. Some owners of patentable trade secrets may elect to run the risk of lawful imitation rather than to make the public disclosure of the invention as is required in order to obtain a patent. The legal monopoly conferred by the patent is only good for 17 years and then anyone can copy the invention.

Patents.   A patent may be granted to any person on any new and useful invention of a (1) process, (2) machine, (3) product, (4) composition of matter, (5) new and useful improvement thereof, (6) a growing plant, or (7) a design. The invention must not have been (1) patented or described in any printed publication in this or any foreign country for more than one year prior to application, (2) known or in use by others in this country prior to its invention, and (3) in public use or sale in this country for more than one year prior to application.

Except for design patents, a patentee gets the exclusive right to utilize, make or sell the patented product, machine, or process for a 17-year period. Design patents may be obtained from 3½ to 14 years depending upon the fee paid. The patent monopoly also includes the right to license others, to utilize the patent, and to control the terms and conditions under which such use is made.

The fact that the U.S. Patent Office has issued a patent does not necessarily mean that the patent is valid. About one third of all patents challenged in court are held to be invalid or unenforceable for various technical reasons. Infringement of a valid patent renders the infringer liable to the patentee for any profits earned, and also for damages suffered by the patentee. In addition, injunctive relief is available to the patentee to prevent future acts of infringement.

Copyrights.   A copyright confers on the holder for a period of 28 years the exclusive right to print, publish, copy, sell or perform books, periodicals, lectures, plays, musical compositions, maps, works of art, drawings of a technical nature, photographs, and motion pictures. The Copyright Act does not impair the common-law protection given to authors or owners of unpublished works. A copyright is obtained by filing an application with the Register of Copyrights, Copyright Office, Library of Congress, Washington, D.C. It can be renewed for an additional 28-year period provided the application for renewal is filed in the copyright office within one year prior to the expiration of the original term.

In general, any form of reproduction of copyrighted material without the consent of the copyright owner may render the copier liable for any actual damages the copyright owner can prove. The court may award from $250 to $5,000 statutory damages if actual damages cannot be proved. The extensive use of copying machines in the academic and business world creates many questions of possible liability under the Copyright Act. There is, however, an ill-defined "fair use" doctrine which may excuse the highly restricted reproduction and distribution of copyrighted material for nonprofit worthwhile purposes. This "fair use" exception is more likely to apply where the circumstances suggest that the copyright owner could not reasonably expect to receive greater royalties if copying of the type under consideration were to be penalized.

Summary

In general, in the absence of a patent, copyright, or trade secret the product of others may be imitated or copied. Liability for "palming off" may occur under trademark law if the consumer is being confused. Trade secrets may be duplicated so long as the method of duplication does not involve misappropriation. Patents give a 17-year legal monopoly to the patentee but many patents are held to be invalid. Copyrights confer the exclusive right to reproduce written material for a period of 28 years.

Sears, Roebuck & Co. v. Stiffel Co.
376 U.S. 225 (1964)

This was an action for unfair competition brought by Stiffel Co. (plaintiff) against Sears (defendant). Sears appealed from a judgment in favor of Stiffel. Reversed.

Stiffel developed a "pole lamp" which proved to be a commercial success. Sears then brought out a substantially identical lamp at a much lower price and Stiffel sued for unfair competition claiming that Sears had caused confusion in the trade as to the source of the lamps thereby engaging in unfair competition under Illinois law.

BLACK, JUSTICE. Pursuant to . . . constitutional authority, Congress in 1790 enacted the first federal patent and copyright law, 1 Stat. 109, and ever since that time has fixed the conditions upon which patents and copyrights shall be granted. These laws, like other laws of the United States enacted pursuant to constitutional authority, are the supreme law of the land. When state law touches upon the area of these federal statutes, it is "familiar doctrine" that the federal policy "may not be set at naught, or its benefits denied" by the state law. This is true, of course, even if the state law is enacted in the exercise of otherwise undoubted state power.

.   .   .   .   .

Thus the patent system is one in which uniform federal standards are carefully used to promote invention while at the same time preserving free competition. Obviously a State could not, consistently with the Supremacy Clause of the Constitution, extend the life of a patent beyond its expiration date or give a patent on an article which lacked the level of invention required for federal patents. . . .

In the present case, the "pole lamp" sold Stiffel has been held not to be entitled to the protection of either a mechanical or a design patent. An unpatentable article, like an article on which the patent has expired, is in the public domain and may be made and sold by whoever chooses to do so. What Sears did was to copy Stiffel's design and to sell lamps almost identical to those sold by Stiffel. This it had every right to do under the federal patent laws. That Stiffel originated the pole lamp and made it popular is immaterial. "Sharing in the goodwill of an article unprotected by patent or trade-mark is the exercise of a right possessed by all—and in the free exercise of which the consuming public is deeply interested." To allow a State by use of its law of unfair competition to prevent the copying of an article which represents too slight an advance to be patented would be to permit the State to block off from the public something which federal law has said belongs to the public. . . .

Sears has been held liable here for unfair competition because of a finding of likelihood of confusion based only on the fact that Sears' lamp was copied from Stiffel's unpatented lamp and that consequently the two looked exactly alike. Of course there could be "confusion" as to who had manufactured these nearly identical articles. But mere inability of the public to tell two identical articles apart is not enough to support an injunction against copying or an award of damages for copying that which the federal patent laws permit to be copied. Doubtless a State may, in appropriate circumstances, require that goods, whether patented or unpatented, be labeled or that other precautionary steps be taken to prevent customers from being misled as to the source, just as it may protect businesses in the use of their trademarks, labels, or distinctive dress in the packaging of goods so as to prevent others, by imitating such markings, from misleading purchasers as to the source of the goods. But because of the federal patent laws a State may not, when the article is unpatented and uncopyrighted, prohibit the copying of the article itself or award damages for such copying. . . .

Atlantic Wool Combing Co. v. *Norfolk Mills, Inc.*
357 F.2d 866 (5th Cir. 1966)

This was an action for misappropriation of a trade secret brought by Atlantic Wool Combing Co. (plaintiff) against Norfolk Mills, Inc. (defendant). Judgment for Norfolk and Atlantic appealed. Reversed.

Throughout most of 1960, the engineer who was Atlantic's director of research devoted full time to the devising of more efficient machinery. The result was a more efficient mechanism which removed a greater percentage of the down than had formerly been recovered.

During the latter part of 1960, Atlantic contracted with Henry Lawton, the owner of a small machine shop, to fabricate the new structures its engineer had devised and to assist in their installation. Atlantic's engineer supplied Lawton with the designs, drawing and instructions essential to the production of the new structures. In addition to manufacturing the essential new parts, Lawton promised the Atlantic that he would not reproduce them for anyone else.

Letoile, one of Atlantic's employees, helped to install the new machinery. He was aware that Atlantic treated the design of its machinery as confidential. In 1962, Norfolk employed Letoile in its new cashmere dehairing plant. At that time the Norfolk people knew in a general way that Atlantic had made some important modifications of its machinery which it regarded as confidential. Letoile informed Norfolk that Atlantic had successfully incorporated a pedal feed mechanism in its operation and that Lawton had made the parts.

Norfolk then approached Lawton to solicit the manufacture of a similar pedal feed dehairing mechanism for it. In so doing, Norfolk supplied no detailed specifications of its needs. After consulting his lawyer concerning his legal position, Lawton manufactured the desired machinery which was duly installed in Norfolk's plant. When Lawton manufactured the machinery for Norfolk he still had Atlantic's designs and blueprints in his possession.

HASTIE, CIRCUIT JUDGE. The district court denied Atlantic's device protection against appropriation because (1) its essential mechanical concepts were already embodied in another well known machine that performed a not very different function, and (2) the adaption of that familiar machine to the exigencies of efficient dehairing of raw cashmere was, in the court's view, a relatively simple undertaking for a competent technician. However, we think these considerations are not decisive against Atlantic's claim. Indeed, the significance accorded them in the court below unduly narrows the scope of trade secret protection.

What some other skilled person could or might have done is not controlling in this type of case, so long as Atlantic did in fact design for its own exclusive use and withheld from general knowledge a new and different machine which embodied an economically valuable advance in the art and process of dehairing raw cashmere. Commercially valuable special knowledge which the plaintiff Atlantic developed through the exercise of skill and ingenuity, through experimentation and through the expenditure of money and effort over a period of time, was embodied in the design and specifications of its new machinery. Moreover, this occurred in a small industry within which the court below found that each company designs and builds its own machinery and traditionally undertakes to keep the details of its process secret, just as Atlantic did here. No more novelty or secrecy than these circumstances establish is needed to bring a proprietor's commercially valuable special knowledge within the area of legally protected trade secrets. . . .

Novelty and invention are not requisite for a trade secret as they are for patentability. . . . The protection is merely against breach of faith and reprehensible means of learning another's secret. For this limited protection it is not appropriate to require also the kind of novelty and invention which is a requisite for patentability. *Restatement,* Torts Sec. 757 comment b.

Within this area the law of torts affords limited protection varying with the circumstances. In general, the essence of the wrong is the obtaining of unjust enrichment and unfair competitive advantage through inequitable conduct, usually a breach of confidence. In particular application of this doctrine, the courts rather consistently impose liability on a proprietor of a business who employs unfair means, characterized by breach of confidence, to acquire otherwise undisclosed plans and specifications for a competitor's distinctive structure or machinery and uses them to produce a similar competitive device for his own use and to his competitor's economic detriment.

.   .   .   .   .

It remains to consider whether the circumstances of Atlantic's disclosure of the details of its machine to Lawton and the circumstances of Lawton's use of that information for the defendant Norfolk's benefit constitute such a breach of confidence as makes Norfolk's appropriation of the Atlantic's special knowledge tortious. Certainly, Lawton was aware that Atlantic's designs were not public knowledge and that they had been entrusted to him for the limited purpose of fabrication for Atlantic's exclusive use. Indeed, Lawton testified that Atlantic "asked me if I would agree not to make the parts for anyone else . . . and that I agreed to." The assumption of fiduciary responsibility by Lawton and his subsequent liability creating breach of Atlantic's confidence are clear.

Norfolk stands in no better position than Lawton. Furnishing Lawton with no plans of its own, it induced him to build for it a machine like Atlantic's, well knowing that the details of the construction of Atlantic's machine were valuable secret information belonging to a competitor. Thus, in legal contemplation, Norfolk was as blameworthy as Lawton and equally responsible.

Interference with Contract or Economic Expectations

Interference with Contract.   In the landmark case *Lumley* v. *Gye* (1853) a court first ruled that an outsider, who maliciously induced one of the two parties to a contract not to perform the contract, would be liable for damages in tort to the other contracting party who was thereby deprived of the benefits of the contract. The doctrine was later extended to protect all types of business contracts from intentional interferences which were without legal justification. Although the cases are not in complete agreement they seem to make a distinction between those situations where the defendant actively *induced* the breach, and those where the defendant's conduct simply *caused* the breach.

Even where a person induces the breach his conduct might be privileged or justifiable on some ground. For example, it was held that a mother who induced a school to exclude a diseased child from her child's private school was not liable to the parents of the diseased child for having induced the school to breach its contract. Business competition only affords a limited justification for interference with contracts. As Prosser states:

The courts have held that the sanctity of the existing contract relation takes precedence over any interest in unrestricted competition, and have enforced as law the ethical precept that one competitor must keep his hands off of the contracts of another. This is true of contracts of employment, where workmen are hired away from an employer, as well as competitive business dealings in general; and it has found particular application in cases of offers of better terms to induce the breach of a contract, and of the violation of exclusive agency agreements and the purchase of goods in derogation of a contract limiting their resale.[1]

Interference with Economic Expectations. The early cases of interference with economic expectations usually involved situations where physical violence was employed to drive off customers or workers. Liability was later extended to cover nonviolent malicious interference and then to unjustifiable intentional interference. Where the intent to interfere is present the liability depends upon the motive and purposes of the defendant and upon the means that he utilizes.

Summary

The unjustifiable interference with the contractual relations of others creates tort liability. The cases consider the motive or purpose of the party inducing the breach and make a distinction between actively inducing breach and simply causing breach. Reasonable economic expectations are also protected but the boundaries of this law are ill-defined.

Bender v. Hearst Corp.

263 F.2d 360 (2nd Cir. 1959)

This was an action brought by Bender (plaintiff) against Hearst Corp. (defendant) for damages for having induced breach of a contract between Bender and Reidl. Judgment for Bender in the amount of $87,500 and Hearst appealed. Affirmed.

In 1953 Bender became a part-time distributor of a loose-leaf reporting service known as Crash Book Service which provided insurance companies, damage appraisers and automobile repair shops with data on the current costs of automobile repairs conveniently displayed in loose-leaf form. The copyright covering the book was held by one Reidl, who traded under the name Crash Book Service. In October 1954 Bender was persuaded by Reidl to give up all other employment and enter an agreement to act as a full-time exclusive distributor of Crash Book Service in an area of the United States generally comprised of the New England and Middle Atlantic States. By October 10, 1956 when this agreement was terminated by the acts of Reidl and Hearst Corporation, Bender employed three full-time and twenty part-time assistants in the distribution of Crash Book Service.

---

[1] William L. Prosser, *Handbook of the Law of Torts* (3rd ed.; St. Paul, Minn.: West Publishing Co., 1964), p. 970.

The distributorship agreement was partly established by letters and partly by oral conversations. It was primarily drafted by Reidl, who, by a letter in September 1955 attempted to integrate it. It included representations by Reidl that by plowing back into the distributorship the commissions on initial sales Bender would profit, in the manner of insurance salesmen, from renewal commissions after a base of initial sales had been established in the first few years. Bender acted upon these representations so that by September 30, 1956, after two years of full-time work, he had sustained a cash loss of a few hundred dollars, but had accounted for more than 3,000 sales, about one half of all sales of Crash Book Service. The agreement also provided prices to the distributor and for resale and certain wholesale discounts. Under it Bender secured a commission of $10 on most initial sales and $5 on renewals, with smaller amounts on bulk sales.

Bender's territory was defined, and it was provided that the agreement would continue in force so long as the distributor remained active in the territory, with activity measured by the maintenance of a reasonable number of subscribers. On the distributor's wrongful conduct all of Reidl's obligations under the contract were to cease, but if the distributor withdrew voluntarily and without wrongful behavior provision was made for him to receive the benefits of the contract for one year. If the distributor died payments were to be made to his family for two years. There was no express provision for the withdrawal of Reidl.

In March 1956 Hearst Corporation determined that its publication, *Motors Manual,* was no longer adequate. It decided to discontinue publication for the two years that would be required to revamp the publication in order to incorporate the advantages that had been suggested by Reidl's design. To avoid the undesirable competitive consequences of a withdrawal of part of its multiple line of publications from the market for so long a time, Hearst Corporation, a publisher with large resources, finally decided to attempt negotiations with Reidl looking to the purchase of his Crash Book Service and its incorporation in Hearst Corporation's line in place of *Motors Manual.*

At about the same time Reidl became concerned over the future of Crash Book Service because of seemingly reliable rumors that Hearst Corporation and others were undertaking revisions of their manuals to incorporate the Crash Book Service advantages, and because these competitors, with their national distribution systems and multiple publications, might prove too much for the small new organization handling Crash Book. The negotiations commenced in May 1956 and resulted in the execution of a written contract for the sale of Crash Book Service to Hearst, executed at Milwaukee, Wisconsin on September 25, 1956, under which Reidl received $42,500 in cash, a contract of employment as editor of the service, and a royalty of 50¢ on all future sales of Crash Book for ten years up to $100,000.

Hearst Corporation knew of Reidl's contract with Bender and was familiar with its terms as well as with the sales and renewals achieved by plaintiff in his territory. Hearst Corporation, as part of the inducement held out to Reidl, agreed to defend him against any suit that Bender might bring, and to reimburse him for any recovery up to $2,500. By this and other inducements Hearst persuaded the reluctant Reidl to repudiate his contract with Bender. By the terms of its contract with Reidl, Hearst Corporation became entitled to receive the profit on subsequent renewals of outstanding subscriptions, and on October 11, 1956 Hearst Corporation took steps to protect this interest by notifying Bender's customers that they were thereafter to deal only with its salesmen. After August 31, 1956 Bender was neither paid nor credited with any of the profit due him on renewals, which averaged 80% of original sales and Bender sued Hearst.

LUMBARD, CIRCUIT JUDGE. Hearst Corporation argues finally that even if the contract did not expressly give Reidl the right to terminate it at will, it is a familiar doctrine of contract law that a manufacturer who agrees to supply an article to a distributor, even to do so for a particular length of time, does not thereby covenant that he will not terminate his business, and therefore Reidl's termination of Bender's interest by sale of the business to Hearst did not involve a breach of the contract. So general a proposition cannot be sustained. While many cases have held that termination by sale is not a breach, they have each determined that the sale of the business was done in "good faith," which has generally, although not uniformly, meant that the owner was unable to continue in business profitably. We have been referred to no case in Wisconsin or elsewhere which has permitted a manufacturer to sell a profitable operating business and to divert to himself profits upon which his distributor was persuaded to rely, on the ground that no covenant to remain in business would be implied. Reidl of course was obligated to deal with Bender in good faith, and we hold that the sale to Hearst without protection of Bender's interest in his distributorship was not a sale in good faith, and was, as the district court found, a breach of his contract.

These latter considerations dispose of Hearst's claim that its inducement to Reidl to commit a breach of his agreement was privileged. Hearst claims that it did not seek Bender's distribution business, but instead sought only to replace a manual whose publication it was forced to suspend with a new and more promising one; that its interest as a publisher was an independent business interest of equal dignity with Bender's; that it did not seek to injure Bender; that therefore the law will not choose between it and Bender, but will hold its assertion of its interest in the acquisition of a new publication privileged. This argument ignores the fact that Hearst deliberately appropriated to itself the commissions on renewals which were Bender's primary profits from his past efforts. Such an appropriation is not "incidental" to its acquisition of a new publication, whose established renewal rate was 80%, and one-half of whose sales had been made by Bender. As against Bender, Hearst stands in no better shoes than would a distributor who had persuaded Reidl to transfer distribution to him. Finally, as recently as 1956 the Wisconsin Supreme Court has held that the "malice" which will subject a defendant to liability may be implied from his knowledge of the plaintiff's contract.

Frank H. Gibson, Inc. v. Omaha Coffee Co.

137 N.W.2d 701 (Sup. Ct. Neb. 1965)

This was an action brought by Frank H. Gibson, Inc. (plaintiff), against Omaha Coffee Company, Conroy Coffee Company, and Kenneth Loseke (defendants) for damages alleged to have resulted from a conspiracy to purchase Gibson, Inc.'s business on their own terms, and if unable to do so, to take over Gibson's sales force, routes, and customers. The trial court jury returned a judgment for Gibson for $20,000 but the court granted a motion for a new trial. Gibson appealed. Reversed and judgment for Gibson reinstated.

Bellows, founder and president, started Gibson, Inc., in 1931 and controlled all but about ten percent of the stock which was held by Loseke, vice president of the company. Thirty years later Gibson, Inc., employed three salesmen and sold a sizable volume of coffee, tea and sundries to restaurants, cafes and factories around Omaha. Gibson, Inc., purchased all of its coffee (about $150,000 per year) from Conroy Coffee Co.

At a meeting, Clark, president of Conroy, and other defendants informed Bellows that they would give him $30,000 for Gibson, Inc. They also told him that if he did not accept the offer that they were prepared to take over his salesmen and customers and to go in business in competition with him on the following Monday. Loseke personally verified the fact that he and the salesmen were prepared to leave Gibson, Inc. In view of this Bellows decided to accept the offer but was told by Clark that he (Clark) had changed his mind and he would not offer as much.

Bellows sold Gibson, Inc., to another firm but Loseke and the three salesmen went over to Conroy Coffee Co. Gibson, Inc., filed suit for damages for conspiracy and unfair competition. Conroy argues that any harm done can be justified by competition.

SPENCER, JUSTICE.   As Conroy pointed out, we said in *Barish* v. *Chrysler Corp.,* "Any person may do business with whomsoever he desires. Also, he may refuse business relations with any person whomsoever. . . . One who causes intended or unintended harm to another by refusing to continue a business relation with him, terminable at his will, is not liable for that harm."

However, in the instant case we have a different situation. We do not have a refusal to do business, but rather an attempt to steal a business by taking unfair advantage of a business relationship. Here we have Clark working with Loseke, a fiduciary, to force a sale to Conroy on its own terms or to destroy the good will of Gibson. Proof of the intent, understanding, or agreement in such instances must usually rest largely on inferences. Here, however, we have direct testimony on the intent of Conroy, corroborated essentially by legitimate inferences from Loseke's actions. Also, the preliminary preparation and the promptness with which the defendants took over the Gibson routes can substantiate the inference of a preconceived plan.

The jury could reasonably find, as it must have done, that Bellows was forced to sell the company because of the conspiracy between Loseke and Conroy, and that this conspiracy entirely destroyed the good will of Gibson.

A legitimate purpose does not justify an unlawful act. It is undisputed in the record that Conroy was not in the retail business; that it had no retail business in the area; that it had no retail sales force available; and that the only way it could accomplish its purpose was by inducing a fiduciary to help to take over Gibson's sales force and by appropriating the use of Gibson's equipment to its own purpose until it could replace it with its own. This is not a matter of competition except as it may be described as unfair competitive practice. It is not a matter of simply hiring Gibson's employees after a sale has been made to a competitor to call on Gibson's former customers. Rather, a proper inference is that it was an agreement made previous to any offer of sale to take over the Gibson business if Conroy could not force a sale on its own terms (and the evidence is that when those terms were met, it changed its terms). It is the preconceived plan to accomplish this purpose which is illegal and which under Gibson's theory forced the sale of the business and destroyed the good will of Gibson's business.

Problem Cases

1. Continental Nut buys various kinds of nuts, processes them, and then resells them. Among the products which it handles are Brazil nuts of a type known as "natural" nuts. Berner is engaged in a similar business, but the Brazil nuts which it imports are not of the "natural" variety but are cured and processed before being imported. Berner published and distributed a letter to its customers under the notation "Important." In the course of the letter, the "natural" nuts bought and resold by Continental were referred to as "green" nuts. Berner claimed that such nuts were "rarely, if ever, properly cured." "[T]he people who buy green Brazil nuts (and most of them won't know they are getting green nuts) will have a shrinkage on their hands and the nuts will develop mould." Berner's customers were further warned that "Food and Drug will be more active than ever" and that "somebody is going to be in trouble" if the Food and Drug inspectors find that the green Brazil nuts do not meet proper standards. At the end of the letter Berner listed Continental Nut among those importers bringing most of the green Brazil nuts into this country.

   Continental sued Berner for libel. Continental alleged an immediate decrease in their gross sales of Brazil nuts and of all other nuts following the publication of the letter. Although not naming the particular customers it lost, Continental listed specific figures of its gross sales before and after the publication and averred that the decrease in sales was the "natural and proximate result" of the letter. Berner contends the statements were not libelous of Continental as a company but at most would be disparagement of the green Brazil nuts, thus requiring allegation and proof of specific special damages. Should Continental's action be dismissed for the reasons stated by Berner?

2. Standard Brands has as a registered trademark "V-8" which it uses on cans containing a combination of eight vegetable juices. Standard also makes and markets several other well-known food products and sells dry vitamin tablets in packages bearing the trademark "Stams." Smidler began selling dry vitamin tablets in an elongated carton on which was printed the symbol "V-8" over the words "Vitamin Tablets" in slightly smaller type. The sentence "These tablets contain 8 vitamins and three minerals" in still smaller type was also on the package. Standard sues to get an injunction against Smidler's use of the "V-8" symbol on the grounds it constitutes an infringement of Standard's trademark and unfair competition. What decision and why?

3. Norwich Pharmacal developed and marketed Pepto-Bismol, a pink-colored medicine for minor stomach disorders, which proved highly successful commercially. Sterling,

one of Norwich's competitors, developed Pepsamar which they also colored pink but which was packaged using a container and label that bore no resemblance to Norwich's packaging. Norwich seeks an injunction barring Sterling from simulating the pink color of Pepto-Bismol in its product Pepsamar and from manufacturing and selling such a product. Should the injunction be issued?

4. In 1893, the predecessor of National Biscuit began producing and marketing a product known as "Shredded Wheat," a pillow-shaped biscuit of wheat. The patented machinery with which National Biscuit had produced the product passed into the public domain prior to the time that Kellogg began producing and marketing "Shredded Wheat." The Kellogg product is clearly marked "Kellogg's" and its cartons are different in size, form, and color from National Biscuit's. National sues Kellogg, alleging unfair competition on the grounds that Kellogg used the name shredded wheat and produced its biscuit in pillow form. Should an injunction be issued enjoining Kellogg's from the sale of this product under this name and in this form?

5. In 1957, O'Day Corporation hired a well-known boat designer to design a safe planing sailboat for family use. In 1958, O'Day began making and selling this boat, the "Day Sailer," and enjoyed commercial success. In early 1959, O'Day hired Bigelow as assistant to its president but Bigelow was discharged after about six months for reasons not relevant to this case. Bigelow decided to manufacture a planing sailboat of his own and studied various boats for a time. In 1960, Bigelow bought a "Day Sailer" and made some changes and alterations in the hull and deck. As modified, this boat was photographed and used in the initial advertising material for Bigelow's boat called the "Explorer." Bigelow had altered the hull so that it would carry an outboard motor without the use of a bracket. A bracket had to be added in order to install a motor on the "Day Sailer."

Bigelow made a mold of the hull of the "Day Sailer" and used this in making the "Explorer." Several new features were added to the Explorer and it enjoyed commercial success.

There was no evidence that customers were confused as to the source of the two boats. Bigelow's boats were plainly marked as to name and origin. There was no evidence that Bigelow used secret information given to him in confidence. O'Day held no design or device patents on the "Day Sailer." O'Day now sues Bigelow and his company asking for damages for unfair competition. What result?

6. Action Comics produced and copyrighted a comic strip series which featured "Superman." Bruns Publication Co. began producing a comic strip which featured "Wonderman." Action Comics claimed that Bruns had infringed their copyright and the judge found that "each publication portrays a man of miraculous strength and speed called 'Superman' in 'Action Comics' and 'Wonderman' in the magazine of Bruns. The attributes and antics of 'Superman' and 'Wonderman' are closely similar. Each at times conceals his strength beneath ordinary clothing but after removing his cloak stands revealed in full panoply in a skin-tight acrobatic costume. The only real difference between them is that 'Superman' wears a blue uniform and 'Wonderman' a red one. Each is termed the champion of the oppressed. Each is shown running toward a full moon 'off into the night,' and each is shown crushing a gun in his powerful hands. 'Superman' is pictured as stopping a bullet with his person and 'Wonderman' as arresting and throwing back shells. Each is depicted as shot at by three men, yet as wholly impervious to the missiles that strike him. 'Superman' is shown as leaping from building to building. 'Superman' and 'Wonderman' are each endowed with sufficient strength to rip open a steel door. Each is described as being

the strongest man in the world and each as battling against 'evil and injustice'." Should Bruns be found guilty of copyright infringement on these facts?

7. Lone Ranger, Inc., owns the copyright to a radio dramatic serial as well as to a comic strip featuring a mythical western cowboy. In addition they have licensed the use of the trademark "Lone Ranger" to vendors of various objects. An actor by the name of Powell and who once played the part of the "Lone Ranger" in a motion picture licensed by Lone Ranger, Inc., has been appearing in a small circus run by Cox. Powell takes the part of a masked man on a white horse, gives the distinctive cry, "Hi, yo, Silver, away!", and is advertised as the "original Lone Ranger" or the "Lone Ranger in person." Lone Ranger, Inc., contends that this is an infringement of their copyright as well as unfair competition. Should an injunction and damages be granted against Powell and Cox on these grounds?

8. Buono Sales held a DeSoto-Plymouth dealership from Chrysler Corporation. When Chrysler discontinued production of DeSotos it sent a letter to all of Buono's DeSoto customers telling them of the discontinuance of the DeSoto line and urging that Dodge dealers were the "best qualified" to provide service on the DeSotos. Buono contends that this constituted tortious interference with business. Is this contention valid?

9. Yocum was employed as a driver-salesman for Colteryahn Dairy for several years before he quit to take a job with another competing dairy. He took no physical customer lists with him but relied on his memory in soliciting his former customers he dealt with while working for Colteryahn. In some cases he told the customers he had been unfairly dismissed by his former employer. There was no clause in Yocum's employment contract which prohibited his solicitations of customers upon termination of his employment with Colteryahn. Colteryahn sues asking that Yocum be enjoined from soliciting their customers and also that he be enjoined from falsely stating the circumstances of his dismissal. What result?

chapter 46. The Sherman Act

Introduction

Legal History. In the 1800's, several English steamship companies combined for the purpose of controlling competition in the shipping business. They jointly reduced rates below cost in certain ports, gave rebates to shippers dealing exclusively with their association, and refused to haul for any shipper who dealt anywhere with a competing shipping company. Several competing carriers brought a tort action claiming that the defendants had intentionally caused the plaintiff great harm without any legal justification.

The English court's ruling in favor of the defendants illustrates how few legal constraints there were on monopolistic business practices at common law. The court ruled that the defendants were only pursuing a "war of competition waged in the interest of their own trade;" and the competitive interest justified the harm inflicted.[1]

With the growth of national markets following the Civil War large industrial combines and trusts engaged in monopolistic practices that soon led to a public outcry for regulation. In 1890, Congress enacted the Sherman Act (26 Stat. 209 [1890] as amended, 15 U.S.C. §§ 1–7.) thereby adopting a public policy calling for the preservation and promotion of free competition within the American economy. Although a number of important exceptions or exemptions have been made, and although additional antitrust laws have been added, this basic competitive policy has been maintained since 1890. The Supreme Court summarized the basis for this belief in competition when it said:

Basic to the faith that a free economy best promotes the public weal is that goods must stand the cold test of competition; that the public, acting through the market's im-

---

[1] *Mogul Steamship Co. Ltd.* v. *McGregor Gow & Co.,* (1889) 23 Q.B.D. 598, Aff'd. (1892) A.C. 25.

personal judgment, shall allocate the Nation's resources and thus direct the course its economic development will take.[2]

Jurisdiction. The Sherman Act applies only to restraints which have a significant impact upon commerce, either domestic or foreign. Local activities are subject to the act if the anticompetitive effect on commerce is present. For example, restraints affecting the local distribution of goods originating in another state may be subject to the act even where the local retailer purchased the goods from a local wholesaler. Purely local restraints on competition are subject to state antitrust laws; but state regulation of anticompetitive practices has been highly sporadic and largely ineffective.

Summary

The Sherman Act attempts to promote and protect free competition as the prime regulating mechanism in our economy. The Sherman Act applies only to restraints which have a significant impact on commerce. Purely local restraints are subject to state regulation.

C. A. Page Publishing Co. v. Work
178 F.Supp. 184 (S.D. Cal. 1959)

This was an action for treble damages under Section 1 of the Sherman Act brought by C. A. Page Publishing Co. (plaintiff) against the Los Angeles News Bureau and others (defendants). Judgment for defendants.

Page Publishing Company owned and published the *Commercial News,* a general business newspaper serving the Los Angeles area. Page brought an antitrust action against a number of community newspapers serving small neighborhoods in and around Los Angeles and the Los Angeles Newspaper Service Bureau together with several of its officers. The Bureau was owned substantially by the defendant newspapers and represented them in the solicitation of legal advertising.

Page claimed that collusive and illegal bidding by defendants caused the *Commercial News* to lose printing contracts for the 1951 and 1954 Los Angeles delinquent tax lists.

SOLOMON, DISTRICT JUDGE. Page argues that a newspaper is by its nature engaged in interstate commerce, and therefore acts which interfere with the normal operation of a newspaper business necessarily affect interstate commerce sufficiently to satisfy the jurisdictional requirements of the Sherman and Clayton Acts.

We may assume that Page and defendant newspapers are engaged in interstate commerce by virtue of (1) their regular purchases of newsprint from sources outside of California, (2) their carriage of some national news and feature items, (3) their carriage of some national advertising, and (4) a few out-of-state subscribers.

However, the test of jurisdiction is not that the acts complained of affect a

---

[2] *Times-Picayune Co.* v. *U.S.,* 345 U.S. 594, 605 (1953).

business engaged in interstate commerce, but that the offensive acts affect the interstate commerce of such business or any business. Furthermore, it is not all economic consequences to interstate commerce which confer jurisdiction but only those anticompetitive consequences which the statutes are designed to prevent.

. . . . .

In *Sears, Roebuck & Company* v. *Blade,* Sears brought a treble damages action against its former Los Angeles advertising manager and several local engravers, arising out of an alleged kick-back arrangement between the manager and his codefendants in the sale to Sears of engravings and mats.

Ample facts appeared to qualify Sears as a business engaged in interstate commerce, and the court so found. Nevertheless, the court dismissed the action on the express ground that the acts complained of were not alleged to have restrained or have tended to restrain these interstate activities in which Sears was engaged.

In every case cited by Page involving news media, a defendant had restrained, or attempted to restrain, competition in the interstate market for national news and advertising.

In each of these cases, newspapers, enjoying dominant positions in local or regional newspaper markets, utilized various methods outlawed by the Sherman Act, to draw advertising from competing news media, in order to drive competitors out of business and to monopolize local markets for interstate news and advertising.

In *Evening News Pub. Co.* v. *Allied Newspaper Carriers of New Jersey* an association of newspaper carriers utilized its dominant position of the home delivery market to force the Evening News to abandon the use of newsboys in order to restrain and monopolize home deliveries of the News. The court held that the dissemination of national news and advertising was "an essential element of [the newspaper's] being," and that home delivery is "an integral part of the interstate operation."

In the present case, the loss of the delinquent tax list contracts was not alleged to have threatened the normal operation of the *Commercial News*—a newspaper of general circulation neither primarily devoted to, nor economically dependent upon legal advertising. Thus, although the *Commercial News* carried substantial amounts of national news and display advertising, there was no interference with the flow of such news and advertising to *Commercial News* readers.

Page asserts that the defendant newspapers were able to destroy the Journal by the exercise of control over the local legal advertising market. But this control could afford them no leverage to gain control of the interstate markets in newsprint, national news, or national display advertising, no matter how successful their monopoly of the legal advertising market, since the major users of these interstate services and commodities, such as the great metropolitan dailies, are not dependent upon the revenues brought by legal advertising.

Sanctions and Remedies

Criminal and Civil Proceedings.   Persons found guilty of violating either Section 1 or 2 of the Sherman Act are subject to criminal prosecution for a misdemeanor and, upon conviction, to a fine not exceeding $50,000, or imprisonment for not more than one year, or both.[3] The Department of Justice also may institute civil proceedings to restrain conduct in violation of the act and ask the court for various remedies including decrees of divorcement, divestiture or, in extreme cases, dissolution.[4]

Any person injured as a result of violations of the act may bring a suit for treble damages against the violators and also recover reasonable attorney's fees. The classic antitrust conviction against General Electric Co. and other electrical equipment manufacturers resulted in the payment of over $200,000,000 in treble damages claims. Criminal fines are not deductible against federal income taxes, but treble damage claims paid may be deducted as business expenses.

A sizable number of the cases brought by the Department of Justice are settled out of court either by consent decrees in civil suits, or pleas of *nolo contendere* in criminal prosecutions. The court decrees are tailored to meet the competitive ills in each situation. On occasion, the defendants may be ordered to license patents on a royalty free basis, file continuing reports showing compliance, or even give aid in the creation of a new competitive firm in the industry.

If a company is adjudged to have violated the Sherman Act this judgment may be used as proof of violation by claimants later filing private treble damage suits. Such claimants would still be required to prove that their losses grew out of the conduct adjudged to be in violation of the Act. The fact that the company charged took a consent decree or filed a plea of *nolo contendere* cannot be used as evidence of violation of the act in subsequent treble damage suits.

Summary

The Sherman Act provides for both civil and criminal proceedings. Treble damage suits may be brought by private parties suffering losses as a result of conduct prohibited under the act. A very large percentage of all cases brought by the government are settled by consent degrees or pleas of *nolo contendere*.

Section 1

Joint Restraints.   Section 1 of the Sherman Act provides:

Every contract, combination in the form of trust or otherwise, or conspiracy, in restraint of trade or commerce among the several states, or with foreign nations is declared to be illegal.

---

[3] Under the Clayton Act, Section 14, corporate officers participating in a corporate violation are liable for a fine up to $5,000 or one year or both.

[4] Divorcement means that the company is separated from some operating function. For example, the meat-packers were divorced from owning or controlling retail outlets. A company may be ordered to divest itself of assets or stock. Du Pont was ordered to divest itself of G.M. stock. Dissolution means that a company must liquidate its assets and go out of business.

The "contract" is the agreement to restrain competition. A "combination" occurs when two or more persons join together for the purpose of carrying out united action. A "conspiracy" is a continuing partnership in restraint of trade. At least two persons are required under all of these forms of joint activity. The departments or divisions of a company are viewed as being parts of one company and intra-company conduct does not violate Section 1. A principal corporation, however, may be found in violation of Section 1 where it conspires with a subsidiary.

Per Se Restraints under Section 1

The Nature of Per Se Restraints.   Certain types of joint activities restraining competition are classed as illegal per se, meaning illegal in and of themselves. These activities are assumed to have such a highly detrimental effect on competition that no arguments in justification of such activities are permitted. Some of the most important restraints of this type include contracts, combinations, or conspiracies to control production, fix or manipulate prices, divide markets or customers, or impose group boycotts.

Restraints on Production.   Under competitive theory, the public is supposed to receive the benefit of an optimum production of goods and services at the lowest possible prices. Joint arrangements among competitors which seek to manipulate production for anticompetitive purposes are per se violations.

Restraints on Pricing.   A majority of the antitrust cases brought by the government under Section 1 involve charges of price fixing. As a general rule, any joint activities fixing or attempting to control prices either horizontally (between competitors) or vertically (between suppliers and distributors) are illegal per se.[5] This prohibition applies regardless of the motive of those fixing, stabilizing, or manipulating prices and applies to setting maximum prices to protect consumers as well as setting minimum prices to protect small firms in a distress industry.

The antitrust agencies often use circumstantial evidence to establish legal pricing arrangements. Nor need there be proof of an outright agreement. As the Supreme Court stated in one case:

It is elementary that an unlawful conspiracy may be and often is formed without simultaneous action or agreement on the part of the conspirators. . . . Acceptance by competitors, without previous agreement, of an invitation to participate in a plan, the necessary consequence of which, if carried out, is restraint of interstate commerce, is sufficient to establish an unlawful conspiracy under the Sherman Act. . . .[6]

---

[5] State "Fair Trade" laws may exempt certain types of vertical price fixing arrangements. This exception to competitive policy is discussed subsequently.

[6] *Interstate Circuit Inc.* v. *U.S.,* 306 U.S. 208, 227 (1939). In dictum in *F.T.C.* v. *Cement Institute,* 333 U.S. 683, 716 n.17 (1948), the Supreme Court said: "It is enough to warrant a

On the other hand, the mere fact that competitors may charge the same prices does not of itself prove a violation. In another case, the Supreme Court stated:

> . . . But this Court has never held that proof of parallel business behavior conclusively establishes agreement or, phrased differently, that such behavior itself constitutes a Sherman Act offense. Circumstantial evidence of consciously parallel behavior may have made heavy inroads into the traditional judicial attitude toward conspiracy; but "conscious parallelism" has not yet read conspiracy out of the Sherman Act entirely.[7]

A manufacturer acting unilaterally, is not prohibited from selling to a dealer and *suggesting* a resale price. Such a manufacturer may, subject to supply contract obligations, discontinue selling to any dealer who refuses to abide by the suggested prices. However, if the manufacturer tries to obtain a price maintenance agreement from any dealer or in any way collaborates with other dealers in seeing that the suggested prices are maintained, Section 1 is violated.

Division of Markets or Customers.   In one of the earliest antitrust cases, several pipe manufacturers were held guilty of per se violations when they apportioned out their market geographically among themselves.[8] It is likewise illegal per se for competitors to allocate customers and agree not to solicit each other's customers.

A manufacturer or supplier may not impose market area or customer restriction agreements on his distributors who are buying goods for resale. A supplier may, however, designate an area of *primary responsibility* for each distributor and may require that each distributor achieve reasonable market penetration in the designated area.

Group Boycotts.   Joint activities by competitors designed to foreclose any competitor's access to a market or to a source of supply are illegal per se. This was held to be true even where dress manufacturers combined to prevent retail stores throughout the nation from dealing with design "pirate" manufacturers who were copying the dress patterns of the "legitimate" dress manufacturers.[9]

Reciprocal Dealing Arrangements.   Large firms typically buy large quantities of goods from suppliers. In many cases, these supplying companies have need of goods of the type manufactured by companies which they supply. Under these circumstances, a large firm may find it very advantageous to use its buying power as a means of "encouraging" its suppliers to purchase all or most of their requirements from the large firm. This use of purchasing power

---

finding of a 'combination' within the meaning of the Sherman Act, if there is evidence that persons, with knowledge that concerted action was contemplated and invited, give adherence to and then participate in a scheme."

[7] *Theatre Enterprises Inc.* v. *Paramount Film Distributing Corp.,* 346 U.S. 537, 540 (1954).

[8] *U.S.* v. *Addyston Pipe & Steel Co.,* 85 F.271 (6th Cir. 1898), Aff'd. 175 U.S. 211 (1899).

[9] *Fashion Originator's Guild* v. *F.T.C.,* 312 U.S. 457 (1941).

to promote sales is called "reciprocity" and may involve serious antitrust consequences.

The case law on reciprocity is very limited. In the 1930's the F.T.C. found that the coercive use of reciprocity was an unfair method of competition which violated Section 5 of the Federal Trade Commission Act. Reciprocity and even the possibility of reciprocity were important considerations in recent cases brought under the merger prohibitions of the Clayton Act (Section 7).[10]

In *United States* v. *General Dynamics*[11] the court indicated that either coercive or mutual patronage reciprocity agreements could constitute per se violations of Section 1 of the Sherman Act. The court stated: "the actual or potential implementation of coercive reciprocity, which presupposes the existence of leverage (i.e., large purchases from, and currently small sales to, the prospect), is inimical to a competitive economic society. 'Mutual patronage' reciprocity, on the other hand, occurs when both parties stand on equal footing with reference to purchasing power inter se, yet agree to purchase from one another. While the former practice certainly is the more offensive, the latter arrangements are equally disruptive of the competitive processes."[12]

Other Per Se Restraints.   Other per se restraints include joint action by competitors to pool profits and losses, refrain from advertising prices, and to refrain from bidding against each other at auctions. Marketing arrangements otherwise legal (i.e., agency distribution or reciprocal dealing) may become illegal per se if a dominant firm exercises coercive control over other firms in creating or operating such arrangement. Also illegal per se are virtually all tying contracts or any activities attempting to extend the antitrust immunities granted in any exceptions or exemptions to the act beyond the strict limitations created for such exceptions or exemptions. The exemptions to the antitrust laws are discussed in Chapter 48.

Summary

Section 1 of the act prohibits joint conduct in restraint of competition. Major per se restraints include agreements to: control production; fix or stabilize prices; divide markets or allocate customers; boycott other competitors; and most tying contracts. Where per se restraints are involved no defenses or justifications for the conduct will be permitted.

Esco Corp. v. *United States*
340 F.2d 1000 (9th Cir. 1965)

Esco and three other distributors of stainless steel pipe were prosecuted for a criminal conspiracy to fix prices under Section 1 of the Sherman Act. The three

---

[10] *FTC* v. *Consolidated Foods*, 380 U.S. 592 (1965).
[11] 258 F. Supp. 36 (S.D. N.Y. 1966).
[12] *Id.* at 59.

other defendants filed pleas of *nolo contendere* and only Esco chose to stand trial. Esco appealed from a jury verdict finding Esco guilty. Affirmed.

BARNES, CIRCUIT JUDGE. While particularly true of price-fixing conspiracies, it is well recognized law that any conspiracy can ordinarily only be proved by inferences drawn from relevant and competent circumstantial evidence, including the conduct of the defendants charged. A knowing wink can mean more than words. Let us suppose five competitors meet on several occasions, discuss their problems, and one finally states—"I won't fix prices with any of you, but here is what I am going to do—put the price of my gidget at X dollars; now you all do what you want." He then leaves the meeting. Competitor number two says—"I don't care whether number one does what he says he's going to do or not; nor do I care what the rest of you do, but I am going to price my gidget at X dollars." Number three makes a similar statement—"My price is X dollars." Number four says not one word. All leave and fix "their" prices at "X" dollars.

We do not say the foregoing illustration *compels* an inference in this case that the competitors' conduct constituted a price-fixing conspiracy, *including an agreement to so conspire,* but neither can we say, as a matter of law, that an inference of no agreement is compelled. As in so many other instances, it remains a question for the trier of fact to consider and determine what inference appeals to it (the jury) as most logical and persuasive, after it has heard all the evidence as to what these competitors had done before such meeting, and what actions they took thereafter, or what actions they did not take.

An accidental or incidental price uniformity, or even "pure" conscious parallelism of prices is, standing alone, not unlawful. Nor is an individual competitor's sole decision to follow a price leadership, standing alone, a violation of law. But we do not find that factual situation here.

Esco then adds a definition to "mutual consent," *i.e.,* "an exchange of assurances to take or refrain from a given course of conduct." With this we disagree, if by it appellant means the existence of specific assurances. Written assurances it concedes, are unnecessary. So are oral assurances, if a course of conduct, or a price schedule, once suggested or outlined by a competitor in the presence of other competitors, is followed by all—generally and customarily—and continuously for all practical purposes, even though there be slight variations.

It is not necessary to find an express agreement, either oral or written, in order to find a conspiracy, but it is sufficient that a concert of action be contemplated and that defendants conform to the arrangement. Mutual consent need not be bottomed on express agreement, for any conformance to an agreed or contemplated pattern of conduct will warrant an inference of conspiracy. Thus not only action, but even a lack of action, may be enough from which to infer a combination or conspiracy.

Applying these rules to the facts at hand, the jury came to an opposite conclusion from that which Esco urges, and the fact that Esco's involvement was in but two of ten allegedly conspirational situations does not absolve Esco from participation in the entire conspiracy if its involvement in the two was unlawful and knowingly and purposely performed.

Theatre Enterprises v. *Paramount Film Distrib. Corp.*

346 U.S. 537 (1954)

This was an action for treble damages under Section 1 of the Sherman Act brought by Theatre Enterprises (plaintiff) against a group of motion picture producers and distributors (the defendants). Judgment for the defendants and Theatre appealed. Affirmed.

Theatre owned the Crest Theatre, located in a neighborhood shopping district some six miles from the downtown shopping center in Baltimore, Maryland. The Crest, possessing the most modern improvements and appointments, opened on February 26, 1949. Before and after the opening, Theatre, through its president, repeatedly sought to obtain first-run features for the theatre. Theatre approached the defendants separately, initially requesting exclusive first-runs later asking for first-runs on a "day and date" basis. But the defendants uniformly rebuffed Theatre's efforts and adhered to an established policy of restricting first-runs in Baltimore to the eight downtown theatres.

CLARK, JUSTICE.   Admittedly there is no direct evidence of illegal agreement between the defendants and no conspiracy is charged as to the independent exhibitors in Baltimore, who account for 63% of first-run exhibitions. The various defendants advanced much the same reasons for denying Theatre's offers. Among other reasons they asserted that day and date first-runs are normally granted only to noncompeting theatres. Since the Crest is in "substantial competition" with the downtown theatres, a day and date arrangement would be economically unfeasible. And even if defendants wished to grant Theatre such a license, no downtown exhibitor would waive his clearance rights over the Crest and agree to a simultaneous showing. As a result, if Theatre were to receive first-runs, the license would have to be an exclusive one. However, an exclusive license would be economically unsound because the Crest is a suburban theatre, located in a small shopping center, and served by limited public transportation facilities; and, with a drawing area of less than one-tenth that of a downtown theatre, it cannot compare with those easily accessible theatres in the power to draw patrons. Hence the downtown theatres offer far greater opportunities for the widespread advertisement and exploitation of newly released features, which is thought necessary to maximize the overall return from subsequent runs as well as first-runs. The defendants, in the light of these conditions, attacked the guaranteed offers of Theatre, one of which occurred during the trial as not being made in good faith. Defendants Loew's and Warner refused Theatre an exclusive license because they owned the three downtown theatres receiving their first-run product.

The crucial question is whether the defendants conduct toward Theatre stemmed from independent decision or from an agreement, tacit or express. To be sure, business behavior is admissible circumstantial evidence from which the fact finder may infer agreement. But this Court has never held that proof of parallel business

behavior conclusively establishes agreement or, phrased differently, that such behavior itself constitutes a Sherman Act offense. Circumstantial evidence of consciously parallel behavior may have made heavy inroads into the traditional judicial
attitude toward conspiracy; but "conscious parallelism" has not yet read conspiracy
out of the Sherman Act entirely. Realizing this, Theatre attempts to bolster its
argument for a directed verdict by urging that the conscious unanimity of action by
defendants should be "measured against the background and findings in the Paramount case." In other words, since the same defendants had conspired in the
Paramount case to impose a uniform system of runs and clearances without adequate explanation to sustain them as reasonable restraints of trade, use of the same
device in the present case should be legally equated to conspiracy. But the Paramount decrees, even if admissible, were only prima facie evidence of a conspiracy
covering the area and existing during the period there involved. Alone or in conjunction with the other proof of Theatre, they would form no basis for a directed
verdict. Here each of the defendants had denied the existence of any collaboration
and in addition had introduced evidence of the local conditions surrounding the
Crest operation which, they contended, precluded it from being a successful first-
run house. They also attacked the good faith of the guaranteed offers of the Theatre
for first-run pictures and attributed uniform action to individual business judgment
motivated by the desire for maximum revenue.

United States v. Parke, Davis & Co.

362 U.S. 29 (1960)

The Government (plaintiff) sought an injunction under the Sherman Act against
Parke, Davis & Company (defendant) on a complaint alleging that Parke Davis
conspired and combined, in violation of Section 1 of the Act, with retail and wholesale druggists in Washington, D.C., and Richmond, Virginia, to maintain the wholesale and retail prices of Parke, Davis pharmaceutical products. The District Court
for the District of Columbia dismissed the complaint and the Government appealed.
Reversed.

Parke Davis makes some 600 pharmaceutical products which it markets nationally through drug wholesalers and drug retailers. The retailers buy these products
from the drug wholesalers or may make large quantity purchases directly from
Parke Davis. Some time before 1956 Parke Davis announced a resale price maintenance policy in its wholesalers' and retailers' catalogues. The wholesalers' catalogue
contained a Net Price Selling Schedule listing suggested minimum resale prices on
Parke Davis products sold by wholesalers to retailers. The catalogue stated that it
was Parke Davis' continuing policy to deal only with drug wholesalers who observed
that schedule and who sold only to drug retailers authorized by law to fill prescriptions. Parke Davis, when selling directly to retailers, quoted the same prices listed
in the wholesalers' Net Price Selling Schedule but granted retailers discounts for
volume purchases. Wholesalers were not authorized to grant similar discounts. The
retailers' catalogue contained a schedule of minimum retail prices applicable in

States with Fair Trade Laws and stated that this schedule was suggested for use also in States not having such laws. These suggested minimum retail prices usually provided a 50% mark-up over cost on Parke Davis products purchased by retailers from wholesalers but, because of the volume discount, often in excess of 100% mark-up over cost on products purchased in large quantities directly from Parke Davis.

There are some 260 drugstores in Washington, D.C., and some 100 in Richmond, Virginia. Many of the stores are units of Peoples' Drug Stores, a large retail drug chain. There are five drug wholesalers handling Parke Davis products in the locality who do business with the drug retailers. The wholesalers observed the resale prices suggested by Parke Davis. However, during the spring and early summer of 1956 drug retailers in the two cities advertised and sold several Parke Davis vitamin products at prices substantially below the suggested minimum retail prices; in some instances the prices apparently reflected the volume discounts on direct purchases from Parke Davis since the products sold below the prices listed in the wholesalers' Net Price Selling Schedule. The Baltimore office manager of Parke Davis in charge of the sales district which included the two cities sought advice from his head office how to handle this situation. The Parke Davis attorney advised that the company could legally "enforce an adopted policy arrived at unilaterally" to sell only to customers who observed the suggested minimum resale prices. He further advised that this meant that "we can lawfully say 'we will sell you only so long as you observe such minimum retail prices' but cannot say 'we will sell you only if you agree to observe such minimum retail prices,' since except as permitted by Fair Trade legislation agreements as to resale price maintenance are invalid." Thereafter in July the branch manager put into effect a program for promoting observance of the suggested minimum retail prices by the retailers involved. The program contemplated the participation of the five drug wholesalers. In order to insure that retailers who did not comply would be cut off from sources of supply, representatives of Parke Davis visited the wholesalers and told them, in effect, that not only would Parke Davis refuse to sell to wholesalers who did not adhere to the policy announced in their catalogue, but also that it would refuse to sell to wholesalers who sold Parke Davis products to retailers who did not observe the suggested minimum retail prices. Each wholesaler was interviewed individually but each was informed that his competitors were also being apprised of this. The wholesalers without exception indicated a willingness to go along.

Representatives called contemporaneously upon the retailers involved, individually, and told each that if he did not observe the suggested minimum retail prices, Parke Davis would refuse to deal with him, and that furthermore he would be unable to purchase any Parke Davis products from the wholesalers. Each of the retailers was also told that his competitors were being similarly informed.

Several retailers refused to give any assurances of compliance and continued after these July interviews to advertise and sell Parke Davis products at prices below the suggested minimum retail prices. Their names were furnished by Parke Davis to the wholesalers. Thereafter Parke Davis refused to fill direct orders from such retailers and the wholesalers likewise refused to fill their orders. This ban was not limited to the Parke Davis products being sold below the suggested minimum prices but included all the company's products, even those necessary to fill prescriptions.

The president of Dart Drug Company, one of the retailers cut off, protested to the assistant branch manager of Parke Davis that Parke Davis was discriminating against him because a drugstore across the street, one of the Peoples' Drug chain, had a sign in its window advertising Parke Davis products at cut prices. The retailer was told that if this were so the branch manager "would see Peoples and try to get them in line." The branch manager later talked to Peoples and they did agree to abide by Parke Davis prices.

Five retailers continued selling Parke Davis products at less than the suggested minimum prices from stocks on hand. Within a few weeks Parke Davis modified its program. Its officials believed that the selling at discount prices would be deterred, and the effects minimized of any isolated instances of discount selling which might continue, if all advertising of such prices were discontinued. In August the Parke Davis representatives again called on the retailers individually. When interviewed, the president of Dart Drug Company indicated that he might be willing to stop advertising, although continuing to sell at discount prices, if shipments to him were resumed. Each of the other retailers was then told individually by Parke Davis representatives that Dart was ready to discontinue advertising. Each thereupon said that if Dart stopped advertising he would also. On August 28 Parke Davis reported this reaction to Dart. Thereafter all of the retailers discontinued advertising of Parke Davis vitamins at less than suggested minimum retail prices and Parke Davis and the wholesalers resumed sales of Parke Davis products to them.

BRENNAN, JUSTICE. The Government concedes for the purposes of this case that under the *Colgate* doctrine a manufacturer, having announced a price maintenance policy, may bring about adherence to it by refusing to deal with customers who do not observe that policy. The Government contends, however, that subsequent decisions of this Court compel the holding that what Parke Davis did here by entwining the wholesalers and retailers in a program to promote general compliance with its price maintenance policy went beyond mere customer selection and created combinations or conspiracies to enforce resale price maintenance in violation of Section 1 of the Sherman Act.

In *Beech-Nut* the company had adopted a policy of refusing to sell its products to wholesalers or retailers who did not adhere to a schedule of resale prices. Beech-Nut later implemented this policy by refusing to sell to wholesalers who sold to retailers who would not adhere to the policy. To detect violations the company utilized code numbers on its products and instituted a system of reporting. When an offender was cut off, he would be reinstated upon the giving of assurances that he would maintain prices in the future. The Court construed the Federal Trade Commission Act to authorize the Commission to forbid practices which had a "dangerous tendency unduly to hinder competition or to create monopoly." The Sherman Act was held to be a guide to what constituted an unfair method of competition. The company had urged that its conduct was entirely legal under the Sherman Act as interpreted by *Colgate*. The Court rejected this contention, saying that "The Beech-Nut system goes far beyond the simple refusal to sell goods to persons who will not sell at stated prices, which in the *Colgate* case was held to be within the legal right of the producer." The Court held further that the nonexistence of contracts covering the practices was irrelevant since "the specific facts found show suppression of the freedom of competition by methods in which the company secures the cooperation of its distributors and customers which are quite as effectual as agreements express or implied intended to accomplish the same purpose." . . .

That *Beech-Nut* narrowly limited *Colgate* and announced principles which subject to Sherman Act liability the producer who secures his customers' adherence to his resale prices by methods which go beyond the simple refusal to sell to customers who will not resell at stated prices, was made clear in *United States* v. *Bausch & Lomb Optical Co.* . . .

Bausch & Lomb, like the instant case, was an action by the United States to restrain alleged violations of Section 1 of the Sherman Act. The Court, relying on *Beech-Nut,* held that a distributor, Soft-Lite Lens Company, Inc., violated the Sherman Act when, as was the case with Parke Davis, the refusal to sell to wholesalers was not used simply to induce acquiescence of the wholesalers in the distributor's published resale price list; the wholesalers "accepted Soft-Lite's proffer of a plan of distribution by cooperating in prices, limitation of sales to and approval of retail licensees. That is sufficient. . . . Whether this conspiracy and combination was achieved by agreement or by acquiescence of the wholesalers coupled with assistance in effectuating its purpose is immaterial." . . . In other words, an unlawful combination is not just such as arises from a price maintenance *agreement,* express or implied; such a combination is also organized if the producer secures adherence to his suggested prices by means which go beyond his mere declination to sell to a customer who will not observe his announced policy.

· · · · ·

The program upon which Parke Davis embarked to promote general compliance with its suggested resale prices plainly exceeded the limitations of the *Colgate* doctrine and under *Beech-Nut* and *Bausch & Lomb* effected arrangements which violated the Sherman Act. Parke Davis did not content itself with announcing its policy regarding retail prices and following this with a simple refusal to have business relations with any retailers who disregarded that policy. Instead Parke Davis used the refusal to deal with the wholesalers in order to elicit their willingness to deny Parke Davis products to retailers and thereby help gain the retailers adherence to its suggested minimum retail prices. The retailers who disregarded the price policy were promptly cut off when Parke Davis supplied the wholesalers with their names. The large retailer who said he would "abide" by the price policy, the multi-unit Peoples' Drug chain, was not cut off. In thus involving the wholesalers to stop the flow of Parke Davis products to the retailers, thereby inducing retailers' adherence to its suggested retail prices. Parke Davis created a combination with the retailers and the wholesalers to maintain retail prices and violated the Sherman Act. . . .

Moreover, Parke Davis also exceeded the "limited dispensation which [*Colgate*] confers," in another way, which demonstrates how far Parke Davis went beyond the limits of the *Colgate* doctrine. With regard to the retailers' suspension of advertising

Park Davis did not rest with the simple announcement to the trade of its policy in that regard followed by a refusal to sell to the retailers who would not observe it. First it discussed the subject with Dart Drug. When Dart indicated willingness to go along the other retailers were approached and Dart's apparent willingness to cooperate was used as the lever to gain their acquiescence in the program. Having secured those acquiescences Parke Davis returned to Dart Drug with the report of that accomplishment. Not until all this was done was the advertising suspended and sales to all the retailers resumed. In this manner Parke Davis sought assurances of compliance and got them, as well as the compliance itself. It was only by actively bringing about substantial unanimity among the competitors that Parke Davis was able to gain adherence to its policy. It must be admitted that a seller's announcement that he will not deal with customers who do not observe his policy may tend to engender confidence in each customer that if he complies his competitors will also. But if a manufacturer is unwilling to rely on individual self-interest to bring about general voluntary acquiescence which has the collateral effect of eliminating price competition, and takes affirmative action to achieve uniform adherence by inducing each customer to adhere to avoid such price competition, the customers' acquiescence is not then a matter of individual free choice prompted alone by the desirability of the product. The product then comes packaged in a competition-free wrapping —a valuable feature in itself—by virtue of concerted action induced by the manufacturer. The manufacturer is thus the organizer of a price-maintenance combination or conspiracy in violation of the Sherman Act.

International Salt Co. v. United States

332 U.S. 392 (1947)

The Government brought this civil action to enjoin the International Salt Company from carrying out provisions of the leases of its patented machines to the effect that lessees would use therein only International's salt products. The restriction is alleged to violate Section 1 of the Sherman Act, and Section 3 of the Clayton Act. Judgment for the government and International appealed. Affirmed.

International is engaged in interstate commerce in salt, of which it is the country's largest producer for industrial uses. It also owns patents on two machines for utilization of salt products. One, the "Lixator," dissolves rock salt into a brine used in various industrial processes. The other, the "Saltomat," injects salt, in tablet form, into canned products during the canning process. The principal distribution of each of these machines is under leases which, among other things, require the lessees to purchase from International all unpatented salt and salt tablets consumed in the leased machines.

International had outstanding 790 leases of an equal number of "Lixators," all of which leases were on International's standard form containing the tying clause and other standard provisions; of 50 other leases which somewhat varied the terms, all but 4 contained the tying clause. It also had in effect 73 leases of 96 "Saltomats," all containing the restrictive clause. In 1944, International sold approximately 119,000 tons of salt, for about $500,000, for use in these machines.

JACKSON, JUSTICE. International's patents confer a limited monopoly of the invention they reward. From them International derives a right to restrain others from making, vending or using the patented machines. But the patents confer no right to restrain use of, or trade in, unpatented salt. By contracting to close this market for salt against competition, International has engaged in a restraint of trade for which its patents afford no immunity from the antitrust laws.

International contends, however, that summary judgment was unauthorized because it precluded trial of alleged issues of fact as to whether the restraint was unreasonable within the Sherman Act or substantially lessened competition or tended to create a monopoly in salt within the Clayton Act. We think the admitted facts left no genuine issue. Not only is price-fixing unreasonable, *per se,* but also it is unreasonable, *per se,* to foreclose competitors from any substantial market. The volume of business affected by these contracts cannot be said to be insignificant or insubstantial, and the tendency of the arrangement to accomplishment of monopoly seems obvious. Under the law, agreements are forbidden which "tend to create a monopoly," and it is immaterial that the tendency is a creeping one rather than one that proceeds at full gallop; nor does the law await arrival at the goal before condemning the direction of the movement.

International contends, however, that the "Lixator" contracts are saved from unreasonableness and from the tendency to monopoly because they provided that if any competitor offered salt of equal grade at a lower price, the lessee should be free to buy in the open market, unless International would furnish the salt at an equal price; and the "Saltomat" agreements provided that the lessee was entitled to the benefit of any general price reduction in lessor's salt tablets. The "Lixator" provision does, of course, afford a measure of protection to the lessee, but it does not avoid the stifling effect of the agreement on competition. International had at all times a priority on the business at equal prices. A competitor would have to undercut appellant's price to have any hope of capturing the market, while International could hold that market by merely meeting competition. We do not think this concession relieves the contract of being a restraint of trade, albeit a less harsh one than would result in the absence of such a provision. The "Saltomat" provision obviously has no effect of legal significance since it gives the lessee nothing more than a right to buy International's salt tablets at International's going price. All purchases must in any event be of International's product.

International also urges that since under the leases it remained under an obligation to repair and maintain the machines, it was reasonable to confine their use to its own salt because its high quality assured satisfactory functioning and low maintenance cost. The International rock salt is alleged to have an average sodium chloride content of 98.2%. Rock salt of other producers, it is said, "does not run consistent in sodium chloride content and in many instances runs as low as 95% of sodium chloride." This greater percentage of insoluble impurities allegedly disturbs the functioning of the "Lixator" machine. A somewhat similar claim is pleaded as to the "Saltomat."

Of course, a lessor may impose on a lessee reasonable restrictions designed in good faith to minimize maintenance burdens and to assure satisfactory operation.

We may assume, as matter of argument, that if the "Lixator" functions best on rock salt of average sodium chloride content of 98.2%, the lessee might be required to use only salt meeting such a specification of quality. But it is not pleaded, nor is it argued, that the machine is allergic to salt of equal quality produced by any one except International. If others cannot produce salt equal to reasonable specifications for machine use, it is one thing; but it is admitted that, at times, at least, competitors do offer such a product. They are, however, shut out of the market by a provision that limits it, not in terms of quality, but in terms of a particular vendor. Rules for use of leased machinery must not be disguised restraints of free competition, though they may set reasonable standards which all suppliers must meet.

Rule of Reason Restraints

Some Examples. Other types of activities are found to be illegal only if the purpose or effect of such activities, in light of all of the economic circumstances, is found to be unreasonably restrictive of competition. Activities of this type include: ancillary covenants not to compete found in employment contracts or in contracts for the purchase of a business; price, customer and marketing territory restrictions imposed by a manufacturer in bona fide consignee-agency selling arrangements; various grantback, pooling, marketing restrictions contained in patent licensing contracts; and exclusive dealing and requirement contract arrangements. These "rule of reason" restraints are treated subsequently.

Simpson v. Union Oil Co. of California
377 U.S. 13 (1964)

This was an action for treble damages under Section 1 of the Sherman Act brought by Simpson (plaintiff) against Union Oil (defendant). Judgment for Union Oil and Simpson appealed. Reversed.

Union Oil required lessees of its retail outlets (including Simpson) to sign product consignment agreements which were one year in duration. The station leases were also for one year. Under the consignment agreement Union retained the title to the gasoline delivered and controlled the retail prices charged. Simpson, however, had the burden of risks, except for acts of God, for gasoline in his possession. Simpson sold some of the gasoline below the price set by Union and Union refused to renew his lease and consignment agreement. Simpson sued claiming that the consignment arrangement violated Section 1 of the Sherman Act.

DOUGLAS, JUSTICE.   We are enlightened on present-day marketing methods by recent congressional investigations. In the automobile field the price is "the manufacturer's suggested retail price," not a price coercively exacted; nor do automobiles go on consignment; they are sold. Resale price maintenance of gasoline through the "consignment" device is increasing. The "consignment" device in the gasoline field is used for resale price maintenance.

Dealers, like Simpson, are independent businessmen; and they have all or most of the indicia of entrepreneurs, except for price fixing. The risk of loss of the gasoline is on them, apart from acts of God. Their return is affected by the rise and fall in the market price, their commissions declining as retail prices drop. Practically the only power they have to be wholly independent businessmen, whose service depends on their own initiative and enterprise, is taken from them by the proviso that they must sell their gasoline at prices fixed by Union Oil. By reason of the lease and "consignment" agreement dealers are coercively laced into an arrangement under which their supplier is able to impose noncompetitive prices on thousands of persons who otherwise might be competitive. The evil of this resale price maintenance program, like that of the requirements contracts held illegal by *Standard Oil Co. of California and Standard Stations* v. *United States,* is its inexorable potentiality for and even certainty in destroying competition in retail sales of gasoline by these nominal "consignees" who are in reality small struggling competitors seeking retail gas customers.

As we have said, an owner of an article may send it to a dealer who may in turn undertake to sell it only at a price determined by the owner. There is nothing illegal about that arrangement. When, however, a "consignment" device is used to cover a vast gasoline distribution system, fixing prices through many retail outlets, the antitrust laws prevent calling the "consignment" an agency, for then the end result of *United States* v. *Socony Vacuum Oil Co.* would be avoided merely by clever manipulation of words, not by differences in substance. The present, coercive "consignment" device, if successful against challenge under the anti-trust laws, furnishes a wooden formula for administering prices on a vast scale.

To allow Union Oil to achieve price fixing in this vast distribution system through this "consignment" device would be to make legality for antitrust purposes turn on clever draftsmanship. We refuse to let a matter so vital to a competitive system rest on such easy manipulation.

Hence on the issue of resale price maintenance under the Sherman Act there is nothing left to try, for there was an agreement for resale price maintenance, coercively employed.

U.S. v. *Arnold, Schwinn & Co.*
388 U.S. 365 (1967)

This was a civil action brought by the Government (plaintiff) against Arnold, Schwinn & Co. (defendant) charging that Schwinn violated Section 1 of the Sherman Act. The Government appealed from certain rulings made by the District Court. Reversed.

Over a period of several years Schwinn suffered a decline in its share of the bicycle market dropping from about 22% of the market down to 13% in 1961.

To reverse these losses, Schwinn adopted a selective franchising system which included assigning exclusive territories to dealers and distributors. Franchised outlets were obligated not to sell outside of their assigned territories and also obligated not to sell to unfranchised reseller customers within their territories. Other distributors and dealers were put on a consignment plan called the "Schwinn-Plan." Similar territory and customer restrictions were imposed. The District Court ruled that the territory restrictions Schwinn imposed on the distributors who bought the bicycles were illegal under Section 1 but refused to order Schwinn to eliminate the customer restrictions. The territory and customer's restrictions were both held valid as to those distributors and dealers operating under the "Schwinn-Plan."

FORTAS, JUSTICE. . . .Schwinn has not appealed from the District Court's order, and, accordingly, we have before us only the Government's pleas: (1) that the decree should not be confined to *sale* transactions between Schwinn and wholesalers but should reach territorial restrictions upon distributors whether they are incident to sale and resale transactions or to consignment, agency or Schwinn-Plan relationship between Schwinn and the distributors; (2) that agreements requiring distributors to limit their distribution to only such retailers as are franchised should be enjoined; and (3) that arrangements preventing franchised retailers from supplying non-franchised retailers, including discount stores, should also be forbidden.

As to point (2), the Government argues that it is illogical and inconsistent to forbid territorial limitations on resales by distributors where the distributor owns the goods, having bought them from Schwinn, and, at the same time, to exonerate arrangements which require distributors to confine resales of the goods they have bought to "franchised" retailers. It argues that requiring distributors, once they have purchased the product, to confine sales to franchised retailers is indistinguishable in law and principle from the division of territory which the decree condemns. Both, the Government argues, are in the nature of restraints upon alienation which are beyond the power of the manufacturer to impose upon its vendees and which, since the nature of the transaction includes an agreement combination or understanding, are violations of Section 1 of the Sherman Act. We agree, and upon remand, the decree should be revised to enjoin any limitation upon the freedom of distributors to dispose of the Schwinn products, which they have bought from Schwinn, where and to whomever they choose. The principle is, of course, equally applicable to sales to retailers, and the decree should similarly enjoin the making of any sales to retailers upon any condition, agreement or understanding limiting the retailer's freedom as to where and to whom it will resell the products.

The government vigorously argues that, since this remedy is confined to situations where the distributor and retailer acquire title to the bicycles, it will provide only partial relief; that to prevent the allocation of territories and confinement to franchised retail dealers, the decree can and should be enlarged to forbid these practices, however effected—whether by sale and resale or by agency, consignment, or the Schwinn Plan. But we are dealing here with a vertical restraint embodying the unilateral program of a single manufacturer. We are not dealing with a combination of manufacturers, as in *Klor's,* or of distributors, as in *General Motors.* We are not dealing with a "division" of territory in the sense of an allocation by and among the distributors, or an agreement among distributors to restrict their competition. We are here concerned with a truly vertical arrangement, raising the fundamental question of the degree to which a manufacturer may not only select the customers to whom he will sell, but also allocate territories for resale and confine access to his product to selected, or franchised, retailers. We conclude that the proper application of Section 1 of the Sherman Act to this problem requires differentiation between the situation where the manufacturer parts with title, dominion, or risk with respect to the article, and where he completely retains ownership and risk of loss.

As the District Court held, where a manufacturer *sells* products to its distributor subject to territorial restrictions upon resale, a *per se* violation of the Sherman Act results. And, as we have held, the same principle applies to restrictions of outlets with which the distributors may deal and to restraints upon retailers to whom the goods are sold. Under the Sherman Act, it is unreasonable without more for a manufacturer to seek to restrict and confine areas or persons with which an article may be traded after the manufacturer has parted with dominion over it. . . . On the other hand, as indicated in *White Motor,* we are not prepared to introduce the inflexibility which a *per se* rule might bring if it were applied to prohibit all vertical restrictions of territory and all franchising, in the sense of designating specified distributors and retailers as the chosen instruments through which the manufacturer, retaining ownership of the goods, will distribute them to the public. Such a rule might severely hamper smaller enterprises resorting to reasonable methods of meeting the competition of giants and of merchandising through independent dealers, and it might sharply accelerate the trend towards vertical integration of the distribution process. But to allow this freedom where the manufacturer has parted with dominion over the goods—the usual marketing situation—would violate the ancient rule against restraints on alienation and open the door to exclusivity of outlets and limitation of territory further than prudence permits.

. . . . . .

On this record, we cannot brand the District Court's finding as clearly erroneous and cannot ourselves conclude that Schwinn's franchising of retailers and its confinement of retail sales to them—so long as it retains all indicia of ownership, including title, dominion, and risk, and so long as the dealings in question are indistinguishable in function from agents or salesmen—constitute an "unreasonable" restraint of trade. Critical in this respect are the facts: (1) that other competitive bicycles are available to distributors and retailers in the marketplace, and there is no showing that they are not in all respects reasonably interchangeable as articles of competitive commerce with the Schwinn product; (2) that Schwinn distributors and retailers handle other brands of bicycles as well as Schwinn's; (3) in the present posture of the case we cannot rule that the vertical restraints are unreasonable because of their intermixture with price fixing; and (4) we cannot disagree with the findings of the trial court that competition made necessary the challenged program; that it was justified by, and went no further than required by, competitive pressures; and that its net effect is to preserve and not to damage competition in the bicycle market. Application of the rule of reason here cannot be confined to intrabrand competition. When we look to the product market as a whole, we cannot conclude that Schwinn's franchise system with respect to products as to which it retains ownership and risk constitutes an unreasonable restraint of trade. This does not, of course, excuse or condone the *per se* violations which, in substance, consist of the control over the resale of Schwinn's products after Schwinn has parted with ownership thereof. Once the manufacturer has parted with title and risk, he has parted with dominion over the product, and his effort thereafter to restrict territory or persons to whom the product may be transferred—whether by explicit agreement or by silent combination or understanding with his vendee—is a *per se* violation of Section 1 of the Sherman Act.

Section 2

Statutory Wording. Section 2 provides:

Every person who shall monopolize, or attempt to monopolize, or combine or conspire with any other person or persons to monopolize any part of the trade or commerce among the several states, or with foreign nations shall be deemed guilty of a misdemeanor. . . .

A single firm (or person) may monopolize or attempt to monopolize. Two or more firms are required in order to combine or conspire to monopolize.

Monopolizing. Monopolizing takes place where a firm acting singly, or a group of firms acting together, have the power to control prices or to exclude competitors from a market. This power to monopolize must be coupled with the intent to exercise it.

Illegal power to control prices or to exclude competitors is measured in relation to the relevant market. The relevant market is determined by defining the product line being monopolized and then by fixing the geographic market for the product line as defined. The product line is determined by including those products which are competitive substitutes for the defendant's products. The geographic scope of the market is measured in terms of the area where the products are customarily made available for purchases. A similar determination of the relevant market is made where services are monopolized rather than products. Economically related services are classed as a "cluster" or trade grouping, and then a geographic market is determined.

The mere existence of monopoly power is not of itself illegal, for a firm may have achieved the power by lawful means such as through a patent or through sheer efficiency. However, the existence of monopolizing power acquired, maintained or used in ways from which an *intent* to exercise such power can be inferred creates the basis for a violation. The acts from which the intent may be inferred need not necessarily be illegal. As was stated in the *Alcoa* Case:

Alcoa insists that it never excluded competitors; but we can think of no more effective exclusion than progressively to embrace each new opportunity as it opened, and to face each newcomer with new capacity already geared to a great organization, having the advantage of experience trade connections and an elite of personnel. Only in case we interpret "exclusion" as limited to maneuvers not honestly industrial, but actuated solely by a desire to prevent competition, can such a course, indefatigably pursued, be deemed not exclusionary. So to limit it would in our judgment emasculate the act.[13]

Summary

Section 2 of the act relates to the crime of monopolizing and may involve one or more firms. Monopolizing entails the power to control prices or exclude competitors in relation to the relevant market. The intent to exercise this monopolizing power must also be proven. This intent must be inferred from conduct aimed at either creating or preserving the power.

U.S. v. Grinnell Corp.
384 U.S. 563 (1966)

This was a civil suit brought by the United States (plaintiff) against Grinnell Corp. (defendant) under Section 2 of the Sherman Act. The district court held for the Government but both Grinnell and the Government appealed. The Government asked for additional relief. Judgment for the Government affirmed and additional relief granted.

Grinnell manufactures plumbing supplies and fire sprinkler systems. It also owns 76% of the stock of ADT, 89% of the stock of AFA, and 100% of the stock of Holmes. ADT provides both burglary and fire protection services; Holmes provides burglary services alone; AFA supplies only fire protection service. Each offers a central station service under which hazard-detecting devices installed on the protected premises automatically transmit an electric signal to a central station. There are other forms of protective services. But the record shows that subscribers to accredited central station service (i.e., that approved by the insurance underwriters) receive reductions in their insurance premiums that are substantially greater than the reduction received by the users of other kinds of protection service. In 1961 accredited companies in the central station service business grossed $65,000,000. ADT, Holmes, and AFA, all controlled by Grinnell, are the three largest companies in the business in terms of revenue with about 87% of the business.

In 1907 Grinnell entered into a series of agreements with the other defendant companies which allocated the major cities and market for central station alarm services in the United States. Each defendant agreed not to compete outside of the market areas allocated.

Over the years the defendants purchased the stock or assets of 30 companies engaged in the business of providing burglar or fire alarm services. After Grinnell

---

[13] *U.S.* v. *Alcoa*, 148 F.2d 416, 431 (2nd Cir. 1945).

acquired control of the other defendants, the latter continued in their attempts to acquire central station companies—offers being made to at least eight companies between the years 1955 and 1961, including four of the five largest nondefendant companies in the business. When the present suit was filed, each of those defendants had outstanding an offer to purchase one of the four largest nondefendant companies.

ADT over the years reduced its minimum basic rates to meet competition and renewed contracts at substantially increased rates in cities where it had a monopoly of accredited central station service. ADT threatened retaliation against firms that contemplated inaugurating central station service.

DOUGLAS, JUSTICE. The offense of monopoly under Section 2 of the Sherman Act has two elements: (1) the possession of monopoly power in the relevant market and (2) the willful acquisition or maintenance of that power as distinguished from growth or development as a consequence of a superior product, business acumen, or historic accident. We shall see that this second ingredient presents no major problem here, as what was done in building the empire was done plainly and explicitly for a single purpose. In *United States* v. *E. I. Du Pont De Nemours & Co.,* we defined monopoly power as "the power to control prices or exclude competition." The existence of such power ordinarily may be inferred from the predominant share of the market. In *American Tobacco Co.* v. *United States,* we said that "over two-thirds of the entire domestic field of cigarettes, and . . . over 80 per cent of the field of comparable cigarettes" constituted "a substantial monopoly." In *United States* v. *Aluminum Co. of America,* 90% of the market constituted monopoly power. In the present case, 87% of the accredited central station service business leaves no doubt that the congeries of these defendants have monopoly power— power which, as our discussion of the record indicates, they did not hesitate to wield —if that business is the relevant market. The only remaining question therefore is, what is the relevant market?

In case of a product it may be of such a character that substitute products must also be considered, as customers may turn to them if there is a slight increase in the price of the main product. That is the teaching of the *du Pont* case, that commodities reasonably interchangeable make up that "part" of trade or commerce which Section 2 protects against monopoly power.

The District Court treated the entire accredited central station service business as a single market and we think it was justified in so doing. Defendants argue that the different central station services offered are so diverse that they cannot under *du Pont* be lumped together to make up the relevant market. For example, burglar alarm services are not interchangeable with fire alarm services. They further urge that *du Pont* requires that protective services other than those of the central station variety be included in the market definition.

But there is here a single use, i.e., the protection of property, through a central station that receives signals. It is that service, accredited, that is unique and that competes with all the other forms of property protection. We see no barrier to combining in a single market a number of different products or services where that combination reflects commercial realities. To repeat, there is here a single basic service—the protection of property through use of a central service station—that must be compared with all other forms of property protection.

There are, to be sure, substitutes for the accredited central station service. But none of them appears to operate on the same level as the central station service so as to meet the interchangeability test of the *du Pont* case.

Defendants earnestly urge that despite these differences, they face competition from these other modes of protection. They seem to us seriously to overstate the degree of competition, but we recognize that (as the District Court found) they "do not have unfettered power to control the price of their services . . . due to the fringe competition of other alarm or watchmen services." What defendants overlook is that the high degree of differentiation between central station protection and the other forms means that for many customers, only central station protection will do.

As the District Court found, the relevant market for determining whether the defendants have monopoly power is not the several local areas which the individual stations serve, but the broader national market that reflects the reality of the way in which they built and conduct their business.

We have said enough about the great hold that the defendants have on this market. The percentage is so high as to justify the finding of monopoly. And, as the facts already related indicate, this monopoly was achieved in large part by unlawful and exclusionary practices. The restrictive agreements that pre-empted for each company a segment of the market where it was free of competition of the others were one device. Pricing practices that contained competitors were another. The acquisition by Grinnell of ADT, AFA, and Holmes were still another. Its control of the three other defendants eliminated any possibility of an outbreak of competition that might have occurred when the 1907 agreements terminated. By those acquisitions it perfected the monopoly power to exclude competitors and fix prices.

[*The court further indicated that the district court should have granted the government relief beyond requiring Grinnell to divest itself of stock in ADT, Holmes and AFA. The monopoly power of ADT in certain cities would have to be broken by divestiture, and the request of the Government for continuing inspection reports, and an injunction was granted.*]

Problem Cases

1. In 1959, Sports Arenas, a national bowling chain, entered into a written agreement with Lieberthal for a 21-year lease of a site and a building, which Lieberthal agreed to construct. Some months later, Sports Arenas, through its local operating subsidiary, served on Lieberthal a notice of termination of the lease, which gave as the reason for termination Lieberthal's failure to complete the required building by March 1, 1959. Lieberthal sued under the Sherman Antitrust Act claiming a conspiracy by Sports Arenas and other bowling chains to prevent opening of the new bowling alley in order to restrain competition with another bowling establishment operated by a competing chain. Since Sports Arenas is a national chain, does the complaint establish a violation based on acts occurring in interstate commerce?

2. East Coast Asphalt was engaged in the business of manufacturing and selling "hot mix asphalt" within the state of Florida. One of the components used by East Coast in its manufacturing process was bitumen, a petroleum product shipped into Florida from Venezuela by importers. The bitumen was temporarily stored in the importers' warehouses pending purchase by East Coast. Hardrives, a Florida paving contractor, brought suit against East Coast and others claiming a conspiracy and price-fixing agreement among the asphalt suppliers. East Coast claimed that the trial court lacked jurisdiction since the bitumen, the only ingredient procured outside Florida, did not meet the statutory "in commerce" test because of the warehousing which interrupted its interstate journey. Does the court have jurisdiction?

3. The Hardwood Manufacturers' Association instituted an optional activity designated the "Open Competition Plan." Of the 400 association members, 365 were members of the plan. While these members operated only 5 percent of the number of hardwood mills in the country, they produced one third of the total production of the United States. The plan provided for detailed pricing and production reports submitted by each member to be compiled and regularly distributed to the membership. There was no agreement to follow the production and pricing practices of others, but an "expert analyst" was employed to counsel the members and the Association acknowledged that "members do naturally follow their most intelligent competitors." The United States brought suit against the individual manufacturers alleging that the concerted action constituted a combination and conspiracy in restraint of interstate commerce. Should the court enjoin such Association activities?

4. The Utah Mechanical Bid Depository was organized for the purpose of eliminating "bid-shopping" and "bid-peddling" by mechanical specialty contractors. Under the terms of the depository's bylaws, members could be fined up to $300 and could be dropped from the association for violation of the bylaws; general contractors who violate the rules are subject to discontinuance of the depository's services.

   The depository eventually suspended its rule requiring contractors to use only depository subcontractors, the rule was actually continued in effect through moral suasion and threatened or actual publication of names of noncomplying contractors. The depository's circulation of violators' names operated as a blacklist fostering the boycott of contractors using nondepository bids.

   Another rule of the depository prohibited subcontract splitting. While that rule may have some beneficial effects, it virtually eliminated mechanical contractors who specialized in one or two phases of subcontracting work. Christiansen, a nonmember contractor, sued the Bid Depository for treble damages. The main defense was that he made a profit during the entire period. Is this a good defense?

5. Continental refused to renew a service station lease and "Supplemental Bailment Agreement" for gasoline with Guidry. The lease was for one year and the "Supplemental Bailment Agreement" was for the same term but in addition was cancelable by either party, without cause, upon 24 hours' written notice. Guidry alleged that the lease and accompanying agreement were not renewed because he refused to comply with Continental demands that he reduce his retail prices for gasoline. Other Continental dealers were asked to cut prices and did so. The person who replaced Guidry agreed to start selling gasoline at reduced prices. Continental claimed that these facts show only a permissible unilateral refusal to deal with Guidry. Can Guidry's claim of resale-price maintenance in violation of the Sherman Act be maintained on these facts?

6. Over a period of years, Pioneer had built up its business and had become the predominant rack jobber in western Kansas and southeastern Colorado. A rack jobber sells nonfood items, such as beauty aids, drugs, toys, household utensils, and like products, to retail merchandisers. The route salesmen for a rack jobber solicit new accounts and service existing accounts by taking orders once or twice a week and are thus crucial to the success of the rack jobber. Perryton entered the rack-jobbing field in 1960, but did not operate in the same area as Pioneer until February, 1961. In May, 1960, Austin, a long-time and trusted employee of Pioneer, left to become sales manager for Perryton. Before and after leaving, Austin tried to persuade other Pioneer employees to come over to Perryton and bring as much of the Pioneer business as possible. In February, 1961, Hink, a route salesman, quit Pioneer and began work for Perryton, calling on the same customers in the same territory which he had serviced for Pioneer. Lehr, Hink's supervisor, knew of these activities and subsequent loss of accounts, but did not inform Pioneer. In June, 1961, Lehr told Pioneer that he was taking a two-week vacation. During that time he visited one of the important Pioneer accounts in an attempt to persuade them to switch to Perryton. He never returned to Pioneer, but entered the employment of Perryton. Can Pioneer claim injunctive relief and damages on the ground that Perryton was guilty of a conspiracy and combination in restraint of trade in violation of the Sherman Act?

7. Perma Life operated a "Midas Muffler Shop" under a sales agreement prepared by Midas, Inc. The agreement obligated Perma Life to purchase all mufflers from Midas, to honor the Midas guarantee on mufflers sold by any dealer, and to sell the mufflers at resale prices fixed by Midas. The agreement also obligated Perma Life to purchase all exhaust system parts from Midas, to carry the complete line of Midas products, and in general to refrain from dealing with any of Midas' competitors. In return Perma Life was given an exclusive right to sell Midas products within a defined territory. Perma Life and other Midas dealers often requested elimination of the restrictive provisions of the selling agreement, but Midas refused and threatened to terminate the agreement should any dealer fail to comply with the restrictions. The dealers all made enormous profits, eagerly sought to acquire additional franchises and voluntarily entered into additional franchise agreements containing the same restrictions. After operating on this basis for several years, Perma Life and other dealers brought an antitrust action against Midas charging a conspiracy between Midas and its parent corporation to restrain competition in violation of the Sherman Act. Can Midas avoid liability by claiming that the dealers were barred from recovery under the *in pari delicto* doctrine, which literally means "of equal fault"?

8. For a period of 15 years, the *Lorain Journal* enjoyed a substantial monopoly of the mass dissemination of both local and national news and advertising in Lorain, Ohio. The *Journal* had enjoyed a 99 percent coverage of Lorain families and became an indispensable medium of advertising for Lorain businesses. *Journal* publishers were justifiably concerned when radio station WEOL was licensed to establish and operate in Elyria, Ohio, 8 miles south of Lorain. In an attempt to regain the desirable situation of times past, publishers of the *Journal* attempted to force an advertising boycott of the competing radio station by refusing to print advertising for those concerns using WEOL. The United States sought an injunction against the *Journal*'s actions, claiming violation of the Sherman Act. Should an injunction be issued?

9. In 1946, U.S. Steel (U.S.S.) a steel supplier and fabricator, agreed to purchase the assets of Consolidated, a steel fabricator with plants in California, Arizona, and Texas. Prior to the acquisition Consolidated completed with U.S.S. in the sale of

structural fabricated products. In the national market, Consolidated's sales of structural steel fabrications amounted to less than 1 percent of total sales; however, in the 11 Western states in which Consolidated sold all of its output, its share was 11 percent of total fabrications sales and U.S.S. had a 13 percent market share in the region. In conjunction with the Consolidated purchase, U.S.S. purchased a government-owned plant in Geneva, Utah, which was intended to be the primary supplier of steel to be used by the Consolidated facilities in fabrication of finished steel products. The Government sought to enjoin the Consolidated purchase claiming a restraint of trade and an attempt to monopolize in violation of the Sherman Act. Should an injunction be issued?

10. Firestone Tire Company, General Motors, and two of the biggest oil companies—Phillips and Standard Oil of California—agreed to furnish capital to three bus companies—National City Lines, Pacific City Lines and American City Lines—on the understanding that these latter companies would then look to the former for their requirements of tires, gasoline, and buses. The capital provided by the four companies would be used to purchase financial interests in or outright control of local transport systems in various parts of the United States; these systems too would then become substantially exclusive markets for the four companies. When the Government brought its case, the three affiliated bus companies operated between them 46 transport systems in 16 different states. It was alleged that there were other agreements, such that the National and Pacific companies would not enter into any new contract for supplies from suppliers outside the defendant group without the express permission of the latter, and that they would not dispose of their interest in any bus-operating company without requiring the purchaser to assume the same obligations. Does this conduct by the four companies supplying the capital violate Section 2?

chapter 47. The Clayton Act

Introduction

History. The continued expansion of large firms after the passage of the Sherman Act led critics of the act, mainly supporters of small local businesses, to argue that additional antitrust legislation was needed. Some believed that the prohibitions in the Sherman Act were too general and vague and others felt that court interpretation had weakened the act. Still others argued for prohibitions that would stop monopoly in its incipiency. The Sherman Act could be brought to bear only against accomplished restraints after the "blood was on the ground."

With the passage of the Clayton Act in 1914 (38 Stat. 730 [1914], as amended, 15 U.S.C. §§ 12–27.), Congress attempted to strike at specific monopolistic practices in their incipiency. Section 2 of the act made certain forms of price discriminations illegal, but since this section was amended and strengthened with the passage of the Robinson-Patman Act in 1936, price discrimination will be treated when that act is discussed in the next chapter. The major prohibitions in the Clayton Act other than those in Section 2 are found in Section 3 (exclusive dealing, requirement and tying contracts), and Section 7 (antimerger).[1]

Section 3. This section makes it unlawful for any person in interstate or foreign commerce, to lease or sell commodities for use, consumption or resale within the United States or its territories, or to fix a price charged therefore:

---

[1] Section 8 of the Clayton Act provides that . . . "no person at the same time shall be a director in any two or more corporations, any one of which has capital, surplus, and undivided profits aggregating more than $1,000,000 . . . if such corporations are or shall have been theretofore competitors, so that the elimination of competition by agreement between them would constitute a violation of any of the provisions of the antitrust laws." The FTC filed only 13 complaints under this section prior to 1964. Only one cease-and-desist order resulted because in other cases the executives simply resigned. There have been a few court cases. See *U.S.* v. *Sears, Roebuck and Co.,* 111 F. Supp. 614 (1953).

. . . on condition, agreement, or understanding that the lessee or purchaser thereof shall not use or deal in the goods . . . or other commodities of a competitor or competitors of the lessor or seller, where the effect of such lease, sale or contract for sale or such condition, agreement, or understanding may be to substantially lessen competition or tend to create a monopoly in any line of commerce.

A sizable number of limitations on the application of Section 3 are to be found in the language employed. First, Section 3 applies only to sales of commodities and not to sales of services. An actual sale or leasing arrangement must have been made. The section does not apply to situations where a seller (or lessor) has refused to deal because the buyer (or lessee) was unwilling to accept otherwise illegal tying or exclusive dealing conditions. The section does not apply where goods are shipped by a principal to an agent on consignment since no sale or lease of commodities would be involved. Nor does it apply unless the agreements or understandings involve conditions designed to prevent buyers (or lessees) from dealing with competing sellers (or lessors). Lastly, there must be a *probability* that the agreements or understandings will lessen competition or tend to create a monopoly in a line of commerce (product market).

Summary

The Clayton Act was enacted to strengthen antitrust enforcement and to stop certain anticompetitive practices in their incipiency before harm was done to competition. Section 3 of the act applies to exclusive dealing contracts and to tying contracts.

Tampa Electric Co. v. Nashville Coal Co.

365 U.S. 320 (1961)

Tampa Electric Co. (plaintiff) brought this action for a declaratory judgment establishing the validity of a contract whereby Tampa agreed to purchase all of its coal requirements for a 20 year period from Nashville Coal Co. (defendant). Tampa appealed from a decision ruling that the contract was illegal under section 3 of the Clayton Act. Reversed.

Tampa Electric is a public utility serving an area of about 1,800 square miles around Tampa, Florida. Tampa Electric entered a 20 year contract whereby it agreed to buy its total requirements of coal for its Gannon Station from Nashville Coal. Co. This purchase obligation also extended to any additional coal using plants Tampa might build at the Gannon Station during the life of the contract. A minimum price for the coal was set with a cost escalation clause. After Tampa had spent approximately $7,500,000 preparing to burn coal instead of oil, Nashville notified Tampa that it would not perform because the contract violated Section 3 of the Clayton Act.

CLARK, JUSTICE.   In practical application, even though a contract is found to be an exclusive-dealing arrangement, it does not violate the section unless the court believes it probable that performance of the contract will foreclose competition in a substantial share of the line of commerce affected. Following the guidelines of earlier decisions, certain considerations must be taken. *First,* the line of commerce, i.e., the type of goods, wares, or merchandise, etc., involved must be determined, where it is in controversy, on the basis of the facts peculiar to the case. *Second,* the area of effective competition in the known line of commerce must be charted by careful selection of the market area in which the seller operates, and to which the purchaser can practicably turn for supplies. In short, the threatened foreclosure of competition must be in relation to the market affected.

To determine substantiality in a given case, it is necessary to weigh the probable effect of the contract on the relevant area of effective competition, taking into account the relative strength of the parties, the proportionate volume of commerce involved in relation to the total volume of commerce in the relevant market area, and the probable immediate and future effects which preemption of that share of the market might have on effective competition therein. It follows that a mere showing that the contract itself involves a substantial number of dollars is ordinarily of little consequence.

In applying these considerations to the facts of the case before us, it appears clear that both the Court of Appeals and the District Court have not given the required effect to a controlling factor in the case—the relevant competitive market area.

Neither the Court of Appeals nor the District Court considered in detail the question of the relevant market. They do seem, however, to have been satisfied with inquiring only as to competition within "Peninsular Florida." By far the bulk of the overwhelming tonnage marketed from the same producing area as serves Tampa is sold outside of Georgia and Florida, and the producers were "eager" to sell more coal in those States. While the relevant competitive market is not ordinarily susceptible to a "metes and bounds" definition, it is of course the area in which respondents and the other 700 producers effectively compete. *Standard Oil Co.* v. *United States, supra.* The record shows that, like the respondents, they sold bituminous coal "suitable for [Tampa's] requirements," mined in parts of Pennsylvania, Virginia, West Virginia, Kentucky, Tennessee, Alabama, Ohio and Illinois. . . . it clearly appears that the proportionate volume of the total relevant coal product as to which the challenged contract pre-empted competition, less than 1 percent, is, conservatively speaking, quite insubstantial. A more accurate figure, even assuming preemption to the extent of the maximum anticipated total requirements, 2,250,000 tons a year, would be .77 percent.

Section 7

Statutory Wording.   As amended in 1950, Section 7 of the Clayton Act prohibits the acquisition by a corporation, in interstate or foreign commerce, unless solely for investment, of:

. . . the whole or any part of the stock . . . or assets of another corporation engaged also in commerce, where in any line of commerce in any section of the country, the effect of such acquisition may be substantially to lessen competition, or to tend to create a monopoly.[2]

Interpretation. In order to determine the legality of a given acquisition under this section the court first must define the product line (line of commerce) and the relevant market area (section of the country) involved. There need only be a *reasonable probability* that anticompetitive effects will be the result of the merger. The Supreme Court has permitted the FTC to define submarkets within both product and area markets. In the *Brown Shoe* case a merger involving only 5 percent of the shoe industry's sales volume was held illegal where the relevant market was defined to include only sales of men's, women's, and children's shoes in cities of 10,000 or more in population.[3]

An acquisition has been invalidated where there are concentration trends in an industry even though fierce and fragmented competition persisted after the acquisition. A merger might be invalidated because of its effect on *potential* competition; or because a large firm might by a product extension merger, enter a different industry and endanger the existing competitive balance within the industry. The possibility that reciprocal trading exchanges arising out of a merger might foreclose other firms from a significant market might be another factor given weight by the court.

Reports on "conglomerate" mergers dominated the business news during the 1960's. There is some confusion as to definition, but the term conglomerate is usually applied to acquisitions where there is no discernible relationship in the nature of the business between the acquiring and the acquired firms.[4] The possible effect of such mergers on the level of competition depends on the particular circumstances involved. It seems apparent, however, that a large firm will not be permitted to make an acquisition in an already concentrated industry which might confront "existing competitors and such potential competitors as existed [with] an even more formidable opponent."[5]

Summary

Section 7 of the act can be enforced against all types of mergers and acquisitions. The U.S. Supreme Court has taken the position that any additional concentration in most industries poses a potential threat to the working of our competitive system. Section 7 has been applied to stop acquisitions even in highly fragmented industries provided concentration trends are found to exist.

---

[2] 38 Stat. 731 (1914), as amended 15 U.S.C. Sec. 18 (1952).

[3] *Brown Shoe Co.* v. *United States,* 370 U.S. 294 (1962).

[4] Sometimes a conglomerate merger is defined as one being neither vertical nor horizontal. See *Antitrust Developments* (Supplement to Report of Attorney General's National Committee to Study the Antitrust Laws, American Bar Association, 1968).

[5] *General Foods* v. *FTC,* 386 F.2d 936, 944 (3d Cir. 1967).

United States v. Pabst Brewing Co.
384 U.S. 546 (1966)

The Government brought this action against Pabst Brewing Company charging that Pabst violated Section 7 of the Clayton Act when it acquired Blatz Brewing Co. in 1958. The District Court dismissed the Government's case on the ground that the Government had failed to show that the effect of the acquisition ". . . may be substantially to lessen competition or to tend to create monopoly in the beer industry in the continental United States, the only relevant geographic market." The Government appealed. Reversed.

BLACK, JUSTICE.   We first take up the court's dismissal based on its conclusion that the Government failed to prove either Wisconsin or the three-state area constituted a "relevant section of the country within the meaning of Section 7." Apparently the District Court thought that in order to show a violation of § 7 it was essential for the Government to show a "relevant geographic market" in the same way the corpus delicti must be proved to establish a crime. But when the Government brings an action under § 7 it must according to the language of the statute, prove no more than that there has been a merger between two corporations engaged in commerce and that the effect of the merger may be substantially to lessen competition or tend to create a monopoly in any line of commerce *"in any section of the country."* (Emphasis supplied.) The language of this section requires merely that the Government prove the merger has a substantial anti-competitive effect somewhere in the United States—"in *any* section" of the United States. This phrase does not call for the delineation of a "section of the country" by metes and bounds as a surveyor would lay off a plot of ground. The Government may introduce evidence which shows that as a result of a merger competition may be substantially lessened throughout the country, or on the other hand it may prove that competition may be substantially lessened only in one or more sections of the country. In either event a violation of § 7 would be proved. Certainly the failure of the Government to prove by an army of expert witnesses what constitutes a relevant "economic" or "geographic" market is not an adequate ground on which to dismiss a § 7 case. . . . Congress did not seem to be troubled about the exact spot competition might be lessened; it simply intended to outlaw mergers which threatened competition in any or all parts of the country. Proof of the section of the country where the anti-competitive effect exists is entirely subsidiary to the crucial question in this and every § 7 case which is whether a merger may substantially lessen competition anywhere in the United States.

The Government's evidence, consisting of documents, statistics, official records, depositions, and affidavits by witnesses, related principally to the competitive position of Pabst and Blatz in the beer industry throughout the Nation, in the three-state area of Wisconsin, Illinois, and Michigan, and in the State of Wisconsin. The record in this case, including admissions by Pabst in its formal answer to the Government's complaint, the evidence introduced by the Government, the findings of fact and opinion of the District Judge, shows among others the following facts. In 1958, the year of the merger, Pabst was the tenth largest brewer in the Nation and Blatz ranked eighteenth. The merger made Pabst the Nation's fifth largest brewer with 4.49% of the industry's total sales. By 1961, three years after the merger, Pabst had increased its share of the beer market to 5.83% and had become the third largest brewer in the country. In the State of Wisconsin, before the merger, Blatz was the leading seller of beer and Pabst ranked fourth. The merger made Pabst the largest seller in the State with 23.95% of all the sales made there. By 1961 Pabst's share of the market had increased to 27.41%. This merger took place in an industry marked by a steady trend toward economic concentration. According to the District Court the number of breweries operating in the United States declined from 714 in 1934 to 229 in 1961, and the total number of different competitors selling beer has fallen from 206 in 1957 to 162 in 1961. In Wisconsin the number of companies selling beer has declined from 77 in 1955 to 54 in 1961. At the same time the number of competitors in the industry were becoming fewer and fewer, the leading brewers were increasing their shares of sales. Between 1957 and 1961 the Nation's 10 leading brewers increased their combined shares of sales from 45.06% to 52.60%. In Wisconsin the four leading sellers accounted for 47.74% of the State's sales in 1957 and by 1961 this share had increased to 58.62%. In the three-state area the evidence showed that in 1957 Blatz was the sixth largest seller with 5.84% of the total sales there and Pabst ranked seventh with 5.48%. As was true in the beer industry throughout the Nation, there was a trend toward concentration in the three-state area. From 1957 to 1961 the number of major brewers selling there dropped from 104 to 86 and during the same period the eight leading sellers increased their combined shares of beer sales from 58.93% to 67.65%.

These facts show a very marked thirty-year decline in the number of brewers and a sharp rise in recent years in the percentage share of the market controlled by the leading brewers. If not stopped, this decline in the number of separate competitors and this rise in the share of the market controlled by the larger beer manufacturers is bound to lead to greater and greater concentration of the beer industry into fewer and fewer hands. The merger of Pabst and Blatz brought together two very large brewers competing against each other in 40 States. In 1957 these two companies had combined sales which accounted for 23.95% of the beer sales in Wisconsin, 11.32% of the sales in the three-state area of Wisconsin, Illinois, and Michigan, and 4.49% of the sales throughout the country. In accord with our prior cases, we hold that the evidence as to the probable effect of the merger on competition in Wisconsin, in the three-state area, and in the entire country was amply sufficient to show a violation of § 7 in each and all of these three areas.

We have not overlooked Pabst's contention that we should not consider the steady trend toward concentration in the beer industry because the Government has not shown that the trend is due to mergers. There is no duty on the Government to make such proof. It would seem fantastic to assume that part of the concentration in the beer industry has not been due to mergers but even if the Government made no such proof, it would not aid Pabst. Congress, in passing § 7 and in amending it with the Celler-Kefauver Anti-Merger Amendment, was concerned with arresting concentration in the American economy, whatever its cause, in its incipiency. To put a halt to what it considered to be a "rising tide" of concentration in American business, Congress, with full power to do so, decided "to clamp down with vigor on mergers." *United States* v. *Von's Grocery Co.* It passed and amended § 7 on the premise that mergers do tend to accelerate concentration in an industry. Many believe that this assumption of Congress is wrong, and that the disappearance of small businesses with a correlative concentration of business in the hands of a few is bound to occur whether mergers are prohibited or not. But it is not for the courts to review the policy decision of Congress that mergers which may substantially lessen competition are forbidden, which in effect the courts would be doing should they now require proof of the congressional premise that mergers are a major cause of concentration. We hold that a trend toward concentration in an industry, whatever its causes, is a highly relevant factor in deciding how substantial the anti-competitive effect of a merger may be.

Reversed and remanded.

FTC v. *Procter & Gamble Co.*

386 U.S. 568 (1967)

This was an action brought by the Federal Trade Commission charging that Procter & Gamble Co. had acquired the assets of Clorox Chemical Co. in violation of Section 7 of the Clayton Act. The FTC ordered divestiture but the Court of Appeals reversed and dismissed the action. The FTC appealed. Reversed.

DOUGLAS, JUSTICE. As indicated by the Commission in its painstaking and illuminating report, it does not particularly aid analysis to talk of this merger in conventional terms, namely, horizontal or vertical or conglomerate. This merger may most appropriately be described as a "product-extension merger," as the Commission stated. The facts are not disputed, and a summary will demonstrate the correctness of the Commission's decision.

At the time of the merger, Clorox was the leading manufacturer in the heavily concentrated household liquid bleach industry. It is agreed that household liquid bleach is the relevant line of commerce. The product is used in the home as a germicide and disinfectant, and more importantly, as a whitening agent in washing clothes and fabrics. It is a distinctive product with no close substitutes. Liquid bleach is a low-price, high-turnover consumer product sold mainly through grocery stores and supermarkets. The relevant geographical market is the Nation and a series of regional markets. Because of high shipping costs and low sales price, it is not feasible to ship the product more than 300 miles from its point of manufacture. Most manufacturers are limited to competition within a single region since they have but one plant. Clorox is the only firm selling nationally; it has 13 plants distributed throughout the Nation. Purex, Clorox's closest competitor in size, does not distribute its bleach in the northeast or middle-Atlantic States; in 1957, Purex's bleach was available in less than 50% of the national market.

At the time of the acquisition, Clorox was the leading manufacturer of household liquid bleach, with 48.8% of the national sales—annual sales of slightly less than $40,000,000. Its market share had been steadily increasing for the five years prior to the merger. The industry is highly concentrated; in 1957, Clorox and Purex accounted for almost 65% of the Nation's household liquid bleach sales, and, together with four other firms, for almost 80%. The remaining 20% was divided among over 200 small producers. Clorox had total assets of $12,000,000; only eight producers had assets in excess of $1,000,000 and very few had assets of more than $75,000.

In light of the territorial limitations on distribution, national figures do not give an accurate picture of Clorox's dominance in the various regions. Thus, Clorox's seven principal competitors did no business in New England, the mid-Atlantic States, or metropolitan New York.

Since all liquid bleach is chemically identical, advertising and sales promotion is vital. In 1957 Clorox spent almost $3,700,000 on advertising, imprinting the value of its bleach in the mind of the consumer. In addition, it spent $1,700,000 for other promotional activities.

Procter is a large, diversified manufacturer of low-price, high-turnover household products sold through grocery, drug and department stores. Prior to its acquisition of Clorox, it did not produce household liquid bleach. Its 1957 sales were in excess of $1,100,000,000 from which it realized profits of more than $67,000,000; its assets were over $500,000,000. Procter has been marked by rapid growth and diversification. It has successfully developed and introduced a number of new products. Its primary activity is in the general area of soaps, detergents, and cleansers; in 1957, of total domestic sales, more than one-half (over $500,000,000) were in this field. Procter was the dominant factor in this area. It accounted for 54.4% of all packaged detergent sales. The industry is heavily concentrated—Procter and its nearest competitors, Colgate-Palmolive and Lever Brothers, account for 80% of the market.

In the marketing of soaps, detergents, and cleansers, as in the marketing of household liquid bleach, advertising and sales promotion are vital. In 1957, Procter was the Nation's largest advertiser, spending more than $80,000,000 on advertising and an additional $47,000,000 on sales promotion. Due to its tremendous volume. Procter receives substantial discounts from the media. As a multi-product producer Procter enjoys substantial advantages in advertising and sales promotion. Thus, it can and does feature several products in its promotions, reducing the printing, mailing, and other costs for each product. It also purchases network programs on behalf of several products, enabling it to give each product network exposure at a fraction of the cost per product that a firm with only one product to advertise would incur.

Prior to the acquisition, Procter was in the course of diversifying into product lines related to its basic detergent-soap-cleanser business. Liquid bleach was a distinct possibility since packaged detergents—Procter's primary product line—and liquid bleach are used complementarily in washing clothes and fabrics, and in general household clothing.

The decision to acquire Clorox was the result of a study conducted by Procter's promotion department designed to determine the advisability of entering the liquid bleach industry. The initial report noted the ascendancy of liquid bleach in the large and expanding household bleach market, and recommended that Procter purchase Clorox rather than enter independently. Since a large investment would be needed to obtain a satisfactory market share, acquisition of the industry's leading firm was attractive.

The Commission found that the acquisition might substantially lessen competition. The findings and reasoning of the Commission need be only briefly summarized. The Commission found that the substitution of Procter with its huge assets and advertising advantages for the already dominant Clorox would dissuade new entrants and discourage active competition from the firms already in the industry due to fear of retaliation by Procter. The Commission thought it relevant that retailers might be induced to give Clorox preferred shelf space since it would be manufactured by Procter, which also produced a number of other products marketed by the retailers. There was also the danger that Procter might underprice Clorox in order to drive out competition, and subsidize the underpricing with revenue from other products. The Commission carefully reviewed the effect of the acquisition on the structure of the industry, noting that "the practical tendency of the . . . merger . . . is to transform the liquid bleach industry into an arena of big business competition only, with the few small firms falling by the wayside, unable to compete with their giant rivals." Further, the merger would seriously diminish potential competition by eliminating Procter as a potential entrant into the industry. Prior to the merger, the Commission found that Procter was the most likely prospective entrant, and absent the merger would have remained on the periphery, restraining Clorox from exercising its market power. If Procter had actually entered, Clorox's dominant position would have been eroded and the concentration of the industry reduced.

Section 7 of the Clayton Act was intended to arrest the anticompetitive effects of market power in their incipiency. The core question is whether a merger may substantially lessen competition, and necessarily requires a prediction of the merger's impact on competition, present and future. And there is certainly no requirement that the anticompetitive power manifest itself in anticompetitive action before § 7 can be called into play. If the enforcement of § 7 turned on the existence of actual anticompetitive practices, the congressional policy of thwarting such practices in their incipiency would be frustrated.

Problem Cases

1. Serum Company was the nation's largest producer of hog serum and had exclusive requirement franchises with all 16 of its wholesalers. The wholesalers could buy from other sources provided they gave up the use of the word "Anchor" in their business. The FTC brought an action under Section 3 of the Clayton Act asking that these restrictions on the use of the word "Anchor" be held illegal. Can Serum Co. impose such restrictions?

2. Window Company issued franchises which required all distributors and dealers of its patented combination storm and screen windows to maintain a sale organization de-

voted exclusively to the sale of such windows. Distributors and dealers also were required not to offer for sale merchandise competitive with any article manufactured or distributed by the Window Company, and to purchase from Window Company materials necessary for the manufacture of special units. A terminated dealer sued Window Company alleging that his plan caused him losses and that he was terminated for handling competitive goods. Has the dealer stated a valid claim under the antitrust laws?

3. Carvel franchised dealers to sell soft ice cream. The franchise provided that Carvel would suggest retail prices. Each dealer was required to buy or lease a number of items of equipment in the franchise package. Some of this equipment was patented and much of it was not. There was evidence that the franchise package as a whole was desired by the retailers as distinguished from patented equipment and the restrictions were aimed at protecting the quality of the food and service. One dealer sued Carvel for treble damages claiming that the leasing or selling of the patented equipment as a package constituted a per se violation of Section 3 of the Clayton Act (illegal tie-in sale). Were the franchise restrictions included as a package with the patent illegal?

4. In 1945, Culligan granted some of its dealers long-term franchises which required these dealers to buy all of their requirements for water-softening services from Culligan. Each dealer was given an exclusive territory in which to sell. The franchise contained standard clauses stipulating that if any part of the franchise was found to be illegal that this should not affect the balance of the contract. In 1956, the FTC issued a complaint against Culligan for violating Section 3 of the Clayton Act (exclusive dealing) and Culligan took a consent decree. Culligan then notified all of its dealers that their old franchises were no longer valid. Culligan sent out new franchises which did not require that the dealer buy all of his requirements from Culligan. In addition, the new franchises were for shorter terms and did not give any dealers exclusive territories. Five filed suit to have their old franchises declared valid except for the exclusive dealing (requirements) provision. They were canceled by Culligan when they refused to accept the new franchises. Can the dealers win?

5. Pillsbury is a leading producer of flour-base mixes. It was the second-largest producer of these products and the third-largest producer of bakery flour. In 1951, Pillsbury purchased the assets of Ballard and of Duff, two competing companies in the industry. With the addition of these two companies, Pillsbury increased its manufacturing capacity by as much as 40 percent in certain product lines. The market share of Pillsbury was increased substantially in the southeastern states where Pillsbury moved from fifth to second place in family flour and made other gains. Did this acquisition violate Section 7?

6. American, a cane-sugar producer with about 7 percent of total sugar sales in a 10-state area, acquired 23 percent of the stock of Cuban Sugar, a company with about 6 percent of the beet-sugar sales in the same area. Cane and beet sugar are highly competitive products. A merger was planned and the resulting company would be the second-largest company in the area. Does this acquisition violate Section 7?

chapter 48. The Robinson-Patman Act

Introduction

Objectives. The two primary objectives of the Robinson-Patman Act (49 Stat. 1526, as amended, 15 U.S.C. § 13.) are: (1) To prevent suppliers from attempting to gain an unfair advantage over their competitors by discriminating among buyers either in price or in providing allowances or services, and (2) to prevent buyers from using their economic power to gain discriminatory prices from suppliers so as to gain an advantage over their own competitors. The overall objective is to promote equality of economic opportunity for businesses selling and buying goods in the channels of commerce.

History. The Robinson-Patman Act amendment of Section 2 of the Clayton Act was enacted in 1936 because of increasing congressional concern for the plight of small retailers confronted with the growth of chain-store competition. The original Section 2 of the Clayton Act was drafted primarily to prohibit the practice, early used by the Standard Oil Company and others, of employing local and territorial price discrimination to drive out competitors in a given area. However, the complaint of grocers, druggists and other retailers, and the wholesalers who supplied them, was that suppliers discriminated in price between different customers, sometimes charging chain stores even less than they did the wholesalers who sold to the small independent stores. The Clayton Act had been interpreted to require an examination only into the competitive effect at the seller's level—not at the customer's level. Furthermore, it was interpreted to permit a seller to meet the price of a competitor even if the competitor's price itself was discriminatory and to permit different prices for different quantities without regard to the cost savings of the seller.

Concern had been brought to a head in 1934 by the report of a thorough investigation of chain stores conducted by the Federal Trade Commission upon the request of Congress. It publicized not only the fact that chains were buying their goods more cheaply than their smaller competitors but that they also frequently received advertising and promotional allowances, payments in lieu of brokerage and other inducements to buy not available to their competitors and often given secretly.

Price Discrimination

The Statute. Section 2(a) of the amended Clayton Act provides:

That it shall be unlawful for any person engaged in commerce, in the course of such commerce, either directly or indirectly, to discriminate in price between different purchasers of commodities of like grade and quality, where either or any of the purchases involved in such discrimination are in commerce, where such commodities are sold for use, consumption, or resale within the United States or any Territory thereof or the District of Columbia or any insular possession or other place under the jurisdiction of the United States, and where the effect of such discrimination may be substantially to lessen competition or tend to create a monopoly in any line of commerce, or to injure, destroy, or prevent competition with any person who either grants or knowingly receives the benefit of such discrimination, or with customers of either of them: *Provided,* That nothing herein contained shall prevent differentials which make only due allowance for differences in the cost of manufacture, sale, or delivery resulting from the differing methods or quantities in which such commodities are to such purchasers sold or delivered: *Provided, however,* That the Federal Trade Commission may, after due investigation and hearing to all interested parties, fix and establish quantity limits, and revise the same as it finds necessary, as to particular commodities or classes of commodities, where it finds that available purchasers in greater quantities are so few as to render differentials on account thereof unjustly discriminatory or promotive of monopoly in any line of commerce; and the foregoing shall then not be construed to permit differentials based on differences in quantities greater than those so fixed and established: *And provided further,* That nothing herein contained shall prevent persons engaged in selling goods, wares, or merchandise in commerce from selecting their own customers in bona fide transactions and not in restraint of trade: *And provided further,* That nothing herein contained shall prevent price changes from time to time where in response to changing conditions affecting the market for or the marketability of the goods concerned, such as but not limited to actual or imminent deterioration of perishable goods, obsolescence of seasonal goods, distress sales under court process, or sales in good faith in discontinuance of business in the goods concerned.

Commerce. This section requires that the discrimination must occur in "commerce" but, unlike the Sherman Act definition, the courts have interpreted this provision to require that the transaction in question involve two or more states or the District of Columbia and a state. The fact that the customers who are discriminated against are located in the same state as those who are favored does not make the act inapplicable if the goods are shipped in from another state. The act also applies where one of the competing buyers is in another state even though the seller and other buyers are in the same state. However, the act does not apply, for example, to an Indiana manufacturer selling to Indiana customers. Only domestic commerce involving transactions by American businessmen are covered by the act.

Discrimination in Price. A price discrimination under the act must involve two or more sales to different purchasers at different prices. One who sells to all buyers at a fixed F.O.B. price would clearly not violate Section 2(a) of the act. The price to be considered is the delivered price—that is, the price at the point where the buyer takes the goods. For two or more sales to be treated as discriminatory, they must be fairly close in point of time. How close depends upon the commodity—longer for pianos than meat or corn, which tend to fluctuate rapidly in price due to perishability or rapidly changing supply and demand factors.

Section 2(a) applies only to different prices between different actual purchasers. Merely quoting a discriminatory price or refusing to sell except at a discriminatory price is not a violation under this section. An actual sale at a discriminatory price must occur before the section applies.

Under certain conditions sales will be attributed, for purposes of the act, to a seller which are not made directly by him. For example, sales by a subsidiary will be attributed to the parent if there is a high degree of control exercised by the parent—likewise, a manufacturer who controls the sales of his customer, a wholesaler, by having his own salesmen take the order and referring it to the wholesaler is the seller.

Commodities of Like Grade and Quality. Section 2's prohibition of price discrimination applies only to goods. It does not cover services. Discriminatory pricing practices in selling advertising space or leasing real estate are not prohibited by the act. What goods are of like grade and quality is a more difficult issue. Different prices cannot be justified merely because the labels on the product are different. It has been held that private labeling of merchandise, such as food products and appliances, does not make them different from the same goods carrying the seller's house brand. If a seller can establish that there is an actual physical difference in grade or quality between two products, then he can justify any differential in price between them he wishes. For this reason establishing a lower priced "fighting" brand is not illegal. The differential in price between different grades or qualities of goods need not, under the act, be proportionate to actual differences in the seller's costs. The magnitude of the difference in quality necessary to permit differential pricing is not clear, although courts have tended to require less difference than has the FTC, nor is it clear the extent to which differences in design permit price differentials. Of course, so long as the seller offers all designs, styles, and qualities to all purchases, he forecloses questions with respect to discrimination when he establishes different prices.

Competitive Effect. Section 2(a) applies only to discriminations which have the reasonable probability of lessening competition. Such an injury may occur to the competition between the sellers, which is called the *primary* level. A classic case was the early Standard Oil practice of cutting prices in one area to drive out a competitor. It is often claimed that a big national firm can finance this "predatory" price cutting by raising prices elsewhere. In such a case there might be no competition between the customers in the price-cutting market and those in the other areas. Or the injury to competition may be at the buyer or *secondary* level, as between a chain grocery and an independent. Often a price discrimination will cause the requisite injury at both levels. Indeed, a third level or *tertiary* competitive injury may occur, as where the effect is on the competition between customers of customers of the seller granting the lower price.

The act does not specifically deal with functional discounts, that is, discounts granted to a buyer, such as a wholesaler, performing certain functions in the distribution system. Therefore, whether a functional price differential is prohibited depends upon its competitive effect. So long as the distribution system is the same for all of the seller's goods distributed in a given area (for example, a manufacturer sells only to wholesalers who in turn supply the retailers) there is little likelihood of violation. However, where a seller sells to a buyer who serves both as a wholesaler and a retailer, injury to competition at the retail level may occur. A competitive advantage may also arise when a wholesaler customer of the seller sells to retailers at a lower price than the seller himself sells to retailers in the same market. Generally, however, the FTC has not questioned lower prices granted to bona fide wholesalers and jobbers.

Defenses. There are two primary defenses a seller may use to justify price differentials. The first is to show that a differential can be justified on the basis of differences in cost to the seller in manufacture, sale, or delivery arising from differences in method or quantities involved. The second defense, appearing in Section 2(b), is to show that a price differential was made in good faith to meet a price of a competitor. In addition, the last of the provisos of Section 2(a) specifically permits differentials in price in response to changing market conditions or changes in the marketability of the goods such as the danger of imminent deterioration of perishable goods or of the obsolescence of seasonal goods. The burden of proving a defense is specifically laid by Section 2(b) upon the person claiming the defense.

Cost Justification. If one buyer purchases the seller's product in reusable containers which may be handled by lift truck and in carload lots at his own warehouse and another buyer requires store door delivery of a few units at a time in small cartons, obviously the cost to the seller will be lower in the first case, although the exact amount of the price differential may be extremely difficult to justify. It is quite unlikely that quantity discounts based upon the annual volume of purchases can be justified on a cost-saving basis. Nor is a seller likely to be able to justify pricing a favored customer on something near to a marginal cost basis because the economies of the additional business would vanish if the other customers were lost. However, the difficulties of cost accounting for a specific product have been recognized and averaging of costs is permitted both by the FTC [1] and the Supreme Court.[2]

Meeting Competition.   Section 2(b) states:

> Upon proof being made, at any hearing on a complaint under this section, that there has been discrimination in price or services or facilities furnished, the burden of rebutting the prima facie case thus made by showing justification shall be upon the person charged with a violation of this section, and unless justification shall be affirmatively shown, the Commission is authorized to issue an order terminating the discrimination: *Provided, however,* That nothing herein contained shall prevent a seller rebutting the prima facie case thus made by showing that his lower price or the furnishing of services or facilities to any purchaser or purchasers was made in good faith to meet an equally low price of a competitor, or the services or facilities furnished by a competitor.

Although meeting a competitor's price is an absolute defense, the FTC has taken a very strict view toward it and has been successful in persuading the courts to limit its application. For example, a seller cannot claim the defense if he knows or should know that the competitor's price which he met was itself an unlawful price discrimination. The seller can only meet, not undercut, the lower price of his competitor, and he cannot use the defense to meet a competitor's price for goods of lower quality or in a larger quantity than those involved in the seller's quotation. Nor can he use a price necessary to meet a specific competitive situation to charge systematically lower prices to a certain customer or customers. The FTC has taken the position that the defense is available only to meet a specific competitor's price in order to keep a specific customer and not to gain new customers by meeting the price of a competitor. This view was rejected by the Seventh Circuit Court, however.[3] Although the seller usually cannot prove that a competitor actually did offer the lower price, he must act upon reasonable belief, and merely taking the word of a customer or even one's own salesman may be held not to be sufficient grounds.[4]

Summary

The objectives of the Robinson-Patman Act, amending the Clayton Act, are to prevent discrimination in price or services by sellers which affect competition among their customers and to prevent discriminatory prices which a seller might use to gain an advantage over his own competitors. It was passed by

---

[1] *Sylvania Electric Product, Inc.,* 51 FTC 282 (1954).
[2] *U.S.* v. *Borden Co.,* 370 U.S. 460 (1962).
[3] *Sunshine Biscuits, Inc.* v. *FTC,* 306 F.2d 48 (7th Cir. 1962).
[4] *FTC* v. *Staley Manufacturing Co.,* 324 U.S. 746 (1945).

Congress primarily in response to complaints that sellers unfairly favored chain stores and other large buyers.

Other discriminatory practices which involve two or more states are covered by the Act, either discrimination between buyers located in different states or discrimination by a seller between customers in a state different from the one in which he is located.

A discrimination in price prohibited in Section 2(a) must involve two or more sales to different purchasers at different prices at the point where the buyer takes the goods. Also a discrimination in price must involve goods of like grade and quality. Different brand names alone have been held insufficient to permit a different price. The discrimination in price must also have an adverse effect on competition among the sellers, their customers or customers further along in the channels of distribution in order to be covered by the Act.

A seller has two defenses to justify differences in price between customers— (1) that the difference in price reflects differences in cost to the seller in manufacture, sale or delivery and (2) that the discriminatory price merely meets a nondiscriminatory price of a competitor for goods of the same quantity and quality.

Ingram v. Phillips Petroleum Co.
259 F.Supp. 176 (D. N.M. 1966)

D. L. Ingram and Edwin H. Ingram (plaintiffs) brought suit against Phillips Petroleum Company (defendant) seeking to enjoin price discrimination alleged to violate Section 2(a) of the Clayton Act as amended by the Robinson-Patman Act. Injunction granted.

The Ingrams were a jobber for Phillips and were assigned a territory in New Mexico surrounding the town of Clovis. Helton was Phillips' wholesaler in an area near Farwell, Texas, which is nine miles east of Clovis. Helton also did business in Texico, New Mexico, which was distinguishable from Farwell only because of the state border. For a long time prior to February, 1965, Helton had purchased gasoline in Farwell from Phillips for one-half cent per gallon less than paid by the Ingrams in Clovis. In early 1965 Phillips made certain price changes in Farwell with the result that the differential favoring Helton increased to 1.8 cents per gallon.

Most of the Ingrams' business was with service stations, with about 25% to consumers, such as farmers, buying at wholesale. The service stations in Clovis had been engaged in an almost continuous price war for three years. During price wars Phillips granted a competitive price allowance or "C.P.A." so as to guarantee a minimum profit margin of 2.5 cents per gallon to the jobber and 5 cents to the retailer. However, the jobber and retailer shared the first one-cent reduction in pump price. Although there had previously been price wars among service stations in Farwell, there was none during early 1965. At this time the pump price at service stations in Clovis was 29.8 cents and 29.9 cents in Farwell. However, because Clovis was treated as having a price war, the Ingrams suffered a net reduction in their margin to service stations of approximately .75 cent while Helton, operating in Farwell where pump prices were considered normal, enjoyed his normal margin.

The Ingrams suffered no loss of service station accounts or reduction in their volume of sales. They had urged their farm customers not to change suppliers until after their suit had been adjudicated and only three or four of these accounts had been lost.

Phillips pointed out that if the requested injunction were granted it would have the effect of extending the Farwell price reductions into New Mexico and that this is contrary to the concept of the entire oil industry that a state line is a proper boundary. It argued that it is customary in the petroleum industry to make price changes within a given state.

DOYLE, DISTRICT JUDGE.   Evidence establishes beyond question a price differential between plaintiffs and Helton, and the question is whether this is an unlawful discrimination which entitled the Ingrams to injunctive relief notwithstanding that they have not suffered a heavy loss.

The elements of a violation of Section 2(a) of the Clayton Act, as amended by the Robinson-Patman Act, are as follows:

1. Price differences between two or more customers of a given seller which amount to a discrimination;
2. A sale involving goods or commodities of like grade and quality;
3. In interstate commerce;
4. For use, consumption, or resale within the United States;
5. Even if each of the above factors is present, a discrimination is not unlawful unless, in addition to the foregoing, its effect may:
   a. Substantially lessen competition in any line of commerce; or
   b. tend to create a monopoly in any line of commerce; or
   c. substantially injure, destroy, or prevent competition:
      (1) with the person who grants the discrimination;
      (2) with any of his customers;
      (3) with the person who knowingly receives the discrimination;
      (4) with any of his customers;
      (5) with the customers of any of them.

· · · · · ·

II. Whether the Price Difference at Bar Can Be Said to Have Had an Adverse Competitive Effect.   Phillips argues that the evidence fails to establish that the Ingrams and Helton are in competition. They say that the Ingrams and Helton are not adversaries in the re-sale market where purchasers [sic] of the products which they buy from Phillips are sold.

We note that this case involves an alleged discrimination at the so-called secondary line level, that is, between purchasers of an allegedly discriminating seller. In such cases a state of competition between the purchasers is essential to actionable price discrimination. The Ingrams and Helton are within the same class. They are wholesalers, are jobbers, and they sell identical products to the same types of customers and so there is no basis for distinction or discrimination between them on the ground that they serve different functions. Moreover, despite the fact that Phillips maintains that they operate in different market areas, we are of the opinion that the Texas-New Mexico state line does not in this instance constitute a trade boundary which separates different trade areas. As a matter of fact, part of Helton's territory is in New Mexico. As previously noted, the towns of Clovis, New Mexico, and Farwell, Texas, are geographically close, and the area is a single homogeneous economic unit held together by its character as agricultural land. . . . The farmers shop in both towns and patronize businesses in both places. In view of these facts, we are constrained to conclude that the Ingrams and Helton are in practical competition.

III. Whether the Evidence Establishes That Competition Has Been Substantially Lessened, Injured, Destroyed or Prevented. Phillips' position as to the deficiency of the Ingrams' proof with respect to injury to competition is that the Ingrams' volume has continued good despite the price difference. The Ingrams have not been required to lower their prices in order to prevent loss of sales. This, however, does not constitute evidence of lack of substantial injury to competition.

In *Standard Motor Products,* discounts were given by an automobile equipment manufacturer to its distributors. Discounts given to certain large distributors and those who were members of cooperative buying groups were larger than those received by the small distributors who were unaffiliated. On the other hand, the distributors sold the equipment at the manufacturer's resale price and there was no evidence of loss of sales. Nevertheless, the Court said that competitive injury was to be inferred from the discount differentials in the light of the narrow profit margins and the competition in the industry. Thus, it was the loss of profits rather than the loss of sales that was regarded as injurious. The smaller distributors were forced to join cooperative buying groups so as to obtain higher discounts. The Court said that this could "tend only to further lessen competition."

. . . . .

IV. Whether Plaintiff Is Entitled to Injunctive Relief Where There Has Been No Measurable Showing of Money Damages. The ultimate question here is whether the evidence establishes a reasonable possibility of substantial injury in the future. In *Standard Oil Co.* v. *Federal Trade Commission* (1945), the Court said:

[I]n the instant case, the Commission went further and showed that the petitioner's discrimination in price to its wholesale customers did have the effect to substantially lessen competition or to injure, destroy, or prevent competition. Note, however, that it would have been necessary for the Commission to prove only that such discrimination in price *may* have that effect. It is not actual injury alone but the prospect reasonably to be expected of injury to competition which the statute seeks to prevent.

Injunctive relief is granted for the purpose of preventing threatened injury. General equitable principles governing the granting of relief in other equity cases apply to the so-called trade cases. Furthermore, actual damages are not a prerequisite to the granting of injunctive relief. In *Continental Baking* the Court noted that a reasonable possibility is more than a mere possibility.

We conclude that the Ingrams' future is much bleaker than is their past and present. The evidence shows that they have persuaded their accounts to await the outcome of this action. It is not reasonable to suppose, however, that these people will continue to buy from Ingrams at the higher price when they can obtain the identical product from Helton at a substantially lower price. The price differential here of 1.8 cents per gallon is sufficiently substantial so that it cannot be regarded as *de minimis*. . . .

V. Whether Defendant May Avail Itself of the Affirmative Defense Provided by Section 2(b) of the Act. Phillips finally contends that the price difference here shown is within the exception recognized by the act as a price made in good faith to meet an equally lower price of a competitor. If applicable, the Section 2(b) provision of the Act is an absolute bar to the granting of relief even though price discrimination injurious to competition has been shown.

It is probable that the price reductions by the independents caused the majors to reduce their prices in Farwell, Texas, during early 1965. It is also clear from the evidence that Phillips reduced its price following the lead of Humble Oil Company, Texaco and Shell Oil Company. Phillips' prices were reduced after the reduction of the prices of the named companies had been reported in the *Oil Daily* and had been certified by the defendant Phillips. There is some evidence that for a time at least Phillips' prices were lower than those of the competitors, but on the whole they were at the same level.

The contention of the Ingrams that Phillips' price reductions were made pursuant to an established pricing system rather than a competitive demand, has merit. If it was pursuant to a pricing system it was not made in genuine response to an individual competitive demand.

We are of the opinion that Phillips' price reduction was more a part of a customary industry pricing system than an individual meeting of competition. The evidence here shows that in the oil industry pump prices are the result of wholesale prices charged by the major oil companies. In the instant case Humble reduced its price in Farwell, Texas, and the other majors, including the defendant Phillips, quickly and automatically followed this lead. Undoubtedly, the retail market had some effect upon this but it is the *system* which is the predominant factor in the price change. Phillips reduced its price in Farwell not to meet any specific competition, but rather because Humble, Texaco and Shell reduced their prices. There was no bargaining and haggling such as that described in *Standard Oil Co.* v. *Federal Trade Commission* (1956). Phillips swiftly and unthinkingly responded to the reduced prices. This was the conscious parallelism system at work. We conclude that this conduct was arbitrary and without regard to any specific competitive demand; rather, it was in accordance with an established method of pricing. Thus it does not fulfill the requirements of Section 2(b) of the Act. Therefore, the 2(b) "good faith" defense must be ruled out.

United Biscuit Co. of America v. FTC

350 F.2d 615 (7th Cir. 1965)

This was a proceeding on petition of United Biscuit Company of America (plaintiff) to review a cease and desist order of the Federal Trade Commission (defendant) issued after the Commission had found United Biscuit had violated Section 2(a) of the Clayton Act as amended by the Robinson-Patman Act. Affirmed.

In 1959 United Biscuit Co. sold its cookies and crackers in the midwest to retail grocery store customers who were divided into those owning or operating only one store (independents) and those owning or operating more than one store (chain). United used graduated monthly discount schedules which allowed discounts up to six percent based on the volume of purchases made by each retail store customer. The discount was calculated on the basis of the aggregated purchases of the store operated by the customer. The larger chains received larger discounts than did the independents.

The Commission's case with respect to the actual operation of United's discount practices was based on the purchases made and the discounts earned during two separate three-month periods of 1959 by thirteen independent stores and by a few chain store outlets located in portions of three communities served by the Sawyer Division—Gary, Indiana; South Bend, Indiana; and Burlington, Wisconsin. Most of the major retail grocery stores and a few of the large independents received a six percent volume discount. Other stores received discounts varying from 1½ percent to five percent. Some received no discount. The Commission found that as a result of the differences in the volume discounts, United charged some customers a higher price for like goods than it charged a competing customer or competing customers.

SWYGERT, CIRCUIT JUDGE. We realize that the dollar amounts representing the discount differentials are small and not as great as those found in many prosecutions for section 2(a) Clayton Act violations. Nevertheless, for reasons hereinafter given, we think there was sufficient evidentiary support for the Commission's finding that there was a likelihood of substantial anticompetitive injury.

. . . . .

The fact that the discounts granted by United increase up to six percent belies the claim that the price differentials as such are insubstantial. The apparent purpose of a graduated discount system is to afford some customers greater profits. As the volume of a customer's purchases grows the percentage of his discount increases, resulting in the opportunity either to realize a greater margin of profit per package or to reduce his retail price in relation to his competitors. There would seem to be no purpose for United to burden itself with maintaining its pricing practices unless it believed that the discounts are sufficiently attractive to induce a greater volume of purchases from its customers. It follows that if the discounts are intended as an inducement, necessarily they must be considered of a substantial character.

United correctly points out, however, that the "substantiality" requirement of the statute relates not to the price differentials, but to their effect upon competition. It then charges that the Commission ignored this distinction by holding that substantial injury to competition may be inferred if the discount to one customer is substantially more than that given his competitors. In other words, United argues that in effect the Commission applied a *per se* test in finding that the anti-competitive effect of petitioner's pricing practices would be substantial rather than minimal. We are convinced, however, that the Commission did not make the finding solely on the basis of the differences in the percentages of the discounts or of the amounts of the discriminations. All of the facts and circumstances of the case, including the amount of the discounts, were considered by the Commission in reaching its conclusion.

Independent store owners testified generally as to the highly competitive nature of the retail food business and that net profits are low; consequently, cash discounts and other allowances are important. One store owner testified "[W]e have to fight not only for pennies but for fractions." Moreover, certain of the independent store witnesses testified that price was a very important, if not the most important, factor in enabling them to compete. There was also testimony from these witnesses to the effect that if they could buy cheaper they could sell for less and that customers will, in the overall picture, buy where the prices are lower. The Commission said that "considering the highly competitive nature of the market and the other factors mentioned, a volume discount of 6% . . . was clearly substantial. Likewise substantial were the lesser discounts shown ranging up to 6%." The Commission concluded that there was sufficient evidence "to find that the competitive opportunities of certain purchasers were injured when they had to pay United substantially more than their competitors had to pay and that the effect may be substantially to injure, destroy or prevent competition with the purchasers receiving the benefit of such discriminations."

Brokerage Payments

Unlawful Brokerage.   Section 2(c) establishes a per se violation of the act in that any type of dummy brokerage payment is prohibited, whether or not paid directly to the buyer. Unlike Section 2(a), no effect on competition need be shown to prove the violation. The section was aimed at price discrimination granted by means of brokerage payments to the buyer or his nominee. To accomplish this objective the courts have, by their interpretation of the section, eliminated the words "except for services rendered." Even when a buyer's broker renders a service such as warehousing or breaking bulk, payment to him has been held to be a violation.[5] Therefore, any commission or allowance to a person directly or indirectly controlled by the buyer is prohibited whether or not any of the payment ever reaches the buyer. It has also been held to be a violation of Section 2(c) if a seller's broker accepts a lower commission and passes the savings to the buyer.

Discriminatory Payments and Services

Introduction.   Sellers and their customers both benefit from merchandising activities carried on by the customer to promote the sale of the goods. These

---

[5] *FTC* v. *Henry Broch & Company,* 368 U.S. 360 (1962).

would include such activities as advertising, displays of the goods, demonstrations and distribution of samples or premiums. Section 2(d) applies primarily to payments made by the seller to his customers to encourage such activities by them. Section 2(e) applies primarily to furnishing such services to the customer by the seller. These sections make either the payment for or the furnishing of a service illegal unless it is made available to all competing customers on proportionately equal terms.

Section 2(d) states:

That it shall be unlawful for any person engaged in commerce to pay or contract for the payment of anything of value to or for the benefit of a customer of such person in the course of such commerce as compensation or in consideration for any services or facilities furnished by or through such customer in connection with the processing, handling, sale or offering for sale of any products or commodities manufactured, sold, or offered for sale by such person, unless such payment or consideration is available on proportionally equal terms to all other customers competing in the distribution of such products or commodities.

Section 2(e) declares:

That it shall be unlawful for any person to discriminate in favor of one purchaser against another purchaser or purchasers of a commodity bought for resale, without or with processing, by contracting to furnish or furnishing, or by contributing to the furnishing of, any services or facilities connected with the processing, handling, sale, or offering for sale of such commodity so purchased upon terms not accorded to all purchasers on proportionally equal terms.

It will be noted that the language of the two sections differs in some respects but they have been interpreted as having substantially the same meaning. They define per se violations, that is, whether the discriminatory allowance or service has the effect of injuring competition is immaterial.

Available. The requirement of availability demands of the seller offering promotional payments or services more than merely not denying the request of a customer to be given a similar payment or service. For example, a seller of coffee who wants to offer a cooperative advertising contract to one of his grocer customers to encourage him to include the seller's branded product in his weekly newspaper advertising must actually make known to his other customers who are in competition with that customer that he will make promotional payments to them on a proportional basis.

To be available the service must be something appropriate to the customer. It is not enough for a seller of coffee to make a payment available only to his customers who advertise in newspapers. The cooperative advertising plan must be flexible enough to permit all competing customers to participate—with handbills or other types of advertising or perhaps even other kinds of promotional devices such as window or counter displays.

On Proportionately Equal Terms. The most common method of proportionalizing is relating payments or services to the quantity of goods purchased.

An example would be a payment of 50 cents per case of coffee purchased. It has been suggested that payments or services, such as furnishing a display case, could be proportionalized by furnishing one case for each of the buyer's stores or payments could be related to the square feet of window space devoted to a display of the seller's product. The fact that it is impracticable to furnish a cosmetics demonstrator for one hour to a small drug store when one is furnished for a full day to a store selling eight times as much of the cosmetics firm's products does not excuse the offering of a proportional service. However, it need not be the same service; it might be quite a different sort of promotional device, such as a demonstration kit.

Summary

Section 2(d) prohibits payments by a seller to a customer for furnishing any service or facility unless such payments are made available on proportionately equal terms to all competing customers. Section 2(e) prohibits the seller from himself furnishing services or facilities which are not available on a proportionalized basis.

The requirement of availability requires that the seller actually make known the offer of the payment of service. The most common way of complying with the requirement that the payment be made or service rendered on proportionately equal terms is by relating them to the quantity of goods sold.

FTC v. Fred Meyer, Inc.
390 U.S. 341 (1968)

This was a proceeding on petition of Fred Meyer, Inc. (petitioner), to review and set aside an order of the Federal Trade Commission (respondent) requiring Meyer to cease and desist from inducing certain suppliers to engage in discriminatory sales promotional activities prohibited by Section 2(d) of the Clayton Act as amended by the Robinson-Patman Act. The Court of Appeals for the Ninth Circuit disagreed in part with the Commissions interpretation of Section 2(d) and directed it to modify the order. Reversed and remanded to the FTC.

Fred Meyer, Inc., operating a chain of 13 supermarkets in the Portland, Oregon, area and making one fourth of the retail food sales in the area, conducted a four week promotional campaign each year. The promotion involved the distribution of a 72 page coupon book to its customers, each coupon good for a special price, often a one-third reduction from the regular price on a specified item carried in the Meyer stores. The coupon book was sold by Meyer to consumers for 10 cents and, in addition, Meyer charged each supplier joining in the promotion $3.50 for each coupon page. The suppliers usually underwrote the promotion further by redeeming coupons for cash or replacing without charge some proportion of the goods sold by Meyer during the promotion.

The proceeding-before the commission involved Tri-Valley Packing Association and Idaho Canning Co. as suppliers who, it was alleged, had violated Section 2(d) in participating in the 1957 promotion. Both paid Meyers $3.50 for the coupon and each agreed to replace for Meyers every third can sold under the offer. Both suppliers also sold to two wholesalers, Hudson House and Wadhams, who resold to a number of Meyer's retail competitors. No comparable promotional allowances had been accorded either of the wholesalers.

Meyer argued that there had been no violation of Section 2(d) because Meyer was not competing with the wholesalers and that the retailers who were competing with Meyer were not customers of Tri-Valley and Idaho Canning but were customers of the wholesalers. The FTC took the view that Meyer's retail competitors buying through the wholesalers were indirect customers of Tri-Valley and Idaho Canning. The FTC ruled that Section 2(d) prohibits a supplier from granting promotional allowances to a direct-buying retailer, such as Meyer, unless the allowances are also made available to wholesalers who purchase from the supplier and resell to retailers who compete with the direct buyer.

WARREN, CHIEF JUSTICE. We agree with the Commission that the proscription of Section 2(d) reaches the kind of discriminatory promotional allowances granted Meyer by Tri-Valley and Idaho Canning. Therefore, we reverse the judgment of the Court of Appeals on this point. However, because we have concluded that Meyer's retail competitors, rather than the two wholesalers, were competing customers under the statute, we also remand the case to the Commission for appropriate modification of its order.

For reasons stated below, we agree with Meyer that, on the facts of this case, Section 2(d) reaches only discrimination between customers competing for resales at the same functional level and, therefore, does not mandate proportional equality between Meyer and the two wholesalers.

Of course, neither the Committee Report nor other parts of the legislative history in so many words defines "customer" to include retailers who purchase through wholesalers and compete with direct buyers in resales. But a narrower reading of Section 2(d) would lead to the following anomalous result. On the one hand, direct-buying retailers like Meyer, who resell large quantities of their suppliers' products and therefore find it feasible to undertake the traditional wholesaling functions for themselves, would be protected by the provision from the granting of discriminatory promotional allowances to their direct-buying competitors. On the other hand, smaller retailers whose only access to suppliers is through independent wholesalers would not be entitled to this protection. Such a result would be diametrically opposed to Congress' clearly stated intent to improve the competitive position of small retailers by eliminating what was regarded as an abusive form of discrimination. If we were to read "customer" as excluding retailers who buy through wholesalers and compete with direct buyers, we would frustrate the purpose of Section 2(d). We effectuate it by holding that the section includes such competing retailers within the protected class.

Given these findings, it was unnecessary for the Commission to resort to the indirect customer doctrine. Whether suppliers deal directly with disfavored competitors or not, they can, and here did, afford a direct buyer the kind of competitive advantage which Section 2(d) was intended to eliminate. In light of our holding that "customer" in Section 2(d) includes retailers who buy through wholesalers and compete with a direct buyer in the resale of the supplier's product, the requirement of direct dealing between the supplier and disfavored competitors imposed by the Court of Appeals rests on too narrow a reading of the statute.

Although we approach the Commission's ruling with the deference due the agency charged with day-to-day administration of the Act, we hold that, at least on the facts before us, Section 2(d) does not require proportional equality between Meyer and the two wholesalers.

The Commission believed it found support for its position in the language of Section 2(d) itself, which requires that promotional allowances be accorded on proportionally equal terms to "customers competing in the distribution" of a supplier's product, rather than merely to customers competing in resales. The majority reasoned that Hudson House and Wadhams, when they resold to Meyer's retail competitors, were competing with Meyer in the distribution of Tri-Valley and Idaho Canning products because the two wholesalers were "seeking exactly the same consumer dollars that respondents are after." While it cannot be doubted that Congress reasonably could have employed such a broad concept of competition in Section 2(d), we do not believe that the use of the word "distribution" rather than "resale" is a clear indication that it did, and what discussion there was of the promotional allowance provision during the congressional hearings indicates that the section was meant to impose proportional equality only where buyers competed on the same functional level.

We recognize that it would be both inappropriate and unwise to attempt to formulate an all-embracing rule applying the elusive language of the section to every system of distribution a supplier might devise for getting his product to the consumer. But, on the concrete facts here presented, it is clear that the direct impact of Meyer's receiving discriminatory promotional allowances is felt by the disfavored retailers with whom Meyer competes in resales. We cannot assume without a clear indication from Congress that Section 2(d) was intended to compel the supplier to pay the allowances to a reseller further up the distributive chain who might or might not pass them onto the level where the impact would be felt directly. We conclude that the most reasonable construction of Section 2(d) is one which places on the supplier the responsibility for making promotional allowances available to those resellers who compete directly with the favored buyer.

The Commission argues here that the view we take of Section 2(d) is impracticable because suppliers will not always find it feasible to bypass their wholesalers and grant promotional allowance directly to their numerous retail outlets. Our decision does not necessitate such bypassing. We hold only that, when a supplier gives allowances to a direct-buying retailer, he must also make them available on comparable terms to those who buy his products through wholesalers and compete with the direct buyer in resales. Nothing we have said bars a supplier, consistently with other provisions of the anti-trust laws, from utilizing his wholesalers to distribute payments or administer a promotional program, so long as the supplier takes responsibility, under rules and guides promulgated by the Commission for the regulation of such practices, for seeing that the allowances are made available to all who compete in the resale of his product.

Vanity Fair Paper Mills v. FTC

311 F.2d 480 (2d Cir. 1962)

This was a petition by Vanity Fair Paper Mills, Inc. (plaintiff), to review an order of the Federal Trade Commission (defendant) directing Vanity Fair to cease and desist from making payments to a customer for advertising or other services or facilities unless such payments were made available to other customers on proportionately equal terms. Commission's order enforced with modification.

Vanity Fair, a manufacturer of household paper products in New York, sold its products to retail and wholesale grocers and druggists in Texas, Louisiana and other states. In 1958 it used a standard Cooperative Advertising Agreement in the Texas-Louisiana area. In addition, because Vanity Fair did not have funds available for extensive advertising, it occasionally participated in special promotions conducted by its customers which featured its products along with other suppliers.

Weingarten, a retail grocery chain operating in Texas and Louisiana and one of Vanity Fair's customers, requested Vanity Fair to participate in its 57th Anniversary Sale in February 1958. It offered Vanity Fair a schedule of promotional services combining an advertisement of Vanity Fair's products in Weingarten's newspaper advertising and special product displays and the "personal enthusiasm" of Weingarten store personnel in one or more of the geographical areas covered by Weingarten stores. The cost of participation, according to the schedule, ranged from $56.05 to $3,995.90. Vanity Fair chose the $215 item which gave it the promotional service in all of Weingarten's Texas and Louisiana stores plus ⅟₁₆ page in the newspapers in Houston, Freeport, Baytown and Texas City. Vanity Fair also participated in October, 1958, in Weingarten's 20th Texas and Louisiana Products Sale.

Childs Big Chain was the only other customer of Vanity Fair which competed with Weingarten in southeastern Texas and southwestern Louisiana which received a special promotional allowance in 1958. None of the other customers requested such an allowance. The combined payments from the standard cooperative advertising contract and the special promotional allowances gave Weingarten 3.4% and Childs 2.2% on Vanity Fair's gross sales to them. The other customers who received no special allowance received allowances ranging from 1.9% to zero.

The commission found that the special allowances to Weingarten violated Section 2(d) of the Robinson-Patman Act.

FRIENDLY, CIRCUIT JUDGE. It is not disputed that Weingarten received from Vanity Fair something of value for services or facilities furnished in the sale of

Vanity Fair's products which was not received by "other customers competing in the distribution of such products or commodities." The issue is whether the Commission was warranted in finding that the "payment or consideration" given to Weingarten was not "available" to all the non-recipients "on proportionally equal terms."

Determination of what a seller must do in order that payments of the sort described in § 2(d) should be "available" to all customers has not been easy. . . .

. . . A promotional allowance is not "available" to all customers if it has been "denied" to some. *Corn Products Refining Co.* v. *FTC* (1945). Neither is it "available" if steps have been taken to conceal it. On the other hand, the legislative history argues against a construction that would require the seller to make an actual "offer" to all customers, including many who might not be interested. Between these polar positions the Commission has shifted uneasily. For some years it tended toward an ever stronger attitude coming perilously close to requiring an offer, as can be seen by comparing earlier cases where the complaint emphasized secrecy and concealment, e.g., *N. Erlanger, Blumgart & Co.,* with the increasingly severe requirements of affirmative and specific notification set forth in *Kay Windsor Frocks, Inc.* Then it made a slight retreat toward a more generalized notification requirement in its 1960 Guides for Advertising Allowances and Other Merchandising Payments and Services, which say:

> The seller should take some action to inform all his customers competing with any participating customer that the plan is available. He can do this by any means he chooses, including letter, telegram, notice on invoices, salesmen, brokers, etc. However, if a seller wants to be able to show later that he did make an offer to a certain customer, he is in a better position to do so if he made it in writing.

Unsatisfactory as the 1960 formulation may be, perhaps it is as much as can be expected when Congress has spoken in such Delphic terms.

A showing here not only that Vanity Fair's sales representatives had been "advised" of its policies with respect to special promotional allowances and "instructed to inform respondent's customers thereof," but also that they had carried out such instructions, would have met the Commission's definition of the statutory standard. However, the stipulation was altogether silent on the latter score. The Commission was entitled to deem the silence significant and to conclude, as it did, that the information had not been generally passed on.

· · · · ·

We also sustain the Commission's alternative position that even if respondent's special promotional allowances were "available" to all customers, they were not available "on proportionally equal terms." . . . Little as the stipulation here tells us of Vanity Fair's "policy," it tells enough to show that the requirement of proportional equality was not satisfied. Even as to identically situated customers, the policy left Vanity Fair free to discriminate both in the quantum of promotional services it would support and in the degree to which it would support them. Altogether consistently with its policy, Vanity Fair could have paid Weingarten as much as $3,995.90 and an identically situated competitor, offering it the same choices as

Weingarten, as little as $56.05. It is true that since Weingarten would have had to furnish more newspaper advertising than its competitor, Vanity Fair would have derived greater benefit from the larger payment, although perhaps not proportionally greater, since both customers would have been furnishing the same displays and "personnel enthusiasm." But Weingarten would have received an enormously greater benefit from Vanity Fair than the equally entitled competitor. Also, even if Vanity Fair chose to support the same advertising space for identical customers, the policy did not require it to pay a uniform proportion of the cost but only "an amount reasonably related" thereto; if the stipulation meant "equal to" or "the same percentage of" the cost, it did not say so. Neither did the policy make any attempt to relate the amount of support accorded different customers to their respective volumes of purchases. To be sure, it was not established that Vanity Fair in fact applied its policy in a discriminatory fashion. But a seller who has paid a special promotional allowance to some customers and not to others does not avoid the proscription of § 2(d) merely because payment *might have been* "available on proportionally equal terms to all other customers competing in the distribution of such products or commodities"; he avoids it only if such payment "is" available. Whatever the statute does or does not require with respect to proportionality, it is not satisfied by a policy as loose as Vanity Fair's.

Buyer Inducement of Discrimination

Inducements Prohibited. Section 2(f) is directed at the buyer and makes it illegal for him to induce or receive knowingly a discrimination in price prohibited by Section 2(a). It states:

> That it shall be unlawful for any person engaged in commerce, in the course of such commerce, knowingly to induce or receive a discrimination in price which is prohibited by this section.

It does not apply to promotional payments or services prohibited by Sections 2(d) and 2(e). A violation occurs only when the buyer knows that the price he receives is lower than that which the seller charges other customers. However, he need not have knowledge that the discrimination actually violates Section 2(a). For example, to be in violation of Section 2(f) the buyer need not be aware of the injury to competition necessary for a violation of Section 2(a).

Enforcement

Types of Proceedings. The various provisions of Section 2 of the Clayton Act as amended by the Robinson-Patman Act may be enforced by four types of proceedings. First, the FTC on its own motion or upon the application of a private party, may make an investigation and issue a complaint which may result in a cease and desist order after proceedings before the Commission. Second, the Attorney General of the United States may bring an injunction suit in a U.S. District Court. Third, an individual or corporation may seek an injunction. Fourth, any individual or corporation who is injured by a violation may bring a suit for triple damages. A substantial number of such treble damage suits have been successful and courts have been relatively liberal in their requirements for proof of damages.

In addition, Section 3 of the Robinson-Patman Act makes it a crime to participate in general price discriminations, in geographical price discriminations seeking to eliminate a competitor in a certain area, and in selling at unreasonably low prices for the purpose of destroying competition or eliminating a competitor. There have been few impositions of criminal penalties under this section.

Ludwig v. American Greetings Corp.
264 F.2d 286 (6th Cir. 1959)

This was an action by William J. Ludwig (plaintiff) to recover treble damages from American Greetings Corporation (defendant) for alleged violation of Section 2 of the Clayton Act as amended by the Robinson-Patman Act. The District Court sustained American Greetings' motion to dismiss the complaint on the grounds that the acts were not such as to permit a private action. Reversed and remanded.

American manufactured greetings cards and related products at Cleveland, Ohio, and distributed them throughout the United States. Ludwig was in the business of purchasing greeting cards from manufacturers and reselling at wholesale in Ohio. Ludwig's complaint alleged that to induce retailers to stock its cards, American bought and destroyed stocks of Ludwig's cards in the hands of retailers, offered to repurchase retailer's greeting card display cabinets and to furnish new ones free of charge, to pay a cash bonus on condition that the retailers switch their business to American, and, in addition, offered to place American's cards with them on a consignment basis. Ludwig claimed he had been injured in his business by reason of such acts in the amount of more than $15,000.

MILLER, CIRCUIT JUDGE. We are of the opinion that placing former retail customers of Ludwig on a consignment basis in order to induce such customers to transfer their business to America, as charged in the complaint, constitutes in substance a prima facie case of indirect price discrimination. It is true that such a prima facie case may be rebutted, but the burden of doing so is upon the person charged with the violation. Section 2(b) of the Act. The District Judge did not reach or pass upon such an issue.

Other types of discrimination are made unlawful under subsections (c), (d) and (e) of the Act. Subsection (c) makes it unlawful to pay or grant a commission or compensation, except for services rendered, in connection with the sale of goods, wares or merchandise. Subsection (d) makes it unlawful to pay anything of value in consideration for any services or facilities furnished by a customer in connection with the handling or offering for sale of any products sold to him, unless such consideration is available on proportionally equal terms to all other customers competing in the distribution of such products. Subsection (e) makes it unlawful to discriminate in favor of one purchaser against another purchaser of a commodity bought for resale by furnishing any services or facilities connected with the handling of such commodity so purchased, upon terms not accorded to all purchasers on proportionally equal terms. We believe that the furnishing by American of new greeting card display cabinets free of charge to retail sellers formerly serviced by Ludwig and the payment of a cash bonus to certain retail customers of Ludwig as an inducement to purchase American's cards instead of Ludwig's, as charged in the complaint, constitute a violation of these sections of the statute. . . .

The opinion of the District Judge indicates that the principal reason for his ruling was because this action was on behalf of a competitor of Ludwig rather than by a customer claiming discrimination between himself and another customer. The present action by a competitor appeared to him to be more in the nature of unfair competition than a violation of the anti-trust laws. It may be that Ludwig might have a cause of action for unfair competition, but such remedy is not an exclusive one. The Act has been construed as giving a right of action to a competitor who is injured in his business as well as to a customer who has been discriminated against.

Problem Cases

1. American Can Co. granted quantity discounts on a scale ranging from 1 percent to 5 percent of annual purchases. The 1 percent discount was granted to customers who purchased between $500,000 and $1,000,000 worth of cans annually. Bruce's Juices purchased approximately $350,000 worth of cans per year and received no discount. Two of its competitors had canneries nearby which used about the same volume of cans but these customers were permitted to pool their purchases with the result that one qualified for the 5 percent discount and the other for a 4 percent discount. The purchases of 98 percent of the customers of American Can were too small to qualify them for any discount. Only three customers received the 5 percent discount. Bruce's brought an action for treble damages against American Can. Is the discount policy a violation of Section 2(a)?

2. Forster, a manufacturer of wooden clothespins, gave a number of distributors in the Pittsburgh market one case of clothespins free for each 10 cases purchased, a deal not available elsewhere. When charged by the FTC with a violation of Section 2(a), Forster's executives testified to the effect that 10 of the 125 clothespin buyers in the Pittsburgh area "reported" that Penley, a competitor seeking to enter the market, was "quoting" or "offering" a 10 percent price concession. There was no testimony that any of these buyers had themselves been made the price reduction offer. Is this a good defense under Section 2(b)?

3. Broch, a broker for Canada Foods and several other food products manufacturers, tried to make a sale to Smucker of apple concentrate processed by Canada Foods.

The regular price was $1.30 per gallon in 50-gallon drums and Canada Foods usually paid Broch a 5 percent commission. Smucker wanted 500 gallons but was willing to pay only $1.25 per gallon. Canada Foods agreed to make the sale at that price if Broch would agree to reduce its brokerage to 3 percent. Thus, in effect, the seller and broker equally shared the price reduction. The sale was completed and subsequent sales were made to Smucker on the same basis. Sales by Broch to other customers continued at $1.30 and 5 percent commission. The FTC charged Broch with a violation of Section 2(c) of the amended Clayton Act. Broch defended on the grounds that it was an independent selling agent, was not covered by Section 2(c) and had not paid anything of value as a commission or other compensation to the buyer. Is Broch's defense good?

4. For two years Blass and Cohn, competing department stores, carried Elizabeth Arden Cosmetics. Arden paid Blass an allowance equal to one half the salary of a clerk-demonstrator to push the products and an allowance equal to the full amount of a demonstrator's salary to Cohn. Sales of Arden's products by the two stores fluctuated— for some periods Blass's sales exceed Cohn's although for the full two years Cohn bought $11,251 and Blass $8,788 of Arden's products. Blass sued Arden, alleging violation of Sections 2(d) and 2(e) of the amended Clayton Act and asked for treble damages based on the difference in allowances made between Blass and Cohn. Arden argued that Section 2(e) was unconstitutional because it was not expressly limited to transactions in interstate commerce and that Blass had made no showing that its business had been injured as a result of the discrimination. Should Blass recover three times the amount of the difference between the allowances to Blass and those to Cohn?

5. During 1959, Nuarc, a manufacturer of printing equipment, spent $32,000 for advertising in *Printing Impressions,* a publication of Foster Publishing Co. Borowsky controlled Foster Publishing Co. He also controlled Foster Type and Equipment Co., a retailer of printing equipment which was a customer of Nuarc. However, nothing in the publication suggested any connection between Foster Publishing and Foster Type. Foster Type also advertised in *Printing Impressions,* paying the same rate as Nuarc and other suppliers and competitors of Foster Type. Nuarc did not make advertising or promotional payments to any other customers competing with Foster Type in the resale of Nuarc products in the area. The FTC ordered Nuarc to cease and desist on the grounds that the advertising payments violated Section 2(d). Nuarc appealed. Is the advertising in *Printing Impressions* a violation of 2(d)?

6. A number of small firms organized themselves into a buying group in order to obtain the economies and volume discounts available to large-scale buyers. The member firms would place their individual orders in the name of their buying group, the American Motor Specialties Co. These orders were sent either directly to the manufacturer or were sent through the group office without any consolidation of member orders. Shipments were made directly to the individual firms, and the rebates were shared on the basis of the proportion the individual members' purchases bore to the group's total purchases. American Motors Specialties defended on the ground that the FTC failed to prove that they had *knowingly* induced or received discriminatory prices. Did American Motors Specialties' buying practice violate Section 2(f)?

7. Pacific Molasses Co., a publicly held company, was engaged in discriminatory pricing practices in the sale of "blackstrap" molasses to certain independent truck distributors. Price concessions granted to favored customers were, in some cases, nearly a 10 percent reduction over prices charged to nonfavored distributor-customers. Doyle at this time was the area sales manager of Pacific and in this capacity advised the president

of Pacific on pricing policies. The ultimate decisions on all pricing were made by the president and then effectuated by Doyle. The FTC found a violation of Section 2(a) of the Robinson-Patman Act and issued a cease and desist order against both Pacific and Doyle. The Commission petitioned the court for enforcement and Doyle objected that the order should not restrain him as an individual. Should Doyle be included in the order?

chapter 49. The Federal Trade Commission Act and Other Laws Relating to Competition

The Federal Trade Commission Act

The Federal Trade Commission Act (38 Stat. 717 1914, as amended, 15 U.S.C. §§ 41–58) like the Clayton Act was enacted because its proponents felt that the Sherman Act had not sufficiently curtailed certain monopolistic practices and tendencies in the American economy. The act created a special bipartisan administrative agency charged with giving expert and continuing enforcement of antitrust policies. Under Section 5 of the act the FTC is given very broad powers to police "unfair methods of competition in commerce, and unfair or deceptive acts or practices in commerce."

While the Federal Trade Commission Act is not technically a part of the antitrust laws and private treble damage actions cannot be brought under Section 5, the act overlaps the Sherman Act in that it also makes illegal as "unfair methods of competition," any of the restraints of trade which are illegal under the Sherman Act. In addition, the powers of the FTC reach incipient anticompetitive practices, false advertising, and other deceptive practices which are not reached by the Sherman Act. The FTC has concurrent jurisdiction with the Department of Justice to enforce the Clayton Act. In practice, the FTC alone has brought the cases under the Robinson-Patman Act amendments to the Clayton Act. The FTC also has jurisdiction in regard to various other acts including: the Webb-Pomerene Act; Wool Products Labeling Act; Federal Drug and Cosmetic Act; Fur Products Labeling Act; Flammable Fabric Act; Lanham Trade-Mark Act; and the Fair Packaging and Labeling Act.

The FTC issues "cease and desist" orders against violations of the act which become final unless appealed to the courts. Businesses which violate these orders are subject to $5,000 fines for each day of continuing violation.

Summary

The FTC has broad powers to stop anticompetitive and deceptive practices. The Commission issues cease and desist orders and also has the power to levy fines. Private treble damage suits are not permitted for violations of the FTC Act.

FTC v. Mary Carter Paint Co.

382 U.S. 46 (1965)

The Federal Trade Commission brought an action under Section 5 of the Federal Trade Commission Act against Mary Carter Paint Co. and issued a cease and desist order. Mary Carter was ordered to stop representing in advertisements that each customer would be given a can of paint "free" for every can of paint purchased. The Commission appealed from a Circuit Court ruling setting aside the cease and desist order. Reversed.

BRENNAN, JUSTICE.   Although there is some ambiguity in the Commission's opinion, we cannot say that its holding constituted a departure from Commission policy regarding the use of the commercially exploitable word "free." Initial efforts to define the term in decisions were followed by "Guides Against Deceptive Prices." These informed businessmen that they might advertise an article as "free," even though purchase of another article was required, so long as the terms of the offer were clearly stated, the price of the article required to be purchased was not increased, and its quality and quantity were not diminished. With specific reference to two-for-the-price-of-one offers, the Guides required that either the sales price for the two be "the advertiser's usual and customary retail price for the single article in the recent, regular course of his business," or where the advertiser has not previously sold the article, the price for two be the "usual and customary" price for one in the relevant trade areas. These, of course, were guides, not fixed rules as such, and were designed to inform businessmen of the factors which would guide Commission decision. Although Mary Carter seems to have attempted to tailor its offer to come within their terms, the Commission found that it failed; the offer complied in appearance only.

The gist of the Commission's reasoning is in the hearing examiner's finding, which it adopted, that

the usual and customary retail price of each can of Mary Carter paint was not, and is not now, the price designated in the advertisement [$6.98] but was, and is now substantially less than such price. The second can of paint was not, and is not now, 'free,' that is, was not, and is not now, given as a gift of gratuity. The offer is, on the contrary, an offer of two cans of paint for the price advertised as or purporting to be the list price or customary and usual price of one can.

In sum, the Commission found that Mary Carter had no history of selling single cans of paint; it was marketing twins, and in allocating what is in fact the price of two cans to one can, yet calling one "free," Mary Carter misrepresented. It is true that respondent was not permitted to show that the quality of its paint matched those paints which usually and customarily sell in the $6.98 range, or that purchasers of paint estimate quality by the price they are charged. If both claims were established, it is arguable that any deception was limited to a representation that Mary Carter has a usual and customary price for single cans of paint, when it has no such price. However, it is not for courts to say whether this violates the Act. "[T]he Commission is often in a better position than are courts to determine when a practice is 'deceptive' within the meaning of the Act." There was substantial evidence in the record to support the Commission's finding; its determination that the practice here was deceptive was neither arbitrary nor clearly wrong. The Court of Appeals should have sustained it.

FTC v. *Texaco, Inc.*
393 U.S. 223 (1968)

The FTC brought this proceeding against Texaco under Section 5 of the FTC Act charging that Texaco's sales commission plan with its dealers constituted an unfair method of competition. The Circuit Court set aside a cease and desist order issued by the Commission and the Commission appealed. Reversed.

BLACK, JUSTICE.   The question presented by this case is whether the FTC was warranted in finding that it was an unfair method of competition in violation of § 5 of the Federal Trade Commission Act for respondent Texaco to undertake to induce its service station dealers to purchase Goodrich tires, batteries, and accessories (hereafter referred to as TBA) in return for a commission paid by Goodrich to Texaco.

The Commission and Texaco agree that the Texaco-Goodrich arrangement for marketing TBA will fall under the rational of our *Atlantic* decision if the Commission was correct in its three ultimate conclusions that (1) Texaco has dominant economic power over its dealers; (2) that Texaco exercises that power over its dealers in fulfilling its agreement to promote and sponsor Goodrich products; and (3) that anticompetitive effects result from the exercise of that power.

That Texaco holds dominant economic power over its dealers is clearly shown by the record in this case. In fact, Texaco does not contest the conclusion of the Court of Appeals below and the Fifth Circuit Court of Appeals in *Shell* that such power is "inherent in the structure and economics of the petroleum distribution system." Nearly 40% of the Texaco dealers lease their stations from Texaco. These dealers typically hold a one-year lease on their stations, and these leases are subject to termination at the end of any year on 10 days' notice. At any time during the year a man's lease on his service station may be immediately terminated by Texaco without advance notice if in Texaco's judgment any of the "house-keeping" provisions of the lease, relating to the use and appearance of the station, are not fulfilled. The contract under which Texaco dealers receive their vital supply of gasoline and other petroleum products also runs from year to year and is terminable on 30 days' notice under Texaco's standard form contract. The average dealer is a man of limited means who has what is for him a sizable investment in his station. He stands to lose much if he incurs the ill will of Texaco. As Judge Wisdom wrote in *Shell,* "A man operating a gas station is bound to be overawed by the great corporation that is his supplier, his banker, and his landlord."

It is against the background of this dominant economic power over the dealers that the sales commission arrangement must be viewed. The Texaco-Goodrich agreement provides that Goodrich will pay Texaco a commission of 10% on all purchases by Texaco service station dealers of Goodrich TBA. In return, Texaco agrees to "promote the sale of Goodrich products" to Texaco dealers. During the five-year period studied by the Commission (1952–1956) $245,000,000 of the Goodrich and Firestone TBA sponsored by Texaco was purchased by Texaco dealers, for which Texaco received almost $22,000,000 in commissions. Evidence before the Commission showed that Texaco carried out its agreement to promote Goodrich products through constantly reminding its dealers of Texaco's desire that they stock and sell the sponsored Goodrich TBA. Texaco emphasizes the importance of TBA and the recommended brands as early as its initial interview with a prospective dealer and repeats its recommendation through a steady flow of campaign materials utilizing Goodrich products. Texaco salesmen, the primary link between Texaco and the dealers, promote Goodrich products in their day-to-day contact with the Texaco dealers. The evaluation of a dealer's station by the Texaco salesman is often an important factor in determining whether a dealer's contract or lease with Texaco will be renewed. Thus the Texaco salesmen, whose favorable opinion is so important to every dealer, are the key men in the promotion of Goodrich products, and on occasion accompany the Goodrich salesmen in their calls on the dealers. Finally, Texaco receives regular reports on the amount of sponsored TBA purchased by each dealer. Texaco contends, however, that these reports are used only for maintaining its accounts with Goodrich and not for policing dealer purchases.

The sales commission system for marketing TBA is inherently coercive. A service station dealer whose very livelihood depends upon the continuing good favor of a major oil company is constantly aware of the oil company's desire that he stock and sell the recommended brand of TBA.

We are similarly convinced that the Commission was correct in determining that this arrangement has an adverse effect on competition in the marketing of TBA. Service stations play an increasingly important role in the marketing of tires, batteries, and other automotive accessories. With five major companies supplying virtually all of the tires that come with new cars, only in the replacement market can the smaller companies hope to compete. Ideally, each service station dealer would stock the brands of TBA that in his judgment were most favored by customers for price and quality. To the extent that dealers are induced to select the sponsored brand in order to maintain the good favor of the oil company upon which they are dependent, to that extent the operation of the competitive market is adversely affected. The nonsponsored brands do not compete on the even terms of price and quality competition; they must overcome, in addition, the influence of the dominant oil company that has been paid to induce its dealers to buy the recommended brand. While the success of this arrangement in foreclosing competitors from the TBA market has not matched that of the direct coercion employed by Atlantic, we feel that the anticompetitive tendencies of such a system are clear, and that the Commission was properly fulfilling the task that Congress assigned it in halting this practice in its incipiency. The Commission is not required to show that a practice it condemns has totally eliminated competition in the relevant market.

The Commission was justified in concluding that more than an insubstantial amount of commerce was involved. Texaco is one of the nation's largest petroleum companies. It sells its products to approximately 30,000 service stations, or about 16.5% of all service stations in the United States. The volume of sponsored TBA purchased by Texaco dealers in the five-year period 1952–1956 was $245,000,000, five times the amount involved in the *Atlantic* case.

Other Laws Affecting Competition

Exceptions and Exemptions to Antitrust.   The 1914 Clayton Act created a broad exemption to the antitrust laws so as to permit the formation of agricultural cooperatives. A similar exemption was created for those engaged in commercial fishing in 1934.

The Clayton Act likewise attempted to exempt the activities of labor unions from the antitrust law but restrictive court interpretations left the unions subject to the laws until the exemption was reinterpreted after the passage of the Norris–LaGuardia Act in 1932.[1] Union activities are now exempt except where unions combine with businesses for the purpose of fixing prices or imposing other illegal restraints on competition.

The Webb-Pomerene Act exempts the activity of exporters engaged in foreign trade provided such activity does not "artificially or intentionally enhance or depress prices within the United States." It is argued that this exemption is necessary so that American firms can compete on an even foot with the many cartels operating in foreign markets.

Many industries are classed as "affected with the public interest" and are subject to varying degrees of regulation by state and federal agencies. Some of these industries including insurance, banking, electric power, airline, telephone, radio and television broadcasting, railroad, pipeline, stock exchange, and ocean shipping are permitted to compete within the varying limits set by the various regulatory commissions; but in general, regulation rather than competition is relied upon to protect the public interest.

Fair-Trade Laws.   One of the most controversial exemptions to the anti-

---

[1] The landmark case exempting unions for most purpose was *U.S.* v. *Hutchenson,* 312 U.S. 219 (1941).

trust laws was created in 1937 with the passage of the Miller-Tydings Act. This statute permits states to enact so-called "fair-trade" laws exempting otherwise illegal vertical price-fixing arrangements from the antitrust laws. The exemption applies only to the sale of trademarked goods which are in "free and open competition with goods of the same general class."

Fair trade permits sellers who are trademark proprietors to contract with their buyers that their trademarked goods will not be resold at less than a specified minimum price. In addition, if the buyer is also a dealer he frequently must agree not to sell to a subvendee unless the latter assents to a similar restriction, namely, vertical price fixing. A more far-reaching provision of most state fair-trade laws is that buyers not a party to such contracts are bound by law to refrain from knowingly and willfully advertising, offering for sale, or selling goods subject to such an agreement at a price below that set in any fair-trade contract in force within that state. These provisions, known as "nonsigner laws," make possible statewide price schedules without individual consent.

Although seemingly designed to validate all provisions of state fair-trade laws as applied to goods in the interstate commerce, the Miller-Tydings Act did not expressly exempt nonsignee provisions from the antitrust laws. Subsequently, the McGuire Act was passed which specifically validated nonsignee provisions of state fair-trade law.

The passage of the McGuire Act enabled the state to establish fair-trade systems, including nonsignee provisions, without fear of federal sanction. Yet, since 1950, state courts have increasingly invalidated their own fair-trade laws, particularly the vital nonsigner provisions, as violative of their state constitutions. Such decisions are frequently grounded on denial of due process and unlawful delegation of legislative power. These courts have evinced a willingness to pass upon matters of substantive economic policy and have held that the law operated not to protect the trademark owner's goodwill, but to benefit the retail merchant by protecting him from the rigors of price competition. Finding no substantial basis for the latter, they have invalidated the law as an unreasonable deprivation of the buyer's property right to sell his goods at whatever price he desires and as an unlawful delegation to private parties of the legislative's power to fix prices. On the other hand, those courts upholding the constitutionality of their fair-trade laws have expressed reluctance to review or interfere with a matter of state substantive economic policy and have deferred to their legislatures.

Fair-trade laws originally existed in 46 states but by 1964, 23 states rendered them inoperative by decisions that either threw them out entirely or nullified the nonsigner clause. An even more serious blow was dealt fair trade in cases holding that price cutters are able to avoid state fair-trade laws by shipping goods in from areas where such laws are not in force. As a consequence, price maintenance was publicly abandoned by the leading manufacturers of electrical appliances and other costly consumers goods.

State Unfair Practices Acts.   Thirty-one states have enacted "unfair practices" acts aimed at preventing sales below cost "for the purpose of injuring competitors or destroying competition." The acts usually attempt to define cost so as to include all costs including all overhead expenses. Some statutes require a definite percentage markup—such as 12 percent over the invoice or replacement cost and provide that any sale below such a figure is prima facie a sale below cost.

These statutes have been successfully challenged on constitutional grounds in a number of states. On the whole they have been rarely enforced and are of little importance.

Summary

There are numerous major exceptions or exemptions to the application of the antitrust laws including: most union activities; agricultural cooperatives; exporters; public utilities and other regulated business; and vertical price fixing under fair-trade laws. Fair-trade, or resale price maintenance, laws are under heavy attack and are now fully effective in only about one half of the states. Closely related to fair-trade laws are the state unfair practices acts, which prohibit sales below cost. On the whole unfair practice acts have been of little importance.

Vornado, Inc. v. *Corning Glass Works*
388 F.2d 117 (3rd Cir. 1968)

Vornado (plaintiff), a dealer, brought this antitrust suit against Corning Glass Works and Schultz and Lehroff, two Corning distributors, (defendants) alleging that the defendants carried on an illegal fair trade program and caused Vornado's franchise to be cancelled in violation of the Sherman Act. Corning counterclaimed asking that Vornado be enjoined from cutting prices below those set in its fair trade contracts. Judgment for Corning and the other defendants and Vornado appealed. Affirmed.

Corning is the manufacturer of a prestige line of ovenware and cookware. These products bear Corning's trademark and are subject to fair trade contracts that have been entered into by Corning in every state where such contracts are permitted by law. Corning has over 3,000 such contracts in New Jersey. Corning publishes its fair trade prices and employs personnel whose duty it is to enforce Corning's fair trade policies through shopping excursions and the warning of price cutters. During the period November 1957 to June 1965, Corning obtained 18 permanent injunctions in New Jersey against violators of its fair trade prices.

Corning sells its products to wholesale-distributors such as Schultz and Lehroff who agreed to resell those products at the fair trade prices established in wholesale fair trade contracts and to sell only to retailers who are franchised Corning dealers: *i.e.,* to those retailers who have signed fair trade agreements with Corning. Such agreements are lawful in New Jersey. Vornado signed such an agreement with Corning and proceeded to purchase Corning Ware from Schultz and Lehroff.

Corning Ware is also sold by Corning to trading stamp companies. Corning's total sales to New Jersey dealers in 1964 were $1,874,000. Of these the sales to trading stamp companies totalled $185,000. These trading stamp companies have redemption centers throughout New Jersey, some in the vicinity of Vornado's retail stores known as "Two Guys from Harrison." The trading stamp companies sell their stamps to retail merchants who customarily give one stamp for each 10 cents of the price of the article purchased. Between $120 and $150's worth of merchandise is required to fill one stamp book, the difference being dependent on which trading company's stamps are employed. At times the retail stores will offer bonus stamps with the purchase of a particular item.

Corning does not require the trading stamp companies to sign fair trade agreements, although Corning suggests values to be put on the stamps used to acquire Corning Ware but the trading stamp companies have not been required to, nor do they, abide by Corning's suggested valuations.

Vornado operates a program whereby its trading stamps are issued on food sales and also are redeemable in merchandise on sale at its retail stores. Unlike other trading stamp companies, Vornado advertises that a completed book containing its stamps is worth $2.25.

In respect to its own trading stamp books, in October of 1962, Vornado commenced a merchandising program for the sale of Corning products which resulted in sales at less than the fair trade prices of the merchandise. Vornado's advertisements stated, to employ an example, that "Your [the purchasing public's] books [are] worth up to $14.50 on these Corning Ware One Book Specials." Below this legend there would be shown a "Corning Ware Homemaker Set", list price $29.95 available at "Two Guys" for $15.75 plus one book. On such sales Vornado often made little or no profit and even took losses, the articles sold being used as "loss leaders." It is stipulated that trading stamp companies never assign such fluctuating values to their stamp books. As noted, the trading stamp companies never permit a combination cash-stamp book purchase.

Corning, upon learning of Vornado's merchandising campaign, sent a telegram to Vornado demanding that it stop such merchandising campaigns. There were some negotiations but no agreement was reached. Corning then terminated Vornado's franchise and so informed its wholesalers-distributors who in turn ceased deliveries to Vornado.

BIGGS, CIRCUIT JUDGE. The prime issues presented are whether Corning forfeited its right to enforce its fair trade program against Vornado because of exemptions Corning has given to trading stamp companies, and further if Corning's exemptions to trading stamp companies be permitted, whether Vornado's own trading stamp program, referred to more particularly hereinafter must also be deemed to be exempt.

The trial judge stated: "The provisions of the Fair Trade Agreements, between Corning and Vornado on the one hand, and Corning and each of its distributors on the other, were in all respects in conformity with the provisions of N.J.S.A. 56:4–5(1) and, therefore, within the exemptive proviso set forth in 15 U.S.C. § 1." This finding by the court below is clearly correct.

The policy of the New Jersey Fair Trade Act, like that of other fair trade acts, is "to prevent a destruction of the producer's good will, which is often established at great cost . . .", it appearing that this good will and "integrity of the product is best preserved in the eyes of the public by regulating the price at which the public can buy the product." "The act introduced into the law the concept that the owner of a trade-marked article retained an interest in his commodity after he parted with ownership and that he was therefore entitled to protect his good will by preventing the resale of his product below a fixed minimum price."

The New Jersey courts have held that a company maintaining a fair trade program may establish exemptions to those programs, provided that such exemptions are reasonable and have a "certain or well-defined meaning." There must be an accommodation of the interests of the public, those of the businessmen subject to the fair trade enforcement and the interests of the fair trader himself. For example in the *Texas Co.* case, the Supreme Court of New Jersey refused to enforce a fair trade program where the exemption granted was too ambiguous for retailers to know who was included in the exemption thereby leaving retailers to sell below fair trade prices at their peril, nearly complete discretion seemingly resting in the fair trader as to the selling prices.

The New Jersey courts also have concluded that the fair trader has abandoned his right to fix prices by using his own fair traded products either alone or with non-fair traded items in promotional combination packages. The New Jersey courts have held that under such circumstances the fair trader has indicated abandonment of his claim to protect the integrity of such fair trade items because of potential injury to retailers.

In another line of decisions New Jersey courts have held it to be no defense in a fair trade enforcement suit that the fair trader does not sell to all persons in the same class. For example, in *Revlon Nail Enamel Corp.* v. *Charmley Drug Shop* (1938), the Court held that a fair trader could sell his items only to beauty shops and retail department stores and nonetheless compel a drug store which had obtained such items in an undisclosed fashion not to sell below fair trade prices. The New Jersey Court held it to be no defense to an enforcement action that the fair trader refused to sell to drug retailers while selling to department stores. We conclude that it cannot be fairly said that Corning's exemption to trading stamp companies is inconsistent with the policy of fair trade. A consumer obtaining a Corning Ware item at a stamp redemption center is unlikely to consider such an acquisition a denigration of the product acquired. As stated above such a consumer has to purchase between $120 and $150 worth of merchandise at the retail store to obtain one book of stamps. It is likely that a family will have to wait three to six months before being able to obtain, for example, a Corning Ware percolator. Moreover, the consumer has little means of comparing the value of the stamps redeemed with the established fair trade value of Corning Ware. As we have said actual valuations are considered to be a trade secret by the stamp companies.

Problem Cases

1. Carter Products, Inc., in advertising "Rise," its shaving cream, on television sought to convince the viewer that its cream remained moist on the skin longer than other creams. For this purpose it used "mockups." To depict ordinary aerated lathers it used "ultra-wet 60L" which came out of an aerosol can with a puff and dried almost immediately. Its own product appeared to remain moist and creamy. A man was shown in great discomfort shaving with what was purported to be a competitor's product in contrast to enjoying a shave with "Rise." The announcer declared, "Instead of drying out on your face . . . Rise wetter lather puts more moisture into whiskers . . . keeps them wet and soft . . . all through your shave. Guards against Razor scratch. . . ."

   The FTC charged Carter under Section 5 of the Federal Trade Commission Act with having falsely represented that shaving creams competing with "Rise" dry out in the course of a shave when, in fact, some of the competing products were made under license from Carter and did not dry out any faster than "Rise." The Commission ordered Carter to cease and desist from disparaging competing products through false and misleading pictures and from representing that pictures depict the superiority of its products when the depiction is not a genuine or accurate comparison. Should the order be enforced?

2. Algoma Lumber Co. and numerous other western lumber manufacturers were selling Ponderoso pine as "California white pine." "White pine" is a name usually applied to the northern white pine coming from the northeastern and Great Lakes states and eastern Canada. It is noted for its durability, resistance to warping and ease of working, while lumber from the yellow pines is considered inferior and sells for a substantially lower price. Ponderoso pine, although one of the yellow pines, is more similar in appearance and characteristics to the northern white pine than southern yellow pine, but is inferior in resistance to decay. "California white pine" was being sold in competition with the northern white pine and many customers were not aware of the differences. Orders for "white pine" by customers expecting to get the northeastern product often were filled with the western product, which frequently resulted in dissatisfaction. The Bureau of Standards of the Department of Commerce had listed "California white pine" as one of the standard commercial names for lumber.

   The FTC ordered Algoma and others to cease and desist using the word "white" in connection with their product, after charging them with unfair competition under Section 5 of the Federal Trade Commission Act. The circuit court, on review, annulled the order. Is the court correct that the use of "Ponderoso white pine" does not violate Section 5?

3. Advertising Service Co. had exclusive contracts with 40 percent of the motion-picture theaters in the area in which it operated, which included 27 states and the District

of Columbia. The majority of the contracts ran for one or two years but some for as long as five years. They provided that the theater would show no advertising films other than those of Advertising Service Co. It and three competitors had exclusive arrangements with approximately three fourths of the theaters in the United States.

The FTC filed a complaint charging Advertising Service Co. with the use of "unfair methods of competition" in violation of Section 5 of the Federal Trade Commission Act. It then entered a cease and desist order limiting the effect of any exclusive agreement to one year from the original date of serve. Should the order be enforced?

4. Motion Picture Advertising Company produced and distributed advertising films and had contracts with exhibitors which contained a provision that the exhibitors would not show any advertising films produced by other companies. M.P.A., the biggest company in the industry, had exclusive contracts of this type with about 40 percent of the theaters in its area of operation. The contracts ran for varying periods up to five years, though the normal period was one year only. The Federal Trade Commission brought a case under Section 5 of the Federal Trade Commission Act charging that the exclusive contracts were an "unfair method of competition." Does this arrangement violate Section 5?

5. Pep Boys, a corporation, operated 52 retail stores selling radios, tubes, radio parts and automobile accessories in seven states and the District of Columbia. It entered into contracts with radio manufacturers to furnish it with radios carrying the brand name "Remington," which it had registered in the U.S. Patent Office as a trademark through an associated corporation. The FTC brought a complaint under Section 5 of the Federal Trade Commission Act charging unfair methods of competition. The FTC issued a cease and desist order. Is the use of "Remington," a name which has been long established and favorably known to the purchasing public (in this case by Remington Rand, Inc. and Remington Arms), an unfair method of competition under Section 5?

6. In 1952, Grand Union accepted a proposal from the owner of a huge sign in the Times Square area of New York City which used timed electric lamps to create animated advertisements. Under the agreement Grand Union leased the sign at $50 per year, provided it found 15 advertisers who would rent time on the sign at the rate of $1,000 per month for 1 minute out of each 20 minutes during which the sign operated. Grand Union could use the other 5 minutes for its own advertisements. The agreement was later revised to eliminate Grand Union's advertisements while giving it 5 percent of the rentals from the first 15 advertisers and all of the rentals of the remaining 5. All or nearly all of the advertisers were suppliers to Grand Union and most were solicited by Grand Union. None of the advertisers knew of the terms of the contract between Grand Union and the owner of the sign or that Grand Union received free advertising or substantial payments for the advertisers' participation in the scheme. The FTC issued a cease and desist order under Section 5 charging that a violation of Section 2(d) of the Robinson-Patman Act also violated Section 5. Is this order valid?

7. Sav-U Chain Store advertised several products showing "manufacturer's list prices" and then offering the products at substantial discounts. The FTC prosecuted the manufacturer under Section 5 of the Federal Trade Commission Act for engaging in unfair or deceptive list price practices. The FTC proved that the products advertised rarely, if ever, were sold to consumers at the prices shown as "manufacturer's list prices." Was the manufacturer subject to a fine and cease and desist order?

8. Retail Package Stores Association tried to persuade all of the liquor wholesalers in the Memphis area to use fair-trade contracts fixing uniform pricing and margins. In addition, the members of the Association worked together to make the manufacturers utilize fair-trade contracts. Retail Package Stores Association and its members were indicted under Section 1 of the Sherman Act. Is the fact that fair-trade contracts were involved a good defense?

9. Esso brought suit to prevent Secatore, a retailer Esso dealer, from cutting his prices below the prices Esso had set in fair-trade contracts in Massachusetts. Secatore defended on the ground that Esso was in competition with Secatore for certain "commercial accounts" and that to permit Esso to fix his (Secatore's) price would in effect amount to nonexempt horizontal price fixing. Is this a good defense?

10. Spark Plug, Inc., supplied spark plugs to T. G. Stores under a contract which required T. G. Stores to charge a stated minimum resale price. The fixed price was authorized by the state fair-trade act so long as the goods were sold under a trademark or trade name in free and open competition with goods of a similar nature. The "fair-trade" contract permitted spark plugs to be sold at reduced minimum prices in sales to "fleet operators." In 1961, the fair-trade contract had defined "fleet operator" in terms of *facilities* for the repair and maintenance of motor vehicles and engines. The 1963 contract definition of "fleet operator" depended on the number of *vehicles* owned by the operator. T. G. Stores sold spark plugs at a price below the fair-trade minimum and Spark Plug, Inc., sued to enjoin further reduced price sales. T. G. Stores defended by claiming the exemption for "fleet operators" was so indefinite that the validity of the fair-trade schedule was destroyed. Spark Plug contended that the term "fleet operator" is well known in the automotive trade and is clearly defined in the fair-trade contracts. However, during the course of trial, Spark Plug's witnesses were not consistent in their testimony as to what they understood a "fleet operator" to be and on at least one occasion the testimonial definition was contrary to the contractual definition. Can Spark Plug enjoin T. G. Stores from cutting prices?

11. City Tobacco sued Weisman asking that Weisman be enjoined from selling cigarettes in violation of a Minnesota statute, entitled the Unfair Cigarette Sales Act, which prohibited below-cost sales of cigarettes. The language of the act indicated that the legislature had found that any sale of cigarettes below cost is with predatory intent, hinders the collection of taxes and fees and otherwise violates public policy. The act specifically exempted four kinds of transactions—isolated sales, clearance sales, the sale of damaged goods, and sales designed to compete with those of competitors. These exemptions were the only defenses allowed to show that the sale was innocently consummated or that there was no injurious effect on competitors or the public. Weisman contended that the Act was unconstitutional under the due process clause of the 14th Amendment. Is the Act constitutional?

Appendixes

The Uniform Commercial Code

ARTICLE 1. General Provisions

SHORT TITLE, CONSTRUCTION, APPLICATION AND SUBJECT MATTER OF THE ACT

§ 1–101. Short Title.

This Act shall be known and may be cited as Uniform Commercial Code.

§ 1–102. Purposes; Rules of Construction; Variation by Agreement.

(1) This Act shall be liberally construed and applied to promote its underlying purposes and policies.

(2) Underlying purposes and policies of this Act are

    (a) to simplify, clarify and modernize the law governing commercial transactions;

    (b) to permit the continued expansion of commercial practices through custom, usage and agreement of the parties;

    (c) to make uniform the law among the various jurisdictions.

(3) The effect of provisions of this Act may be varied by agreement, except as otherwise provided in this Act and except that the obligations of good faith, diligence, reasonableness and care prescribed by this Act may not be disclaimed by agreement but the parties may by agreement determine the standards by which the performance of such obligations is to be measured if such standards are not manifestly unreasonable.

(4) The presence in certain provisions of this Act of the words "unless otherwise agreed" or words of similar import does not imply that the effect of other provisions may not be varied by agreement under subsection (3).

(5) In this Act unless the context otherwise requires

    (a) words in the singular number include the plural, and in the plural include the singular;

    (b) words of the masculine gender include the feminine and the neuter, and when the sense so indicates words of the neuter gender may refer to any gender.

§ 1–103. Supplementary General Principles of Law Applicable.

Unless displaced by the particular provisions of this Act, the principles of law and equity, including the law merchant and the law relative to capacity to contract, principal and agent, estoppel, fraud, misrepresentation, duress, coercion, mistake, bankruptcy, or other validating cause shall supplement its provisions.

§ 1–104. Construction Against Implicit Repeal.

This Act being a general act intended as a unified coverage of its subject matter, no part of it shall be deemed to be impliedly repealed by subsequent legislation if such construction can reasonably be avoided.

§ 1–105. Territorial Application of the Act; Parties' Power to Choose Applicable Law.

(1) Except as provided hereafter in this section, when a transaction bears a reasonable relation to this state and also to another state or nation the parties may agree that the law either of this state or of such other state or nation shall govern their rights and duties. Failing such agreement this Act applies to transactions bearing an appropriate relation to this state.

(2) Where one of the following provisions of this Act specifies the applicable law, that provision governs and a contrary agreement is effective only to the extent permitted by the law (including the conflict of laws rules) so specified:

Rights of creditors against sold goods. Section 2–402.

Applicability of the Article on Bank Deposits and Collections. Section 4–102.

Bulk transfers subject to the Article on Bulk Transfers. Section 6–102.

Applicability of the Article on Investment Securities. Section 8–106.

Policy and scope of the Article on Secured Transactions. Sections 9–102 and 9–103.

§ 1–106. Remedies to Be Liberally Administered.

(1) The remedies provided by this Act shall be liberally administered to the end that the aggrieved party may be put in as good a position as if the other party had fully performed but neither consequential or special nor penal damages may be had except as specifically provided in this Act or by other rule of law.

(2) Any right or obligation declared by this Act is enforceable by action unless the provision declaring it specifies a different and limited effect.

§ 1–107. Waiver or Renunciation of Claim or Right After Breach.

Any claim or right arising out of an alleged breach can be discharged in whole or in part without consideration by a written waiver or renunciation signed and delivered by the aggrieved party.

§ 1–108. Severability.

If any provision or clause of this Act or application thereof to any person or circumstances is held invalid, such invalidity shall not affect other provisions or applications of the Act which can be given effect without the invalid provision or application, and to this end the provisions of this Act are declared to be severable.

§ 1–109. Section Captions.

Section captions are parts of this Act.

PART 2
GENERAL DEFINITIONS AND PRINCIPLES OF INTERPRETATION

§ 1–201. General Definitions.

Subject to additional definitions contained in the subsequent Articles of this Act which are applicable to specific Articles or Parts thereof, and unless the context otherwise requires, in this Act:

(1) "Action" in the sense of a judicial proceeding includes recoupment, counterclaim, set-off, suit in equity and any other proceedings in which rights are determined.

(2) "Aggrieved party" means a party entitled to resort to a remedy.

(3) "Agreement" means the bargain of the parties in fact as found in their language or by implication from other circumstances including course of dealing or usage of trade or course of performance as provided in this Act (Sections 1–205 and 2–208). Whether an agreement

has legal consequences is determined by the provisions of this Act, if applicable; otherwise by the law of contracts (Section 1–103). (Compare "Contract".)

(4) "Bank" means any person engaged in the business of banking.

(5) "Bearer" means the person in possession of an instrument, document of title, or security payable to bearer or indorsed in blank.

(6) "Bill of lading" means a document evidencing the receipt of goods for shipment issued by a person engaged in the business of transporting or forwarding goods, and includes an airbill. "Airbill" means a document serving for air transportation as a bill of lading does for marine or rail transportation, and includes an air consignment note or air waybill.

(7) "Branch" includes a separately incorporated foreign branch of a bank.

(8) "Burden of establishing" a fact means the burden of persuading the triers of fact that the existence of the fact is more probable than its non-existence.

(9) "Buyer in ordinary course of business" means a person who in good faith and without knowledge that the sale to him is in violation of the ownership rights or security interest of a third party in the goods buys in ordinary course from a person in the business of selling goods of that kind but does not include a pawnbroker. "Buying" may be for cash or by exchange of other property or on secured or unsecured credit and includes receiving goods or documents of title under a pre-existing contract for sale but does not include a transfer in bulk or as security for or in total or partial satisfaction of a money debt.

(10) "Conspicuous": A term or clause is conspicuous when it is so written that a reasonable person against whom it is to operate ought to have noticed it. A printed heading in capitals as: (NON-NEGOTIABLE BILL OF LADING) is conspicuous. Language in the body of a form is "conspicuous" if it is in larger or other contrasting type or color. But in a telegram any stated term is "conspicuous". Whether a term or clause is "conspicuous" or not is for decision by the court.

(11) "Contract" means the total legal obligation which results from the parties' agreement as affected by this Act and any other applicable rules of law. (Compare "Agreement".)

(12) "Creditor" includes a general creditor, a secured creditor, a lien creditor and any representative of creditors, including an assignee for the benefit of creditors, a trustee in bankruptcy, a receiver in equity and an executor or administrator of an insolvent debtor's assignor's estate.

(13) "Defendant" includes a person in the position of defendant in a cross-action or counterclaim.

(14) "Delivery" with respect to instruments, documents of title, chattel paper or securities means voluntary transfer of possession.

(15) "Document of title" includes bill of lading, dock warrant, dock receipt, warehouse receipt or order for the delivery of goods, and also any other document which in the regular course of business or financing is treated as adequately evidencing that the person in possession of it is entitled to receive, hold and dispose of the document and the goods it covers. To be a document of title a document must purport to be issued by or addressed to a bailee and purport to cover goods in the bailee's possession which are either identified or are fungible portions of an identified mass.

(16) "Fault" means wrongful act, omission or breach.

(17) "Fungible" with respect to goods or securities means goods or securities of which any unit is, by nature or usage of trade, the equivalent of any other like unit. Goods which are not fungible shall be deemed fungible for the purposes of this Act to the extent that under a particular agreement or document unlike units are treated as equivalents.

(18) "Genuine" means free of forgery or counterfeiting.

(19) "Good faith" means honesty in fact in the conduct or transaction concerned.

(20) "Holder" means a person who is in possession of a document of title or an instrument or an investment security drawn, issued or indorsed to him or to his order or to bearer or in blank.

(21) To "honor" is to pay or to accept and pay, or where a credit so engages to purchase or discount a draft complying with the terms of the credit.

(22) "Insolvency proceedings includes any assignment for the benefit of creditors or other proceedings intended to liquidate or rehabilitate the estate of the person involved.

(23) A person is "insolvent who either has ceased to pay his debts in the ordinary course of business or cannot pay his debts as they become due or is insolvent within the meaning of the federal bankruptcy law.

(24) "Money means a medium of exchange authorized or adopted by a domestic or foreign government as a part of its currency.

(25) A person has "notice" of a fact when

(a) he has actual knowledge of it; or

(b) he has received a notice or notification of it; or

(c) from all the facts and circumstances known to him at the time in question he has reason to know that it exists.

A person "knows" or has "knowledge" of a fact when he has actual knowledge of it. "Discover" or "learn" or a word or phrase of similar import refers to knowledge rather than to reason to know. The time and circumstances under which a notice or notification may cease to be effective are not determined by this Act.

(26) A person "notifies" or "gives" a notice or notification to another by taking such steps as may be reasonably required to inform the other in ordinary course whether or not such other actually comes to know of it. A person "receives" a notice or notification when

(a) it comes to his attention; or

(b) it is duly delivered at the place of business through which the contract was made or at any other place held out by him as the place for receipt of such communications.

(27) Notice, knowledge or a notice or notification received by an organization is effective for a particular transaction from the time when it is brought to the attention of the individual conducting that transaction, and in any event from the time when it would have been brought to his attention if the organization had exercised due diligence. An organization exercises due diligence if it maintains reasonable routines for communicating significant information to the person conducting the transaction and there is reasonable compliance with the routines. Due diligence does not require an individual acting for the organization to communicate information unless such communication is part of his regular duties or unless he has reason to know of the transaction and that the transaction would be materially affected by the information.

(28) "Organization" includes a corporation, government or governmental subdivision or agency, business trust, estate, trust, partnership or association, two or more persons having a joint or common interest, or any other legal or commercial entity.

(29) "Party," as distinct from "third party," means a person who has engaged in a transaction or made an agreement within this Act.

(30) "Person" includes an individual or an organization (See Section 1–102).

(31) "Presumption" or "presumed" means that the trier of fact must find the existence of the fact presumed unless and until evidence is introduced which would support a finding of its nonexistence.

(32) "Purchase" includes taking by sale, discount, negotiation, mortgage, pledge, lien, issue or re-issue, gift or any other voluntary transaction creating an interest in property.

(33) "Purchaser" means a person who takes by purchase.

(34) "Remedy" means any remedial right to which an aggrieved party is entitled with or without resort to a tribunal.

(35) "Representative" includes an agent, an officer of a corporation or association, and a trustee, executor or administrator of an estate, or any other person empowered to act for another.

(36) "Rights" includes remedies.

(37) "Security interest" means an interest in personal property or fixtures which secures payment or performance of an obligation. The retention or reservation of title by a seller of goods notwithstanding shipment or delivery to the buyer (Section 2–401) is limited in effect to a reservation of a "security interest." The term also includes any interest of a buyer of accounts, chattel paper, or contract rights which is subject to Article 9. The special property

interest of a buyer of goods on identification of such goods to a contract for sale under Section 2–401 is not a "security interest," but a buyer may also acquire a "security interest" by complying with Article 9. Unless a lease or consignment is intended as security, reservation of title thereunder is not a "security interest" but a consignment is in any event subject to the provisions on consignment sales (Section 2–326). Whether a lease is intended as security is to be determined by the facts of each case; however, (a) the inclusion of an option to purchase does not of itself make the lease one intended for security, and (b) an agreement that upon compliance with the terms of the lease the lessee shall become or has the option to become the owner of the property for no additional consideration or for a nominal consideration does make the lease one intended for security.

(38) "Send" in connection with any writing or notice means to deposit in the mail or deliver for transmission by any other usual means of communication with postage or cost of transmission provided for and properly addressed and in the case of an instrument to an address specified thereon or otherwise agreed, or if there be none to any address reasonable under the circumstances. The receipt of any writing or notice within the time at which it would have arrived if properly sent has the effect of a proper sending.

(39) "Signed" includes any symbol executed or adopted by a party with present intention to authenticate a writing.

(40) "Surety" includes guarantor.

(41) "Telegram" includes a message transmitted by radio, teletype, cable, any mechanical method of transmission, or the like.

(42) "Term" means that portion of an agreement which relates to a particular matter.

(43) "Unauthorized" signature or indorsement means one made without actual, implied or apparent authority and includes a forgery.

(44) "Value." Except as otherwise provided with respect to negotiable instruments and bank collections (Sections 3–303, 4–208 and 4–209) a person gives "value" for rights if he acquires them

    (a) in return for a binding commitment to extend credit or for the extension of immediately available credit whether or not drawn upon and whether or not a chargeback is provided for in the event of difficulties in collection; or

    (b) as security for or in total or partial satisfaction of a pre-existing claim; or

    (c) by accepting delivery pursuant to a pre-existing contract for purchase; or

    (d) generally, in return for any consideration sufficient to support a simple contract.

(45) "Warehouse receipt" means a receipt issued by a person engaged in the business of storing goods for hire.

(46) "Written" or "writing" includes printing, typewriting or any other intentional reduction to tangible form.

§ 1–202. Prima Facie Evidence by Third Party Documents.

A document in due form purporting to be a bill of lading, policy or certificate of insurance, official weigher's or inspector's certificate, consular invoice, or any other document authorized or required by the contract to be issued by a third party shall be prima facie evidence of its own authenticity and genuineness and of the facts stated in the document by the third party.

§ 1–203. Obligation of Good Faith.

Every contract or duty within this Act imposes an obligation of good faith in its performance or enforcement.

§ 1–204. Time; Reasonable Time; "Seasonably."

(1) Whenever this Act requires any action to be taken within a reasonable time, any time which is not manifestly unreasonable may be fixed by agreement.

(2) What is a reasonable time for taking any action depends on the nature, purpose and circumstances of such action.

(3) An action is taken "seasonably" when it is taken at or within the time agreed or if no time is agreed at or within a reasonable time.

§ 1–205. Course of Dealing and Usage of Trade.

(1) A course of dealing is a sequence of previous conduct between the parties to a particular transaction which is fairly to be regarded as establishing a common basis of understanding for interpreting their expressions and other conduct.

(2) A usage of trade is any practice or method of dealing having such regularity of observance in a place, vocation or trade as to justify an expectation that it will be observed with respect to the transaction in question. The existence and scope of such a usage are to be proved as facts. If it is established that such a usage is embodied in a written trade code or similar writing the interpretation of the writing is for the court.

(3) A course of dealing between parties and any usage of trade in the vocation or trade in which they are engaged or of which they are or should be aware give particular meaning to and supplement or qualify terms of an agreement.

(4) The express terms of an agreement and an applicable course of dealing or usage of trade shall be construed wherever reasonable as consistent with each other; but when such construction is unreasonable express terms control both course of dealing and usage of trade and course of dealing controls usage of trade.

(5) An applicable usage of trade in the place where any part of performance is to occur shall be used in interpreting the agreement as to that part of the performance.

(6) Evidence of a relevant usage of trade offered by one party is not admissible unless and until he has given the other party such notice as the court finds sufficient to prevent unfair surprise to the latter.

§ 1–206. Statute of Frauds for Kinds of Personal Property Not Otherwise Covered.

(1) Except in the cases described in subsection (2) of this section a contract for the sale of personal property is not enforceable by way of action or defense beyond five thousand dollars in amount or value of remedy unless there is some writing which indicates that a contract for sale has been made between the parties at a defined or stated price, reasonably identifies the subject matter, and is signed by the party against whom enforcement is sought or by his authorized agent.

(2) Subsection (1) of this section does not apply to contracts for the sale of goods (Section 2–201) nor of securities (Section 8–319) nor to security agreements (Section 9–203).

§ 1–207. Performance or Acceptance Under Reservation of Rights.

A party who with explicit reservation of rights performs or promises performance or assents to performance in a manner demanded or offered by the other party does not thereby prejudice the rights reserved. Such words as "without prejudice," "under protest" or the like are sufficient.

§ 1–208. Option to Accelerate at Will.

A term providing that one party or his successor in interest may accelerate payment or performance or require collateral or additional collateral "at will" or "when he deems himself insecure" or in words of similar import shall be construed to mean that he shall have power to do so only if he in good faith believes that the prospect of payment or performance is impaired. The burden of establishing lack of good faith is on the party against whom the power has been exercised.

ARTICLE 2. Sales

PART 1
SHORT TITLE, CONSTRUCTION AND SUBJECT MATTER

§ 2–101. Short Title.

This Article shall be known and may be cited as Uniform Commercial Code—Sales.

§ 2–102. Scope; Certain Security and Other Transactions Excluded From This Article.

Unless the context otherwise requires, this Article applies to transactions in goods; it does not apply to any transaction which although in the form of an unconditional contract to sell or present sale is intended to operate only as a security transaction nor does this Article impair or repeal any statute regulating sales to consumers, farmers or other specified classes of buyers.

§ 2–103. Definitions and Index of Definitions.

(1) In this Article unless the context otherwise requires

    (a) "Buyer" means a person who buys or contracts to buy goods.

    (b) "Good faith" in the case of a merchant means honesty in fact and the observance of reasonable commercial standards of fair dealing in the trade.

    (c) "Receipts" of goods means taking physical possession of them.

    (d) "Seller" means a person who sells or contracts to sell goods.

(2) Other definitions applying to this Article or to specified Parts thereof, and the sections in which they appear are:

"Acceptance." Section 2–606.
"Banker's credit." Section 2–325.
"Between merchants." Section 2–104.
"Cancellation." Section 2–106(4).
"Commercial unit." Section 2–105.
"Confirmed credit." Section 2–325.
"Conforming to contract." Section 2–106.
"Contract for sale." Section 2–106.
"Cover." Section 2–712.
"Entrusting." Section 2–403.
"Financing agency." Section 2–104.
"Future goods." Section 2–105.
"Goods." Section 2–105.
"Identification." Section 2–501.
"Installment contract." Section 2–612.
"Letter of Credit." Section 2–325.
"Lot." Section 2–105.
"Merchant." Section 2–104.
"Overseas." Section 2–323.
"Person in position of seller." Section 2–707.
"Present sale." Section 2–106.
"Sale." Section 2–106.
"Sale on approval." Section 2–326.
"Sale or return." Section 2–326.
"Termination." Section 2–106.

(3) The following definitions in other Articles apply to this Article:

"Check." Section 3–104.
"Consignee." Section 7–102.
"Consignor." Section 7–102.
"Consumer goods." Section 9–109.
"Dishonor." Section 3–507.
"Draft." Section 3–104.

(4) In addition Article 1 contains general definitions and principles of construction and interpretation applicable throughout this Article.

§ 2–104. Definitions: "Merchant"; "Between Merchants"; "Financing Agency."

(1) "Merchant" means a person who deals in goods of the kind or otherwise by his occupation holds himself out as having knowledge or skill peculiar to the practices or goods involved in the transaction or to whom such knowledge or skill may be attributed by his employment

of an agent or broker or other intermediary who by his occupation holds himself out as having such knowledge or skill.

(2) "Financing agency" means a bank, finance company or other person who in the ordinary course of business makes advances against goods or documents of title or who by arrangement with either the seller or the buyer intervenes in ordinary course to make or collect payment due or claimed under the contract for sale, as by purchasing or paying the seller's draft or making advances against it or by merely taking it for collection whether or not documents of title accompany the draft. "Financing agency" includes also a bank or other person who similarly intervenes between persons who are in the position of seller and buyer in respect to the goods (Section 2–707).

(3) "Between merchants" means in any transaction with respect to which both parties are chargeable with the knowledge or skill of merchants.

§ 2–105. Definitions: Transferability; "Goods"; "Future" Goods; "Lot"; "Commercial Unit."

(1) "Goods" means all things (including specially manufactured goods) which are movable at the time of identification to the contract for sale other than the money in which the price is to be paid, investment securities (Article 8) and things in action. "Goods" also includes the unborn young of animals and growing crops and other identified things attached to realty as described in the section on goods to be severed from realty (Section 2–107).

(2) Goods must be both existing and identified before any interest in them can pass. Goods which are not both existing and identified are "future" goods. A purported present sale of future goods or of any interest therein operates as a contract to sell.

(3) There may be a sale of a part interest in existing identified goods.

(4) An undivided share in an identified bulk of fungible goods is sufficiently identified to be sold although the quantity of the bulk is not determined. Any agreed proportion of such a bulk or any quantity thereof agreed upon by number, weight or other measure may to the extent of the seller's interest in the bulk be sold to the buyer who then becomes an owner in common.

(5) "Lot" means a parcel or a single article which is the subject matter of a separate sale or delivery, whether or not it is sufficient to perform the contract.

(6) "Commercial unit" means such a unit of goods as by commercial usage is a single whole for purposes of sale and division of which materially impairs its character or value on the market or in use. A commercial unit may be a single article (as a machine) or a set of articles (as a suite of furniture or an assortment of sizes) or a quantity (as a bale, gross, or carload) or any other unit treated in use or in the relevant market as a single whole.

§ 2–106. Definitions: "Contract"; "Agreement"; "Contract for Sale"; "Sale"; "Present Sale"; "Conforming" to Contract; "Termination"; "Cancellation."

(1) In this Article unless the context otherwise requires "contract" and "agreement" are limited to those relating to the present or future sale of goods. "Contract for sale" includes both a present sale of goods and a contract to sell goods at a future time. A "sale" consists in the passing of title from the seller to the buyer for a price (Section 2–401). A "present sale" means a sale which is accomplished by the making of the contract.

(2) Goods or conduct including any part of a performance are "conforming" or conform to the contract when they are in accordance with the obligations under the contract.

(3) "Termination" occurs when either party pursuant to a power created by agreement or law puts an end to the contract otherwise than for its breach. On "termination" all obligations which are still executory on both sides are discharged but any right based on prior breach or performance survives.

(4) "Cancellation" occurs when either party puts an end to the contract for breach by the other and its effect is the same as that of "termination" except that the cancelling party also retains any remedy for breach of the whole contract or any unperformed balance.

§ 2–107. Goods to Be Severed From Realty: Recording.

(1) A contract for the sale of timber, minerals or the like or a structure or its materials to be removed from realty is a contract for the sale of goods within this Article if they are to

be severed by the seller but until severance a purported present sale thereof which is not effective as a transfer of an interest in land is effective only as a contract to sell.

(2) A contract for the sale apart from the land of growing crops or other things attached to realty and capable of severance without material harm thereto but not described in subsection (1) is a contract for the sale of goods within this Article whether the subject matter is to be severed by the buyer or by the seller even though it forms part of the realty at the time of contracting, and the parties can by identification effect a present sale before severance.

(3) The provisions of this section are subject to any third party rights provided by the law relating to realty records, and the contract for sale may be executed and recorded as a document transferring an interest in land and shall then constitute notice to third parties of the buyer's rights under the contract for sale.

PART 2
FORM, FORMATION AND READJUSTMENT OF CONTRACT

§ 2–201. Formal Requirements; Statute of Frauds.

(1) Except as otherwise provided in this section a contract for the sale of goods for the price of $500 or more is not enforceable by way of action or defense unless there is some writing sufficient to indicate that a contract for sale has been made between the parties and signed by the party against whom enforcement is sought or by his authorized agent or broker. A writing is not insufficient because it omits or incorrectly states a term agreed upon but the contract is not enforceable under this paragraph beyond the quantity of goods shown in such writing.

(2) Between merchants if within a reasonable time a writing in confirmation of the contract and sufficient against the sender is received and the party receiving it has reason to know its contents, it satisfies the requirements of subsection (1) against such party unless written notice of objection to its contents is given ten days after it is received.

(3) A contract which does not satisfy the requirements of subsection (1) but which is valid in other respects is enforceable

(a) if the goods are to be specially manufactured for the buyer and are not suitable for sale to others in the ordinary course of the seller's business and the seller, before notice of repudiation is received and under circumstances which reasonably indicate that the goods are for the buyer, has made either a substantial beginning of their manufacture or commitments for their procurement; or

(b) if the party against whom enforcement is sought admits in his pleading, testimony or otherwise in court that a contract for sale was made, but the contract is not enforceable under this provision beyond the quantity of goods admitted; or

(c) with respect to goods for which payment has been made and accepted or which have been received and accepted (Sec. 2–606).

§ 2–202. Final Written Expression: Parol or Extrinsic Evidence.

Terms with respect to which the confirmatory memoranda of the parties agree or which are otherwise set forth in a writing intended by the parties as a final expression of their agreement with respect to such terms as are included therein may not be contradicted by evidence of any prior agreement or of a contemporaneous oral agreement but may be explained or supplemented

(a) by course of dealing or usage of trade (Section 1–205) or by course of performance (Section 2–208); and

(b) by evidence of consistent additional terms unless the court finds the writing to have been intended also as a complete and exclusive statement of the terms of the agreement.

§ 2–203. Seals Inoperative.

The affixing of a seal to a writing evidencing a contract for sale or an offer to buy or sell goods does not constitute the writing a sealed instrument and the law with respect to sealed instruments does not apply to such a contract or offer.

§ 2–204. Formation in General.

(1) A contract for sale of goods may be made in any manner sufficient to show agreement, including conduct by both parties which recognizes the existence of such a contract.

(2) An agreement sufficient to constitute a contract for sale may be found even though the moment of its making is undetermined.

(3) Even though one or more terms are left open a contract for sale does not fail for indefiniteness if the parties have intended to make a contract and there is a reasonably certain basis for giving an appropriate remedy.

§ 2–205. Firm Offers.

An offer by a merchant to buy or sell goods in a signed writing which by its terms gives assurance that it will be held open is not revocable, for lack of consideration, during the time stated or if no time is stated for a reasonable time, but in no event may such period of irrevocability exceed three months; but any such term of assurance on a form supplied by the offeree must be separately signed by the offeror.

§ 2–206. Offer and Acceptance in Formation of Contract.

(1) Unless otherwise unambiguously indicated by the language or circumstances
   (a) an offer to make a contract shall be construed as inviting acceptance in any manner and by any medium reasonable in the circumstances;
   (b) an order or other offer to buy goods for prompt or current shipment shall be construed as inviting acceptance either by a prompt promise to ship or by the prompt or current shipment of conforming or nonconforming goods, but such a shipment of non-conforming goods does not constitute an acceptance if the seller seasonably notifies the buyer that the shipment is offered only as an accommodation to the buyer.

(2) Where the beginning of a requested performance is a reasonable mode of acceptance an offeror who is not notified of acceptance within a reasonable time may treat the offer as having lapsed before acceptance.

§ 2–207. Additional Terms in Acceptance or Confirmation.

(1) A definite and seasonable expression of acceptance or a written confirmation which is sent within a reasonable time operates as an acceptance even though it states terms additional to or different from those offered or agreed upon, unless acceptance is expressly made conditional on assent to the additional or different terms.

(2) The additional terms are to be construed as proposals for addition to the contract. Between merchants such terms become part of the contract unless:
   (a) the offer expressly limits acceptance to the terms of the offer;
   (b) they materially alter it; or
   (c) notification of objection to them has already been given or is given within a reasonable time after notice of them is received.

(3) Conduct by both parties which recognizes the existence of a contract is sufficient to establish a contract for sale although the writings of the parties do not otherwise establish a contract. In such case the terms of the particular contract consist of those terms on which the writings of the parties agree, together with any supplementary terms incorporated under any other provisions of this Act.

§ 2–208. Course of Performance or Practical Construction.

(1) Where the contract for sale involves repeated occasions for performance by either party with knowledge of the nature of the performance and opportunity for objection to it by the other, any course of performance accepted or acquiesced in without objection shall be relevant to determine the meaning of the agreement.

(2) The express terms of the agreement and any such course of performance, as well as any course of dealing and usage of trade, shall be construed whenever reasonable as consistent with

each other; but when such construction is unreasonable, express terms shall control course of performance and course of performance shall control both course of dealing and usage of trade (Section 1–205).

(3) Subject to the provisions of the next section on modification and waiver, such course of performance shall be relevant to show a waiver or modification of any term inconsistent with such course of performance.

§ 2–209. Modification, Rescission and Waiver.

(1) An agreement modifying a contract within this Article needs no consideration to be binding.

(2) A signed agreement which excludes modification or rescission except by a signed writing cannot be otherwise modified or rescinded, but except as between merchants such a requirement on a form supplied by the merchant must be separately signed by the other party.

(3) The requirements of the statute of frauds section of this Article (Section 2–201) must be satisfied if the contract as modified is within its provisions.

(4) Although an attempt at modification or rescission does not satisfy the requirements of subsection (2) or (3) it can operate as a waiver.

(5) A party who has made a waiver affecting an executory portion of the contract may retract the waiver by reasonable notification received by the other party that strict performance will be required of any term waived, unless the retraction would be unjust in view of a material change of position in reliance on the waiver.

§ 2–210. Delegation of Performance; Assignment of Rights.

(1) A party may perform his duty through a delegate unless otherwise agreed or unless the other party has a substantial interest in having his original promisor perform or control the acts required by the contract. No delegation of performance relieves the party delegating of any duty to perform or any liability for breach.

(2) Unless otherwise agreed all rights of either seller or buyer can be assigned except where the assignment would materially change the duty of the other party, or increase materially the burden or risk imposed on him by his contract, or impair materially his chance of obtaining return performance. A right to damages for breach of the whole contract or a right arising out of the assignor's due performance of his entire obligation can be assigned despite agreement otherwise.

(3) Unless the circumstances indicate the contrary a prohibition of assignment of "the contract" is to be construed as barring only the delegation to the assignee of the assignor's performance.

(4) An assignment of "the contract" or of "all my rights under the contract" or an assignment in similar general terms is an assignment of rights and unless the language or the circumstances (as in an assignment for security) indicate the contrary, it is a delegation of performance of the duties of the assignor and its acceptance by the assignee constitutes a promise by him to perform those duties. This promise is enforceable by either the assignor or the other party to the original contract.

(5) The other party may treat any assignment which delegates performance as creating reasonable grounds for insecurity and may without prejudice to his rights against the assignor demand assurances from the assignee (Section 2–609).

PART 3
GENERAL OBLIGATION AND CONSTRUCTION OF CONTRACT

§ 2–301. General Obligations of Parties.

The obligation of the seller is to transfer and deliver and that of the buyer is to accept and pay in accordance with the contract.

§ 2–302. Unconscionable Contract or Clause.

(1) If the court as a matter of law finds the contract or any clause of the contract to have been unconscionable at the time it was made the court may refuse to enforce the contract, or

it may enforce the remainder of the contract without the unconscionable clause, or it may so limit the application of any unconscionable clause as to avoid any unconscionable result.

(2) When it is claimed or appears to the court that the contract or any clause thereof may be unconscionable the parties shall be afforded a reasonable opportunity to present evidence as to its commercial setting, purpose and effect to aid the court in making the determination.

§ 2–303. Allocation or Division of Risks.

Where this Article allocates a risk or a burden as between the parties "unless otherwise agreed," the agreement may not only shift the allocation but may also divide the risk or burden.

§ 2–304. Price Payable in Money, Goods, Realty, or Otherwise.

(1) The price can be made payable in money or otherwise. If it is payable in whole or in part in goods each party is a seller of the goods which he is to transfer.

(2) Even though all or part of the price is payable in an interest in realty the transfer of the goods and the seller's obligations with reference to them are subject to this Article, but not the transfer of the interest in realty or the transferor's obligations in connection therewith.

§ 2–305. Open Price Term.

(1) The parties if they so intend can conclude a contract for sale even though the price is not settled. In such a case the price is a reasonable price at the time for delivery if

(a) nothing is said as to price; or

(b) the price is left to be agreed by the parties and they fail to agree; or

(c) the price is to be fixed in terms of some agreed market or other standard as set or recorded by a third person or agency and it is not so set or recorded.

(2) A price to be fixed by the seller or by the buyer means a price for him to fix in good faith.

(3) When a price left to be fixed otherwise than by agreement of the parties fails to be fixed through fault of one party the other may at his option treat the contract as cancelled or himself fix a reasonable price.

(4) Where, however, the parties intend not to be bound unless the price be fixed or agreed and it is not fixed or agreed there is no contract. In such a case the buyer must return any goods already received or if unable so to do must pay their reasonable value at the time of delivery and the seller must return any portion of the price paid on account.

§ 2–306. Output, Requirements and Exclusive Dealings.

(1) A term which measures the quantity by the output of the seller or the requirements of the buyer means such actual output or requirements as may occur in good faith, except that no quantity unreasonably disproportionate to any stated estimate or in the absence of a stated estimate to any normal or otherwise comparable prior output or requirements may be tendered or demanded.

(2) A lawful agreement by either the seller or the buyer for exclusive dealing in the kind of goods concerned imposes unless otherwise agreed an obligation by the seller to use best efforts to supply the goods and by the buyer to use best efforts to promote their sale.

§ 2–307. Delivery in Single Lot or Several Lots.

Unless otherwise agreed all goods called for by a contract for sale must be tendered in a single delivery and payment is due only on such tender but where the circumstances give either party the right to make or demand delivery in lots the price if it can be apportioned may be demanded for each lot.

§ 2–308. Absence of Specified Place for Delivery.

Unless otherwise agreed

(a) the place for delivery of goods is the seller's place of business or if he has none his residence; but

(b) in a contract for sale of identified goods which to the knowledge of the parties at the time of contracting are in some other place, that place is the place for their delivery; and

(c) documents of title may be delivered through customary banking channels.

§ 2–309. Absence of Specific Time Provisions; Notice of Termination.

(1) The time for shipment or delivery or any other action under a contract if not provided in this Article or agreed upon shall be a reasonable time.

(2) Where the contract provides for successive performances but is indefinite in duration it is valid for a reasonable time but unless otherwise agreed may be terminated at any time by either party.

(3) Termination of a contract by one party except on the happening of an agreed event requires that reasonable notification be received by the other party and an agreement dispensing with notification is invalid if its operation would be unconscionable.

§ 2–310. Open Time for Payment or Running of Credit; Authority to Ship Under Reservation.

Unless otherwise agreed

(a) payment is due at the time and place at which the buyer is to receive the goods even though the place of shipment is the place of delivery; and

(b) if the seller is authorized to send the goods he may ship them under reservation, and may tender the documents of title, but the buyer may inspect the goods after their arrival before payment is due unless such inspection is inconsistent with the terms of the contract (Section 2–513); and

(c) if delivery is authorized and made by way of documents of title otherwise than by subsection (b) then payment is due at the time and place at which the buyer is to receive the documents regardless of where the goods are to be received; and

(d) where the seller is required or authorized to ship the goods on credit the credit period runs from the time of shipment but post-dating the invoice or delaying its dispatch will correspondingly delay the starting of the credit period.

§ 2–311. Options and Cooperation Respecting Performance.

(1) An agreement for sale which is otherwise sufficiently definite (subsection (3) of Section 2–204) to be a contract is not made invalid by the fact that it leaves particulars of performance to be specified by one of the parties. Any such specification must be made in good faith and within limits set by commercial reasonableness.

(2) Unless otherwise agreed specifications relating to assortment of the goods are at the buyer's option and except as otherwise provided in subsections (1) (c) and (3) of Section 2–319 specifications or arrangements relating to shipment are at the seller's option.

(3) Where such specification would materially affect the other party's performance but is not seasonably made or where one party's cooperation is necessary to the agreed performance of the other but is not seasonably forthcoming, the other party in addition to all other remedies

(a) is excused for any resulting delay in his own performance; and

(b) may also either proceed to perform in any reasonable manner or after the time for a material part of his own performance treat the failure to specify or to cooperate as a breach by failure to deliver or accept the goods.

§ 2–312. Warranty of Title and Against Infringement; Buyer's Obligation Against Infringement.

(1) Subject to subsection (2) there is in a contract for sale a warranty by the seller that

(a) the title conveyed shall be good, and its transfer rightful; and

(b) the goods shall be delivered free from any security interest or other lien or encumbrance of which the buyer at the time of contracting has no knowledge.

(2) A warranty under subsection (1) will be excluded or modified only by specific language or by circumstances which give the buyer reason to know that the person selling does not claim title in himself or that he is purporting to sell only such right or title as he or a third person may have.

(3) Unless otherwise agreed a seller who is a merchant regularly dealing in goods of the kind warrants that the goods shall be delivered free of the rightful claim of any third person by way of infringement or the like but a buyer who furnishes specifications to the seller must hold the seller harmless against any such claim which arises out of compliance with the specifications.

§ 2–313. Express Warranties by Affirmation, Promise, Description, Sample.

(1) Express warranties by the seller are created as follows:
   (a) Any affirmation of fact or promise made by the seller to the buyer which relates to the goods and becomes part of the basis of the bargain creates an express warranty that the goods shall conform to the affirmation or promise.
   (b) Any description of the goods which is made part of the basis of the bargain creates an express warranty that the goods shall conform to the description.
   (c) Any sample or model which is made part of the basis of the bargain creates an express warranty that the whole of the goods shall conform to the sample or model.
(2) It is not necessary to the creation of an express warranty that the seller use formal words such as "warrant" or "guarantee" or that he have a specific intention to make a warranty, but an affirmation merely of the value of the goods or a statement purporting to be merely the seller's opinion or commendation of the goods does not create a warranty.

§ 2–314. Implied Warranty: Merchantability; Usage of Trade.

(1) Unless excluded or modified (Section 2–316), a warranty that the goods shall be merchantable is implied in a contract for their sale if the seller is a merchant with respect to goods of that kind. Under this section the serving for value of food or drink to be consumed either on the premises or elsewhere is a sale.
(2) Goods to be merchantable must be at least such as
   (a) pass without objection in the trade under the contract description; and
   (b) in the case of fungible goods, are of fair average quality within the description; and
   (c) are fit for the ordinary purposes for which such goods are used; and
   (d) run, within the variations permitted by the agreement, of even kind, quality and quantity within each unit and among all units involved; and
   (e) are adequately contained, packaged, and labeled as the agreement may require; and
   (f) conform to the promises or affirmations of fact made on the container or label if any.
(3) Unless excluded or modified (Section 2–316) other implied warranties may arise from course of dealing or usage of trade.

§ 2–315. Implied Warranty: Fitness for Particular Purpose.

Where the seller at the time of contracting has reason to know any particular purpose for which the goods are required and that the buyer is relying on the seller's skill or judgment to select or furnish suitable goods, there is unless excluded or modified under the next section an implied warranty that the goods shall be fit for such purpose.

§ 2–316. Exclusion or Modification of Warranties.

(1) Words or conduct relevant to the creation of an express warranty and words or conduct tending to negate or limit warranty shall be construed wherever reasonable as consistent with each other; but subject to the provisions of this Article on parol or extrinsic evidence (Section 2–202) negation or limitation is inoperative to the extent that such construction is unreasonable.
(2) Subject to subsection (3), to exclude or modify the implied warranty of merchantability or any part of it the language must mention merchantability and in case of a writing must be conspicuous, and to exclude or modify any implied warranty of fitness the exclusion must be by a writing and conspicuous. Language to exclude all implied warranties of fitness is sufficient if it states, for example, that "There are no warranties which extend beyond the description on the face hereof."

(3) Notwithstanding subsection (2)

    (a) unless the circumstances indicate otherwise, all implied warranties are excluded by expressions like "as is," "with all faults" or other language which in common understanding calls the buyer's attention to the exclusion of warranties and makes plain that there is no implied warranty; and

    (b) when the buyer before entering into the contract has examined the goods or the sample or model as fully as he desired or has refused to examine the goods there is no implied warranty with regard to defects which an examination ought in the circumstances to have revealed to him; and

    (c) an implied warranty can also be excluded or modified by course of dealing or course of performance or usage of trade.

(4) Remedies for breach of warranty can be limited in accordance with the provisions of this Article on liquidation or limitation of damages and on contractual modification of remedy (Sections 2–718 and 2–719).

§ 2–317. Cumulation and Conflict of Warranties Express or Implied.

Warranties whether express or implied shall be construed as consistent with each other and as cumulative, but if such construction is unreasonable the intention of the parties shall determine which warranty is dominant. In ascertaining that intention the following rules apply:

    (a) Exact or technical specifications displace an inconsistent sample or model or general language of description.

    (b) A sample from an existing bulk displaces inconsistent general language of description.

    (c) Express warranties displace inconsistent implied warranties other than an implied warranty of fitness for a particular purpose.

§ 2–318. Third Party Beneficiaries of Warranties Express or Implied.

A seller's warranty whether express or implied extends to any natural person who is in the family or household of his buyer or who is a guest in his home if it is reasonable to expect that such person may use, consume or be affected by the goods and who is injured in person by breach of the warranty. A seller may not exclude or limit the operation of this section.

§ 2–319. F.O.B. and F.A.S Terms

(1) Unless otherwise agreed the term F.O.B. (which means "free on board") at a named place, even though used only in connection with the stated price, is a delivery term under which

    (a) when the term is F.O.B. the place of shipment, the seller must at that place ship the goods in the manner provided in this Article (Section 2–504) and bear the expense and risk of putting them into the possession of the carrier; or

    (b) when the term is F.O.B. the place of destination, the seller must at his own expense and risk transport the goods to that place and there tender delivery of them in the manner provided in this Article (Section 2–503);

    (c) when under either (a) or (b) the term is also F.O.B. vessel, car or other vehicle, the seller must in addition at his own expense and risk load the goods on board. If the term is F.O.B. vessel the buyer must name the vessel and in an appropriate case the seller must comply with the provisions of this Article on the form of bill of lading (Section 2–323).

(2) Unless otherwise agreed the term F.A.S. vessel (which means "free alongside") at a named port, even though used only in connection with the stated price, is a delivery term under which the seller must

    (a) at his own expense and risk deliver the goods alongside the vessel in the manner usual in that port or on a dock designated and provided by the buyer; and

    (b) obtain and tender a receipt for the goods in exchange for which the carrier is under a duty to issue a bill of lading.

(3) Unless otherwise agreed in any case falling within subsection (1) (a) or (c) or subsection (2) the buyer must seasonably give any needed instructions for making delivery, including when the term is F.A.S. or F.O.B. the loading berth of the vessel and in an appropriate

case its name and sailing date. The seller may treat the failure of needed instructions as a failure of cooperation under this Article (Section 2–311). He may also at his option move the goods in any reasonable manner preparatory to delivery or shipment.

(4) Under the term F.O.B. vessel or F.A.S. unless otherwise agreed the buyer must make payment against tender of the required documents and the seller may not tender nor the buyer demand delivery of the goods in substitution for the documents.

§ 2–320 C.I.F. and C. & F. Terms.

(1) The term C.I.F. means that the price includes in a lump sum the cost of the goods and the insurance and freight to the named destination. The term C. & F. or C.F. means that the price so includes cost and freight to the named destination.

(2) Unless otherwise agreed and even though used only in connection with the stated price and destination, the term C.I.F. destination or its equivalent requires the seller at his own expense and risk to

> (a) put the goods into the possession of a carrier at the port for shipment and obtain a negotiable bill or bills of lading covering the entire transportation to the named destination; and
>
> (b) load the goods and obtain a receipt from the carrier (which may be contained in the bill of lading) showing that the freight has been paid or provided for; and
>
> (c) obtain a policy or certificate of insurance, including any war risk insurance, of a kind and on terms then current at the port of shipment in the usual amount, in the currency of the contract, shown to cover the same goods covered by the bill of lading and providing for payment of loss to the order of the buyer or for the account of whom it may concern; but the seller may add to the price the amount of the premium for any such war risk insurance; and
>
> (d) prepare an invoice of the goods and procure any other documents required to effect shipment or to comply with the contract; and
>
> (e) forward and tender with commercial promptness all the documents in due form and with any indorsement necessary to perfect the buyer's rights.

(3) Unless otherwise agreed the term C. & F. or its equivalent has the same effect and imposes upon the seller the same obligations and risks as a C.I.F. term except the obligation as to insurance.

(4) Under the term C.I.F. or C. & F. unless otherwise agreed the buyer must make payment against tender of the required documents and the seller may not tender nor the buyer demand delivery of the goods in substitution for the documents.

§ 2–321. C.I.F. or C. & F.: "Net Landed Weights"; "Payment on Arrival"; Warranty of Condition on Arrival.

Under a contract containing a term C.I.F. or C. & F.

(1) Where the price is based on or is to be adjusted according to "net landed weights," "delivered weights," "out turn" quantity or quality or the like, unless otherwise agreed the seller must reasonably estimate the price. The payment due on tender of the documents called for by the contract is the amount so estimated, but after final adjustment of the price a settlement must be made with commercial promptness.

(2) An agreement described in subsection (1) or any warranty of quality or condition of the goods on arrival places upon the seller the risk of ordinary deterioration, shrinkage and the like in transportation but has no effect on the place or time of identification to the contract for sale or delivery or on the passing of the risk of loss.

(3) Unless otherwise agreed where the contract provides for payment on or after arrival of the goods the seller must before payment allow such preliminary inspection as is feasible; but if the goods are lost delivery of the documents and payment are due when the goods should have arrived.

§ 2–322. Delivery "Ex-Ship."

(1) Unless otherwise agreed a term for delivery of goods "ex-ship" (which means from the carrying vessel) or in equivalent language is not restricted to a particular ship and requires

delivery from a ship which has reached a place at the named port of destination where goods of the kind are usually discharged.

(2) Under such a term unless otherwise agreed

(a) the seller must discharge all liens arising out of the carriage and furnish the buyer with a direction which puts the carrier under a duty to deliver the goods; and

(b) the risk of loss does not pass to the buyer until the goods leave the ship's tackle or are otherwise properly unloaded.

§ 2–323. Form of Bill of Lading Required in Overseas Shipment; "Overseas."

(1) Where the contract contemplates overseas shipment and contains a term C.I.F. or C. & F. or F.O.B. vessel, the seller unless otherwise agreed must obtain a negotiable bill of lading stating that the goods have been loaded on board or, in the case of a term C.I.F. or C. & F., received for shipment.

(2) Where in a case within subsection (1) a bill of lading has been issued in a set of parts, unless otherwise agreed if the documents are not to be sent from abroad the buyer may demand tender of the full set; otherwise only one part of the bill of lading need be tendered. Even if the agreement expressly requires a full set

(a) due tender of a single part is acceptable within the provisions of this Article on cure of improper delivery (subsection (1) of Section 2–508); and

(b) even though the full set is demanded, if the documents are sent from abroad the person tendering an incomplete set may nevertheless require payment upon furnishing an indemnity which the buyer in good faith deems adequate.

(3) A shipment by water or by air or a contract contemplating such shipment is "overseas" insofar as by usage of trade or agreement it is subject to the commercial, financing or shipping practices characteristic of international deep water commerce.

§ 2–324. "No Arrival, No Sale" Term.

Under a term "no arrival, no sale" or terms of like meaning, unless otherwise agreed,

(a) the seller must properly ship conforming goods and if they arrive by any means he must tender them on arrival but he assumes no obligation that the goods will arrive unless he has caused the non-arrival; and

(b) where without fault of the seller the goods are in part lost or have so deteriorated as no longer to conform to the contract or arrive after the contract time, the buyer may proceed as if there had been casualty to identified goods (Section 2–613).

§ 2–325. "Letter of Credit" Term; "Confirmed Credit."

(1) Failure of the buyer seasonably to furnish an agreed letter of credit is a breach of the contract for sale.

(2) The delivery to seller of a proper letter of credit suspends the buyer's obligation to pay. If the letter of credit is dishonored, the seller may on seasonable notification to the buyer require payment directly from him.

(3) Unless otherwise agreed the term "letter of credit" or "banker's credit" in a contract for sale means an irrevocable credit issued by a financing agency of good repute and, where the shipment is overseas, of good international repute. The term "confirmed credit" means that the credit must also carry the direct obligation of such an agency which does business in the seller's financial market.

§ 2–326. Sale on Approval and Sale or Return; Consignment Sales and Rights of Creditors.

(1) Unless otherwise agreed, if delivered goods may be returned by the buyer even though they conform to the contract, the transaction is

(a) a "sale on approval" if the goods are delivered primarily for use, and

(b) a "sale or return" if the goods are delivered primarily for resale.

(2) Except as provided in subsection (3), goods held on approval are not subject to the claims of the buyer's creditors until acceptance; goods held on sale or return are subject to such claims while in the buyer's possession.

(3) Where goods are delivered to a person for sale and such person maintains a place of business at which he deals in goods of the kind involved, under a name other than the name of the person making delivery, then with respect to claims of creditors of the person conducting the business the goods are deemed to be on sale or return. The provisions of this subsection are applicable even though an agreement purports to reserve title to the person making delivery until payment or resale or uses such words as "on consignment" or "on memorandum." However, this subsection is not applicable if the person making delivery

   (a) complies with an applicable law providing for a consignor's interest or the like to be evidenced by a sign, or

   (b) establishes that the person conducting the business is generally known by his creditors to be substantially engaged in selling the goods of others, or

   (c) complies with the filing provisions of the Article on Secured Transactions (Article 9).

(4) Any "or return" term of a contract for sale is to be treated as a separate contract for sale within the statute of frauds section of this Article (Section 2–201) and as contradicting the sale aspect of the contract within the provisions of this Article on parol or extrinsic evidence (Section 2–202).

§ 2–327. Special Incidents of Sale on Approval and Sale or Return.

(1) Under a sale on approval unless otherwise agreed

   (a) although the goods are identified to the contract the risk of loss and the title do not pass to the buyer until acceptance; and

   (b) use of the goods consistent with the purpose of trial is not acceptance but failure seasonably to notify the seller of election to return the goods is acceptance, and if the goods conform to the contract acceptance of any part is acceptance of the whole; and

   (c) after due notification of election to return, the return is at the seller's risk and expense but a merchant buyer must follow any reasonable instructions.

(2) Under a sale or return unless otherwise agreed

   (a) the option to return extends to the whole or any commercial unit of the goods while in substantially their original condition, but must be exercised seasonably; and

   (b) the return is at the buyer's risk and expense.

§ 2–328. Sale by Auction.

(1) In a sale by auction if goods are put up in lots each lot is the subject of a separate sale.

(2) A sale by auction is complete when the auctioneer so announces by the fall of the hammer or in other customary manner. Where a bid is made while the hammer is falling in acceptance of a prior bid the auctioneer may in his discretion reopen the bidding or declare the goods sold under the bid on which the hammer was falling.

(3) Such a sale is with reserve unless the goods are in explicit terms put up without reserve. In an auction with reserve the auctioneer may withdraw the goods at any time until he announces completion of the sale. In an auction without reserve, after the auctioneer calls for bids on an article or lot, that article or lot cannot be withdrawn unless no bid is made within a reasonable time. In either case a bidder may retract his bid until the auctioneer's announcement of completion of the sale, but a bidder's retraction does not revive any previous bid.

(4) If the auctioneer knowingly receives a bid on the seller's behalf or the seller makes or procures such a bid, and notice has not been given that liberty for such bidding is reserved, the buyer may at his option avoid the sale or take the goods at the price of the last good faith bid prior to the completion of the sale.

PART 4
TITLE, CREDITORS AND GOOD FAITH PURCHASERS

§ 2–401. Passing of Title; Reservation for Security; Limited Application of This Section.

Each provision of this Article with regard to the rights, obligations and remedies of the seller, the buyer, purchasers or other third parties applies irrespective of title to the goods except where the provision refers to such title. Insofar as situations are not covered by the other provisions of this Article and matters concerning title became material the following rules apply:

(1) Title to goods cannot pass under a contract for sale prior to their identification to the contract (Section 2–501), and unless otherwise explicitly agreed the buyer acquires by their identification a special property as limited by this Act. Any retention or reservation by the seller of the title (property) in goods shipped or delivered to the buyer is limited in effect to a reservation of a security interest. Subject to these provisions and to the provisions of the Article on Secured Transactions (Article 9), title to goods passes from the seller to the buyer in any manner and on any conditions explicitly agreed on by the parties.

(2) Unless otherwise explicitly agreed title passes to the buyer at the time and place at which the seller completes his performance with reference to the physical delivery of the goods, despite any reservation of a security interest and even though a document of title is to be delivered at a different time or place; and in particular and despite any reservation of a security interest by the bill of lading.

    (a) if the contract requires or authorizes the seller to send the goods to the buyer but does not require him to deliver them at destination, title passes to the buyer at the time and place of shipment; but

    (b) if the contract requires delivery at destination, title passes on tender there.

(3) Unless otherwise explicitly agreed where delivery is to be made without moving the goods,

    (a) if the seller is to deliver a document of title, title passes at the time when and the place where he delivers such documents; or

    (b) if the goods are at the time of contracting already identified and no documents are to be delivered, title passes at the time and place of contracting.

(4) A rejection or other refusal by the buyer to receive or retain the goods, whether or not justified, or a justified revocation of acceptance revests title to the goods in the seller. Such revesting occurs by operation of law and is not a "sale."

§ 2–402. Rights of Seller's Creditors Against Sold Goods.

(1) Except as provided in subsections (2) and (3), rights of unsecured creditors of the seller with respect to goods which have been identified to a contract for sale are subject to the buyer's rights to recover the goods under this Article (Sections 2–502 and 2–716).

(2) A creditor of the seller may treat a sale or an identification of goods to a contract for sale as void if as against him a retention of possession by the seller is fraudulent under any rule of law of the state where the goods are situated, except that retention of possession in good faith and current course of trade by a merchant-seller for a commercially reasonable time after a sale or identification is not fraudulent.

(3) Nothing in this Article shall be deemed to impair the rights of creditors of the seller

    (a) under the provisions of the Article on Secured Transactions (Article 9); or

    (b) where identification to the contract or delivery is made not in current course of trade but in satisfaction of or as security for a pre-existing claim for money, security or the like and is made under circumstances which under any rule of law of the state where the goods are situated would apart from this Article constitute the transaction a fraudulent transfer or voidable preference.

§ 2–403. Power to Transfer; Good Faith Purchase of Goods; "Entrusting."

(1) A purchaser of goods acquires all title which his transferor had or had power to transfer except that a purchaser of a limited interest acquires rights only to the extent of the interest purchased. A person with voidable title has power to transfer a good title to a good faith purchaser for value. When goods have been delivered under a transaction of purchase the purchaser has such power even though

    (a) the transferor was deceived as to the identity of the purchaser, or

    (b) the delivery was in exchange for a check which is later dishonored, or

    (c) it was agreed that the transaction was to be a "cash sale," or

(d) the delivery was procured through fraud punishable as larcenous under the criminal law.

(2) Any entrusting of possession of goods to a merchant who deals in goods of that kind gives him power to transfer all rights of the entruster to a buyer in ordinary course of business.

(3) "Entrusting" includes any delivery and any acquiescence in retention of possession regardless of any condition expressed between the parties to the delivery or acquiescence and regardless of whether the procurement of the entrusting or the possessor's disposition of the goods have been such as to be larcenous under the criminal law.

(4) The rights of other purchasers of goods and of lien creditors are governed by the Articles on Secured Transactions (Article 9), Bulk Transfers (Article 6) and Documents of Title (Article 7).

PART 5
PERFORMANCE

§ 2–501. Insurable Interest in Goods; Manner of Identification of Goods.

(1) The buyer obtains a special property and an insurable interest in goods by identification of existing goods as goods to which the contract refers even though the goods so identified are non-conforming and he has an option to return or reject them. Such identification can be made at any time and in any manner explicitly agreed to by the parties. In the absence of explicit agreement identification occurs

(a) when the contract is made if it is for the sale of goods already existing and identified;

(b) if the contract is for the sale of future goods other than those described in paragraph (c), when goods are shipped, marked or otherwise designated by the seller as goods to which the contract refers;

(c) when the crops are planted or otherwise become growing crops or the young are conceived if the contract is for the sale of unborn young to be born within twelve months after contracting or for the sale of crops to be harvested within twelve months or the next normal harvest season after contracting whichever is longer.

(2) The seller retains an insurable interest in goods so long as title to or any security interest in the goods remains in him and where the identification is by the seller alone he may until default or insolvency or notification to the buyer that the identification is final substitute other goods for those identified.

(3) Nothing in this section impairs any insurable interest recognized under any other statute or rule of law.

§ 2–502. Buyer's Right to Goods on Seller's Insolvency.

(1) Subject to subsection (2) and even though the goods have not been shipped a buyer who has paid a part or all of the price of goods in which he has a special property under the provisions of the immediately preceding section may on making and keeping good a tender of any unpaid portion of their price recover them from the seller if the seller becomes insolvent within ten days after receipt of the first installment on their price.

(2) If the identification creating his special property has been made by the buyer he acquires the right to recover the goods only if they conform to the contract for sale.

§ 2–503. Manner of Seller's Tender of Delivery.

(1) Tender of delivery requires that the seller put and hold conforming goods at the buyer's disposition and give the buyer any notification reasonably necessary to enable him to take delivery. The manner, time and place for tender are determined by the agreement and this Article, and in particular

(a) tender must be at a reasonable hour, and if it is of goods they must be kept available for the period reasonably necessary to enable the buyer to take possession; but

(b) unless otherwise agreed the buyer must furnish facilities reasonably suited to the receipt of the goods.

(2) Where the case is within the next section respecting shipment tender requires that the seller comply with its provisions.

(3) Where the seller is required to deliver at a particular destination tender requires that he comply with subsection (1) and also in any appropriate case tender documents as described in subsections (4) and (5) of this section.

(4) Where goods are in the possession of a bailee and are to be delivered without being moved

    (a) tender requires that the seller either tender a negotiable document of title covering such goods or procure acknowledgment by the bailee of the buyer's right to possession of the goods; but

    (b) tender to the buyer of a non-negotiable document of title or of a written direction to the bailee to deliver is sufficient tender unless the buyer seasonably objects, and receipt by the bailee of notification of the buyer's rights fixes those rights as against the bailee and all third persons; but risk of loss of the goods and of any failure by the bailee to honor the non-negotiable document of title or to obey the direction remains on the seller until the buyer has had a reasonable time to present the document or direction, and a refusal by the bailee to honor the document or to obey the direction defeats the tender.

(5) Where the contract requires the seller to deliver documents

    (a) he must tender all such documents in correct form, except as provided in this Article with respect to bills of lading in a set (subsection (2) of Section 2–323); and

    (b) tender through customary banking channels is sufficient and dishonor of a draft accompanying the documents constitutes non-acceptance or rejection.

§ 2–504. Shipment by Seller.

Where the seller is required or authorized to send the goods to the buyer and the contract does not require him to deliver them at a particular destination, then unless otherwise agreed he must

    (a) put the goods in the possession of such a carrier and make such a contract for their transportation as may be reasonable having regard to the nature of the goods and other circumstances of the case; and

    (b) obtain and promptly deliver or tender in due form any document necessary to enable the buyer to obtain possession of the goods or otherwise required by the agreement or by usage of trade; and

    (c) promptly notify the buyer of the shipment.

Failure to notify the buyer under paragraph (c) or to make a proper contract under paragraph (a) is a ground for rejection only if material delay or loss ensues.

§ 2–505. Seller's Shipment Under Reservation.

(1) Where the seller has identified goods to the contract by or before shipment:

    (a) his procurement of a negotiable bill of lading to his own order or otherwise reserves in him a security interest in the goods. His procurement of the bill to the order of a financing agency or of the buyer indicates in addition only the seller's expectation of transferring that interest to the person named.

    (b) a non-negotiable bill of lading to himself or his nominee reserves possession of the goods as security but except in a case of conditional delivery (subsection (2) of Section 2–507) a non-negotiable bill of lading naming the buyer as consignee reserves no security interest even though the seller retains possession of the bill of lading.

(2) When shipment by the seller with reservation of a security interest is in violation of the contract for sale it constitutes an improper contract for transportation within the preceding section but impairs neither the rights given to the buyer by shipment and identification of the goods to the contract nor the seller's powers as a holder of a negotiable document.

§ 2–506. Rights of Financing Agency.

(1) A financing agency by paying or purchasing for value a draft which relates to a ship-rights under the draft and any document of title securing it any rights of the shipper in the goods including the right to stop delivery and the shipper's right to have the draft honored by ment of goods acquires to the extent of the payment or purchase and in addition to its own the buyer.

(2) The right to reimbursement of a financing agency which has in good faith honored or purchased the draft under commitment to or authority from the buyer is not impaired by subsequent discovery of defects with reference to any relevant document which was apparently regular on its face.

§ 2–507. Effect of Seller's Tender; Delivery on Condition.

(1) Tender of delivery is a condition to the buyer's duty to accept the goods and, unless otherwise agreed, to his duty to pay for them. Tender entitles the seller to acceptance of the goods and to payment according to the contract.

(2) Where payment is due and demanded on the delivery to the buyer of goods or documents of title, his right as against the seller to retain or dispose of them is conditional upon his making the payment due.

§ 2–508. Cure by Seller of Improper Tender or Delivery; Replacement.

(1) Where any tender or delivery by the seller is rejected because non-conforming and the time for performance has not yet expired, the seller may seasonably notify the buyer of his intention to cure and may then within the contract time make a conforming delivery.

(2) Where the buyer rejects a non-conforming tender which the seller had reasonable grounds to believe would be acceptable with or without money allowance the seller may if he seasonably notifies the buyer have a further reasonable time to substitute a conforming tender.

§ 2–509. Risk of Loss in the Absence of Breach.

(1) Where the contract requires or authorizes the seller to ship the goods by carrier
- (a) if it does not require him to deliver them at a particular destination, the risk of loss passes to the buyer when the goods are duly delivered to the carrier even though the shipment is under reservation (Section 2-505); but
- (b) if it does require him to deliver them at a particular destination and the goods are there duly tendered while in the possession of the carrier, the risk of loss passes to the buyer when the goods are there duly so tendered as to enable the buyer to take delivery.

(2) Where the goods are held by a bailee to be delivered without being moved, the risk of loss passes to the buyer
- (a) on his receipt of a negotiable document of title covering the goods; or
- (b) on acknowledgment by the bailee of the buyer's right to possession of the goods; or
- (c) after his receipt of a non-negotiable document of title or other written direction to deliver, as provided in subsection (4) (b) of Section 2–503.

(3) In any case not within subsection (1) or (2), the risk of loss passes to the buyer on his receipt of the goods if the seller is a merchant; otherwise the risk passes to the buyer on tender of delivery.

(4) The provisions of this section are subject to contrary agreement of the parties and to the provisions of this Article on sale on approval (Section 2–327) and on effect of breach on risk of loss (Section 2–510).

§ 2–510. Effect of Breach on Risk of Loss.

(1) Where a tender or delivery of goods so fails to conform to the contract as to give a right of rejection the risk of their loss remains on the seller until cure or acceptance.

(2) Where the buyer rightfully revokes acceptance he may to the extent of any deficiency

in his effective insurance coverage treat the risk of loss as having rested on the seller from the beginning.

(3) Where the buyer as to conforming goods already identified to the contract for sale repudiates or is otherwise in breach before risk of their loss has passed to him, the seller may to the extent of any deficiency in his effective insurance coverage treat the risk of loss as resting on the buyer for a commercially reasonable time.

§ 2–511. Tender of Payment by Buyer; Payment by Check.

(1) Unless otherwise agreed tender of payment is a condition to the seller's duty to tender and complete any delivery.

(2) Tender of payment is sufficient when made by any means or in any manner current in the ordinary course of business unless the seller demands payment in legal tender and gives any extension of time reasonably necessary to procure it.

(3) Subject to the provisions of this Act on the effect of an instrument on an obligation (Section 3–802), payment by check is conditional and is defeated as between the parties by dishonor of the check on due presentment.

§ 2–512. Payment by Buyer Before Inspection.

(1) Where the contract requires payment before inspection non-conformity of the goods does not excuse the buyer from so making payment unless
- (a) the non-conformity appears without inspection; or
- (b) despite tender of the required documents the circumstances would justify injunction against honor under the provisions of this Act (Section 5–114).

(2) Payment pursuant to subsection (1) does not constitute an acceptance of goods or impair the buyer's right to inspect or any of his remedies.

§ 2–513. Buyer's Right to Inspection of Goods.

(1) Unless otherwise agreed and subject to subsection (3), where goods are tendered or delivered or identified to the contract for sale, the buyer has a right before payment or acceptance to inspect them at any reasonable place and time and in any reasonable manner. When the seller is required or authorized to send the goods to the buyer, the inspection may be after their arrival.

(2) Expenses of inspection must be borne by the buyer but may be recovered from the seller if the goods do not conform and are rejected.

(3) Unless otherwise agreed and subject to the provisions of this Article on C.I.F. contracts (subsection (3) of Section 2–321), the buyer is not entitled to inspect the goods before payment of the price when the contract provides
- (a) for delivery "C.O.D." or on other like terms; or
- (b) for payment against documents of title, except where such payment is due only after the goods are to become available for inspection.

(4) A place or method of inspection fixed by the parties is presumed to be exclusive but unless otherwise expressly agreed it does not postpone identification or shift the place for delivery or for passing the risk of loss. If compliance becomes impossible, inspection shall be as provided in this section unless the place or method fixed was clearly intended as an indispensable condition failure of which avoids the contract.

§ 2–514. When Documents Deliverable on Acceptance; When on Payment.

Unless otherwise agreed documents against which a draft is drawn are to be delivered to the drawee on acceptance of the draft if it is payable more than three days after presentment; otherwise, only on payment.

§ 2–515. Preserving Evidence of Goods in Dispute.

In furtherance of the adjustment of any claim or dispute
- (a) either party on reasonable notification to the other and for the purpose of ascer-

taining evidence has the right to inspect, test and sample the goods including such of them as may be in the possession or control of the other; and

(b) the parties may agree to a third party inspection or survey to determine the conformity or condition of the goods and may agree that the findings shall be binding upon them in any sebsequent litigation or adjustment.

PART 6
BREACH, REPUDIATION AND EXCUSE

§ 2–601. Buyer's Rights on Improper Delivery.

Subject to the provisions of this Article on breach in installment contracts (Section 2–612) and unless otherwise agreed under the sections on contractual limitations of remedy (Sections 2–718 and 2–719), if the goods or the tender of delivery fail in any respect to conform to the contract, the buyer may

(a) reject the whole; or

(b) accept the whole; or

(c) accept any commercial unit or units and reject the rest.

§ 2–602. Manner and Effect of Rightful Rejection.

(1) Rejection of goods must be within a reasonable time after their delivery or tender. It is ineffective unless the buyer seasonably notifies the seller.

(2) Subject to the provisions of the two following sections on rejected goods (Sections 2–603 and 2–604),

(a) after rejection any exercise of ownership by the buyer with respect to any commercial unit is wrongful as against the seller; and

(b) if the buyer has before rejection taken physical possession of goods in which he does not have a security interest under the provisions of this Article (subsection (3) of Section 2–711), he is under a duty after rejection to hold them with reasonable care at the seller's disposition for a time sufficient to permit the seller to remove them; but

(c) the buyer has no further obligations with regard to goods rightfully rejected.

(3) The seller's rights with respect to goods wrongfully rejected are governed by the provisions of this Article on seller's remedies in general (Section 2–703).

§ 2–603. Merchant Buyer's Duties as to Rightfully Rejected Goods.

(1) Subject to any security interest in the buyer (subsection (3) of Section 2–711), when the seller has no agent or place of business at the market of rejection a merchant buyer is under a duty after rejection of goods in his possession or control to follow any reasonable instructions received from the seller with respect to the goods and in the absence of such instructions to make reasonable efforts to sell them for the seller's account if they are perishable or threaten to decline in value speedily. Instructions are not reasonable if on demand indemnity for expenses is not forthcoming.

(2) When the buyer sells goods under subsection (1), he is entitled to reimbursement from the seller or out of the proceeds for reasonable expenses of caring for and selling them, and if the expenses include no selling commission then to such commission as is usual in the trade or if there is none to a reasonable sum not exceeding ten per cent on the gross proceeds.

(3) In complying with this section the buyer is held only to good faith and good faith conduct hereunder is neither acceptance nor conversion nor the basis of an action for damages.

§ 2–604. Buyer's Options as to Salvage of Rightfully Rejected Goods.

Subject to the provisions of the immediately preceding section on perishables if the seller gives no instructions within a reasonable time after notification of rejection the buyer may store the rejected goods for the seller's account or reship them to him or resell them for the seller's account with reimbursement as provided in the preceding section. Such action is not acceptance or conversion.

§ 2–605. Waiver of Buyer's Objections by Failure to Particularize.

(1) The buyer's failure to state in connection with rejection a particular defect which is ascertainable by reasonable inspection precludes him from relying on the unstated defect to justify rejection or to establish breach

   (a) where the seller could have cured it if stated seasonably; or

   (b) between merchants when the seller has after rejection made a request in writing for a full and final written statement of all defects on which the buyer proposes to rely.

(2) Payment against documents made without reservation of rights precludes recovery of the payment for defects apparent on the face of the documents.

§ 2–606. What Constitutes Acceptance of Goods.

(1) Acceptance of goods occurs when the buyer

   (a) after a reasonable opportunity to inspect the goods signifies to the seller that the goods are conforming or that he will take or retain them inspite of their nonconformity; or

   (b) fails to make an effective rejection (subsection (1) of Section 2–602), but such acceptance does not occur until the buyer has had a reasonable opportunity to inspect them; or

   (c) does any act inconsistent with the seller's ownership; but if such act is wrongful as against the seller it is an acceptance only if ratified by him.

(2) Acceptance of a part of any commercial unit is acceptance of that entire unit.

§ 2–607. Effect of Acceptance; Notice of Breach; Burden of Establishing Breach After Acceptance; Notice of Claim or Litigation to Person Answerable Over.

(1) The buyer must pay at the contract rate for any goods accepted.

(2) Acceptance of goods by the buyer precludes rejection of the goods accepted and if made with knowledge of a non-conformity cannot be revoked because of it unless the acceptance was on the reasonable assumption that the non-conformity would be seasonably cured but acceptance does not of itself impair any other remedy provided by this Article for nonconformity.

(3) Where a tender has been accepted.

   (a) the buyer must within a reasonable time after he discovers or should have discovered any breach notify the seller of breach or be barred from any remedy; and

   (b) if the claim is one for infringement or the like (subsection (3) of Section 2–312) and the buyer is sued as a result of such a breach he must so notify the seller within a reasonable time after he receives notice of the litigation or be barred from any remedy over for liability established by the litigation.

(4) The burden is on the buyer to establish any breach with respect to the goods accepted.

(5) Where the buyer is sued for breach of a warranty or other obligation for which his seller is answerable over

   (a) he may give his seller written notice of the litigation. If the notice states that the seller may come in and defend and that if the seller does not do so he will be bound in any action against him by his buyer by any determination of fact common to the two litigations, then unless the seller after seasonable receipt of the notice does come in and defend he is so bound.

   (b) if the claim is one for infringement or the like (subsection (3) of Section 2–312) the original seller may demand in writing that his buyer turn over to him control of the litigation including settlement or else be barred from any remedy over and if he also agrees to bear all expense and to satisfy any adverse judgment, then unless the buyer after seasonable receipt of the demand does turn over control the buyer is so barred.

(6) The provisions of subsections (3), (4) and (5) apply to any obligation of a buyer to hold the seller harmless against infringement or the like (subsection (3) of Section 2–312).

§ 2–608. Revocation of Acceptance in Whole or in Part.

(1) The buyer may revoke his acceptance of a lot or commercial unit whose non-conformity substantially impairs its value to him if he has accepted it
  (a) on the reasonable assumption that its non-conformity would be cured and it has not been seasonably cured; or
  (b) without discovery of such non-conformity if his acceptance was reasonably induced either by the difficulty of discovery before acceptance or by the seller's assurances.

(2) Revocation of acceptance must occur within a reasonable time after the buyer discovers or should have discovered the ground for it and before any substantial change in condition of the goods which is not caused by their own defects. It is not effective until the buyer notifies the seller of it.

(3) A buyer who so revokes has the same rights and duties with regard to the goods involved as if he had rejected them.

§ 2–609. Right to Adequate Assurance of Performance.

(1) A contract for sale imposes an obligation on each party that the other's expectation of receiving due performance will not be impaired. When reasonable grounds for insecurity arise with respect to the performance of either party the other may in writing demand adequate assurance of due performance and until he receives such assurance may if commercially reasonable suspend any performance for which he has not already received the agreed return.

(2) Between merchants the reasonableness of grounds for insecurity and the adequacy of any assurance offered shall be determined according to commercial standards.

(3) Acceptance of any improper delivery or payment does not prejudice the aggrieved party's right to demand adequate assurance of future performance.

(4) After receipt of a justified demand failure to provide within a reasonable time not exceeding thirty days such assurance of due performance as is adequate under the circumstances of the particular case is a repudiation of the contract.

§ 2–610. Anticipatory Repudiation.

When either party repudiates the contract with respect to a performance not yet due the loss of which will substantially impair the value of the contract to the other, the aggrieved party may
  (a) for a commercially reasonable time await performance by the repudiating party; or
  (b) resort to any remedy for breach (Section 2–703 or Section 2–711), even though he has notified the repudiating party that he would await the latter's performance and has urged retraction; and
  (c) in either case suspend his own performance or proceed in accordance with the provisions of this Article on the seller's right to identify goods to the contract notwithstanding breach or to salvage unfinished goods. (Section 2–704).

§ 2–611. Retraction of Anticipatory Repudiation.

(1) Until the repudiating party's next performance is due he can retract his repudiation unless the aggrieved party has since the repudiation cancelled or materially changed his position or otherwise indicated that he considers the repudiation final.

(2) Retraction may be by any method which clearly indicates to the aggrieved party that the repudiating party intends to perform, but must include any assurance justifiably demanded under the provisions of this Article (Section 2–609).

(3) Retraction reinstates the repudiating party's rights under the contract with due excuse and allowance to the aggrieved party for any delay occasioned by the repudiation.

§ 2–612. "Installment Contract"; Breach.

(1) An "installment contract" is one which requires or authorizes the delivery of goods in separate lots to be separately accepted, even though the contract contains a clause "each delivery is a separate contract" or its equivalent.

(2) The buyer may reject any installment which is non-conforming if the non-conformity substantially impairs the value of that installment and cannot be cured or if the non-conformity is a defect in the required documents; but if the non-conformity does not fall within subsection (3) and the seller gives adequate assurance of its cure the buyer must accept that installment.

(3) Whenever non-conformity or default with respect to one or more installments substantially impairs the value of the whole contract there is a breach of the whole. But the aggrieved party reinstates the contract if he accepts a non-conforming installment without seasonably notifying of cancellation or if he brings an action with respect only to past installments or demands performance as to future installments.

§ 2–613. Casualty to Identified Goods.

Where the contract requires for its performance goods identified when the contract is made, and the goods suffer casualty without fault of either party before the risk of loss passes to the buyer, or in a proper case under a "no arrival, no sale" term (Section 2–324) then

  (a) if the loss is total the contract is avoided; and
  (b) if the loss is partial or the goods have so deteriorated as no longer to conform to the contract the buyer may nevertheless demand inspection and at his option either treat the contract as avoided or accept the goods with due allowance from the contract price for the deterioration or the deficiency in quantity but without further right against the seller.

§ 2–614. Substituted Performance.

(1) Where without fault of either party the agreed berthing, loading, or unloading facilities fail or an agreed type of carrier becomes unavailable or the agreed manner of delivery otherwise becomes commercially impracticable but a commercially reasonable substitute is available, such substitute performance must be tendered and accepted.

(2) If the agreed means or manner of payment fails because of domestic or foreign government regulation, the seller may withhold or stop delivery unless the buyer provides a means or manner of payment which is commercially a substantial equivalent. If delivery has already been taken, payment by the means or in the manner provided by the regulation discharges the buyer's obligation unless the regulation is discriminatory, oppressive or predatory.

§ 2–615. Excuse by Failure of Presupposed Conditions.

Except so far as a seller may have assumed a greater obligation and subject to the preceding section on substituted performance:

  (a) Delay in delivery or non-delivery in whole or in part by a seller who complies with paragraphs (b) and (c) is not a breach of his duty under a contract for sale if performance as agreed has been made impracticable by the occurrence of a contingency the non-occurrence of which was a basic assumption on which the contract was made or by compliance in good faith with any applicable foreign or domestic governmental regulation or order whether or not it later proves to be invalid.
  (b) Where the causes mentioned in paragraph (a) affect only a part of the seller's capacity to perform, he must allocate production and deliveries among his customers but may at his option include regular customers not then under contract as well as his own requirements for further manufacture. He may so allocate in any manner which is fair and reasonable.
  (c) The seller must notify the buyer seasonably that there will be delay or non-delivery and, when allocation is required under paragraph (b), of the estimated quota thus made available for the buyer.

§ 2–616. Procedure on Notice Claiming Excuse.

(1) Where the buyer receives notification of a material or indefinite delay or an allocation justified under the preceding section he may by written notification to the seller as to any delivery concerned, and where the prospective deficiency substantially impairs the value of the

whole contract under the provisions of this Article relating to breach of installment contracts (Section 2–612), then also as to the whole,

(a) terminate and thereby discharge any unexecuted portion of the contract; or

(b) modify the contract by agreeing to take his available quota in substitution.

(2) If after receipt of such notification from the seller the buyer fails so to modify the contract within a reasonable time not exceeding thirty days the contract lapses with respect to any deliveries affected.

(3) The provisions of this section may not be negated by agreement except in so far as the seller has assumed a greater obligation under the preceding section.

PART 7
REMEDIES

§ 2–701. Remedies for Breach of Collateral Contracts Not Impaired.

Remedies for breach of any obligation or promise collateral or ancillary to a contract for sale are not impaired by the provisions of this Article.

§ 2–702. Seller's Remedies on Discovery of Buyer's Insolvency.

(1) Where the seller discovers the buyer to be insolvent he may refuse delivery except for cash including payment for all goods theretofore delivered under the contract, and stop delivery under this Article (Section 2–705).

(2) Where the seller discovers that the buyer has received goods on credit while insolvent he may reclaim the goods upon demand made within ten days after the receipt, but if misrepresentation of solvency has been made to the particular seller in writing within three months before delivery the ten day limitation does not apply. Except as provided in this subsection the seller may not base a right to reclaim goods on the buyer's fraudulent or innocent misrepresentation of solvency or of intent to pay.

(3) The seller's right to reclaim under subsection (2) is subject to the rights of a buyer in ordinary course or other good faith purchaser or lien creditor under this Article (Section 2–403). Successful reclamation of goods excludes all other remedies with respect to them.

§ 2–703. Seller's Remedies in General.

Where the buyer wrongfully rejects or revokes acceptance of goods or fails to make a payment due on or before delivery or repudiates with respect to a part or the whole, then with respect to any goods directly affected and, if the breach is of the whole contract (Section 2–612), then also with respect to the whole undelivered balance, the aggrieved seller may

(a) withhold delivery of such goods;

(b) stop delivery by any bailee as hereafter provided (Section 2–705);

(c) proceed under the next section respecting goods still unidentified to the contract;

(d) resell and recover damages as hereafter provided (Section 2–706);

(e) recover damages for non-acceptance (Section 2–708) or in a proper case the price (Section 2–709);

(f) cancel.

§ 2–704. Seller's Right to Identify Goods to the Contract Notwithstanding Breach or to Salvage Unfinished Goods.

(1) An aggrieved seller under the preceding section may

(a) identify to the contract conforming goods not already identified if at the time he learned of the breach they are in his possession or control;

(b) treat as the subject of resale goods which have demonstrably been intended for the particular contract even though those goods are unfinished.

(2) Where the goods are unfinished an aggrieved seller may in the exercise of reasonable commercial judgment for the purposes of avoiding loss and of effective realization either complete the manufacture and wholly identify the goods to the contract or cease manufacture and resell for scrap or salvage value or proceed in any other reasonable manner.

§ 2–705. Seller's Stoppage of Delivery in Transit or Otherwise.

(1) The seller may stop delivery of goods in the possession of a carrier or other bailee when he discovers the buyer to be insolvent (Section 2–702) and may stop delivery of carload, truckload, planeload or larger shipments of express or freight when the buyer repudiates or fails to make a payment due before delivery or if for any other reason the seller has a right to withhold or reclaim the goods.

(2) As against such buyer the seller may stop delivery until

    (a) receipt of the goods by the buyer; or

    (b) acknowledgment to the buyer by any bailee of the goods except a carrier that the bailee holds the goods for the buyer; or

    (c) such acknowledgment to the buyer by a carrier by reshipment or as warehouseman; or

    (d) negotiation to the buyer of any negotiable document of title covering the goods.

(3) (a) To stop delivery the seller must so notify as to enable the bailee by reasonable diligence to prevent delivery of the goods.

    (b) After such notification the bailee must hold and deliver the goods according to the directions of the seller but the seller is liable to the bailee for any ensuing charges or damages.

    (c) If a negotiable document of title has been issued for goods the bailee is not obliged to obey a notification to stop until surrender of the document.

    (d) A carrier who has issued a non-negotiable bill of lading is not obliged to obey a notification to stop received from a person other than the consignor.

§ 2–706. Seller's Resale Including Contract for Resale.

(1) Under the conditions stated in Section 2–703 on seller's remedies, the seller may resell the goods concerned or the undelivered balance thereof. Where the resale is made in good faith and in a commercially reasonable manner the seller may recover the difference between the resale price and the contract price together with any incidental damages allowed under the provisions of this Article (Section 2–710), but less expenses saved in consequence of the buyer's breach.

(2) Except as otherwise provided in subsection (3) or unless otherwise agreed resale may be at public or private sale including sale by way of one or more contracts to sell or of identification to an existing contract of the seller. Sale may be as a unit or in parcels and at any time and place and on any terms but every aspect of the sale including the method, manner, time, place and terms must be commercially reasonable. The resale must be reasonably identified as referring to the broken contract, but it is not necessary that the goods be in existence or that any or all of them have been identified to the contract before the breach.

(3) Where the resale is at private sale the seller must give the buyer reasonable notification of his intention to resell.

(4) Where the resale is at public sale

    (a) only identified goods can be sold except where there is a recognized market for a public sale of futures in goods of the kind; and

    (b) it must be made at a usual place or market for public sale if one is reasonably available and except in the case of goods which are perishable or threaten to decline in value speedily the seller must give the buyer reasonable notice of the time and place of the resale; and

    (c) if the goods are not to be within the view of those attending the sale the notification of sale must state the place where the goods are located and provide for their reasonable inspection by prospective bidders; and

    (d) the seller may buy.

(5) A purchaser who buys in good faith at a resale takes the goods free of any rights of the original buyer even though the seller fails to comply with one or more of the requirements of this section.

(6) The seller is not accountable to the buyer for any profit made on any resale. A person

in the position of a seller (Section 2–707) or a buyer who has rightfully rejected or justifiably revoked acceptance must account for any excess over the amount of his security interest, as hereinafter defined (subsection (3) of Section 2–711).

§ 2–707. "Person in the Position of a Seller."

(1) A "person in the position of a seller" includes as against a principal an agent who has paid or become responsible for the price of goods on behalf of his principal or anyone who otherwise holds a security interest or other right in goods similar to that of a seller.

(2) A person in the position of a seller may as provided in this Article withhold or stop delivery (Section 2–705) and resell (Section 2–706) and recover incidental damages (Section 2–710).

§ 2–708. Seller's Damages for Non-acceptance or Repudiation.

(1) Subject to subsection (2) and to the provisions of this Article with respect to proof of market price (Section 2–723), the measure of damages for non-acceptance or repudiation by the buyer is the difference between the market price at the time and place for tender and the unpaid contract price together with any incidental damages provided in this Article (Section 2–710), but less expenses saved in consequence of the buyer's breach.

(2) If the measure of damages provided in subsection (1) is inadequate to put the seller in as good a position as performance would have done then the measure of damages is the profit (including reasonable overhead) which the seller would have made from full performance by the buyer, together with any incidental damages provided in this Article (Section 2–710), due allowance for costs reasonably incurred and due credit for payments or proceeds of resale.

§ 2–709. Action for the Price.

(1) When the buyer fails to pay the price as it becomes due the seller may recover, together with any incidental damages under the next section, the price
   (a) of goods accepted or of conforming goods lost or damaged within a commerically reasonable time after risk of their loss has passed to the buyer; and
   (b) of goods identified to the contract if the seller is unable after reasonable effort to resell them at a reasonable price or the circumstances reasonably indicate that such effort will be unavailing.

(2) Where the seller sues for the price he must hold for the buyer any goods which have been identified to the contract and are still in his control except that if resale becomes possible he may resell them at any time prior to the collection of the judgment. The net proceeds of any such resale must be credited to the buyer and payment of the judgment entitles him to any goods not resold.

(3) After the buyer has wrongfully rejected or revoked acceptance of the goods or has failed to make a payment due or has repudiated (Section 2–610), a seller who is held not entitled to the price under this section shall nevertheless be awarded damages for non-acceptance under the preceding section.

§ 2–710. Seller's Incidental Damages.

Incidental damages to an aggrieved seller include any commercially reasonable charges, expenses or commissions incurred in stopping delivery, in the transportation, care and custody of goods after the buyer's breach, in connection with return or resale of the goods or otherwise resulting from the breach.

§ 2–711 Buyer's Remedies in General; Buyer's Security Interest in Rejected Goods.

(1) Where the seller fails to make delivery or repudiates or the buyer rightfully rejects or justifiably revokes acceptance then with respect to any goods involved, and with respect to the whole if the breach goes to the whole contract (Section 2–612), the buyer may cancel and whether or not he has done so may in addition to recovering so much of the price as has been paid

(a) "cover" and have damages under the next section as to all the goods affected whether or not they have been identified to the contract; or

(b) recover damages for non-delivery as provided in this Article (Section 2–713).

(2) Where the seller fails to deliver or repudiates the buyer may also

(a) if the goods have been identified recover them as provided in this Article (Section 2–502); or

(b) in a proper case obtain specific performance or replevy the goods as provided in this Article (Section 2–716).

(3) On rightful rejection or justifiable revocation of acceptance a buyer has a security interest in goods in his possession or control for any payments made on their price and any expenses reasonably incurred in their inspection, receipt, transportation, care and custody and may hold such goods and resell them in like manner as an aggrieved seller (Section 2–706).

§ 2–712. "Covert"; Buyer's Procurement of Substitute Goods.

(1) After a breach within the preceding section the buyer may "cover" by making in good faith and without unreasonable delay any reasonable purchase of or contract to purchase goods in substitution for those due from the seller.

(2) The buyer may recover from the seller as damages the difference between the cost of cover and the contract price together with any incidental or consequential damages as hereinafter defined (Section 2–715), but less expenses saved in consequence of the seller's breach.

(3) Failure of the buyer to effect cover within this section does not bar him from any other remedy.

§ 2–713. Buyer's Damages for Non-Delivery or Repudiation.

(1) Subject to the provisions of this Article with respect to proof of market price (Section 2–723), the measure of damages for non-delivery or repudiation by the seller is the difference between the market price at the time when the buyer learned of the breach and the contract price together with any incidental and consequential damages provided in this Article (Section 2–715), but less expenses saved in consequence of the seller's breach.

(2) Market price is to be determined as of the place for tender or, in cases of rejection after arrival or revocation of acceptance, as of the place of arrival.

§ 2–714. Buyer's Damages for Breach in Regard to Accepted Goods.

(1) Where the buyer has accepted goods and given notification (subsection (3) of Section 2–607) he may recover as damages for any non-conformity of tender the loss resulting in the ordinary course of events from the seller's breach as determined in any manner which is reasonable.

(2) The measure of damages for breach of warranty is the difference at the time and place of acceptance between the value of the goods accepted and the value they would have had if they had been as warranted, unless special circumstances show proximate damages of a different amount.

(3) In a proper case any incidental and consequential damages under the next section may also be recovered.

§ 2–715. Buyer's Incidental and Consequential Damages.

(1) Incidental damages resulting from the seller's breach include expenses reasonably incurred in inspection, receipt, transportation and care and custody of goods rightfully rejected, any commercially reasonable charges, expenses or commissions in connection with effecting cover and any other reasonable expense incident to the delay or other breach.

(2) Consequential damages resulting from the seller's breach include

(a) any loss resulting from general or particular requirements and needs of which the seller at the time of contracting had reason to know and which could not reasonably be prevented by cover or otherwise; and

(b) injury to person or property proximately resulting from any breach of warranty.

§ 2–716. Buyer's Right to Specific Performance or Replevin.

(1) Specific performance may be decreed where the goods are unique or in other proper circumstances.

(2) The decree for specific performance may include such terms and conditions as to payment of the price, damages, or other relief as the court may deem just.

(3) The buyer has a right of replevin for goods identified to the contract if after reasonable effort he is unable to effect cover for such goods or the circumstances reasonably indicate that such effort will be unavailing or if the goods have been shipped under reservation and satisfaction of the security interest in them has been made or tendered.

§ 2–717. Deduction of Damages From the Price.

The buyer on notifying the seller of his intention to do so may deduct all or any part of the damages resulting from any breach of the contract from any part of the price still due under the same contract.

§ 2–718. Liquidation or Limitation of Damages; Deposits.

(1) Damages for breach by either party may be liquidated in the agreement but only at an amount which is reasonable in the light of the anticipated or actual harm caused by the breach, the difficulties of proof of loss, and the inconvenience or nonfeasibility of otherwise obtaining an adequate remedy. A term fixing unreasonably large liquidated damages is void as a penalty.

(2) Where the seller justifiably withholds delivery of goods because of the buyer's breach, the buyer is entitled to restitution of any amount by which the sum of his payments exceeds

  (a) the amount to which the seller is entitled by virtue of terms liquidating the seller's damages in accordance with subsection (1), or

  (b) in the absence of such terms, twenty per cent of the value of the total performance for which the buyer is obligated under the contract or $500, whichever is smaller.

(3) The buyer's right to restitution under subsection (2) is subject to offset to the extent that the seller establishes

  (a) a right to recover damages under the provisions of this Article other than subsection (1), and

  (b) the amount or value of any benefits received by the buyer directly or indirectly by reason of the contract.

(4) Where a seller has received payment in goods their reasonable value or the proceeds of their resale shall be treated as payments for the purposes of subsection (2); but if the seller has notice of the buyer's breach before reselling goods received in part performance, his resale is subject to the conditions laid down in this Article on resale by an aggrieved seller (Section 2–706).

§ 2–719. Contractual Modification or Limitation of Remedy.

(1) Subject to the provisions of subsections (2) and (3) of this section and the preceding section on liquidation and limitation of damages,

  (a) the agreement may provide for remedies in addition to or in substitution for those provided in this Article and may limit or alter the measure of damages recoverable under this Article, as by limiting the buyer's remedies to return of the goods and repayment of the price or to repair and replacement of non-conforming goods or parts; and

  (b) resort to a remedy as provided is optional unless the remedy is expressly agreed to be exclusive, in which case it is the sole remedy.

(2) Where circumstances cause an exclusive or limited remedy to fail of its essential purpose, remedy may be had as provided in this Act.

(3) Consequential damages may be limited or excluded unless the limitation or exclusion is unconscionable. Limitation of consequential damages for injury to the person in the case of consumer goods is prima facie unconscionable but limitation of damages where the loss is commercial is not.

§ 2–720. Effect of "Cancellation" or "Rescission" on Claims for Antecedent Breach.

Unless the contrary intention clearly appears, expressions of "cancellation" or "rescission" of the contract or the like shall not be construed as a renunciation or discharge of any claim in damages for an antecedent breach.

§ 2–721. Remedies for Fraud.

Remedies for material misrepresentation or fraud include all remedies available under this Article for non-fraudulent breach. Neither rescission or a claim for rescission of the contract for sale nor rejection or return of the goods shall bar or be deemed inconsistent with a claim for damages or other remedy.

§ 2–722. Who Can Sue Third Parties for Injury to Goods.

Where a third party so deals with goods which have been identified to a contract for sale as to cause actionable injury to a party to that contract

(a) a right of action against the third party is in either party to the contract for sale who has title to or a security interest or a special property or an insurable interest in the goods; and if the goods have been destroyed or converted a right of action is also in the party who either bore the risk of loss under the contract for sale or has since the injury assumed that risk as against the other;

(b) if at the time of the injury the party plaintiff did not bear the risk of loss as against the other party to the contract for sale and there is no arrangement between them for disposition of the recovery, his suit or settlement is, subject to his own interest, as a fiduciary for the other party to the contract;

(c) either party may with the consent of the other sue for the benefit of whom it may concern.

§ 2–723. Proof of Market Price: Time and Place.

(1) If an action based on anticipatory repudiation comes to trial before the time for performance with respect to some or all of the goods, any damages based on market price (Section 2–708 or Section 2–713) shall be determined according to the price of such goods prevailing at the time when the aggrieved party learned of the repudiation.

(2) If evidence of a price prevailing at the times or places described in this Article is not readily available the price prevailing within any reasonable time before or after the time described or at any other place which in commercial judgment or under usage of trade would serve as a reasonable substitute for the one described may be used, making any proper allowance for the cost of transporting the goods to or from such other place.

(3) Evidence of a relevant price prevailing at a time or place other than the one described in this Article offered by one party is not admissible unless and until he has given the other party such notice as the court finds sufficient to prevent unfair surprise.

§ 2–724. Admissibility of Market Quotations.

Whenever the prevailing price or value of any goods regularly bought and sold in any established commodity market is in issue, reports in official publications or trade journals or in newspapers or periodicals of general circulation published as the reports of such market shall be admissible in evidence. The circumstances of the preparation of such a report may be shown to affect its weight but not its admissibility.

§ 2–725. Statute of Limitations in Contracts for Sale.

(1) An action for breach of any contract for sale must be commenced within four years after the cause of action has accrued. By the original agreement the parties may reduce the period of limitation to not less than one year but may not extend it.

(2) A cause of action accrues when the breach occurs, regardless of the aggrieved party's lack of knowledge of the breach. A breach of warranty occurs when tender of delivery is

made, except that where a warranty explicitly extends to future performance of the goods and discovery of the breach must await the time of such performance the cause of action accrues when the breach is or should have been discovered.

(3) Where an action commenced within the time limited by subsection (1) is so terminated as to leave available a remedy by another action for the same breach such other action may be commenced after the expiration of the time limited and within six months after the termination of the first action unless the termination resulted from voluntary discontinuance or from dismissal for failure or neglect to prosecute.

(4) This section does not alter the law on tolling of the statute of limitations nor does it apply to causes of action which have accrued before this Act becomes effective.

ARTICLE 3. Commercial Paper

PART 1
SHORT TITLE, FORM AND INTERPRETATION

§ **3–101. Short Title.**

This Article shall be known and may be cited as Uniform Commercial Code—Commercial Paper.

§ **3–102. Definitions and Index of Definitions.**

(1) In this Article unless the context otherwise requires
- (a) "Issue" means the first delivery of an instrument to a holder or a remitter.
- (b) An "order" is a direction to pay and must be more than an authorization or request. It must identify the person to pay with reasonable certainty. It may be addressed to one or more such persons jointly or in the alternative but not in succession.
- (c) A "promise" is an undertaking to pay and must be more than an acknowledgment of an obligation.
- (d) "Secondary party" means a drawer or endorser.
- (e) "Instrument" means a negotiable instrument.

(2) Other definitions applying to this Article and the sections in which they appear are:
"Acceptance." Section 3–410.
"Accommodation party." Section 3–415.
"Alteration." Section 3–407.
"Certificate of deposit." Section 3–104.
"Certification." Section 3–411.
"Check." Section 3–104.
"Definite time." Section 3–109.
"Dishonor." Section 3–507.
"Draft." Section 3–104.
"Holder in due course." Section 3–302.
"Negotiation." Section 3–202.
"Note." Section 3–104.
"Notice of dishonor." Section 3–508.
"On demand." Section 3–108.
"Presentment." Section 3–504.
"Protest." Section 3–509.
"Restrictive Indorsement." Section 3–205.
"Signature." Section 3–401.

(3) The following definitions in other Articles apply to this Article:
"Account." Section 4–104.
"Banking Day." Section 4–104.
"Clearing house." Section 4–104.

"Collecting bank." Section 4–105.
"Customer." Section 4–104.
"Depositary Bank." Section 4–105.
"Documentary Draft." Section 4–104.
"Intermediary Bank." Section 4–105.
"Item." Section 4–104.
"Midnight deadline." Section 4–104.
"Payor bank." Section 4–105.

(4) In addition Article 1 contains general definitions and principles of construction and interpretation applicable throughout this Article.

§ 3–103. Limitations on Scope of Article.

(1) This Article does not apply to money, documents of title or investment securities.

(2) The provisions of this Article are subject to the provisions of the Article on Bank Deposits and Collections (Article 4) and Secured Transactions (Article 9).

§ 3–104. Form of Negotiable Instruments; "Draft"; "Check"; "Certificate of Deposit"; "Note."

(1) Any writing to be a negotiable instrument within this Article must
  (a) be signed by the maker or drawer; and
  (b) contain an unconditional promise or order to pay a sum certain in money and no other promise, order, obligation or power given by the maker or drawer except as authorized by this Article; and
  (c) be payable on demand or at a definite time; and
  (d) be payable to order or to bearer.

(2) A writing which complies with the requirements of this section is
  (a) a "draft" ("bill of exchange") if it is an order;
  (b) a "check" if it is a draft drawn on a bank and payable on demand;
  (c) a "certificate of deposit" if it is an acknowledgment by a bank of receipt of money with an engagement to repay it;
  (d) a "note" if it is a promise other than a certificate of deposit.

(3) As used in other Articles of this Act, and as the context may require, the terms "draft," "check," "certificate of deposit" and "note" may refer to instruments which are not negotiable within this Article as well as to instruments which are so negotiable.

§ 3–105. When Promise or Order Unconditional.

(1) A promise or order otherwise unconditional is not made conditional by the fact that the instrument
  (a) is subject to implied or constructive conditions; or
  (b) states its consideration, whether performed or promised, or the transaction which gave rise to the instrument, or that the promise or order is made or the instrument matures in accordance with or "as per" such transaction; or
  (c) refers to or states that it arises out of a separate agreement or refers to a separate agreement for rights as to prepayment or acceleration; or
  (d) states that it is drawn under a letter of credit; or
  (e) states that it is secured, whether by mortgage, reservation of title or otherwise; or
  (f) indicates a particular account to be debited or any other fund or source from which reimbursement is expected; or
  (g) is limited to payment out of a particular fund or the proceeds of a particular source, if the instrument is issued by a government or governmental agency or unit; or
  (h) is limited to payment out of the entire assets of a partnership, unincorporated association, trust or estate by or on behalf of which the instrument is issued.

(2) A promise or order is not unconditional if the instrument
  (a) states that it is subject to or governed by any other agreement; or
  (b) states that it is to be paid only out of a particular fund or source except as provided in this section.

§ 3–106. Sum Certain.

(1) The sum payable is a sum certain even though it is to be paid

    (a) with stated interest or by stated installments; or

    (b) with stated different rates of interest before and after default or a specified date; or

    (c) with a stated discount or addition if paid before or after the date fixed for payment; or

    (d) with exchange or less exchange, whether at a fixed rate or at the current rate; or

    (e) with costs of collection or an attorney's fee or both upon default.

(2) Nothing in this section shall validate any term which is otherwise illegal.

§ 3–107. Money.

(1) An instrument is payable in money if the medium of exchange in which it is payable is money at the time the instrument is made. An instrument payable in "currency" or "current funds" is payable in money.

(2) A promise or order to pay a sum stated in a foreign currency is for a sum certain in money and, unless a different medium of payment is specified in the instrument, may be satisfied by payment of that number of dollars which the stated foreign currency will purchase at the buying sight rate for that currency on the day on which the instrument is payable or, if payable on demand, on the day of demand. If such an instrument specifies a foreign currency as the medium of payment the instrument is payable in that currency.

§ 3–108. Payable on Demand.

Instruments payable on demand include those payable at sight or on presentation and those in which no time for payment is stated.

§ 3–109. Definite Time.

(1) An instrument is payable at a definite time if by its terms it is payable

    (a) on or before a stated date or at a fixed period after a stated date; or

    (b) at a fixed period after sight; or

    (c) at a definite time subject to any acceleration; or

    (d) at a definite time subject to extension at the option of the holder, or to extension to a further definite time at the option of the maker or acceptor or automatically upon or after a specified act or event.

(2) An instrument which by its terms is otherwise payable only upon an act or event uncertain as to time of occurrence is not payable at a definite time even though the act or event has occurred.

§ 3–110. Payable to Order.

(1) An instrument is payable to order when by its terms it is payable to the order or assigns of any person therein specified with reasonable certainty, or to him or his order, or when it is conspicuously designated on its face as "exchange" or the like and names a payee. It may be payable to the order of

    (a) the maker or drawer; or

    (b) the drawee; or

    (c) a payee who is not maker, drawer or drawee; or

    (d) two or more payees together or in the alternative; or

    (e) an estate, trust or fund, in which case it is payable to the order of the representative of such estate, trust or fund or his successors; or

    (f) an office, or an officer by his title as such in which case it is payable to the principal but the incumbent of the office or his successors may act as if he or they were the holder; or

    (g) a partnership or unincorporated association, in which case it is payable to the partnership or association and may be indorsed or transferred by any person thereto authorized.

(2) An instrument not payable to order is not made so payable by such words as "payable upon return of this instrument properly indorsed."

(3) An instrument made payable both to order and to bearer is payable to order unless the bearer words are handwritten or typewritten.

§ 3–111. Payable to Bearer.

An instrument is payable to bearer when by its terms it is payable to
- (a) bearer or the order of bearer; or
- (b) a specified person or bearer; or
- (c) "cash" or the order of "cash," or any other indication which does not purport to designate a specific payee.

§ 3–112. Terms and Omissions Not Affecting Negotiability.

(1) The negotiability of an instrument is not affected by
- (a) the omission of a statement of any consideration or of the place where the instrument is drawn or payable; or
- (b) a statement that collateral has been given to secure obligations either on the instrument or otherwise of an obligor on the instrument or that in case of default on those obligations the holder may realize on or dispose of the collateral; or
- (c) a promise or power to maintain or protect collateral or to give additional collateral; or
- (d) a term authorizing a confession of judgment on the instrument if it is not paid when due; or
- (e) a term purporting to waive the benefit of any law intended for the advantage or protection of any obligor; or
- (f) a term in a draft providing that the payee by indorsing or cashing it acknowledges full satisfaction of an obligation of the drawer; or
- (g) a statement in a draft drawn in a set of parts (Section 3–801) to the effect that the order is effective only if no other part has been honored.

(2) Nothing in this section shall validate any term which is otherwise illegal.

§ 3–113. Seal.

An instrument otherwise negotiable is within this Article even though it is under a seal.

§ 3–114. Date, Antedating, Postdating.

(1) The negotiability of an instrument is not affected by the fact that it is undated, antedated or postdated.

(2) Where an instrument is antedated or postdated the time when it is payable is determined by the stated date if the instrument is payable on demand or at a fixed period after date.

(3) Where the instrument or any signature thereon is dated, the date is presumed to be correct.

§ 3–115. Incomplete Instruments.

(1) When a paper whose contents at the time of signing show that it is intended to become an instrument is signed while still incomplete in any necessary respect it cannot be enforced until completed, but when it is completed in accordance with authority given it is effective as completed.

(2) If the completion is unauthorized the rules as to material alteration apply (Section 3–407), even though the paper was not delivered by the maker or drawer; but the burden of establishing that any completion is unauthorized is on the party so asserting.

§ 3–116. Instruments Payable to Two or More Persons.

An instrument payable to the order of two or more persons
- (a) if in the alternative is payable to any one of them and may be negotiated, discharged or enforced by any of them who has possession of it;

(b) if not in the alternative is payable to all of them and may be negotiated, discharged or enforced only by all of them.

§ 3–117. Instruments Payable With Words of Description.

An instrument made payable to a named person with the addition of words describing him
- (a) as agent or officer of a specified person is payable to his principal but the agent or officer may act as if he were the holder;
- (b) as any other fiduciary for a specified person or purpose is payable to the payee and may be negotiated, discharged or enforced by him;
- (a) in any other manner is payable to the payee unconditionally and the additional words are without effect on subsequent parties.

§ 3–118. Ambiguous Terms and Rules of Construction.

The following rules apply to every instrument:
- (a) Where there is doubt whether the instrument is a draft or a note the holder may treat it as either. A draft drawn on the drawer is effective as a note.
- (b) Handwritten terms control typewritten and printed terms, and typewritten control printed.
- (c) Words control figures except that if the words are ambiguous figures control.
- (d) Unless otherwise specified a provision for interest means interest at the judgment rate at the place of payment from the date of the instrument, or if it is undated from the date of issue.
- (e) Unless the instrument otherwise specifies two or more persons who sign as maker, acceptor or drawer or indorser and as a part of the same transaction are jointly and severally liable even though the instrument contains such words as "I promise to pay."
- (f) Unless otherwise specified consent to extension authorizes a single extension for not longer than the original period. A consent to extension, expressed in the instrument, is binding on secondary parties and accommodation makers. A holder may not exercise his option to extend an instrument over the objection of a maker or acceptor or other party who in accordance with Section 3–604 tenders full payment when the instrument is due.

§ 3–119. Other Writings Affecting Instrument.

(1) As between the obligor and his immediate obligee or any transferee the terms of an instrument may be modified or affected by any other written agreement executed as a part of the same transaction, except that a holder in due course is not affected by any limitation of his rights arising out of the separate written agreement if he had no notice of the limitation when he took the instrument.

(2) A separate agreement does not affect the negotiability of an instrument.

§ 3–120. Instruments "Payable Through" Bank.

An instrument which states that it is "payable through" a bank or the like designates that bank as a collecting bank to make presentment but does not of itself authorize the bank to pay the instrument.

§ 3–121. Instruments Payable at Bank.

Note: *If this Act is introduced in the Congress of the United States this section should be omitted. (States to select either alternative)*

Alternative A—A note or acceptance which states that it is payable at a bank is the equivalent of a draft drawn on the bank payable when it falls due out of any funds of the maker or acceptor in current account or otherwise available for such payment.

Alternative B—A note or acceptance which states that it is payable at a bank is not of itself an order or authorization to the bank to pay it.

§ 3–122. Accrual of Cause of Action.

(1) A cause of action against a maker or an acceptor accrues

(a) in the case of a time instrument on the day after maturity;

(b) in the case of a demand instrument upon its date or, if no date is stated, on the date of issue.

(2) A cause of action against the obligor of a demand or time certificate of deposit accrues upon demand, but demand on a time certificate may not be made until on or after the date of maturity.

(3) A cause of action against a drawer of a draft or an indorser of any instrument accrues upon demand following dishonor of the instrument. Notice of dishonor is a demand.

(4) Unless an instrument provides otherwise, interest runs at the rate provided by law for a judgment

(a) in the case of a maker, acceptor or other primary obligor of a demand instrument, from the date of demand;

(b) in all other cases from the date of accrual of the cause of action.

PART 2
TRANSFER AND NEGOTIATION

§ 3–201. Transfer: Right to Indorsement.

(1) Transfer of an instrument vests in the transferee such rights as the transferor has therein, except that a transferee who has himself been a party to any fraud or illegality affecting the instrument or who as a prior holder had notice of a defense or claim against it cannot improve his position by taking from a later holder in due course.

(2) A transfer of a security interest in an instrument vests the foregoing rights in the transferee to the extent of the interest transferred.

(3) Unless otherwise agreed any transfer for value of an instrument not then payable to bearer gives the transferee the specifically enforceable right to have the unqualified indorsement of the transferor. Negotiation takes effect only when the indorsement is made and until that time there is no presumption that the transferee is the owner.

§ 3–202. Negotiation.

(1) Negotiation is the transfer of an instrument in such form that the transferee becomes a holder. If the instrument is payable to order it is negotiated by delivery with any necessary indorsement; if payable to bearer it is negotiated by delivery.

(2) An indorsement must be written by or on behalf of the holder and on the instrument or on a paper so firmly affixed thereto as to become a part thereof.

(3) An indorsement is effective for negotiation only when it conveys the entire instrument or any unpaid residue. If it purports to be of less it operates only as a partial assignment.

(4) Words of assignment, condition, waiver, guaranty, limitation or disclaimer of liability and the like accompanying an indorsement do not affect its character as an indorsement.

§ 3–203. Wrong or Misspelled Name.

Where an instrument is made payable to a person under a misspelled name or one other than his own he may indorse in that name or his own or both but signature in both names may be required by a person paying or giving value for the instrument.

§ 3–204. Special Indorsement; Blank Indorsement.

(1) A special indorsement specifies the person to whom or to whose order it makes the instrument payable. Any instrument specially indorsed becomes payable to the order of the special indorsee and may be further negotiated only by his indorsement.

(2) An indorsement in blank specifies no particular indorsee and may consist of a mere signature. An instrument payable to order and indorsed in blank becomes payable to bearer and may be negotiated by delivery alone until specially indorsed.

(3) The holder may convert a blank indorsement into a special indorsement by writing over the signature of the indorser in blank any contract consistent with the character of the indorsement.

§ 3–205. Restrictive Indorsements.

An indorsement is restrictive which either
  (a) is conditional; or
  (b) purports to prohibit further transfer of the instrument; or
  (c) includes the words "for collection," "for deposit," "pay any bank," or like terms signifying a purpose of deposit or collection; or
  (d) otherwise states that it is for the benefit or use of the indorser or of another person.

§ 3–206. Effect of Restrictive Indorsement.

(1) No restrictive indorsement prevents further transfer or negotiation of the instrument.

(2) An intermediary bank, or a payor bank which is not the depositary bank, is neither given notice nor otherwise affected by a restrictive indorsement of any person except the bank's immediate transferor or the person presenting for payment.

(3) Except for an intermediary bank, any transferee under an indorsement which is conditional or includes the words "for collection," "for deposit," "pay any bank," or like terms (subparagraphs (a) and (c) of Section 3–205) must pay or apply any value given by him for or on the security of the instrument consistently with the indorsement and to the extent that he does so he becomes a holder for value. In addition such transferee is a holder in due course if he otherwise complies with the requirements of Section 3–302 on what constitutes a holder in due course.

(4) The first taker under an indorsement for the benefit of the indorser or another person (subparagraph (d) of Section 3–205) must pay or apply any value given by him for or on the security of the instrument consistently with the indorsement and to the extent that he does so he becomes a holder for value. In addition such taker is a holder in due course if he otherwise complies with the requirements of Section 3–302 on what constitutes a holder in due course. A later holder for value is neither given notice nor otherwise affected by such restrictive indorsement unless he has knowledge that a fiduciary or other person has negotiated the instrument in any transaction for his own benefit or otherwise in breach of duty (subsection (2) of Section 3–304).

§ 3–207. Negotiation Effective Although It May Be Rescinded.

(1) Negotiation is effective to transfer the instrument although the negotiation is
  (a) made by an infant, a corporation exceeding its powers, or any other person without capacity; or
  (b) obtained by fraud, duress or mistake of any kind; or
  (c) part of an illegal transaction; or
  (d) made in breach of duty.

(2) Except as against a subsequent holder in due course such negotiation is in an appropriate case subject to rescission, the declaration of a constructive trust or any other remedy permitted by law.

§ 3–208. Reacquisition.

Where an instrument is returned to or reacquired by a prior party he may cancel any indorsement which is not necessary to his title and reissue or further negotiate the instrument, but any intervening party is discharged as against the reacquiring party and subsequent holders not in due course and if his indorsement has been cancelled is discharged as against subsequent holders in due course as well.

PART 3

RIGHTS OF A HOLDER

§ 3–301. Rights of a Holder.

The holder of an instrument whether or not he is the owner may transfer or negotiate it and, except as otherwise provided in Section 3–603 on payment or satisfaction, discharge it or enforce payment in his own name.

§ 3–302. Holder in Due Course.

(1) A holder in due course is a holder who takes the instrument
    (a) for value; and
    (b) in good faith; and
    (c) without notice that it is overdue or has been dishonored or of any defense against or claim to it on the part of any person.
(2) A payee may be a holder in due course.
(3) A holder does not become a holder in due course of an instrument:
    (a) by purchase of it at judicial sale or by taking it under legal process; or
    (b) by acquiring it in taking over an estate; or
    (c) by purchasing it as part of a bulk transaction not in regular course of business of the transferor.
(4) A purchaser of a limited interest can be a holder in due course only to the extent of the interest purchased.

§ 3–303. Taking for Value.

A holder takes the instrument for value
    (a) to the extent that the agreed consideration has been performed or that he acquires a security interest in or a lien on the instrument otherwise than by legal process; or
    (b) when he takes the instrument in payment of or as security for an antecedent claim against any person whether or not the claim is due; or
    (c) when he gives a negotiable instrument for it or makes an irrevocable commitment to a third person.

§ 3–304. Notice to Purchaser.

(1) The purchaser has notice of a claim or defense if
    (a) the instrument is so incomplete, bears such visible evidence of forgery or alteration, or is otherwise so irregular as to call into question its validity, terms of ownership or to create an ambiguity as to the party to pay; or
    (b) the purchaser has notice that the obligation of any party is voidable in whole or in part, or that all parties have been discharged.
(2) The purchaser has notice of a claim against the instrument when he has knowledge that a fiduciary has negotiated the instrument in payment of or as security for his own debt or in any transaction for his own benefit or otherwise in breach of duty.
(3) The purchaser has notice that an instrument is overdue if he has reason to know
    (a) that any part of the principal amount is overdue or that there is an uncured default in payment of another instrument of the same series; or
    (b) that acceleration of the instrument has been made; or
    (c) that he is taking a demand instrument after demand has been made or more than a reasonable length of time after its issue. A reasonable time for a check drawn and payable within the states and territories of the United States and the District of Columbia is presumed to be thirty days.
(4) Knowledge of the following facts does not of itself give the purchaser notice of a defense or claim
    (a) that the instrument is antedated or postdated;
    (b) that it was issued or negotiated in return for an executory promise or accompanied by a separate agreement, unless the purchaser has notice that a defense or claim has arisen from the terms thereof;
    (c) that any party has signed for accommodation;
    (d) that an incomplete instrument has been completed, unless the purchaser has notice of any improper completion;
    (e) that any person negotiating the instrument is or was a fiduciary;

(f) that there has been default in payment of interest on the instrument or in payment of any other instrument, except one of the same series.

(5) The filing or recording of a document does not of itself constitute notice within the provisions of this Article to a person who would otherwise be a holder in due course.

(6) To be effective notice must be received at such time and in such manner as to give a reasonable opportunity to act on it.

§ 3–305. Rights of a Holder in Due Course.

To the extent that a holder is a holder in due course he takes the instrument free from
(1) all claims to it on the part of any person; and
(2) all defenses of any party to the instrument with whom the holder has not dealt except
  (a) infancy, to the extent that it is a defense to a simple contract; and
  (b) such other incapacity, or duress, or illegality of the transaction, as renders the obligation of the party a nullity; and
  (c) such misrepresentation as has induced the party to sign the instrument with neither knowledge nor reasonable opportunity to obtain knowledge of its character or its essential terms; and
  (d) discharge in insolvency proceedings; and
  (e) any other discharge of which the holder has notice when he takes the instrument.

§ 3–306. Rights of One Not Holder in Due Course.

Unless he has the rights of a holder in due course any person takes the instrument subject to
  (a) all valid claims to it on the part of any person; and
  (b) all defenses of any party which would be available in an action on a simple contract; and
  (c) the defenses of want or failure of consideration, nonperformance of any condition precedent, non-delivery, or delivery for a special purpose (Section 3–408); and
  (d) the defense that he or a person through whom he holds the instrument acquired it by theft, or that payment or satisfaction to such holder would be inconsistent with the terms of a restrictive indorsement. The claim of any third person to the instrument is not otherwise available as a defense to any party liable thereon unless the third person himself defends the action for such party.

§ 3–307. Burden of Establishing Signatures, Defenses and Due Course.

(1) Unless specifically denied in the pleadings each signature on an instrument is admitted. When the effectiveness of a signature is put in issue
  (a) the burden of establishing it is on the party claiming under the signature; but
  (b) the signature is presumed to be genuine or authorized except where the action is to enforce the obligation of a purported signer who has died or become incompetent before proof is required.

(2) When signatures are admitted or established, production of the instrument entitles a holder to recover on it unless the defendant establishes a defense.

(3) After it is shown that a defense exists a person claiming the rights of a holder in due course has the burden of establishing that he or some person under whom he claims is in all respects a holder in due course.

PART 4

LIABILITY OF PARTIES

§ 3–401. Signature.

(1) No person is liable on an instrument unless his signature appears thereon.

(2) A signature is made by use of any name, including any trade or assumed name, upon an instrument, or by any word or mark used in lieu of a written signature.

§ 3–402. Signature in Ambiguous Capacity.

Unless the instrument clearly indicates that a signature is made in some other capacity it is an indorsement.

§ 3–403. Signature by Authorized Representative.

(1) A signature may be made by an agent or other representative, and his authority to make it may be established as in other cases of representation. No particular form of appointment is necessary to establish such authority.

(2) An authorized representative who signs his own name to an instrument

(a) is personally obligated if the instrument neither names the person represented nor shows that the representative signed in a representative capacity;

(b) except as otherwise established between the immediate parties, is personally obligated if the instrument names the person represented but does not show that the representative signed in a representative capacity, or if the instrument does not name the person represented but does show that the representative signed in a representative capacity.

(3) Except as otherwise established the name of an organization preceded or followed by the name and office of an authorized individual is a signature made in a representative capacity.

§ 3–404. Unauthorized Signatures.

(1) Any unauthorized signature is wholly inoperative as that of the person whose name is signed unless he ratifies it or is precluded from denying it but it operates as the signature of the unauthorized signer in favor of any person who in good faith pays the instrument or takes it for value.

(2) Any unauthorized signature may be ratified for all purposes of this Article. Such ratification does not of itself affect any rights of the person ratifying against the actual signer.

§ 3–405. Imposters; Signature in Name of Payee.

(1) An indorsement by any person in the name of a named payee is effective if

(a) an imposter by use of the mails or otherwise has induced the maker or drawer to issue the instrument to him or his confederate in the name of the payee; or

(b) a person signing as or on behalf of a maker or drawer intends the payee to have no interest in the instrument; or

(c) an agent or employee of the maker or drawer has supplied him with the name of the payee intending the latter to have no such interest.

(2) Nothing in this section shall affect the criminal or civil liability of the person so indorsing.

§ 3–406. Negligence Contributing to Alteration or Unauthorized Signature.

Any person who by his negligence substantially contributes to a material alteration of the instrument or to the making of an unauthorized signature is precluded from asserting the alteration or lack of authority against a holder in due course or against a drawee or other payor who pays the instrument in good faith and in accordance with the reasonable commercial standards of the drawee's or payor's business.

§ 3–407. Alteration.

(1) Any alteration of an instrument is material which changes the contract of any party thereto in any respect, including any such change in

(a) the number or relations of the parties; or

(b) an incomplete instrument, by completing it otherwise than as authorized; or

(c) the writing as signed, by adding to it or by removing any part of it.

(2) As against any person other than a subsequent holder in due course

(a) alteration by the holder which is both fraudulent and material discharges any party whose contract is thereby changed unless that party assents or is precluded from asserting the defense;

(b) no other alteration discharges any party and the instrument may be enforced according to its original tenor, or as to incomplete instruments according to the authority given.

(3) A subsequent holder in due course may in all cases enforce the instrument according to its original tenor, and when an incomplete instrument has been completed, he may enforce it as completed.

§ 3–408. Consideration.

Want or failure of consideration is a defense as against any person not having the rights of a holder in due course (Section 3–305), except that no consideration is necessary for an instrument or obligation thereon given in payment of or as security for an antecedent obligation of any kind. Nothing in this section shall be taken to displace any statute outside this Act under which a promise is enforceable notwithstanding lack or failure of consideration. Partial failure of consideration is a defense pro tanto whether or not the failure is in an ascertained or liquidated amount.

§ 3–409. Draft Not an Assignment.

(1) A check or other draft does not of itself operate as an assignment of any funds in the hands of the drawee available for its payment, and the drawee is not liable on the instrument until he accepts it.

(2) Nothing in this section shall affect any liability in contract, tort or otherwise arising from any letter of credit or other obligation or representation which is not an acceptance.

§ 3–410. Definition and Operation of Acceptance.

(1) Acceptance is the drawee's signed engagement to honor the draft as presented. It must be written on the draft, and may consist of his signature alone. It becomes operative when completed by delivery or notification.

(2) A draft may be accepted although it has not been signed by the drawer or is otherwise incomplete or is overdue or has been dishonored.

(3) Where the draft is payable at a fixed period after sight and the acceptor fails to date his acceptance the holder may complete it by supplying a date in good faith.

§ 3–411. Certification of a Check.

(1) Certification of a check is acceptance. Where a holder procures certification the drawer and all prior indorsers are discharged.

(2) Unless otherwise agreed a bank has no obligation to certify a check.

(3) A bank may certify a check before returning it for lack of proper indorsement. If it does so the drawer is discharged.

§ 3–412. Acceptance Varying Draft.

(1) Where the drawee's proffered acceptance in any manner varies the draft as presented the holder may refuse the acceptance and treat the draft as dishonored in which case the drawee is entitled to have his acceptance cancelled.

(2) The terms of the draft are not varied by an acceptance to pay at any particular bank or place in the United States, unless the acceptance states that the draft is to be paid only at such bank or place.

(3) Where the holder assents to an acceptance varying the terms of the draft each drawer and indorser who does not affirmatively assent is discharged.

§ 3–413. Contract of Maker, Drawer and Acceptor.

(1) The maker or acceptor engages that he will pay the instrument according to its tenor at the time of his engagement or as completed pursuant to Section 3–115 on incomplete instruments.

(2) The drawer engages that upon dishonor of the draft and any necessary notice of dishonor or protest he will pay the amount of the draft to the holder or to any indorser who takes it up. The drawer may disclaim this liability by drawing without recourse.

(3) By making, drawing or accepting the party admits as against all subsequent parties including the drawee the existence of the payee and his then capacity to indorse.

§ 3–414. Contract of Indorser; Order of Liability.

(1) Unless the indorsement otherwise specifies (as by such words as "without recourse") every indorser engages that upon dishonor and any necessary notice of dishonor and protest he will pay the instrument according to its tenor at the time of his indorsement to the holder or to any subsequent indorser who takes it up, even though the indorser who takes it up was not obligated to do so.

(2) Unless they otherwise agree indorsers are liable to one another in the order in which they indorse, which is presumed to be the order in which their signatures appear on the instrument.

§ 3–415. Contract of Accommodation Party.

(1) An accommodation party is one who signs the instrument in any capacity for the purpose of lending his name to another party to it.

(2) When the instrument has been taken for value before it is due the accommodation party is liable in the capacity in which he has signed even though the taker knows of the accommodation.

(3) As against a holder in due course and without notice of the accommodation oral proof of the accommodation is not admissible to give the accommodation party the benefit of discharges dependent on his character as such. In other cases the accommodation character may be shown by oral proof.

(4) An indorsement which shows that it is not in the chain of title is notice of its accommodation character.

(5) An accommodation party is not liable to the party accommodated, and if he pays the instrument has a right of recourse on the instrument against such party.

§ 3–416. Contract of Guarantor.

(1) "Payment guaranteed" or equivalent words added to a signature mean that the signer engages that if the instrument is not paid when due he will pay it according to its tenor without resort by the holder to any other party.

(2) "Collection guaranteed" or equivalent words added to a signature mean that the signer engages that if the instrument is not paid when due he will pay it according to its tenor, but only after the holder has reduced his claim against the maker or acceptor to judgment and execution has been returned unsatisfied, or after the maker or acceptor has become insolvent or it is otherwise apparent that it is useless to proceed against him.

(3) Words of guaranty which do not otherwise specify guarantee payment.

(4) No words of guaranty added to the signature of a sole maker or acceptor affect his liability on the instrument. Such words added to the signature of one of two or more makers or acceptors create a presumption that the signature is for the accommodation of the others.

(5) When words of guaranty are used presentment, notice of dishonor and protest are not necessary to charge the user.

(6) Any guaranty written on the instrument is enforcible not withstanding any statute of frauds.

§ 3–417. Warranties on Presentment and Transfer.

(1) Any person who obtains payment or acceptance and any prior transferor warrants to a person who in good faith pays or accepts that
      (a) he has a good title to the instrument or is authorized to obtain payment or acceptance on behalf of one who has a good title; and
      (b) he has no knowledge that the signature of the maker or drawer is unauthorized,

except that this warranty is not given by a holder in due course acting in good faith

    (i) to a maker with respect to the maker's own signature; or

    (ii) to a drawer with respect to the drawer's own signature, whether or not the drawer is also the drawee; or

    (iii) to an acceptor of a draft if the holder in due course took the draft after the acceptance or obtained the acceptance without knowledge that the drawer's signature was unauthorized; and

(c) the instrument has not been materially altered, except that this warranty is not given by a holder in due course acting in good faith

    (i) to the maker of a note or

    (ii) to the drawer of a draft whether or not the drawer is also the drawee or

    (iii) to the acceptor of a draft with respect to an alteration made prior to the acceptance if the holder in due course took the draft after the acceptance, even though the acceptance provided "payable as originally drawn" or equivalent terms; or

    (iv) to the acceptor of a draft with respect to an alteration made after the acceptance.

(2) Any person who transfers an instrument and receives consideration warrants to his transferee and if the transfer is by indorsement to any subsequent holder who takes the instrument in good faith that

(a) he has a good title to the instrument or is authorized to obtain payment or acceptance on behalf of one who has a good title and the transfer is otherwise rightful; and

(b) all signatures are genuine or authorized; and

(c) the instrument has not been materially altered; and

(d) no defense of any party is good against him; and

(e) he has no knowledge of any insolvency proceeding instituted with respect to the maker or acceptor or the drawer of an unaccepted instrument.

(3) By transferring "without recourse" the transferor limits the obligation stated in subsection (2) (d) to a warranty that he has no knowledge of such a defense.

(4) A selling agent or broker who does not disclose the fact that he is acting only as such gives the warranties provided in this section, but if he makes such disclosure warrants only his good faith and authority.

§ 3–418. Finality of Payment or Acceptance.

Except for recovery of bank payments as provided in the Article on Bank Deposits and Collections (Article 4) and except for liability for breach of warranty on presentment under the preceding section, payment or acceptance of any instrument is final in favor of a holder in due course, or a person who has in good faith changed his position in reliance on the payment.

§ 3–419. Conversion of Instrument; Innocent Representative.

(1) An instrument is converted when

(a) a drawee to whom it is delivered for acceptance refuses to return it on demand or

(b) any person to whom it is delivered for payment refuses on demand either to pay or to return it; or

(c) it is paid on a forged indorsement.

(2) In an action against a drawee under subsection (1) the measure of the drawee's liability is the face amount of the instrument. In any other action under subsection (1) the measure of liability is presumed to be the face amount of the instrument.

(3) Subject to the provisions of this Act concerning restrictive indorsements a representative, including a depositary or collecting bank, who has in good faith and in accordance with the reasonable commercial standards applicable to the business of such representative dealt with an instrument or its proceeds on behalf of one who was not the true owner is not liable in conversion or otherwise to the true owner beyond the amount of any proceeds remaining in his hands.

(4) An intermediary bank or payor bank which is not a depositary bank is not liable in conversion solely by reason of the fact that proceeds of an item indorsed restrictively (Sections 3–205 and 3–206) are not paid or applied consistently with the restrictive indorsement of an indorser other than its immediate transferor.

PART 5

PRESENTMENT, NOTICE OF DISHONOR AND PROTEST

§ 3–501. When Presentment, Notice of Dishonor, and Protest Necessary or Permissible.

(1) Unless excused (Section 3–511) presentment is necessary to charge secondary parties as follows:

- (a) presentment for acceptance is necessary to charge the drawer and indorsers of a draft where the draft so provides, or is payable elsewhere than at the residence or place of business of the drawee, or its date of payment depends upon such presentment. The holder may at his option present for acceptance any other draft payable at a stated date;
- (b) presentment for payment is necessary to charge any indorser;
- (c) in the case of any drawer, the acceptor of a draft payable at a bank or the maker of a note payable at a bank, presentment for payment is necessary, but failure to make presentment discharges such drawer, acceptor or maker only as stated in Section 3–502(1) (b).

(2) Unless excused (Section 3–511)

- (a) notice of any dishonor is necessary to charge any indorser;
- (b) in the case of any drawer, the acceptor of a draft payable at a bank or the maker of a note payable at a bank, notice of any dishonor is necessary, but failure to give such notice discharges such drawer, acceptor or maker only as stated in Section 3–502(1) (b).

(3) Unless excused (Section 3–511) protest of any dishonor is necessary to charge the drawer and indorsers of any draft which on its face appears to be drawn or payable outside of the states and territories of the United States and the District of Columbia. The holder may at his option make protest of any dishonor of any other instrument and in the case of a foreign draft may on insolvency of the acceptor before maturity make protest for better security.

(4) Notwithstanding any provision of this section, neither presentment nor notice of dishonor nor protest is necessary to charge an indorser who has indorsed an instrument after maturity.

§ 3–502. Unexcused Delay; Discharge.

(1) Where without excuse any necessary presentment or notice of dishonor is delayed beyond the time when it is due

- (a) any indorser is discharged; and
- (b) any drawer or the acceptor of a draft payable at a bank or the maker of a note payable at a bank who because the drawee or payor bank becomes insolvent during the delay is deprived of funds maintained with the drawee or payor bank to cover the instrument may discharge his liability by written assignment to the holder of his rights against the drawee or payor bank in respect of such funds, but such drawer, acceptor or maker is not otherwise discharged.

(2) Where without excuse a necessary protest is delayed beyond the time when it is due any drawer or indorser is discharged.

§ 3–503. Time of Presentment.

(1) Unless a different time is expressed in the instrument the time for any presentment is determined as follows:

- (a) where an instrument is payable at or a fixed period after a stated date any presentment for acceptance must be made on or before the date it is payable;

(b) where an instrument is payable after sight it must either be presented for acceptance or negotiated within a reasonable time after date or issue whichever is later;

(c) where an instrument shows the date on which it is payable presentment for payment is due on that date;

(d) where an instrument is accelerated presentment for payment is due within a reasonable time after the acceleration;

(e) with respect to the liability of any secondary party presentment for acceptance or payment of any other instrument is due within a reasonable time after such party becomes liable thereon.

(2) A reasonable time for presentment is determined by the nature of the instrument, any usage of banking or trade and the facts of the particular case. In the case of an uncertified check which is drawn and payable within the United States and which is not a draft drawn by a bank the following are presumed to be reasonable periods within which to present for payment or to initiate bank collection:

(a) with respect to the liability of the drawer, thirty days after date or issue whichever is later; and

(b) with respect to the liability of an indorser, seven days after his indorsement.

(3) Where any presentment is due on a day which is not a full business day for either the person making presentment or the party to pay or accept, presentment is due on the next following day which is a full business day for both parties.

(4) Presentment to be sufficient must be made at a reasonable hour, and if at a bank during its banking day.

§ 3–504. How Presentment Made.

(1) Presentment is a demand for acceptance or payment made upon the maker, acceptor, drawee or other payor by or on behalf of the holder.

(2) Presentment may be made

(a) by mail, in which event the time of presentment is determined by the time of receipt of the mail; or

(b) through a clearing house; or

(c) at the place of acceptance or payment specified in the instrument or if there be none at the place of business or residence of the party to accept or pay. If neither the party to accept or pay nor anyone authorized to act for him is present or accessible at such place presentment is excused.

(3) It may be made

(a) to any one of two or more makers, acceptors, drawees or other payors; or

(b) to any person who has authority to make or refuse the acceptance or payment.

(4) A draft accepted or a note made payable at a bank in the United States must be presented at such bank.

(5) In the cases described in Section 4–210 presentment may be made in the manner and with the result stated in that section.

§ 3–505. Rights of Party to Whom Presentment Is Made.

(1) The party to whom presentment is made may without dishonor require

(a) exhibition of the instrument; and

(b) reasonable identification of the person making presentment and evidence of his authority to make it if made for another; and

(c) that the instrument be produced for acceptance or payment at a place specified in it, or if there be none at any place reasonable in the circumstances; and

(d) a signed receipt on the instrument for any partial or full payment and its surrender upon full payment.

(2) Failure to comply with any such requirement invalidates the presentment but the person presenting has a reasonable time in which to comply and the time for acceptance or payment runs from the time of compliance.

§ 3–506. Time Allowed for Acceptance or Payment.

(1) Acceptance may be deferred without dishonor until the close of the next business day following presentment. The holder may also in a good faith effort to obtain acceptance and without either dishonor of the instrument or discharge of secondary parties allow postponement of acceptance for an additional business day.

(2) Except as a longer time is allowed in the case of documentary drafts drawn under a letter of credit, and unless an earlier time is agreed to by the party to pay, payment of an instrument may be deferred without dishonor pending reasonable examination to determine whether it is properly payable, but payment must be made in any event before the close of business on the day of presentment.

§ 3–507. Dishonor; Holder's Right of Recourse; Term Allowing Re-Presentment.

(1) An instrument is dishonored when

    (a) a necessary or optional presentment is duly made and due acceptance or payment is refused or cannot be obtained within the prescribed time or in case of bank collections the instrument is seasonably returned by the midnight deadline (Section 4–301); or

    (b) presentment is excused and the instrument is not duly accepted or paid.

(2) Subject to any necessary notice of dishonor and protest, the holder has upon dishonor an immediate right of recourse against the drawers and indorsers.

(3) Return of an instrument for lack of proper indorsement is not dishonor.

(4) A term in a draft or an indorsement thereof allowing a stated time for re-presentment in the event of any dishonor of the draft by nonacceptance if a time draft or by nonpayment if a sight draft gives the holder as against any secondary party bound by the term an option to waive the dishonor without affecting the liability of the secondary party and he may present again up to the end of the stated time.

§ 3–508. Notice of Dishonor.

(1) Notice of dishonor may be given to any person who may be liable on the instrument by or on behalf of the holder or any party who has himself received notice, or any other party who can be compelled to pay the instrument. In addition an agent or bank in whose hands the instrument is dishonored may give notice to his principal or customer or to another agent or bank from which the instrument was received.

(2) Any necessary notice must be given by a bank before its midnight deadline and by any other person before midnight of the third business day after dishonor or receipt of notice of dishonor.

(3) Notice may be given in any reasonable manner. It may be oral or written and in any terms which identify the instrument and state that it has been dishonored. A misdescription which does not mislead the party notified does not vitiate the notice. Sending the instrument bearing a stamp, ticket or writing stating that acceptance or payment has been refused or sending a notice of debit with respect to the instrument is sufficient.

(4) Written notice is given when sent although it is not received.

(5) Notice to one partner is notice to each although the firm has been dissolved.

(6) When any party is in insolvency proceedings instituted after the issue of the instrument notice may be given either to the party or to the representative of his estate.

(7) When any party is dead or incompetent notice may be sent to his last known address or given to his personal representative.

(8) Notice operates for the benefit of all parties who have rights on the instrument against the party notified.

§ 3–509. Protest; Noting for Protest.

(1) A protest is a certificate of dishonor made under the hand and seal of a United States consul or vice consul or a notary public or other person authorized to certify dishonor by the

law of the place where dishonor occurs. It may be made upon information satisfactory to such person.

(2) The protest must identify the instrument and certify either that due presentment has been made or the reason why it is excused and that the instrument has been dishonored by nonacceptance or nonpayment.

(3) The protest may also certify that notice of dishonor has been given to all parties or to specified parties.

(4) Subject to subsection (5) any necessary protest is due by the time that notice of dishonor is due.

(5) If, before protest is due, an instrument has been noted for protest by the officer to make protest, the protest may be made at any time thereafter as of the date of the noting.

§ 3–510. Evidence of Dishonor and Notice of Dishonor.

The following are admissible as evidence and create a presumption of dishonor and of any notice of dishonor therein shown:

(a) a document regular in form as provided in the preceding section which purports to be a protest;

(b) the purported stamp or writing of the drawee, payor bank or presenting bank on the instrument or accompanying it stating that acceptance or payment has been refused for reasons consistent with dishonor;

(c) any book or record of the drawee, payor bank, or any collecting bank kept in the usual course of business which shows dishonor, even though there is no evidence of who made the entry.

§ 3–511. Waived or Excused Presentment, Protest or Notice of Dishonor or Delay Therein.

(1) Delay in presentment, protest or notice of dishonor is excused when the party is without notice that it is due or when the delay is caused by circumstances beyond his control and he exercises reasonable diligence after the cause of the delay ceases to operate.

(2) Presentment or notice or protest as the case may be is entirely excused when

(a) the party to be charged has waived it expressly or by implication either before or after it is due; or

(b) such party has himself dishonored the instrument or has countermanded payment or otherwise has no reason to expect or right to require that the instrument be accepted or paid; or

(c) by reasonable diligence the presentment or protest cannot be made or the notice given.

(3) Presentment is also entirely excused when

(a) the maker, acceptor or drawee of any instrument except a documentary draft is dead or in insolvency proceedings instituted after the issue of the instrument; or

(b) acceptance or payment is refused but not for want of proper presentment.

(4) Where a draft has been dishonored by nonacceptance a later presentment for payment and any notice of dishonor and protest for nonpayment are excused unless in the meantime the instrument has been accepted.

(5) A waiver of protest is also a waiver of presentment and of notice of dishonor even though protest is not required.

(6) Where a waiver of presentment or notice or protest is embodied in the instrument itself it is binding upon all parties; but where it is written above the signature of an indorser it binds him only.

PART 6

DISCHARGE

§ 3–601. Discharge of Parties.

(1) The extent of the discharge of any party from liability on an instrument is governed by the sections on

(a) payment or satisfaction (Section 3–603); or

(b) tender of payment (Section 3–604); or

(c) cancellation or renunciation (Section 3–605); or

(d) impairment of right of recourse or of collateral (Section 3–606); or

(e) reacquisition of the instrument by a prior party (Section 3–208); or

(f) fraudulent and material alteration (Section 3–407); or

(g) certification of a check (Section 3–411); or

(h) acceptance varying a draft (Section 3–412); or

(i) unexcused delay in presentment or notice of dishonor or protest (Section 3–502).

(2) Any party is also discharged from his liability on an instrument to another party by any other act or agreement with such party which would discharge his simple contract for the payment of money.

(3) The liability of all parties is discharged when any party who has himself no right of action or recourse on the instrument

(a) reacquires the instrument in his own right; or

(b) is discharged under any provision of this Article, except as otherwise provided with respect to discharge for impairment of recourse or of collateral (Section 3–606).

§ 3–602. Effect of Discharge Against Holder in Due Course.

No discharge of any party provided by this Article is effective against a subsequent holder in due course unless he has notice thereof when he takes the instrument.

§ 3–603. Payment or Satisfaction.

(1) The liability of any party is discharged to the extent of his payment or satisfaction to the holder even though it is made with knowledge of a claim of another person to the instrument unless prior to such payment or satisfaction the person making the claim either supplies indemnity deemed adequate by the party seeking the discharge or enjoins payment or satisfaction by order of a court of competent jurisdiction in an action in which the adverse claimant and the holder are parties. This subsection does not, however, result in the discharge of the liability

(a) of a party who in bad faith pays or satisfies a holder who acquired the instrument by theft or who (unless having the rights of a holder in due course) holds through one who so acquired it; or

(b) of a party (other than an intermediary bank or a payor bank which is not a depositary bank) who pays or satisfies the holder of an instrument which has been restrictively indorsed in a manner not consistent with the terms of such restrictive indorsement.

(2) Payment or satisfaction may be made with the consent of the holder by any person including a stranger to the instrument. Surrender of the instrument to such a person gives him the rights of a transferee (Section 3–201).

§ 3–604. Tender of Payment.

(1) An party making tender of full payment to a holder when or after it is due is discharged to the extent of all subsequent liability for interest, costs and attorney's fees.

(2) The holder's refusal of such tender wholly discharges any party who has a right of recourse against the party making the tender.

(3) Where the maker or acceptor of an instrument payable otherwise than on demand is able and ready to pay at every place of payment specified in the instrument when it is due, it is equivalent to tender.

§ 3–605. Cancellation and Renunciation.

(1) The holder of an instrument may even without consideration discharge any party

(a) in any manner apparent on the face of the instrument or the indorsement, as by intentionally cancelling the instrument or the party's signature by destruction or mutilation, or by striking out the party's signature; or

(b) by renouncing his rights by a writing signed and delivered or by surrender of the instrument to the party to be discharged.

(2) Neither cancellation nor renunciation without surrender of the instrument affects the title thereto.

§ 3–606. Impairment of Recourse or of Collateral.

(1) The holder discharges any party to the instrument to the extent that without such party's consent the holder

(a) without express reservation of rights releases or agrees not to sue any person against whom the party has to the knowledge of the holder a right of recourse or agrees to suspend the right to enforce against such person the instrument or collateral or otherwise discharges such person, except that failure or delay in effecting any required presentment, protest or notice of dishonor with respect to any such person does not discharge any party as to whom presentment, protest or notice of dishonor is effective or unnecessary; or

(b) unjustifiably impairs any collateral for the instrument given by or on behalf of the party or any person against whom he has a right of recourse.

(2) By express reservation of rights against a party with a right of recourse the holder preserves

(a) all his rights against such party as of the time when the instrument was originally due; and

(b) the right of the party to pay the instrument as of that time; and

(c) all rights of such party to recourse against others.

PART 7
ADVICE OF INTERNATIONAL SIGHT DRAFT

§ 3–701. Letter of Advice of International Sight Draft.

(1) A "letter of advice" is a drawer's communication to the drawee that a described draft has been drawn.

(2) Unless otherwise agreed when a bank receives from another bank a letter of advice of an international sight draft the drawee bank may immediately debit the drawer's account and stop the running of interest pro tanto. Such a debit and any resulting credit to any account covering outstanding drafts leaves in the drawer full power to stop payment or otherwise dispose of the amount and creates no trust or interest in favor of the holder.

(3) Unless otherwise agreed and except where a draft is drawn under a credit issued by the drawee, the drawee of an international sight draft owes the drawer no duty to pay an unadvised draft but if it does so and the draft is genuine, may appropriately debit the drawer's account.

PART 8
MISCELLANEOUS

§ 3–801. Drafts in a Set.

(1) Where a draft is drawn in a set of parts, each of which is numbered and expressed to be an order only if no other part has been honored, the whole of the parts constitutes one draft but a taker of any part may become a holder in due course of the draft.

(2) Any person who negotiates, indorses or accepts a single part of a draft drawn in a set thereby becomes liable to any holder in due course of that part as if it were the whole set, but as between different holders in due course to whom different parts have been negotiated the holder whose title first accrues has all rights to the draft and its proceeds.

(3) As against the drawee the first presented part of a draft drawn in a set is the part entitled to payment, or if a time draft to acceptance and payment. Acceptance of any subsequently presented part renders the drawee liable thereon under subsection (2). With respect both to a holder and to the drawer payment of a subsequently presented part of a draft payable

at sight has the same effect as payment of a check notwithstanding an effective stop order (Section 4–407).

(4) Except as otherwise provided in this section, where any part of a draft in a set is discharged by payment or otherwise the whole draft is discharged.

§ 3–802. Effect of Instrument on Obligation for Which It Is Given.

(1) Unless otherwise agreed where an instrument is taken for an underlying obligation

    (a) the obligation is pro tanto discharged if a bank is drawer, maker or acceptor of the instrument and there is no recourse on the instrument against the underlying obligor; and

    (b) in any other case the obligation is suspended pro tanto until the instrument is due or if it is payable on demand until its presentment. If the instrument is dishonored action may be maintained on either the instrument or the obligation; discharge of the underlying obligor on the instrument also discharges him on the obligation.

(2) The taking in good faith of a check which is not postdated does not of itself so extend the time on the original obligation as to discharge a surety.

§ 3–803. Notice to Third Party.

Where a defendant is sued for breach of an obligation for which a third person is answerable over under this Article he may give the third person written notice of the litigation, and the person notified may then give similar notice to any other person who is answerable over to him under this Article. If the notice states that the person notified may come in and defend and that if the person notified does not do so he will in any action against him by the person giving the notice be bound by any determination of fact common to the two litigations, then unless after seasonable receipt of the notice the person notified does come in and defend he is so bound.

§ 3–804. Lost, Destroyed or Stolen Instruments.

The owner of an instrument which is lost, whether by destruction, theft or otherwise, may maintain an action in his own name and recover from any party liable thereon upon due proof of his ownership, the facts which prevent his production of the instrument and its terms. The court may require security indemnifying the defendant against loss by reason of further claims on the instrument.

§ 3–805. Instruments Not Payable to Order or to Bearer.

This Article applies to any instrument whose terms do not preclude transfer and which is otherwise negotiable within this Article but which is not payable to order or to bearer, except that there can be no holder in due course of such an instrument.

ARTICLE 4. Bank Deposits and Collections

PART 1
GENERAL PROVISIONS AND DEFINITIONS

§ 4–101. Short Title.

This Article shall be known and may be cited as Uniform Commercial Code—Bank Deposits and Collections.

§ 4–102. Applicability.

(1) To the extent that items within this Article are also within the scope of Articles 3 and 8, they are subject to the provisions of those Articles. In the event of conflict the provisions of this Article govern those of Article 3 but the provisions of Article 8 govern those of this Article.

(2) The liability of a bank for action or non-action with respect to any item handled by it

for purposes of presentment, payment or collection is governed by the law of the place where the bank is located. In the case of action or non-action by or at a branch or separate office of a bank, its liability is governed by the law of the place where the branch or separate office is located.

§ 4–103. Variation by Agreement; Measure of Damages; Certain Action Constituting Ordinary Care.

(1) The effect of the provisions of this Article may be varied by agreement except that no agreement can disclaim a bank's responsibility for its own lack of good faith or failure to exercise ordinary care or can limit the measure of damages for such lack or failure; but the parties may by agreement determine the standards by which such responsibility is to be measured if such standards are not manifestly unreasonable.

(2) Federal Reserve regulations and operating letters, clearing house rules, and the like, have the effect of agreements under subsection (1), whether or not specifically assented to by all parties interested in items handled.

(3) Action or non-action approved by this Article or pursuant to Federal Reserve regulations or operating letters constitutes the exercise of ordinary care and, in the absence of special instructions, action or non-action consistent with clearing house rules and the like or with a general banking usage not disapproved by this Article, prima facie constitutes the exercise of ordinary care.

(4) The specification or approval of certain procedures by this Article does not constitute disapproval of other procedures which may be reasonable under the circumstances.

(5) The measure of damages for failure to exercise ordinary care in handling an item is the amount of the item reduced by an amount which could not have been realized by the use of ordinary care, and where there is bad faith it includes other damages, if any, suffered by the party as a proximate consequence.

§ 4–104. Definitions and Index of Definitions.

(1) In this Article unless the context otherwise requires

    (a) "Account" means any account with a bank and includes a checking, time, interest or savings account;

    (b) "Afternoon" means the period of a day between noon and midnight;

    (c) "Banking day" means that part of any day on which a bank is open to the public for carrying on substantially all of its banking functions;

    (d) "Clearing house" means any association of banks or other payors regularly clearing items;

    (e) "Customer" means any person having an account with a bank or for whom a bank has agreed to collect items and includes a bank carrying an account with another bank;

    (f) "Documentary draft" means any negotiable or nonnegotiable draft with accompanying documents, securities or other papers to be delivered against honor of the draft;

    (g) "Item" means any instrument for the payment of money even though it is not negotiable but does not include money;

    (h) "Midnight deadline" with respect to a bank is midnight on its next banking day following the banking day on which it receives the relevant item or notice or from which the time for taking action commences to run, whichever is later;

    (i) "Properly payable" includes the availability of funds for payment at the time of decision to pay or dishonor;

    (j) "Settle" means to pay in cash, by clearing house settlement, in a charge or credit or by remittance, or otherwise as instructed. A settlement may be either provisional or final;

    (k) "Suspends payments" with respect to a bank means that it has been closed by order of the supervisory authorities, that a public officer has been appointed to take it over or that it ceases or refuses to make payments in the ordinary course of business.

(2) Other definitions apply to this Article and the sections in which they appear are:

"Collecting bank"	Section 4–105
"Depository bank"	Section 4–105
"Intermediary bank"	Section 4–105
"Payor bank"	Section 4–105
"Presenting bank"	Section 4–105
"Remitting bank"	Section 4–105

(3) The following definitions in other Articles apply to this Article:

"Acceptance"	Section 3–410
"Certificate of deposit"	Section 3–104
"Certification"	Section 3–411
"Check"	Section 3–104
"Draft"	Section 3–104
"Holder in due course"	Section 3–302
"Notice of dishonor"	Section 3–508
"Presentment"	Section 3–504
"Protest"	Section 3–509
"Secondary party"	Section 3–102

(4) In addition Article 1 contains general definitions and principles of construction and interpretation applicable throughout this Article.

§ 4–105. "Depository Bank"; "Intermediary Bank"; "Collecting Bank"; "Payor Bank"; "Presenting Bank"; "Remitting Bank."

In this Article unless the context otherwise requires:

(a) "Depository bank" means the first bank to which an item is transferred for collection even though it is also the payor bank;

(b) "Payor bank" means a bank by which an item is payable as drawn or accepted;

(c) "Intermediary bank" means any bank to which an item is transferred in course of collection except the depository or payor bank;

(d) "Collecting bank" means any bank handling the item for collection except the payor bank;

(e) "Presenting bank" means any bank presenting an item except a payor bank;

(f) "Remitting bank" means any payor or intermediary bank remitting for an item.

§ 4–106. Separate Office of a Bank.

A branch or separate office of a bank [maintaining its own deposit ledgers] is a separate bank for the purpose of computing the time within which and determining the place at or to which action may be taken or notices or orders shall be given under this Article and under Article 3.

Note: *The brackets are to make it optional with the several states whether to require a branch to maintain its own deposit ledgers in order to be considered to be a separate bank for certain purposes under Article 4. In some states "maintaining its own deposit ledgers" is a satisfactory test. In others branch banking practices are such that this test would not be suitable.*

§ 4–107. Time of Receipt of Items.

(1) For the purpose of allowing time to process items, prove balances and make the necessary entries on its books to determine its position for the day, a bank may fix an afternoon hour of two P.M. or later as a cut-off hour for the handling of money and items and the making of entries on its books.

(2) Any item or deposit of money received on any day after a cut-off hour so fixed or after the close of the banking day may be treated as being received at the opening of the next banking day.

§ 4–108. Delays.

(1) Unless otherwise instructed, a collecting bank in a good faith effort to secure payment may, in the case of specific items and with or without the approval of any person involved,

waive, modify or extend time limits imposed or permitted by this Act for a period not in excess of an additional banking day without discharge of secondary parties and without liability to its transferor or any prior party.

(2) Delay by a collecting bank or payor bank beyond time limits prescribed or permitted by this Act or by instructions is excused if caused by interruption of communication facilities, suspension of payments by another bank, war, emergency conditions or other circumstances beyond the control of the bank provided it exercises such diligence as the circumstances require.

§ 4–109. Process of Posting.

The "process of posting" means the usual procedure followed by a payor bank in determining to pay an item and in recording the payment including one or more of the following or other steps as determined by the bank:

(a) verification of any signature;

(b) ascertaining that sufficient funds are available;

(c) affixing a "paid" or other stamp;

(d) entering a charge or entry to a customer's account;

(e) correcting or reversing an entry or erroneous action with respect to the item.

PART 2
COLLECTION OF ITEMS: DEPOSITORY AND COLLECTING BANKS

§ 4–201. Presumption and Duration of Agency Status of Collecting Banks and Provisional Status of Credits; Applicability of Article; Item Indorsed "Pay Any Bank."

(1) Unless a contrary intent clearly appears and prior to the time that a settlement given by a collecting bank for an item is or becomes final (subsection (3) of Section 4–211 and Section 4–212 and 4–213) the bank is an agent or sub-agent of the owner of the item and any settlement given for the item is provisional. This provision applies regardless of the form of indorsement or lack of indorsement and even though credit given for the item is subject to immediate withdrawal as of right or is in fact withdrawn; but the continuance of ownership of an item by its owner and any rights of the owner to proceeds of the item are subject to rights of a collecting bank such as those resulting from outstanding advances on the item and valid rights of setoff. When an item is handled by banks for purposes of presentment, payment and collection, the relevant provisions of this Article apply even though action of parties clearly establishes that a particular bank has purchased the item and is the owner of it.

(2) After an item has been indorsed with the words "pay any bank" or the like, only a bank may acquire the rights of a holder

(a) until the item has been returned to the customer initiating collection; or

(b) until the item has been specially indorsed by a bank to a person who is not a bank.

§ 4–202. Responsibility for Collection; When Action Seasonable.

(1) A collecting bank must use ordinary care in

(a) presenting an item or sending it for presentment; and

(b) sending notice of dishonor or non-payment or returning an item other than a documentary draft to the bank's transferor [or directly to the depositary bank under subsection (2) of Section 4–212 *(see note to Section 4–212)* after learning that the item has not been paid or accepted as the case may be; and

(c) settling for an item when the bank receives final settlement; and

(d) making or providing for any necessary protest; and

(e) notifying its transferor of any loss or delay in transit within a reasonable time after discovery thereof.

(2) A collecting bank taking proper action before its midnight deadline following receipt of an item, notice or payment acts seasonably; taking proper action within a reasonably longer time may be seasonable but the bank has the burden of so establishing.

(3) Subject to subsection (1) (a), a bank is not liable for the insolvency, neglect, misconduct, mistake or default of another bank or person or for loss or destruction of an item in transit or in the possession of others.

§ 4–203. Effect of Instructions.

Subject to the provisions of Article 3 concerning conversion of instruments (Section 3–419) and the provisions of both Article 3 and this Article concerning restrictive indorsements only a collecting bank's transferor can give instructions which affect the bank or constitute notice to it and a collecting bank is not liable to prior parties for any action taken pursuant to such instructions or in accordance with any agreement with its transferor.

§ 4–204. Methods of Sending and Presenting; Sending Direct to Payor Bank.

(1) A collecting bank must send items by reasonably prompt method taking into consideration any relevant instructions, the nature of the item, the number of such items on hand, and the cost of collection involved and the method generally used by it or others to present such items.

(2) A collecting bank may send
  (a) any item direct to the payor bank;
  (b) any item to any non-bank payor if authorized by its transferor; and
  (c) any item other than documentary drafts to any non-bank payor, if authorized by Federal Reserve regulation or operating letter, clearing house rule or the like.

(3) Presentment may be made by a presenting bank at a place where the payor bank has requested that presentment be made.

§ 4–205. Supplying Missing Indorsement; No Notice from Prior Indorsement.

(1) A depositary bank which has taken an item for collection may supply any indorsement of the customer which is necessary to title unless the item contains the words "payee's indorsement required" or the like. In the absence of such a requirement a statement placed on the item by the depositary bank to the effect that the item was deposited by a customer or credited to his account is effective as the customer's indorsement.

(2) An intermediary bank, or payor bank which is not a depositary bank, is neither given notice nor otherwise affected by a restrictive indorsement of any person except the bank's immediate transferor.

§ 4–206. Transfer Between Banks.

Any agreed method which identifies the transferor bank is sufficient for the item's further transfer to another bank.

§ 4–207. Warranties of Customer and Collecting Bank on Transfer or Presentment of Items; Time for Claims.

(1) Each customer or collecting bank who obtains payment or acceptance of an item and each prior customer and collecting bank warrants to the payor bank or other payor who in good faith pays or accepts the item that
  (a) he has a good title to the item or is authorized to obtain payment or acceptance on behalf of one who has a good title; and
  (b) he has no knowledge that the signature of the maker or drawer is unauthorized, except that this warranty is not given by any customer or collecting bank that is a holder in due course and acts in good faith
    (i) to a maker with respect to the maker's own signature; or
    (ii) to a drawer with respect to the drawer's own signature, whether or not the drawer is also the drawee; or
    (iii) to an acceptor of an item if the holder in due course took the item after the acceptance or obtained the acceptance without knowledge that the drawer's signature was unauthorized; and
  (c) the item has not been materially altered, except that this warranty is not given by any customer or collecting bank that is a holder in due course and acts in good faith
    (i) to the maker of a note; or
    (ii) to the drawer of a draft whether or not the drawer is also the drawee; or

(iii) to the acceptor of an item with respect to an alteration made prior to the acceptance if the holder in due course took the item after the acceptance, even though the acceptance provided "payable as originally drawn" or equivalent terms; or

(iv) to the acceptor of an item with respect to an alteration made after the acceptance.

(2) Each customer and collecting bank who transfers an item and receives a settlement or other consideration for it warrants to his transferee and to any subsequent collecting bank who takes the item in good faith that

(a) he has a good title to the item or is authorized to obtain payment or acceptance on behalf of one who has a good title and the transfer is otherwise rightful; and

(b) all signatures are genuine or authorized; and

(c) the item has not been materially altered; and

(d) no defense of any party is good against him; and

(e) he has no knowledge of any insolvency proceeding instituted with respect to the maker or acceptor or the drawer of an unaccepted item.

In addition each customer and collecting bank so transferring an item and receiving a settlement or other consideration engages that upon dishonor and any necessary notice of dishonor and protest he will take up the item.

(3) The warranties and the engagement to honor set forth in the two preceding subsections arise notwithstanding the absence of indorsement or words of guaranty or warranty in the transfer or presentment and a collecting bank remains liable for their breach despite remittance to its transferor. Damages for breach of such warranties or engagement to honor shall not exceed the consideration received by the customer or collecting bank responsible plus finance charges and expenses related to the item, if any.

(4) Unless a claim for breach of warranty under this section is made within a reasonable time after the person claiming learns of the breach, the person liable is discharged to the extent of any loss caused by the delay in making claim.

§ 4–208. Security Interest of Collecting Bank in Items, Accompanying Documents and Proceeds.

(1) A bank has a security interest in an item and any accompanying documents or the proceeds of either

(a) in case of an item deposited in an account to the extent to which credit given for the item has been withdrawn or applied;

(b) in case of an item for which it has given credit available for withdrawal as of right, to the extent of the credit given whether or not the credit is drawn upon and whether or not there is a right of charge-back; or

(c) if it makes an advance on or against the item.

(2) When credit which has been given for several items received at one time or pursuant to a single agreement is withdrawn or applied in part the security interest remains upon all the items, any accompanying documents or the proceeds of either. For the purpose of this section, credits first given are first withdrawn.

(3) Receipt by a collecting bank of a final settlement for an item is a realization on its security interest in the item, accompanying documents and proceeds. To the extent and so long as the bank does not receive final settlement for the item or give up possession of the item or accompanying documents for purposes other than collection, the security interest continues and is subject to the provisions of Article 9 except that

(a) no security agreement is necessary to make the security interest enforceable (subsection (1) (b) of Section 9–203); and

(b) no filing is required to perfect the security interest; and

(c) the security interest has priority over conflicting perfected security interests in the item, accompanying documents or proceeds.

§ 4–209. When Bank Gives Value for Purposes of Holder in Due Course.

For purposes of determining its status as a holder in due course, the bank has given value to the extent that it has a security interest in an item provided that the bank otherwise complies with the requirements of Section 3–302 on what constitutes a holder in due course.

§ 4–210. Presentment by Notice of Item Not Payable by, Through or at a Bank; Liability of Secondary Parties.

(1) Unless otherwise instructed, a collecting bank may present an item not payable by, through or at a bank by sending to the party to accept or pay a written notice that the bank holds the item for acceptance or payment. The notice must be sent in time to be received on or before the day when presentment is due and the bank must meet any requirement of the party to accept or pay under Section 3–505 by the close of the bank's next banking day after it knows of the requirement.

(2) Where presentment is made by notice and neither honor nor request for compliance with a requirement under Section 3–505 is received by the close of business on the day after maturity or in the case of demand items by the close of business on the third banking day after notice was sent, the presenting bank may treat the item as dishonored and charge any secondary party by sending him notice of the facts.

§ 4–211. Media of Remittance; Provisional and Final Settlement in Remittance Cases.

(1) A collecting bank may take in settlement of an item
   (a) a check of the remitting bank or of another bank on any bank except the remitting bank; or
   (b) a cashier's check or similar primary obligation of a remitting bank which is a member of or clears through a member of the same clearing house or group as the collecting bank; or
   (c) appropriate authority to charge an account of the remitting bank or of another bank with the collecting bank; or
   (d) if the item is drawn upon or payable by a person other than a bank, a cashier's check, certified check or other bank check or obligation.

(2) If before its midnight deadline the collecting bank properly dishonors a remittance check or authorization to charge on itself or presents or forwards for collection a remittance instrument of or on another bank which is of a kind approved by subsection (1) or has not been authorized by it, the collecting bank is not liable to prior parties in the event of the dishonor of such check, instrument or authorization.

(3) A settlement for an item by means of a remittance instrument or authorization to charge is or becomes a final settlement as to both the person making and the person receiving the settlement
   (a) if the remittance instrument or authorization to charge is of a kind approved by subsection (1) or has not been authorized by the person receiving the settlement and in either case the person receiving the settlement acts seasonably before its midnight deadline in presenting, forwarding for collection or paying the instrument or authorization,—at the time the remittance instrument or authorization is finally paid by the payor by which it is payable;
   (b) if the person receiving the settlement has authorized remittance by a non-bank check or obligation or by a cashier's check or similar primary obligation of or a check upon the payor or other remitting bank which is not of a kind approved by subsection (1) (b),—at the time of the receipt of such remittance check or obligation; or
   (c) if in a case not covered by sub-paragraphs (a) or (b) the person receiving the settlement fails to seasonably present, forward for collection, pay or return a remittance instrument or authorization to it to charge before its midnight deadline,—at such midnight deadline.

§ 4–212. Right of Charge-Back or Refund.

(1) If a collecting bank has made provisional settlement with its customer for an item and itself fails by reason of dishonor, suspension of payments by a bank or otherwise to receive a settlement for the item which is or becomes final, the bank may revoke the settlement given by it, charge back the amount of any credit given for the item to its customer's account

or obtain refund from its customer whether or not it is able to return the items if by its midnight deadline or within a longer reasonable time after it learns the facts it returns the item or sends notification of the facts. These rights to revoke, charge-back and obtain refund terminate if and when a settlement for the item received by the bank is or becomes final (subsection (3) of Section 4–211 and subsections (2) and (3) of Section 4–213).

[(2) Within the time and manner prescribed by this section and Section 4–301, an intermediary or payor bank, as the case may be, may return an unpaid item directly to the despositary bank and may send for collection a draft on the depositary bank and obtain reimbursement. In such case, if the depositary bank has received provisional settlement for the item, it must reimburse the bank drawing the draft and any provisional credits for the item between banks shall become and remain final.]

Note: *Direct returns is recognized as an innovation that is not yet established bank practice, and therefore, Paragraph 2 has been bracketed. Some lawyers have doubts whether it should be included in legislation or left to development by agreement.*

(3) A depositary bank which is also the payor may charge-back the amount of an item to its customer's account or obtain refund in accordance with the section governing return of an item received by a payor bank for credit on its books (Section 4–301).

(4) The right to charge-back is not affected by

    (a) prior use of the credit given for the item; or

    (b) failure by any bank to exercise ordinary care with respect to the item but any bank so failing remains liable.

(5) A failure to charge-back or claim refund does not affect other rights of the bank against the customer or any other party.

(6) If credit is given in dollars as the equivalent of the value of an item payable in a foreign currency the dollar amount of any charge-back or refund shall be calculated on the basis of the buying sight rate for the foreign currency prevailing on the day when the person entitled to the charge-back or refund learns that it will not receive payment in ordinary course.

§ 4–213. Final Payment of Item by Payor Bank; When Provisional Debits and Credits Become Final; When Certain Credits Become Available for Withdrawal.

(1) An item is finally paid by a payor bank when the bank has done any of the following, whichever happens first:

    (a) paid the item in cash; or

    (b) settled for the item without reserving a right to revoke the settlement and without having such right under statute, clearing house rule or agreement; or

    (c) completed the process of posting the item to the indicated account of the drawer, maker or other person to be charged therewith; or

    (d) made a provisional settlement for the item and failed to revoke the settlement in the time and manner permitted by statute, clearing house rule or agreement.

Upon a final payment under subparagraphs (b), (c) or (d) the payor bank shall be accountable for the amount of the item.

(2) If provisional settlement for an item between the presenting and payor banks is made through a clearing house or by debits or credits in an account between them, then to the extent that provisional debits or credits for the item are entered in accounts between the presenting and payor banks or between the presenting and successive prior collecting banks seriatim, they become final upon final payment of the item by the payor bank.

(3) If a collecting bank receives a settlement for an item which is or becomes final (subsection (3) of Section 4–211, subsection (2) of Section 4–213) the bank is accountable to its customer for the amount of the item and any provisional credit given for the item in an account with its customer becomes final.

(4) Subject to any right of the bank to apply the credit to an obligation of the customer, credit given by a bank for an item in an account with its customer becomes available for withdrawal as of right

(a) in any case where the bank has received a provisional settlement for the item,—when such settlement becomes final and the bank has had a reasonable time to learn that the settlement is final;

(b) in any case where the bank is both a depositary bank and a payor bank and the item is finally paid,—at the opening of the bank's second banking day following receipt of the item.

(5) A deposit of money in a bank is final when made but, subject to any right of the bank to apply the deposit to an obligation of the customer, the deposit becomes available for withdrawal as of right at the opening of the bank's next banking day following receipt of the deposit.

§ 4–214. Insolvency and Preference.

(1) Any item in or coming into the possession of a payor or collecting bank which suspends payment and which item is not finally paid shall be returned by the receiver, trustee or agent in charge of the closed bank to the presenting bank or the closed bank's customer.

(2) If a payor bank finally pays an item and suspends payments without making a settlement for the item with its customer or the presenting bank which settlement is or becomes final, the owner of the item has a preferred claim against the payor bank.

(3) If a payor bank gives or a collecting bank gives or receives a provisional settlement for an item and thereafter suspends payments, the suspension does not prevent or interfere with the settlement becoming final if such finality occurs automatically upon the lapse of certain time or the happening of certain events (subsection (3) of Section 4–211, subsections (1) (d), (2) and (3) of Section 4–213).

(4) If a collecting bank receives from subsequent parties settlement for an item which settlement is or becomes final and suspends payments without making a settlement for the item with its customer which is or becomes final, the owner of the item has a preferred claim against such collecting bank.

PART 3
COLLECTION OF ITEMS: PAYOR BANKS

§ 4–301. Deferred Posting; Recovery of Payment by Return of Items; Time of Dishonor.

(1) Where an authorized settlement for a demand item (other than a documentary draft) received by a payor bank otherwise than for immediate payment over the counter has been made before midnight of the banking day of receipt the payor bank may revoke the settlement and recover any payment if before it has made final payment (subsection (1) of Section 4–213) and before its midnight deadline it

(a) returns the item; or

(b) sends written notice of dishonor or nonpayment if the item is held for protest or is otherwise unavailable for return.

(2) If a demand item is received by a payor bank for credit on its books it may return such item or send notice of dishonor and may revoke any credit given or recover the amount thereof withdrawn by its customer, if it acts within the time limit and in the manner specified in the preceding subsection.

(3) Unless previous notice of dishonor has been sent an item is dishonored at the time when for purposes of dishonor it is returned or notice sent in accordance with this section.

(4) An item is returned:

(a) as to an item received through a clearing house, when it is delivered to the presenting or last collecting bank or to the clearing house or is sent or delivered in accordance with its rules; or

(b) in all other cases, when it is sent or delivered to the bank's customer or transferor or pursuant to his instructions.

§ 4–302. Payor Bank's Responsibility for Late Return of Item.

In the absence of a valid defense such as breach of a presentment warranty (subsection (1) of Section 4–207), settlement effected or the like, if an item is presented on and received by a payor bank the bank is accountable for the amount of

(a) a demand item other than a documentary draft whether properly payable or not if the bank, in any case where it is not also the depositary bank, retains the item beyond midnight of the banking day of receipt without settling for it or, regardless of whether it is also the depositary bank, does not pay or return the item or send notice of dishonor until after its midnight deadline; or

(b) any other properly payable item unless within the time allowed for acceptance or payment of that item the bank either accepts or pays the item or returns it and accompanying documents.

§ 4–303. When Items Subject to Notice, Stop-Order, Legal Process or Setoff; Order in Which Items May Be Charged or Certified.

(1) Any knowledge, notice or stop-order received by, legal process served upon or setoff exercised by a payor bank, whether or not effective under other rules of law to terminate, suspend or modify the bank's right or duty to pay an item or to charge its customer's account for the item, comes too late to so terminate, suspend or modify such right or duty if the knowledge, notice, stop-order or legal process is received or served and a reasonable time for the bank to act thereon expires or the setoff is exercised after the bank has done any of the following:

(a) accepted or certified the item;

(b) paid the item in cash;

(c) settled for the item without reserving a right to revoke the settlement and without having such right under statute, clearing house rule or agreement;

(d) completed the process of posting the item to the indicated account of the drawer, maker or other person to be charged therewith or otherwise has evidenced by examination of such indicated account and by action its decision to pay the item; or

(e) become accountable for the amount of the item under subsection (1) (d) of Section 4–213 and Section 4–302 dealing with the payor bank's responsibility for late return of items.

(2) Subject to the provisions of subsection (1) items may be accepted, paid, certified or charged to the indicated account of its customer in any order convenient to the bank.

PART 4
RELATIONSHIP BETWEEN PAYOR BANK AND ITS CUSTOMER

§ 4–401. When Bank May Charge Customer's Account.

(1) As against its customer, a bank may charge against his account any item which is otherwise properly payable from that account even though the charge creates an overdraft.

(2) A bank which in good faith makes payment to a holder may charge the indicated account of its customer according to

(a) the original tenor of his altered item; or

(b) the tenor of his completed item, even though the bank knows the item has been completed unless the bank has notice that the completion was improper.

§ 4–402. Bank's Liability to Customer for Wrongful Dishonor.

A payor bank is liable to its customer for damages proximately caused by the wrongful dishonor of an item. When the dishonor occurs through mistake liability is limited to actual damages proved. If so proximately caused and proved damages may include damages for an arrest or prosecution of the customer or other consequential damages. Whether any consequential damages are proximately caused by the wrongful dishonor is a question of fact to be determined in each case.

§ 4–403. Customer's Right to Stop Payment; Burden of Proof of Loss.

(1) A customer may by order to his bank stop payment of any item payable for his account but the order must be received at such time and in such manner as to afford the bank a reason-

able opportunity to act on it prior to any action by the bank with respect to the item described in Section 4–303.

(2) An oral order is binding upon the bank only for fourteen calendar days unless confirmed in writing within that period. A written order is effective for only six months unless renewed in writing.

(3) The burden of establishing the fact and amount of loss resulting from the payment of an item contrary to a binding stop payment order is on the customer.

§ 4–404. Bank Not Obligated to Pay Check More Than Six Months Old.

A bank is under no obligation to a customer having a checking account to pay a check, other than a certified check, which is presented more than six months after its date, but it may charge its customer's account for a payment made thereafter in good faith.

§ 4–405. Death or Incompetence of Customer.

(1) A payor or collecting bank's authority to accept, pay or collect an item or to account for proceeds of its collection if otherwise effective is not rendered ineffective by incompetence of a customer of either bank existing at the time the item is issued or its collection is undertaken if the bank does not know of an adjudication of incompetence. Neither death nor incompetence of a customer revokes such authority to accept, pay, collect or account until the bank knows of the fact of death or of an adjudication of incompetence and has reasonable opportunity to act on it.

(2) Even with knowledge a bank may for ten days after the date of death pay or certify checks drawn on or prior to that date unless ordered to stop payment by a person claiming an interest in the account.

§ 4–406. Customer's Duty to Discover and Report Unauthorized Signature or Alteration.

(1) When a bank sends to its customer a statement of account accompanied by items paid in good faith in support of the debit entries or holds the statement and items pursuant to a request or instructions of its customer or otherwise in a reasonable manner makes the statement and items available to the customer, the customer must exercise reasonable care and promptness to examine the statement and items to discover his unauthorized signature or any alteration on an item and must notify the bank promptly after discovery thereof.

(2) If the bank establishes that the customer failed with respect to an item to comply with the duties imposed on the customer by subsection (1) the customer is precluded from asserting against the bank

   (a) his unauthorized signature or any alteration on the item if the bank also establishes that it suffered a loss by reason of such failure; and

   (b) an authorized signature or alteration by the same wrongdoer on any other item paid in good faith by the bank after the first item and statement was available to the customer for a reasonable period not exceeding fourteen calendar days and before the bank receives notification from the customer of any such unauthorized signature or alteration.

(3) The preclusion under subsection (2) does not apply if the customer establishes lack of ordinary care on the part of the bank in paying the item(s).

(4) Without regard to care or lack of care of either the customer or the bank a customer who does not within one year from the time the statement and items are made available to the customer (subsection (1)) discover and report his unauthorized signature or any alteration on the face or back of the item or does not within three years from that time discover and report any unauthorized indorsement is precluded from asserting against the bank such unauthorized signature or indorsement or such alteration.

(5) If under this section a payor bank has a valid defense against a claim of a customer upon or resulting from payment of an item and waives or fails upon request to assert the defense the bank may not assert against any collecting bank or other prior party presenting or transferring the item a claim based upon the unauthorized signature or alteration giving rise to the customer's claim.

§ 4–407. Payor Bank's Right to Subrogation on Improper Payment.

If a payor bank has paid an item over the stop payment order of the drawer or maker or otherwise under circumstances giving a basis for objection by the drawer or maker, to prevent unjust enrichment and only to the extent necessary to prevent loss to the bank by reason of its payment of the item, the payor bank shall be subrogated to the rights

   (a) of any holder in due course on the item against the drawer or maker; and

   (b) of the payee or any other holder of the item against the drawer or maker either on the item or under the transaction out of which the item arose; and

   (c) of the drawer or maker against the payee or any other holder of the item with respect to the transaction out of which the item arose.

PART 5
COLLECTION OF DOCUMENTARY DRAFTS

§ 4–501. Handling of Documentary Drafts; Duty to Send for Presentment and to Notify Customer of Dishonor.

A bank which takes a documentary draft for collection must present or send the draft and accompanying documents for presentment and upon learning that the draft has not been paid or accepted in due course must seasonably notify its customer of such fact even though it may have discounted or bought the draft or extended credit available for withdrawal as of right.

§ 4–502. Presentment of "On Arrival" Drafts.

When a draft or the relevant instructions require presentment "on arrival," "when goods arrive" or the like, the collecting bank need not present until in its judgment a reasonable time for arrival of the goods has expired. Refusal to pay or accept because the goods have not arrived is not dishonor; the bank must notify its transferor of such refusal but need not present the draft again until it is instructed to do so or learns of the arrival of the goods.

§ 4–503. Responsibility of Presenting Bank for Documents and Goods; Report of Reasons for Dishonor; Referee in Case of Need.

Unless otherwise instructed and except as provided in Article 5 a bank presenting a documentary draft

   (a) must deliver the documents to the drawee on acceptance of the draft if it is payable more than three days after presentment; otherwise, only on payment; and

   (b) upon dishonor, either in the case of presentment for acceptance or presentment for payment, may seek and follow instructions from any referee in case of need designated in the draft or if the presenting bank does not choose to utilize his services it must use diligence and good faith to ascertain the reason for dishonor, must notify its transferor of the dishonor and of the results of its effort to ascertain the reasons therefor and must request instructions.

But the presenting bank is under no obligation with respect to goods represented by the documents except to follow any reasonable instructions seasonably received; it has a right to reimbursement for any expense incurred in following instructions and to prepayment of or indemnity for such expenses.

§ 4–504. Privilege of Presenting Bank to Deal With Goods; Security Interest for Expenses.

(1) A presenting bank which, following the dishonor of a documentary draft, has seasonably requested instructions but does not receive them within a reasonable time may store, sell, or otherwise deal with the goods in any reasonable manner.

(2) For its reasonable expenses incurred by action under subsection (1) the presenting bank has a lien upon the goods or their proceeds, which may be foreclosed in the same manner as an unpaid seller's lien.

ARTICLE 5. Letters of Credit

§ 5–101. Short Title.

This Article shall be known and may be cited as Uniform Commercial Code—Letters of Credit.

§ 5–102. Scope.

(1) This Article applies
- (a) to a credit issued by a bank if the credit requires a documentary draft or a documentary demand for payment; and
- (b) to a credit issued by a person other than a bank if the credit requires that the draft or demand for payment be accompanied by a document of title; and
- (c) to a credit issued by a bank or other person if the credit is not within subparagraphs (a) or (b) but conspicuously states that it is a letter of credit or is conspicuously so entitled.

(2) Unless the engagement meets the requirements of subsection (1), this Article does not apply to engagements to make advances or to honor drafts or demands for payment, to authorities to pay or purchase, to guarantees or to general agreements.

(3) This Article deals with some but not all of the rules and concepts of letters of credit as such rules or concepts have developed prior to this act or may hereafter develop. The fact that this Article states a rule does not by itself require, imply or negate application of the same or a converse rule to a situation not provided for or to a person not specified by this Article.

§ 5–103. Definitions.

(1) In this Article unless the context otherwise requires
- (a) "Credit" or "letter of credit" means an engagement by a bank or other person made at the request of a customer and of a kind within the scope of this Article (Section 5–102) that the issuer will honor drafts or other demands for payment upon compliance with the conditions specified in the credit. A credit may be either revocable or irrevocable. The engagement may be either an agreement to honor or a statement that the bank or other person is authorized to honor.
- (b) A "documentary draft" or a "documentary demand for payment" is one honor of which is conditioned upon the presentation of a document or documents. "Document" means any paper including document of title, security, invoice, certificate, notice of default and the like.
- (c) An "issuer" is a bank or other person issuing a credit.
- (d) A "beneficiary" of a credit is a person who is entitled under its terms to draw or demand payment.
- (e) An "advising bank" is a bank which gives notification of the issuance of a credit by another bank.
- (f) A "confirming bank" is a bank which engages either that it will itself honor a credit already issued by another bank or that such a credit will be honored by the issuer or a third bank.
- (g) A "customer" is a buyer or other person who causes an issuer to issue a credit. The term also includes a bank which procures issuance or confirmation on behalf of that bank's customer.

(2) Other definitions applying to this Article and the sections in which they appear are:

"Notation of Credit"	Section 5–108
"Presenter"	Section 5–112(3)

(3) Definitions in other Articles applying to this Article and the sections in which they appear are:

"Accept" or "Acceptance"	Section 3–410
"Contract for sale"	Section 2–106
"Draft"	Section 3–104
"Holder in due course"	Section 3–302
"Midnight deadline"	Section 4–104
"Security"	Section 8–102

(4) In addition, Article 1 contains general definitions and principles of construction and interpretation applicable throughout this Article.

§ 5–104. Formal Requirements; Signing.

(1) Except as otherwise required in subsection (1) (c) of Section 5–102 on scope, no particular form of phrasing is required for a credit. A credit must be in writing and signed by the issuer and a confirmation must be in writing and signed by the confirming bank. A modification of the terms of a credit or confirmation must be signed by the issuer or confirming bank.

(2) A telegram may be a sufficient signed writing if it identifies its sender by an authorized authentication. The authentication may be in code and the authorized naming of the issuer in an advice of credit is a sufficient signing.

§ 5–105. Consideration.

No consideration is necessary to establish a credit or to enlarge or otherwise modify its terms.

§ 5–106. Time and Effect of Establishment of Credit.

(1) Unless otherwise agreed a credit is established

    (a) as regards the customer as soon as a letter of credit is sent to him or the letter of credit or an authorized written advice of its issuance is sent to the beneficiary and

    (b) as regards the beneficiary when he receives a letter of credit or an authorized written advice of its issuance.

(2) Unless otherwise agreed once an irrevocable credit is established as regards the customer it can be modified or revoked only with the consent of the customer and once it is established as regards the beneficiary it can be modified or revoked only with his consent.

(3) Unless otherwise agreed after a revocable credit is established it may be modified or revoked by the issuer without notice to or consent from the customer or beneficiary.

(4) Notwithstanding any modification or revocation of a revocable credit any person authorized to honor or negotiate under the terms of the original credit is entitled to reimbursement for or honor of any draft or demand for payment duly honored or negotiated before receipt of notice of the modification or revocation and the issuer in turn is entitled to reimbursement from its customer.

§ 5–107. Advice of Credit; Confirmation; Error in Statement of Terms.

(1) Unless otherwise specified an advising bank by advising a credit issued by another bank does not assume any obligation to honor drafts drawn or demands for payment made under the credit but it does assume obligation for the accuracy of its own statement.

(2) A confirming bank by confirming a credit becomes directly obligated on the credit to the extent of its confirmation as though it were its issuer and acquires the rights of an issuer.

(3) Even though an advising bank incorrectly advises the terms of a credit it has been authorized to advise the credit is established as against the issuer to the extent of its original terms.

(4) Unless otherwise specified the customer bears as against the issuer all risks of transmission and reasonable translation or interpretation of any message relating to a credit.

§ 5–108. "Notation Credit"; Exhaustion of Credit.

(1) A credit which specifies that any person purchasing or paying drafts drawn or demands for payment made under it must note the amount of the draft or demand on the letter or advice of credit is a "notation credit."

(2) Under a notation credit

    (a) a person paying the beneficiary or purchasing a draft or demand for payment from him acquires a right to honor only if the appropriate notation is made and by transferring or forwarding for honor the documents under the credit such a person warrants to the issuer that the notation has been made; and

    (b) unless the credit or a signed statement that an appropriate notation has been made accompanies the draft or demand for payment the issuer may delay honor until evidence of notation has been procured which is satisfactory to it but its obligation and that of its customer continue for a reasonable time not exceeding thirty days to obtain such evidence.

(3) If the credit is not a notation credit

    (a) the issuer may honor complying drafts or demands for payment presented to it in the order in which they are presented and is discharged pro tanto by honor of any such draft or demand;

    (b) as between competing good faith purchasers of complying drafts or demands the person first purchasing has priority over a subsequent purchaser even though the later purchased draft or demand has been first honored.

§ 5–109. Issuer's Obligation to Its Customer.

(1) An issuer's obligation to its customer includes good faith and observance of any general banking usage but unless otherwise agreed does not include liability or responsibility

    (a) for performance of the underlying contract for sale or other transaction between the customer and the beneficiary; or

    (b) for any act or omission of any person other than itself or its own branch or for loss or destruction of a draft, demand or document in transit or in the possession of others; or

    (c) based on knowledge or lack of knowledge of any usage of any particular trade.

(2) An issuer must examine documents with care so as to ascertain that on their face they appear to comply with the terms of the credit but unless otherwise agreed assumes no liability or responsibility for the genuineness, falsification or effect of any document which appears on such examination to be regular on its face.

(3) A non-bank issuer is not bound by any banking usage of which it has no knowledge.

§ 5–110. Availability of Credit in Portions; Presenter's Reservation of Lien or Claim.

(1) Unless otherwise specified a credit may be used in portions in the discretion of the beneficiary.

(2) Unless otherwise specified a person by presenting a documentary draft or demand for payment under a credit relinquishes upon its honor all claims to the documents and a person by transferring such draft or demand or causing such presentment authorizes such relinquishment. An explicit reservation of claim makes the draft or demand non-complying.

§ 5–111. Warranties on Transfer and Presentment.

(1) Unless otherwise agreed the beneficiary by transferring or presenting a documentary draft or demand for payment warrants to all interested parties that the necessary conditions of the credit have been complied with. This is in addition to any warranties arising under Articles 3, 4, 7 and 8.

(2) Unless otherwise agreed a negotiating, advising, confirming, collecting or issuing bank presenting or transferring a draft or demand for payment under a credit warrants only the matters warranted by a collecting bank under Article 4 and any such bank transferring a document warrants only the matters warranted by an intermediary under Articles 7 and 8.

§ 5–112. Time Allowed for Honor or Rejection; Withholding Honor or Rejection by Consent; "Presenter."

(1) A bank to which a documentary draft or demand for payment is presented under a credit may without dishonor of the draft, demand or credit

    (a) defer honor until the close of the third banking day following receipt of the documents; and

    (b) further defer honor if the presenter has expressly or impliedly consented thereto.

Failure to honor within the time here specified constitutes dishonor of the draft or demand and of the credit [except as otherwise provided in subsection (4) of Section 5–114 on conditional payment].

Note: *The bracketed language in the last sentence of subsection (1) should be included only if the optional provisions of Section 5–114(4) and (5) are included.*

(2) Upon dishonor the bank may unless otherwise instructed fulfill its duty to return the draft or demand and the documents by holding them at the disposal of the presenter and sending him an advice to that effect.

(3) "Presenter" means any person presenting a draft or demand for payment for honor under a credit even though that person is a confirming bank or other correspondent which is acting under an issuer's authorization.

§ 5–113. Indemnities.

(1) A bank seeking to obtain (whether for itself or another) honor, negotiation or reimbursement under a credit may give an indemnity to induce such honor, negotiation or reimbursement.

(2) An indemnity agreement inducing honor, negotiation or reimbursement

    (a) unless otherwise explicitly agreed applies to defects in the documents but not in the goods; and

    (b) unless a longer time is explicitly agreed expires at the end of ten business days following receipt of the documents by, the ultimate customer unless notice of objection is sent before such expiration date. The ultimate customer may send notice of objection to the person from whom he received the documents and any bank receiving such notice is under a duty to send notice to its transferor before its midnight deadline.

§ 5–114. Issuer's Duty and Privilege to Honor; Right to Reimbursement.

(1) An issuer must honor a draft or demand for payment which complies with the terms of the relevant credit regardless of whether the goods or documents conform to the underlying contract for sale or other contract between the customer and the beneficiary. The issuer is not excused from honor of such a draft or demand by reason of an additional general term that all documents must be satisfactory to the issuer, but an issuer may require that specified documents must be satisfactory to it.

(2) Unless otherwise agreed when documents appear on their face to comply with the terms of a credit but a required document does not in fact conform to the warranties made on negotiation or transfer of a document of title (Section 7–507) or of a security (Section 8–306) or is forged or fraudulent or there is fraud in the transaction

    (a) the issuer must honor the draft or demand for payment if honor is demanded by a negotiating bank or other holder of the draft or demand which has taken the draft or demand under the credit and under circumstances which would make it a holder in due course (Section 3–302) and in an appropriate case would make it a person to whom a document of title has been duly negotiated (Section 7–502) or a bona fide purchaser of a security (Section 8–302); and

    (b) in all other cases as against its customer, an issuer acting in good faith may honor the draft or demand for payment despite notification from the customer of fraud, forgery or other defect not apparent on the face of the documents but a court of appropriate jurisdiction may enjoin such honor.

(3) Unless otherwise agreed an issuer which has duly honored a draft or demand for payment is entitled to immediate reimbursement of any payment made under the credit and to be put in effectively available funds not later than the day before maturity of any acceptance made under the credit.

[(4) When a credit provides for payment by the issuer on receipt of notice that the required documents are in the possession of a correspondent or other agent of the issuer

    (a) any payment made on receipt of such notice is conditional; and

    (b) the issuer may reject documents which do not comply with the credit if it does so within three banking days following its receipt of the documents; and

    (c) in the event of such rejection, the issuer is entitled by charge back or otherwise to return of the payment made.]

[(5) In the case covered by subsection (4) failure to reject documents within the time specified in sub-paragraph (b) constitutes acceptance of the documents and makes the payment final in favor of the beneficiary.]

Note: *Subsections (4) and (5) are bracketed as optional. If they are included the bracketed language in the last sentence of Section 5–112(1) should also be included.*

§ 5–115. Remedy for Improper Dishonor or Anticipatory Repudiation.

(1) When an issuer wrongfully dishonors a draft or demand for payment presented under a credit the person entitled to honor has with respect to any documents the rights of a person in the position of a seller (Section 2–707) and may recover from the issuer the face amount of the draft or demand together with incidental damages under Section 2–710 on seller's incidental damages and interest but less any amount realized by resale or other use or disposition of the subject matter of the transaction. In the event no resale or other utilization is made the documents, goods or other subject matter involved in the transaction must be turned over to the issuer on payment of judgment.

(2) When an issuer wrongfully cancels or otherwise repudiates a credit before presentment of a draft or demand for payment drawn under it the beneficiary has the rights of a seller after anticipatory repudiation by the buyer under Section 2–610 if he learns of the repudiation in time reasonably to avoid procurement of the required documents. Otherwise the beneficiary has an immediate right of action for wrongful dishonor.

§ 5–116. Transfer and Assignment.

(1) The right to draw under a credit can be transferred or assigned only when the credit is expressly designated as transferable or assignable.

(2) Even though the credit specifically states that it is nontransferable or nonassignable the beneficiary may before performance of the conditions of the credit assign his right to proceeds. Such an assignment is an assignment of a contract right under Article 9 on Secured Transactions and is governed by that Article except that

    (a) the assignment is ineffective until the letter of credit or advice of credit is delivered to the assignee which delivery constitutes perfection of the security interest under Article 9; and

    (b) the issuer may honor drafts or demands for payment drawn under the credit until it receives a notification of the assignment signed by the beneficiary which reasonably identifies the credit involved in the assignment and contains a request to pay the assignee; and

    (c) after what reasonably appears to be such a notification has been received the issuer may without dishonor refuse to accept or pay even to a person otherwise entitled to honor until the letter of credit or advice of credit is exhibited to the issuer.

(3) Except where the beneficiary has effectively assigned his right to draw or his right to proceeds, nothing in this section limits his right to transfer or negotiate drafts or demands drawn under the credit.

§ 5–117. Insolvency of Bank Holding Funds for Documentary Credit.

(1) Where an issuer or an advising or confirming bank or a bank which has for a customer procured issuance of a credit by another bank becomes insolvent before final payment under the credit and the credit is one to which this Article is made applicable by paragraphs (a) or (b) of Section 5–102(1) on scope, the receipt or allocation of funds or collateral to secure or meet obligations under the credit shall have the following results:

(a) to the extent of any funds or collateral turned over after or before the insolvency as indemnity against or specifically for the purpose of payment of drafts or demands for payment drawn under the designated credit, the drafts or demands are entitled to payment in preference over depositors or other general creditors of the issuer or bank; and

(b) on expiration of the credit or surrender of the beneficiary's rights under it unused any person who has given such funds or collateral is similarly entitled to return thereof; and

(c) a charge to a general or current account with a bank if specifically consented to for the purpose of indemnity against or payment of drafts or demands for payment drawn under the designated credit falls under the same rules as if the funds had been drawn out in cash and then turned over with specific instructions.

(2) After honor or reimbursement under this section the customer or other person for whose account the insolvent bank has acted is entitled to receive the documents involved.

ARTICLE 6. Bulk Transfers

§ 6–101. Short Title.

This Article shall be known and may be cited as Uniform Commercial Code—Bulk Transfers.

§ 6–102. "Bulk Transfer"; Transfers of Equipment; Enterprises Subject to This Article; Bulk Transfers Subject to This Article.

(1) A "bulk transfer" is any transfer in bulk and not in the ordinary course of the transferor's business of a major part of the materials, supplies, merchandise or other inventory (Section 9–109) of an enterprise subject to this Article.

(2) A transfer of a substantial part of the equipment (Section 9–109) of such an enterprise is a bulk transfer if it is made in connection with a bulk transfer of inventory, but not otherwise.

(3) The enterprises subject to this Article are all those whose principal business is the sale of merchandise from stock, including those who manufacture what they sell.

(4) Except as limited by the following section all bulk transfers of goods located within this state are subject to this Article.

§ 6–103. Transfers Excepted From This Article.

The following transfers are not subject to this Article:

(1) Those made to give security for the performance of an obligation;

(2) General assignments for the benefit of all the creditors of the transferor, and subsequent transfers by the assignee thereunder;

(3) Transfers in settlement or realization of a lien or other security interest;

(4) Sales by executors, administrators, receivers, trustees in bankruptcy, or any public officer under judicial process;

(5) Sales made in the course of judicial or administrative proceedings for the dissolution or reorganization of a corporation and of which notice is sent to the creditors of the corporation pursuant to order of the court or administrative agency;

(6) Transfers to a person maintaining a known place of business in this State who becomes

bound to pay the debts of the transferor in full and gives public notice of that fact, and who is solvent after becoming so bound;

(7) A transfer to a new business enterprise organized to take over and continue the business, if public notice of the transaction is given and the new enterprise assumes the debts of the transferor and he receives nothing from the transaction except an interest in the new enterprise junior to the claims of creditors;

(8) Transfers of property which is exempt from execution.

Public notice under subsection (6) or subsection (7) may be given by publishing once a week for two consecutive weeks in a newspaper of general circulation where the transferor had its principal place of business in this state an advertisement including the names and addresses of the transferor and transferee and the effective date of the transfer.

§ 6–104. Schedule of Property, List of Creditors.

(1) Except as provided with respect to auction sales (Section 6–108), a bulk transfer subject to this Article is ineffective against any creditor of the transferor unless:

(a) The transferee requires the transferor to furnish a list of his existing creditors prepared as stated in this section; and

(b) The parties prepare a schedule of the property transferred sufficient to identify it; and

(c) The transferee preserves the list and schedule for six months next following the transfer and permits inspection of either or both and copying therefrom at all reasonable hours by any creditor of the transferor, or files the list and schedule in (*a public office to be here identified*).

(2) The list of creditors must be signed and sworn to or affirmed by the transferor or his agent. It must contain the names and business addresses of all creditors of the transferor, with the amounts when known, and also the names of all persons who are known to the transferor to assert claims against him even though such claims are disputed. If the transferor is the obligor of an outstanding issue of bonds, debentures or the like as to which there is an indenture trustee, the list of creditors need include only the name and address of the indenture trustee and the aggregate outstanding principal amount of the issue.

(3) Responsibility for the completeness and accuracy of the list of creditors rests on the transferor, and the transfer is not rendered ineffective by errors or omissions therein unless the transferee is shown to have had knowledge.

§ 6–105. Notice to Creditors.

In addition to the requirements of the preceding section, any bulk transfer subject to this Article except one made by auction sale (Section 6–108) is ineffective against any creditor of the transferor unless at least ten days before he takes possession of the goods or pays for them, whichever happens first, the transferee gives notice of the transfer in the manner and to the persons hereafter provided (Section 6–107).

[§ 6–106. Application of the Proceeds.

In addition to the requirements of the two preceding sections:

(1) Upon every bulk transfer subject to this Article for which new consideration becomes payable except those made by sale at auction it is the duty of the transferee to assure that such consideration is applied so far as necessary to pay those debts of the transferor which are either shown on the list furnished by the transferor (Section 6–104) or filed in writing in the place stated in the notice (Section 6–107) within thirty days after the mailing of such notice. This duty of the transferee runs to all the holders of such debts, and may be enforced by any of them for the benefit of all.

(2) If any of said debts are in dispute the necessary sum may be withheld from distribution until the dispute is settled or adjudicated.

(3) If the consideration payable is not enough to pay all of the said debts in full distribution shall be made pro rata.]

Note: *This section is bracketed to indicate division of opinion as to whether or not it is a wise provision, and to suggest that this is a point on which State enactments may differ without serious damage to the principle of uniformity.*

In any State where this section is omitted, the following parts of sections, also bracketed in the text, should also be omitted, namely:

Section 6–107(2) (e).

   6–108(3) (c)

   6–109(2).

In any State where this section is enacted, these other provisions should be also.

Optional Subsection (4)

[(4) The transferee may within ten days after he takes possession of the goods pay the consideration into the (*specify court*) in the county where the transferor had its principal place of business in this state and thereafter may discharge his duty under this section by giving notice by registered or certified mail to all the persons to whom the duty runs that the consideration has been paid into that court and that they should file their claims there. On motion of any interested party, the court may order the distribution of the consideration to the persons entitled to it.]

Note: *Optional subsection (4) is recommended for those states which do not have a general statute providing for payment of money into court.*

§ 6–107. The Notice.

(1) The notice to creditors (Section 6–105) shall state:

(a) that a bulk transfer is about to be made; and

(b) the names and business addresses of the transferor and transferee, and all other business names and addresses used by the transferor within three years last past so far as known to the transferee; and

(c) whether or not all the debts of the transferor are to be paid in full as they fall due as a result of the transaction, and if so, the address to which creditors should send their bills.

(2) If the debts of the transferor are not to be paid in full as they fall due or if the transferee is in doubt on that point then the notice shall state further:

(a) the location and general description of the property to be transferred and the estimated total of the transferor's debts;

(b) the address where the schedule of property and list of creditors (Section 6–104) may be inspected;

(c) whether the transfer is to pay existing debts and if so the amount of such debts and to whom owing;

(d) whether the transfer is for new consideration and if so the amount of such consideration and the time and place of payment; [and]

[(e) if for new consideration the time and place where creditors of the transferor are to file their claims.]

(3) The notice in any case shall be delivered personally or sent by registered or certified mail to all the persons shown on the list of creditors furnished by the transferor (Section 6–104) and to all other persons who are known to the transferee to hold or assert claims against the transferor.

§ 6–108. Auction Sales; "Auctioneer."

(1) A bulk transfer is subject to this Article even though it is by sale at auction, but only in the manner and with the results stated in this section.

(2) The transferor shall furnish a list of his creditors and assist in the preparation of a schedule of the property to be sold, both prepared as before stated (Section 6–104).

(3) The person or persons other than the transferor who direct, control or are responsible for the auction are collectively called the "auctioneer." The auctioneer shall:

(a) receive and retain the list of creditors and prepare and retain the schedule of property for the period stated in this Article (Section 6–104);

(b) give notice of the auction personally or by registered or certified mail at least ten days before it occurs to all persons shown on the list of creditors and to all other persons who are known to him to hold or assert claims against the transferor; [and]

[(c) assure that the net proceeds of the auction are applied as provided in this Article (Section 6–106).]

(4) Failure of the auctioneer to perform any of these duties does not affect the validity of the sale or the title of the purchasers, but if the auctioneer knows that the auction constitutes a bulk transfer such failure renders the auctioneer liable to the creditors of the transferor as a class for the sums owing to them from the transferor up to but not exceeding the net proceeds of the auction. If the auctioneer consists of several persons their liability is joint and several.

§ 6–109. What Creditors Protected; [Credit for Payment to Particular Creditors].

(1) The creditors of the transferor mentioned in this Article are those holding claims based on transactions or events occurring before the bulk transfer, but creditors who become such after notice to creditors is given (Sections 6–105 and 6–107) are not entitled to notice.

[(2) Against the aggregate obligation imposed by the provisions of this Article concerning the application of the proceeds (Section 6–106 and subsection (3) (c) of 6–108) the transferee or auctioneer is entitled to credit for sums paid to particular creditors of the transferor, not exceeding the sums believed in good faith at the time of the payment to be properly payable to such creditors.]

§ 6–110. Subsequent Transfers.

When the title of a transferee to property is subject to a defect by reason of his non-compliance with the requirements of this Article, then:

(1) a purchaser of any of such property from such transferee who pays no value or who takes with notice of such non-compliance takes subject to such defect, but

(2) a purchaser for value in good faith and without such notice takes free of such defect.

§ 6–111. Limitation of Actions and Levies.

No action under this Article shall be brought nor levy made more than six months after the date on which the transferee took possession of the goods unless the transfer has been concealed. If the transfer has been concealed, actions may be brought or levies made within six months after its discovery.

Note to Article 6: *Section 6–106 is bracketed to indicate division of opinion as to whether or not it is a wise provision, and to suggest that this is a point on which State enactments may differ without serious damage to the principle of uniformity.*

In any State where Section 6–106 is not enacted, the following parts of sections, also bracketed in the text, should also be omitted, namely:

Section 6–107(2) (e).

6–108(3) (c)

6–109(2).

In any State where Section 6–106 is enacted, these other provisions should be also.

ARTICLE 7. Warehouse Receipts, Bills of Lading and Other Documents of Title

PART 1

GENERAL

§ 7–101. Short Title.

This Article shall be known and may be cited as Uniform Code—Documents of Title.

§ 7–102. Definitions and Index of Definitions.

(1) In this Article, unless the context otherwise requires:

(a) "Bailee" means the person who by a warehouse receipt, bill of lading or other document of title acknowledges possession of goods and contracts to deliver them.

(b) "Consignee" means the person named in a bill to whom or to whose order the bill promises delivery.

(c) "Consignor" means the person named in a bill as the person from whom the goods have been received for shipment.

(d) "Delivery order" means a written order to deliver goods directed to a warehouseman, carrier or other person who in the ordinary course of business issues warehouse receipts or bills of lading.

(e) "Document" means document of title as defined in the general definitions in Article 1 (Section 1–201).

(f) "Goods" means all things which are treated as movable for the purposes of a contract of storage or transportation.

(g) "Issuer" means a bailee who issues a document except that in relation to an unaccepted delivery order it means the person who orders the possessor of goods to deliver. Issuer includes any person for whom an agent or employee purports to act in issuing a document if the agent or employee has real or apparent authority to issue documents, notwithstanding that the issuer received no goods or that the goods were misdescribed or that in any other respect the agent or employee violated his instructions.

(h) "Warehouseman" is a person engaged in the business of storing goods for hire.

(2) Other definitions applying to this Article or to specified Parts thereof, and the sections in which they appear are:

"Duly negotiate." Section 7–501.

"Person entitled under the document." Section 7–403(4).

(3) Definitions in other Articles applying to this Article and the sections in which they appear are:

"Contract for sale." Section 2–106.

"Overseas." Section 2–323.

"Receipt" of goods. Section 2–103.

(4) In addition Article 1 contains general definitions and principles of construction and interpretation applicable throughout this Article.

§ 7–103. Relation of Article to Treaty, Statute, Tariff, Classification or Regulation.

To the extent that any treaty or statute of the United States, regulatory statute of this State or tariff, classification or regulation filed or issued pursuant thereto is applicable, the provisions of this Article are subject thereto.

§ 7–104. Negotiable and Non-Negotiable Warehouse Receipt, Bill of Lading or Other Document of Title.

(1) A warehouse receipt, bill of lading or other document of title is negotiable

(a) if by its terms the goods are to be delivered to bearer or to the order of a named person; or

(b) where recognized in overseas trade, if it runs to a named person or assigns.

(2) Any other document is non-negotiable. A bill of lading in which it is stated that the goods are consigned to a named person is not made negotiable by a provision that the goods are to be delivered only against a written order signed by the same or another named person.

§ 7–105. Construction Against Negative Implication.

The omission from either Part 2 or Part 3 of this Article of a provision corresponding to a provision made in the other Part does not imply that a corresponding rule of law is not applicable.

PART 2

WAREHOUSE RECEIPTS: SPECIAL PROVISIONS

§ 7–201. Who May Issue a Warehouse Receipt; Storage Under Government Bond.

(1) A warehouse receipt may be issued by any warehouseman.

(2) Where goods including distilled spirits and agricultural commodities are stored under a statute requiring a bond against withdrawal or a license for the issuance of receipts in the nature of warehouse receipts, a receipt issued for the goods has like effect as a warehouse receipt even though issued by a person who is the owner of the goods and is not a warehouseman.

§ 7–202. Form of Warehouse Receipt; Essential Terms; Optional Terms.

(1) A warehouse receipt need not be in any particular form.

(2) Unless a warehouse receipt embodies within its written or printed terms each of the following, the warehouseman is liable for damages caused by the omission to a person injured thereby:

(a) the location of the warehouse where the goods are stored;

(b) the date of issue of the receipt;

(c) the consecutive number of the receipt;

(d) a statement whether the goods received will be delivered to the bearer, to a specified person, or to a specified person or his order;

(e) the rate of storage and handling charges, except that where goods are stored under a field warehousing arrangement a statement of that fact is sufficient on a non-negotiable receipt;

(f) a description of the goods or of the packages containing them;

(g) the signature of the warehouseman, which may be made by his authorized agent;

(h) if the receipt is issued for goods of which the warehouseman is owner, either solely or jointly or in common with others, the fact of such ownership; and

(i) a statement of the amount of advances made and of liabilities incurred for which the warehouseman claims a lien or security interest (Section 7–209). If the precise amount of such advances made or of such liabilities incurred is, at the time of the issue of the receipt, unknown to the warehouseman or to his agent who issues it, a statement of the fact that advances have been made or liabilities incurred and the purpose thereof is sufficient.

(3) A warehouseman may insert in his receipt any other terms which are not contrary to the provisions of this Act and do not impair his obligation of delivery (Section 7–403) or his duty of care (Section 7–204). Any contrary provisions shall be ineffective.

§ 7–203. Liability for Non-Receipt or Misdescription.

A party to or purchaser for value in good faith of a document of title other than a bill of lading relying in either case upon the description therein of the goods may recover from the issuer damages caused by the non-receipt or misdescription of the goods, except to the extent that the document conspicuously indicates that the issuer does not know whether any part or all of the goods in fact were received or conform to the description, as where the description is in terms of marks or labels or kind, quantity or condition, or the receipt or description is qualified by "contents, condition and quality unknown," "said to contain" or the like, if such indication be true, or the party or purchaser otherwise has notice.

§ 7–204. Duty of Care; Contractual Limitation of Warehouseman's Liability.

(1) A warehouseman is liable for damages for loss of or injury to the goods caused by his failure to exercise such care in regard to them as a reasonably careful man would exercise under like circumstances but unless otherwise agreed he is not liable for damages which could not have been avoided by the exercise of such care.

(2) Damages may be limited by a term in the warehouse receipt or storage agreement limiting the amount of liability in case of loss or damage, and setting forth a specific liability per

article or item, or value per unit of weight, beyond which the warehouseman shall not be liable; provided, however, that such liability may on written request of the bailor at the time of signing such storage agreement or within a reasonable time after receipt of the warehouse receipt be increased on part or all of the goods thereunder, in which event increased rates may be charged based on such increased valuation, but that no such increase shall be permitted contrary to a lawful limitation of liability contained in the warehouseman's tariff, if any. No such limitation is effective with respect to the warehouseman's liability for conversion to his own use.

(3) Reasonable provisions as to the time and manner of presenting claims and instituting actions based on the bailment may be included in the warehouse receipt or tariff.

(4) This section does not impair or repeal . . .

Note: Insert in subsection (4) a reference to any statute which imposes a higher responsibility upon the warehouseman or invalidates contractual limitations which would be permissible under this Article.

§ 7–205. Title Under Warehouse Receipt Defeated in Certain Cases.

A buyer in the ordinary course of business of fungible goods sold and delivered by a warehouseman who is also in the business of buying and selling such goods takes free of any claim under a warehouse receipt even though it has been duly negotiated.

§ 7–206. Termination of Storage at Warehouseman's Option.

(1) A warehouseman may on notifying the person on whose account the goods are held and any other person known to claim an interest in the goods require payment of any charges and removal of the goods from the warehouse at the termination of the period of storage fixed by the document, or, if no period is fixed, within a stated period not less than thirty days after the notification. If the goods are not removed before the date specified in the notification, the warehouseman may sell them in accordance with the provisions of the section on enforcement of a warehouseman's lien (Section 7–210).

(2) If a warehouseman in good faith believes that the goods are about to deteriorate or decline in value to less than the amount of his lien within the time prescribed in subsection (1) for notification, advertisement and sale, the warehouseman may specify in the notification any reasonable shorter time for removal of the goods and in case the goods are not removed, may sell them at public sale held not less than one week after a single advertisement or posting.

(3) If as a result of a quality or condition of the goods of which the warehouseman had no notice at the time of deposit the goods are a hazard to other property or to the warehouse or to persons, the warehouseman may sell the goods at public or private sale without advertisement on reasonable notification to all persons known to claim an interest in the goods. If the warehouseman after a reasonable effort is unable to sell the goods he may dispose of them in any lawful manner and shall incure no liability by reason of such disposition.

(4) The warehouseman must deliver the goods to any person entitled to them under this Article upon due demand made at any time prior to sale or other disposition under this section.

(5) The warehouseman may satisfy his lien from the proceeds of any sale or disposition under this section but must hold the balance for delivery on the demand of any person to whom he would have been bound to deliver the goods.

§ 7–207. Goods Must Be Kept Separate; Fungible Goods.

(1) Unless the warehouse receipt otherwise provides, a warehouseman must keep separate the goods covered by each receipt so as to permit at all times identification and delivery of those goods except that different lots of fungible goods may be commingled.

(2) Fungible goods so commingled are owned in common by the persons entitled thereto and the warehouseman is severally liable to each owner for that owner's share. Where because of overissue a mass of fungible goods is insufficient to meet all the receipts which the warehouseman has issued against it, the persons entitled include all holders to whom overissued receipts have been duly negotiated.

§ 7–208. Altered Warehouse Receipts.

Where a blank in a negotiable warehouse receipt has been filled in without authority, a purchaser for value and without notice of the want of authority may treat the insertion as authorized. Any other unauthorized alteration leaves any receipt enforceable against the issuer according to its original tenor.

§ 7–209. Lien of Warehouseman.

(1) A warehouseman has a lien against the bailor on the goods covered by a warehouse receipt or on the proceeds thereof in his possession for charges for storage or transportation (including demurrage and terminal charges), insurance, labor, or charges present or future in relation to the goods, and for expenses necessary for preservation of the goods or reasonably incurred in their sale pursuant to law. If the person on whose account the goods are held is liable for like charges or expenses in relation to other goods whenever deposited and it is stated in the receipt that a lien is claimed for charges and expenses in relation to other goods, the warehouseman also has a lien against him for such charges and expenses whether or not the other goods have been delivered by the warehouseman. But against a person to whom a negotiable warehouse receipt is duly negotiated a warehouseman's lien is limited to charges in an amount or at a rate specified on the receipt or if no charges are so specified then to a reasonable charge for storage of the goods covered by the receipt subsequent to the date of the receipt.

(2) The warehouseman may also reserve a security interest against the bailor for a maximum amount specified on the receipt for charges other than those specified in subsection (1), such as for money advanced and interest. Such a security interest is governed by the Article on Secured Transactions (Article 9).

(3) A warehouseman's lien for charges and expenses under subsection (1) or a security interest under subsection (2) is also effective against any person who so entrusted the bailor with possession of the goods that a pledge of them by him to a good faith purchaser for value would have been valid but is not effective against a person as to whom the document confers no right in the goods covered by it under Section 7–503.

(4) A warehouseman loses his lien on any goods which he voluntarily delivers or which he unjustifiably refuses to deliver.

§ 7–210. Enforcement of Warehouseman's Lien.

(1) Except as provided in subsection (2), a warehouseman's lien may be enforced by public or private sale of the goods in bloc or in parcels, at any time or place and on any terms which are commercially reasonable, after notifying all persons known to claim an interest in the goods. Such notification must include a statement of the amount due, the nature of the proposed sale and the time and place of any public sale. The fact that a better price could have been obtained by a sale at a different time or in a different method from that selected by the warehouseman is not of itself sufficient to establish that the sale was not made in a commercially reasonable manner. If the warehouseman either sells the goods in the usual manner in any recognized market therefor, or if he sells at the price current in such market at the time of his sale, or if he has otherwise sold in conformity with commercially reasonable practices among dealers in the type of goods sold, he has sold in a commercially reasonable manner. A sale of more goods than apparently necessary to be offered to insure satisfaction of the obligation is not commercially reasonable except in cases covered by the preceding sentence.

(2) A warehouseman's lien on goods other than goods stored by a merchant in the course of his business may be enforced only as follows:

    (a) All persons known to claim an interest in the goods must be notified.

    (b) The notification must be delivered in person or sent by registered or certified letter to the last known address of any person to be notified.

    (c) The notification must include an itemized statement of the claim, a description of the goods to the lien, a demand for payment within a specified time not less than ten days after receipt of the notification, and a conspicuous statement that unless the claim is paid within the time the goods will be advertised for sale and sold by auction at a specified time and place.

(d) The sale must conform to the terms of the notification.

(e) The sale must be held at the nearest suitable place to that where the goods are held or stored.

(f) After the expiration of the time given in the notification, an advertisement of the sale must be published once a week for two weeks consecutively in a newspaper of general circulation where the sale is to be held. The advertisement must include a description of the goods, the name of the person on whose account they are being held, and the time and place of the sale. The sale must take place at least fifteen days after the first publication. If there is no newspaper of general circulation where the sale is to be held, the advertisement must be posted at least ten days before the sale in not less than six conspicuous places in the neighborhood of the proposed sale.

(3) Before any sale pursuant to this section any person claiming a right in the goods may pay the amount necessary to satisfy the lien and the reasonable expenses incurred under this section. In that event the goods must not be sold, but must be retained by the warehouseman subject to the terms of the receipt and this Article.

(4) The warehouseman may buy at any public sale pursuant to this section.

(5) A purchaser in good faith of goods sold to enforce a warehouseman's lien takes the goods free of any rights of persons against whom the lien was valid, despite noncompliance by the warehouseman with the requirements of this section.

(6) The warehouseman may satisfy his lien from the proceeds of any sale pursuant to this section but must hold the balance, if any, for delivery on demand to any person to whom he would have been bound to deliver the goods.

(7) The rights provided by this section shall be in addition to all other rights allowed by law to a creditor against his debtor.

(8) Where a lien is on goods stored by a merchant in the course of his business the lien may be enforced in accordance with either subsection (1) or (2).

(9) The warehouseman is liable for damages caused by failure to comply with the requirements for sale under this section and in case of willful violation is liable for conversion.

PART 3
BILLS OF LADING: SPECIAL PROVISIONS

§ 7–301. Liability for Non-Receipt or Misdescription; "Said to Contain"; "Shipper's Load and Count"; Improper Handling.

(1) A consignee of a non-negotiable bill who has given value in good faith or a holder to whom a negotiable bill has been duly negotiated relying in either case upon the description therein of the goods, or upon the date therein shown, may recover from the issuer damages caused by the misdating of the bill or the non-receipt or misdescription of the goods, except to the extent that the document indicates that the issuer does not know whether any part or all of the goods in fact were received or conform to the description, as where the description is in terms of marks or labels or kind, quantity, or condition or the receipt or description is qualified by "contents or condition of contents of packages unknown," "said to contain," "shipper's weight, load and count" or the like, if such indication be true.

(2) When goods are loaded by an issuer who is a common carrier, the issuer must count the packages of goods if package freight and ascertain the kind and quantity if bulk freight. In such cases "shipper's weight, load and count" or other words indicating that the description was made by the shipper are ineffective except as to freight concealed by packages.

(3) When bulk freight is loaded by a shipper who makes available to the issuer adequate facilities for weighing such freight, an issuer who is a common carrier must ascertain the kind and quantity within a reasonable time after receiving the written request of the shipper to do so. In such cases "shipper's weight" or other words of like purport are ineffective.

(4) The issuer may by inserting in the bill the words "shipper's weight, load and count"

or other words of like purport indicate that the goods were loaded by the shipper; and if such statement be true the issuer shall not be liable for damages caused by the improper loading. But their omission does not imply liability for such damages.

(5) The shipper shall be deemed to have guaranteed to the issuer the accuracy at the time of shipment of the description, marks, labels, number, kind, quantity, condition and weight, as furnished by him; and the shipper shall indemnify the issuer against damage caused by inaccuracies in such particulars. The right of the issuer to such indemnity shall in no way limit his responsibility and liability under the contract of carriage to any person other than the shipper.

§ 7–302. Through Bills of Lading and Similar Documents.

(1) The issuer of a through bill of lading or other document embodying an undertaking to be performed in part by persons acting as its agents or by connecting carriers is liable to anyone entitled to recover on the document for any breach by such other persons or by a connecting carrier of its obligation under the document but to the extent that the bill covers an undertaking to be performed overseas or in territory not contiguous to the continental United States or an undertaking including matters other than transportation this liability may be varied by agreement of the parties.

(2) Where goods covered by a through bill of lading or other document embodying an undertaking to be performed in part by persons other than the issuer are received by any such person, he is subject with respect to his own performance while the goods are in his possession to the obligation of the issuer. His obligation is discharged by delivery of the goods to another such person pursuant to the document, and does not include liability for breach by any other such persons or by the issuer.

(3) The issuer of such through bill of lading or other document shall be entitled to recover from the connecting carrier or such other person in possession of the goods when the breach of the obligation under the document occurred, the amount it may be required to pay to anyone entitled to recover on the document therefor, as may be evidenced by any receipt, judgment, or transcript thereof, and the amount of any expense reasonably incurred by it in defending any action brought by anyone entitled to recover on the document therefor.

§ 7–303. Diversion; Reconsignment; Change of Instructions.

(1) Unless the bill of lading otherwise provides, the carrier may deliver the goods to a person or destination other than that stated in the bill or may otherwise dispose of the goods on instructions from

(a) the holder of a negotiable bill; or

(b) the consignor on a non-negotiable bill notwithstanding contrary instructions from the consignee; or

(c) the consignee on a non-negotiable bill in the absence of contrary instructions from the consignor, if the goods have arrived at the billed destination or if the consignee is in possession of the bill; or

(d) the consignee on a non-negotiable bill if he is entitled as against the consignor to dispose of them.

(2) Unless such instructions are noted on a negotiable bill of lading, a person to whom the bill is duly negotiated can hold the bailee according to the original terms.

§ 7–304. Bills of Lading in a Set.

(1) Except where customary in overseas transportation, a bill of lading must not be issued in a set of parts. The issuer is liable for damages caused by violation of this subsection.

(2) Where a bill of lading is lawfully drawn in a set of parts, each of which is numbered and expressed to be valid only if the goods have not been delivered against any other part, the whole of the parts constitute one bill.

(3) Where a bill of lading is lawfully issued in a set of parts and different parts are negotiated to different persons, the title of the holder to whom the first due negotiation is made prevails as to both the document and the goods even though any later holder may have re-

ceived the goods from the carrier in good faith and discharged the carrier's obligation by surrender of his part.

(4) Any person who negotiates or transfers a single part of a bill of lading drawn in a set is liable to holders of that part as if it were the whole set.

(5) The bailee is obliged to deliver in accordance with Part 4 of this Article against the first presented part of a bill of lading lawfully drawn in a set. Such delivery discharges the bailee's obligation on the whole bill.

§ 7–305. Destination Bills.

(1) Instead of issuing a bill of lading to the consignor at the place of shipment a carrier may at the request of the consignor procure the bill to be issued at destination or at any other place designated in the request.

(2) Upon request of anyone entitled as against the carrier to control the goods while in transit and on surrender of any outstanding bill of lading or other receipt covering such goods, the issuer may procure a substitute bill to be issued at any place designated in the request.

§ 7–306. Altered Bills of Lading.

An unauthorized alteration or filling in of a blank in a bill of lading leaves the bill enforceable according to its original tenor.

§ 7–307. Lien of Carrier.

(1) A carrier has a lien on the goods covered by a bill of lading for charges subsequent to the date of its receipt of the goods for storage or transportation (including demurrage and terminal charges) and for expenses necessary for preservation of the goods incident to their transportation or reasonably incurred in their sale pursuant to law. But against a purchaser for value of a negotiable bill of lading a carrier's lien is limited to charges stated in the bill or the applicable tariffs, or if no charges are stated then to a reasonable charge.

(2) A lien for charges and expenses under subsection (1) on goods which the carrier was required by law to receive for transportation is effective against the consignor or any person entitled to the goods unless the carrier had notice that the consignor lacked authority to subject the goods to such charges and expenses. Any other lien under subsection (1) is effective against the consignor and any person who permitted the bailor to have control or possession of the goods unless the carrier had notice that the bailor lacked such authority.

(3) A carrier loses his lien on any goods which he voluntarily delivers or which he unjustifiably refuses to deliver.

§ 7–308. Enforcement of Carrier's Lien.

(1) A carrier's lien may be enforced by public or private sale of the goods, in bloc or in parcels, at any time or place and on any terms which are commercially reasonable, after notifying all persons known to claim an interest in the goods. Such notification must include a statement of the amount due, the nature of the proposed sale and the time and place of any public sale. The fact that a better price could have been obtained by a sale at a different time or in a different method from that selected by the carrier is not of itself sufficient to establish that the sale was not made in a commercially reasonable manner. If the carrier either sells the goods in the usual manner in any recognized market therefor or if he sells at the price current in such market at the time of his sale or if he has otherwise sold in conformity with commercially reasonable practices among dealers in the type of goods he has sold in a commercially reasonable manner. A sale of more goods than apparently necessary to be offered to ensure satisfaction of the obligation is not commercially reasonable except in cases covered by the preceding sentence.

(2) Before any sale pursuant to this section any person claiming a right in the goods may pay the amount necessary to satisfy the lien and the reasonable expenses incurred under this section. In that event the goods must not be sold, but must be retained by the carrier subject to the terms of the bill and this Article.

(3) The carrier may buy at any public sale pursuant to this section.

(4) A purchaser in good faith of goods sold to enforce a carrier's lien takes the goods free of any rights of persons against whom the lien was valid, despite noncompliance by the carrier with the requirements of this section.

(5) The carrier may satisfy his lien from the proceeds of any sale pursuant to this section but must hold the balance, if any, for delivery on demand to any person to whom he would have been bound to deliver the goods.

(6) The rights provided by this section shall be in addition to all other rights allowed by law to a creditor against his debtor.

(7) A carrier's lien may be enforced in accordance with either subsection (1) or the procedure set forth in subsection (2) of Section 7–210.

(8) The carrier is liable for damages caused by failure to comply with the requirements for sale under this section and in case of willful violation is liable for conversion.

§ 7–309. Duty of Care; Contractual Limitation of Carrier's Liability.

(1) A carrier who issues a bill of lading whether negotiable or non-negotiable must exercise the degree of care in relation to the goods which a reasonably careful man would exercise under like circumstances. This subsection does not repeal or change any law or rule of law which imposes liability upon a common carrier for damages not caused by its negligence.

(2) Damages may be limited by a provision that the carrier's liability shall not exceed a value stated in the document if the carrier's rates are dependent upon value and the consignor by the carrier's tariff is afforded an opportunity to declare a higher value or a value as lawfully provided in the tariff, or where no tariff is filed he is otherwise advised of such opportunity; but no such limitation is effective with respect to the carrier's liability for conversion to its own use.

(3) Reasonable provisions as to the time and manner of presenting claims and instituting actions based on the shipment may be included in a bill of lading or tariff.

PART 4

WAREHOUSE RECEIPTS AND BILLS OF LADING: GENERAL OBLIGATIONS

§ 7–401. Irregularities in Issue of Receipt or Bill or Conduct of Issuer.

The obligations imposed by this Article on an issuer apply to a document of title regardless of the fact that
  (a) the document may not comply with the requirements of this Article or of any other law or regulation regarding its issue, form or content; or
  (b) the issuer may have violated laws regulating the conduct of his business; or
  (c) the goods covered by the document were owned by the bailee at the time the document was issued; or
  (d) the person issuing the document does not come within the definition of warehouseman if it purports to be a warehouse receipt.

§ 7–402. Duplicate Receipt or Bill; Overissue.

Neither a duplicate nor any other document of title purporting to cover goods already represented by an outstanding document of the same issuer confers any right in the goods, except as provided in the case of bills in a set, overissue of documents for fungible goods and substitutes for lost, stolen or destroyed documents. But the issuer is liable for damages caused by his overissue or failure to identify a duplicate document as such by conspicuous notation on its face.

§ 7–403. Obligation of Warehouseman or Carrier to Deliver; Excuse.

(1) The bailee must deliver the goods to a person entitled under the document who complies with subsections (2) and (3), unless and to the extent that the bailee establishes any of the following:

(a) delivery of the goods to a person whose receipt was rightful as against the claimant;

(b) damage to or delay, loss or destruction of the goods for which the bailee is not liable [but the burden of establishing negligence in such cases is on the person entitled under the document];

Note: *The brackets in (1) (b) indicate that State enactments may differ on this point without serious damage to the principle of uniformity.*

(c) previous sale or other disposition of the goods in lawful enforcement of a lien or on warehouseman's lawful termination of storage;

(d) the exercise by a seller of his right to stop delivery pursuant to the provisions of the Article on Sales (Section 2–705);

(e) a diversion, reconsignment or other disposition pursuant to the provisions of this Article (Section 7–303) or tariff regulating such right;

(f) release, satisfaction or any other fact affording a personal defense against the claimant;

(g) any other lawful excuse.

(2) A person claiming goods covered by a document of title must satisfy the bailee's lien where the bailee so requests or where the bailee is prohibited by law from delivering the goods until the charges are paid.

(3) Unless the person claiming is one against whom the document confers no right under Section 7–503(1), he must surrender for cancellation or notation of partial deliveries any outstanding negotiable document covering the goods, and the bailee must cancel the document or conspicuously note the partial delivery thereon or be liable to any person to whom the document is duly negotiated.

(4) "Person entitled under the document" means holder in the case of a negotiable document, or the person to whom delivery is to be made by the terms of or pursuant to written instructions under a non-negotiable document.

§ 7–404. No Liability for Good Faith Delivery Pursuant to Receipt or Bill.

A bailee who in good faith including observance of reasonable commercial standards has received goods and delivered or otherwise disposed of them according to the terms of the document of title or pursuant to this Article is not liable therefor. This rule applies even though the person from whom he received the goods had no authority to procure the document or to dispose of the goods and even though the person to whom he delivered the goods had no authority to receive them.

PART 5

WAREHOUSE RECEIPTS AND BILLS OF LADING: NEGOTIATION AND TRANSFER

§ 7–501. Form of Negotiation and Requirements of "Due Negotiation."

(1) A negotiable document of title running to the order of a named person is negotiated by his indorsement and delivery. After his indorsement in blank or to bearer any person can negotiate it by delivery alone.

(2) (a) A negotiable document of title is also negotiated by delivery alone when by its original terms it runs to bearer.

(b) When a document running to the order of a named person is delivered to him the effect is the same as if the document had been negotiated.

(3) Negotiation of a negotiable document of title after it has been indorsed to a specified person requires indorsement by the special indorsee as well as delivery.

(4) A negotiable document of title is "duly negotiated" when it is negotiated in the manner stated in this section to a holder who purchases it in good faith without notice of any defense against or claim to it on the part of any person and for value, unless it is established that the negotiation is not in the regular course of business or financing or involves receiving the document in settlement or payment of a money obligation.

(5) Indorsement of a non-negotiable document neither makes it negotiable nor adds to the transferee's rights.

(6) The naming in a negotiable bill of a person to be notified of the arrival of the goods does not limit the negotiability of the bill nor constitute notice to a purchaser thereof of any interest of such person in the goods.

§ 7–502. Rights Acquired by Due Negotiation.

(1) Subject to the following section and to the provisions of Section 7–205 on fungible goods, a holder to whom a negotiable document of title has been duly negotiated acquires thereby:

(a) title to the document;

(b) title to the goods;

(c) all rights accruing under the law of agency or estoppel, including rights to goods delivered to the bailee after the document was issued; and

(d) the direct obligation of the issuer to hold or deliver the goods according to the terms of the document free of any defense or claim by him except those arising under the terms of the document or under this Article. In the case of a delivery order the bailee's obligation accrues only upon acceptance and the obligation acquired by the holder is that the issuer and any indorser will procure the acceptance of the bailee.

(2) Subject to the following section, title and rights so acquired are not defeated by any stoppage of the goods represented by the document or by surrender of such goods by the bailee, and are not impaired even though the negotiation or any prior negotiation constituted a breach of duty or even though any person has been deprived of possession of the document by misrepresentation, fraud, accident, mistake, duress, loss, theft or conversion, or even though a previous sale or other transfer of the goods or document has been made to a third person.

§ 7–503. Document of Title to Goods Defeated in Certain Cases.

(1) A document of title confers no right in goods against a person who before issuance of the document had a legal interest or a perfected security interest in them and who neither

(a) delivered or entrusted them or any document of title covering them to the bailor or his nominee with actual or apparent authority to ship, store or sell or with power to obtain delivery under this Article (Section 7–403) or with power of disposition under this Act (Sections 2–403 and 9–307) or other statute or rule of law; nor

(b) acquiesced in the procurement by the bailor or his nominee of any document of title.

(2) Title to goods based upon an unaccepted delivery order is subject to the rights of anyone to whom a negotiable warehouse receipt or bill of lading covering the goods has been duly negotiated. Such a title may be defeated under the next section to the same extent as the rights of the issuer or a transferee from the issuer.

(3) Title to goods based upon a bill of lading issued to a freight forwarder is subject to the rights of anyone to whom a bill issued by the freight forwarder is duly negotiated; but delivery by the carrier in accordance with Part 4 of this Article pursuant to its own bill of lading discharges the carrier's obligation to deliver.

§ 7–504. Rights Acquired in the Absence of Due Negotiation; Effect of Diversion; Seller's Stoppage of Delivery.

(1) A transferee of a document, whether negotiable or nonnegotiable, to whom the document has been delivered but not duly negotiated, acquires the title and rights which his transferor had or had actual authority to convey.

(2) In the case of a non-negotiable document, until but not after the bailee receives notification of the tansfer, the rights of the transferee may be defeated.

(a) by those creditors of the transferor who could treat the sale as void under Section 2–402; or

(b) by a buyer from the transferor in ordinary course of business if the bailee has delivered the goods to the buyer or received notification of his rights; or

(c) as against the bailee by good faith dealings of the bailee with the transferor.

(3) A diversion or other change of shipping instructions by the consignor in a non-negotiable bill of lading which causes the bailee not the deliver to the consignee defeats the consignee's title to the goods if they have been delivered to a buyer in ordinary course of business and in any event defeats the consignee's rights against the bailee.

(4) Delivery pursuant to a non-negotiable document may be stopped by a seller under Section 2–705, and subject to the requirement of due notification there provided. A bailee honoring the seller's instructions is entitled to be indemnified by the seller against any resulting loss or expense.

§ 7–505. Indorser Not a Guarantor for Other Parties.

The indorsement of a document of title issued by a bailee does not make the indorser liable for any default by the bailee or by previous indorsers.

§ 7–506. Delivery Without Indorsement: Right to Compel Indorsement.

The transferee of a negotiable document of title has a specifically enforceable right to have his transferor supply any necessary indorsement but the transfer becomes a negotiation only as of the time the indorsement is supplied.

§ 7–507. Warranties on Negotiation or Transfer of Receipt or Bill.

Where a person negotiates or transfers a document of title for value otherwise than as a mere intermediary under the next following section, then unless otherwise agreed he warrants to his immediate purchaser only in addition to any warranty made in selling the goods
   (a) that the document is genuine; and
   (b) that he has no knowledge of any fact which would impair its validity or worth; and
   (c) that his negotiation or transfer is rightful and fully effective with respect to the title to the document and the goods it represents.

§ 7–508. Warranties of Collecting Bank as to Documents.

A collecting bank or other intermediary known to be entrusted with documents on behalf of another or with collection of a draft or other claim against delivery of documents warrants by such delivery of the documents only its own good faith and authority. This rule applies even though the intermediary has purchased or made advances against the claim or draft to be collected.

§ 7–509. Receipt or Bill: When Adequate Compliance With Commercial Contract.

The question whether a document is adequate to fulfill the obligations of a contract for sale or the conditions of a credit is governed by the Articles on Sales (Article 2) and on Letters of Credit (Article 5).

PART 6
WAREHOUSE RECEIPTS AND BILLS OF LADING: MISCELLANEOUS PROVISIONS

§ 7–601. Lost and Missing Documents.

(1) If a document has been lost, stolen or destroyed, a court may order delivery of the goods or issuance of a substitute document and the bailee may without liability to any person comply with such order. If the document was negotiable the claimant must post security approved by the court to indemnify any person who may suffer loss as a result of non-surrender of the document. If the document was not negotiable, such security may be required at the discretion of the court. The court may also in its discretion order payment of the bailee's reasonable costs and counsel fees.

(2) A bailee who without court order delivers goods to a person claiming under a missing negotiable document is liable to any person injured thereby, and if the delivery is not in good faith becomes liable for conversion. Delivery in good faith is not conversion if made in accordance with a filed classification or tariff or, where no classification or tariff is filed,

if the claimant posts security with the bailee in an amount at least double the value of the goods at the time of posting to indemnify any person injured by the delivery who files a notice of claim within one year after the delivery.

§ 7–602. Attachment of Goods Covered by a Negotiable Document.

Except where the document was originally issued upon delivery of the goods by a person who had no power to dispose of them, no lien attaches by virtue of any judicial process to goods in the possession of a bailee for which a negotiable document of title is outstanding unless the document be first surrendered to the bailee or its negotiation enjoined, and the bailee shall not be compelled to deliver the goods pursuant to process until the document is surrendered to him or impounded by the court. One who purchases the document for value without notice of the process or injunction takes free of the lien imposed by judicial process.

§ 7–603. Conflicting Claims; Interpleader.

If more than one person claims title or possession of the goods, the bailee is excused from delivery until he has had a reasonable time to ascertain the validity of the adverse claims or to bring an action to compel all claimants to interplead and may compel such interpleader, either in defending an action for non-delivery of the goods, or by original action, whichever is appropriate.

ARTICLE 8. Investment Securities

PART 1
SHORT TITLE AND GENERAL MATTERS

§ 8–101. Short Title.

This Article shall be known and may be cited as Uniform Commercial Code—Investment Securities.

§ 8–102. Definitions and Index of Definitions.

(1) In this Article unless the context otherwise requires
    (a) A "security" is an instrument which
        (i) is issued in bearer or registered form; and
        (ii) is of a type commonly dealt in upon securities exchanges or markets or commonly recognized in any area in which it is issued or dealt in as a medium for investment; and
        (iii) is either one of a class or series or by its terms is divisible into a class or series of instruments; and
        (iv) evidences a share, participation or other interest in property or in an enterprise or evidences an obligation of the issuer.
    (b) A writing which is a security is governed by this Article and not by Uniform Commercial Code–Commercial Paper even though it also meets the requirements of that Article. This Article does not apply to money.
    (c) A security is in "registered form" when it specifies a person entitled to the security or to the rights it evidences and when its transfer may be registered upon books maintained for that purpose by or on behalf of an issuer or the security so states.
    (d) A security is in "bearer form" when it runs to bearer according to its terms and not by reason of any indorsement.
(2) A "subsequent purchaser" is a person who takes other than by original issue.
(3) A "clearing corporation" is a corporation all of the capital stock of which is held by or for a national securities exchange or association registered under a statute of the United States such as the Securities Exchange Act of 1934.

(4) A "custodian bank" is any bank or trust company which is supervised and examined by state or federal authority having supervision over banks and which is acting as custodian for a clearing corporation.

(5) Other definitions applying to this Article or to specified Parts thereof and the sections in which they appear are:

"Adverse claim"	Section 8–301
"Bona fide purchaser"	Section 8–302
"Broker"	Section 8–303
"Guarantee of the signature"	Section 8–402
"Intermediary Bank"	Section 4–105
"Issuer"	Section 8–201
"Overissue"	Section 8–104

(6) In addition Article 1 contains general definitions and principles of construction and interpretation applicable throughout this Article.

§ 8–103 Issuer's Lien.

A lien upon a security in favor of an issuer thereof is valid against a purchaser only if the right of the issuer to such lien is noted conspicuously on the security.

§ 8–104 Effect of Overissue; "Overissue."

(1) The provisions of this Article which validate a security or compel its issue or reissue do not apply to the extent that validation, issue or reissue would result in overissue; but

    (a) if an identical security which does not constitute an overissue is reasonably available for purchase, the person entitled to issue or validation may compel the issuer to purchase and deliver such a security to him against surrender of the security, if any, which he holds; or

    (b) if a security is not so available for purchase, the person entitled to issue or validation may recover from the issuer the price he or the last purchaser for value paid for it with interest from the date of his demand.

(2) "Overissue" means the issue of securities in excess of the amount which the issuer has corporate power to issue.

§ 8–105. Securities Negotiable; Presumptions.

(1) Securities governed by this Article are negotiable instruments.

(2) In any action on a security

    (a) unless specifically denied in the pleadings, each signature on the security or in a necessary indorsement is admitted;

    (b) when the effectiveness of a signature is put in issue the burden of establishing it is on the party claiming under the signature but the signature is presumed to be genuine or authorized;

    (c) when signatures are admitted or established production of the instrument entitles a holder to recover on it unless the defendant establishes a defense or a defect going to the validity of the security; and

    (d) after it is shown that a defense or defect exists the plaintiff has the burden of establishing that he or some person under whom he claims is a person against whom the defense or defect is ineffective (Section 8–202).

§ 8–106. Applicability.

The validity of a security and the rights and duties of the issuer with respect to registration of transfer are governed by the law (including the conflict of laws rules) of the jurisdiction of organization of the issuer.

§ 8–107. Securities Deliverable; Action for Price.

(1) Unless otherwise agreed and subject to any applicable law or regulation respecting short sales, a person obligated to deliver securities may deliver any security of the specified issue in bearer form or registered in the name of the transferee or indorsed to him or in blank.

(2) When the buyer fails to pay the price as it comes due under a contract of sale the seller may recover the price

   (a) of securities accepted by the buyer; and

   (b) of other securities if efforts at their resale would be unduly burdensome or if there is no readily available market for their resale.

PART 2
ISSUE—ISSUER

§ 8–201. "Issuer."

(1) With respect to obligations on or defenses to a security "issuer" includes a person whom

   (a) places or authorizes the placing of his name on a security (otherwise than as authenticating trustee, registrar, transfer agent or the like) to evidence that it represents a share, participation or other interest in his property or in an enterprise or to evidence his duty to perform an obligation evidenced by the security; or

   (b) directly or indirecting creates fractional interests in his rights or property which fractional interests are evidenced by securities; or

   (c) becomes responsible for or in place of any other person described as an issuer in this section.

(2) With respect to obligations on or defenses to a security a guarantor is an issuer to the extent of his guaranty whether or not his obligation is noted on the security.

(3) With respect to registration of transfer (Part 4 of this Article) "issuer" means a person on whose behalf transfer books are maintained.

§ 8–202. Issuer's Responsibility and Defenses; Notice of Defect or Defense.

(1) Even against a purchaser for value and without notice, the terms of a security include those stated on the security and those made part of the security by reference to another instrument, indenture or document or to a constitution, statute, ordinance, rule, regulation, order or the like to the extent that the terms so referred to do no conflict with the stated terms. Such a reference does not of itself charge a purchaser for value with notice of a defect going to the validity of the security even though the security expressly states that a person accepting it admits such notice.

   (2) (a) A security other than one issued by a government or governmental agency or unit even though issued with a defect going to its validity is valid in the hands of a purchaser for value and without notice of the particular defect unless the defect involves a violation of constitutional provisions in which case the security is valid in the hands of a subsequent purchaser for value and without notice of the defect.

   (b) The rule of subparagraph (a) applies to an issuer which is a government or governmental agency or unit only if either there has been substantial compliance with the legal requirements governing the issue or the issuer has received a substantial consideration for the issue as a whole or for the particular security and a stated purpose of the issue is one for which the issuer has power to borrow money or issue the security.

(3) Except as otherwise provided in the case of certain unauthorized signatures on issue (Section 8–205), lack of genuineness of a security is a complete defense even against a purchaser for value and without notice.

(4) All other defenses of the issuer including nondelivery and conditional delivery of the security are ineffective against a purchaser for value who has taken without notice of the particular defense.

(5) Nothing in this section shall be construed to affect the right of a party to a "when, as and if issued" or a "when distributed" contract to cancel the contract in the event of a material change in the character of the security which is the subject of the contract or in the plan or arrangement pursuant to which such security is to be issued or distributed.

§ 8–203. Staleness as Notice of Defects or Defenses.

(1) After an act or event which creates a right to immediate performance of the principal

obligation evidenced by the security or which sets a date on or after which the security is to be presented or surrendered for redemption or exchange, a purchaser is charged with notice of any defect in its issue or defense of the issuer

    (a) if the act or event is one requiring the payment of money or the delivery of securities or both on presentation or surrender of the security and such funds or securities are available on the date set for payment or exchange and he takes the security more than one year after that date; and

    (b) if the act or event is not covered by paragraph (a) and he takes the security more than two years after the date set for surrender or presentation or the date on which such performance became due.

(2) A call which has been revoked is not within subsection (1).

§ 8–204. Effect of Issuer's Restrictions on Transfer.

Unless noted conspicuously on the security a restriction on transfer imposed by the issuer even though otherwise lawful is ineffective except against a person with actual knowledge of it.

§ 8–205. Effect of Unauthorized Signature on Issue.

An unauthorized signature placed on a security prior to or in the course of issue is ineffective except that the signature is effective in favor of a purchaser for value and without notice of the lack of authority if the signing has been done by

    (a) an authenticating trustee, registrar, transfer agent or other person entrusted by the issuer with the signing of the security or of similar securities or their immediate preparation for signing; or

    (b) an employee of the issuer or of any of the foregoing entrusted with responsible handling of the security.

§ 8–206. Completion or Alteration of Instrument.

(1) Where a security contains the signatures necessary to its issue or transfer but is incomplete in any other respect

    (a) any person may complete it by filling in the blanks as authorized; and

    (b) even though the blanks are incorrectly filled in, the security as completed is enforceable by a purchaser who took it for value and without notice of such incorrectness.

(2) A complete security which has been improperly altered even though fraudulently remains enforceable but only according to its original terms.

§ 8–207. Rights of Issuer With Respect to Registered Owners.

(1) Prior to due presentment for registration of transfer of a security in registered form the issuer or indenture trustee may treat the registered owner as the person exclusively entitled to vote, to receive notifications and otherwise to exercise all the rights and powers of an owner.

(2) Nothing in this Article shall be construed to affect the liability of the registered owner of a security for calls, assessments or the like.

§ 8–208. Effect of Signature of Authenticating Trustee, Registrar or Transfer Agent.

(1) A person placing his signature upon a security as authenticating trustee, registrar, transfer agent or the like warrants to a purchaser for value without notice of the particular defect that

    (a) the security is genuine; and

    (b) his own participation in the issue of the security is within his capacity and within the scope of the authorization received by him from the issuer; and

    (c) he has reasonable grounds to believe that the security is in the form and within the amount the issuer is authorized to issue.

(2) Unless otherwise agreed, a person by so placing his signature does not assume responsibility for the validity of the security in other respects.

PART 3
PURCHASE

§ 8–301. Rights Acquired by Purchaser; "Adverse Claim"; Title Acquired by Bona Fide Purchaser.

(1) Upon delivery of a security the purchaser acquires the rights in the security which his transferor had or had actual authority to convey except that a purchaser who has himself been a party to any fraud or illegality affecting the security or who as a prior holder had notice of an adverse claim cannot improve his position by taking from a later bona fide purchaser. "Adverse claim" includes a claim that a transfer was or would be wrongful or that a particular adverse person is the owner of or has an interest in the security.

(2) A bona fide purchaser in addition to acquiring the rights of a purchaser also acquires the security free of any adverse claim.

(3) A purchaser of a limited interest acquires rights only to the extent of the interest purchased.

§ 8–302. "Bona Fide Purchaser."

A "bona fide purchaser" is a purchaser for value in good faith and without notice of any adverse claim who takes delivery of a security in bearer form or of one in registered form issued to him or indorsed to him or in blank.

§ 8–303. "Broker."

"Broker" means a person engaged for all or part of his time in the business of buying and selling securities, who in the transaction concerned acts for, or buys a security from or sells a security to a customer. Nothing in this Article determines the capacity in which a person acts for purposes of any other statute or rule to which such person is subject.

§ 8–304. Notice to Purchaser of Adverse Claims.

(1) A purchaser (including a broker for the seller or buyer but excluding an intermediary bank) of a security is charged with notice of adverse claims if
- (a) the security whether in bearer or registered form has been indorsed "for collection" or "for surrender" or for some other purpose not involving transfer; or
- (b) the security is in bearer form and has on it an unambiguous statement that it is the property of a person other than the transferor. The mere writing of a name on a security is not such a statement.

(2) The fact that the purchaser (including a broker for the seller or buyer) has notice that the security is held for a third person or is registered in the name of or indorsed by a fiduciary does not create a duty of inquiry into the rightfulness of the transfer or constitute notice of adverse claims. If, however, the purchaser (excluding an intermediary bank) has knowledge that the proceeds are being used or that the transaction is for the individual benefit of the fiduciary or otherwise in breach of duty, the purchaser is charged with notice of adverse claims.

§ 8–305. Staleness as Notice of Adverse Claims.

An act or event which creates a right to immediate performance of the principal obligation evidenced by the security or which sets a date on or after which the security is to be presented or surrendered for redemption or exchange does not of itself constitute any notice of adverse claims except in the case of a purchase
- (a) after one year from any date set for such presentment or surrender for redemption or exchange; or
- (b) after six months from any date set for payment of money against presentation or surrender of the security if funds are available for payment on that date.

§ 8–306. Warranties on Presentment and Transfer.

(1) A person who presents a security for registration of transfer or for payment or exchange warrants to the issuer that he is entitled to the registration, payment or exchange. But a pur-

chaser for value without notice of adverse claims who receives a new, reissued or re-registered security on registration of transfer warrants only that he has no knowledge of any unauthorized signature (Section 8–311) in a necessary indorsement.

(2) A person by transferring a security to a purchaser for value warrants only that

    (a) his transfer is effective and rightful; and

    (b) the security is genuine and has not been materially altered; and

    (c) he knows no fact which might impair the validity of the security.

(3) Where a security is delivered by an intermediary known to be entrusted with delivery of the security on behalf of another or with collection of a draft or other claim against such delivery, the intermediary by such delivery warrants only his own good faith and authority even though he has purchased or made advances against the claim to be collected against the delivery.

(4) A pledgee or other holder for security who redelivers the security received, or after payment and on order of the debtor delivers that security to a third person makes only the warranties of an intermediary under subsection (3).

(5) A broker gives to his customer and to the issuer and a purchaser the warranties provided in this section and has the rights and privileges of a purchaser under this section. The warranties of and in favor of the broker acting as an agent are in addition to applicable warranties given by and in favor of his customer.

§ 8–307. Effect of Delivery Without Indorsement; Right to Compel Indorsement.

Where a security in registered form has been delivered to a purchaser without a necessary indorsement he may become a bona fide purchaser only as of the time the indorsement is supplied, but against the transferor the transfer is complete upon delivery and the purchaser has a specifically enforceable right to have any necessary indorsement supplied.

§ 8–308. Indorsement, How Made; Special Indorsement; Indorser Not a Guarantor; Partial Assignment.

(1) An indorsement of a security in registered form is made when an appropriate person signs on it or on a separate document an assignment or transfer of the security or a power to assign or transfer it or when the signature of such person is written without more upon the back of the security.

(2) An indorsement in blank includes an indorsement to bearer. A special indorsement specifies the person to whom the security is to be transferred, or who has power to transfer it. A holder may convert a blank indorsement into a special indorsement.

(3) "An appropriate person" in subsection (1) means

    (a) the person specified by the security or by special indorsement to be entitled to the security; or

    (b) where the person so specified is described as a fiduciary but is no longer serving in the described capacity,—either that person or his successor; or

    (c) where the security or indorsement so specifies more than one person as fiduciaries and one or more are no longer serving in the described capacity,—the remaining fiduciary or fiduciaries, whether or not a successor has been appointed or qualified; or

    (d) where the person so specified is an individual and is without capacity to act by virtue of death, incompetence, infancy or otherwise,—his executor, administrator, guardian or like fiduciary; or

    (e) where the security or indorsement so specifies more than one person as tenants by the entirety or with right of survivorship and by reason of death all cannot sign,—the survivor or survivors; or

    (f) a person having power to sign under applicable law or controlling instrument; or

    (g) to the extent that any of the foregoing persons may act through an agent,—his authorized agent.

(4) Unless otherwise agreed the indorser by his indorsement assumes no obligation that the security will be honored by the issuer.

(5) An indorsement purporting to be only of part of a security representing units intended by the issuer to be separately transferable is effective to the extent of the indorsement.

(6) Whether the person signing is appropriate is determined as of the date of signing and an indorsement by such a person does not become unauthorized for the purposes of this Article by virtue of any subsequent change of circumstances.

(7) Failure of a fiduciary to comply with a controlling instrument or with the law of the state having jurisdiction of the fiduciary relationship, including any law requiring the fiduciary to obtain court approval of the transfer, does not render his indorsement unauthorized for the purposes of this Article.

§ 8–309. Effect of Indorsement Without Delivery.

An indorsement of a security whether special or in blank does not constitute a transfer until delivery of the security on which it appears or if the indorsement is on a separate document until delivery of both the document and the security.

§ 8–310. Indorsement of Security in Bearer Form.

An indorsement of a security in bearer form may give notice of adverse claims (Section 8–304) but does not otherwise affect any right to registration the holder may possess.

§ 8–311. Effect of Unauthorized Indorsement.

Unless the owner has ratfiied an unauthorized indorsement or is otherwise precluded from asserting its ineffectiveness
- (a) he may assert its ineffectiveness against the issuer or any purchaser other than a purchaser for value and without notice of adverse claims who has in good faith received a new, re-issued or re-registered security on registration of transfer; and
- (b) an issuer who registers the transfer of a security upon the unauthorized indorsement is subject to liability for improper registration (Section 8–404).

§ 8–312. Effect of Guaranteeing Signature or Indorsement.

(1) Any person guaranteeing a signature of an indorser of a security warrants that at the time of signing
- (a) the signature was genuine; and
- (b) the signer was an appropriate person to indorse (Section 8–308); and
- (c) the signer had legal capacity to sign.

But the guarantor does not otherwise warrant the rightfulness of the particular transfer.

(2) Any person may guarantee an indorsement of a security and by so doing warrants not only the signature (subsection 1) but also the rightfulness of the particular transfer in all respects. But no issuer may require a guarantee of indorsement as a condition to registration of transfer.

(3) The foregoing warranties are made to any person taking or dealing with the security in reliance on the guarantee and the guarantor is liable to such person for any loss resulting from breach of the warranties.

§ 8–313. When Delivery to the Purchaser Occurs; Purchaser's Broker as Holder.

(1) Delivery to a purchaser occurs when
- (a) he or a person designated by him acquires possession of a security; or
- (b) his broker acquires possession of a security specially indorsed to or issued in the name of the purchaser; or
- (c) his broker sends him confirmation of the purchase and also by book entry or otherwise identifies a specific security in the broker's possession as belonging to the purchaser; or
- (d) with respect to an identified security to be delivered while still in the possession of a third person when that person acknowledges that he holds for the purchaser.
- (e) appropriate entries on the books of a clearing corporation are made under Section 8–320.

(2) The purchaser is the owner of a security held for him by his broker, but is not the holder except as specified in subparagraphs (b), (c) and (e) of subsection (1). Where a security is part of a fungible bulk the purchaser is the owner of a proportionate property interest in the fungible bulk.

(3) Notice of an adverse claim received by the broker or by the purchaser after the broker takes delivery as a holder for value is not effective either as to the broker or as to the purchaser. However, as between the broker and the purchaser the purchaser may demand delivery of an equivalent security as to which no notice of an adverse claim has been received.

§ 8–314. Duty to Deliver, When Completed.

(1) Unless otherwise agreed where a sale of a security is made on an exchange or otherwise through brokers
  (a) the selling customer fulfills his duty to deliver when he places such a security in the possession of the selling broker or of a person designated by the broker or if requested causes an acknowledgment to be made to the selling broker that it is held for him; and
  (b) the selling broker including a correspondent broker acting for a selling customer fulfills his duty to deliver by placing the security or a like security in the possession of the buying broker or a person designated by him or by effecting clearance of the sale in accordance with the rules of the exchange on which the transaction took place.

(2) Except as otherwise provided in this section and unless otherwise agreed, a transferor's duty to deliver a security under a contract of purchase is not fulfilled until he places the security in form to be negotiated by the purchaser in the possession of the purchaser or of a person designated by him or at the purchaser's request causes an acknowledgment to be made to the purchaser that it is held for him. Unless made on an exchange a sale to a broker purchasing for his own account is within this subsection and not within subsection (1).

§ 8–315. Action Against Purchaser Based Upon Wrongful Transfer.

(1) Any person against whom the transfer of a security is wrongful for any reason, including his incapacity, may against any one except a bona fide purchaser reclaim possession of the security or obtain possession of any new security evidencing all or part of the same rights or have damages.

(2) If the transfer is wrongful because of an unauthorized indorsement, the owner may also reclaim or obtain possession of the security or new security even from a bona fide purchaser if the ineffectiveness of the purported indorsement can be asserted against him under the provisions of this Article on unauthorized indorsements (Section 8–311).

(3) The right to obtain or reclaim possession of a security may be specifically enforced and its transfer enjoined and the security impounded pending the litigation.

§ 8–316. Purchaser's Right to Requisites for Registration of Transfer on Books.

Unless otherwise agreed the transferor must on due demand supply his purchaser with any proof of his authority to transfer or with any other requisite which may be necessary to obtain registration of the transfer of the security but if the transfer is not for value a transferor need not do so unless the purchaser furnishes the necessary expenses. Failure to comply with a demand made within a reasonable time gives the purchaser the right to reject or rescind the transfer.

§ 8–317. Attachment or Levy Upon Security.

(1) No attachment or levy upon a security or any share or other interest evidenced thereby which is outstanding shall be valid until the security is actually seized by the officer making the attachment or levy but a security which has been surrendered to the issuer may be attached or levied upon at the source.

(2) A creditor whose debtor is the owner of a security shall be entitled to such aid from courts of appropriate jurisdiction, by injunction or otherwise, in reaching such security or in

satisfying the claim by means thereof as is allowed at law or in equity in regard to property which cannot readily be attached or levied upon by ordinary legal process.

§ 8–318. No Conversion by Good Faith Delivery.

An agent or bailee who in good faith (including observance of reasonable commercial standards if he is in the business of buying, selling or otherwise dealing with securities) has received securities and sold, pledged or delivered them according to the instructions of his principal is not liable for conversion or for participation in breach of fiduciary duty although the principal had no right to dispose of them.

§ 8–319. Statute of Frauds.

A contract for the sale of securities is not enforceable by way of action or defense unless
- (a) there is some writing signed by the party against whom enforcement is sought or by his authorized agent or broker sufficient to indicate that a contract has been made for sale of a stated quantity of described securities at a defined or stated price; or
- (b) delivery of the security has been accepted or payment has been made but the contract is enforceable under this provision only to the extent of such delivery or payment; or
- (c) within a reasonable time a writing in confirmation of the sale or purchase and sufficient against the sender under paragraph (a) has been received by the party against whom enforcement is sought and he has failed to send written objection to its contents within ten days after its receipt; or
- (d) the party against whom enforcement is sought admits in his pleading, testimony or otherwise in court that a contract was made for sale of a stated quantity of described securities at a defined or stated price.

§ 8–320. Transfer or Pledge within a Central Depository System.

(1) If a security
- (a) is in the custody of a clearing corporation or of a custodian bank or a nominee of either subject to the instructions of the clearing corporation; and
- (b) is in bearer form or indorsed in blank by an appropriate person or registered in the name of the clearing corporation or custodian bank or a nominee of either; and
- (c) is shown on the account of a transferor or pledgor on the books of the clearing corporation;

then, in addition to other methods, a transfer or pledge of the security or any interest therein may be effected by the making of appropriate entries on the books of the clearing corporation reducing the account of the transferor or pledgor and increasing the account of the transferee or pledgee by the amount of the obligation or the number of shares or rights transferred or pledged.

(2) Under this section entries may be with respect to like securities or interests therein as a part of a fungible bulk and may refer merely to a quantity of a particular security without reference to the name of the registered owner, certificate or bond number or the like and, in appropriate cases, may be on a net basis taking into account other transfers or pledges of the same security.

(3) A transfer or pledge under this section has the effect of a delivery of a security in bearer form or duly indorsed in blank (Section 8–301) representing the amount of the obligation or the number of shares or rights transferred or pledged. If a pledge or the creation of a security interest is intended, the making of entries has the effect of a taking of delivery by the pledgee or a secured party (Sections 9–304 and 9–305). A transferee or pledgee under this section is a holder.

(4) A transfer or pledge under this section does not constitute a registration of transfer under Part 4 of this Article.

(5) That entries made on the books of the clearing corporation as provided in subsection (1) are not appropriate does not affect the validity or effect of the entries nor the liabilities or obligations of the clearing corporation to any person adversely affected thereby.

PART 4

REGISTRATION

§ 8–401. Duty of Issuer to Register Transfer.

(1) Where a security in registered form is presented to the issuer with a request to register transfer, the issuer is under a duty to register the transfer as requested if

    (a) the security is indorsed by the appropriate person or persons (Section 8–308); and

    (b) reasonable assurance is given that those indorsements are genuine and effective (Section 8–402); and

    (c) the issuer has no duty to inquire into adverse claims or has discharged any such duty (Section 8–403); and

    (d) any applicable law relating to the collection of taxes has been complied with; and

    (e) the transfer is in fact rightful or is to a bona fide purchaser.

(2) Where an issuer is under a duty to register a transfer of a security the issuer is also liable to the person presenting it for registration or his principal for loss resulting from any unreasonable delay in registration or from failure or refusal to register the transfer.

§ 8–402. Assurance that Indorsements are Effective.

(1) The issuer may require the following assurance that each necessary indorsement (Section 8–308) is genuine and effective

    (a) in all cases, a guarantee of the signature (subsection (1) of Section 8–312) of the person indorsing; and

    (b) where the indorsement is by an agent, appropriate assurance of authority to sign;

    (c) where the indorsement is by a fiduciary, appropriate evidence of appointment or incumbency;

    (d) where there is more than one fiduciary, reasonable assurance that all who are required to sign have done so;

    (e) where the indorsement is by a person not covered by any of the foregoing, assurance appropriate to the case corresponding as nearly as may be to the foregoing.

(2) A "guarantee of the signature" in subsection (1) means a guarantee signed by or on behalf of a person reasonably believed by the issuer to be responsible. The issuer may adopt standards with respect to responsibility provided such standards are not manifestly unreasonable.

(3) "Appropriate evidence of appointment or incumbency" in subsection (1) means

    (a) in the case of a fiduciary appointed or qualified by a court, a certificate issued by or under the direction or supervision of that court or an officer thereof and dated within sixty days before the date of presentation for transfer; or

    (b) in any other case, a copy of a document showing the appointment or a certificate issued by or on behalf of a person reasonably believed by the issuer to be responsible or, in the absence of such a document or certificate, other evidence reasonably deemed by the issuer to be appropriate. The issuer may adopt standards with respect to such evidence provided such standards are not manifestly unreasonable. The issuer is not charged with notice of the contents of any document obtained pursuant to this paragraph (b) except to the extent that the contents relate directly to the appointment or incumbency.

(4) The issuer may elect to require reasonable assurance beyond that specified in this section but if it does so and for a purpose other than that specified in subsection 3(b) both requires and obtains a copy of a will, trust, indenture, articles of co-partnership, by-laws or other controlling instrument it is charged with notice of all matters contained therein affecting the transfer.

§ 8–403. Limited Duty of Inquiry.

(1) An issuer to whom a security is presented for registration is under a duty to inquire into adverse claims if

    (a) a written notification of an adverse claim is received at a time and in a manner which affords the issuer a reasonable opportunity to act on it prior to the issuance of a new, reissued or re-registered security and the notification identifies the claimant, the registered owner and the issue of which the security is a part and provides an address for communications directed to the claimant; or

(b) the issuer is charged with notice of an adverse claim from a controlling instrument which it has elected to require under subsection (4) of Section 8–402.

(2) The issuer may discharge any duty of inquiry by any reasonable means, including notifying an adverse claimant by registered or certified mail at the address furnished by him or if there be no such address at his residency or regular place of business that the security has been presented for registration of transfer by a named person, and that the transfer will be registered unless within thirty days from the date of mailing the notification, either

(a) an appropriate restraining order, injunction or other process issues from a court of competent jurisdiction; or

(b) an indemnity bond sufficient in the issuer's judgment to protect the issuer and any transfer agent, registrar or other agent of the issuer involved, from any loss which it or they may suffer by complying with the adverse claim is filed with the issuer.

(3) Unless an issuer is charged with notice of an adverse claim from a controlling instrument which it has elected to require under subsection (4) of Section 8–402 or receives notification of an adverse claim under subsection (1) of this section, where a security presented for registration is indorsed by the appropriate person or persons the issuer is under no duty to inquire into adverse claims. In particular

(a) an issuer registering a security in the name of a person who is a fiduciary or who is described as a fiduciary is not bound to inquire into the existence, extent, or correct description of the fiduciary relationship and thereafter the issuer may assume without inquiry that the newly registered owner continues to be the fiduciary until the issuer receives written notice that the fiduciary is no longer acting as such with respect to the particular security;

(b) an issuer registering transfer on an indorsement by a fiduciary is not bound to inquire whether the transfer is made in compliance with a controlling instrument or with the law of the state having jurisdiction of the fiduciary relationship, including any law requiring the fiduciary to obtain court approval of the transfer; and

(c) the issuer is not charged with notice of the contents of any court record or file or other recorded or unrecorded document even though the document is in its possession and even though the transfer is made on the indorsement of a fiduciary to the fiduciary himself or to his nominee.

§ 8–404. Liability and Non-Liability for Registration.

(1) Except as otherwise provided in any law relating to the collection of taxes, the issuer is not liable to the owner or any other person suffering loss as a result of the registration of a transfer of a security if

(a) there were on or with the security the necessary indorsements (Section 8–308); and

(b) the issuer had no duty to inquire into adverse claims or has discharged any such duty (Section 8–403).

(2) Where an issuer has registered a transfer of a security to a person not entitled to it the issuer on demand must deliver a like security to the true owner unless

(a) the registration was pursuant to subsection (1); or

(b) the owner is precluded from asserting any claim for registering the transfer under subsection (1) of the following section; or

(c) such delivery would result in overissue, in which case the issuer's liability is governed by Section 8–104.

§ 8–405. Lost, Destroyed and Stolen Securities.

(1) Where a security has been lost, apparently destroyed or wrongfully taken and the owner fails to notify the issuer of that fact within a reasonable time after he has notice of it and the issuer registers a transfer of the security before receiving such a notification, the owner is pre-

cluded from asserting against the issuer any claim for registering the transfer under the preceding section or any claim to a new security under this section.

(2) Where the owner of a security claims that the security has been lost, destroyed or wrongfully taken, the issuer must issue a new security in place of the original security if the owner

(a) so requests before the issuer has notice that the security has been acquired by a bona fide purchaser; and

(b) files with the issuer a sufficient indemnity bond; and

(c) satisfies any other reasonable requirements imposed by the issuer.

(3) If, after the issue of the new security, a bona fide purchaser of the original security presents it for registration of transfer, the insurer must register the transfer unless registration would result in overissue, in which event the issuer's liability is governed by Section 8–104. In addition to any rights on the indemnity bond, the issuer may recover the new security from the person to whom it was issued or any person taking under him except a bona fide purchaser.

§ 8–406. Duty of Authenticating Trustee, Transfer Agent or Registrar.

(1) Where a person acts as authenticating trustee, transfer agent, registrar, or other agent for an issuer in the registration of transfers of its securities or in the issue of new securities or in the cancellation of surrendered securities

(a) he is under a duty to the issuer to exercise good faith and due diligence in performing his functions; and

(b) he has with regard to the particular functions he performs the same obligation to the holder or owner of the security and has the same rights and privileges as the issuer has in regard to those functions.

(2) Notice to an authenticating trustee, transfer agent, registrar or other such agent is notice to the issuer with respect to the functions performed by the agent.

ARTICLE 9. Secured Transactions; Sales of Accounts, Contract Rights and Chattel Paper

PART 1
SHORT TITLE, APPLICABILITY AND DEFINITIONS

§ 9–101. Short Title.

This Article shall be known and may be cited as Uniform Commercial Code—Secured Transactions.

§ 9–102. Policy and Scope of Article.

(1) Except as otherwise provided in Section 9–103 on multiple state transactions and in Section 9–104 on excluded transactions, this Article applies so far as concerns any personal property and fixtures within the jurisdiction of this state

(a) to any transaction (regardless of its form) which is intended to create a security interest in personal property or fixtures including goods, documents, instruments, general intangibles, chattel paper, accounts or contract rights; and also

(b) to any sale of accounts, contract rights or chattel paper.

(2) This Article applies to security interests created by contract including pledge, assignment, chattel mortgage, chattel trust, trust deed, factor's lien, equipment trust, conditional sale, trust receipt, other lien or title retention contract and lease or consignment intended as security. This Article does not apply to statutory liens except as provided in Section 9–310.

(3) The application of this Article to a security interest in a secured obligation is not affected by the fact that the obligation is itself secured by a transaction or interest to which this Article does not apply.

Note: *The adoption of this Article should be accompanied by the repeal of existing statutes dealing with conditional sales, trust receipts, factor's liens where the factor is given a non-possessory lien, chattel mortgages, crop mortgages, mortgages on railroad equipment, assignment of accounts and generally statutes regulating security interests in personal property.*

Where the state has a retail installment selling act or small loan act, that legislation should be carefully examined to determine what changes in those acts are needed to conform them to this Article. This Article primarily sets out rules defining rights of a secured-party against persons dealing with the debtor; it does not prescribe regulations and controls which may be necessary to curb abuses arising in the small loan business or in the financing of consumer purchases on credit. Accordingly, there is no intention to repeal existing regulatory acts in those fields. See Section 9–203(2) and the Note thereto.

§ 9–103. Accounts, Contract Rights, General Intangibles and Equipment Relating to Another Jurisdiction; and Incoming Goods Already Subject to a Security Interest.

(1) If the office where the assignor of accounts or contract rights keeps his records concerning them is in this state, the validity and perfection of a security interest therein and the possibility and effect of proper filing is governed by this Article; otherwise by the law (including the conflict of laws rules) of the jurisdiction where such office is located.

(2) If the chief place of business of a debtor is in this state, this Article governs the validity and perfection of a security interest and the possibility and effect of proper filing with regard to general intangibles or with regard to goods of a type which are normally used in more than one jurisdiction (such as automotive equipment, rolling stock, airplanes, road building equipment, commercial harvesting equipment, construction machinery and the like) if such goods are classified as equipment or classified as inventory by reason of their being leased by the debtor to others. Otherwise, the law (including the conflict of laws rules) of the jurisdiction where such chief place of business is located shall govern. If the chief place of business is located in a jurisdiction which does not provide for perfection of the security interest by filing or recording in that jurisdiction, then the security interest may be perfected by filing in this state. [For the purpose of determining the validity and perfection of a security interest in an airplane, the chief place of business of a debtor who is a foreign air carrier under the Federal Aviation Act of 1958, as amended, is the designated office of the agent upon whom service of process may be made on behalf of the debtor.]

(3) If personal property other than that governed by subsections (1) and (2) is already subject to a security interest when it is brought into this state, the validity of the security interest in this state is to be determined by the law (including the conflict of laws rules) of the jurisdiction where the property was when the security interest attached. However, if the parties to the transaction understood at the time that the security interest attached that the property would be kept in this state and it was brought into this state within 30 days after the security interest attached for purposes other than transportation through this state, then the validity of the security interest in this state is to be determined by the law of this state. If the security interest was already perfected under the law of the jurisdiction where the property was when the security interest attached and before being brought into this state, the security interest continues perfected in this state for four months and also thereafter if within the four month period it is perfected in this state. The security interest may also be perfected in this state after the expiration of the four month period; in such case perfection dates from the time of perfection in this state. If the security interest was not perfected under the law of the jurisdiction where the property was when the security interest attached and before being brought into this state, it may be perfected in this state; in such case perfection dates from the time of perfection in this state.

(4) Notwithstanding subsections (2) and (3), if personal property is covered by a certificate of title issued under a statute of this state or any other jurisdiction which requires indication on a certificate of title of any security interest in the property as a condition of perfection, then the perfection is governed by the law of the jurisdiction which issued the certificate.

[(5) Notwithstanding subsection (1) and Section 9–302, if the office where the assignor of accounts or contract rights keeps his records concerning them is not located in a jurisdiction which is a part of the United States, its territories or possessions, and the accounts or contract rights are within the jurisdiction of this state or the transaction which creates the security interest otherwise bears an appropriate relation to this state, this Article governs the validity and perfection of the security interest and the security interest may only be perfected by notification to the account debtor.]

Note: *The last sentence of subsection (2) and subsection (5) are bracketed to indicate optional enactment. In states engaging in financing of airplanes of foreign carriers and of international open accounts receivable bracketed language will be of value. In other states not engaging in financing of this type, the bracketed language may not be considered necessary.*

§ 9–104. Transactions Excluded From Article.

This Article does not apply

- (a) to a security interest subject to any statute of the United States such as the Ship Mortgage Act, 1920, to the extent that such statute governs the rights of parties to and third parties affected by transactions in particular types of property; or
- (b) to a landlord's lien; or
- (c) to a lien given by statute or other rule of law for services or materials except as provided in section 9–310 on priority of such liens; or
- (d) to a transfer of a claim for wages, salary or other compensation of an employee; or
- (e) to an equipment trust covering railway rolling stock; or
- (f) to a sale of accounts, contract rights or chattel paper as part of a sale of the business out of which they arose, or an assignment of accounts, contract rights or chattel paper which is for the purpose of collection only, or a transfer of a contract right to an assignee who is also to do the performance under the contract; or
- (g) to a transfer of an interest or claim in or under any policy of insurance; or
- (h) to a right represented by a judgment; or
- (i) to any right of setoff; or
- (j) except to the extent that provision is made for fixtures in Section 9–313, to the creation or transfer of an interest in or lien on real estate, including a lease or rents thereunder; or
- (k) to a transfer in whole or in part of any of the following: any claim arising out of tort; any deposit, savings, passbook or like account maintained with a bank, savings and loan association, credit union or like organization.

§ 9–105. Definitions and Index of Definitions.

(1) In this Article unless the context otherwise requires:

- (a) "Account debtor" means the person who is obligated on an account, chattel paper, contract right or general intangible;
- (b) "Chattel paper" means a writing or writings which evidence both a monetary obligation and a security interest in or a lease of specific goods. When a transaction is evidenced both by such a security agreement or a lease and by an instrument or a series of instruments, the group of writings taken together constitutes chattel paper;
- (c) "Collateral" means the property subject to a security interest, and includes accounts, contract rights and chattel paper which have been sold;
- (d) "Debtor" means the person who owes payment or other performance of the obligation secured, whether or not he owns or has rights in the collateral, and includes the seller of accounts, contract rights or chattel paper. Where the debtor and the owner of the collateral are not the same person, the term "debtor" means the owner of the collateral in any provision of the Article dealing with the collateral, the obligor in any provision dealing with the obligation, and may include both where the context so requires;
- (e) "Document" means document of title as defined in the general definitions of Article 1 (Section 1–201);
- (f) "Goods" includes all things which are movable at the time the security interest attaches or which are fixtures (Section 9–313), but does not include money, docu-

ments, instruments, accounts, chattel paper, general intangibles, contract rights and other things in action. "Goods" also include the unborn young of animals and growing crops;

    (g) "Instrument" means a negotiable instrument (defined in Section 3–104), or a security (defined in Section 8–102) or any other writing which evidences a right to the payment of money and is not itself a security agreement or lease and is of a type which is in ordinary course of business transferred by delivery with any necessary indorsement or assignment;

    (h) "Security agreement" means an agreement which creates or provides for a security interest;

    (i) "Secured party" means a lender, seller or other person in whose favor there is a security interest, including a person to whom accounts, contract rights or chattel paper have been sold. When the holders of obligations issued under an indenture of trust, equipment trust agreement or the like are represented by a trustee or other person, the representative is the secured party.

(2) Other definitions applying to this Article and the sections in which they appear are:

"Account"	Section 9–106
"Consumer goods"	Section 9–109 (1)
"Contract right"	Section 9–106
"Equipment"	Section 9–109 (2)
"Farm products"	Section 9–109 (3)
"General intangibles"	Section 9–106
"Inventory"	Section 9–109 (4)
"Lien creditor"	Section 9–301 (3)
"Proceeds"	Section 9–306 (1)
"Purchase money security interest"	Section 9–107

(3) The following definitions in other Articles apply to this Article:

"Check"	Section 3–104
"Contract for sale"	Section 2–106
"Holder in due course"	Section 3–302
"Note"	Section 3–104
"Sale"	Section 2–106

    (4) In addition Article 1 contains general definitions and principles of construction and interpretation applicable throughout this Article.

§ 9–106. Definitions: "Account"; "Contract Right"; "General Intangibles."

"Account" means any right to payment for goods sold or leased or for services rendered which is not evidenced by an instrument or chattel paper. "Contract right" means any right to payment under a contract not yet earned by performance and not evidenced by an instrument or chattel paper. "General intangibles" means any personal property (including things in action) other than goods, accounts, contract rights, chattel paper, documents and instruments.

§ 9–107. Definitions: "Purchase Money Security Interest."

A security interest is a "purchase money security interest" to the extent that it is

    (a) taken or retained by the seller of the collateral to secure all or part of its price; or

    (b) taken by a person who by making advances or incurring an obligation gives value to enable the debtor to acquire rights in or the use of collateral if such value is in fact so used.

§ 9–108. When After-Acquired Collateral Not Security for Antecedent Debt.

Where a secured party makes an advance, incurs an obligation, releases a perfected security interest, or otherwise gives new value which is to be secured in whole or in part by after-acquired property his security interest in the after-acquired collateral shall be deemed to be taken for new value and not as security for an antecedent debt if the debtor acquires his rights in such collateral either in the ordinary course of his business or under a contract of purchase made pursuant to the security agreement within a reasonable time after new value is given.

§ 9–109. Classification of Goods; "Consumer Goods"; "Equipment"; "Farm Products"; "Inventory."

Goods are

(1) "consumer goods" if they are used or bought for use primarily for personal, family or household purposes;

(2) "equipment" if they are used or bought for use primarily in business (including farming or a profession) or by a debtor who is a non-profit organization or a governmental subdivision or agency or if the goods are not included in the definitions of inventory, farm products or consumer goods;

(3) "farm products" if they are crops or livestock or supplies used or produced in farming operations or if they are products of crops or livestock in their unmanufactured states (such as ginned cotton, wool-clip, maple syrup, milk and eggs), and if they are in the possession of a debtor engaged in raising, fattening, grazing or other farming operations. If goods are farm products they are neither equipment nor inventory.

(4) "inventory" if they are held by a person who holds them for sale or lease or to be furnished under contracts of service or if he has so furnished them, or if they are raw materials, work in process or materials used or consumed in a business. Inventory of a person is not to be classified as his equipment.

§ 9–110. Sufficiency of Description.

For the purposes of this Article any description of personal property or real estate is sufficient whether or not it is specific if it reasonably identifies what is described.

§ 9–111. Applicability of Bulk Transfer Laws.

The creation of a security interest is not a bulk transfer under Article 6(see Section 6–103).

§ 9–112. Where Collateral Is Not Owned by Debtor.

Unless otherwise agreed, when a secured party knows that collateral is owned by a person who is not the debtor, the owner of the collateral is entitled to receive from the secured party any surplus under Section 9–502(2) or under Section 9–504(1), and is not liable for the debt or for any deficiency after resale, and he has the same right as the debtor

(a) to receive statements under Section 9–208;

(b) to receive notice of and to object to a secured party's proposal to retain the collateral in satisfaction of the indebtedness under Section 9–505;

(c) to redeem the collateral under Section 9–506;

(d) to obtain injunctive or other relief under Section 9–507(1); and

(e) to recover losses caused to him under Section 9–208(2).

§ 9–113. Security Interests Arising Under Article on Sales.

A security interest arising solely under the Article on Sales (Article 2) is subject to the provisions of this Article except that to the extent that and so long as the debtor does not have or does not lawfully obtain possession of the goods

(a) no security agreement is necessary to make the security interest enforceable; and

(b) no filing is required to perfect the security interest; and

(c) the rights of the secured party on default by the debtor are governed by the Article on Sales (Article 2).

PART 2
VALIDITY OF SECURITY AGREEMENT AND RIGHTS OF PARTIES THERETO

§ 9–201. General Validity of Security Agreement.

Except as otherwise provided by this Act a security agreement is effective according to its terms between the parties, against purchasers of the collateral and against creditors. Nothing in this Article validates any charge or practice illegal under any statute or regulation thereunder governing usury, small loans, retail installment sales, or the like, or extends the application of any such statute or regulation to any transaction not otherwise subject thereto.

§ 9–202. Title to Collateral Immaterial.

Each provision of this Article with regard to rights, obligations and remedies applies whether title to collateral is in the secured party or in the debtor.

§ 9–203. Enforceability of Security Interest; Proceeds, Formal Requisites.

Subject to the provisions of Section 4–208 on the security interest of a collecting bank and Section 9–113 on a security interest arising under the Article on Sales, a security interest is not enforceable against the debtor or third parties unless

  (a) the collateral is in the possession of the secured party; or
  (b) the debtor has signed a security agreement which contains a description of the collateral and in addition, when the security interest covers crops or oil, gas or minerals to be extracted or timber to be cut, a description of the land concerned. In describing collateral, the word "proceeds" is sufficient without further description to cover proceeds of any character.

(2) A transaction, although subject to this Article, is also subject to ————*, and in the case of conflict between the provisions of this Article and any such statute, the provisions of such statute control. Failure to comply with any applicable statute has only the effect which is specified therein.

Note: *At * in subsection (2) insert reference to any local statute regulating small loans, retail installment sales and the like.*

The foregoing subsection (2) is designed to make it clear that certain transactions, although subject to this Article, must also comply with other applicable legislation.

This Article is designed to regulate all the "security" aspects of transactions within its scope. There is, however, much regulatory legislation, particularly in the consumer field, which supplements this Article and should not be repealed by its enactment. Examples are small loan acts, retail installment selling acts and the like. Such acts may provide for licensing and rate regulation and may prescribe particular forms of contract. Such provisions should remain in force despite the enactment of this Article. On the other hand if a Retail Installment Selling Act contains provisions on filing, rights on default, etc., such provisions should be repealed as inconsistent with this Article.

§ 9–204. When Security Interest Attaches; After-Acquired Property; Future Advances.

(1) A security interest cannot attach until there is agreement (subsection (3) of Section 1–201) that it attach and value is given and the debtor has rights in the collateral. It attaches as soon as all of the events in the preceding sentence have taken place unless explicit agreement postpones the time of attaching.

(2) For the purposes of this section the debtor has no rights
  (a) in crops until they are planted or otherwise become growing crops, in the young of livestock until they are conceived;
  (b) in fish until caught, in oil, gas or minerals until they are extracted, in timber until it is cut;
  (c) in a contract right until the contract has been made;
  (d) in an account until it comes into existence.

(3) Except as provided in subsection (4) a security agreement may provide that collateral whenever acquired, shall secure all obligations covered by the security agreement.

(4) No security interest attaches under an after-acquired property clause
  (a) to crops which become such more than one year after the security agreement is executed except that a security interest in crops which is given in conjunction with a lease or a land purchase or improvement transaction evidenced by a contract, mortgage or deed of trust may if so agreed attach to crops to be grown on the land concerned during the period of such real estate transaction;

(b) to consumer goods other than accessions (Section 9–314) when given as additional security unless the debtor acquires rights in them within ten days after the secured party gives value.

(5) Obligations covered by a security agreement may include future advances or other value whether or not the advances or value are given pursuant to commitment.

§ 9–205. Use or Disposition of Collateral Without Accounting Permissible.

A security interest is not invalid or fraudulent against creditors by reason of liberty in the debtor to use, commingle or dispose of all or part of the collateral (including returned or repossessed goods) or to collect or compromise accounts, contract rights or chattel paper, or to accept the return of goods or make repossessions, or to use, commingle or dispose of proceeds, or by reason of the failure of the secured party to require the debtor to account for proceeds or replace collateral. This section does not relax the requirements of possession where perfection of a security interest depends upon possession of the collateral by the secured or by a bailee.

§ 9–206. Agreement Not to Assert Defenses Against Assignee; Modification of Sales Warranties Where Security Agreement Exists.

(1) Subject to any statute or decision which establishes a different rule for buyers or lessees of consumer goods, an agreement by a buyer or lessee that he will not assert against an assignee any claim or defense which he may have against the seller or lessor is enforceable by an assignee who takes his assignment for value, in good faith and without notice of a claim or defense, except as to defenses of a type which may be asserted against a holder in due course of a negotiable instrument under the Article on Commercial Paper (Article 3). A buyer who as part of one transaction signs both a negotiable instrument and a security agreement makes such an agreement.

(2) When a seller retains a purchase money security interest in goods the Article on Sales (Article 2) governs the sale and any disclaimer, limitation or modification of the seller's warranties.

§ 9–207. Rights and Duties When Collateral Is in Secured Party's Possession.

(1) A secured party must use reasonable care in the custody and preservation of collateral in his possession. In the case of an instrument or chattel paper reasonable care includes taking necessary steps to preserve rights against prior parties unless otherwise agreed.

(2) Unless otherwise agreed, when collateral is in the secured party's possession

    (a) reasonable expenses (including the cost of any insurance and payment of taxes or other charges) incurred in the custody, preservation, use or operation of the collateral are chargeable to the debtor and are secured by the collateral;

    (b) the risk of accidental loss or damage is on the debtor to the extent of any deficiency in any effective insurance coverage;

    (c) the secured party may hold as additional security any increase or profits (except money) received from the collateral, but money so received, unless remitted to the debtor, shall be applied in reduction of the secured obligation;

    (d) the secured party must keep the collateral identifiable but fungible collateral may be commingled;

    (e) the secured party may repledge the collateral upon terms which do not impair the debtor's right to redeem it.

(3) A secured party is liable for any loss caused by his failure to meet any obligation imposed by the preceding subsections but does not lose his security interest.

(4) A secured party may use or operate the collateral for the purpose of preserving the collateral or its value or pursuant to the order of a court of appropriate jurisdiction or, except in the case of consumer goods, in the manner and to the extent provided in the security agreement.

§ 9–208. Request for Statement of Account or List of Collateral.

(1) A debtor may sign a statement indicating what he believes to be the aggregate amount of unpaid indebtedness as of a specified date and may send it to the secured party with a request

that the statement be approved or corrected and returned to the debtor. When the security agreement or any other record kept by the secured party identifies the collateral a debtor may similarly request the secured party to approve or correct a list of the collateral.

(2) The secured party must comply with such a request within two weeks after receipt by sending a written correction or approval. If the secured party claims a security interest in all of a particular type of collateral owned by the debtor he may indicate that fact in his reply and need not approve or correct an itemized list of such collateral. If the secured party without reasonable excuse fails to comply he is liable for any loss caused to the debtor thereby; and if the debtor has properly included in his request a good faith statement of the obligation or a list of the collateral or both the secured party may claim a security interest only as shown in the statement against persons misled by his failure to comply. If he no longer has an interest in the obligation or collateral at the time the request is received he must disclose the name and address of any successor in interest known to him and he is liable for any loss caused to the debtor as a result of failure to disclose. A successor in interest is not subject to this section until a request is received by him.

(3) A debtor is entitled to such a statement once every six months without charge. The secured party may require payment of a charge not exceeding $10 for each additional statement furnished.

PART 3
RIGHTS OF THIRD PARTIES; PERFECTED AND UNPERFECTED SECURITY INTERESTS; RULES OF PRIORITY

§ 9–301. Persons Who Take Priority Over Unperfected Security Interests; "Lien Creditor."

(1) Except as otherwise provided in subsection (2), an unperfected security interest is subordinate to the rights of
  (a) persons entitled to priority under Section 9–312;
  (b) a person who becomes a lien creditor without knowledge of the security interest and before it is perfected;
  (c) in the case of goods, instruments, documents, and chattel paper, a person who is not a secured party and who is a transferee in bulk or other buyer not in ordinary course of business to the extent that he gives value and receives delivery of the collateral without knowledge of the security interest and before it is perfected;
  (d) in the case of accounts, contract rights, and general intangibles, a person who is not a secured party and who is a transferee to the extent that he gives value without knowledge of the security interest and before it is perfected.

(2) If the secured party files with respect to a purchase money security interest before or within ten days after the collateral comes into possession of the debtor, he takes priority over the rights of a transferee in bulk or of a lien creditor which arise between the time the security interest attaches and the time of filing.

(3) A "lien creditor" means a creditor who has acquired a lien on the property involved by attachment, levy or the like and includes an assignee for benefit of creditors from the time of assignment, and a trustee in bankruptcy from the date of the filing of the petition or a receiver in equity from the time of appointment. Unless all the creditors represented had knowledge of the security interest such a representative of creditors is a lien creditor without knowledge even though he personally has knowledge of the security interest.

§ 9–302. When Filing Is Required to Perfect Security Interest; Security Interests to Which Filing Provisions of This Article Do Not Apply.

(1) A financing statement must be filed to perfect all security interests except the following:
  (a) a security interest in collateral in possession of the secured party under Section 9–305;
  (b) a security interest temporarily perfected in instruments or documents without delivery under Section 9–304 or in proceeds for a 10 day period under Section 9–306;
  (c) a purchase money security interest in farm equipment having a purchase price not

in excess of $2500; but filing is required for a fixture under Section 9–313 or for a motor vehicle required to be licensed;

(d) a purchase money security interest in consumer goods; but filing is required for a fixture under Section 9–313 or for a motor vehicle required to be licensed;

(e) an assignment of accounts or contract rights which does not alone or in conjunction with other assignments to the same assignee transfer a significant part of the outstanding accounts or contract rights of the assignor;

(f) a security interest of a collecting bank (Section 4–208) or arising under the Article on Sales (see Section 9–313) or covered in subsection (3) of this section.

(2) If a secured party assigns a perfected security interest, no filing under this Article is required in order to continue the perfected status of the security interest against creditors of and transferees from the original debtor.

(3) The filing provisions of this Article do not apply to a security interest in property subject to a statute

(a) of the United States which provides for a national registration or filing of all security interests in such property; or

Note: *States to select either Alternative A or Alternative B.*
Alternative A—

(b) of this state which provides for central filing of, or which requires indication on a certificate of title of, such security interests in such property.

Alternative B—

(b) of this state which provides for central filing of security interests in such property, or in a motor vehicle which is not inventory held for sale for which a certificate of title is required under the statutes of this state if a notation of such a security interest can be indicated by a public official on a certificate or a duplicate thereof.

(4) A security interest in property covered by a statute described in subsection (3) can be perfected only by registration or filing under that statute or by indication of the security interest on a cerificate of title or a duplicate thereof by a public official.

§ 9–303. When Security Interest Is Perfected; Continuity of Perfection.

(1) A security interest is perfected when it has attached and when all of the applicable steps required for perfection have been taken. Such steps are specified in Sections 9–302, 9–304, 9–305 and 9–306. If such steps are taken before the security interest attaches, it is perfected at the time when it attaches.

(2) If a security interest is originally perfected in any way permitted under this Article and is subsequently perfected in some other way under this Article, without an intermediate period when it was unperfected, the security interest shall be deemed to be perfected continuously for the purposes of this Article.

§ 9–304. Perfection of Security Interest in Instruments, Documents, and Goods Covered by Documents; Perfection by Permissive Filing; Temporary Perfection Without Filing or Transfer of Possession.

(1) A security interest in chattel paper or negotiable documents may be perfected by filing. A security interest in instruments (other than instruments which constitute part of chattel paper) can be perfected only by the secured party's taking possession, except as provided in subsections (4) and (5).

(2) During the period that goods are in the possession of the issuer of a negotiable document therefor, a security interest in the goods is perfected by perfecting a security interest in the document, and any security interest in the goods otherwise perfected during such period is subject thereto.

(3) A security interest in goods in the possession of a bailee other than one who has issued a negotiable document therefor is perfected by issuance of a document in the name of the secured party or by the bailee's receipt of notification of the secured party's interest or by filing as to the goods.

(4) A security interest in instruments or negotiable documents is perfected without filing or the taking of possession for a period of 21 days from the time it attaches to the extent that it arises for new value given under a written security agreement.

(5) A security interest remains perfected for a period of 21 days without filing where a secured party having a perfected security interest in an instrument, a negotiable document or goods in possession of a bailee other than one who has issued a negotiable document therefor

    (a) makes available to the debtor the goods or documents representing the goods for the purpose of ultimate sale or exchange or for the purpose of loading, unloading, storing, shipping, transshipping, manufacturing, processing or otherwise dealing with them in a manner preliminary to their sale or exchange; or

    (b) delivers the instrument to the debtor for the purpose of ultimate sale or exchange or of presentation, collection, renewal or registration of transfer.

(6) After the 21 day period in subsections (4) and (5) perfection depends upon compliance with applicable provisions of this Article.

§ 9–305. When Possession by Secured Party Perfects Security Interest Without Filing.

A security interest in letters of credit and advices of credit (subsection (2) (a) of Section 5–116), goods, instruments, negotiable documents or chattel paper may be perfected by the secured party's taking possession of the collateral. If such collateral other than goods covered by a negotiable document is held by a bailee, the secured party is deemed to have possession from the time the bailee receives notification of the secured party's interest. A security interest is perfected by possession from the time possession is taken without relation back and continues only so long as possession is retained, unless otherwise specified in this Article. The security interest may be otherwise perfected as provided in this Article before or after the period of possession by the secured party.

§ 9–306. "Proceeds"; Secured Party's Rights on Disposition of Collateral.

(1) "Proceeds" includes whatever is received when collateral or proceeds is sold, exchanged, collected or otherwise disposed of. The term also includes the account arising when the right to payment is earned under a contract right. Money, checks and the like are "cash proceeds." All other proceeds are "non-cash proceeds."

(2) Except where this Article otherwise provides, a security interest continues in collateral notwithstanding sale, exchange or other disposition thereof by the debtor unless his action was authorized by the secured party in the security agreement or otherwise, and also continues in any identifiable proceeds including collections received by the debtor.

(3) The security interest in proceeds is a continuously perfected security interest if the interest in the original collateral was perfected but it ceases to be a perfected security interest and becomes unperfected ten days after receipt of the proceeds by the debtor unless

    (a) a filed financing statement covering the original collateral also covers proceeds; or

    (b) the security interest in the proceeds is perfected before the expiration of the ten day period.

(4) In the event of insolvency proceedings instituted by or against a debtor, a secured party with a perfected security interest in proceeds has a perfected security interest

    (a) in identifiable non-cash proceeds;

    (b) in identifiable cash proceeds in the form of money which is not commingled with other money or deposited in a bank account prior to the insolvency proceedings;

    (c) in identifiable cash proceeds in the form of checks and the like which are not deposited in a bank account prior to the insolvency proceedings; and

    (d) in all cash and bank accounts of the debtor, if other cash proceeds have been commingled or deposited in a bank account, but the perfected security interest under this paragraph (d) is

        (i) subject to any right of setoff; and

        (ii) limited to an amount not greater than the amount of any cash proceeds received by the debtor within ten days before the institution of the insolvency proceedings and commingled or deposited in a bank account prior to the insolvency proceedings less the amount of cash proceeds received by the debtor and paid over to the secured party during the ten day period.

(5) If a sale of goods results in an account or chattel paper which is transferred by the seller to a secured party, and if the goods are returned to or are repossessed by the seller or the secured party, the following rules determine priorities:

    (a) If the goods were collateral at the time of sale for an indebtedness of the seller which is still unpaid, the original security interest attaches again to the goods and continues as a perfected security interest if it was perfected at the time when the goods were sold. If the security interest was originally perfected by a filing which is still effective, nothing further is required to continue the perfected status; in any other case, the secured party must take possession of the returned or repossessed goods or must file.

    (b) An unpaid transferee of the chattel paper has a security interest in the goods against the transferor. Such security interest is prior to a security interest asserted under paragraph (a) to the extent that the transferee of the chattel paper was entitled to priority under Section 9–308.

    (c) An unpaid transferee of the account has a security interest in the goods against the transferor. Such security interest is subordinate to a security interest asserted under paragraph (a).

    (d) A security interest of an unpaid transferee asserted under paragraph (b) or (c) must be perfected for protection against creditors of the transferor and purchasers of the returned or repossessed goods.

§ 9–307. Protection of Buyers of Goods.

(1) A buyer in ordinary course of business (subsection (9) of Section 1–201) other than a person buying farm products from a person engaged in farming operations takes free of a security interest created by his seller even though the security interest is perfected and even though the buyer knows of its existence.

(2) In the case of consumer goods and in the case of farm equipment having an original purchase price not in excess of $2500 (other than fixtures, see Section 9–313), a buyer takes free of a security interest even though perfected if he buys without knowledge of the security interest, for value and for his own personal, family or household purposes or his own farming operations unless prior to the purchase the secured party has filed a financing statement covering such goods.

§ 9–308. Purchase of Chattel Paper and Non-Negotiable Instruments.

A purchaser of chattel paper or a non-negotiable instrument who gives new value and takes possession of it in the ordinary course of his business and without knowledge that the specific paper or instrument is subject to a security interest has priority over a security interest which is perfected under Section 9–304 (permissive filing and temporary perfection). A purchaser of chattel paper who gives new value and takes possession of it in the ordinary course of his business has priority over a security interest in chattel paper which is claimed merely as proceeds of inventory subject to a security interest (Section 9–306), even though he knows that the specific paper is subject to the security interest.

§ 9–309. Protection of Purchasers of Instruments and Documents.

Nothing in this Article limits the rights of a holder in due course of a negotiable instrument (Section 3–302) or a holder to whom a negotiable document of title has been duly negotiated (Section 7–501) or a bona fide purchaser of a security (Section 8–301) and such holders or purchasers take priority over an earlier security interest even though perfected. Filing under this Article does not constitute notice of the security interest to such holders or purchasers.

§ 9–310. Priority of Certain Liens Arising by Operation of Law.

When a person in the ordinary course of his business furnishes services or materials with respect to goods subject to a security interest, a lien upon goods in the possession of such person given by statute or rule of law for such materials or services takes priority over a perfected security interest unless the lien is statutory and the statute expressly provides otherwise.

§ 9–311. Alienability of Debtor's Rights: Judicial Process.

The debtor's rights in collateral may be voluntarily or involuntarily transferred (by way of sale, creation of a security interest, attachment, levy, garnishment or other judicial process) notwithstanding a provision in the security agreement prohibiting any transfer or making the transfer constitute a default.

§ 9–312. Priorities Among Conflicting Security Interests in the Same Collateral.

(1) The rules of priority stated in the following sections shall govern where applicable; Section 4–208 with respect to the security interest of collecting banks in items being collected, accompanying documents and proceeds; Section 9–301 on certain priorities; Section 9–304 on goods covered by documents; Section 9–306 on proceeds and repossessions; Section 9–307 on buyers of goods; Section 9–308 on possessory against nonpossessory interests in chattel paper or non-negotiable instruments; Section 9–309 on security interests in negotiable instruments, documents or securities; Section 9–310 on priorities between perfected security interests and liens by operation of law; Section 9–313 on security interests in fixtures as against interests in real estate; Section 9–314 on security interests in accessions as against interest in goods; Section 9–315 on conflicting security interests where goods lose their identity or become part of a product; and Section 9–316 on contractual subordination.

(2) A perfected security interest in crops for new value given to enable the debtor to produce the crops during the production season and given not more than three months before the crops become growing crops by planting or otherwise takes priority over an earlier perfected security interest to the extent that such earlier interest secures obligations due more than six months before the crops become growing crops by planting or otherwise, even though the person giving new value had knowledge of the earlier security interest.

(3) A purchase money security interest in inventory collateral has priority over a conflicting security interest in the same collateral if

    (a) the purchase money security interest is perfected at the time the debtor receives possession of the collateral; and

    (b) any secured party whose security interest is known to the holder of the purchase money security interest or who, prior to the date of the filing made by the holder of the purchase money security interest, had filed a financing statement covering the same items or type of inventory, has received notification of the purchase money security interest before the debtor receives possession of the collateral covered by the purchase money security interest; and

    (c) such notification states that the person giving the notice has or expects to acquire a purchase money security interest in inventory of the debtor, describing such inventory by item or type.

(4) A purchase money security interest in collateral other than inventory has priority over a conflicting security interest in the same collateral if the purchase money security interest is perfected at the time the debtor receives possession of the collateral or within ten days thereafter.

(5) In all cases not governed by other rules stated in this section (including cases of purchase money security interests which do not qualify for the special priorities set forth in subsections (3) and (4) of this section), priority between conflicting security interests in the same collateral shall be determined as follows:

    (a) in the order of filing if both are perfected by filing, regardless of which security interest attached first under Section 9–204(1) and whether it attached before or after filing;

    (b) in the order of perfection unless both are perfected by filing, regardless of which security interest attached first under Section 9–204(1) and, in the case of a filed security interest, whether it attached before or after filing; and

(c) in the order of attachment under Section 9–204(1) so long as neither is perfected.

(6) For the purpose of the priority rules of the immediately preceding subsection, a continuously perfected security interest shall be treated at all times as if perfected by filing if it was originally so perfected and it shall be treated at all times as if perfected otherwise than by filing if it was originally perfected otherwise than by filing.

§ 9–313. Priority of Security Interests in Fixtures.

(1) The rules of this section do not apply to goods incorporated into a structure in the manner of lumber, bricks, tile, cement, glass, metal work and the like and no security interest in them exists under this Article unless the structure remains personal property under applicable law. The law of this state other than this Act determines whether and when other goods become fixtures. This Act does not prevent creation of an encumbrance upon fixtures or real estate pursuant to the law applicable to real estate.

(2) A security interest which attaches to goods before they become fixtures takes priority as to the goods over the claims of all persons who have an interest in the real estate except as stated in subsection (4).

(3) A security interest which attaches to goods after they become fixtures is valid against all persons subsequently acquiring interests in the real estate except as stated in subsection (4) but is invalid against any person with an interest in the real estate at the time the security interest attaches to the goods who has not in writing consented to the security interest or disclaimed an interest in the goods as fixtures.

(4) The security interests described in subsections (2) and (3) do not take priority over

    (a) a subsequent purchaser for value of any interest in the real estate; or

    (b) a creditor with a lien on the real estate subsequently obtained by judicial proceedings; or

    (c) a creditor with a prior encumbrance of record on the real estate to the extent that he makes subsequent advances

if the subsequent purchase is made, the lien by judicial proceedings is obtained, or the subsequent advance under the prior encumbrance is made or contracted for without knowledge of the security interest and before it is perfected. A purchaser of the real estate at a foreclosure sale other than an encumbrancer purchasing at his own foreclosure sale is a subsequent purchaser within this section.

(5) When under subsections (2) or (3) and (4) a secured party has priority over the claims of all persons who have interests in the real estate, he may, on default, subject to the provisions of Part 5, remove his collateral from the real estate but he must reimburse any encumbrancer or owner of the real estate who is not the debtor and who has not otherwise agreed for the cost of repair of any physical injury, but not for any diminution in value of the real estate caused by the absence of the goods removed or by any necessity for replacing them. A person entitled to reimbursement may refuse permission to remove until the secured party gives adequate security for the performance of this obligation.

§ 9–314. Accessions.

(1) A security interest in goods which attaches before they are installed in or affixed to other goods takes priority as to the goods installed or affixed (called in this section "accessions") over the claims of all persons to the whole except as stated in subsection (3) and subject to Section 9–315(1).

(2) A security interest which attaches to goods after they become part of a whole is valid against all persons subsequently acquiring interests in the whole except as stated in subsection (3) but is invalid against any person with an interest in the whole at the time the security interest attaches to the goods who has not in writing consented to the security interest or disclaimed an interest in the goods as part of the whole.

(3) The security interests described in subsections (1) and (2) do not take priority over

    (a) a subsequent purchaser for value of any interest in the whole; or

    (b) a creditor with a lien on the whole subsequently obtained by judicial proceedings; or

    (c) a creditor with a prior perfected security interest in the whole to the extent that he makes subsequent advances if the subsequent purchase is made, the lien by judicial proceedings obtained or the subsequent advance under the prior perfected security interest is made or contracted for without knowledge of the security interest and before it is perfected. A purchaser of the whole at a foreclosure sale other than the holder of a perfected security interest purchasing at his own foreclosure sale is a subsequent purchaser within this section.

(4) When under subsections (1) or (2) and (3) a secured party has an interest in accessions which has priority over the claims of all persons who have interests in the whole, he may on default subject to the provisions of Part 5 remove his collateral from the whole but he must reimburse any encumbrancer or owner of the whole who is not the debtor and who has not otherwise agreed for the cost of repair of any physical injury but not for any diminution in value of the whole caused by the absence of the goods removed or by any necessity for replacing them. A person entitled to reimbursement may refuse permission to remove until the secured party gives adequate security for the performance of this obligation.

§ 9–315. Priority When Goods Are Commingled or Processed.

(1) If a security interest in goods was perfected and subsequently the goods or a part thereof have become part of a product or mass, the security interest continues in the product or mass if
  (a) the goods are so manufactured, processed, assembled or commingled that their identity is lost in the product or mass; or
  (b) a financing statement covering the original goods also covers the product into which the goods have been manufactured, processed or assembled.
In a case to which paragraph (b) applies, no separate security interest in that part of the original goods which has been manufactured, processed or assembled into the product may be claimed under Section 9–314.

(2) When under subsection (1) more than one security interest attaches to the product or mass, they rank equally according to the ratio that the cost of the goods to which each interest originally attached bears to the cost of the total product or mass.

§ 9–316. Priority Subject to Subordination.

Nothing in this Article prevents subordination by agreement by any person entitled to priority.

§ 9–317. Secured Party Not Obligated on Contract of Debtor.

The mere existence of a security interest or authority given to the debtor to dispose of or use collateral does not impose contract or tort liability upon the secured party for the debtor's acts or omissions.

§ 9–318. Defenses Against Assignee; Modification of Contract After Notification of Assignment Ineffective; Identification and Proof of Assignment.

(1) Unless an account debtor has made an enforceable agreement not to assert defenses or claims arising out of a sale as provided in Section 9–206 the rights of an assignee are subject to
  (a) all the terms of the contract between the account debtor and assignor and any defense or claim arising therefrom; and
  (b) any other defense or claim of the account debtor against the assignor which accrues before the account debtor receives notification of the assignment.

(2) So far as the right to payment under an assigned contract right has not already become an account, and notwithstanding notification of the assignment, any modification of or substitution for the contract made in good faith and in accordance with reasonable commercial standards is effective against an assignee unless the account debtor has otherwise agreed but the assignee acquires corresponding rights under the modified or substituted contract. The assignment may provide that such modification or substitution is a breach by the assignor.

(3) The account debtor is authorized to pay the assignor until the account debtor receives notification that the account has been assigned and that payment is to be made to the assignee. A notification which does not reasonably identify the rights assigned is ineffective. If requested

by the account debtor, the assignee must seasonably furnish reasonable proof that the assignment has been made and unless he does so the account debtor may pay the assignor.

(4) A term in any contract between an account debtor and an assignor which prohibits assignment of an account or contract right to which they are parties is ineffective.

PART 4
FILING

§ 9–401. Place of Filing; Erroneous Filing; Removal of Collateral.

First Alternative Subsection (1)

(1) The proper place to file in order to perfect a security interest is as follows:

(a) when the collateral is goods which at the time the security interest attaches are or are to become fixtures, then in the office where a mortgage on the real estate concerned would be filed or recorded;

(b) in all other cases, in the office of the [Secretary of State].

Second Alternative Subsection (1)

(1) The proper place to file in order to perfect a security interest is as follows:

(a) when the collateral is equipment used in farming operations, or farm products, or accounts, contract rights or general intangibles arising from or relating to the sale of farm products by a farmer, or consumer goods, then in the office of the _____ in the county of the debtor's residence or if the debtor is not a resident of this state then the office of the _____ in the county where the goods are kept, and in addition when the collateral is crops in the office of the _____ in the county where the land on which the crops are growing or to be grown is located;

(b) when the collateral is goods which at the time the security interest attaches are or are to become fixtures, then in the office where a mortgage on the real estate concerned would be filed or recorded;

(c) in all other cases, in the office of the [Secretary of State].

Third Alternative Subsection (1)

(1) The proper place to file in order to perfect a security interest is as follows:

(a) when the collateral is equipment used in farming operations, or farm products, or accounts, contract rights or general intangibles arising from or relating to the sale of farm products by a farmer, or consumer goods, then in the office of the _____ in the county of the debtor's residence or if the debtor is not a resident of this state then in the office of the _____ in the county where the goods are kept, and in addition when the collateral is crops in the office of the _____ in the county where the land on which the crops are growing or to be grown is located;

(b) when the collateral is goods which at the time the security interest attaches are or are to become fixtures, then in the office where a mortgage on the real estate concerned would be filed or recorded;

(c) in all other cases, in the office of the [Secretary of State] and in addition, if the debtor has a place of business in only one county of this state, also in the office of _____ of such county, or, if the debtor has no place of business in this state, but resides in the state, also in the office of _____ of the county in which he resides.

Note: *One of the three alternatives should be selected as subsection (1).*

(2) A filing which is made in good faith in an improper place or not in all of the places required by this section is nevertheless effective with regard to any collateral as to which the filing complied with the requirements of this Article and is also effective with regard to collateral covered by the financing statement against any person who has knowledge of the contents of such financing statement.

(3) A filing which is made in the proper place in this state continues effective even though the debtor's residence or place of business or the location of the collateral or its use, whichever controlled the original filing, is thereafter changed.

Alternative Subsection (3)

[(3) A filing which is made in the proper county continues effective for four months after a change to another county of the debtor's residence or place of business or the location of the collateral, whichever controlled the original filing. It becomes ineffective thereafter unless a copy of the financing statement signed by the secured party is filed in the new county within said period. The security interest may also be perfected in the new county after the expiration of the four-month period, in such case perfection dates from the time of perfection in the new county. A change in the use of the collateral does not impair the effectiveness of the original filing.]

(4) If collateral is brought into this state from another jurisdiction, the rules stated in Section 9–103 determine whether filing is necessary in this state.

§ 9–402. Formal Requisites of Financing Statement; Amendments.

(1) A financing statement is sufficient if it is signed by the debtor and the secured party, gives an address of the secured party from which information concerning the security interest may be obtained, gives a mailing address of the debtor and contains a statement indicating the types, or describing the items, of collateral. A financing statement may be filed before a security agreement is made or a security interest otherwise attaches. When the financing statement covers crops growing or to be grown or goods which are or are to become fixtures, the statement must also contain a description of the real estate concerned. A copy of the security agreement is sufficient as a financing statement if it contains the above information and is signed by both parties.

(2) A financing statement which otherwise complies with subsection (1) is sufficient although it is signed only by the secured party when it is filed to perfect a security interest in

    (a) collateral already subject to a security interest in another jurisdiction when it is brought into this state. Such a financing statement must state that the collateral was brought into this state under such circumstances.

    (b) proceeds under Section 9–30 if the security interest in the original collateral was perfected. Such a financing statement must describe the original collateral.

(3) A form substantially as follows is sufficient to comply with subsection (1):

Name of debtor (or assignor) ——————————————————————————

Address ——————————————————————————————————————

Name of secured party (or assignee) ————————————————————————

Address ——————————————————————————————————————

1. This financing statement covers the following types (or items) of property:
       (Describe) ————————————————————————————————
2. (If collateral is crops) The above described crops are growing or are to be grown on:
       (Describe Real Estate) ————————————————————————————
3. (If collateral is goods which are or to become fixtures) The above described goods are affixed or to be affixed to:
       (Describe Real Estate) ————————————————————————————
4. (If proceeds or products of collateral are claimed) Proceeds—Products of the collateral are also covered.
       Signature of Debtor (or Assignor) ——————————————————————
       Signature of Secured Party (or Assignee) ————————————————————

(4) The term "financing statement" as used in this Article means the original financing statement and any amendments but if any amendment adds collateral, it is effective as to the added collateral only from the filing date of the amendment.

(5) A financing statement substantially complying with the requirements of this section is effective even though it contains minor errors which are not seriously misleading.

§ 9–403. What Constitutes Filing; Duration of Filing; Effect of Lapsed Filing; Duties of Filing Officer.

(1) Presentation for filing of a financing statement and tender of the filing fee or acceptance of the statement by the filing officer constitutes filing under this Article.

(2) A filed financing statement which states a maturity date of the obligation secured of five years or less is effective until such maturity date and thereafter for a period of sixty days. Any other filed financing statement is effective for a period of five years from the date of filing. The effectiveness of a filed financing statement lapses on the expiration of such sixty day period after a stated maturity date or on the expiration of such five year period, as the case may be, unless a continuation statement is filed prior to the lapse. Upon such lapse the security interest becomes unperfected. A filed financing statement which states that the obligation secured is payable on demand is effective for five years from the date of filing.

(3) A continuation statement may be filed by the secured party (i) within six months before and sixty days after a stated maturity date of five years or less, and (ii) otherwise within six months prior to the expiration of the five year period specified in subsection (2). Any such continuation statement must be signed by the secured party, identify the original statement by file number and state that the original statement is still effective. Upon timely filing of the continuation statement, the effectiveness of the original statement is continued for five years after the last date to which the filing was effective whereupon it lapses in the same manner as provided in subsection (2) unless another continuation statement is filed prior to such lapse. Succeeding continuation statements may be filed in the same manner to continue the effectiveness of the original statement. Unless a statute on disposition of public records provides otherwise, the filing officer may remove a lapsed statement from the files and destroy it.

(4) A filing officer shall mark each statement with a consecutive file number and with the date and hour of filing and shall hold the statement for public inspection. In addition the filing officer shall index the statements according to the name of the debtor and shall note in the index the file number and the address of the debtor given in the statement.

(5) The uniform fee for filing, indexing and furnishing filing data for an original or a continuation statement shall be $_____.

§ 9–404. Termination Statement.

(1) Whenever there is no outstanding secured obligation and no commitment to make advances, incur obligations or otherwise give value, the secured party must on written demand by the debtor send the debtor a statement that he no longer claims a security interest under the financing statement, which shall be identified by file number. A termination statement signed by a person other than the secured party of record must include or be accompanied by the assignment or a statement by the secured party of record that he has assigned the security interest to the signer of the termination statement. The uniform fee for filing and indexing such an assignment or statement thereof shall be $_____. If the affected secured party fails to send such a termination statement within ten days after proper demand therefor he shall be liable to the debtor for one hundred dollars, and in addition for any loss caused to the debtor by such failure.

(2) On presentation to the filing officer of such a termination statement he must note it in the index. The filing officer shall remove from the files, mark "terminated" and send or deliver to the secured party the financing statement and any continuation statement, statement of assignment or statement of release pertaining thereto.

(3) The uniform fee for filing and indexing a termination statement including sending or delivering the financing statement shall be $_____.

§ 9–405. Assignment of Security Interest; Duties of Filing Officer; Fees.

(1) A financing statement may disclose an assignment of a security interest in the collateral described in the statement by indication in the statement of the name and address of the assignee or by an assignment itself or a copy thereof on the face or back of the statement. Either the original secured party or the assignee may sign this statement as the secured party. On presentation to the filing officer of such a financing statement the filing officer shall mark the same as provided in Section 9–403(4). The uniform fee for filing, indexing and furnishing filing data for a financing statement so indicating an assignment shall be $_____.

(2) A secured party may assign of record all or a part of his rights under a financing state-

ment by the filing of a separate written statement of assignment signed by the secured party of record and setting forth the name of the secured party of record and the debtor, the file number and the date of filing of the financing statement and the name and address of the assignee and containing a description of the collateral assigned. A copy of the assignment is sufficient as a separate statement if it complies with the preceding sentence. On presentation to the filing officer of such a separate statement, the filing officer shall mark such separate statement with the date and hour of the filing. He shall note the assignment on the index of the financing statement. The uniform fee for filing, indexing and furnishing filing data about such a separate statement of assignment shall be $_____.

(3) After the disclosure or filing of an assignment under this section, the assignee is the secured party of record.

§ 9–406. Release of Collateral; Duties of Filing Officer; Fees.

A secured party of record may by his signed statement release all or a part of any collateral described in a filed financing statement. The statement of release is sufficient if it contains a description of the collateral being released, the name and address of the debtor, the name and address of the secured party, and the file number of the financing statement. Upon presentation of such a statement to the filing officer he shall mark the statement with the hour and date of filing and shall note the same upon the margin of the index of the filing of the financing statement. The uniform fee for filing and noting such a statement of release shall be $_____.

§ 9–407. Information From Filing Officer.

[(1) If the person filing any financing statement, termination statement, statement of assignment, or statement of release, furnishes the filing officer a copy thereof, the filing officer shall upon request note upon the copy the file number and date and hour of the filing of the original and deliver or send the copy to such person.

(2) Upon request of any person, the filing officer shall issue his certificate showing whether there is on file on the date and hour stated therein, any presently effective financing statement naming a particular debtor and any statement of assignment thereof and if there is, giving the date and hour of filing of each such statement and the names and addresses of each secured party therein. The uniform fee for such a certificate shall be $_____ plus $_____ for each financing statement and for each statement of assignment reported therein. Upon request the filing officer shall furnish a copy of any filed financing statement or statement of assignment for a uniform fee of $_____ per page.]

Note: *This new section is proposed as an optional provision to require filing officers to furnish certificates. Local law and practices should be consulted with regard to the advisability of adoption.*

PART 5

DEFAULT

§ 9–501. Default; Procedure When Security Agreement Covers Both Real and Personal Property.

(1) When a debtor is in default under a security agreement, a secured party has the rights and remedies provided in this Part and except as limited by subsection (3) those provided in the security agreement. He may reduce his claim to judgment, foreclose or otherwise enforce the security interest by any available judicial procedure. If the collateral is documents the secured party may proceed either as to the documents or as to the goods covered thereby. A secured party in possession has the rights, remedies and duties provided in Section 9–207. The rights and remedies referred to in this subsection are cumulative.

(2) After default, the debtor has the rights and remedies provided in this Part, those provided in the security agreement and those provided in Section 9–207.

(3) To the extent that they give rights to the debtor and impose duties on the secured party, the rules stated in the subsections referred to below may not be waived or varied except

as provided with respect to compulsory disposition of collateral (subsection (1) of Section 9–505) and with respect to redemption of collateral (Section 9–506) but the parties may by agreement determine the standards by which the fulfillment of these rights and duties is to be measured if such standards are not manifestly unreasonable:

    (a) subsection (2) of Section 9–502 and subsection (2) of Section 9–504 insofar as they require accounting for surplus proceeds of collateral;

    (b) subsection (3) of Section 9–504 and subsection (1) of Section 9–505 which deal with disposition of collateral;

    (c) subsection (2) of Section 9–505 which deals with acceptance of collateral as discharge of obligation;

    (d) Section 9–506 which deals with redemption of collateral; and

    (e) subsection (1) of Section 9–507 which deals with the secured party's liability for failure to comply with this Part.

(4) If the security agreement covers both real and personal property, the secured party may proceed under this Part as to the personal property or he may proceed as to both the real and the personal property in accordance with his rights and remedies in respect of the real property in which case the provisions of this Part do not apply.

(5) When a secured party has reduced his claim to judgment the lien of any levy which may be made upon his collateral by virtue of any execution based upon the judgment shall relate back to the date of the perfection of the security interest in such collateral. A judicial sale, pursuant to such execution, is a foreclosure of the security interest by judicial procedure within the meaning of this section, and the secured party may purchase at the sale and thereafter hold the collateral free of any other requirements of this Article.

§ 9–502. Collection Rights of Secured Party.

(1) When so agreed and in any event on default the secured party is entitled to notify an account debtor or the obligor on an instrument to make payment to him whether or not the assignor was theretofore making collections on the collateral, and also to take control of any proceeds to which he is entitled under Section 9–306.

(2) A secured party who by agreement is entitled to charge back uncollected collateral or otherwise to full or limited recourse against the debtor and who undertakes to collect from the account debtors or obligors must proceed in a commercially reasonable manner and may deduct his reasonable expenses of realization from the collections. If the security agreement secures an indebtedness, the secured party must account to the debtor for any surplus, and unless otherwise agreed, the debtor is liable for any deficiency. But, if the underlying transaction was a sale of accounts, contract rights, or chattel paper, the debtor is entitled to any surplus or is liable for any deficiency only if the security agreement so provides.

§ 9–503. Secured Party's Right to Take Possesssion After Default.

Unless otherwise agreed a secured party has on default the right to take possession of the collateral. In taking possession a secured party may proceed without judicial process if this can be done without breach of the peace or may proceed by action. If the security agreement so provides the secured party may require the debtor to assemble the collateral and make it available to the secured party at a place to be designated by the secured party which is reasonably convenient to both parties. Without removal a secured party may render equipment unusable, and may dispose of collateral on the debtor's premises under Section 9–504.

§ 9–504. Secured Party's Right to Dispose of Collateral After Default; Effect of Disposition.

(1) A secured party after default may sell, lease or otherwise dispose of any or all of the collateral in its then condition or following any commercially reasonable preparation or processing. Any sale of goods is subject to the Article on Sales (Article 2). The proceeds of disposition shall be applied in the order following to

    (a) the reasonable expenses of retaking, holding, preparing for sale, selling and the like and, to the extent provided for in the agreement and not prohibited by law, the reasonable attorneys' fees and legal expenses incurred by the secured party;

    (b) the satisfaction of indebtedness secured by the security interest under which the disposition is made;

    (c) the satisfaction of indebtedness secured by any subordinate security interest in the collateral if written notification of demand therefor is received before distribution of the proceeds is completed. If requested by the secured party, the holder of a subordinate security interest must seasonably furnish reasonable proof of his interest, and unless he does so, the secured party need not comply with his demand.

(2) If the security interest secures an indebtedness, the secured party must account to the debtor for any surplus, and, unless otherwise agreed, the debtor is liable for any deficiency. But if the underlying transaction was a sale of accounts, contract rights, or chattel paper, the debtor is entitled to any surplus or is liable for any deficiency only if the security agreement so provides.

(3) Disposition of the collateral may be by public or private proceedings and may be made by way of one or more contracts. Sale or other disposition may be as a unit or in parcels and at any time and place and on any terms but every aspect of the disposition including the method, manner, time, place and terms must be commercially reasonable. Unless collateral is perishable or threatens to decline speedily in value or is of a type customarily sold on a recognized market, reasonable notification of the time and place of any public sale or reasonable notification of the time after which any private sale or other intended disposition is to be made shall be sent by the secured party to the debtor, and except in the case of consumer goods to any other person who has a security interest in the collateral and who has duly filed a financing statement indexed in the name of the debtor in this state or who is known by the secured party to have a security interest in the collateral. The secured party may buy at any public sale and if the collateral is of a type customarily sold in a recognized market or is of a type which is the subject of widely distributed standard price quotations he may buy at private sale.

(4) When collateral is disposed of by a secured party after default, the disposition transfers to a purchaser for value all of the debtor's rights therein, discharges the security interest under which it is made and any security interest or lien subordinate thereto. The purchaser takes free of all such rights and interests even though the secured party fails to comply with the requirements of this Part or of any judicial proceedings

    (a) in the case of a public sale, if the purchaser has no knowledge of any defects in the sale and if he does not buy in collusion with the secured party, other bidders or the person conducting the sale; or

    (b) in any other case, if the purchaser acts in good faith.

(5) A person who is liable to a secured party under a guaranty, indorsement, repurchase agreement or the like and who receives a transfer of collateral from the secured party or is subrogated to his rights has thereafter the rights and duties of the secured party. Such a transfer of collateral is not a sale or disposition of the collateral under this Article.

§ 9–505. Compulsory Disposition of Collateral; Acceptance of the Collateral as Discharge of Obligation.

(1) If the debtor has paid sixty per cent of the cash price in the case of a purchase money security interest in consumer goods or sixty per cent of the loan in the case of another security interest in consumer goods, and has not signed after default a statement renouncing or modifying his rights under this Part a secured party who has taken possession of collateral must dispose of its under Section 9–504 and if he fails to do so within ninety days after he takes possession the debtor at his option may recover in conversion or under Section 9–507(1) on secured party's liability.

(2) In any other case involving consumer goods or any other collateral a secured party in possession may, after default, propose to retain the collateral in satisfaction of the obligation. Written notice of such proposal shall be sent to the debtor and except in the case of consumer goods to any other secured party who has a security interest in the collateral and who has duly filed a financing statement indexed in the name of the debtor in this state or is known by the secured party in possession to have a security interest in it. If the debtor or other person entitled to receive notification objects in writing within thirty days from the receipt of the notification or

if any other secured party objects in writing within thirty days after the secured party obtains possession the secured party must dispose of the collateral under Section 9–504. In the absence of such written objection the secured party may retain the collateral in satisfaction of the debtor's obligation.

§ 9–506. Debtor's Right to Redeem Collateral.

At any time before the secured party has disposed of collateral or entered into a contract for its disposition under Section 9–504 or before the obligation has been discharged under Section 9–505(2) the debtor or any other secured party may unless otherwise agreed in writing after default redeem the collateral by tendering fulfillment of all obligations secured by the collateral as well as the expenses reasonably incurred by the secured party in retaking, holding and preparing the collateral for disposition, in arranging for the sale, and to the extent provided in the agreement and not prohibited by law, his reasonable attorneys' fees and legal expenses.

§ 9–507. Secured Party's Liability for Failure to Comply With This Part.

(1) If it is established that the secured party is not proceeding in accordance with the provisions of this Part disposition may be ordered or restrained on appropriate terms and conditions. If the disposition has occurred the debtor or any person entitled to notification or whose security interest has been made known to the secured party prior to the disposition has a right to recover from the secured party any loss caused by a failure to comply with the provision of this Part. If the collateral is consumer goods, the debtor has a right to recover in any event an amount not less than the credit service charge plus ten per cent of the principal amount of the debt or the time price differential plus ten per cent of the cash price.

(2) The fact that a better price could have been obtained by a sale at a different time or in a different method from that selected by the secured party is not of itself sufficient to establish that the sale was not made in a commercially reasonable manner. If the secured party either sells the collateral in the usual manner in any recognized market therefor or if he sells at the price current in such market at the time of his sale or if he has otherwise sold in conformity with reasonable commercial practices among dealers in the type of property sold he has sold in a commercially reasonable manner. The principles stated in the two preceding sentences with respect to sales also apply as may be appropriate to other types of disposition. A disposition which has been approved in any judicial proceeding or by any bona fide creditors' committee or representative of creditors shall conclusively be deemed to be commercially reasonable, but this sentence does not indicate that any such approval must be obtained in any case nor does it indicate that any disposition not so approved is not commercially reasonable.

ARTICLE 10
EFFECTIVE DATE AND REPEALER

§ 10–101. Effective Date.

This Act shall become effective at midnight on December 31st following its enactment. It applies to transactions entered into and events occurring after that date.

§ 10–102. Specific Repealer; Provision for Transition.

(1) The following acts and all other acts and parts of acts inconsistent here with are hereby repealed:

(Here should follow the acts to be specifically repealed including the following:

    Uniform Negotiable Instruments Act

    Uniform Warehouse Receipts Act

    Uniform Sales Act

    Uniform Bills of Lading Act

    Uniform Stock Transfer Act

    Uniform Conditional Sales Act

Uniform Trust Receipts Act
Also any acts regulating:
     Bank collections
     Bulk sales
     Chattel mortgages
     Conditional sales
     Factor's lien acts
     Farm storage of grain and similar acts
     Assignment of accounts receivable)

(2) Transactions validly entered into before the effective date specified in Section 10–101 and the rights, duties and interests flowing from them remain valid thereafter and may be terminated, completed, consummated or enforced as required or permitted by any statute or other law amended or repealed by this Act as though such repeal or amendment had not occurred.

Note: *Subsection (1) should be separately prepared for each state. The foregoing is a list of statutes to be checked.*

§ 10–103. General Repealer.

Except as provided in the following section, all acts and parts of acts inconsistent with this Act are hereby repealed.

§ 10–104. Laws Not Repealed.

(1) The Article on Documents of Title (Article 7) does not repeal or modify any laws prescribing the form or contents of documents of title or the services or facilities to be afforded by bailees, or otherwise regulating bailees' businesses in respects not specifically dealt with herein; but the fact that such laws are violated does not affect the status of a document of title which otherwise complies with the definition of a document of title (Secion 1–201).

[(2) This Act does not repeal _____*, cited as the Uniform Act for the Simplification of Fiduciary Security Transfers, and if in any respect there is any inconsistency between that Act and the Article of this Act on investment securities (Article 8) the provisions of the former Act shall control.]

Note: *At * in subsection (2) insert the statutory reference to the Uniform Act for the Simplification of Fiduciary Security Transfers if such Act has previously been enacted. If it has not been enacted, omit subsection (2).*

Uniform Partnership Act

PRELIMINARY PROVISIONS

Sec. 1. (Name of Act.) This act may be cited as Uniform Partnership Act.

Sec. 2. (Definition of Terms.) In this act, "Court" includes every court and judge having jurisdiction in the case.

"Business" includes every trade, occupation, or profession.

"Person" includes individuals, partnerships, corporations, and other associations.

"Bankrupt" includes bankrupt under the Federal Bankruptcy Act or insolvent under any state insolvent act.

"Conveyance" includes every assignment, lease, mortgage, or encumbrance.

"Real property" includes land and any interest or estate in land.

Sec. 3. (Interpretation of Knowledge and Notice.) (1) A person has "knowledge" of a fact within the meaning of this act not only when he has actual knowledge thereof, but also when he has knowledge of such other facts as in the circumstances shows bad faith.

(2) A person has "notice" of a fact within the meaning of this act when the person who claims the benefit of the notice

(a) States the fact to such person, or

(b) Delivers through the mail, or by other means of communication, a written statement of the fact to such person or to a proper person at his place of business or residence.

Sec. 4. (Rules of Construction.) (1) The rule that statutes in derogation of the common law are to be strictly construed shall have no application to this act.

(2) The law of estoppel shall apply under this act.

(3) The law of agency shall apply under this act.

(4) This act shall be so interpreted and construed as to effect its general purpose to make uniform the law of those states which enact it.

(5) This act shall not be construed so as to impair the obligations of any contract existing when the act goes into effect, nor to affect any action or proceedings begun or right accrued before this act takes effect.

Sec. 5. (Rules for Cases Not Provided for in this Act.) In any case not provided for in this act the rules of law and equity, including the law merchant, shall govern.

PART II

NATURE OF PARTNERSHIP

Sec. 6. (Partnership Defined.) (1) A partnership is an association of two or more persons to carry on as co-owners a business for profit.

(2) But any association formed under any other statute of this state, or any statute adopted by authority, other than the authority of this state, is not a partnership under this act, unless such association would have been a partnership in this state prior to the adopion of this act; but this act shall apply to limited partnerships except in so far as the statutes relating to such partnerships are inconsistent herewith.

Sec. 7. (Rules for Determining the Existence of a Partnership.) In determining whether a partnership exists, these rules shall apply:

(1) Except as provided by Section 16 persons who are not partners as to each other are not partners as to third persons.

(2) Joint tenancy, tenancy in common, tenancy by the entireties, joint property, common property, or part ownership does not of itself establish a partnership, whether such co-owners do or do not share any profits made by the use of the property.

(3) The sharing of gross returns does not of itself establish a partnership, whether or not the persons sharing them have a joint or common right or interest in any property from which the returns are derived.

(4) The receipt by a person of a share of the profits of a business is prima facie evidence that he is a partner in the business, but no such inference shall be drawn if such profits were received in payment:

    (a) As a debt by installments or otherwise,

    (b) As wages of an employee or rent to a landlord,

    (c) As an annuity to a widow or representative of a deceased partner,

    (d) As interest on a loan, though the amount of payment vary with the profits of the business,

    (e) As the consideration for the sale of a good-will of a business or other property by installments or otherwise.

Sec. 8. (Partnership Property.) (1) All property originally brought into the partnership stock or subsequently acquired by purchase or otherwise, on account of the partnership, is partnership property.

(2) Unless the contrary intention appears, property acquired with partnership funds is partnership property.

(3) Any estate in real property may be acquired in the partnership name. Title so acquired can be conveyed only in the partnership name.

(4) A conveyance to a partnership in the partnership name, though without words of inheritance, passes the entire estate of the grantor unless a contrary intent appears.

PART III

RELATIONS OF PARTNERS TO PERSONS DEALING WITH THE PARTNERSHIP

Sec. 9. (Partner Agent of Partnership as to Partnership Business.) (1) Every partner is an agent of the partnership for the purpose of its business, and the act of every partner, including the execution in the partnership name of any instrument, for apparently carrying on in the usual way the business of the partnership of which he is a member binds the partnership, unless the partner so acting has in fact no authority to act for the partnership in the particular matter, and the person with whom he is dealing has knowledge of the fact that he has no such authority.

(2) An act of a partner which is not apparently for the carrying on of the business of the

partnership in the usual way does not bind the partnership unless authorized by the other partners.

(3) Unless authorized by the other partners or unless they have abandoned the business, one or more but less than all the partners have no authority to:

(a) Assign the partnership property in trust for creditors or on the assignee's promise to pay the debts of the partnership,

(b) Dispose of the good-will of the business,

(c) Do any other act which would make it impossible to carry on the ordinary business of a partnership,

(d) Confess a judgment,

(e) Submit a partnership claim or liability to arbitration or reference.

(4) No act of a partner in contravention of a restriction on authority shall bind the partnership to persons having knowledge of the restriction.

Sec. 10. (Conveyance of Real Property of the Partnership.) (1) Where title to real property is in the partnership name, any partner may convey title to such property by a conveyance executed in the partnership name; but the partnership may recover such property unless the partner's act binds the partnership under the provisions of paragraph (1) of section 9 or unless such property has been conveyed by the grantee or a person claiming through such grantee to a holder for value without knowledge that the partner, in making the conveyance, has exceeded his authority.

(2) Where title to real property is in the name of the partnership, a conveyance executed by a partner, in his own name, passes the equitable interest of the partnership, provided the act is one within the authority of the partner under the provisions of paragraph (1) of section 9.

(3) Where title to real property is in the name of one or more but not all the partners, and the record does not disclose the right of the partnership, the partners in whose name the title stands may convey title to such property, but the partnership may recover such property if the partners' act does not bind the partnership under the provisions of paragraph (1) of section 9, unless the purchaser or his assignee, is a holder for value, without knowledge.

(4) Where the title to real property is in the name of one or more or all the partners, or in a third person in trust for the partnership, a conveyance executed by a partner in the partnership name, or in his own name, passes the equitable interest of the partnership, provided the act is one within the authority of the partner under the provisions of paragraph (1) of section 9.

(5) Where the title to real property is in the names of all the partners a conveyance executed by all the partners passes all their rights in such property.

Sec. 11. (Partnership Bound by Admission of Partner.) An admission or representation made by any partner concerning partnership affairs within the scope of his authority as conferred by this act is evidence against the partnership.

Sec. 12. (Partnership Charged with Knowledge of or Notice to Partner.) Notice to any partner of any matter relating to partnership affairs, and the knowledge of the partner acting in the particular matter, acquired while a partner or then present to his mind, and the knowledge of any other partner who reasonably could and should have communicated it to the acting partner, operate as notice to or knowledge of the partnership, except in the case of a fraud on the partnership committed by or with the consent of that partner.

Sec. 13. (Partnership Bound by Partner's Wrongful Act.) Where, by any wrongful act or omission of any partner acting in the ordinary course of the business of the partnership or with the authority of his co-partners, loss or injury is caused to any person, not being a partner in the partnership, or any penalty is incurred, the partnership is liable therefor to the same extent as the partner so acting or omitting to act.

Sec. 14. (Partnership Bound by Partner's Breach of Trust.) The partnership is bound to make good the loss:

(a) Where one partner acting within the scope of his apparent authority receives money or property of a third person and misapplies it; and

(b) Where the partnership in the course of its business receives money or property of a third person and the money or property so received is misapplied by any partner while it is in the custody of the partnership.

Sec. 15. (Nature of Partner's Liability.) All partners are liable:
  (a) Jointly and severally for everything chargeable to the partnership under sections 13 and 14,
  (b) Jointly for all other debts and obligations of the partnership; but any partner may enter into a separate obligation to perform a partnership contract.

Sec. 16. (Partner by Estoppel.) (1) When a person, by words spoken or written or by conduct, represents himself, or consents to another representing him to any one, as a partner in an existing partnership or with one or more persons not actual partners, he is liable to any such person to whom such representation has been made, who has, on the faith of such representation, given credit to the actual or apparent partnership, and if he has made such representation or consented to its being made in a public manner he is liable to such person, whether the representation has or has not been made or communicated to such person so giving credit by or with the knowledge of the apparent partner making the representation or consenting to its being made.
  (a) When a partnership liability results, he is liable as though he were an actual member of the partnership.
  (b) When no partnership liability results, he is liable jointly with the other persons, if any, so consenting to the contract or representation as to incur liability, otherwise separately.
  (2) When a person has been thus represented to be a partner in an existing partnership, or with one or more persons not actual partners, he is an agent of the persons consenting to such representation to bind them to the same extent and in the same manner as though he were a partner in fact, with respect to persons who rely upon the representation. Where all the members of the existing partnership consent to the representation, a partnership act or obligation results; but in all other cases it is the joint act or obligation of the person acting and the persons consenting to the representation.

Sec. 17. (Liability of Incoming Partner.) A person admitted as a partner into an existing partnership is liable for all the obligations of the partnership arising before his admission as though he had been a partner when such obligations were incurred, except that this liability shall be satisfied only out of partnership property.

PART IV

RELATIONS OF PARTNERS TO ONE ANOTHER

Sec. 18. (Rules Determining Rights and Duties of Partners.) The rights and duties of the partners in relation to the partnership shall be determined, subject to any agreement between them, by the following rules:
  (a) Each partner shall be repaid his contributions, whether by way of capital or advances to the partnership property and share equally in the profits and surplus remaining after all liabilities, including those to partners, are satisfied; and must contribute towards the losses, whether of capital or otherwise, sustained by the partnership according to his share in the profits.
  (b) The partnership must indemnify every partner in respect of payments made and personal liabilities reasonably incurred by him in the ordinary and proper conduct of its business, or for the preservation of its business or property.
  (c) A partner, who in aid of the partnership makes any payment or advance beyond the amount of capital which he agreed to contribute, shall be paid interest from the date of the payment or advance.
  (d) A partner shall receive interest on the capital contributed by him only from the date when repayment should be made.

(e) All partners have equal rights in the management and conduct of the partnership business.

(f) No partner is entitled to remuneration for acting in the partnership business, except that a surviving partner is entitled to reasonable compensation for his services in winding up the partnership affairs.

(g) No person can become a member of a partnership without the consent of all the partners.

(h) Any difference arising as to ordinary matters connected with the partnership business may be decided by a majority of the partners; but no act in contravention of any agreement between the partners may be done rightfully without the consent of all the partners.

Sec. 19. (Partnership Books.) The partnership books shall be kept, subject to any agreement between the partners, at the principal place of business of the partnership, and every partner shall at all times have access to and may inspect and copy any of them.

Sec. 20. (Duty of Partners to Render Information.) Partners shall render on demand true and full information of all things affecting the partnership to any partner or the legal representative of any deceased partner or partner under legal disability.

Sec. 21. (Partner Accountable as a Fiduciary.) (1) Every partner must account to the partnership for any benefit, and hold as trustee for it any profits derived by him without the consent of the other partners from any transaction connected with the formation, conduct, or liquidation of the partnership or from any use by him of its property.

(2) This section applies also to the representatives of a deceased partner engaged in the liquidation of the affairs of the partnership as the personal representatives of the last surviving partner.

Sec. 22. (Right to an Account.) Any partner shall have the right to a formal account as to partnership affairs:

(a) If he is wrongfully excluded from the partnership business or possession of its property by his co-partners,

(b) If the right exists under the terms of any agreement,

(c) As provided by section 21,

(d) Whenever other circumstances render it just and reasonable.

Sec. 23. (Continuation of Partnership Beyond Fixed Term.) (1) When a partnership for a fixed term or particular undertaking is continued after the termination of such term or particular undertaking without any express agreement, the rights and duties of the partners remain the same as they were at such termination, so far as is consistent with a partnership at will.

(2) A continuation of the business by the partners or such of them as habitually acted therein during the term, without any settlement or liquidation of the partnership affairs, is prima facie evidence of a continuation of the partnership.

PART V

PROPERTY RIGHTS OF A PARTNER

Sec. 24. (Extent of Property Rights of a Partner.) The property rights of a partner are (1) his rights in specific partnership property, (2) his interest in the partnership, and (3) his right to participate in the management.

Sec. 25. (Nature of a Partner's Right in Specific Partnership Property.) (1) A partner is co-owner with his partners of specific partnership property holding as a tenant in partnership.

(2) The incidents of this tenancy are such that:

(a) A partner, subject to the provisions of this act and to any agreement between the partners, has an equal right with his partners to possess specific partnership property for partnership purposes; but he has no right to possess such property for any other purpose without the consent of his partners.

(b) A partner's right in specific partnership property is not assignable except in connection with the assignment of rights of all the partners in the same property.

(c) A partner's right in specific partnership property is not subject to attachment or execution, except on a claim against the partnership. When partnership property is attached for a partnership debt the partners, or any of them, or the representatives of a deceased partner, cannot claim any right under the homestead or exemption laws.

(d) On the death of a partner his right in specific partnership property vests in the surviving partner or partners, except where the deceased was the last surviving partner, when his right in such property vests in his legal representative. Such surviving partner or partners, or the legal representative of the last surviving partner, has no right to possess the partnership property for any but a partnership purpose.

(e) A partner's right in specific partnership property is not subject to dower, curtesy, or allowances to widows, heirs, or next of kin.

Sec. 26. (Nature of Partner's Interest in the Partnership.) A partner's interest in the partnership is his share of the profits and surplus, and the same is personal property.

Sec. 27. (Assignment of Partner's Interest.) (1) A conveyance by a partner of his interest in the partnership does not of itself dissolve the partnership, nor, as against the other partners in the absence of agreement, entitle the assignee, during the continuance of the partnership to interfere in the management or administration of the partnership business or affairs, or to require any information or account of partnership transactions, or to inspect the partnership books; but it merely entitles the assignee to receive in accordance with his contract the profits to which the assigning partner would otherwise be entitled.

(2) In case of a dissolution of the partnership, the assignee is entitled to receive his assignor's interest and may require an account from the date only of the last account agreed to by all the partners.

Sec. 28. (Partner's Interest Subject to Charging Order.) (1) On due application to a competent court by any judgment creditor of a partner, the court which entered the judgment, order, or decree, or any other court, may charge the interest of the debtor partner with payment of the unsatisfied amount of such judgment debt with interest thereon; and may then or later appoint a receiver of his share of the profits, and of any other money due or to fall due to him in respect of the partnership, and make all other orders, directions, accounts and inquiries which the debtor partner might have made, or which the circumstances of the case may require.

(2) The interest charged may be redeemed at any time before foreclosure, or in case of a sale being directed by the court may be purchased without thereby causing a dissolution:

(a) With separate property, by any one or more of the partners, or

(b) With partnership property, by any one or more of the partners with the consent of all the partners whose interests are not so charged or sold.

(3) Nothing in this act shall be held to deprive a partner of his right, if any, under the exemption laws, as regards his interest in the partnership.

PART VI

DISSOLUTION AND WINDING UP

Sec. 29. (Dissolution Defined.) The dissolution of a partnership is the change in the relation of the partners caused by any partner ceasing to be associated in the carrying on as distinguished from the winding up of the business.

Sec. 30. (Partnership Not Terminated by Dissolution.) On dissolution the partnership is not terminated, but continues until the winding up of partnership affairs is completed.

Sec. 31. (Causes of Dissolution.) Dissolution is caused: (1) Without voliation of the agreement between the partners,

(a) By the termination of the definite term or particular undertaking specified in the agreement,

(b) By the express will of any partner when no definite term or particular undertaking is specified,

(c) By the express will of all the partners who have not assigned their interest or suffered them to be charged for their separate debts, either before or after the termination of any specified term or particular undertaking,

(d) By the expulsion of any partner from the business bona fide in accordance with such a power conferred by the agreement between the partners;

(2) In contravention of the agreement between the partners, where the circumstances do not permit a dissolution under any other provision of this section, by the express will of any partner at any time;

(3) By any event which makes it unlawful for the business of the partnership to be carried on or for the members to carry it on in partnership;

(4) By the death of any partner;

(5) By the bankruptcy of any partner or the partnership;

(6) By decree of court under section 32.

Sec. 32. (Dissolution by Decree of Court.) (1) On application by or for a partner the court shall decree a dissolution whenever:

(a) A partner has been declared a lunatic in any judicial proceeding or is shown to be of unsound mind,

(b) A partner becomes in any other way incapable of performing his part of the partnership contract,

(c) A partner has been guilty of such conduct as tends to affect prejudicially the carrying on of the business,

(d) A partner wilfully or persistently commits a breach of the partnership agreement, or otherwise so conducts himself in matters relating to the partnership business that it is not reasonably practicable to carry on the business in partnership with him,

(e) The business of the partnership can only be carried on at a loss,

(f) Other circumstances render a dissolution equitable.

(2) On the application of the purchaser of a partner's interest under sections 27 or 28:

(a) After the termination of the specified term or particular undertaking,

(b) At any time if the partnership was a partnership at will when the interest was assigned or when the charging order was issued.

Sec. 33. (General Effect of Dissolution on Authority of Partner.) Except so far as may be necessary to wind up partnership affairs or to complete transactions begun but not then finished, dissolution terminates all authority of any partner to act for the partnership,

(1) With respect to the partners,

(a) When the dissolution is not by the act, bankruptcy or death of a partner; or

(b) When the dissolution is by such act, bankruptcy or death of a partner, in cases where section 34 so requires.

(2) With respect to persons not partners, as declared in section 35.

Sec. 34. (Right of Partner to Contribution From Copartners After Dissolution.) Where the dissolution is caused by the act, death or bankruptcy of a partner, each partner is liable to his copartners for his share of any liability created by any partner acting for the partnership as if the partnership had not been dissolved unless:

(a) The dissolution being by act of any partner, the partner acting for the partnership had knowledge of the dissolution, or

(b) The dissolution being by the death or bankruptcy of a partner, the partner acting for the partnership had knowledge or notice of the death or bankruptcy.

Sec. 35. (Power of Partner to Bind Partnership to Third Persons After Dissolution.) (1) After dissolution a partner can bind the partnership except as provided in Paragraph (3):

(a) By any act appropriate for winding up partnership affairs or completing transactions unfinished at dissolution;

(b) By any transaction which would bind the partnership if dissolution had not taken place, provided the other party to the transaction:

(I) Had extended credit to the partnership prior to dissolution and had no knowledge or notice of the dissolution; or

(II) Though he had not so extended credit, had nevertheless known of the partnership prior to dissolution, and, having no knowledge or notice of dissolution, the fact of dissolution had not been advertised in a newspaper of general circulation in the place (or in each place if more than one) at which the partnership business was regularly carried on.

(2) The liability of a partner under paragraph (1b) shall be satisfied out of partnership assets alone when such partner had been prior to dissolution:

(a) Unknown as a partner to the person with whom the contract is made; and

(b) So far unknown and inactive in partnership affairs that the business reputation of the partnership could not be said to have been in any degree due to his connection with it.

(3) The partnership is in no case bound by any act of a partner after dissolution:

(a) Where the partnership is dissolved because it is unlawful to carry on the business, unless the act is appropriate for winding up partnership affairs; or

(b) Where the partner has become bankrupt; or

(c) Where the partner has no authority to wind up partnership affairs; except by a transaction with one who:

(I) Had extended credit to the partnership prior to dissolution and had no knowledge or notice of his want of authority; or

(II) Had not extended credit to the partnership prior to dissolution, and, having no knowledge or notice of his want of authority, the fact of his want of authority has not been advertised in the manner provided for advertising the fact of dissolution in paragraph (1bII).

(4) Nothing in this section shall affect the liability under section 16 of any person who after dissolution represents himself or consents to another representing him as a partner in a partnership engaged in carrying on business.

Sec. 36. (Effect of Dissolution on Partner's Existing Liability.) (1) The dissolution of the partnership does not of itself discharge the existing liability of any partner.

(2) A partner is discharged from any existing liability upon dissolution of the partnership by an agreement to that effect between himself, the partnership creditor and the person or partnership continuing the business; and such agreement may be inferred from the course of dealing between the creditor having knowledge of the dissolution and the person or partnership continuing the business.

(3) Where a person agrees to assume the existing obligations of a dissolved partnership, the partners whose obligations have been assumed shall be discharged from any liability to any creditor of the partnership who, knowing of the agreement, consents to a material alteration in the nature or time of payment of such obligations.

(4) The individual property of a deceased partner shall be liable for all obligations of the partnership incurred while he was a partner but subject to the prior payment of his separate debts.

Sec. 37. (Right to Wind Up.) Unless otherwise agreed the partners who have not wrongfully dissolved the partnership or the legal representative of the last surviving partner, not bankrupt, has the right to wind up the partnership affairs; provided, however, that any partner, his legal representative or his assignee, upon cause shown, may obtain winding up by the court.

Sec. 38. (Rights of Partners to Application of Partnership Property.) (1) When dissoution is caused in any way, except in contravention of the partnership agreement, each partner as against his co-partners and all persons claiming through them in respect of their interests in the partnership, unless otherwise agreed, may have the partnership property applied to discharge its liabilities, and the surplus applied to pay in cash the net amount owing to the respective partners.

But if dissolution is caused by expulsion of a partner, bona fide under the partnership agreement and if the expelled partner is discharged from all partnership liabilities, either by payment or agreement under section 36(2), he shall receive in cash only the net amount due him from the partnership.

(2) When dissolution is caused in contravention of the partnership agreement the rights of the partners shall be as follows:

    (a) Each partner who has not caused dissolution wrongfully shall have:

        (I) All the rights specified in paragraph (1) of this section, and

        (II) The right, as against each partner who has caused the dissolution wrongfully, to damages for breach of the agreement.

    (b) The partners who have not caused the dissolution wrongfully, if they all desire to continue the business in the same name, either by themselves or jointly with others, may do so, during the agreed term for the partnership and for that purpose may possess the partnership property, provided they secure the payment by bond approved by the court, or pay to any partner who has caused the dissolution wrongfully, the value of his interest in the partnership at the dissolution, less any damages recoverable under clause (2aII) of the section, and in like manner indemnify him against all present or future partnership liabilities.

    (c) A partner who has caused the dissolution wrongfully shall have:

        (I) If the business is not continued under the provisions of paragraph (2b) all the rights of a partner under paragraph (1), subject to clause (2aII), of this section.

        (II) If the business is continued under paragraph (2b) of this section the right as against his co-partners and all claiming through them in respect of their interests in the partnership, to have the value of his interest in the partnership, less any damages caused to his co-partners by the dissolution, ascertained and paid to him in cash, or the payment secured by bond approved by the court, and to be released from all existing liabilities of the partnership; but in ascertaining the value of the partner's interest the value of the good-will of the business shall not be considered.

Sec. 39. (Rights Where Partnership is Dissolved for Fraud or Misrepresentation.) Where a partnership contract is rescinded on the ground of the fraud or misrepresentation of one of the parties thereto, the party entitled to rescind is, without prejudice to any other right, entitled,

    (a) To a lien on, or right of retention of, the surplus of the partnership property after satisfying the partnership liabilities to third persons for any sum of money paid by him for the purchase of an interest in the partnership and for any capital or advances contributed by him; and

    (b) To stand, after all liabilities to third persons have been satisfied, in the place of the creditors of the partnership for any payments made by him in respect of the partnership liabilities; and

    (c) To be indemnified by the person guilty of the fraud or making the representation against all debts and liabilities of the partnership.

Sec. 40. (Rules for Distribution.) In settling accounts between the partners after dissolution, the following rules shall be observed, subject to any agreement to the contrary:

    (a) The assets of the partnership are:

        (I) The partnership property,

        (II) The contributions of the partners necessary for the payment of all the liabilities specified in clause (b) of this paragraph.

    (b) The liabilities of the partnership shall rank in order of payment, as follows:

        (I) Those owing to creditors other than partners,

        (II) Those owing to partners other than for capital and profits,

        (III) Those owing to partners in respect of capital,

        (IV) Those owing to partners in respect of profits.

    (c) The assets shall be applied in the order of their declaration in clause (a) of this paragraph to the satisfaction of the liabilities.

(d) The partners shall contribute, as provided by section 18(a) the amount necessary to satisfy the liabilities; but if any, but not all, of the partners are insolvent, or, not being subject to process, refuse to contribute, the other parties shall contribute their share of the liabilities, and, in the relative proportions in which they share the profits, the additional amount necessary to pay the liabilities.

(e) An assignee for the benefit of creditors or any person appointed by the court shall have the right to enforce the contributions specified in clause (d) of this paragraph.

(f) Any partner or his legal representative shall have the right to enforce the contributions specified in clause (d) of this paragraph, to the extent of the amount which he has paid in excess of his share of the liability.

(g) The individual property of a deceased partner shall be liable for the contributions specified in clause (d) of this paragraph.

(h) When partnership property and the individual properties of the partners are in possession of a court for distribution, partnership creditors shall have priority on partnership property and separate creditors on individual property saving the rights of lien or secured creditors as heretofore.

(i) Where a partner has become bankrupt or his estate is insolvent the claims against his separate property shall rank in the following order:

(I) Those owing to separate creditors,

(II) Those owing to partnership creditors,

(III) Those owing to partners by way of contribution.

Sec. 41. (Liability of Persons Continuing the Business in Certain Cases.) (1) When any new partner is admitted into an existing partnership, or when any partner retires and assigns (or the representative of the deceased partner assigns) his rights in partnership property to two or more of the partners, or to one or more of the partners and one or more third persons, if the business is continued without liquidation of the partnership affairs, creditors of the first or dissolved partnership are also creditors of the partnership so continuing the business.

(2) When all but one partner retire and assign (or the representative of a deceased partner assigns) their rights in partnership property to the remaining partner, who continues the business without liquidation of partnership affairs, either alone or with others, creditors of the dissolved partnership are also creditors of the person or partnership so continuing the business.

(3) When any partner retires or dies and the business of the dissolved partnership is continued as set forth in paragraphs (1) and (2) of this section, with the consent of the retired partners or the representative of the deceased partner, but without any assignment of his right in partnership property, rights of creditors of the dissolved partnership and of the creditors of the person or partnership continuing the business shall be as if such assignment had been made.

(4) When all the partners or their representatives assign their rights in partnership property to one or more third persons who promise to pay the debts and who continue the business of the dissolved partnership, creditors of the dissolved partnership are also creditors of the person or partnership continuing the business.

(5) When any partner wrongfully causes a dissolution and the remaining partners continue the business under the provisions of section 38(2b), either alone or with others, and without liquidation of the partnership affairs, creditors of the dissolved partnership are also creditors of the person or partnership continuing the business.

(6) When a partner is expelled and the remaining partners continue the business either alone or with others, without liquidation of the partnership affairs, creditors of the dissolved partnership are also creditors of the person or partnership continuing the business.

(7) The liability of a third person becoming a partner in the partnership continuing the business, under this section, to the creditors of the dissolved partnership shall be satisfied out of partnership property only.

(8) When the business of a partnership after dissolution is continued under any conditions set forth in this section the creditors of the dissolved partnership, as against the separate creditors of the retiring or deceased partner or the representative of the deceased partner, have a prior right to any claim of the retired partner or the representative of the deceased partner against the person or partnership continuing the business, on account of the retired or deceased partner's

interest in the dissolved partnership or on account of any consideration promised for such interest or for his right in partnership property.

(9) Nothing in this section shall be held to modify any right of creditors to set aside any assignment on the ground of fraud.

(10) The use by the person or partnership continuing the business of the partnership name, or the name of a deceased partner as part thereof, shall not of itself make the individual property of the deceased partner liable for any debts contracted by such person or partnership.

Sec. 42. (Rights of Retiring or Estate of Deceased Partner When the Business is Continued.) When any partner retires or dies, and the business is continued under any of the conditions set forth in section 41(1, 2, 3, 5, 6), or section 38(2b), without any settlement of accounts as between him or his estate and the person or partnership continuing the business, unless otherwise agreed, he or his legal representative as against such persons or partnership may have the value of his interest at the date of dissolution ascertained, and shall receive as an ordinary creditor an amount equal to the value of his interest in the dissolved partnership with interest, or, at his option or at the option of his legal representative, in lieu of interest, the profits attributable to the use of his right in the property of the dissolved partnership; provided that the creditors of the dissolved partnership as against the separate creditors, or the representative of the retired or deceased partner, shall have priority on any claim arising under this section, as provided by section 41(8) of this act.

Sec. 43. (Accrual of Actions.) The right to an account of his interest shall accrue to any partner, or his legal representative, as against the winding up partners or the surviving partners or the person or partnership continuing the business, at the date of dissolution, in the absence of any agreement to the contrary.

PART VII

MISCELLANEOUS PROVISIONS

Sec. 44. (When Act Takes Effect.) This act shall take effect on the _____ day of _____ one thousand nine hundred and _____.

Sec. 45. (Legislation Repealed.) All acts or parts of acts inconsistent with this act are hereby repealed.

Model Business Corporation Act

§ **1. Short Title.**

This Act shall be known and may be cited as the "_____* Business Corporation Act."

§ **2. Definitions.**

As used in this Act, unless the context otherwise requires, the term:

(a) "Corporation" or "domestic corporation" means a corporation for profit subject to the provisions of this Act, except a foreign corporation.

(b) "Foreign corporation" means a corporation for profit organized under laws other than the laws of this State for a purpose or purposes for which a corporation may be organized under this Act.

(c) "Articles of incorporation" means the original or restated articles of incorporation or articles of consolidation and all amendments thereto including articles of merger.

(d) "Shares" means the units into which the proprietary interests in a corporation are divided.

(e) "Subscriber" means one who subscribes for shares in a corporation, whether before or after incorporation.

(f) "Shareholder" means one who is a holder of record of shares in a corporation.

(g) "Authorized shares" means the shares of all classes which the corporation is authorized to issue.

(h) "Treasury shares" means shares of a corporation which have been issued, have been subsequently acquired by and belong to the corporation, and have not, either by reason of the acquisition or thereafter, been cancelled or restored to the status of authorized but unissued shares. Treasury shares shall be deemed to be "issued" shares, but not "outstanding" shares.

(i) "Net assets" means the amount by which the total assets of a corporation, excluding treasury shares, exceed the total debts of the corporation.

(j) "Stated capital" means, at any particular time, the sum of (1) the par value of all shares of the corporation having a par value that have been issued, (2) the amount of the consideration received by the corporation for all shares of the corporation without par value that have been issued, except such part of the consideration therefor as may have been allocated to capital surplus in a manner permitted by law, and (3) such amounts not included in clauses (1) and (2) of this paragraph as have been transferred to stated capital of the corporation, whether upon the issue of shares as a share dividend or otherwise, minus all reductions from such sum as have been effected in a manner permitted by law. Irrespective of the manner of designation

---

* Insert name of state.

thereof by the laws under which a foreign corporation is organized, the stated capital of a foreign corporation shall be determined on the same basis and in the same manner as the stated capital of a domestic corporation, for the purpose of computing fees, franchise taxes and other charges imposed by this Act. Earned surplus shall include also any portion of surplus allocated to earned surplus in mergers, consolidations or acquisitions of all or substantially all of the outstanding shares or of the property and assets of another corporation, domestic or foreign.

(k) "Surplus" means the excess of the net assets of a corporation over its stated capital.

(l) "Earned surplus" means the portion of the surplus of a corporation equal to the balance of its net profits, income, gains and losses from the date of incorporation, or from the latest date when a deficit was eliminated by an application of its capital surplus or stated capital or otherwise, after deducting subsequent distributions to shareholders and transfers to stated capital and capital surplus to the extent such distributions and transfers are made out of earned surplus.

(m) "Capital surplus" means the entire surplus of a corporation other than its earned surplus.

(n) "Insolvent" means inability of a corporation to pay its debts as they become due in the usual course of its business.

§ 3. Purposes.

Corporations may be organized under this Act for any lawful purpose or purposes, except for the purpose of banking or insurance.

§ 4. General Powers.

Each corporation shall have power:

(a) To have perpetual succession by its corporation name unless a limited period of duration is stated in its articles of incorporation.

(b) To sue and be sued, complain and defend, in its corporate name.

(c) To have a corporate seal which may be altered at pleasure, and to use the same by causing it, or a facsimile thereof, to be impressed or affixed or in any other manner reproduced.

(d) To purchase, take, receive, lease, or otherwise acquire, own, hold, improve, use and otherwise deal in and with, real or personal property or any interest therein wherever situated.

(e) To sell convey, mortgage, pledge, lease, exchange, transfer and otherwise dispose of all or any part of its property and assets.

(f) To lend money to its employees other than its officers and directors, and otherwise assist its employees, officers and directors.

(g) To purchase, take, receive, subscribe for, or otherwise acquire, own, hold, vote, use, employ, sell, mortgage, lend, pledge, or otherwise dispose of, and otherwise use and deal in and with, shares or other interests in, or obligations of, other domestic or foreign corporations, associations partnerships or individuals, or direct or indirect obligations of the United States or of any other government, state, territory, governmental district or municipality or of any instrumentality thereof.

(h) To make contracts and guarantees and incur liabilities, borrow money at such rates of interest as the corporation may determine, issue its notes, bonds, and other obligations, and secure any of its obligations by mortgage or pledge of all or any of its property, franchises and income.

(i) To lend money for its corporate purposes, invest and reinvest its funds, and take and hold real and personal property as security for the payment of funds so loaned or invested.

(j) To conduct its business, carry on its operations, and have offices and exercise the powers granted by this Act in any state, territory, district, or possession of the United States, or in any foreign country.

(k) To elect or appoint officers and agents of the corporation, and define their duties and fix their compensation.

(l) To make and alter by-laws, not inconsistent with its articles of incorporation or with the laws of this State, for the administration and regulation of the affairs of the corporation.

(m) To make donations for the public welfare or for charitable, scientific or educational purposes; and in time of war to make donations in aid of war activities.

(n) In time of war to transact any lawful business in aid of the United States in the prosecution of the war.

(o) To indemnify any director or officer or former director or officer of the corporation, or any person who may have served at its request as a director or officer of another corporation in which it owns shares of capital stock or of which it is a creditor, against expenses actually and necessarily incurred by him in connection with the defense of any action, suit or proceeding, civil or criminal, in which he is made a party by reason of being or having been such director or officer, except in relation to matters as to which he shall be adjudged in such action, suit or proceeding to be liable for negligence or misconduct in the performance of duty to the corporation; and to make any other indemnification that shall be authorized by the articles of incorporation or by any by-law or resolution adopted by the shareholders after notice.

(p) To pay pensions and establish pension plans, pension trusts, profit-sharing plans, stock bonus plans, stock option plans and other incentive plans for any or all of its directors, officers and employees.

(q) To cease its corporate activities and surrender its corporate franchise.

(r) To have and exercise all powers necessary or convenient to effect any or all of the purposes for which the corporation is organized.

§ 5. Right of Corporation to Acquire and Dispose of Its Own Shares.

A corporation shall have the right to purchase, take, receive or otherwise acquire, hold, own, pledge, transfer or otherwise dispose of its own shares, but purchases of its own shares, whether direct or indirect, shall be made only to the extent of unreserved and unrestricted earned surplus available therefor, and, if the articles of incorporation so permit or with the affirmative vote of the holders of at least two-thirds of all shares entitled to vote thereon, to the extent of unreserved and unrestricted capital surplus available therefor.

To the extent that earned surplus or capital surplus is used as the measure of the corporation's right to purchase its own shares, such surplus shall be restricted so long as such shares are held as treasury shares, and upon the disposition or cancellation of any such shares the restriction shall be removed pro tanto.

Notwithstanding the foregoing limitation, a corporation may purchase or otherwise acquire its own shares for the purpose of:

(a) Eliminating fractional shares.

(b) Collecting or compromising indebtedness to the corporation.

(c) Paying dissenting shareholders entitled to payment for their shares under the provisions of this Act.

(d) Effecting, subject to the other provisions of this Act, the retirement of its redeemable shares by redemption or by purchase at not to exceed the redemption price.

No purchase of or payment for its own shares shall be made at a time when the corporation is insolvent or when such purchase or payment would make it insolvent.

§ 6. Defense of Ultra Vires.

No act of a corporation and no conveyance or transfer of real or personal property to or by a corporation shall be invalid by reason of the fact that the corporation was without capacity or power to do such act or to make or receive such conveyance or transfer, but such lack of capacity or power may be asserted:

(a) In a proceeding by a shareholder against the corporation to enjoin the doing of any act or acts or the transfer of real or personal property by or to the corporation. If the unauthorized acts or transfer sought to be enjoined are being, or are to be, performed or made pursuant to any contract to which the corporation is a party, the court may, if all of the parties to the contract are parties to the proceeding and if it deems the same to be equitable, set aside and enjoin the performance of such contract, and in so doing may allow to the corporation or to the other parties to the contract, as the case may be, compensation for the loss or damage sustained by either of them which may result from the action of the court in setting aside and enjoining the performance of such contract, but anticipated profits to be derived from the performance of the contract shall not be awarded by the court as a loss or damage sustained.

(b) In a proceeding by the corporation, whether acting directly or through a receiver, trustee, or other legal representative, or through shareholders in a representative suit, against the incumbent or former officers or directors of the corporation.

(c) In a proceeding by the Attorney General, as provided in this Act, to dissolve the corporation, or in a proceeding by the Attorney General to enjoin the corporation from the transaction of unauthorized business.

§ 7. Corporate Name.

The corporate name:

(a) Shall contain the word "corporation," "company," "incorporated" or "limited," or shall contain an abbreviation of one of such words.

(b) Shall not contain any word or phrase which indicates or implies that it is organized for any purpose other than one or more of the purposes contained in its articles of incorporation.

(c) Shall not be the same as, or deceptively similar to, the name of any domestic corporation existing under the laws of this State or any foreign corporation authorized to transact business in this State, or a name the exclusive right to which is, at the time, reserved in the manner provided in this Act, or the name of a corporation which has in effect a registration of its corporate name as provided in this Act.

§ 8. Reserved Name.

The exclusive right to the use of a corporate name may be reserved by:

(a) Any person intending to organize a corporation under this Act.

(b) Any domestic corporation intending to change its name.

(c) Any foreign corporation intending to make application for a certificate of authority to transact business in this State.

(d) Any foreign corporation authorized to transact business in this State and intending to change its name.

(e) Any person intending to organize a foreign corporation and intending to have such corporation make application for a certificate of authority to transact business in this State.

The reservation shall be made by filing with the Secretary of State an application to reserve a specified corporate name, executed by the applicant. If the Secretary of State finds that the name is available for corporate use, he shall reserve the same for the exclusive us of the applicant for a period of one hundred and twenty days.

The right to the exclusive use of a specified corporate name so reserved may be transferred to any other person or corporation by filing in the office of the Secretary of State a notice of such transfer, executed by the applicant for whom the name was reserved, and specifying the name and address of the transferee.

§ 9. Registered Name.

Any corporation organized and existing under the laws of any state or territory of the United States may register its corporate name under this Act, provided its corporate name is not the same as, or deceptively similar to, the name of any domestic corporation existing under the laws of this State, or the name of any foreign corporation authorized to transact business in this State, or any corporate name reserved or registered under this Act.

Such registration shall be made by:

(a) Filing with the Secretary of State (1) an application for registration executed by the corporation by an officer thereof, setting forth the name of the corporation, the state or territory under the laws of which it is incorporated, the date of its incorporation, a statement that it is carrying on or doing business, and a brief statement of the business in which it is engaged, and (2) a certificate setting forth that such corporation is in good standing under the laws of the state or territory wherein it is organized, executed by the Secretary of State of such state or territory or by such other official as may have custody of the records pertaining to corporations, and

(b) Paying to the Secretary of State a registration fee in the amount of one dollar for each month, or fraction thereof, between the date of filing such application and December 31st of the calendar year in which such application is filed.

Such registration shall be effective until the close of the calendar year in which the application for registration is filed.

§ 10. Renewal of Registered Name.

A corporation which has in effect a registration of its corporate name, may renew such registration from year to year by annually filing an application for renewal setting forth the facts required to be set forth in an original application for registration and a certificate of good standing as required for the original registration and by paying a fee of ten dollars. A renewal application may be filed between the first day of October and the thirty-first day of December in each year, and shall extend the registration for the following calendar year.

§ 11. Registered Office and Registered Agent.

Each corporation shall have and continuously maintain in this State:

(a) A registered office which may be, but need not be, the same as its place of business.

(b) A registered agent, which agent may be either an individual resident in this State whose business office is identical with such registered office, or a domestic corporation, or a foreign corporation authorized to transact business in this State, having a business office identical with such registered office.

§ 12. Change of Registered Office or Registered Agent.

A corporation may change its registered office or change its registered agent, or both, upon filing in the office of the Secretary of State a statement setting forth:

(a) The name of the corporation.

(b) The address of its then registered office.

(c) If the address of its registered office be changed, the address to which the registered office is to be changed.

(d) The name of its then registered agent.

(e) If its registered agent be changed, the name of its successor registered agent.

(f) That the address of its registered office and the address of the business office of its registered agent, as changed, will be identical.

(g) That such change was authorized by resolution duly adopted by its board of directors.

Such statement shall be executed by the corporation by its president or a vice president, and verified by him, and delivered to the Secretary of State. If the Secretary of State finds that such statement conforms to the provisions of this Act, he shall file such statement in his office, and upon such filing the change of address of the registered office, or the appointment of a new registered agent, or both, as the case may be, shall become effective.

Any registered agent of a corporation may resign as such agent upon filing a written notice thereof, executed in duplicate, with the Secretary of State, who shall forthwith mail a copy thereof to the corporation at its registered office. The appointment of such agent shall terminate upon the expiration of thirty days after receipt of such notice by the Secretary of State.

If a registered agent changes his or its business address to another place within the same _____,* he or it may change such address and the address of the registered office of any corporations of which he or it is registered agent by filing a statement as required above except that it need be signed only by the registered agent and need not be responsive to (e) or (g) and must recite that a copy of the statement has been mailed to each such corporation.

§ 13. Service of Process on Corporation.

The registered agent so appointed by a corporation shall be an agent of such corporation upon whom any process, notice or demand required or permitted by law to be served upon the corporation may be served.

---

* Supply designation of jurisdiction, such as county, etc., in accordance with local practice.

Whenever a corporation shall fail to appoint or maintain a registered agent in this State, or whenever its registered agent cannot with reasonable diligence be found at the registered office, then the Secretary of State shall be an agent of such corporation upon whom any such process, notice, or demand may be served. Service on the Secretary of State of any such process, notice, or demand shall be made by delivering to and leaving with him, or with any clerk having charge of the corporation department of his office, duplicate copies of such process, notice or demand. In the event any such process, notice or demand is served on the Secretary of State, he shall immediately cause one of the copies thereof to be forwarded by registered mail, addressed to the corporation at its registered office. Any service so had on the Secretary of State shall be returnable in not less than thirty days.

The Secretary of State shall keep a record of all processes, notices and demands served upon him under this section, and shall record therein the time of such service and his action with reference thereto.

Nothing herein contained shall limit or affect the right to serve any process, notice or demand required or permitted by law to be served upon a corporation in any other manner now or hereafter permitted by law.

§ 14. Authorized Shares.

Each corporation shall have power to create and issue the number of shares stated in its articles of incorporation. Such shares may be divided into one or more classes, any or all of which classes may consist of shares with par value or shares without par value, with such designations, preferences, limitations, and relative rights as shall be stated in the articles of incorporation. The articles of incorporation may limit or deny the voting rights of or provide special voting rights for the shares of any class to the extent not inconsistent with the provisions of this Act.

Without limiting the authority herein contained, a corporation, when so provided in its articles of incorporation, may issue shares of preferred or special classes:

(a) Subject to the right of the corporation to redeem any of such shares at the price fixed by the articles of incorporation for the redemption thereof.

(b) Entitling the holders thereof to cumulative, noncumulative or partially cumulative dividends.

(c) Having preference over any other class or classes of shares as to the payment of dividends.

(d) Having preference in the assets of the corporation over any other class or classes of shares upon the voluntary or involuntary liquidation of the corporation.

(e) Convertible into shares of any other class or into shares of any series of the same or any other class, except a class having prior or superior rights and preferences as to dividends or distribution of assets upon liquidation, but shares without par value shall not be converted into shares with par value unless that part of the stated capital of the corporation represented by such shares without par value is, at the time of conversion, at least equal to the aggregate par value of the shares into which the shares without par value are to be converted.

§ 15. Issuance of Shares of Preferred or Special Classes in Series.

If the articles of incorporation so provide, the shares of any preferred or special class may be divided into and issued in series. If the shares of any such class are to be issued in series, then each series shall be so designated as to distinguish the shares thereof from the shares of all other series and classes. Any or all of the series of any such class and the variations in the relative rights and preferences as between different series may be fixed and determined by the articles of incorporation, but all shares of the same class shall be identical except as to the following relative rights and preferences, as to which there may be variations between different series:

A. The rate of dividend.

B. Whether shares may be redeemed and, if so, the redemption price and the terms and conditions of redemption.

C. The amount payable upon shares in event of voluntary and involuntary liquidation.

D. Sinking fund provisions, if any, for the redemption or purchase of shares.

E. The terms and conditions, if any, on which shares may be converted.

If the articles of incorporation shall expressly vest authority in the board of directors, then, to the extent that the articles of incorporation shall not have established series and fixed and determined the variations in the relative rights and preferences as between series, the board of directors shall have authority to divide any or all of such classes into series and, within the limitations set forth in this section and in the articles of incorporation, fix and determine the relative rights and preferences of the shares of any series so established.

In order for the board of directors to establish a series, where authority so to do is contained in the articles of incorporation, the board of directors shall adopt a resolution setting forth the designation of the series and fixing and determining the relative rights and preferences thereof, or so much thereof as shall not be fixed and determined by the articles of incorporation.

Prior to the issue of any shares of a series established by resolution adopted by the board of directors, the corporation shall file in the office of the Secretary of State a statement setting forth:

(a) The name of the corporation.

(b) A copy of the resolution establishing and designating the series, and fixing and determining the relative rights and preferences thereof.

(c) The date of adoption of such resolution.

(d) That such resolution was duly adopted by the board of directors.

Such statement shall be executed in duplicate by the corporation by its president or a vice president and by its secretary or an assistant secretary, and verified by one of the officers signing such statement, and shall be delivered to the Secretary of State. If the Secretary of State finds that such statement conforms to law, he shall, when all franchise taxes and fees have been paid as in this Act prescribed:

(1) Endorse on each of such duplicate originals the word "Filed," and the month, day, and year of the filing thereof.

(2) File one of such duplicate originals in his office.

(3) Return the other duplicate original to the corporation or its representative.

Upon the filing of such statement by the Secretary of State, the resolution establishing and designating the series and fixing and determining the relative rights and preferences thereof shall become effective and shall constitute an amendment of the articles of incorporation.

§ 16. Subscriptions for Shares.

A subscription for shares of a corporation to be organized shall be irrevocable for a period of six months, unless otherwise provided by the terms of the subscription agreement or unless all of the subscribers consent to the revocation of such subscription.

Unless otherwise provided in the subscription agreement, subscriptions for shares, whether made before or after the organization of a corporation, shall be paid in full at such time, or in such installments and at such times, as shall be determined by the board of directors. Any call made by the board of directors for payment on subscriptions shall be uniform as to all shares of the same class or as to all shares of the same series, as the case may be. In case of default in the payment of any installment or call when such payment is due, the corporation may proceed to collect the amount due in the same manner as any debt due the corporation. The by-laws may prescribe other penalties for failure to pay installments or calls that may become due, but no penalty working a forfeiture of a subscription, or of the amounts paid thereon, shall be declared as against any subscriber unless the amount due thereon shall remain unpaid for a period of twenty days after written demand has been made therefor. If mailed, such written demand shall be deemed to be made when deposited in the United States mail in a sealed envelope addressed to the subscriber at his last post-office address known to the corporation, with postage thereon prepaid. In the event of the sale of any shares by reason of any forfeiture, the excess of proceeds realized over the amount due and unpaid on such shares shall be paid to the delinquent subscriber or to his legal representative.

§ 17. Consideration for Shares.

Shares having a par value may be issued for such consideration expressed in dollars, not less than the par value thereof, as shall be fixed from time to time by the board of directors.

Shares without par value may be issued for such consideration expressed in dollars as may be fixed from time to time by the board of directors unless the articles of incorporation reserve to the shareholders the right to fix the consideration. In the event that such right be reserved as to any shares, the shareholders shall, prior to the issuance of such shares, fix the consideration to be received for such shares by a vote of the holders of a majority of all shares entitled to vote thereon.

Treasury shares may be disposed of by the corporation for such consideration expressed in dollars as may be fixed from time to time by the board of directors.

That part of the surplus of a corporation which is transferred to stated capital upon the issuance of shares as a share dividend shall be deemed to be the consideration for the issuance of such shares.

In the event of a conversion of shares, or in the event of an exchange of shares with or without par value for the same or a different number of shares with or without par value, whether of the same or a different class or classes, the consideration for the shares so issued in exchange or conversion shall be deemed to be (1) the stated capital then represented by the shares so exchanged or converted, and (2) that part of surplus, if any, transferred to stated capital upon the issuance of shares for the shares so exchanged or converted, and (3) any additional consideration paid to the corporation upon the issuance of shares for the shares so exchanged or converted.

§ 18. Payment for Shares.

The consideration for the issuance of shares may be paid, in whole or in part, in money, in other property, tangible or intangible, or in labor or services actually performed for the corporation. When payment of the consideration for which shares are to be issued shall have been received by the corporation, such shares shall be deemed to be fully paid and nonassessable.

Neither promissory notes nor future services shall constitute payment or part payment, for shares of a corporation.

In the absence of fraud in the transaction, the judgment of the board of directors or the shareholders, as the case may be, as to the value of the consideration received for shares shall be conclusive.

[Optional] § 18A. Stock Rights and Options.

Subject to any provisions in respect thereof set forth in its articles of incorporation, a corporation may create and issue, whether or not in connection with the issuance and sale of any of its shares or other securities, rights or options entitling the holders thereof to purchase from the corporation shares of any class or classes. Such rights or options shall be evidenced in such manner as the board of directors shall approve and, subject to the provisions of the articles of incorporation, shall set forth the terms upon which, the time or times within which and the price or prices at which such shares may be purchased from the corporation upon the exercise of any such right or option. If such rights or options are to be issued to directors, officers or employees as such of the corporation or of any subsidiary thereof, and not to the shareholders generally, their issuance shall be approved by the affirmative vote of the holders of a majority of the shares entitled to vote thereon or shall be authorized by and consistent with a plan theretofore approved by such a vote of shareholders and set forth or incorporated by reference in the instrument evidencing each such right or option. In the absence of fraud in the transaction, the judgment of the board of directors as to the adequacy of the consideration received for such rights or options shall be conclusive. The price or prices to be received for any shares having a par value, other than treasury shares to be issued upon the exercise of such rights or options, shall not be less than the par value thereof.

§ 19. Determination of Amount of Stated Capital.

In case of the issuance by a corporation of shares having par value, the consideration received therefor shall constitute stated capital to the extent of the par value of such shares, and the excess, if any, of such consideration shall constitute capital surplus.

In case of the issuance by a corporation of shares without par value, the entire consideration received therefor shall constitute stated capital unless the corporation shall determine as provided in this section that only a part thereof shall be stated capital. Within a period of sixty days after the issuance of any shares without par value, the board of directors may allocate to capital surplus any portion of the consideration received for the issuance of such shares. No such allocation shall be made of any portion of the consideration received for shares without par value having a preference in the assets of the corporation in the event of involuntary liquidation except the amount, if any, of such consideration in excess of such preference.

If shares have been or shall be issued by a corporation in merger or consolidation or in acquisition of all or substantially all of the outstanding shares or of the property and assets of another corporation, whether domestic or foreign, any amount that would otherwise constitute capital surplus under the foregoing provisions of this section may instead be allocated to earned surplus by the board of directors of the issuing corporation except that its aggregate earned surplus shall not exceed the sum of the earned surpluses as defined in this Act of the issuing corporation and of all other corporations, domestic or foreign, that were merged or consolidated or of which the shares or assets were acquired.

The stated capital of a corporation may be increased from time to time by resolution of the board of directors directing that all or a part of the surplus of the corporation be transferred to stated capital. The board of directors may direct that the amount of the surplus so transferred shall be deemed to be stated capital in respect of any designated class of shares.

§ 20. Expenses of Organization, Reorganization and Financing.

The reasonable charges and expenses of organization or reorganization of a corporation, and the reasonable expenses of and compensation for the sale or underwriting of its shares, may be paid or allowed by such corporation out of the consideration received by it in payment for its share without thereby rendering such shares not fully paid or assessable.

§ 21. Certificates Representing Shares.

The shares of a corporation shall be represented by certificates signed by the president or a vice president and the secretary or an assistant secretary of the corporation, and may be sealed with the seal of the corporation or a facsimile thereof. The signatures of the president or vice president and the secretary or assistant secretary upon a certificate may be facsimiles if the certificate is countersigned by a transfer agent, or registered by a registrar, other than the corporation itself or an employee of the corporation. In case any officer who has signed or whose facsimile signature has been placed upon such certificate shall have ceased to be such officer before such certificate is issued, it may be issued by the corporation with the same effect as if he were such officer at the date of its issue.

Every certificate representing shares issued by a corporation which is authorized to issue shares of more than one class shall set forth upon the face or back of the certificate, or shall state that the corporation will furnish to any shareholder upon request and without charge, a full statement of the designations, preferences, imitations, and relative rights of the shares of each class authorized to be issued and, if the corporation is authorized to issue any preferred or special class in series, the variations in the relative rights and preferences between the shares of each such series so far as the same have been fixed and determined and the authority of the board of directors to fix and determine the relative rights and preferences of subsequent series.

Each certificate representing shares shall state upon the face thereof:

(a) That the corporation is organized under the laws of this State.

(b) The name of the person to whom issued.

(c) The number and class of shares, and the designation of the series, if any, which such certificate represents.

(d) The par value of each share represented by such certificate, or a statement that the shares are without par value.

No certificate shall be issued for any share until such share is fully paid.

§ 22. Issuance of Fractional Shares or Scrip.

A corporation may, but shall not be obliged to, issue a certificate for a fractional share, and, by action of its board of directors, may issue in lieu thereof scrip in registered or bearer form which shall entitle the holder to receive a certificate for a full share upon the surrender of such scrip aggregating a full share. A certificate for a fractional share shall, but scrip shall not unless otherwise provided therein, entitle the holder to exercise voting rights, to receive dividends thereon, and to participate in any of the assets of the corporation in the event of liquidation. The board of directors may cause such scrip to be issued subject to the condition that it shall become void if not exchanged for certificates representing full shares before a specified date, or subject to the condition that the shares for which such scrip is exchangeable may be sold by the corporation and the proceeds thereof distributed to the holders of such scrip, or subject to any other conditions which the board of directors may deem advisable.

§ 23. Liability of Subscribers and Shareholders.

A holder of or subscriber to shares of a corporation shall be under no obligation to the corporation or its creditors with respect to such shares other than the obligation to pay to the corporation the full consideration for which such shares were issued or to be issued.

Any person becoming an assignee or transferee of shares or of a subscription for shares in good faith and without knowledge or notice that the full consideration therefor has not been paid shall not be personally liable to the corporation or its creditors for any unpaid portion of such consideration.

An executor, administrator, conservator, guardian, trustee, assignee for the benefit of creditors, or receiver shall not be personally liable to the corporation as a holder of or subscriber to shares of a corporation but the estate and funds in his hands shall be so liable.

No pledgee or other holder of shares as collateral security shall be personally liable as a shareholder.

§ 24. Shareholders' Preemptive Rights.

The preemptive right of a shareholder to acquire unissued or treasury shares of a corporation may be limited or denied to the extent provided in the articles of incorporation.

Unless otherwise provided by its articles of incorporation, any corporation may issue and sell its shares to its officers or employees or to the officers or employees of any subsidiary corporation, without first offering such shares to its shareholders, for such consideration and upon such terms and conditions as shall be approved by the holders of a majority of all shares entitled to vote thereon or by its board of directors pursuant to like approval of the shareholders.

Alternative § 24. Shareholders' Preemptive Rights.

The shareholders of a corporation shall have no preemptive right to acquire unissued or treasury shares of the corporation, or obligations of the corporation convertible into such shares, except to the extent, if any, that such right is provided in the articles of incorporation.

§ 25. By-Laws.

The initial by-laws of a corporation shall be adopted by its board of directors. The power to alter, amend or repeal the by-laws or adopt new by-laws shall be vested in the board of directors unless reserved to the shareholders by the articles of incorporation. The by-laws may contain any provisions for the regulation and management of the affairs of the corporation not inconsistent with law or the articles of incorporation.

§ 25A. By-Laws and Other Powers in Emergency.

(Optional) The board of directors of any corporation may adopt emergency by-laws, subject to repeal or change by action of the shareholders, which shall, notwithstanding any different provision elsewhere in this Act or in the articles of incorporation or by-laws, be operative during any emergency in the conduct of the business of the corporation resulting from an attack on the United States or any nuclear or atomic disaster. The emergency by-laws may make any provision that may be practical and necessary for the circumstances of the emergency, including provisions that:

(a) A meeting of the board of directors may be called by any officer or director in such manner and under such conditions as shall be prescribed in the emergency by-laws;

(b) The director or directors in attendance at the meeting, or any greater number fixed by the emergency by-laws, shall constitute a quorum; and

(c) The officers or other persons designated on a list approved by the board of directors before the emergency, all in such order of priority and subject to such conditions and for such period of time (not longer than reasonably necessary after the termination of the emergency) as may be provided in the emergency by-laws or in the resolution approving the list, shall, to the extent required to provide a quorum at any meeting of the board of directors, be deemed directors for such meeting.

The board of directors, either before or during any such emergency, may provide, and from time to time modify, lines of succession in the event that during such an emergency any or all officers or agents of the corporation shall for any reason be rendered incapable of discharging their duties.

The board of directors, either before or during any such emergency, may, effective in the emergency, change the head office or designate several alternative head offices or regional offices, or authorize the officers so to do.

To the extent not inconsistent with any emergency by-laws so adopted, the by-laws of the corporation shall remain in effect during any such emergency and upon its termination the emergency by-laws shall cease to be operative.

Unless otherwise provided in emergency by-laws, notice of any meeting of the board of directors during any such emergency may be given only to such of the directors as it may be feasible to reach at the time and by such means as may be feasible at the time, including publication or radio.

To the extent required to constitute a quorum at any meeting of the board of directors during any such emergency, the officers of the corporation who are present shall, unless otherwise provided in emergency by-laws, be deemed, in order of rank and within the same rank in order of seniority, directors for such meeting.

No officer, director or employee acting in accordance with any emergency by-laws shall be liable except for willful misconduct. No officer, director or employee shall be liable for any action taken by him in good faith in such an emergency in furtherance of the ordinary business affairs of the corporation even though not authorized by the by-laws then in effect.

§ 26. Meetings of Shareholders.

Meetings of shareholders may be held at such place, either within or without this State, as may be provided in the by-laws. In the absence of any such provision, all meetings shall be held at the registered office of the corporation.

An annual meeting of the shareholders shall be held at such time as may be provided in the by-laws. Failure to hold the annual meeting at the designated time shall not work a forfeiture or dissolution of the corporation.

Special meetings of the shareholders may be called by the president, the board of directors, the holders of not less than one-tenth of all the shares entitled to vote at the meeting, or such other officers or persons as may be provided in the articles of incorporation or the by-laws.

§ 27. Notice of Shareholders' Meetings.

Written notice stating the place, day and hour of the meeting and, in case of a special meeting, the purpose or purposes for which the meeting is called, shall be delivered not less than ten nor more than fifty days before the date of the meeting, either personally or by mail, by or at the direction of the president, the secretary, or the officer or persons calling the meeting, to each shareholder of record entitled to vote at such meeting. If mailed, such notice shall be deemed to be delivered when deposited in the United States mail addressed to the shareholder at his address as it appears on the stock transfer books of the corporation, with postage thereon prepaid.

§ 28. Closing of Transfer Books and Fixing Record Date.

For the purpose of determining shareholders entitled to notice of or to vote at any meeting of shareholders or any adjournment thereof, or entitled to receive payment of any dividend, or in order to make a determination of shareholders for any other proper purpose, the board of directors of a corporation may provide that the stock transfer books shall be closed for a stated period but not to exceed, in any case, fifty days. If the stock transfer books shall be closed for the purpose of determining shareholders entitled to notice of or to vote at a meeting of shareholders, such books shall be closed for at least ten days immediately preceding such meeting. In lieu of closing the stock transfer books, the by-laws, or in the absence of an applicable by-law the board of directors, may fix in advance a date as the record date for any such determination of shareholders, such date in any case to be not more than fifty days and, in case of a meeting of shareholders, not less than ten days prior to the date on which the particular action, requiring such determination of shareholders, is to be taken. If the stock transfer books are not closed and no record date is fixed for the determination of shareholders entitled to notice of or to vote at a meeting of shareholders, or shareholders entitled to receive payment of a dividend, the date on which notice of the meeting is mailed or the date on which the resolution of the board of directors declaring such dividend is adopted, as the case may be, shall be the record date for such determination of shareholders. When a determination of shareholders entitled to vote at any meeting of shareholders has been made as provided in this section, such determination shall apply to any adjournment thereof.

§ 29. Voting List.

The officer or agent having charge of the stock transfer books for shares of a corporation shall make a complete list of the shareholders entitled to vote at such meeting or any adjournment thereof, arranged in alphabetical order, with the address of and the number of shares held by each. Such list shall be produced and kept open at the time and place of the meeting and shall be subject to the inspection of any shareholder during the whole time of the meeting for the purposes thereof.

Failure to comply with the requirements of this section shall not affect the validity of any action taken at such meeting.

An officer or agent having charge of the stock transfer books who shall fail to prepare the list of shareholders, or produce and keep it open for inspection at the meeting, as provided in this section, shall be liable to any shareholder suffering damage on account of such failure, to the extent of such damage.

§ 30. Quorum of Shareholders.

Unless otherwise provided in the articles of incorporation, a majority of the shares entitled to vote, represented in person or by proxy, shall constitute a quorum at a meeting of shareholders, but in no event shall a quorum consist of less than one-third of the shares entitled to vote at the meeting. If a quorum is present, the affirmative vote of the majority of the shares represented at the meeting and entitled to vote on the subject matter shall be the act of the shareholders, unless the vote of a greater number or voting by classes is required by this Act or the articles of incorporation or by-laws.

§ 31. Voting of Shares.

Each outstanding share, regardless of class, shall be entitled to one vote on each matter submitted to a vote at a meeting of shareholders, except to the extent that the voting rights of the shares of any class or classes are limited or denied by the articles of incorporation as permitted by this Act.

Neither treasury shares, nor shares held by another corporation if a majority of the shares entitled to vote for the election of directors of such other corporation is held by the corporation, shall be voted at any meeting or counted in determining the total number of outstanding shares at any given time.

A shareholder may vote either in person or by proxy executed in writing by the shareholder or by his duly authorized attorney-in-fact. No proxy shall be valid after eleven months from the date of its execution, unless otherwise provided in the proxy.

(Either of the following prefatory phrases may be inserted here: "The articles of incorporation may provide that" or "Unless the articles of incorporation otherwise provide") . . . at each election for directors every shareholder entitled to vote at such election shall have the right to vote, in person or by proxy, the number of shares owned by him for as many persons as there are directors to be elected and for whose election he has a right to vote, or to cumulate his votes by giving one candidate as many votes as the number of such directors multiplied by the number of his shares shall equal, or by distributing such votes on the same principle among any number of such candidates.

Shares standing in the name of another corporation, domestic or foreign, may be voted by such officer, agent or proxy as the by-laws of such corporation may prescribe, or, in the absence of such provision, as the board of directors of such corporation may determine.

Shares held by an administrator, executor, guardian or conservator may be voted by him, either in person or by proxy, without a transfer of such shares into his name. Shares standing in the name of a trustee may be voted by him, either in person or by proxy, but no trustee shall be entitled to vote shares held by him without a transfer of such shares into his name.

Shares standing in the name of a receiver may be voted by such receiver, and shares held by or under the control of a receiver may be voted by such receiver without the transfer thereof into his name if authority so to do be contained in an appropriate order of the court by which such receiver was appointed.

A shareholder whose shares are pledged shall be entitled to vote such shares until the shares have been transferred into the name of the pledgee, and thereafter the pledgee shall be entitled to vote the shares so transferred.

On and after the date on which written notice of redemption of redeemable shares has been mailed to the holders thereof and a sum sufficient to redeem such shares has been deposited with a bank or trust company with irrevocable instruction and authority to pay the redemption price to the holders thereof upon surrender of certificates therefor, such shares shall not be entitled to vote on any matter and shall not be deemed to be outstanding shares.

§ 32. Voting Trust.

Any number of shareholders of a corporation may create a voting trust for the purpose of conferring upon a trustee or trustees the right to vote or otherwise represent their shares, for a period of not to exceed ten years, by entering into a written voting trust agreement specifying the terms and conditions of the voting trust, by depositing a counterpart of the agreement with the corporation at its registered office, and by transferring their shares to such trustee or trustees for the purposes of the agreement. The counterpart of the voting trust agreement so deposited with the corporation shall be subject to the same right of examination by a shareholder of the corporation, in person or by agent or attorney, as are the books and records of the corporation, and shall be subject to examination by any holder of a beneficial interest in the voting trust, either in person or by agent or attorney, at any reasonable time for any proper purpose.

§ 33. Board of Directors.

The business and affairs of a corporation shall be managed by a board of directors. Directors need not be residents of this State or shareholders of the corporation unless the articles of incorporation or by-laws so require. The articles of incorporation or by-laws may prescribe other qualifications for directors. The board of directors shall have authority to fix the compensation of directors unless otherwise provided in the articles of incorporation.

§ 34. Number and Election of Directors.

The number of directors of a corporation shall be not less than three. Subject to such limitation, the number of directors shall be fixed by the by-laws, except as to the number constituting the initial board of directors, which number shall be fixed by the articles of incorporation. The number of directors may be increased or decreased from time to time by amendment to the by-laws, but no decrease shall have the effect of shortening the term of any incumbent director. In the absence of a by-law fixing the number of directors, the number shall be the same as that stated in the articles of incorporation. The names and addresses of the members of the first board of directors shall be stated in the articles of incorporation. Such persons shall hold office until the first annual meeting of shareholders, and until their successors shall have been elected and qualified. At the first annual meeting of shareholders and at each annual meeting thereafter the shareholders shall elect directors to hold office until the next succeeding annual meeting, except in case of the classification of directors as permitted by this Act. Each director shall hold office for the term for which he is elected and until his successor shall have been elected and qualified.

§ 35. Classification of Directors.

When the board of directors shall consist of nine or more members, in lieu of electing the whole number of directors annually, the articles of incorporation may provide that the directors be divided into either two or three classes, each class to be as nearly equal in number as possible, the term of office of directors of the first class to expire at the first annual meeting of shareholders after their election, that of the second class to expire at the second annual meeting after their election, and that of the third class, if any, to expire at the third annual meeting after their election. At each annual meeting after such classification the number of directors equal to the number of the class whose term expires at the time of such meeting shall be elected to hold office until the second succeeding annual meeting, if there be two classes, or until the third succeeding annual meeting, if there be three classes. No classification of directors shall be effective prior to the first annual meeting of shareholders.

§ 36. Vacancies.

Any vacancy occurring in the board of directors may be filled by the affirmative vote of a majority of the remaining directors though less than a quorum of the board of directors. A director elected to fill a vacancy shall be elected for the unexpired term of his predecessor in office. Any directorship to be filled by reason of an increase in the number of directors may be filled by the board of directors for a term of office continuing only until the next election of directors by the shareholders.

[Optional] § 36A. Removal of Directors.

At a meeting called expressly for that purpose, directors may be removed in the manner provided in this section. The entire board of directors may be removed, with or without cause, by a vote of the holders of a majority of the shares then entitled to vote at an election of directors.

† If less than the entire board is to be removed, no one of the directors may be removed if the votes cast against his removal would be sufficient to elect him if then cumulatively voted at an election of the entire board of directors, or, if there be classes of directors, at an election of the class of directors of which he is a part.

Whenever the holders of the shares of any class are entitled to elect one or more directors by the provisions of the articles of incorporation, the provisions of this section shall apply, in respect of the removal of a director or directors so elected, to the vote of the holders of the outstanding shares of that class and not to the vote of the outstanding shares as a whole.

---

† If cumulative voting is permissive, the sentence should begin with the phrase "In the case of a corporation having cumulative voting,".

§ 37. Quorum of Directors.

A majority of the number of directors fixed by the by-laws, or in the absence of a by-law fixing the number of directors, then of the number stated in the articles of incorporation, shall constitute a quorum for the transaction of business unless a greater number is required by the articles of incorporation or the by-laws. The act of the majority of the directors present at a meeting at which a quorum is present shall be the act of the board of directors, unless the act of a greater number is required by the articles of incorporation or the by-laws.

§ 38. Executive and Other Committees.

If the articles of incorporation or the by-laws so provide, the board of directors, by resolution adopted by a majority of the full board of directors, may designate from among its members an executive committee and one or more other committees each of which, to the extent provided in such resolution or in the articles of incorporation or the by-laws of the corporation, shall have and may exercise all the authority of the board of directors, but no such committee shall have the authority of the board of directors in reference to amending the articles of incorporation, adopting a plan of merger or consolidation, recommending to the shareholders the sale, lease, exchange, or other disposition of all or substantially all the property and assets of the corporation otherwise than in the usual and regular course of its business, recommending to the shareholders a voluntary dissolution of the corporation or a revocation thereof, or amending the by-laws of the corporation.

§ 39. Place and Notice of Directors' Meetings.

Meetings of the board of directors, regular or special, may be held either within or without this State.

Regular meetings of the board of directors may be held with or without notice as prescribed in the by-laws. Special meetings of the board of directors shall be held upon such notice as is prescribed in the by-laws. Attendance of a director at a meeting shall constitute a waiver of notice of such meeting, except where a director attends a meeting for the express purpose of objecting to the transaction of any business because the meeting is not lawfully called or convened. Neither the business to be transacted at, nor the purpose of, any regular or special meeting of the board of directors need be specified in the notice or waiver of notice of such meeting unless required by the by-laws.

[Optional] § 39A. Action by Directors Without a Meeting.

Unless otherwise provided by the articles of incorporation or by-laws, any action required by this Act to be taken at a meeting of the directors or of a committee, may be taken without a meeting if a consent in writing, setting forth the action so to be taken, shall be signed before such action by all of the directors, or all of the members of the committee, as the case may be. Such consent shall have the same effect as a unanimous vote.

§ 40. Dividends.

The board of directors of a corporation may, from time to time, declare and the corporation may pay dividends on its outstanding shares in cash, property, or its own shares, except when the corporation is insolvent or when the payment thereof would render the corporation insolvent or when the declaration or payment thereof would be contrary to any restrictions contained in the articles of incorporation, subject to the following provisions:

(a) Dividends may be declared and paid in cash or property only out of the unreserved and unrestricted earned surplus of the corporation, except as otherwise provided in this section.

(a) (Alternative) Dividends may be declared and paid in cash or property only out of the unreserved and unrestricted earned surplus of the corporation, or out of the unreserved and unrestricted net earnings of the current fiscal year and the next preceding fiscal year taken as a single period.

(b) If the articles of incorporation of a corporation engaged in the business of exploiting natural resources so provide, dividends may be declared and paid in cash out of the depletion reserves, but each such dividend shall be identified as a distribution of such reserves and the amount per share paid from such reserves shall be disclosed to the shareholders receiving the same concurrently with the distribution thereof.

(c) Dividends may be declared and paid in its own shares out of any treasury shares that have been reacquired out of surplus of the corporation.

(d) Dividends may be declared and paid in its own authorized but unissued shares out of any unreserved and unrestricted surplus of the corporation upon the following conditions:

(1) If a dividend is payable in its own shares having a par value, such shares shall be issued at not less than the par value thereof and there shall be transferred to stated capital at the time such dividend is paid an amount of surplus at least equal to the aggregate par value of the shares to be issued as a dividend.

(2) If a dividend is payable in its own shares without par value, such shares shall be issued at such stated value as shall be fixed by the board of directors by resolution adopted at the time such dividend is declared, and there shall be transferred to stated capital at the time such dividend is paid an amount of surplus equal to the aggregate stated value so fixed in respect of such shares; and the amount per share so transferred to stated capital shall be disclosed to the shareholders receiving such dividend concurrently with the payment thereof.

(e) No dividend payable in shares of any class shall be paid to the holders of shares of any other class unless the articles of incorporation so provide or such payment is authorized by the affirmative vote or the written consent of the holders of at least a majority of the outstanding shares of the class in which the payment is to be made.

A split-up or division of the issued shares of any class into a greater number of shares of the same class without increasing the stated capital of the corporation shall not be construed to be a share dividend within the meaning of this section.

§ 41. Distributions from Capital Surplus.

The board of directors of a corporation may, from time to time, distribute to its shareholders out of capital surplus of the corporation a portion of its assets, in cash or property, subject to the following provisions:

(a) No such distribution shall be made at a time when the corporation is insolvent or when such distribution would render the corporation insolvent.

(b) No such distribution shall be made unless the articles of incorporation so provide or such distribution is authorized by the affirmative vote of the holders of a majority of the outstanding shares of each class whether or not entitled to vote thereon by the provisions of the articles of incorporation of the corporation.

(c) No such distribution shall be made to the holders of any class of shares unless all cumulative dividends accrued on all preferred or special classes of shares entitled to preferential dividends shall have been fully paid.

(d) No such distribution shall be made to the holders of any class of shares which would reduce the remaining net assets of the corporation below the aggregate preferential amount payable in event of voluntary liquidation to the holders of shares having preferential rights to the assets of the corporation in the event of liquidation.

(e) Each such distribution, when made, shall be identified as a distribution from capital surplus and the amount per share disclosed to the shareholders receiving the same concurrently with the distribution thereof.

The board of directors of a corporation may also, from time to time, distribute to the holders of its outstanding shares having a cumulative preferential right to receive dividends, in discharge of their cumulative dividend rights, dividends payable in cash out of the capital surplus of the corporation, if at the time the corporation has no earned surplus and is not insolvent and would not thereby be rendered insolvent. Each distribution, when made, shall be identified as a payment of cumulative dividends out of capital surplus.

§ 42. Loans.

No loans shall be made by a corporation to its officers or directors, and no loans shall be made by a corporation secured by its shares.

§ 43. Liability of Directors in Certain Cases.

In addition to any other liabilities imposed by law upon directors of a corporation:

(a) Directors of a corporation who vote for or assent to the declaration of any dividend or other distribution of the assets of a corporation to its shareholders contrary to the provisions of this Act or contrary to any restrictions contained in the articles of incorporation, shall be jointly and severally liable to the corporation for the amount of such dividend which is paid or the value of such assets which are distributed in excess of the amount of such dividend or distribution which could have been paid or distributed without a violation of the provisions of this Act or the restrictions in the articles of incorporation.

(b) Directors of a corporation who vote for or assent to the purchase of its own shares contrary to the provisions of this Act shall be jointly and severally liable to the corporation for the amount of consideration paid for such shares which is in excess of the maximum amount which could have been paid therefor without a violation of the provisions of this Act.

(c) The directors of a corporation who vote for or assent to any distribution of assets of a corporation to its shareholders during the liquidation of the corporation without the payment and discharge of, or making adequate provision for, all known debts, obligations, and liabilities of the corporation shall be jointly and severally liable to the corporation for the value of such assets which are distributed, to the extent that such debts, obligations and liabilities of the corporation are not thereafter paid and discharged.

(d) The directors of a corporation who vote for or assent to the making of a loan to an officer or director of the corporation, or the making of any loan secured by shares of the corporation, shall be jointly and severally liable to the corporation for the amount of such loan until the repayment thereof.

(e) If a corporation shall commence business before it has received at least one thousand dollars as consideration for the issuance of shares, the directors who assent thereto shall be jointly and severally liable to the corporation for such part of one thousand dollars as shall not have been received before commencing business, but such liability shall be terminated when the corporation has actually received one thousand dollars as consideration for the issuance of shares.

A director of a corporation who is present at a meeting of its board of directors at which action on any corporate matter is taken shall be presumed to have assented to the action taken unless his dissent shall be entered in the minutes of the meeting or unless he shall file his written dissent to such action with the person acting as the secretary of the meeting before the adjournment thereof or shall forward such dissent by registered mail to the secretary of the corporation immediately after the adjournment of the meeting. Such right to dissent shall not apply to a director who voted in favor of such action.

A director shall not be liable under subparagraphs (a), (b) or (c) of this section if he relied and acted in good faith upon financial statements of the corporation represented to him to be correct by the president or the officer of such corporation having charge of its books of account, or stated in a written report by an independent public or certified public accountant or firm of such accountants fairly to reflect the financial condition of such corporation, nor shall he be so liable if in good faith in determining the amount available for any such dividend or distribution he considered the assets to be of their book value.

Any director against whom a claim shall be asserted under or pursuant to this section for the payment of a dividend or other distribution of assets of a corporation and who shall be held liable thereon, shall be entitled to contribution from the shareholders who accepted or received any such dividend or assets, knowing such dividend or distribution to have been made in violation of this Act, in proportion to the amounts received by them respectively.

Any director against whom a claim shall be asserted under or pursuant to this section shall be entitled to contribution from the other directors who voted for or assented to the action upon which the claim is asserted.

[Optional] § 43A. Provisions Relating to Actions by Shareholders.

No action shall be brought in this State by a shareholder in the right of a domestic or foreign corporation unless the plaintiff was a holder of record of shares or of voting trust certificates therefor at the time of the transaction of which he complains, or his shares or voting trust certificates thereafter devolved upon him by operation of law from a person who was a holder of record at such time.

In any action hereafter instituted in the right of any domestic or foreign corporation by the holder or holders of record of shares of such corporation or of voting trust certificates therefor, the court having jurisdiction, upon final judgment and a finding that the action was brought without reasonable cause, may require the plaintiff or plaintiffs to pay to the parties named as defendant the reasonable expenses, including fees of attorneys, incurred by them in the defense of such action.

In any action now pending or hereafter instituted or maintained in the right of any domestic or foreign corporation by the holder or holders of record of less than five per cent of the outstanding shares of any class of such corporation or of voting trust certificates therefor, unless the shares or voting trust certificates so held have a market value in excess of twenty-five thousand dollars, the corporation in whose right such action is brought shall be entitled at any time before final judgment to require the plaintiff or plaintiffs to give security for the reasonable expenses, including fees of attorneys, that may be incurred by it in connection with such action or may be incurred by other parties named as defendant for which it may become legally liable. Market value shall be determined as of the date that the plaintiff institutes the action or, in the case of an intervener, as of the date that he becomes a party to the action. The amount of such security may from time to time be increased or decreased, in the discretion of the court, upon showing that the security provided has or may become inadequate or is excessive. The corporation shall have recourse to such security in such amount as the court having jurisdiction shall determine upon the termination of such action, whether or not the court finds the action was brought without reasonable cause.

§ 44. Officers.

The officers of a corporation shall consist of a president, one or more vice presidents as may be prescribed by the by-laws, a secretary, and a treasurer, each of whom shall be elected by the board of directors at such time and in such manner as may be prescribed by the by-laws. Such other officers and assistant officers and agents as may be deemed necessary may be elected or appointed by the board of directors or chosen in such other manner as may be prescribed by the by-laws. Any two or more offices may be held by the same person, except the offices of president and secretary.

All officers and agents of the corporation, as between themselves and the corporation, shall have such authority and perform such duties in the management of the corporation as may be provided in the by-laws, or as may be determined by resolution of the board of directors not inconsistent with the by-laws.

§ 45. Removal of Officers.

Any officer or agent may be removed by the board of directors whenever in its judgment the best interests of the corporation will be served thereby, but such removal shall be without prejudice to the contract rights, if any, of the person so removed. Election or appointment of an officer or agent shall not of itself create contract rights.

§ 46. Books and Records.

Each corporation shall keep correct and complete books and records of account and shall keep minutes of the proceedings of its shareholders and board of directors; and shall keep at its registered office or principal place of business, or at the office of its transfer agent or registrar, a record of its shareholders, giving the names and addresses of all shareholders and the number and class of the shares held by each.

Any person who shall have been a shareholder of record for at least six months immediately preceding his demand or who shall be the holder of record of at least five per cent of all the outstanding shares of a corporation, upon written demand stating the purpose thereof, shall have the right to examine, in person, or by agent or attorney, at any reasonable time or times, for any proper purpose, its books and records of account, minutes and record of shareholders and to make extracts therefrom.

Any officer or agent who, or a corporation which, shall refuse to allow any such shareholder, or his agent or attorney, so to examine and make extracts from its books and records of account, minutes, and record of shareholders, for any proper purpose, shall be liable to such shareholder in a penalty of ten per cent of the value of the shares owned by such shareholder, in addition to any other damages or remedy afforded him by law. It shall be a defense to any action for penalties under this section that the person suing therefor has within two years sold or offered for sale any list of shareholders of such corporation or any other corporation or has aided or abetted any person in procuring any list of shareholders for any such purpose, or has improperly used any information secured through any prior examination of the books and records of account, or minutes, or record of shareholders of such corporation or any other corporation, or was not acting in good faith or for a proper purpose in making his demand.

Nothing herein contained shall impair the power of any court of competent jurisdiction, upon proof by a shareholder of proper purpose, irrespective of the period of time during which such shareholder shall have been a shareholder of record, and irrespective of the number of shares held by him, to compel the production for examination by such shareholder of the books and records of account, minutes, and record of shareholders of a corporation.

Upon the written request of any shareholder of a corporation, the corporation shall mail to such shareholder its most recent financial statements showing in reasonable detail its assets and liabilities and the results of its operations.

§ 47. Incorporators.

One or more persons, or a domestic or foreign corporation, may act as incorporator or incorporators of a corporation by signing and delivering in duplicate to the Secretary of State articles of incorporation for such corporation.

§ 48. Articles of Incorporation.

The articles of incorporation shall set forth:

(a) The name of the corporation.

(b) The period of duration, which may be perpetual.

(c) The purpose or purposes for which the corporation is organized.

(d) The aggregate number of shares which the corporation shall have authority to issue; if such shares are to consist of one class only, the par value of each of such shares, or a statement that all of such shares are without par value; or, if such shares are to be divided into classes, the number of shares of each class, and a statement of the par value of the shares of each such class or that such shares are to be without par value.

(e) If the shares are to be divided into classes, the designation of each class and a statement of the preferences, limitations and relative rights in respect of the shares of each class.

(f) If the corporation is to issue the shares of any preferred or special class in series, then the designation of each series and a statement of the variations in the relative rights and preferences as between series in so far as the same are to be fixed in the articles of incorporation, and a statement of any authority to be vested in the board of directors to establish series and fix and determine the variations in the relative rights and preferences as between series.

(g) A statement that the corporation will not commence business until consideration of the value of at least one thousand dollars has been received for the issuance of shares.

(h) Any provision limiting or denying to shareholders the preemptive right to acquire additional or treasury shares of the corporation.

(i) Any provision, not inconsistent with law, which the incorporators elect to set forth in the articles of incorporation for the regulation of the internal affairs of the corporation, including any provision restricting the transfer of shares and any provision which under this Act is required or permitted to be set forth in the by-laws.

(j) The address of its initial registered office, and the name of its initial registered agent at such address.

(k) The number of directors constituting the initial board of directors and the names and addresses of the persons who are to serve as directors until the first annual meeting of shareholders or until their successors be elected and qualify.

(1) The name and address of each incorporator.

It shall not be necessary to set forth in the articles of incorporation any of the corporate powers enumerated in this Act.

§ 49. Filing of Articles of Incorporation.

Duplicate originals of the articles of incorporation shall be delivered to the Secretary of State. If the Secretary of State finds that the articles of incorporation conform to law, he shall, when all fees have been paid as in this Act prescribed:

(1) Endorse on each of such duplicate originals the word "Filed," and the month, day and year of the filing thereof.

(2) File one of such duplicate originals in his office.

(3) Issue a certificate of incorporation to which he shall affix the other duplicate original.

The certificate of incorporation, together with the duplicate original of the articles of incorporation affixed thereto by the Secretary of State, shall be returned to the incorporators or their representative.

§ 50. Effect of Issuance of Certificate of Incorporation.

Upon the issuance of the certificate of incorporation, the corporate existence shall begin, and such certificate of incorporation shall be conclusive evidence that all conditions precedent required to be performed by the incorporators have been complied with and that the corporation has been incorporated under this Act, except as against this State in a proceeding to cancel or revoke the certificate of incorporation or for involuntary dissolution of the corporation.

§ 51. Requirement before Commencing Business.

A corporation shall not transact any business or incur any indebtedness, except such as shall be incidental to its organization or to obtaining subscriptions to or payment for its shares, until there has been paid in for the issuance of shares consideration of the value of at least one thousand dollars.

§ 52. Organization Meeting of Directors.

After the issuance of the certificate of incorporation an organization meeting of the board of directors named in the articles of incorporation shall be held, either within or without this State, at the call of a majority of the incorporators, for the purpose of adopting by-laws, electing officers and the transaction of such other business as may come before the meeting. The incorporators calling the meeting shall give at least three days' notice thereof by mail to each director so named, which notice shall state the time and place of the meeting.

§ 53. Right to Amend Articles of Incorporation.

A corporation may amend its articles of incorporation, from time to time, in any and as many respects as may be desired, so long as its articles of incorporation as amended contain only such provisions as might be lawfully contained in original articles of incorporation at the time of making such amendment, and, if a change in shares or the rights of shareholders, or an exchange, reclassification or cancellation of shares or rights of shareholders is to be made, such provisions as may be necessary to effect such change, exchange, reclassification or cancellation.

In particular, and without limitation upon such general power of amendment, a corporation may amend its articles of incorporation from time to time, so as:

(a) To change its corporate name.

(b) To change its period of duration.

(c) To change, enlarge or diminish its corporate purposes.

(d) To increase or decrease the aggregate number of shares, or shares of any class, which the corporation has authority to issue.

(e) To increase or decrease the par value of the authorized shares of any class having a par value, whether issued or unissued.

(f) To exchange, classify, reclassify or cancel all or any part of its shares, whether issued or unissued.

(g) To change the designation of all or any part of its shares, whether issued or unissued, and to change the preferences, limitations, and the relative rights in respect of all or any part of its shares, whether issued or unissued.

(h) To change shares having a par value, whether issued or unissued, into the same or a different number of shares without par value, and to change shares without par value, whether issued or unissued, into the same or a different number of shares having a par value.

(i) To change the shares of any class, whether issued or unissued, and whether with or without par value, into a different number of shares of the same class or into the same or a different number of shares, either with or without par value, of other classes.

(j) To create new classes of shares having rights and preferences either prior and superior or subordinate and inferior to the shares of any class then authorized, whether issued or unissued.

(k) To cancel or otherwise affect the right of the holders of the shares of any class to receive dividends which have accrued but have not been declared.

(l) To divide any preferred or special class of shares, whether issued or unissued, into series and fix and determine the designations of such series and the variations in the relative rights and preferences as between the shares of such series.

(m) To authorize the board of directors to establish, out of authorized but unissued shares, series of any preferred or special class of shares and fix and determine the relative rights and preferences of the shares of any series so established.

(n) To authorize the board of directors to fix and determine the relative rights and preferences of the authorized but unissued shares of series theretofore established in respect of which either the relative rights and preferences have not been fixed and determined or the relative rights and preferences theretofore fixed and determined are to be changed.

(o) To revoke, diminish, or enlarge the authority of the board of directors to establish series out of authorized but unissued shares of any preferred or special class and fix and determine the relative rights and preferences of the shares of any series so established.

(p) To limit, deny or grant to shareholders of any class the preemptive right to acquire additional or treasury shares of the corporation, whether then or thereafter authorized.

§ 54. Procedure to Amend Articles of Incorporation.

Amendments to the articles of incorporation shall be made in the following manner:

(a) The board of directors shall adopt a resolution setting for the proposed amendment and directing that it be submitted to a vote at a meeting of shareholders, which may be either an annual or a special meeting.

(b) Written notice setting forth the proposed amendment or a summary of the changes to be effected thereby shall be given to each shareholder of records entitled to vote thereon within the time and in the manner provided in this Act for the giving of notice of meetings of shareholders. If the meeting be an annual meeting, the proposed amendment or such summary may be included in the notice of such annual meeting.

(c) At such meeting a vote of the shareholders entitled to vote thereon shall be taken on the proposed amendment. The proposed amendment shall be adopted upon receiving the affirmative vote of the holders of two-thirds of the shares entitled to vote thereon, unless any class of shares is entitled to vote thereon as a class, in which event the proposed amendment shall be adopted upon receiving the affirmative vote of the holders of two-thirds of the shares of each class of shares entitled to vote thereon as a class and of the total shares entitled to vote thereon.

Any number of amendments may be submitted to the shareholders, and voted upon by them, at one meeting.

§ 55. Class Voting on Amendments.

The holders of the outstanding shares of a class shall be entitled to vote as a class upon a proposed amendment, whether or not entitled to vote thereon by the provisions of the articles of incorporation, if the amendment would:

(a) Increase or decrease the aggregate number of authorized shares of such class.

(b) Increase or decrease the par value of the shares of such class.

(c) Effect an exchange, reclassification or cancellation of all or part of the shares of such class.

(d) Effect an exchange, or create a right of exchange, of all or any part of the shares of another class into the shares of such class.

(e) Change the designations, preferences, limitations or relative rights of the shares of such class.

(f) Change the shares of such class, whether with or without par value, into the same or a different number of shares, either with or without par value, of the same class or another class or classes.

(g) Create a new class of shares having rights and preferences prior and superior to the shares of such class, or increase the rights and preferences of any class having rights and preferences prior or superior to the shares of such class.

(h) In the case of a preferred or special class of shares, divide the shares of such class into series and fix and determine the designation of such series and the variations in the relative rights and preferences between the shares of such series, or authorize the board of directors to do so.

(i) Limit or deny the existing preemptive rights of the shares of such class.

(j) Cancel or otherwise affect dividends on the shares of such class which have accrued but have not been declared.

§ 56. Articles of Amendment.

The articles of amendment shall be executed in duplicate by the corporation by its president or a vice president and by its secretary or an assistant secretary, and verified by one of the officers signing such articles, and shall set forth:

(a) The name of the corporation.

(b) The amendment so adopted.

(c) The date of the adoption of the amendment by the shareholders.

(d) The number of shares outstanding, and the number of shares entitled to vote thereon, and if the shares of any class are entitled to vote thereon as a class, the designation and number of outstanding shares entitled to vote thereon of each such class.

(e) The number of shares voted for and against such amendment, respectively, and, if the shares of any class are entitled to vote thereon as a class, the number of shares of each such class voted for and against such amendment, respectively.

(f) If such amendment provides for an exchange, reclassification or cancellation of issued shares, and if the manner in which the same shall be effected is not set forth in the amendment, then a statement of the manner in which the same shall be effected.

(g) If such amendment effects a change in the amount of stated capital, then a statement of the manner in which the same is effected and a statement, expressed in dollars, of the amount of stated capital as changed by such amendment.

§ 57. Filing of Articles of Amendment.

Duplicate originals of the articles of amendment shall be delivered to the Secretary of State. If the Secretary of State finds that the articles of amendment conform to law, he shall, when all fees and franchise taxes have been paid as in this Act prescribed:

(1) Endorse on each of such duplicate originals the word "Filed," and the month, day and year of the filing thereof.

(2) File one of such duplicate originals in his office.

(3) Issue a certificate of amendment to which he shall affix the other duplicate original.

The certificate of amendment, together with the duplicate original of the articles of amendment affixed thereto by the Secretary of State, shall be returned to the corporation or its representative.

§ 58. Effect of Certificate of Amendment.

Upon the issuance of the certificate of amendment by the Secretary of State, the amendment shall become effective and the articles of incorporation shall be deemed to be amended accordingly.

No amendment shall affect any existing cause of action in favor of or against such corporation, or any pending suit to which such corporation shall be a party, or the existing rights of persons other than shareholders; and, in the event the corporate name shall be changed by amendment, no suit brought by or against such corporation under its former name shall abate for that reason.

§ 59. Restated Articles of Incorporation.

A domestic corporation may at any time restate its articles of incorporation as theretofore amended, in the following manner:

(A) The board of directors shall adopt a resolution setting forth the proposed restated articles of incorporation and directing that they be submitted to a vote at a meeting of shareholders, which may be either an annual or a special meeting.

(B) Written notice setting forth the proposed restated articles shall be given to each shareholder of record entitled to vote thereon within the time and in the manner provided in this Act for the giving of notice of meetings of shareholders. If the meeting be an annual meeting, the proposed restated articles may be included in the notice of such annual meeting.

(C) At such meeting a vote of the shareholders entitled to vote thereon shall be taken on the proposed restated articles. The proposed restated articles shall be adopted upon receiving the affirmative vote of the holders of a majority of the shares entitled to vote thereon.

Upon such approval, restated articles of incorporation shall be executed in duplicate by the corporation by its president or a vice president and by its secretary or assistant secretary, and verified by one of the officers signing such articles, and shall set forth:

(a) The name of the corporation.

(b) The period of its duration.

(c) The purpose or purposes which the corporation is then authorized to pursue.

(d) The aggregate number of shares which the corporation has authority to issue; if such shares consist of one class only, the par value of each of such shares, or a statement that all of such shares are without par value; or, if such shares are divided into classes, the number of shares of each class, and a statement of the par value of the shares of each such class or that such shares are without par value.

(e) If the shares are divided into classes, the designation of each class and a statement of the preferences, limitations and relative rights in respect of the shares of each class.

(f) If the shares of any preferred or special class are issuable in series, the designation of each series and a statement of the variations in the relative rights and preferences as between series in so far as the same have been fixed, and a statement of any authority vested in the board of directors to establish series and fix and determine the variations in the relative rights and preferences as between series.

(g) Any existing provision limiting or denying to shareholders the preemptive right to acquire additional or treasury shares of the corporation.

(h) Any provisions, not inconsistent with law, which are then set forth in the articles of incorporation as theretofore amended, for the regulation of the internal affairs of the corporation.

(i) A statement that the restated articles of incorporation correctly set forth without change the corresponding provisions of the articles of incorporation as theretofore amended, and that the restated articles of incorporation supersede the original articles of incorporation and all amendments thereto.

Duplicate originals of the restated articles of incorporation shall be delivered to the Secretary of State. If the Secretary of State finds that such restated articles of incorporation conform to law, he shall, when all fees and franchise taxes have been paid as in this Act prescribed:

(1) Endorse on each of such duplicate originals the word "Filed," and the month, day and year of the filing thereof.

(2) File one of such duplicate originals in his office.

(3) Issue a restated certificate of incorporation to which he shall affix the other duplicate original.

The restated certificate of incorporation, together with the duplicate original of the restated articles of incorporation affixed thereto by the Secretary of State, shall be returned to the corporation or its representative.

Upon the issuance of the restated certificate of incorporation by the Secretary of State, the restated articles of incorporation shall become effective and shall supersede the original articles of incorporation and all amendments thereto.

[Optional] § 59A. Amendment of Articles of Incorporation in Reorganization Proceedings.

Whenever a plan of reorganization of a corporation has been confirmed by decree or order of a court of competent jurisdiction in proceedings for the reorganization of such corporation, pursuant to the provisions of any applicable statute of the United States relating to reorganizations of corporations, the articles of incorporation of the corporation may be amended, in the manner provided in this section, in as many respects as may be necessary to carry out the plan and put it into effect, so long as the articles of incorporation as amended contain only such provisions as might be lawfully contained in original articles of incorporation at the time of making such amendment.

In particular and without limitation upon such general power of amendment, the articles of incorporation may be amended for such purpose so as to:

(a) Change the corporate name, period of duration or corporate purposes of the corporation.

(b) Repeal, alter or amend the by-laws of the corporation;

(c) Change the aggregate number of shares, or shares of any class, which the corporation has authority to issue;

(d) Change the preferences, limitations and relative rights in respect of all or any part of the shares of the corporation, and classify, reclassify or cancel all or any part thereof, whether issued or unissued;

(e) Authorize the issuance of bonds, debentures or other obligations of the corporation, whether or not convertible into shares of any class or bearing warrants or other evidences of optional rights to purchase or subscribe for shares of any class, and fix the terms and conditions thereof; and

(f) Constitute or reconstitute and classify or reclassify the board of directors of the corporation, and appoint directors and officers in place of or in addition to all or any of the directors or officers then in office.

Amendments to the articles of incorporation pursuant to this section shall be made in the following manner:

(a) Articles of amendment approved by decree or order of such court shall be executed and verified in duplicate by such person or persons as the court shall designate or appoint for the purpose, and shall set forth the name of the corporation, the amendments of the articles of incorporation approved by the court, the date of the decree or order approving the articles of amendment, the title of the proceedings in which the decree or order was entered, and a statement that such decree or order was entered by a court having jurisdiction of the proceedings for the reorganization of the corporation pursuant to the provisions of an applicable statute of the United States.

(b) Duplicate originals of the articles of amendment shall be delivered to the Secretary of State. If the Secretary of State finds that the articles of amendment conform to law, he shall, when all fees and franchise taxes have been paid as in this Act prescribed:

(1) Endorse on each of such duplicate originals the word "Filed," and the month, day and year of the filing thereof.

(2) File one of such duplicate originals in his office.

(3) Issue a certificate of amendment to which he shall affix the other duplicate original.

The certificate of amendment, together with the duplicate original of the articles of amendment affixed thereto by the Secretary of State, shall be returned to the corporation or its representative.

Upon the issuance of the certificate of amendment by the Secretary of State, the amendment shall become effective and the articles of incorporation shall be deemed to be amended accordingly, without any action thereon by the directors or shareholders of the corporation and with the same effect as if the amendments had been adopted by unanimous action of the directors and shareholders of the corporation.

§ 60. Restriction on Redemption or Purchase of Redeemable Shares.

No redemption or purchase of redeemable shares shall be made by a corporation when it is insolvent or when such redemption or purchase would render it insolvent, or which would reduce the net assets below the aggregate amount payable to the holders of shares having prior or equal rights to the assets of the corporation upon involuntary dissolution.

§ 61. Cancellation of Redeemable Shares by Redemption or Purchase.

When redeemable shares of a corporation are redeemed or purchased by the corporation, the redemption or purchase shall effect a cancellation of such shares, and a statement of cancellation shall be filed as provided in this section. Thereupon such shares shall be restored to the status of authorized but unissued shares, unless the articles of incorporation provide that such shares when redeemed or purchased shall not be reissued, in which case the filing of the statement of cancellation shall constitute an amendment to the articles of incorporation and shall reduce the number of shares of the class so cancelled which the corporation is authorized to issue by the number of shares so cancelled.

The statement of cancellation shall be executed in duplicate by the corporation by its president or a vice president and by its secretary or an assistant secretary, and verified by one of the officers signing such statement, and shall set forth:

(a) The name of the corporation.

(b) The number of redeemable shares cancelled through redemption or purchase, itemized by classes and series.

(c) The aggregate number of issued shares, itemized by classes and series, after giving effect to such cancellation.

(d) The amount, expressed in dollars, of the stated capital of the corporation after giving effect of such cancellation.

(e) If the articles of incorporation provide that the cancelled shares shall not be reissued, then the number of shares which the corporation has authority to issue, itemized by classes and series, after giving effect to such cancellation.

Duplicate originals of such statement shall be delivered to the Secretary of State. If the Secretary of State finds that such statement conforms to law, he shall, when all fees and franchise taxes have been paid as in this Act prescribed:

(1) Endorse on each of such duplicate originals the word "Filed," and the month, day and year of the filing thereof.

(2) File one of such duplicate originals in his office.

(3) Return the other duplicate original to the corporation or its representative.

Upon the filing of such statement of cancellation, the stated capital of the corporation shall be deemed to be reduced by that part of the stated capital which was, at the time of such cancellation, represented by the shares so cancelled.

Nothing contain in this section shall be construed to forbid a cancellation of shares or a reduction of stated capital in any other manner permitted by this Act.

§ 62. Cancellation of Other Reacquired Shares.

A corporation may at any time, by resolution of its board of directors, cancel all or any part of the shares of the corporation of any class reacquired by it, other than redeemable shares redeemed or purchased, and in such event a statement of cancellation shall be filed as provided in this section.

The statement of cancellation shall be executed in duplicate by the corporation by its president or a vice president and by its secretary or an assistant secretary, and verified by one of the officers signing such statement, and shall set forth:

(a) The name of the corporation.

(b) The number of reacquired shares cancelled by resolution duly adopted by the board of directors, itemized by classes and series, and the date of its adoption.

(c) The aggregate number of issued shares, itemized by classes and series, after giving effect to such cancellation.

(d) The amount, expressed in dollars, of the stated capital of the corporation after giving effect to such cancellation.

Duplicate originals of such statement shall be delivered to the Secretary of State. If the Secretary of State finds that such statement conforms to law, he shall, when all fees and franchise taxes have been paid as in this Act prescribed:

(1) Endorse on each of such duplicate originals the word "Filed," and the month, day and year of the filing thereof.

(2) File one of such duplicate originals in his office.

(3) Return the other duplicate original to the corporation or its representative.

Upon the filing of such statement of cancellation, the stated capital of the corporation shall be deemed to be reduced by that part of the stated capital which was, at the time of such cancellation, represented by the shares so cancelled, and the shares so cancelled shall be restored to the status of authorized but unissued shares.

Nothing contained in this section shall be construed to forbid a cancellation of shares or a reduction of stated capital in any other manner permitted by this Act.

§ 63. Reduction of Stated Capital in Certain Cases.

A reduction of the stated capital of a corporation, where such reduction is not accompanied by any action requiring an amendment of the articles of incorporation and not accompanied by a cancellation of shares, may be made in the following manner:

(A) The board of directors shall adopt a resolution setting forth the amount of the proposed reduction and the manner in which the reduction shall be effected, and directing that the question of such reduction be submitted to a vote at a meeting of shareholders, which may be either an annual or a special meeting.

(B) Written notice, stating that the purpose or one of the purposes of such meeting is to consider the question of reducing the stated capital of the corporation in the amount and manner proposed by the board of directors, shall be given to each shareholder of record entitled to vote thereon within the time and in the manner provided in this Act for the giving of notice of meetings of shareholders.

(C) At such meeting a vote of the shareholders entitled to vote thereon shall be taken on the question of approving the proposed reduction of stated capital, which shall require for its adoption the affirmative vote of the holders of a majority of the shares entitled to vote thereon.

When a reduction of the stated capital of a corporation has been approved as provided in this section, a statement shall be executed in duplicate by the corporation by its president or a vice president and by its secretary or an assistant secretary, and verified by one of the officers signing such statement, and shall set forth:

(a) The name of the corporation.

(b) A copy of the resolution of the shareholders approving such reduction, and the date of its adoption.

(c) The number of shares outstanding, and the number of shares entitled to vote thereon.

(d) The number of shares voted for and against such reduction, respectively.

(e) A statement of the manner in which such reduction is effected, and a statement, expressed in dollars, of the amount of stated capital of the corporation after giving effect to such reduction.

Duplicate originals of such statement shall be delivered to the Secretary of State. If the Secretary of State finds that such statement conforms to law, he shall, when all fees and franchise taxes have been paid as in this Act prescribed:

(1) Endorse on each of such duplicate originals the word "Filed," and the month, day and year of the filing thereof.

(2) File one of such duplicate originals in his office.

(3) Return the other duplicate original to the corporation or its representative.

Upon the filing of such statement, the stated capital of the corporation shall be reduced as therein set forth.

No reduction of stated capital shall be made under the provisions of this section which would reduce the amount of the aggregate stated capital of the corporation to an amount equal to or less than the aggregate preferential amounts payable upon all issued shares having a preferential right in the assets of the corporation in the event of involuntary liquidation, plus the aggregate par value of all issued shares having a par value but no preferential right in the assets of the corporation in the event of involuntary liquidation.

§ 64. Special Provisions Relating to Surplus and Reserves.

The surplus, if any, created by or arising out of a reduction of the stated capital of a corporation shall be capital surplus.

The capital surplus of a corporation may be increased from time to time by resolution of the board of directors directing that all or a part of the earned surplus of the corporation be transferred to capital surplus.

A corporation may, by resolution of its board of directors, apply any part or all of its capital surplus to the reduction or elimination of any deficit arising from losses, however incurred, but only after first eliminating the earned surplus, if any, of the corporation by applying such losses against earned surplus and only to the extent that such losses exceed the earned surplus, if any. Each such application of capital surplus shall, to the extent thereof, effect a reduction of capital surplus.

A corporation may, by resolution of its board of directors, create a reserve or reserves out of its earned surplus for any proper purpose or purposes, and may abolish any such reserve in the same manner. Earned surplus of the corporation to the extent so reserved shall not be available for the payment of dividends or other distributions by the corporation except as expressly permitted by this Act.

§ 65. Procedure for Merger.

Any two or more domestic corporations may merge into one of such corporations pursuant to a plan of merger approved in the manner provided in this Act.

The board of directors of each corporation shall, by resolution adopted by each such board, approve a plan of merger setting forth:

(a) The names of the corporations proposing to merge, and the name of the corporation into which they propose to merge, which is hereinafter designated as the surviving corporation.

(b) The terms and conditions of the proposed merger.

(c) The manner and basis of converting the shares of each merging corporation into shares or other securities or obligations of the surviving corporation.

(d) A statement of any changes in the articles of incorporation of the surviving corporation to be effected by such merger.

(e) Such other provisions with respect to the proposed merger as are deemed necessary or desirable.

§ 66. Procedure for Consolidation.

Any two or more domestic corporations may consolidate into a new corporation pursuant to a plan of consolidation approved in the manner provided in this Act.

The board of directors of each corporation shall, by a resolution adopted by each such board, approve a plan of consolidation setting forth:

(a) The names of the corporations proposing to consolidate, and the name of the new corporation into which they propose to consolidate, which is hereinafter designated as the new corporation.

(b) The terms and conditions of the proposed consolidation.

(c) The manner and basis of converting the shares of each corporation into shares or other securities or obligations of the new corporation.

(d) With respect to the new corporation, all of the statements required to be set forth in articles of incorporation for corporations organized under this Act.

(e) Such other provisions with respect to the proposed consolidation as are deemed necessary or desirable.

§ 67. Approval by Shareholders.

The board of directors of each corporation, upon approving such plan of merger or plan of consolidation, shall, by resolution, direct that the plan be submitted to a vote at a meeting of shareholders, which may be either an annual or a special meeting. Written notice shall be given to each shareholder of record, whether or not entitled to vote at such meeting, not less than twenty days before such meeting, in the manner provided in this Act for the giving of notice of meetings of shareholders, and whether the meeting be an annual or a special meeting, shall state that the purpose or one of the purposes is to consider the proposed plan of merger or consolidation.

At each such meeting, a vote of the shareholders shall be taken on the proposed plan of merger or consolidation. The plan of merger or consolidation shall be approved upon receiving the affirmative vote of the holders of two-thirds of the shares entitled to vote thereon of each such corporation, unless any class of shares of any such corporation is entitled to vote thereon as a class, in which event, as to such corporation, the plan of merger or consolidation shall be approved upon receiving the affirmative vote of the holders of two-thirds of the shares of each class of shares entitled to vote thereon as a class and of the total shares entitled to vote thereon. Any class of shares of any such corporation shall be entitled to vote as a class if the plan of merger or consolidation, as the case may be, contains any provision which, if contained in a proposed amendment to articles of incorporation, would entitle such class of shares to vote as a class.

After such approval by a vote of the shareholders of each corporation, and at any time prior to the filing of the articles of merger or consolidation, the merger or consolidation may be abandoned pursuant to provisions therefor, if any, set forth in the plan of merger or consolidation.

§ 68. Articles of Merger or Consolidation.

Upon such approval, articles of merger or articles of consolidation shall be executed in duplicate by each corporation by its president or a vice president and by its secretary or an assistant secretary, and verified by one of the officers of each corporation signing such articles and shall set forth:

(a) The plan of merger or the plan of consolidation.

(b) As to each corporation, the number of shares outstanding, and, if the shares of any class are entitled to vote as a class, the designation and number of outstanding shares of each such class.

(c) As to each corporation, the number of shares voted for and against such plan, respectively, and, if the shares of any class are entitled to vote as a class, the number of shares of each such class voted for and against such plan, respectively.

Duplicate originals of the articles of merger or articles of consolidation shall be delivered to the Secretary of State. If the Secretary of State finds that such articles conform to law, he shall, when all fees and franchise taxes have been paid as in this Act prescribed:

(1) Endorse on each of such duplicate originals the word "Filed," and the month, day and year of the filing thereof.

(2) File one of such duplicate originals in his office.

(3) Issue a certificate of merger or a certificate of consolidation to which he shall affix the other duplicate original.

The certificate of merger or certificate of consolidation, together with the duplicate original of the articles of merger or articles of consolidation affixed thereto by the Secretary of State, shall be returned to the surviving or new corporation, as the case may be, or its representative.

[Optional] § 68A. Merger of Subsidiary Corporation.

Any corporation owning at least ninety-five per cent of the outstanding shares of each class of another corporation may merge such other corporation into itself without approval by a vote of the shareholders of either corporation. Its board of directors shall, by resolution, approve a plan of merger setting forth:

(a) The name of the subsidiary corporation and the name of the corporation owning at least ninety-five per cent of its shares, which is hereinafter designated as the surviving corporation.

(b) The manner and basis of converting the shares of the subsidiary corporation into shares or other securities or obligations of the surviving corporation or the cash or other consideration to be paid or delivered upon surrender of each share of the subsidiary corporation.

A copy of such plan of merger shall be mailed to each shareholder of record of the subsidiary corporation.

Articles of merger shall be executed in duplicate by the surviving corporation by its president or a vice president and by its secretary or an assistant secretary, and verified by one of its officers signing such articles, and shall set forth:

(a) The plan of merger;

(b) The number of outstanding shares of each class of the subsidiary corporation and the number of such shares of each class owned by the surviving corporation; and

(c) The date of the mailing to shareholders of the subsidiary corporation of a copy of the plan of merger.

On and after the thirtieth day after the mailing of a copy of the plan of merger to shareholders of the subsidiary corporation or upon the waiver thereof by the holders of all outstanding shares duplicate originals of the articles of merger shall be delivered to the Secretary of State. If the Secretary of State finds that such articles conform to law, he shall, when all fees and franchise taxes have been paid as in this Act prescribed:

(1) Endorse on each of such duplicate originals the word "Filed," and the month, day and year of the filing thereof;

(2) File one of such duplicate originals in his office; and

(3) Issue a certificate of merger to which he shall affix the other duplicate original.

The certificate of merger, together with the duplicate original of the articles of merger affixed thereto by the Secretary of State, shall be returned to the surviving corporation or its representative.

§ 69. Effect of Merger or Consolidation.

Upon the issuance of the certificate of merger or the certificate of consolidation by the Secretary of State, the merger or consolidation shall be effected.

When such merger or consolidation has been effected:

(a) The several corporations parties to the plan of merger or consolidation shall be a single corporation, which, in the case of a merger, shall be that corporation designated in the plan of merger as the surviving corporation, and, in the case of a consolidation, shall be the new corporation provided for in the plan of consolidation.

(b) The separate existence of all corporations parties to the plan of merger or consolidation, except the surviving or new corporation, shall cease.

(c) Such surviving or new corporation shall have all the rights, privileges, immunities and powers and shall be subject to all the duties and liabilities of a corporation organized under this Act.

(d) Such surviving or new corporation shall thereupon and thereafter possess all the rights, privileges, immunities, and franchises, as well of a public as of a private nature, of each of the merging or consolidating corporations; and all property, real, personal and mixed, and all debts due on whatever account, including subscriptions to shares, and all other choses in action, and all and every other interest of or belonging to or due to each of the corporations so merged or consolidated, shall be taken and deemed to be transferred to and vested in such single corporation without further act or deed; and the title to any real estate, or any interest therein, vested in any of such corporations shall not revert or be in any way impaired by reason of such merger or consolidation.

(e) Such surviving or new corporation shall thenceforth be responsible and liable for all the liabilities and obligations of each of the corporations so merged or consolidated; and any claim existing or action or proceeding pending by or against any of such corporations may be prosecuted as if such merger or consolidation had not taken place, or such surviving or new corporation may be substituted in its place. Neither the rights of creditors nor any liens upon the property of any such corporation shall be impaired by such merger or consolidation.

(f) In the case of a merger, the articles of incorporation of the surviving corporation shall be deemed to be amended to the extent, if any, that changes in its articles of incorporation are stated in the plan of merger; and, in the case of a consolidation, the statements set forth in the articles of consolidation and which are required or permitted to be set forth in the articles of incorporation of corporations organized under this Act shall be deemed to be the original articles of incorporation of the new corporation.

§ 70. Merger or Consolidation of Domestic and Foreign Corporations.

One or more foreign corporations and one or more domestic corporations may be merged or consolidated in the following manner, if such merger or consolidation is permitted by the laws of the state under which each such foreign corporation is organized:

(a) Each domestic corporation shall comply with the provisions of this Act with respect to the merger or consolidation, as the case may be, of domestic corporations and each foreign corporation shall comply with the applicable provisions of the laws of the state under which it is organized.

(b) If the surviving or new corporation, as the case may be, is to be governed by the laws of any state other than this State, it shall comply with the provisions of this Act with respect to foreign corporations if it is to transact business in this State, and in every case it shall file with the Secretary of State of this State:

(1) an agreement that it may be served with process in this State in any proceeding for the enforcement of any obligation of any domestic corporation which is a party to such merger or consolidation and in any proceeding for the enforcement of the rights of a dissenting shareholder of any such domestic corporation against the surviving or new corporation;

(2) an irrevocable appointment of the Secretary of State of this State as its agent to accept service of process in any such proceeding; and

(3) an agreement that it will promptly pay to the dissenting shareholders of any such domestic corporation the amount, if any, to which they shall be entitled under the provisions of this Act with respect to the rights of dissenting shareholders.

The effect of such merger or consolidation shall be the same as in the case of the merger or consolidation of domestic corporations, if the surviving or new corporation is to be governed by the laws of this State. If the surviving or new corporation is to be governed by the laws of any state other than this State, the effect of such merger or consolidation shall be the same as in the case of the merger or consolidation of domestic corporations except in so far as the laws of such other state provide otherwise.

At any time prior to the filing of the articles of merger or consolidation, the merger or consolidation may be abandoned pursuant to provisions therefor, if any, set forth in the plan of merger or consolidation.

§ 71. Sale or Mortgage of Assets in Regular Course of Business.

The sale, lease, exchange, or other disposition of all, or substantially all, the property and assets of a corporation in the usual and regular course of its business and the mortgage or pledge of any or all property and assets of a corporation whether or not in the usual and regular course of business may be made upon such terms and conditions and for such consideration, which may consist in whole or in part of money or property, real or personal, including shares of any other corporation, domestic or foreign, as shall be authorized by its board of directors; and in any such case no authorization or consent of the shareholders shall be required.

§ 72. Sale or Mortgage of Assets Other Than in Regular Course of Business.

A sale, lease, exchange, or other disposition of all, or substantially all, the property and assets, with or without the good will, of a corporation, if not in the usual and regular course of its business, may be made upon such terms and conditions and for such consideration, which may consist in whole or in part of money or property, real or personal, including shares of any other corporation, domestic or foreign, as may be authorized in the following manner:

(a) The board of directors shall adopt a resolution recommending such sale, lease, exchange, or other disposition and directing the submission thereof to a vote at a meeting of shareholders, which may be either an annual or a special meeting.

(b) Written notice shall be given to each shareholder of record, whether or not entitled to vote at such meeting, not less than twenty days before such meeting, in the manner provided in this Act for the giving of notice of meetings of shareholders, and, whether the meeting be an annual or a special meeting, shall state that the purpose, or one of the purposes, is to consider the proposed sale, lease, exchange, or other disposition.

(c) At such meeting the shareholders may authorize such sale, lease, exchange, or other disposition and may fix, or may authorize the board of directors to fix, any or all of the terms and conditions thereof and the consideration to be received by the corporation therefor. Such authorization shall require the affirmative vote of the holders of two-thirds of the shares of the corporation, entitled to vote thereon, unless any class of shares is entitled to vote thereon as a class, in which event such authorization shall require the affirmative vote of the holders of two-thirds of the shares of each class of shares entitled to vote as a class thereon and of the total shares entitled to vote thereon.

(d) After such authorization by a vote of shareholders, the board of directors nevertheless, in its discretion, may abandon such sale, lease, exchange, or other disposition of assets, subject to the rights of third parties under any contracts relating thereto, without further action or approval by shareholders.

§ 73. Right of Shareholders to Dissent.

Any shareholder of a corporation shall have the right to dissent from any of the following corporate actions:

(a) any plan of merger or consolidation to which the corporation is a party; or

(b) any sale or exchange of all or substantially all of the property and assets of the corporation not made in the usual and regular course of its business, including a sale in dissolution, but not including a sale pursuant to an order of a court having jurisdiction in the premises or a sale for cash on terms requiring that all or substantially all of the net proceeds of sale be distributed to the shareholders in accordance with their respective interests within one year after the date of the sale.

A shareholder may dissent as to less than all of the shares registered in his name. In that event, his rights shall be determined as if the shares as to which he has dissented and his other shares were registered in the names of different shareholders.

The provisions of this section shall not apply to the shareholders of the surviving corporation in a merger if such corporation is on the date of the filing in the articles of merger the owner of all the outstanding shares of the other corporations, domestic or foreign, which are parties to the merger.*

§ 74. Rights of Dissenting Shareholders.

Any shareholder electing to exercise such right of dissent shall file with the corporation, prior to or at the meeting of shareholders at which such proposed corporate action is submitted to a vote, a written objection to such proposed corporate action. If such proposed corporate action be approved by the required vote and such shareholder shall not have voted in favor thereof, such shareholder may, within ten days after the date on which the vote was taken † make written demand on the corporation, or, in the case of a merger or consolidation, on the surviving or new corporation, domestic or foreign, for payment of the fair value of such share-

---

* If optional Section 68A is included, there should be added, "or if a vote of the shareholders of such corporation is not necessary to authorize such merger."

† If optional Section 68A is included, there should be inserted "or if a corporation is to be merged without a vote of its shareholders into another corporation, any of its shareholders may, within fifteen days after the plan of such merger shall have been mailed to such shareholders,".

holder's shares, and, if such proposed corporate action is effected, such corporation shall pay to such shareholder, upon surrender of the certificate or certificates representing such shares, the fair value thereof as of the day prior to the date on which the vote was taken approving the proposed corporate action, excluding any appreciation or depreciation in anticipation of such corporate action. Any shareholder failing to make demand within the ten day period shall be bound by the terms of the proposed corporate action. Any shareholder making such demand shall thereafter be entitled only to payment as in this section provided and shall not be entitled to vote or to exercise any other rights of a shareholder.

No such demand may be withdrawn unless the corporation shall consent thereto. If, however, such demand shall be withdrawn upon consent, or if the proposed corporate action shall be abandoned or rescinded or the shareholders shall revoke the authority to effect such action, or if, in the case of a merger, on the date of the filing of the articles of merger the surviving corporation is the owner of all the outstanding shares of the other corporations, domestic and foreign, that are parties to the merger, or if no demand or petition for the determination of fair value by a court shall have been made or filed within the time provided in this section, or if a court of competent jurisdiction shall determine that such shareholder is not entitled to the relief provided by this secton, then the right of such shareholder to be paid the fair value of his shares shall cease and his status as a shareholder shall be restored, without prejudice to any corporate proceedings which may have been taken during the interim.

Within ten days after such corporate action is effected, the corporation, or, in the case of a merger or consolidation, the surviving or new corporation, domestic or foreign, shall give written notice thereof to each dissenting shareholder who has made demand as herein provided, and shall make a written offer to each such shareholder to pay for such shares at a specified price deemed by such corporation to be the fair value thereof. Such notice and offer shall be accompanied by a balance sheet of the corporation the shares of which the dissenting shareholder holds, as of the latest available date and not more than twelve months prior to the making of such offer, and a profit and loss statement of such corporation for the twelve months' period ended on the date of such balance sheet.

If within thirty days after the date on which such corporate action was effected the fair value of such shares is agreed upon between any such dissenting shareholder and the corporation, payment therefor shall be made within ninety days after the date on which such corporate action was effected, upon surrender of the certificate or certificates representing such shares. Upon payment of the agreed value the dissenting shareholder shall cease to have any interest in such shares.

If within such period of thirty days a dissenting shareholder and the corporation do not so agree, then the corporation, within thirty days after receipt of written demand from any dissenting shareholder given within sixty days after the date on which such corporate action was effected, shall, or at its election at any time within such period of sixty days may, file a petition in any court of competent jurisdiction in the county in this state where the registered office of the corporation is located praying that the fair value of such shares be found and determined. If, in the case of a merger or consolidation, the surviving or new corporation is a foreign corporation without a registered office in this state, such petition shall be filed in the county where the registered office of the domestic corporation was last located. If the corporation shall fail to institute the proceeding as herein provided, any dissenting shareholder may do so in the name of the corporation. All dissenting shareholders, wherever residing, shall be made parties to the proceeding as an action against their shares quasi in rem. A copy of the petition shall be served on each dissenting shareholder who is a resident of this state and shall be served by registered or certified mail on each dissenting shareholder who is a nonresident. Service on nonresidents shall also be made by publication as provided by law. The jurisdiction of the court shall be plenary and exclusive. All shareholders who are parties to the proceeding shall be entitled to judgment against the corporation for the amount of the fair value of their shares. The court may, if it so elects, appoint one or more persons as appraisers to receive evidence and recommend a decision on the question of fair value. The appraisers shall have such power and authority as shall be specified in the order of their appointment or an amendment thereof. The judgment shall be payable only upon and concurrently with the surrender to the corporation of the certificate or certificates representing such shares. Upon payment of the judgment, the dissenting shareholder shall cease to have any interest in such shares.

The judgment shall include an allowance for interest at such rate as the court may find to be fair and equitable in all the circumstances, from the date on which the vote was taken on the proposed corporate action to the date of payment.

The costs and expenses of any such proceeding shall be determined by the court and shall be assessed against the corporation, but all or any part of such costs and expenses may be apportioned and assessed as the court may deem equitable against any or all of the dissenting shareholders who are parties to the proceeding to whom the corporation shall have made an offer to pay for the shares if the court shall find that the action of such shareholders in failing to accept such offer was arbitrary or vexatious or not in good faith. Such expenses shall include reasonable compensation for and reasonable expenses of the appraisers, but shall exclude the fees and expenses of counsel for and experts employed by any party; but if the fair value of the shares as determined materially exceeds the amount which the corporation offered to pay therefor, or if no offer was made, the court in its discretion may award to any shareholder who is a party to the proceeding such sum as the court may determine to be reasonable compensation to any expert or experts employed by the shareholder in the proceeding.

Within twenty days after demanding payment for his shares, each shareholder demanding payment shall submit the certificate or certificates representing his shares to the corporation for notation thereon that such demand has been made. His failure to do so shall, at the option of the corporation, terminate his rights under this section unless a court of competent jurisdiction, for good and sufficent cause shown, shall otherwise direct. If shares represented by a certificate on which notation has been so made shall be transferred, each new certificate issued therefor shall bear similar notation, together with the name of the original dissenting holder of such shares, and a transferee of such shares shall acquire by such transfer no rights in the corporation other than those which the original dissenting shareholder had after making demand for payment of the fair value thereof.

Shares acquired by a corporation pursuant to payment of the agreed value therefor or to payment of the judgment entered therefor, as in this section provided, may be held and disposed of by such corporation as in the case of other treasury shares, except that, in the case of a merger or consolidation, they may be held and disposed of as the plan of merger or consolidation may otherwise provide.

§ 75. Voluntary Dissolution by Incorporators.

A corporation which has not commenced business and which has not issued any shares may be voluntarily dissolved by its incorporators at any time within two years after the date of the issuance of its certificate of incorporation, in the following manner:

(A) Articles of dissolution shall be executed in duplicate by a majority of the incorporators, and verified by them, and shall set forth:

(a) The name of the corporation.

(b) The date of issuance of its certificate of incorporation.

(c) That none of its shares has been issued.

(d) That the corporation has not commenced business.

(e) That the amount, if any, actually paid in on subscriptions for its shares, less any part thereof disbursed for necessary expenses, has been returned to those entitled thereto.

(f) That no debts of the corporation remain unpaid.

(g) That a majority of the incorporators elect that the corporation be dissolved.

(B) Duplicate originals of the articles of dissolution shall be delivered to the Secretary of State. If the Secretary of State finds that the articles of dissolution conform to law, he shall, when all fees and franchise taxes have been paid as in this Act prescribed:

(1) Endorse on each of such duplicate originals the word "Filed," and the month, day and year of the filing thereof.

(2) File one of such duplicate originals in his office.

(3) Issue a certificate of dissolution to which he shall affix the other duplicate original.

The certificate of dissolution, together with the duplicate original of the articles of dissolution affixed thereto by the Secretary of State, shall be returned to the incorporators or their representative. Upon the issuance of such certificate of dissolution by the Secretary of State, the existence of the corporation shall cease.

§ 76. Voluntary Dissolution by Consent of Shareholders.

A corporation may be voluntarily dissolved by the written consent of all of its shareholders.

Upon the execution of such written consent, a statement of intent to dissolve shall be executed in duplicate by the corporation by its president or a vice president and by its secretary or an assistant secretary, and verified by one of the officers signing such statement, which statement shall set forth:

(a) The name of the corporation.

(b) The names and respective addresses of its officers.

(c) The names and respective addresses of its directors.

(d) A copy of the written consent signed by all shareholders of the corporation.

(e) A statement that such written consent has been signed by all shareholders of the corporation or signed in their names by their attorneys thereunto duly authorized.

§ 77. Voluntary Dissolution by Act of Corporation.

A corporation may be dissolved by the act of the corporation, when authorized in the following manner:

(1) The board of directors shall adopt a resolution recommending that the corporation be dissolved, and directing that the question of such dissolution be submitted to a vote at a meeting of shareholders, which may be either an annual or a special meeting.

(2) Written notice shall be given to each shareholder of record entitled to vote at such meeting within the time and in the manner provided in this Act for the giving of notice of meetings of shareholders, and, whether the meeting be an annual or special meeting, shall state that the purpose, or one of the purposes, of such meeting is to consider the advisability of dissolving the corporation.

(3) At such meeting a vote of shareholders entitled to vote thereat shall be taken on a resolution to dissolve the corporation. Such resolution shall be adopted upon receiving the affirmative vote of the holders of two-thirds of the shares of the corporation entitled to vote thereon, unless any class of shares is entitled to vote thereon as a class, in which event the resolution shall be adopted upon receiving the affirmative vote of the holders of two-thirds of the shares of each class of shares entitled to vote thereon as a class and of the total shares entitled to vote thereon.

(4) Upon the adoption of such resolution, a statement of intent to dissolve shall be executed in duplicate by the corporation by its president or a vice president and by its secretary or an assistant secretary, and verified by one of the officers signing such statement, which statement shall set forth:

(a) The name of the corporation.

(b) The names and respective addresses of its officers.

(c) The names and respective addresses of its directors.

(d) A copy of the resolution adopted by the shareholders authorizing the dissolution of the corporation.

(e) The number of shares outstanding, and, if the shares of any class are entitled to vote as a class, the designation and number of outstanding shares of each such class.

(f) The number of shares voted for and against the resolution, respectively, and, if the shares of any class are entitled to vote as a class, the number of shares of each such class voted for and against the resolution, respectively.

§ 78. Filing of Statement of Intent to Dissolve.

Duplicate originals of the statement of intent to dissolve, whether by consent of shareholders or by act of the corporation, shall be delivered to the Secretary of State. If the Secretary of State finds that such statement conforms to law, he shall, when all fees and franchise taxes have been paid as in this Act prescribed:

(1) Endorse on each of such duplicate originals the word "Filed," and the month, day and year of the filing thereof.

(2) File one of such duplicate originals in his office.

(3) Return the other duplicate original to the corporation or its representative.

§ 79. Effect of Statement of Intent to Dissolve.

Upon the filing by the Secretary of State of a statement of intent to dissolve, whether by consent of shareholders or by act of the corporation, the corporation shall cease to carry on its business, except in so far as may be necessary for the winding up thereof, but its corporate existence shall continue until a certificate of dissolution has been issued by the Secretary of State or until a decree dissolving the corporation has been entered by a court of competent jurisdiction as in this Act provided.

§ 80. Procedure After Filing of Statement of Intent to Dissolve.

After the filing by the Secretary of State of a statement of intent to dissolve:

(a) The corporation shall immediately cause notice thereof to be mailed to each known creditor of the corporation.

(b) The corporation shall proceed to collect its assets, convey and dispose of such of its properties as are not to be distributed in kind to its shareholders, pay, satisfy and discharge its liabilities and obligations and do all other acts required to liquidate its business and affairs, and, after paying or adequately providing for the payment of all its obligations, distribute the remainder of its assets, either in cash or in kind, among its shareholders according to their respective rights and interests.

(c) The corporation, at any time during the liquidation of its business and affairs, may make application to a court of competent jurisdiction within the state and judicial subdivision in which the registered office or principal place of business of the corporation is situated, to have the liquidation continued under the supervision of the court as provided in this Act.

§ 81. Revocation of Voluntary Dissolution Proceedings by Consent of Shareholders.

By the written consent of all of its shareholders, a corporation may, at any time prior to the issuance of a certificate of dissolution by the Secretary of State, revoke voluntary dissolution proceedings theretofore taken, in the following manner:

Upon the execution of such written consent, a statement of revocation of voluntary dissolution proceedings shall be executed in duplicate by the corporation by its president or a vice president and by its secretary or an assistant secretary, and verified by one of the officers signing such statement, which statement shall set forth:

(a) The name of the corporation.

(b) The names and respective addresses of its officers.

(c) The names and respective addresses of its directors.

(d) A copy of the written consent signed by all shareholders of the corporation revoking such voluntary dissolution proceedings.

(e) That such written consent has been signed by all shareholders of the corporation or signed in their names by their attorneys thereunto duly authorized.

§ 82. Revocation of Voluntary Dissolution Proceedings by Act of Corporation.

By the act of the corporation, a corporation may, at any time prior to the issuance of a certificate of dissolution by the Secretary of State, revoke voluntary dissolution proceedings theretofore taken, in the following manner:

(1) The board of directors shall adopt a resolution recommending that the voluntary dissolution proceedings be revoked, and directing that the question of such revocation be submitted to a vote at a special meeting of shareholders.

(2) Written notice, stating that the purpose or one of the purposes of such meeting is to consider the advisability of revoking the voluntary dissolution proceedings, shall be given to each shareholder of record entitled to vote at such meeting within the time and in the manner provided in this Act for the giving of notice of special meetings of shareholders.

(3) At such meeting a vote of the shareholders entitled to vote thereat shall be taken on a resolution to revoke the voluntary dissolution proceedings which shall require for its adoption the affirmative vote of the holders of two-thirds of the shares entitled to vote thereon.

(4) Upon the adoption of such resolution, a statement of revocation of voluntary dissolution proceedings shall be executed in duplicate by the corporation by its president or a vice president and by its secretary or an assistant secretary, and verified by one of the officers signing such statement, which statement shall set forth:

(a) The name of the corporation.

(b) The names and respective addresses of its officers.

(c) The names and respective addresses of its directors.

(d) A copy of the resolution adopted by the shareholders revoking the voluntary dissolution proceedings.

(e) The number of shares outstanding.

(f) The number of shares voted for and against the resolution, respectively.

§ 83. Filing of Statement of Revocation of Voluntary Dissolution Proceedings.

Duplicate originals of the statement of revocation of voluntary dissolution proceedings, whether by consent of shareholders or by act of the corporation, shall be delivered to the Secretary of State. If the Secretary of State finds that such statement conforms to law, he shall, when all fees and franchise taxes have been paid as in this Act prescribed:

(1) Endorse on each of such duplicate originals the word "Filed," and the month, day and year of the filing thereof.

(2) File one of such duplicate originals in his office.

(3) Return the other duplicate original to the corporation or its representative.

§ 84. Effect of Statement of Revocation of Voluntary Dissolution Proceedings.

Upon the filing by the Secretary of State of a statement of revocation of voluntary dissolution proceedings, whether by consent of shareholders or by act of the corporation, the revocation of the voluntary dissolution proceedings shall become effective and the corporation may again carry on its business.

§ 85. Articles of Dissolution.

If voluntary dissolution proceedings have not been revoked, then when all debts, liabilities and obligations of the corporation have been paid and discharged, or adequate provision has been made therefor, and all of the remaining property and assets of the corporation have been distributed to its shareholders, articles of dissolution shall be executed in duplicate by the corporation by its president or a vice president and by its secretary or an assistant secretary, and verified by one of the officers signing such statement, which statement shall set forth:

(a) The name of the corporation.

(b) That the Secretary of State has theretofore filed a statement of intent to dissolve the corporation, and the date on which such statement was filed.

(c) That all debts, obligations and liabilities of the corporation have been paid and discharged or that adequate provision has been made therefor.

(d) That all the remaining property and assets of the corporation have been distributed among its shareholders in accordance with their respective rights and interests.

(e) That there are no suits pending against the corporation in any court, or that adequate provision has been made for the satisfaction of any judgment, order or decree which may be entered against it in any pending suit.

§ 86. Filing of Articles of Dissolution.

Duplicate originals of such articles of dissolution shall be delivered to the Secretary of State. If the Secretary of State finds that such articles of dissolution conform to law, he shall, when all fees and franchise taxes have been paid as in this Act prescribed:

(1) Endorse on each of such duplicate originals the word "Filed," and the month, day and year of the filing thereof.

(2) File one of such duplicate originals in his office.

(3) Issue a certificate of dissolution to which he shall affix the other duplicate original.

The certificate of dissolution, together with the duplicate original of the articles of dissolution affixed thereto by the Secretary of State, shall be returned to the representative of the dissolved corporation. Upon the issuance of such certificate of dissolution the existence of the corporation shall cease, except for the purpose of suits, other proceedings and appropriate corporate action by shareholders, directors, and officers as provided in this Act.

§ 87. Involuntary Dissolution.

A corporation may be dissolved involuntarily by a decree of the _____ court in an action filed by the Attorney General when it is established that:

(a) The corporation has failed to file its annual report within the time required by this Act, or has failed to pay its franchise tax on or before the first day of August of the year in which such franchise tax becomes due and payable; or

(b) The corporation procured its articles of incorporation through fraud; or

(c) The corporation has continued to exceed or abuse the authority conferred upon it by law; or

(d) The corporation has failed for thirty days to appoint and maintain a registered agent in this State; or

(e) The corporation has failed for thirty days after change of its registered office or registered agent to file in the office of the Secretary of State a statement of such change.

§ 88. Notification to Attorney General.

The Secretary of State, on or before the last day of December of each year, shall certify to the Attorney General the names of all corporations which have failed to file their annual reports or to pay franchise taxes in accordance with the provisions of this Act, together with the facts pertinent thereto. He shall also certify, from time to time, the names of all corporations which have given other cause for dissolution as provided in this Act, together with the facts pertinent thereto. Whenever the Secretary of State shall certify the name of a corporation to the Attorney General as having given any cause for dissolution, the Secretary of State shall concurrently mail to the corporation at its registered office a notice that such certification has been made. Upon the receipt of such certification, the Attorney General shall file an action in the name of the State against such corporation for its dissolution. Every such certificate from the Secretary of State to the Attorney General pertaining to the failure of a corporation to file an annual report or pay a franchise tax shall be taken and received in all courts as prima facie evidence of the facts therein stated. If, before action is filed, the corporation shall file its annual report or pay its franchise tax, together with all penalties thereon, or shall appoint or maintain a registered agent as provided in this Act, or shall file with the Secretary of State the required statement of change of registered office or registered agent, such fact shall be forthwith certified by the Secretary of State to the Attorney General and he shall not file an action against such corporation for such cause. If, after action is filed, the corporation shall file its annual report or pay its franchise tax, together with all penalties thereon, or shall appoint or maintain a registered agent as provided in this Act, or shall file with the Secretary of State the required statement of change of registered office or registered agent, and shall pay the costs of such action, the action for such cause shall abate.

§ 89. Venue and Process.

Every action for the involuntary dissolution of a corporation shall be commenced by the Attorney General either in the _____ court of the county in which the registered office of the corporation is situated, or in the _____ court of _____ county. Summons shall issue and be served as in other civil actions. If process is returned not found, the Attorney General shall cause publication to be made as in other civil cases in some newspaper published in the county where the registered office of the corporation is situated, containing a notice of the pendency of such action, the title of the court, the title of the action, and the date on or after which default may be entered. The Attorney General may include in one notice the names of any number of corporations against which actions are then pending in the same court. The Attorney General shall cause a copy of such notice to be mailed to the corporation at its registered office within ten days after the first publication thereof. The certificate of the Attorney General of the mailing of such notice shall be prima facie evidence thereof. Such notice shall be published at least once each week for two successive weeks, and the first publication thereof may begin at any time after the summons has been returned. Unless a corporation shall have been served with summons, no default shall be taken against it earlier than thirty days after the first publication of such notice.

§ 90. Jurisdiction of Court to Liquidate Assets and Business of Corporation.

The _____ courts shall have full power to liquidate the assets and business of a corporation:

(a) In an action by a shareholder when it is established:

(1) That the directors are deadlocked in the management of the corporate affairs and the shareholders are unable to break the deadlock, and that irreparable injury to the corporation is being suffered or is threatened by reason thereof; or

(2) That the acts of the directors or those in control of the corporation are illegal, oppressive or fraudulent; or

(3) That the shareholders are deadlocked in voting power, and have failed, for a period which includes at least two consecutive annual meeting dates, to elect successors to directors whose terms have expired or would have expired upon the election of their successors; or

(4) That the corporate assets are being misapplied or wasted.

(b) In an action by a creditor:

(1) When the claim of the creditor has been reduced to judgment and an execution thereon returned unsatisfied and it is established that the corporation is insolvent; or

(2) When the corporation has admitted in writing that the claim of the creditor is due and owing and it is established that the corporation is insolvent.

(c) Upon application by a corporation which has filed a statement of intent to dissolve, as provided in this Act, to have its liquidation continued under the supervision of the court.

(d) When an action has been filed by the Attorney General to dissolve a corporation and it is established that liquidation of its business and affairs should precede the entry of a decree of dissolution.

Proceedings under clause (a), (b) or (c) of this section shall be brought in the county in which the registered office or the principal office of the corporation is situated.

It shall not be necessary to make shareholders parties to any such action or proceeding unless relief is sought against them personally.

§ 91. Procedure in Liquidation of Corporation by Court.

In proceedings to liquidate the assets and business of a corporation the court shall have power to issue injunctions, to appoint a receiver or receivers pendente lite, with such powers and duties as the court, from time to time, may direct, and to take such other proceedings as may be requisite to preserve the corporate assets wherever situated, and carry on the business of the corporation until a full hearing can be had.

After a hearing had upon such notice as the court may direct to be given to all parties to the proceedings and to any other parties in interest designated by the court, the court may appoint a liquidating receiver or receivers with authority to collect the assets of the corporation, including all amounts owing to the corporation by shareholders on account of any unpaid portion of the consideration for the issuance of shares. Such liquidating receiver or receivers shall have authority, subject to the order of the court, to sell, convey and dispose of all or any part of the assets of the corporation wherever situated, either at public or private sale. The assets of the corporation or the proceeds resulting from a sale, conveyance or other disposition thereof shall be applied to the expenses of such liquidation and to the payment of the liabilities and obligations of the corporation, and any remaining assets or proceeds shall be distributed among its shareholders according to their respective rights and interests. The order appointing such liquidating receiver or receivers shall state their powers and duties. Such powers and duties may be increased or diminished at any time during the proceedings.

The court shall have power to allow from time to time as expenses of the liquidation compensation to the receiver or receivers and to attorneys in the proceeding, and to direct the payment thereof out of the assets of the corporation or the proceeds of any sale or disposition of such assets.

A receiver of a corporation appointed under the provisions of this section shall have authority to sue and defend in all courts in his own name as receiver of such corporation. The court appointing such receiver shall have exclusive jurisdiction of the corporation and its property, wherever situated.

§ 92. Qualifications of Receivers.

A receiver shall in all cases be a citizen of the United States or a corporation authorized to act as receiver, which corporation may be a domestic corporation or a foreign corporation authorized to transact business in this State, and shall in all cases give such bond as the court may direct with such sureties as the court may require.

§ 93. Filing of Claims in Liquidation Proceedings.

In proceedings to liquidate the assets and business of a corporation the court may require all creditors of the corporation to file with the clerk of the court or with the receiver, in such form as the court may prescribe, proofs under oath of their respective claims. If the court requires the filing of claims it shall fix a date, which shall be not less than four months from the date of the order, as the last day for the filing of claims, and shall prescribe the notice that shall be given to creditors and claimants of the date so fixed. Prior to the date so fixed, the court may extend the time for the filing of claims. Creditors and claimants failing to file proofs of claim on or before the date so fixed may be barred, by order of court, from participating in the distribution of the assets of the corporation.

§ 94. Discontinuance of Liquidation Proceedings.

The liquidation of the assets and business of a corporation may be discontinued at any time during the liquidation proceedings when it is established that cause for liquidation no longer exists. In such event the court shall dismiss the proceedings and direct the receiver to redeliver to the corporation all its remaining property and assets.

§ 95. Decree of Involuntary Dissolution.

In proceedings to liquidate the assets and business of a corporation, when the costs and expenses of such proceedings and all debts, obligations and liabilities of the corporation shall have been paid and discharged and all of its remaining property and assets distributed to its shareholders, or in case its property and assets are not sufficient to satisfy and discharge such costs, expenses, debts and obligations, all the property and assets have been applied so far as they will go to their payment, the court shall enter a decree dissolving the corporation, whereupon the existence of the corporation shall cease.

§ 96. Filing of Decree of Dissolution.

In case the court shall enter a decree dissolving a corporation, it shall be the duty of the clerk of such court to cause a certified copy of the decree to be filed with the Secretary of State. No fee shall be charged by the Secretary of State for the filing thereof.

§ 97. Deposit with State Treasurer of Amount Due Certain Shareholders.

Upon the voluntary or involuntary dissolution of a corporation, the portion of the assets distributable to a creditor or shareholder who is unknown or cannot be found, or who is under disability and there is no person legally competent to receive such distributive portion, shall be reduced to cash and deposited with the State Treasurer and shall be paid over to such creditor or shareholder or to his legal representative upon proof satisfactory to the State Treasurer of his right thereto.

§ 98. Survival of Remedy After Dissolution.

The dissolution of a corporation either (1) by the issuance of a certificate of dissolution by the Secretary of State, or (2) by a decree of court when the court has not liquidated the assets and business of the corporation as provided in this Act, or (3) by expiration of its period of duration, shall not take away or impair any remedy available to or against such corporation, its directors, officers, or shareholders, for any right or claim existing, or any liability incurred, prior to such dissolution if action or other proceeding thereon is commenced within two years after the date of such dissolution. Any such action or proceeding by or against the corporation may be prosecuted or defended by the corporation in its corporate name. The shareholders, directors and officers shall have power to take such corporate or other action as shall be appropriate to protect such remedy, right or claim. If such corporation was dissolved by the expiration of its period of duration, such corporation may amend its articles of incorporation at any time during such period of two years so as to extend its period of duration.

§ 99. Admission of Foreign Corporation.

No foreign corporation shall have the right to transact business in this State until it shall have procured a certificate of authority so to do from the Secretary of State. No foreign corporation shall be entitled to procure a certificate of authority under this Act to transact in this State any business which a corporation organized under this Act is not permitted to transact. A foreign corporation shall not be denied a certificate of authority by reason of the fact that the laws of the state or country under which such corporation is organized governing its organization and internal affairs differ from the laws of this State, and nothing in this Act contained shall be construed to authorize this State to regulate the organization or the internal affairs of such corporation.

Without excluding other activities which may not constitute transacting business in this State, a foreign corporation shall not be considered to be transacting business in this State, for the purposes of this Act, by reason of carrying on in this State any one or more of the following activities:

(a) Maintaining or defending any action or suit or any administrative or arbitration proceeding, or effecting the settlement thereof or the settlement of claims or disputes.

(b) Holding meetings of its directors or shareholders or carrying on other activities concerning its internal affairs.

(c) Maintaining bank accounts.

(d) Maintaining offices or agencies for the transfer, exchange and registration of its securities, or appointing and maintaining trustees or depositaries with relation to its securities.

(e) Effecting sales through independent contractors.

(f) Soliciting or procuring orders, whether by mail or through employees or agents or otherwise, where such orders require acceptance without this State before becoming binding contracts.

(g) Creating evidences of debt, mortgages or liens on real or personal property.

(h) Securing or collecting debts or enforcing any rights in property securing the same.

(i) Transacting any business in interstate commerce.

(j) Conducting an isolated transaction completed within a period of thirty days and not in the course of a number of repeated transactions of like nature.

§ 100. Powers of Foreign Corporation.

A foreign corporation which shall have received a certificate of authority under this Act shall, until a certificate of revocation or of withdrawal shall have been issued as provided in this Act, enjoy the same, but no greater, rights and privileges as a domestic corporation organized for the purposes set forth in the application pursuant to which such certificate of authority is issued; and, except as in this Act otherwise provided, shall be subject to the same duties, restrictions, penalties and liabilities now or hereafter imposed upon a domestic corporation of like character.

§ 101. Corporate Name of Foreign Corporation.

No certificate of authority shall be issued to a foreign corporation unless the corporate name of such corporation:

(a) Shall contain the word "corporation," "company," "incorporated," or "limited," or shall contain an abbreviation of one of such words, or such corporation shall, for use in this State, add at the end of its name one of such words or an abbreviation thereof.

(b) Shall not contain any word or phrase which indicates or implies that it is organized for any purpose other than one or more of the purposes contained in its articles of incorporation or that it is authorized or empowered to conduct the business of banking or insurance.

(c) Shall not be the same as, or deceptively similar to, the name of any domestic corporation existing under the laws of this State or any foreign corporation authorized to transact business in this State or a name the exclusive right to which is, at the time, reserved in the manner provided in this Act, or the name of a corporation which has in effect a registration of its name as provided in this Act.

§ 102. Change of Name by Foreign Corporation.

Whenever a foreign corporation which is authorized to transact business in this State shall change its name to one under which a certificate of authority would not be granted to it on application therefor, the certificate of authority of such corporation shall be suspended and it shall not thereafter transact any business in this State until it has changed its name to a name which is available to it under the laws of this State.

§ 103. Application for Certificate of Authority.

A foreign corporation, in order to procure a certificate of authority to transact business in this State, shall make application therefor to the Secretary of State, which application shall set forth:

(a) The name of the corporation and the state or county under the laws of which it is incorporated.

(b) If the name of the corporation does not contain the word "corporation," "company," "incorporated," or "limited," or does not contain an abbreviation of one of such words, then the name of the corporation with the word or abbreviation which it elects to add thereto for use in this State.

(c) The date of incorporation and the period of duration of the corporation.

(d) The address of the principal office of the corporation in the state or country under the laws of which it is incorporated.

(e) The address of the proposed registered office of the corporation in this State, and the name of its proposed registered agent in this State at such address.

(f) The purpose or purposes of the corporation which it proposes to pursue in the transaction of business in this State.

(g) The names and respective addresses of the directors and officers of the corporation.

(h) A statement of the aggregate number of shares which the corporation has authority to issue, itemized by classes, par value of shares, shares without par value, and series, if any, within a class.

(i) A statement of the aggregate number of issued shares itemized by classes, par value of shares, shares without par value, and series, if any, within a class.

(j) A statement, expressed in dollars, of the amount of stated capital of the corporation, as defined in this Act.

(k) An estimate, expressed in dollars, of the value of all property to be owned by the corporation for the following year, wherever located, and an estimate of the value of the property of the corporation to be located within this State during such year, and an estimate, expressed in dollars, of the gross amount of business which will be transacted by the corporation during such year, and an estimate of the gross amount thereof which will be transacted by the corporation at or from places of business in this State during such year.

(l) Such additional information as may be necessary or appropriate in order to enable the Secretary of State to determine whether such corporation is entitled to a certificate of authority to transact business in this State and to determine and assess the fees and franchise taxes payable as in this Act prescribed.

Such application shall be made on forms prescribed and furnished by the Secretary of State and shall be executed in duplicate by the corporation by its president or a vice president and by its secretary or an assistant secretary, and verified by one of the officers signing such application.

§ 104. Filing of Application for Certificate of Authority.

Duplicate originals of the application of the corporation for a certificate of authority shall be delivered to the Secretary of State, together with a copy of its articles of incorporation and all amendments thereto, duly authenticated by the proper officer of the state or country under the laws of which it is incorporated.

If the Secretary of State finds that such application conforms to law, he shall, when all fees and franchise taxes have been paid as in this Act prescribed:

(1) Endorse on each of such documents the word "Filed," and the month, day and year of the filing thereof.

(2) File in his office one of such duplicate originals of the application and the copy of the articles of incorporation and amendments thereto.

(3) Issue a certificate of authority to transact business in this State to which he shall affix the other duplicate original application.

The certificate of authority, together with the duplicate original of the application affixed thereto by the Secretary of State, shall be returned to the corporation or its representative.

§ 105. Effect of Certificate of Authority.

Upon the issuance of a certificate of authority by the Secretary of State, the corporation shall be authorized to transact business in this State for those purposes set forth in its application, subject, however, to the right of this State to suspend or to revoke such authority as provided in this Act.

§ 106. Registered Office and Registered Agent of Foreign Corporation.

Each foreign corporation authorized to transact business in this State shall have and continuously maintain in this State:

(a) A registered office which may be, but need not be, the same as its place of business in this State.

(b) A registered agent, which agent may be either an individual resident in this State whose business office is identical with such registered office, or a domestic corporation, or a foreign corporation authorized to transact business in this State, having a business office identical with such registered office.

§ 107. Change of Registered Office or Registered Agent of Foreign Corporation.

A foreign corporation authorized to transact business in this State may change its registered office or change its registered agent, or both, upon filing in the office of the Secretary of State a statement setting forth:

(a) The name of the corporation.

(b) The address of its then registered office.

(c) If the address of its registered office be changed, the address to which the registered office is to be changed.

(d) The name of its then registered agent.

(e) If its registered agent be changed, the name of its successor registered agent.

(f) That the address of its registered office and the address of the business office of its registered agent, as changed, will be identical.

(g) That such change was authorized by resolution duly adopted by its board of directors.

Such statement shall be executed by the corporation by its president or a vice president, and verified by him, and delivered to the Secretary of State. If the Secretary of State finds that such statement conforms to the provisions of this Act, he shall file such statement in his office, and upon such filing the change of address of the registered office, or the appointment of a new registered agent, or both, as the case may be, shall become effective.

Any registered agent of a foreign corporation may resign as such agent upon filing a written notice thereof, executed in duplicate, with the Secretary of State, who shall forthwith mail a copy thereof to the corporation at its principal office in the state or country under the laws of which it is incorporated. The appointment of such agent shall terminate upon the expiration of thirty days after receipt of such notice by the Secretary of State.

If a registered agent changes his or its business address to another place within the same _____,* he or it may change such address and the address of the registered office of any corporations of which he or it is registered agent by filing a statement as required above except that it need be signed only by the registered agent and need not be responsive to (e) or (g) and must recite that a copy of the statement has been mailed to each such corporation.

§ 108. Service of Process on Foreign Corporation.

The registered agent so appointed by a foreign corporation authorized to transact business in this State shall be an agent of such corporation upon whom any process, notice or demand required or permitted by law to be served upon the corporation may be served.

Whenever a foreign corporation authorized to transact business in this State shall fail to appoint or maintain a registered agent in this State, or whenever any such registered agent cannot with reasonable diligence be found at the registered office, or whenever the certificate of authority of a foreign corporation shall be suspended or revoked, then the Secretary of State shall be an agent of such corporation upon whom any such process, notice, or demand may be served. Service on the Secretary of State of any such process, notice, or demand shall be made by delivering to and leaving with him, or with any clerk having charge of the corporation department of his office, duplicate copies of such process, notice or demand. In the event any such process, notice or demand is served on the Secretary of State, he shall immediately cause one of such copies thereof to be forwarded by registered mail, addressed to the corporation at its principal office in the state or country under the laws of which it is incorporated. Any service so had on the Secretary of State shall be returnable in not less than thirty days.

The Secretary of State shall keep a record of all processes, notices and demands served upon him under this section, and shall record therein the time of such service and his action with reference thereto.

Nothing herein contained shall limit or affect the right to serve any process, notice or demand, required or permitted by law to be served upon a corporation in any other manner now or hereafter permitted by law.

§ 109. Amendment to Articles of Incorporation of Foreign Corporation.

Whenever the articles of incorporation of a foreign corporation authorized to transact business in this State are amended, such foreign corporation shall, within thirty days after such amendment becomes effective, file in the office of the Secretary of State a copy of such amendment duly authenticated by the proper officer of the state or country under the laws of which it is incorporated; but the filing thereof shall not of itself enlarge or alter the purpose or purposes which such corporation is authorized to pursue in the transaction of business in this State, nor authorize such corporation to transact business in this State under any other name than the name set forth in its certificate of authority.

---

* Supply designation of jurisdiction, such as county, etc., in accordance with local practice.

§ 110. Merger of Foreign Corporation Authorized to Transact Business in This State.

Whenever a foreign corporation authorized to transact business in this State shall be a party to a statutory merger permitted by the laws of the state or country under the laws of which it is incorporated, and such corporation shall be the surviving corporation, it shall, within thirty days after such merger becomes effective, file with the Secretary of State a copy of the articles of merger duly authenticated by the proper officer of the state or country under the laws of which such statutory merger was effected; and it shall not be necessary for such corporation to procure either a new or amended certificate of authority to transact business in this State unless the name of such corporation be changed thereby or unless the corporation desires to pursue in this State other or additional purposes than those which it is then authorized to transact in this State.

§ 111. Amended Certificate of Authority.

A foreign corporation authorized to transact business in this State shall procure an amended certificate of authority in the event it changes its corporate name, or desires to pursue in this State other or additional purposes than those set forth in its prior application for a certificate of authority, by making application therefor to the Secretary of State.

The requirements in respect to the form and contents of such application, the manner of its execution, the filing of duplicate originals thereof with the Secretary of State, the issuance of an amended certificate of authority and the effect thereof, shall be the same as in the case of an original application for a certificate of authority.

§ 112. Withdrawal of Foreign Corporation.

A foreign corporation authorized to transact business in this State may withdraw from this State upon procuring from the Secretary of State a certificate of withdrawal. In order to procure such certificate of withdrawal, such foreign corporation shall deliver to the Secretary of State an application for withdrawal, which shall set forth:

(a) The name of the corporation and the state or country under the laws of which it is incorporated.

(b) That the corporation is not transacting business in this State.

(c) That the corporation surrenders its authority to transact business in this State.

(d) That the corporation revokes the authority of its registered agent in this State to accept service of process and consents that service of process in any action, suit or proceeding based upon any cause of action arising in this State during the time the corporation was authorized to transact business in this State may thereafter be made on such corporation by service thereof on the Secretary of State.

(e) A post-office address to which the Secretary of State may mail a copy of any process against the corporation that may be served on him.

(f) A statement of the aggregate number of shares which the corporation has authority to issue, itemized by classes, par value of shares, shares without par value, and series, if any, within a class, as of the date of such application.

(g) A statement of the aggregate number of issued shares, itemized by classes, par value of shares, shares without par value, and series, if any, within a class, as of the date of such application.

(h) A statement, expressed in dollars, of the amount of stated capital of the corporation, as of the date of such application.

(i) Such additional information as may be necessary or appropriate in order to enable the Secretary of State to determine and assess any unpaid fees or franchise taxes payable by such foreign corporation as in this Act prescribed.

The application for withdrawal shall be made on forms prescribed and furnished by the Secretary of State and shall be executed by the corporation by its president or a vice president and by its secretary or an assistant secretary, and verified by one of the officers signing the application, or, if the corporation is in the hands of a receiver or trustee, shall be executed on behalf of the corporation by such receiver or trustee and verified by him.

§ 113. Filing of Application for Withdrawal.

Duplicate originals of such application for withdrawal shall be delivered to the Secretary of State. If the Secretary of State finds that such application conforms to the provisions of this Act, he shall, when all fees and franchise taxes have been paid as in this Act prescribed:

(1) Endorse on each of such duplicate originals the word "Filed," and the month, day and year of the filing thereof.

(2) File one of such duplicate originals in his office.

(3) Issue a certificate of withdrawal to which he shall affix the other duplicate original.

The certificate of withdrawal, together with the duplicate original of the application for withdrawal affixed thereto by the Secretary of State, shall be returned to the corporation or its representative. Upon the issuance of such certificate of withdrawal, the authority of the corporation to transact business in this State shall cease.

§ 114. Revocation of Certificate of Authority.

The certificate of authority of a foreign corporation to transact business in this State may be revoked by the Secretary of State upon the conditions prescribed in this section when:

(a) The corporation has failed to file its annual report within the time required by this Act, or has failed to pay any fees, franchise taxes or penalties prescribed by this Act when they have become due and payable; or

(b) The corporation has failed to appoint and maintain a registered agent in this State as required by this Act; or

(c) The corporation has failed, after change of its registered office or registered agent, to file in the office of the Secretary of State a statement of such change as required by this Act; or

(d) The corporation has failed to file in the office of the Secretary of State any amendment to its articles of incorporation or any articles of merger within the time prescribed by this Act; or

(e) A misrepresentation has been made of any material matter in any application, report, affidavit, or other document submitted by such corporation pursuant to this Act.

No certificate of authority of a foreign corporation shall be revoked by the Secretary of State unless (1) he shall have given the corporation not less than sixty days notice thereof by mail addressed to its registered office in this State, and (2) the corporation shall fail prior to revocation to file such annual report, or pay such fees, franchise taxes or penalties, or file the required statement of change of registered agent or registered office, or file such articles of amendment or articles of merger, or correct such misrepresentation.

§ 115. Issuance of Certificate of Revocation.

Upon revoking any such certificate of authority, the Secretary of State shall:

(1) Issue a certificate of revocation in duplicate.

(2) File one of such certificates in his office.

(3) Mail to such corporation at its registered office in this State a notice of such revocation accompanied by one of such certificates.

Upon the issuance of such certificate of revocation, the authority of the corporation to transact business in this State shall cease.

§ 116. Application to Corporations Heretofore Authorized to Transact Business in This State.

Foreign corporations which are duly authorized to transact business in this State at the time this Act takes effect, for a purpose or purposes for which a corporation might secure such authority under this Act, shall, subject to the limitations set forth in their respective certificates of authority, be entitled to all the rights and privileges applicable to foreign corporations procuring certificates of authority to transact business in this State under this Act, and from the time this Act takes effect such corporations shall be subject to all the limitations, restrictions, liabilities, and duties prescribed herein for foreign corporations procuring certificates of authority to transact business in this State under this Act.

§ 117. Transacting Business Without Certificate of Authority.

No foreign corporation transacting business in this State without a certificate of authority shall be permitted to maintain any action, suit or proceeding in any court of this State, until such corporation shall have obtained a certificate of authority. Nor shall any action, suit or proceeding be maintained in any court of this State by any successor or assignee of such corporation on any right, claim or demand arising out of the transaction of business by such corporation in this State, until a certificate of authority shall have been obtained by such corporation or by a corporation which has acquired all or substantially all of its assets.

The failure of a foreign corporation to obtain a certificate of authority to transact business in this State shall not impair the validity of any contract or act of such corporation, and shall not prevent such corporation from defending any action, suit or proceeding in any court of this State.

A foreign corporation which transacts business in this State without a certificate of authority shall be liable to this State, for the years or parts thereof during which it transacted business in this State without a certificate of authority, in an amount equal to all fees and franchise taxes which would have been imposed by this Act upon such corporation had it duly applied for and received a certificate of authority to transact business in this State as required by this Act and thereafter filed all reports required by this Act, plus all penalties imposed by this Act for failure to pay such fees and franchise taxes. The Attorney General shall bring proceedings to recover all amounts due this State under the provisions of this Section.

§ 118. Annual Report of Domestic and Foreign Corporations.

Each domestic corporation, and each foreign corporation authorized to transact business in this State, shall file, within the time prescribed by this Act, an annual report setting forth:

(a) The name of the corporation and the state or country under the laws of which it is incorporated.

(b) The address of the registered office of the corporation in this State, and the name of its registered agent in this State at such address, and, in the case of a foreign corporation, the address of its principal office in the state or country under the laws of which it is incorporated.

(c) A brief statement of the character of the business in which the corporation is actually engaged in this State.

(d) The names and respective addresses of the directors and officers of the corporation.

(e) A statement of the aggregate number of shares which the corporation has authority to issue, itemized by classes, par value of shares, shares without par value, and series, if any, within a class.

(f) A statement of the aggregate number of issued shares, itemized by classes, par value of shares, shares without par value, and series, if any, within a class.

(g) A statement, expressed in dollars, of the amount of stated capital of the corporation, as defined in this Act.

(h) A statement, expressed in dollars, of the value of all the property owned by the corporation, wherever located, and the value of the property of the corporation located within this State, and a statement, expressed in dollars, of the gross amount of business transacted by the corporation for the twelve months ended on the thirty-first day of December preceding the date herein provided for the filing of such report and the gross amount thereof transacted by the corporation at or from places of business in this State. If, on the thirty-first day of December preceding the time herein provided for the filing of such report, the corporation had not been in existence for a period of twelve months, or in the case of a foreign corporation had not been authorized to transact business in this State for a period of twelve months, the statement with respect to business transacted shall be furnished for the period between the date of incorporation or the date of its authorization to transact business in this State, as the case may be, and such thirty-first day of December. If all the property of the corporation is located in this State and all of its business is transacted at or from places of business in this State, or if the corporation elects to pay the annual franchise tax on the basis of its entire stated capital, then the information required by this subparagraph need not be set forth in such report.

(i) Such additional information as may be necessary or appropriate in order to enable the Secretary of State to determine and assess the proper amount of franchise taxes payable by such corporation.

Such annual report shall be made on forms prescribed and furnished by the Secretary of State, and the information therein contained shall be given as of the date of the execution of the report, except as to the information required by subparagraphs (g), (h) and (i) which shall be given as of the close of business on the thirty-first day of December next preceding the date herein provided for the filing of such report. It shall be executed by the corporation by its president, a vice president, secretary, an assistant secretary, or treasurer, and verified by the officer executing the report, or, if the corporation is in the hands of a receiver or trustee, it shall be executed on behalf of the corporation and verified by such receiver or trustee.

§ 119. Filing of Annual Report of Domestic and Foreign Corporations.

Such annual report of a domestic or foreign corporation shall be delivered to the Secretary of State between the first day of January and the first day of March of each year, except that the first annual report of a domestic or foreign corporation shall be filed between the first day of January and the first day of March of the year next succeeding the calendar year in which its certificate of incorporation or its certificate of authority, as the case may be, was issued by the Secretary of State. Proof to the satisfaction of the Secretary of State that prior to the first day of March such report was deposited in the United States mail in a sealed envelope, properly addressed, with postage prepaid, shall be deemed a compliance with this requirement. If the Secretary of State finds that such report conforms to the requirements of this Act, he shall file the same. If he finds that it does not so conform, he shall promptly return the same to the corporation for any necessary corrections, in which event the penalties hereinafter prescribed for failure to file such report within the time hereinabove provided shall not apply, if such report is corrected to conform to the requirements of this Act and returned to the Secretary of State within thirty days from the date on which it was mailed to the corporation by the Secretary of State.

§ 120. Fees, Franchise Taxes and Charges to Be Collected by Secretary of State.

The Secretary of State shall charge and collect in accordance with the provisions of this Act:

(a) Fees for filing documents and issuing certificates.

(b) Miscellaneous charges.

(c) License fees.

(d) Franchise taxes.

§ 121. Fees for Filing Documents and Issuing Certificates.

The Secretary of State shall charge and collect for:

(a) Filing articles of incorporation and issuing a certificate of incorporation, twenty dollars.

(b) Filing articles of amendment and issuing a certificate of amendment, twenty dollars.

(c) Filing restated articles of incorporation, twenty dollars.

(d) Filing articles of merger or consolidation and issuing a certificate of merger or consolidation, twenty dollars.

(e) Filing an application to reserve a corporate name, five dollars.

(f) Filing a notice of transfer of a reserved corporate name, five dollars.

(g) Filing a statement of change of address of registered office or change of registered agent, or both, one dollar.

(h) Filing a statement of the establishment of a series of shares, five dollars.

(i) Filing a statement of cancellation of shares, five dollars.

(j) Filing a statement of reduction of stated capital, five dollars.

(k) Filing a statement of intent to dissolve, one dollar.

(l) Filing a statement of revocation of voluntary dissolution proceedings, one dollar.

(m) Filing articles of dissolution, one dollar.

(n) Filing an application of a foreign corporation for a certificate of authority to transact business in this State and issuing a certificate of authority, twenty dollars.

(o) Filing an application of a foreign corporation for an amended certificate of authority to transact business in this State and issuing an amended certificate of authority, twenty dollars.

(p) Filing a copy of an amendment to the articles of incorporation of a foreign corporation holding a certificate of authority to transact business in this State, ten dollars.

(q) Filing a copy of articles of merger of a foreign corporation holding a certificate of authority to transact business in this State, twenty dollars.

(r) Filing an application for withdrawal of a foreign corporation and issuing a certificate of withdrawal, five dollars.

(s) Filing any other statement or report, except an annual report, of a domestic or foreign corporation, one dollar.

§ 122. Miscellaneous Charges.

The Secretary of State shall charge and collect:

(a) For furnishing a certified copy of any document, instrument, or paper relating to a corporation, thirty-five cents per page and one dollar for the certificate and affixing the seal thereto.

(b) At the time of any service of process on him as resident agent of a corporation, five dollars, which amount may be recovered as taxable costs by the party to the suit or action causing such service to be made if such party prevails in the suit or action.

§ 123. License Fees Payable by Domestic Corporations.

The Secretary of State shall charge and collect from each domestic corporation license fees, based upon the number of shares which it will have authority to issue or the increase in the number of shares which it will have authority to issue, at the time of:

(a) Filing articles of incorporation;

(b) Filing articles of amendment increasing the number of authorized shares; and

(c) Filing articles of merger or consolidation increasing the number of authorized shares which the surviving or new corporation, if a domestic corporation, will have authority to issue above the aggregate number of shares which the constituent domestic corporations and constituent foreign corporations authorized to transact business in this State had authority to issue.

The license fees shall be at the rate of one cent per share up to and including the first 10,000 authorized shares, one-half cent per share for each authorized share in excess of 10,000 shares up to and including 100,000 shares, and one-fifth cent per share for each authorized share in excess of 100,000 shares, whether the shares are of par value or without par value.

The license fees payable on an increase in the number of authorized shares shall be imposed only on the increased number of shares, and the number of previously authorized shares shall be taken into account in determining the rate applicable to the increased number of authorized shares.

§ 124. License Fees Payable by Foreign Corporations.

The Secretary of State shall charge and collect from each foreign corporation license fees, based upon the proportion represented in this State of the number of shares which it has authority to issue or the increase in the number of shares which it has authority to issue, at the time of:

(a) Filing an application for a certificate of authority to transact business in this State;

(b) Filing articles of amendment which increased the number of authorized shares; and

(c) Filing articles of merger or consolidation which increased the number of authorized shares which the surviving or new corporation, if a foreign corporation, has authority to issue above the aggregate number of shares which the constituent domestic corporations and constituent foreign corporations authorized to transact business in this State had authority to issue.

The license fees shall be at the rate of one per cent per share up to and including the first 10,000 authorized shares represented in this State, one-half cent per share for each authorized share in excess of 10,000 shares up to and including 100,000 shares represented in this State, and one-fifth cent per share for each authorized share in excess of 100,000 shares represented in this State, whether the shares are of par value or without par value.

The license fees payable on an increase in the number of authorized shares shall be imposed only on the increased number of such shares represented in this State, and the number of previously authorized shares represented in this State shall be taken into account in determining the rate applicable to the increased number of authorized shares.

The number of authorized shares represented in this State shall be that proportion of its total authorized shares which the sum of the value of its property located in this State and the gross amount of business transacted by it at or from places of business in this State bears to the sum of the value of all of its property, wherever located, and the gross amount of its business, wherever transacted. Such proportion shall be determined from information contained in the application for a certificate of authority to transact business in this State until the filing of an annual report and thereafter from information contained in the latest annual report filed by the corporation.

§ 125. Franchise Taxes Payable by Domestic Corporations.

The Secretary of State shall charge and collect from each domestic corporation an initial franchise tax at the time of filing its articles of incorporation at the rate of one-twelfth of one-half of the license fee payable by such corporation under the provisions of this Act at the time of filing its articles of incorporation, for each calendar month, or fraction thereof, between the date of the issuance of the certificate of incorporation by the Secretary of State and the first day of July of the next succeeding calendar year.

The Secretary of State shall charge and collect from each domestic corporation an annual franchise tax, payable in advance for the period from July 1 in each year to July 1 in the succeeding year, beginning July 1 in the calendar year in which such corporation is required to file its first annual report under this Act, at the rate of one-twentieth of one per cent of the amount represented in this State of the stated capital of the corporation, as disclosed by the latest annual report filed by the corporation with the Secretary of State.

The amount represented in this State of the stated capital of the corporation shall be that proportion of its stated capital which the sum of the value of its property located in this State and the gross amount of business transacted by it at or from places of business in this State bears to the sum of the value of all of its property, wherever located, and the gross amount of its business, wherever transacted, except as follows:

(a) If the corporation elects in its annual report in any year to pay its annual franchise tax on its entire stated capital, all franchise taxes accruing against the corporation after the filing of such annual report shall be assessed accordingly until the corporation elects otherwise in an annual report for a subsequent year.

(b) If the corporation fails to file its annual report in any year within the time prescribed by this Act, the proportion of its stated capital represented in this State shall be deemed to be its entire stated capital, unless its annual report is thereafter filed and its franchise tax thereafter adjusted by the Secretary of State in accordance with the provisions of this Act, in which case the proportion shall likewise be adjusted to the same proportion that would have prevailed if the corporation had filed its annual report within the time prescribed by this Act.

§ 126. Franchise Taxes Payable by Foreign Corporations.

The Secretary of State shall charge and collect from each foreign corporation authorized to transact business in this State an initial franchise tax at the time of filing its application for a certificate of authority at the rate of one-twelfth of one-half of the license fee payable by such corporation under the provisions of this Act at the time of filing such application, for each month, or fraction thereof, between the date of the issuance of the certificate of authority by the Secretary of State and the first day of July of the next succeeding calendar year.

The Secretary of State shall charge and collect from each foreign corporation authorized to transact business in this State an annual franchise tax, payable in advance for the period from July 1 in each year to July 1 in the succeeding year, beginning July 1 in the calendar year in which such corporation is required to file its first annual report under this Act, at the rate of one-twentieth of one per cent of the amount represented in this State of the stated capital of the corporation, as disclosed by the latest annual report filed by the corporation with the Secretary of State.

The amount represented in this State of the stated capital of the corporation shall be that proportion of its stated capital which the sum of the value of its property located in this State and the gross amount of business transacted by it at or from places of business in this State bears to the sum of the value of all of its property, wherever located, and the gross amount of its business, wherever transacted, except as follows:

(a) If the corporation elects in its annual report in any year to pay its annual franchise tax on its entire stated capital, all franchise taxes accruing against the corporation after the filing of such annual report shall be assessed accordingly until the corporation elects otherwise in an annual report for a subsequent year.

(b) If the corporation fails to file its annual report in any year within the time prescribed by this Act, the proportion of its stated capital represented in this State shall be deemed to be its entire stated capital, unless its annual report is thereafter filed and its franchise tax thereafter adjusted by the Secretary of State in accordance with the provisions of this Act, in which case the proportion shall likewise be adjusted to the same proportion that would have prevailed if the corporation had filed its annual report within the time prescribed by this Act.

§ 127. Assessment and Collection of Annual Franchise Taxes.

It shall be the duty of the Secretary of State to collect all annual franchise taxes and penalties imposed by, or assessed in accordance with, this Act.

Between the first day of March and the first day of June of each year, the Secretary of State shall assess against each corporation, domestic and foreign, required to file an annual report in such year, the franchise tax payable by it for the period from July 1 of such year to July 1 of the succeeding year in accordance with the provisions of this Act, and, if it has failed to file its annual report within the time prescribed by this Act, the penalty imposed by this Act upon such corporation for its failure so to do; and shall mail a written notice to each corporation against which such tax is assessed, addressed to such corporation at its registered office in this State, notifying the corporation (1) of the amount of franchise tax assessed against it for the ensuing year and the amount of penalty, if any, assessed against it for failure to file its annual report; (2) that objections, if any, to such assessment will be heard by the officer making the assessment on or before the fifteenth day of June of such year, upon receipt of a request from the corporation; and (3) that such tax and penalty shall be payable to the Secretary of State on the first day of July next succeeding the date of the notice. Failure to receive such notice shall not relieve the corporation of its obligation to pay the tax and any penalty assessed, or invalidate the assessment thereof.

The Secretary of State shall have power to hear and determine objections to any assessment of franchise tax at any time after such assessment and, after hearing, to change or modify any such assessment. In the event of any adjustment of franchise tax with respect to which a penalty has been assessed for failure to file an annual report, the penalty shall be adjusted in accordance with the provisions of this Act imposing such penalty.

All annual franchise taxes and all penalties for failure to file annual reports shall be due and payable on the first day of July of each year. If the annual franchise tax assessed against any corporation subject to the provisions of this Act, together with all penalties assessed thereon, shall not be paid to the Secretary of State on or before the thirty-first day of July of the year in which such tax is due and payable, the Secretary of State shall certify such fact to the Attorney General on or before the fifteenth day of November of such year, whereupon the Attorney General may institute an action against such corporation in the name of this State, in any court of competent jurisdiction, for the recovery of the amount of such franchise tax and penalties, together with the cost of suit, and prosecute the same to final judgment.

For the purpose of enforcing collection, all annual franchise taxes assessed in accordance with this Act, and all penalties assessed thereon and all interest and costs that shall accrue in connection with the collection thereof, shall be a prior and first lien on the real and personal property of the corporation from and including the first day of July of the year when such franchise taxes become due and payable until such taxes, penalties, interest, and costs shall have been paid.

§ 128. Penalties Imposed Upon Corporations.

Each corporation, domestic or foreign, that fails or refuses to file its annual report for any year within the time prescribed by this Act shall be subject to a penalty of ten per cent of the amount of the franchise tax assessed against it for the period beginning July 1 of the year in which such report should have been filed. Such penalty shall be assessed by the Secretary of State at the time of the assessment of the franchise tax. If the amount of the franchise tax as originally assessed against such corporation be thereafter adjusted in accordance with the provisions of this Act, the amount of the penalty shall be likewise adjusted to ten per cent of the amount of the adjusted franchise tax. The amount of the franchise tax and the amount of the penalty shall be separately stated in any notice to the corporation with respect thereto.

If the franchise tax assessed in accordance with the provisions of this Act shall not be paid on or before the thirty-first day of July, it shall be deemed to be delinquent, and there shall be added a penalty of one per cent for each month or part of month that the same is delinquent, commencing with the month of August.

Each corporation, domestic or foreign, that fails or refuses to answer truthfully and fully within the time prescribed by this Act interrogatories propounded by the Secretary of State in accordance with the provisions of this Act, shall be deemed to be guilty of a misdemeanor and upon conviction thereof may be fined in any amount not exceeding five hundred dollars.

§ 129. Penalties Imposed Upon Officers and Directors.

Each officer and director of a corporation, domestic or foreign, who fails or refuses within the time prescribed by this Act to answer truthfully and fully interrogatories propounded to him by the Secretary of State in accordance with the provisions of this Act, or who signs any articles, statement, report, application or other document filed with the Secretary of State which is known to such officer or director to be false in any material respect, shall be deemed to be guilty of a misdemeanor, and upon conviction thereof may be fined in any amount not exceeding five hundred dollars.

§ 130. Interrogatories by Secretary of State.

The Secretary of State may propound to any corporation, domestic or foreign, subject to the provisions of this Act, and to any officer or director thereof, such interrogatories as may be reasonably necessary and proper to enable him to ascertain whether such corporation has complied with all the provisions of this Act applicable to such corporation. Such interrogatories shall be answered within thirty days after the mailing thereof, or within such additional time as shall be fixed by the Secretary of State, and the answers thereto shall be full and complete and shall be made in writing and under oath. If such interrogatories be directed to an individual they shall be answered by him, and if directed to a corporation they shall be answered by the president, vice president, secretary or assistant secretary thereof. The Secretary of State need not file any document to which such interrogatories relate until such interrogatories be answered as herein provided, and not then if the answers thereto disclose that such document is not in conformity with the provisions of this Act. The Secretary of State shall certify to the Attorney General, for such action as the Attorney General may deem appropriate, all interrogatories and answers thereto which disclose a violation of any of the provisions of this Act.

§ 131. Information Disclosed by Interrogatories.

Interrogatories propounded by the Secretary of State and the answers thereto shall not be open to public inspection nor shall the Secretary of State disclose any facts or information obtained therefrom except in so far as his official duty may require the same to be made public or in the event such interrogatories or the answers thereto are required for evidence in any criminal procedings or in any other action by this State.

§ 132. Powers of Secretary of State.

The Secretary of State shall have the power and authority reasonably necessary to enable him to administer this Act efficiently and to perform the duties therein imposed upon him.

§ 133. Appeal from Secretary of State.

If the Secretary of State shall fail to approve any articles of incorporation, amendment, merger, consolidation or dissolution, or any other document required by this Act to be approved by the Secretary of State before the same shall be filed in his office, he shall, within ten days after the delivery thereof to him, give written notice of his disapproval to the person or corporation, domestic or foreign, delivering the same, specifying the reasons therefor. From such disapproval such person or corporation may appeal to the _____ court of the county in which the registered office of such corporation is, or is proposed to be, situated by filing with the clerk of such court a petition setting forth a copy of the articles or other document sought to be filed and a copy of the written disapproval thereof by the Secretary of State; whereupon the matter shall be tried de novo by the court, and the court shall either sustain the action of the Secretary of State or direct him to take such action as the court may ·deem proper.

If the Secretary of State shall revoke the certificate of authority to transact business in this State of any foreign corporation, pursuant to the provisions of this Act, such foreign corporation may likewise appeal to the _____ court of the county where the registered office of such corporation in this State is situated, by filing with the clerk of such court a petition setting forth a copy of its certificate of authority to transact business in this State and a copy of the notice of revocation given by the Secretary of State; whereupon the matter shall be tried de novo by the court, and the court shall either sustain the action of the Secretary of State or direct him to take such action as the court may deem proper.

Appeals from all final orders and judgments entered by the _____ court under this section in review of any ruling or decision of the Secretary of State may be taken as in other civil actions.

§ 134. Certificates and Certified Copies to Be Received in Evidence.

All certificates issued by the Secretary of State in accordance with the provisions of this Act, and all copies of documents filed in his office in accordance with the provisions of this Act when certified by him, shall be taken and received in all courts, public offices, and official bodies as prima facie evidence of the facts therein stated. A certificate by the Secretary of State under the great seal of this State, as to the existence or non-existence of the facts relating to corporations shall be taken and received in all courts, public offices, and official bodies as prima facie evidence of the existence or non-existence of the facts therein stated.

§ 135. Forms to Be Furnished by Secretary of State.

All reports required by this Act to be filed in the office of the Secretary of State shall be made on forms which shall be prescribed and furnished by the Secretary of State. Forms for all other documents to be filed in the office of the Secretary of State shall be furnished by the Secretary of State on request therefor, but the use thereof, unless otherwise specifically prescribed in this Act, shall not be mandatory.

§ 136. Greater Voting Requirements.

Whenever, with respect to any action to be taken by the shareholders of a corporation, the articles of incorporation require the vote or concurrence of the holders of a greater proportion of the shares, or of any class or series thereof, than required by this Act with respect to such action, the provisions of the articles of incorporation shall control.

§ 137. Waiver of Notice.

Whenever any notice is required to be given to any shareholder or director of a corporation under the provisions of this Act or under the provisions of the articles of incorporation or by-laws of the corporation, a waiver thereof in writing signed by the person or persons entitled to such notice, whether before or after the time stated therein, shall be equivalent to the giving of such notice.

§ 138. Action by Shareholders Without a Meeting.

Any action required by this Act to be taken at a meeting of the shareholders of a corporation, or any action which may be taken at a meeting of the shareholders, may be taken without a meeting if a consent in writing, setting forth the action so taken, shall be signed by all of the shareholders entitled to vote with respect to the subject matter thereof.

Such consent shall have the same effect as a unanimous vote of shareholders, and may be stated as such in any articles or document filed with the Secretary of State under this Act.

§ 139. Unauthorized Assumption of Corporate Powers.

All persons who assume to act as a corporation without authority so to do shall be jointly and severally liable for all debts and liabilities incurred or arising as a result thereof.

§ 140. Application to Existing Corporations.

The provisions of this Act shall apply to all existing corporations organized under any general act of this State providing for the organization of corporations for a purpose or purposes for which a corporation might be organized under this Act, where the power has been reserved to amend, repeal or modify the act under which such corporation was organized and where such act is repealed by this Act.

§ 141. Application to Foreign and Interstate Commerce.

The provisions of this Act shall apply to commerce with foreign nations and among the several states only in so far as the same may be permitted under the provisions of the Constitution of the United States.

§ 142. Reservation of Power.

The _____* shall at all times have power to prescribe such regulations, provisions and limitations as it may deem advisable, which regulations, provisions and limitations shall be binding upon any and all corporations subject to the provisions of this Act, and the _____* shall have power to amend, repeal or modify this Act at pleasure.

§ 143. Effect of Repeal of Prior Acts.

The repeal of a prior act by this Act shall not affect any right accrued or established, or any liability or penalty incurred, under the provisions of such act, prior to the repeal thereof.

§ 144. Effect of Invalidity of Part of This Act.

If a court of competent jurisdiction shall adjudge to be invalid or unconstitutional any clause, sentence, paragraph, section or part of this Act, such judgment or decree shall not affect, impair, invalidate or nullify the remainder of this Act, but the effect thereof shall be confined to the clause, sentence, paragraph, section or part of this Act so adjudged to be invalid or unconstitutional.

---

* Insert name of legislative body.

Glossary of Legal Terms and Definitions

abatable nuisance. A nuisance which may be terminated either by the party injured or by suit instituted by him for that purpose.

abatement. A reduction, decrease, diminution. To put a final end to a suit.

abet. To abet is to assist. Abeting imparts a positive act in the aid of the commission of an offense.

ab initio. From the beginning. A contract which is void ab initio is void from its inception.

able buyer. A buyer is able who actually has the money to meet the cash payments demanded by the seller.

abrogate. To repeal; to make void; to annul.

absolute acceptance. The unqualified assent to liability by the drawee on a bill of exchange.

absque injuria. Without violation of a legal right.

abstract of title. A summary of the conveyances, transfers, and other facts relied on as evidence of title, together with all such facts appearing of record which may impair the validity. It should contain a brief but complete history of the title.

abutting owners. Those owners whose lands touch.

acceleration. The shortening of the time for the performance of a contract or the payment of a note by the operation of some provision in the contract or note itself.

acceptance. The actual or implied receipt and retention of that which is tendered or offered. The acceptance of an offer is the assent to an offer which is requisite to the formation of a contract. It is either express or evidenced by circumstances from which such assent may be implied.

accession. In its legal meaning it is generally used to signify the acquisition of property by its incorporation or union with other property.

accommodation paper. Ordinarily a note or other form of negotiable instrument made for the purpose of enabling the payee to obtain credit, and as such it has no validity until it passes into the hands of a holder for value.

accord. A mutual agreement between debtor and creditor as to the allowance or disallowance of their respective claims and as to the balance struck upon the final adjustment of their accounts and demands on both sides.

accord and satisfaction. The adjustment of a disagreement as to what is due from one person to another, and the payment of the agreed amount.

account stated. An account which has been rendered by one to another and which purports to state the true balance due and which balance is either expressly or impliedly admitted to be due by the debtor.

acknowledgment. A form for authenticating instruments conveying property or otherwise conferring rights. It is a public declaration by the grantor that the act evidenced by the instrument is his act and deed. Also an admission or confirmation.

acquit. To set free or judicially to discharge from an accusation; to release from a debt, duty, obligation, charge or suspicion of guilt.

action, common law. The formal demand of one's right from another person or party made and insisted on in a court of justice. At common law certain formal proceedings were followed in bringing suit to enforce such demands. The ordinary common law actions were:

covenant. The remedy which the law assigns for all breaches of a contract under seal.

debt. Action which lies for the recovery of a fixed and definite sum of money.

ejectment. Originally ejectment was brought to recover the possession of corporeal hereditaments. By statute in some states it is an action to recover immediate possession of real estate.

replevin. An action by which an owner recovers the possession of his own goods.

trover. An action for the recovery of damages for the conversion of personal property. In some jurisdictions it includes any action in which the rights of individuals in a personal chattel are determined.

actionable. Remedial by an action at law.

action ex contractu. An action arising out of the breach of a contract.

action ex delicto. An action arising out of the violation of a duty or obligation created by positive law independent of contract. An action in tort.

adequate remedy at law. A remedy at law which is complete and which is the substantial equivalent of the equitable relief.

adjacent. Usually used to designate property which is in the neighborhood of other property but which does not actually touch such other property. Sometimes used to mean "touching" or "contiguous."

adjudge. To give judgment; to decide; to sentence.

adjudicate. To adjudge; to settle by judicial decree; to hear or try and determine, as a court.

adjust. To settle or to come to a satisfactory agreement so that the parties are in accord in the result. To adjust accounts.

ad litem. During the pendency of the action or proceeding.

administrator. A person appointed by a probate court to settle the estate of a deceased person. His duties are customarily defined by statute. If a woman is appointed she is called the administratrix.

advisement. When a court takes a case under advisement it delays its decision until it has examined and considered the questions involved.

affidavit. A statement or declaration reduced to writing and sworn or affirmed to before an officer who has authority to administer an oath or affirmation.

affirm. To confirm a former judgment or order of a court. Also to declare solemnly instead of making a sworn statement.

agent. An agent is the substitute or representative of his principal and derives his authority from him.

aggrieved. One whose legal rights have been invaded by the act of another is said to be aggrieved. Also one whose pecuniary interest is directly affected by a judgment, or whose right of property may be divested thereby, is to be considered a party aggrieved.

aleatory contract. A contract is aleatory or hazardous when there is a risk on one side or both and when all risks appertaining to the contract and not excepted are assumed by the parties.

alias. Otherwise; also known as; at another time; as formerly.

alibi. Literally the word means "elsewhere." An alibi as used in the criminal law indicates that the defendant will prove that he did not commit and could not have committed the crime because he was not at the scene of the crime at the time of its commission.

alienation. The voluntary act or acts by which one person transfers his own property to another.

aliquot. Strictly, forming an exact proper divisor, but treated as meaning fractional when applied to trusts, etc.

allegation. A declaration, a formal averment or statement of a party to an action in a declaration or pleading of what he intends to prove.

allege. To make a statement of fact; to plead.

allocate. To allow an appropriate proportion; to apportion; to allot.

allonge. A paper attached to and made a part of a promissory note, on which paper an endorsement is written.

ambiguity. Doubtfulness or uncertainty especially in the meaning of language arising from its admitting of more than one meaning.

amend. To improve; to make better by change or modification.

amortize. In modern usage the word means to provide for the payment of a debt by creating a sinking fund or paying in installments.

ancillary. Auxiliary to. An ancillary receiver is a receiver who has been appointed in aid of, and in subordination to, the primary receiver.

answer. The pleading of a defendant in which he may deny any or all the facts set out in the plaintiff's declaration or complaint.

anticipatory breach. The doctrine of the law of contracts that when the promisor has repudiated the contract before the time of performance has arrived the promisee may sue forthwith.

appeal and error. An appeal brings up questions of fact as well as of law, but upon a writ of error only questions of law apparent on the record can be considered, and there can be no inquiry whether there was error in dealing with questions of fact.

appear. To give notice of appearance in an action.

appearance. The first act of the defendant in court.

appellant. A person who files an appeal.

appellate jurisdiction. Jurisdiction to revise or correct the work of a subordinate court.

appellee. A party against whom a cause is appealed from a lower court to a higher court. He is called the "respondent" in some jurisdictions.

applicant. A petitioner; one who files a petition or application.

appurtenances. An appurtenance is that which belongs to another thing, but which has not belonged to it immemorially; e.g., buildings would be appurtenant to the land.

arbitrate. To submit some disputed matter to selected persons and to accept their decision or award as a substitute for the decision of a judicial tribunal.

argument. The discussion by counsel for the respective parties of their contentions on the law and the facts of the case being tried in order to aid the jury in arriving at a correct and just conclusion.

as per. Commonly used and understood to mean in accordance with, or in accordance with the terms of, or as by the contract authorized. The term is not susceptible of literal translation.

assault. A demonstration of an unlawful intent by one person to inflict immediate injury on the person of another then present.

assent. To give or express one's concurrence or approval of something done. Assent does not include consent.

assignable. Capable of being lawfully assigned or transferred; transferable; negotiable. Also capable of being specified or pointed out as an assignable error.

assignee. A person to whom an assignment is made.

assignment. A transfer or setting over of property or some right or interest therein, from one person to another. In its ordinary application the word is limited to the transfer of choses in action, e.g., the assignment of a contract.

assignor. The maker of an assignment.

assumpsit. The form of action brought if one

failed to perform a parol agreement either express or implied. The form of action is now brought if one fails to perform any undertaking promissory in its nature.

attachment. Taking property into the legal custody of an officer by virtue of the directions contained in a writ of attachment. A seizure under a writ of a debtor's property.

attest. To bear witness to; to affirm; to be true or genuine.

attorney-in-fact. A person who is authorized by his principal, either for some particular purpose, or to do a particular act, not of a legal character.

authentication. Such official attestation of a written instrument as will render it legally admissible in evidence.

authority. Judicial or legislative precedent; delegated power; warrant.

averment. A positive statement of fact made in a pleading.

avoidable. Capable of being nullified or made void.

bad faith. The term imparts a person's actual intent to mislead or deceive another; an intent to take an unfair and unethical advantage of another.

bail. The release of a person from custody upon the undertaking of one or more persons for him and also upon his own recognizance, that he shall appear to answer the charge against him at the time appointed; the delivery or bailment of a person to his sureties, so that he is placed in their friendly custody instead of remaining in prison.

bailee. The person to whom a bailment is made.

bailment. A delivery of personal property by one person to another in trust for a specific purpose, with a contract, express or implied, that the trust shall be faithfully executed and the property returned or duly accounted for when the special purpose is accomplished, or kept until the bailor reclaims it.

bailor. The maker of a bailment; one who delivers personal property to another to be held in bailment.

banc. A bench; a meeting of all the judges of a court.

bankable. Capable of being discounted or receivable as cash by a bank.

bank check. An instrument by which a depositor seeks to withdraw funds from a bank.

bankruptcy. The state of a person who is unable to pay his debts without respect to time; one whose liabilities exceed his assets.

bar. As a collective noun it is used to include those persons who are admitted to practice law, members of the bar. The court itself. A plea or peremptory exception of a defendant sufficient to destroy the plaintiff's action.

barratry. The habitual stirring up of quarrels and suits; a single act would not constitute the offense.

barter. To exchange one commodity for another; to negotiate for the acquisition of a thing.

bearer. The designation of the bearer as the payee of a negotiable instrument signifies that the instrument is payable to the person who seems to be the holder.

bench. A court; the judges of a court; the seat upon which the judges of a court are accustomed to sit while the court is in session.

beneficiaries, third party. A person who is not a party to a contract, agreement or instrument but is, by the terms of the contract, agreement, or written instrument, to receive the promised consideration or some portion of it.

    donee beneficiary. A person who is not a party to a contract yet is to receive the consideration promised by way of gift.

    creditor beneficiary. A person who is not a party to a contract yet is to receive the consideration contracted for by the promisee in discharge of a debt owed by the promisee to the creditor beneficiary.

benefit of clergy. The exemption of clergymen from trial or punishment for crime excepting before the ecclesiastical court.

bequeath. Commonly used to denote a testamentary gift of real estate; synonymous to "to devise."

bid. To make an offer at an auction or at a judicial sale. As a noun it means an offer.

bilateral contract. A contract in which the promise of one of the parties forms the consideration for the promise of the other; a contract formed by an offer requiring a reciprocal promise.

bill of exchange. An unconditional order in writing by one person to another, signed by the person giving it, requiring the person to whom it is addressed to pay on demand or at a fixed or determinable future time a sum certain in money to order or to bearer.

bill of lading. A written acknowledgment of the receipt of goods to be transported to a designated place and delivery to a named person or to his order.

bill of sale. A written agreement by which one person assigns or transfers his interests or rights in personal property to another.

binder. Also called a binding slip—a brief memorandum or agreement issued by an insurer as a temporary policy for the convenience of all the parties, constituting a present insurance in the amount specified, to continue in force until the execution of a formal policy.

blacklist. A document whereby, either voluntarily or in pursuance of a previous arrangement, one person communicates to another or other persons information about a third person which is likely to prevent them from entering into business relations with that third person.

"blue sky" laws. A popular name for statutes regulating the sale of securities and intended to protect investors against fraudulent and visionary schemes.

bogus. Spurious, fictitious, or sham. A bogus check is a check given by a person upon a bank in which he has no funds.

bona fide. Good faith.

bond. An obligation under seal.

breach of contract. The failure of a party to a contract to comply with the duty he has assumed by the obligation of the contract.

breaking bulk. The division or separation of the contents of a package or container.

brief. A statement of a party's case; usually an abridgment of either the plaintiff's or defendant's case prepared by his attorneys for use of counsel on a trial at law. Also an abridgment of a reported case.

broker. An agent who bargains or carries on negotiations in behalf of his principal as an intermediary between the latter and third persons in transacting business relative to the acquisition of contractual rights, or to the sale or purchase of property the custody of which is not intrusted to him for the purpose of discharging his agency.

burden of proof. The necessity or obligation of affirmatively proving the fact or facts in dispute on an issue raised in a suit in court.

buyer's risk. In sales, the risk follows the title and if title to the goods has passed to the buyer the risk of loss or damage to the goods while in transit rests on the buyer.

bylaw. A rule or law of a corporation for its government. It includes all self-made regulations of a corporation affecting its business and members which do not operate on third persons, or in any way affect their rights.

call. A notice of a meeting to be held by the stockholders or board of directors of a corporation. Also a demand for payment.

cancellation. The act of crossing out a writing.

The operation of destroying a written instrument.

canon. A law; commonly used to indicate a law of the church. Also a church officer who took revenue for conducting service.

capacity. A person's ability to understand the nature and effect of the art in which he is engaged and the business which he is transacting.

capias. A writ issued for the purpose of securing the person or property of a defendant in a civil action.

caption. A taking; a seizure; the heading or title of a document.

carte blanche. A signed blank instrument intended by the signer to be filled in and used by another person without restriction.

case. A contested question in a court of justice.

case law. The law as laid down in the decisions of the courts. The law extracted from decided cases.

cashier's check. A bill of exchange, drawn by a bank upon itself, and accepted by the act of issuance.

casualty. Chance; accident; contingency. A fatal or serious accident.

cause of action. A right of action at law arises from the existence of a primary right in the plaintiff, and an invasion of that right by some delict on the part of the defendant, and that the facts which establish the existence of that right and that delict constitute the cause of action.

caveat emptor. Let the buyer beware. This maxim expresses the general idea that the buyer purchases at his peril, and that there are no warranties, either express or implied, made by the seller.

caveat venditor. Let the seller beware. It is not accepted as a rule of law in the law of sales.

certainty. Distinctness and accuracy of statement.

certification. The return of a writ; a formal attestation of a matter of fact; the appropriate marking of a certified check.

certified check. A check which has been "accepted" by the drawee bank and has been so marked or certified that it indicates such acceptance.

cestui que trust. The person for whose benefit property is held in trust by a trustee.

challenge. An objection; an exception; to object; to take exception to.

champerty. The purchase of an interest in a matter in dispute so as to take part in the litigation.

chancellor. A judge of a court of chancery.

chancery. Equity or a court of equity.

charge. To charge a jury is to instruct the jury

as to the essential law of the case. The first step in the prosecution of a crime is to formally accuse the offender or charge him with the crime.

charter. An instrument or authority from the sovereign power bestowing the right or power to do business under the corporate form of organization. Also the organic law of a city or town, and representing a portion of the statute law of the state.

chattel interest. Any interest in land of a less dignity than a freehold estate.

chattel morgage. An instrument whereby the owner of chattels transfers the title to such property to another as security for the performance of an obligation subject to be defeated on the performance of the obligation. Under the U.C.C. called merely a security interest.

chattel real. Interests in real estate less than a freehold, such as an estate for years.

chattels. Goods both movable and immovable except such as are in the nature of freehold or a part of a freehold.

check. A written order on a bank or banker payable on demand to the person named or his order or bearer and drawn by virtue of credits due the drawer from the bank created by money deposited with the bank.

chose in action. A personal right not reduced to possession but recoverable by a suit at law.

c.i.f. An abbreviation for cost, freight, and insurance, used in mercantile transactions, especially in import transactions.

circuit. A judge's journey in holding court in different places; the district of a judge thus traveling.

citation. A writ issued out of a court of competent jurisdiction, commanding the person therein named to appear on a day named to do something therein mentioned.

citation of authorities. The reference to legal authorities such as reported cases or treatises to support propositions advanced.

civil action. An action brought to enforce a civil right.

claim and delivery. A statutory action which partakes of the common law action of replevin in that its objective is the recovery of specific property when possible.

claimant. One who makes a claim. A voluntary applicant for justice.

class action. An action brought on behalf of other persons similarly situated.

clause. A sentence or paragraph in a written instrument. One of the subdivisions of a written or printed document.

close corporation. A corporation wherein a major part of the persons to whom the corporate powers have been granted have the right to fill vacancies occurring in their ranks. Also used to refer to any corporation whose stock is not freely traded and whose shareholders are personally known to each other.

c. o. d. "Cash on delivery." When goods are delivered to a carrier for a cash on delivery shipment the carrier must not deliver without receiving payment of the amount due.

code. A system of law; a systematic and complete body of law.

codicil. Some addition to or qualification of one's last will and testament.

coercion. The compulsion actual or presumed by which one is actually or presumably forced to do an act which he would not have done of his own free will and choice.

cognovit. To acknowledge an action. A cognovit note is a promissory note which contains an acknowledgment clause.

collateral attack. An attempt to impeach a decree, a judgment or other official act in a proceeding which has not been instituted for the express purpose of correcting or annulling or modifying the decree, judgment or official act.

comaker. A person who with another or others signs a negotiable instrument on its face and thereby becomes primarily liable for its payment.

commercial law. The law which relates to the rights of property and persons engaged in trade or commerce.

commission merchant. A person who sells goods in his own name at his own store, and on commission, from sample. Also one who buys and sells goods for a principal in his own name and without disclosing his principal.

common carrier. One who undertakes, for hire or reward, to transport the goods of such of the public as choose to employ him.

compact. Synonymous to contract.

compensatory damages. Damages which will compensate a party for an injury suffered and nothing more.

complaint. A form of legal process which usually consists of a formal allegation or charge against a party, made or presented to the appropriate court or officer. The technical name of a bill in chancery by which the complainant sets out his cause of action.

composition with creditors. An agreement between creditors and their common debtor and between themselves whereby the creditors agree to accept the sum or security stipulated in full payment of their claims.

concurrent. Running with, simultaneous with. The word is used in different senses. In contracts concurrent conditions are conditions which must be performed simultaneously by the mutual acts required by each of the parties.

condemn. To appropriate land for public use. To adjudge a person guilty; to pass sentence upon a person convicted of a crime.

condition. A provision or clause in a contract which operates to suspend or rescind the principal obligation. A qualification or restriction annexed to a conveyance of lands, whereby it is provided that in the case a particular event does or does not happen, or in case the grantor or grantees do or omit to do a particular act, an estate shall commence, be enlarged or be defeated.

condition precedent. A condition which must happen before either party is bound by the principal obligation of a contract; e.g., one agrees to purchase goods if they are delivered before a stated day. Delivery before the stated day is a condition precedent to one's obligation to purchase.

condition subsequent. A condition which operates to relieve or discharge one from his obligation under a contract.

conditional acceptance. An acceptance of a bill of exchange containing some qualification limiting or altering the acceptor's liability on the bill.

conditional sale. The term is most frequently applied to a sale wherein the seller reserves the title to the goods, though the possession is delivered to the buyer, until the purchase price is paid in full.

confession of judgment. An entry of judgment upon the admission or confession of the debtor without the formality, time, or expense involved in an ordinary proceeding.

confusion. The mingling of goods of different owners into a common mass.

conservator (of an insane person). A person appointed by a competent court to take care of and oversee the person and estate of an idiot or other incompetent person.

consideration. An essential of a valid contract. It consists of either a benefit to the promisor or a detriment to the promisee.

consignee. A person to whom goods are consigned, shipped, or otherwise transmitted, either for sale or for safe-keeping.

consignment. A bailment for sale. The consignee does not undertake the absolute obligation to sell or pay for the goods.

consignor. One who sends goods to another on consignment; a shipper or transmitter of goods.

construe. To read a statute or document for the purpose of ascertaining its meaning and effect but in doing so the law must be regarded.

contempt. Conduct in the presence of a legislative or judicial body tending to disturb its proceedings, or impair the respect due to its authority or a disobedience to the rules or orders of such a body which interferes with the due administration of law.

contra. Otherwise; disagreeing with; contrary to.

contra bonos moris. Contrary to good morals.

contribution. A payment made by each, or by any, of several having a common interest or liability of his share in the loss suffered, or in the money necessarily paid by one of the parties in behalf of the others.

conversion. Any distinct act of dominion wrongfully exerted over another's personal property in denial of or inconsistent with his rights therein. That tort which is committed by a person who deals with chattels not belonging to him in a manner which is inconsistent with the ownership of the lawful owner.

conveyance. In its common use it refers to a written instrument transferring the title to land or some interest therein from one person to another. It is sometimes applied to the transfer of the property in personality.

copartnership. A partnership.

corporation. An artificial being, invisible, intangible and existing only in contemplation of law. It is exclusively the work of the law, and the best evidence of its existence is the grant of corporate powers by the commonwealth.

corporation de facto. A corporation in fact. An organization which has made a bona fide attempt to organize a corporation under an existing law and which has done business as a corporation but which failed to comply with all the requirements of the law under which it attempted to incorporate.

corporation de jure. A corporation which has, in its organization, complied with all the requirements of the law under which it is incorporated and would not be vulnerable to an attack by the state in a quo warranto proceeding.

corporeal. Possessing physical substance; tangible; perceptible to the senses.

counterclaim. A claim which, if established, will defeat or in some way qualify a judgment to which the plaintiff is otherwise entitled.

counter-offer. A cross offer made by the offeree to the offeror.

court of appeals. A court in which appeals from a lower court are heard and disposed of.

court of claims. A Federal tribunal established to hear and investigate claims against the United States. Its opinion is merely advisory.

covenant. The word is used in its popular sense as synonymous to contract. In its specific sense it ordinarily imparts an agreement reduced to writing, and executed by a sealing and delivery.

covenantor. A person who covenants; the maker of a covenant.

coverture. The condition of a married woman.

credible. As applied to a witness the word means competent.

culpable. Censurable, also sometimes used to mean criminal.

cumulative. Adding to or added to something else; by way of increase.

cumulative voting. A method of voting by which an elector entitled to vote for several candidates for the same office may cast more than one vote for the same candidate, distributing among the candidates as he chooses a number of votes equal to the number of candidates to be elected.

curtesy. Under the early English land law if a man married a woman who had an interest in real estate, and issue was born, the man was entitled to a life estate in his wife's real estate. This life estate was known as curtesy.

custodia legis. The custody of the law. When property is lawfully taken, by virtue of legal process, it is in the custody of the law.

custody. The bare control or care of a thing as distinguished from the possession of it.

custom. Something which has by its universality and antiquity acquired the force and effect of law, in a particular place or country, in respect to the subject matter to which it relates; practice which is judicially noticed without proof.

damages. Indemnity to the person who suffers loss or harm from an injury; a sum recoverable as amends for a wrong. An adequate compensation for the loss suffered or the injury sustained.

    consequential. Damages which are not produced without the concurrence of some other event attributable to the same origin or cause.

    liquidated. Damages made certain by the prior agreement of the parties.

    nominal. Damages which are recoverable where a legal right is to be vindicated against an invasion which has produced no actual present loss.

date of issue. As the term is applied to notes, bonds, etc., of a series, it usually means the arbitrary date fixed as the beginning of the term for which they run, without reference to the precise time when convenience or the state of the market may permit of their sale or delivery.

deal. To engage in mutual intercourse or transactions of any kind.

debenture. A written acknowledgment of a debt; specifically an instrument under seal for the repayment of money lent.

debtor. A person who owes another anything, or who is under obligation, arising from express agreement, implication of law, or from the principles of natural justice, to render and pay a sum of money to another.

deceit. A specie of fraud; actual fraud consisting of any false representations or contrivance whereby one person overreaches and misleads another to his hurt.

decide. To weigh the reasons for and against and see which preponderates and to be governed by that preponderance.

decision. A decision is the judgment of a court, while the opinion represents merely the reasons for that judgment.

declaration. The pleadings by which a plaintiff in an action at law sets out his cause of action. An admission or statement subsequently used as evidence in the trial of an action.

declaratory. Explanatory affirmative; tending to remove doubt.

decree. An order or sentence of a court of equity determining some right or adjudicating some matter affecting the merits of the cause.

deed. A writing, sealed and delivered by the parties; an instrument conveying real property.

de facto. In fact as distinguished from "de jure," by right.

defalcation. The word includes both embezzlement and misappropriation and is a broader term than either.

default. Fault; neglect; omission; the failure of a party to an action to appear when properly served with process; the failure to perform a duty or obligation; the failure of a person to pay money when due or when lawfully demanded.

defeasible (of title to property). Capable of being defeated. A title to property which is open to attack or which may be defeated by the performance of some act.

defend. To oppose a claim or action; to plead in defense of an action; to contest an action suit or proceeding.

defendant. A party sued in a personal action.

defendant in error. Any of the parties in whose favor a judgment was rendered which the losing party seeks to have reversed or modified by writ of error and whom he names as adverse parties.

deficiency. That part of a debt which a mortgage was made to secure, not realized by the liquidation of the mortgaged property. Something which is lacking.

defraud. To deprive another of a right by deception or artifice. To cheat; to wrong another by fraud.

dehors. Outside of; disconnected with, unrelated to.

de jure. By right; complying with the law in all respects.

del credere agent. An agent who guarantees his principal against the default of those with whom contracts are made.

deliver. To surrender property to another person.

demand. A claim; a legal obligation; a request to perform an alleged obligation; a written statement of a claim.

de minimis non curat lex. The law is not concerned with trifles. The maxim has been applied to exclude the recovery of nominal damages where no unlawful intent or disturbance of a right of possession is shown, and where all possible damage is expressly disproved.

demurrage. A compensation for the delay of a vessel beyond the time allowed for loading, unloading, or sailing. It is also applied to the compensation for the similar delay of a railroad car.

demurrer. An objection made by one party to his opponents pleading, alleging that he ought not to answer it, for some defect in law in the pleading.

de novo, trial. Anew; over again; a second time. A trial de novo is a new trial in which the entire case is retried in all its detail.

dependent covenants. Covenants made by two parties to a deed or agreement which are such that the thing covenanted or promised to be done on each part enters into the whole consideration for the covenant or promise on the part of the other, or such covenants as are concurrent, and to be performed at the same time. Neither party to such a covenant can maintain an action against the other without averring and proving performance on his part.

deposition. An affidavit; an oath; the written testimony of a witness given in the course of a judicial proceeding, either at law or in equity, in response to interrogatories either oral or written, and where an opportunity is given for cross-examination.

deputy. A person subordinate to a public officer whose business and object is to perform the duties of the principal.

derivative action. A suit by a shareholder to enforce a corporate cause of action.

descent. Hereditary succession. It is the title whereby a man on the death of his ancestor acquires his estate by right of representation as his heir at law, an heir being one upon whom the law casts the estate immediately at the death of the ancestor, the estate so descending being the inheritance.

detinue. A common law action, now seldom used, which lies where a party claims the specific recovery of goods and chattels unlawfully detained from him.

detriment. A detriment is any act or forebearbearance by a promisee. A loss or harm suffered in person or property.

dictum. The opinion of a judge which does not embody the resolution or determination of the court and is made without argument, or full consideration of the point, and is not the professed deliberation of the judge himself.

directed verdict. A verdict which the jury returns as directed by the court. The court may thus withdraw the case from the jury whenever there is no competent, relevent and material evidence to support the issue.

discharge. To unload or deliver a cargo from a vessel. To set a person at liberty who has been in custody. The release or performance of a contract or other obligation.

discharge in bankruptcy. An order or decree rendered by a court in bankruptcy proceedings, the effect of which is to satisfy all debts provable against the estate of the bankrupt as of the time when the bankruptcy proceedings were initiated.

discount. A loan upon an evidence of debt, where the compensation for the use of the money until the maturity of the debt is deducted from the principal and retained by the lender at the time of making the loan.

dismiss. To discontinue; to order a cause, motion, or prosecution to be discontinued or quashed.

diverse citizenship. A term of frequent use in the interpretation of the federal constitutional provision for the jurisdiction of the federal courts which extends it to controversies between citizens of different states.

divided court. A court is so described when there has been a division of opinion between its members on a matter which has been submitted to it for decision.

dividend. A gain or profit. A fund which a corporation sets apart from its profits to be divided among its members.

document. Any matter expressed or described upon any substance by means of letters, figures or marks or by more than one of these means intended to be used, or which may be used, for the purpose of recording that matter.

domain. The ownership of land; immediate or absolute ownership. The public lands of a state are frequently termed the public domain.

domicile. A place where a person lives or has his home; in a strict legal sense, the place where he has his true, fixed, permanent home and principal establishment, and to which place he has whenever he is absent, the intention of returning.

dominion (property). The rights of dominion or property are those rights which a man may acquire in and to such external things as are unconnected with his body.

donee. A person to whom a gift is made.

donor. A person who makes a gift.

dower. The legal right or interest which his wife acquires by marriage in the real estate of her husband.

draft. A written order drawn upon one person by another, requesting him to pay money to a designated third person. A bill of exchange payable on demand.

drawee. A person upon whom a draft or bill of exchange is drawn by the drawer.

drawer. The maker of a draft or bill of exchange.

drummer. A person who drums up business; a solicitor of customers or business.

due bill. An acknowledgment of a debt in writing, not made payable to order.

dummy. One posing or represented as acting for himself, but in reality acting for another. A tool or straw man for the real parties in interest.

duress. Overpowering of the will of a person by force or fear.

earnest. Something given as part of the purchase price to bind the bargain.

easement. A liberty, privilege or advantage in land without profit, existing distinct from the ownership of the soil; the right which one person has to use the land of another for a specific purpose.

edict. A command or prohibition promulgated by a sovereign and having the effect of law.

effects. As used in wills, the word is held equivalent to personal property. It denotes property in a more extensive sense than goods and includes all kinds of personal property but will be held not to include real property, unless the context discloses an intention on the part of the testator to dispose of his realty by the use of the word.

e.g. An abbreviation for "exempli gratia," meaning for or by the way of example.

ejectment. By statute in some states, it is an action to recover the immediate possession of real property. At common law, it was a purely possessory action, and as modified by statute, though based upon title, it is still essentially a possessory action.

eleemosynary corporation. A corporation created for a charitable purpose or for charitable purposes, such as are constituted for the perpetual distribution of free alms to such purposes as their founders and supporters have directed.

emancipate. To release; to set free. Where a father expressly or impliedly by his conduct waives his right generally to the services of his minor child, the child is said to be emancipated and he may sue on contracts made by him for his services.

embezzlement. A statutory offense consisting of the fraudulent conversion of another's personal property by one to whom it has been intrusted, with the intention of depriving the owner thereof, the gist of the offense being usually the violation of relations of fiduciary character.

encumbrance. An encumbrance on land is a right in a third person in the land to the diminution of the value of the land, though consistent with the passing of the fee by the deed of conveyance.

endorsement. Writing on the back of an instrument; the contract whereby the holder of a bill or note transfers to another person his right to such instrument and incurs the liabilities incident to the transfer.

entity. An existence; a being actual or artificial.

entry. Recordation; noting in a record; going upon land; taking actual possession of land. Literally, the act of going into a place after a breach has been effected.

eo nominee. By or in that name or designation.

equitable defense. Any matter which would authorize an application to a court of chancery for relief against a legal liability, but which at law could not be pleaded in bar.

equity. That which in human transactions is founded in natural justice, in honesty and right, and which arises in equity and good conscience; that portion of remedial justice which is exclusively administered by a court of equity, as counterdistinguished from that portion of remedial justice which is exclusively administered by a court of common law.

error. A mistake of law or fact; a mistake of the court in the trial of an action.

escheat. The revision of land to the state in the event there is no person competent to inherit it.

estate. Technically the word refers only to an interest in land.

estate at will. A lease of lands or tenements to be held at the will of the lessor. Such can be determined by either party.

estate for a term. An estate less than a freehold which is in fact a contract for the possession of land or tenements for some determinate period.

estate for life. An estate created by deed or grant conveying land or tenements to a person to hold for the term of his own life or for the life of any other person or for more lives than one.

estate in fee simple. An absolute inheritance, clear of any conditions, limitations or restrictions to particular heirs. It is the highest estate known to the law and necessarily implies absolute dominion over the land.

estate per autre vie. An estate which is to endure for the life of another person than the grantee, or for the lives of more than one, in either of which cases the grantee is called the tenant for life.

estoppel. That state of affairs which arises when one is forbidden by law from alleging or denying a fact because of his previous action or inaction.

et al. An abbreviation for the Latin "et alius" meaning, and another; also of "et alii" meaning, and others.

et ux. An abbreviation for the Latin "et uxor" meaning, and his wife.

eviction. Originally, as applied to tenants, the word meant depriving the tenant of the possession of the demised premises, but technically, it is the disturbance of his possession, depriving him of the enjoyment of the premises demised or any portion thereof by title paramount or by entry and act of the landlord.

evidence. That which makes clear or ascertains the truth of the fact or point in issue either on the one side or the other; those rules of law whereby we determine what testimony is to be admitted and what rejected in each case and what is the weight to be given to the testimony admitted.

exception. An objection; a reservation; a contradiction.

exchange. An executed contract which operates by itself as a reciprocal conveyance of the thing given and the thing received in exchange, each of the parties being individually considered in the double light of vendor and vendee. A transfer of money from one person to another at a place more or less distant at an agreed rate of exchange or at the customary rate.

ex delicto. From or out of a wrongful act; tortious; tortiously.

executed. When applied to written instruments the word is sometimes used as synonymous with the word "signed" and means no more than that, but more frequently it imports that everything has been done to complete the transaction; that is that the instrument has been signed, sealed, and delivered. An executed contract is one in which the object of the contract is performed.

execution. A remedy in the form of a writ or process afforded by law for the enforcement of a judgment. The final consummation of a contract of sale, including only those acts which are necessary to the full completion of an instrument, such as the signature of the seller, the affixing of his seal and its delivery to the buyer.

executor. A person who is designated in a will as one who is to administer the estate of the testator.

executory. Not yet executed; not yet fully performed, completed, fulfilled or carried out; to be performed wholly or in part.

executrix. Feminine of executor.

exemption. A release from some burden, duty or obligation; a grace; a favor; an immunity; taken out from under the general rule, not to be like others who are not exempt.

exhibit. A copy of a written instrument on which a pleading is founded, annexed to the pleading and by reference made a part of it. Any paper or thing offered in evidence and marked for identification.

ex industria. On purpose; purposely; intentionally.

exports. Goods exported from the United States to a foreign country.

extension. A lengthening; a continuance; a grant of further time.

ex vi termini. By the force of the term; by the intrinsic import of the term or expression.

face value. The nominal or par value of an instrument as expressed on its face; in the case of a bond this is the amount really due, including interest.

factor. An agent who is employed to sell goods for a principal, usually in his own name, and who is given possession of the goods.

f.a.s. An abbreviation for the expression "free alongside steamer."

fee simple absolute. Same as fee simple. See estates.

felony. As a general rule all crimes punishable by death or by imprisonment in a state prison are felonies.

feme covert. A married woman.

feme sole. An unmarried woman.

feoffment. The transfer of a fee, a freehold or a corporeal hereditament by livery of seisin. It operated on the possession, and effected the transmutation thereof.

fiction. An assumption made by the law that something is true which is or may be false.

fiduciary. One who holds goods in trust for another or one who holds a position of trust and confidence.

fieri facias. You cause to be made—an ordinary writ of execution whereby the officer is commanded to levy and sell and to "make," if he can, the amount of the judgment creditors demand.

fiscal. The fiscal affairs of a county are the business transactions of the county, the performance of such duties as the law has defined and placed upon the county board, or such as uniformly pertain to the office of its members.

fixture. A thing which was originally a personal chattel and which has been actually or constructively affixed to the soil itself or to some structure legally a part of such soil; an article which was once a chattel, but which by being physically annexed or affixed to the realty has become accessory to it and part and parcel of it.

f.o.b. An abbreviation of "free on board."

forced sale. The term generally applies to a sale made under the authority of any legal proceedings whether at law or in equity, which seek to appropriate the property to the payment of debt.

foreman. The spokesman and presiding member of a jury who is usually elected to that position by the jury itself, but sometimes is appointed by the court.

forfeiture. A forfeiture implies a penalty and the word forfeit is often used synonymously with penalty, but in its strict sense a forfeiture implies a divestiture of property without compensation, in consequence of a default or offense.

forwarder. A person who, having no interest in goods and no ownership or interest in the means of their carriage, undertakes, for hire, to forward them by a safe carrier to their destination.

franchise. A special privilege conferred by government upon individuals, and which does not belong to the citizens of a country generally, of common right. Also a contractual relationship establishing a means of marketing goods or services giving certain elements of control to the supplier (franchiser) in return for the right of the franchisee to use the supplier's tradename or trademark, usually in a specific marketing area.

fraud. Conduct which operates prejudicially on the rights of others, and is so intended; deception practiced to induce another to part with property, or surrender some legal right, and which accomplished the end desired.

freehold. Any estate of inheritance or for life in either a corporeal or incorporeal hereditament existing in or arising from real property of free tenure.

fungible goods. Goods any unit of which is from its nature or by mercantile custom treated as the equivalent of any other unit.

futures. Contracts for the sale and future delivery of stocks or commodities, wherein either party may waive delivery, and receive or pay, as the case may be, the difference in market price at the time set for delivery.

garnishee. As a noun, the term signifies the person upon whom a garnishment is served, usually a debtor of the defendant in the action. As a verb, the word means to institute garnishment proceedings; to cause a garnishment to be levied on the garnishee.

garnishment. The term denotes a proceeding whereby property, money, or credits of a debtor in possession of another, the garnishee, are applied to the payment of the debts by means of process against the debtor and the garnishee. It is a statutory proceeding based upon contract relations, and can only be resorted to where it is authorized by statute.

general issue. A plea of the defendant amounting to a denial of every material allegation of fact in the plaintiff's complaint or declaration.

going business. An establishment which is still continuing to transact its ordinary business, though it may be insolvent.

good faith. An honest intention to abstain from taking an unconscientious advantage of another.

grantee. A person to whom a grant is made.

grantor. A person who makes a grant.

gravamen. Gist, essence; substance. The grievance complained of; the substantial cause of the action.

guarantor. A person who promises to answer for the debt, default or miscarriage of another.

guaranty. An undertaking by one person to be answerable for the payment of some debt, or the due performance of some contract or duty by another person, who himself remains liable to pay or perform the same.

guardian. A person (in some rare cases a corporation) to whom the law has entrusted the custody and control of the person, or estate, or both, of an infant, lunatic or incompetent person.

habeas corpus. Any of several common law writs having as their object to bring a party before the court or judge. The only issue it presents is whether the prisoner is restrained of his liberty by due process.

habendum. The second part of a deed or conveyance following that part which names the grantee. It describes the estate conveyed and to what use. It is no longer essential and if included in a modern deed is a mere useless form.

hearing. The supporting of one's contentions by argument and if need be by proof. It is an absolute right and if denied to a contestant it would amount to the denial of one of his constitutional rights.

hedging. A market transaction wherein a party buys a certain quantity of a given commodity at the price current on the date of the purchase and sells an equal quantity of the same commodity for future delivery, thereby protecting himself against loss due to fluctuation in the market; for if the price goes down he gains on futures and if the price advances he loses on futures, but, in either event, he is secure in the profit he has gained on the price of the commodity at the time he purchased it.

heirs. Those persons appointed by law to succeed to the real estate of a decedent, in case of intestacy.

hereditaments. A larger and more comprehensive word than either "land" or "tenements," and meaning anything capable of being inherited, whether it be corporeal, incorporeal, real, personal, or mixed.

hinder and delay creditors. To impede creditors in their lawful efforts to subject the property of their debtor to the payment of their claims, whether done innocently or with intent to hinder and delay them. A debtors sale of his property for less than its fair value may be such a hindrance and delay, although innocently made.

holder in due course. A holder who has taken a negotiable instrument under the following conditions:

(1) That it is complete and regular on its face; (2) that he became the holder of it before it was overdue, and without notice that it had been previously dishonored, if such was the fact; (3) that he took it in good faith and for value; (4) that at the time it was negotiated to him he had no notice of any infirmity in the instrument or defect in the title of the person negotiating it.

holding company. A corporation the purpose of which is in many instances to circumvent antitrust laws and, by which, combination among competing corporations is sought to be effected through the absolute transfer of the stocks of the constituent companies to the central "holding" company. This plan is executed by organizing a corporation, often under the laws of a foreign state, to hold the shares of the stock of the constituent companies, their shareholders receiving, upon an agreed basis of value, shares in the holding corporation in exchange therefor.

homestead. In a legal sense the word means the real estate occupied as a home and also the right to have it exempt from levy and forced sale. It is the land, not exceeding the prescribed amount, upon which the dwelling house, or residence, or habitation, or abode of the owner thereof and his family resides, and includes the dwelling house as an indispensable part.

illusory. Deceiving or intending to deceive, as by false appearances; fallacious. An illusory promise is a promise which appears to be binding but which in fact does not bind the promisor.

immunity. A personal favor granted by law, contrary to the general rule.

impanel. To place the names of the jurors on a panel; to make a list of the names of those persons who have been selected for jury duty; to go through the process of selecting a jury which is to try a cause.

implied. Contained in substance or essence or by fair inference but not actually expressed; deductible by inference or implication.

implied warranty. An implied warranty arises by operation of law and exists without any intention of the seller to create it. It is a conclusion or inference of law, pronounced by the court, on facts admitted or proved before the jury.

inalienable. Incapable of being alienated, transferred, or conveyed; nontransferrable.

in banc. With all the judges of the court sitting.

incapacity. In its legal meaning it applies to one's legal disability, such as infancy, want of authority, or other personal incapacity to alter legal relationship.

inception. Initial stage. The word does not refer to a state of actual existence but to a condition of things or circumstances from which the thing may develop; as the beginning of work on a building.

inchoate. Imperfect; incipient; not completely formed.

incorporeal. Having no body or substances; intangible; without physical existence.

indemnity. An obligation or duty resting on one person to make good any loss or damage another has incurred while acting at his request or for his benefit. By a contract of indemnity one may agree to save another from a legal consequence of the conduct of one of the parties or of some other person.

indenture. Indentures were deeds which originally were made in two parts formed by cutting or tearing a single sheet across the middle in a jagged or indented line, so that the two parts might be subsequently matched; and they were executed by both grantor and grantee. Later the indenting of the deed was discontinued, yet the term came to be applied to all deeds which were executed by both parties.

independent contractor. One who, exercising an independent employment, contracts to do a piece of work according to his own methods, and without being subject to the control of his employer except as to the result of his work; one who contracts to perform the work at his own risk and cost, the workmen being his servants, and he being liable for their misconduct.

indictment. An accusation founded on legal testimony of a direct and positive character, and the concurring judgment of at least 12 of the grand jurors that upon the evidence presented to them the defendant is guilty.

indorsement. See endorsement.

information. A written accusation of crime preferred by a public prosecuting officer without the intervention of a grand jury.

injunction. A restraining order issued by a court of equity; a prohibitory writ restraining a person from committing or doing an act, other than a criminal act, which appears to be against equity and conscience. There is also the mandatory injunction which commands an act to be done or undone and compels the performance of some affirmative act.

in pari delicto. Equally at fault in tort or crime; in equal fault or guilt.

in personam. Against the person.

in re. In the matter; in the transaction.

in rem. Against a thing and not against a person; concerning the condition or status of a thing.

insolvency. The word has two distinct meanings. It may be used to denote the insufficiency of the entire property and assets of an individual to pay his debts, which is its general meaning and its meaning as used in the National Bankruptcy Act; but in a more restricted sense, it expresses the inability of a party to pay his debts as they become due in the regular course of his business, and it is so used when traders and merchants are said to be insolvent.

in statu quo. In the situation in which he was.

instrument. In its broadest sense, the term includes formal or legal documents in writing, such as contracts, deeds, wills, bonds, leases, and mortgages. In the law of evidence it has still a wider meaning and includes not merely documents, but witnesses and things animate and inanimate which may be presented for inspection.

insurable interest. Any interest in property the owner of which interest derives a benefit from the existence of the property or would suffer a loss from its destruction. It is not necessary, to constitute an insurable interest, that the interest is such that the event insured against would necessarily subject the insured to loss; it is sufficient that it might do so.

inter alia. Among other things or matters.

interlocutory. In law, that is interlocutory which does not decide the cause, but only settles some intervening matter relating to the cause. The matter thus settled is brought before the court by special motion.

interpleader. An equitable remedy which lies when two or more persons severally claim the same thing under different titles or in separate interests from another, who, not claiming any title or interest therein himself, and not knowing to which of the claimants he ought in right to render the debt or duty claimed or to deliver the property in his custody, is either molested in an action or actions brought against him, or fears that he may suffer injury from the conflicting claims of the parties.

intervention. A proceeding by which one not originally made a party to an action or suit is permitted, on his own application, to appear therein and join one of the original parties in maintaining his cause of action or defense, or to assert some cause of action against some or all of the parties to the proceeding as originally instituted.

intestate. A person who has died without leaving a valid will disposing of his property and estate.

in toto. In the whole, altogether; wholly.

in transitu. On the journey. Goods are as a rule considered as in transitu while they are in the possession of a carrier, whether by land or water, until they arrive at the ultimate place of their destination and are delivered into the actual possession of the buyer, whether or not the carrier has been named or designated by the buyer.

ipso facto. By the fact itself; by the very fact; by the act itself.

irreparable injury. As applied to the law of injunctions, the term means that which cannot be repaired, restored, or adequately compensated for in money or where the compensation cannot be safely measured.

irrevocable. Never to be revoked; never to be abrogated, annulled, or withdrawn. A court will not so interpret the word when such a construction would be unreasonably harsh.

joint. The word joint imparts unity.

joint bank account. A bank account of two persons so fixed that they shall be joint owners thereof during their mutual lives, and the survivor shall take the whole on the death of other.

jointly. Acting together or in concert or co-operating; holding in common or interdependently, not separately. Persons are "jointly bound" in a bond or note when both or all must be sued in one action for its enforcement, not either one at the election of the creditor.

jointly and severally. Persons who find themselves "jointly and severally" in a bond or note may all be sued together for its enforcement, or the creditor may select any one or more as the object of his suit.

joint tenancy. An estate held by two or more jointly, with an equal right in all to share in the enjoyments of the land during their lives. Four requisites must exist to constitute a joint tenancy, viz.: the tenants must have one and the same interest; the interest must accrue by one and the same conveyance; they must commence at one and the same time; and the property must be held by one and the same undivided possession. If any one of these four elements is lacking, the estate will not be one of joint tenancy. An incident of joint tenancy is the right of survivorship.

judgment. The sentence of the law upon the record; the application of the law to the facts and pleadings. The last word in the judicial controversy; the final consideration and determination of a court of competent jurisdiction upon matters submitted to it in an action or proceeding.

judgment lien. The statutory lien upon the real property of a judgment debtor which is created by the judgment itself. At common law a judgment imposes no lien upon the real property of the judgment debtor, and to subject the property of the debtor to the judgment it was necessary to take out an elegit.

judgment n.o.v. (judgment non obstante veredicto). Judgment notwithstanding the verdict. Under certain circumstances the judge has the power to enter a judgment which is contrary to the verdict of the jury. Such a judgment is a judgment non obstante veredicto.

jurisdiction. The right to adjudicate concerning the subject matter in a given case. The modern tendency is to make the word include not only the power to hear and determine, but also the power to render the particular judgment in the particular case.

jury. A body of laymen, selected by lot, or by some other fair and impartial means, to ascertain, under the guidance of the judge, the truth in questions of fact arising either in civil litigation or a criminal process.

justification. A valid defense to an action; a proof made by sureties that they are responsible in the amount of the bond which they have executed.

kite. To secure the temporary use of money by issuing or negotiating worthless paper and then redeeming such paper with the proceeds of similar paper. The word is also used as a noun, meaning the worthless paper thus employed.

laches. The established doctrine of equity that, apart from any question of statutory limitation, its courts will discourage delay and sloth in the enforcement of rights. Equity demands conscience, good faith, and reasonable diligence.

lawful age. The age at which one attains majority, that is, 21 years in England and in most of the United States, and 18 for girls in some states.

law merchant. The custom of merchants, or lex mercatorio, which grew out of the necessity and convenience of business, and which, although different from the general rules of the common law, was engrafted into it and became a part of it. It was founded on the custom and usage of merchants and it is today the combined result of reason and experience slowly modified by the necessities and changes in commercial affairs.

leading case. A case often referred to by the courts and by counsel as having finally settled and determined a point of law.

leading questions. Those questions which suggest to the witness the answer desired, those which assume a fact to be proved which is not proved, or which, embodying a material fact, admit of an answer by a simple negative or affirmative.

lease. A contract for the possession and profits of land on one side, and a recompense of rent or other income on the other; a conveyance to a person for life, or years, or at will in consideration of a return of rent or other recompense.

legacy. A bequest; a testamentary gift of personal property. Sometimes incorrectly ap-

plied to a testamentary gift of real property.

legal. According to the principles of law; according to the method required by statute; by means of judicial proceedings; not equitable.

legitimacy. A person's status embracing his right to inherit from his ancestors, to be inherited from, and to bear the name and enjoy the support of his father.

letter of attorney. A power of attorney; a formal document authorizing some act which shall have a binding effect upon the person who grants the authority. It is usually under seal, and while the want of a seal might not invalidate the instrument as a power of attorney, it is not true that every paper conferring authority upon another is a letter of attorney.

letter of credit. An instrument containing a request (general or special) to pay to the bearer or person named money, or sell him some commodity on credit or give him something of value and look to the drawer of the letter for recompense. It partakes of the nature of a negotiable instrument, but the rules governing bills of exchange and promissory notes are always the same, while letters of credit are to be construed with reference to the particular and often varying terms in which they may be expressed, the circumstances and intention of the parties to them, and the usage of the particular trade or business contemplated.

levy. At common law a levy on goods consisted of an officer's entering the premises where they were and either leaving an assistant in charge of them or removing them after taking an inventory. Today courts differ as to what is a valid levy, but by the weight of authority there must be an actual or constructive seizure of the goods. In most states, a levy on land must be made by some unequivocal act of the officer indicating his intention of singling out certain real estate for the satisfaction of the debt.

license. A personal privilege to do some act or series of acts upon the land of another, without possessing any estate therein. A permit or authorization to do what, without a license, would be unlawful.

lien. In its most extensive meaning it is a charge upon property for the payment or discharge of a debt or duty; a qualified right; a proprietary interest which, in a given case, may be exercised over the property of another.

life estate. An estate created by deed or grant conveying lands or tenements to a person to hold for the term of his own life, or for the life of any other person, or for more lives than one.

lineal. In direct line. Lineal heirs are heirs who are related to the deceased in a direct ascending or descending line, as children and grandchildren, parents and grandparents.

lis pendens. A pending suit. As applied to the doctrine of lis pendens it is the jurisdiction, power, or control which courts acquire over property involved in a suit, pending the continuance of the action, and until its final judgment therein.

listing contract. A so-called contract whereby an owner of real property employs a broker to procure a purchaser without giving the broker exclusive right to sell. Under such an agreement, it is generally held that the employment may be terminated by the owner at will, and that a sale of the property by the owner terminates the employment.

livery. Delivery. The act of delivering legal possession of property, as of lands or tenements.

long arm statute. A statute subjecting a foreign corporation to jurisdiction although it may have committed only a single act within the state.

magistrate. A word commonly applied to the lower judicial officers, such as justices of the peace, police judges, town recorders, and other local judicial functionaries. In a broader sense, a magistrate is a public civil officer invested with some part of the legislative, executive, or judicial power given by the Constitution. The President of the United States is the chief magistrate of the nation.

maker. A person who makes or executes an instrument, the signer of an instrument.

mala fides. Bad faith.

malfeasance. The doing of an act which a person ought not to do at all. It is to be distinguished from misfeasance, which is the improper doing of an act which a person might lawfully do.

malum in se. Evil in and of itself. An offense or act is malum in se which is naturally evil as adjudged by the senses of a civilized community. Acts malum in se are usually criminal acts, but not necessarily so.

malum prohibitum. An act which is wrong because it is made so by statute.

mandamus. We command. It is a command issuing from a competent jurisdiction, in the name of the state or sovereign, directed to some inferior court, officer, corporation, or person, requiring the performance of a particular duty therein specified, which duty results from the official station of the party to whom it is directed, or from operation of law.

margin. A deposit by a buyer in stocks with a seller or a stockbroker, as security to cover fluctuations in the market in reference to stocks which the buyer has purchased, but for which he has not paid. Commodities are also traded in on margin.

marshals. Ministerial officers belonging to the executive department of the federal government, who with their deputies have the same powers of executing the laws of the United States in each state as the sheriffs and their deputies in such state may have in executing the law of that state.

mechanic's lien. A claim created by law for the purpose of securing a priority of payment of the price or value of work performed and materials furnished in erecting or repairing a building or other structure; as such it attaches to the land as well as to the buildings erected therein.

mens rea. A guilty mind, criminal intent.

merchantable. Of good quality and salable, but not necessarily the best. As applied to articles sold, the word requires that the article shall be such as is usually sold in the market, of medium quality and bringing the average price.

merger. To merge means to sink or disappear in something else; to be swallowed up; to lose identity or individuality.

minor. A person who has not reached the age at which the law recognizes a general contractual capacity, usually 21 years.

misdemeanor. Any crime which is punishable neither by death nor by imprisonment in a state prison.

mistrial. An invalid trial due to lack of jurisdiction, error in selection of jurors or some other fundamental requirement.

mitigation of damages. A term relating only to exemplary damages and their reduction by extenuating circumstances such as provocation or malice. The theory of such mitigation is based on the regard of the law for the frailty of human passions, since it looks with some indulgence upon violations of good order which are committed in a moment of irritation and excitement.

moiety. One half.

monopoly. In its broadest meaning, the word signifies the sole power of dealing in an article or doing a specified thing, either generally or in a particular place.

mortgage. A conveyance of property to secure the performance of some obligation, the conveyance to be void on the due performance thereof.

motive. The cause or reason that induced a person to commit a crime.

movables. A word derived from the civil law and usually understood to signify the utensils which are to furnish or ornament a house, but it would seem to comprehend personal property generally.

mutuality. That essential of every contract to make it binding upon both parties at the same time. It is a rule of law that there must be mutuality in a contract; that is, it must be binding upon both parties at the same time, if it is to be deemed valid and enforceable as to either.

necessaries. With reference to an infant, the word includes whatever is reasonably necessary for his proper and suitable maintenance, in view of his means and prospects, and the customs of the social circle in which he moves and is likely to move.

negligence. The word has been defined as the omission to do something which a reasonable man, guided by those considerations which ordinarily regulate human affairs, would do, or doing something which a prudent and reasonable man would not do.

negotiability. A technical term derived from the usage of merchants and bankers in transferring, primarily, bills of exchange and, afterward, promissory notes. At common law no contract was assignable, so as to give to an assignee a right to enforce it by suit in his own name. To this rule, bills of exchange and promissory notes, payable to order or bearer, have been admitted exceptions, made such by the adoption of the law merchant.

negotiable instrument. An instrument which may be transferred or negotiated, so that the holder may maintain an action thereon in his own name.

no arrival, no sale. A sale of goods "to arrive" or "on arrival," per or ex a certain ship, has been construed to be a sale subject to a double condition precedent, namely, that the ship arrives in port and that when she arrives the goods are on board, and if either of these conditions fails, the contract becomes nugatory.

no-par value stock. Stock of a corporation having no face or par value.

nolo contendere. A plea in a criminal action which has the same effect as a guilty plea except that it does not bind the defendant in a civil suit on the same wrong.

nominal damages. Damages which are recoverable where a legal right is to be vindicated against an invasion that has produced no actual present loss of any kind, or where there has been a breach of a contract and no actual damages whatever have

been or can be shown, or where, under like conditions, there has been a breach of legal duty.

non age. Underage; under majority; infancy.

non compus mentis. Totally and positively incompetent. The term denotes a person entirely destitute or bereft of his memory or understanding.

nonfeasance. In the law of agency, it is the total omission or failure of an agent to enter upon the performance of some distinct duty or undertaking which he has agreed with his principal to do. It is not every omission or failure to perform a duty that will constitute a nonfeasance, but only an omission to perform such distinct duties as he owes to his principal, as distinguished from those which he owes to third persons or to the public in general, as a member of society.

non obstante veredicto. Notwithstanding the verdict of the jury. See judgment non obstante veredicto.

nonsuit. A judgment given against the plaintiff when he is unable to prove a case, or when he refuses or neglects to proceed to the trial of the cause after it has been put at issue without determining such issue.

noting protest. The act of making a memorandum on a bill or note at the time of, and embracing the principal facts attending, its dishonor. The object is to have a record from which the instrument of protest may be written, so that a notary need not rely on his memory for the fact.

novation. Under the civil law, a mode of extinguishing one obligation by another. Under common law, it was at first a transaction whereby a debtor was discharged from his liability to his original creditor by contracting a new obligation in favor of a new creditor by the order of the original creditor. In modern law, it is a mutual agreement, between all parties concerned, for the discharge of a valid existing obligation by the substitution of a new valid obligation on the part of the debtor or another, or a like agreement for the discharge of a debtor to his creditor by the substitution of a new creditor.

nudum pactum. A naked promise, a promise for which there is no consideration.

nuisance. In legal parlance, the words extend to everything that endangers life or health, gives offense to the senses, violates the laws of decency, or obstructs the reasonable and comfortable use of property.

oath. Any form of attestation by which a person signifies that he is bound in conscience to perform an act faithfully and truthfully. It involves the idea of calling on God to witness what is averred as truth, and it is supposed to be accompanied with an invocation of His vengeance, or a renunciation of His favor, in the event of falsehood.

obiter dictum. That which is said in passing; a rule of law set forth in a court's opinion, but not involved in the case; what is said by the court outside the record or on a point not necessarily involved therein.

objection. In the trial of a case it is the formal remonstrance made by counsel to something which has been said or done, in order to obtain the court's ruling thereon; and when the court has ruled, the alleged error is preserved by the objector's exception to the ruling, which exception is noted in the record.

obligee. A person to whom another is bound by a promise or other obligation; a promisee.

obligor. A person who is bound by a promise or other obligation; a promisor.

offer. A proposal by one person to another which is intended of itself to create legal relations on acceptance by the person to whom it is made.

offeree. A person to whom an offer is made.

offeror. A person who makes an offer.

opinion. The opinion of the court represents merely the reasons for its judgment, while the decision of the court is the judgment itself.

option. A contract whereby the owner of property agrees with another person that he shall have the right to buy the property at a fixed price within a certain time. There are two elements in an option contract: First, the offer to sell, which does not become a contract until accepted; second, the completed contract to leave the offer open for a specified time. These elements are wholly independent and cannot be treated together without great liability to confusion and error. The offer must be considered wholly independent of the contract to leave it open in determining whether or not it had itself ripened into a contract, and the question whether or not there was a valid contract to leave the offer open is wholly immaterial if the offer was in fact accepted before it was withdrawn.

oral. By word of mouth; verbal; spoken as opposed to written.

ordinance. A legislative enactment of a county or an incorporated city or town.

ostensible authority. Such authority as a principal, either intentionally or by want of ordinary care, causes or allows a third person to believe the agent to possess. If a principal by his acts has led others to believe that he has conferred authority upon his agent, he cannot be heard to assert, as

against third persons who have relied thereon, in good faith, that he did not intend such power.

ostensible partners. Members of a partnership whose names are made known and appear to the world as partners, and who in reality are such.

overdraft. The withdrawal from a bank by a depositor of money in excess of the amount of money he has on deposit there.

overdraw. A depositor overdraws his account at a bank when he obtains on his check or checks from the bank more money than he deposited in the account.

overplus. That which remains; a balance left over.

owner's risk. A term employed by common carriers in bills of lading and shipping receipts to signify that the carrier does not assume responsibility for the safety of the goods.

oyer. To hear. To demand oyer or to crave oyer was a demand as of right to hear an instrument read. The modern practice is usually to demand the privilege of inspecting the document or to demand a copy of it.

par. Par means equal, and par value means a value equal to the face of a bond or a stock certificate. A sale of bonds at par is a sale at the rate of one dollar in money for one dollar in bonds. This is the accepted meaning in the mercantile world.

parol. Oral; verbal; by word of mouth; spoken as opposed to written.

particeps criminis. A party to the crime. The term, which, in common acceptance, means an act that may be visited by an indictment or other criminal prosecution, but it applies to other transactions contrary to good morals, whether they be immoral per se, or prohibited by statute under penalty, or by a simple prohibition, or as militating against the policy of a statute, or fraud, or other corrupt contract.

parties. All persons who are interested in the subject matter of an action and who have a right to make defense, control the proceedings, examine and cross-examine witnesses, and appeal from the judgment.

partition. A proceeding the object of which is to enable those who own property as joint tenants or tenants in common, to put an end to the tenancy so as to vest in each a sole estate in specific property or an allotment of the lands and tenements. If a division of the estate is impracticable the estate ought to be sold, and the proceeds divided.

partners. Those persons who contribute property, money, or services to carry on a joint business for their common benefit, and who own and share the profits thereof in certain proportions; the members of a partnership.

partnership. An association of two or more persons to carry on as co-owners a business for profit.

passbook. The bankbook of a depositor of a bank, in which the cashier or teller, whenever a deposit is made, enters the amount and date thereof.

patent. A patent for land is a conveyance of title to government lands by the government; a patent of an invention is the right of monopoly secured by statute to those who invent or discover new and useful devices and processes.

pawn. A pledge; a bailment of personal property as security for some debt or engagement, redeemable on certain terms, and with an implied power of sale on default.

payee. A person to whom a payment is made or is made payable.

pecuniary. Financial; pertaining or relating to money; capable of being estimated, computed, or measured by money value.

penal. The words "penal" and "penalty" have many different meanings. Strictly and primarily, they denote punishment, whether corporeal or pecuniary, imposed and enforced by the state for a crime or offense against its laws. But they are also commonly used as including an extraordinary liability to which the law subjects a wrongdoer in favor of the person wronged, not limited to the damages suffered. They are also applied to cases of private contract as when one speaks of the "penal sum" or "penalty" of a bond.

penalty. A word which when used in a contract is sometimes construed as meaning liquidated damages, as where the sum named is reasonable, and the actual damages are uncertain in amount and difficult of proof. If, however, it is called a penalty in the contract, it will be held to be a penalty if there is nothing in the nature of the contract to show a contrary intent. An exaction in the nature of a punishment for the nonperformance of an act, or the performance of an unlawful act, and involving the idea of punishment, whether enforced by a civil or criminal action or proceeding.

per curiam. By the court; by the court as a whole.

peremptory challenge. A challenge to a proposed juror which a defendant in a criminal case may make as an absolute right, and which cannot be questioned by either opposing counsel or the court.

performance. As the word implies, it is such a thorough fulfillment of a duty as puts an end to obligations by leaving nothing to be done. The chief requisite of performance is that it shall be exact.

perjury. The willful and corrupt false swearing or affirming, after an oath lawfully administered, in the course of a judicial or quasi judicial proceeding as to some matter material to the issue or point in question.

per se. The expression means by or through itself; simply, as such; in its own relations.

petition. In equity pleading, a petition is in the nature of a pleading (at least when filed by a stranger to the suit) and forms a basis for independent action.

pie-powder court. The court of dusty foot, a court which was held in England by the steward of each fair or market.

plaintiff. A person who brings a suit, action, bill, or complaint.

plaintiff in error. The unsuccessful party to the action who prosecutes a writ of error in a higher court.

plea. A plea is an answer to a declaration or complaint or any material allegation of fact therein which if untrue would defeat the action. In criminal procedure, a plea is the matter which the accused, on his arraignment, alleges in answer to the charge against him.

pledge. A pawn; a bailment of personal property as security for some debt or engagement, redeemable on certain terms, and with an implied power of sale on default.

pledgee. A person to whom personal property is pledged by a pledgor.

pledgor. A person who makes a pledge of personal property to a pledgee.

positive law. Laws actually and specifically enacted or adopted by proper authority for the government of a jural society as distinguished from principles of morality or laws of honor.

possession. Respecting real property, possession involves exclusive dominion and control such as owners of like property usually exercise over it. The existence of such possession is largely a question of fact dependent on the nature of the property and the surrounding circumstances.

power of attorney. A written authorization to an agent to perform specified acts in behalf of his principal. The writing by which the authority is evidenced is termed a letter of attorney and is dictated by the convenience and certainty of business.

praecipe. An order; a command; a writ ordering a person to do some act or to show cause why he should not do it.

precedent. A previous decision relied upon as authority. The doctrine of stare decisis, commonly called the doctrine of precedents, has been firmly established in the law. It means that we should adhere to decided cases and settled principles, and not disturb matters which have been established by judicial determination.

preference. The act of a debtor in paying or securing one or more of his creditors in a manner more favorable to them than to other creditors or to the exclusion of such other creditors. In the absence of statute, a preference is perfectly good, but to be legal it must be bona fide, and not a mere subterfuge of the debtor to secure a future benefit to himself or to prevent the application of his property to his debts.

prerogative. A special power, privilege, or immunity, usually used in reference to an official or his office.

presumption. A term used to signify that which may be assumed without proof, or taken for granted. It is asserted as a self-evident result of human reason and experience.

prima facie. At first view or appearance of the business, as a holder of a bill of exchange, endorsed in blank, is prima facie its owner. Prima facie evidence of fact is in law suffiicient to establish the fact, unless rebutted.

privies. Persons connected together or having mutual interests in the same action or thing by some relation other than actual contract between them.

privilege. A right peculiar to an individual or body.

probate. The word originally meant merely "relating to proof," and later "relating to the proof of wills," but in American law it is now a general name or term used to include all matters of which probate courts have jurisdiction which in many states are the estates of deceased persons and of persons under guardianship.

proffer. To offer for acceptance or to make a tender of.

promise. A declaration which gives to the person to whom it is made a right to expect or claim the performance or nonperformance of some particular thing.

promisee. The person to whom a promise is made.

promisor. A person who makes a promise to another; a person who promises.

promoters. The persons who bring about the incorporation and organization of a corporation.

pro rata. According to the rate, proportion, or allowance. A creditor of an insolvent estate is to be paid pro rata with creditors of the same class. According to a certain rule or proportion.

prospectus. An introductory proposal for a contract in which the representations may or may not form the basis of the contract actually made; it may contain promises which are to be treated as a sort of floating obligation to take effect when appropriated by persons to whom they are addressed, and amount to a contract when assented to by any person who invests his money on the faith of them.

pro tanto. For so much; to such an extent.

proximate cause. That cause of an injury which, in natural and continuous sequence, unbroken by any efficient intervening cause, produces the injury, and without which the injury would not have occurred.

qualified acceptance. A conditional or modified acceptance. In order to create a contract an acceptance must accept the offer substantially as made; hence a qualified acceptance is no acceptance at all, is treated by the courts as a rejection of the offer made, and is in effect an offer by the offeree, which the offeror may, if he chooses, accept and thus create a contract.

quantum meruit. One of the common counts in assumpsit which lies for the value of services rendered.

quasi contract. Sometimes called a contract implied in law, but more properly known as a quasi contract or constructive contract. It is a contract in the sense that it is remediable by the contractual remedy of assumpsit. The promise is purely fictitious and is implied in order to fit the actual cause of action to the remedy. The liability under it exists from an implication of law that arises from the facts and circumstances independent of agreement or presumed intention.

quasi judicial. The acts of an officer which are executive or administrative in their character and which call for the exercise of that officer's judgment and discretion are not ministerial acts, and his authority to perform such acts is quasi judicial.

quitclaim deed. A deed conveying only the right, title, and interest of the grantor in the property described, as distinguished from a deed conveying the property itself.

quorum. That number of persons, shares represented, or officers who may lawfully transact the business of a meeting called for that purpose.

quo warranto. By what authority. The name of a writ (and also of the whole pleading) by which the government commences an action to recover an office or franchise from the person or corporation in possession of it.

raising a check. A class of forgery where the signatures on the check are all genuine, but the amount of the check has been increased by the forger's alteration.

ratification. The adoption by one in whose name an unauthorized act has been performed by another upon the assumption of authority to act as his agent, even though without any precedent authority whatever, which adoption or ratification relates back, supplies the original authority to do the act, binding the principal so adopting or ratifying to the same extent as if the act had been done in the first instance—by his previous authority. The act of an infant upon reaching his majority affirming a voidable contract made by him during his infancy and giving it the same force and effect as if it had been valid from the beginning.

rebuttal. Testimony addressed to evidence produced by the opposite party; rebutting evidence.

receiver. An indifferent person between the parties to a cause, appointed by the court to receive and preserve the property or funds in litigation, and receive its rents, issues, and profits, and apply or dispose of them at the direction of the court, when it does not seem reasonable that either party should hold them.

recognizance. At common law, an obligation entered into before some court of record or magistrate duly authorized, with a condition to do some particular act, usually to appear and answer to a criminal accusation. Being taken in open court and entered upon the order book, it was valid without the signature or seal of any of the obligors.

recorder. A public officer of a town or county charged with the duty of keeping the record books required by law to be kept in his office and of receiving and causing to be copied in such books such instruments as by law are entitled to be recorded.

recoupment. The doctrine under which in an action for breach of contract the defendant may show that the plaintiff has not performed the same contract on his part, and may recoup his damages for such breach in the same action, whether liquidated or not.

redemption. The buying back of one's property after it has been sold. The right to redeem property sold under an order or decree of court is purely a privilege conferred by, and does not exist independently of, statute.

redress. Remedy; indemnity; reparation.

rejected. A claim of a creditor is said to have been rejected when, after having been presented in due form to the proper officer for allowance or approval as a valid claim, it has been disallowed by that officer in the manner provided at law.

release. The giving up or abandoning of a claim or right to a person against whom the claim exists or the right is to be enforced or exercised. It is the discharge of a debt by the act of the party in distinction from an extinguishment which is a discharge by operation of law.

relevancy. The logical relation between proposed evidence and the fact to be established.

remainderman. One who is entitled to the remainder of the estate after a particular estate carved out of it has expired.

remedy. The appropriate legal form of relief by which a remediable right may be enforced.

remit. To pardon; to remand for a new trial or for future proceedings; to transmit. To remit means to send back.

remittitur. The certificate of reversal issued by an appellate court upon reversing the order or judgment appealed from.

replevin. A proceeding by which the owner recovers possession of his own goods.

res. The thing; the subject matter of a suit; the property involved in the litigation; a matter; property; the business; the affair; the transaction.

res adjudicata. A matter which has been adjudicated; that which is definitely settled by a judical decision.

rescind. As the word is applied to contracts, to rescind in some cases means to terminate the contract as to future transactions, while in others it means to annul the contract from the beginning.

residue. All that portion of the estate of a testator of which no effectual disposition has been made by his will otherwise than in the residuary clause.

respondent. The defendant in an action; a party adverse to an appellant in an action which is appealed to a higher court. The person against whom a bill in equity was exhibited.

reversal. An annulment or setting aside; as the word is used in connection with judgments, its usual meaning contemplates only a reversal by an appellate court, that is, by a court authorized to set aside the judgment.

reversed and remanded. Where the judgment of an appellate court concludes with the words, "judgment reversed and cause remanded," unless it is apparent from the opinion of the court that the adjudication was intended to be a final disposition of the cause, the effect of the reversal is only to set aside the judgment of the lower court that a new trial may be had.

reversion. The residue of a fee simple remaining in the grantor, to commence in possession after the determination of some particular estate granted out by him. The estate of a landlord during the existence of the outstanding leasehold estate.

reversioner. A person who is entitled to a reversion.

revocation. A withdrawal; a recall; an annulment; a repudiation.

right. When we speak of a person having a right, we must necessarily refer to a civil right as distinguished from the elemental idea of a right absolute. We must have in mind a right given and protected by law, and a person's enjoyment thereof is regulated entirely by the law which creates it.

riparian. From the Latin word "riparius," of or belonging to the bank of a river, in turn derived from "ripa," a bank, and defined as "pertaining to or situated on the bank of a river"; the word has reference to the bank and not to the bed of the stream.

sanction. The part of a law which signifies the evil or penalty which will be incurred by the wrongdoer for his breach of it.

satisfaction. A performance of the terms of an accord. If such terms require a payment of a sum of money, then "satisfaction" means that such payment has been made.

schedule in bankruptcy. An inventory filed by the bankrupt in bankruptcy proceedings, containing a list of all his property and his credits.

scienter. In cases of fraud and deceit, the word means knowledge on the part of the person making the representations, at the time when they are made, that they are false. In an action for deceit it is generally held that scienter must be proved.

scintilla of evidence. The least particle of evidence. A slight amount of evidence supporting a material issue.

seal. At common law, a seal is an impression on wax or some other tenacious material, but in modern practice the letters "l.s." (locus sigilli) or the word "seal" enclosed in a scroll, either written, or printed, and acknowledged in the body of the instrument to be a seal, are often used as substitutes.

secular. Temporal; pertaining to temporal things, things of the world; worldly; opposed to spiritual, holy.

security. That which makes the enforcement of a promise more certain than the mere personal obligation of the debtor or promisor, whatever may be his possessions or financial standing. It may be a pledge of property or an additional personal obligation; but it means more than the mere promise of the debtor with property liable to general execution.

security agreement. An agreement which creates or provides a security interest or lien on personal property. A term used in the U.C.C. including a wide range of transactions in the nature of chattel mortgages, conditional sales, etc.

seizin. In a legal sense, the word means possession of premises with the intention of asserting a claim to a freehold estate therein; it is pactically the same thing as ownership; it is a possession of a freehold estate, such as by the common law is created by livery of seizen.

seller's lien. A lien which the vendor of goods has at common law for the whole or the unpaid portion of the purchase price of the goods, where he has parted with title but not with possession. It is in the nature of a pledge raised or created by law upon the happening of the insolvency of the buyer, to secure the unpaid purchase money to the seller.

service. As applied to a process of courts, the word ordinarily implies something in the nature of an act or proceeding adverse to the party served, or of a notice to him.

setoff. A setoff both at law and in equity is that right which exists between two parties, each of whom, under an independent contract, owes an ascertained amount to the other, to set off their respective debts by way of mutual deduction, so that, in any action brought for the larger debt, the residue only, after such deduction, shall be recovered.

severable contract. A contract which is not entire or indivisible. If the consideration is single, the contract is entire; but if it is expressly or by necessary implication apportioned, the contract is severable. The question is ordinarily determined by inquiring whether the contract embraces one or more subject matters, whether the obligation is due at the same time to the same person, and whether the consideration is entire or apportioned.

several. Separate; distinct; exclusive; individual; appropriated. In this sense it is opposed to common; and it has been held that the word could not be construed as equivalent to respective. More than two but not many.

shareholder. It is generally held that one who holds shares on the books of the corporation is a shareholder and that one who merely holds a stock certificate is not. Shareholders may become such either by original subscription, by direct purchase from the corporation, or by subsequent transfer from the original holder.

share of stock. The right which its owner has in the management, profits and ultimate assets of the corporation. The tangible property of a corporation and the shares of stock therein are separate and distinct kinds of property and belong to different owners, the first being the property of an artificial person—the corporation—the latter the property of the individual owner.

sheriff. The office is a most ancient one, dating back at least to the time of Alfred, King of England, and the holder thereof has always been the chief executive officer and conservator of the peace in his shire or county.

sight. A term signifying the date of the acceptance or that of protest for the non-acceptance of a bill of exchange; for example, 10 days after sight.

sine qua non. Without which it is not; an indispensable requisite.

situs. Location; local position; the place where a person or thing is, is his situs. Intangible property has no actual situs, but it may have a legal situs, and for the purpose of taxation its legal situs is at the place where it is owned and not at the place where it is owed.

specific performance. The actual accomplishment of a contract by the party bound to fulfill it; the name of an equitable remedy of very ancient origin the object of which is to secure a decree to compel the defendant specifically to perform his contract, which is nothing more or less than a means of compelling a party to do precisely what he ought to have done without being coerced by a court.

stare decisis. The doctrine or principle that the decisions of the court should stand as precedents for future guidance.

status quo. The situation in which he was.

stipulation. An agreement between opposing counsel in a pending action, usually required to be made in open court and entered on the minutes of the court, or else to be in writing and filed in the action, ordinarily entered into for the purpose of avoiding delay, trouble, or expense in the conduct of the action.

stockholder. See shareholder.

stoppage in transitu. A right which the vendor of goods on credit has to recall them, or retake them, on the discovery of the insolvency of the vendee. It continues so long as the carrier remains in the possession and control of the goods or until there has been an actual or constructive delivery to the vendee, or some third person has acquired a bona fide right in them.

subpoena. A process the purpose of which is to compel the attendance of a person whom it is desired to use as a witness.

subrogation. The substitution of one person in the place of another with reference to a lawful claim or right, frequently referred to as the doctrine of substitution. It is a device adopted or invented by equity to compel the ultimate discharge of a debt or obligation by him who in good conscience ought to pay it. It is the machinery by which the equity of one man is worked out through the legal rights of another.

sui generis. Of its own kind; peculiar to itself.

summary proceedings. Proceedings, usually statutory, in the course of which many formalities are dispensed with. But such proceedings are not concluded without proper investigation of the facts, or without notice, or an opportunity to be heard by the person alleged to have committed the act, or whose property is sought to be affected.

summons. A writ or process issued and served upon a defendant in a civil action for the purpose of securing his appearance in the action. In modern practice, the summons serves the same purpose, but it also usually notifies the defendant that if he does not appear within the time specified in the summons, judgment by default will be entered against him.

supra. Above; above mentioned; in addition to.

surety. One who by accessory agreement called a contract of suretyship binds himself with another, called the principal, for the performance of an obligation in respect to which such other person is already bound and primarily liable for such performance.

tacit law. The law which arises out of the silent consent and the custom and usages of the people.

tacking. The adding together of successive periods of adverse possession of persons in privity with each other, in order to constitute one continuous adverse possession for the time required by the statute, to establish title.

tangible. Capable of being possessed or realized; readily apprehensible by the mind; real; substantial; evident.

tariff. A schedule or tabulated list of rates.

tenancy. A tenancy exists when one has let real estate to another to hold of him as landlord. When duly created and the tenant put into possession, he is the owner of an estate for the time being, and has all the usual rights and remedies to defend his possession.

tender. An unconditional offer of payment, consisting in the actual production in money or legal tender of a sum not less than the amount due.

tender offer. An offer to security holders to acquire their securities in exchange for money or other securities.

tenement. A word commonly used in deeds which passes not only lands and other inheritances but also offices, rents, commons, and profits arising from lands. Usually it is applied exclusively to land, or what is ordinarily denominated real property.

tenor. The tenor of an instrument is an exact copy of the instrument. Under the rule that an indictment for forgery must set out in the instrument according to its "tenor," the word imports an exact copy—that the instrument is set forth in the very words and figures.

tenure. In its technical sense, the word means the manner whereby lands or tenements are holden, or the service that the tenant owes his lord. In the latter case there can be no tenure without some service, because the service makes the tenure. The word is also used as signifying the estate in land. The most common tenure by which lands are held in the United States is "fee simple."

testament. Redfield, in his work on wills, defined a last will and testament as the disposition of one's property to take effect after death.

testator. A deceased person who died leaving a will.

testatrix. Feminine of testator.

testimony. In some contexts the word bears the same import as the word "evidence," but in most connections it has a much narrower meaning. Testimony is the words heard from the witness in court, and evidence is what the jury considers it worth.

tort. An injury or wrong committed, either with or without force, to the person or property of another. Such injury may arise by nonfeasance, or by the malfeasance or the misfeasance of the wrongdoer.

tort-feasor. A person who commits a tort; a wrongdoer.

tortious. Partaking of the nature of a tort; wrongful; injurious.

trade fixtures. Articles of personal property which have been annexed to the freehold and which are necessary to the carrying on of a trade.

transcript. A copy of a writing.

transferee. A person to whom a transfer is made.

transferor. A person who makes a transfer.

treasury shares. Shares of stock of a corporation which have been issued as fully paid to shareholders and subsequently acquired by the corporation.

trespass. Every unauthorized entry on another's property is a trespass and any person who makes such an entry is a trespasser. In its widest signification, trespass means any violation of law. In its most restricted sense, it signifies an injury intentionally inflicted by force either on the person or property of another.

trial. An examination before a competent tribunal, according to the law of the land, of the facts or law put in issue in a cause, for the purpose of determining such issue. When the court hears and determines any issue of fact or law for the purpose of determining the rights of the parties, it may be considered a trial.

trust. A confidence reposed in one person, who is termed trustee, for the benefit of another, who is called the cestui que trust, respecting property, which is held by the trustee for the benefit of the cestui que trust. As the word is used in the law pertaining to unlawful combinations and monopolies, a trust in its original and typical form is a combination formed by an agreement among the shareholders in a number of competing corporations to transfer their shares to an unincorporated board of trustees, and to receive in exchange trust certificates in some agreed proportion to their shareholdings.

trustee. A person in whom property is vested in trust for another.

trustee in bankruptcy. The Federal bankruptcy act defines the term as an officer, and he is an officer of the courts in a certain restricted sense, but not in any such sense as a receiver. He takes the legal title to the property of the bankrupt and in respect to suits stands in the same general position as a trustee of an express trust or an executor. His duties are fixed by statute. He is to collect and reduce to money the property of the estate of the bankrupt.

ultra vires act. An act of a corporation which is beyond the powers conferred upon the corporation.

undertaking. A promise to perform some act; a bond; a recognizance.

unilateral contract. A contract formed by an

offer or a promise on one side for an act to be done on the other, and a doing of the act by the other by way of acceptance of the offer or promise; that is, a contract wherein the only acceptance of the offer that is necessary is the performance of the act.

usury. The taking more than the law allows upon a loan or for forbearance of a debt. Illegal interest; interest in excess of the rate allowed by law.

utter. As applied to counterfeiting, to utter and publish is to declare or assert, directly or indirectly, by words or actions, that the money or note is good. Thus to offer it in payment is an uttering or publishing. To utter and publish a document is to offer directly or indirectly, by words or actions, such document as good and valid. There need be no acceptance by the offeree to constitute an uttering.

valid. Effective; operative; not void; subsisting; sufficient in law.

vendee. A purchaser of property. The word is more commonly applied to a purchaser of real property, the word "buyer" being more commonly applied to the purchaser of personal property.

vendor. A person who sells property to a vendee. The words "vendor" and "vendee" are more commonly applied to the seller and purchaser of real estate, and the words "seller" and "buyer" are more commonly applied to the seller and purchaser of personal property.

vendue. A sale; a sale at auction.

venire. The name of a writ by which a jury is summoned.

venue. The word originally was employed to indicate the county from which the jurors were to come who were to try a case, but in modern times it refers to the county in which a case is to be tried.

veracity. The words truth, veracity, and honesty are almost synonyms each of the other.

verbal. By word of mouth; spoken; oral; parol.

verdict. The answer of a jury given to the court concerning the matters of fact committed to their trial and examination; it makes no precedent, and settles nothing but the present controversy to which it relates. It is the decision made by the jury and reported to the court, and as such it is an elemental entity which cannot be divided by the judge.

verification. The affidavit of a party annexed to his pleadings which states that the pleading is true of his own knowledge except as to matters which are therein stated on his information or belief, and as to those matters, that he believes it to be true. A sworn statement of the truth of the facts stated in the instrument verified.

versus. Against. Versus and vs. have become ingrafted upon the English language; their meaning is as well understood and their use quite as appropriate as the word "against" could be.

vest. To give an immediate fixed right of present or future enjoyment.

void. That which is entirely null. A void act is one which is not binding on either party, and which is not susceptible of ratification.

voidable. Capable of being made void; not utterly null, but annullable, and hence that may be either voided or confirmed.

voucher. A written instrument which attests, warrants, maintains, and bears witness.

waive. To throw away; to relinquish voluntarily, as a right which one may enforce, if he chooses.

waiver. The intentional relinquishment of a known right. It is a voluntary act and implies an election by the party to dispense with something of value, or to forego some advantage which he might at his option have demanded and insisted on.

warrant. An order authorizing a payment of money by another person to a third person. Also an option to purchase a security. As a verb, the word means to defend; to guarantee; to enter into an obligation of warranty.

warrant of arrest. A legal process issued by competent authority, usually directed to regular officers of the law, but occasionally issued to private persons named in it, directing the arrest of a person or persons upon grounds stated therein.

warranty. In the sale of a commodity, an undertaking by the seller to answer for the defects therein is construed as a warranty. In a contract of insurance, as a general rule, any statement or description, or any undertaking on the part of the insured on the face of the policy or in another instrument properly incorporated in the policy, which relates to the risk, is a warranty.

wash sales. A stock exchange term designating sales which are merely bets upon the market, in which it is understood between the parties that neither is bound to deliver or accept delivery.

waste. The destruction or material alteration of any part of a tenement by a tenant for life or years, to the injury of the person entitled to the inheritance; an unlawful act or omission of duty on the part of the tenant which results in permanent injury to the inheritance; any spoil or destruction done or permitted with respect to land, houses, gardens, trees, or other corporeal hereditaments, by the tenant thereof, to the prejudice of him in reversion or remainder, or, in other words to the lasting injury of the inheritance.

watered stock. Stock issued by a corporation as fully paid up, when in fact it is not fully paid up.

writ. A mandatory precept, issued by the authority and in the name of the sovereigns or the state, for the purpose of compelling the defendant to do something therein mentioned. It is issued by a court or other competent jurisdiction and is returnable to the same. It is to be under seal and tested by the proper officer and is directed to the sheriff or other officer lawfully authorized to execute the same.

Year Books. The earliest reports of the decisions of the courts of England. The reports are extant in a regular series from the reign of Edward the Second, inclusive. From his time to that of Henry the Eighth the decisions were taken down by the prothonotaries, or chief scribes of the court, at the expense of the crown, and were published annually, and hence they are known as Year Books.

zone. As a verb, the word is comparatively new and "to zone" means to separate the commercial or industrial districts of a city from the residence district or districts, and to prohibit the establishment of places of business in any designated residence district.

Indexes

Index of Cases

General Index

This book has been set in 11, 10, and 9 point Times Roman, leaded 2 points. Part numbers and titles and chapter numbers and titles are in 14 point Helvetica. The size of the type page is 30 by 47 picas.